How Tobacco Smoke Causes Disease: The Biology and Behavioral Basis for Smoking-Attributable Disease

A Report of the Surgeon General

2010

U.S. DEPARTMENT OF HEALTH AND HUMAN SERVICES
Public Health Service
Office of the Surgeon General
Rockville, MD

National Library of Medicine Cataloging in Publication

How tobacco smoke causes disease: the biology and behavioral basis for smoking-attributable disease : a report of the Surgeon General. – Rockville, MD : Dept. of Health and Human Services, Public Health Service, Office of Surgeon General, 2010.
p. 704
Includes bibliographical references.

1. Tobacco – adverse effects. 2. Smoking – adverse effects. 3. Disease – etiology. 4. Tobacco Use Disorder – complications. 5. Tobacco Smoke Pollution – adverse effects. I. United States. Public Health Service. Office of the Surgeon General. II. United States. Office on Smoking and Health.

QV 137 H847 2010

U.S. Department of Health and Human Services
Centers for Disease Control and Prevention
National Center for Chronic Disease Prevention and Health Promotion
Office on Smoking and Health

This publication is available on the World Wide Web at
http://www.surgeongeneral.gov/library

Suggested Citation

U.S. Department of Health and Human Services. *How Tobacco Smoke Causes Disease: The Biology and Behavioral Basis for Smoking-Attributable Disease: A Report of the Surgeon General.* Atlanta, GA: U.S. Department of Health and Human Services, Centers for Disease Control and Prevention, National Center for Chronic Disease Prevention and Health Promotion, Office on Smoking and Health, 2010.

For sale by the Superintendent of Documents, U.S. Government Printing Office, Washington, DC 20402. ISBN 978-0-16-084078-4

Message from Kathleen Sebelius
Secretary of Health and Human Services

Tobacco use imposes enormous public health and financial costs on this nation—costs that are completely avoidable. Until we end tobacco use, more people will become addicted, more people will become sick, more families will be devastated by the loss of loved ones, and the nation will continue to incur damaging medical and lost productivity costs. Now is the time to fully implement proven and effective interventions that reduce tobacco-caused death and disease and to help end this public health epidemic once and for all.

Cigarettes are responsible for approximately 443,000 deaths—one in every five deaths—each year in the United States. The chronic diseases caused by tobacco use lead the causes of death and disability in the United States and unnecessarily strain our health care system. The economic burden of cigarette use includes more than $193 billion annually in health care costs and loss of productivity.

We can prevent the staggering toll that tobacco takes on individuals, families, and communities. This new Surgeon General's report focuses on cigarettes and cigarette smoke to provide further evidence on how cigarettes cause addiction and premature death. It identifies better approaches to helping people stop smoking and brings to light new ideas for how to lower the incidence of smoking-caused disease.

Twenty years of successful state efforts show that the more states invest in tobacco control programs, the greater the reductions in smoking, and the longer states maintain such programs, the greater and faster the impact. The largest impacts come when we increase tobacco prices, ban smoking in public places, offer affordable and accessible cessation treatments and services, and combine media campaigns with other initiatives. We have outlined a level of state investment in comprehensive tobacco control and prevention efforts that, if implemented, would result in an estimated five million fewer smokers over the next five years. Hundreds of thousands of premature deaths caused by tobacco use could be prevented, and many fewer of the nations' children would be deprived by premature death of their aunts, uncles, parents, and grandparents. Importantly, in 2009 the U.S. Food and Drug Administration received statutory authority to regulate tobacco products. This has the potential to lead to even greater progress in reducing morbidity and mortality from tobacco use.

Tobacco prevention and control efforts need to be commensurate with the harm caused by tobacco use. Otherwise, tobacco use will remain the largest cause of preventable illness and death in our nation for decades to come. When we help Americans quit tobacco use and prevent our youth from ever starting, we all benefit. Now is the time for comprehensive public health and regulatory approaches to tobacco control. We have the knowledge and tools to largely eliminate tobacco caused disease. If we seize this moment, we will make a difference in all of our communities and in the lives of generations to come.

Foreword

In 1964, the first Surgeon General's report on the effects of smoking on health was released. In the nearly 50 years since, extensive data from thousands of studies have consistently substantiated the devastating effects of smoking on the lives of millions of Americans. Yet today in the United States, tobacco use remains the single largest preventable cause of death and disease for both men and women. Now, this 2010 report of the Surgeon General explains beyond a shadow of a doubt how tobacco smoke causes disease, validates earlier findings, and expands and strengthens the science base. Armed with this irrefutable data, the time has come to mount a full-scale assault on the tobacco epidemic.

More than 1,000 people are killed every day by cigarettes, and one-half of all long-term smokers are killed by smoking-related diseases. A large proportion of these deaths are from early heart attacks, chronic lung diseases, and cancers. For every person who dies from tobacco use, another 20 Americans continue to suffer with at least one serious tobacco-related illness. But the harmful effects of smoking do not end with the smoker. Every year, thousands of nonsmokers die from heart disease and lung cancer, and hundreds of thousands of children suffer from respiratory infections because of exposure to secondhand smoke. There is no risk-free level of exposure to tobacco smoke, and there is no safe tobacco product.

This new Surgeon General's report describes in detail the ways tobacco smoke damages every organ in the body and causes disease and death. We must build on our successes and more effectively educate people about the health risks of tobacco use, prevent youth from ever using tobacco products, expand access to proven cessation treatments and services, and reduce exposure to secondhand smoke. Putting laws and other restrictions in place, including making tobacco products progressively less affordable, will ultimately lead to our goal of a healthier America by reducing the devastating effects of smoking.

The Centers for Disease Control and Prevention (CDC), the U.S. Food and Drug Administration (FDA), and other federal agencies are diligently working toward this goal by implementing and supporting policies and regulations that strengthen our resolve to end the tobacco epidemic. CDC has incorporated the World Health Organization's MPOWER approach into its actions at the local, state, and national levels. MPOWER consists of six key interventions proven to reduce tobacco use that can prevent millions of deaths. CDC, along with federal, state, and local partners, is committed to monitoring the tobacco epidemic and prevention policies; protecting people from secondhand smoke where they live, work, and play; offering quit assistance to current smokers; warning about the dangers of tobacco; enforcing comprehensive restrictions on tobacco advertising, promotion, and sponsorship; and raising taxes and prices on tobacco products.

In 2009, the *Family Smoking Prevention and Tobacco Control Act* was enacted, giving FDA explicit regulatory authority over tobacco products to protect and promote the health of the American public. Among other things, this historic legislation gave the agency the authority to require companies to reveal all of the ingredients in tobacco products—including the amount of nicotine—and to prohibit the sale of tobacco products labeled as "light," "mild," or "low." Further, with this new regulatory mandate, FDA will regulate tobacco advertising and require manufacturers to use more effective warning labels, as well as restrict the access of young people to their products. FDA will also assess and regulate modified risk products, taking into account the impact their availability and marketing has on initiation and cessation of tobacco use.

Reducing the tremendous toll of disease, disability, and death caused by tobacco use in the United States is an urgent need and a shared responsibility. All public health agencies need to partner together to develop common strategies to combat the dangers of smoking and tobacco use and defeat this epidemic for good.

This 2010 Surgeon General's report represents another important step in the developing recognition, both in this nation and around the world, that tobacco use is devastating to public health. Past investments in research and in comprehensive tobacco control programs—combined with the findings presented by this new report—provide the foundation, evidence, and impetus to increase the urgency of our actions to end the epidemic of tobacco use.

Thomas R. Frieden, M.D., M.P.H.
Director
Centers for Disease Control and Prevention
and
Administrator
Agency for Toxic Substances and Disease Registry

Margaret A. Hamburg, M.D.
Commissioner of Food and Drugs
U.S. Food and Drug Administration

Preface

from the Surgeon General,
United States Public Health Service

In 1964, the Surgeon General released a landmark report on the dangers of smoking. During the intervening 45 years, 29 Surgeon General's reports have documented the overwhelming and conclusive biologic, epidemiologic, behavioral, and pharmacologic evidence that tobacco use is deadly. Our newest report, How Tobacco Smoke Causes Disease, is a comprehensive, scientific discussion of how mainstream and secondhand smoke exposures damage the human body. Decades of research have enabled scientists to identify the specific mechanisms of smoking-related diseases and to characterize them in great detail. Those biologic processes of cigarette smoke and disease are the focus of this report.

One-third of people who have ever tried smoking become daily smokers. This report investigates how and why smokers become addicted and documents how nicotine compares with heroin and cocaine in its hold on users and its effects on the brain. The way tobacco is grown, mixed, and processed today has made cigarettes more addictive than ever before. Because of this, the majority of smokers who try to quit on their own typically require many attempts. It is imperative that we use this information to prevent initiation, make tobacco products less addictive, and provide access to treatments and services to help smokers quit successfully.

This new report also substantiates the evidence that there is no safe level of exposure to cigarette smoke. When individuals inhale cigarette smoke, either directly or secondhand, they are inhaling more than 7,000 chemicals: hundreds of these are hazardous, and at least 69 are known to cause cancer. The chemicals are rapidly absorbed by cells in the body and produce disease-causing cellular changes. This report explains those changes and identifies the mechanisms by which the major classes of the chemicals in cigarette smoke contribute to specific disease processes. In addition, the report discusses how chemicals in cigarette smoke impair the immune system and cause the kind of cellular damage that leads to cancer and other diseases. Insight is provided as to why smokers are far more likely to suffer from chronic disease than are nonsmokers.

By learning how tobacco smoke causes disease, we learn more about how chemicals harm cells, how genes may make us susceptible, and how tobacco users become addicted to nicotine. The answers to these questions will help us to more effectively prevent tobacco addiction and treat tobacco-caused disease. Understanding the complexity of genetic, biochemical, and other influences discussed in this report offers the promise of reducing the disease burden from tobacco use through earlier detection and better treatment; however, even with all of the science presented here, it currently remains true that the only proven strategies to reduce the risks of tobacco-caused disease are preventing initiation, facilitating cessation, and eliminating exposure to secondhand smoke.

My priority as Surgeon General is the health of the American people. Although we have made great strides in tobacco control, more than 440,000 deaths each year are caused by smoking and exposure to secondhand smoke. The cost to the nation is tremendous: a staggering amount is spent on medical care and lost productivity. But most importantly there is immeasurable cost in human suffering and loss.

In 1964, Surgeon General Luther Terry called for "appropriate remedial actions" to address the adverse effects of smoking. With this report, the devastating effects of smoking have been characterized in great detail and the need for appropriate remedial action is even more apparent. The harmful effects of tobacco smoke do not end with the users of tobacco. There is no safe level of exposure to tobacco smoke. Every inhalation of tobacco smoke exposes our children, our families, and our loved ones to dangerous chemicals that can damage their bodies and result in life-threatening diseases such as cancer and heart disease. And, although not a focus of this report, we know that smokeless tobacco causes cancer and has other adverse health effects. The science is now clear that "appropriate remedial actions" include protecting everyone in the country from having to breathe secondhand smoke; making all tobacco products progressively less affordable; expanding access to proven cessation treatments and services; taking actions at the federal, state, and local levels to counteract the influence of tobacco advertising, promotions, and sponsorship; and ensuring that all adults and children clearly understand that the result of tobacco use is addiction, suffering, reduced quality of life, and all too often, early death. Forty-five years after Surgeon General Terry called on this nation to act, I say, if not now, when? The health of our nation depends on it.

Regina Benjamin, M.D., M.B.A.
Surgeon General

Acknowledgments

This report was prepared by the U.S. Department of Health and Human Services under the general direction of the Centers for Disease Control and Prevention, National Center for Chronic Disease Prevention and Health Promotion, Office on Smoking and Health.

Vice Admiral Regina Benjamin, M.D., M.B.A., Surgeon General, U.S. Public Health Service, Office of the Assistant Secretary for Health, Office of the Surgeon General, Office of the Secretary, U.S. Department of Health and Human Services, Washington, D.C.

Rear Admiral Boris Lushniak, M.D., M.P.H., Deputy Surgeon General, U.S. Public Health Service, Office of the Assistant Secretary for Health, Office of the Surgeon General, Office of the Secretary, U.S. Department of Health and Human Services, Washington, D.C.

Rear Admiral Christopher Halliday, D.D.S., M.P.H., Chief of Staff, U.S. Public Health Service, Office of the Assistant Secretary for Health, Office of the Surgeon General, Office of the Secretary, U.S. Department of Health and Human Services, Washington, D.C.

Mary Beth Bigley, Dr.P.H., M.S.N., A.N.P., Acting Director of the Office of Science and Communication, Office of the Surgeon General, Office of the Assistant Secretary for Health, Office of the Secretary, U.S. Department of Health and Human Services, Washington, D.C.

Rear Admiral (Retired) Steven K. Galson, M.D., M.P.H., former Acting Surgeon General, U.S. Public Health Service, Office of the Surgeon General, Office of the Assistant Secretary for Health, Office of the Secretary, U.S. Department of Health and Human Services, Washington, D.C.

Rear Admiral (Retired) Kenneth P. Moritsugu, M.D., M.P.H., former Acting Surgeon General, U.S. Public Health Service, Office of the Surgeon General, Office of Public Health and Science, Office of the Secretary, U.S. Department of Health and Human Services, Washington, D.C.

Rear Admiral (Retired) Carol A. Romano, Ph.D., R.N., F.A.A.N., former Acting Deputy Surgeon General, U.S. Public Health Service, Office of the Surgeon General, Office of Public Health and Science, Office of the Secretary, U.S. Department of Health and Human Services, Washington, D.C.

Rear Admiral (Retired) David Rutstein, M.D., M.P.H., former Acting Deputy Surgeon General, U.S. Public Health Service, Office of the Assistant Secretary for Health, Office of the Surgeon General, Office of the Secretary, U.S. Department of Health and Human Services, Washington, D.C.

Rear Admiral (Retired) Robert C. Williams, P.E., D.E.E., former Acting Deputy Surgeon General, U.S. Public Health Service, Office of the Surgeon General, Office of the Assistant Secretary for Health, Office of the Secretary, U.S. Department of Health and Human Services, Washington, D.C.

Thomas R. Frieden, M.D., M.P.H., Director, Centers for Disease Control and Prevention, Atlanta, Georgia.

Ursula Bauer, Ph.D., Director, National Center for Chronic Disease Prevention and Health Promotion, Centers for Disease Control and Prevention, Atlanta, Georgia.

Barbara Bowman, Ph.D., Associate Director for Science, National Center for Chronic Disease Prevention and Health Promotion, Centers for Disease Control and Prevention, Atlanta, Georgia.

Samuel F. Posner, Ph.D., Associate Director for Science (Acting), National Center for Chronic Disease Prevention and Health Promotion, Centers for Disease Control and Prevention, Atlanta, Georgia.

Tim A. McAfee, M.D., M.P.H., Director, Office on Smoking and Health, National Center for Chronic Disease Prevention and Health Promotion, Centers for Disease Control and Prevention, Atlanta, Georgia.

Terry F. Pechacek, Ph.D., Associate Director for Science, Office on Smoking and Health, National Center for Chronic Disease Prevention and Health Promotion, Centers for Disease Control and Prevention, Atlanta, Georgia.

The editors of the report were

David Sidransky, M.D., Senior Scientific Editor, Professor, Otolaryngology-Head & Neck Surgery, Oncology, Pathology, Urology, Cellular and Molecular Medicine, and Director, Head and Neck Cancer Research, The Johns Hopkins University School of Medicine, Johns Hopkins Medical Institutions, Baltimore, Maryland.

Leslie A. Norman, Managing Editor, Office on Smoking and Health, National Center for Chronic Disease Prevention and Health Promotion, Centers for Disease Control and Prevention, Atlanta, Georgia.

Anne McCarthy, Technical Editor, Northrop Grumman supporting National Center for Health Marketing, Division of Creative Services, Centers for Disease Control and Prevention, Atlanta, Georgia.

Peter L. Taylor, M.B.A., Technical Editor, Senior Editor, Palladian Partners, Silver Spring, Maryland.

Contributing editors were

David L. Ashley, Ph.D., Chief, Emergency Response and Air Toxicants Branch, Division of Laboratory Sciences, National Center for Environmental Health, Centers for Disease Control and Prevention, Atlanta, Georgia.

Neal L. Benowitz, M.D., Professor of Medicine and Biopharmaceutical Sciences and Chief, Division of Clinical Pharmacology and Experimental Therapeutics, University of California, San Francisco, California.

Dorothy Hatsukami, Ph.D., Forster Family Professor in Cancer Prevention, Professor of Psychiatry, University of Minnesota Tobacco Use Research Center, University of Minnesota, Minneapolis, Minnesota.

Stephen S. Hecht, Ph.D., Wallin Professor of Cancer Prevention, Masonic Cancer Center, University of Minnesota, Minneapolis, Minnesota.

Jack E. Henningfield, Ph.D., Vice President Research and Health Policy, Pinney Associates, Bethesda, Maryland; and Professor, Adjunct, Department of Psychiatry and Behavioral Sciences, The Johns Hopkins University School of Medicine, Baltimore, Maryland.

Patricia Richter, Ph.D., DABT, Toxicologist, Office on Smoking and Health, National Center for Chronic Disease Prevention and Health Promotion, Centers for Disease Control and Prevention, Atlanta, Georgia.

Jonathan M. Samet, M.D., M.S., Professor and Chairman, Department of Epidemiology, Bloomberg School of Public Health, The Johns Hopkins University, Baltimore, Maryland (1994–2008); and Director, USC Institute for Global Health, and Chairman, Department of Preventive Medicine, Keck School of Medicine, University of Southern California, Los Angeles, California (2008–present).

Gayle C. Windham, Ph.D., M.S.P.H., Research Scientist Supervisor, Chief, Environmental Surveillance Unit, Division of Environmental and Occupational Disease Control, California Department of Public Health, Richmond, California.

Contributing authors were

David L. Ashley, Ph.D., Chief, Emergency Response and Air Toxicants Branch, Division of Laboratory Sciences, National Center for Environmental Health, Centers for Disease Control and Prevention, Atlanta, Georgia.

Timothy B. Baker, Ph.D., Professor of Medicine, University of Wisconsin School of Medicine and Public Health, Madison, Wisconsin.

Steve A. Belinsky, Ph.D., Director, Lung Cancer Program, Senior Scientist, Lovelace Respiratory Research Institute, Albuquerque, New Mexico.

Neal L. Benowitz M.D., Professor of Medicine and Biopharmaceutical Sciences and Chief, Division of Clinical Pharmacology and Experimental Therapeutics, University of California, San Francisco, California.

Tomoku Betsuyaku, M.D., Ph.D., Associate Professor, First Department of Medicine, Hokkaido University School of Medicine, Sapporo, Japan.

Ann M. Bode, Ph.D., Research Professor and Associate Director, The Hormel Institute, University of Minnesota, Austin, Minnesota.

Anne Burke, M.D., Assistant Professor of Medicine, Gastroenterology Division, University of Pennsylvania School of Medicine, Philadelphia, Pennsylvania.

David M. Burns, M.D., Professor Emeritus, Department of Family and Preventive Medicine, School of Medicine, University of California, San Diego, California.

Rebecca Buus, Ph.D., Health Scientist, Maternal and Infant Health Branch, Division of Reproductive Health, National Center for Chronic Disease Prevention and Health Promotion, Centers for Disease Control and Prevention, Atlanta, Georgia.

Laurie Chassin, Ph.D., Regents Professor of Psychology, Psychology Department, Arizona State University, Tempe, Arizona.

David Christiani, M.D., M.P.H., Professor, Departments of Environmental Health and Epidemiology, Harvard School of Public Health, Harvard University, Boston, Massachusetts.

Pamela I. Clark, M.S.P.H., Ph.D., Research Professor, School of Public Health, University of Maryland, College Park, Maryland.

John P. Cooke, M.D., Ph.D., Professor of Medicine, Stanford University, Stanford, California.

Adolfo Correa, M.D., Ph.D., M.P.H., Medical Officer, Division of Birth Defects and Developmental Disabilities, National Center on Birth Defects and Developmental Disabilities, Centers for Disease Control and Prevention, Atlanta, Georgia.

Johannes Czernin, M.D., Professor, Molecular and Medical Pharmacology, and Chief, Ahmanson Biological Imaging Division, David Geffen School of Medicine, University of California, Los Angeles, California.

Gerald N. DeLorenze, Ph.D., Research Scientist, Division of Research, Kaiser Permanente Northern California, Oakland, California.

David M. DeMarini, Ph.D., Genetic Toxicologist, Integrated Systems Toxicology Division, U.S. Environmental Protection Agency, Research Triangle Park, North Carolina.

Delia Dempsey, M.D., M.S., Assistant Professor, Pediatrics, Medicine and Clinical Pharmacology, Division of Clinical Pharmacology, University of California, San Francisco, San Francisco, California.

Phillip A. Dennis, M.D., Ph.D., Senior Investigator, Medical Oncology Branch, Center for Cancer Research, National Cancer Institute, National Institutes of Health, Bethesda, Maryland.

Yan Shirley Ding, Ph.D., Senior Service Fellow, Emergency Response and Air Toxicants Branch, Division of Laboratory Sciences, National Center for Environmental Health, Centers for Disease Control and Prevention, Atlanta, Georgia.

Mirjana V. Djordjevic, Ph.D., Program Director, Tobacco Control Research Branch, Behavioral Research Program, Division of Cancer Control and Population Sciences, National Cancer Institute, National Institutes of Health, Bethesda, Maryland.

Zigang Dong, M.D., M.S., Dr.P.H., Professor, The Hormel Institute, University of Minnesota, Austin, Minnesota.

Björn Eliasson, M.D., Ph.D., Associate Professor, Department of Internal Medicine, Sahlgrenska University Hospital, Göteborg, Sweden.

Lucinda England, M.D., M.S.P.H., Medical Epidemiologist, Maternal and Infant Health Branch, Division of Reproductive Health, National Center for Chronic Disease Prevention and Health Promotion, Centers for Disease Control and Prevention, Atlanta, Georgia.

Reginald Fant, Ph.D., Senior Scientist and Director, Pinney Associates, Bethesda, Maryland.

Garret A. FitzGerald, M.D., Chair, Department of Pharmacology, and Director, Institute for Translational Medicine and Therapeutics, University of Pennsylvania School of Medicine, Philadelphia, Pennsylvania.

Mari S. Golub, Ph.D., Staff Toxicologist, Office of Environmental Health Hazard Assessment, California Environmental Protection Agency, Sacramento, California.

Dorothy Hatsukami, Ph.D., Forster Family Professor in Cancer Prevention, Professor of Psychiatry, University of Minnesota Tobacco Use Research Center, University of Minnesota, Minneapolis, Minnesota.

Stephen S. Hecht, Ph.D., Wallin Professor of Cancer Prevention, Masonic Cancer Center, University of Minnesota, Minneapolis, Minnesota.

Marc K. Hellerstein, M.D., Ph.D., Professor (DH Calloway Chair in Human Nutrition), Department of Nutritional Sciences, University of California, Berkeley, California; and Professor of Endocrinology, Metabolism and Nutrition, Department of Medicine, University of California, San Francisco, California.

Jack E. Henningfield, Ph.D., Vice President Research and Health Policy, Pinney Associates, Bethesda, Maryland; and Professor, Adjunct, Department of Psychiatry and Behavioral Sciences, The Johns Hopkins University School of Medicine, Baltimore, Maryland.

Brian Hitsman, Ph.D., Assistant Professor, Department of Preventive Medicine, Northwestern University, Chicago, Illinois.

James C. Hogg, M.D., Ph.D., Emeritus Professor of Pathology and Lab Medicine, iCAPTURE Centre for Cardiovascular and Pulmonary Research, University of British Columbia and St. Paul's Hospital, Vancouver, British Columbia, Canada.

Anne M. Joseph, M.D., M.P.H., Wexler Professor of Medicine, and Director, Applied Clinical Research Program, University of Minnesota Medical School, Minneapolis, Minnesota.

Caryn Lerman, Ph.D., Mary W. Calkins Professor, Department of Psychiatry and Annenberg Public Policy Center; and Director, Tobacco Use Research Center, Scientific Director, Abramson Cancer Center, University of Pennsylvania, Philadelphia, Pennsylvania.

William MacNee, Professor, ELEGI Colt Research Labs, MRC Centre for Inflammation Research, The Queen's Medical Research Institute, University of Edinburgh, Edinburgh, Scotland, United Kingdom.

Athina Markou, Ph.D., Professor, Department of Psychiatry, School of Medicine, University of California, San Diego, La Jolla, California.

Robert Merritt, M.A., Branch Chief, Epidemiology and Surveillance Branch, Division of Heart Disease and Stroke Prevention, National Center for Chronic Disease Prevention and Health Promotion, Centers for Disease Control and Prevention, Atlanta, Georgia.

Dennis L. Molfese, Ph.D., Distinguished University Scholar and Professor, Birth Defects Center, University of Louisville, Louisville, Kentucky.

Masaaki Moriya, Ph.D., Research Professor, Laboratory of Chemical Biology, Department of Pharmacological Sciences, University at Stony Brook, The State University of New York, Stony Brook, New York.

Marcus Munafò, M.A., M.Sc., Ph.D., Reader in Biological Psychology, Department of Experimental Psychology, University of Bristol, Bristol, United Kingdom.

Sharon E. Murphy, Ph.D., Professor, Biochemistry, Molecular Biology and BioPhysics, Masonic Cancer Center, University of Minnesota, Minneapolis, Minnesota.

Raymond Niaura, Ph.D., Professor, Department of Psychiatry and Human Behavior, The Warren Alpert Medical School of Brown University; and Director, Transdisciplinary Research, Butler Hospital, Providence, Rhode Island.

James Pankow, Ph.D., Professor, Department of Chemistry, and Department of Civil and Environmental Engineering, Portland State University, Portland, Oregon.

Steve Pappas, Ph.D., Research Chemist, Emergency Response and Air Toxicants Branch, Division of Laboratory Sciences, National Center for Environmental Health, Centers for Disease Control and Prevention, Atlanta, Georgia.

Terry F. Pechacek, Ph.D., Associate Director for Science, Office on Smoking and Health, National Center for Chronic Disease Prevention and Health Promotion, Centers for Disease Control and Prevention, Atlanta, Georgia.

Kenneth A. Perkins, Ph.D., Professor of Psychiatry, Western Psychiatric Institute and Clinic, University of Pittsburgh School of Medicine, Pittsburgh, Pennsylvania.

Lisa A. Peterson, Ph.D., Professor, Masonic Cancer Center and the Division of Environmental Health Sciences, University of Minnesota, Minneapolis, Minnesota.

Gerd P. Pfeifer, Ph.D., Professor and Chair, Division of Biology, Beckman Research Institute, City of Hope National Medical Center, Duarte, California.

Halit Pinar, M.D., Director, Division of Perinatal and Pediatric Pathology, Women and Infants Hospital of Rhode Island; and Professor, Department of Pathology and Laboratory Medicine, Brown University Alpert School of Medicine, Providence, Rhode Island.

Gregory Polzin, Ph.D., Research Chemist, Emergency Response and Air Toxicants Branch, Division of Laboratory Sciences, National Center for Environmental Health, Centers for Disease Control and Prevention, Atlanta, Georgia.

Patricia Richter, Ph.D., DABT, Toxicologist, Office on Smoking and Health, National Center for Chronic Disease Prevention and Health Promotion, Centers for Disease Control and Prevention, Atlanta, Georgia.

Nancy Rigotti, M.D., Professor of Medicine, Harvard Medical School; and Director, Tobacco Research and Treatment Center, Massachusetts General Hospital, Boston, Massachusetts.

Wendie A. Robbins, Ph.D., Associate Professor, UCLA Schools of Nursing and Public Health, University of California, Los Angeles, California.

Andrew G. Salmon, M.A., D.Phil., Senior Toxicologist, Office of Environmental Health Hazard Assessment, California Department of Health Services, Oakland, California.

Jonathan M. Samet, M.D., M.S., Professor and Chairman, Department of Epidemiology, Bloomberg School of Public Health, The Johns Hopkins University, Baltimore, Maryland (1994–2008); and Director, USC Institute for Global Health, and Chairman, Department of Preventive Medicine, Keck School of Medicine, University of Southern California, Los Angeles, California (2008–present).

Robert M. Senior, M.D., Professor of Pulmonary Medicine, Cell Biology & Physiology, Division of Pulmonary and Critical Care, Washington University School of Medicine, St. Louis, Missouri.

Edwin K. Silverman, M.D., Ph.D., Associate Professor of Medicine, Harvard Medical School, Harvard University; and Associate Physician, Brigham and Women's Hospital, Boston, Massachusetts.

Margaret R. Spitz, M.D., M.P.H., Professor and Chair, Department of Epidemiology, The University of Texas, M. D. Anderson Cancer Center, Houston, Texas.

Stephen B. Stanfill, M.S., Chemist, Emergency Response and Air Toxicants Branch, National Center for Environmental Health, Centers for Disease Control and Prevention, Atlanta, Georgia.

Prudence Talbot, Ph.D., Professor of Cell Biology, Department of Cell Biology and Neuroscience, University of California, Riverside, California.

Anne Thorndike, M.D., M.P.H., Instructor in Medicine, General Medicine Unit, Massachusetts General Hospital, Boston, Massachusetts.

Clifford H. Watson, Ph.D., Lead Research Chemist, Emergency Response and Air Toxicants Branch, National Center for Environmental Health, Centers for Disease Control and Prevention, Atlanta, Georgia.

Gayle C. Windham, Ph.D., M.S.P.H., Research Scientist Supervisor, Chief, Environmental Surveillance Unit, Division of Environmental and Occupational Disease Control, California Department of Public Health, Richmond, California.

Weija (William) Wu, Ph.D., Senior Service Fellow, Emergency Response and Air Toxicants Branch, Division of Laboratory Sciences, National Center for Environmental Health, Centers for Disease Control and Prevention, Atlanta, Georgia.

Mitchell Zeller, J.D., Vice President for Policy and Strategic Communications, Pinney Associates, Bethesda, Maryland.

Reviewers were

Erik M. Augustson, Ph.D., M.P.H., Behavioral Scientist/ Psychologist, Tobacco Control Research Branch, Behavioral Research Program, Division of Cancer Control and Population Sciences, National Cancer Institute, National Institutes of Health, Bethesda, Maryland.

Cathy L. Backinger, Ph.D., M.P.H., Chief, Tobacco Control Research Branch, Behavioral Research Program, Division of Cancer Control and Population Sciences, National Cancer Institute, National Institutes of Health, Bethesda, Maryland.

Neal L. Benowitz M.D., Professor of Medicine and Biopharmaceutical Sciences and Chief, Division of Clinical Pharmacology and Experimental Therapeutics, University of California, San Francisco, California.

Mary Beth Bigley, Dr.P.H., M.S.N., A.N.P., Acting Director of the Office of Science and Communication, Office of the Surgeon General, Office of Public Health and Science, Office of the Secretary, U.S. Department of Health and Human Services, Washington, D.C.

Michele Bloch, M.D., Ph.D., Medical Officer, Tobacco Control Research Branch, Behavioral Research Program, Division of Cancer Control and Population Sciences, National Cancer Institute, National Institutes of Health, Bethesda, Maryland.

Naomi Breslau, Ph.D., Professor, Department of Epidemiology, Michigan State University, East Lansing, Michigan.

Klaus D. Brunnemann, M.S., Research Associate, New York Medical College, Valhalla, New York.

David M. Burns, M.D., Professor Emeritus, Department of Family and Preventive Medicine, School of Medicine, University of California, San Diego, California.

Pamela I. Clark, M.S.P.H., Ph.D., Research Professor, School of Public Health, University of Maryland, College Park, Maryland.

Gregory N. Connolly, D.M.D., M.P.H., Professor, Department of Society, Human Development, and Health, Harvard School of Public Health, Harvard University, Boston, Massachusetts.

William A. Corrigall, Ph.D., Professor of Psychiatry, University of Minnesota; and Senior Scientist, Minneapolis Medical Research Foundation, Minneapolis, Minnesota.

James D. Crapo, M.D., Professor of Medicine, National Jewish Health, Denver, Colorado.

Michael Criqui, M.D., M.P.H., Professor and Chief, Division of Preventive Medicine, Department of Family and Preventive Medicine; and Professor, Department of Medicine, School of Medicine, University of California, San Diego, La Jolla, California.

K. Michael Cummings, Ph.D., M.P.H., Senior Research Scientist, Chair, Department of Health Behavior, Division of Cancer Prevention and Population Sciences, Roswell Park Cancer Institute, Buffalo, New York.

Mirjana V. Djordjevic, Ph.D., Program Director, Tobacco Control Research Branch, Behavioral Research Program, Division of Cancer Control and Population Sciences, National Cancer Institute, National Institutes of Health, Bethesda, Maryland.

Erik Dybing, M.D., Ph.D., Division Director and Professor (retired), Division of Environmental Health, Norwegian Institute of Public Health, Oslo, Norway.

Michael Eriksen, Sc.D., Professor, and Director, Institute of Public Health, Georgia State University, Atlanta, Georgia.

Jefferson Fowles, Ph.D., Toxicologist, LyondellBasell Industries, Rotterdam, The Netherlands.

Adi F. Gazdar, M.D., Professor, Department of Pathology, University of Texas Southwestern Medical Center, Dallas, Texas.

Gary A. Giovino, Ph.D., M.S., Professor and Chair, Department of Health Behavior, School of Public Health and Health Professions, University at Buffalo, The State University of New York, Buffalo, New York.

Stanton Glantz, Ph.D., Professor of Medicine, Division of Cardiology, University of California, San Francisco, California.

Michael R. Guerin, Ph.D., Associate Division Director (retired), Oak Ridge National Laboratory, Knoxville, Tennessee.

Dorothy Hatsukami, Ph.D., Forster Family Professor in Cancer Prevention, Professor of Psychiatry, University of Minnesota Tobacco Use Research Center, University of Minnesota, Minneapolis, Minnesota.

Jack E. Henningfield, Ph.D., Vice President Research and Health Policy, Pinney Associates, Bethesda, Maryland; and Professor, Adjunct, Department of Psychiatry and Behavioral Sciences, The Johns Hopkins University School of Medicine, Baltimore, Maryland.

Allison Chausmer Hoffman, Ph.D., Program Director, National Institute on Drug Abuse, National Institutes of Health, Bethesda, Maryland.

John R. Hoidal, M.D., Professor and Chairman of Medicine, School of Medicine, University of Utah Health Sciences Center, Salt Lake City, Utah.

John E. Hokanson, Ph.D., Associate Professor and Chair, Department of Epidemiology, Colorado School of Public Health, University of Colorado, Denver, Aurora, Colorado.

John Hughes, M.D., Professor, Department of Psychiatry, University of Vermont, Burlington, Vermont.

Richard D. Hurt, M.D., Professor of Medicine, Mayo Clinic College of Medicine, Rochester, Minnesota.

Jared B. Jobe, Ph.D., FABMR, Program Director, Clinical Applications and Prevention Branch, Division of Prevention and Population Sciences, National Heart, Lung, and Blood Institute, National Institutes of Health, Bethesda, Maryland.

Rachel Kaufmann, Ph.D., M.P.H., Deputy Associate Director for Science, Office on Smoking and Health, National Center for Chronic Disease Prevention and Health Promotion, Centers for Disease Control and Prevention, Atlanta, Georgia.

Karl T. Kelsey, M.D., M.O.H., Professor, Community Health and Pathology and Laboratory Medicine, Director, Center for Environmental Health and Technology, Brown University, Providence, Rhode Island.

Juliette Kendrick, M.D., Medical Officer, Division of Reproductive Health, National Center for Chronic Disease Prevention and Health Promotion, Centers for Disease Control and Prevention, Atlanta, Georgia.

Martin Kharrazi, Ph.D., Chief, Program Research and Demonstration Section, Genetic Disease Screening Program, California Department of Public Health, Richmond, California.

Taline V. Khroyan, Ph.D., Behavioral Pharmacologist, SRI International, Center for Health Sciences, Menlo Park, California.

Walther N.M. Klerx, Food and Consumer Product Safety Authority, Eindhoven, The Netherlands.

Philip Lazarus, Ph.D., Professor of Pharmacology, College of Medicine, Pennsylvania State University, Milton S. Hershey Medical Center, Hershey, Pennsylvania.

Scott Leischow, Ph.D., Associate Director for Behavioral and Social Sciences Research, Arizona Cancer Center, The University of Arizona, Tucson, Arizona.

Christina N. Lessov-Schlaggar, Ph.D., Research Assistant Professor, Department of Psychiatry, Washington University School of Medicine, St. Louis, Missouri.

Catherine Lorraine, Director, Policy Development and Coordination Staff, Food and Drug Administration, Silver Spring, Maryland.

Cathy Melvin, Ph.D., M.P.H., Director, Child Health Services Program, Cecil G. Sheps Center for Health Services Research, University of North Carolina, Chapel Hill, North Carolina.

John D. Minna, M.D., Director, Hamon Center for Therapeutic Oncology Research, University of Texas Southwestern Medical Center, Dallas, Texas.

Joshua E. Muscat, Ph.D., Professor, Department of Public Health Sciences, College of Medicine, Pennsylvania State University, Milton S. Hershey Medical Center, Hershey, Pennsylvania.

Mark Parascandola, Ph.D., M.P.H., Epidemiologist, Tobacco Control Research Branch, Behavioral Research Program, Division of Cancer Control and Population Sciences, National Cancer Institute, National Institutes of Health, Bethesda, Maryland.

Wallace Pickworth, Ph.D., Health Research Leader, Battelle Centers for Public Health Research and Evaluation, Baltimore, Maryland.

John M. Pinney, President, Pinney Associates, Bethesda, Maryland.

Britt C. Reid, D.D.S., Ph.D., Chief, Modifiable Risk Factors Branch, Epidemiology and Genetics Research Program, Division of Cancer Control and Population Sciences, National Cancer Institute, National Institutes of Health, Bethesda, Maryland.

John E. Repine, M.D., Director, Webb-Waring Center, Waring Professor of Medicine and Pediatrics, School of Medicine, University of Colorado, Denver, Colorado.

William Rickert, Ph.D., Chief Executive Officer, Labstat International ULC, Kitchener, Ontario, Canada.

David J. Riley, M.D., Professor, Department of Medicine, University of Medicine and Dentistry of New Jersey, Robert Wood Johnson Medical School, Piscataway, New Jersey.

Scott Rogers, M.P.H., Public Health Advisor, Epidemiology and Genetics Research Program, Division of Cancer Control and Population Sciences, National Cancer Institute, National Institutes of Health, Bethesda, Maryland.

Dale P. Sandler, Ph.D., Chief, Epidemiology Branch, National Institute of Environmental Health Sciences, National Institutes of Health, Research Triangle Park, North Carolina.

David A. Scott, Ph.D., Associate Professor, Oral Health and Systemic Disease Research Group, University of Louisville, Louisville, Kentucky.

Harold E. Seifried, Ph.D., DABT, Chemist, Toxicologist, Industrial Hygienist (retired), Program Director, Nutritional Sciences Research Group, Division of Cancer Prevention, National Cancer Institute, National Institutes of Health, Bethesda, Maryland.

Peter G. Shields, M.D., Professor of Medicine and Oncology, Deputy Director, Lombardi Comprehensive Cancer Center, Georgetown University Medical Center, Washington, D.C.

Saul Shiffman, Ph.D., Research Professor, Psychology and Psychiatry, University of Pittsburgh; and Senior Scientific Advisor, Pinney Associates, Pittsburgh, Pennsylvania.

Donald R. Shopland, Sr., U.S. Public Health Service (retired), Ringgold, Georgia.

Stephen Sidney, M.D., M.P.H., Associate Director for Clinical Research, Division of Research, Kaiser Permanente, Oakland, California.

Gary D. Stoner, Ph.D., Professor Emeritus, Department of Internal Medicine, The Ohio State University, Columbus, Ohio.

Gary E. Swan, Ph.D., Director, Center for Health Sciences, SRI International Fellow, SRI International, Center for Health Sciences, Menlo Park, California.

Michael J. Thun, M.D., M.S., Vice President Emeritus, Epidemiology and Surveillance Research, American Cancer Society, Atlanta, Georgia.

Robert B. Wallace, M.D., M.Sc., Irene Ensminger Stecher Professor of Epidemiology and Internal Medicine, Department of Epidemiology, University of Iowa College of Public Health, Iowa City, Iowa.

Deborah M. Winn, Ph.D., Deputy Director, Epidemiology and Genetics Research Program, Division of Cancer Control and Population Sciences, National Cancer Institute, National Institutes of Health, Bethesda, Maryland.

Other contributors were

Charlotte Gerczak, M.L.A., Communications Associate, Department of Epidemiology, Bloomberg School of Public Health, The Johns Hopkins University, Baltimore, Maryland.

Roberta B. Gray, Administrative Supervisor to Dr. Jonathan M. Samet, Department of Epidemiology, Bloomberg School of Public Health, The Johns Hopkins University, Baltimore, Maryland.

Marta Gwinn, M.D., M.P.H., Medical Officer, Office of Public Health Genomics, National Center for Chronic Disease Prevention and Health Promotion, Centers for Disease Control and Prevention, Atlanta, Georgia.

Nancy Leonard, Administrative Coordinator to Dr. Jonathan M. Samet, Department of Epidemiology, Bloomberg School of Public Health, The Johns Hopkins University, Baltimore, Maryland.

Deborah Williams, Desktop Publishing Specialist to Dr. Jonathan M. Samet, Department of Epidemiology, Bloomberg School of Public Health, The Johns Hopkins University, Baltimore, Maryland.

How Tobacco Smoke Causes Disease: The Biology and Behavioral Basis for Smoking-Attributable Disease

Chapter 1
Introduction, Evaluation of Evidence on Mechanisms of Disease Production, and Summary

Introduction

Since the first of the series in 1964, reports of the Surgeon General have provided definitive syntheses of the evidence on smoking and health. The topics have ranged widely, including comprehensive coverage of the health effects of active and passive smoking (U.S. Department of Health, Education, and Welfare [USDHEW] 1979; U.S. Department of Health and Human Services [USDHHS] 1986, 2004, 2006), the impact of tobacco control policies (USDHHS 2000), and addiction (USDHHS 1988). A goal of these reports has been to synthesize available evidence for reaching conclusions on causality that have public health implications. In reaching conclusions on causation, the reports have followed a model that originated with the 1964 report: compilation of all relevant lines of scientific evidence, critical assessment of the evidence, evaluation of the strength of evidence by using guidelines for evidence evaluation, and a summary conclusion on causation (USDHEW 1964; USDHHS 2004). The 2004 Surgeon General's report provides a review of this approach and gives a set of ordered categories for classifying the strength of evidence for causality that was used in the 2004 and 2006 reports on active and involuntary smoking, respectively (Table 1.1). The Surgeon General's reports have established a long list of health consequences and diseases caused by tobacco use and exposure to tobacco smoke (Figure 1.1).

This report considers the biologic and behavioral mechanisms that may underlie the pathogenicity of tobacco smoke. Many Surgeon General's reports have considered research findings on mechanisms in assessing the biologic plausibility of associations observed in epidemiologic studies. Mechanisms of disease are important because they may provide plausibility, which is one of the guideline criteria for assessing evidence on causation. The 1964 report, for example, gave extensive consideration to the presence of carcinogens in tobacco smoke and the findings of animal models (USDHEW 1964). This new report, however, specifically reviews the evidence on the potential mechanisms by which smoking causes diseases and

considers whether a mechanism is likely to be operative in the production of human disease by tobacco smoke. This evidence is important to understand how smoking causes disease, to identify those who may be particularly susceptible, and to assess the potential risks of tobacco products. In addition, this evidence is relevant to achieving the tobacco-related goals and objectives in the Healthy People initiative—the nation's disease prevention and health promotion agenda—and to developing the interventions for our nation's tobacco cessation targets for the year 2020 (USDHHS 2009).

In the planning of this report, the diseases and other adverse outcomes causally linked to smoking served to define the scope of issues considered in each of the chapters. Because sufficient biologic plausibility had been established in prior reports for all causal conclusions, the evidence on biologic and behavioral mechanisms reviewed in this report complements and supports the causal conclusions established earlier. The report is *not* focused on whether the evidence supports the plausibility of a causal association of smoking with a particular disease. In fact, most of the diseases and other adverse outcomes considered in this report have long been causally linked to smoking. This report focuses on the health consequences caused by exposure to tobacco smoke and does not review the evidence on the mechanisms of how smokeless tobacco causes disease.

The determination of whether a particular mechanism figures in the causation of disease by tobacco smoke has potential implications for prevention, diagnosis, and treatment. A general schema for the causation of disease by tobacco smoke is provided in Figure 1.2. The assumption is that disease may be a consequence of one or more pathways, each possibly having one or more component mechanisms. The figure shows multiple pathways, each comprised potentially of multiple mechanisms. Moreover, the same mechanism might figure into several different pathways. For example, mutations of genes are likely to

Table 1.1   Four-level hierarchy for classifying the strength of causal inferences from available evidence

Level 1	Evidence is **sufficient** to infer a causal relationship
Level 2	Evidence is **suggestive but not sufficient** to infer a causal relationship
Level 3	Evidence is **inadequate** to infer the presence or absence of a causal relationship (which encompasses evidence that is sparse, of poor quality, or conflicting)
Level 4	Evidence is **suggestive of no causal relationship**

Source: U.S. Department of Health and Human Services 2004, 2006.

Figure 1.1   The health consequences causally linked to smoking and exposure to secondhand smoke

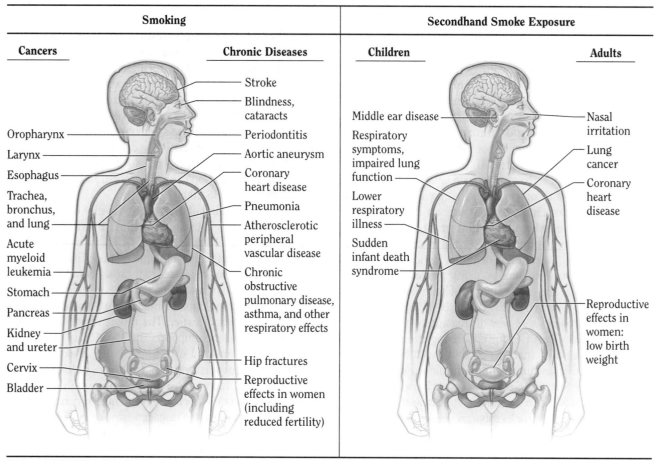

Source: USDHHS 2004, 2006.

figure into several different pathways for the causation of cancer. As a complex mixture with many different toxic components, tobacco smoke is likely to act through multiple pathways in causing disease, and multiple genes may be involved. Genes may modulate the activity of these pathways, and there may also be connections between the pathways. Other environmental factors may act through the same pathways as tobacco smoke or through different pathways and, thereby, augment the contribution of smoking to disease incidence. For example, the combined effects of smoking and radon may contribute to causing lung cancer (National Research Council 1998).

Pathways and mechanisms by which active and passive smoking contribute to causation of cardiovascular disease are illustrated in Figure 1.3 (Ambrose and Barua 2004). This depiction of cigarette components in the "tar phase" and "gas phase" shows their action through several interacting pathways, indicating a role for genetic as well as other factors.

The characterization of mechanisms by which smoking causes disease could lead to applications of this knowledge to public health by (1) assessing tobacco products for their potential to cause injury through a particular mechanism, (2) developing biomarkers of injury to identify smokers at early stages of disease development, (3) identifying persons at risk on a genetic basis through the operation of a particular mechanism, (4) providing a basis for preventive therapies that block or reverse the underlying process of injury, and (5) identifying the contribution of smoking to causation of diseases with multiple etiologic factors. Consequently, research continues on the mechanisms by which smoking causes disease, even though the evidence has long been sufficient to infer that active smoking and exposure to secondhand smoke cause numerous diseases (USDHHS 2004, 2006). In addition, the resulting understanding of mechanisms is likely to prove applicable to diseases caused not only by

Figure 1.2   General schema for the causation of disease by tobacco smoke

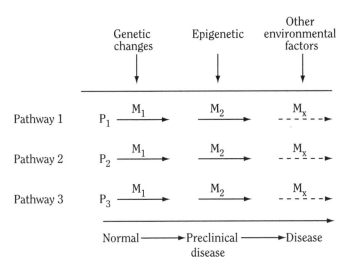

Note: **M** = disease mechanisms; **P** = disease pathways.

smoking but by other agents that may act through some of the same mechanisms.

This report is written at a time when new research methods have facilitated exploration of the mechanisms by which smoking causes disease at a depth not previously possible. With the powerful methods of molecular and cellular research, disease pathogenesis can now be studied at the molecular level, and animal models can be developed to explore specific pathways of injury. Consequently, the range of evidence considered in this report is broad, coming from clinical studies, animal models, and in vitro systems. The coverage extends from research at the molecular level to population-level biomarker studies.

Evaluation of Evidence on Mechanisms of Disease Production

Approaches for evaluation and synthesis of evidence on mechanisms have not been previously proposed in Surgeon General's reports, although substantial emphasis has been placed on biologic mechanisms. The 1964 report indicated that three lines of evidence would be reviewed: animal experiments, clinical and autopsy studies, and population studies. It further commented on the essential nature of all three lines of evidence in reaching conclusions on causality. That report and subsequent reports of the Surgeon General, however, have given only general guidance on assessing biologic plausibility (USDHEW

1964; USDHHS 2004). The 1964 report used the term "coherence of the association" as one of the criteria for causality (Table 1.2). In addressing lung cancer, the report stated: "A final criterion for the appraisal of causal significance of an association is its coherence with known facts in the natural history and biology of the disease" (USDHEW 1964, p. 185).

The 1982 report of the Surgeon General noted:

Coherence is clearly established when the actual mechanism of disease production is defined. Coherence exists, nonetheless, although of a lesser magnitude, when there is enough evidence to support a plausible mechanism, but not a detailed understanding of each step in the chain of events by which a given etiologic agent produces disease (USDHHS 1982, p. 20).

The 2004 report discussed coherence, plausibility, and analogy together, commenting:

Although the original definitions of these criteria were subtly different, in practice they have been treated essentially as one idea: that a proposed causal relationship not violate known scientific principles, and that it be consistent with experimentally demonstrated biologic mechanisms and other relevant data, such as ecologic patterns of disease…. In addition, if biologic understanding can be used to set aside explanations other than a causal association, it offers further support for causality. Together, these criteria can serve both to support a causal claim (by supporting the proposed mechanism) or refute it (by showing that the proposed mechanism is unlikely) (USDHHS 2004, p. 22).

Hill (1965) listed both plausibility and coherence among his nine criteria but did not offer a sharp distinction between the two. He commented on the linkage of the concept of plausibility to the contemporary state of knowledge, and his views of coherence were largely consistent with statements in the 1964 Surgeon General's report.

Current evidence on mechanisms of disease causation raises issues that could not have been anticipated at the time of the 1964 report. With advances in laboratory research over the last several decades, researchers are challenged to interpret molecular and cellular evidence on mechanisms and causation. The need for new approaches to interpret such evidence has been recognized in several research areas including infectious diseases and cancer. Approaches have been proposed by agencies and researchers that assess carcinogens.

Figure 1.3   Potential pathways and mechanisms for cardiovascular dysfunction mediated by cigarette smoking

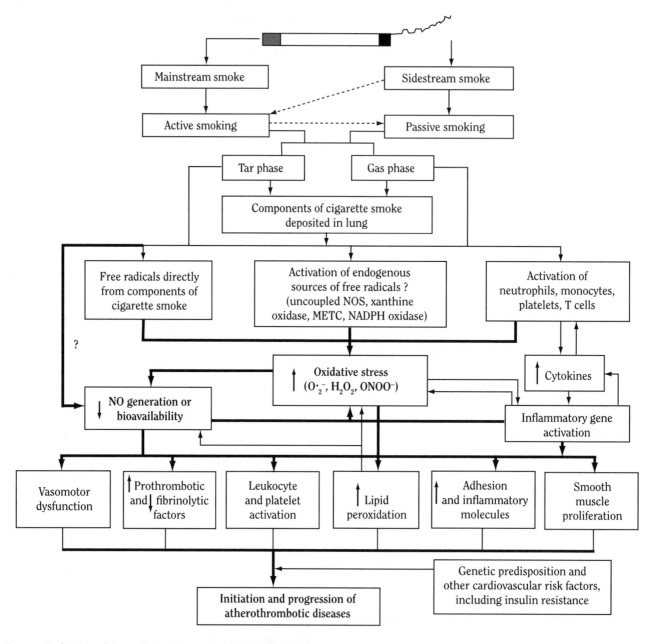

Source: Ambrose and Barua 2004. Reprinted with permission from Elsevier, © 2004.
Note: The bold boxes and arrows in the flow diagram represent the probable central mechanisms in the complex pathophysiology of atherothrombotic disease mediated by cigarette smoking. H_2O_2 = hydrogen peroxide; **METC** = mitochondrial electron transport chain; **NADPH** = reduced nicotinamide adenine dinucleotide phosphate; **NO** = nitric oxide; **NOS** = nitric oxide synthase; $O_2^{\cdot-}$ = superoxide anion; **ONOO$^-$** = peroxynitrite.

In infectious disease research, the arrival of molecular techniques for studying microbes led to a recognition that extensions of Koch's postulates were needed to accommodate this new type of information (Falkow 1988; Fredericks and Relman 1996). Falkow (1988) proposed "molecular Koch's postulates" for considering the role of specific microbial genes in pathogenicity. Fredericks and Relman (1996) listed seven criteria for evaluating whether a disease could be attributed to a putatively identified pathogen, found by sequence-based methods. They emphasized that "coherence and plausibility are important" (p. 30). Pagano and colleagues (2004) also acknowledged the complexities of causally linking cancer to infectious agents.

Research has broadened and increased the literature on mechanisms of carcinogenesis and has contributed to a similar rationale for developing approaches to review information on mechanisms. Approaches have been proposed by the International Agency for Research on Cancer (IARC) and the U.S. Environmental Protection Agency (EPA).

In the preamble to its monographs on carcinogenicity, IARC describes its approach for characterizing the strength of evidence regarding mechanisms relevant to the agent being evaluated (IARC 2006). For animal experiments, IARC offers a four-level classification of the strength of evidence, which parallels the categories of the 2004 Surgeon General's report: *sufficient evidence of carcinogenicity, limited evidence of carcinogenicity, inadequate evidence of carcinogenicity,* and *evidence suggesting lack of carcinogenicity.* The strength of evidence on mechanisms is described with terms such as "weak," "moderate," or "strong." The IARC working group preparing the monographs is also charged with assessing whether the mechanism is operative in humans. Guidance is given for evaluating the role of a mechanism in experimental animals. Emphasis is placed on consistency across experimental systems and on biologic plausibility and coherence.

EPA covers the identification of a "mode of action" in its *Guidelines for Carcinogen Risk Assessment* (USEPA 2005). Mode of action refers to the process by which an agent causes disease but at a less detailed and specific level than is intended by mechanism of action. In these guidelines, EPA modified the Hill (1965) criteria, offering its framework for evaluating evidence on mode of action. The steps for evaluating a hypothesized mode of action include (1) description of the hypothesized mode of action, (2) discussion of the experimental support for this mode of action, (3) consideration of the possibility of other modes of action, and (4) conclusions about the hypothesized mode of action. In regard to evaluating the experimental support, the *Guidelines* list strength, consistency, and specificity of association as considerations. The finding of dose-response is given weight as is proper temporal ordering. Finally, the *Guidelines* call for biologic plausibility and coherence: "It is important that the hypothesized mode of action and the events that are part of it be based on contemporaneous understanding of the biology of cancer to be accepted" (pp. 2–46). Standard descriptors for the strength of evidence are not mentioned.

Mechanisms of Action: Necessary, Sufficient, or Neither

For many of the diseases caused by smoking, multiple mechanisms are likely to be involved. For example, study results indicate that general and specific DNA injury and repair processes contribute to carcinogenesis. Causal agents have been classified as "necessary," "sufficient," or "neither necessary nor sufficient" (Rothman 1976). A necessary cause is requisite for occurrence of the disease;

Table 1.2   Causal criteria

1964 Report of the Advisory Committee to the U.S. Surgeon General	Austin Bradford Hill's criteria
1. Consistency of the association	1. Strength
2. Strength of the association	2. Consistency
3. Specificity of the association	3. Specificity
4. Temporal relationship of the association	4. Temporality
5. Coherence of the association	5. Biological gradient
	6. Plausibility
	7. Coherence
	8. Experiment
	9. Analogy

Source: U.S. Department of Health, Education, and Welfare 1964; Hill 1965.

severe acute respiratory syndrome (SARS), for example, cannot occur without infection with the SARS coronavirus. Exposure to a sufficient cause is invariably followed by occurrence of the disease. For chronic diseases, many causal factors are in the category "neither necessary nor sufficient"; cigarette smoking, for example, does not cause lung cancer in all smokers, and some cases occur among lifetime nonsmokers.

A similar formulation of "necessary" and "sufficient" might be extended to considering the mechanisms of disease production. If there is only one pathway to a disease, and a particular mechanism is included in that pathway, then the mechanism is required for the development of the disease and would be considered "necessary." A mechanism that is a component of one or more but not all pathways would be considered "sufficient." Application of this type of classification would require a depth of understanding of the interplay of mechanisms that has not been reached for the pathogenesis of most diseases caused by tobacco smoking. Consequently, the chapters of this report largely address mechanisms of disease causation one by one without placing them into categories of necessary, sufficient, or neither.

Description of Evidence on Mechanisms of Disease Production

Because evidence related to mechanisms of diseases caused by smoking is still evolving, this report uses a descriptive approach in reviewing and presenting the evidence. The chapters are based on review of the most relevant studies at the time they were written. A summary is given on the basis of the strength of evidence for each mechanism considered.

As for causal inference in regard to smoking and disease, the finding that a particular mechanism plays a role in the production of disease by smoking has implications. The finding could point to a biomarker indicating that the pathway is active, or it could indicate the possibility of new preventive therapies to obviate the particular pathway.

Scientific Basis of the Report

The statements and conclusions throughout this report are documented by citation of studies published in the scientific literature. For the most part, this report cites peer-reviewed journal articles, including reviews that integrate findings from numerous studies, and books by recognized experts. When a study has been accepted for publication but the publication has not yet been issued, owing to the delay between acceptance and final publication, the study is referred to as "in press." This report also refers, on occasion, to unpublished research such as a presentation at a professional meeting or a personal communication from the researcher. These personal references are to acknowledge experts whose research is in progress.

Development of the Report

This report of the Surgeon General was prepared by the Office on Smoking and Health, National Center for Chronic Disease Prevention and Health Promotion, Centers for Disease Control and Prevention, USDHHS. Initial chapters were written by 64 experts selected because of their knowledge of and familiarity with the topics presented here. These contributions are summarized in seven chapters evaluated by more than 30 peer reviewers. The entire manuscript was then sent to more than 20 scientists and other experts, who examined it for scientific integrity. After each review cycle, the drafts were revised by the editors on the basis of the reviewers' comments. Subsequently, the report was reviewed by various institutes and agencies within USDHHS. Publication lags, even short ones, prevent an up-to-the-minute inclusion of all recently published articles and data. Therefore, by the time the public reads this report, additional studies or data may have been published.

Throughout this report, genes are represented by their abbreviations in italics. In many cases, proteins and enzymes related to these genes have the same abbreviation, presented in roman type. Definitions, alternative genetic symbols, related proteins and enzymes, and polymorphisms and variant genotypes are listed alphabetically by gene abbreviation in the table at the end of this report, "Definitions and Alternative Nomenclature of Genetic Symbols Used in This Report."

On June 22, 2009, President Barack Obama signed into law legislation granting authority to the U.S. Food and Drug Administration to regulate all tobacco products (Family Smoking Prevention and Tobacco Control Act 2009 [Public Law 111-31]). Terms used in this report reflect terms in the scientific literature and may not meet the definitions under the Tobacco Control Act.

Major Conclusions

The scientific evidence supports the following major conclusions:

1. The evidence on the mechanisms by which smoking causes disease indicates that there is no risk-free level of exposure to tobacco smoke.

2. Inhaling the complex chemical mixture of combustion compounds in tobacco smoke causes adverse health outcomes, particularly cancer and cardiovascular and pulmonary diseases, through mechanisms that include DNA damage, inflammation, and oxidative stress.

3. Through multiple defined mechanisms, the risk and severity of many adverse health outcomes caused by smoking are directly related to the duration and level of exposure to tobacco smoke.

4. Sustained use and long-term exposures to tobacco smoke are due to the powerfully addicting effects of tobacco products, which are mediated by diverse actions of nicotine and perhaps other compounds, at multiple types of nicotinic receptors in the brain.

5. Low levels of exposure, including exposures to secondhand tobacco smoke, lead to a rapid and sharp increase in endothelial dysfunction and inflammation, which are implicated in acute cardiovascular events and thrombosis.

6. There is insufficient evidence that product modification strategies to lower emissions of specific toxicants in tobacco smoke reduce risk for the major adverse health outcomes.

Chapter Conclusions

Chapter 2. The Changing Cigarette

1. The evidence indicates that changing cigarette designs over the last five decades, including filtered, low-tar, and "light" variations, have not reduced overall disease risk among smokers and may have hindered prevention and cessation efforts.

2. There is insufficient evidence to determine whether novel tobacco products reduce individual and population health risks.

3. The overall health of the public could be harmed if the introduction of novel tobacco products encourages tobacco use among people who would otherwise be unlikely to use a tobacco product or delays cessation among persons who would otherwise quit using tobacco altogether.

Chapter 3. Chemistry and Toxicology of Cigarette Smoke and Biomarkers of Exposure and Harm

1. In spite of uncertainties concerning whether particular cigarette smoke constituents are responsible for specific adverse health outcomes, there is broad scientific agreement that several of the major classes of chemicals in the combustion emissions of burned tobacco are toxic and carcinogenic.

2. The design characteristics of cigarettes, including ventilation features, filters, and paper porosity, have a significant influence on the levels of toxic and carcinogenic chemicals in the inhaled smoke.

3. The different types of tobacco lamina (e.g., bright, burley, or oriental) that are combined to produce a specific tobacco blend have a significant influence on the levels of toxic and carcinogenic chemicals in the combustion emissions of burned tobacco.

4. There is no available cigarette machine-smoking method that can be used to accurately predict doses of the chemical constituents of tobacco smoke received when using tobacco products.

5. Tobacco-specific biomarkers (nicotine and its metabolites and the tobacco-specific nitrosamines) have been validated as quantitative measures of exposure to tobacco smoke among smokers of cigarettes of similar design who do not use other tobacco-containing products.

6. Although biomarkers of potential harm exist for most tobacco-related diseases, many are not specific to tobacco and levels are also influenced by diet, occupation, or other lifestyle or environmental factors.

Chapter 4. Nicotine Addiction: Past and Present

1. Nicotine is the key chemical compound that causes and sustains the powerful addicting effects of commercial tobacco products.

2. The powerful addicting effects of commercial tobacco products are mediated by diverse actions of nicotine at multiple types of nicotinic receptors in the brain.

3. Evidence is suggestive that there may be psychosocial, biologic, and genetic determinants associated with different trajectories observed among population subgroups as they move from experimentation to heavy smoking.

4. Inherited genetic variation in genes such as *CYP2A6* contributes to the differing patterns of smoking behavior and smoking cessation.

5. Evidence is consistent that individual differences in smoking histories and severity of withdrawal symptoms are related to successful recovery from nicotine addiction.

Chapter 5. Cancer

1. The doses of cigarette smoke carcinogens resulting from inhalation of tobacco smoke are reflected in levels of these carcinogens or their metabolites in the urine of smokers. Certain biomarkers are associated with exposure to specific cigarette smoke carcinogens, such as urinary metabolites of the tobacco-specific nitrosamine 4-(methylnitrosamino)-1-(3-pyridyl)-1-butanone and hemoglobin adducts of aromatic amines.

2. The metabolic activation of cigarette smoke carcinogens by cytochrome P-450 enzymes has a direct effect on the formation of DNA adducts.

3. There is consistent evidence that a combination of polymorphisms in the *CYP1A1* and *GSTM1* genes leads to higher DNA adduct levels in smokers and higher relative risks for lung cancer than in those smokers without this genetic profile.

4. Carcinogen exposure and resulting DNA damage observed in smokers results directly in the numerous cytogenetic changes present in lung cancer.

5. Smoking increases the frequency of DNA adducts of cigarette smoke carcinogens such as benzo[a]pyrene and tobacco-specific nitrosamines in the lung and other organs.

6. Exposure to cigarette smoke carcinogens leads to DNA damage and subsequent mutations in *TP53* and *KRAS* in lung cancer.

7. There is consistent evidence that smoking leads to the presence of promoter methylation of key tumor suppressor genes such as *P16* in lung cancer and other smoking-caused cancers.

8. There is consistent evidence that smoke constituents such as nicotine and 4-(methylnitrosamino)-1-(3-pyridyl)-1-butanone can activate signal transduction pathways directly through receptor-mediated events, allowing the survival of damaged epithelial cells that would normally die.

9. There is consistent evidence for an inherited susceptibility of lung cancer with some less common genotypes unrelated to a familial clustering of smoking behaviors.

10. Smoking cessation remains the only proven strategy for reducing the pathogenic processes leading to cancer in that the specific contribution of many tobacco carcinogens, alone or in combination, to the development of cancer has not been identified.

Chapter 6. Cardiovascular Diseases

1. There is a nonlinear dose response between exposure to tobacco smoke and cardiovascular risk, with a sharp increase at low levels of exposure (including exposures from secondhand smoke or infrequent cigarette smoking) and a shallower dose-response relationship as the number of cigarettes smoked per day increases.

2. Cigarette smoking leads to endothelial injury and dysfunction in both coronary and peripheral arteries. There is consistent evidence that oxidizing chemicals and nicotine are responsible for endothelial dysfunction.

3. Tobacco smoke exposure leads to an increased risk of thrombosis, a major factor in the pathogenesis of smoking-induced cardiovascular events.

4. Cigarette smoking produces a chronic inflammatory state that contributes to the atherogenic disease processes and elevates levels of biomarkers of inflammation, known powerful predictors of cardiovascular events.

5. Cigarette smoking produces an atherogenic lipid profile, primarily due to an increase in triglycerides and a decrease in high-density lipoprotein cholesterol.

6. Smoking cessation reduces the risk of cardiovascular morbidity and mortality for smokers with or without coronary heart disease.

7. The use of nicotine or other medications to facilitate smoking cessation in people with known cardiovascular disease produces far less risk than the risk of continued smoking.

8. The evidence to date does not establish that a reduction of cigarette consumption (that is, smoking fewer cigarettes per day) reduces the risks of cardiovascular disease.

9. Cigarette smoking produces insulin resistance and chronic inflammation, which can accelerate macrovascular and microvascular complications, including nephropathy.

Chapter 7. Pulmonary Diseases

1. Oxidative stress from exposure to tobacco smoke has a role in the pathogenetic process leading to chronic obstructive pulmonary disease.

2. Protease-antiprotease imbalance has a role in the pathogenesis of emphysema.

3. Inherited genetic variation in genes such as *SERPINA3* is involved in the pathogenesis of tobacco-caused chronic obstructive pulmonary disease.

4. Smoking cessation remains the only proven strategy for reducing the pathogenetic processes leading to chronic obstructive pulmonary disease.

Chapter 8. Reproductive and Developmental Effects

1. There is consistent evidence that links smoking in men to chromosome changes or DNA damage in sperm (germ cells), affecting male fertility, pregnancy viability, and anomalies in offspring.

2. There is consistent evidence for association of periconceptional smoking to cleft lip with or without cleft palate.

3. There is consistent evidence that increases in follicle-stimulating hormone levels and decreases in estrogen and progesterone are associated with cigarette smoking in women, at least in part due to effects of nicotine on the endocrine system.

4. There is consistent evidence that maternal smoking leads to transient increases in maternal heart rate and blood pressure (primarily diastolic), probably mediated by the release of norepinephrine and epinephrine into the circulatory system.

5. There is consistent evidence that links maternal smoking to interference in the physiological transformation of spiral arteries and thickening of the villous membrane in forming the placenta; placental problems could lead to fetal loss, preterm delivery, or low birth weight.

6. There is consistent evidence of the presence of histopathologic changes in the fetus from maternal smoking, particularly in the lung and brain.

7. There is consistent evidence that suggests smoking leads to immunosuppressive effects, including dysregulation of the inflammatory response, that may lead to miscarriage and preterm delivery.

8. There is consistent evidence that suggests a role for polycyclic aromatic hydrocarbons from tobacco smoke in the adverse effects of maternal smoking on a variety of reproductive and developmental endpoints.

9. There is consistent evidence that tobacco smoke exposure leads to diminished oviductal functioning, which could impair fertilization.

10. There is consistent evidence that links prenatal smoke exposure and genetic variations in metabolizing enzymes such as GSTT1 with increased risk of adverse pregnancy outcomes such as lowered birth weight and reduced gestation.

11. There is consistent evidence that genetic polymorphisms, such as variants in transforming growth factor-alpha, modify the risks of oral clefting in offspring related to maternal smoking.

12. There is consistent evidence that carbon monoxide leads to birth weight deficits and may play a role in neurologic deficits (cognitive and neurobehavioral endpoints) in the offspring of smokers.

References

Ambrose JA, Barua RS. The pathophysiology of cigarette smoking and cardiovascular disease: an update. *Journal of the American College of Cardiology* 2004; 43(10):1731–7.

Falkow S. Molecular Koch's postulates applied to microbial pathogenicity. *Reviews of Infectious Diseases* 1988; 10(Suppl 2):S274–S276.

Fredericks DN, Relman DA. Sequence-based identification of microbial pathogens; a reconsideration of Koch's postulates. *Clinical Microbiology Reviews* 1996; 9(1):18–33.

Hill AB. The environment and disease: association or causation? *Proceedings of the Royal Society of Medicine* 1965;58:295–300.

International Agency for Research on Cancer. IARC Monographs on the Evaluation of Carcinogenic Risk to Humans: Preamble, 2006; <http://monographs.iarc.fr/ENG/Preamble/CurrentPreamble.pdf>; accessed: December 10, 2008.

National Research Council. *Research Priorities for Airborne Particulate Matter. I: Immediate Priorities and a Long-Range Research Portfolio.* Washington: National Academy Press, 1998.

Pagano JS, Blaser M, Buendia M-A, Damania B, Khalili K, Raab-Traub N, Roizman B. Infectious agents and cancer: criteria for a causal relation. *Seminars in Cancer Biology* 2004;14(6):453–71.

Rothman KJ. Causes. *American Journal of Epidemiology* 1976;104(6):587–92.

U.S. Department of Health and Human Services. *The Health Consequences of Smoking: Cancer. A Report of the Surgeon General.* Rockville (MD): U.S. Department of Health and Human Services, Public Health Service, Office on Smoking and Health, 1982. DHHS Publication No. (PHS) 82-50179.

U.S. Department of Health and Human Services. *The Health Consequences of Involuntary Smoking. A Report of the Surgeon General.* Rockville (MD): U.S. Department of Health and Human Services, Public Health Service, Centers for Disease Control, Center for Health Promotion and Education, Office on Smoking and Health, 1986. DHHS Publication No. (CDC) 87-8398.

U.S. Department of Health and Human Services. *The Health Consequences of Smoking: Nicotine Addiction. A Report of the Surgeon General.* Atlanta: U.S. Department of Health and Human Services, Public Health Service, Centers for Disease Control, National Center for Chronic Disease Prevention and Health Promotion, Office on Smoking and Health, 1988. DHHS Publication No. (CDC) 88-8406.

U.S. Department of Health and Human Services. *Reducing Tobacco Use. A Report of the Surgeon General.* Atlanta: U.S. Department of Health and Human Services, Centers for Disease Control and Prevention, National Center for Chronic Disease Prevention and Health Promotion, Office on Smoking and Health, 2000.

U.S. Department of Health and Human Services. *The Health Consequences of Smoking: A Report of the Surgeon General.* Atlanta: U.S. Department of Health and Human Services, Centers for Disease Control and Prevention, National Center for Chronic Disease Prevention and Health Promotion, Office on Smoking and Health, 2004.

U.S. Department of Health and Human Services. *The Health Consequences of Involuntary Exposure to Tobacco Smoke: A Report of the Surgeon General.* Atlanta: U.S. Department of Health and Human Services, Centers for Disease Control and Prevention, Coordinating Center for Health Promotion, National Center for Chronic Disease Prevention and Health Promotion, Office on Smoking and Health, 2006.

U.S. Department of Health and Human Services. Healthy People, 2009; <http://www.healthypeople.gov>; accessed: September 28, 2009.

U.S. Department of Health, Education, and Welfare. *Smoking and Health: Report of the Advisory Committee to the Surgeon General of the Public Health Service.* Washington: U.S. Department of Health, Education, and Welfare, Public Health Service, Center for Disease Control, 1964. PHS Publication No. 1103.

U.S. Department of Health, Education, and Welfare. *Smoking and Health: A Report of the Surgeon General.* Washington: U.S. Department of Health, Education, and Welfare, Public Health Service, Office of the Assistant Secretary for Health, Office on Smoking and Health, 1979. DHEW Publication No. (PHS) 79-50066.

U.S. Environmental Protection Agency. *Guidelines for Carcinogen Risk Assessment.* Washington: U.S. Environmental Protection Agency, Risk Assessment Forum, 2005. EPA Publication No. EPA/630/P-013/001F.

Chapter 2
The Changing Cigarette

Introduction

Cigarettes are the most common form of tobacco used in most of the world (World Health Organization [WHO] 2006) and cause 443,000 deaths in the United States each year (U.S. Department of Health and Human Services [USDHHS] 1986, 1988; National Cancer Institute [NCI] 1997; Centers for Disease Control and Prevention [CDC] 2008). The primary short- and long-range strategies for reducing deaths associated with tobacco use are cessation and prevention, respectively, along with reduction of secondhand smoke exposure (Warner et al. 1998; USDHHS 2000; Stratton et al. 2001; WHO 2003a). Another concept that has been considered is changing the cigarette itself to make it less toxic. The concept of modifying conventional cigarettes to be potentially less harmful is not new. Beginning in the 1950s, the tobacco industry embarked on efforts to modify cigarettes in response to growing public awareness of the health hazards of tobacco use, primarily through reducing machine-measured tar and nicotine content (NCI 1996). However, evidence now demonstrates that these modifications did not reduce the risk of cigarette smoking and in addition may have undermined efforts to prevent tobacco use and promote cessation (NCI 2001). In recent years, a range of new products have been introduced and marketed to smokers as an alternative to conventional cigarettes, sometimes accompanied by messages, explicit or implied, that they offer reduced exposure to toxic substances or risk of disease (Pederson and Nelson 2007). The focus of this chapter is on the health consequences of changes in cigarette design over time. Coverage of novel cigarette products is not intended to be comprehensive or current, because this market is rapidly evolving.

Cigarette Design Changes over the Years

The history of tobacco product design and marketing has been discussed elsewhere and need not be repeated (Reynolds and Shachtman 1989; Goodman 1993, 2004; Hilts 1996; Kluger 1996; Tate 1999; Brandt 2007). However, the tobacco industry's internal memoranda and other documents make it clear that the core concept and function of the cigarette has changed little since its invention in the early part of the nineteenth century; namely, it is a tobacco-derived product for delivering nicotine to the user (University of California at San Francisco [UCSF] 2008).

By the early 1950s, mounting scientific evidence began to implicate cigarette smoking in the development of serious respiratory, heart, and neoplastic diseases (Royal College of Physicians of London 1962; U.S. Department of Health, Education, and Welfare [USDHEW] 1964). This evidence created a new force in cigarette design that has remained prominent to this day: to design cigarettes that could be marketed as addressing the health concerns of both cigarette smokers and health professionals by reducing toxicants (Slade and Henningfield 1998; Stratton et al. 2001). Early efforts to reduce toxicants focused on efforts to reduce the overall tar (e.g., total particulate matter minus nicotine and water content) and nicotine yields of cigarettes.

The first major design change to reduce tar and nicotine yields was the introduction of filters in the 1950s.

Before 1950, only 0.6 percent of cigarettes were filtered, but the increasing lay press coverage of the potential dangers of smoking led to an explosion of filter development and marketing. By 1960, filtered cigarettes represented 51 percent of the cigarette market (USDHHS 1989). By 2005, they represented 99 percent of the market. Major design efforts to reduce machine-measured tar and nicotine yields continued throughout the 1960s and 1970s with the introduction of "light" and low-tar cigarettes. Efforts to further reduce machine-measured tar and nicotine yields included the use of porous cigarette paper, reconstituted tobacco, filter tip ventilation, and the use of expanded tobacco (Hoffmann et al. 1996).

The initial focus on reduction of tar and nicotine yields was supported by early case-control studies suggesting that cancer risks were reduced by increased use of filters and decreased machine-measured tar delivery, and laboratory studies appeared to confirm this dose-response relationship. This research led to the seemingly reasonable conclusion that cigarettes with lower machine-measured tar and nicotine might pose fewer hazards, assuming that smokers did not increase the number of cigarettes they smoked per day or otherwise change their smoking behaviors (USDHEW 1967, 1969, 1971, 1974; USDHHS 1981; Stratton et al. 2001). Thus, it was widely accepted that declining tar and nicotine levels could lead to decreased disease risk. The concept that reduced exposure to toxicants could reduce disease risk was supported by previous Surgeon General's reports (USDHEW 1969). In 1966, the U.S. Public Health Service recommended "the progressive reduction of the 'tar' and nicotine content of cigarette smoke" (USDHEW 1966, p. 2), and the Federal Trade Commission (FTC) announced that it would generally permit cigarette companies to make marketing claims about tar and nicotine yields as long as those statements were based on a uniform machine-based test method for measuring tar and nicotine yields, subsequently known as "the FTC method" (Peeler 1996; Pillsbury 1996).

Efforts to reduce tar and nicotine yields as measured on the basis of machine-smoking conditions were successful. The sales-weighted deliveries in U.S. cigarette smoke decreased from 38 milligrams (mg) of tar and 2.7 mg of nicotine in 1954 to 12 mg of tar and 0.95 mg of nicotine in 1993 (Hoffmann et al. 1996). Machine measurements of tar have shown little change since then, and machine measurements of nicotine delivery have remained at approximately 0.9 mg per cigarette since 1981 (*Federal Register* 1995, 1996; Slade et al. 1995; Hurt and Robertson 1998; Kessler 2001).

Unfortunately, with the accrual and evaluation of additional data, the evidence today does not demonstrate that efforts to lower machine-measured tar and nicotine yields actually decreased the health risks of smoking, primarily because these changes did not reduce smokers' actual exposure to tobacco toxicants (NCI 2001; USDHHS 2004). Indeed, to the extent that filters and other efforts to reduce machine-measured tar and nicotine reduced smokers' health concerns, and thereby delayed quitting and/or increased cigarette use, they may have contributed to an overall increase in cigarette-caused mortality (Stratton et al. 2001).

As mentioned above, for example, the first effort to change the design of cigarettes was the addition of the filter. In theory, use of filter technologies can remove substantial amounts of a wide variety of toxicants (Browne 1990; Hoffmann and Hoffmann 1997). In fact, however, evidence on the ability of filters to reduce harm is not clear (Slade 1993; NCI 2001; Stratton et al. 2001). And, some novel filter designs may introduce new toxicants such as asbestos (Slade 1993), carbon (Pauly et al. 1997), and glass (Pauly et al. 1998). The wide variation in filter technology across brands and over time precludes general conclusions about whether filters increased or decreased exposure of smokers to toxicants.

Similarly, a variety of design features made it possible for cigarette smokers to compensate, that is, easily ingest severalfold higher amounts of tar and nicotine than the yields obtained when using the machine-based FTC method (Djordjevic et al. 2000; NCI 2001; Stratton et al.

2001; WHO 2003c). Most important was the introduction of ventilation holes in the cigarette filters, which allowed smoke to escape during machine testing. In the 1980s, researchers discovered that smokers covered these ventilation holes with their fingers, negating the effect of the holes in reducing smoke exposure (Kozlowski et al. 1980, 2002, 2006). Moreover, subsequent research demonstrated that the use of ventilation holes produced higher levels of free-base nicotine, which led to a more addictive product as well as deeper lung inhalation of cooler and less harsh smoke (Stratton et al. 2001; Pankow et al. 2003a,b; Watson et al. 2004). Driven by nicotine addiction and enabled by cigarettes that delivered smoother, cooler smoke diluted by ambient air, smokers could easily compensate for reduced delivery of nicotine by increasing smoke intake per cigarette and per day, thus maintaining high levels of disease risk (NCI 2001; Thun and Burns 2001).

Tobacco industry documents, many of which are available at the Legacy Tobacco Documents Library at UCSF, clearly demonstrate that at least by the mid-1970s the tobacco industry well understood the importance of creating health reassurance messages in order to alleviate health concerns, and that one important method of doing so was through claims of low deliveries of tar. For example, a 1977 British American Tobacco marketing report concluded, "All work in this area should be directed towards providing *consumer reassurance (emphasis in original)* about cigarettes and the smoking habit. This can be provided in different ways, e.g. by claimed low deliveries, by the perception of low deliveries and by the perception of 'mildness'" (Short 1977, p. 3). At the same time, tobacco company documents also clearly demonstrate that the industry understood that smokers would not achieve the claimed deliveries because of smoker compensation. For example, a 1975 Philip Morris memo noted: "In effect, the Marlboro 85 smokers in this study did not achieve any reduction in smoke intake by smoking a cigarette (Marlboro Lights) normally considered lower in delivery" (Goodman 1975, p. 3).

In contrast to industry awareness, the various ways that cigarettes were physically modified and the nature and level of compensation in response to design changes were not well understood by parties outside of the tobacco industry itself. Public health officials had little basis to anticipate the degree to which manufacturers could design cigarettes to allow smokers to draw more smoke and nicotine from cigarettes than was represented by machine-measured yields of tar and nicotine (NCI 2001; Parascandola 2005).

It was not until the turn of the twenty-first century that it became increasingly clear that no relationship existed between machine-measured tar and nicotine levels and risks for most categories of cigarette-related diseases.

In 1994, an expert committee convened by NCI concluded: "The smoking of cigarettes with lower *machine-measured* yields has a small effect in reducing the risk of cancer caused by smoking, no effect on the risk of cardiovascular diseases, and an uncertain effect on the risk of pulmonary disease" (NCI 1996, p. vi). Moreover, whereas squamous cell carcinomas had been the predominant form of lung cancer, by the late twentieth century adenocarcinoma of the lung was becoming increasingly common, presumably reflecting deeper inhalation of smoke that was facilitated by ventilated filters as well as other factors such as changes in agricultural practices, tobacco curing, and cigarette manufacturing processes that could lead to increased concentrations of tobacco-specific nitrosamines (NCI 2001; Stratton et al. 2001) (see Chapter 5, "Cancer"). By 2001, NCI concluded that "measurements of tar and nicotine yields using the FTC method do not offer smokers meaningful information on the amount of tar and nicotine they will receive from a cigarette" (NCI 2001, p. 10). The 2001 review also concluded that the evidence "...does not indicate a benefit to public health from changes in cigarette design and manufacturing over the last fifty years" (NCI 2001, p. 10). Today, there is a scientific consensus that changes in cigarette designs from the 1950s to the 1980s to reduce machine-measured tar yields

did not result in decreased morbidity and mortality (NCI 2001; Thun and Burns 2001). In sum, it took decades to recognize that changes to reduce machine-measured tar and nicotine yields in cigarettes did not have a measurable beneficial impact on public health (NCI 2001). In 2008, FTC rescinded its 1966 guidance that generally permitted statements concerning tar and nicotine yield if they were based on the Cambridge filter method (sometimes called the FTC method) (FTC 2008).

Other changes during the past 50 years have included efforts that potentially have made cigarettes more addicting through the use of flavors, chemical treatments to alter the smell and appearance of cigarette smoke, methods to mask noxious sensory effects, and control of the nicotine dose (see Chapter 4, "Nicotine Addiction: Past and Present"). These approaches included new types of filters, tobacco blends, and ingredients; cigarette ventilation; control of pH; and efforts to reduce various volatile organic compounds in tobacco and smoke. These product modifications have the potential to increase the risk of addiction by contributing to increased risk of initiating use of the product, increased ease of smoke inhalation, decreased noxiousness of the smoke, and possibly increased brain nicotine exposure (WHO 2007; Chapter 4, "Nicotine Addiction: Past and Present").

New Cigarette Products

Cigarette smoke contains more than 7,000 chemicals, including at least 69 known carcinogens and many other toxicants implicated in major diseases (International Agency for Research on Cancer [IARC] 2004; Borgerding and Klus 2005; Rodgman and Perfetti 2009), and because the potency of toxicants and mechanisms of action differ, reducing concentrations of individual toxicants might have only a negligible effect on disease risk from smoking (Fowles and Dybing 2003; Pankow et al. 2007; Burns et al. 2008). Despite these challenges, Brown & Williamson (acquired by R.J. Reynolds in 2004), Vector Tobacco, and Philip Morris have all developed cigarettes that purport to deliver lower levels of specific toxicants (e.g., carcinogenic nitrosamines) as determined by standard machine-smoking methods. This reduction in toxicant levels has been accomplished by use of new technologies in tobacco curing and/or by adding carbon or other materials to cigarette filters (Hoffmann et al. 2001; IARC 2004). However, the extent to which exposure to toxicants is actually reduced in smokers is not known because reduced machine-measured yields of toxicants do not necessarily reflect actual human exposure. A smoker

who switches to a brand with lower machine-measured toxicants may smoke these cigarettes in a more intense fashion or may consume more cigarettes per day than previously. Either change could result in greater human exposure to toxicants and no decrease in risk of disease.

For example, Brown & Williamson introduced Advance as a new cigarette with the claim that levels of tobacco-specific nitrosamines (TSNAs) were 70 percent lower than those in leading "light" brands (Star Scientific 2005). Preliminary laboratory studies of cigarette smokers provide mixed evidence for the possibility that use of this cigarette substitute would result in reduced exposure to tobacco toxicants (Breland et al. 2002, 2003). Omni, manufactured by Vector Tobacco, is a conventional cigarette for which the marketers claimed lower levels of carcinogenic polycyclic aromatic hydrocarbons, nitrosamines, and catechols (Vector Group 2001). Preliminary studies in which Omni is smoked instead of the smokers' usual brand of cigarettes provide little evidence for reduced exposure to toxicants (Hatsukami et al. 2004b; Hughes et al. 2004).

Low-Nicotine Cigarettes

In theory, gradually reducing the content and yield of nicotine in cigarettes over a period of many years, using design features that make compensation difficult or impossible, might lessen smokers' dependence on nicotine. Low-nicotine cigarettes have also been proposed as a method to prevent new smokers (primarily youth) from ever establishing nicotine dependence (Benowitz and Henningfield 1994; Henningfield et al. 1998; Benowitz et al. 2007; Zeller et al. 2009). However, the potential role of nicotine analogues in maintaining addiction is poorly understood.

A commercial cigarette with very low nicotine content was introduced in test markets in 1989 under the brand name Next (Butschky et al. 1995). The nicotine content of Next appeared to be lower than the levels hypothesized by Benowitz and Henningfield (1994) to be the addictive threshold. The test market ended in 1991 when Philip Morris withdrew the product from the market. Quest was a low-nicotine cigarette developed by Vector Tobacco (Rose and Behm 2004; Vector Tobacco 2004). Three products were available: (1) a cigarette with 0.6 mg of nicotine and 10 mg of tar per cigarette, as determined by FTC machine measurements; (2) a cigarette with 0.3 mg of nicotine and 10 mg of tar per cigarette; and (3) a "nicotine-free" cigarette with no more than 0.05 mg of nicotine and 10 mg of tar per cigarette (Vector Tobacco 2004). It was unclear how long and how often smokers would use the "nicotine-free" version rather than versions that contained higher levels of nicotine and whether the two versions with nicotine would hinder the desire and ability to stop smoking.

Cigarette-Like Products

In 1988, R.J. Reynolds launched a new era of novel products with Premier, a nicotine-delivering product similar in size and appearance to a conventional cigarette but consisting of an aluminum canister that contained alumina beads impregnated with glycerin, propylene glycol, and a nicotine-rich tobacco extract (Slade 1993; Slade and Henningfield 1998). Heat from a carbon fuel element vaporized material adjacent to the alumina beads, and these vapors condensed into more proximal segments to form the aerosol that was puffed and inhaled by the consumer (Slade and Henningfield 1998). Compared with conventional cigarettes, Premier delivered similar doses of nicotine, higher levels of carbon monoxide (CO), and reduced levels of many other toxicants (WHO 2001). Premier was test marketed in the United States in 1988 but was soon withdrawn because of poor sales (Slade and Henningfield 1998).

More recently, tobacco companies have developed several other novel cigarette-like products that deliver nicotine to the consumer (Stratton et al. 2001; Slade et al. 2002). Eclipse (R.J. Reynolds) uses a technology similar to that developed for Premier (Slade and Henningfield 1998; Slade et al. 2002): the heat source is a carbon fuel element, and nicotine and glycerin are vaporized from an aluminum-lined chamber filled with what the manufacturer described as "highly processed tobacco" and mixed with glycerin. Both human and machine-testing data indicate that these products provide no clear benefit to users over conventional cigarettes. A report commissioned by the Commonwealth of Massachusetts Department of Public Health found that intensive machine smoking of Eclipse delivered levels of key lung and cancer-causing toxicants (e.g., acrolein, CO) similar to, or higher than, those from two commercial cigarette brands (Labstat 2000). A complication in evaluating the toxicity of Eclipse is that several prototypes were test marketed (Slade et al. 2002). It is not clear whether changes not disclosed by the manufacturer account for the variability across studies (Stapleton et al. 1998; Lee et al. 2004; Breland et al. 2006). Nonetheless, it appears that volunteers who had been exposed to Eclipse (Shiffman et al. 2004; Hughes et al. 2005) or had heard of it believed it to be less harmful than conventional cigarettes. Furthermore, concerns have been raised that Eclipse and Premier could be modified to deliver other drugs, including illicit drugs (Cone and Henningfield 1989; Steckley et al. 2002).

Accord (Philip Morris) consists of a specially designed "cigarette" used in combination with an ignition system (Slade and Henningfield 1998). The handheld, battery-operated, microchip-controlled product heats a cigarette-like tobacco roll when it is puffed (Slade and Henningfield 1998). Although actual-use studies of Accord have not been performed, preliminary laboratory studies with volunteers suggest the possibility that actual human exposure to nicotine and toxicants might substantially exceed that predicted by Philip Morris' tests (Buchhalter et al. 2001; Breland et al. 2002; Philip Morris USA 2005).

Evaluation of New Cigarette Products

The health consequences of new cigarette products have not been demonstrated in scientific studies. The challenges include a need for development and validation of testing methods for new products (WHO 2004b). Extended nonlaboratory studies under natural conditions with a broader range of biomarkers of toxicants are required to determine whether novel products result in overall reduction of exposure to toxicants, and still longer and more extensive studies would be required to determine whether or not the disease risk of the individual or population harm are decreased (WHO 2004a, 2007; Hatsukami et al. 2007). For example, products delivering lower levels of nitrosamines might theoretically reduce cancer risks, but because many of these products still deliver nicotine and CO, cardiovascular risks may remain unchanged or may even increase. In addition, if TSNAs are removed, other potent carcinogens may sustain overall high levels of exposure to carcinogens (Fowles and Dybing 2003).

There are substantial risks that the marketing of novel cigarettes could lead to increased tobacco use in current smokers, relapse in former smokers, and initiation in those who never smoked, particularly youth (Henningfield et al. 2003; Hatsukami et al. 2004a, 2005). For example, in a survey of 1,000 current cigarette smokers and 499 former smokers older than 18 years of age, 91 percent thought Eclipse was safer than regular cigarettes, 24 percent believed Eclipse was completely safe, and 57.4 percent were interested in using the product (Shiffman et al. 2004). Interest was greatest among those who were contemplating smoking cessation, and exposure to Eclipse's claims was followed by a reduced interest in cessation. Those interested in using Eclipse included 6.2 percent of all former smokers and 15.2 percent of young adults 18 through 25 years of age who had stopped smoking within the past two years. Further extending these findings, Hamilton and colleagues (2004) found that advertisements for light cigarettes were perceived to imply that their use is healthier than use of regular cigarettes, partly because consumers wrongly believed that the advertisements must be approved and endorsed by a government agency.

In addition, products designed or marketed to be used in places where smoking is not allowed may defeat public health efforts to reduce smoking rates. For example, studies have found that having a 100-percent smoke-free workplace reduced smoking prevalence by 6 to 22 percent and average daily consumption by up to 14 percent among smokers compared with workers subject to minimal or no restrictions (Farrelly et al. 1999; NCI 2000; USDHHS 2000; Bonnie et al. 2007). Products that enable nicotine consumption in the workplace and other places could reverse these potential reductions in smoking prevalence through use of one product in the workplace and continued smoking outside, that is, dual product use (Henningfield et al. 2002; European Commission 2007). Moreover, the dual use of tobacco products is likely to result in greater exposure to toxicants than does use of either product type alone (Henningfield et al. 2002).

Balancing the risks and benefits of new cigarette products is challenging because of the diversity of products, their associated potential risks and benefits on the multitude of tobacco-related diseases, and the dearth of empirical data on their effects. The 2001 Institute of Medicine (IOM) report (Stratton et al. 2001) and a report from the University of Minnesota Transdisciplinary Tobacco Use Research Center raised a series of questions about these and similar products (Hughes 2000; Stratton et al. 2001; Hatsukami and Hecht 2005; Hatsukami et al. 2005). WHO developed similar scientific questions, as well as recommendations for research and product testing (WHO 2003d, 2004a, 2006, 2007). Although all the questions raised by these organizations merit consideration, the following questions are a critical starting point for evaluating new cigarette or cigarette-like products:

- Does use of the product decrease individual and population exposure to the harmful substances in tobacco smoke?

- Is this decreased exposure associated with a decrease in individual and population risk of disease?

- Are there surrogate indicators of disease risk that could be measured in a timeframe of sufficient duration for product evaluation?

- What are the public health implications of products that may reduce exposure to toxicants in tobacco smoke? Specifically, do these products increase initiation of tobacco use, decrease cessation, promote relapse among those who have quit, or lead to dual product use?

New Oversight of Tobacco Products

On June 22, 2009, President Barack Obama signed into law the Family Smoking Prevention and Tobacco Control Act (Public Law 111-31). The Tobacco Control Act grants the U.S. Food and Drug Administration (FDA) the authority to regulate tobacco products to protect the public's health and recognizes FDA as the primary federal regulatory authority with respect to the manufacture, marketing, and distribution of tobacco products. Key elements of the act include, among other things, creation of a new Center for Tobacco Products, prohibition of the sale of cigarettes containing certain characterizing flavors, the requirement that manufacturers and importers report to FDA the ingredients and additives in their products, strengthened warning labels with graphic images of the adverse effects of cigarette use, and oversight of the tobacco industry's efforts to develop and market potential reduced-exposure tobacco products. The Tobacco Control Act also requires FDA to reissue the agency's 1996 regulation aimed at reducing young people's access to tobacco products and curbing the appeal of tobacco to the young. Although some provisions of the act went into effect shortly after the statute was enacted, such as the ban on flavored cigarettes, others will be implemented over time.

Sections 910 and 911 of the Tobacco Control Act provide that premarket review of certain tobacco products by FDA is required before the products may be marketed. Section 910 requires manufacturers of new tobacco products (those not commercially marketed as of February 15, 2007, or modified after that date) to submit an application containing specified manufacturing and ingredient information, as well as studies of the product's health risks, for FDA review. After reviewing the application, the agency will issue an order either permitting the product to be marketed or denying its marketing according to specified bases for its action. New tobacco products determined by FDA to be substantially equivalent to products already on the market as of February 15, 2007, are not required to undergo premarket review.

Section 911 provides that "modified risk tobacco products" may only be marketed if FDA determines, after reviewing a product application, that the product will significantly reduce the risk of tobacco-related disease to individual users, and benefit the health of the population as a whole, taking into account the impact on both users and nonusers of tobacco products. Section 911 recognizes so-called special rule products, which also require premarket approval. Such products may be marketed for up to five years (subject to renewal) if the agency determines that the applicant has met specified criteria, the applicant agrees to conduct certain postmarket surveillance and studies, and other specified findings regarding the relative harm of the product are made. Under this section, FDA must issue guidance or regulations on the scientific evidence required for the assessment and ongoing review of modified-risk tobacco products in consultation with IOM.

Summary

To reduce smoking-attributable death and disease, public health efforts since the 1964 Surgeon General's report on smoking and health have focused on reducing the prevalence of tobacco use. Reduced prevalence has been achieved through efforts to prevent tobacco use and promote cessation; this effort has been termed one of the "ten great public health achievements of the twentieth century" (CDC 1999). At the time the adverse effects of smoking were being recognized, the tobacco industry developed cigarettes with low machine-measured yields of tar and nicotine, and public health authorities encouraged consumers to select them (Peeler 1996; Shopland 2001). Unfortunately, it took public health researchers and federal authorities many years to discover what the tobacco industry knew much earlier: the health benefits of reductions of tar and nicotine intakes were negligible at best for persons using these products (*Federal Register* 1995, 1996; NCI 2001; WHO 2001; *U.S. v. Philip Morris* No. 449 F. Supp. 2d 1, 430–75 [D.D.C. 2006]). In 2001, an NCI report concluded: "There is no convincing evidence that changes in cigarette design between 1950 and the mid 1980s have resulted in an important decrease in the disease burden caused by cigarette use either for smokers as a group or for the entire population" (NCI 2001, p. 146). Thus, by the twenty-first century, it was apparent that five decades of evolving cigarette design had not reduced overall disease risk among smokers, and new designs were used by the tobacco industry as a tool to undermine prevention and cessation efforts (NCI 2001; Stratton et al. 2001; WHO 2001, 2003a,b,c; USDHHS 2004).

Similarly, informative and comprehensive scientific evaluations do not exist for any of the other new products developed ostensibly to reduce toxicants in cigarette smoke. This lack of data limits any conclusions that can be drawn about potential health risks or benefits.

The well-documented risks of cigarette design changes must be weighed against any potential benefits (Stratton et al. 2001). As this chapter makes clear, substantial risks may be associated with new tobacco products: (1) smokers who might have otherwise stopped smoking may continue to smoke because of perceived reduction in risk with use of new products; (2) former smokers may resume smoking because of perceived reduction in risk with use of new products; and (3) nonsmokers, particularly youth, may start to use new products because of their perceived safety. The theoretical benefit of cigarette design changes is to reduce exposure to toxicants sufficiently to reduce the risk of disease and death. However, if these products are used by persons otherwise unlikely to use a tobacco product, which would undermine efforts to prevent tobacco use, or if the products delay cessation among persons who would otherwise stop using tobacco, the overall health of the population would be harmed.

There is little doubt that new tobacco products will continue to be developed. Consequently, there is a critical need to conduct independent research on the design, composition, and health effects of new cigarette products and to put in place a comprehensive surveillance system to understand consumers' knowledge, attitudes, and behaviors regarding these products.

Conclusions

1. The evidence indicates that changing cigarette designs over the last five decades, including filtered, low-tar, and "light" variations, have not reduced overall disease risk among smokers and may have hindered prevention and cessation efforts.

2. There is insufficient evidence to determine whether novel tobacco products reduce individual and population health risks.

3. The overall health of the public could be harmed if the introduction of novel tobacco products encourages tobacco use among people who would otherwise be unlikely to use a tobacco product or delays cessation among persons who would otherwise quit using tobacco altogether.

References

Benowitz NL, Hall SM, Stewart S, Wilson M, Dempsey D, Jacob P III. Nicotine and carcinogen exposure with smoking of progressively reduced nicotine content cigarette. *Cancer Epidemiology, Biomarkers & Prevention* 2007;16(11):2479–85.

Benowitz NL, Henningfield JE. Establishing a nicotine threshold for addiction: the implications for tobacco regulation. *New England Journal of Medicine* 1994; 331(2):123–5.

Bonnie RJ, Stratton K, Wallace RB, editors. *Ending the Tobacco Problem: A Blueprint for the Nation.* Washington: National Academies Press, 2007.

Borgerding M, Klus H. Analysis of complex mixtures—cigarette smoke. *Experimental and Toxicologic Pathology* 2005;57(Suppl 1):43–73.

Brandt AM. *The Cigarette Century: The Rise, Fall, and Deadly Persistence of the Product That Defined America.* New York: Basic Books, 2007.

Breland AB, Acosta MC, Eissenberg T. Tobacco specific nitrosamines and potential reduced exposure products for smokers: a preliminary evaluation of Advance. *Tobacco Control* 2003;12(3):317–21.

Breland AB, Buchhalter AR, Evans SE, Eissenberg T. Evaluating acute effects of potential reduced-exposure products for smokers: clinical laboratory methodology. *Nicotine & Tobacco Research* 2002;4(Suppl 2):S131–S140.

Breland AB, Kleykamp BA, Eissenberg T. Clinical laboratory evaluation of potential reduced exposure products for smokers. *Nicotine & Tobacco Research* 2006;8(6):727–38.

Browne CL. *The Design of Cigarettes.* 3rd ed. Charlotte (NC): Hoechst Celanese Corporation, 1990.

Buchhalter AR, Schrinel L, Eissenberg T. Withdrawal suppressing effects of a novel smoking system: comparison with own brand, not own brand, and de-nicotinized cigarettes. *Nicotine & Tobacco Research* 2001;3(2):111–8.

Burns DM, Dybing E, Gray N, Hecht S, Anderson C, Sanner T, O'Connor R, Djordjevic M, Dresler C, Hainaut P, et al. Mandated lowering of toxicants in cigarette smoke: a description of the World Health Organization TobReg proposal. *Tobacco Control* 2008;17(2):132–41.

Butschky MF, Bailey D, Henningfield JE, Pickworth WB. Smoking without nicotine delivery decreases withdrawal in 12-hour abstinent smokers. *Pharmacology, Biochemistry, and Behavior* 1995;50(1):91–6.

Centers for Disease Control and Prevention. Ten great public health achievements—United States, 1900–1999. *Morbidity and Mortality Weekly Report* 1999;48(12):241–3.

Centers for Disease Control and Prevention. Smoking attributable mortality, years of potential life lost, and productivity losses—United States, 2000–2004. *Morbidity and Mortality Weekly Report* 2008;57(45): 1226–8.

Cone EJ, Henningfield JE. Premier "smokeless cigarettes" can be used to deliver crack [letter]. *JAMA: the Journal of the American Medical Association* 1989;261(1):41.

Djordjevic MV, Stellman SD, Zang E. Doses of nicotine and lung carcinogens delivered to cigarette smokers. *Journal of the National Cancer Institute* 2000;92(2): 106–11.

European Commission. Health Effects of Smokeless Tobacco Products Preliminary Report. Brussels: European Commission, Scientific Committee on Emerging and Newly Identified Health Risks, 2007; <http://ec.europa.eu/health/ph_risk/committees/04scenihr/docs/scenihr_o_009.pdf>.

Family Smoking Prevention and Tobacco Control Act, Public Law 111-31, *U.S. Statutes at Large* 123 (2009):1776

Farrelly MC, Evans WN, Sfekas AE. The impact of workplace smoking bans: results from a national survey. *Tobacco Control* 1999;8(3):272–7.

Federal Register. U.S. Department of Health and Human Services, Food and Drug Administration. Regulations restricting the sale and distribution of cigarettes and smokeless tobacco products to protect children and adolescents; proposed rule analysis regarding FDA's jurisdiction over nicotine-containing cigarettes and smokeless tobacco products; notice. 60 *Fed. Reg.* 41314–792 (1995).

Federal Register. U.S. Department of Health and Human Services, Food and Drug Administration. Regulations restricting the sale and distribution of cigarettes and smokeless tobacco to protect children and adolescents; final rule (21 CFR Parts 801, 803, 804, 807, 820, and 897). 61 *Fed. Reg.* 44396–5318 (1996).

Federal Trade Commission. FTC rescinds guidance from 1966 on statements concerning tar and nicotine yields [press release]. Washington: Federal Trade Commission, Office of Public Affairs, November 26, 2008.

Fowles J, Dybing E. Application of toxicological risk assessment principles to the chemical constituents of cigarette smoke. *Tobacco Control* 2003;12(4):424–30.

Goodman B. Marlboro - Marlboro Lights study delivery data. 1975. Philip Morris Collection. Bates No. 2077992557. <http://legacy.library.ucsf.edu/tid/Awa18c00>.

Goodman J. *Tobacco in History: the Cultures of Dependence*. New York: Routledge, 1993.

Goodman J, editor in chief. *Tobacco in History and Culture: An Encyclopedia*. 2 Vol. Scribner Turning Points Library. Detroit: Charles Scribner's Sons, 2004.

Hamilton WL, Norton G, Ouellette TK, Rhodes WM, Kling R, Connolly GN. Smokers' responses to advertisements for regular and light cigarettes and potential reduced-exposure tobacco products. *Nicotine & Tobacco Research* 2004;6(Suppl 3):S353–S362.

Hatsukami D, Hecht S. *Hope or Hazard? What Research Tells Us about "Potentially Reduced Exposure" Tobacco Products*. Minneapolis: University of Minnesota Transdisciplinary Tobacco Use Research Center, 2005.

Hatsukami DK, Giovino GA, Eissenberg T, Clark PI, Lawrence D, Leischow S. Methods to assess potential reduced exposure products. *Nicotine & Tobacco Research* 2005;7(6):827–44.

Hatsukami DK, Henningfield JE, Kotlyar M. Harm reduction approaches to reducing tobacco-related mortality. *Annual Review of Public Health* 2004a;25:377–95.

Hatsukami DK, Joseph AM, Lesage M, Jensen J, Murphy SE, Pentel PR, Kotlyar M, Borgida E, Le C, Hecht SS. Developing the science base for reducing tobacco harm. *Nicotine & Tobacco Research* 2007;9(Suppl 4): S537–S553.

Hatsukami DK, Lemmonds C, Zhang Y, Murphy SE, Le C, Carmella SG, Hecht SS. Evaluation of carcinogen exposure in people who used "reduced exposure" tobacco products. *Journal of the National Cancer Institute* 2004b;96(11):844–52.

Henningfield JE, Benowitz NL, Slade J, Houston TP, Davis RM, Deitchman SD. Reducing the addictiveness of cigarettes. *Tobacco Control* 1998;7(3):281–93.

Henningfield JE, Moolchan ET, Zeller M. Regulatory strategies to reduce tobacco addiction in youth. *Tobacco Control* 2003;12(Suppl 1):i14–i24.

Henningfield JE, Rose CA, Giovino GA. Brave new world of tobacco disease prevention: promoting dual product use? *American Journal of Preventive Medicine* 2002;23(3):226–8.

Hilts PJ. *Smoke Screen: The Truth Behind the Tobacco Industry Cover-Up*. New York: Addison-Wesley Publishing Company, 1996.

Hoffmann D, Djordjevic MV, Brunnemann KD. Changes in Cigarette Design and Composition Over Time and How They Influence the Yields of Smoke Constituents. In:

The FTC Cigarette Test Method for Determining Tar, Nicotine, and Carbon Monoxide Yields of U.S. Cigarettes. Report of the NCI Expert Committee. Smoking and Tobacco Control Monograph No. 7. Bethesda (MD): U.S. Department of Health and Human Services, Public Health Service, National Institutes of Health, National Cancer Institute, 1996:15–37. NIH Publication No. 96-4028.

Hoffmann D, Hoffmann I. The changing cigarette, 1950–1995. *Journal of Toxicology and Environmental Health* 1997;50(4):307–64.

Hoffmann D, Hoffmann I, El-Bayoumy K. The less harmful cigarette: a controversial issue. A tribute to Ernst L. Wynder. *Chemical Research in Toxicology* 2001;14(7):767-90.

Hughes JR. Reduced smoking: an introduction and review of the evidence. *Addiction* 2000;95(Suppl 1):S3–S7.

Hughes JR, Hecht SS, Carmella SG, Murphy SE, Callas P. Smoking behaviour and toxin exposure during six weeks use of a potential reduced exposure product: Omni. *Tobacco Control* 2004;13(2):175–9.

Hughes JR, Keely JP, Callas PW. Ever users versus never users of a "less risky" cigarette. *Psychology of Addictive Behaviors* 2005;19(4):439–42.

Hurt RD, Robertson CR. Prying open the door to the tobacco industry's secrets about nicotine: the Minnesota Tobacco Trial. *JAMA: the Journal of the American Medical Association* 1998;280(13):1173–81.

International Agency for Research on Cancer. *IARC Monographs on the Evaluation of Carcinogenic Risks to Humans: Tobacco Smoke and Involuntary Smoking*. Vol. 83. Lyon (France): International Agency for Research on Cancer, 2004.

Kessler D. *A Question of Intent: A Great American Battle with a Deadly Industry*. New York: Public Affairs, 2001.

Kluger R. *Ashes to Ashes: America's Hundred-Year Cigarette War, the Public Health, and the Unabashed Triumph of Philip Morris*. New York: Alfred A. Knopf, 1996.

Kozlowski LT, Frecker RC, Khouw V, Pope MA. The misuse of 'less-hazardous' cigarettes and its detection: hole blocking of ventilated filters. *American Journal of Public Health* 1980;70(11):1202–3.

Kozlowski LT, O'Connor RJ. Cigarette filter ventilation is a defective design because of misleading taste, bigger puffs, and blocked vents. *Tobacco Control* 2002;11(Suppl 1):I40–I50.

Kozlowski LT, O'Connor RJ, Giovino GA, Whetzel CA, Pauly J, Cummings KM. Maximum yields might improve public health—if filter vents were banned: a lesson from the history of vented filters. *Tobacco Control* 2006;15(3):262–6.

Labstat International. Project Identifier: GC7 Labstat International Inc. Test Report. Prepared for the Commonwealth of Massachusetts, Department of Public Health. Kitchener (Canada): Labstat International. 2000. RJ Reynolds Collection. Bates No. 525005136/5153. http://legacy.library.ucsf.edu/tid/xqv27a00.

Lee EM, Malson JL, Moolchan ET, Pickworth WB. Quantitative comparisons between a nicotine delivery device (Eclipse) and conventional cigarette smoking. *Nicotine & Tobacco Research* 2004;6(1):95–102.

National Cancer Institute. *The FTC Cigarette Test Method for Determining Tar, Nicotine, and Carbon Monoxide Yields of U.S. Cigarettes. Report of the NCI Expert Committee.* Smoking and Tobacco Control Monograph No. 7. Bethesda (MD): U.S. Department of Health and Human Services, Public Health Service, National Institutes of Health, National Cancer Institute, 1996. NIH Publication No. 96-4028.

National Cancer Institute. *Changes in Cigarette-Related Disease Risks and Their Implications for Prevention and Control.* Smoking and Tobacco Control Monograph No. 8. Bethesda (MD): U.S. Department of Health and Human Services, Public Health Service, National Institutes of Health, National Cancer Institute, 1997. NIH Publication No. 97-4213.

National Cancer Institute. *Population Based Smoking Cessation: Proceedings of a Conference on What Works to Influence Cessation in the General Population.* Smoking and Tobacco Control Monograph No. 12. Bethesda (MD): U.S. Department of Health and Human Services, Public Health Service, National Institutes of Health, National Cancer Institute, 2000. NIH Publication No. 00-4892.

National Cancer Institute. *Risks Associated with Smoking Cigarettes with Low Machine-Measured Yields of Tar and Nicotine.* Smoking and Tobacco Control Monograph No. 13. Bethesda (MD): U.S. Department of Health and Human Services, Public Health Service, National Institutes of Health, National Cancer Institute, 2001. NIH Publication No. 02-5047.

Pankow JF, Barsanti KC, Peyton DH. Fraction of free-base nicotine in fresh smoke particulate matter from the Eclipse "cigarette" by 1H NMR spectroscopy. *Chemical Research in Toxicology* 2003a;16(1):23–7.

Pankow JF, Tavakoli AD, Luo W, Isabelle LM. Percent free base nicotine in the tobacco smoke particulate matter of selected commercial and reference cigarettes. *Chemical Research in Toxicology* 2003b;16(8):1014–8.

Pankow JF, Watanabe KH, Toccalino PL, Luo W, Austin DF. Calculated cancer risks for conventional and "potentially reduced exposure product" cigarettes. *Cancer Epidemiology, Biomarkers and Prevention* 2007;16(3):584–92.

Parascandola M. Lessons from the history of tobacco harm reduction: the National Cancer Institute's Smoking and Health Program and the "less hazardous cigarette." *Nicotine & Tobacco Research* 2005;7(5):779–89.

Pauly JL, Lee HJ, Hurley EL, Cummings KM, Lesses JD, Streck RJ. Glass fiber contamination of cigarette filters: an additional health risk to the smoker? *Cancer Epidemiology, Biomarkers & Prevention* 1998;7(11):967–79.

Pauly JL, Stegmeier SJ, Mayer AG, Lesses JD, Streck RJ. Release of carbon granules from cigarettes with charcoal filters. *Tobacco Control* 1997;6(1):33–40.

Pederson LL, Nelson DE. Literature review and summary of perceptions, attitudes, beliefs, and marketing of potentially reduced exposure products: communication implications. *Nicotine & Tobacco Research* 2007;9(5):525–34.

Peeler CL. Cigarette testing and the Federal Trade Commission: a historical overview. In: *The FTC Cigarette Test Method for Determining Tar, Nicotine, and Carbon Monoxide Yields of U.S. Cigarettes. Report of the NCI Expert Committee.* Smoking and Tobacco Control Monograph No. 7. Bethesda (MD): U.S. Department of Health and Human Services, Public Health Service, National Institutes of Health, National Cancer Institute, 1996:1–8. NIH Publication No. 96-4028.

Philip Morris USA. Product facts: tar and nicotine numbers, 2005; <http://www.philipmorrisusa.com/en/product_facts/tar_nicotine/tar_nicotine_numbers.asp>; accessed: July 7, 2005.

Pillsbury HC. Review of the Federal Trade Commission Method for determining cigarette tar and nicotine yield. In: *The FTC Cigarette Test Method for Determining Tar, Nicotine, and Carbon Monoxide Yields of U.S. Cigarettes. Report of the NCI Expert Committee.* Smoking and Tobacco Control Monograph No. 7. Bethesda (MD): U.S. Department of Health and Human Services, Public Health Service, National Institutes of Health, National Cancer Institute, 1996:9–14. NIH Publication No. 96-4028.

Reynolds P, Shachtman T. *The Gilded Leaf: Triumph, Tragedy, and Tobacco—Three Generations of the R. J. Reynolds Family and Fortune.* Boston: Little, Brown, 1989.

Rodgman A, Perfetti TA. *The Chemical Components of Tobacco and Tobacco Smoke.* Boca Raton (FL): CRC Press, Taylor & Francis Group, 2009.

Rose, JE, Behm FM. Effects of low nicotine content cigarettes on smoke intake. *Nicotine & Tobacco Research* 2004;6(2):309-19.

Royal College of Physicians. *Smoking and Health.* London: Pitman Medical Publishing, 1962.

Shiffman S, Pillitteri JL, Burton SL, Di Marino ME. Smoker and ex-smoker reactions to cigarettes claiming reduced risk. *Tobacco Control* 2004;13(1):78–84.

Shopland DR. Historical perspective: the low tar lie. *Tobacco Control* 2001;10(Suppl 1):i1–i3.

Short PL. Smoking and health item 7: the effect on marketing, April 28, 1977; <http://library.ucsf.edu/tobacco/batco/html/13300/13388/>; accessed: July 7, 2005.

Slade J. Nicotine delivery devices. In: Orleans CT, Slade J, editors. *Nicotine Addiction: Principles and Management.* New York: Oxford University Press, 1993:3–23.

Slade J, Bero LA, Hanauer P, Barnes DE, Glantz SA. Nicotine and addiction: the Brown & Williamson documents. *JAMA: the Journal of the American Medical Association* 1995;274(3):225–33.

Slade J, Connolly GN, Lymperis D. Eclipse: does it live up to its health claims? *Tobacco Control* 2002;11(Suppl 2): ii64–ii70.

Slade J, Henningfield JE. Tobacco product regulation: context and issues. *Food and Drug Law Journal* 1998;53(Suppl):43–74.

Stapleton JA, Russell MAH, Sutherland G, Feyerabend C. Nicotine availability from Eclipse tobacco-heating cigarette. *Psychopharmacology* 1998;139(3):288–90.

Star Scientific. Test marketed advance low tsna cigarette with dalmatian type activated charcoal/acetate filter: ADVANCE Onsert A; <http://www.starscientific.com/066745321909/OnsertA.html>; accessed: July 7, 2005.

Steckley SL, Darwin WD, Henningfield JE, Huestis MA, Pickworth WB. Eclipse can deliver crack cocaine. *Nicotine & Tobacco Research* 2002;4(Suppl 2):S189–S190.

Stratton K, Shetty P, Wallace R, Bondurant S, editors. Clearing the Smoke: Assessing the Science Base for Tobacco Harm Reduction. Washington: National Academy Press, 2001.

Tate C. *Cigarette Wars: The Triumph of the "Little White Slaver."* New York: Oxford University Press, 1999.

Thun MJ, Burns DM. Health impact of "reduced yield" cigarettes: a critical assessment of the epidemiological evidence. *Tobacco Control* 2001;10(Suppl 1):i4–i11.

U.S. v. Philip Morris, 449 F. Supp 2d 1 (D.D.C. 2006), *aff'd in part and vacated in part,* 566 F. 3d 1095 (D.C. Cir. 2009) *(per curiam), petitions for cert. filed,* Nos. 09–976 through 09–980, 09–994, 09–1012 (Feb. 19, 2010).

U.S. Department of Health and Human Services. *The Health Consequences of Smoking: The Changing Cigarette. A Report of the Surgeon General.* Rockville (MD): U.S. Department of Health and Human Services, Public Health Service, Office on Smoking and Health, 1981. DHHS Publication No. (PHS) 81-50156.

U.S. Department of Health and Human Services. *The Health Consequences of Using Smokeless Tobacco.*

A Report of the Advisory Committee to the Surgeon General of the Public Health Service. Bethesda (MD): U.S. Department of Health and Human Services, Public Health Service, 1986. NIH Publication No. (CDC) 86-2874.

U.S. Department of Health and Human Services. *The Health Consequences of Smoking: Nicotine Addiction. A Report of the Surgeon General.* Atlanta: U.S. Department of Health and Human Services, Public Health Service, Centers for Disease Control, National Center for Chronic Disease Prevention and Health Promotion, Office on Smoking and Health, 1988. DHHS Publication No. (CDC) 88-8406.

U.S. Department of Health and Human Services. *Reducing the Health Consequences of Smoking: 25 Years of Progress. A Report of the Surgeon General.* Rockville (MD): U.S. Department of Health and Human Services, Public Health Service, Centers for Disease Control, National Center for Chronic Disease Prevention and Health Promotion, Office on Smoking and Health, 1989. DHHS Publication No. (CDC) 89-8411.

U.S. Department of Health and Human Services. *Reducing Tobacco Use. A Report of the Surgeon General.* Atlanta: U.S. Department of Health and Human Services, Centers for Disease Control and Prevention, National Center for Chronic Disease Prevention and Health Promotion, Office on Smoking and Health, 2000.

U.S. Department of Health and Human Services. *The Health Consequences of Smoking: A Report of the Surgeon General.* Atlanta: U.S. Department of Health and Human Services, Centers for Disease Control and Prevention, National Center for Chronic Disease Prevention and Health Promotion, Office on Smoking and Health, 2004.

U.S. Department of Health, Education, and Welfare. *Smoking and Health: Report of the Advisory Committee to the Surgeon General of the Public Health Service.* Washington: U.S. Department of Health, Education, and Welfare, Public Health Service, Center for Disease Control, 1964. PHS Publication No. 1103.

U.S. Department of Health, Education, and Welfare. Technical Report on "Tar" and Nicotine. Washington: U.S. Department of Health, Education, and Welfare, Public Health Service. 1966. Brown & Williamson Collection. Bates No. 680236352/6355. <http://legacy.library.ucsf.edu/tid/kaq04f00>.

U.S. Department of Health, Education, and Welfare. *The Health Consequences of Smoking: A Public Service Review: 1967.* Washington: U.S. Department of Health, Education, and Welfare, Public Health Service, Health Services and Mental Health Administration, 1967. PHS Publication No. 1696.

U.S. Department of Health, Education, and Welfare. *The Health Consequences of Smoking. 1969 Supplement to the 1967 Public Health Service Review*. Washington: U.S. Department of Health, Education, and Welfare, Public Health Service, 1969. DHEW Publication No. 1696-2.

U.S. Department of Health, Education, and Welfare. *The Health Consequences of Smoking. A Report of the Surgeon General: 1971*. Washington: U.S. Department of Health, Education, and Welfare, Public Health Service, Health Services and Mental Health Administration, 1971. DHEW Publication No. (HSM) 71-7513.

U.S. Department of Health, Education, and Welfare. *The Health Consequences of Smoking. A Report of the Surgeon General, 1974*. Washington: U.S. Department of Health, Education, and Welfare, Public Health Service, Center for Disease Control, 1974. DHEW Publication No. (CDC) 74-8704.

University of California at San Francisco. Tobacco Documents Bibliography, June 2008; <http://www.library.ucsf.edu/tobacco/docsbiblio.html>; accessed: September 15, 2008.

Vector Group. Reduced carcinogen cigarette now available; Vector Tobacco launches Omni nationwide [press release]. 2001. RJ Reynolds. Bates No. 528810104/0105. <http://legacy.library.ucsf.edu/tid/dyh93a00>.

Vector Tobacco. What is Quest? 2004; <http://www.vector-tobacco.com/prodInfo.asp>; accessed: July 7, 2005.

Warner KE, Peck CC, Woosley RL, Henningfield JE, Slade J. Tobacco dependence: innovative regulatory approaches to reduce death and disease [preface]. *Food and Drug Law Journal* 1998;53(Suppl):1–8.

Watson CH, Trommel JS, Ashley DL. Solid-phase microextraction-base approach to determine free-base nicotine in trapped mainstream cigarette smoke total particulate matter. *Journal of Agricultural and Food Chemistry* 2004;52(24):7240–5.

World Health Organization. *Advancing Knowledge on Regulating Tobacco Products*. Geneva: World Health Organization, 2001:47–55.

World Health Organization. Policy Recommendations for Smoking Cessation and Treatment of Tobacco Dependence. Geneva: World Health Organization, 2003a.

World Health Organization. *Recommendation on Health Claims Derived from ISO/FTC Method to Measure Cigarette Yield*. Geneva: World Health Organization, Scientific Advisory Committee on Tobacco Product Regulation, 2003b.

World Health Organization. *Recommendation on Nicotine and the Regulation in Tobacco and non-Tobacco Products*. Geneva: World Health Organization, Scientific Advisory Committee on Tobacco Product Regulation, 2003c.

World Health Organization. *Statement of Principles: Guiding the Evaluation of New or Modified Tobacco Products*. Geneva: World Health Organization, Scientific Advisory Committee on Tobacco Product Regulation, 2003d.

World Health Organization. *Guiding Principles for the Development of Tobacco Product Research and Testing Capacity and Proposed Protocols for the Initiation of Tobacco Product Testing*. Geneva: World Health Organization, Study Group on Tobacco Product Regulation, 2004a; <http://www.who.int/tobacco/global_interaction/tobreg/TobReg1finalfortfiweb.pdf>; accessed July 13, 2007.

World Health Organization. *Recommendations and Statement of Principles*. Geneva: World Health Organization, 2004b; <http://www.who.int/tobacco/sactob/recommendations/en/>; accessed: September 16, 2008.

World Health Organization. *Tobacco: Deadly in Any Form or Disguise*. Geneva: World Health Organization, 2006; <http://www.who.int/tobacco/communications/events/wntd/2006/Tfi_Rapport.pdf>; accessed: July 13, 2007.

World Health Organization. *The Scientific Basis of Tobacco Product Regulation. Report of a WHO Study Group*. Geneva: World Health Organization, 2007. WHO Technical Report Series No. 945.

Zeller M, Hatsukami D, Backinger C, Benowitz N, Biener L, Burns D, Clark P, Connolly G, Djordjevic M, Eissenberg T, et al. The strategic dialogue on tobacco harm reduction: a vision and blueprint for action in the United States. *Tobacco Control* 2009;doi:10.1136/tc.2008.027318.

Chapter 3
Chemistry and Toxicology of Cigarette Smoke and Biomarkers of Exposure and Harm

Introduction

This chapter summarizes the state of knowledge about the chemistry and toxicology of cigarette smoke and provides data relevant to the evaluations and conclusions presented in the disease-specific chapters of this report. The literature reviewed in this chapter is limited to manufactured cigarettes and does not include publications on handmade ("roll your own") cigarettes or other products that contain nicotine. The next section, "Chemistry," includes a brief description of technologies used by cigarette manufacturers in a limited number of cigarette brands marketed as "reduced-exposure" or "lower-yield" products. These commercial products have not been met with widespread consumer acceptance. The following section, "Biomarkers," focuses on the manufactured tobacco-burning cigarette consumed by the majority of smokers in the United States and elsewhere.

The section on "Chemistry" describes the chemical components of cigarette smoke and addresses aspects of product design that alter the components of cigarette smoke and factors affecting delivery of smoke to the smoker. In most cases, the data reported for chemical levels in mainstream smoke were derived under standard smoking conditions described by the U.S. Federal Trade Commission (FTC) and the International Organization for Standardization (ISO). These standard conditions are puff volume of 35 milliliters (mL), two-second puff duration, one-minute puff frequency, and butt length defined as either 23 millimeters (mm) for nonfilter cigarettes or the length of the filter overwrap paper plus 3 mm. When alternative smoking regimens are used, levels of potentially harmful substances in smoke emissions usually differ from those measured under standard conditions. (For more details, see "Delivery of Chemical Constituents into Tobacco Smoke" later in this chapter.) When people smoke, they do not use the puff volume and puff frequency programmed into smoking machines, and smoking habits vary significantly from person to person and cigarette to cigarette. Consequently, actual exposures to and doses of components of smoke cannot be derived from values obtained with machine smoking.

The section on "Biomarkers" offers an overview of in vitro and in vivo data on genotoxicity and cytotoxicity and a review of the literature on animal bioassays, in addition to general concepts of biomarkers of exposure, of biologically effective dose, and of potential harm, as an introduction to more detailed descriptions of biomarkers in subsequent chapters of this Surgeon General's report.

Cigarette smoke is a complex mixture of chemical compounds that are bound to aerosol particles or are free in the gas phase. Chemical compounds in tobacco can be distilled into smoke or can react to form other constituents that are then distilled to smoke. Researchers have estimated that cigarette smoke has 7,357 chemical compounds from many different classes (Rodgman and Perfetti 2009). In assessing the nature of tobacco smoke, scientists must consider chemical composition, concentrations of components, particle size, and particle charge (Dube and Green 1982). These characteristics vary with the cigarette design and the chemical nature of the product.

Fowles and Dybing (2003) suggested an approach to identify the chemical components in tobacco smoke with the greatest potential for toxic effects. They considered the risk for cancer, cardiovascular disease, and heart disease. Using this approach, these investigators found that 1,3-butadiene presented by far the most significant cancer risk; acrolein and acetaldehyde had the greatest potential to be respiratory irritants; and cyanide, arsenic, and the cresols were the primary sources of cardiovascular risk. Other chemical classes of concern include other metals, *N*-nitrosamines, and polycyclic aromatic hydrocarbons (PAHs). This evaluation, along with the Hoffmann list of biologically active chemicals (Hoffmann and Hoffmann 1998), was used to select the chemicals reviewed in this chapter. Other chemical components with potential for harm will be identified as analysis of tobacco smoke becomes more complete and cigarette design and additives change.

Chemistry

Phases of Tobacco Smoke

Smoke from a burning cigarette is a "concentrated aerosol of liquid particles suspended in an atmosphere consisting mainly of nitrogen, oxygen, carbon monoxide and carbon dioxide" (Guerin 1980, p. 201). Researchers have also described cigarette smoke as a "lightly charged, highly concentrated matrix of submicron particles contained in a gas with each particle being a multicompositional collection of compounds arising from distillation, pyrolysis, and combustion of tobacco" (Dube and Green 1982, p. 42). Tobacco smoke is a complex and dynamic chemical mixture. Researchers have analyzed whole smoke or used chemical and physical means to separately examine the gas and particulate portions of tobacco smoke. The gas phase is defined as the portion of smoke that passes through a glass fiber filter of specified physical parameters, and the particulate phase refers to all matter captured by the glass fiber filter (Pillsbury 1969). Standard methods for analysis of tobacco smoke separate the two phases by using Cambridge glass fiber filters designed to collect aerosol particles of 0.3 micrometers (µm) or larger with an efficiency not less than 99 percent (Pillsbury 1969). Although these separate phases are an artificial construct, they are useful for describing the results of analysis of the components of cigarette smoke typically obtained by machine smoking. When people smoke cigarettes, the continuum of physical characteristics in smoke does not include the differentiation into specific fractions. The diameter of cigarette smoke particles constantly changes, and as the particles coalesce after their formation, they grow in diameter. However, in diluted smoke, loss of a volatile chemical matrix or other components may cause particles to shrink and changes in the particle size may alter the relative amounts of certain chemicals in the gas and particle phases (Guerin 1980).

Smoke formation occurs when the cigarette is lit and a puff is taken or when the cigarette smolders between puffs. Mainstream smoke is released from the butt end of the burning cigarette during puffing, and sidestream smoke emanates from the burning cigarette coal when it smolders (Guerin 1980). The air in the immediate vicinity of an active smoker contains a mixture of sidestream smoke, exhaled mainstream smoke, and any smoke that passes through the porous paper surrounding the tobacco (Löfroth 1989). A greater quantity of sidestream smoke is generated when the amount of tobacco burned during smoldering increases relative to the amount burned

during puffing (Johnson et al. 1973b; Perfetti et al. 1998). Thus, the way the cigarette is smoked (e.g., puff volume and time between puffs) can alter the relative levels of mainstream and sidestream smoke (Perfetti et al. 1998).

In addition, the ratio of the levels of chemical components in sidestream smoke to their levels in mainstream smoke can be altered by differences among cigarettes (Perfetti et al. 1998). These differences are related to the tobacco blend or type, the tobacco preparation (e.g., cut width, additives, and moisture level), the dimensions of the cigarette, the weight of the tobacco rod, the porosity of the paper, the presence of a filter, and the type of filter. Studies using a machine that simulates human smoking have determined that the change in the ratio of sidestream to mainstream smoke components after introducing a filter and ventilation primarily resulted from a decrease in the amount of mainstream smoke, because the amount of sidestream smoke does not change substantially with alterations in cigarette design (Perfetti et al. 1998). Examination of chemicals with similar properties revealed that those with a low boiling point had higher ratios of levels in sidestream smoke to levels in mainstream smoke and that compounds with a high boiling point had lower ratios (Sakuma et al. 1984). Studies indicate that compared with mainstream smoke collected under standard FTC/ISO smoking parameters, sidestream smoke has higher levels of PAHs (Grimmer et al. 1987; Evans et al. 1993); nitrosamines (Brunnemann et al. 1977a, 1980; Hoffmann et al. 1979a; Rühl et al. 1980); aza-arenes (Dong et al. 1978; Grimmer et al. 1987); aromatic amines (Patrianakos and Hoffmann 1979); carbon monoxide (CO) (Hoffmann et al. 1979b; Rickert et al. 1984); nicotine (Rickert et al. 1984; Pakhale et al. 1997); ammonia (Brunnemann and Hoffmann 1975); pyridine (Johnson et al. 1973b; Brunnemann et al. 1978; Sakuma et al. 1984); and the gas phase components 1,3-butadiene, acrolein, isoprene, benzene, and toluene (Brunnemann et al. 1990). With increased puffing intensity, the toxicant ratios of sidestream to mainstream smoke decrease (Borgerding et al. 2000).

The increase in the amount of tobacco burned during smoldering compared with tobacco burned during puffing is not the only factor influencing differences in the chemical content of sidestream and mainstream smoke. The burning conditions that generate sidestream and mainstream smoke also differ (Guerin 1987). Temperatures reach 900°C during a puff and fall to about 400°C between puffs (Guerin 1987). Puffing burns the tobacco on the periphery of the cigarette, and tobacco in the core burns between puffs (Johnson 1977; Hoffmann et al. 1979a). Thus, mainstream smoke depends on the chemical composition of the combustible portion of the cigarette near the periphery of the rod, whereas chemicals at higher concentrations in the central portion of the rod have higher levels in sidestream smoke than in mainstream smoke (Johnson 1977). Sidestream smoke is produced during conditions with less available oxygen (Guerin et al. 1987) and higher alkalinity and water content than those for mainstream smoke (Brunnemann and Hoffmann 1974; Adams et al. 1987; Guerin 1987). Ammonia levels are significantly higher in sidestream smoke, resulting in a more alkaline pH (Adams et al. 1987). Thus, the composition and levels of chemical species in mainstream smoke differ from those in sidestream smoke.

Levels of some compounds are higher in mainstream smoke than in sidestream smoke, and this difference may reflect chemical influences that are more complex than just changes in puff frequency. For example, mainstream smoke contains considerably more cyanide than sidestream smoke does (Johnson et al. 1973b; Brunnemann et al. 1977a; Norman et al. 1983). Sakuma and colleagues (1983) measured a series of semivolatile compounds in tobacco smoke and found that levels of phenol, cresol, xylenols, guiacol, formic acid, and acetic acid were higher in sidestream smoke, whereas levels of catechol and hydroquinone were higher in mainstream smoke.

Individual chemical constituents may be found in the particulate phase, the gas phase, or both (Guerin 1980). As cigarette smoke dissipates, chemicals may pass between the particulate and gas phases (Löfroth 1989). The gas phase contains gases and chemical constituents that are sufficiently volatile to remain in the gas phase long enough to pass through the Cambridge glass fiber filter (Guerin 1980), but as the filter becomes wet during the first puffs, hydrophilic compounds tend to adhere to it. The gas phase of cigarette smoke includes nitrogen (N_2), oxygen (O_2), carbon dioxide (CO_2), CO, acetaldehyde, methane, hydrogen cyanide (HCN), nitric acid, acetone, acrolein, ammonia, methanol, hydrogen sulfide (H_2S), hydrocarbons, gas phase nitrosamines, and carbonyl compounds (Borgerding and Klus 2005; Rodgman and Perfetti 2009). Constituents in the particulate phase include carboxylic acids, phenols, water, humectants, nicotine, terpenoids, paraffin waxes, tobacco-specific nitrosamines (TSNAs), PAHs, and catechols. Mainstream smoke contains only a small amount of nicotine in the gas phase (Johnson et al. 1973b; Pakhale et al. 1997), but the fraction of nicotine in the gas phase is higher in sidestream smoke because of the higher pH (Johnson et al. 1973b; Brunnemann and Hoffmann 1974; Adams et al. 1987; Pakhale et al. 1997). Brunnemann and colleagues (1977b) studied both mainstream and sidestream smoke

and found that the gas phase of mainstream smoke contained more cyanide than did the particulate phase. Johnson and colleagues (1973b), however, showed that in sidestream smoke, cyanide is present almost exclusively in the particulate phase. Guerin (1980) concluded that both formaldehyde and cyanide may be present in both phases, and Spincer and Chard (1971) found formaldehyde in both the particulate and gas phases. The PAHs in the gas phase were only 1 percent of total PAHs, and the PAH distribution between gas and particulate phases varied with the boiling point of the PAHs (Grimmer et al. 1987). Because physical and chemical changes occur after tobacco smoke is drawn from the cigarette, some of the reported differences in PAH levels could result from differences in measurement techniques.

In summary, cigarette smoke is a complex and dynamic system. The concentration of smoke and the time after it leaves the cigarette can cause changes in particle size that may alter the relative amounts of certain chemicals in the gas and particle phases. Also, specific properties of the tobacco, the physical design of the cigarette, and the machine-smoking method that is employed to generate mainstream smoke for analyes can have a significant impact on the levels of both mainstream and sidestream emissions.

Nicotine and Free Nicotine

The tobacco leaf contains many alkaloid chemicals; nicotine is the most abundant. Nicotine content varies, among other factors, by the leaf position on the tobacco stalk and also by the blend or leaf type used in a given cigarette or cigar (Tso 1990; Kozlowski et al. 2001). Plants such as tobacco that are characterized by high alkaloid content often possess a natural pharmacologic defense against microorganisms, insects, and vertebrates. For example, nicotine is toxic to many insects and, for many years, has been extracted from tobacco for use as a commercial pesticide (Domino 1999). Nicotine is addictive in humans because a portion of the nicotine molecule is similar to acetylcholine, an important brain neurotransmitter (Brody et al. 2006).

The alkaloids in tobacco leaf include anatabine, anabasine, nornicotine, *N*-methylanabasine, anabaseine, nicotine, nicotine *N'*-oxide, myosmine, β-nicotyrine, cotinine, and 2,3'-bipyridyl (Figure 3.1). In commercial tobacco products, nicotine concentrations range from 6 to 18 milligrams per gram (mg/g) (0.6 to 1.8 percent by weight) (International Agency for Research on Cancer [IARC] 2004; Counts et al. 2005). Together, the sum of the concentrations of anatabine, anabasine, and nornicotine equals approximately 5 percent of the nicotine

Figure 3.1   Tobacco alkaloids

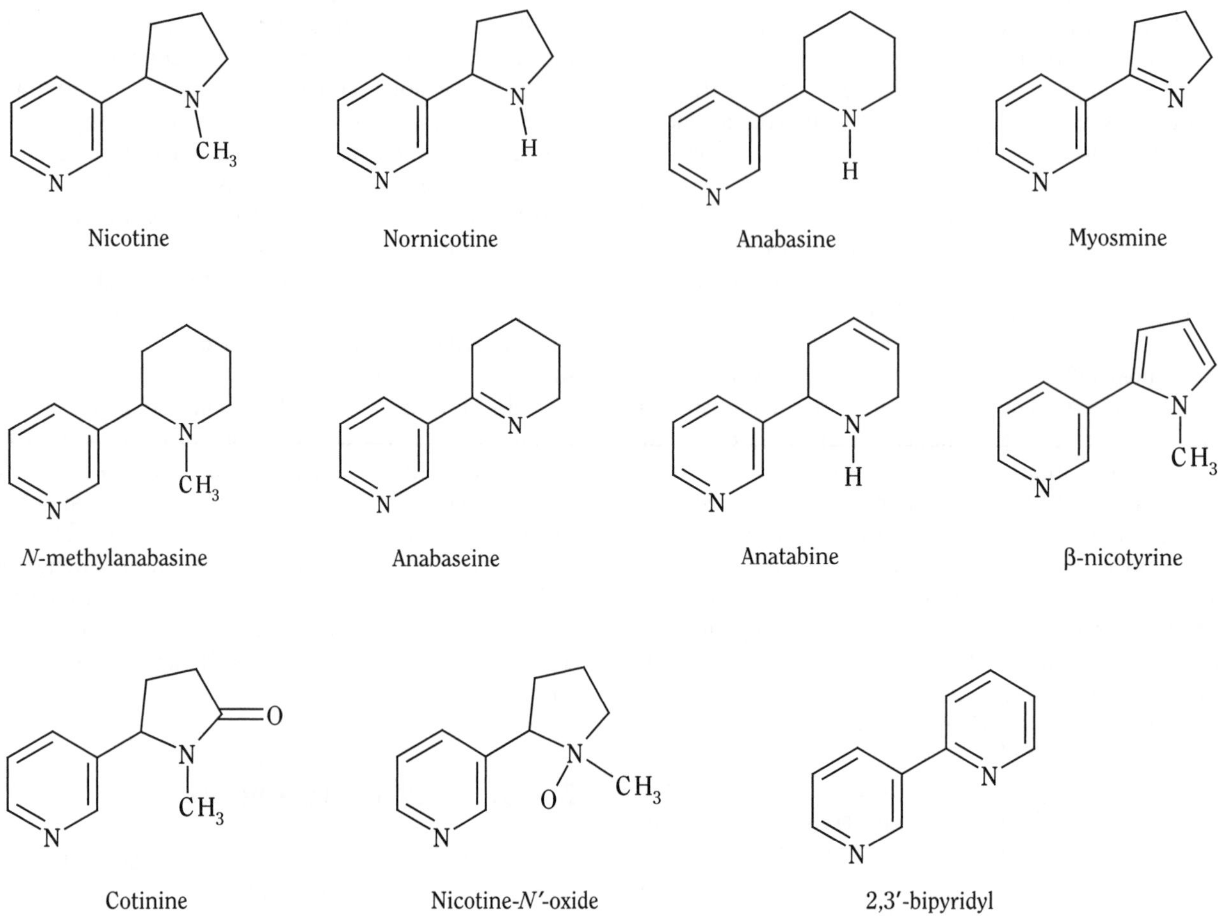

Nicotine   Nornicotine   Anabasine   Myosmine

N-methylanabasine   Anabaseine   Anatabine   β-nicotyrine

Cotinine   Nicotine-*N'*-oxide   2,3'-bipyridyl

concentration (Jacob et al. 1999). Many minor tobacco alkaloids are pharmacologically active in humans in one or more ways. Clark and colleagues (1965) observed that some of these alkaloids had physiological effects in a variety of animal tests. Lefevre (1989) reviewed the evidence and concluded that anabasine and nornicotine had demonstrated effects on smooth muscle fiber, blood pressure, and enzyme inhibition. The literature on potentially addictive properties of these minor alkaloids is limited. *S*(-)-nicotine, which is present in the tobacco leaf, is structurally similar to forms of several minor alkaloids also found in the tobacco leaf, such as *S*(-)-*N*-methylanabasine (Figure 3.2). Moreover, Dwoskin and colleagues (1995) reported that in the rat, anatabine, anabasine, *N*-methylanabasine, anabaseine, and nornicotine all release dopamine from striatal brain tissue. Overall, it is likely that some of the minor tobacco alkaloids could (1) be addictive if delivered alone at sufficiently high levels and (2) act together with

nicotine during tobacco use to generate effects that are difficult to discern because nicotine levels are so much higher. In addition to addictiveness, both nicotine and minor secondary amine alkaloids are precursors of carcinogenic TSNAs (IARC 2004, 2007).

The unprotonated nicotine molecule contains two nitrogen atoms with basic properties. The unprotonated nicotine molecule can thus add one proton to form a monoprotonated species or two protons to form the diprotonated species (Figure 3.3) (Brunnemann and Hoffmann 1974). The first proton added to nicotine attaches predominantly to the nitrogen on the five-membered (pyrrolidine) ring, because that nitrogen is significantly more basic than the nitrogen on the six-membered (pyridine) ring. Although protonated nicotine is not volatile, unprotonated nicotine is volatile and is able to enter the gas phase and readily pass into lipid membranes. Unprotonated nicotine is therefore free of the limitations that come with carrying an ionic charge, and the scientific literature and tobacco industry documents frequently refer to nicotine in this form as both "free nicotine" and "free-base nicotine." In the tobacco plant and in the dried leaf, nicotine largely exists in its ionic forms; otherwise, it would be rapidly lost to the surrounding atmosphere.

In water or in the droplets of particulate matter in tobacco smoke, the distribution of nicotine among its three forms depends on the pH of the solution. Increasing acidity of the solution increases the fraction of protonated molecules; conversely, increasing basicity increases the fraction in the unprotonated (free base) form (Figure 3.3). Because all forms of nicotine are highly soluble in water, all of the nicotine entering the respiratory tract from one puff of tobacco smoke easily dissolves in lung fluids and blood. However, because unprotonated nicotine from tobacco smoke particles is volatile, whereas protonated nicotine is not, a higher percentage of unprotonated nicotine in a puff results in a higher rate of nicotine deposition in the respiratory tract (Pankow 2001; Henningfield et al. 2004). The exact nature and effects of the increased rate of deposition depends on the chemical composition and the size of particles in the tobacco smoke, as well as topographic characteristics of smoking, such as puff size and duration and depth of inhalation. Increased rates of deposition in the respiratory tract lead to increased rates of nicotine delivery to the brain, which intensify the addictive properties of a drug (Henningfield et al. 2004). The conventional view has been that a sample of particulate matter from tobacco smoke is not usually so acidic that the diprotonated form becomes important. In water at room temperature, the approximate dividing line between dominance by protonated forms or by the unprotonated form is a pH of 8 (González et al. 1980). At higher pH, the fraction of unprotonated nicotine (α_{fb}) is greater than the fraction of protonated nicotine (Pankow 2001). At pH 8, the two fractions are present in equal percentages. At any lower pH, the fraction of protonated nicotine is greater.

Figure 3.2   Structures of nicotine and minor alkaloid S(-)-N-methylanabasine in tobacco leaf

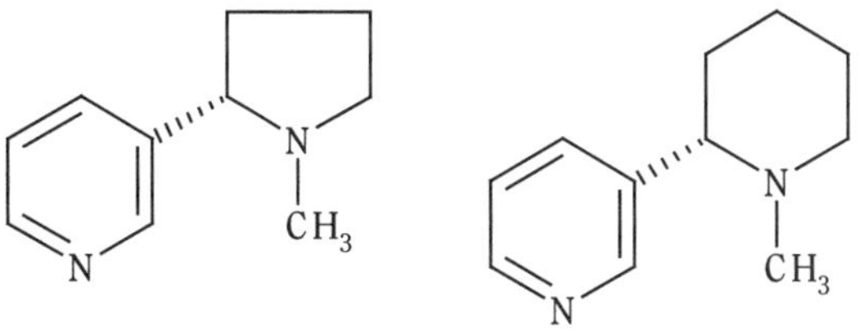

S(-)-nicotine   S(-)-N-methylanabasine

Because a typical sample of particulate matter from tobacco smoke collected from a cigarette or cigar is mostly nonaqueous liquid, it is not possible to take conventional pH measurements to determine nicotine distribution between the monoprotonated and unprotonated forms (Pankow 2001). However, it is possible to measure the concentration of unprotonated nicotine in a sample of tobacco smoke particulate ($c_{p,u}$), because that level produces a directly proportional concentration of unprotonated nicotine in the gas phase, which is measurable (Pankow et al. 1997, 2003; Watson et al. 2004). Measuring the concentration of nicotine in a sample of tobacco smoke in the particulate phase ($c_{p,t}$) allows calculation of the fraction of unprotonated nicotine: $\alpha_{fb} = c_{p,u}/c_{p,t}$ (Pankow et al. 2003). To simplify the discussion of α_{fb} values in tobacco smoke, Pankow (2001) introduced the term "effective pH" (pH_{eff}), which refers to the pH needed in water to obtain the α_{fb} value in a sample of particulate matter from smoke. Reported values of α_{fb} for smoke from commercial cigarettes at 20°C were 0.006 to 0.36 (Pankow et al. 2003; Watson et al. 2004), which corresponds to pH_{eff} values at 20°C in the range of 5.8 to 7.8.

Figure 3.3   Three forms of nicotine

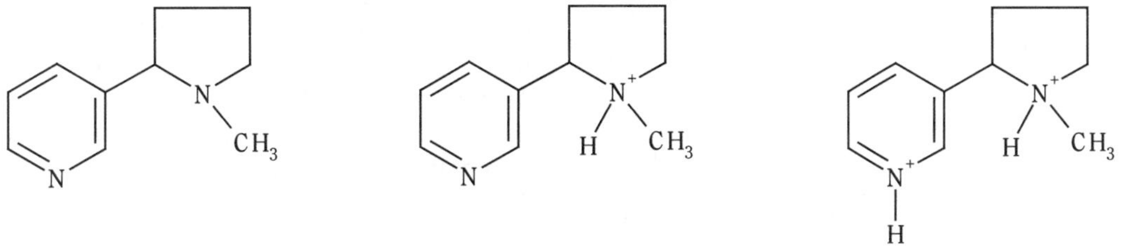

Unprotonated (free base)   Monoprotonated   Diprotonated

The fraction α_{fb} for particulate matter in tobacco smoke is important because the rapidity with which inhaled nicotine from tobacco smoke evaporates from the particulate phase and deposits on the linings of the respiratory tract is directly proportional to the α_{fb} value for the smoke (Pankow et al. 2003). According to numerous tobacco industry documents, increasing levels of unprotonated nicotine in tobacco smoke was known to increase smoke "strength," "impact," "kick," and/or "harshness" (Backhurst 1965; Dunn 1973; Teague 1974; Ingebrethsen and Lyman 1991). Because of similar mechanisms, nicotine replacement therapy delivering gaseous nicotine caused throat irritation at delivery levels per puff that were similar to those reached by smoking a cigarette rated by using the FTC regimen at approximately 1 mg of total nicotine delivery; thus, cigarette design is focused on a balance between smoke "impact" and irritation. Some researchers have suggested that the irritation and harshness of smoke at higher pH makes it harder for smokers to inhale this smoke into the lungs (Brunnemann and Hoffmann 1974).

The value of α_{fb} for particulate matter in each puff of smoke from one brand of cigarette or cigar strongly depends on the overall proportion of acids to bases in the puff (Pankow et al. 1997). As already noted, nicotine itself is a base. The natural acids in tobacco smoke (e.g., formic acid, acetic acid, and propionic acid) can protonate nicotine and tend to reduce α_{fb} from its maximum of 1.0. The natural bases (e.g., ammonia) tend to neutralize the acids and keep more nicotine in the unprotonated form.

Variability in the acid-base nature of commercially available tobacco leaf is considerable. Flue-cured ("bright") tobacco is typically viewed as producing acidic smoke. Air-cured ("burley") tobacco is typically viewed as producing basic smoke. Simple adjustment of the tobacco blend can therefore produce a considerable range of acid or base content in tobacco smoke. In acidic smoke, α_{fb} can be 0.01 or lower (e.g., 1-percent unprotonated nicotine), and in basic smoke, the α_{fb} can be relatively high (e.g., 0.36 [36-percent unprotonated nicotine]) (Pankow et al. 2003; Watson et al. 2004).

Tobacco additives that are bases increase α_{fb} values in mainstream smoke, and these additives are discussed extensively in tobacco industry documents (Henningfield et al. 2004). The documents reveal that a variety of basic additives have been considered, including ammonia and ammonia precursors. Conversely, some manufacturers also were interested in reducing harshness to a minimum and investigated acidic additives such as levulinic acid as "smoothing" agents. In that context, the natural basicity of a specific blend and the harshness of the smoke can be reduced by acidic additives such as levulinic acid, which tend to reduce α_{fb} (Guess 1980; Stewart and Lawrence 1988).

In summary, nicotine in cigarette smoke exists in either a protonated or unprotonated form, depending on a number of factors, including the presence of natural acids and bases, the tobacco blend, tip ventilation, and the use of additives. Cigarette design ensures that the smoke has enough unprotonated nicotine to rapidly transfer nicotine into the body but not so much of it as to be too harsh for the smoker to continue to smoke.

N-Nitrosamines

N-nitrosamines are a class of chemical compounds containing a nitroso group attached to an amine nitrogen. There are two types of nitrosamines in tobacco and tobacco smoke: volatile and nonvolatile, including TSNAs (Hoffmann et al. 1981; Tricker et al. 1991; Spiegelhalder and Bartsch 1996; IARC 2007). The volatile nitrosamines include N-nitrosodimethylamine, N-nitrosoethylmethylamine, N-nitrosodiethylamine, N-nitro-sopyrrolidine, and N-nitrosomorpholine. The nonvolatile nitrosamines are 4-(N-nitroso-N-methylamino)butyric acid, N-nitrosopipecolic acid, N-nitrososarcosine, 3-(N-nitroso-N-methylamino)propionic acid, N-nitrosoproline, and N-nitrosodiethanolamine. The nonvolatile TSNAs (Figure 3.4) have been examined extensively in tobacco and tobacco smoke. They include N'-nitrosonornicotine (NNN), 4-(methylnitrosamino)-1-(3-pyridyl)-1-butanone (NNK), N'-nitrosoanatabine (NATB), and N'-nitrosoanabasine (NAB). The levels of nitrosamines in tobacco products are higher than are those in other consumer products, such as cooked bacon and beer (Hecht and Hoffmann 1988), and smokers are exposed to higher levels of TSNAs than of the other nitrosamines (Hoffmann et al. 1981; IARC 2007).

Studies have been conducted to identify precursors of nitrosamines and to determine the conditions required for their formation in tobacco. The primary intent of this research was to identify ways to reduce nitrosamine levels in tobacco and tobacco smoke. Secondary and tertiary amines in tobacco, including the alkaloids, react with nitrosating agents to form N-nitrosamines (Hecht and Hoffmann 1988). Hecht and colleagues (1978) showed that both nicotine and nornicotine can react with sodium nitrite under controlled conditions to form carcinogenic NNN and NNK, but nicotine is considered more important because of its higher level in tobacco products. TSNAs are not present at trace levels in freshly harvested tobacco, but they are predominantly formed during processing, curing, and storage (Hoffmann et al. 1974, 1981;

Figure 3.4   Tobacco-specific nitrosamines

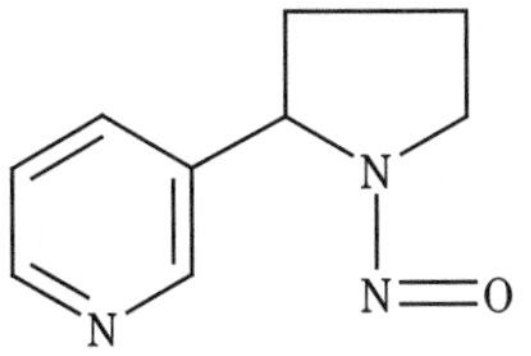

N'-nitrosonornicotine

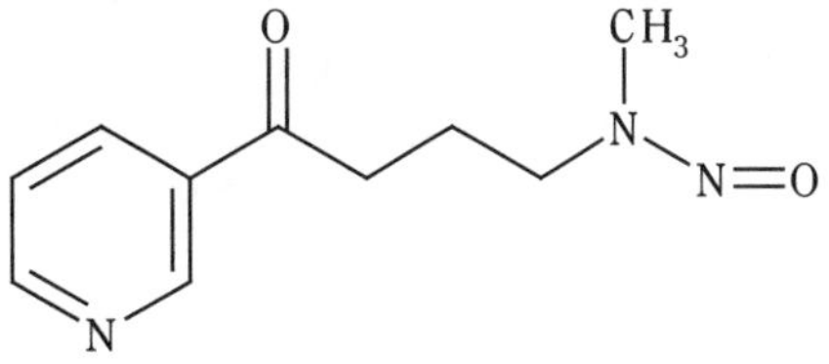

4-(methylnitrosamino)-1-
(3-pyridyl)-1-butanone

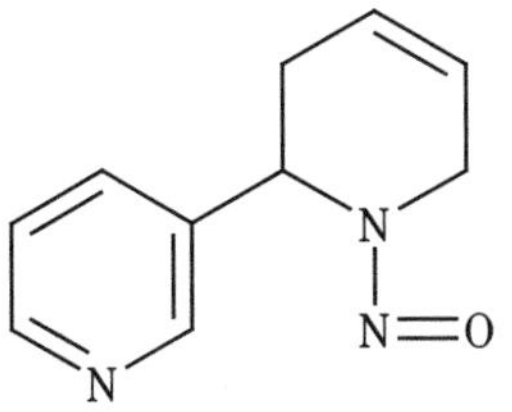

N'-nitrosoanatabine

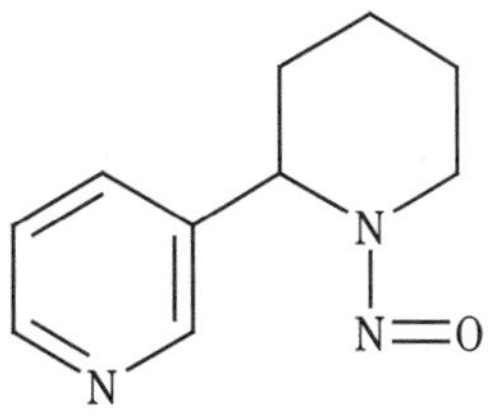

N'-nitrosoanabasine

Chamberlain et al. 1984; Andersen and Kemp 1985; Bhide et al. 1987; Djordjevic et al. 1989; Fischer et al. 1989b; Fisher 2000a). Aerobic bacteria play a major role in TSNA formation in air-cured tobacco (Hecht et al. 1975; Hoffmann et al. 1981; Parsons et al. 1986). In flue-cured tobacco, the curing conditions alter levels of nitrosamines (Fisher 2000a). Before the late 1960s and early 1970s, direct-fire curing in the United States did not produce high levels of TSNAs. When propane gas was introduced as the combustion source (Fisher 2000a), nitrogen oxides from the exhaust gases in tobacco barns reacted with alkaloids in the tobacco plant to form TSNAs. Hoffmann and colleagues (Hoffmann et al. 1981; Brunnemann and Hoffmann 1991) also revealed that *N*-nitrosodiethanolamine is formed from the diethanolamine used in the formulation of maleic hydrazide, which is applied to regulate suckers on tobacco plants.

Volatile nitrosamines are found primarily in the gas phase of tobacco smoke, and TSNAs are almost exclusively found in the particulate phase (Guerin 1980). Researchers suggest that about one-half of the nitrosamines in tobacco smoke are transferred unchanged from the tobacco to the smoke and that the remainder is formed from pyrosynthesis during smoking (Hoffmann et al. 1977; Adams et al. 1983). Other researchers have concluded that almost all TSNAs are transferred directly from the tobacco (Fischer et al. 1990b).

It is difficult to determine whether TSNAs are pyrosynthesized or transferred intact, because the most

important factors in nitrosamine formation such as concentrations of preformed TSNA in tobacco or their precursor, as well as chemical and physical processes during smoking, could affect either mechanism. Morie and Sloan (1973) reported that the nitrate and amine content in tobacco determined the amount of *N*-nitrosodimethylamine formed in tobacco smoke. This finding has been widely duplicated by researchers looking at other nitrosamines (Hecht et al. 1975; Brunnemann et al. 1977a, 1983; Hoffmann et al. 1981; Adams et al. 1983, 1984; Fischer et al. 1989b; Tricker et al. 1991; Atawodi et al. 1995; Spiegelhalder and Bartsch 1996). Other factors that influence nitrate concentrations in tobacco can also indirectly influence nitrosamine concentrations. Because TSNA content is strongly influenced by the use of stems that are naturally high in TSNAs in the cigarette rod, the increased use of stems leads to higher nitrosamines in the smoke (Brunnemann et al. 1983). Researchers have also found that the use of nitrogen fertilizer can contribute to the concentration of nitrosamines in tobacco and ultimately in the smoke (Johnson and Rhoades 1972; Tso et al. 1975; Brunnemann et al. 1977a; Chamberlain et al. 1984, 1986). Other influential factors identified were tobacco growth conditions, storage times, storage temperatures (Andersen et al. 1982; Andersen and Kemp 1985), and the stalk positions from which the tobacco leaves are harvested (Chamberlain et al. 1986).

Another factor contributing to nitrosamine concentrations in tobacco is the type of tobacco used (Johnson and Rhoades 1972; Brunnemann et al. 1983; Fischer et al. 1989b,c). Oriental tobaccos are lowest in both nitrates and TSNAs (Fischer et al. 1989b), whereas burley tobacco contains the highest TSNA concentrations (Fischer et al. 1989b,c). The nitrosamine concentrations in bright tobacco are between those in oriental and burley and depend on the curing practices described earlier (Tso et al. 1975; Hoffmann et al. 1979a). The TSNA concentrations are higher in blended cigarettes than in those made from bright tobacco, because burley is included in the blend (Fischer et al. 1990a). In most tobaccos, NNN concentrations exceed NNK concentrations (Fischer et al. 1989b), but in bright tobacco, NNK concentrations exceed those of NNN (Fischer et al. 1989b, 1990a).

The preformed concentration of nitrosamines in tobacco leaves and stems is a major determinant of the levels in tobacco smoke (Fischer et al. 1990c; Spiegelhalder and Bartsch 1996). However, for cigarettes that have the same concentrations of nitrosamines in the tobacco, the nitrosamine levels in the smoke were largely determined by the degree of ventilation and the use of cellulose-acetate filter tips in the cigarette. After examining machine-generated smoke, by the FTC/ISO method, from cigarettes containing the same type of tobacco, whether blended or bright only, researchers found that nitrosamine levels are correlated with tar delivery, which is primarily a function of filter ventilation (Adams et al. 1987; Fischer et al. 1990a). However, studies of cigarettes with different blends of tobacco have shown that tar is not an accurate measure of nitrosamine levels (Fischer et al. 1989c; Spiegelhalder and Bartsch 1996; Counts et al. 2004). Studies have also shown that cellulose-acetate filter tips remove both volatile nitrosamines and TSNAs (Morie and Sloan 1973; Brunnemann et al. 1980; Rühl et al. 1980; Hoffmann et al. 1981). These findings indicate the importance of measuring TSNA levels in smoke, rather than using measured levels of tar or nicotine to predict levels of TSNAs in smoke on the basis of an average relationship between tar or nicotine and TSNAs.

Nitrosamine levels measured in the tobacco and the smoke from cigarettes that were purchased around the world vary widely because of the differences cited above. Historically, the ranges of levels of NNN (2 to 12,454 nanograms [ng] per cigarette), NAB+NATB (109 to 1,033 ng), and NNK (55 to 10,745 ng) in cigarette tobacco were wide (Hoffmann et al. 1974; Fischer et al. 1989b, 1990a,c; Tricker et al. 1991; Atawodi et al. 1995; IARC 2004, 2007). More recent analyses have given more consistent results that depend on the blend of tobacco (NNN + NNK: 87 to 1,900 ng/g) (Ashley et al. 2003). Levels in mainstream tobacco smoke, as reported by the FTC/ISO machine-smoking method, have been reported at an order of magnitude lower than those in tobacco (NNN = 4 to 1,353 ng

generated per cigarette); NAB+NATB = 10 to 82 ng; and NNK = 5 to 1,749 ng (Fischer et al. 1989b, 1990a,c; Tricker et al. 1991; Atawodi et al. 1995; Mitacek et al. 1999).

Using the ISO, Massachusetts (MDPH; 45-mL puff volume, 30-second puff interval, 50 percent of ventilation holes blocked) and Canadian Intense (CAN; 55-mL puff volume, 30-second puff interval, 100 percent of ventilation holes blocked) smoking regimens, Counts and colleagues (2005) reported the levels of TSNAs in mainstream smoke from Philip Morris cigarettes sold internationally. The investigators found that in mainstream smoke, NNN levels were 5.0 to 195.3 ng generated per cigarette for ISO, 16.3 to 374.2 ng for MDPH, and 20.6 to 410.6 ng for CAN. NNK levels were 12.4 to 107.8 ng generated per cigarette for ISO, 25.8 to 206.6 ng for MDPH, and 39.1 to 263.0 ng for CAN. NATB levels were 8.0 to 160.4 ng generated per cigarette for ISO, 31.9 to 295.3 ng for MDPH, and 43.5 to 345.1 ng for CAN.

The combined levels of NNN and NNK reported by Wu and associates (2005) are in good agreement with the ranges reported by Counts and colleagues (2005). This finding suggests that the more advanced analytical methods used in these later studies yielded more accurate measures for current cigarettes than did previous measures. Levels of volatile nitrosamines in mainstream tobacco smoke are typically lower than those of the TSNAs (dimethylnitrosamine = 0.1 to 97 ng generated per cigarette; methylethylnitrosamine = 0.1 to 9.1 ng; and N-nitrosopyrrolidine = 1.5 to 64.5 ng) (Brunnemann et al. 1977a, 1980; Adams et al. 1987).

Ashley and colleagues (2003) compared TSNA concentrations in tobacco from Marlboro cigarettes with those in locally popular, non-U.S. brands of cigarettes in 13 countries. For most of the countries, TSNA concentrations in the tobacco from Marlboro cigarettes were higher than those in tobacco from locally popular brands from that country. TSNA concentrations varied widely (20-fold overall) between and within brands from the same country and differed significantly from country to country. This study confirmed earlier work showing wide variations in TSNA levels in tobacco and smoke from products within a country and between countries (Hecht et al. 1975; Fischer et al. 1990c; Spiegelhalder and Bartsch 1996; Gray et al. 2000). The basic findings from this study were confirmed by work from Wu and colleagues (2005), who examined combined levels of NNN and NNK in the mainstream smoke from cigarettes from the same 13 countries and also found a wide variation in this matrix.

Identification of growing, curing, and blending practices that alter nitrosamine levels in tobacco and smoke have led researchers to agree that low TSNA levels in smoke can be achieved by using particular varieties of tobacco and carefully controlling the factors leading to formation and transfer of TSNAs from tobacco into smoke (Brunnemann et al. 1977a; Hoffmann et al. 1977; Hecht et al. 1978; Rühl et al. 1980; Andersen and Kemp 1985; Hecht and Hoffmann 1988; Fischer et al. 1990c; Spiegelhalder and Bartsch 1996; Mitacek et al. 1999; Ashley et al. 2003; Burns et al. 2008). To reduce TSNAs, tobacco curing in the United States is undergoing a transition, and nitrosamine levels may change as curing and blending practices change (Counts et al. 2004; O'Connor et al. 2008).

In summary, nitrosamines are found in tobacco and tobacco smoke at high levels compared with other consumer products. The levels of these compounds, which are formed during tobacco processing, curing, and storage, can be minimized by breeding and selecting tobacco lines with lower propensity for TSNA formation, and limiting the use of nitrogen fertilizer, the levels of nitrogen oxides in the atmosphere during curing, the amount of burley tobacco in the blend, and storage times. The impact of different practices is clearly seen by the wide global range of TSNA levels in tobacco and smoke.

Polycyclic Aromatic Hydrocarbons

PAHs are chemical compounds with two or more condensed aromatic and other cyclic rings of carbon and hydrogen atoms (Douben 2003). Recent studies (Rodgman and Perfetti 2006) have identified at least 539 PAHs in tobacco smoke. The U.S. Environmental Protection Agency (EPA) has identified 16 priority environmental PAHs on the basis of evidence that they cause or may cause cancer: acenaphthylene, acenaphthene, anthracene, benz[*a*] anthracene, benzo[*a*]pyrene (B[*a*]P), benzo[*b*]fluoranthene (B[*b*]F), benzo[*k*]fluoranthene (B[*k*]F), benzo[*g,h,i*] perylene, chrysene, dibenz[*a,h*]anthracene, fluoranthene, fluorene, indeno[1,2,3-*cd*]pyrene, naphthalene, phenanthrene, and pyrene (Figure 3.5) (USEPA 1980, 1986). The 16 PAHs, which have two to six fused rings and molecular weights of 128 to 278, were detected in the particulate matter of tobacco smoke (IARC 1986, 2004; Ding et al. 2006, 2007). PAHs range from highly volatile to relatively nonvolatile, and their distribution in the particulate and gas phases of tobacco smoke varies with the boiling point (Grimmer et al. 1987). However, the gas phase contained only an estimated 1 percent of the total PAHs found in tobacco smoke. The composition of PAHs in mainstream smoke is different from that in sidestream smoke (Grimmer et al. 1987), and the lipophilic characteristics range from moderate to high (Douben 2003).

PAHs are formed by incomplete combustion of natural organic matter such as wood, petroleum, and tobacco and are found throughout the environment (Evans et al. 1993; Douben 2003). In the burning cone

at the tip of the tobacco rod, various pyrolysis reactions occur to form methylidyne (CH) radicals that are precursors to the pyrosynthesis of PAHs. Hoffmann and Wynder (1967) were the first to show that adding nitrate to tobacco reduced B[*a*]P levels. During smoking, nitrates form O_2 and nitric oxide (NO), which intercept radicals and reduce PAH levels (Johnson et al. 1973a; Hoffmann and Hoffmann 1997). Other researchers also reported that the presence of nitrate in tobacco decreases B[*a*]P levels in the smoke (Torikai et al. 2005). The pyrolytic conditions also favor the formation of PAHs from certain isoprenoids such as solanesol (IARC 1986), although other findings have disagreed with this assessment (Torikai et al. 2005). B[*a*]P is the most widely known and studied PAH (IARC 2004).

Differences in tobacco type can affect levels of PAHs in the smoke. Flue-cured (bright) or sun-cured (oriental) tobaccos have lower nitrate content than does air-cured (burley) tobacco. Pyrosynthesis of PAHs generates higher PAH levels in smoke from cigarettes made exclusively with flue-cured or sun-cured tobaccos than in smoke from cigarettes made with burley tobaccos (Hoffmann and Hoffmann 1997; Ding et al. 2005). Cigarettes made from reconstituted tobacco with cellulose fiber as an additive yield significantly reduced PAH levels. Evans and colleagues (1993) measured PAHs in mainstream and sidestream smoke and found that B[*a*]P, B[*b*]F, and B[*k*]F levels are related to tar yields in cigarette smoke that result from differences in cigarette ventilation.

Some studies reported the levels of B[*a*]P alone as a surrogate for the total PAH content. Ding and colleagues (2005) observed that total PAH levels in mainstream smoke from commercial cigarette brands varied from 1 to 1.6 µg generated per cigarette under FTC machine-smoking conditions. In the same study, individual PAHs ranged from less than 10 ng generated per cigarette (B[*k*]F) to approximately 500 ng (naphthalene) (Ding et al. 2005). Other researchers reported levels of B[*b*]F at 10.4 ng, B[*k*]F at 5.1 ng, and B[*a*]P at 13.4 ng generated per cigarette (Evans et al. 1993). In four of five brands tested, B[*a*]P concentrations in cigarette tar were about 0.5 ng/mg of tar (Tomkins et al. 1985). Kaiserman and Rickert (1992) reported the levels of B[*a*]P in smoke from 35 brands of Canadian cigarettes by using the ISO method; mean levels were 3.36 to 28.39 ng generated per cigarette. Although B[*a*]P levels were linearly related to declared tar values, the tar values and the B[*a*]P levels did not change at the same relative rate. In a study of PAHs in mainstream smoke from cigarettes from 14 countries, Ding and colleagues (2006) showed a significant global variation in levels. They also demonstrated an inverse relationship with TSNA levels at high PAH and low TSNA levels, possibly as a result of differences in nitrate levels.

Figure 3.5   Priority environmental polycyclic aromatic hydrocarbons

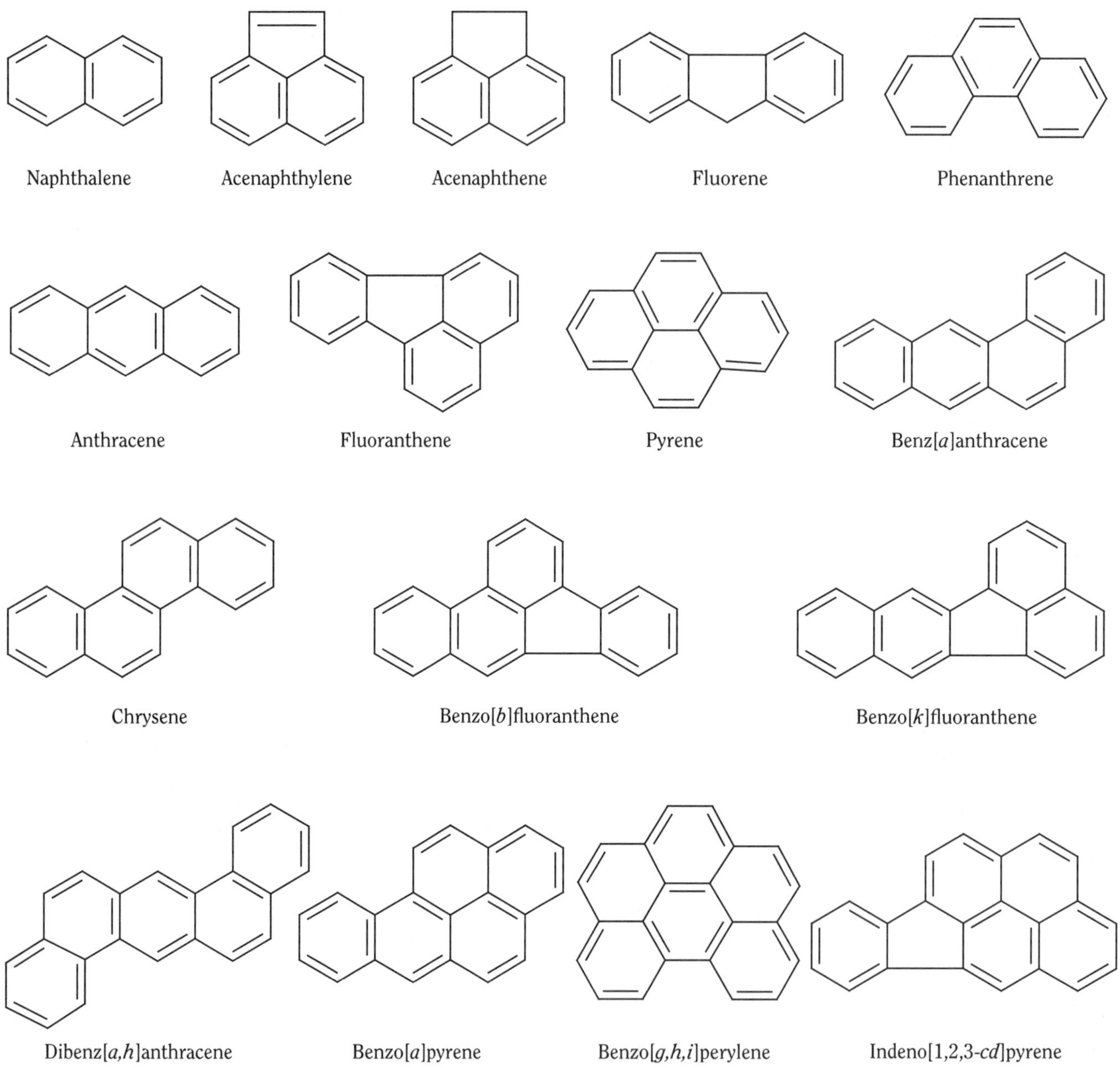

Naphthalene   Acenaphthylene   Acenaphthene   Fluorene   Phenanthrene

Anthracene   Fluoranthene   Pyrene   Benz[*a*]anthracene

Chrysene   Benzo[*b*]fluoranthene   Benzo[*k*]fluoranthene

Dibenz[*a,h*]anthracene   Benzo[*a*]pyrene   Benzo[*g,h,i*]perylene   Indeno[1,2,3-*cd*]pyrene

In summary, PAHs result from the burning of biologic material, so they are present in the smoke from any form of burning tobacco. Factors that can affect PAH levels in tobacco smoke include the type of tobacco and its nitrate content. Because of divergent pyrosynthetic mechanisms, factors that increase the nitrate content of tobacco decrease PAH levels but may increase TSNA levels in cigarette smoke. However, a substantial reduction in PAH levels in cigarette smoke will be a challenge as long as tobacco smoke is generated from burning tobacco.

Volatile Compounds Including Aldehydes

When a cigarette is smoked, chemicals partition between the particulate and gas phases on the basis of physical properties including volatility and solubility (Hoffmann and Hoffmann 1997). Complete partitioning of any chemical to the gas phase of cigarette smoke is generally limited to the gaseous products of combustion, such as the oxides of nitrogen, carbon, and sulfur, and the extremely volatile low-molecular-weight organic compounds. There are between 400 and 500 volatile gases and other compounds in the gas phase (Hoffmann and Hoffmann 1997). The nearly complete combustion of the cigarette tobacco filler generates an effluent stream of gaseous chemicals residing almost exclusively in the gas phase portion of mainstream cigarette smoke. These chemicals, on the basis of weight, account for most of the mainstream smoke. In order by prevalence, these chemicals include N_2, O_2, CO_2, CO, nitrogen oxides, and the sulfur-containing gaseous compounds.

CO and CO_2 result from the combustion of tobacco. Other than N_2 and O_2, CO and CO_2 are the most abundant compounds in mainstream cigarette smoke, representing nearly 15 percent of the weight of the gas phase. CO_2 levels (approximately 50 mg generated per cigarette) are more abundant than are CO levels (approximately 20 mg), as determined by the FTC machine-smoking method.

Nitrogen oxide gases are formed by the combustion of nitrogen-containing amino acids and proteins in the tobacco leaf (Hoffmann and Hoffmann 1997). Mainstream cigarette smoke contains mostly NO with traces of nitrogen dioxide (NO_2) and nitrous oxide. The formation of nitrogen oxides is amplified by combustion with nitrate salts, and the amount formed is directly related to the nitrate concentration of the tobacco leaf (MacKown et al. 1999). The mainstream cigarette smoke contains approximately 500 µg of NO generated per cigarette. Although fresh smoke contains little NO_2, the aging of the smoke converts the reactive NO to NO_2, which has an estimated half-life of 10 minutes (Borland et al. 1985; Rickert et al. 1987). These gases react with water and other components in cigarette smoke to form nitrate particles and acidic constituents.

Sulfur-containing gases result from the combustion of sulfur-containing amino acids and proteins (Horton and Guerin 1974). In mainstream cigarette smoke, H_2S is the most abundant of these gases (approximately 85 µg generated per cigarette), and both sulfur dioxide and carbon disulfide are present in smaller quantities (approximately 2 µg).

In addition to the volatile gases, mainstream cigarette smoke contains a wide range of volatile organic compounds (VOCs) (Counts et al. 2005; Polzin et al. 2007). The formation of these VOCs results from the incomplete combustion of tobacco during and between puffs. The generation of VOCs, as well as the previously mentioned volatile gases, is directly related to the tar delivery of the cigarette, as evidenced by machine smoking under the FTC regimen (Hoffmann and Hoffmann 1997; Polzin et al. 2007). Therefore, factors altering the yield of tar (e.g., tobacco blend, cigarette filter, filter ventilation, paper

porosity, and tobacco weight) directly affect the yield of VOCs. Under certain machine-smoking conditions, the use of charcoal filters (Williamson et al. 1965; Counts et al. 2005; Laugesen and Fowles 2006; Polzin et al. 2008), variations in the temperature in the burning zone, and the presence or absence of O_2 can substantially alter the levels of VOCs generated in cigarette smoke (Torikai et al. 2004). The VOCs in mainstream cigarette smoke, as a result of their high biologic activity and levels, are among the most hazardous chemicals in cigarette smoke (Fowles and Dybing 2003; IARC 2004). In developed countries, the combined exposure of smokers to mainstream cigarette smoke and nonsmokers to secondhand smoke constitutes a significant portion of the population's total exposure to certain VOCs. For example, more than one-half of the U.S. population's exposure to benzene is from cigarette smoking (U.S. Department of Health and Human Services [USDHHS] 2002). The roughly 500 VOCs in the gas phase of mainstream cigarette smoke can be subclassified by structure. Among the most significant classes are the aromatic hydrocarbons, carbonyls, aliphatic hydrocarbons, and nitriles. Although other classes of volatile compounds (e.g., acids and bases) are present, these four classes of VOCs have been the most widely studied, because of their biologic activity and overall higher levels.

Aromatics are a class of compounds defined by their structural similarity to benzene. These compounds result from incomplete combustion of the organic matter of the cigarette, most notably sugars and cellulose (Chortyk and Schlotzhauer 1973). The most abundant aromatic compounds in mainstream smoke generated from full-flavored cigarettes with use of the FTC/ISO smoking regimen are toluene (approximately 5 to 80 µg generated per cigarette), benzene (approximately 4 to 60 µg), total xylenes (approximately 2 to 20 µg), styrene (approximately 0.5 to 10 µg), and ethylbenzene (approximately 1 to 8 µg) (Counts et al. 2005; Polzin et al. 2007).

Carbonyl compounds include the ketones and aldehydes. These compounds are studied because of their reactivity and levels, which approach 1 mg generated per cigarette. The most prevalent aldehydes in mainstream smoke from cigarettes, generated using the ISO regimen, are acetaldehyde (approximately 30 to 650 µg generated per cigarette), acrolein (approximately 2.5 to 60 µg), and formaldehyde (approximately 2 to 50 µg) (Counts et al. 2005). The most prevalent ketones in mainstream cigarette smoke, generated by using the FTC/ISO smoking regimen, are acetone (approximately 50 to 550 µg generated per cigarette) and 2-butanone (approximately 10 to 130 µg) (Counts et al. 2005; Polzin et al. 2007). Spincer and Chard (1971) identified formaldehyde in both the particulate and gas phases of tobacco smoke and found that much of the formaldehyde was associated with total particulate matter (TPM). These investigators determined that formaldehyde delivery was higher in smoke from bright tobacco than in that from burley tobacco.

On the basis of total mass, hydrocarbons represent the largest VOC class in mainstream cigarette smoke (Hoffmann and Hoffmann 1997). Both saturated hydrocarbons and olefins result from the incomplete combustion of cigarette tobacco. The most abundant hydrocarbons in cigarette smoke are methane, ethane, and propane, which represent nearly 1 percent of the total cigarette effluent. Unsaturated hydrocarbons are also present in significant quantities in mainstream cigarette smoke, as evidenced by using the ISO regimen, but the olefins isoprene (approximately 70 to 480 µg generated per cigarette) and 1,3-butadiene (approximately 6.5 to 55 µg) are the most abundant unsaturated hydrocarbons (Counts et al. 2005).

The volatile nitriles, which include compounds such as HCN, acetonitrile, and acrylonitrile, are important because of their toxic effects. The most abundant nitriles in mainstream smoke generated from cigarettes by using the ISO regimen are HCN (approximately 3 to 200 µg generated per cigarette), acetonitrile (approximately 100 µg), and acrylonitrile (approximately 1 to 12 µg) (Counts et al. 2005).

In summary, cigarette smoke is composed primarily of gaseous and volatile compounds. Thus, levels of these compounds are critical in determining the overall toxicity of tobacco smoke. Differences in the design of the cigarette can have a substantial effect on the levels determined in smoke, which makes the reproducibility of results challenging, but provides knowledge of possible mechanisms to reduce the exposure of smokers.

Heavy Metals

Metals and metalloids are among the many substances contained in tobacco smoke; they are often loosely called "heavy metals" without regard to whether they are light- or heavy-mass metals or metalloids. Their chemical properties span a wide range. These substances are found as pure metals or as metals naturally associated or chemically bound to other elements that can significantly alter the chemical properties of the metals.

Although metals can be deposited on tobacco leaves from particles in the air and some fungicides and pesticides containing toxic metals have been sprayed on tobacco leaves or soils in the past (Frank et al. 1977), most of the metals present in plants are absorbed from the soil (Schwartz and Hecking 1991; Cheng 2003; Xiao et al. 2004a,b). Soils, therefore, including any amendments to the soil, such as sludge, fertilizers, or irrigation with polluted water have been the predominant source

of metals found in tobacco grown in various geographic areas (Bache et al. 1985; Mulchi et al. 1987, 1991, 1992; Adamu et al. 1989; Bell et al. 1992; Rickert and Kaiserman 1994; Stephens et al. 2005). Cadmium and lead content in tobacco and smoke have been correlated with the content in the soil in which the tobacco was grown, after adjustment for the amendments to the soil (Bache et al. 1985; Adamu et al. 1989; Mulchi et al. 1991, 1992; Bell et al. 1992; Rickert and Kaiserman 1994; Stephens et al. 2005). In addition, Rickert and Kaiserman (1994) showed that heavy metals in the air can be important. For example, significant changes in the lead concentrations in the air between 1974 and 1988 accounted for most of the changes in lead levels in tobacco during that period. Researchers have associated the mercury content in tobacco with environmental factors and soil in geographic areas where the tobacco was grown (Rickert and Kaiserman 1994). Mulchi and colleagues (1992) have also suggested that consideration of soil pH is important to understanding the relationship between metals in the soil and metals in the tobacco leaf. Because of differences in the soil, air, and metal uptake by the tobacco plant, the metal content of tobaccos varies widely.

Most metals and metalloids are not volatile at room temperature. Pure metallic mercury is volatile, but only a few forms are volatile at temperatures lower than 100°C. The temperature of tobacco that burns at the tip of a cigarette may reach 900°C (Baker 1981). A burning cigarette tip is hot enough to volatilize many metals into the gas phase, but by the time the smoke is inhaled or rises in a plume from the cigarette as secondhand smoke, most of the metals have condensed and moved into the particulate portion of the smoke aerosol (Baker 1981; Chang et al. 2003).

The range of levels of toxic metals found in tobacco smoke reflects differences in cigarette manufacturing processes, ventilation, additives, concentrations in the tobacco, and the efficiency with which the metal transfers from the leaf to the smoke. The transfer rate of metals from tobacco into smoke also depends on the properties of the metal (Krivan et al. 1994). Because tobacco plants easily absorb and accumulate cadmium from the soil, cadmium is found at relatively high concentrations in tobacco leaves. This accumulation, along with the high percentage of transfer from the leaves into the smoke (Schneider and Krivan 1993), yields high cadmium levels in tobacco smoke (Chiba and Masironi 1992). Kalcher and colleagues (1993) developed a model for the behavior of metals in mainstream smoke and found that most of the cadmium in tobacco smoke is in the particulate phase, whereas lead is equally partitioned between the particulate and gas phases. Cadmium levels have been reported to range from 10 to 250 ng generated per cigarette in the particulate phase (Allen and Vickroy 1976; Bache et al. 1985; Nitsch et al. 1991; Schneider and Krivan 1993; Krivan et al. 1994; Rhoades and White 1997; Csalári and Szántai 2002; Torrence et al. 2002) to a lower level of 1 to 31 ng in the gas phase (Nitsch et al. 1991). More recent studies of cadmium levels in particulate matter in smoke from commercial cigarettes smoked under FTC/ ISO conditions reported a range of 1.6 to 101.0 ng generated per cigarette (Counts et al. 2005; Pappas et al. 2006). Not surprisingly, Counts et al. (2005) also showed that levels of cadmium in smoke generated using more intense smoking regimens such as MDPH (12.7 to 178.3 ng generated per cigarette) and CAN (43.5 to 197.1 ng generated per cigarette) were higher than when using FTC/ISO. This increase was also seen with other metals tested. These studies also demonstrated that changes in cigarette design, such as introducing filter ventilation, reduces the delivery of metals under FTC/ISO smoking conditions. In counterfeit cigarettes, levels of cadmium in particulate matter from mainstream smoke can be significantly higher, ranging from 40 to 300 ng generated per cigarette, under FTC smoking conditions (Pappas et al. 2007).

Lead also transfers well from tobacco to smoke (Schneider and Krivan 1993); measurements range from 18 to 83 ng generated per cigarette in the particulate phase (Allen and Vickroy 1976; Nitsch et al. 1991; Schneider and Krivan 1993; Krivan et al. 1994; Csalári and Szántai 2002; Torrence et al. 2002; Baker et al. 2004) and from 6 to 149 ng in the gas phase (Nitsch et al. 1991). More recent studies of lead levels in particulate matter in smoke from commercial cigarettes smoked under FTC/ISO conditions reported a range of 4 to 39 ng generated per cigarette (Counts et al. 2005; Pappas et al. 2006). Studies of cigarettes in the United Kingdom have documented concentrations of heavy metals in a number of counterfeit cigarette brands that were higher than those in domestic products (Stephens et al. 2005). These metals included arsenic, cadmium, and lead. In counterfeit cigarettes, levels of lead in mainstream cigarette smoke can be significantly higher, ranging up to 330 ng generated per cigarette, under FTC smoking conditions (Pappas et al. 2007). Studies have also found similar levels of nickel in both phases: particulate levels range from 1.1 to 78.5 ng generated per cigarette (Bache et al. 1985; Nitsch et al. 1991; Schneider and Krivan 1993; Torjussen et al. 2003), and gas phase levels range from 3 to 57 ng (Nitsch et al. 1991).

Tobacco smoke also contains lower levels of other metals. The range of levels found in the particulate phase includes cobalt, 0.012 to 48.0 ng generated per cigarette; arsenic, 1.5 to 21.0 ng; chromium, 1.1 to 1.7 ng; antimony, 0.10 to 0.13 ng; thallium, 0.6 to 2.4 ng; and mercury, 0.46 to 6.5 ng (Allen and Vickroy 1976; Suzuki et al. 1976; Nitsch et al. 1991; Schneider and Krivan 1993;

Krivan et al. 1994; Rhoades and White 1997; Milnerowicz et al. 2000; Shaikh et al. 2002; Torrence et al. 2002; Baker et al. 2004; Pappas et al. 2006). Gas phase levels depend on the volatility of the metals or metal complexes. Cobalt levels range from less than 1 to 10 ng generated per cigarette, and mercury levels range from 5.0 to 7.4 ng generated per cigarette (Nitsch et al. 1991; Chang et al. 2002). In a limited analysis, Chang and colleagues (2003) found arsenic and antimony in the gas phase but did not provide quantitative results.

Studies have identified radioactive elements in tobacco and tobacco smoke. Lead 210, a product of radioactive decay of radon, was found in tobacco (Peres and Hiromoto 2002) and is transported at low levels in tobacco smoke (Skwarzec et al. 2001). Most of the lead in tobacco smoke is the nonradioactive isotopes. Polonium, an element found only in radioactive forms, is also a product of radioactive decay of radon. Some researchers have found polonium 210 in tobacco (Skwarzec et al. 2001; Peres and Hiromoto 2002; Khater 2004), and others estimated transfer of 11 to 30 percent of the amount in tobacco to tobacco smoke (Ferri and Baratta 1966). The presence of a filter and the type of filter used can alter the amount of polonium transferred into mainstream smoke; some filters remove 33 to 50 percent of the polonium from the smoke (Ferri and Baratta 1966).

In summary, the levels of metals in tobacco smoke are primarily a function of their content in the soil in which the tobacco is grown, added substances such as fertilizer, and the design of the cigarette. Study findings indicate that (1) growing conditions for tobacco contribute to the levels of metals in cigarettes manufactured worldwide and (2) some counterfeit cigarettes have higher levels of metals than do domestic commercial cigarettes. This evidence has proved that tobacco-growing conditions can alter the concentrations of metals in cigarette tobacco and therefore the levels in the smoke.

Aromatic Amines

Aromatic amines and their derivatives are used in the preparation of dyes, pharmaceuticals, pesticides, and plastics (Brougham et al. 1986; Bryant et al. 1994; Centers for Disease Control and Prevention [CDC] 1994) and in the rubber industry as antioxidants and accelerators (Parmeggiani 1983). Because of their widespread use, aromatic amines are prevalent and may be found as contaminants in some color additives, paints, food colors, and leather and textile dyes and in the fumes from heating oils and fuels. Studies that measured aromatic amines in the ambient environment detected their presence and determined concentrations in air, water, and soil (Birner and

Neumann 1988; Del Santo et al. 1991; Ward et al. 1991; Skipper et al. 1994; Sabbioni and Beyerbach 1995). Aromatic amines consist of at least one hydrocarbon ring and one amine-substituted ring, but these agents have diverse chemical structures. Chemically, aromatic amines act as bases and most exist as solids at room temperature.

Some scientists have suggested that aromatic amines are present in unburned tobacco (Schmeltz and Hoffmann 1977) and are also formed as combustion products in the particulate phase of tobacco smoke (Patrianakos and Hoffmann 1979). Investigators determined levels of aromatic amines in both mainstream and sidestream smoke (Hoffmann et al. 1969; Patrianakos and Hoffmann 1979; Grimmer et al. 1987; Luceri et al. 1993; Stabbert et al. 2003a). The identified compounds include aniline; 1-, 2-, 3-, 4-toluidine; 2-, 3-, 4-ethylaniline; 2,3-, 2,4-, 2,5-, 2,6-dimethylaniline; 1-, 2-naphthylamine; 2-, 3-, 4-aminobiphenyl; and 2-methyl-1-naphthylamine. The most commonly studied compounds from this class are shown in Figure 3.6. Stabbert and colleagues (2003a) found that aromatic amines reside primarily in the particulate phase of smoke, except for the more volatile amines such as *o*-toluidine; only 3 percent of *o*-toluidine was found in the gas phase. Studies have reported that sidestream smoke contains substantially higher levels of aromatic amines than does mainstream smoke, but these levels depend on the parameters for puffing the cigarette (Patrianakos and Hoffmann 1979; Grimmer et al. 1987; Luceri et al. 1993). For mainstream smoke, the levels of aromatic amines were reported to be 200 to 1,330 ng generated per cigarette (Luceri et al. 1993; Stabbert et al. 2003a), but studies have reported much higher levels in sidestream smoke (Luceri et al. 1993). More recently, one study reported the following levels of aromatic amines in mainstream cigarette smoke (Counts et al. 2005). Using the ISO regimen, these investigators determined that levels were 3 to 27 ng generated per cigarette for 1-aminonaphthalene; 2 to 17 ng for 2-aminonaphthalene; 0.6 to 4.2 ng for 3-aminobiphenyl; and 0.5 to 3.3 ng for 4-aminobiphenyl. These levels increased on average by approximately 115

percent when the MDPH smoking regimen was used and by approximately 130 percent under the CAN smoking regimen.

Levels of aromatic amines in tobacco smoke are influenced by both the chemical constituents in the tobacco and the chemical and physical processes of the burning cigarette. Levels of aromatic amines in smoke from cigarettes made with dark tobacco are higher than those in cigarettes made from light tobacco (Luceri et al. 1993). For typical U.S.-blended cigarettes, there is a linear correlation between levels of aromatic amines and tar in the smoke (Stabbert et al. 2003a).

Sources of nitrogen in the tobacco also significantly influence levels of aromatic amines in tobacco smoke. Nitrate is a primary factor in altering the level of aromatic amines in tobacco smoke, and its presence is influenced by the use of nitrogen fertilizers (Patrianakos and Hoffmann 1979; Stabbert et al. 2003a). Protein in tobacco is known to be a good source of biologic nitrogen, and studies have reported that higher nitrogen content from elevated protein in tobacco increased the yields of 2-naphthylamine and 4-aminobiphenyl (Patrianakos and Hoffmann 1979; Torikai et al. 2005). Cigarette smoke from bright tobacco had lower aromatic amine levels than expected compared with the smoke of U.S. blended cigarettes, possibly because of the lower nitrogen content in bright tobacco (Stabbert et al. 2003a). Combustion temperature is also a factor in the generation of aromatic amines in tobacco smoke, because lower temperatures yielded lower levels of aromatic amines in smoke (Stabbert et al. 2003b). Other investigators have suggested that increased cellulose levels in tobacco can decrease aromatic amines in the smoke (Torikai et al. 2005), and in another study, cellulose-acetate filters removed a substantial portion of aromatic amines from mainstream smoke (Luceri et al. 1993).

In summary, it appears that the nitrogen content in tobacco, either from protein levels or use of nitrogen fertilizer, is a primary determinant of aromatic amine levels in tobacco smoke. The type of tobacco used in the cigarette filler also alters these levels in tobacco smoke.

Figure 3.6   Commonly studied aromatic amines in tobacco smoke

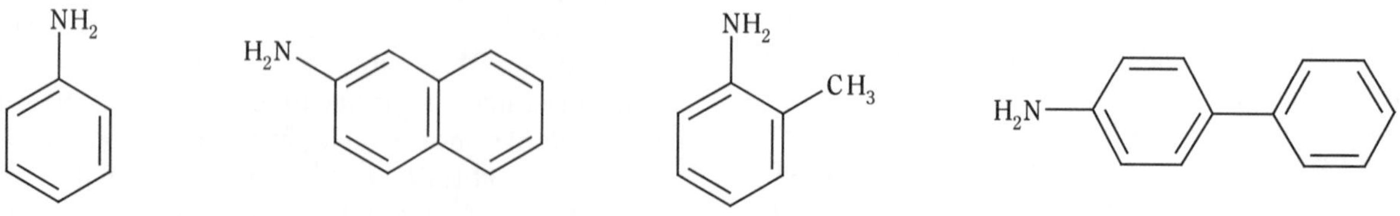

Aniline   2-aminonaphthalene   2-toluidine   4-aminobiphenyl

Figure 3.7   Primary heterocyclic amines in tobacco smoke

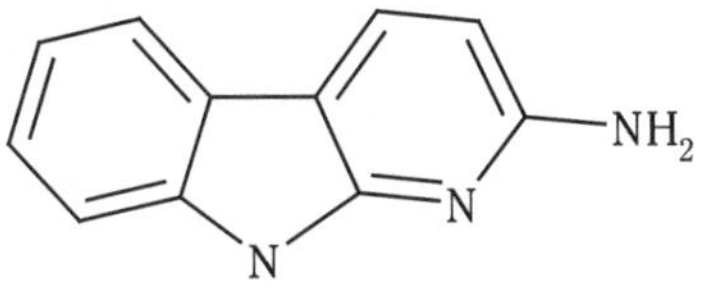

2-amino-9*H*-pyrido[2,3-*b*]
indole

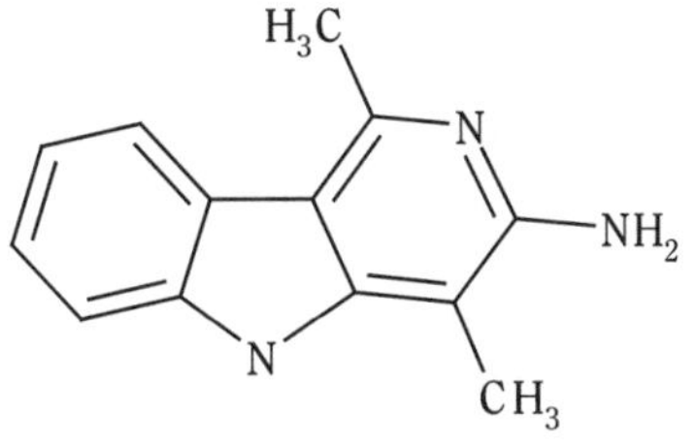

3-amino-1,4-dimethyl-5*H*-
pyrido[3,4-*b*]indole

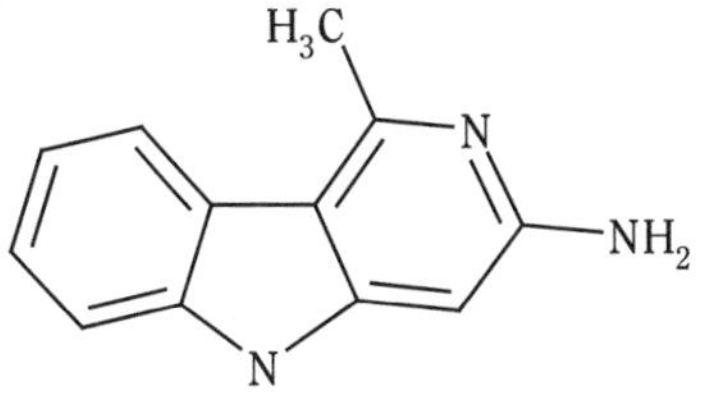

3-amino-1-methyl-5*H*-
pyrido[3,4-*b*]indole

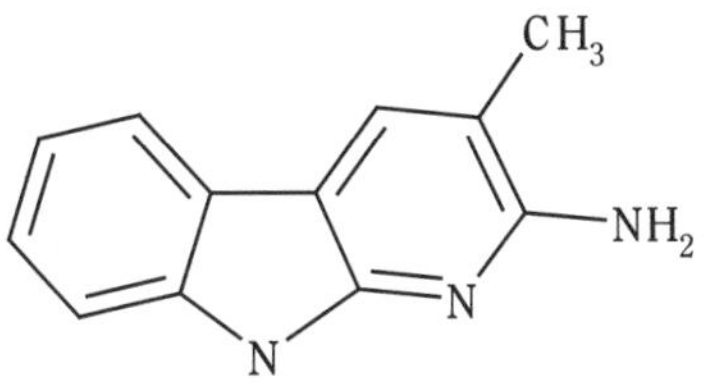

2-amino-3-methyl-9*H*-
pyrido[2,3-*b*]indole

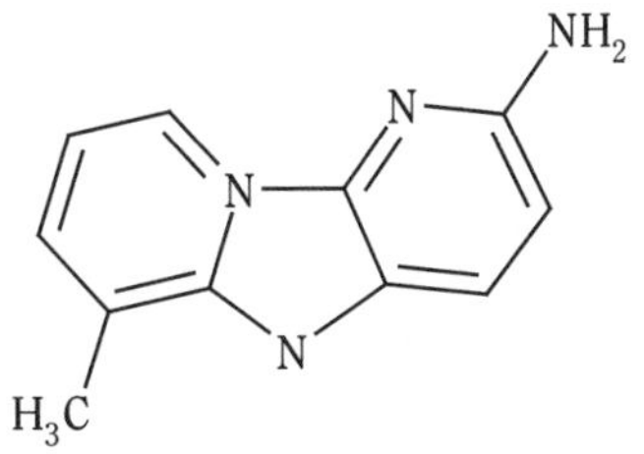

2-amino-6-methylpyrido
[1,2-*a*:3′,2′-*d*]imidazole

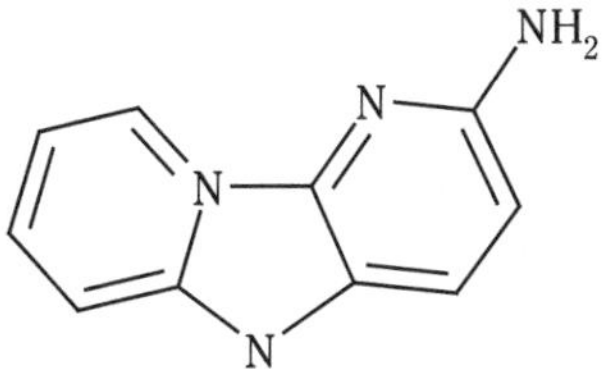

2-aminodipyrido[1,2-*a*:3′,2′-*d*]
imidazole

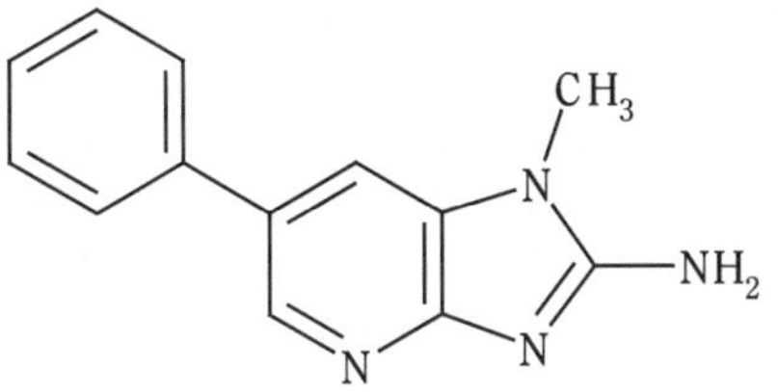

2-amino-1-methyl-6-phenylimidazo
[4,5-*b*]pyridine

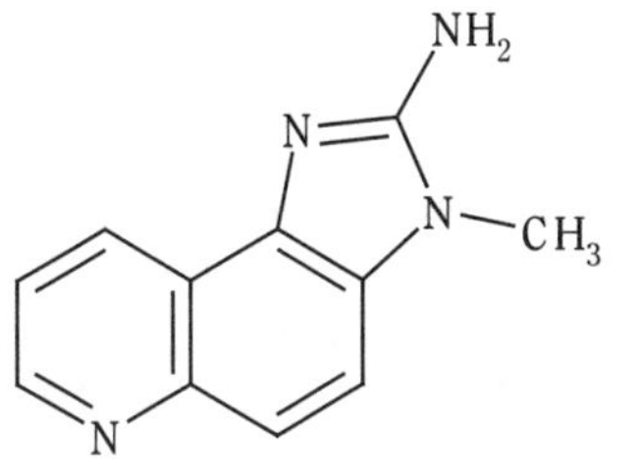

2-amino-3-methylimidazo
[4,5-*f*]quinoline

Heterocyclic Amines

Heterocyclic amines (HCAs) are a class of chemical compounds that contain at least one cyclic ring and an amine-substituted ring. HCAs act as basic compounds because of the amine functional group. HCAs can occur in food stuff, such as grilled meats, poultry, fish, and tobacco smoke (Sugimura et al. 1977; Sugimura 1997; Skog et al. 1998; Murkovic 2004). HCAs are classified in two groups: one is produced by the pyrolysis of amino acids and proteins through radical reactions, and the other is generated by heating mixtures of creatinine, sugars, and amino acids (Sugimura 1997; Murkovic 2004). The first group dominates when the pyrolysis temperature

is high, whereas the second group is predominant at low temperatures commonly used to cook meat (Sugimura 1997). In tobacco smoke, the primary HCAs are 2-amino-9*H*-pyrido[2,3-*b*]indole; 2-amino-3-methyl-9*H*-pyrido[2,3-*b*]indole; 3-amino-1,4-dimethyl-5*H*-pyrido[4,3-*b*]indole (Trp-P-1); 3-amino-1-methyl-5*H*-pyrido[4,3-*b*]indole (Trp-P-2); 2-amino-3-methylimidazo[4,5-*f*]quinoline; 2-amino-6-methyldipyrido[1,2-*a*:3′,2′-*d*]imidazole (Glu-P-1); 2-aminodipyrido[1,2-*a*:3′,2′-*d*]imidazole; and 2-amino-1-methyl-6-phenylimidazo[4,5-*b*]pyridine (PhIP) (Figure 3.7) (Kataoka et al. 1998).

HCAs are not found in unburned tobacco; they are present in tobacco smoke as a result of pyrolysis and are found in the particulate phase (Manabe and Wada 1990).

The chemical composition of amino acids, protein, sugars, and creatine/creatinine in the tobacco filler influences the final HCA levels in the smoke. Other components that may alter the pyrolysis of amino acids can also change HCA levels in smoke. The usual levels of HCAs in tobacco smoke were reported to be 0.3 to 260.0 ng generated per cigarette (Hoffmann et al. 2001). Manabe and Wada (1990) reported levels of 0.29 to 0.31 ng of Trp-P-1 generated per cigarette and 0.51 to 0.66 ng for Trp-P-2 in smoke condensate from five types of cigarettes. Manabe and colleagues (1991) determined an average level of 16.4 ng generated per cigarette for PhIP in tobacco smoke condensate from cigarettes purchased in Japan, the United Kingdom, and the United States.

In summary, although HCAs are not specific to tobacco products, they are found at levels in tobacco smoke particulate that must be considered when assessing the harm from the use of burned tobacco. The concentration of nitrogen-containing compounds in tobacco influences the levels of HCAs that are found in the smoke, and reducing the nitrogen content may be a means of reducing HCAs.

Effect of Additives on Tobacco Smoke

Chemical additives are introduced into cigarette tobacco for a variety of specific purposes, including pH adjustment, maintenance of moisture (humectants), amelioration of the harshness of smoke, control of the burn rate, and impartation of desirable flavor to the smoke (Penn 1997). The taste and flavor of cigarette smoke is affected primarily by the tobacco blend and is further modified with additives. Specific additives are applied to mask the harshness of lower-quality tobacco (*World Tobacco* 2000). Early in the processing of burley and flue-cured tobaccos, a solution called "casing" is added to the shreds of tobacco lamina. The casing is a slurry containing humectants (e.g., glycerol and propylene glycol) and flavor ingredients with low volatility (e.g., cocoa, honey, licorice, and fruit extracts) that lend a pleasant aroma. After the tobacco is aged, a top-flavoring solution is added to the finished cigarette blend. Top flavoring is generally an alcohol- or rum-based mixture containing volatile compounds (e.g., menthol) and other ingredients (e.g., aromatic compounds, essential oils, and extracts) that are added immediately before packaging (Penn 1997; Fisher 1999).

Even though the specific ingredients added to individual cigarette brands are proprietary, a collective list of 599 additives used in U.S. cigarettes has been published on the World Wide Web (Indiana Prevention Resource Center 2005). The "599 list" contains individual chemical compounds and complex additives, such as essential oils, juices, powders, oleoresins, and extracts. Included in the list are complex natural extracts and essential oils, such as anise, cassia, cedarwood, chocolate, cinnamon, ginger, lavender, licorice, nutmeg, peppermint, valerian, and vanilla. The list also includes individual organic chemical compounds, such as 1-menthol, 3-methyl pentanoic acid, anethole, β-caryophyllene, caffeine, ethyl acetate, γ-decalactone, isoamyl acetate, methyl cinnamate, sucrose, and vanillin. The compounds in the 599 list have been approved by the U.S. Food and Drug Administration as generally recognized as safe for use in foods (Hoffmann and Hoffmann 1997). Virtually any material with this approval as a food additive is used in cigarette manufacturing (*World Tobacco* 2000). However, this use is based on the broad assumption that additives designated as safe for ingestion are safe to burn and inhale in cigarette smoke. Because of the detoxifying action of the liver on blood coming directly from the digestive tract and the movement of blood from the lungs into the general circulation without first passing through the liver, the toxic effects associated with ingesting a compound can differ from the toxic effects of breathing it. Studies indicated that eugenol, a compound found in many natural extracts and used as an additive in clove cigarettes, had an LD_{50} 200 times lower in Fischer rats when administered intratracheally compared with gavage (LaVoie et al. 1986). Although this did not simulate inhalation, it did raise concern about increased toxicity of this compound to the lung.

Cigarette tobacco is a complex physicochemical mixture containing several types of tobacco and numerous additives (Hoffmann and Hoffmann 1997). The flavor compounds in tobacco can be transferred into the smoke by distillation, combustion, or pyrolysis (Green et al. 1989). Newly emerging flavored "dessert" cigarettes marketed under names such as Midnight Berry, Mandarin Mint, and Mocha Taboo (Carpenter et al. 2005) may represent new sources of exposure to harmful substances, but the qualitative and quantitative differences in smoke from these cigarettes have not been described.

One of the most common tobacco additives is menthol, a monoterpene alcohol (Burdock 1995) first used in cigarettes in the mid-1920s (Reynolds 1981) and subsequently added to most cigarettes (Eccles 1994). Natural sources of menthol include plants in the mint family, namely, peppermint (*Mentha piperita*) and corn mint (*Mentha arvensis*) (Burdock 1995). Flavorants derived from natural sources generally contain a mix of compounds, in contrast to flavoring compounds that are chemically synthesized. If menthol added to the tobacco is derived from natural sources, such as peppermint, constituents such as pulegone may also be present at low concentrations. Submicrogram concentrations of pulegone (0.024 to 0.29 µg/g) were measured in 12 mentholated brands but were not detected in nonmentholated brands (Stanfill and Ashley 1999). Menthol can be added on the tobacco, the filter, or the foil pack (Wayne and Connolly 2004). Menthol levels in smoke have ranged between 0.15 and 0.58 mg generated per cigarette for several brands (Cantrell 1990). Unlike most nonmentholated cigarettes, menthol cigarettes usually contain more flue-cured and less burley tobacco, along with reconstituted tobacco made without added ammonia.

Although they generally are regarded as safe for use in foods, certain flavor-related chemicals added to cigarettes and found in cigarette smoke (Stanfill and Ashley 1999) have known toxic properties. In an analysis of 12 flavor compounds in tobacco fillers from 68 U.S. cigarette brands, concentrations of compounds were 0.0018 to 43.0 µg/g (Stanfill and Ashley 1999). Also, 62 percent of the 68 brands contained detectable levels of 1 or more of the 12 flavor compounds. Piperonal and myristicin were present at the highest concentrations. Anethole, myristicin, and safrole were found in 20 percent or more of the brands; pulegone, piperonal, and methyleugenol were each present in at least 10 percent of the brands. In four brands, safrole, myristicin, and elemicin were found together, which strongly suggests the presence of flavorings such as nutmeg or mace (*Myristica fragrans*) in the tobacco. Coumarin is a benzopyrone compound found in the tobacco of one menthol brand at a concentration of 0.39 µg/g. Pulegone, a monoterpene ketone found in peppermint, was present only in mentholated brands. Tentative identification of other compounds suggested the use of flavor agents such as cinnamon and ginger (Stanfill and Ashley 1999). In addition to tobacco analysis, mainstream smoke particulates from several brands were also analyzed for six flavor compounds: eugenol, isoeugenol, methyleugenol, myristicin, elemicin, and piperonal (Stanfill and Ashley 2000). Levels of these compounds in the smoke from eight U.S. cigarette brands were 0.0066 to 4.21 µg generated per cigarette. The measurements suggested that a portion of eugenol and isoeugenol in smoke from some cigarettes could be a by-product of the burning tobacco. Also, when filter ventilation holes in the cigarette were partially or fully blocked, the transfer of these compounds from tobacco filler to mainstream smoke particulates increased twofold to sevenfold.

In summary, the impact of flavor-related additives on the toxicity, carcinogenicity, and addictive properties of tobacco products has not been thoroughly studied. In addition to the known harmful properties of these compounds, they may potentiate the effects of other known smoke constituents or alter the way people smoke cigarettes. These additives may also increase the initiation and continuation of smoking in the population.

Delivery of Chemical Constituents into Tobacco Smoke

Various tobacco types are used in the manufacture of cigarettes and other tobacco products. Lamina from bright, burley, and oriental tobacco varieties, along with reconstituted tobacco sheet, is the main filler component used in cigarettes (Hoffmann and Hoffmann 1997). In addition to lamina, cigarette filler often contains puffed or expanded tobacco, tobacco stems, humectants, and various flavor additives (Hoffmann and Hoffmann 1997; Abdallah 2003a). One tobacco variety such as bright can be used, or several varieties can be mixed together in products with specific tobacco blends. Most commercial cigarettes are constructed primarily from bright tobacco or from a blend of mainly bright, burley, and oriental tobaccos, usually referred to as an American blend (Browne 1990). However, a few small geographic areas outside the United States (e.g., France) have regional preferences for cigarettes made exclusively from dark, air-cured tobacco (Akehurst 1981; Tso et al. 1982). Each type of tobacco has unique properties that influence packing density (Artho et al. 1963), burn rate (Muramatsu 1981), tar and nicotine delivery (Griest and Guerin 1977), and flavor and aroma (Davis 1976; Enzell 1976; Leffingwell 1976). Bright tobacco, also known as flue-cured or Virginia tobacco, has lower nitrogen content (i.e., less protein) and higher sugar content than do the other varieties. Burley and Maryland tobaccos are air cured and typically have higher nicotine content but reduced sugar content.

Sakuma and colleagues (1984) measured the smoke components in mainstream and sidestream smoke and found that nitrogen-containing compounds were abundant in smoke from burley tobacco, whereas the non-nitrogen-containing compounds were more abundant in smoke from bright and oriental tobaccos. Oriental tobacco is often included in blended varieties because of its unique aromatic properties (Browne 1990). Cigarettes such as light or ultralight varieties that deliver low yields of tar and nicotine by FTC/ISO machine measurement often contain puffed or expanded tobacco lamina with higher "filling power" (Kertsis and Sun 1984; Lewis 1990; Kramer 1991), which lowers the density of the tobacco rod, thus lowering the amount of tobacco in each cigarette. Several types of reconstituted tobacco sheet are also used to manufacture cigarettes (Abdallah 2003b).

Development of reconstituted tobacco was an attempt at 100-percent utilization of tobacco (Abdallah

2003b). Stems, ribs, and scrap lamina are combined with various binders and other additives to form a "reconstituted" sheet approximating the physical and chemical characteristics of a tobacco leaf (Browne 1990; Blackard 1997; Abdallah 2003b). A common additive in reconstituted tobacco is diammonium hydrogen phosphate, which is used as a pectin release agent that facilitates cross-linkage to form stable sheet material (Hind and Seligman 1967, 1969; Hind 1968). Reconstituted tobacco sheet containing this additive selectively adsorbs nicotine from surrounding lamina and enriches it in an environment abundant in ammonia precursors (Larson at al. 1980).

The stages of manufacturing a cigarette include processing the tobacco lamina and reconstituted tobacco materials and slicing them into shreds of a specific cut width. Tobacco cut widths vary from approximately 1.5 mm for a coarse cut to 0.4 mm for a fine cut (Hoffmann and Hoffmann 1997). Alternatively, the cut width may be expressed in units of cuts per inch, which range from approximately 14 to 48. Cigarettes made from fine-cut tobacco have faster static burn rates resulting in fewer puffs (Resnik et al. 1977). A consequence of using tobacco filler with a fine-cut width is that the ratio of filler surface area to void volume increases and may increase the efficiency of the tobacco column to filter large aerosol particles (Keith and Derrick 1960).

The papers used in cigarettes are generally flax or linen fiber and may contain additives (Browne 1990). Salts often are added to the cigarette paper as optical whiteners to achieve a target static burn rate and to mask the appearance of sidestream smoke (Schur and Rickards 1960; Owens 1978; Durocher 1984). A key physical property of the paper wrapper is its porosity. Papers with high porosity facilitate diffusion of gases in and out of the tobacco rod (Newsome and Keith 1965; Owen and Reynolds 1967). Volatile smoke constituents such as CO readily diffuse through a porous wrapper, so delivery to the smoker is lower than that with less volatile constituents. High-porosity papers also permit more O_2 to diffuse inward, which increases the static burn rate and the airflow through the tobacco column that dilutes the smoke. A faster-burning cigarette yields fewer puffs, reducing tar and nicotine delivery per cigarette (Durocher 1984). Porosity of the paper, filler cut width, filter efficiency, and tobacco density all make important contributions to reduction of pressure drop in the tobacco rod, which is a key index related to acceptance by smokers (Norman 1999). Smokers prefer a cigarette on which they do not have to draw too hard because of changes in pressure drop as a result of design. A separate but related parameter, filter pressure drop, is directly related to smoke delivery and filter efficiency (Norman 1999).

In 2006, cigarette lengths generally fell into one of four categories in the U.S. market: king-size filter cigarettes (79–88 mm; accounting for 62 percent of the market); long (94–101 mm; 34 percent of the market); ultra long (110–121 mm; 2 percent of the market); and regular, nonfilter cigarettes (68–72 mm; 1 percent of the market) (FTC 2009). The usual diameter of a conventional cigarette is 7.5 to 8.0 mm (Norman 1999), although some "slims" have diameters of 5 to 6 mm. The amount of tobacco consumed varies with the circumference of the cigarette, and in cigarettes with smaller circumference, delivery of constituents in the smoke to the smoker decreases accordingly (Ohlemiller et al. 1993). The greater surface of the wrapper in long cigarettes increases the opportunity for gaseous diffusion out of the cigarette, which can (1) reduce delivery of highly volatile constituents of mainstream smoke to the smoker, but increase delivery to the nonsmoker and (2) increase the static burn rate as more O_2 diffuses inward (Moore and Bock 1968). However, long cigarettes generally facilitate delivery of higher tar and nicotine levels, because more tobacco mass is burned.

Before the 1950s, most cigarettes were about 70 mm long and unfiltered (Hoffmann and Hoffmann 1997). The addition of a filter tip to a cigarette can greatly reduce delivery of many chemical constituents of mainstream smoke as determined by the FTC/ISO machine-smoking method (Fordyce et al. 1961; Williamson et al. 1965). This reduction was attributed to filtering of the smoke particulate and reducing the amount of tobacco in each cigarette. Cost savings are also achieved because the filter material is less expensive than the tobacco (Browne 1990). Filters provide a firm mouthpiece and permit the smoker to avoid direct contact with the tobacco. Cigarettes with modern cellulose-acetate filter tips gained about 96 percent of the market share by the 1970s (Hoffmann and Hoffmann 1997). In the United States, cellulose-acetate filter tips are the most popular and can selectively remove certain constituents of the smoke, including phenols and alkylphenols (Hoffmann and Wynder 1963; Spears 1963; Baggett and Morie 1973; Morie et al. 1975). Typically, a bonding agent such as triacetin or glycerol triacetate is used to facilitate filter manufacturing (Browne 1990). The filtration efficiency is proportional to the length, diameter, size, and number of fiber strands and the packing density of the cigarette (Keith 1975, 1978; Eaker 1990). Flavoring agents or other materials can also be incorporated into the filter design.

Extensive research from the 1960s has examined the use of activated charcoal in the cigarette filter to efficiently remove volatile compounds (Newsome and Keith 1965; Williamson et al. 1965; Keith et al. 1966). The addition of activated charcoal significantly reduced levels of volatile compounds, such as formaldehyde, cyanide, and acrolein (Williamson et al. 1965; Spincer and Chard 1971). Charcoal filters reduced the delivery of H_2S to mainstream smoke (Horton and Guerin 1974). Both cellulose-acetate and charcoal filters removed some of the volatile pyridines (Brunnemann et al. 1978). Coatings with metallic oxides were extremely efficient at removing acidic gases (Keith et al. 1966). Filter designs can also be tailored to selectively pass and not trap certain classes of targeted compounds. For instance, inclusion of alkaline materials in the filter inhibits filtration of gaseous nicotine (Browne 1990).

One key technology used to reduce FTC/ISO machine-measured tar and nicotine delivery is the inclusion of microscopic ventilation holes in the paper wrapper (Harris 1890) or the filter paper. These holes cause the mainstream smoke to become diluted with air (Norman 1974). Filter ventilation holes are usually located in one or more rings about 12 mm from the mouth end of the filter (Baker and Lewis 1997). The amount of filter ventilation ranges from about 10 percent in some full-flavored varieties to 80 percent in brands measured as having very low delivery by using the FTC smoking regimen (CDC 1997). Filter ventilation also contributes to control of the burn rate (Durocher 1984). The tiny perforations can be made by mechanical means, electrostatic sparking, or laser ablation. Paper permeability can also be used to increase air dilution, although as the cigarette is consumed, this effect becomes less important. Delivery of lower levels of the constituents of mainstream smoke, as measured under FTC machine-smoking conditions, occurs when smoke drawn through the cigarette rod mixes and is diluted with air drawn through filter ventilation holes. Under FTC machine-smoking conditions, filter ventilation is highly effective in reducing delivery of chemical constituents (Norman 1974). However, the fingers or lips of smokers may cover vent holes when they smoke cigarettes and reduce the amount of air available for dilution, which results in delivery that is higher than expected (Kozlowski et al. 1982, 1996).

Cigarette smoke is formed by (1) the condensation of chemicals formed by the combustion of tobacco, (2) pyrolysis and pyrosynthesis, and (3) distillation products that form an aerosol in the cooler region directly behind the burning coal (Browne 1990). During a puff, the coal temperature reaches 800°C to 900°C, and the temperature of the aerosol drops rapidly to slightly above room temperature as it travels down the tobacco rod (Touey and Mumpower 1957; Lendvay and Laszlo 1974). As the smoke cools, compounds with lower volatility condense first, and many of the very volatile gaseous constituents, such as CO, remain in the gas phase. The cooler tobacco rod acts as a filter itself, and some portions of the smoke condense

(Dobrowsky 1960) as the smoke is drawn through the tobacco column during a puff.

Torikai and colleagues (2004) examined the influence of the temperature, the pyrolysis environment, and the pH of the tobacco leaf on the formation of a wide variety of constituents of tobacco smoke. Their findings showed that, in general, the yields of the chemical constituents in tobacco smoke that present health concerns increased as the temperature increased from 300°C to 1,000°C, but some compounds (e.g., acrolein and formaldehyde) reached their maximum yield at 500°C and the yield remained approximately the same at higher temperatures. The presence of O_2 in the pyrolysis atmosphere increased the yield of acrolein and other volatile organic compounds but lowered the levels of cyanide, phenol, and 1-aminonaphthalene. The pH of the tobacco had a mixed effect on the levels of toxic chemicals in tobacco smoke. Levels of B[*a*]P, cyanide, quinoline, resorcinol, and acrylonitrile increased with a lower pH, and hydroquinone and 1-naphthylamine levels increased with higher pH. The effects of the pH and pyrolysis atmosphere combine to influence the radical reactions that generate many constituents in tobacco smoke.

In summary, design features of the cigarette have a major influence on the yield of the constituents in smoke. Altering the tobacco blend, filter type and length, cut width, paper porosity, ventilation, and chemical additives alters the levels of many constituents of smoke.

Delivery of Chemicals to Smokers

In addition to cigarette design, the major factors that influence the delivery of chemicals to smokers are characteristics of puffing (puff volume, duration, and frequency), cigarette length smoked, and blocking air dilution holes on the filter tips of ventilated cigarettes (e.g., with the mouth or fingers). Testing cigarettes by using smoking machines or smokers in a laboratory setting can elucidate how certain design factors and smoking characteristics can influence the chemical components in smoke. However, the results obtained in a laboratory cannot be directly applied to populations of smokers because many factors influence the way a person smokes each cigarette.

In a laboratory setting, Fischer and colleagues (1989a) investigated the influence of smoking parameters on the delivery of TSNAs in mainstream smoke for six cigarette brands. The research included filter-tipped cigarettes with very-low-to-medium ISO/FTC yields of constituents of smoke and unfiltered cigarettes with high and very high ISO smoke yields. The major finding was that the puff profile and duration had no remarkable influence on TSNA delivery, but puff volume and frequency significantly increased TSNA yields. The dependency of TSNA delivery on the volume of smoke emitted from one cigarette (puff volume × number of puffs) was almost linear up to a total volume of approximately 500 mL. TSNA yield was equivalent for the same total volume whether the total volume was from a change in puff volume or puff frequency. Thus, the total volume drawn through a cigarette was the main factor responsible for delivery of TSNAs in mainstream smoke.

In another study, average levels of tar, nicotine, and CO per liter of smoke and per cigarette were determined for 10 brands of cigarettes smoked under 27 machine-smoking conditions (Rickert et al. 1986). Yields per cigarette were highly variable across smoking conditions, because of differences in the total volume of smoke. The results of a simple linear regression analysis indicated that up to 95 percent of the variation in tar yield per cigarette could be explained by variation in the total volume of smoke produced per cigarette. Puffing behavior (topography), especially the interpuff interval and total smoke volume per cigarette, which were influenced by puff volume, number of puffs, and length of the cigarette smoked, were the primary determinants of blood levels of constituents of cigarette smoke (Bridges et al. 1990).

The influence of machine-smoking parameters on levels of chemical constituents measured in smoke is well illustrated in the work of Counts and colleagues (2005). This research was performed according to the ISO, MDPH, and CAN regimens described earlier. The study examined levels of 44 chemicals emitted in cigarette smoke. Not surprisingly, the more intense smoking regimens resulted in higher levels of constituents in cigarette smoke. However, in some cases, the emissions of the constituents did not maintain their relative levels as a result of different burning properties of the tobacco under different regimens and because of breakthrough in charcoal filters in the more intense smoking regimens. Because the intensity of smoking changes, the delivery of chemicals to the smoker varies and cannot be assessed by using a single smoking regimen.

In studies of 129 female and 128 male smokers of contemporary cigarettes, Melikian and colleagues (2007a,b) reported data on smoking topography and exposure to toxic substances in mainstream smoke of cigarettes that deliver a wide range of nicotine as reported by the FTC/ISO method. Exposure was determined by the delivered dose and urinary biomarkers. The first study focused on whether differences in gender and ethnicity affect delivered doses of select toxicants in mainstream cigarette smoke, as a result of differences in smoking behavior or type of cigarettes smoked (Melikian et al. 2007b). Smoking topography differed significantly between females and males. Compared with men, women

drew more (13.5 versus 12.0; p = 0.001) but smaller puffs (37.6 versus 45.8 mL; p = 0.0001) of shorter duration (1.33 versus 1.48 seconds; p = 0.002). Women also smoked a smaller portion of the cigarettes (36.3-mm butts [40.2 percent of cigarette length] versus 34.3-mm butts [39.2 percent of cigarette length]; p = 0.01). Although smoke volume per cigarette did not differ between women and men (p = 0.06), the daily dose of smoke was significantly higher in men (9.3 versus 8.0 liters [L]; p = 0.02), because men consume a greater number of cigarettes per day.

When data were stratified by race, no difference was found in puffing characteristics between European American and African American female and male smokers, except that African American women and men smoked equal lengths of the cigarettes (34.5- versus 33.9-mm butts; p = 0.93). However, African Americans smoked fewer cigarettes, so the daily smoke volume was significantly higher among European American smokers (8.61 versus 7.45 L for women; 10.6 versus 7.8 L for men). The emissions of select toxicants per cigarette, as determined by use of machine-smoking regimens that mimicked each smoker, were consistently greater among male smokers than among the female smokers, and they correlated significantly with delivered smoke volume per cigarette. The geometric means of emissions of nicotine from cigarettes were 1.92 mg per cigarette for women versus 2.2 mg for men (p = 0.005). Cigarettes smoked by women yielded 139.5 ng of NNK per cigarette compared with 170.3 ng for men (p = 0.0007). B[*a*]P emissions were 18.0 ng per cigarette for women and 20.5 ng for men (p = 0.01). Differences between women and men in delivery of toxicants in cigarette smoke to the smoker were more profound in European Americans than in African Americans. On average, African American men's smoking behavior produced the highest emissions of select toxicants from cigarettes, and European American female smokers received the lowest amounts of toxicants.

The second study by Melikian and colleagues (2007a) investigated urinary concentrations of biomarkers in relation to levels of select toxicants in mainstream cigarette smoke, as determined by using machine-smoking regimens that mimicked the smoking behavior of each smoker. In this study of 257 smokers, the researchers determined levels of nicotine, NNK, and B[*a*]P in mainstream smoke and concentrations of the respective urinary metabolites: cotinine, 4-(methylnitrosamino)-1-(3-pyridyl)-1-butanol (NNAL), and 1-hydroxypyrene (1-HOP). The smokers were assigned to groups according to the FTC yield of toxic substances in the cigarettes they smoked: low yield (0.1 to 0.8 mg of nicotine generated per cigarette, medium yield (0.9 to 1.2 mg), and high yield (>1.3 mg). Concentrations of urinary metabolites, expressed per level of parent compound delivered decreased with increased smoke emissions. In smokers of low-, medium-, and high-yield cigarettes, as measured by FTC methods, the respective ratios of cotinine (nanograms per milligram of creatinine) to nicotine (milligrams per day) were 89.4, 77.8, and 57.1 (low versus high; p = 0.06). Ratios of NNAL (picomoles per milligram of creatinine) to NNK (nanograms per day) were 0.81, 0.55, and 0.57 (low versus high; p = 0.05). Ratios of 1-HOP (picograms per milligram of creatinine) to B[a]P (nanograms per day) were 1.55, 1.13, and 0.97 (low versus high; p = 0.008). Similarly, for smokers who consumed fewer than 20 cigarettes per day, the means of cotinine per unit of delivered nicotine were 3.5-fold higher than those for smokers of more than 20 cigarettes per day. Likewise, a negative correlation was observed between ratios of cotinine to nicotine and delivered doses of nicotine in subgroups of smokers who used the identical brand of cigarettes, namely a filter-tipped, vented Marlboro (r = -0.59), which is a popular brand among European Americans, and Newport (r = -0.37), a menthol-flavored cigarette without filter-tip vents that is preferred by African Americans. The researchers concluded that the intensity of smoking and the mouth levels of smoke constituents significantly affect the concentrations of urinary biomarkers of exposure and should be taken into account in evaluating human exposure to toxic substances in cigarette smoke.

Regarding the influence of cigarette type on urinary biomarkers of exposure to toxic substances in mainstream smoke, there is a slight difference in puff volume and puff frequency among smokers of low-FTC-yield versus medium-FTC-yield cigarettes, as measured under FTC conditions (Djordjevic et al. 2000). Smokers of low-FTC-yield brands drew somewhat larger puffs (48.6 versus 44.1 mL) and inhaled more smoke both per cigarette (615 versus 523 mL) and daily (9.5 versus 8.2 L). However, delivered doses of NNK and B[a]P were marginally higher among smokers of medium-yield cigarettes (NNK: 250.9 versus 186.5 ng per cigarette; B[a]P: 21.4 versus 17.9 ng). On the other hand, Hecht and colleagues (2005) found no differences in urinary biomarkers of exposure to NNK and B[a]P among smokers of regular, light, or ultralight cigarettes.

Researchers have also suggested that blocking ventilation holes during smoking can result in increased delivery of smoke constituents. For example, when puff and inhalation parameters were allowed to vary, participants took significantly more and larger puffs from cigarettes with unblocked ventilation than from those with completely blocked ventilation (Zacny et al. 1986; Sweeney et al. 1999). Hoffmann and colleagues (1983) found that blocking air-dilution holes in seven brands of commercial filter-tipped cigarettes increased nicotine yields by 69 percent, tar yields by 51 percent, and CO yields by 147 percent. Another study examined a cigarette brand with tar and nicotine yields of 4.0 and 0.4 mg, respectively,

under various conditions of machine smoking intended to reflect the wide range of smoking behaviors (Rickert et al. 1983). The researchers studied three levels of five smoking parameters (butt length, puff duration, puff interval, puff volume, and ventilation occlusion) and the effects on the number of puffs and TPM, and they estimated gas phase, particulate phase, and total yields of HCN. The HCN and TPM yields varied significantly under different smoking conditions. Ventilation occlusion had the most pronounced effect, accounting for 34 percent of the response variation in TPM yields and 42 percent of the response variation in total HCN yields.

Comparison of normal lip contact during smoking, which partially blocked filter vents, and smoking through a cigarette holder, which avoided blocking, showed higher nicotine boosts with normal lip contact (Höfer et al. 1991). Exposure to other smoke constituents may vary with the degree of blocking. Sweeney and colleagues (1999) found that blocking the filter vents of cigarettes with ventilation levels of at least 66 percent led to significant increases in CO exposure. The same manipulation of filter vents in cigarettes with filter ventilation levels of 56 percent or lower appeared to have negligible consequences for CO exposure. In another report, CO exposure from completely blocked filter vents was twice as high as from the unblocked vents (8.96 versus 4.32 parts per million [ppm]) (Zacny et al. 1986). Blocking filter vents also resulted in higher CO exposure in a study by Höfer and associates (1991). Blocking filter ventilation holes is not the only element of smoking topography that influences filter efficiency. More rapid or intense puffing increases flow rates, which results in less effective filtration, because the smoke passes through the tobacco column and filter material more quickly with less opportunity for adsorption on the filter's fibers. This smoking behavior also reduced the time for highly volatile gaseous materials to diffuse outward through the cigarette's paper wrapper.

An "elastic" cigarette is one that shows low levels of tar and nicotine when it is tested on a smoking machine but can potentially yield higher levels of emissions to smokers (Kozlowski et al. 2001). When cigarettes are elastic, smokers can extract as much nicotine as they need by changing their pattern of puffing on the cigarette. Analysis of tobacco from commercial American blend cigarettes purchased in the United States in 1990 revealed that the nicotine content did not differ substantially among brands that delivered a wide range of FTC-measured yields (Kozlowski et al. 1998). This cigarette design allowed delivery of virtually any amount of nicotine, depending on puffing behavior. Because there are similar amounts of other constituents in tobacco (e.g., TSNAs, metals, nitrates, and nitrites), regardless of the FTC ranking of the cigarette brand, more intense smoking to obtain a desired dose of nicotine leads to higher exposure to carcinogens. Historically, smokers have refused to use brands designed to reduce delivery of nicotine. For example, one company experimented with a modified cigarette containing denicotinized tobacco and a tar yield of 9.3 mg generated per cigarette but a nicotine yield of only 0.08 mg, as determined by using the FTC regimen, but this product was not successfully marketed (Rickert 2000).

Not all of the smoke volume delivered in the puff is inhaled by the smoker. Some escapes during mouth holding before inhalation. The depth of inhalation may be important for some smoke constituents but not for others, which is not surprising because of the complexity of the physics related to particle size that is involved with smoking and respiration. Finally, even very brief breath holding at peak inspiration can theoretically contribute to increased diffusion of some smoke constituents across alveolar membranes, as the intra-alveolar pressure increases.

There are considerable individual differences in inhalation patterns. In one study, inhaled smoke volume was measured by tracing the smoke with an isotope of the inert gas krypton (Woodman et al. 1986). The percentage of inhaled smoke (total inhaled smoke volume per total puff volume) averaged between 46 and 85 percent among persons in the study. Neither the mean inhaled smoke volume per puff nor the total inhaled smoke volume per cigarette was significantly correlated with any of the indices for puffing.

Evidence on the importance of inhalation patterns to total smoke exposure is mixed (Woodman et al. 1986; Zacny et al. 1987; Zacny and Stitzer 1996). Variations in results may be related to the small number of persons tested and to the difficulties inherent in accurately capturing the relationship between puffing indices and total inhaled smoke. Methods used include pneumography using a mercury strain gauge, whole-body (head and arms out) plethysmography, impedance plethysmography, inductive plethysmography, and inert gas radiotracers. The method most commonly used in U.S. laboratories that study smoking is inductive plethysmography, in which chest and abdominal expansions are measured by bands applied around the rib cage and the abdomen. Significant practical limitations include difficulties in accurate calibration of the systems and adequate integration of chest and abdominal expansions, especially because men tend to have greater abdominal expansion than women do. Measurement artifacts created by movement during measurement are another limitation. Studies of the accuracy of the systems have shown fair results in adults (Zacny et al. 1987). Errors in volume measurements were typically approximately 100 mL over a large number of respiratory cycles. Unfortunately, the attributes of the systems

have not been well studied for the puff-by-puff evaluation of human smoking behaviors. In addition, the most useful information will come from integrating puff analyses with inhalation parameters on a puff-by-puff basis to assess mouth holding and breath holding at peak inhalation. Studies such as those cited above have shown that mechanical testing regimens cannot mimic the way people smoke cigarettes. These findings suggest the importance of expressing the levels of toxic constituents as a ratio with nicotine or puff volume in the denominator (Rickert et al. 1985; Burns et al. 2008).

The size of particles containing chemical species can affect their retention in the lung. Cigarette smoke is an aerosol formed as the vapors generated in the pyrolysis zone cool and condense. Cigarette design has been shown to control particle-size distribution in an aerosol, so particles become easier or more difficult to inhale (Stöber 1982; Ingebrethsen 1986; McRae 1990; Wayne et al. 2008). Burning finer-cut tobacco creates an aerosol with smaller particles, which are easier to inhale. Thus, changing the filler cut width can change the distribution of particle size in the aerosol and the chemistry. Particle size is also altered by air dilution. Dilution reduces the aerosol concentration and, thus, the coagulation rate. The particle size of the smoke is increased by increasing the coagulation rate or by condensing the moisture produced during combustion onto the smoke particles. According to Ishizu and colleagues (1987), the timed average particle size (equivalent diameter) for major chemical components in tobacco smoke was 0.03 to 0.5 μm, and constituents with higher boiling points tended toward larger particle sizes. Very small particles are more likely to be retained in the lungs. The overall equivalent diameter of particles of crude tar in tobacco smoke was 0.21 μm. Nicotine was usually present in small particles (e.g., 0.08 μm). Particle size influences how fast chemicals are transferred to tissue. Particles larger than 0.3 μm are more likely than smaller particles to be absorbed in the mouth and throat than in the lungs (Wayne et al. 2008).

Accurate measurement of particle size distribution in cigarette smoke is important for estimating deposition in the lung (Anderson et al. 1989). Most earlier studies (1960–1982) reported a median diameter of 0.3 to 0.5 μm, including a few ultrafine particles (<0.1 μm). Using the electrical aerosol analyzer, Anderson and colleagues (1989) reported similar values for median diameter (0.36 to 0.4 μm) for the particles emitted in smoke from U.S. commercial filter-tipped cigarettes. But, there were also distinctly smaller particles, with a median diameter of 0.096 to 0.11 μm. This finding indicated the presence of many more ultrafine particles in the smoke than was previously recognized. It is notable that the low- and ultralow-yield filter-tipped cigarettes Merit and Carlton emitted smaller particles than did the full-flavored Marlboro cigarettes. Ultrafine particles are of toxicologic importance because their deposition in the respiratory tract was significantly higher than that of the 0.3- to 0.5-μm particles. Also, the relatively large surface-to-volume ratio of the ultrafine particles could facilitate adsorption and delivery of potentially toxic gases to the lung.

An alternative analysis of the impact of particle size on deposition in the lung suggested that growth in particle size may accelerate deposition in the respiratory tract (Martonen and Musante 2000). Because of their hygroscopicity, inhaled smoke particles may grow to several times their original diameter. This study suggested that mainstream cigarette smoke could behave aerodynamically as a large cloud (e.g., 20 μm in diameter) rather than as submicrometer constituent particles. The effect of cloud motion on deposition is pronounced. For example, an aerosol with a mass median aerodynamic diameter of 0.443 μm and a geometric standard deviation of 1.44 would have the following deposition fractions: lung, 0.14; tracheobronchial, 0.03; and pulmonary, 0.11. When cloud motion is simulated, the total deposition is concentrated in the tracheobronchial compartment, especially in the upper bronchi, and pulmonary deposition is negligible. Cloud motion produces a heterogeneous deposition resulting in increased exposure of underlying airway cells to toxic and carcinogenic substances. The deposition sites correlate with the incidence of cancers in vivo.

Although most of the smoke particles deposit in the periphery of the lung, the surface concentrations of deposited particles are not significantly greater in the periphery than in centrally located airways (Muller et al. 1990). Concentrations on the surface of the central airway are relatively independent of breathing patterns and airway geometry. This finding suggests that the effects of deposition of particles from cigarette smoke cannot be greatly reduced by changing the pattern of smoke inhalation. Efforts to manipulate particle size in smoke have been described in greater detail in a report by Wayne and colleagues (2008). Their study draws on internal tobacco company documents to assess industry consideration of the role of smoke particle size as a potential controlling influence over inhalation patterns and exposure of lungs to harmful substances. The researchers reported that tobacco manufacturers evaluated manipulation of particle size to control physical and sensory attributes of tobacco products and to reduce health hazards related to exposure to tobacco smoke. Examples of design features of tobacco products that relate to potential effects on generation of particle size and distribution of particles include puff flow rate, tobaccos and experimental blends, combustion, circumference, rod length, and ventilation (Wayne et al. 2008).

In summary, smoking behavior (puff volume, number of puffs per cigarette, and percentage of ventilation holes blocked) has a major impact on the levels of toxic, carcinogenic, and addictive compounds delivered to the smoker in cigarette smoke. The puffing patterns of smokers vary considerably from person to person. To completely understand the effect of specific harmful chemical constituents on smokers, further research is needed to explore how cigarette design and the chemical makeup of cigarettes influence use of the product.

Biomarkers

General Concepts

Accurate prediction of health risks from cigarette use is complicated by several factors, including the chemical complexity of cigarette smoke, significant variations among the dose-response relationships for the many diseases associated with exposure to cigarette smoke, qualitative and quantitative changes in the dose of cigarette smoke received by smokers throughout their smoking histories, and the long latencies between the initiation of exposure and the onset of some diseases, such as various cancers, caused by smoking cigarettes. Prediction is also hampered by the ever-changing number and types of tobacco products available to consumers, as well as fluctuations in the composition of the products (Stratton et al. 2001).

Before the term "biomarker" was coined, biomedical researchers used the appearance of unique markers such as carcinoembryonic antigens (Burtin et al. 1972) to diagnose and monitor cancer or panels of metabolic or physiological risk factors (e.g., serum cholesterol, maternal serum α-fetoprotein, and serum angiotensin-converting enzyme) to predict the clinical course of adverse effects on health. During the 1980s, the National Research Council (NRC) issued a series of reports that covered the conceptual basis for using biomarkers and reviewing biomarkers related to major organ systems and diseases (Committee on Biological Markers of the NRC 1987). In an early comprehensive discussion of biomarkers as risk assessment tools, Hattis (1986) described their value in characterizing dose-response relationships, estimating internal dose, extrapolating across species, and assessing interindividual variability (DeCaprio 1997). At about the same time, Prignot (1987) published a summary of existing chemical markers of tobacco exposure that could be used to assess individual exposure to tobacco and exposure to secondhand tobacco smoke as well as to validate successful smoking cessation.

In the framework for considering biomarkers proposed by the NRC Committee on Biological Markers (1987), a set of still useful definitions was offered. In brief, exposure involves contact with the agent of concern. Dose refers to the material that enters the body. Internal dose refers to the amount of material entering the body, and biologically effective dose refers to the amount of the agent that reaches the target site(s) within the body. Markers of health effects reflect preclinical changes short of those reached when clinical disease occurs. Markers of susceptibility are linked to increased risk on exposure.

The long latency of most diseases caused by cigarette use indicates the need for predictive markers of future risk that could identify those people already experiencing preclinical effects of smoking. However, the first widely accepted tobacco biomarkers were indicators of exposure rather than predictors of disease risk. Breath CO, saliva thiocyanate (Jaffe et al. 1981), serum thiocyanate (Foulds et al. 1968), and nicotine and nicotine metabolites (Watson 1977) were prominent in the early literature for assessing exposure to cigarette smoke, and they remain in use today.

In comparison with the framework and definitions used for exposure and dose generally, a somewhat distinct set of terms has been applied to exposure to cigarette smoke. The 2001 report, *Clearing the Smoke*, published by the Institute of Medicine defines a biomarker of exposure as a tobacco constituent or metabolite that is measured in a biologic fluid or tissue and has the potential to interact with a biologic macromolecule (Stratton et al. 2001). The definition notes that such biomarkers are also considered as measures of internal dose. A biomarker of a biologically effective dose is defined as the amount of a tobacco constituent or a metabolite that binds to or alters a macromolecule. A biomarker of a biologic event with the potential to lead to harm is defined as a measurement of an effect attributable to exposure, including early biologic effects; alterations in morphology, structure, or function; and clinical symptoms consistent with harm. In the more general formulation, such biomarkers constitute markers of health effects.

Validated biomarkers of tobacco exposure exist, and progress has been made in developing biomarkers of biologically effective dose. The biologically effective dose represents the net effect of metabolic activation and the rate of detoxification in a target biologic tissue or bodily fluid. Many tobacco-related toxicants and carcinogens are biologically inactive until transformed by metabolic enzymes such as cytochrome P-450s into reactive intermediates. Reactive metabolic intermediates bind to macromolecules such as DNA and protein and disrupt their normal function. Not all binding to, or alteration of, a macromolecule leads to an adverse health effect. Consequently, the amount of material bound to a target macromolecule provides only an estimate of the biologically effective dose (Stratton et al. 2001). Polymorphisms of the metabolic enzymes may modify the balance of activation and detoxification and thus the potency and response of a biomarker (Norppa 2003).

Biomarkers of biologic events with the potential to lead to harm reflect changes in a cell or in cellular macromolecules that result from exposure to tobacco. These biomarkers can range from isolated changes with or without effects on function to events that clearly lead to illness or are symptoms of illness (e.g., cough). Measurable biomarkers of biologic events with the potential to lead to harm are relatively nonspecific (Stratton et al. 2001).

Few specific biomarkers have been validated as predictors of disease development (Stratton et al. 2001), although some studies indicated that DNA and protein adduct levels are associated with cancer risk (Hecht 2003). The application of biomarkers in tobacco-related disease is described in detail throughout this report and discussed briefly here.

Biomarkers of Exposure

There are diverse biomarkers of exposure. The least intrusive measurements are of chemicals and metabolic products in the breath. Levels of exhaled CO, nitric oxide, 2,5-dimethylfuran, and volatile organic compounds (e.g., benzene and toluene) are higher in the breath of smokers than in the breath of nonsmokers (Gordon et al. 2002; IARC 2004). One study showed that volatile compounds such as benzene and 1,3-butadiene have a short residence time in the body and that their concentrations in breath were a function of the number of cigarettes smoked and the time between when the smoker takes a puff and when the breath sample is collected (Gordon et al. 2002). Saliva is another biologic material that is readily accessible and inexpensive to collect. Cotinine, a metabolite of nicotine (Bernert et al. 2000), and thiocyanate, a metabolite of cyanide (Prignot 1987), can be measured in saliva; levels of both metabolites can be used to distinguish between smokers and nonsmokers.

Urinary compounds are useful markers of the uptake and metabolic processing of constituents of cigarette smoke (IARC 2004). Urinary markers of exposure to cigarette smoke are nicotine and nicotine metabolites including cotinine; minor tobacco alkaloids such as anatabine and anabasine; 1-HOP; 1- and 2-naphthol; hydroxyphenanthrenes and phenanthrene dihydrodiols; aromatic amines; heterocyclic amines; *N*-nitrosoproline; and NNAL (Hoffmann and Brunnemann 1983; Jacob et al. 1999; Hecht 2002; Murphy et al. 2004), thiocyanate (Prignot 1987), acetonitrile (Pinggera et al. 2005), and methylhippuric acids (Buratti et al. 1999). Nicotine and its metabolites and NNAL are specific to tobacco exposure, and compounds such as thiocyanate and 1-HOP reflect environmental sources of exposure including diet (Van Rooij et al. 1994; Sithisarankul et al. 1997; Hecht et al. 2004). In one study, levels of total NNAL, total cotinine, and 1-HOP increased with the number of cigarettes smoked per day (Joseph et al. 2005). The highest rates of increase were observed at low levels of cigarette use (1 to 10 cigarettes per day), and levels in urine plateaued at 25 to 35 cigarettes per day.

Some urinary metabolites provide information on metabolic activation and detoxification, as well as the dose (Hecht 2002, 2003). Examples are *trans,trans*-muconic acid and *S*-phenylmercapturic acid (benzene metabolites), NNAL and its glucuronides (metabolites of the TSNA NNK) (Melikian et al. 1993, 1994; Hecht 2002, 2003), and 1-HOP (a pyrene metabolite) (Hecht et al. 2004). Studies reported that concentrations of urinary 1-HOP glucuronide (Sithisarankul et al. 1997) and total 1-HOP (free and conjugated) (Van Rooij et al. 1994) correlated well with the number of cigarettes smoked per day. In one study, there appeared to be no significant difference in the urinary concentration of 1-HOP glucuronide in smokers of cigarettes containing blond (flue-cured) tobacco versus smokers of black (air-cured) tobacco (Sithisarankul et al. 1997). Other studies found that in most smokers, more than 80 percent of the nicotine dose received was accounted for by urine content of nicotine, nicotine glucuronide, cotinine, cotinine glucuronide, and *trans*-3'-hydroxycotinine (Benowitz et al. 1994; Davis and Curvall 1999). Total cotinine (free and conjugated) is considered the most reliable urinary marker of nicotine exposure (Murphy et al. 2004).

Examination of the blood of smokers shows elevated carboxyhemoglobin, thiocyanate, cadmium, acetonitrile, 2,5-dimethylfuran, VOCs (e.g., benzene, toluene, and styrene), the presence of nicotine and its metabolite cotinine, and NNAL (Ashley et al. 1996; Houeto et al. 1997; IARC 2004). In addition, investigators found a positive correlation between carboxyhemoglobin and exhaled CO for several hours after smoking (Hopkins et al. 1984), and

serum cotinine and blood cadmium levels correlated with the number of cigarettes smoked per day (Telišman et al. 1997; Caraballo et al. 1998). The correlation between acetonitrile concentrations and the number of cigarettes smoked per day was shown to be weak (Houeto et al. 1997).

Markers of tobacco smoke exposure that were measured in other biologic tissues include PAH compounds in lung tissue, B[*a*]P and TSNAs in cervical mucus (IARC 2004), and TSNAs in pancreatic juice (Prokopczyk et al. 2002). Also, researchers observed that pregnant smokers had higher placental levels of cadmium than did pregnant women who did not smoke (Ronco et al. 2005a,b). In another study, cadmium was detected in the seminal fluid of smokers at higher levels than in that of nonsmokers, and the levels correlated with the number of cigarettes smoked per day (Telišman et al. 1997).

Biomarkers of Biologically Effective Dose

For cancer, a common assessment of the biologically effective dose is measurement of levels of carcinogen-DNA adducts. Strong data from animal experiments and some human studies indicate relationships among the levels of constituents of tobacco smoke, formation of carcinogen-DNA adducts, and cancer risk (Stratton et al. 2001). Levels of DNA adducts potentially provide the most direct measure of tobacco-induced DNA damage, and many studies reported higher levels in the tissues of smokers than in those of nonsmokers (Hecht 2003). In one study, most cancers causally associated with tobacco smoking showed positive evidence of increased adduct levels (Phillips 2005). However, human data on adduct formation suggested that saturation may occur at high levels of exposure (i.e., >20 cigarettes per day), causing the dose-response curve to plateau and reducing the proportional relationship between exposure and adduct levels (Godschalk et al. 2003). Little is known about the temporal variability of DNA adducts within a target or surrogate tissue. One investigator reported that levels of carcinogen-DNA adducts are indicators of carcinogenic hazards but not of quantifiable risks (Phillips 2005).

Carcinogen-DNA adducts can be measured in target or surrogate tissues. For example, they were measured in human lung tissue, exfoliated bladder cells, oral mucosa, exfoliated oral cells, and cervical cells—all sites of tobacco-derived cancers—and in surrogate tissues (e.g., carcinogen–peripheral blood lymphocyte DNA adducts) (Mancini et al. 1999; Romano et al. 1999; Stratton et al. 2001). The assumption that levels of DNA adducts in a surrogate tissue or cell reflect those in a target tissue has principally been supported by studies of animals treated with single carcinogens, but results in human biomonitoring studies have been mixed (Phillips 2005).

Additional biomarkers of biologically effective dose are (1) protein adducts, in that most carcinogen metabolites that react with DNA also react with proteins, and (2) oxidized damage to DNA bases. Protein adducts present at higher levels in smokers than in nonsmokers include hemoglobin adducts of TSNAs, 3-aminobiphenyl, 4-aminobiphenyl, *o*-toluidine, *p*-toluidine, and 2,4-dimethylaniline, as well as adducts from ethylation or methylation of the *N*-terminal valine of hemoglobin (Branner et al. 1998; Thier et al. 2001; Hecht 2003). The lung tissues of smokers have higher levels of acrolein-derived DNA lesions, one of which was identified as the mutagenic guanine adduct α-hydroxy-2'-deoxyguanosine. This lesion blocks DNA replication, potentially leading to G→T and G→A base substitution mutations (Yang et al. 2002; Zhang et al. 2007; Zaliznyak et al. 2009). The repair products of oxidative DNA lesions are water soluble and are generally excreted into urine without further metabolism. Because of extensive and rapid DNA repair, urine excretion of the oxidative DNA repair lesions reflects the average rate of oxidative DNA damage in all the cells in the body (Loft and Poulsen 1998). Levels of 8-hydroxy-2'-deoxyguanosine (8-OH-dG) (Gackowski et al. 2003) and 8-nitroguanine (Hsieh et al. 2002), both shown to indicate oxidative DNA damage, were found to be higher in the DNA of leukocytes of smokers than in those of nonsmokers. Tobacco smoking was consistently shown to increase the urinary excretion rate of 8-OH-dG by 30 to 50 percent, and levels in urine decreased after smoking cessation (Loft and Poulsen 1998). In addition, both healthy smokers and smokers with cancer had urine levels of 8-hydroxyguanine that were higher than those in healthy nonsmokers (Gackowski et al. 2003). The oxidatively modified DNA base, 8-hydroxyguanine, is also a marker of oxidative stress. There is no epidemiologic evidence that high levels of oxidative DNA modification in tissue or high levels of oxidatively modified nucleic acid products in urine are predictors of cancer development in humans (Poulsen 2005).

Many mutagens and carcinogens are metabolically activated in vivo to electrophilic forms capable of interaction with cellular macromolecules (van Doorn et al. 1981). One of the mechanisms used by an organism to combat electrophilic attack is conjugation of the reactive chemical moiety with reduced glutathione, a nucleophile. This reaction causes an increase in more polar thioether conjugates, which are excreted from the body in urine and bile. Urinary thioether concentrations are used as a non-specific indicator of exposure to alkylating agents. Cigarette smoking was found to cause a dose-related increase in the urinary excretion of thioethers. Chemicals present in cigarette smoke and excreted in urine as thioethers include benzene, styrene, and vinyl chloride (van Doorn

et al. 1981; Goldstein and Faletto 1993; Fisher 2000b). Increased concentrations of alkyladenines and alkylguanines from the reaction of alkylating agents with DNA were also observed in the urine of smokers (Hecht 2002). All three types of carcinogen biomarkers (thioethers, alkyladenines, and alkylguanines) reflect chemical uptake and the balance between activation and detoxification (Hecht 2003).

Biomarkers of Biologic Events with the Potential to Lead to Harm

Stratton and colleagues (2001) have reviewed a large number of biomarkers of biologic events with the potential to lead to harm. This review and more recent publications are summarized here. On an organ or system level, signs and symptoms of potential biologic events with the potential to lead to harm include osteoporosis, cough, hyperplasia, dysplasia, abnormal serum lipid concentrations, alterations in levels of blood coagulants, periodontal disease, and abnormal results for glucose tolerance tests (Stratton et al. 2001). On a molecular level, relevant measurements in target tissues of smokers include changes in RNA or protein expression, somatic mutations or loss of heterozygosity, alterations in promoter methylation, and mitochondrial mutations. In surrogate tissues, biomarkers of biologic events with the potential to lead to harm among smokers include leukocytosis, *HPRT* mutations, chromosomal aberrations, and changes in circulating lymphocytes.

Studies have identified biomarkers of biologic events with the potential to lead to harm related to cigarette smoking that are addressed in this Surgeon General's report. For example, a significant association and a dose-response relationship were shown for chromosomal aberrations induced by B[*a*]P diol epoxide at locus 3p21.3 in peripheral blood lymphocytes and for risk of squamous cell carcinoma of the head and neck (Zhu et al. 2002). Also, study findings suggested the frequency of promoter methylation in tumor-suppressor genes (P14, P16, P53) as a biomarker for risk of non-small-cell lung cancer among current and former smokers and cervical squamous cell cancer among smokers (Jarmalaite et al. 2003; Lea et al. 2004).

Cigarette smoking is a risk factor for bladder cancer. The increased mutagenicity of smokers' urine was first shown in 1977 by testing the brand XAD/acetone-extractable organics from urine in the *Salmonella* (Ames test) mutagenicity assay (Yamasaki and Ames 1977). Studies using essentially the same methods confirmed this observation (DeMarini 2004). Peak mutagenic activity of the urine occurs 4 to 5 hours after the start of smoking and decreases to pre-smoking levels in approximately 12 to 18 hours (Kado et al. 1985). Findings suggested that the mutagens are absorbed rapidly (in 3 to 5 hours).

Urinary mutagenicity generally correlates with the number of cigarettes smoked, and the level of urinary mutagenicity was found to be similar regardless of the tar level of the cigarettes smoked (Tuomisto et al. 1986; Kuenemann-Migeot et al. 1996). However, the urine from smokers of black tobacco was reported to be twice as mutagenic as that from smokers of blond tobacco, which correlated with the known increased risk for bladder cancer among smokers of black versus blond tobacco (Malaveille et al. 1989). In addition, smoking-associated urinary mutagenicity correlated with external measures of exposure (e.g., daily intake of chemicals from tobacco smoke) and with internal measures of exposure (e.g., urinary 1-pyrenol) (Pavanello et al. 2002).

Aromatic amines, heterocyclic amines, and PAHs appear to be the chemicals responsible for smoking-related urinary mutagenicity, as detected in the Salmonella assay (IARC 2004). Studies showed that urinary mutagenicity correlated with the levels of a 4-aminobiphenyl-DNA adduct in exfoliated urothelial cells from smokers (Talaska et al. 1991). Chemical analyses of urine from smokers with exceptionally high urinary mutagenicity revealed the presence of the mutagen 2-amino-7-naphthol, a metabolite of the bladder carcinogen 2-aminonaphthalene (β-naphthylamine) (Connor et al. 1983).

Although studies have described several biomarkers for risk of cardiovascular disease, no biomarker was specific to cigarette smoking. These biomarkers include changes in blood lipid concentrations, urine thromboxane A2 metabolites, blood F2-isoprostanes, vascular cell adhesion molecule-1, reduced platelet survival, atherosclerosis or calcium formation, and possibly elevated blood pressure (Stratton et al. 2001; Cavusoglu et al. 2004; Morrow 2005).

Symptoms and signs of biologic events with the potential to lead to harm to the respiratory system include late-occurring symptoms (cough, chronic phlegm production, wheeze, and shortness of breath) and decrements in pulmonary function, such as a notable decline in forced expiratory volume in one second (Carrell 1984; Ogushi et al. 1991; Stratton et al. 2001). Other biomarkers of biologic events with the potential to lead to harm are declines in alveolar neutrophil and macrophage counts and declines in neutrophil elastase α1-antiprotease complexes.

Some of the general markers described here can be considered as biomarkers of potential reproductive or developmental effects from maternal cigarette smoking during pregnancy. Findings in one study indicated that increased levels of F2-isoprostane in cord blood may serve as a biomarker of oxidative stress (Obwegeser et al. 1999).

Another study reported biomarkers in cord blood of offspring of women who smoked during pregnancy and in maternal blood (İşcan et al. 1997). The markers included reduced levels of high-density lipoprotein cholesterol (HDLc) and apolipoprotein A-I (APO A-I) and elevated ratios of total cholesterol to HDLc, low-density lipoprotein cholesterol (LDLc) to HDLc, and APO B to APO A-I. Proteomics allows study of changes to proteins following environmental exposures. A recent comparison of up- and downregulated proteins in blood cord sera from the offspring of women who smoked during pregnancy with that of offspring of nonsmokers suggests that infants exposed in utero undergo changes in protein expression similar to those of smoke-exposed adults and animal models (Colquhoun et al. 2009). Among the changes were markers of inflammation (α2-macroglobulin), altered lipid metabolism (APO A-I), and α-fetoprotein, which is associated with fetal growth retardation (Colquhoun et al. 2009). These findings indicate that serum and cord blood lipid panels may provide biomarkers of biologic events with the potential to lead to harm to fetal metabolism of lipids.

Smoking interferes with absorption of vitamins B6, B12, and C and folic acid (Cogswell et al. 2003). Study findings indicate that lower plasma concentrations of vitamins (folate and B12) and nitric oxide from maternal smoking may result in hyperhomocysteinemia in pregnant women, a known risk factor for pregnancy-induced hypertension, abruptio placentae, and intrauterine growth restriction (Obwegeser et al. 1999; Özerol et al. 2004; Steegers-Theunissen et al. 2004). Women who smoke during pregnancy have an increased risk of delivering a low-birth-weight infant (USDHHS 2004). Decreases in birth weight were dose related to the number of cigarettes smoked (Abel 1980). Researchers reported that low concentrations of maternal serum folate and vitamin B12 were associated with higher risk of preterm delivery and low birth weight, and low-birth-weight infants had significantly lower concentrations of vitamins A, B2, E, and folate (Navarro et al. 1984; Fréry et al. 1992; Scholl et al. 1996). In other studies, placental cadmium levels were strongly correlated with birth weight in newborns of mothers who smoked (Ronco et al. 2005a). Cotinine concentrations in maternal serum and urine were also useful in predicting birth weight (Stratton et al. 2001).

In summary, several biomarkers provide an accurate assessment of exposure to toxic chemicals in cigarette smoke. Still to be determined is how accurately they can characterize differences in exposure between tobacco-burning cigarettes and the variety of potentially reduced-exposure products introduced into the market during the last few years. Biomarkers of biologically effective doses for mutagenic and carcinogenic chemicals can provide an estimate of the interaction between chemicals in smoke and target biologic tissues or bodily fluids. Genetic polymorphisms of the enzymes involved in the metabolic activation of the chemicals may influence the net balance of activation and detoxification in a target biologic tissue and complicate interpretation of the dose-response relationship between exposure and binding with macromolecular targets. Despite the large number of biomarkers of biologic events with the potential to lead to harm, most are not specific to exposure to cigarette smoke and require additional testing to establish their specificity, sensitivity, and reliability when smoking behaviors or product characteristics vary. In addition, not all biomarkers of biologic events with the potential to lead to harm may be sufficient for determining population-level effects of the product.

Genotoxicity

Cigarette Smoke Condensate

Condensate from cigarette smoke is mutagenic in a variety of systems (DeMarini 1983, 2004; IARC 1986, 2004). Most studies have used condensate generated from the smoke of reference cigarettes such as those available from the University of Kentucky, Lexington, Kentucky. Researchers using the bacterial *Salmonella* mutagenicity assay reported that the average mutagenicity of cigarette smoke condensates prepared from the mainstream smoke from U.S. commercial cigarettes and K1R4F reference cigarettes was not significantly different among cigarettes representing more than 70 percent of the U.S. market (Steele et al. 1995). These findings suggested that such reference cigarettes are acceptable standards for comparative mutagenicity of condensates from cigarettes purchased typically in the United States. The genotoxicity of 10 cigarette smoke condensate samples from a diverse set of cigarettes (including the K2R4F reference cigarette) and produced under different smoking-machine conditions was studied in four short-term assays: the *Salmonella* mutagenicity assay in frameshift strains TA98 and YG1041, the micronucleus and comet assays in L5178YTk ± 7.3.2C mouse lymphoma cells, and an assay for chromosomal aberrations in CHO-K1 cells (DeMarini et al. 2008). All 10 condensate samples were mutagenic in both strains of *Salmonella* and induced micronuclei, and 9 samples induced DNA damage or chromosome aberrations. While their mutagenic potencies in *Salmonella* spanned 7-fold when expressed as revertants per gram of condensate, they spanned 158-fold when expressed as revertants per milligram of nicotine. The range of genotoxic potencies of the condensates in the other assays was similar regardless of how the data were expressed. The overall conclusion was that there was no relation among the genotoxic potencies of the cigarette smoke condensates across the assays (DeMarini et al. 2008).

Several lines of evidence indicated that the primary sources of mutagenic activity detected in the *Salmonella* mutagenicity assay are aromatic amines and heterocyclic amine protein pyrolysate products (IARC 1986). Most of this activity resides in the basic or base/neutral fraction of the condensates, which contains the aromatic and heterocyclic amines. At the molecular level, the mutation spectrum of cigarette smoke condensate in the *Salmonella* frameshift strain TA98 was identical to that of the heterocyclic amine Glu-P-1 (DeMarini et al. 1995). The finding suggested that this class of compounds is responsible for most of the frameshift mutagenic activity of cigarette smoke condensate detected in TA98. A frameshift mutation is the insertion into or deletion from DNA of a number of nucleotides that are not three or multiples of three. In contrast, most of the mutations induced by cigarette smoke condensate in the base-substitution strain TA100 were shown to be transversions of GC→TA (78 percent), which resembled most closely the mutation spectrum of B[*a*]P, the model PAH (DeMarini et al. 1995). The GC→TA transversions, a common class of base substitutions found in lung tumors of smokers, were also induced by cigarette smoke condensate at the *HPRT* locus in human B-lymphoblastoid MCL-5 cells (Krause et al. 1999).

Study findings indicated that most of the ability of cigarette smoke condensate to induce sister chromatid exchange (SCE) in mammalian cells may reside in the neutral and acidic/neutral fractions, suggesting that this activity is attributable to PAHs and acidic compounds, such as catechol, hydroquinone, alkylphenols, and benzaldehyde (Jansson et al. 1988).

Nicotine and its metabolites were not mutagenic in *Salmonella* and did not induce SCEs in mammalian cells in culture, and nicotine did not produce mutagenic urine in rats (Doolittle et al. 1995). Burning tobacco produced mutagenic chemicals, and cigarette smoke condensate contained a variety of agents exhibiting a wide range of toxic effects. Varying the amounts of 300 to 400 ingredients added to typical commercially blended test cigarettes did not alter the inherent mutagenicity or cytotoxicity of the resulting condensates or the toxic effects of inhalation of the smoke of the resulting cigarettes (Carmines 2002; Baker et al. 2004). Many of the pyrolysis products from the cigarette ingredients identified as "biologically active" were volatile compounds (e.g., benzene, toluene, and styrene) (Baker et al. 2004) and would presumably reside primarily in the gas phase of the cigarette smoke rather than in the condensate used in most in vitro assays.

DNA Damage

Many studies have demonstrated that cigarette smoke and its condensate can produce DNA strand breaks in rodents, in mammalian cells in culture, or in DNA in vitro (IARC 2004). Collectively, results of these studies are consistent with the demonstrated clastogenicity (chromosome-breaking ability) of cigarette smoke and condensate and cigarette smoke in experimental systems and in humans. Several of these studies (IARC 2004) indicated that reactive oxygen or nitrogen species may be the primary cause of the breaks in DNA strands.

Cytogenetic Effects in Rodents

Exposure of rodents to cigarette smoke by inhalation has generally produced an increased frequency of SCE in the bone marrow (IARC 1986). However, such exposure produced some negative studies and one positive study of induction of chromosomal aberrations in lung cells (DeMarini 2004). Nonetheless, this exposure consistently produced micronuclei in bone marrow, peripheral blood erythrocytes, and lung cells (IARC 2004).

Transplacental Effects in Rodents

Mice born to dams exposed to cigarette smoke by inhalation during pregnancy had elevated levels of micronuclei in the liver and peripheral blood (Balansky and Blagoeva 1989), and such exposure induced SCEs in the liver of fetal mice (Karube et al. 1989). Intraperitoneal injection of pregnant Syrian golden hamsters with the tobacco carcinogen NNK also induced micronuclei in fetal liver (Alaoui-Jamali et al. 1989), and intraperitoneal injection of pregnant mice with NNK induced oxidative damage, as determined by measurement of concentrations of 8-OH-dG DNA adducts in the fetuses (Sipowicz et al. 1997).

Studies in Humans

HPRT *Mutations*

In general, smoking was shown to increase the frequency of *HPRT* mutants in peripheral blood lymphocytes by approximately 50 percent. However, the increases did not reach statistical significance in some studies, probably because of the large interindividual variability (DeMarini 2004). An increase in transversions, in particular GC→TA, was noted frequently among smokers (IARC 2004). However, some analyses found no difference in the mutation spectrum at *HPRT* in smokers and nonsmokers (Curry et al. 1999). GC→TA transversions are the primary class of base substitution induced by PAHs, and an excess of this class of mutation in the *HPRT* mutation spectrum

for smokers is consistent with exposure to PAHs in cigarette smoke.

Genotoxic Effects in Reproductive Tissues and Fluids and in Children of Smokers

Lymphocytes from pregnant women who smoked either tobacco cigarettes or marijuana cigarettes had elevated frequencies of *HPRT* mutants, as determined by the autoradiographic *HPRT* assay, and analyses of cord blood indicated that lymphocytes from the newborns also had elevated frequencies of *HPRT* mutants (IARC 2004; DeMarini and Preston 2005). No differences in frequencies of *HPRT* mutants were observed in T lymphocytes from newborns of smokers compared with those from newborns of nonsmokers, as determined by the T-cell cloning assay. However, the mutation spectra for these two groups of newborns differed significantly from those for newborns of smokers who had an increase in "illegitimate" genomic deletions mediated by V(D)J recombinase. These findings suggested alteration in the *HPRT* mutation spectrum and possible increase in the frequency of *HPRT* mutant cells in newborns of mothers who smoked compared with those in newborns of mothers who did not smoke. Another study reported that in utero exposure to cigarette smoke also resulted in increases of translocation frequencies in newborns (Pluth et al. 2000). Other evidence indicated that smoking by the mother may lead to DNA strand breaks in lymphocytes of newborns (Şardaş et al. 1995). Amniocytes from mothers who smoked may show an increase in chromosomal mutations compared with those from nonsmokers (de la Chica et al. 2005); however, researchers raised concerns about this study, such as the lack of exposure assessment, the small sample size, and the fact that the chromosomal aberrations identified were of the chromatid type, which is a type that could have been formed in the petri dish during culturing and were not present in the amniotic fluid initially (DeMarini and Preston 2005).

Reviews indicated that the cervical mucus and amniotic fluid of smokers were mutagenic and that cervical epithelial cells from smokers had higher frequencies of micronuclei compared with those from nonsmokers (IARC 2004). Findings also suggested that smoking may induce chromosomal mutations and DNA damage in sperm or ova of smokers. The evidence that smoking induced oxidative damage to sperm DNA was found in elevated concentrations of 8-OH-dG in sperm DNA of smokers compared with that of nonsmokers (Shen et al. 1997). In addition, seminal fluid from infertile male smokers showed more oxidative damage than did that from infertile nonsmokers (Saleh et al. 2002). Consistent with these observations was the finding that sperm from smokers had higher concentrations of DNA strand breaks than did sperm from nonsmokers (Potts et al. 1999). Concentrations of DNA adducts in sperm, measured by the ^{32}P-postlabeling assay were also higher among current smokers than among lifetime nonsmokers (Horak et al. 2003). Collectively, these data from studies of humans are consistent with the recent demonstration that exposure to cigarette smoke by inhalation resulted in germ-cell mutations in male mice (Yauk et al. 2007).

Cytogenetic Effects

Micronuclei. Many studies have examined the influence of smoking on the frequency of micronuclei in peripheral lymphocytes; the results were mixed (Bonassi et al. 2003). A reanalysis of pooled data from 24 databases from the Human MicroNucleus international collaborative project showed that smokers did not have an overall increase in micronuclei frequency in lymphocytes. However, a significant increase in micronucleus frequency was found in heavy smokers (i.e., those smoking 30 cigarettes or more per day) who were not exposed occupationally to genotoxic agents. Studies also found elevated micronuclei frequencies in the tracheobronchial epithelium of smokers (Lippman et al. 1990).

Sister chromatid exchange. In contrast to frequency of micronuclei, SCE frequencies in peripheral lymphocytes are generally higher among smokers than among nonsmokers. Numerous studies of SCE frequencies in peripheral lymphocytes showed that cigarette smoking induced SCEs, which can then be a confounding factor in occupational studies (IARC 2004). The findings indicated that of all the cytogenetic endpoints, SCE is the most sensitive to the effect of smoking.

Chromosomal aberrations. Studies of large populations with use of chromosome banding techniques to assess chromosomal aberrations have had mixed results. One study reported that the frequency of chromosomal aberration was not increased by smoking (Bender et al. 1988), and another reported that smoking caused a 10- to 20-percent increase in the frequency (*Mutation Research* 1990). Smaller studies and those using molecular cytogenetic techniques also had mixed results; in some, smoking increased the frequency of chromosomal aberrations in peripheral lymphocytes, and in others, this finding was not observed (DeMarini 2004).

Mechanistic considerations include the observation that smokers had lower concentrations of folate in red blood cells than did nonsmokers, which may play a role in the higher frequency of chromosomal aberrations detected in smokers (Chen et al. 1989). Other studies found that exposure of peripheral lymphocytes from smokers to mutagens in vitro resulted in a higher frequency of chromosomal aberrations than did similar exposure of lymphocytes from nonsmokers (IARC 2004). Collectively, findings of these studies suggested that cells of smokers, especially males, were less able to repair DNA damage and that concentrations of DNA repair enzymes, fragile sites in chromosomes, and telomeric associations could be affected by recent mutagenic exposures such as smoking (DeMarini 2004). These effects of smoking varied among individuals, and were influenced by exposures other than smoking.

A large international study showed that an elevated frequency of chromosomal aberrations in lymphocytes predicted cancer risk independently of exposure to carcinogens, including cigarette smoke (Bonassi et al. 2000). However, many studies demonstrated an association between smoking and certain genetic changes that are specific predictors of various types of tumors. For example, lymphocytes of smokers had a higher frequency of fragile sites in chromosomes and metaphases with extensive breakage, as well as overexpression of fragile sites at chromosomal breakpoints associated with cancer and oncogene sites on chromosomes (Kao-Shan et al. 1987). Smoking was associated with chromosomal instability in lymphocytes as a biomarker for predisposition to oral premalignant lesions (Wu et al. 2002). In addition, smoking was associated with mutagen sensitivity of lymphocytes as a predictor of cancer of the upper aerodigestive tract. An analysis of normal bronchial epithelium using a molecular cytogenetic technique found a significant percentage of trisomy 7 in cancer-free tobacco smokers (Lechner et al. 1997). Another study reported a significant increase in the loss of heterozygosity involving microsatellite DNA at three specific chromosomal sites containing putative tumor-suppressor genes in histologically normal bronchial epithelium from long-term smokers (Mao et al. 1997; Wistuba et al. 1997). The frequency of chromosomal aberrations was much higher in lung tumors from smokers (48 percent) than in those from nonsmokers (11 percent), suggesting that lung cancer in smokers is a result of genetic alterations distinct from those in nonsmokers (Sanchez-Cespedes et al. 2001).

Studies also associated alterations in chromosome 9 in bladder tumors with cigarette smoking, and cytogenetic changes and smoking were associated with risk for leukemia and other myelodysplastic syndromes (IARC 2004).

DNA strand breaks and oxidative damage. A review by DeMarini (2004) reported that lymphocytes, buccal cells, and urothelial cells of smokers had higher frequencies of DNA strand breaks than those in nonsmokers, as measured by the single-cell gel electrophoresis (comet) assay, which detects broken DNA that separates from whole nuclear DNA when exposed to an electric current. Oxidative damage measured by concentrations of 7-hydroxy-8-oxo-2'-deoxyguanosine (8-oxo-dG) (a marker of oxidative damage) was elevated in lymphocytes and leukocytes, urine, and lung tissue of smokers. In vitro studies, including some in human cells, also found that cigarette smoke or its components induced DNA or oxidative damage. Collectively, these studies suggested that smoking induced oxidative DNA damage.

Mutations in tumors associated with smoking. In a review of studies in 2004, IARC noted that the *TP53* gene was mutated most frequently in lung tumors associated with smoking, and the details of this observation were reviewed extensively (Pfeifer et al. 2002; Pfeifer and Hainaut 2003; IARC 2004). Mutations in the *TP53* gene were more common in smokers than in nonsmokers, and a direct relationship existed between the frequency of *TP53* mutations and the number of cigarettes smoked. *TP53* mutations were found in preneoplastic lesions of the lung, indicating that they were early events linked temporally to DNA damage from smoking.

Among the mutations of the *TP53* gene in lung tumors of smokers, 30 percent were GC→TA transversions, whereas only 10 percent of the *TP53* mutations in lung tumors of nonsmokers or in other tumors were of this type. The sites at which these mutations occurred in the *TP53* gene corresponded with the sites of DNA adducts remaining after cells were exposed to diol epoxides of PAHs and allowed to undergo a period of DNA repair (Smith et al. 2000). The mutations in the tumors were targeted at methylated CpG sites on chromosomes, and there was a bias for most of the mutated guanines of the GC→TA mutations to be on the nontranscribed DNA strand in lung tumors from smokers, which is attributable to the preferential repair of DNA adducts on the transcribed strand (Yoon et al. 2001).

Mutations in the *KRAS* gene (codons 12, 13, or 61) were shown to occur in approximately 30 percent of lung adenocarcinomas of smokers and are primarily GC→TA transversions, as seen in the *TP53* gene (Gealy et al. 1999). As with the *TP53* gene, the site at which the majority of a particular type of PAH adducts are formed in the *KRAS* gene (the first position of codon 12) corresponded with the position where a high frequency of GC→TA transversions occur in lung tumors associated with smoking (Tretyakova et al. 2002). Similar to *TP53* mutations, *KRAS* mutations occurred early in carcinogenesis of the lung, and 66 percent of the mutations in the *KRAS* gene in smoking-associated lung tumors were GC→TA transversions (Keohavong et al. 2001).

These observations, along with substantially more data, suggest that the *TP53* and *KRAS* mutations in lung tumors of smokers are due to the direct DNA damage resulting from the carcinogens in cigarette smoke, especially PAHs (Pfeifer and Hainaut 2003). Researchers have suggested that other factors, especially selection, may also play a role in the observed mutation spectrum in smoking-associated lung tumors (Rodin and Rodin 2005).

Cytotoxicity

Cytotoxicity refers to a specific destructive action on cells. The cytotoxicity of cigarette smoke has been shown to manifest as several pathological conditions including irritation and inflammation, cell proliferation and hyperplasia, oxidative stress and damage, and decreased organ function (Andreoli et al. 2003). Studies demonstrated the presence of cytotoxic agents in the gas and particulate phases of cigarette smoke, and HCN and acrolein were identified as specific cytotoxic agents in the gas phase (Thayer and Kensler 1964; Battista 1976a). In the particulate phase, nonvolatile and semivolatile fractions, especially semivolatile acidic and neutral fractions, were found to demonstrate cytotoxic activity (Curvall et al. 1984, 1985; Matsukura et al. 1991).

Study findings indicate that cytotoxicity may play a role in several tobacco-related chronic diseases, including emphysema, carcinogenesis, and atherosclerosis (Bombick et al. 1998; Andreoli et al. 2003). For example, injury to cells of the respiratory system by cigarette smoke is thought to be mediated by smoke-induced inflammation and damage from free radicals (Churg and Cherukupalli 1993). Thus, the usefulness of in vitro cytotoxicity tests lies in their ability to measure indicators of cellular injury that may correlate with or predict inflammation (Stratton et al. 2001).

Many early cytotoxicity studies focused on damage to ciliated organisms (paramecium), clam gill epithelium, and animal trachea (Wang 1963; Weiss and Weiss 1964; Wynder et al. 1965; Dalhamn 1970; Battista 1976a,b; Donnelly et al. 1981a,b; Curvall et al. 1984), as well as cells such as adipocytes, macrophages, and human tumor cell lines (Thayer and Kensler 1964; Thayer 1976a,b; Drath et al. 1981; Curvall et al. 1984, 1985). Ciliatoxicity assays measure the time to incapacitation of ciliated cells or the time required by ciliated respiratory cells to transport inert particles when exposed to cigarette smoke. Impaired ciliary function and mucus transport in an intact respiratory system precede metaplasia in bronchial epithelium. Assays with isolated or cultured cells typically assess inhibition of metabolic activity or cellular growth in the presence of cigarette smoke or damage to the cell membrane (Wynder and Hoffmann 1967).

Subsequent research on the cytotoxicity of cigarette smoke has frequently used the neutral red incorporation assay to evaluate smoke from different types of cigarettes or tobaccos (Bombick et al. 1997a,b, 1998; Foy et al. 2004). This assay is based on the uptake of neutral red dye into the lysosomes of viable cells. Injury to the plasma membrane or lysosomal membrane was shown to decrease uptake and retention of the dye (Babich and Borenfreund 1987). One study demonstrated that flue-cured tobacco produced smoke condensate that was significantly more cytotoxic in the neutral red incorporation assay than was condensate from burley tobacco smoke (Bombick et al. 1998). In addition, no difference was found in the cytotoxicity of smoke condensate from reference cigarettes representing commercial ultralow-tar (1R5F), low-tar (1R4F), or unfiltered full-flavored (2R1) cigarettes. In contrast, with this assay, whole mainstream smoke and the vapor phase of mainstream smoke from a 2R1 cigarette were more cytotoxic than those from a 1R4F cigarette, and those from a 1R4F cigarette were more cytotoxic than those from a 1R5F cigarette (Bombick et al. 1997a). In addition, sidestream smoke (whole smoke and vapor phase) was more cytotoxic than mainstream smoke, as determined in the neutral red incorporation assay. The same laboratory reported that neither a low-nitrogen tobacco blend with a cellulose-acetate filter (11.6 mg tar in mainstream smoke) nor a traditional U.S. tobacco blend with a charcoal filter (10.4 mg tar in mainstream smoke) reduced the cytotoxicity of the condensate of full-flavored, low-tar cigarettes in the neutral red incorporation assay (Bombick et al. 1997b).

In more recent studies, researchers reported that heating the tobacco at a low temperature instead of burning it reduced the cytotoxicity of the smoke, as determined by the neutral red incorporation assay (Tewes et al. 2003). However, the reduction was greater in the particulate phase than in the gas phase (Patskan and Reininghaus 2003). Less frequently used in vitro assays for cytotoxicity include the dye exclusion assay (Hopkin et al. 1981; Hopkin and Evans 1984); the lactate dehydrogenase release assay; the 3-(4,5-dimethylthiazol-2-yl)-2,5-diphenyltetrazolium bromide (MTT) uptake assay; and the kenacid blue binding assay (Putnam et al. 2002).

Smoking-machine conditions are a determinant of the cytotoxicity of cigarette smoke condensate (Foy et al. 2004; Roemer et al. 2004). Smoke condensates from U.S. commercial cigarettes ranging from very low or ultralow tar to full flavor as ranked by the FTC/ISO method, and also experimental reference cigarettes ranging from ultralow tar to low tar to full flavor, demonstrated a higher level of cytotoxicity when produced under smoking-machine conditions that generated higher smoke yields. The increase in cytotoxicity was measured in both the particulate and the gas phases expressed on a per cigarette

basis. The increase in cytotoxicity measured in smoke produced under more intense smoking conditions was greatest for the particulate phase of the full-flavored commercial cigarettes and least for the ultralight varieties. This pattern was not as evident for cytotoxicity induced in the gas phase (Roemer et al. 2004).

The cytotoxicity of machine-generated mainstream smoke from the 2R1 reference cigarette to cultured mouse fibroblast L-929 cells was reduced by increasing the age of the smoke and the amounts of charcoal in an acetate filter (versus acetate alone) (Sonnenfeld et al. 1985). Investigators showed that cytotoxic effects on lung epithelial cells were attributable to oxidants and aldehydes present in the volatile phase of the smoke or formed in the cells on exposure to the smoke (Hoshino et al. 2001). In one study, selective reduction of compounds in the gas phase by an activated carbon filter decreased the cytotoxicity of the gas phase of the smoke from a commercial cigarette to lung epithelial cells (Pouli et al. 2003). (The compounds were acetaldehyde, acetone, acetonitrile, acrolein, acrylonitrile, benzene, 1,3-butadiene, 2-butanone, 2,5-dimethylfuran, ethylbenzene, furan, isobutyraldehyde, isoprene, methacrolein, methanol, 1,3-pentadiene, propionaldehyde, propionitrile, toluene, and *m*-xylene.) However, in other research, a decrease in intracellular concentrations of reduced glutathione in a human type II–like cultured lung cell line (A549) exposed to whole smoke was significantly greater than that produced by smoke filtered through a Cambridge filter pad (Ritter et al. 2004). This finding suggests that chemicals in the particulate phase of cigarette smoke produce an immediate depletion of an important cellular antioxidant. The A549 cell line has been extensively used to study human lung damage by single chemicals and complex chemical mixtures. This cell line may be more useful for studying substances that are active in their administered form, rather than for studying those that require biotransformation to reactive metabolites, because some cytochrome P-450 isoforms are not expressed in A549 cells (Castell et al. 2005).

Recent mechanistic studies identified apoptosis and necrosis as important mechanisms of cytotoxicity of cigarette smoke to cultured mammalian lung cells (Hoshino et al. 2001; Piperi et al. 2003; Pouli et al. 2003). In one study, the viability of alveolar type 2 A549 cells was reduced by smoke extract from a commercial cigarette in a time- and concentration-dependent manner, as measured by the reduction of MTT (Hoshino et al. 2001). In another study, the viability of mouse lung LA-4 cells was reduced by the gas phase of commercial cigarette smoke in a concentration-dependent manner, as measured by lactate dehydrogenase leakage and reduced metabolic activity (WST-1 assay) (Piperi et al. 2003). In both studies, apoptosis was seen at low concentrations of smoke and necrosis was seen at higher concentrations. One of the studies found that smoke extract increased intracellular oxidative activity (Hoshino et al. 2001). The other study observed a dose-dependent reduction in reduced cellular glutathione levels (Piperi et al. 2003). In addition, cells exposed to cigarette smoke showed increased protein modification (nitrotyrosine immunoreactivity) and activation of mitogen-activated protein kinase pathways. Aoshiba and colleagues (2001) reported that toxic effects on isolated alveolar macrophages from the smoke of an unfiltered commercial cigarette involved oxidative stress, an important mediator of cell death through both necrosis and apoptosis. This effect was associated with accumulation of BAX protein, mitochondrial dysfunction, and release of mitochondrial cytochrome *c*, but it was independent of the *TP53* gene, FAS, and caspase activation. Sublethal concentrations of unfiltered extract from mainstream smoke from a commercial cigarette produced evidence of senescence in alveolar epithelial cells—A549 cells and alveolar type 2 cells isolated from normal human lungs. The senescence was characterized by dose- and time-dependent increases in β-galactosidase activity, changes in cell morphology, accumulation of lipofuscin, overexpression of the P21$^{CIP1/WAF1/SDI1}$ protein, and irreversible growth arrest (Tsuji et al. 2004).

Scientists reported that the limitation of past and current in vitro tests for cytotoxicity is that the results are based on the response of single cell types or isolated tissues and do not include the influence of the whole-body system on the response (Stratton et al. 2001). However, in vitro cytotoxicity assays are useful in determining the contribution of different tobacco blends or cigarette components (e.g., the filter) to the overall cytotoxicity of the smoke and in identifying causative cytotoxic agents in smoke and mechanistic pathways. Although in vitro assays are not able to replace all conventional animal bioassays, they are increasingly seen as alternatives to animal testing of drugs and chemicals, in the European Union, the United States, and elsewhere (Höfer et al. 2004; Interagency Coordinating Committee on the Validation of Alternative Methods 2004). Many cellular pathways are activated similarly in vitro and in vivo (Devlin et al. 2005). In 2005, the Canadian government implemented a regulation requiring performance of three in vitro tests of toxicity (mutagenicity, clastogenicity, and cytotoxicity) on emissions for all cigarettes sold in Canada and that the results be reported to the Minister of Health (*Canada Gazette* 2005). Quantitative in vitro dose-response data could eliminate the need for use of a large number of experimental animals to achieve appropriate statistical power in an in vivo study (Parry et al. 2005).

Animal Bioassays

Researchers have tested the carcinogenic ability of tar in cigarette smoke in laboratory animals for more than nine decades and in animal inhalation studies of machine-generated cigarette smoke for more than five decades (Wynder and Hoffmann 1967). The first successful induction of cancer in a laboratory animal with a tobacco product was reported by Wynder and colleagues (1953, 1957) with the application of cigarette tar to mouse skin. They observed a clear dose-response trend between the amount of tar applied to the skin of the mice and the percentage of animals bearing skin papilloma and carcinoma in the test group. Skin-painting studies typically used condensate from cigarette smoke produced under standard FTC or ISO conditions, allowing comparisons among studies. More recent studies showed that smoking-machine conditions influence the measures of in vitro mutagenicity and cytotoxicity of smoke condensate, expressed on a per cigarette or per milligram of tar basis (Roemer et al. 2004; Rickert et al. 2007). However, skin-painting studies typically focused on product characteristics such as tobacco filler, paper, and additives rather than on smoke condensate produced under different smoking-machine conditions. One study demonstrated that tobacco blend, filter type, and flavoring materials are determinants of the composition of mainstream smoke, whereas the amount of tobacco in the cigarette, the dimensions of the cigarette, and the filter type influence smoke yield (Borgerding and Klus 2005). Future skin-painting studies will likely use condensates produced by different smoking-machine conditions, because some countries have begun to mandate cigarette testing with alternative smoking-machine conditions.

The use of experimental animal studies to predict cancer risk is more qualitative than quantitative (Stratton et al. 2001). Most animals used in laboratory studies with smoke are obligate nose breathers. Furthermore, Wynder and Hoffman (1967) reported that the respiratory systems of laboratory animals differ qualitatively and quantitatively from those of humans in surface area, in the development of mucous membranes, and in having an enhanced glandular system that increases the fluid in the nasal passages. Despite these limitations, animal studies provide information that is not available from in vitro systems because animal studies permit the use of an intact host system with a full complement of endocrine, hormone, and immune effects and hepatic and extrahepatic metabolism (Eaton and Klaassen 2001). Animal studies are often used to confirm positive findings or to resolve conflicting results from in vitro assays and to study organ-specific effects. Animal studies provide valuable data in terms of biologic plausibility, mechanisms of action, and causality. Animal studies of chronic diseases such as cancer can be less expensive than human clinical studies, and they also allow the use of invasive procedures (Devlin et al. 2005).

The smoke and smoke condensate animal bioassay literature is extensive and was reviewed by IARC in 2004. A synopsis follows of similar literature with a focus on studies made available since the publication of that review.

Dermal Application of Cigarette Smoke Condensate

Studies have used mouse skin as the test tissue in experiments carried out during the past 35 years, and the results from various laboratories have been similar with respect to the overall degree of carcinogenic activity of cigarette smoke condensate and the major differences in activity from cigarettes with different designs. Cigarette smoke condensate produces both benign and malignant tumors on mouse skin. The induced tumors are usually of epidermal origin. The carcinogenic potency of the cigarette smoke condensate depends on the tobacco variety, the composition of the cigarette paper, and the presence of additives. Subtle differences in smoking techniques, storage conditions for cigarette smoke condensate, and procedures for animal exposure do not appear to critically affect the results (IARC 2004). Researchers also conducted a limited number of skin-painting studies in other animal species including Syrian golden hamsters (Bernfeld and Homburger 1983) and rabbits (Graham et al. 1957).

In early skin-painting experiments with mice, researchers examined the tumorigenic activity of smoke condensates from reference cigarettes, from cigarettes made with different reconstituted tobacco sheets, or from mixtures of smoke condensates from reference cigarettes and reconstituted tobacco sheets made with 8-percent sodium nitrate as a tobacco additive (Dontenwill et al. 1972). Three preparations were tested: smoke condensate, dry smoke condensate without volatile smoke components, and condensate from vapor phase smoke. The smoke and the dry smoke condensates were equivalent in their ability to induce tumors, but the condensate from vapor phase smoke was nearly ineffective. The manufacturing process used to prepare the reconstituted tobacco sheet was a factor in the tumorigenic activity of the smoke condensate. Sodium nitrate reduced the tumorigenic activity of smoke condensate when added to the tobacco, to the reference cigarettes, or to the reconstituted tobacco sheet.

Subsequent studies continued to evaluate reference and experimental cigarettes constructed of tobacco-derived materials in dermal tumor promotion studies with female SENCAR mice (Meckley et al. 2004a,b). Cigarette smoke condensate from 1R4F reference cigarettes, which

was applied to the skin of mice three times per week for 29 weeks, produced significant, dose-dependent increases in both the number of tumor-bearing animals and in the total number of tumors in mice treated first (initiated) with the carcinogen 7,12-dimethylbenz[a]anthracene (DMBA). The tumors were papillomas and squamous cell carcinomas; papillomas were still progressing toward carcinomas at the end of the study. Animals in the high-dose group demonstrated treatment-related damage to the treated dorsal skin. The damage was described as peeling skin, erythema, and sores. The effects on the dorsal skin occurred at a lower incidence in the middle-dose group. Dose-dependent histologic changes in nonneoplastic skin at the treatment site were characterized by increased epidermal thickness (acanthosis) and hyperkeratosis. Significant increases were reported in the ratios of organ to body weight for the kidneys, liver, and spleen and in organ weight and ratios of organ weight to brain weight for the liver and spleen in the mid- and high-dose groups compared with those for the control group, which was initiated with DMBA but not promoted with condensate. Histologic examinations revealed an increase in extramedullary hematopoiesis of the spleen in the high-dose group.

To increase the filling power of tobacco, manufacturers developed processes to impregnate shredded tobacco with volatile materials and then rapidly remove them to expand the cellular structure of the leaf, thereby reducing the density of the tobacco filler. The expanded tobacco was shown to have a high burn rate and irritating smoke (Browne 1990). The reduced cigarette weight, increased filling power, and increased burn rate reduced the number of puffs, which, in turn, reduced delivery of tar and nicotine (Abdallah 2003a). Expanded tobacco is included in commercial cigarettes, and the amount of expanded tobacco as a percentage of the tobacco mass increases from approximately 15 percent in full-flavored cigarettes to 50 percent in ultralight brands (Theophilus et al. 2004). Other scientists reported that concentrations of most chemicals measured in the smoke of cigarettes with puffed, expanded, or freeze-dried tobacco were significantly reduced compared with those in control cigarettes (Hoffmann et al. 2001).

In a study by Theophilus and colleagues (2003b), condensates from the smoke of cigarettes constructed with 100-percent tobacco expanded with dry ice or Freon-11 (trichlorofluoromethane) produced similar numbers of tumor-bearing animals and total tumors in DMBA-initiated mice. Animals in the group treated with a low dose of condensate from smoke of tobacco expanded with Freon had a significantly longer median time to onset of tumors and significantly more total tumors than animals in the group treated with a low dose of condensate from smoke of tobacco expanded with dry ice. No biologically significant nonneoplastic changes were observed in internal organs or treated dorsal skin. Smoke from the tobacco expanded with dry ice contained significantly higher concentrations of CO_2, acetone, formaldehyde, catechol, nitric oxide, and NATB than did smoke from the Freon-expanded tobacco.

In other research, Theophilus and colleagues (2003a) studied smoke from cigarettes constructed with 100-percent propane-expanded tobacco. They found that the smoke had significantly higher concentrations of total particulate matter, nicotine, tar, CO, CO_2, ammonia, catechol, hydroquinone, phenol, *p*- and *m*-cresol, nitric oxide, NATB, and NNK than did the smoke from Freon-expanded tobacco. No biologically significant nonneoplastic differences in internal organs or treated dorsal skin were observed among animals treated with condensate from cigarettes containing propane-expanded tobacco compared with animals treated with condensate from cigarettes containing Freon-expanded tobacco. Smoke condensates from cigarettes made with Freon- or propane-expanded tobacco produced similar numbers of tumor-bearing animals and total tumors in DMBA-initiated mice.

In another study, Theophilus and colleagues (2004) treated mice with smoke condensate from cigarettes constructed with increasing percentages of expanded shredded tobacco stems. In general, there was a pattern of increasing numbers of tumor-bearing animals and total tumors with increasing doses of tar among groups of mice treated with low, medium, or high concentrations of expanded shredded tobacco stems. This pattern was not present across these groups at a given tar level. The control group treated with condensate from cigarettes without expanded shredded tobacco stems showed a dose-dependent increase in the percentage of animals with tumors and in the total number of tumors compared with DMBA-initiated animals in the solvent (vehicle) control group not treated with smoke condensate. Cigarettes containing expanded shredded tobacco stems produced lower concentrations of some chemicals in mainstream smoke than did cigarettes that did not contain expanded shredded tobacco stems, but the concentrations were not consistently reduced in a dose-dependent manner.

In vivo and in vitro analyses support the hypothesis that short-term measures such as cytotoxicity, cellular proliferation (hyperplasia), generation of free radicals, and inflammation are involved in tumor promotion produced by cigarette smoke condensate (Curtin et al. 2004a). Other studies found that in addition to promoting tumors, cigarette smoke condensate and its fractions can act as tumor initiators, tumor accelerators, and cocarcinogens when applied together with other chemicals such as B[*a*]P and

complete carcinogens (Wynder and Hoffmann 1961; Hoffmann and Wynder 1971; Hecht 2005).

The results from studies of dermal application of cigarette smoke condensate suggest a tissue-specific response to the chemicals in cigarette smoke that undergo covalent binding to DNA. Investigators have detected adducts in the skin, lung, heart, kidney, liver, and spleen of female ICR mice treated topically with cigarette smoke condensate from a commercial U.S.-blended unfiltered cigarette (Randerath et al. 1986, 1988; Reddy and Randerath 1990). In one study, dermal application of condensate from the smoke of 1R4F reference cigarettes three times per week for one or four weeks induced DNA adducts in the skin and lung tissue of male CD-1 mice (Lee et al. 1992). The relative adduct labeling values in skin were highest after one week of exposure and did not increase after four weeks. DNA adduct levels in the lung increased between one week and four weeks of treatment with condensate. Skin adducts declined to less than one-half the values of the first week by four weeks after cessation of exposure to condensate. In contrast, adduct levels in the lung continued to increase during the four weeks after cessation of exposure. Adduct levels increased with the total amount of tar applied weekly. The dose-response relationship was especially evident in lung tissue. In another study, treatments three times per week with similar concentrations of condensate from 1R4F cigarettes for 29 weeks resulted in an increase in DNA adducts in skin and dose- and time-dependent increases in DNA adducts in lung and heart tissues of female SENCAR mice (Brown et al. 1998).

Inhalation Studies with Cigarette Smoke

Historically, animals have not proven to be good models for the type of lung tumors induced by cigarette smoke in humans. Inhalation exposure to cigarette smoke leads to a reduction in the respiratory rate, and nontransgenic animals and animal strains with a low background incidence of lung tumors often do not develop an excess of lung tumors of any type. Researchers have attempted to induce lung cancer by exposure to cigarette smoke in several animal species, including rabbits, monkeys, dogs, and hamsters and other rodents. Hamsters developed laryngeal tumors but not tumors in the lower respiratory tract, and dogs developed epidermoid and bronchioloalveolar carcinomas (Coggins 2002; IARC 2004; Witschi 2005). Rodents tended to develop adenomas arising in the periphery of the lung rather than bronchial tumors arising centrally (Stratton et al. 2001). A study by Hutt and associates (2005) was the first to describe successful induction of lung tumors in mice after a lifetime whole-body exposure to mainstream cigarette smoke. Many animal studies used exposure chambers that permit whole-body exposure to cigarette smoke. Modern nose-only exposure tubes that allow body heat to dissipate are regarded by some as superior to whole-body exposure chambers because they eliminate dosing by nonrespiratory routes and allow the test concentration delivered to the animal to be closer to the concentration delivered to the system, by avoiding loss of the test compound on the walls, loss on the skin and fur of the animals, sedimentation and impaction of aerosol particles in the chamber, and chemical reactivity in

the chamber (Pauluhn 2005). Table 3.1 contains data on lung tumor incidence from studies of carcinogenicity in rodents that used inhalation exposure to cigarette smoke.

Mouse. Witschi and colleagues (1997a) demonstrated that mouse lung tumors developed in the peripheral lung as areas of hyperplasia that progress to adenocarcinomas. In subsequent research, Witschi and colleagues (2002) studied male Balb/c and SWR mice exposed to a mixture of 89-percent sidestream smoke and

Table 3.1   Selected chronic carcinogenicity studies in mice and rats with inhalation exposure to cigarette smoke

Study	Strain	Gender	Concentration	Exposure duration/ administration route	Lung tumor incidence (%)
Mouse					
Witschi et al. 2002	Balb/c and SWR	Male	Average TSP concentration of 122 mg/m^3 from 1R4F reference cigarette sidestream/mainstream smoke mixture	6 hours/day, 5 days/week for 5 months/whole body	Balb/c: 9/27 (33) Controls: 6/30 (20) SWR: 6/31 (19) Controls: 1/26 (4)
Witschi et al. 2004	A/J	Male	Average TSP concentrations of 176 mg/m^3 (high dose), 120 mg/m^3 (medium dose), 99 mg/m^3 (low dose) from 2R4F reference cigarette sidestream/ mainstream smoke mixture	6 hours/day, 5 days/week for 5 months/whole body	High: 18/22 (82)[a] Medium: 23/25 (92)[a] Low: 18/25 (72)[a] Controls: 10/25 (40)
Hutt et al. 2005	B6C3F$_1$	Female	Average daily TPM concentration of 254 ± 27 mg/m^3 from a 2R1 reference cigarette	6 hours/day, 5 days/week for 30 months/whole body	148/330 (44.8)* Controls: 31/326 (9.5)
Rat					
Dalbey et al. 1980	F-344	Female	10% smoke concentration from unfiltered experimental cigarettes (NCI code 16)	8 hours/day, 5 days/week for 126 to 128 weeks/nose only	7/80 (9)[a,b] Controls: 1/93 (1)
Mauderly et al. 2004	F-344	Female, male	Low dose (100 mg/m^3 [6%]) and high dose (250 mg/m^3 [14%]) from a 1R3 reference cigarette	6 hours/day, 5 days/week for up to 30 months/whole body	Female Low: 4/175 (2.3) High: 4/81 (4.9)[a] Controls: 0/119 (0) Male Low: 1/178 (0.6) High: 5/82 (6.1) Controls: 3/118 (2.5)

Note: **mg/m^3** = milligrams per cubic meter; **NCI** = National Cancer Institute; **TPM** = total particulate matter; **TSP** = total suspended particulate.
[a]Significantly different (p <0.05) from controls.
[b]Respiratory tumors consisted of 8 in the lung (5 adenomas, 2 alveologenic carcinomas, 1 squamous carcinoma) and 2 nasal tumors (adenocarcinoma and squamous-cell carcinoma).
*p <0.001.

11-percent mainstream smoke from 1R4F reference cigarettes (Witschi et al. 2002). As reported in the previous studies (Witschi et al. 1997a,b), the investigators included a four-month recovery period to increase the development of lung tumors. In both strains, they observed increases in lung tumor multiplicities (average number of tumors per lung) (0.44 ± 0.13 and 0.35 ± 0.14, respectively) and lung tumor incidences (number of tumor-bearing mice per total number of treated mice) (33% in treated Balb/c mice versus 20% in controls and 19% of treated SWR mice versus 4% in controls, respectively) (Table 3.1) after exposure to cigarette smoke. Only the lung tumor multiplicity in treated SWR mice was statistically different from that in SWR controls exposed to air only. These investigators found that strain A/J mice were more susceptible to carcinogen-induced lung tumors than were Balb/c or SWR mice (Witschi et al. 2002). The same exposure regimen showed that in male strain A/J mice, the lung tumor multiplicity was significantly higher among the exposed mice than among the air-only controls, and there was a good correlation between exposure (average concentration of cigarette smoke multiplied by exposure duration) and lung tumor multiplicity (Witschi et al. 2002). Proliferative pulmonary lesions were categorized as focal alveolar epithelial hyperplasia, alveolobronchiolar adenomas, and alveolobronchiolar adenocarcinomas. Although it was possible to achieve a dose-related increase in lung tumor multiplicity in A/J mice with this exposure protocol, mice exposed to cigarette smoke had fewer adenomas with carcinomatous foci or adenocarcinomas (malignant tumors) than did air-only controls (Witschi et al. 2002).

In a later study, Witschi and colleagues (2004) used a similar exposure regimen with five months of whole-body exposure to smoke from 2R4F reference cigarettes (89-percent sidestream and 11-percent mainstream smoke), followed by a four-month recovery period. This regimen produced a significant increase in lung tumor multiplicity and tumor incidence compared with the air-only controls although the response to the high dose was slightly less than to the medium dose (Table 3.1) in male strain A/J mice. The authors attribute the flat dose-response curve to the weak lung carcinogenicity of cigarette smoke in mice. The tumors were described as bronchioloalveolar adenomas.

Curtin and associates (2004b) studied effects of subchronic exposure to mainstream smoke from 1R4F reference cigarettes in male *RasH2* transgenic mice, which carry the human *C-HA-RAS* oncogene, and A/J mice. Mice had whole-body exposure for 20 weeks or nose-only exposure for 28 weeks. Results indicated that whole-body exposure may be more effective than nose-only exposure for inducing statistically significant changes in tumor multiplicity and tumor incidence. One concentration of cigarette smoke was used in the whole-body experiments, and three concentrations were used in the nose-only experiments. Both exposure regimens included a 16-week recovery period. With whole-body exposure, microscopically confirmed tumor incidence and tumor multiplicity were significantly greater in the exposed animals than in the sham-exposed animals in both mouse strains.

Hutt and colleagues (2005) developed a model that achieved a 10-fold increase in hyperplastic lesions, a 4.6-fold increase in adenomas and papilloma, a 7.25-fold increase in adenocarcinomas, and a 5-fold increase in metastatic pulmonary adenocarcinomas in mice with lifetime whole-body exposure to cigarette smoke compared with lesions in air-only sham controls. The $B6C3F_1$ strain of mice used in this study have low background incidence of lung tumors compared with that for A/J mice used in other studies. The female mice were exposed to mainstream smoke from an unfiltered 2R1 reference cigarette for 30 months. An increase in lung hyperplasia and neoplasia was first seen in mice exposed to TPM that died spontaneously between 540 and 720 days after the initial exposure. At the end of the study, the survival of mice exposed to smoke was significantly longer than that of the sham-exposed controls possibly because of reduced food consumption leading to lower body weight and a lower incidence and delayed onset of other types of cancers. Animals exposed to TPM also had a statistically significant increase in incidence of benign and malignant proliferative lesions in the nasal cavity. In contrast to other studies using a mouse model, this study achieved a significantly greater incidence of adenocarcinomas in treated animals (67 of 330, 20.3 percent) than in sham-exposed controls (9 of 326, 2.8 percent).

Rat. Female Fischer-344 (F-344) rats received daily nose-only exposure to the smoke of experimental cigarettes for 126 to 128 weeks (7 cigarettes per 8-hour day, 5 days per week) (Dalbey et al. 1980). The mean delivery of smoke particulate from 85-mm unfiltered cigarettes (National Cancer Institute, code 16) was 18.4 mg per cigarette. The exposure chamber consisted of holding tubes attached to the side of a 350-mL chamber containing a mixture of cigarette smoke and room air. The two control groups consisted of unexposed and sham-exposed controls. Survival in the smoke-exposed rats was similar to that of the two control groups combined. Animals in the group exposed to smoke had significantly more tumors of the respiratory tract than did the combined control groups (Table 3.1). Compared with controls, rats exposed to cigarette smoke had significantly fewer tumors in the hypophysis, hematopoietic and lymphoid system, uterus, and ovary. The number of adrenal tumors and oral tumors in treated animals increased, but the changes did not reach statistical significance. Animals exposed to smoke also had a significant increase in dermal tumors (subcutaneous sarcomas) near ulcers on the front feet from pushing against the holding tubes during exposure compared with animals in the control groups.

In the same study of lifetime exposure, researchers observed nonneoplastic tumors throughout the respiratory tract of animals exposed to smoke (Dalbey et al. 1980). These lesions included hyperplastic and metaplastic areas in the epithelium of the upper airways (nasal turbinates, larynx, and trachea) and areas of the lung with focal alveolitis (accumulations of pigmented macrophages, alveolar epithelial hyperplasia, and alveolar fibrosis).Lesions in control animals were much smaller and less severe. Researchers observed fibrosis and thickening of arterioles in the papillary muscle of the heart. No other organ systems showed evidence of smoke-related pathology.

One study also used chronic whole-body exposure in an attempt to achieve higher lung doses of cigarette smoke in F-344 rats (Mauderly et al. 2004). Low (100 mg TPM/cubic meter [m^3]) and high (250 mg TPM/m^3) concentrations of mainstream cigarette smoke were used for exposures up to 30 months. Cigarette smoke was produced from unfiltered 1R3 reference cigarettes machine puffed twice per minute using a 70-mL, two-second puff and then diluted with air cleaned by a high-efficiency particulate air filter. Exposure to cigarette smoke significantly increased the incidences of nonneoplastic and neoplastic, proliferative lung lesions in female rats. Trends with exposure for all neoplastic lung lesions were highly significant for female rats. No trend with exposure was significant for males. Time to first observation of hyperplastic lesions was shortened by exposure among female but not male rats. Both benign and malignant neoplasms were observed earlier in high-exposure female rats than in low-exposure female rats. Hyperplastic responses consisted primarily of focal alveolar epithelial hyperplasia. Benign neoplasms were bronchioloalveolar adenomas, and malignant neoplasms were bronchioloalveolar carcinomas. Mean absolute weights of lungs in male and female rats exposed to high concentrations of smoke were significantly greater than those in animals in the control groups. Nonproliferative changes more common in animals in high-exposure groups than in low-exposure groups were ciliated cuboidal cell metaplasia and squamous metaplasia in alveolar ducts. There was no consistent difference by sex in development of proliferative nasal lesions, and the incidence of nasal cavity neoplasms increased significantly in both male and female rats exposed to high concentrations of smoke. Most of the nasal cavity tumors were epithelial in origin, and the benign epithelial tumors were

adenomas. Histologic changes in the nasal cavity, such as squamous metaplasia of transitional and respiratory epithelium, mucous cell metaplasia and hyperplasia, and inflammatory infiltrates, were more common or more severe in the rats exposed to high concentrations of smoke.

Carcinogenicity bioassays should be conducted for a major portion of the test animal's lifetime. Short-term (subchronic) exposure studies are primarily performed to provide information on target organs of repeated exposure. Short-term, nose-only exposures to mainstream smoke produced treatment-related histopathologic changes in the respiratory tract and in clinical chemistry parameters in male and female Sprague-Dawley rats (Coggins et al. 1989; Ayres et al. 2001; Terpstra et al. 2003). Animals exposed to cigarette smoke had significantly more chronic active inflammation, epithelial hyperplasia, atrophy of the olfactory epithelium, and squamous metaplasia of the nasal passages and larynx. Other histopathologic changes included increased counts of intra-alveolar brown-gold macrophages and bronchial goblet cells. There was a dose-dependent trend toward increased severity of the effects with increased exposure. Some of the effects such as laryngeal squamous metaplasia were not completely reversed during a recovery period.

A U.S.-tobacco-blend cigarette containing the additive 1-menthol and other conventional processing aids and flavoring ingredients was compared with a reference cigarette comprised of a similar tobacco blend in a 13-week inhalation study of toxicity in male and female F-344 rats (Gaworski et al. 1997). Only one concentration of 1-menthol (5,000 ppm) was used. Three dose levels of cigarette smoke were tested for each cigarette. Both cigarette varieties produced similar dose-related histologic changes in the respiratory tract and increases in ratios of lung weight to body weight. The researchers noted that although lesions in the trachea and larynx related to cigarette smoke were similar in incidence, the degree of the response was slightly more severe in some groups of female rats exposed to mentholated cigarette smoke than it was in those exposed to nonmentholated cigarette smoke.

Theophilus and colleagues (2003a,b, 2004) performed several 13-week nose-only inhalation studies with Sprague-Dawley rats to evaluate the toxic effects of expanded materials derived from tobacco (Theophilus 2003a,b, 2004). The exposure regimen consisted of one hour of exposure per day, five days per week, for 13 weeks, followed by a 13-week recovery period. Male and female rats were exposed to mainstream smoke from cigarettes constructed of 100-percent tobacco expanded with dry ice or Freon-11 (Theophilus et al. 2003b) or tobacco expanded with propane or Freon-11 (Theophilus et al. 2003a). Animals exposed to cigarette smoke demonstrated chronic active inflammation and epithelial hyperplasia of nasal tissues and ventral squamous metaplasia of the larynx that appeared to increase in severity with increasing doses. Treated animals also had significantly more non-pigmented macrophages and brown-gold macrophages and evidence of chronic active inflammation of the larynx than did air-only controls. Most of the histologic changes resolved after a 13-week recovery period (Theophilus et al. 2003a,b). A separate study was conducted to evaluate the toxic effects of different percentages of expanded shredded tobacco stems (Theophilus et al. 2004). Overall, exposure to mainstream smoke from cigarettes constructed of 9.25-percent, 18.5-percent, or 25-percent expanded shredded stems failed to produce signs of increased or decreased toxicity relative to the control cigarettes that did not contain expanded shredded stems. At the highest dose, animals in all the groups exposed to expanded shredded stems had significant increases in the severity of nonpigmented macrophages in left and apical regions of the lung compared with those in unexposed animals. Treatment groups with the medium (18.5 percent) and high (25 percent) content of expanded shredded stems also had a significant increase in the severity of nonpigmented macrophages and goblet cells in the right diaphragmatic region of the lung at the highest dose compared with animals treated with smoke from control cigarettes containing zero-percent expanded shredded stems. Theophilus and colleagues did not describe the composition or tobacco blend in the control cigarettes or in the cigarettes made with expanded shredded stems. They stated that the tobacco blend and cigarette configuration were comparable between test and control cigarettes and that the main difference was the percentage of expanded shredded stems in the test cigarettes.

Cardiovascular and Cerebrovascular Studies in Animals

Some animal models show promise for studying the development of cardiovascular disease induced by cigarette smoke. For example, researchers have proposed an elastase-perfusion mouse model for aortic aneurysms induced by cigarette smoke (Buckley et al. 2004). Another example is the cockerel as a model for arteriosclerosis (Penn et al. 1983, 1992, 1996; Penn and Snyder 1988). Cockerels are sensitive to the plaque-promoting effects of chemicals administered by inhalation or injection. Inhalation of mainstream cigarette smoke or the vapor phase smoke component, 1,3-butadiene, was shown to promote plaque development in cockerels, but CO or an injection of NNK or solubilized concentrated cigarette smoke condensate from an unventilated 2R1 reference cigarette did not promote plaque development in cockerels. At high

doses, intramuscular injections of PAH compounds with different carcinogenic potencies also led to arteriosclerotic plaque formation. Sidestream smoke was more effective than mainstream smoke in stimulating aortic plaque development in the cockerel model.

Investigators reported that tissue injury induced by oxidative stress, altered serum lipids, increased blood pressure, and endothelial damage were other possible factors in cardiovascular injury from cigarette smoking (Stratton et al. 2001). In another study, inhalation exposure to cigarette smoke produced evidence of oxidative stress in the hearts of Balb/c mice (Koul et al. 2003). After 10 weeks of whole-body exposure for 60 minutes per day to the smoke from five commercial filter-tipped cigarettes, mice had significantly lower concentrations of glutathione and higher concentrations of lipid peroxides, glutathione peroxidase, glutathione reductase, and catalase than did unexposed mice. Serum triglycerides, total cholesterol, LDLc, and the ratio of total cholesterol to HDLc were also significantly higher, and HDL and the ratio of HDLc to LDLc were significantly lower in the group exposed to smoke. Concomitant administration of α-tocopherol prevented some of the smoke-induced changes.

In one study, whole-body exposure to smoke from a 2R1 reference cigarette three times per day for 30 days resulted in a significant increase in the formation of 8-oxo-dG, a marker of oxidative damage, in the heart tissue of male Sprague-Dawley rats, compared with the concentration in unexposed controls (Park et al. 1998). Cigarettes were smoked for 15 to 20 minutes to a fixed butt length in a 500-mL flask with air pumped into the flask. The reduced glutathione content and the oxidative state of glutathione in heart tissue were not significantly different from those in controls. In another study, whole-body exposure to low concentrations of cigarette smoke resulted in impaired oxidative function in cardiac mitochondrial cells; increased intracellular, low-molecular-weight iron that can play a role in redox reactions; and reduced α-tocopherol during cardiac ischemia and reperfusion in female Sprague-Dawley rats (van Jaarsveld et al. 1992). These findings suggested a mechanism involving oxidant radicals. Twice a day for two months, smoke was introduced by inserting a lit cigarette into a hole in the exposure chamber and allowing smoke to be drawn into the chamber for 5 seconds, followed by room air for 55 seconds. This procedure was repeated until the cigarette extinguished (approximately 10 minutes). Carboxyhemoglobin concentrations in rats exposed to smoke or air were not statistically different.

Scientists reported that hepatic uptake of chylomicrons was significantly lower in Sprague-Dawley rats with whole-body exposure to the smoke of two unfiltered, king-size, GPC-brand cigarettes (35 to 40 mL per puff, 20 puffs per cigarette) than was uptake in sham-exposed controls (Pan et al. 1993). Animals were exposed to the smoke for 10 minutes, four times per day, for 10 days. In addition, more chylomicrons remained in the hearts of rats exposed to smoke than in the hearts of controls. Hepatic uptake and residence time in heart tissues also changed when chylomicrons were administered to unexposed animals that had been previously exposed to smoke. Smoke exposure increased the thiobarbituric acid reactive substance measurement in chylomicrons, a measure of lipid peroxidation. In a subsequent series of experiments, whole-body exposure to the smoke of two 2R1 reference cigarettes (35 to 40 mL per puff, 20 puffs per cigarette) for 10 minutes, six times per day, for 10 days, significantly increased postprandial serum triglyceride and chylomicron concentrations, decreased hepatic uptake of chylomicron remnants, and increased plasma postheparin lipoprotein lipase activity. Hepatic lipase activity was similar in rats exposed to smoke and controls (Pan et al. 1997). In another study, subchronic (14 or 90 days) but not acute (1 day) whole-body inhalation exposure to cigarette smoke resulted in significantly increased cholesterol, triglyceride, and phospholipid levels in the serum, hearts, aortas, and lungs of male Sprague-Dawley rats (Latha et al. 1988). Changes in serum lipoproteins included decreases in HDLc, triglycerides, and phospholipids and increases in LDL and very-low-density lipoprotein cholesterol, triglycerides, and phospholipids. Other alterations in lipid metabolism included increased hydroxymethylglutaryl-CoA reductase activity, decreased lipoprotein lipase activity in heart tissue, and increased lipoprotein lipase in adipose tissue.

Research in male hypercholesterolemic *ApoE* *-/*- mice suggested that five weeks of exposure to 1R4F cigarette smoke led to an increase in oxidized LDL immunoglobulin M (IgM) and antiphosphorylcholine IgM antibodies and a decrease in oxidized LDL IgG and lymphotoxin-β messenger ribonucleic acid (mRNA) expression in the spleen (Tani et al. 2004). Both IgM changes were associated with an increase in thickness of arterial intima. Animals were acclimated to cigarette smoke produced by a vacuum pump until smoke from one cigarette per day was tolerated. Mice exposed to cigarette smoke had significantly higher serum carboxyhemoglobin concentrations than those of air-only controls.

Researchers examined the aortic endothelium from male Sprague-Dawley rats by scanning and transmission electron microscopy after inhalation exposure to the smoke of two medium-tar cigarettes (19 mg of tar and 1.5 mg of nicotine) (Pittilo et al. 1982, 1990). Smoking-machine conditions were not provided in the description of study methods. Animals were anesthetized before

exposure. The exposure was repeated 5 days per week during a 25-day period. Compared with sham-exposed controls, the rats exposed to smoke demonstrated marked morphologic evidence of endothelial damage that included increased blebs, microvillus-like projections, plasmalemmal vesicles, and Weibel-Palade bodies that store von Willebrand factor protein. No endothelial abnormalities were seen in rats that received nicotine by subcutaneous injections or by continuous subcutaneous pumps. These observations suggest that components of cigarette smoke other than nicotine are responsible for the endothelial cell changes associated with smoking. Researchers reported that male Sprague-Dawley rats with exposure to the smoke of five low-nicotine (1 mg) cigarettes for 20 to 30 minutes per day for four to six weeks had significantly higher mean arterial blood pressure after bilateral occlusion of the common carotid artery than did the sham-exposed controls (Bennett and Richardson 1990). Additionally, the time required to reach a maximum mean arterial blood pressure after occlusion was significantly less in the animals exposed to cigarette smoke versus the sham-exposed controls. Only one smoke concentration was used in this study. Using anesthetized, mechanically ventilated rats as an in vivo model, researchers showed that cigarette smoke produced a biphasic change in the diameter of the cerebral arterioles and an increase in mean arterial blood pressure in rats (Iida et al. 1998). An initial vasoconstriction was seen in animals breathing the smoke but not in animals receiving an intravenous infusion of nicotine. These findings led researchers to conclude that a smoke constituent other than nicotine was responsible for the early vascular change. Thromboxane A_2 was proposed as the agent responsible for the vasoconstriction. Others have determined that cigarette smoking, but not the use of transdermal nicotine or smokeless tobacco, increased concentrations of thromboxane A_2 (Wennmalm et al. 1991; Benowitz et al. 1993).

Cardiovascular changes were observed in several studies of short-term and lifetime inhalation cigarette smoke exposure in rodents. Investigators studied male Wistar rats with whole-body exposure to the smoke of an unidentified commercial cigarette for 30 days. They observed a significant increase in left ventricular systolic diameter and a significant reduction in systolic shortening fraction and ejection fraction compared with those in unexposed controls (de Paiva et al. 2003). No change in heart rate or heart weight was seen under the exposure conditions of this study. Another study demonstrated a significant increase in heart weight in female, but not male, Sprague-Dawley rats with 13 weeks of daily nose-only inhalation exposure to the smoke of a custom-blended experimental cigarette smoked under FTC conditions (Coggins et al. 1989). Other investigators conducted a 13-week inhalation study of male and female F-344 rats exposed to smoke of mentholated or nonmentholated cigarettes. Male rats exposed to medium or high doses and female rats exposed to high doses of smoke from mentholated cigarettes, machine smoked under FTC conditions, developed a significant increase in the ratio of heart weight to body weight (Gaworski et al. 1997). Male and female rats exposed to high doses of smoke from nonmentholated cigarettes also had a significant increase in cardiomegaly (high ratio of heart weight to body weight). The difference between treated and control animals was no longer significant after a six-week recovery period. Dalbey and colleagues (1980) observed fibrosis and thickening of arterioles in the heart papillary muscle of female F-344 rats with daily nose-only inhalation exposure for 126 to 128 weeks to smoke from unfiltered experimental cigarettes. No smoke-related pathologic changes to the large vessels were detected from the one concentration of smoke (10 percent) that was used.

Studies using dermal applications of smoke condensate or inhalation exposure to cigarette smoke demonstrated that chemicals in cigarette smoke underwent covalent binding to heart tissue DNA in laboratory animals (Randerath et al. 1986, 1988; Reddy and Randerath 1990; Brown et al. 1998; Gupta et al. 1999). Studies of cigarette smokers showed that the heart tissue contained more DNA adducts than that from nonsmokers or former smokers (Van Schooten et al. 1998). They also demonstrated a linear relationship between DNA adduct levels and daily cigarette smoking. Furthermore, higher DNA adduct levels were associated with a higher degree of coronary artery disease.

Respiratory Studies in Animals

Exposure to chemicals in cigarette smoke affects the function of the respiratory system in laboratory animals and humans. Notably, exposure to cigarette smoke affected airway mucociliary function (Shephard 1978; Wanner 1985; Finch et al. 1995). Another researcher demonstrated that exposure resulted in a dose-dependent inhibition of lung clearance and increased absorption of components of the inhaled smoke through the tracheobronchial airways, especially where particle deposition occurred and mucociliary clearance was less efficient, specifically at the ridges within bifurcations and in posterior sections of tubular airways (Martonen 1992). Studies have shown that the activity of xenobiotic metabolizing (cytochrome P-450) enzymes in human lung tissue is likely sufficient to cause in situ activation of pulmonary toxicants (Castell et al. 2005). Species differences in enzyme activities have led some to question the use of animal data to predict toxic effects in humans from chemicals requiring bioactivation to reactive metabolites (Castell et al. 2005). Short-term assays to evaluate the components of cigarette smoke that impair mucociliary function were described in the "Cytotoxicity" section earlier in this chapter.

Persistent pulmonary inflammation from repeated exposure to cigarette smoke may lead to more severe alterations in the structure and function of the lung (Stratton et al. 2001). For example, researchers concluded that emphysema in cigarette smokers reflects a low-level, chronic inflammatory process in the lower respiratory tract with an imbalance of protease and antiprotease activities leading to the degradation of connective tissue (Churg et al. 2002).

Syrian golden hamsters have been used extensively to study the pathogenesis of emphysema. They show a pattern of inflammatory airway response and impaired activity of antioxidants (superoxide dismutase and catalase)—a pattern similar to that in humans with repeated exposure to cigarette smoke (Hoidal and Niewoehner 1982; McCusker and Hoidal 1990). Rat strains were shown to be more resistant to the induction of emphysema by exposure to cigarette smoke, but susceptibility in mice was strain specific (Groneberg and Chung 2004). Research on emphysema induced by cigarette smoke in animals has not consistently demonstrated progression of the disease (March et al. 1999). In a comparative study of $B6C3F_1$ mice and F-344 rats, the mouse strain displayed more morphometric changes (parenchymal air-space enlargement, volume density of alveolar air space, and loss of alveolar tissue) and significantly more neutrophils within inflammatory lesions in the lung. Morphometric differences in the mice at 13 months were greater than those at 7 months. This finding suggests that in mice, emphysema induced by cigarette smoke may be progressive. Animals received a whole-body exposure to the smoke of 2R1 reference cigarettes that were machine smoked (two 70-mL puffs per minute) and diluted with filtered air to achieve a chamber concentration of 250 mg of TPM/m^3. The exposure duration was six hours per day, five days per week. The investigators concluded that the type of inflammatory response may be a determining factor for differences in susceptibility to emphysema induction by cigarette smoke among test species.

Animal models can readily be used to detect and quantitate the pulmonary inflammatory response to inhaled compounds or mixtures, and the literature in this area was reviewed (Stratton et al. 2001; IARC 2004). An analysis of bronchoalveolar lavage (BAL) fluid for cellular and biochemical indicators of inflammation allows quantitation of the pulmonary inflammatory response of rodents to inhaled cigarette smoke (Churg et al. 2002; Shapiro et al. 2003). The differential cell count and the functioning of cells obtained by the BAL technique can be used to classify the type of inflammatory response, and the biochemical content of the BAL fluid can be used to detect release of various cytokines and alterations in pulmonary surfactant (Stratton et al. 2001; Miller et al. 2002).

Response of inflammatory cells, cytokine profiles, enlargement of air space, and mechanical properties of the lung (elastance) differed among mouse strains after exposure to cigarette smoke (Guerassimov et al. 2004). In one study, emphysema-resistant (ICR) and emphysema-sensitive (C57BL/6) mouse strains showed differences in BAL cytokine and chemokine responses following a nose-only inhalation exposure to 2R1 reference cigarette mainstream smoke (two-second, 35-mL puff, once per minute) for two hours per day for seven days (Obot et al. 2004). Test concentrations were achieved by diluting mainstream smoke with fresh, conditioned air. There was a significant dose response for chemokines and cytokines (KC, JE, MIP-1α, MIP-2, RANTES, interleukin (IL)-17, SDF-1β) that recruit or activate neutrophils and other cell types in ICR mice, and a significant dose-response change in thymus- and activation-regulated chemokines was noted in C57BL/6 mice. Other researchers found that in contrast to emphysema-resistant ICR mice, emphysema-sensitive mouse strains (DBA/2 and C57BL/6J) showed a decrease in BAL antioxidant capacity after acute whole-body exposure to smoke (five cigarettes in 20 minutes) from a commercial, Virginia-tobacco-type cigarette (Cavarra et al. 2001). The animals that had lifetime exposure to the smoke (three cigarettes per day for 90 minutes, five days per week, for seven months) had decreased lung elastin content and developed emphysema. In a study of male ICR mice exposed five days per week for two weeks to mainstream smoke from commercial, unfiltered, high-tar cigarettes (1-second puff of 20-mL volume at 10-second intervals and 45 puffs per cigarette), the lungs showed evidence of senescence of alveolar epithelial cells (increased β-galactosidase activity, lipofuscin accumulation, and P21$^{CIP1/WAF1/SDI1}$ protein in type II cells) (Tsuji et al. 2004). The researchers proposed that the senescence prohibited lung epithelial cells from proliferating and repopulating epithelial cells lost to apoptosis during emphysema.

Bartalesi and associates (2005) also studied whole-body exposure to cigarette smoke from three commercial, filter-tipped, Virginia-tobacco cigarettes per day, five days per week, for up to 10 months. This exposure produced epithelial cell injury, loss of cilia in the airways, and a positive reaction for mouse neutrophil elastase. The findings suggested degradation of lung elastin in emphysema-sensitive (C57BL/6J and DBA/2) mouse strains. The C57 strain of mice is moderately deficient in serum α1-proteinase. Overt emphysema in the C57 strain was

characterized by disseminated foci of severe emphysema interspersed by normal parenchyma. In DBA/2 mice, the foci of emphysema were scattered in a network of uniformly dilated parenchyma. Other differences were a greater fibrotic reaction and faster development of emphysema in DBA/2 mice (three months versus six months in C57 mice), and more extensive goblet cell metaplasia and immunohistochemical reaction for IL-4, IL-13, and MUC5AC (a secreted mucin) in C57 mice.

Further research with genetically modified mice explored the role of α1-antitrypsin (AAT), elastases, and tumor necrosis factor-alpha (TNFα) in emphysema induced by cigarette smoke. In one study, mice deficient in AAT (C57BL/6J *pa/*pa [pallid]) developed diffuse, panlobular emphysema affecting the entire air space, and C57 mice with normal concentrations of AAT developed more localized centrilobular emphysema (Takubo et al. 2002). Other more evident changes in the pallid mice with low concentrations of AAT after daily subchronic exposure (six months) to 2R1 cigarette smoke were increased T-cell inflammation in the alveolar wall and a reduced ability of the lungs to distend under pressure (compliance). Other investigators studied mice deficient in *NE*-/*-* or *MMP-12*-/*-*. The animals failed to develop air-space enlargement after six months of exposure to cigarette smoke from an unfiltered reference cigarette (Hautamaki et al. 1997; Shapiro et al. 2003). The investigators concluded that neutrophil elastase is required for recruitment of neutrophils and macrophages and for activation of MMP, which solubilizes extracellular matrix proteins including elastin. Other investigators reported that mice deficient in *MMP* (*MMP*-/*-*) that had a single exposure to the whole smoke of four 2R1 reference cigarettes did not show the same early elevations in lavage neutrophils, desmosine, or hydroxyproline that are seen in mice with normal levels of *MMP* activity (*MMP*+/*+*) (Churg et al. 2002). In a later study, these investigators reported that the absence of TNFα receptors is protective against infiltration of inflammatory cells, breakdown of lung matrix, and air-space enlargement in mice lacking P55 and P75 TNFα receptors (TNFRKO mice) after exposure to whole smoke from four 2R1 reference cigarettes five days per week for six months (Churg et al. 2004).

Several studies have shown that subchronic and chronic exposure to cigarette smoke produced evidence of respiratory tract toxicity that leads to emphysema in rats. In one study, the total glutathione, reduced glutathione, and protein-bound glutathione content in lung tissue of Sprague-Dawley rats with whole-body exposure to smoke from 2R1 reference cigarettes for 30 days, three times per day, were significantly lower than those in unexposed controls (Park et al. 1998). Oxidized glutathione increased significantly in rats exposed to smoke. Smoke exposure also produced a treatment-related increase in 8-oxo-dG DNA levels in the lungs. Cigarettes were smoked for 15 to 20 minutes to a fixed butt length in a 500-mL flask with air pumped into the flask.

Researchers found increased lung IL-4 and MMP-12 levels and decreased interferon-γ levels in Wistar rats after daily whole-body exposure to the smoke of 20 commercial unfiltered cigarettes six hours per day, five days per week, for three and one-half months (Xu et al. 2004). The changes were accompanied by pathologic evidence of emphysema in the form of inflammation, damage to airway epithelium and cilia, reduced mean alveolar number, air-space enlargement, and changes in pulmonary function.

Chronic nose-only exposure of female Sprague-Dawley rats to smoke from 2R1 reference cigarettes twice per day significantly reduced the disaturated phosphatidylcholine and surfactant protein levels in BAL fluid, but not in lung tissues, and significantly increased the albumin content of BAL fluid (Subramaniam et al. 1995). The researchers also observed increased surface compressibility and decreased respreading on expansion (respreadability index) of organic extracts of the BAL fluid from treated rats compared with those for room controls and sham-treated controls. Total levels of total lung phospholipids were not significantly different among the groups.

In selective reviews of the literature, Coggins (1998, 2002) summarized other nonneoplastic histopathologic changes observed in animals exposed to cigarette smoke:

- pulmonary fibrosis in C57 mice accompanied by accumulation of lymphocytes and macrophages in the peribronchiolar and perivascular regions;

- alveolar fibrosis, alveolitis, and bronchiolitis with accumulation of macrophages in F-344 rats;

- granulomas in alveolar spaces and adjacent interstitial areas of all lobes of the lung in F-344 rats;

- perivascular or peribronchiolar accumulation of lymphoreticular cells, fibrosis and cellular enlargement of peribronchiolar septa, hyperplasia of type II cells and septal fibrosis, and air-space enlargement in F-344 rats;

- pulmonary edema, bronchial pneumonia, pulmonary fibrosis, emphysema, and cor pulmonale in beagle dogs that had tracheotomy; and

- pleural thickening, alveolar fibrosis, and subpleural inflammation in beagle dogs without tracheotomy.

Reproductive and Developmental Studies in Animals

Fertility and Conception

Animal studies have suggested altered gonadotropin release, decreased luteinizing hormone surge, inhibition of prolactin release, altered tubal motility, and motility and impairment of blastocyst formation and implantation as possible mechanisms of fertility impairment among smokers (Stratton et al. 2001). In one study, male and female Sprague-Dawley rats received nose-only exposure to the smoke of 1R4F reference cigarettes (two-second puff, one puff per minute, 35-mL puff) for two hours per day, seven days per week, for four weeks before and during mating for males, and for two weeks before mating, during mating, and through gestation day 20 for females (Carmines et al. 2003). The investigators observed a statistically significant decrease in weight of seminal vesicles for males exposed to a low concentration or a medium concentration of smoke. Weight gains during pregnancy and mean uterine weight were significantly reduced in the female rats exposed to a high concentration of smoke. Fertility and conception endpoints unaffected by exposure to smoke were sperm count, motility, and morphology in males and corpora lutea, resorptions, implantation sites, and mortality in females. In another study, three months of whole-body inhalation exposure to mainstream smoke for two hours a day from a commercial, filter-tipped, high-tar cigarette mechanically smoked with a 50-mL syringe did not lead to a reduction in uterine weight or estrous cycle but did result in decreased estradiol concentration in rat uterine tissue compared with that in uterine tissues of sham-exposed control rats (Berstein et al 1999). The proliferation index and proportion of uterine tissue cells in S and G_2/M phases were increased at three weeks of exposure for two hours per day. By three months, the differences in values from those of controls were no longer statistically different, but they were significantly lower than at three weeks, which the investigators attributed to a decline in the intensity of cell division.

In another study, Wistar rats received whole-body exposure to the smoke of a commercial cigarette from conception until parturition. Rats were exposed to cigarette smoke six hours per day, five days per week, for 11 weeks: 6 weeks before mating, 2 weeks during mating, and 3 weeks during pregnancy (Florek and Marszalek 1999). Three concentrations of cigarette smoke were monitored by CO concentration, and exposure was assessed by the determination of carboxyhemoglobin. Offspring were mated to produce two subsequent generations. The researchers observed an apparent dose-dependent reduction in the mating index, fertility index, and the number of pregnant rats, but no influence on the duration of pregnancy. This exposure regimen also resulted in a dose-dependent decrease in the mean number of animals rearing pups on the 21st postnatal day (Florek et al. 1999).

Researchers reported that the transport of preimplantation embryos through the oviduct was retarded in golden hamsters with nose-only exposure to mainstream or sidestream smoke of unfiltered 2R1 reference cigarettes (DiCarlantonio and Talbot 1999). Low, medium, and high doses were produced by generating smoke from two, four, or six cigarettes. They observed that doses used in the study produced serum concentrations of cotinine within the range of those in women actively or involuntarily exposed to cigarette smoke during pregnancy. Animals were exposed to cigarette smoke (one puff per minute, 35-mL puff) 7 days per week, beginning 14 days before mating and continuing through day 3 of pregnancy. In females exposed to mainstream smoke, the increased percentage of embryos recovered from the oviducts on day three of pregnancy was dose dependent. The difference in these percentages for the hamsters in the medium- and high-dose groups and the control hamsters, who breathed only air, was statistically significant. The number of embryos retained in the oviducts of hamsters in all three groups exposed to sidestream smoke was significantly different from that for controls, but the researchers did not observe a dose-dependent pattern. The contraction rate of the oviductal muscle also decreased significantly during a single exposure to either mainstream or sidestream smoke and did not return to initial values during a 25-minute recovery period.

Researchers have evaluated the effects of individual components of cigarette smoke on reproduction in hamster oviducts in vitro. Many components act in a dose-response manner and inhibit oviduct function at concentrations found in cigarette smoke. Talbot and colleagues (1998) showed that cyanide concentrations in 2R1 cigarette smoke were sufficient to inhibit the ciliary beat frequency and time needed for an oocyte cumulus complex to travel through the oviduct to the ostium (oocyte cumulus pickup rate) in golden hamsters. Other constituents of cigarette smoke (acrolein, formaldehyde, phenol, and acetaldehyde) produced these alterations at concentrations that were 3 to 50 times higher than the corresponding concentrations in the smoke of an experimental 2R1 reference cigarette that was machine smoked under a single set of conditions (two-second puff, one puff per minute, 40-mL puff). All chemicals acted in a dose-dependent manner, and inhibition of the ciliary beat frequency for all except acrolein was at least partially reversible. The beat frequency of cilia treated with acrolein continued to decrease after the chemical was flushed out of the perfusion chamber. Tested individually, indole, 5-methylindole, quinoline, isoquinoline, hydroquinone, and substituted phenols (compounds present in the mainstream smoke of cigarettes), at picomolar to micromolar concentrations, inhibited oviductal functioning (ciliary beat frequency, oocyte pickup rate, and the contraction rate of infundibular smooth muscle) of golden hamster oviduct explants. Substitution of an ethyl or methyl group greatly increased the potency of the phenolic derivatives over that of the parent compound (Riveles et al. 2005). A recent study compared follicle loss and markers of apoptosis in the ovaries of mice exposed to mainstream cigarette smoke or B[a]P (Tuttle et al. 2009). Female mice received a nose-only exposure to mainstream smoke for eight weeks at a level equal to a pack-a-day habit in humans. Compared with mice exposed only to air, smoke-exposed mice had a significant reduction in the number of follicles. There was no increase in apoptotic follicles or other markers of cell death in response to cigarette smoke exposure. In vitro treatment of cultured ovaries with B[a]P did not increase apoptosis. The authors concluded that smoke exposure selectively reduced follicles in the primordial and transitional stages but that the loss was not due to apoptosis (Tuttle et al. 2009).

Fetal Effects

Researchers have demonstrated fetotoxicity from cigarette smoke exposure by reporting reduced fetal weight in rats and mice exposed during gestation. Reduced fetal weight is one of the most reproducible treatment-related effects. In utero exposure of fetal Sprague-Dawley rats to smoke from a king-size, filter-tipped, commercial cigarette on days 1 through 20 of gestation produced a significant reduction in fetal weight (Leichter 1989). For more than two hours, the adult female rats were exposed to the smoke of 10 lit cigarettes with the burning end of the cigarette placed inside a whole-body-exposure chamber. Litter size and placental weights were not different between rats exposed to smoke and pair-fed controls given the amount of food equal to that consumed by the smoke-exposed group. The increase in resorptions of implanted embryos in the group exposed to smoke was not significantly different from that in the controls. In a study of mainstream smoke from 1R4F cigarettes (two-second puff, one puff per minute, 35-mL puff), male Sprague-Dawley rats had nose-only exposure for four weeks before and during mating and female rats had nose-only exposure for two weeks before mating, during mating, and through gestation day 20 (Carmines et al. 2003). Researchers identified a significant decrease in mean fetal weight compared with that of the sham-exposed controls. The number of live and dead fetuses was unaffected by smoke exposure. A series of experiments with smoke from research cigarettes that varied in levels of nicotine, condensate, and CO demonstrated that the weight and length of fetuses from Sprague-Dawley rats was dependent on the intensity and duration of smoke inhalation (Reznik and Marquard 1980). All cigarettes were machine smoked with one set of conditions (two-second puff, one puff per minute, 35-mL puff). The number of exposures per day, the duration of the exposure in days, the number of puffs per cigarette, and the volume of air used to dilute the smoke were varied to create different exposure groups. The mean fetal weight and length decreased with increasing smoke concentrations, and fetuses of rats exposed to cigarette smoke two, three, or four times a day had significant reductions in weights and lengths compared with the fetuses of rats exposed for one period per day. Growth retardation was more extensive when smoke exposure occurred during the second half of pregnancy, but the reduction was less severe in the fetuses of rats exposed during the entire pregnancy. These effects could not be attributed to the CO concentration in the smoke alone, because the effects were more pronounced with exposure to the whole smoke than with exposure to the gas phase. The number of resorbed fetuses was not influenced by smoke exposure.

In one study, mice with the autosomal recessive curly-tail gene received nose-only exposure to the mainstream smoke of a commercial low-tar or high-tar cigarette for 20 minutes, once a day from day zero to day eight of pregnancy (Seller et al. 1992). Both cigarette varieties were smoked under the same smoking-machine conditions (two-second, 35-mL puff). The scientists observed similar levels of increased embryonic loss and retardation in embryonic development. The decrease in the mean somite number in the treated animals compared with that in the sham-exposed mice was statistically significant. Longer exposures (day 0 through day 17 of pregnancy) to smoke from the low-tar cigarettes resulted in a fivefold increase in intrauterine embryonic deaths, and live embryos weighed significantly less than those from the sham-treated group. Differences between the groups exposed to smoke from the high- or low-tar cigarettes were evident when exposure (10 minutes, three times a day) was restricted to days six, seven, and eight of pregnancy. The scientists reported that differences between the high-tar and low-tar treatment groups disappeared when the dose of the smoke from the low-tar cigarettes was increased. Weight loss in the treated pregnant mice was statistically significant, and weight loss was not dose dependent. Findings indicated a dose-response trend in the various dosing regimens, and the effect on embryonic

survival and growth rate from exposure to the smoke of six cigarettes was greater than that of two cigarettes.

Curly-tail and C57BL strain mice received nose-only exposure on days six, seven, and eight of pregnancy to the smoke of a commercial low-tar or high-tar cigarette (Bnait and Seller 1995). One set of smoking-machine conditions (two-second puff, one puff per minute, 35-mL puff) was used to generate smoke from the low-tar and high-tar cigarettes, which was puffed over the noses of the test animals in individual chambers. Mice in both treatment groups were sacrificed on day nine. The embryos were removed, and embryonic cells from the fetal plate, surface ectoderm, pericardium, and heart were examined by scanning and transmission electron microscopy. In both strains, the morphology of the exterior of the neural cells, the surface ectoderm, the pericardium, and the heart were the same. Cells from embryos of females in the high-tar exposure group showed evidence of depressed metabolic activity, suggesting anoxic damage that persisted 20 hours after the exposure had ceased. In embryos from the low-tar group, changes were also present but were less marked than in embryos of mice in the high-tar group. No change occurred in the total cell number or in the number of dead cells or alteration in the mitotic index with either type of cigarette, but C57BL embryos of mice in the low-tar group had a significant reduction in the mitotic index compared with embryos of sham-treated controls.

Developmental Effects

Animal studies have suggested that even brief exposures from maternal smoking are detrimental to the very early embryo (Bassi et al. 1984; Collins et al. 1985; Lichtenbeld and Vidíc 1989; Moessinger 1989; Seller and Bnait 1995). Prenatal exposure to cigarette smoke resulted in impaired growth and maturation of fetal lung, including reduced lung volume, lower internal surface area, fewer and larger alveoli, decreased lung interstitium and parenchymal elastic tissue, increased density of parenchymal interstitium, and apparent reduction in synthesis of surfactant.

Investigators in one study reported that a single four-hour, whole-body exposure to smoke from filter-tipped or unfiltered cigarettes (one puff per minute, 35-mL puff) and a single intranasal administration of cigarette smoke condensate induced DNA deletions in fetal C57BL/6J mice homozygous for the pink-eyed unstable mutation (Jalili et al. 1998). The phenotypic expression of the DNA deletions was development of dark spots on the gray fur of the offspring. Spotting frequency did not increase with an increase in smoke concentration. The investigators reported that chemicals in the particulate phase of cigarette smoke that are possibly responsible for the

DNA deletions are B[*a*]P, cadmium, acetamide, aniline, *o*-toluidine, acrylonitrile, and catechol. (For a description of transplacental genotoxic effects in rodents, see the section on "Genotoxicity" earlier in this chapter.)

Developmental effects from exposure to cigarette smoke were further studied in the curly-tail mouse and in the C57BL strain, a strain not predisposed to neural tube defects (Seller and Bnait 1995). Mice received nose-only exposure to smoke from commercial low-tar or high-tar cigarettes from day 0 through day 17. Six cigarettes were smoked during each exposure, using one set of smoking-machine conditions (two-second, 35-mL puff). Mice in both treatment groups were sacrificed on day 18, and the embryos were removed and examined for gross congenital malformations. Treated mice (low tar and high tar) showed significant reduction in number of ossification centers in seven regions compared with sham-treated controls. Changes were consistently more marked in the animals exposed to low tar, but the differences were not significantly different from those produced by exposure to smoke from the high-tar cigarettes. One rib abnormality occurred in the C57BL mice, but no major congenital malformations were observed. In the curly-tail mice, a modest increase in the frequency of open spina bifida and exencephaly was observed. The researchers proposed that although cigarette smoke is not a potent teratogen in mice, it may have minor effects in mice that are genetically predisposed to an abnormality.

In a study of pregnancy-related adverse health outcomes from exposure to cigarette smoke, fetuses of Sprague-Dawley rats were examined for abnormalities of the skull, extremities, and other parts of the body (Reznik and Marquard 1980). The exposure regimens varied in the number of exposures per day, in the period of exposure during gestation, and in smoke concentrations from research cigarettes with different yields of nicotine, condensate, and CO. All cigarettes were machine smoked with one set of smoking-machine conditions (two-second puff, one puff per minute, 35-mL puff). None of the regimens produced an increase in malformations.

A study of developmental toxicity in the fetuses of male and female Sprague-Dawley rats exposed to cigarette smoke identified an incomplete supraoccipital ossification and unossified sternebrae significantly more often in smoke-exposed animals than in sham controls (Carmines et al. 2003). The number of skeletal variations was dose dependent. Fetal external and visceral variations in treated animals and controls were not significantly different. The exposure regimen consisted of nose-only inhalation for two hours per day, seven days per week, for four weeks before and during mating for males, and for two weeks before mating, during mating, and through gestation day 20 for females. Three concentrations of mainstream smoke were generated from 1R4F reference cigarettes (two-second puff, one puff per minute, 35-mL puff) by diluting the smoke with filtered, conditioned air. No deaths among male rats were associated with exposure to smoke. Occasional diarrhea, salivation, and red material around the eyes and nose were noted among male rats exposed to smoke and the sham controls. One female rat died of causes unrelated to exposure during the study. Females exposed to cigarette smoke also had diarrhea, salivation, and red material around eyes and nose. The decrease in maternal body weight during gestation days 0 through 20, mean maternal body weight at termination, and mean uterine weight in the group exposed to high smoke concentration (600 mg TPM/m^3) were statistically significant compared with those in sham-control female rats.

In another study, two-day-old pups born to Sprague-Dawley rats with nose-only daily exposure to mainstream cigarette smoke from day 2 to day 22 of pregnancy had selective reductions in protein kinase C gamma and delta isoforms and neuronal nitric oxide synthase within the dorsocaudal brainstem, a region relevant to respiratory and other autonomic functions (Hasan et al. 2001). One concentration of cigarette smoke exposure (1,000 mL = 10-mL puff × 10 puffs per cigarette × 10 cigarettes per day at hourly intervals) was used in this study.

Other Health Effects

Immune System

Habitual use of cigarettes results in repeated contact with thousands of chemicals. Researchers have shown that antigens in tobacco and cigarette smoke are capable of stimulating an immune response (Becker et al. 1976; Romanski and Broda 1977; Lehrer et al. 1978, 1980; Francus et al. 1988). Experimental data suggest that nicotine itself can affect the immune system, and at least one researcher has identified an allergic reaction to nicotine in a person exposed to cigarette smoke (Lee et al. 1998; McAllister-Sistilli et al. 1998). In addition to nicotine, other immunologically active chemicals are found in cigarette smoke, including the common additive menthol (Rappaport and Hoffman 1941; McGowan 1966; Becker et al. 1976; Johnson et al. 1990; Mudzinski 1993; Li et al. 1997). Research into mechanisms underlying allergic sensitization induced by cigarette smoke suggests that exposure to cigarette smoke suppresses the normal tolerance to common inhaled allergenic matter (Moerloose et al. 2006). Exposure to ovalbumin, an inert antigen, and mainstream smoke from five unfiltered 2R4F reference cigarettes produced a significant increase in ovalbumin-specific IgE and airway inflammation rich in eosinophils and goblet cells in male Balb/c mice. In mice exposed to ovalbumin and cigarette smoke, levels of cytokine IFN-γ and thymus and activation-regulated chemokine were significantly higher, as were the number of dendritic cells, which are specialized for antigen capture, migration, and T-cell stimulation; activated CD4-positive and CD8-positive T lymphocytes; and peribronchial infiltrates with eosinophils. Mice exposed only to cigarette smoke did not have increased serum IgE, increased total numbers of cells in BAL fluid, goblet cell hyperplasia in lung tissue, or increased levels of cytokines and chemokines in BAL fluid supernatant.

A body of evidence suggests that exposure to cigarette smoke produces changes in cellular and humoral immune function in humans and laboratory animals (Johnson et al. 1990). The immune and host defense systems are highly conserved across species; thus, organs and cells of the immune system in humans, mice, and rats are similar (Selgrade et al. 1995). However, the effect of cigarette smoke on the immune system depends on the species, the duration, and the level of exposure. Short-term, low-level exposures generally do not affect the immune system or may be stimulatory, whereas long-term exposures (six months or more) or high levels of exposure were found to be immunosuppressive (Thomas et al. 1974; Holt et al. 1978; Gregson and Prentice 1981; Sopori et al. 1985; Johnson et al. 1990). Smoking-related changes in the peripheral immune system in humans were observed (Stratton et al. 2001). These changes included high white blood cell counts; high counts of cytotoxic or suppressor T cells; low counts of inducer or helper T cells; slight suppression of T-lymphocyte activity; significantly lower activity of natural killer cells; low titers of circulating immunoglobulin, except for elevated titers of IgE; and increased susceptibility to infection. Researchers observed similar effects in animals. More recently, researchers reported decreased immune response and resistance to transplanted tumor cells in mice with prenatal exposure to cigarettes (Ng et al. 2006).

Animals exposed to cigarette smoke for extended periods were more susceptible to challenges with tumor cells and infectious agents than were unexposed animals (Johnson et al. 1990). Scientists studied male C57BL/6J mice with 26 weeks of exposure to the smoke of a king-size, filter-tipped cigarette, with seven to eight minutes of exposure to the smoke of 30 cigarettes per day on five consecutive days per week and subcutaneous inoculation with tumor cells (Chalmer et al. 1975). Tumors in the mice had a significantly higher mean volume, which is a measure of tumor growth rate, than did unexposed controls. This group also had larger and significantly more lung metastases. Animals exposed for only 10 weeks had a significantly lower mean tumor volume than did control mice. In a study of female C57BL/6 mice, toxic effects to

the cellular immune system induced by cigarette smoke resulted in decreased viral neutralization, which was reflected in significant decreases in levels of antibody to serum adenovirus and a decrease in activated CD4 T cells in the lung after adenovirus administration (Robbins et al. 2004). The subchronic daily regimen, which consisted of exposure to mainstream smoke from 1R1 or 1R3 reference cigarettes, also significantly reduced the number of dendritic cells in the lung. Exposure inhibited CD4 T-cell expansion and maximal activation and reduced numbers of activated CD4 and CD8 T cells in response to adenovirus administration. Animals exposed to smoke had percentages of lung macrophages, B cells, and CD4 and CD8 cells similar to those of controls without exposure to cigarette smoke. CD8 cytotoxic T lymphocytes are major effector cells involved in immunologically specific tumor destruction in vivo, and CD4 T cells are essential for controlling CD8 T-cell-dependent eradication of tumors (Shiku 2003).

In another study, tumor cells were injected into offspring of female mice exposed to cigarette smoke and air-only controls (Ng et al. 2006). Litter size, but not body weight of offspring, was significantly reduced by prenatal exposure to cigarette smoke. Male offspring injected with tumor cells at 5 or 10 weeks of age and female offspring injected at 5 weeks had a significant increase in tumor incidence compared with that of offspring of mice exposed to air only. Tumors grew significantly faster in the male offspring with prenatal exposure to cigarette smoke. The scientists observed no treatment-related effect on time to tumor formation. Activity of cytotoxic T lymphocytes in male pups exposed to cigarette smoke was significantly reduced, but no effects on natural killer cell activity, cytokine levels, histology of lymphoid organs, or subpopulations of immune cells were observed. Scientists studied adult mice that were susceptible (A/J strain) or resistant (C3H strain) to lung tumors and were exposed to the tobacco carcinogen NNK (Razani-Boroujerdi and Sopori 2007). The findings suggest that differences in immune response to chemical carcinogens predicted differences in tumor response to the carcinogens. In A/J mice, but not in C3H mice, intraperitoneal treatment with NNK suppressed anti–sheep red blood cell antibody plaque-forming cells; T-cell proliferation induced by concanavalin A; and the rise in intracellular calcium induced by anti–CD3/CD28 antibody. NNK also stimulated a significantly higher expression of cyclooxygenase-2 and of α7 nicotinic acetylcholine receptors in the lungs of A/J mice than in the lungs of C3H mice. The NNK treatments administered in this study resulted in lung tumors in all A/J mice but not in C3H mice.

Subchronic (14 weeks) exposure to a 6-percent concentration of the smoke of filtered medium-tar cigarettes (two-second puff, one puff per minute, 35-mL puff) resulted in increased alveolar macrophage activity in Wistar rats (Gregson and Prentice 1981). The macrophage activity and the increase in levels of macrophage acid phosphatase were dose and time dependent. In a study of Sprague-Dawley rats, exposures of 21 or more weeks to the mainstream smoke of 2R1 reference cigarettes led to significant inhibition of antibody production in lymph node cells associated with the lung (Sopori et al. 1989). Longer exposures of 35 to 39 weeks significantly reduced the plaque-forming response of cells in other lymphoid tissues. The plaque-forming response of lymph node cells associated with the lung to a T-cell-independent antigen was markedly reduced compared with the response of cells from control rats. Proliferative responses of lymphoid tissue associated with the lung to T-cell mitogens were unaffected by this exposure, by the relative amounts of T and B cells in lymph node cells associated with the lung or in the spleen, or by macrophage function in the spleen.

In another study of the immunosuppressive effects of exposure to cigarette smoke in female F-344 rats, chronic, daily whole-body exposures of up to 30 months to mainstream smoke from 1R3 reference cigarettes (two-second puff, two puffs per minute, 70-mL puff) reduced proliferation mediated by T-cell antigen and led to constitutive activation of enzymes involved in activation of the T-cell antigen receptor, tyrosine phosphorylase, and phospholipase C-γ1 (Kalra et al. 2000). At eight months, T-cell proliferation in the spleen was significantly reduced in response to anti–CD3 antibody, which directly binds the T-cell antigen receptor and causes T-cell proliferation in the absence of activation of CD28 on T cells. Other treatment-related evidence of altered antigen-mediated T-cell signaling were depleted calcium stores sensitive to inositol-1,4,5-triphosphate and decreased calcium mobilization in spleen cells after ligation of the T-cell antigen receptor.

Endocrine and Other Effects

Changes in blood glucose were noted in several rodent bioassays. Single but not repeated exposure to mainstream cigarette smoke produced a significant increase in blood glucose levels in anesthetized, mechanically ventilated Sprague-Dawley rats. The smoke was inspired through a tracheal cannula (Iida et al. 1998). In another study, subchronic nose-only inhalation exposure to the mainstream smoke of mentholated or nonmentholated cigarettes (two-second puff, one puff per minute, 35-mL puff) resulted in a significant decrease in blood glucose levels in a high-dose group of F-344 rats exposed to smoke from menthol cigarettes or nonmenthol cigarettes compared with unexposed control animals

(Gaworski et al. 1997). Similarly, subchronic nose-only exposure to mainstream smoke from 1R4F reference cigarettes (one puff per minute, 35-mL puff) produced a significant decrease in glucose level in a high-dose group of male Sprague-Dawley rats and in the two groups of female rats with highest doses (Terpstra et al. 2003).

Andersson and colleagues (1985) studied acute, nose-only, intermittent exposure to smoke from one, two, or four unfiltered 1R1 reference cigarettes. This exposure resulted in dose-dependent increases in catecholamine utilization in the dopamine and noradrenaline nerve terminal systems in the hypothalamus of Sprague-Dawley male rats. Luteinizing hormone, prolactin, and thyroid-stimulating hormone were significantly lower in a dose-dependent manner in treated rats than in controls. Corticosterone was significantly increased in rats with the highest exposure. Follicle-stimulating hormone, adrenocorticotropic hormone (ACTH), and vasopressin were not affected by exposure to cigarette smoke. Treated animals received nose-only exposure, but controls were exposed only to air.

In a subsequent study, these investigators reported that, in contrast, acute, nose-only continuous exposure of male Sprague-Dawley rats to the smoke of one, two, or four unfiltered 1R1 reference cigarettes produced smaller reductions in catecholamine levels and increases in catecholamine turnover and did not produce an increase in dopamine utilization in the median eminence (Andersson et al. 1987). The researchers proposed that intermittent exposure to cigarette smoke produced stronger euphoric and neuroendocrine-related effects than did continuous exposure to cigarette smoke. As with male rats, diestrus female Sprague-Dawley rats with intermittent 30 minutes of nose-only exposure to the smoke of one, two, or four unfiltered 1R1 reference cigarettes had decreased catecholamine levels and increased catecholamine utilization in hypothalamic and preoptic noradrenaline nerve terminal systems and decreased serum prolactin and luteinizing hormone (Andersson et al. 1985). The effects were dose and time dependent. In contrast to findings in male rats (Andersson et al. 1985), for female rats, exposure to cigarette smoke caused lower dopamine and noradrenaline levels in the median eminence and lower ACTH levels (Andersson et al. 1988). Exposure to cigarette smoke did not inhibit secretion of the thyroid-stimulating hormone in female rats as it did in male rats. Catecholamine levels were measured in male Sprague-Dawley rats for 48 hours, 72 hours, or 7 days after an exposure regimen that consisted of a daily 2-hour exposure to the smoke of two 1R1 unfiltered reference cigarettes for 10 days (Andersson et al. 1989). At 48 hours after exposure, significantly lower levels of serum corticosterone and serum prolactin were noted and were attributed to maintained activation in dopamine utilization. At 72 hours, serum prolactin levels were still significantly lower than those in controls. Brain regions of increased catecholamine utilization in rats exposed to cigarette smoke decreased with time and were absent by seven days after exposure. Levels of ACTH were not changed relative to those in controls exposed only to air.

Jansson and colleagues (1992) found that age of onset of postnatal endocrine changes varied by the duration of exposure to cigarette smoke. Male Sprague-Dawley rats were exposed daily to the smoke of two 1R1 reference cigarettes, beginning on day 1 after birth and continuing for 5, 10, or 20 days. The rats were sacrificed 24 hours after the 10- or 20-day exposure. Rat pups had a significant increase in serum levels of luteinizing hormone compared with levels in control pups exposed only to air. Animals sacrificed seven months after the 20-day exposure had a significant increase in serum prolactin levels. Pups sacrificed 24 hours after a 20-day exposure had a significant increase in catecholamine utilization in the medial palisade zone of the median eminence and a substantial reduction in catecholamine utilization in the parvocellular and magnocellular parts of the paraventricular hypothalamic nucleus. Changes in catecholamine utilization were not seen in animals sacrificed seven months after the 20-day exposure to cigarette smoke. Serum corticosterone levels and dopamine and norepinephrine utilization in the hypothalamus were not significantly different for rats exposed to smoke and controls.

Other researchers noted statistically significant increases in the weight of the adrenal gland relative to body weight in Sprague-Dawley rats after subchronic inhalation exposure to the smoke of 1R4F reference cigarettes (one puff per minute, 35-mL puff) (Terpstra et al. 2003).

Compared with the sham controls, the weight of the left adrenal gland increased for males in the two groups with the highest doses, whereas females had an increase in the weight of the left and right adrenal glands in the two groups with the highest doses.

An inverse relationship exists between smoking and body weight in humans, and nicotine is believed to be the chemical mediator (Chen et al. 2005). Direct nicotine administration to humans or animals decreases body weight and caloric intake. Scientists designed a study to determine the effect of short-term exposure to cigarette smoke on appetite control in male Balb/c mice. Inhalation exposure to the smoke of three commercial cigarettes a day for four days led to a significant decrease in plasma concentrations of leptin, a hormone that signals satiety (Chen et al. 2005). Animals exposed to smoke had a decrease in mRNA expression of white adipose tissue UCP1 (a mitochondrial uncoupling protein involved in energy metabolism) and an increase in mRNA expression of brown adiposise tissue UCP3. Food intake and body weight were significantly decreased in the animals exposed to smoke compared with those in the sham controls, even though plasma concentrations of corticosterone were unchanged. Concentrations of hypothalamic neuropeptide Y, which stimulates feeding behavior, were not affected by the acute exposure regimen. Only one concentration of smoke was used in this study, and details on smoking-machine conditions were not provided. Other animal studies with longer durations of exposure to cigarette smoke also documented either weight loss or reduced weight gain in treated animals compared with those in unexposed controls (Ayres et al. 2001; Carmines et al. 2003; Witschi et al. 2004).

Summary

This chapter discusses a wide variety of chemicals found in cigarette smoke. These chemicals extend across a broad spectrum of volatility, lipophilicity, and reactivity, and include compounds that are known or suspected to be carcinogenic, toxic, and addictive. Some of these compounds also promote the carcinogenicity, toxicity, or addictiveness of the other constituents of cigarette smoke. Despite uncertainties about which chemical constituents are responsible for specific adverse health outcomes, there is broad scientific agreement about which chemicals in conventional tobacco-burning cigarettes could be harmful to individuals' health. Less is known about, and research is needed on, the potentially harmful chemicals in smoke from new and emerging cigarette technologies. Cigarette characteristics that influence either nicotine delivery to the smoker or smoke constituents that interact with nicotine deserve special consideration, because nicotine maintains the addiction and thereby leads to ongoing exposures of smokers to chemical compounds with known adverse health effects.

The levels of the chemical constituents in cigarette smoke are influenced by many different factors. The levels of the metals and nitrogen-containing compounds in the tobacco are highly influenced by the soil in which it is grown and the fertilizers used to promote growth of the plant. Many of the chemicals of direct concern vary with the different types of tobacco (e.g., bright, burley, or oriental) that are combined to produce a specific tobacco blend. Within a type of tobacco, the position of the leaf on the stalk can also influence the chemical levels in harvested tobacco leaves that will eventually affect the levels in smoke. The inclusion of reconstituted and expanded tobacco in cigarette fillers can also alter the chemistry of cigarette smoke. After the tobacco is harvested, the method of curing and the addition of humectants, sugars, and flavor-related compounds will change the chemical composition of the tobacco that goes into the cigarette. Different tobacco blends, filters, filter paper, additives, and design innovations employed in cigarette manufacturing have a profound influence on the levels of toxicants transferred from tobacco into the mainstream smoke with every single puff.

It is well documented that cigarettes are not smoked with the same puffing profile. The differences in smoking patterns, including the number of puffs, the puff volume, and whether the smoker blocks the ventilation holes greatly influence the delivery of smoke constituents to the smoker. An individual smoker consumes each cigarette differently, depending on the time of day, on individual stress levels, and on the time since the last nicotine use. The smoker will change the number of puffs taken, the depth of the puff, and the degree to which ventilation holes are blocked, depending on the individual circumstances occurring at that time. In addition, the rate of metabolism of the chemicals after they enter the smoker's body, in addition to other enzymatic and genetic effects, can influence how long the chemical species of concern remains in the smoker's system. It is broadly understood that there is not a single machine-smoking method that can be used to project the levels of chemical constituents that are found in the human body.

Validated biomarkers of exposure that correlate with dose (the number of cigarettes smoked per day) or that provide information on metabolic activation and detoxification have been reported in the literature. Additional research is needed to determine levels of reduction of these chemicals in cigarette smoke that would produce measurable decreases in the dose delivered to the smoker. Although some biomarkers (nicotine and its metabolites and the TSNAs) are specific to tobacco exposure, most are not specific to tobacco and are influenced by diet, occupation, or other environmental factors. Also, although biomarkers typically represent only recent exposures, the strongest determinant of risk for many diseases (e.g., lung cancer) caused by tobacco use is the duration of smoking (IARC 2004). Carcinogen adducts as biomarkers of biologically effective doses are the most direct measure of tobacco-induced damage at cancer sites in smokers.

Surrogate measures such as DNA oxidative repair lesions in urine and thioether levels respond in a dose-related manner to exposure to cigarette smoke and reflect an ongoing state of oxidative stress in the body of a smoker. Biomarkers of potential harm exist for all major tobacco-related diseases. The predictive value of these biomarkers is lessened by their nonspecific nature.

In vitro assays using mammalian or bacterial cellular systems show that cigarette smoke is mutagenic and cytotoxic. Genetic damage to the cell and altered metabolic activities probably play a role in tobacco-related chronic diseases such as cancer and cardiovascular disease. Notably, oxidative DNA damage and markers of oxidative stress are represented by increased levels of oxidatively modified DNA bases in urine, white blood cells, and lung tissue and by oxidative damage to sperm DNA and seminal fluid; increased oxidation of cell membrane lipids (F_2-isoprostanes) in adult and cord blood; and decreased levels of reduced glutathione in lung cells and heart tissue. In addition, short-term mutagenicity and cytotoxicity assays have led to the identification of several potentially causative chemical agents in cigarette smoke (e.g., aromatic amines and heterocyclic amine protein pyrolysate products in the *Salmonella* mutagenicity assay and HCN and acrolein in cytotoxicity assays). Future in vitro research on mutagenicity and cytotoxicity will likely involve cigarette smoke produced under smoking-machine conditions that more closely mimic human smoking behavior, rather than one standard set of conditions such as the FTC or ISO methods.

Many smoking-related effects in humans can be reproduced in experimental animals. Some of the most promising animal models are those for emphysema and cardiovascular disease induced by cigarette smoke. In contrast, animals have not proven to be good models for the type of lung tumors induced by cigarette smoke in humans. In the absence of a widely accepted animal model for tobacco carcinogenesis, ample data show that cigarette smoke and its condensate are tumorigenic in several animal species and are mutagenic in a variety of systems. Current animal studies have attempted to demonstrate a dose-response relationship by using either the smoke or the condensate from one cigarette type diluted to produce several concentrations or the smoke or condensate from cigarettes from different yield categories. In either instance, researchers have used one set of smoking-machine conditions to produce the cigarette smoke or condensate. Standardized smoking-machine conditions such as the FTC or ISO methods are useful for comparisons between cigarettes but are less relevant to the exposure of human smokers. Future studies will likely incorporate alternative smoking-machine conditions required by some countries or designed to mimic human smoking patterns.

In general, an absence of human data requires researchers to use the results of experiments with laboratory animals and nonanimal systems to estimate human risk. The sum of several decades of laboratory research lends experimental support to the epidemiologic observations that cancer, respiratory disease, cardiovascular disease, and other adverse health outcomes are causally related to cigarette smoking. Although some topics were not a primary focus of this chapter, of note are the instances when sidestream smoke, frequently used as a surrogate for environmental tobacco smoke or secondhand smoke, proved to be more toxic than mainstream smoke, which is inhaled directly by the smoker—for example, in the neutral red cytotoxicity assay and in the development of aortic plaque in the cockerel. Many chemicals of concern to public health are present in higher concentrations in sidestream smoke, the main contributor to secondhand smoke exposure, than in mainstream smoke: 1,3-butadiene, ammonia, aromatic amines, benzene, CO, isoprene, nicotine, nitrosamines, PAHs, pyridine, and toluene.

Perhaps the greatest utility of toxicity testing of cigarette smoke and condensate comes from the ability to explore mechanisms by which tobacco and the constituents of its smoke cause disease, to identify better biomarkers of potential disease risk for use in both clinical and population-based studies, and possibly to evaluate the relative contribution of cigarette components and design features (e.g., additives, tobacco blends, nontobacco components, and filter ventilations) to the inherent toxicity and addictiveness of the product.

The uncertainties in understanding all of the factors involved in the delivery and uptake of toxic, carcinogenic, and addictive chemicals in cigarette smoke and the mechanisms of toxicity induced by cigarette smoke should not impede efforts to lower the concentrations of these chemicals in cigarette smoke. There are ways to lower the concentrations of toxic constituents in cigarette smoke, although additional research is needed to determine the levels of reduction required for achievement of measurable and biologically relevant decreases in delivery of these constituents to the smoker. Such approaches include controls over tobacco growing and curing; the types of tobacco used in the filler, including the use of reconstituted tobacco; the use of additives such as menthol; and the design of the cigarette.

Conclusions

1. In spite of uncertainties concerning whether particular cigarette smoke constituents are responsible for specific adverse health outcomes, there is broad scientific agreement that several of the major classes of chemicals in the combustion emissions of burned tobacco are toxic and carcinogenic.

2. The design characteristics of cigarettes, including ventilation features, filters, and paper porosity, have a significant influence on the levels of toxic and carcinogenic chemicals in the inhaled smoke.

3. The different types of tobacco lamina (e.g., bright, burley, or oriental) that are combined to produce a specific tobacco blend have a significant influence on the levels of toxic and carcinogenic chemicals in the combustion emissions of burned tobacco.

4. There is no available cigarette machine-smoking method that can be used to accurately predict doses of the chemical constituents of tobacco smoke received when using tobacco products.

5. Tobacco-specific biomarkers (nicotine and its metabolites and the tobacco-specific nitrosamines) have been validated as quantitative measures of exposure to tobacco smoke among smokers of cigarettes of similar design who do not use other tobacco-containing products.

6. Although biomarkers of potential harm exist for most tobacco-related diseases, many are not specific to tobacco and levels are also influenced by diet, occupation, or other lifestyle or environmental factors.

References

Abdallah F. Processing techniques: leaf conditioning, casing, expansion and flavoring. *Tobacco Reporter* 2003a;130(7):64–70.

Abdallah F. Recon's new role: contributions of a new-generation recon sheet to tobacco products. *Tobacco Reporter* 2003b;130(6):58–61.

Abel EL. Smoking during pregnancy: a review of effects on growth and development of offspring. *Human Biology* 1980;52(4):593–625.

Adams JD, Lee SJ, Hoffmann D. Carcinogenic agents in cigarette smoke and the influence of nitrate on their formation. *Carcinogenesis* 1984;5(2):221–3.

Adams JD, Lee SJ, Vinchkoski N, Castonguay A, Hoffmann D. On the formation of the tobacco-specific carcinogen 4-(methylnitrosamino)-1-(3-pyridyl)-1-butanone during smoking. *Cancer Letters* 1983;17(3):339–46.

Adams JD, O'Mara-Adams J, Hoffmann D. Toxic and carcinogenic agents in undiluted mainstream smoke and sidestream smoke of different types of cigarettes. *Carcinogenesis* 1987;8(5):729–31.

Adamu CA, Bell PF, Mulchi C, Chaney R. Residual metal concentrations in soils and leaf accumulations in tobacco a decade following farmland application of municipal sludge. *Environmental Pollution* 1989;56(2):113–26.

Akehurst BC. *Tobacco*. 2nd ed. New York: Longman, 1981.

Alaoui-Jamali MA, Rossignol G, Schuller HM, Castonguay A. Transplacental genotoxicity of a tobacco-specific *N*-nitrosamine, 4-(methylnitrosamino)-1-(3-pyridyl)-1-butanone, in Syrian golden hamster. *Mutation Research* 1989;223(1):65–72.

Allen RE, Vickroy DG. The characterization of cigarette smoke from Cytrel smoking products and its comparison to smoke from flue-cured tobacco. III: particulate phase analysis. *Beiträge zur Tabakforschung International* 1976;8(7):430–7.

Andersen RA, Kasperbauer MJ, Burton HR, Hamilton JL, Yoder EE. Changes in chemical composition of homogenized leaf-cured and air cured Burley tobacco stored in controlled environments. *Journal of Agricultural and Food Chemistry* 1982;30(4):663–8.

Andersen RA, Kemp TR. Accumulation of 4-(*N*-methyl-*N*-nitrosamino)-1-(3-pyridy)-1-butanone in alkaloid genotypes of Burley tobacco during postharvest processing: comparisons with *N*′-nitrosonornicotine and probable nitrosamine precursors. *Cancer Research* 1985;45(11 Pt 1):5287–93.

Anderson PJ, Wilson JD, Hiller FC. Particle size distribution of mainstream tobacco and marijuana smoke: analysis using the electrical aerosol analyzer. *American Review of Respiratory Disease* 1989;140(1):202–5.

Andersson K, Eneroth P, Fuxe K, Härfstrand A. Effects of acute intermittent exposure to cigarette smoke on hypothalamic and preoptic catecholamine nerve terminal systems and on neuroendocrine function in the diestrus rat. *Naunyn-Schmiedeberg's Archives of Pharmacology* 1988;337(2):131–9.

Andersson K, Fuxe K, Eneroth P, Agnati LF, Härfstrand A. Effects of acute continuous exposure of the rat to cigarette smoke on amine levels and utilization in discrete hypothalamic catecholamine nerve terminal systems and on neuroendocrine function. *Naunyn-Schmiedeberg's Archives of Pharmacology* 1987;335(5):521–8.

Andersson K, Fuxe K, Eneroth P, Jansson A, Härfstrand A. Effects of withdrawal from chronic exposure to cigarette smoke on hypothalamic and preoptic catecholamine nerve terminal systems and on the secretion of pituitary hormones in the male rat. *Naunyn-Schmiedeberg's Archives of Pharmacology* 1989;339(4):387–96.

Andersson K, Fuxe K, Eneroth P, Mascagni F, Agnati LF. Effects of acute intermittent exposure to cigarette smoke on catecholamine levels and turnover in various types of hypothalamic DA and NA nerve terminal systems as well as on the secretion of adenohypophyseal hormones and corticosterone. *Acta Physiologica Scandinavica* 1985;124(2):277–85.

Andreoli C, Gigante D, Nunziata A. A review of in vitro methods to assess the biological activity of tobacco smoke with the aim of reducing the toxicity of smoke. *Toxicology in Vitro* 2003;17(5–6):587–94.

Aoshiba K, Tamaoki J, Nagai A. Acute cigarette smoke exposure induces apoptosis of alveolar macrophages. *American Journal of Physiology – Lung Cellular and Molecular Physiology* 2001;281(6):L1392–L1401.

Artho AJ, Monroe RJ, Weybrew JA. Physical characteristics of cured tobacco. I: simplified procedures for measuring specific volume and fragility. *Tobacco Science* 1963;7:191–7.

Ashley DL, Beeson MD, Johnson DR, McCraw JM, Richter P, Pirkle JL, Pechacek TF, Song S, Watson CH. Tobacco-specific nitrosamines in tobacco from U.S. brand and non-U.S. brand cigarettes. *Nicotine & Tobacco Research* 2003;5(3):323–31.

Ashley DL, Bonin MA, Hamar B, McGeehin M. Using the blood concentration of 2,5-dimethylfuran as a marker for smoking. *International Archives of Occupational and Environmental Health* 1996;68(3):183–7.

Atawodi SE, Preussmann R, Spiegelhalder B. Tobacco-specific nitrosamines in some Nigerian cigarettes. *Cancer Letters* 1995;97(1):1–6.

Ayres PH, Hayes JR, Higuchi MA, Mosberg AT, Sagartz JW. Subchronic inhalation by rats of mainstream smoke from a cigarette that primarily heats tobacco compared to a cigarette that burns tobacco. *Inhalation Toxicology* 2001;13(2):149–86.

Babich H, Borenfreund E. Structure-activity relationship (SAR) models established *in vitro* with the neutral red cytotoxicity assay. *Toxicology in Vitro* 1987;1(1):3–9.

Bache CA, Lisk DJ, Doss GJ, Hoffmann D, Adams JD. Cadmium and nickel in mainstream particulates of cigarettes containing tobacco grown on a low-cadmium soil-sludge mixture. *Journal of Toxicology and Environmental Health* 1985;16(3–4):547–52.

Backhurst JD. Relation between the "strength" of a cigarette and the "extractable nicotine" in the smoke. Brown and Williamson Collection. Research and Development Establishment – Southhampton. 1965. Bates No. 570340734/0758. <http://legacy.library.ucsf.edu/tid/xud51f00>.

Baggett MS, Morie GP. Quantitative determination of phenol and alkylphenols in cigarette smoke and their removal by various filters. *Tobacco Science* 1973;17:30–2.

Baker RR. Product formation mechanisms inside a burning cigarette. *Progress in Energy and Combustion Science* 1981;7(2):135–53.

Baker RR, Lewis LS. Filter ventilation—has there been a "cover up"? *Recent Advances in Tobacco Science* 1997;23:152–96.

Baker RR, Massey ED, Smith G. An overview of the effects of tobacco ingredients on smoke chemistry and toxicity. *Food and Chemical Toxicology* 2004;42(Suppl):S53–S83.

Balansky RM, Blagoeva PM. Tobacco smoke-induced clastogenicity in mouse fetuses and in newborn mice. *Mutation Research* 1989;223(1):1–6.

Bartalesi B, Cavarra E, Fineschi S, Lucattelli M, Lunghi B, Martorana PA, Lungarella G. Different lung responses to cigarette smoke in two strains of mice sensitive to oxidants. *European Respiratory Journal* 2005;25(1):15–22.

Bassi JA, Rosso P, Moessinger AC, Blanc WA, James LS. Fetal growth retardation due to maternal tobacco smoke exposure in the rat. *Pediatric Research* 1984;18(2):127–30.

Battista SP. Cilia toxic components of cigarette smoke. In: Wynder EL, Hoffmann D, Gori GB, editors. *Smoking and Health 1. Modifying the Risk to the Smoker*. Proceedings of the 3rd World Conference on Smoking and Health; June 2–5, 1975; New York. Washington: U.S. Department of Health, Education, and Welfare, Public Health Service, National Institutes of Health, National Cancer Institute, 1976a:517–34. DHEW Publication No. (NIH) 76-1221.

Battista SP. Ciliatoxicity. In: Gori GB, editor. *Toward Less Hazardous Cigarettes. The First Set of Experimental Cigarettes*. Report No. 1. Washington: U.S. Department of Health, Education, and Welfare, Public Health Service, National Institutes of Health, 1976b:96–103. DHEW Publication No. (NIH) 76-905.

Becker CG, Dubin T, Wiedemann HP. Hypersensitivity to tobacco antigen. *Proceedings of the National Academy of Sciences of the United States of America* 1976;73(5):1712–6.

Bell PF, Mulchi CL, Chaney RL. Microelement concentrations in Maryland air-cured tobacco. *Communications in Soil Science and Plant Analysis* 1992;23(13–14):1617–28.

Bender MA, Preston RJ, Leonard RC, Pyatt BE, Gooch PC, Shelby MD. Chromosomal aberration and sister-chromatid exchange frequencies in peripheral blood lymphocytes of a large human population sample. *Mutation Research* 1988;204(3);421–33.

Bennett CH, Richardson DR. Time-dependent changes in cardiovascular regulation caused by chronic tobacco smoke exposure. *Journal of Applied Physiology* 1990;68(1):248–52.

Benowitz NL, Fitzgerald GA, Wilson M, Zhang Q. Nicotine effects on eicosanoid formation and hemostatic function: comparison of transdermal nicotine and cigarette smoking. *Journal of the American College of Cardiology* 1993;22(4):1159–67.

Benowitz NL, Jacob P III, Fong I, Gupta S. Nicotine metabolic profile in man: comparison of cigarette smoking and transdermal nicotine. *Journal of Pharmacology and Experimental Therapeutics* 1994;268(1):296–303.

Bernert JT Jr, McGuffey JE, Morrison MA, Pirkle JL. Comparison of serum and salivary cotinine measurements by a sensitive high-performance liquid chromatography–tandem mass spectrometry method as an indicator of exposure to tobacco smoke among smokers and nonsmokers. *Journal of Analytical Toxicology* 2000;24(5):333–9.

Bernfeld P, Homburger F. Skin painting studies in Syrian hamsters. *Progress in Experimental Tumor Research* 1983;26:128–53.

Berstein LM, Tsyrlina EV, Gamajunova VB, Bychkova NV, Krjukova OG, Dzhumasultanova SV, Kovalenko IG, Kolesnik OS. Study of tobacco smoke influence on content of estrogens and DNA flow cytometry data in uterine tissue of rats of different age. *Hormone and Metabolic Research* 1999;31(1):27–30.

Bhide SV, Nair J, Maru GB, Nair UJ, Rao BV, Chakraborty MK, Brunnemann KD. Tobacco-specific *N*-nitrosamines [TSNA] in green mature and processed tobacco leaves from India. *Beiträge zur Tabakforschung International* 1987;14(1):29–32.

Birner G, Neumann H-G. Biomonitoring of aromatic amines. II: hemoglobin binding of some monocyclic aromatic amines. *Archives of Toxicology* 1988;62(2–3):110–5.

Blackard CZ. Cigarette design: reconstituted tobacco isn't just cheap recycling, it's a tool for lowering tar and optimizing taste. *Tobacco Reporter* 1997;124(10):51–3.

Bnait KS, Seller MJ. Ultrastructural changes in 9-day old mouse embryos following maternal tobacco smoke inhalation. *Experimental and Toxicologic Pathology* 1995;47(6):453–61.

Bombick DW, Ayres PH, Doolittle DJ. Cytotoxicity assessment of whole smoke and vapor phase of mainstream and sidestream cigarette smoke from three Kentucky reference cigarettes. *Toxicology Methods* 1997a;7(3):177–90.

Bombick DW, Bombick BR, Ayres PH, Putnam K, Avalos J, Borgerding MF, Doolittle DJ. Evaluation of the genotoxic and cytotoxic potential of mainstream whole smoke and smoke condensate from a cigarette containing a novel carbon filter. *Fundamental and Applied Toxicology* 1997b;39(1):11–7.

Bombick DW, Putnam K, Doolittle DJ. Comparative cytotoxicity studies of smoke condensates from different types of cigarettes and tobaccos. *Toxicology in Vitro* 1998;12(3):241–9.

Bonassi S, Hagmar L, Strömberg U, Montagud AH, Tinnerberg H, Forni A, Heikkilä P, Wanders S, Wilhardt P, Hansteen I-L, et al. Chromosomal aberrations in lymphocytes predict human cancer independently of exposure to carcinogens. *Cancer Research* 2000;60(6):1619–25.

Bonassi S, Neri M, Lando C, Ceppi M, Lin Y-P, Chang WP, Holland N, Kirsch-Volders M, Zeiger E, Fenech M. Effect of smoking habit on the frequency of micronuclei in human lymphocytes: results from the Human MicroNucleus project. *Mutation Research* 2003;543(2):155–66.

Borgerding MF, Bodnar JA, Wingate DE. *The 1999 Massachusetts Benchmark Study: Final Report.* 2000. Brown & Williamson Collection. Bates No. 569670588/0712. <http://legacy.library.ucsf.edu/tid/yek21c00>.

Borgerding M, Klus H. Analysis of complex mixtures—cigarette smoke. *Experimental and Toxicologic Pathology* 2005;57(Suppl 1):43–73.

Borland CDR, Chamberlain AT, Higenbottam TW, Barber RW, Thrush BA. A comparison between the rate of reaction of nitric oxide in the gas phase and in whole cigarette smoke. *Beiträge zur Tabakforschung International* 1985;13(2):67–73.

Branner B, Kutzer C, Zwickenpflug W, Scherer G, Heller W-D, Richter E. Haemoglobin adducts from aromatic amines and tobacco-specific nitrosamines in pregnant smoking and non-smoking women. *Biomarkers* 1998;3(1):35–47.

Bridges RB, Combs JG, Humble JW, Turbek JA, Rehm SR, Haley NJ. Puffing topography as a determinant of smoke exposure. *Pharmacology, Biochemistry, and Behavior* 1990;37(1):29–39.

Brody AL, Mandelkern MA, London ED, Olmstead RE, Farahi J, Scheibal D, Jou J, Allen V, Tiongson E, Chefer SI, et al. Cigarette smoking saturates brain $\alpha_4\beta_2$ nicotinic acetylcholine receptors. *Archives of General Psychiatry* 2006;63(8):808–16.

Brougham LR, Cheng H, Pittman KA. Sensitive high-performance liquid chromatographic method for the determination of chlorhexidine in human serum and urine. *Journal of Chromatography B: Biomedical Sciences and Applications* 1986;383(2):365–73.

Brown B, Kolesar J, Lindberg K, Meckley D, Mosberg A, Doolittle D. Comparative studies of DNA adduct formation in mice following dermal application of smoke condensates from cigarettes that burn or primarily heat tobacco. *Mutation Research* 1998;414(1–3):21–30.

Browne CL. *The Design of Cigarettes.* 3rd ed. Charlotte (NC): Hoechst Celanese Corporation, 1990.

Brunnemann KD, Fink W, Moser F. Analysis of volatile *N*-nitrosamines in mainstream and sidestream smoke from cigarettes by GLC-TEA. *Oncology* 1980;37(4):217–22.

Brunnemann KD, Hoffmann D. The pH of tobacco smoke. *Food and Cosmetic Toxicology* 1974;12(1):115–24.

Brunnemann KD, Hoffmann D. Chemical studies on tobacco smoke. XXXIV: gas chromatographic determination of ammonia in cigarette and cigar smoke. *Journal of Chromatographic Sciences* 1975;13(4):159–63.

Brunnemann KD, Hoffmann D. Decreased concentrations of *N*-nitrosodiethanolamine and *N*-nitrosomorpholine in commercial tobacco products. *Journal of Agricultural and Food Chemistry* 1991;39(1):207–8.

Brunnemann KD, Kagan MR, Cox JE, Hoffmann D. Analysis of 1,3-butadiene and other selected gas-phase components in cigarette mainstream and sidestream smoke by gas chromatography–mass selective detection. *Carcinogenesis* 1990;11(10):1863–8.

Brunnemann KD, Masaryk J, Hoffmann D. Role of tobacco stems in the formation of *N*-nitrosamines in tobacco and cigarette mainstream and sidestream smoke. *Journal of Agricultural and Food Chemistry* 1983;31(6):1221–4.

Brunnemann KD, Stahnke G, Hoffmann D. Chemical studies on tobacco smoke. LXI: volatile pyridines: quantitative analysis in mainstream and sidestream smoke of cigarettes and cigars. *Analytical Letters* 1978;A11(7):545–60.

Brunnemann KD, Yu L, Hoffmann D. Assessment of carcinogenic volatile *N*-nitrosamines in tobacco and in mainstream and sidestream smoke from cigarettes. *Cancer Research* 1977a;37(9):3218–22.

Brunnemann KD, Yu L, Hoffmann D. Chemical studies on tobacco smoke. XLIX: gas chromatographic determination of hydrogen cyanide and cyanogen in tobacco smoke. *Journal of Analytical Toxicology* 1977b;1: 38–42.

Bryant MS, Simmons HF, Harrell RE, Hinson JA. 2,6-Dimethylaniline – hemoglobin adducts from lidocaine in humans. *Carcinogenesis* 1994;15(10):2287–90.

Buckley C, Wyble CW, Borhani M, Ennis TL, Kobayashi DK, Curci JA, Shapiro SD, Thompson RW. Accelerated enlargement of experimental abdominal aortic aneurysms in a mouse model of chronic cigarette smoke exposure. *Journal of the American College of Surgeons* 2004;199(6):896–903.

Buratti M, Pellegrino O, Valla C, Fustinoni S, Brambilla G, Colombi A. Gas chromatography–electron-capture detection of urinary methylhippuric acid isomers as biomarkers of environmental exposure to xylene. *Journal of Chromatography B: Biomedical Sciences and Applications* 1999;723(1–2):95–104.

Burdock GA, editor. *Fenaroli's Handbook of Flavor Additives*. 3rd ed., vol. II. Boca Raton (FL): CRC Press, 1995:199, 251, 470.

Burns DM, Dybing E, Gray N, Hecht S, Anderson C, Sanner T, O'Connor R, Djordjevic M, Dresler C, Hainaut P, et al. Mandated lowering of toxicants in cigarette smoke: a description of the World Health Organization TobReg proposal. *Tobacco Control* 2008;17(2):132–41.

Burtin P, Buffe D, Von Kleist S. The carcinoembryonic antigens of human tumours. *Triangle* 1972;11(4): 123–9.

Canada Gazette. Tobacco Act: regulations amending the tobacco reporting regulations. P.C. 2005-1126 June 7, 2005. Statutory instruments 2005. Ottawa: *Canada Gazette* Part II, 139(13), Wednesday, June 29, 2005.

Cantrell D. Various aspects of menthol product development, March 1990; Bates No. 584100123; <http://tobaccodocuments.org/product_design/967595.html>; accessed: May 24, 2005.

Caraballo RS, Giovino GA, Pechacek TF, Mowery PD, Richter PA, Strauss WJ, Sharp DJ, Eriksen MP, Pirkle JL, Maurer KR. Racial and ethnic differences in serum cotinine levels of cigarette smokers: Third National Health and Nutrition Examination Survey, 1988–1991.

JAMA: the Journal of the American Medical Association 1998;280(2):135–9.

Carmines EL. Evaluation of the potential effects of ingredients added to cigarettes. Part 1: cigarette design, testing approach, and review of results. *Food and Chemical Toxicology* 2002;40(1):77–91.

Carmines EL, Gaworski CL, Faqi AS, Rajendran N. *In utero* exposure to 1R4F reference cigarette smoke: evaluation of developmental toxicity. *Toxicological Sciences* 2003;75(1):134–47.

Carpenter CM, Wayne GF, Pauly JL, Koh HK, Connolly GN. New cigarette brands with flavors that appeal to youth: tobacco marketing strategies. *Health Affairs* 2005;24(6):1601–10.

Carrell RW. α1-Antitrypsin, emphysema and smoking. *New Zealand Medical Journal* 1984;97(756):327–8.

Castell JV, Donato MT, Gómez-Lechón MJ. Metabolism and bioactivation of toxicants in the lung: the in vitro cellular approach. *Experimental and Toxicologic Pathology* 2005;57(Suppl 1):189–204.

Cavarra E, Bartalesi B, Lucattelli M, Fineschi S, Lunghi B, Gambelli F, Ortiz LA, Martorana PA, Lungarella G. Effects of cigarette smoke in mice with different levels of α_1-proteinase inhibitor and sensitivity to oxidants. *American Journal of Respiratory and Critical Care Medicine* 2001;164(5):886–90.

Cavusoglu Y, Timuralp B, Us T, Akgün Y, Kudaiberdieva G, Gorenek B, Unalir A, Goktekin O, Ata N. Cigarette smoking increases plasma concentrations of vascular cell adhesion molecule-1 in patients with coronary artery disease. *Angiology* 2004;55(4):397–402.

Centers for Disease Control and Prevention. Prilocaine-induced methemoglobinemia—Wisconsin, 1993. *Morbidity and Mortality Weekly Report* 1994;272(18): 1403–4.

Centers for Disease Control and Prevention. Filter ventilation levels in selected U.S. cigarettes, 1997. *Morbidity and Mortality Weekly Report* 1997;46(44):1043–7.

Chalmer J, Holt PG, Keast D. Cell-mediated immune responses to transplanted tumors in mice chronically exposed to cigarette smoke. *Journal of the National Cancer Institute* 1975;55(5):1129–34.

Chamberlain WJ, Baker JL, Chortyk OT, Stephenson MG. Studies on the reduction of nitrosamines in tobacco. *Tobacco Science* 1986;30:81–2.

Chamberlain WJ, Severson RF, Stephenson MG. Levels of N-nitrosonornicotine in tobaccos grown under varying agronomic conditions. *Tobacco Science* 1984;28: 156–8.

Chang MJ, McDaniel RL, Naworal JD, Self DA. A rapid method for the determination of mercury in mainstream cigarette smoke by two-stage amalgamation cold vapor atomic absorption spectrometry. *Journal of Analytical Atomic Spectrometry* 2002;17(7):710–5.

Chang MJ, Naworal JD, Walker K, Connell CT. Investigations on the direct introduction of cigarette smoke for trace elements analysis by inductively coupled plasma mass spectrometry. *Spectrochimica Acta Part B, Atomic Spectroscopy* 2003;58(11):1979–96.

Chen ATL, Reidy JA, Annest JL, Welty TK, Zhou H-G. Increased chromosome fragility as a consequence of blood folate levels, smoking status, and coffee consumption. *Environmental and Molecular Mutagenesis* 1989;13(4):319–24.

Chen H, Vlahos R, Bozinovski S, Jones J, Anderson GP, Morris MJ. Effect of short-term cigarette smoke exposure on body weight, appetite and brain neuropeptide Y in mice. *Neuropsychopharmacology* 2005;30(4):713–9.

Cheng S. Heavy metal pollution in China: origin, pattern and control. *Environmental Science and Pollution Research International* 2003;10(3):192–8.

Chiba M, Masironi R. Toxic and trace elements in tobacco and tobacco smoke. *Bulletin of the World Health Organization* 1992;70(2):269–75.

Chortyk OT, Schlotzhauer WS. Studies on the pyrogenesis of tobacco smoke constituents (a review). *Beiträge zur Tabakforschung* 1973;7(3):165–78.

Churg A, Cherukupalli K. Cigarette smoke causes rapid lipid peroxidation of rat tracheal epithelium. *International Journal of Experimental Pathology* 1993; 74(2):127–32.

Churg A, Wang RD, Tai H, Wang X, Xie C, Wright JL. Tumor necrosis factor-α drives 70% of cigarette smoke–induced emphysema in the mouse. *American Journal of Respiratory and Critical Care Medicine* 2004;170(5):492–8.

Churg A, Zay K, Shay S, Xie C, Shapiro SD, Hendricks R, Wright JL. Acute cigarette smoke–induced connective tissue breakdown requires both neutrophils and macrophage metalloelastase in mice. *American Journal of Respiratory Cell and Molecular Biology* 2002;27(3):368–74.

Clark MSG, Rand MJ, Vanov S. Comparison of pharmacological activity of nicotine and related alkaloids occurring in cigarette smoke. *Archives of International Pharmacodynamics* 1965;156(2):363–79.

Coggins CRE. A review of chronic inhalation studies with mainstream cigarette smoke in rats and mice. *Toxicologic Pathology* 1998;26(3):307–14.

Coggins CRE. A minireview of chronic animal inhalation studies with mainstream cigarette smoke. *Inhalation Toxicology* 2002;14(10):991–1002.

Coggins CRE, Ayres PH, Mosberg AT, Sagartz JW, Burger GT, Hayes AW. Ninety-day inhalation study in rats, comparing smoke from cigarettes that heat tobacco with those that burn tobacco. *Fundamental and Applied Toxicology* 1989;13(3):460–83.

Cogswell ME, Weisberg P, Spong C. Cigarette smoking, alcohol use and adverse pregnancy outcomes: implications for micronutrient supplementation. *Journal of Nutrition* 2003;133(5 Suppl 2):1722S–1731S.

Collins MH, Moessinger AC, Kleinerman J, Bassi J, Rosso P, Collins AM, James LS, Blanc WA. Fetal lung hypoplasia associated with maternal smoking: a morphometric analysis. *Pediatric Research* 1985;19(4):408–12.

Colquhoun DR, Goldman LR, Cole RN, Gucek M, Mansharamani M, Witter FR, Apelberg BJ, Halden RU. Global screening of human cord blood proteomes for biomarkers of toxic exposure and effect, *Environmental Health Perspectives* 2009;117(5):832-8.

Committee on Biological Markers of the National Research Council. Biological markers in environmental health research. *Environmental Health Perspectives* 1987;74: 3–9.

Connor TH, Ramanujam VMS, Ward JB Jr, Legaor MS. The identification and characterization of a urinary mutagen resulting from cigarette smoke. *Mutation Research* 1983;113(2):161–72.

Counts ME, Hsu FS, Laffoon SW, Dwyer RW, Cox RH. Mainstream smoke constituent yields and predicting relationships from a worldwide market sample of cigarette brands: ISO smoking conditions. *Regulatory Toxicology and Pharmacology* 2004;39(2):111–34.

Counts ME, Morton MJ, Laffoon SW, Cox RH, Lipowicz PJ. Smoke composition and predicting relationships for international commercial cigarettes smoked with three machine-smoking conditions. *Regulatory Toxicology and Pharmacology* 2005;41(3):185–227.

Csalári J, Szántai K. Transfer rate of cadmium, lead, zinc and iron from the tobacco-cut of the most popular Hungarian cigarette brands to the combustion products. *Acta Alimentaria* 2002;31(3):279–88.

Curry J, Karnaoukhova L, Guenette GC, Glickman BW. Influence of sex, smoking and age on human *hprt* mutation frequencies and spectra. *Genetics* 1999; 152(3):1065–77.

Curtin GM, Hanausek M, Walaszek Z, Mosberg AT, Slaga TJ. Short-term *in vitro* and *in vivo* analyses for assessing the tumor-promoting potentials of cigarette smoke condensates. *Toxicological Sciences* 2004a;81(1): 14–25.

Curtin GM, Higuchi MA, Ayres PH, Swauger JE, Mosberg AT. Lung tumorigenicity in A/J and rasH2 transgenic mice following mainstream tobacco smoke inhalation. *Toxicological Sciences* 2004b;81(1):26–34.

Curvall M, Enzell CR, Jansson T, Pettersson B, Thelestam M. Evaluation of the biological activity of cigarette-smoke condensate fractions using six *in vitro* short-term tests. *Journal of Toxicology and Environmental Health* 1984;14(2–3):163–80.

Curvall M, Jansson T, Pettersson B, Hedin A, Enzell CR. In vitro studies of biological effects of cigarette smoke condensate. I: genotoxic and cytotoxic effects of neutral, semivolatile constituents. *Mutation Research* 1985;157(2–3):169–80.

Dalbey WE, Nettesheim P, Griesemer R, Caton JE, Guerin MR. Lifetime exposures of rats to cigarette tobacco smoke. In: Sanders CL, Cross FT, Dagle GE, Mahaffey JA, editors. *Pulmonary Toxicology of Respirable Particles.* Proceedings of the Nineteenth Annual Hanford Life Sciences Symposium; October 22–24, 1979; Springfield (VA): U.S. Department of Energy, 1980;522–35.

Dalhamn T. In vivo and in vitro ciliotoxic effects of tobacco smoke. *Archives of Environmental Health* 1970;21(5):633–4.

Davis DL. Waxes and lipids in leaf and their relationship to smoking quality and aroma. In: *Recent Advances in Tobacco Science, Vol 2. Leaf Composition and Physical Properties in Relation to Smoking Quality and Aroma.* The 30th Tobacco Chemists' Research Conference, Oct. 18, 1976. Brown and Williamson Collection. Bates No. 501010394/0535. <http://legacy.library.ucsf.edu/tid/vvr10f00>.

Davis RA, Curvall M. Determination of nicotine and its metabolites in biological fluids: in vivo studies. In: Gorrod JW, Jacob P III, editors. *Analytical Determination of Nicotine and Related Compounds and Their Metabolites.* New York: Elsevier Science, 1999:583–643.

de la Chica RA, Ribas I, Giraldo J, Egozcue J, Fuster C. Chromosomal instability in amniocytes from fetuses of mothers who smoke. *JAMA: The Journal of the American Medical Association* 2005;293(10):1212–22.

de Paiva SAR, Zornoff LAM, Okoshi MP, Okoshi K, Cicogna AC, Campana AO. Behavior of cardiac variables in animals exposed to cigarette smoke. *Arquivos Brasileiros de Cardiologia* 2003;81(3):225–8.

DeCaprio AP. Biomarkers: coming of age for environmental health and risk assessment. *Environmental Science & Technology* 1997;31(7):1837–48.

Del Santo P, Moneti G, Salvadori M, Saltutti C, Delle Rose A, Dolara P. Levels of the adducts of 4-aminobiphenyl to hemoglobin in control subjects and bladder carcinoma patients. *Cancer Letters* 1991;60(3):245–51.

DeMarini DM. Genotoxicity of tobacco smoke and tobacco smoke condensate. *Mutation Research* 1983;114(1):59–89.

DeMarini DM. Genotoxicity of tobacco smoke and tobacco smoke condensate: a review. *Mutation Research* 2004;567(2–3):447–74.

DeMarini DM, Gudi R, Szkudlinska A, Rao M, Recio L, Kehl M, Kirby PE, Polzin G, Richter PA. Genotoxicity of 10 cigarette smoke condensates in four test systems: comparisons between assays and condensates. *Mutation Research* 2008;650(1):15–29.

DeMarini DM, Preston RJ. Smoking while pregnant: transplacental mutagenesis of the fetus by tobacco smoke. *JAMA: The Journal of the American Medical Association* 2005;293(10):1264–5.

DeMarini DM, Shelton ML, Levine JG. Mutation spectrum of cigarette smoke condensate in *Salmonella*: comparison to mutations in smoking-associated tumors. *Carcinogenesis* 1995;16(10):2535–42.

Devlin RB, Frampton ML, Ghio AJ. In vitro studies: what is their role in toxicology? *Experimental and Toxicologic Pathology* 2005;57(Suppl 1):183–8.

DiCarlantonio G, Talbot P. Inhalation of mainstream and sidestream cigarette smoke retards embryo transport and slows muscle contraction in oviducts of hamsters (*Mesocricetus auratus*). *Biology of Reproduction* 1999;61(3):651–6.

Ding YS, Ashley DL, Watson CH. Determination of 10 carcinogenic polycyclic aromatic hydrocarbons in mainstream cigarette smoke. *Journal of Agricultural and Food Chemistry* 2007;55(15):5966–73.

Ding YS, Trommel JS, Yan XJ, Ashley D, Watson CH. Determination of 14 polycyclic aromatic hydrocarbons in mainstream smoke from domestic cigarettes. *Environmental Science & Technology* 2005;39(2):471–8.

Ding YS, Yan XJ, Jain RB, Lopp E, Tavakoli A, Polzin GM, Stanfill SB, Ashley DL, Watson CH. Determination of 14 polycyclic hydrocarbons in mainstream smoke from U.S. brand and non-U.S. brand cigarettes. *Environmental Science & Technology* 2006;40(4):1133–8.

Djordjevic MV, Gay SL, Bush LP, Chaplin JF. Tobacco-specific nitrosamine accumulation and distribution in flue-cured tobacco alkaloid isolines. *Journal of Agricultural and Food Chemistry* 1989;37(3):752–6.

Djordjevic MV, Stellman SD, Zang E. Doses of nicotine and lung carcinogens delivered to cigarette smokers. *Journal of the National Cancer Institute* 2000;92(2):106–11.

Dobrowsky A. The adsorption of tobacco smoke: how far is a cigarette its own filter? *Tobacco Science* 1960;4:126–9.

Domino EF. Pharmacological significance of nicotine. In: Gorrod JW, Jacob P III, editors. *Analytical Determination of Nicotine and Related Compounds and Their Metabolites.* New York: Elsevier, 1999:1–11.

Dong M, Schmeltz I, Jacobs E, Hoffmann D. Aza-arenes in tobacco smoke. *Journal of Analytical Toxicology* 1978;2(1):21–5.

Donnelly GM, McKean HE, Heird CS, Green J. Bioassay of a cigarette smoke fraction. I: examination of dose-response relations and dilution bioassay assumptions in a ciliostasis system. *Journal of Toxicology and Environmental Health* 1981a;7(3–4):405–17.

Donnelly GM, McKean HE, Heird CS, Green J. Bioassay of a cigarette smoke fraction. II: experimental design and potency estimations. *Journal of Toxicology and Environmental Health* 1981b;7(3–4):419–44.

Dontenwill W, Chevalier H-J, Harke H-P, Klimisch H-J, Lafrenz U, Reckzeh G, Fleischman B, Keller W. Experimental studies on tumorigenic activity of cigarette smoke condensate on mouse skin. IV: comparative studies of condensates from different reconstituted tobacco leaves, the effect of NaNO$_3$ as additive to tobacco or reconstituted tobacco sheets, the effect of volatile constituents of smoke, the effect of initial treatment with DMBA. *Zeitschrift fur Krebsforschung und Klinische Onkologie* 1972;78(3):236–64.

Doolittle DJ, Winegar R, Lee CK, Caldwell WS, Hayes AW, deBethizy JD. The genotoxic potential of nicotine and its major metabolites. *Mutation Research* 1995;344 (3–4):95–102.

Douben PET, editor. *PAHs: An Ecotoxicological Perspective.* Hoboken (NJ): John Wiley & Sons, 2003.

Drath DB, Shorey JM, Huber GL. Functional and metabolic properties of alveolar macrophages in response to the gas phase of tobacco smoke. *Infection and Immunity* 1981;34(1):11–5.

Dube MF, Green CR. Methods of collection of smoke for analytical purposes. *Recent Advances in Tobacco Science: Formation, Analysis, and Composition of Tobacco Smoke* 1982;8:42–102.

Dunn WL. Nicotine and inhalation impact. Philip Morris Collection. 1973. Bates No. 1003295309/5310. <http://legacy.library.ucsf.edu/tid/ies74e00>.

Durocher FD. The choice of paper components for low tar cigarettes. *Recent Advances in Tobacco Science* 1984;10:52–71.

Dwoskin LP, Teng L, Buxton ST, Ravard A, Deo N, Crooks PA. Minor alkaloids of tobacco release [^{3}H]dopamine from superfused rat striatal slices. *European Journal of Pharmacology* 1995;276(1–2):195–9.

Eaker DW. Dynamic behavior and filtration of mainstream smoke in tobacco column and filter. *Recent Advances in Tobacco Science* 1990;16:103–87.

Eaton DL, Klaassen CD. Principles of toxicology. In: Klaassen CD, editor. *Casarett & Doull's Toxicology. The Basic Science of Poisons.* 6th ed. New York: McGraw-Hill, 2001:11–34.

Eccles R. Menthol and related cooling compounds. *Journal of Pharmacy and Pharmacology* 1994;46(8): 618–30.

Enzell CF. Terpenoid components of leaf and their relationship to smoking quality and aroma. *Recent Advances in Tobacco Science* 1976;2:32–60.

Evans WH, Thomas NC, Boardman MC, Nash SJ. Relationships of polycyclic aromatic hydrocarbon yields with particulate matter (water and nicotine free) yields in mainstream and sidestream cigarette smoke. *Science of the Total Environment* 1993;136(1–2):101–9.

Fairchild A, Colgrove J. Out of the ashes: the life, death, and rebirth of the "safer" cigarette in the United States. *American Journal of Public Health* 2004;94(2): 192–204.

Federal Trade Commission. *Federal Trade Commission Cigarette Report for 2006.* Washington: Federal Trade Commission, 2009.

Ferri ES, Baratta EJ. Polonium-210 in tobacco products and human tissues. *Radiological Health Data Report* 1966;7(9):485–8.

Finch GL, Nikula KJ, Chen BT, Barr EB, Chang I-Y, Hobbs CH. Effect of chronic cigarette smoke exposure on lung clearance of tracer particles inhaled by rats. *Fundamental and Applied Toxicology* 1995;24(1):76–85.

Fischer S, Castonguay A, Kaiserman M, Spiegelhalder B, Preussmann R. Tobacco-specific nitrosamines in Canadian cigarettes. *Journal of Cancer Research and Clinical Oncology* 1990a;116(6):563–8.

Fischer S, Spiegelhalder B, Eisenbarth J, Preussmann R. Investigations on the origin of tobacco-specific nitrosamines in mainstream smoke of cigarettes. *Carcinogenesis* 1990b;11(5):723–30.

Fischer S, Spiegelhalder B, Preussmann R. Influence of smoking parameters on the delivery of tobacco-specific nitrosamines in cigarette smoke—a contribution to relative risk evaluation. *Carcinogenesis* 1989a; 10(6):1059–66.

Fischer S, Spiegelhalder B, Preussmann R. Preformed tobacco-specific nitrosamines in tobacco—role of nitrate and influence of tobacco type. *Carcinogenesis* 1989b;10(8):1511–7.

Fischer S, Spiegelhalder B, Preussmann R. Tobacco-specific nitrosamines in mainstream smoke of West German cigarettes—tar alone is not a sufficient index for carcinogenic potential of cigarette smoke. *Carcinogenesis* 1989c;10(1):169–73.

Fischer S, Spiegelhalder B, Preussmann R. Tobacco-specific nitrosamines in European and USA cigarettes. *Archiv für Geschwulstforschung* 1990c;60(3):169–76.

Fisher B. Curing the TSNA problem: major efforts are underway to eliminate tobacco-specific nitrosamines in U.S. flue-cured tobacco. *Tobacco Reporter* 2000a; 127(8):1–6.

Fisher B. Unraveling smoke: as cigarette makers face new challenges, the pressure to understand tobacco smoke is greater than ever. *Tobacco Reporter* 2000b;127(9): 24–29.

Fisher P. Cigarette manufacture. In: Davis DL, Neilson MT, editors. *World Agricultural Series. Tobacco: Production, Chemistry and Technology.* Ames (IA): Blackwell Publishing, 1999:350–1.

Florek E, Marszalek A. An experimental study of the influences of tobacco smoke on fertility and reproduction. *Human & Experimental Toxicology* 1999;18(4):272–8.

Florek E, Marszalek A, Biczysko W, Szymanowski K. The experimental investigations of the toxic influence of tobacco smoke affecting progeny during pregnancy. *Human & Experimental Toxicology* 1999; 18(4):245–51.

Fordyce WB, Hughes IW, Ivinson MG. The filtration of cigarette smoke. *Tobacco Science* 1961;5:70–5.

Foulds WS, Bronte-Stewart JM, Chisholm IA. Serum thiocyanate concentrations in tobacco amblyopia. *Nature* 1968;218(141):586.

Fowles J, Dybing E. Application of toxicological risk assessment principles to the chemical constituents of cigarette smoke. *Tobacco Control* 2003;12(4):424–30.

Foy JWD, Bombick BR, Bombick DW, Doolittle DJ, Mosberg AT, Swauger JE. A comparison of in vitro toxicities of cigarette smoke condensate from Eclipse cigarettes and four commercially available ultra low-"tar" cigarettes. *Food and Chemical Toxicology* 2004;42(2): 237–43.

Francus T, Klein RF, Staiano-Coico L, Becker CG, Siskind GW. Effects of tobacco glycoprotein (TGP) on the immune system. II: TGP stimulates the proliferation of human T cells and the differentiation of human B cells into Ig secreting cells. *Journal of Immunology* 1988;140(6):1823–9.

Frank R, Braun HE, Holdrinet M, Stonefield KI, Elliot JM, Zilkey B, Vickery L, Chang HH. Metal contents and insecticide residues in tobacco soils and cured tobacco leaves collected in southern Ontario. *Tobacco Science* 1977;21:74–80.

Fréry N, Huel G, Leroy M, Moreau T, Savard R, Blot P, Lellouch J. Vitamin B12 among parturients and their newborns and its relationship with birthweight. *European Journal of Obstetrics, Gynecology, and Reproductive Biology* 1992;45(3):155–63.

Gackowski D, Speina E, Zielinska M, Kowalewski J, Rozalski R, Siomek A, Paciorek T, Tudke B, Olinski R. Products of oxidative DNA damage and repair as possible biomarkers of susceptibility to lung cancer. *Cancer Research* 2003;63(16):4899–902.

Gaworski CL, Dozier MM, Gerhart JM, Rajendran N, Brennecke LH, Aranyi C, Heck JD. 13-Week inhalation toxicity study of menthol cigarette smoke. *Food and Chemical Toxicology* 1997;35(7):683–92.

Gealy R, Zhang L, Siegfried JM, Luketich JD, Keohavong P. Comparison of mutations in the p53 and K-ras genes in lung carcinomas from smoking and nonsmoking women. *Cancer Epidemiology, Biomarkers & Prevention* 1999;8(4 Pt 1):297–302.

Godschalk RWL, Van Schooten F-J, Bartsch H. A critical evaluation of DNA adducts as biological markers for human exposure to polycyclic aromatic compounds. *Journal of Biochemistry and Molecular Biology* 2003; 36(1):1–11.

Goldstein JA, Faletto MB. Advances in mechanisms of activation and deactivation of environmental chemicals. *Environmental Health Perspectives* 1993;100:169–76.

González E, Monge C, Whittembury J. Ionization constants of 5,5' – dimethyl – 2,4 – oxazolidinedione (DMO) and nicotine at temperatures and NaCl concentrations of biological interest. *Acta Científica Venezolana* 1980;31(2):128–30.

Gordon SM, Wallace LA, Brinkman MC, Callahan PJ, Kenny DV. Volatile organic compounds as breath biomarkers for active and passive smoking. *Environmental Health Perspectives* 2002;110(7):689–98.

Graham EA, Croninger AB, Wynder EL. Experimental production of carcinoma with cigarette tar. IV: successful experiments with rabbits. *Cancer Research* 1957;17(11):1058–66.

Gray N, Zaridze D, Robertson C, Krivosheeva L, Sigacheva N, Boyle P, the International Cigarette Variation Group. Variation within global cigarette brands in tar, nicotine, and certain nitrosamines: analytic study. *Tobacco Control* 2000;9(3):351.

Green JD, Chalmers J, Kinnard PJ. The transfer of tobacco additives to cigarette smoke: examination of the possible contribution of pyrolysis products to mainstream smoke composition. *Beiträge zur Tabakforschung International* 1989;14(5):283–8.

Gregson RL, Prentice DE. Aspects of the immunotoxicity of chronic tobacco smoke exposure of the rat. *Toxicology* 1981;22(1):23–31.

Griest WH, Guerin MR. Influence of tobacco type on smoke composition. *Recent Advances in Tobacco Science* 1977;3:121–44.

Grimmer G, Naujack K-W, Dettbarn G. Gas chromatographic determination of polycyclic aromatic hydrocarbons, aza-arenes, aromatic amines in the particle and vapor phase of mainstream and sidestream smoke of cigarettes. *Toxicology Letters* 1987;35(1):117–24.

Groneberg DA, Chung KF. Models of chronic obstructive pulmonary disease. *Respiratory Research* 2004;5(18).

Guerassimov A, Hoshino Y, Takubo Y, Turcotte A, Yama-moto M, Ghezzo H, Triantafillopoulos A, Whittaker K, Hoidal JR, Cosio MG. The development of emphysema in cigarette smoke-exposed mice is strain dependent. *American Journal of Respiratory and Critical Care Medicine* 2004;170(9):974–80.

Guerin MR. Chemical composition of cigarette smoke. In: Gori GB, Bock FG, editors. *Banbury Report No. 3: A Safe Cigarette?* Cold Spring Harbor (NY): Cold Spring Harbor Laboratory, 1980:191–204.

Guerin MR. Formation and physiochemical nature of sidestream smoke. In: O'Neill IK, Brunnemann KD, Dodet B, Hoffmann D, editors. *Environmental Carcinogens: Methods of Analysis and Exposure Measurement*, Volume 9–Passive Smoking. Lyon: International Agency for Research on Cancer, 1987: 11–23. IARC Scientific Publications No. 81.

Guerin MR, Higgins CE, Jenkins RA. Measuring environmental emissions from tobacco combustion: sidestream cigarette smoke literature review. *Atmospheric Environment* 1987;21(2):291–7.

Guess HE. pH control via weak acid/conjugate base system (common ion effect) in filter. RJ Reynolds Collection. 1980. Bates No. 504168860/8861. <http://legacy.library.ucsf.edu/tid/ydu58d00>.

Gupta RC, Arif JM, Gairola CG. Enhancement of preexisting DNA adducts in rodents exposed to cigarette smoke. *Mutation Research* 1999;424(1–2):195–205.

Harris EM. Cigarette. 1890. U.S. Patent 439,004, filed Nov. 29, 1889, and issued Oct. 21, 1890.

Hasan SU, Simakajornboon N, MacKinnon Y, Gozal D. Prenatal cigarette smoke exposure selectively alters protein kinase C and nitric oxide synthase expression within the neonatal rat brainstem. *Neuroscience Letters* 2001;301(2):135–8.

Hattis DB. The promise of molecular epidemiology for quantitative risk assessment. *Risk Analysis* 1986; 6(2):181–93.

Hautamaki RD, Kobayashi DK, Senior RM, Shapiro SD. Requirement for macrophage elastase for cigarette smoke-induced emphysema in mice. *Science* 1997; 277(5334):2002–4.

Hecht SS. Human urinary carcinogen metabolites: biomarkers for investigating tobacco and cancer. *Carcinogenesis* 2002;23(6):907–22.

Hecht SS. Tobacco carcinogens, their biomarkers and tobacco-induced cancer. *Nature Reviews* 2003;3(10): 733–44.

Hecht SS. Carcinogenicity studies of inhaled cigarette smoke in laboratory animals: old and new. *Carcinogenesis* 2005;26(9):1488–92.

Hecht SS, Carmella SG, Le K-A, Murphy SE, Li YS, Le C, Jensen J, Hatsukami DK. Effects of reduced cigarette smoking on levels of 1-hydroxypyrene in urine. *Cancer Epidemiology, Biomarkers & Prevention* 2004; 13(5):834–42.

Hecht SS, Chen CB, Hirota N, Ornaf RM, Tso TC, Hoffmann D. Tobacco-specific nitrosamines: formation from nicotine in vitro and during tobacco curing and carcinogenicity in strain A mice. *Journal of the National Cancer Institute* 1978;60(4):819–24.

Hecht SS, Hoffmann D. Tobacco-specific nitrosamines, an important group of carcinogens in tobacco and tobacco smoke. *Carcinogenesis* 1988;9(6):875–84.

Hecht SS, Murphy SE, Carmella SG, Li S, Jensen J, Le C, Joseph AM, Hatsukami DK. Similar uptake of lung carcinogens by smokers of regular, light, and ultralight cigarettes. *Cancer Epidemiology, Biomarkers & Prevention* 2005;14(3):693–8.

Hecht SS, Ornaf RM, Hoffmann D. Chemical studies on tobacco smoke. XXXIII: N'-nitrosonornicotine in tobacco: analysis of possible contributing factors and biologic implications. *Journal of the National Cancer Institute* 1975;54(5):1237–44.

Henningfield JE, Pankow JF, Garrett BE. Ammonia and other chemical base tobacco additives and cigarette nicotine delivery: issues and research needs. *Nicotine & Tobacco Research* 2004;6(2):199–205.

Hind JD. Method of making a reconstituted tobacco sheet. 1968. U.S. Patent 3,386,449, filed June 16, 1966, and issued June 4, 1968.

Hind JD, Seligman RB. Tobacco sheet material. 1967. U.S. Patent 3,353,541, filed June 16, 1966, and issued Nov. 21, 1967.

Hind JD, Seligman RB. Method of preparing a reconstituted tobacco sheet employing a pectin adhesive. 1969. U.S. Patent 3,420,241, filed June 16, 1966, and issued Jan. 7, 1969.

Höfer I, Nil R, Bättig K. Ultralow-yield cigarettes and type of ventilation: the role of ventilation blocking. *Pharmacology, Biochemistry, and Behavior* 1991;40(4): 907–14.

Höfer T, Gerner I, Gundert-Remy U, Liebsch M, Schulte A, Spielmann H, Vogel R, Wettig K. Animal testing and alternative approaches for the human health risk assessment under the proposed new European chemicals regulation. *Archives of Toxicology* 2004; 78(10):549–64.

Hoffmann D, Adams JD, Brunnemann KD, Hecht SS. Assessment of tobacco-specific N-nitrosamines in tobacco products. *Cancer Research* 1979a;39(7 Pt 1): 2505–9.

Hoffmann D, Adams JD, Brunnemann KD, Hecht SS. Formation, occurrence, and carcinogenicity of N-nitrosamines in tobacco products. *American Chemical Society Symposium Series* 1981;174:247–73.

Hoffmann D, Adams JD, Haley NJ. Reported cigarette smoke values: a closer look. *American Journal of Public Health* 1983;73(9):1050–3.

Hoffmann D, Adams JD, Wynder EL. Formation and analysis of carbon monoxide in cigarette mainstream and sidestream smoke. *Preventive Medicine* 1979b; 8(3):344–50.

Hoffmann D, Brunnemann KD. Endogenous formation of N-nitrosoproline in cigarette smokers. *Cancer Research* 1983;43(11):5570–4.

Hoffmann D, Djordjevic MV, Hoffmann I. The changing cigarette. *Preventive Medicine* 1997;26(4):427–34.

Hoffmann D, Dong M, Hecht SS. Origin in tobacco smoke of N'-nitrosonornicotine, a tobacco-specific carcinogen: brief communication. *Journal of the National Cancer Institute* 1977;58(6):1841–4.

Hoffmann D, Hecht SS, Ornaf RM, Wynder EL. N'-nitrosonornicotine in tobacco. *Science* 1974;186(4160): 265–7.

Hoffmann D, Hoffmann I. The changing cigarette, 1950–1995. *Journal of Toxicology and Environmental Health* 1997;50(4):307–64.

Hoffmann D, Hoffmann I. Tobacco smoke components [letter]. *Beiträge zur Tabakforschung International* 1998;18(1):49–52.

Hoffmann D, Hoffmann I, El-Bayoumy K. The less harmful cigarette: a controversial issue. A tribute to Ernst L. Wynder. *Chemical Research in Toxicology* 2001;14(7):767–90.

Hoffmann D, Masuda Y, Wynder EL. α-Naphthylamine and β-naphthylamine in cigarette smoke. *Nature* 1969;221(5177):254–6.

Hoffmann D, Wynder EL. Filtration of phenols from cigarette smoke. *Journal of the National Cancer Institute* 1963;30:67–84.

Hoffmann D, Wynder EL. The reduction of the tumorigenicity of cigarette smoke condensate by addition of sodium nitrate to tobacco. *Cancer Research* 1967;27(1):172–4.

Hoffmann D, Wynder EL. A study of tobacco carcinogenesis. XI: tumor initiators, tumor accelerators, and tumor promoting activity of condensate fractions. *Cancer* 1971;27(4):848–64.

Hoidal JR, Niewoehner DE. Lung phagocyte recruitment and metabolic alterations induced by cigarette smoke in humans and hamsters. *American Review of Respiratory Disease* 1982;126(3):548–52.

Holt PG, Keast D, Mackenzie JS. Immunosuppression in the mouse induced by long-term exposure to cigarette smoke. *American Journal of Pathology* 1978; 90(1):281–4.

Hopkin JM, Evans HU. Cellular effects of smoke from "safer" cigarettes. *British Journal of Cancer* 1984;49(3):333–6.

Hopkin JM, Tomlinson VS, Jenkins RM. Variation in response to cytotoxicity of cigarette smoke. *BMJ (British Medical Journal)* 1981;283(6301):1209–11.

Hopkins R, Wood LE, Sinclair NM. Evaluation of methods to estimate cigarette smoke uptake. *Clinical Pharmacology and Therapeutics* 1984;36(6):788–95.

Horak S, Polanska J, Widlak P. Bulky DNA adducts in human sperm: relationship with fertility semen quality, smoking, and environmental factors. *Mutation Research* 2003;537(1):53–65.

Horton AD, Guerin MR. Quantitative determination of sulfur compounds in the gas phase of cigarette smoke. *Journal of Chromatography A* 1974;90(1):63–70.

Hoshino Y, Mio T, Nagai S, Miki H, Ito I, Izumi T. Cytotoxic effects of cigarette smoke extract on an alveolar type II cell-derived cell line. *American Journal of Physiology – Lung Cellular and Molecular Physiology* 2001;281(2):L509–L516.

Houeto P, Hoffman JR, Got P, Dang Vu B, Baud FJ. Acetonitrile as a possible marker of current cigarette smoking. *Human & Experimental Toxicology* 1997;16(11): 658–61.

Hsieh Y-S, Chen B-C, Shiow S-J, Wang H-C, Hsu J-D, Wang C-J. Formation of 8-nitroguanine in tobacco cigarette smokers and in tobacco smoke-exposed Wistar rats. *Chemico-Biological Interactions* 2002;140(1):67–80.

Hutt JA, Vuillemenot BR, Barr EB, Grimes MJ, Hahn FF, Hobbs CH, March TH, Gigliotti AP, Seilkop SK, Finch GL, et al. Life-span inhalation exposure to mainstream cigarette smoke induces lung cancer in B6C3F1 mice through genetic and epigenetic pathways. *Carcinogenesis* 2005;26(11):1999–2009.

Iida M, Iida H, Dohi S, Takenaka M, Fujiwara H. Mechanisms underlying cerebrovascular effects of cigarette smoking in rats in vivo. *Stroke* 1998;29(8):1656–65.

Indiana Prevention Resource Center. Additives found in American cigarettes, Dec. 8, 2005; <http://www.drugs.indiana.edu/resources/druginfo/drugs/tobaccoadditives.html>; accessed: December 31, 2005.

Ingebrethsen BJ. Aerosol studies of cigarette smoke. *Recent Advances in Tobacco Science: Advances in the Analytical Methodology of Leaf and Smoke* 1986;12: 54–142.

Ingebrethsen B, Lyman C. Evaporative deposition as a mechanism of sensory stimulation. RJ Reynolds Collection. 1991. Bates No. 508297971/7997. <http://legacy.library.ucsf.edu/tid/jgx93d00>.

Interagency Coordinating Committee on the Validation of Alternative Methods. ICCVAM mission, vision and strategic priorities, February 11, 2004; <http://

iccvam.niehs.nih.gov/docs/about_docs/MisVisStrat. pdf>; accessed: April 30, 2007.

International Agency for Research on Cancer. *IARC Monographs on the Evaluation of Carcinogenic Risks to Humans: Tobacco Smoking*. Vol. 38. Lyon (France): International Agency for Research on Cancer, 1986.

International Agency for Research on Cancer. *IARC Monographs on the Evaluation of the Carcinogenic Risks to Humans: Tobacco Smoke and Involuntary Smoking*. Vol. 83. Lyon (France): International Agency for Research on Cancer, 2004.

International Agency for Research on Cancer. *IARC Monographs on the Evaluation of Carcinogenic Risks to Humans: Smokeless Tobacco and Some Tobacco-specific N-Nitrosamines*. Vol. 89. Lyon (France): International Agency for Research on Cancer, 2007.

İşcan A, Yiğitoğlu MR, Ece A, Ari Z, Akyildiz M. The effect of cigarette smoking during pregnancy on cord blood lipid, lipoprotein and apolipoprotein levels. *Japanese Heart Journal* 1997;38(4):497–502.

Ishizu Y, Kaneki K, Okada T. A new method to determine the relation between the particle size and chemical composition of tobacco smoke particles. *Journal of Aerosol Science* 1987;18(2):123–9.

Jacob P III, Yu L, Shulgin AT, Benowitz NL. Minor tobacco alkaloids as biomarkers for tobacco use: comparison of users of cigarettes, smokeless tobacco, cigars, and pipes. *American Journal of Public Health* 1999;89(5):731–6.

Jaffe JH, Kanzler M, Friedman L, Stunkard AJ, Verebey K. Carbon monoxide and thiocyanate levels in low tar-nicotine smokers. *Addictive Behaviors* 1981;6(4): 337–44.

Jalili T, Murthy GG, Schiestl RH. Cigarette smoke induces DNA deletions in the mouse embryo. *Cancer Research* 1998;58(12):2633–8.

Jansson A, Andersson K, Bjelke B, Eneroth P, Fuxe K. Effects of a postnatal exposure to cigarette smoke on hypothalamic catecholamine nerve terminal systems and on neuroendocrine function in the postnatal and adult male rat: evidence for long-term modulation of anterior pituitary function. *Acta Physiologica Scandinavica* 1992;144(4):453–62.

Jansson T, Curvall M, Hedin A, Enzell CR. In vitro studies of the biological effects of cigarette smoke condensate. III: induction of SCE by some phenolic and related constituents derived from cigarette smoke. A study of structure-activity relationships. *Mutation Research* 1988;206(1):17–24.

Jarmalaite S, Kannio A, Anttila S, Lazutka JR, Husgafvel-Pursiainen K. Aberrant *p16* promoter methylation in smokers and former smokers with nonsmall cell lung cancer. *International Journal of Cancer* 2003; 106(6):913–8.

Johnson WR. The pyrogenesis and physicochemical nature of tobacco smoke. *Recent Advances in Tobacco Science* 1977;3:1–27.

Johnson DE, Rhoades JW. *N*-nitrosamines in smoke condensate from several varieties of tobacco. *Journal of the National Cancer Institute* 1972;48(6):1845–7.

Johnson JD, Houchens DP, Kluwe WM, Craig DK, Fisher GL. Effects of mainstream and environmental tobacco smoke on the immune system in animals and humans: a review. *Critical Reviews in Toxicology* 1990; 20(5):369–95.

Johnson WR, Hale RW, Clough SC, Chen PH. Chemistry of the conversion of nitrate nitrogen to smoke products. *Nature* 1973a;243(5404):223–5.

Johnson WR, Hale RW, Nedlock JW, Grubbs HJ, Powell DH. The distribution of products between mainstream and sidestream smoke. *Tobacco Science* 1973b;17:141–4.

Joseph AM, Hecht SS, Murphy SE, Carmella SG, Le CT, Zhang Y, Han S, Hatsukami DK. Relationships between cigarette consumption and biomarkers of tobacco toxin exposure. *Cancer Epidemiology, Biomarkers & Prevention* 2005;14(12):2963–8.

Kado NY, Manson C, Eisenstadt E, Hsieh DHP. The kinetics of mutagen excretion in the urine of cigarette smokers. *Mutation Research* 1985;157(2–3):227–33.

Kaiserman MJ, Rickert WS. Carcinogens in tobacco smoke: benzo[*a*]pyrene from Canadian cigarettes and cigarette tobacco. *American Journal of Public Health* 1992;82(7):1023–6.

Kalcher K, Kern W, Pietsch R. Cadmium and lead in the smoke of a filter cigarette. *Science of the Total Environment* 1993;128(1):21–35.

Kalra R, Singh SP, Savage SM, Finch GL, Sopori ML. Effects of cigarette smoke on immune response: chronic exposure to cigarette smoke impairs antigen-mediated signaling in T cells and depletes IP3-sensitive Ca^{2+} stores. *Journal of Pharmacology and Experimental Therapeutics* 2000;293(1):166–71.

Kao-Shan C-S, Fine RL, Whang-Peng J, Lee EC, Chabner BA. Increased fragile sites and sister chromatid exchanges in bone marrow and peripheral blood of young cigarette smokers. *Cancer Research* 1987; 47(23):6278–82.

Karube T, Odagiri Y, Takemoto K, Watanabe S. Analyses of transplacentally induced sister chromatid exchanges and micronuclei in mouse fetal liver cells following maternal exposure to cigarette smoke. *Cancer Research* 1989;49(13):3550–2.

Kataoka H, Kijima K, Maruo G. Determination of mutagenic heterocyclic amines in combustion smoke samples. *Bulletin of Environmental Contamination and Toxicology* 1998;60(1):60–7.

Keith CH. Experimental and theoretical aspects of ciga-rette smoke filtration. *American Chemical Society Symposium Series* 1975;17:79–90.

Keith CH. Physical mechanisms of smoke filtration. *Recent Advances in Tobacco Science* 1978;4:25–45.

Keith CH, Derrick JC. Measurement of the particle size distribution and concentration of cigarette smoke by the "conifuge." *Tobacco Science* 1960;4:84–91.

Keith CH, Norman V, Bates WW Jr. Tobacco smoke fil-ter. 1966. U.S. Patent 3251365, filed Mar. 4, 1963, and issued May 17, 1966.

Keohavong P, Mady HH, Gao WM, Siegfried JM, Luketich JD, Melhem MF. Topographic analysis of K-*ras* muta-tions in histologically normal lung tissues and tumours of lung cancer patients. *British Journal of Cancer* 2001;85(2):235–41.

Kertsis GD, Sun HH. Philip Morris: increasing the fill-ing power of tobacco lamina filler. *Tobacco Reporter* 1984;110(10):92.

Khater AEM. Polonium-210 budget in cigarettes. *Journal of Environmental Radioactivity* 2004;71(1):33–41.

Koul A, Singh A, Sandhir R. Effect of α-tocopherol on the cardiac antioxidant defense system and atherogenic lip-ids in cigarette smoke-inhaling mice. *Inhalation Toxi-cology* 2003;15(5):513–22.

Kozlowski LT, Mehta NY, Sweeney CT, Schwartz SS, Vogler GP, Jarvis MJ, West RJ. Filter ventilation and nicotine content of tobacco in cigarettes from Canada, the United Kingdom, and the United States. *Tobacco Control* 1998;7(4):369–75.

Kozlowski LT, O'Connor RJ, Sweeney CT. Cigarette design. In: *Risks Associated with Smoking Cigarettes with Low Machine-Measured Yields of Tar and Nicotine.* Smok-ing and Tobacco Control Monograph No. 13. Bethesda (MD): U.S. Department of Health and Human Services, Public Health Service, National Institutes of Health, National Cancer Institute, 2001:13–37. NIH Publica-tion No. 02-5047.

Kozlowski LT, Rickert WS, Pope MA, Robinson JC, Frek-ker RC. Estimating the yield to smokers of tar, nico-tine, and carbon monoxide from the 'lowest yield' ventilated filter-cigarettes. *British Journal of Addiction* 1982;77(2):159–65.

Kozlowski LT, Sweeny CT, Pillitteri JL. Blocking cigarette filter vent with lips more than doubles carbon monox-ide intake from ultra-low tar cigarettes. *Experimental and Clinical Psychopharmacology* 1996;4(4):404–8.

Kramer AI. R.J. Reynolds: method of expanding tobacco. *Tobacco Reporter* 1991;118(9):66.

Krause G, Garganta F, Vrieling H, Schere G. Spontaneous and chemically induced point mutations in *HPRT* cDNA

of the metabolically competent human lymphoblas-toid cell line, MCL-5. *Mutation Research* 1999;431(2): 417–28.

Krivan V, Schneider G, Baumann H, Reus U. Multi-element characterization of tobacco smoke conden-sate. *Fresenius' Journal of Analytical Chemistry* 1994;348(3):218–25.

Kuenemann-Migeot C, Callais F, Momas I, Festy B. Uri-nary promutagens of smokers: comparison of concen-tration methods and relation to cigarette consumption. *Mutation Research* 1996;368(2):141–7.

Larson TM, Moring TB, Ireland MS. Nicotine transfer pro-cess. 1980. U.S. Patent 4,215,706, filed Oct. 13, 1978, and issued Aug. 5, 1980.

Latha MS, Vijayammal PL, Kurup PA. Effect of exposure of rats to cigarette smoke on the metabolism of lipids. *Atherosclerosis* 1988;70(3):225–31.

Laugesen M, Fowles J. Marlboro Ultrasmooth: a potentially reduced exposure cigarette? *Tobacco Control* 2006; 15(6):430–5.

LaVoie EJ, Adams JD, Reinhardt J, Rivenson A, Hoffmann D. Toxicity studies on clove cigarette smoke and con-stituents of clove: determination of LD_{50} of eugenol by intratracheal installation in rats and hamsters. *Archives of Toxicology* 1986;59(2):78-81.

Lea JS, Coleman R, Kurien A, Schorge JO, Miller DS, Minna JD, Muller CY. Aberrant *p16* methylation is a biomarker for tobacco exposure in cervical squamous cell carcinogenesis. *American Journal of Obstetrics and Gynecology* 2004;190(3):674–9.

Lechner JF, Neft RE, Gilliland FD, Crowell RE, Belinsky SA. Molecular identification of individuals at high risk for lung cancer. *Radiation Oncology Investigations* 1997;5(3):103–5.

Lee CK, Brown BG, Reed EA, Hejtmancik M, Mosberg AT, Doolittle DJ, Hayes AW. DNA adduct formation in mice following dermal application of smoke condensates from cigarettes that burn or heat tobacco. *Environ-mental and Molecular Mutagenesis* 1992;20(4):313–9.

Lee IW, Ahn SK, Choi EH, Lee SH. Urticarial reaction fol-lowing the inhalation of nicotine in tobacco smoke. *British Journal of Dermatology* 1998;138(3):486–8.

Lefevre PJ. Pharmacology of minor alkaloids of tobacco [French]. *Journée de la Dépendance Tabagique* 1989; 65(40):2424–32.

Leffingwell JC. Nitrogen components of leaf and their relationship to smoking quality and aroma. *Recent Advances in Tobacco Science* 1976;2:1–31.

Lehrer SB, Wilson MR, Salvaggio JE. Immunogenic prop-erties of tobacco smoke. *Journal of Allergy and Clinical Immunology* 1978;62(6):368–70.

Lehrer SB, Wilson MR, Salvaggio JE. Immunogenicity of tobacco smoke components in rabbits and mice. *International Archives of Allergy and Applied Immunology* 1980;62(1):16–22.

Leichter J. Growth of fetuses of rats exposed to ethanol and cigarette smoke during gestation. *Growth, Development, and Aging* 1989;53(3):129–34.

Lendvay AT, Laszlo TS. Cigarette peak coal temperature measurements. *Beiträge zur Tabakforschung International* 1974;7(5):276–81.

Lewis CL. The effect of cigarette construction parameter on smoke generation and yield. *Recent Advances in Tobacco Science* 1990;16:73–101.

Li Q, Aubrey MT, Christian T, Freed BM. Differential inhibition of DNA synthesis in human T cells by the cigarette tar components hydroquinone and catechol. *Fundamental and Applied Toxicology* 1997;38(2):158–65.

Lichtenbeld H, Vidić B. Effect of maternal exposure to smoke on gas diffusion capacity in neonatal rat. *Respiration Physiology* 1989;75(2):129–40.

Lippman SM, Peters EJ, Wargovich MJ, Stadnyk AN, Dixon DO, Dekmezian RH, Loewy JW, Morice RC, Cunningham JE, Hong KW. Bronchial micronuclei as a marker of an early stage of carcinogenesis in the human tracheobronchial epithelium. *International Journal of Cancer* 1990;45(5):811–5.

Löfroth G. Environmental tobacco smoke: overview of chemical composition and genotoxic components. *Mutation Research* 1989;222(2):73–80.

Loft S, Poulsen HE. Estimation of oxidative DNA damage in man from urinary excretion of repair products. *Acta Biochimica Polonica* 1998;45(1):133–44.

Luceri F, Pieraccini G, Moneti G, Dolara P. Primary aromatic amines from side-stream cigarette smoke are common contaminants of indoor air. *Toxicology and Industrial Health* 1993;9(3):405–13.

MacKown CT, Crafts-Brandner SJ, Sutton TG. Tobacco production - relationships among soil nitrate, leaf nitrate, and leaf yield of burley tobacco: effects of nitrogen management. *Agronomy Journal* 1999;91(4):613–21.

Malaveille C, Vineis P, Estéve J, Ohshima H, Brun G, Hautefeuille A, Gallet P, Ronco G, Terracini B, Bartsch H. Levels of mutagens in the urine of smokers of black and blond tobacco correlate with their risk of bladder cancer. *Carcinogenesis* 1989;10(3):577–86.

Manabe S, Tohyama K, Wada O, Aramaki T. Detection of a carcinogen, 2-amino-1-methyl-6-phenylimidazo[4,5-*b*] pyridine (PhIP), in cigarette smoke condensate. *Carcinogenesis* 1991;12(10):1945–7.

Manabe S, Wada O. Carcinogenic tryptophan pyrolysis products in cigarette smoke condensate and cigarette

smoke-polluted indoor air. *Environmental Pollution* 1990;64(2):121–32.

Mancini R, Romano G, Sgambato A, Flamini G, Giovagnoli MR, Boninsegna A, Carraro C, Vecchione A, Cittadini A. Polycyclic aromatic hydrocarbon–DNA adducts in cervical smears of smokers and nonsmokers. *Gynecologic Oncology* 1999;75(1):68–71.

Mao L, Lee JS, Kurie JM, Fan YH, Lippman SM, Lee JJ, Ro YJ, Broxson A, Yu R, Morice RC, et al. Clonal genetic alterations in the lungs of current and former smokers. *Journal of the National Cancer Institute* 1997;89(12):857–62.

March TH, Barr EB, Finch GL, Hahn FF, Hobbs CH, Ménache MG, Nikula KJ. Cigarette smoke exposure produces more evidence of emphysema in B6C3F1 mice than in F344 rats. *Toxicological Sciences* 1999;51(2):289–99.

Martonen TB. Deposition patterns of cigarette smoke in human airways. *American Industrial Hygiene Association Journal* 1992;53(1):6–18.

Martonen TB, Musante CJ. Importance of cloud motion on cigarette smoke deposition in lung airways. *Inhalation Toxicology* 2000;12(Suppl 4):261–80.

Matsukura N, Willey J, Miyashita M, Taffe B, Hoffmann D, Waldren C, Puck TT, Harris CC. Detection of direct mutagenicity of cigarette smoke condensate in mammalian cells. *Carcinogenesis* 1991;12(4):685–9.

Mauderly JL, Gigliotti AP, Barr EB, Bechtold WE, Belinksy SA, Hahan FF, Hobbs CA, March TH, Seilkop SK, Finch GL. Chronic inhalation exposure to mainstream cigarette smoke increases lung and nasal tumor incidence in rats. *Toxicological Sciences* 2004;81(2):280–92.

McAllister-Sistilli CG, Caggiula AR, Knopf S, Rose CA, Miller AL, Donny EC. The effects of nicotine on the immune system. *Psychoneuroendocrinology* 1998;23(2):175–87.

McCusker K, Hoidal J. Selective increase of antioxidant enzyme activity in the alveolar macrophages from cigarette smokers and smoke-exposed hamsters. *American Review of Respiratory Disease* 1990;141(3):678–82.

McGowan EM. Menthol urticaria. *Archives of Dermatology* 1966;94(1):62–3.

McRae DD. The physical and chemical nature of tobacco smoke. *Recent Advances in Tobacco Science: The Formation and Evolution of Cigarette Smoke* 1990;16;233–323.

Meckley D, Hayes JR, Van Kampen KR, Mosberg AT, Swauger JE. A responsive, sensitive, and reproducible dermal tumor promotion assay for the comparative evaluation of cigarette smoke condensates. *Regulatory Toxicology and Pharmacology* 2004a;39(2):135–49.

Meckley DR, Hayes JR, Van Kampen KR, Ayres PH, Mosberg AT, Swauger JE. Comparative study of smoke condensates from 1R4F cigarettes that burn tobacco versus ECLIPSE cigarettes that primarily heat tobacco in the SENCAR mouse dermal tumor promotion assay. *Food and Chemical Toxicology* 2004b;42(5):851–63.

Melikian AA, Djordjevic MV, Chen S, Richie J Jr, Stellman SD. Effect of delivered dosage of cigarette smoke toxins on the levels of urinary biomarkers of exposure. *Cancer Epidemiology, Biomarkers & Prevention* 2007a;16(7):1408–15.

Melikian AA, Djordjevic MV, Hosey J, Zhang J, Chen S, Zang E, Muscat J, Stellman SD. Gender differences relative to smoking behavior and emissions of toxins from mainstream cigarette smoke. *Nicotine & Tobacco Research* 2007b;9(3):377–87.

Melikian AA, Prahalad AK, Hoffmann D. Urinary *trans, trans*-muconic acid as an indicator of exposure to benzene in cigarette smokers. *Cancer Epidemiology, Biomarkers & Prevention* 1993;2(1):47–51.

Melikian AA, Prahalad AK, Secker-Walker RH. Comparison of the levels of the urinary benzene metabolite *trans, trans*-muconic acid in smokers and nonsmokers and the effects of pregnancy. *Cancer Epidemiology, Biomarkers & Prevention* 1994;3(3):239–44.

Miller LM, Foster WM, Dambach DM, Doebler D, McKinnon M, Killar L, Longphre M. A murine model of cigarette smoke-induced pulmonary inflammation using intranasally administered smoke-conditioned medium. *Experimental Lung Research* 2002;28(6):435–55.

Milnerowicz H, Zalewski J, Geneja R, Milnerowicz-Nabzdyk E, Zaslawski R, Woyton J. Effects of exposure to tobacco smoke in pregnancies complicated by oligohydraminos and premature rupture of the membranes. I: concentration of Cd and Pb in blood and Zn, Cu, Cd and Pb in amniotic fluid. *International Journal of Occupational Medicine and Environmental Health* 2000;13(3):185–93.

Mitacek EJ, Brunnemann KD, Hoffmann D, Limsila T, Suttajit M, Martin N, Caplan LS. Volatile nitrosamines and tobacco-specific nitrosamines in the smoke of Thai cigarettes: a risk factor for lung cancer and a suspected risk factor for liver cancer in Thailand. *Carcinogenesis* 1999;20(1):133–7.

Moerloose KB, Robays LJ, Maes T, Brusselle GG, Tournoy KG, Joos GF. Cigarette smoke exposure facilitates allergic sensitization in mice. *Respiratory Research* 2006; 7:49.

Moessinger AC. Mothers who smoke and the lungs of their offspring. *Annals of the New York Academy of Sciences* 1989;562:101–4.

Moore GE, Bock FG. "Tar" and nicotine levels of American cigarettes. *Journal of the National Cancer Institute Monographs* 1968;28:89–94.

Morie GP, Sloan CH. Determination of N-nitrosodimethylamine in the smoke of high-nitrate tobacco cigarettes. *Beiträge zur Tabakforschung International* 1973; 7(2):61–6.

Morie GP, Sloan CH, Baggett MS. Parameters affecting the selective filtration of certain tobacco smoke components. *Beiträge zur Tabakforschung International* 1975;8(3):145–9.

Morrow JD. Quantification of isoprostanes as indices of oxidant stress and the risk of atherosclerosis in humans. *Arteriosclerosis, Thrombosis, and Vascular Biology* 2005;25(2):279–86.

Mudzinski SP. Effects of benzo[*a*]pyrene on concanavalin A-stimulated human peripheral blood mononuclear cells *in vitro*: inhibition of proliferation but no effect on parameters related to the G_1 phase of the cell cycle. *Toxicology and Applied Pharmacology* 1993; 119(2):166–74.

Mulchi CL, Adamu CA, Bell PF, Chaney RL. Residual heavy metal concentrations in sludge-amended coastal plain soils. I: comparison of extractants. *Communications in Soil Science and Plant Analysis* 1991;22(9–10):919–41.

Mulchi CL, Adamu CA, Bell PF, Chaney RL. Residual heavy metal concentrations in sludge-amended coastal plain soils. II: predicting metal concentrations in tobacco from soil test information. *Communications in Soil Science and Plant Analysis* 1992;23(9–10):1053–69.

Mulchi CL, Bell PF, Adamu C, Chaney R. Long term availability of metals in sludge amended acid soils. *Journal of Plant Nutrition* 1987;10(9–16):1149–61.

Muller WJ, Hess GD, Scherer PW. A model of cigarette smoke particle deposition. *American Industrial Hygiene Association Journal* 1990;51(5):245–56.

Muramatsu M. *Studies on the Transport Phenomena in Naturally Smoldering Cigarettes*. Translated by D. Jackson. Japan Tobacco Monopoly Research Corporation, Scientific Papers of the Central Research Institute. 1981. Brown and Williamson Collection. Bates No. 650329128/9236. <legacy.library.ucsf.edu/tid/eyI00f00>.

Murkovic M. Chemistry, formation and occurrence of genotoxic heterocyclic aromatic amines in fried products. *European Journal of Lipid Science and Technology* 2004;106(11):777–85.

Murphy SE, Link CA, Jensen J, Le C, Puumala SS, Hecht SS, Carmella SG, Losey L, Hatsukami DK. A comparison of urinary biomarkers of tobacco and carcinogen exposure in smokers. *Cancer Epidemiology, Biomarkers & Prevention* 2004;13(10):1617–23.

Mutation Research. A Nordic data base on somatic chromosome damage in humans. Nordic Study Group on the Health Risk of Chromosome Damage. *Mutation Research* 1990;241(3):325–37.

National Center for Health Statistics. Summary health statistics for U.S. adults: National Health Interview Survey, 2007. *Vital and Health Statistics*. Series 10, No. 240. Hyattsville (MD): U.S. Department of Health and Human Services, Centers for Disease Control and Prevention, National Center for Health Statistics, 2007. DHHS Publication No. (PHS) 2008-1563.

Navarro J, Causse MB, Desquilbet N, Hervé F, Lallemand D. The vitamin status of low birth weight infants and their mothers. *Journal of Pediatric Gastroenterology and Nutrition* 1984;3(5):744–8.

Newsome JR, Keith CH. Variation of the gas phase composition within a burning cigarette. *Tobacco Science* 1965;9:65–9.

Ng SP, Silverstone AE, Lai ZW, Zelikoff JT. Effects of prenatal exposure to cigarette smoke on offspring tumor susceptibility and associated immune mechanisms. *Toxicological Sciences* 2006;89(1):135–44.

Nitsch A, Kalcher K, Greschonig H, Pietsch R. Heavy metals in tobacco smoke. II: trace metals cadmium, lead, copper, cobalt and nickel in Austrian cigarettes and in particle phase and smoke gas. *Beiträge zur Tabakforschung International* 1991;15(1):19–32.

Norman A. Cigarette design and materials. In: Davis DL, Nielsen MT, editors. *Tobacco Production, Chemistry, and Technology*. Malden (MA): Blackwell Science, 1999:353–87.

Norman V. The effect of perforated tipping paper on the yield of various smoke components. *Beiträge zur Tabakforschung International* 1974;7(5):282–7.

Norman V, Ihrig AM, Larson TM, Moss BL. The effect of some nitrogenous blend components on NO/NO$_x$ and HCN levels in mainstream and sidestream smoke. *Beiträge zur Tabakforschung International* 1983; 12(2):55–62.

Norppa H. Genetic susceptibility, biomarker responses, and cancer. *Mutation Research* 2003;544(2–3):339–48.

Obot CJ, Lee KM, Fuciarelli AF, Renne RA, McKinney WJ. Characterization of mainstream cigarette smoke-induced biomarker responses in ICR and C57Bl/6 mice. *Inhalation Toxicology* 2004;16(10):701–19.

Obwegeser R, Oguogho A, Ulm M, Berghammer P, Sinzinger H. Maternal cigarette smoking increases F$_2$-isoprostanes and reduces prostacyclin and nitric oxide in umbilical vessels. *Prostaglandins & Other Lipid Mediators* 1999;57(4):269–79.

O'Connor RJ, Hurley PJ. Existing technologies to reduce specific toxicant emissions in cigarette smoke. *Tobacco Control* 2008;17(Suppl 1):i39–i48.

Ogushi F, Hubbard RC, Vogelmeier C, Fells GA, Crystal RG. Risk factors for emphysema: cigarette smoking is associated with a reduction in the association rate constant of lung α1-antitrypsin for neutrophil elastase. *Journal of Clinical Investigation* 1991;87(3):1060–5.

Ohlemiller TJ, Villia KM, Braun E, Eberhardt KR, Harris RH Jr, Lawson JR, Gann RG. *Test Methods for Quantifying the Propensity of Cigarettes to Ignite Soft Furnishings*. Washington: U.S. Department of Commerce, U.S. National Institute of Standards and Technology, 1993. NIST Special Publication 851.

Owen WC, Reynolds ML. The diffusion of gasses through cigarette paper during smoking. *Tobacco Science* 1967; 11:14–20.

Owens WF Jr. Effect of cigarette paper on smoke yield and composition. *Recent Advances in Tobacco Science* 1978;4:3–24.

Özerol E, Özerol I, Gökdeniz R, Temel I, Akyol O. Effect of smoking on serum concentrations of total homocysteine, folate, vitamin B$_{12}$, and nitric oxide in pregnancy: a preliminary study. *Fetal Diagnosis and Therapy* 2004;19(2):145–8.

Pakhale SS, Dolas SS, Maru GB. The distribution of total particulate matter (TPM) and nicotine between mainstream and sidestream smoke in bidis and cigarettes. *Analytical Letters* 1997;30(2):383–94.

Pan X-M, Staprans I, Hardman DA, Rapp JH. Exposure to cigarette smoke delays the plasma clearance of chylomicrons and chylomicron remnants in rats. *American Journal of Physiology* 1997;273(1 Pt 1):G158–G163.

Pan X-M, Staprans I, Read TE, Rapp JH. Cigarette smoke alters chylomicron metabolism in rats. *Journal of Vascular Surgery* 1993;18(2):161–9.

Pankow JF. A consideration of the role of gas/particle partitioning in the deposition of nicotine and other tobacco smoke compounds in the respiratory tract. *Chemical Research in Toxicology* 2001;14(11):1465–81.

Pankow JF, Mader BT, Isabelle LM, Luo W, Pavlick A, Liang C. Conversion of nicotine in tobacco smoke to its volatile and available free-base form through the action of gaseous ammonia. *Environmental Science & Technology* 1997;31(8):2428–33.

Pankow JF, Tavakoli AD, Luo W, Isabelle LM. Percent free base nicotine in the tobacco smoke particulate matter of selected commercial and reference cigarettes. *Chemical Research in Toxicology* 2003;16(8):1014–8.

Pappas RS, Polzin GM, Watson CH, Ashley DL. Cadmium, lead, and thallium in smoke particulate from counterfeit cigarettes compared to authentic US brands. *Food and Chemical Toxicology* 2007;45(2):202–9.

Pappas RS, Polzin GM, Zhang L, Watson CH, Paschal DC, Ashley DL. Cadmium, lead, and thallium in mainstream tobacco smoke particulate. *Food and Chemical Toxicology* 2006;44(5):714–23.

Park E-M, Park Y-M, Gwak Y-S. Oxidative damage in tissues of rats exposed to cigarette smoke. *Free Radical Biology & Medicine* 1998;25(1):79–86.

Parmeggiani L, editor. *Encyclopedia of Occupational Health and Safety*. 3rd (revised) ed., vol. 1. Geneva: International Labour Office, 1983.

Parry JM, Parry EM, Johnson G, Quick E, Waters EM. The detection of genotoxic activity and the quantitative and qualitative assessment of the consequences of exposures. *Experimental and Toxicologic Pathology* 2005;57(Suppl 1):205–12.

Parsons LL, Smith MS, Hamilton JL, Mackown CT. Nitrate reduction during curing and processing of Burley tobacco. *Tobacco Science* 1986;30:100–3.

Patrianakos C, Hoffmann D. Chemical studies on tobacco smoke. LXIV: on the analysis of aromatic amines in cigarette smoke. *Journal of Analytical Toxicology* 1979; 3(4):150–4.

Patskan G, Reininghaus W. Toxicological evaluation of an electrically heated cigarette. Part 1: overview of technical concepts and summary of findings. *Journal of Applied Toxicology* 2003;23(5):323–8.

Pauluhn J. Overview of inhalation exposure techniques: strengths and weaknesses. *Experimental and Toxicologic Pathology* 2005;57(Suppl 1):111–28.

Pavanello S, Simioli P, Carrieri M, Gregorio P, Clonfero E. Tobacco-smoke exposure indicators and urinary mutagenicity. *Mutation Research* 2002;521(1–2):1–9.

Penn RN. Tobacco flavoring: an overview. *Perfumer & Flavorist* 1997;22:21–8.

Penn A, Butler J, Snyder C, Albert RE. Cigarette smoke and carbon monoxide do not have equivalent effects upon development of arteriosclerotic lesions. *Artery* 1983;12(2):117–31.

Penn A, Currie J, Snyder C. Inhalation of carbon monoxide does not accelerate arteriosclerosis in cockerels. *European Journal of Pharmacology* 1992;228(2–3):155–64.

Penn A, Keller K, Snyder C, Nadas A, Chen LC. The tar fraction of cigarette smoke does not promote arteriosclerotic plaque development. *Environmental Health Perspectives* 1996;104(10):1108–13.

Penn A, Snyder CA. Arteriosclerotic plaque development is "promoted" by polynuclear aromatic hydrocarbons. *Carcinogenesis* 1988;9(12):2185–9.

Peres AC, Hiromoto G. Evaluation of ^{210}Pb and [210]Po in cigarette tobacco produced in Brazil. *Journal of Environmental Radioactivity* 2002;62(1):115–9.

Perfetti TA, Coleman WM III, Smith WS. Determination of mainstream and sidestream cigarette smoke components for cigarettes of different tobacco types and a set

of reference cigarettes. *Beiträge zur Tabakforschung International* 1998;18(3):95–113.

Pfeifer GP, Denissenko MF, Olivier M, Tretyakova N, Hecht SS, Hainaut P. Tobacco smoke carcinogens, DNA damage and p53 mutations in smoking-associated cancers. *Oncogene* 2002;21(48):7435–51.

Pfeifer GP, Hainaut P. On the origin of G→T transversions in lung cancer. *Mutation Research* 2003;526(1–2): 39–43.

Phillips DH. DNA adducts as markers of exposure and risk. *Mutation Research* 2005;577(1–2):284–92.

Pillsbury HC, Bright CC, O'Connor KJ, Irish FW. Tar and nicotine in cigarette smoke. *Journal of the Association of Official Analytical Chemists* 1969;52(3):458–62.

Pinggera G-M, Lirk P, Bodogri F, Herwig R, Steckel-Berger G, Bartsch G, Rieder J. Urinary acetonitrile concentrations correlate with recent smoking behaviour. *BJU International* 2005;95(3):306–9.

Piperi C, Pouli AE, Katerelos NA, Hatzinikolaou DG, Stavridou A, Psallidopoulos MC. Study of the mechanisms of cigarette smoke gas phase cytotoxicity. *Anticancer Research* 2003;23(3A):2185–90.

Pittilo RM, Bull HA, Gulati S, Rowles PM, Blow CM, Machin SJ, Woolf N. Nicotine and cigarette smoking: effects on the ultrastructure of aortic endothelium. *International Journal of Experimental Pathology* 1990; 71(4):573–86.

Pittilo RM, Mackie IJ, Rowles PM, Machin SJ, Woolf N. Effects of cigarette smoking on the ultrastructure of rat thoracic aorta and its ability to produce prostacyclin. *Thrombosis and Haemostasis* 1982;48(2):173–6.

Pluth JM, Ramsey MJ, Tucker JD. Role of maternal exposures and newborn genotypes on newborn chromosome aberration frequencies. *Mutation Research* 2000;465(1–2):101–11.

Polzin GM, Kosa-Maines RE, Ashley DL, Watson CH. Analysis of volatile organic compounds in mainstream cigarette smoke. *Environmental Science & Technology* 2007;41(4):1297–1302.

Polzin GM, Zhang L, Hearn BA, Tavakoli AD, Vaughan C, Ding YS, Ashley DL, Watson CH. Effect of charcoal-containing cigarette filters on gas phase volatile organic compounds in mainstream cigarette smoke. *Tobacco Control* 2008;17(Suppl 1):i10–i16.

Potts RJ, Newbury CJ, Smith G, Notarianni LJ, Jefferies TM. Sperm chromatin damage associated with male smoking. *Mutation Research* 1999;423(1–2):103–11.

Pouli AE, Hatzinikolaou DG, Piperi C, Stavridou A, Psallidopoulos MC, Stavrides JC. The cytotoxic effect of volatile organic compounds of the gas phase of cigarette smoke on lung epithelial cells. *Free Radical Biology & Medicine* 2003;34(3):345–55.

Poulsen HE. Oxidative DNA modifications. *Experimental and Toxicologic Pathology* 2005;57(Suppl 1):161–9.

Prignot J. Quantification and chemical markers of tobacco-exposure. *European Journal of Respiratory Disease* 1987;70(1):1–7.

Prokopczyk B, Hoffmann D, Bologna M, Cunningham AJ, Trushin N, Akerkar S, Boyiri T, Amin S, Desai D, Colosimo S, et al. Identification of tobacco-derived compounds in human pancreatic juice. *Chemical Research in Toxicology* 2002;15(5):677–85.

Putnam KP, Bombick DW, Doolittle DJ. Evaluation of eight in vitro assays for assessing the cytotoxicity of cigarette smoke condensate. *Toxicology in Vitro* 2002; 16(5):599–607.

R.J. Reynolds. Menthol, November 25, 1981; <http://tobaccodocuments.org/product_design/504331475–1477.html>; accessed: May 24, 2005.

Randerath E, Avitts TA, Reddy MV, Miller RH, Everson RB, Randerath K. Comparative ^{32}P-analysis of cigarette smoke-induced DNA damage in human tissues and mouse skin. *Cancer Research* 1986;46(11):5869–77.

Randerath E, Mittal D, Randerath K. Tissue distribution of covalent DNA damage in mice treated dermally with cigarette 'tar': preference for lung and heart DNA. *Carcinogenesis* 1988;9(1):75–80.

Rappaport BZ, Hoffman MM. Urticaria due to aliphatic aldehydes. *JAMA: The Journal of the American Medical Association* 1941;116(24):2656–9.

Razani-Boroujerdi S, Sopori ML. Early manifestations of NNK-induced lung cancer: role of lung immunity in tumor susceptibility. *American Journal of Respiratory Cell and Molecular Biology* 2007;36(1):13–19.

Reddy MV, Randerath K. A comparison of DNA adduct formation in white blood cells and internal organs of mice exposed to benzo[a]pyrene, dibenzo[c,g]carbazole, safrole and cigarette smoke condensate. *Mutation Research* 1990;241(1):37–48.

Resnik FE, Houck WG, Geiszler WA, Wickham JE. Factors affecting static burning rate. *Tobacco Science* 1977; 21:103–7.

Reznik G, Marquard G. Effect of cigarette smoke inhalation during pregnancy in Sprague-Dawley rats. *Journal of Environmental Pathology and Toxicology* 1980; 4(5–6):141–52.

Rhoades CB Jr, White RT Jr. Mainstream smoke collection by electrostatic precipitation for acid dissolution in a microwave digestion system prior to trace metal determination. *Journal of AOAC International* 1997; 80(6):1320–31.

Rickert W. Today's cigarettes: steps towards reducing the health impact. In: Ferrence R, Slade J, Room R, Pope M, editors. *Nicotine and Public Health*. Washington: American Public Health Association, 2000:135–58.

Rickert WS, Collishaw NE, Bray DF, Robinson JC. Estimates of maximum or average cigarette tar, nicotine, and carbon monoxide yields can be obtained from yields under standard conditions. *Preventive Medicine* 1986;15(1):82–91.

Rickert WS, Kaiserman MJ. Levels of lead, cadmium, and mercury in Canadian cigarette tobacco as indicators of environmental change: results of a 21-year study (1968–1988). *Environmental Science & Technology* 1994;28(5):924–7.

Rickert WS, Robinson JC, Bray DF, Rogers B, Collishaw NE. Characterization of tobacco products: a comparative study of the tar, nicotine, and carbon monoxide yields of cigars, manufactured cigarettes, and cigarettes made from fine-cut tobacco. *Preventive Medicine* 1985;14(2):226–33.

Rickert WS, Robinson JC, Collishaw N. Yields of tar, nicotine, and carbon monoxide in the sidestream smoke from 15 brands of Canadian cigarettes. *American Journal of Public Health* 1984;74(3):228–31.

Rickert WS, Robinson JC, Collishaw NE. A study of the growth and decay of cigarette smoke NOx in ambient air under controlled conditions. *Environment International* 1987;13(6):399–408.

Rickert WS, Robinson JC, Collishaw NE, Bray DF. Estimating the hazards of "less hazardous" cigarettes. III: a study of the effect of various smoking conditions on yields of hydrogen cyanide and cigarette tar. *Journal of Toxicology and Environmental Health* 1983;12(1): 39–54.

Rickert WS, Trivedi AH, Momin RA, Wright WG, Lauterbach JH. Effect of smoking conditions and methods of collection on the mutagenicity and cytotoxicity of cigarette mainstream smoke. *Toxicological Sciences* 2007;96(2):285–93.

Ritter D, Knebel JW, Aufderheide M. Comparative assessment of toxicities of mainstream smoke from commercial cigarettes. *Inhalation Toxicology* 2004;16(10): 691–700.

Riveles K, Roza R, Talbot P. Phenols, quinolines, indoles, benzene, and 2-cyclopenten-1-ones are oviductal toxicants in cigarette smoke. *Toxicological Sciences* 2005; 86(1):141–51.

Robbins CS, Dawe DE, Goncharova SI, Pouladi MA, Drannik AG, Swirski FK, Cox G, Stämpfli MR. Cigarette smoke decreases pulmonary dendritic cells and impacts antiviral immune responsiveness. *American Journal of Respiratory Cell and Molecular Biology* 2004;30(2):202–11.

Rodgman A, Perfetti TA. The composition of cigarette smoke: a catalogue of the polycyclic aromatic hydrocarbons. *Beiträge zur Tabakforschung International* 2006;22(1):13–69.

Rodgman A, Perfetti TA. *The Chemical Components of Tobacco and Tobacco Smoke*. Boca Raton (FL): CRC Press, Taylor & Francis Group, 2009.

Rodin SN, Rodin AS. Origins and selection of p53 mutations in lung carcinogenesis. *Seminars in Cancer Biology* 2005;15(2):103–12.

Roemer E, Stabbert R, Rustemeier K, Veltel DJ, Meisgen TJ, Reininghaus W, Carchman RA, Gaworski CL, Podraza KF. Chemical composition, cytotoxicity and mutagenicity of smoke from US commercial and reference cigarettes smoked under two sets of machine smoking conditions. *Toxicology* 2004;15;195(1):31–52.

Romano G, Sgambato A, Boninsegna A, Flamini G, Cerigliano G, Yang Q, La Gioia V, Signorelli C, Ferro A, Capelli G, et al. Evaluation of polycyclic aromatic hydrocarbon-DNA adducts in exfoliated oral cells by an immunohistochemical assay. *Cancer Epidemiology, Biomarkers & Prevention* 1999;8(1):91–6.

Romanski B, Broda S. The immunological response to tobacco antigens in the smoker. I: specific precipitins against tobacco antigens in the serum of healthy cigarette smokers. *Allergologia et Immunophathologia* 1977;5(6):659–62.

Ronco AM, Arguello G, Munoz L, Gras N, Llanos M. Metals content in placentas from moderate cigarette consumers: correlation with newborn birth weight. *Biometals* 2005a;18(3):233–41.

Ronco AM, Arguello G, Suazo M, Llanos MN. Increased levels of metallothionein in placenta of smokers. *Toxicology* 2005b;208(1):133–9.

Rühl C, Adams JD, Hoffmann D. Chemical studies on tobacco smoke. LXVI: comparative assessment of volatile and tobacco-specific N-nitrosamines in the smoke of selected cigarettes from the U.S.A., West Germany and France. *Journal of Analytical Toxicology* 1980; 4(5):255–9.

Sabbioni G, Beyerbach A. Determination of hemoglobin adducts of arylamines in humans. *Journal of Chromatography B: Biomedical Sciences and Applications* 1995;667(1):75–83.

Sakuma H, Kusana M, Munakata S, Ohsumi T, Sugawara S. The distribution of cigarette smoke components between mainstream and sidestream smoke. I: acidic components. *Beiträge zur Tabakforschung International* 1983;12(2):63–71.

Sakuma H, Kusama M, Yamaguchi K, Sugawara S. The distribution of cigarette smoke components between mainstream and sidestream smoke. III: middle and higher boiling compounds. *Beiträge zur Tabakforschung International* 1984;12(5):251–8.

Saleh RA, Agarwal A, Sharma RK, Nelson DR, Thomas AJ Jr. Effect of cigarette smoking on levels of seminal oxidative stress in infertile men: a prospective study. *Fertility and Sterility* 2002;78(3):491–9.

Sanchez-Cespedes M, Ahrendt SA, Piantadosi S, Rosell R, Monzo M, Wu L, Westra WH, Yang SC, Jen J, Sidransky D. Chromosomal alterations in lung adenocarcinoma from smokers and nonsmokers. *Cancer Research* 2001; 61(4):1309–13.

Şardaş S, Walker D, Akyol D, Karakaya AE. Assessment of smoking-induced DNA damage in lymphocytes of smoking mothers of newborn infants using the alkaline single-cell gel electrophoresis technique. *Mutation Research* 1995;335(3):213–7.

Schmeltz I, Hoffmann D. Nitrogen-containing compounds in tobacco and tobacco smoke. *Chemical Reviews* 1977;77(3):295–311.

Schneider G, Krivan V. Multi-element analysis of tobacco and smoke condensate by instrumental neutron activation analysis and atomic absorption spectrometry. *International Journal of Environmental Analytical Chemistry* 1993;53(2):87–100.

Scholl TO, Hediger ML, Schall JI, Khoo C-S, Fischer RL. Dietary and serum folate: their influence on the outcome of pregnancy. *American Journal of Clinical Nutrition* 1996;63(4):520–5.

Schur MO, Rickards JC. The design of low yield cigarettes. *Tobacco Science* 1960;4:69–77.

Schwartz RS, Hecking LT. Determination of geographic origin of agricultural products by multivariate analysis of trace element composition. *Journal of Analytical Atomic Spectrometry* 1991;6(8):637–42.

Selgrade MJK, Cooper KD, Devlin RB, van Loveren H, Biagini RE, Luster MI. Immunotoxicity—bridging the gap between animal research and human health effects. *Fundamental and Applied Toxicology* 1995;24(1): 13–21.

Seller MJ, Bnait KS. Effects of tobacco smoke inhalation on the developing mouse embryo and fetus. *Reproductive Toxicology* 1995;9(5):449–59.

Seller MJ, Bnait KS, Cairns NJ. Effects of maternal tobacco smoke inhalation on early embryonic growth. In: Poswillo D, Alberman E, editors. *Effects of Smoking on the Fetus, Neonate, and Child*. New York: Oxford University Press, 1992:45–59.

Shaikh AN, Negi BS, Sadasivan S. Characterization of Indian cigarette tobacco and its smoke aerosol by nuclear and allied techniques. *Journal of Radioanalytical and Nuclear Chemistry* 2002;253(2):231–4.

Shapiro SD, Goldstein NM, Houghton AM, Kobayashi DK, Kelley D, Belaaouaj A. Neutrophil elastase contributes to cigarette smoke-induced emphysema in mice. *American Journal of Pathology* 2003;163(6):2329–35.

Shen H-M, Chia S-E, Ni Z-Y, New A-L, Lee B-L, Ong C-N. Detection of oxidative DNA damage in human sperm and the association with cigarette smoking. *Reproductive Toxicology* 1997:11(5):675–80.

Shephard RJ. Cigarette smoking and reactions to air pollutants. *Canadian Medical Association Journal* 1978; 118(4):379–81, 383, 392.

Shiku H. Importance of CD4+ helper T-cells in antitumor immunity. *International Journal of Hematology* 2003;77(5):435–8.

Sipowicz MA, Amin S, Desai D, Kasprzak KS, Anderson LM. Oxidative DNA damage in tissues of pregnant female mice and fetuses caused by the tobacco-specific nitrosamine, 4-(methylnitrosamino)-1-(3-pyridyl)-1-butanone (NNK). *Cancer Letters* 1997:117(1):87–91.

Sithisarankul P, Vineis P, Kang D, Rothman N, Caporaso N, Strickland P. Association of 1-hydroxypyrene-glucuronide in human urine with cigarette smoking and broiled or roasted meat consumption. *Biomarkers* 1997;2(4):217–21.

Skipper PL, Peng X, Soohoo CK, Tannenbaum SR. Protein adducts as biomarkers of human carcinogen exposure. *Drug Metabolism Reviews* 1994;26(1–2):111–24.

Skog KI, Johansson MAE, Jägerstad MI. Carcinogenic heterocyclic amines in model systems and cooked foods: a review on formation, occurrence and intake. *Food and Chemical Toxicology* 1998;36(9–10):879–96.

Skwarzec B, Ulatowski J, Struminska DI, Boryło A. Inhalation of ^{210}Po and ^{210}Pb from cigarette smoking in Poland. *Journal of Environmental Radioactivity* 2001; 57(3):221–30.

Smith LE, Denissenko MF, Bennett WP, Li H, Amin S, Tang M-S, Pfeifer GP. Targeting of lung cancer mutational hotspots by polycyclic aromatic hydrocarbons. *Journal of the National Cancer Institute* 2000;92(10):803–11.

Sonnenfeld G, Griffith RB, Hudgens RW. The effect of smoke generation and manipulation variables on the cytotoxicity of mainstream and cigarette sidestream smoke to monolayer cultures of L-929 cells. *Archives of Toxicology* 1985;58(2):120–2.

Sopori ML, Cherian S, Chilukuri R, Shopp GM. Cigarette smoke causes inhibition of the immune response to intratracheally administered antigens. *Toxicology and Applied Pharmacology* 1989;97(3):489–99.

Sopori ML, Gairola CC, DeLucia AJ, Bryant LR, Cherian S. Immune responsiveness of monkeys exposed chronically to cigarette smoke. *Clinical Immunology and Immunopathology* 1985;36(3):338–44.

Spears AW. Selective filtration of volatile phenolic compounds from cigarette smoke. *Tobacco Science* 1963; 7:76–80.

Spiegelhalder B, Bartsch H. Tobacco-specific nitrosamines. *European Journal of Cancer Prevention* 1996; 5(Suppl 1):33–8.

Spincer D, Chard BC. The determination of formaldehyde in cigarette smoke. *Beiträge zur Tabakforschung International* 1971;6(2):74–8.

Stabbert R, Schäfer K-H, Biefel C, Rustemeier K. Analysis of aromatic amines in cigarette smoke. *Rapid Communications in Mass Spectrometry* 2003a;17(18):2125–32.

Stabbert R, Voncken P, Rustemeier K, Haussmann H-J, Roemer E, Schaffernicht H, Patskan G. Toxicological evaluation of an electrically heated cigarette. Part 2: chemical composition of mainstream smoke. *Journal of Applied Toxicology* 2003b;23(5):329–39.

Stanfill SB, Ashley DL. Solid phase microextraction of alkenylbenzenes and other flavor-related compounds from tobacco for analysis by selected ion monitoring gas chromatography–mass spectrometry. *Journal of Chromatography A* 1999;858(1):79–89.

Stanfill SB, Ashley DL. Quantitation of flavor-related alkenylbenzenes in tobacco smoke particulate by selected ion monitoring gas chromatography-mass spectrometry. *Journal of Agricultural and Food Chemistry* 2000; 48(4):1298–306.

Steegers-Theunissen RP, Van Iersel CA, Peer PG, Nelen WL, Steegers EA. Hyperhomocysteinemia, pregnancy complications, and the timing of investigation. *Obstetrics and Gynecology* 2004;104(2):336–43.

Steele RH, Payne VM, Fulp CW, Rees DC, Lee CK, Doolittle DJ. A comparison of the mutagenicity of the mainstream cigarette smoke condensates from a representative sample of the U.S. cigarette market with a Kentucky reference cigarette (K1R4F). *Mutation Research* 1995;342(3–4):179–90.

Stephens WE, Calder A, Newton J. Source and health implications of high toxic metal concentrations in illicit tobacco products. *Environmental Science & Technology* 2005;39(2):479–88.

Stewart CA, Lawrence BM. Project XGT: effects of levulinic acid, tobacco essence and nicotine salts on smoke pH. Project No. 0113. 1988. RJ Reynolds Collection. Bates No.507869978/9986. <http://legacy.library.ucsf.edu/tid/ggk14d00>.

Stober W. Generation, size distribution and composition of tobacco smoke aerosols. *Recent Advances in Tobacco Science: Formation, Analysis, and Composition of Tobacco Smoke* 1982;8:3–41.

Stratton K, Shetty P, Wallace R, Bonderant S, editors. *Clearing the Smoke: Assessing the Science Base for Tobacco Harm Reduction*. Washington: National Academy Press, 2001.

Subramaniam S, Bummer P, Gairola CG. Biochemical and biophysical characterization of pulmonary surfactant in rats exposed chronically to cigarette smoke. *Fundamental and Applied Toxicology* 1995;27(1):63–9.

Sugimura T. Overview of carcinogenic heterocyclic amines. *Mutation Research* 1997;376(1–2):211–9.

Sugimura T, Nagao M, Kawachi T, Honda M, Yahagi T, Seino Y, Sato S, Matsukura N, Matsushima T, Shirai A, et al. Mutagen-carcinogens in food, with special reference to highly mutagenic pyrolytic products in broiled foods. In: Hiatt HH, Watson JD, Winsten JA, editors. *Origins of Human Cancer.* Book C, Human Risk Assessment, Section 17. New York: Cold Spring Harbor Press, 1977:1561–77.

Suzuki T, Shishido S, Urushiyama K. Mercury in cigarettes. *Tohoku Journal of Experimental Medicine* 1976; 119(4):353–6.

Sweeney CT, Kozlowski LT, Parsa P. Effect of filter vent blocking on carbon monoxide exposure from selected lower tar cigarette brands. *Pharmacology, Biochemistry, and Behavior* 1999;63(1):167–73.

Takubo Y, Guerassimov A, Ghezzo H, Triantafillopoulos A, Bates JHT, Hoidal JR, Cosio MG. α_1-antitrypsin determines the pattern of emphysema and function in tobacco smoke–exposed mice: parallels with human disease. *American Journal of Respiratory and Critical Care Medicine* 2002;166(12 Pt 1):1596–603.

Talaska G, Schamer M, Skipper P, Tannenbaum S, Caporaso N, Unruh L, Kadlubar FF, Bartsch H, Malaveille C, Vineis P. Detection of carcinogen-DNA adducts in exfoliated urothelial cells of cigarette smokers: association with smoking, hemoglobin adducts, and urinary mutagenicity. *Cancer Epidemiology, Biomarkers & Prevention* 1991;1(1):61–6.

Talbot P, DiCarlantonio G, Knoll M, Gomez C. Identification of cigarette smoke components that alter functioning of hamster (*Mesocricetus auratus*) oviducts in vitro. *Biology of Reproduction* 1998;58(4):1047–53.

Tani S, Dimayuga PC, Anazawa T, Chyu K-Y, Li H, Shah PK, Cercek B. Aberrant antibody responses to oxidized LDL and increased intimal thickening in apoE–/– mice exposed to cigarette smoke. *Atherosclerosis* 2004;175(1):7–14.

Teague CE Jr. Implications and activities arising from correlation of smoke pH with nicotine impact, other smoke qualities, and cigarette sales. 1974. RJ Reynolds Collection. Bates No. 511223463/3484. <http://legacy.library.ucsf.edu/tid/rte53d00>.

Telišman S, Jurasović J, Pizent A, Cvitković P. Cadmium in the blood and seminal fluid of nonoccupationally exposed adult male subjects with regard to smoking habits. *International Archives of Occupational and Environmental Health* 1997;70(4):243–8.

Terpstra PM, Teredesai A, Vanscheeuwijck PM, Verbeeck J, Schepers G, Radtke F, Kuhl P, Gomm W, Anskeit E, Patskan G. Toxicological evaluation of an electrically heated cigarette. Part 4: subchronic inhalation toxicology. *Journal of Applied Toxicology* 2003;23(5):349–62.

Tewes FJ, Meisgen TJ, Veltel DJ, Roemer E, Patskan G. Toxicological evaluation of an electrically heated cigarette. Part 3: genotoxicity and cytotoxicity of mainstream smoke. *Journal of Applied Toxicology* 2003;23(5): 341–8.

Thayer PS. Inhibition of cell culture. In: Gori GB, editor. *Toward Less Hazardous Cigarettes. The First Set of Experimental Cigarettes.* Report No. 1. Washington: U.S. Department of Health, Education, and Welfare, Public Health Service, National Institutes of Health, National Cancer Institute, Smoking and Health Program, 1976a:107–8. DHEW Publication No. (NIH) 76-905.

Thayer PS. Inhibition of macrophages. In: Gori GB editor. *Toward Less Hazardous Cigarettes. The First Set of Experimental Cigarettes.* Report No. 1. Washington: U.S. Department of Health, Education, and Welfare, Public Health Service, National Institutes of Health, National Cancer Institute, Smoking and Health Program, 1976b:104–6. DHEW Publication No. (NIH) 76-905.

Thayer PS, Kensler CJ. Cigarette smoke: charcoal filters reduce components that inhibit growth of cultured human cells. *Science* 1964;146(3644):642–4.

Theophilus EH, Bombick BR, Meckley DR, Higuchi MA, Borgerding MF, Morton MJ, Mosberg AT, Swauger JE. Toxicological evaluation of propane expanded tobacco. *Food and Chemical Toxicology* 2003a;41(12):1771–80.

Theophilus EH, Pence DH, Meckley DR, Higuchi MA, Bombick BR, Borgerding MF, Ayres PH, Swauger JE. Toxicological evaluation of expanded shredded tobacco stems. *Food and Chemical Toxicology* 2004;42(4): 631–9.

Theophilus EH, Poindexter DB, Meckley DR, Bombick BR, Borgerding MF, Higuchi MA, Ayres PH, Morton MJ, Mosberg AT, Swauger JE. Toxicological evaluation of dry ice expanded tobacco. *Toxicology Letters* 2003b;145(2):107–19.

Thier R, Lewalter J, Selinski S, Bolt HM. Re-evaluation of the effect of smoking on the methylation of *N*-terminal valine in haemoglobin. *Archives of Toxicology* 2001;75(5):270–3.

Thomas WR, Holt PG, Keast D. Antibody production in mice chronically exposed to fresh cigarette smoke. *Experientia* 1974;30(12):1469–70.

Tomkins BA, Jenkins RA, Griest WH, Reagan RR, Holladay SK. Liquid chromatography determination of benzo[*a*]pyrene in total particulate matter of cigarette smoke.

Journal of the Association of Official Analytical Chemists 1985;68(5):935–40.

Torikai K, Uwano Y, Nakamori T, Tarora W, Takahashi H. Study on tobacco components involved in the pyrolytic generation of selected smoke constituents. *Food Chemistry and Toxicology* 2005;43(4):559–68.

Torikai K, Yoshida S, Takahashi H. Effects of temperature, atmosphere and pH on the generation of smoke compounds during tobacco pyrolysis. *Food and Chemical Toxicology* 2004;42(9):1409–17.

Torjussen W, Zachariasen H, Andersen I. Cigarette smoking and nickel exposure. *Journal of Environmental Monitoring* 2003;5(2):198–201.

Torrence KM, McDaniel RL, Self DA, Chang MJ. Slurry sampling for the determination of arsenic, cadmium, and lead in mainstream cigarette smoke condensate by graphite furnace–atomic absorption spectrometry and inductively coupled plasma–mass spectrometry. *Analytical and Bioanalytical Chemistry* 2002;372 (5–6):723–31.

Touey GP, Mumpower RC. Measurement of the combustion-zone temperature of cigarettes. *Tobacco Science* 1957;1:33–7.

Tretyakova N, Matter B, Jones R, Shallop A. Formation of benzo[*a*]pyrene diol epoxide–DNA adducts at specific guanines within *K-ras* and *p53* gene sequences: stable isotope-labeling mass spectrometry approach. *Biochemistry* 2002;41(30):9535–44.

Tricker AR, Ditrich C, Preussmann R. *N*-nitroso compounds in cigarette tobacco and their occurrence in mainstream tobacco smoke. *Carcinogenesis* 1991; 12(2):257–61.

Tso TC. Ch. 21–Organic metabolism–alkaloids. In: *Production and Biochemistry of Tobacco Plant*. Beltsville (MD): Ideals, Inc., 1990.

Tso TC, Chaplin JF, Adams JD, Hoffmann D. Simple correlation and multiple regression among leaf and smoke characteristics of burley tobaccos. *Beiträge zur Tabakforschung International* 1982;11(3):141–50.

Tso TC, Sims JL, Johnson DE. Some agronomic factors affecting N-dimethylnitrosamine content in cigarette smoke. *Beiträge zur Tabakforschung International* 1975;8(1):34–8.

Tsuji T, Aoshiba K, Nagai A. Cigarette smoke induces senescence in alveolar epithelial cells. *American Journal of Respiratory Cell and Molecular Biology* 2004; 31(6):643–9.

Tuomisto J, Kolonen S, Sorsa M, Einistö P. No difference between urinary mutagenicity in smokers of low-tar and medium-tar cigarettes: a double-blind cross-over study. *Archives of Toxicology* 1986;Suppl 9:115–9.

Tuttle AM, Stämpfli M, Foster WG. Cigarette smoke causes follicle loss in mice ovaries at concentrations representative of human exposure. *Human Reproduction* 2009;24(6):1452–9.

U.S. Department of Health and Human Services. *10th Report on Carcinogens*. Research Triangle Park (NC): U.S. Department of Health and Human Services, Public Health Service, National Toxicology Program, 2002.

U.S. Department of Health and Human Services. *The Health Consequences of Smoking: A Report of the Surgeon General*. Atlanta: U.S. Department of Health and Human Services, Centers for Disease Control and Prevention, National Center for Chronic Disease Prevention and Health Promotion, Office on Smoking and Health, 2004.

U.S. Environmental Protection Agency. *Ambient Water Quality Criteria for Polynuclear Aromatic Hydrocarbons*. Washington: U.S. Environmental Protection Agency, Office of Water Regulations and Standards, 1980. Publication No. EPA 440/5-80-069.

U.S. Environmental Protection Agency. *Quality Criteria for Water 1986*. Washington: U.S. Environmental Protection Agency, Office of Water Regulations and Standards, 1986. Publication No. EPA 440/5-86-001.

van Doorn R, Leujdekkers CM, Bos RP, Brouns RME, Henderson PT. Detection of human exposure to electrophilic compounds by assay of thioether detoxification products in urine. *Annals of Occupational Hygiene* 1981;24(1):77–92.

van Jaarsveld H, Kuyl JM, Alberts DW. Exposure of rats to low concentration of cigarette smoke increases myocardial sensitivity to ischaemia/reperfusion. *Basic Research in Cardiology* 1992;87(4):393–9.

Van Rooij JGM, Veeger MMS, Bodelier-Bade MM, Scheepers PTJ, Jongeneelen FJ. Smoking and dietary intake of polcyclic aromatic hydrocarbons as sources of interindividual variability in the baseline excretion of 1-hydroxypyrene in urine. *International Archives of Occupational and Environmental Health* 1994;66(1): 55–65.

Van Schooten FJ, Hirvonen A, Maas LM, De Mol BA, Kleinjans JCS, Bell DA, Durrer JD. Putative susceptibility markers of coronary artery disease: association between *VDR* genotype, smoking, and aromatic DNA adduct levels in human right atrial tissue. *FASEB Journal* 1998;12(13):1409–17.

Wang H. Differential responses of *Paramecium aurelia* to cigarette smoke. *Nature* 1963;197(4871):946–8.

Wanner A. A review of the effects of cigarette smoke on airway mucosal function. *European Journal of Respiratory Disease* 1985;66(Suppl 139):49–53.

Ward E, Carpenter A, Markowitz S, Roberts D, Halperin W. Excess number of bladder cancers in workers exposed to ortho-toluidine and aniline. *Journal of the National Cancer Institute* 1991;83(7):501–6.

Watson ID. Rapid analysis of nicotine and cotinine in the urine of smokers by isocratic high-performance liquid chromatography. *Journal of Chromatography B* 1977;143(2):203–6.

Watson CH, Trommel JS, Ashley DL. Solid-phase microextraction-based approach to determine free-base nicotine in trapped mainstream cigarette smoke total particulate matter. *Journal of Agricultural and Food Chemistry* 2004;52(24):7240–5.

Wayne GF, Connolly GN. Application, function, and effects of menthol in cigarettes: a survey of tobacco industry documents. *Nicotine & Tobacco Research* 2004;6 (Suppl 1):S43–S54.

Wayne GF, Connolly GN, Henningfield JE, Farone WA. Tobacco industry research and efforts to manipulate particle size: implications for product regulation. *Nicotine & Tobacco Research* 2008;10(4):613–25.

Weiss W, Weiss WA. Effect of tobacco smoke solutions on Paramecium. *Archives of Environmental Health* 1964; 9:500–4.

Wennmalm Å, Benthin G, Granström EF, Persson L, Petersson A-S, Winell S. Relation between tobacco use and urinary excretion of thromboxane A_2 and prostacyclin metabolites in young men. *Circulation* 1991; 83(5):1698–704.

Williamson JT, Graham JF, Allman DR. The modification of cigarette smoke by filter tips. *Beiträge zur Tabakforschung International* 1965;3(3):233–42.

Wistuba II, Lam S, Behrens C, Virmani AK, Fong KM, LeRiche J, Samet JM, Srivastava S, Minna JD, Gazdar AF. Molecular damage in the bronchial epithelium of current and former smokers. *Journal of the National Cancer Institute* 1997;89(18):1366–73.

Witschi H. A/J mouse as a model for lung tumorigenesis caused by tobacco smoke: strengths and weaknesses. *Experimental Lung Research* 2005;31(1):3–18.

Witschi H, Espiritu I, Dance ST, Miller MS. A mouse lung tumor model of tobacco smoke carcinogenesis. *Toxicological Sciences* 2002;68(2):322–30.

Witschi H, Espiritu I, Maronpot RR, Pinkerton KE, Jones AD. The carcinogenic potential of the gas phase of environmental tobacco smoke. *Carcinogenesis* 1997a; 18(11):2035–42.

Witschi H, Espiritu I, Peake JL, Wu K, Maronpot RR, Pinkerton KE. The carcinogenicity of environmental tobacco smoke. *Carcinogenesis* 1997b;18(3):575–86.

Witschi H, Espiritu I, Uyeminami D, Suffia M, Pinkerton KE. Lung tumor response in strain A mice exposed to tobacco smoke: some dose-effect relationships. *Inhalation Toxicology* 2004;16(1):27–32.

Woodman G, Newman SP, Pavia D, Clarke SW. Inhaled smoke volume, puffing indices and carbon monoxide uptake in asymptomatic cigarette smokers. *Clinical Science (London)* 1986;71(4):421–7.

World Tobacco Staff. Tobacco's essential partner. *World Tobacco*, March 2000;174:21–2.

Wu W, Zhang L, Jain RB, Ashley DL, Watson CH. Determination of carcinogenic tobacco-specific nitrosamines in mainstream smoke from U.S.-brand and non-U.S.-brand cigarettes from 14 countries. *Nicotine & Tobacco Research* 2005;7(3):443–51.

Wu X, Lippmann SM, Lee JJ, Zhu Y, Wei QV, Thomas M, Hong WK, Spitz MR. Chromosome instability in lymphocytes: a potential indicator of predisposition to oral premalignant lesions. *Cancer Research* 2002;62(10):2813–8.

Wynder EL, Goodman DA, Hoffmann D. Ciliatoxic components in cigarette smoke. 3: in vitro comparison of different smoke components. *Cancer* 1965;18(12):1652–8.

Wynder EL, Graham EA, Croninger AB. Experimental production of carcinoma with cigarette tar. *Cancer Research* 1953;13(12):855–64.

Wynder EL, Hoffmann D. A study of tobacco carcinogenesis. VIII: the role of the acidic fractions as promoters. *Cancer* 1961;14(6):1306–15.

Wynder EL, Hoffmann D. *Tobacco and Tobacco Smoke: Studies in Experimental Carcinogenesis.* New York: Academic Press, 1967.

Wynder EL, Kopf P, Ziegler H. A study of tobacco carcinogenesis. II: dose-response studies. *Cancer* 1957; 10(6):1193–200.

Xiao T, Guha J, Boyle D, Liu C-Q, Chen J. Environmental concerns related to high thallium levels in soils and thallium uptake by plants in southwest Guizhou, China. *Science of the Total Environment* 2004a;318 (1–3):223–44.

Xiao T, Guha J, Boyle D, Liu C-Q, Zheng B, Wilson GC, Rouleau A, Chen J. Naturally occurring thallium: a hidden geoenvironmental health hazard? *Environment International* 2004b;30(4):501–7.

Xu L, Cai B-Q, Zhu Y-J. Pathogenesis of cigarette smoke-induced chronic obstructive pulmonary disease and therapeutic effects of glucocorticoids and N-acetylcysteine in rats. *Chinese Medical Journal* 2004; 117(11):1611–9.

Yamasaki E, Ames BN. Concentration of mutagens from urine by adsorption with the nonpolar resin XAD-2: cigarette smokers have mutagenic urine. *Proceedings of the National Academy of Sciences of the United States of America* 1977;74(8):3555–9.

Yang IY, Chan G, Miller H, Huang Y, Torres MC, Johnson F, Moriya M. Mutagenesis by acrolein-derived propano-deoxyguanosine adducts in human cells. *Biochemistry* 2002;41(46):13826–32.

Yauk CL, Berndt ML, Williams A, Rowan-Carroll A, Douglas GR, Stampfli MR. Mainstream tobacco smoke causes paternal germ-line DNA mutations. *Cancer Research* 2007;67(11):5103–6.

Yoon J-H, Smith LE, Feng Z, Tang M-S, Lee C-S, Pfeifer GP. Methylated CpG dinucleotides are the preferential targets for G-to-T transversion mutations induced by benzo[*a*]pyrene diol epoxide in mammalian cells: similarities with the p53 mutation spectrum in smoking-associated lung cancers. *Cancer Research* 2001; 61(19):7110–7.

Zacny JP, Stitzer ML. Human smoking patterns. In: *The FTC Cigarette Test Method for Determining Tar, Nicotine, and Carbon Monoxide Yields of U.S. Cigarettes.* Report of the NCI Expert Committee Panel. Smoking and Tobacco Control Monograph No. 7. Bethesda (MD): U.S. Department of Health and Human Services, Public Health Service, National Institutes of Health, National Cancer Institute, 1996:151–60. NIH Publication No. 96-4028.

Zacny JP, Stitzer ML, Brown FJ, Yingling JE, Griffiths RR. Human cigarette smoking: effects of puff and inhalation parameters on smoke exposure. *Journal of Pharmacology and Experimental Therapeutics* 1987;240(2): 554–64.

Zacny JP, Stitzer ML, Yingling JE. Cigarette filter vent blocking: effects on smoking topography and carbon monoxide exposure. *Pharmacology, Biochemistry, and Behavior* 1986;25(6):1245–52.

Zaliznyak T, Bonala R, Attaluri S, Johnson F, de los Santos C. Solution structure of DNA containing α-OH-PdG: the mutagenic adduct produced by acrolein. *Nucleic Acids Research* 2009;37(7):2153–63.

Zhang S, Villalta PW, Wang M, Hecht SS. Detection and quantitation of acrolein-derived $1,N^2$-propanodeoxy-guanosine adducts in human lung by liquid chromatography-electrospray ionization-tandem mass spectrometry. *Chemical Research in Toxicology* 2007; 20(4):565–71.

Zhu Y, Spitz MR, Zheng Y-L, Hong WK, Wu X. BPDE-induced lymphocytic 3p21.3 aberrations may predict head and neck carcinoma risk. *Cancer* 2002;95(3): 563–8.

Chapter 4
Nicotine Addiction: Past and Present

Introduction

Nicotine addiction is the fundamental reason that individuals persist in using tobacco products, and this persistent tobacco use contributes to many diseases described in this report. The 1988 report, *The Health Consequences of Smoking: Nicotine Addiction: A Report of the Surgeon General* (U.S. Department of Health and Human Services [USDHHS] 1988, p. 9), describes the pharmacologic basis of tobacco addiction and arrives at three major conclusions:

1. Cigarettes and other forms of tobacco are addicting.

2. Nicotine is the drug in tobacco that causes addiction.

3. The pharmacologic and behavioral processes that determine tobacco addiction are similar to those that determine addiction to drugs such as heroin and cocaine.

Tobacco addiction remains a substantial problem in the United States and worldwide. Of those individuals who have ever tried smoking, about one-third become daily smokers (USDHHS 1994, p. 67). Of those smokers who try to quit, less than 5 percent are successful at any one time (Centers for Disease Control and Prevention [CDC] 2002, 2004). Although not all smokers become nicotine dependent, the prevalence of individuals diagnosed as nicotine dependent is higher than that for any other substance abuse disorder (Anthony et al. 1994; CDC 1995b;

Kandel et al. 1997). Any efforts to reduce tobacco-related disease must take into account the addiction potential of a tobacco product.

Since the 1988 Surgeon General's report was published, significant advances have been made in understanding the physiological effects of nicotine and the basis for addiction:

1. identifying specific genotypes and receptor subtypes that may contribute to and play an important role in nicotine addiction,

2. observing sensitivities and responses to nicotine in adolescents that might make them more susceptible to nicotine addiction than adults are and recognizing the different trajectories for the development of nicotine dependence,

3. developing a greater awareness of the important role of associative learning in addiction,

4. recognizing the strong associations between smoking and comorbid psychiatric disorders, and

5. achieving a better understanding of the relapse and recovery processes.

The goals of this chapter are to describe these advances and their implications and to discuss future directions.

Definition of Nicotine Addiction

The crux of understanding the pathophysiology of tobacco addiction and its measurement relies on the identification of critical characteristics and the definition of addiction. This area continues to evolve, and significant gaps in research are evident. There is no established consensus on criteria for diagnosing nicotine addiction. However, researchers have identified several symptoms as indicators of addiction. The 1988 Surgeon General's report lists the following general "criteria for drug dependence," including nicotine dependence (USDHHS 1988, p. 7):

Primary Criteria
- Highly controlled or compulsive use
- Psychoactive effects
- Drug-reinforced behavior

Additional Criteria
- Addictive behavior, often involves:
  - stereotypic patterns of use
  - use despite harmful effects
  - relapse following abstinence
  - recurrent drug cravings

- Dependence-producing drugs often produce:
  - tolerance
  - physical dependence
  - pleasant (euphoriant) effects

These criteria are consistent with those for a diagnosis of dependence provided in the *Diagnostic and Statistical Manual of Mental Disorders,* 4th ed. (*DSM-IV*) (American Psychiatric Association [APA] 2000) and the *International Classification of Diseases, Tenth Revision* (*ICD-10*) (Table 4.1) (World Health Organization [WHO] 1992). The diagnosis of dependence using these diagnostic systems depends on the person experiencing a specific number of these symptoms. The relevance of some of these symptoms to nicotine addiction may be questionable because the *DSM* criteria are used across different drugs of abuse. For example, one symptom of addiction is that a great deal of time is spent in activities necessary to obtain the substance or recover from its effect. This criterion may not be as relevant to the diagnosis of nicotine addiction compared with other abused substances. Another prominent instrument that researchers have used to determine the degree or severity of dependence in smokers is the Fagerström Tolerance Questionnaire (FTQ) (Fagerström 1978; Fagerström and Schneider 1989), and a later, modified version, the Fagerström Test for Nicotine Dependence (FTND) (Heatherton et al. 1991). The items on these scales, which describe the extent of nicotine exposure, the impaired control over use, and the urgency for use, are listed in Table 4.2. The first item, time to first cigarette after waking, is by itself a stronger predictor of relapse than is any other self-report measure of dependence (Baker et al. 2007). The 1988 Surgeon General's report describes the general characteristics and criteria for drug dependence, *DSM-IV* and *ICD-10* describe the criteria necessary for diagnosis of dependence, and the FTQ and FTND can be used to determine the degree of dependence. The core features across these diagnostic methods include (1) repeated and compulsive self-administration; (2) impaired control over use (e.g., repeated unsuccessful attempts to stop use or continued use despite known harmful consequences); (3) high motivation to seek the drug, because of cravings, regulation of affect (e.g., smoking to ease a depressed mood, for relaxation, or for stimulation), or other reasons associated with the psychoactive effects of the drug; (4) judgment of greater value from

Table 4.1   Criteria for substance (nicotine) dependence

DSM-IV	*ICD-10*
A maladaptive pattern of substance use, leading to clinically significant impairment or distress, as manifested by 3 or more of the following criteria, occurring at any time in the same 12-month period	
• Tolerance—need increased amounts of substance to achieve desired effect, or diminished effect with continued use of same amount	• Increased tolerance
• Withdrawal symptoms	• Physical withdrawal at times
• Substance often taken in larger amounts or over longer period than intended	• Strong desire to take drug
• Persistent desire or unsuccessful efforts to cut down or control substance use	• Difficulty controlling use
• Great deal of time spent in activities necessary to obtain substance, use substance, or recover from its effects	
• Important social, occupational, or recreational activities given up or reduced because of substance use	• Higher priority given to drug use than to other activities and obligations
• Substance use continued despite knowledge of having persistent or recurrent physical or psychological problem likely to have been caused or exacerbated by substance	• Persistent use despite harmful consequences

Source: Adapted from Royal College of Physicians of London 2000 with permission from Royal College of Physicians, © 2000.
Note: **DSM-IV** = *Diagnostic and Statistical Manual of Mental Disorders,* 4th ed.; **ICD-10** = *International Classification of Diseases, Tenth Revision.*

Table 4.2   Questions, answers, and scoring for Fagerström Test for Nicotine Dependence and Fagerström Tolerance Questionnaire

Questions	Answers	Points
Fagerström Test for Nicotine Dependence[a]		
How soon after you wake up do you smoke your first cigarette?	Within 5 minutes	3
	6–30 minutes	2
	31–60 minutes	1
	After 60 minutes	0
Do you find it difficult to refrain from smoking in places where it is forbidden (e.g., in church, at the library, in the cinema, etc.)?	Yes	1
	No	0
Which cigarette would you hate most to give up?	The first one in the morning	1
	All others	0
How many cigarettes/day do you smoke?	≤10	0
	11–20	1
	21–30	2
	≥31	3
Do you smoke more frequently during the first hours after waking up than during the rest of the day?	Yes	1
	No	0
Do you smoke if you are so ill that you are in bed most of the day?	Yes	1
	No	0
Fagerström Tolerance Questionnaire[b]		
How soon after you wake up do you smoke your first cigarette?	Within 30 minutes	1
	After 30 minutes	0
Do you find it difficult to refrain from smoking in places where it is forbidden (e.g., in church, at the library, in the cinema, etc.)?	Yes	1
	No	0
Which cigarette would you hate to give up?	The first one in the morning	1
	Any other	0
How many cigarettes/day do you smoke?	≤15	0
	16–25	1
	≥26	2
Do you smoke more during the morning than during the rest of the day?	Yes	1
	No	0
Do you smoke if you are so ill that you are in bed most of the day?	Yes	1
	No	0
What is the nicotine level of your usual brand of cigarette?	≤0.9 mg	0
	1.0–1.2 mg	1
	≥1.3 mg	2
Do you inhale?	Never	0
	Sometimes	1
	Always	2

Note: **mg** = milligrams.
[a]Data are from Heatherton et al. 1991.
[b]Data are from Fagerström and Schneider 1989.

use of the drug over other reinforcers or activities; and (5) manifestation of physical dependence, as evidenced by withdrawal or tolerance.

Despite acknowledgment of these core features, the current diagnostic criteria for nicotine addiction have certain limitations. Beginning in 2005, a group of scientists have worked to delineate the various issues surrounding the measurement of nicotine dependence. The results of this work were published in June 2009 (National Cancer Institute [NCI] 2009). These issues included the following:

1. whether nicotine addiction is categorical, dimensional, or emergent (changing over time) and, if emergent, whether different aspects of dependence are observed early or late in the process of dependence, for example, aspects more related to social, sensory, and associational learning versus a more physical dimension with a longer duration of drug use;

2. whether nicotine addiction is unidimensional or multidimensional and, if multidimensional, whether symptoms or dimensions warrant weighting or are additive;

3. whether a threshold of severity or a certain number or specific types of symptoms are needed for diagnosis of nicotine addiction;

4. whether motivations or cognitive processes for seeking a drug are important components of the addiction;

5. whether multiple profiles, patterns, and pathways of addiction exist; and

6. whether the quantity and frequency of use play a critical role in addiction.

Other current measures of nicotine addiction or tobacco dependence are shown in Table 4.3 that are beginning to consider and address some of the limitations of current definitions of addiction and that consider nicotine addiction to be comprised of more than one phenotype (expression of a trait on the basis of genetic and environmental influences). Developing valid measures of the various phenotypes of dependence is critical for research that (1) examines how these phenotypes are related to the trajectory and cessation of smoking behaviors and (2) determines whether these phenotypes are related to specific neurobiologic measures of addiction or to specific genes.

In this chapter, the terms "dependence" and "addiction" have been used interchangeably. For some disciplines, dependence has been primarily associated with physiological manifestations of repeated tobacco use, but compulsive drug seeking is typically at the core of both the technical term "dependence" and the more general term "addiction." Furthermore, the terms "nicotine dependence" and "tobacco dependence" are used interchangeably. Nicotine is the drug in tobacco that leads to compulsive drug seeking or addiction. However, several lines of epidemiologic and laboratory evidence presented in this chapter indicate that tobacco-delivered nicotine is substantially more addictive than are pure nicotine forms. Other tobacco constituents, delivery methods, and processes may play a critical supporting role.

Factors contributing to nicotine or tobacco addiction include the following:

1. the effects of the product itself, including the addictive constituents, their pharmacokinetics and pharmacodynamics, and the design of the product that delivers the addictive constituents (see Chapter 3, "Chemistry and Toxicology of Cigarette Smoke and Biomarkers of Exposure and Harm");

2. the response of the host, including genetic susceptibility and physiological response; and

3. the environmental setting that determines the availability of, accessibility to, and norms for use of the product.

Like the 1988 Surgeon General's report on nicotine addiction, this chapter focuses primarily on the effects of the product and the response of the host.

Table 4.3   Measures of nicotine addiction

Measures	Characteristics
Fagerström Tolerance Questionnaire (FTQ) (Fagerström 1978; Fagerström and Schneider 1989) Fagerström Test for Nicotine Dependence (FTND) (Heatherton et al. 1991)	Unidimensional and continuous scale that measures behavioral and physiological aspects of addiction (e.g., rate of smoking, morning smoking, and difficulty refraining from smoking) and was developed to measure physical dependence. Both FTQ and FTND show limited internal consistency (Pomerleau et al. 1990; Etter et al. 1999). FTND is a multidimensional scale (≤ 2 factors) summarized as single score (Haddock et al. 1999; Breteler et al. 2004). Adequate test-retest reliability, particularly with FTND (Pomerleau et al. 1994). Modestly correlates with levels of carbon monoxide, nicotine, and cotinine; weak predictor of withdrawal symptoms (Hughes and Hatsukami et al. 1986; Shiffman et al. 2004a; Etter et al. 2005); and modest or weak predictor of treatment outcome (Pinto et al. 1987; Silagy et al. 1994; Haddock et al. 1999; Etter et al. 2003a, 2005; Piper et al. 2006). Moderates efficacy of nicotine medications (Shiffman and Paton 1999). Does not have incremental value compared with measures of number of cigarettes/day (Razavi et al. 1999; Dale et al. 2001). A single item—time to first cigarette—is a good predictor of cessation success and reflects a pattern of heavy, uninterrupted, and automatic smoking (Transdisciplinary Tobacco Use Research Center et al. 2007). FTQ was modified for adolescents (Prokhorov et al. 1996, 2000). One item was eliminated—brand of cigarette or number of cigarettes per day—depending on study. Most items were changed to 4-point rating scales. One factor accounted for 41–53% of the variance. Interitem and item-to-total score correlations were weak to moderate. Internal consistency was adequate, with good test-retest reliability. Modest correlations were observed with amount smoked and between scales for individual items (except inhalation item) and cotinine levels. Stanford Dependence Index is also modified FTQ with only 5 items that are assessed on a 4- to 6-point scale. This measure was used in adults (Killen et al. 1990) and adolescents (Rojas et al. 1998). Adequate test-retest reliability was observed for both populations. In the adolescent population, total scores were significantly related to smoking rate, cotinine levels, and self-reported severity of withdrawal in past attempts to stop smoking.
Heaviness of Smoking Index (Heatherton et al. 1989)	Two items from FTQ: time to first cigarette of day and number of cigarettes/day.
Diagnostic and Statistical Manual of Mental Disorders, 4th ed. (*DSM-IV*) (APA 1994)	Categorical (nicotine dependent and not nicotine dependent) diagnostic resource that measures cognitive, behavioral, and physiological aspects of addiction. Criteria are consensus driven rather than theory driven and involve pattern of repeated drug use that results in withdrawal, tolerance, and compulsive drug taking despite negative consequences. *DSM* diagnosis is assessed by structured and semistructured interviews, such as Diagnostic Interview Schedule (DIS) (Robins et al. 1990) or Composite International Diagnostic Interview Substance Abuse Module (Robins et al. 1990). DIS results in 2-factor structure (Radzius et al. 2004). Diagnosis of dependence is also made by surveys, such as National Comorbidity Survey and National Survey on Drug Use & Health [formerly the National Household Survey on Drug Abuse], or by self-reported measures such as Tobacco Dependence Screener (TDS) (Kawakami et al. 1999). TDS has a continuous score and acceptable internal consistency. *DSM-IV* diagnoses assessed in epidemiologic surveys are associated with heavier smoking and predict persistence in smoking (Breslau et al. 2001). *DSM-IV* diagnosis is a stronger predictor of cessation than FTND, but weaker than number of cigarettes/day (Breslau and Johnson 2000), and it is poorly correlated with FTND (Moolchan et al. 2002). TDS is associated with number of cigarettes/day, carbon monoxide levels, and duration of smoking (Kawakami et al. 1999; Piper et al. 2006). Limitation: dichotomous diagnostic classification does not capture dependence that varies in degree, assumes unidimensionality, and masks heterogeneity (e.g., diagnosis can be met by endorsement of any of several criteria).

Table 4.3   Continued

Measures	Characteristics
Hooked on Nicotine Checklist (DiFranza et al. 2002a)	Unidimensional, continuous, 10-item measure to stop smoking theoretically derived on the basis of theory of loss of autonomy. Items measure inability to stop smoking, difficulty refraining from smoking in prohibited places, craving and need for cigarette, and withdrawal and feeling addicted. One-factor solution explains 60% of variance. Strong internal reliability, moderate-to-strong test-retest reliability of individual items and total score (O'Loughlin et al. 2002), and strong positive relationship to maximum frequency of smoking and maximum amount smoked. Weak correlation with duration of smoking. Significantly associated (those who endorsed at least 1 item on the scale) with failed attempt at smoking cessation, continued smoking until end of follow-up, and progression to daily smoking. High rate of symptom endorsement even in persons who ever used tobacco.
Cigarette Dependence Scale (CDS) (Etter et al. 2003a, 2005)	Unidimensional, continuous measure and empirically derived scale (single-factor structure) that covers main criteria for *DSM-IV* and *International Statistical Classification of Diseases and Related Health Problems, Tenth Revision*. Definitions for dependence include compulsion, withdrawal symptoms, loss of control, time allocation (the amount of time spent smoking), neglect of other activities, and persistence despite harm, but exclude tolerance. This scale has 2 forms, CDS-12 and CDS-5, with 12 and 5 items, respectively. Both scales have high test-retest reliability and moderate-to-strong internal consistency. CDS-12 scores were higher in daily smokers than in occasional smokers and were associated with strength of urge to smoke on last attempt to stop smoking and saliva cotinine levels. Both CDS-12 and CDS-5 scores decreased with reduction in cigarette smoking, but neither scale predicted smoking abstinence at follow-up. In a subsequent study, higher CDS-12 scores predicted smoking abstinence at 1 month after cessation. Higher baseline CDS-12 scores weakly predicted higher withdrawal ratings at follow-up, with the exception of appetite. Performs better than FTND on many of these measures.
Wisconsin Inventory of Smoking Dependence Motives (WISDM) (Piper et al. 2006)	Multidimensional, 68 items with 13 theory-based subscales: (1) affiliative attachment (to smoking); (2) automaticity (smoking without awareness or intention); (3) behavioral choice/amelioration (smoking despite constraints or alternative reinforcers); (4) cognitive enhancement; (5) craving; (6) cue exposure/associative process (reflects basic learning process); (7) loss of control; (8) negative reinforcement; (9) positive reinforcement; (10) social/environmental goads (potency of social stimuli that model or invite smoking); (11) taste/sensory properties; (12) tolerance; and (13) weight control. Identifies motivational dependence process that influences dependence criteria. Some subscales are highly correlated, indicating overlapping dimensions. All scales except social/environmental goads were weakly to strongly correlated with FTND and moderately to strongly correlated with the TDS. Total WISDM score was moderately predictive of number of cigarettes/day and carbon monoxide level, with variability of strength of prediction for subscales. Total WISDM score did not significantly predict relapse, whereas combination of subscales was predictive (e.g., automaticity, behavioral choice/amelioration, cognitive enhancement, and negative reinforcement).
Nicotine Dependence Syndrome Scale (NDSS) (Shiffman et al. 2004a; Shiffman and Sayette 2005)	Multidimensional, theoretically derived scale with 5 subscales: drive (craving and withdrawal, withdrawal avoidance, and subjective compulsion to smoke), tolerance (reduced sensitivity to effects of smoking), continuity (regularity of smoking rate), stereotypy (rigid patterns of tobacco use), and priority (preference for smoking over other reinforcers). Continuous factor scores and single total score can be obtained. Most of the reliability and validity testing were not conducted on the final 19 items that comprise this scale. Internal consistency of subscales is moderate to strong. Test-retest is modest to strong. In persons who did not stop smoking, NDSS scores modestly correlated with number of cigarettes smoked, difficulty in abstaining, and severity of past withdrawal symptoms. In treatment-seeking population, scales are modestly predictive of urges during smoking and during abstinence, acute withdrawal symptoms (except negative affect), and cessation outcome. Subscales show independent predictive usefulness (e.g., differential correlation with indices of dependence). NDSS strongly discriminates nonnicotine-dependent smokers who smoke a maximum of 5 cigarettes/day (chippers) from regular smokers. Scales also discriminated levels of intake and dependence among chippers. Relationship between NDSS remained even when controlled for FTQ score.

Note: Description and results on scales are illustrative and not comprehensive.

Tobacco Constituents and Pharmacokinetics

Nicotine and Other Tobacco Constituents

Tobacco products contain more than 4,000 chemicals, some of which could contribute to dependence. However, there is little debate that nicotine is a major tobacco component responsible for addiction (USDHHS 1988; Stolerman and Jarvis 1995; Royal College of Physicians of London 2000; Balfour 2004). Nicotine, 3-(1-methyl-2-pyrrolidinyl)pyridine, is a volatile alkaloid (pKa = 8.5) with a molecular weight of 162.23. The absorption and renal excretion of nicotine are highly dependent on pH. At a high (alkaline) pH, nicotine is in the nonionized state, which is associated with the ability to more easily pass through lipoprotein membranes (Stratton et al. 2001). Nicotine can be rapidly absorbed in the lungs through cigarette smoking because of the large surface area of the alveoli and small airways and the dissolution of nicotine in pulmonary fluid, which has a physiological pH that facilitates absorption. Similarly, nicotine from oral products that have an alkaline pH can be readily but more gradually absorbed through the oral mucosa. In addition, nicotine can be well absorbed in the small intestine, because of its more alkaline pH and large surface area. However, nicotine is poorly absorbed from the stomach, because of its acidic environment resulting in greater ionized nicotine. Unlike when it is swallowed, nicotine's bioavailability is greater through the lung or through the oral mucosa because nicotine reaches systemic circulation before passing through the liver (first-pass metabolism).

Earlier studies that examined a wide range of animal species have shown that nicotine alone can lead to self-administration in preference to an inert control substance (Henningfield and Goldberg 1983; USDHHS 1988; Swedberg et al. 1990; Rose and Corrigall 1997; Royal College of Physicians of London 2000). Humans have also demonstrated a preference for nicotine over a control substance in studies examining intravenous administration (Henningfield and Goldberg 1983; Harvey et al. 2004), nasal administration (Perkins et al. 1996a), and use of medicinal gum (Hughes et al. 1990a). Furthermore, if levels of nicotine in the body are altered, smokers tend to compensate or titrate their dose by (1) smoking more if the levels of nicotine are reduced or blocked by a nicotinic receptor antagonist or (2) smoking less if exogenous nicotine or higher levels of nicotine are administered (USDHHS 1988; NCI 1996, 2001). Titration of the level of nicotine in the body during smoking involves adjusting smoking behaviors by changing the (1) number of puffs on a cigarette, (2) duration of the puffs, (3) interpuff intervals, and/or (4) number of cigarettes smoked (Griffiths et al. 1982). For example, researchers observed this compensatory smoking behavior in smokers who had either switched from cigarettes with a high machine-determined yield of nicotine to cigarettes with a low yield (Scherer 1999; NCI 2001) or reduced the number of cigarettes smoked (Fagerström and Hughes 2002; Hecht et al. 2004). The resulting levels of cotinine and other biochemical indicators of exposure to tobacco were proportionately lower than expected, considering the reduction in the nicotine yield of the cigarette or the number of cigarettes smoked.

Researchers have observed that ingredients besides nicotine in tobacco or tobacco smoke (e.g., nornicotine and acetaldehyde) have either synergistic effects with nicotine or reinforcing effects of their own. Several pharmacologically active metabolites of nicotine were observed in the central nervous system (CNS) after acute administration of nicotine (Crooks and Dwoskin 1997). Nornicotine is both a metabolite of nicotine and a minor tobacco alkaloid. According to a review by Crooks and Dwoskin (1997), $S(-)$-nornicotine evokes concentration-dependent and calcium-ion (Ca^{2+})-dependent increases in endogenous release of dopamine from rat striatal slices and from mouse striatal synaptosomes. At low nornicotine concentrations, nicotinic receptor antagonists, such as mecamylamine and [^{3}H]-dihydro-β-erythroidine (DHβE), inhibit dopamine release evoked by $S(-)$-nornicotine. At high nornicotine doses, this inhibition is not observed, thereby indicating that at high doses, nonselective mechanisms may be associated with the release of dopamine. In addition, $S(-)$-nornicotine, $R(+)$-nornicotine, and nicotine appear to activate the neural mechanisms responsible for behavioral sensitization. For example, administration of $S(-)$-nornicotine desensitized nicotine receptors, but at a potency 12-fold lower than that of nicotine. $S(-)$-nornicotine also showed cross-desensitization with nicotine; that is, receptors desensitized by nicotine were also desensitized by $S(-)$-nornicotine. This result suggests the involvement of common subtypes of nicotinic receptors (Dwoskin et al. 2001).

Researchers have observed similar behavioral effects from nicotine and nornicotine. In one study examining acute or chronic (repeated) administration of $S(-)$-nicotine, $R(+)$-nornicotine, and $S(-)$-nornicotine on locomotor activity, the effects of both nornicotine enantiomers were qualitatively different from that of the $S(-)$-nicotine enantiomer after acute administration (Dwoskin et al. 1999a). Unlike $S(-)$-nicotine, neither nornicotine enantiomer produced hyperactivity following acute injection with the doses used in the study. However, long-term administration of a nornicotine enantiomer, specifically S(-)-nornicotine, showed patterns of effects similar to those of nicotine. Furthermore, long-term pretreatment with either nornicotine enantiomer produced cross-sensitization to the locomotor stimulant effects after a nicotine challenge.

Studies in rats show that (-)-nornicotine substitutes for (-)-nicotine in a drug-discrimination paradigm (Goldberg et al. 1989) and partially substitutes for (+)-amphetamine as a discriminative stimulus, although it is less potent than (-)-nicotine (Bardo et al. 1997). In a study of self-administration by rats (Bardo et al. 1999), S(-)-nicotine and RS(±)-nornicotine produced a number of responses on a lever to obtain these drugs that was higher than the number on a lever to obtain an inactive or saline infusion used as a control. Furthermore, response decreased when saline was substituted for nornicotine, confirming that the animals were responding for nornicotine. Response increased when nornicotine was again available. In another study, pretreatment with (±)-nornicotine produced a dose-dependent decrease in nicotine self-administration (Green et al. 2000).

These results indicate that nornicotine functions as a positive reinforcer but has less potency than that of nicotine. Researchers have speculated that this reduced effect may be attributable to (1) the longer half-life of nornicotine; (2) the use of RS(±)-nornicotine rather than the pure S(-)-nornicotine, which is considered more potent in evoking dopamine release in the brain; or (3) the reduced potency of nornicotine in the release of dopamine (Bardo et al. 1999). Because nornicotine is present only as a minor metabolite, it is unclear whether it would have any significant pharmacologic effect in smokers.

Less data are available on cotinine, which is a major metabolite of nicotine (Benowitz and Jacob 1994). Studies suggest that cotinine is available in the CNS and stimulates nicotinic receptors to evoke the release of dopamine in a calcium-dependent manner from superfused rat striatal slices but that it is much less potent than nicotine or S(-)-nornicotine (Dwoskin et al. 1999b). (In superfusion, artificial central spinal fluid is poured over thin slices of brain tissue to maintain function and enable in vitro studies.) Other studies indicated that cotinine has a low affinity for nicotinic receptors (Abood et al. 1981, 1985) and may be associated with increased serotonin (5HT) levels (De Clercq and Truhaut 1963; Yamamoto and Domino 1965; Essman 1973; Rosencrans and Chance 1977; Fuxe et al. 1979; Risner et al. 1985; Goldberg et al. 1989; Takada et al. 1989; Erenmemisoglu and Tekol 1994). Studies in animals and humans have shown that cotinine is psychoactive and behaviorally active (Hatsukami et al. 1997, 1998a), but

most studies showed this effect only with high cotinine doses. In human clinical studies, cotinine demonstrates effects opposite those of nicotine, indicating that cotinine may function as a nicotine antagonist (Keenan et al. 1994; Hatsukami et al. 1998a,b).

Acetaldehyde, a constituent in tobacco smoke that results from burning sugars and other materials in the tobacco leaf, may play a role in increasing the reinforcing effects of nicotine (DeNoble and Mele 1983). In a later study, acetaldehyde enhanced the acquisition of nicotine self-administration among adolescent rats but not among adult rats (Belluzzi et al. 2005). The authors point out that adolescence may be a time of particular sensitivity to the effects of nicotine. This observation is supported by the fact that even a limited exposure to nicotine during adolescence may lead to symptoms of dependence (Kandel and Chen 2000; DiFranza et al. 2002b). In animals, nicotine treatment during adolescence leads to neurochemical changes in the brain that differ from those observed in adults (Adriani et al. 2002; Slotkin 2002). Furthermore, studies show an increased sensitivity to the rewarding effects of nicotine in adolescent compared with adult rodents (Adriani et al. 2002; Levin et al. 2003; Belluzzi et al. 2004). Further research is needed to understand the mechanism(s) by which acetaldehyde enhances the reinforcing effects and other effects of nicotine.

Fowler and colleagues (2003) point out that compared with nonsmokers and former smokers, current smokers had lower levels of MAOA, which preferentially oxidizes norepinephrine and serotonin, and of MAOB, which preferentially oxidizes phenethylamine. Both forms of MAO also oxidize dopamine, tyramine, and octopamine. Because former smokers showed normal MAO levels, the low levels in smokers appear to result from the pharmacologic effects of tobacco use, rather than from an inherent characteristic of smokers. Low levels of MAO may contribute to the reinforcing effects of tobacco use, because of the resulting higher levels of catecholamines. Nicotine does not appear to be responsible for this effect. Rather, the responsible constituents appear to be extracts (2,3,6-dimethyl-benzoquinone and 2-naphthylamine) from flue-cured tobacco leaves (Khalil et al. 2000; Hauptmann and Shih 2001). Animal studies with rats and mice have also shown that cigarette smoke and solutions of cigarette smoke (Yu and Boulton 1987; Carr and Basham 1991), as well as cigarette tobacco extract (Yu and Boulton 1987), inhibit MAO activity in the brain. The MAO inhibition in smokers is partial, with reductions at about 30 and 40 percent for MAOA and MAOB, respectively (Fowler et al. 2003). The reduction in MAOB levels does not appear to be rapidly reversible, as demonstrated by a study that showed no difference in MAOB levels when smokers were scanned by positron emission tomography (PET) at 10 minutes or

11 hours after smoking a cigarette (Fowler et al. 2000). One study found that the intensity of the withdrawal symptoms was inversely related to platelet MAO activity (Rose et al. 2001a); that is, smokers with low platelet activity at baseline experienced the most severe withdrawal symptoms.

In summary, nicotine is the most potent constituent associated with the reinforcing effects of tobacco. However, researchers have identified other constituents in tobacco and tobacco smoke that may be reinforcing or facilitate reinforcing effects of tobacco. Nicotine metabolites have also been identified as potential reinforcers or enhancers of the reinforcing effects of nicotine. Researchers have observed that in addition to nicotine and other constituents of tobacco and tobacco smoke, sensory aspects of nicotine and environmental stimuli also have a significant role in maintaining smoking behavior (Rose et al. 1993; Shahan et al. 1999; Caggiula et al. 2001, 2002b; Perkins et al. 2001d) (for details, see "Learning and Conditioning" later in this chapter).

Pharmacokinetics

Nicotine addiction depends on the amount of nicotine delivered and the way in which it is delivered, which can either enhance or reduce its potential for abuse: the faster the delivery, rate of absorption, and attainment of high concentrations of nicotine, the greater is the potential for addiction (Henningfield and Keenan 1993; deWit and Zacny 1995; Stitzer and de Wit 1998).

Nicotine can be readily absorbed in the lung, oral mucosa, and nose, and through the skin. Table 4.4 shows (1) the bioavailability and amount of nicotine absorbed per unit dose of products containing nicotine and (2) the time to reach maximum blood concentrations of nicotine (T_{max}). Figure 4.1 shows the concentrations of nicotine in venous blood and the peak concentrations across the products containing nicotine. The mean peak concentrations of nicotine are higher with use of tobacco products than with use of nicotine replacement products, and cigarette smoking produced both the highest peak concentration and most rapid rate of nicotine absorption. Venous concentrations of nicotine from smoking are lower than arterial concentrations. Ratios of arterial concentrations to venous concentrations ranged from 2.3 to 10 across studies (Henningfield et al. 1993; Gourlay and Benowitz 1997; Rose et al. 1999). What accounts for the variability in arterial to venous nicotine concentration ratios observed across studies is unclear but may be a function of the study procedures and cigarette brands that were tested. In one study, lower-than-expected arterial nicotine concentrations were observed. The low concentration was attributed to the distribution of nicotine into the lungs and the slow release of nicotine into arterial circulation (Rose et al. 1999). The greater reinforcing efficacy of rapid delivery of nicotine was therefore thought to be due to both direct effects on the CNS and to stimulation of nicotinic receptors in the lung. These results would also suggest that neuronal nicotinic receptors associated with reinforcing effects of nicotine may be sensitive to low concentrations of nicotine. Clearly, more studies are needed to resolve the issues related to arterial concentrations of nicotine and consequent physiological effects.

Oral use of smokeless tobacco products results in high venous concentrations of nicotine equal to those for use of cigarettes. Although the T_{max} for delivery of nicotine in nasal spray appears to be less (faster) than that for

Table 4.4   Bioavailability and amount of nicotine absorbed per unit dose and time to maximum venous blood concentration of nicotine by product

Product	Bioavailability per dose	Time to maximum concentration
Cigarette	1–2 mg	Within 5 minutes
Nicotine gum (2 mg, 4 mg)	1 mg, 2 mg	30 minutes
Nicotine inhaler	2 mg/cartridge	20–30 minutes
Nicotine nasal spray	0.5 mg	10 minutes
Nicotine patch	15–22 mg (during 16–24 hours)	4–9 hours
Smokeless tobacco	3.6–4.5 mg	20–30 minutes

Source: Data are from Benowitz 1988; Fant et al. 1999a; Fagerström 2000; Medical Economics Company 2000. Table is adapted from Stratton et al. 2001 with permission from the National Academies Press, © 2001, National Academy of Sciences.
Note: **mg** = milligrams.

Figure 4.1   Venous blood concentrations of nicotine over time for various nicotine delivery systems

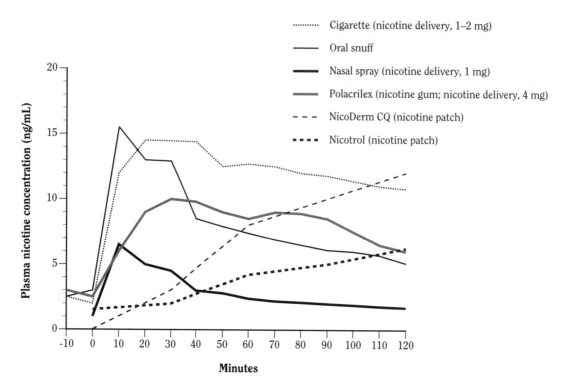

.... Cigarette (nicotine delivery, 1–2 mg)

——— Oral snuff

━━━ Nasal spray (nicotine delivery, 1 mg)

━━━ Polacrilex (nicotine gum; nicotine delivery, 4 mg)

- - - NicoDerm CQ (nicotine patch)

▪▪▪▪ Nicotrol (nicotine patch)

Source: Adapted from Fant et al. 1999b with permission from Elsevier, © 1999.
Note: **mg** = milligrams; **ng/mL** = nanograms per milliliter.

smokeless tobacco products, the addiction potential may be higher for smokeless tobacco than for nicotine nasal spray, because the rate of nicotine absorption for smokeless tobacco is faster. Within 10 minutes after administration of a smokeless tobacco product, a nicotine boost of 10 nanograms per milliliter can be achieved (Holm et al. 1992) compared with two to three times longer after administration of nasal spray. However, the rise of arterial concentrations from nicotine nasal spray compared with smokeless tobacco is unknown. A further complication is that the rate and amount of nicotine absorption vary across smokeless tobacco products (Figure 4.2). This variability results from the processing and pH of the smokeless tobacco product. Cigarettes also vary in nicotine content. The tobacco plant, the curing process, and the additives can determine the pH of the tobacco and tobacco smoke (see Chapter 3, "Chemistry and Toxicology of Cigarette Smoke and Biomarkers of Exposure and Harm").

Nonetheless, although the pharmacokinetics of some smokeless tobacco products may overlap with those of medicinal nicotine products, medicinal products tend to have a slower rate and a lower amount of nicotine

absorption than do the most popular brands of conventional smokeless tobacco products (Kotlyar et al. 2007). Among the medicinal nicotine products, nicotine nasal spray has the fastest rate of nicotine absorption, followed by nicotine gum, the nicotine lozenge, and the nicotine patch.

Together, these results demonstrate that the nicotine pharmacokinetics associated with cigarette smoking is likely to lead to high potential for addiction, whereas medicinal nicotine products have relatively minimal potential for addiction. For example, the extent of liking, and therefore the addiction potential for these products, are related to the speed of nicotine delivery (Henningfield and Keenan 1993). Nicotine delivered through cigarette smoking and intravenously shows the greatest dose-related liking for the drug, and nicotine delivered transdermally is associated with the least liking (Henningfield and Keenan 1993; Stratton et al. 2001).

The pharmacokinetic profile of a drug can determine the user's pattern of drug delivery. Cigarette smoking results in rapidly rising arterial concentrations of nicotine that reach the brain in about 10 to 19 seconds (Benowitz

1990). The peak levels decline quickly as nicotine is taken up by peripheral tissues, followed by an elimination of nicotine from the body (Benowitz et al. 1988). This profile enables the smoker to finely control the nicotine dose to obtain the desired effect and enables frequent doses. These characteristics facilitate the addiction potential of cigarettes (Benowitz 1999). In contrast, oral nicotine products such as smokeless tobacco result in a more gradual rate of nicotine absorption and the nicotine levels are more sustained, resulting in a reduced ability of the smoker to manipulate the nicotine dose and less frequent dosing. The nicotine patch is the extreme example of slow absorption and once-a-day dosing, which results in a minimal potential for addiction.

Nicotine metabolism may also play a role in the reinforcing effects of nicotine. Researchers have hypothesized that the rate of nicotine metabolism should be related to smoking behaviors and that faster elimination of nicotine is associated with increased smoking and nicotine dependence (Benowitz 1999). Although surprisingly few published studies have tested this hypothesis, the research evidence has given some support to it (see "Genetics" later in this chapter). However, the evidence is modest. The rate of nicotine metabolism accounts for less than 16 percent of variation in the number of cigarettes smoked per day (Benowitz et al. 2003; Johnstone et al. 2006), and there is no significant variance in the FTND (Benowitz et al. 2003; Johnstone et al. 2006; Kandel et al. 2007) or in scoring

on the Horn-Russell Scale (Johnstone et al. 2006). Kandel and colleagues (2007) found no significant association between the rate of metabolism and the number of cigarettes per day or nicotine dependence as measured by the FTND in a sample of young (18 through 26 years of age), less dependent, light smokers (average of 12 cigarettes per day). Possible reasons for the apparent disconnect between rate of metabolism and nicotine dependence include the following: (1) The questionnaire measures of adult nicotine dependence used may not be the most sensitive measures of the rate of metabolism (Benowitz et al. 2003; Johnstone et al. 2006). (2) The rate of metabolism may be related to nicotine dependence only during the transition from experimentation to "addicted" smoking (Benowitz et al. 2003). (3) The rate of metabolism is not an important determinant of smoking behavior in young smokers because of a low level of smoking (Kandel et al. 2007).

One of the reasons metabolism per se may not be directly related to measures of nicotine dependence is that the pharmacokinetics of nicotine metabolism are one step removed from the pharmacodynamics of nicotine, that is, from the impact (1) on neurotransmitters in the reward pathway, (2) on central effects, as measured by electroencephalography and cerebral blood flow, and (3) on peripheral effects such as cardiovascular responses. Both central and peripheral effects contribute to subjective reactions to nicotine and the subsequent likelihood

Figure 4.2   Mean plasma nicotine concentrations after administration of each of four smokeless tobacco products or mint snuff

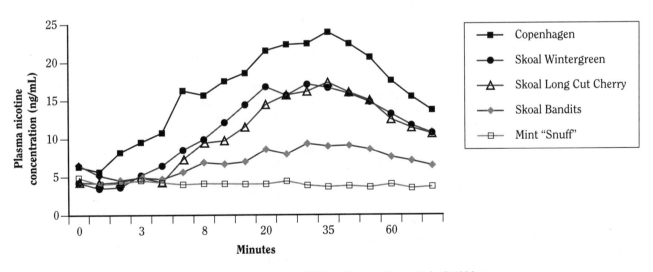

Source: Adapted from Fant et al. 1999a with permission from BMJ Publishing Group Ltd., © 1999.
Note: **ng/mL** = nanograms per milliliter.

of continued smoking. (For discussion of the pharmaco-dynamics of nicotine in the brain, see "Pathophysiology of Nicotine Addiction" later in this chapter.)

The factors contributing to the high addiction potential of tobacco products are undoubtedly multiple and have complex interrelationships, making it a challenge to parse their relative contributions. In addition, smoking results in rapid delivery of nicotine by cigarette smoke and in exposure to chemicals other than nicotine that have central and sensory effects, including taste and draw resistance, as well as stimuli associated with smoking (Scherer 1999; Caggiula et al. 2002a; Rose 2006).

Relatively few studies have been conducted outside the tobacco industry to determine how features of the cigarette are engineered to increase its addictive potential. However, tobacco industry documents suggest that more than nicotine dosing and pharmacokinetics are important in determining the overall addiction potential of modern cigarettes (Slade et al. 1995; Hurt and Robertson 1998; Wayne et al. 2004). (For description of design features that can enhance nicotine delivery and absorption rate, see Chapter 3, "Chemistry and Toxicology of Cigarette Smoke and Biomarkers of Exposure and Harm.")

Components of Nicotine Addiction

What are the effects of nicotine, and how does it cause addiction? The factors that may contribute to addictive behaviors include (1) neuroadaptations that occur with the persistent use of nicotine (e.g., tolerance), (2) withdrawal symptoms experienced when intake of the drug is stopped, and (3) the effects of nicotine that reinforce dependence. The primary reinforcing effects can entail the rewarding (psychoactive or psychostimulant) effects of nicotine (positive reinforcement) and/or the alleviation of aversive or negative states or stimuli—for example, relief from withdrawal symptoms (negative reinforcement). Nicotine may also enhance the reinforcing values of other reinforcers or stimuli, which may also contribute to its reinforcing effects.

Strong learning processes also contribute to addictive behaviors. These learning processes include conditioning in which stimuli associated with drug use evoke responses that are similar to the effects from the drug or similar to withdrawal symptoms or that may modulate drug effects. One hypothesis is that incentive sensitization can occur, in which some of the conditioned stimuli (CSs) are given priority in the allocation of attention and become a strong source of motivation to seek the drug (Robinson and Berridge 2001). Incentive sensitization consists of neuroadaptations from repeated use of a drug that render brain-reward systems hypersensitive (sensitized) to drug-associated stimuli. Also, nicotine's ability to be a secondary reinforcer of CSs to other reinforcers strengthens its addictive effects. Nicotine tolerance, withdrawal, and reinforcement in humans are examined in the next section, which is followed by a section on learning and conditioning in nicotine addiction.

Physiological Mechanisms and Indicators: Nicotine Tolerance, Withdrawal, and Reinforcement

Chronic Tolerance

Tolerance is a reduced responsiveness to a drug as a function of earlier exposure to that drug. This reduction in responsiveness is a consequence of drug use (Kalant et al. 1971). Therefore, tolerance should be distinguished from innate differences in drug responses that may relate to an initial risk of dependence, such as responses attributable to genetic or other constitutional factors (see "Genetics" later in this chapter). Sensitization, the opposite of tolerance, is an enhanced responsiveness to nicotine as a function of earlier exposure to the drug (Kalant et al. 1971). Sensitization is not addressed here, because it has not been clearly demonstrated in clinical studies. However, animal research suggests that sensitization occurs in response to locomotor activity and other physical and behavioral effects of exposure to nicotine (Le Foll et al. 2003; Samaha et al. 2005).

Tolerance and sensitization can be characterized on the basis of the time course of the adaptation involved. Acute tolerance develops within minutes after the initial exposure of the day (e.g., first few cigarettes) and is generally lost with overnight abstinence from smoking (Perkins et al. 1995). Acute tolerance may help to explain patterns of smoking during the course of a day (Balfour et al. 2000), but researchers think it is less important than chronic tolerance for an understanding of dependence (Di Chiara 2000). Chronic tolerance develops over weeks, months, or years (Kalant et al. 1971). Tolerance can also be distinguished on the basis of mechanisms. Pharmacokinetic tolerance is a reduced response to a drug because of an increase in drug clearance or metabolism that results in a smaller concentration of the drug in the body for a given administered dose. This type of tolerance is not discussed here, because clinical studies showed no evidence of a pharmacokinetic tolerance to nicotine in humans (Benowitz and Jacob 1993). However, innate differences in nicotine metabolism are well known (see "Genetics" later in this chapter). Pharmacodynamic tolerance is a reduced response to a given concentration of a drug in the body that results from changes in tissue sensitivity. The following discussion focuses on the association between chronic pharmacodynamic tolerance to nicotine and dependence on nicotine.

Chronic Tolerance to Nicotine

Chronic tolerance to nicotine or to most drugs is difficult to examine in clinical studies for practical and ethical reasons. The time required for the onset of chronic tolerance generally precludes longitudinal studies of changes in tolerance. Thus, the study of chronic tolerance usually requires cross-sectional comparisons between groups that differ in past histories of smoking, which can require administering nicotine to nonsmokers. Such comparisons may also introduce potential bias due to self-selection of drug history and because smoking history may covary with many other important differences that affect responses to nicotine, such as history of other drug use and psychiatric history (Hughes et al. 2000; Richter et al. 2002).

Despite methodologic limitations, studies have clearly shown a chronic tolerance for many self-reported responses to nicotine, such as a subjective mood. For example, smokers show fewer responses than do nonsmokers to the same amount of nicotine, as evidenced by measures of subjective stimulation that may be viewed as pleasurable, such as arousal, vigor, and a subjective experience often referred to as "head rush" or "buzz," as well as some experiences that may be viewed as aversive, including tension and nausea (Perkins et al. 2001b). However, chronic tolerance is less apparent for many other effects of nicotine, including cardiovascular responses (Perkins et al. 2001b). Chronic tolerance is virtually absent for simple psychomotor effects such as finger-tapping speed and Stroop task performance (Perkins et al. 2001b). This research is reviewed in detail elsewhere (Perkins 2002).

Association of Nicotine Tolerance with Dependence in Adults

Chronic tolerance to some effects of nicotine develops after long-term smoking. However, tolerance appears to be a nonsensitive marker for dependence among those with any history of extensive smoking (Perkins 2002). Perkins hypothesized that if a close association exists between tolerance and the level of dependence, then (1) more dependent smokers would show tolerance greater than that of less dependent smokers, (2) tolerance to nicotine before smoking cessation would predict the success of a subsequent attempt to stop smoking, and (3) tolerance would decrease with a longer duration of abstinence after cessation, indicating loss of dependence. However, the limited evidence suggests no such links between tolerance and dependence (Perkins 2002).

First, some research (Shiffman et al. 1992; Perkins et al. 2001b) shows little or no difference in tolerance to most effects of nicotine between dependent smokers and a subset of smokers who do not meet dependence criteria—for example, smokers of up to five cigarettes per day who do not experience withdrawal symptoms and who often go for long periods without smoking (Shiffman et al. 1992). Second, the magnitude of tolerance to nicotine before smoking cessation does not predict the severity of withdrawal or the duration of abstinence after an attempt to stop smoking, although a measure of nicotine reinforcement predicts both (Perkins et al. 2002a). Third, longitudinal studies show no change in chronic tolerance within one week or one month of smoking cessation and no difference in tolerance between former smokers who stopped smoking for 1 to 4 years or 6 to 19 years (Perkins et al. 2001c).

The conclusion that tolerance among smokers is not a good index of dependence warrants additional research (Perkins 2002). Most of these studies compared responses at low doses of nicotine to avoid aversive effects in groups with histories of limited smoking. Even so, tolerance to higher doses of nicotine may be associated with indices of dependence. Moreover, the acute effects of nicotine that explain its reinforcing quality are still not understood fully, so chronic tolerance to responses that were not assessed in this earlier research may be tied closely to dependence. In addition, chronic tolerance may be more critical during the onset of dependence in the adolescent years than it is in adults (Kandel and Chen 2000), because tolerance to the aversive effects of nicotine must occur for adolescents to escalate from one to two cigarettes per day to one pack per day (see "Epidemiology of Tobacco Use and Nicotine Dependence in Adults" later in this chapter). However, chronic tolerance may no longer be important after the onset of dependence.

Withdrawal

In tobacco-dependent smokers, a reliable consequence of abstaining from smoking for more than a few hours is the onset of distress indicated by self-reported behavioral, cognitive, and physiological symptoms and by clinical signs (APA 2000; Shiffman et al. 2004b; Hughes 2007). The subjective symptoms of withdrawal are manifested by affective disturbance, including irritability and anger, anxiety, and a depressed mood. The behavioral symptoms include restlessness, sleep disturbance, and an increased appetite, typically assessed by self-reports. Cognitive disturbances usually center on difficulty concentrating (Shiffman et al. 2004b; Hughes 2007). Researchers believe these symptoms—known collectively as withdrawal—are major factors that impair the ability to remain abstinent from smoking (Patten and Martin 1996; see "Trajectory of Recovery or Relapse" later in this chapter). The management of withdrawal and craving symptoms (e.g., the urge to smoke) is a primary treatment strategy to maintain smoking cessation. Withdrawal symptoms typically emerge within a few hours after the last cigarette is smoked, peak within a few days to one week, and return to precessation baseline levels after two to four weeks (Shiffman et al. 2004b). However, individual variability in the time course of withdrawal may be substantial and clinically significant (see "Trajectory of Recovery or Relapse" later in this chapter).

Individual withdrawal symptoms are often viewed as different manifestations of the same underlying process. One approach suggests that symptoms should be tightly linked in terms of pattern, intensity, time course, relationship to relapse, and neurobiologic factors. Another-approach suggests that symptoms should be assessed individually instead of by aggregating symptom scores into one total score (Shiffman et al. 2004b) (see "Pathophysiology of Nicotine Addiction" and "Trajectory of Recovery or Relapse" later in this chapter).

Unlike nicotine tolerance, the severity of withdrawal is more strongly related to some of the indices of nicotine dependence (such as cessation). For example, although nicotine-dependent and nonnicotine-dependent smokers generally do not differ in tolerance to nicotine, nicotine-dependent smokers are more likely to experience more severe withdrawal during initial abstinence (Shiffman 1989b). The observation that withdrawal but not tolerance is associated with dependence has also been noted for other drugs of abuse, especially alcohol (Schuckit et al. 1999; Hasin et al. 2000; O'Neill and Sher 2000).

Individual Differences in Withdrawal

Individual differences in the severity and pattern of withdrawal are topics of major clinical interest (see "Trajectory of Recovery or Relapse" later in this chapter). A history of major depression may exacerbate withdrawal after smoking cessation (Pomerleau et al. 2004) and may

increase the risk of relapse in women but perhaps not in men (Hall et al. 1998). The role of a major depressive disorder in relapse has been inconsistent and may be related to how depression is defined (see "Trajectory of Recovery or Relapse" later in this chapter), and few other characteristics have been associated with differences in withdrawal for men and women. For example, even though women generally have more difficulty than do men in maintaining abstinence from smoking, the severity of withdrawal in men and women does not appear to differ (Benowitz and Hatsukami 1998). However, withdrawal severity may be moderated by the phase of the menstrual cycle in women, with more severe withdrawal and depressed mood among women who stop smoking during the luteal phase than among those who stop during the follicular phase (Allen et al. 1996; Perkins et al. 2000). Other than studies of the effects of medication to relieve withdrawal symptoms, few researchers have examined other factors that acutely modify withdrawal.

Reinforcement

In behavioral psychology, a stimulus is considered reinforcing if it increases a response or behavior resulting in obtaining that stimulus. Thus, a drug is reinforcing if it is self-administered more than an inert substance used for comparison (e.g., placebo). "Reward," on the other hand, is a less specific term defined as an index of subjective hedonic effects of substance use (Everitt and Robbins 2005), and it is typically assessed after drug intake by ratings such as "liking" and "good effects." Ratings of drug reward may help to explain reinforcement, but they should be kept distinct from measures of reinforcement, which are inherently behavioral.

After a drug is established to be reinforcing, research can then focus on the neurobiologic or behavioral underpinnings of the reinforcing effects. (For discussion of research on the neurobiology of nicotine reinforcement, see "Pathophysiology of Nicotine Addiction" later in this chapter.) Behavioral or subjective effects of nicotine that may be reinforcing have not been definitively identified. Methodologic issues complicate the study of what makes nicotine either positively or negatively reinforcing. Pleasurable effects indicate positive reinforcement, whereas reductions in negative effects, such as relief from withdrawal, indicate negative reinforcement. These distinctions are important because exploration of positively reinforcing effects may be critical to understanding why adolescents begin to smoke cigarettes (i.e., onset of addiction) and why persons relapse after an attempt to stop smoking. Negatively reinforcing effects may be specific to relief from acute withdrawal and thus relevant only to relapse and not to the initiation of smoking or the onset of addiction. Some research in nonsmokers links acute self-administration of nicotine with pleasurable subjective responses of increased vigor and arousal, suggesting that positive reinforcement occurs with initial experience with nicotine (Perkins et al. 2001a). Similar research should focus on whether initial nicotine reinforcement is linked to relief from preexisting aversive symptoms, such as depressive symptoms.

Other effects of nicotine may also reinforce its use, but their links with self-administration have not been clearly established. These effects include modulating negative affect (e.g., reducing fatigue, anxiety, or sadness) (Kassel et al. 2003), enhancing attention and concentration during cognitively demanding tasks (Heishman et al. 1994), and perhaps preventing hunger and maintaining a lower body weight (Perkins 1993). Evidence suggests that these effects are observed largely in abstinent smokers experiencing withdrawal and are thus examples of negative rather than positive reinforcement.

Finally, animal research indicates that nicotine may have a secondary reinforcing function, aside from the direct (primary) reinforcing effects noted here. These studies, conducted mostly by Caggiula, Donny, and colleagues (e.g., Chaudhri et al. 2006), show that nicotine can enhance the reinforcing value of other reinforcers not associated with nicotine intake. Primary reinforcing effects require rapid administration of nicotine and are contingent on a response, whereas other reinforcement-enhancing effects can occur regardless of the speed of nicotine delivery or the contingency of response. Although recent work suggests the occurrence of reinforcement-enhancing effects of nicotine (Barr et al. 2008), the clinical research is insufficient to warrant extensive discussion of how this influence promotes nicotine dependence. However, this influence may help to explain why smoking appears to acutely increase consumption of other reinforcers, such as alcohol (Mitchell et al. 1995), and it may facilitate understanding of the difficulties involved in smoking cessation. If nicotine has reinforcement-enhancing effects, then smoking cessation removes these effects, leading to a lessening of reinforcement from many other reinforcers and not just the loss of reinforcement from smoking.

Smoking Frequency and Tobacco Addiction

The most common index of reinforcement in research on tobacco or nicotine addiction is the number of cigarettes smoked per day (smoking frequency). That is, drugs that are highly reinforcing will tend to be self-administered to a greater extent. Typically, the number of cigarettes smoked per day is assessed by self-report. Biochemical measures of the amount of smoking exposure include blood, salivary, and urinary levels of cotinine, the main metabolite of nicotine. Smoking frequency is related to a variety of dependence measures including scores on scales of nicotine dependence such as the widely used FTND (Hughes et al. 2004a). Higher frequency of smoking was found to predict a more severe withdrawal and a faster relapse after an attempt to stop smoking (Ockene et al. 2000), which are both important clinical indices of addiction. Higher frequency of smoking is also associated with early lapses after smoking cessation, such as smoking on the first day of cessation or within the first two weeks, which are each strongly associated with an increased risk of relapse (Kenford et al. 1994). Other indices of smoking reinforcement or persistence are related to a high level of addiction. These indices include a longer duration of smoking, young age at smoking initiation, no previous attempt to stop smoking, and a shorter duration of abstinence during previous attempts to stop smoking (Ockene et al. 2000) (see "Trajectory of Recovery or Relapse" later in this chapter).

Acute Measures of Reinforcement

Reinforcement is often assessed in basic research studies by analyzing regular, or extent of, smoking behavior over a period of time. This is usually determined by the number of cigarettes smoked per day but occasionally by microtopographic measures of puffing behaviors, blood nicotine levels, or the percentage of carbon monoxide in expired air (Lee et al. 2003), a biochemical index of acute smoking exposure. Smoking behavior in such short-term studies has been sensitive to a variety of manipulations of nicotine exposure, demonstrating the reinforcing effects of nicotine. For example, the intensity of acute smoking behavior increases when the nicotine yield of the cigarette is lowered, which is a compensation to maintain nicotine intake (Zacny and Stitzer 1988). The increase in plasma concentrations of nicotine from smoking is greater after pretreatment with mecamylamine, a nicotine receptor antagonist. The increase is probably a result of more intense puffing in an attempt to overcome the blockade of nicotine receptors (Rose et al. 2001b). Factors have been observed to moderate the reinforcing effects of tobacco. Some studies have shown increased smoking reinforcement after pretreatment with alcohol (Nil et al. 1984; Mitchell et al. 1995) or with stimulant drugs such as *d*-amphetamine (Tidey et al. 2000), methylphenidate (Rush et al. 2005), or cocaine (Roll et al. 1997), but not with other stimulants such as caffeine (Nil et al. 1984; Lane and Rose 1995). The increase in smoking reinforcement from acute pretreatment with drugs may help to explain the association between a history of drug use and nicotine dependence (Richter et al. 2002).

Several other procedures provide sensitive and acute measures of smoking or nicotine reinforcement. These procedures include performance on a task (operant responding) on various schedules of reinforcement for puffs on a cigarette and the choice of nicotine or nonnicotine cigarettes. Instances of working for puffs on a cigarette and choosing nicotine over nonnicotine cigarettes increase with smoking abstinence (Perkins et al. 1994, 1996b). The operant response to obtain puffs on a cigarette increases when the required number of responses per reinforcer is changed and access to alternative reinforcers is reduced, showing regulation of smoking intake (Johnson and Bickel 2003). A slightly different procedure—responding for puffs on a progressive-ratio schedule by gradually increasing the response requirements after each earned puff—may also provide a sensitive measure of the reinforcing value of smoking (Perkins et al. 2002b). However, few findings have related this measure to nicotine dependence.

Separation of Nicotine Reinforcement from Smoking Reinforcement

Nicotine dependence generally involves the intake of nicotine by tobacco use, especially cigarette smoking. Therefore, the contribution of the many nonnicotine aspects of tobacco associated with smoking cigarettes should be distinguished from the influence of nicotine per se. The self-administration of cigarette smoke is not the same as the self-administration of nicotine. Among many differences between nicotine delivery through smoking and delivery in other forms, the smoke stimuli that typically accompany nicotine from cigarette smoking may acquire conditioned reinforcing effects that maintain smoking behavior (Caggiula et al. 2001) (see "Learning and Conditioning" in the next section).

Nevertheless, some of the manipulations that alter smoking behavior also alter the self-administration of novel nicotine formulations. Nicotine alone, isolated from tobacco smoke, is reinforcing in humans (Perkins et al. 1996a; Harvey et al. 2004). The choice of nicotine nasal spray instead of a placebo nasal spray increases with smoking abstinence (Perkins et al. 1996b) and subsequently predicts a more severe withdrawal and a faster relapse during an attempt to stop smoking without medication (Perkins et al. 2002a). Blocking the effects of nicotine with mecamylamine pretreatment increases the intravenous self-administration of nicotine (Rose et al. 2003a). Also, under the same conditions of assessment, the amount of nicotine spray used voluntarily is correlated with the amount of voluntary smoking (Perkins et al. 1997). This finding indicates a generalizability between nicotine reinforcement through smoking and reinforcement through at least one novel form of nicotine delivery.

Individual Differences in Nicotine Reinforcement

Individual differences in nicotine reinforcement may provide direction for the study of individual differences in nicotine addiction and in approaches to treating addiction. In some studies, the reinforcing effects of nicotine tend to be less in women than in men, but the reinforcing effects of nonnicotine stimuli related to tobacco smoke (e.g., "cues") tend to be greater in women than in men (Perkins et al. 2001d, 2002b). In light of the generally greater difficulty most women have with smoking cessation, this observation suggests that the influence of nonnicotine stimuli can be important to the persistence of smoking behavior (i.e., dependence) (Caggiula et al. 2001; Rose 2006). Other characteristics that may be associated with greater reinforcement from smoking or from nicotine include comorbid psychiatric disorders (Lasser et al. 2000), a history of alcohol dependence (Keenan et al. 1990; Hughes et al. 2000), and perhaps other drug dependence (Richter et al. 2002), as well as other subgroups associated with a high prevalence of smoking and low rates of cessation. Similarly, smokers who are not obese may find the nicotine in cigarettes more reinforcing than do obese smokers (Blendy et al. 2005).

Learning and Conditioning

Nicotine and Secondary Reinforcement

Perhaps as powerful as the direct effects of smoking and nicotine on neural functioning are the associative processes that develop with repeated tobacco use (Caggiula et al. 2002a; Hyman 2005). The classic conditioning paradigm provides an important conceptual and theoretical framework for consideration of the powerful associative learning processes that, according to Bevins and Palmatier (2004), develop in a specific manner. Smoking serves as the unconditioned stimulus (US), and the subjective and physiological effects of smoking and exposure to nicotine serve as unconditioned responses. Exteroceptive (environmental) and interoceptive (internal) stimuli that occur repeatedly in temporal proximity to smoking become CSs. CSs include smoking paraphernalia (e.g., an ashtray), sensory aspects of smoking (e.g., cigarette smell or taste), and/or situational cues (e.g., smoking in the car while driving to work). The acquired response evoked by CSs becomes a conditioned response. With longer-term smoking, conditioned responses include urges to smoke. Repeated pairings of these CSs with cigarette smoking result in the CSs alone (before smoking) triggering urges to smoke (to want and to seek a cigarette) (Niaura 2000; Berridge and Robinson 2003).

Nicotine as a Conditioned Stimulus

Bevins and Palmatier (2004) have extended the associative learning model of nicotine dependence by hypothesizing that nicotine also has important actions as a CS of smoking behavior (the conditioned response) (Figure 4.3). The traditional role of nicotine has been limited to serving as a US. As a CS, nicotine acquires new or additional affective properties through being paired repeatedly with other stimuli such as coffee. In other words, nicotine enhances the salience of these and numerous other stimuli, which strengthens the associative bond and increases smoking behavior.

Nicotine as a Modifier of Associative Processes

In addition to serving as a CS, nicotine modifies associative processes in conditioned and unconditioned manners (Bevins and Palmatier 2004). As a conditioned modulator (Figure 4.3), the interoceptive cuing of nicotine serves as a contextual stimulus that "sets the occasion" for an association between a discrete CS in the environment and smoking (Bevins and Palmatier 2004). The CS-US association is conditioned on the drug state (context). Examples include smoking while drinking alcohol to relax and smoking during a break at work to cope with distress. As an unconditioned modulator, nicotine

may enhance the salience of other stimuli that have incentive values to the person (Bevins and Palmatier 2004). For example, as depicted in connector "a" (solid line) of Figure 4.3, nicotine enhances the incentive or reward value of alcohol, which has its own significant reward value. This "incentive amplification" is unconditioned because the effects of nicotine do not depend on a contingent association between smoking and the motivational stimulus. "Incentive amplification" by nicotine is not limited to other drug reinforcers. Nicotine also enhances the reinforcing effects of nondrug reinforcers, such as light stimulus (Palmatier et al. 2007).

Positive Reinforcement and Learning

The positive reinforcing action of nicotine is attributable in large part to its influence on the brain regions associated with reward processes (e.g., the mesolimbic dopaminergic system) (Balfour 2004). In a review of positive-reinforcement theory as applied to nicotine addiction, Glautier (2004) suggests several mechanisms underlying positive-reinforcement processes. Besides exerting a direct reinforcing action through its effects on core brain-reward centers, nicotine may enhance the reinforcing efficacy of smoking-related cues as a result of priming the smoker to selectively attend to those stimuli. In addition, nicotine acquires indirect reinforcing actions through its

Figure 4.3   Associative learning processes in nicotine addiction

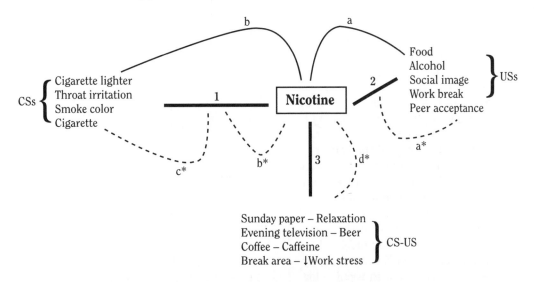

Source: Adapted from Bevins and Palmatier 2004 with permission from Sage Publications Inc. Journals, © 2004.
Note: Connections 1, 2, and 3 reflect the role of the unconditioned stimuli (USs), conditioned stimuli (CSs), and occasion setter, respectively. Solid lines "a" and "b" refer to nicotine's ability to amplify incentive salience. Dashed lines ("a*" through "d*") denote potentially interesting feedback functions in which conditioned associations may be strengthened.

effect on other behaviors. According to Hogarth and Duka (2006), considerable evidence suggests that nicotine-conditioned effects are mediated by a smoker's expectations of the effects of nicotine coupled with an appetitive emotional response that reflects the positive value of nicotine to the smoker (e.g., pleasure or relaxation).

Although clearly influential, positive reinforcement is not a likely primary motivational influence on persistence in smoking (Baker et al. 2004), except possibly in the case of occasional smoking (Shiffman and Paty 2006). Unlike expectations of negative reinforcement, such as smoking to relieve stress, expectations of positive reinforcement do not predict the likelihood of a relapse after smoking cessation. This finding indicates that positive-reinforcement processes may have less motivational significance for relapse than do negative-reinforcement processes (Wetter et al. 1994). Relapse is less likely to occur during positive-affect states than during negative-affect states (Shiffman et al. 1996c) (see "Trajectory of Recovery or Relapse" later in this chapter).

Negative Reinforcement and Learning

Negative reinforcement refers to processes by which smoking or nicotine reduces aversive states, such as pain, craving, difficulty concentrating, and the negative-affect states generally associated with nicotine withdrawal. Nicotine addiction is maintained in part because persons learn during the early stages of smoking that tobacco use allows them to escape aversive states associated with smoking abstinence or because they learn later that it helps them to avoid these aversive states (Eissenberg 2004). These states include irritability and an anxious or depressed mood. With continued use of cigarettes by smokers over time, the associative link between tobacco use and the relief of withdrawal-associated aversive states is strengthened. Tiffany and colleagues (2004) hypothesize that a crucial phase in the development of nicotine addiction may be the transition from experimental smoking to smoking to reduce the experience of negative states.

Baker and colleagues (2004) extend the conceptualization of this negative-reinforcement model of tobacco dependence by focusing on the role of negative affect. Within this reformulation of negative reinforcement, negative affect is the core symptom of the nicotine withdrawal syndrome that drives a person to smoke to relieve aversive states. Traditional negative-reinforcement models have emphasized the role of environmental cues, such as interpersonal conflict, but not internal cues, such as physiological symptoms that signal impending withdrawal-related states of negative affect. With repeated pairings of nicotine withdrawal and smoking to relieve withdrawal, persons addicted to nicotine may learn over time to detect internal cues at a level that is not in the immediate awareness of the smoker, especially cues associated with negative-affect states, regardless of whether they are related to withdrawal (Baker et al. 2004). Nicotine operates on both aversive withdrawal states and distress associated with external stressors, according to Baker and colleagues (2004). However, nicotine may be less effective in reducing negative affect associated with distress from external stressors. Consistent with this view, cigarette smoking has not been found to attenuate experimentally induced negative affect in the laboratory setting (Conklin and Perkins 2005). Studies of smoking in real-world settings have found little or no association between subjective negative affect and smoking behavior (Piasecki 2006). Baker and colleagues (2004) further hypothesize that smokers acquire a "motivational-processing sequence in which interoceptive signals of negative affect engage drug self-administration response sequences and may induce awareness of the desire or urge to use a drug without awareness of the affective origins or setting events for the desire" (p. 47).

The finding that negative-reinforcement processes may not be consciously accessible (Baker et al. 2004) could contribute to the difficulty smokers experience in trying to stop smoking. When negative affect or external stressors become sufficiently strong, the person becomes aware of them, and the negative affect leads to biases in information processing. One example is attentional bias for negative affect cues that trigger smoking (Baker et al. 2004). Although it is provocative, Baker and colleagues' model of negative reinforcement should be viewed as provisional and requiring validation. Related individual differences, such as the inability to tolerate distress, may influence learning and conditioning processes (Brown et al. 2005). Using momentary ecological assessment, Shiffman and Waters (2004) found that rapid increases in negative affect exert especially strong influence in precipitating lapses to smoking (see "Trajectory of Recovery or Relapse" later in this chapter for a more detailed discussion of smoking relapse).

Environmental Context

Animal studies confirm the powerful role that environmental stimuli play in nicotine self-administration. When environmental stimuli are paired with nicotine self-administration, the extinguished drug-seeking behavior is reinstated (Le Foll and Goldberg 2005). The important role of environmental context in nicotine addiction is observed in its effect on relapse. (For more description, see "Trajectory of Recovery or Relapse" later in this chapter.) Studies of smokers consistently report an association among exposure to smoking cues, craving, and positive and negative affective states, which could be construed as emotional cues followed by return to smoking after an attempt to stop (Shiffman 1982; Marlatt and Gordon 1985). These studies, however, rely on subjectively recalled events that may be prone to several types of memory bias. Using methods of ecological momentary assessment in an electronic diary, Shiffman and colleagues (1996c) confirmed that lapses in smoking abstinence were strongly associated with being in situations in which smoking was permitted, cigarettes were available, and other persons were smoking.

Clinical studies have used a cue-exposure paradigm to explore the association of smoking cues with craving and physiological and behavioral responses. These studies are premised on the assumption that they yield insights into how environmental and internal stimuli play a role in provoking smoking and relapse (Niaura et al. 1988; Caggiula et al. 2001; Chiamulera 2005). Stimuli are presented in a variety of modes, including photographic and video, auditory, in vivo (presence of cigarette paraphernalia or smoking by another person), and the use of imagery (e.g., request to imagine specific situations). In a meta-analytic review, Carter and Tiffany (1999) found that exposure to smoking cues increased craving most reliably, followed in order by sweat gland activity and heart rate changes. Sweating and changes in heart rate probably reflect an increased arousal of the sympathetic nervous system. Other researchers have noted cue effects on an increase in reaction time (Sayette and Hufford 1994), cognitive interference on the Stroop test (Munafò et al. 2003), and similar paradigms used to assess attentional interference (Mogg and Bradley 2002). Imaging studies of cue responses also suggest that neural activity is greatest in brain areas involved in emotion and reward, including the prefrontal cortex, limbic lobe (anterior cingulate, posterior hippocampus, and right posterior amygdala), medial thalamus, and midbrain structures (ventral tegmentum) (Due et al. 2002; McClernon and Gilbert 2004; David et al. 2005).

Exposure to smoking cues among smokers also decreases the prepulse inhibition of the acoustic startle reflex, an effect associated with an increase in dopaminergic activity in the ventral tegmental brain region (Hutchison et al. 1999b). The effects of smoking cues on neural responses and craving are also moderated by factors such as the perceived availability of cigarettes. After cue exposure, craving increased more when there is an expectation of the opportunity to smoke (perceived availability) than when there is perceived unavailability (Carter and Tiffany 1999). Exposure to a cigarette cue under the condition of perceived availability is associated with an increase in activation of the ventromedial prefrontal cortex and a decrease in activation of the dorsolateral prefrontal cortex

compared with exposure to a neutral cue (Wilson et al. 2004). This pattern of neural activation with corresponding increases in craving can be seen as setting the stage for behaviors that culminate in smoking.

Responses to cues in laboratory experiments are associated with responses to smoking cessation treatments. For example, acute increases in heart rate assessed among smokers in response to a cue exposure at the end of a treatment protocol were related to a later relapse to smoking (Niaura et al. 1989). An acute deceleration in heart rate assessed when smokers observed a cigarette being lit during the cue-exposure procedure also predicted relapse. Heart rate deceleration in this context may reflect a greater attention paid to the stimulus (e.g., a lit cigarette). Subsequently, Waters and colleagues (2004) found that a cue-provoked craving before treatment predicted relapse, but only among those who were treated with an active nicotine patch instead of a placebo patch, suggesting inconsistent results or uncertainty in the link between cue-provoked craving in the laboratory and relapse.

If cue-provoked responses assessed in the laboratory are associated with smoking relapse, then treatments that decrease or blunt these responses may increase the likelihood of successful smoking cessation. A review by Conklin and Tiffany (2002) suggests that conventional extinction-type treatments, such as exposure to smoking-related cues unaccompanied by the reinforcing effects of nicotine or exposure with response-prevention treatments, are ineffective in helping persons to stop smoking. This finding may relate to the possibility that stimulus-response pairing, if sufficiently strong, cannot be forgotten or unlearned (LaBar and LeDoux 2001; Conklin and Tiffany 2002; Niaura 2002). In addition, the large number of potential cues likely serves to maintain smoking behavior or the state-dependent learning processes. However, methods such as use of denicotinized cigarettes or antagonists (e.g., mecamylamine) show significant effects on reducing the rewarding value of smoking cues and have the potential to enhance smoking cessation (Rose and Behm 2004; Rose 2006). Other cognitive or behavioral methods based in modern learning theory may also show more promise in suppressing the stimulus-response bond. Pharmacologic treatments show some promise in decreasing cue reactivity. Compared with a placebo gum, nicotine polacrilex gum diminished the craving response to smoking cues more rapidly (Shiffman et al. 2003). In a study using the same cue-exposure paradigm, a more recent formulation of a rapid-release nicotine gum reduced craving more than did conventional nicotine polacrilex gum (Niaura et al. 2005). Nicotine polacrilex gum is an effective smoking cessation aid (Silagy et al. 2004). Its efficacy may be associated with its ability to diminish a cue-provoked craving.

Other rapid-release formulations of nicotine replacement therapy (NRT), including gum and nasal spray, may similarly help persons to stop smoking, in part because these formulations decrease the craving response to cues. In contrast, although slower-releasing NRT formulations (e.g., a nicotine patch) appear to lower absolute levels of craving, these formulations do not blunt cue-provoked craving (Tiffany et al. 2000; Waters et al. 2004). One study has suggested that treatment with bupropion blunts cue-provoked craving, but the study did not control for abstinence status (Brody et al. 2004a). Other nonnicotine compounds (e.g., naltrexone and olanzapine) also may blunt cue-provoked craving (Hutchison et al. 1999a, 2004). This finding suggests that the cue-exposure paradigm may be a useful screening tool for testing pharmacologic aids to smoking cessation; however, further studies need to be conducted to better understand why some medications affect cue-induced cravings and others do not.

Summary and Future Directions

Long-term exposure to nicotine produces biologic adaptations leading to reduced sensitivity to some of the effects of nicotine (tolerance) and symptoms of distress soon after cessation of drug use (withdrawal). Tolerance of nicotine in adolescent smokers may be related to onset of drug dependence, even though tolerance in adult smokers does not appear to be related to different indices of nicotine addiction. Withdrawal symptoms, especially self-reported cravings and negative affect, are related to some indices of addiction. A narrower focus on the individual withdrawal symptoms most strongly related to relapse, such as negative affect (e.g., depressed mood), may increase understanding of the underlying mechanisms associated with the maintenance of nicotine addiction and requires further study.

Positive reinforcement from nicotine may play a more significant role in the initiation of smoking, and negative reinforcement, particularly relief from withdrawal, is an important contributor to the persistence of smoking and relapse. Measures of nicotine's reinforcing effects, especially the most common measure—self-reported number of cigarettes smoked per day—are consistently related to other indices of addiction, including the risk of relapse. However, other objective measures of nicotine's reinforcing effects, especially those reflecting persistence in smoking behavior, may provide even stronger markers of addiction for predicting clinical outcomes and for testing the efficacy of new treatments or tobacco products. Such measures may also be useful as endophenotypes of dependence for future research into the etiology of addiction, including the influence of a person's genetic composition. Therefore, the development of these validated markers and measures for nicotine and smoking reinforcement is critical for future research examining the etiology and treatments for nicotine addiction and for tobacco product testing.

Nicotine addiction results not only from the pharmacodynamic effects of nicotine but also from associative learning and conditioning. Nicotine serves not only as a US, but can also serve as a CS and a modifier of associative processes. Motivational influences on persistent smoking are more likely tied to negative reinforcement than to positive reinforcement.

Interoceptive (internal) cues of negative affect have been linked to craving and relapse, whereas positive affective states are less likely to lead to relapse. Exteroceptive (environmental) cues also play an important role in eliciting craving and relapse. Reactivity to both internal and environmental cues may provide another measure of nicotine addiction. Factors such as age, gender, and psychiatric comorbid history are important to consider in future research, because they have or may have an important role in moderating responses to nicotine (see "Epidemiology of Tobacco Use and Nicotine Dependence in Adults" later in this chapter). Because of the importance of learning in the development and maintenance of nicotine addiction, this is an area that requires more extensive research.

Pathophysiology of Nicotine Addiction

Because nicotine is one of the primary constituents responsible for tobacco addiction, research to promote an understanding of the neurobiology of tobacco addiction focuses on the mechanisms mediating nicotine addiction. As noted previously, dependence on nicotine is characterized by both the persistence of a drug-taking behavior and the emergence of withdrawal symptoms on abrupt cessation of nicotine administration (Wikler 1973; Levine 1974; Stewart et al. 1984; Ludwig 1986; O'Brien et al. 1990; Hughes and Hatsukami 1992; Koob et al. 1993; Markou et al. 1993, 1998; APA 1994; Kenny and Markou 2001). Therefore, both the neurosubstrates (brain structures, pathways, and systems) mediating the reinforcing effects of acute administration of nicotine and those mediating the nicotine withdrawal syndrome are relevant to drug dependence. The physiological systems that develop adaptations to repeated nicotine administration and lead to the emergence of withdrawal signs on cessation of nicotine administration are likely to intersect with systems that mediate the acute effects of nicotine (Markou et al. 1998; Kenny and Markou 2001). That is, drug dependence develops as a neurobiologic adaptation to chronic drug exposure.

Accordingly, this section first reviews the systems and pathways mediating the reinforcing effects of nicotine and then discusses the neuroadaptations that occur because of chronic nicotine exposure. These neurobiologic adaptations mediate the tolerance to and effects of withdrawal from nicotine that are interlinked in most theoretical conceptualizations. Researchers have hypothesized that the sensitization to the locomotor-activating effects of drugs, including effects observed after repeated nicotine administrations, reflect a progressive augmentation in the motivation to self-administer the drug (Robinson and Berridge 1993). (The locomotor-activating effects consist of progressively increased locomotor responses to repeated drug-challenge injections.) However, no direct evidence suggests that sensitization to the locomotor-activating effects of nicotine reflects any aspect of dependence on nicotine. Therefore, sensitization is not covered in this section. If sensitization to the reinforcing effects of nicotine develops, it will most likely be relevant to early phases of tobacco use involving the acquisition of tobacco smoking as a continuing behavior.

The final discussion focuses on the comorbidity of nicotine dependence and psychiatric disorders in the context of shared substrates that mediate nicotine dependence and depression-like aspects of psychiatric disorders (Markou et al. 1998; Markou and Kenny 2002; Paterson and Markou 2007).

Nicotinic Acetylcholine Receptors

Nicotine, an alkaloid in concentrations of approximately 1 to 3 percent in tobacco (Browne 1990), is an agonist at the nicotinic acetylcholine receptors (nAChRs) expressed both in the peripheral nervous system and the CNS (Henningfield et al. 1996; Vidal 1996; Holladay et al. 1997; Paterson and Norberg 2000). Similar to other ligand-gated ion channels, neuronal nAChRs are composed of five membrane-spanning subunits that combine to form a functional receptor (Lindstrom et al. 1996; Role and Berg 1996; Albuquerque et al. 1997; Lèna and Changeux 1998, 1999; Dani 2000; Gotti et al. 2006). Neuronal nAChR subunits are arranged in different combinations to form nAChRs with distinct pharmacologic and kinetic

properties. The neuronal α subunit exists in nine isoforms (α2 through α10), whereas the neuronal β subunit exists in three isoforms (β2, β3, and β4) (Arneric et al. 1995; Wonnacott 1997; Elgoyhen et al. 2001). Study of oocyte expression systems injected with pairwise combinations of different neuronal α and β subunits indicate that these subunits combine with a stoichiometry of 2α:3β to produce a functional neuronal nicotinic hetero-oligomeric receptor (Deneris et al. 1991; Conroy and Berg 1995; Colquhoun and Patrick 1997). In contrast, α7, α8, and α9 subunits form homo-oligomeric complexes composed of five α subunits and no β subunits (Chen et al. 1998). Only the α7 pentamer is expressed in the CNS.

Neuronal nAChRs in rats are divided broadly into three classes: (1) those with a high-affinity binding site for racemic nicotine—the nAChRs containing α4, of which the α4β2 combination is the most abundant (Flores et al. 1992; Picciotto et al. 1995); (2) those with a high affinity for the radioiodine $[^{125}I]$α-bungarotoxin that correspond to the homomeric α7 nAChRs (Clarke 1992); and (3) those with a high affinity for neuronal bungarotoxin—the α3-containing nAChRs (Schulz et al. 1991). The precise combinations of nAChR subunits that constitute active brain nAChRs in vivo have been primarily inferred from their pharmacologic profile (Sershen et al. 1997; Kaiser et al. 1998; Luo et al. 1998; Sharples et al. 2000). However, advances have identified nAChR subunits expressed by individual neurons in specific brain regions (Lèna et al. 1999; Sheffield et al. 2000).

The predominant role of nAChRs in the brain is the modulation of neurotransmitter release, because nAChRs are situated primarily on presynaptic terminals (Wonnacott 1997). Nevertheless, nAChRs are also found at somatodendritic, axonal, and postsynaptic sites (Sargent 1993). As a result of actions at the nAChR sites, nicotine stimulates the release of most neurotransmitters throughout the brain (Araujo et al. 1988; Toide and Arima 1989; McGehee and Role 1995; Gray et al. 1996; Role and Berg 1996; Wilkie et al. 1996; Albuquerque et al. 1997; Alkondon et al. 1997; Kenny et al. 2000; Grady et al. 2001). Therefore, as discussed in the next section, various transmitter systems are likely to be involved in the rewarding effects of nicotine and in the adaptations that occur in response to chronic exposure to nicotine, which give rise to dependence and withdrawal responses.

Neurosubstrates of Nicotine Reinforcement

The mesocorticolimbic brain system in the midbrain of mammals is composed of interconnected brain structures. This system has been shown to be critically involved in the effects of drugs of abuse (Koob 2008). Among the main components of this system are the dopaminergic neurons originating in the ventral tegmental area (VTA) and projecting to the nucleus accumbens and the frontal cortex. The activity of these VTA dopamine neurons is regulated by the release of the excitatory neurotransmitter glutamate from neuronal projections originating from several sites, including the nucleus accumbens and the frontal cortex. Other inputs that also regulate activity of the mesolimbic system are (1) γ-aminobutyric acid (GABA) inhibitory interneurons located within the VTA and the nucleus accumbens and (2) cholinergic projections from brainstem nuclei to the VTA. These cholinergic projections release the endogenous neurotransmitter acetylcholine, which acts on excitatory nAChRs located on glutamate and GABA neuronal terminals in the VTA (Figure 4.4). Extensive investigations over decades have conclusively demonstrated a critical role of the mesocorticolimbic system and its connections in several behavioral and affective responses to drugs of abuse.

Dopamine and Nicotinic Acetylcholine Receptors

As with other drugs of abuse, it has been demonstrated that the mesolimbic dopaminergic system and nAChRs within that system are critically involved in the reinforcing properties of nicotine (Watkins et al. 2000; Picciotto and Corrigall 2002; Balfour 2004). Acute administration of nicotine increased the firing rate of dopaminergic neurons in the VTA (Grenhoff et al. 1986; Pidoplichko et al. 1997) and elevated dialysate levels of dopamine in the shell of the nucleus accumbens (Imperato et al. 1986; Damsma et al. 1989; Mifsud et al. 1989; Benwell and Balfour 1992; Pontieri et al. 1996; Nisell et al. 1997; Carboni et al. 2000). These effects of nicotine may occur through excitatory actions at nAChRs on the mesolimbic dopaminergic neurons in both the VTA and the nucleus accumbens and at nAChRs located on local neuronal circuitry within these brain regions (McGehee and Role 1996; Nisell et al. 1997; Teng et al. 1997). The nAChRs in the VTA play a more important role than those in the nucleus accumbens in the effects of nicotine on the release of dopamine from the nucleus accumbens (Nisell et al. 1994a,b, 1997).

Several findings support the conclusion that nAChRs located within the VTA are involved in nicotine reinforcement. Intravenous nicotine self-administration is a procedure that allows the assessment of the reinforcing effects of nicotine by measuring the number of infusions a rat chooses to receive intravenously through an indwelling permanent catheter by pressing a lever during one-hour daily sessions in a testing chamber. Each of four factors decreased intravenous nicotine self-administration in rats

(Picciotto and Corrigall 2002). The factors were (1) injections of the competitive nAChR antagonist DHβE into the VTA (Williams and Robinson 1984) but not the nucleus accumbens (Corrigall et al. 1994), (2) development of lesions of the mesolimbic dopaminergic projections from the VTA to the nucleus accumbens (Corrigall et al. 1992), (3) development of cholinergic lesions of the brainstem pedunculopontine tegmental nucleus that project to the VTA (Lança et al. 2000), and (4) systemic administration of dopamine receptor antagonists (Corrigall and Coen 1991b). Studies suggest an involvement of the nAChR subtypes containing α4β2 in both the nicotine-induced release of dopamine and nicotine reinforcement (Picciotto et al. 1998; Schilström et al. 1998b; Watkins et al. 1999; Grillner and Svensson 2000; Sharples et al. 2000). In addition, mutant mice with hypersensitive α4 nAChRs show a 50-fold increase in sensitivity to the reinforcing effects of nicotine measured by a place-preference procedure (Tapper et al. 2004). A place-preference procedure assesses the rewarding effects of a drug by measuring the preference a rat exhibits for a compartment previously associated with the effects of a drug instead of a compartment associated with an injection of saline. The place-preference finding by Tapper and colleagues (2004) further indicates a critical role of α4 nAChRs in nicotine reinforcement. The α7 homomeric receptors may be involved in the reinforcing effects of nicotine. Methyllycaconitine, an antagonist with limited selectivity for the α7 nAChR, decreased the intravenous nicotine self-administration procedure in rats (Markou and Paterson 2001), although another study with rats showed no effects of this antagonist on nicotine-induced hyperactivity or nicotine self-administration (Grottick et al. 2000). Finally, both the α4β2 and α7 subtypes are implicated in the effects of nicotine on memory (Levin et al. 1999; Bancroft and Levin 2000) and the anxiolytic effects of nicotine (Gordon 1999; Cheeta et al. 2001), which also contribute to persistent tobacco use (USDHHS 1988).

Glutamate

Other mechanisms by which nicotine may elevate striatal dopamine levels include increases in excitatory glutamatergic inputs from the frontal cortex to the nucleus accumbens and/or excitatory glutamatergic inputs to VTA dopaminergic neurons projecting to the striatum. Nicotine increases the release of glutamate by agonist actions at excitatory presynaptic nAChRs on glutamatergic terminals in various brain sites, including the VTA (Fu et al. 2000; Grillner and Svensson 2000; Mansvelder and McGehee 2000), nucleus accumbens (Reid et al. 2000), prefrontal cortex (Gioanni et al. 1999), and hippocampus (Gray et al. 1996). In the VTA, nicotine acts

Figure 4.4 Neural pathways for γ-aminobutyric acid, glutamate, dopamine, and excitatory neurotransmitters

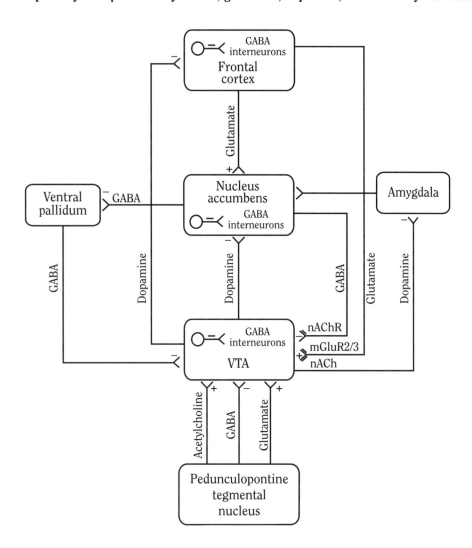

Source: Markou 2006. Reprinted with permission from Wiley-Blackwell, © 2006.
Note: The circular symbol with the reverse arrow attached to it depicts a neuron. The circle is the cell body, and the reverse arrow is the terminal that releases neurotransmitter(s) out of its open site into the synapse at the indicated projection brain site. The minus sign (-) indicates inhibitory input of the neurotransmitter, and the plus sign (+) indicates excitatory input of the neurotransmitter. Some neurons are interneurons projecting within a particular brain site, and other neurons project from one brain site to another distant brain site. **GABA** = γ-aminobutyric acid; **nAChR** = nicotinic acetylcholine receptor; **mGluR2/3** = metabotropic glutamate 2/3 receptor; **VTA** = ventral tegmental area.

at presynaptic α7 nAChRs located on glutamate neurons (neurons that release glutamate as the primary neurotransmitter). Activation of these α7 nAChRs on glutamate neurons (Mansvelder and McGehee 2000) increases the release of glutamate in the VTA. This activity, in turn, stimulates the release of dopamine in the nucleus accumbens (Nisell et al. 1994a,b; Schilström et al. 1998a,b; Fu et al. 2000; Mansvelder and McGehee 2000). That is, this

increased release of glutamate acts at metabotropic and ionotropic glutamate receptors located on postsynaptic dopamine neurons (neurons that have dopamine as the primary neurotransmitter). Activation of these glutamate receptors leads to excitation of the dopamine neurons that results in increased release of dopamine in terminal brain sites where these neurons project, such as the nucleus accumbens, the amygdala, and the frontal cortex.

Ionotropic antagonists of *N*-methyl-D-aspartate receptors blocked (prevented) tolerance to the locomotor depressant effects of acute nicotine administration (Shoaib and Stolerman 1992; Shoaib et al. 1994) and blocked sensitization to the locomotor stimulant effects of chronic nicotine administration (Shoaib and Stolerman 1992). Most relevant to addiction is the finding that blockade of the postsynaptic metabotropic glutamate receptor subtype 5 (mGluR5) with 2-methyl-6-(phenylethynyl)pyridine (MPEP) decreased intravenous nicotine self-administration in rats and mice (Paterson et al. 2003) and decreased the motivation to self-administer nicotine (Paterson and Markou 2005). These effects are likely mediated by decreasing the nicotine-stimulated release of dopamine in the mesolimbic system. At doses that blocked nicotine self-administration, MPEP had no effect on response for food (Paterson et al. 2003). The progressive-ratio schedule of reinforcement, which gradually increases the response requirements after each earned reward, allows the assessment of the motivation for reinforcers, such as nicotine or food, by evaluating the maximal number of responses emitted by the rat (i.e., breaking point) to receive a single intravenous infusion of nicotine or a single food reward. In this schedule, MPEP had a greater effect on motivation for nicotine than on motivation for food, even when the magnitudes of reinforcer value were equated to support equal breaking points for nicotine and food under baseline conditions (Paterson and Markou 2005). This selectivity of the MPEP effects for nicotine reinforcement versus food reinforcement suggests that MPEP selectively blocks the reinforcing effects of nicotine without affecting motor performance or food reinforcement. Furthermore, evidence suggests a potential role of ionotropic glutamate receptors in the effects of nicotine. Animals that self-administered nicotine chronically exhibited an increase in ionotropic glutamate receptor subunits in brain regions, such as the VTA and the frontal cortex, that are implicated in the reinforcing effects of nicotine (Wang et al. 2007).

γ-Aminobutyric Acid

GABA is the major inhibitory transmitter in the brain and is another transmitter system critically involved in the reinforcing effects of acute nicotine administration. Several factors inhibit the release of mesolimbic dopamine, including inhibitory GABA transmission on ascending afferents to dopaminergic VTA neurons from the pedunculopontine tegmental nucleus (Walaas and Fonnum 1980; Yim and Mogenson 1980), descending GABA-ergic inputs from the ventral pallidum and the nucleus accumbens, GABA interneurons within the VTA, and medium spiny GABA neurons in the nucleus accumbens (Walaas and Fonnum 1979; Heimer and Alheid 1991;

Churchill et al. 1992; Dewey et al. 1992; Kalivas et al 1992; Klitenick et al. 1992; Sugita et al. 1992; Engberg et al. 1993). As suggested by this neuroanatomy and extensive electrophysiological studies, interactions between the GABA, dopaminergic, and glutamatergic systems in the VTA are complex (Mansvelder and McGehee 2000; Mansvelder et al. 2002). Glutamate afferents to the VTA excite dopamine neurons, and GABA-ergic afferents to the VTA inhibit dopamine neurons. Excitatory nAChRs are located on both glutamate and GABA-ergic neurons. The nAChRs on GABA neurons desensitize quickly to chronic administration of nicotine, but the nAChRs on glutamate neurons require higher doses of nicotine for desensitization. This delicate balance leads to a nicotine-induced increase in the release of dopamine in the nucleus accumbens, the terminal area of VTA neurons (Schilström et al. 1998b; Mansvelder and McGehee 2000). Similar transmitter interactions may also occur in other brain sites.

Increased GABA-ergic transmission abolishes both the nicotine-induced increases in dopamine in the nucleus accumbens and the reinforcing effects of nicotine (Dewey et al. 1999; Brebner et al. 2002). Systemic injections of γ-vinyl GABA (vigabatrin) increased GABA levels and decreased nicotine self-administration in rats (Paterson and Markou 2002). Vigabatrin is an irreversible inhibitor of GABA transaminase, the primary enzyme involved in GABA metabolism (Jung et al. 1977; Lippert et al. 1977). Systemic injections of vigabatrin also abolished the expression and acquisition of nicotine-induced conditioned place preference (Dewey et al. 1998). The administration of vigabatrin also lowered nicotine-induced increases in dopamine in the nucleus accumbens in both untreated rats and those receiving long-term treatment with nicotine in a dose- and time-dependent manner measured by in vivo microdialysis. In addition, vigabatrin abolished nicotine-induced increases in striatal dopamine in primates, as determined by PET scan (Brebner et al. 2002).

The use of receptor-selective agonists in animals suggests the involvement of GABA$_B$ receptors in the reinforcing effects of nicotine. Systemic injections or microinjections of baclofen or CGP44532 [(3-amino-2[S]-hydroxypropyl)-methylphosphinic acid]—two GABA$_B$ receptor agonists—into the nucleus accumbens shell, the VTA, or the pedunculopontine tegmental nucleus that sends cholinergic, GABA-ergic, and glutamatergic projections to the VTA decreased the reinforcing effects of nicotine (Shoaib et al. 1998; Corrigall et al. 2000, 2001; Fattore et al. 2002; Paterson et al. 2004). However, injections into the caudate-putamen did not have these effects. The decreases in nicotine self-administration persisted even after administration of CGP44532 for 14 days, indicating little tolerance to this effect of the $GABA_B$ receptor agonist with this duration of treatment (Paterson et al. 2005b); that is, the reduction in nicotine self-administration persisted over time. The issue of tolerance is important because long-term administration of drug therapies is necessary to achieve smoking cessation. However, in studies of rats, vigabatrin and $GABA_B$ receptor agonists also decreased response for food, although at doses higher than the threshold doses for inducing decreases in nicotine self-administration (Paterson and Markou 2002; Paterson et al. 2004, 2005b). These effects on response for food may reflect nonspecific effects on performance by GABA-ergic compounds or specific effects on food intake. The possibility of effects on food intake is intriguing, because weight gain associated with abstinence from smoking is often a concern for smokers, especially women, who want to stop smoking cigarettes.

Thus, increased GABA transmission through the activation of $GABA_B$ receptors blocks the reinforcing effects of nicotine. However, a clinical study shows that one dose of baclofen had no effect on either the number of cigarettes smoked or the craving for nicotine (Cousins et al. 2001). Nevertheless, other clinical studies show that long-term administration of baclofen reduced abuse of cocaine and alcohol, as well as cue-induced brain activation (Ling et al. 1998; Addolorato et al. 2000, 2002a,b). Therefore, long-term treatment with these GABA-ergic drugs may first be required to reduce tobacco smoking.

Opioid, Endocannabinoid, and Serotonin Systems

The data on the possible role of opioid systems in the rewarding effects of nicotine remain inconclusive. Nicotine did not induce a conditioned place preference in μ-opioid receptor *NULL*-mutant mice, but it did so in wild-type animals (Berrendero et al. 2002). Similarly, nicotine induced a conditioned place preference in wild-type but not in preproenkephalin *NULL*-mutant mice. A nicotine-induced elevation in dopamine overflow in the nucleus accumbens was absent in *NULL* mutants (Berrendero et al. 2005). However, systemic or intra-VTA administration of the opiate receptor antagonist naltrexone or the opiate receptor agonist D-Ala^2,N-Me-Phe^4-Gly-ol-enkephalin, respectively, had limited or no effects on nicotine self-administration in rats (Corrigall and Coen 1991a; Corrigall et al. 2000).

In humans, acute and short-term nicotine administration leads to the release of β-endorphins, endogenous opioid peptides that have reinforcing effects (Davenport et al. 1990; Boyadjieva and Sarkar 1997). Furthermore, in humans, the acute administration of naltrexone decreased the reinforcing value of nicotine in a procedure involving choice between puffs on nicotinized versus denicotinized cigarettes (i.e., compared with placebo, naltrexone significantly reduced the number of nicotine cigarette choices) (Rukstalis et al. 2005). This result is consistent with a previous finding that acute administration of naltrexone significantly decreased the total number of choice cigarettes smoked (e.g., subjects were given a choice to smoke four cigarettes in a two-hour period of time) (Epstein and King 2004). However, a randomized, double-blind trial of naltrexone for smoking cessation found only a nonsignificant trend toward increased cessation rates, and the effect disappeared at 12 months after cessation (Covey et al. 1999). Other clinical trials examining the effects of naltrexone versus placebo in smokers who were assigned nicotine patches to aid cessation have also observed no significant effects of naltrexone on improving treatment outcomes (King et al. 2006; O'Malley et al. 2006). Thus, the possible involvement of the opiate system in the reinforcing effects of nicotine remains at best unclear, and the use of opiate antagonists as treatments for dependence on tobacco smoking appears unwarranted. A Cochrane review in 2001 concluded that opioid antagonists failed to significantly increase long-term abstinence from smoking on the basis that the limited evidence was insufficient to support a conclusive finding on whether naltrexone is an aid to smoking cessation (David et al. 2006). Although one study suggested an effect of gender, women benefited more than men from treatment with naltrexone (King et al. 2006).

The evidence is much stronger for the role of serotonin in the reinforcing effects of nicotine. Acute administration of nicotine elevated extracellular serotonin in the nucleus accumbens (Schiffer et al. 2001) and the VTA (Singer et al. 2004). Serotonin was also implicated in a neurochemical sensitization to nicotine, which some researchers hypothesize to be relevant to aspects of nicotine dependence. The administration of the serotonin ($5HT_2$) receptor agonist (±)-2,5-dimethoxy-4-iodoamphetamine (Olausson et al. 2001) or the $5HT_{2C}$ receptor agonist (S)-2-(chloro-5-fluoro-indol-1-yl)-1-methylethylamine fumarate (Di Matteo et al. 2004) blocked the increased overflow of serotonin observed after a nicotine challenge in nicotine-treated rats. In addition, nicotine increased serotonin overflow in cortical areas (Toth et al. 1992; Ribeiro et al. 1993; Summers and Giacobini 1995; Singer et al. 2004) and in the dorsal hippocampus (Singer et al. 2004). In contrast, Balfour and Ridley (2000) found a decrease in the serotonin overflow after acute administration of nicotine. However, Singer and colleagues (2004) used anesthetized rats, and Balfour and Ridley (2000) used in vivo microdialysis in conscious rats. In addition, administration of nicotine for at least 20 days was associated with decreased serotonin levels in the dorsal hippocampus (Benwell and Balfour 1979; Balfour and Ridley

2000). However, nicotine administration for 14 days was associated with increased serotonin levels (Takada et al. 1995). Nicotine infusion into the ventromedial nuclei or the lateral hypothalamic area increased the release of serotonin in this area (Yang et al. 1999; Ramos et al. 2004). Together, the findings suggest that acute administration of nicotine increases serotonin levels but that long-term administration leads to decreases in serotonin levels that may mediate the affective aspects of nicotine dependence and withdrawal (Harrison et al. 2001).

Studies provide conflicting evidence on the role of cannabinoid subtype 1 (CB_1) receptors in modulating the reinforcing effects of nicotine. CB_1 knockout mice (i.e., mice genetically engineered to lack CB_1 receptors) self-administered nicotine (Cossu et al. 2001) but did not exhibit conditioned place preference to nicotine (Castañe et al. 2002). Furthermore, the CB_1 receptor antagonist rimonabant (SR141716) decreased nicotine seeking and self-administration of nicotine induced by the presentation of conditioned cues and also attenuated a nicotine-induced release of dopamine in the nucleus accumbens shell (Cohen et al. 2002, 2005; De Vries et al. 2005). Thus, the data from experimental studies of rodents on the role of the cannabinoid system are inconclusive and so are the clinical data (Le Foll and Goldberg 2005). However, an analysis of data pooled from three clinical trials of rimonabant compared with a placebo showed modest success at the end of treatment (Cinciripini et al. 2006).

Norepinephrine

Data also suggest a role of norepinephrine in the effects of nicotine. Acute nicotine administration increases extracellular norepinephrine in the nucleus accumbens, the hippocampus, and the cortex in rats (Brazell et al. 1991; Mitchell et al. 1993; Summers and Giacobini 1995; Benwell and Balfour 1997; Schiffer et al. 2001). Nicotine-evoked hippocampal release of norepinephrine in vivo was attenuated by α-bungarotoxin but was unaffected by either of the nAChR antagonists mecamylamine or DHβE, implicating $\alpha7$ nAChRs, rather than $\alpha4\beta2$ nAChRs associated with the release of norepinephrine in this region of the brain (Fu et al. 1999). However, norepinephrine release from hippocampal synaptosomes in rats was sensitive to mecamylamine, DHβE, and methyllycaconitine suggesting that the release of norepinephrine may not be specific to $\alpha7$ nAChRs (Clarke and Reuben 1996). Additional studies suggest the role of norepinephrine in nicotine's effects. Intravenous self-administration of nicotine increased norepinephrine concentrations in the amygdala and the hypothalamic paraventricular nucleus (Fu et al. 2001,

2003). In vitro studies indicated that nicotine increased release of norepinephrine in (1) prefrontal cortex slices of rats (Rao et al. 2003) and (2) locus coeruleus neurons of fetal rats grown in cultures (Gallardo and Leslie 1998).

Consistent with these neurochemical findings, short-term or long-term administration of reboxetine, the selective noradrenaline reuptake inhibitor, decreased nicotine self-administration in rats (Rauhut et al. 2002). However, reboxetine also decreased sucrose-maintained response, although to a lesser degree than nicotine-maintained response. Reboxetine acts as a noncompetitive nAChR antagonist, in addition to blocking noradrenaline reuptake (Miller et al. 2002). Thus, it is not conclusive that the effects of reboxetine on nicotine self-administration are attributable to its effects on noradrenaline reuptake rather than to its actions as an nAChR antagonist.

Bupropion, a smoking cessation aid, also inhibits reuptake of norepinephrine, as well as dopamine (Ferris et al. 1983). Administration of bupropion increased extracellular concentrations of dopamine and epinephrine in the nucleus accumbens, hypothalamus, and prefrontal cortex (Nomikos et al. 1989, 1992; Li et al. 2002). Furthermore, electrophysiological studies indicated that bupropion decreased the firing rates of dopamine neurons in the nucleus accumbens and noradrenergic neurons in the locus coeruleus but had no effect on firing of serotonin dorsal raphe neurons (neurons located in the dorsal raphe firing) (Cooper et al. 1994).

Despite the demonstrated effects of bupropion on neurotransmitter and receptor systems that appear to mediate the effects of nicotine, bupropion had inconsistent effects on nicotine self-administration in rats. Some studies showed a decrease in nicotine self-administration in fixed-ratio schedules of reinforcement but had no effects in a progressive-ratio schedule (Glick et al. 2002; Bruijnzeel and Markou 2003). In contrast, another study (Shoaib et al. 2003) indicated that repeated daily administration of bupropion increased nicotine self-administration in a fixed-ratio schedule, but the results were not significant (Shoaib et al. 2003). Finally, Rauhut and coworkers (2003) showed that low doses of bupropion increased and high doses of bupropion decreased nicotine self-administration and response for sucrose.

In summary, these findings suggest a strong effect of nicotine on transmission of norepinephrine, but bupropion, which inhibits the reuptake of both dopamine and norepinephrine, has inconsistent effects on nicotine self-administration in rodents. Thus, other properties of bupropion, such as relief from withdrawal symptoms, may contribute to its efficacy as an aid to smoking cessation.

Neurosubstrates of Nicotine Dependence and Withdrawal

Nicotine Withdrawal Syndrome in Rodents

Smoking cessation leads to an aversive withdrawal syndrome lasting one to four weeks after cessation (Shiffman et al. 2004b). As noted previously, this withdrawal syndrome has affective, behavioral, somatic, and cognitive components (see "Physiological Mechanisms and Indicators: Nicotine Tolerance, Withdrawal, and Reinforcement" earlier in this chapter). The nicotine withdrawal syndrome is considered an important motivational factor that contributes to the perpetuation of nicotine dependence and continuing behaviors related to tobacco smoking (Markou et al. 1998; Kenny and Markou 2001). Withdrawal signs are often opposite to the acute effects of the drug (e.g., improved concentration versus poor concentration), probably reflecting the finding that the development of nicotine dependence leads to changes in brain function to counteract the acute effects of nicotine (e.g., increase in receptor number).

One of the first and most widely used measures developed to investigate the neurobiology of the nicotine withdrawal syndrome and nicotine dependence is the frequency of somatic signs reliably observed in rats, but less reliably observed in mice (Malin et al. 1992; Epping-Jordan et al. 1998; Hildebrand et al. 1999; Isola et al. 1999; Carboni et al. 2000; Malin 2001; Semenova and Markou 2003; Salas et al. 2004). The most prominent somatic signs in rats are abdominal constrictions (writhes), gasps, ptosis, facial fasciculation, and eyeblinks. These somatic signs are both centrally and peripherally mediated (Hildebrand et al. 1999; Carboni et al. 2000; Watkins et al. 2000; Malin 2001; Cryan et al. 2003).

The somatic components of nicotine withdrawal are unpleasant. However, avoidance of the negative affect and depression-like components of withdrawal may play a more important role in the maintenance of nicotine dependence than do the somatic aspects of withdrawal (Hughes 1992; Kenny and Markou 2001). In rodents, a valid and reliable measure of the affective and motivational aspects of drug withdrawal is the elevation of brain-reward thresholds observed after cessation of long-term administration of nicotine (Epping-Jordan et al. 1998; Harrison et al. 2001; Cryan et al. 2003; Semenova and Markou 2003). Elevations of reward thresholds are an operational measure of "diminished interest or pleasure" in rewarding stimuli (i.e., anhedonia), which is a symptom of nicotine withdrawal and a core symptom of depression (APA 1994). Similar threshold elevations are observed

during withdrawal from all major drugs of abuse in rodents (Kokkinidis et al. 1980; Markou and Koob 1991; Schulteis et al. 1994, 1995; Paterson et al. 2000; Spielewoy and Markou 2003). Several dissociations have been identified between the threshold elevations and the somatic signs of nicotine withdrawal, and these observations are similar to those in clinical studies (see "Physiological Mechanisms and Indicators: Nicotine Tolerance, Withdrawal, and Reinforcement" earlier in this chapter). These findings suggest that the various aspects of withdrawal are mediated by different substrates (Epping-Jordan et al. 1998; Watkins et al. 2000; Harrison et al. 2001; Semenova and Markou 2003). Other rodent models that may be relevant to the disruption of behavioral performance in humans involve (1) disruptions induced by termination of administration of nicotine on behavioral responses maintained by food (Carroll et al. 1989); (2) increases in the acoustic startle response in rats (Helton et al. 1993); and (3) decreases in prepulse inhibition (i.e., decrease in the adaptation response to a stronger stimuli after presentation of a prior weaker stimuli) in mice (Semenova et al. 2003).

Important study data indicate that rats with threshold elevations reflecting a reward deficit associated with nicotine withdrawal can become conditioned to previously neutral environmental stimuli (Kenny and Markou 2005) (see "Learning and Conditioning" earlier in this chapter). Nicotine-dependent rats were presented with a light and tone CS and received injections of the nicotinic receptor antagonist DHβE for four consecutive days before an assessment of brain-reward thresholds. This procedure led to elevations of brain-reward thresholds in the nicotine-dependent rats. When the rats were presented with just the light and tone CS on the test day, thresholds were again elevated, reflecting a conditioned state of negative affect. This type of conditioned affective response may lead to a relapse to tobacco smoking to alleviate this conditioned state of negative affect. This finding may partly explain the relapse observed months or even years after a person last smoked a cigarette.

Subsequent data suggest that the experience of nicotine withdrawal in male adolescent rats may differ from that in adult rats. At the time of this review, no females have been tested. The evidence for this hypothesis is threefold. First, male adolescent rats displayed fewer somatic signs of nicotine withdrawal than did adult males. Second, although male adolescent rats displayed a conditioned place aversion produced by nicotine withdrawal, it was less robust than that seen in adult males. Third, adolescent male rats did not display the decreases in brain-reward function seen in adult rats experiencing withdrawal (O'Dell et al. 2006, 2007).

Neurochemical Correlates of Nicotine Withdrawal

Several experimental approaches are used to investigate the neuronal substrates of nicotine dependence and withdrawal. In vivo microdialysis studies provide information about the neurochemical changes occurring in specific brain sites with nicotine dependence. The precipitation of nicotine withdrawal in nicotine-treated rats, but not in controls, with administration of drugs that probe various transmitter systems and receptors suggests that chronic exposure to nicotine induces adaptations in specific transmitter systems and receptors. The combination of the in vivo microdialysis technique with the precipitated nicotine withdrawal technique indicates that the circuits mediating the acute effects of nicotine develop adaptations with nicotine dependence that lead to the withdrawal syndrome (Figure 4.4 depicts the brain structures and their interconnections forming circuits discussed in this chapter).

During nicotine withdrawal precipitated by systemic or intra-VTA administration of the nAChR antagonist mecamylamine in nicotine-treated rats, dialysate levels of dopamine were decreased in the nucleus accumbens (Fung et al. 1996; Hildebrand et al. 1998; Carboni et al. 2000) and in the central nucleus of the amygdala (Panagis et al. 2000). These mecamylamine injections into the VTA also produced, in a dose-dependent manner, most of the somatic signs of nicotine withdrawal (Hildebrand et al. 1999). This finding suggests the involvement of nAChRs in the VTA in the expression of the somatic signs of nicotine withdrawal. Most important, similar decreases in levels of dopamine in the nucleus accumbens were observed in rats allowed to self-administer nicotine for 25 days, beginning 24 to 48 hours after the last session for self-administration of nicotine (Rahman et al. 2004). Decreases in dopamine levels in the nucleus accumbens are also associated with withdrawal from other drugs of abuse, such as ethanol, morphine, cocaine, and amphetamine (Rossetti et al. 1992). In contrast, the increases in dialysate dopamine levels observed in the frontal cortex (Hildebrand et al. 1998; Carboni et al. 2000) were similar to those observed during withdrawal from other drugs of abuse (Imperato et al. 1986). Thus, it appears that common substrates are involved in the mediation of the withdrawal signs associated with different drugs of abuse that involve alterations in dopamine transmission in the nucleus accumbens and the frontal cortex.

The smoking cessation aid bupropion, an atypical antidepressant, acts at least partly by inhibiting the neuronal uptake of dopamine, which thereby increases dopamine transmission (Nomikos et al. 1992). Bupropion reverses both the threshold elevations and the somatic signs associated with nicotine withdrawal (Cryan

et al. 2003) in rats, although its effects on nicotine self-administration are inconsistent (Glick et al. 2002; Bruijnzeel and Markou 2003; Shoaib et al. 2003). Taken together, the above data strongly suggest that a decrease in mesolimbic dopaminergic transmission mediates aspects of nicotine withdrawal.

Another transmitter system that may be involved in nicotine dependence and withdrawal is the norepinephrine system. However, to date, the role of this system in nicotine dependence has not been investigated as extensively as that of the dopamine system. Acute administration of nicotine elevates extracellular noradrenaline levels in the nucleus accumbens (Schiffer et al. 2001), hippocampus (Brazell et al. 1991; Mitchell et al. 1993; Benwell and Balfour 1997), cortex (Summers and Giacobini 1995), amygdala, and hypothalamic paraventricular nucleus (Fu et al. 2001). These findings indicate that nicotine withdrawal may be characterized by a decrease in noradrenergic transmission. This hypothesis is supported by evidence for the beneficial effects on smoking cessation of nortriptyline, a norepinephrine reuptake inhibitor (Hughes et al. 2004b) and the ameliorative effects of the α2-adrenoceptor agonist clonidine on nicotine withdrawal in double-blind, placebo-controlled studies (Covey and Glassman 1991).

Other neurotransmitter systems such as serotonin, endocannabinoid, or opioid may also be involved in withdrawal, but research on these systems is limited. A few studies suggest the involvement of the opioid system. For example, naloxone precipitates somatic signs of withdrawal in nicotine-dependent rats (Malin et al. 1993; Watkins et al. 1999). Some studies also demonstrate the involvement of the serotonin system (see "Antidepressant and Antipsychotic Drugs and Nicotine Withdrawal" later in this chapter).

Receptors and Behavioral Signs of Nicotine Withdrawal

Studies document that administration of a variety of nAChR antagonists induces behavioral signs of withdrawal in addition to the neurochemical effects of withdrawal in nicotine-treated rats. Systemic or intra-VTA administration of mecamylamine or systemic or intraventricular administration of chlorisondamine induced somatic signs and/or elevation of reward threshold in nicotine-dependent rats only (Hildebrand et al. 1999; Watkins et al. 2000). Administration of the nAChR antagonist DHβE, which is selective for high-affinity nAChRs containing α4 (Harvey and Luetje 1996), induced threshold elevations (Epping-Jordan et al. 1998; Bruijnzeel and Markou 2004) but did not induce increases in somatic signs in nicotine-dependent rats (Epping-Jordan et al. 1998). This finding demonstrates that the threshold elevations are not due to nonspecific performance effects of the antagonists. Together, these results illustrate the involvement of nAChRs in the VTA in both the somatic and affective aspects of withdrawal.

In addition, work in knockout mice demonstrates a critical role of β4 but not β2 nAChRs in the somatic signs of withdrawal (Salas et al. 2004; Jackson et al. 2008). β2 nAChRs are critical for the reinforcing effects of nicotine (Picciotto and Corrigall 2002) and for the affective signs of nicotine withdrawal, as reflected in anxiety-like behavior and conditioned place aversion (Jackson et al. 2008). The α7 homomeric nAChRs may be involved in the reinforcing effects of nicotine (Markou and Paterson 2001) and perhaps only in some somatic aspects but not in the affective aspects of nicotine withdrawal (Markou and Paterson 2001; Jackson et al. 2008). Specifically, administration of the α7 nAChR antagonist methyllycaconitine did not precipitate either the typical somatic signs of nicotine withdrawal or the reward deficits reflected in threshold elevations in nicotine-dependent rats (Markou and Paterson 2001). However, in α7 knockout mice, no hyperalgesia was present during nicotine withdrawal, an effect seen in wild-type mice during nicotine withdrawal (Jackson et al. 2008). However, these α7 knockout mice showed normal levels of somatic and affective signs of nicotine withdrawal. Thus, the role of α7 nAChRs may be limited to some somatic signs, including hyperalgesia, of nicotine withdrawal. Finally, α4 nAChRs have been shown to be involved in the reinforcing effects of nicotine (Tapper et al. 2004). Their role in nicotine withdrawal has not been clearly delineated, but it may influence both affective and somatic withdrawal effects (Salas et al. 2004; Gonzales et al. 2006; Jorenby et al. 2006; Jackson et al. 2008). Overall, the observation that nAChR antagonists precipitate the behavioral and neurochemical signs of withdrawal in nicotine-dependent rats, but not in controls, suggests that chronic exposure to nicotine induces a compensatory reduction in endogenous cholinergic tone that leads to the nicotine withdrawal syndrome.

Because glutamate stimulates dopamine release (Schilström et al. 1998a; Mansvelder and McGehee 2000), decreased glutamate transmission may mediate nicotine withdrawal. Systemic or intra-VTA administration of the mGluR subtype 2/3 (mGluR2/3) agonist LY314582 led to withdrawal-like threshold elevations in nicotine-dependent rats but not in control rats (Kenny et al. 2003). These mGluR2/3 receptors are found primarily presynaptically (i.e., on the transmitting neuron at the synaptic terminal that extends to the synapse, and the released transmitters target the postsynaptic neuron), where they inhibit glutamate transmission (Cartmell and Schoepp 2000; Kenny and Markou 2004). The increased sensitivity of nicotine-dependent rats to an agonist at the presynaptic inhibitory mGluR2/3 suggests that nicotine dependence is characterized by increased inhibition of glutamate transmission through these receptors, resulting in decreases in the release of glutamate when nicotine is no longer present to stimulate glutamate release. Consistent with this hypothesis, the mGluR2/3 antagonist LY341495 reversed the threshold elevations observed in rats that had spontaneous nicotine withdrawal (Kenny et al. 2003). Similarly, activity decreased in postsynaptic α-amino-3-hydroxy-5-methyl-4-isoxazole proprionic/kainate receptors, although no adaptations in mGluR5 receptors were observed in nicotine-dependent rats (Kenny et al. 2003). This result was somewhat surprising considering the important role found for this receptor in the reinforcing effects of nicotine (Paterson et al. 2003; Paterson and Markou 2005). Taken together, all of the above findings indicate that decreased glutamate transmission resulting from adaptations in presynaptic and postsynaptic receptors may contribute to the affective aspects of nicotine withdrawal.

These data on the lack of adaptations in mGluR5 activity highlight the finding that not all systems involved in the reinforcing effects of nicotine develop changes with long-term exposure to nicotine. This notion is also supported by data demonstrating that there are no changes in GABA transmission, GABA$_B$ receptor activity, or α7 nAChR activity in nicotine-dependent rats, despite the important role of the GABA$_B$ receptor and possibly the α7 nAChR in the reinforcing effects of nicotine (Markou and Paterson 2001; Paterson and Markou 2002; Paterson et al. 2004, 2005a,b).

Molecular Mechanisms

Activated nAChRs are permeable to both sodium ions and Ca^{2+}, which lead to activation of the neurons and thus the release of many transmitters (Wonnacott et al. 2005). The widespread brain activation induced by acute or long-term administration of nicotine is shown by the expression of *C-FOS* in areas such as the amygdala, bed nucleus of the stria terminalis, lateral septum, hypothalamic nuclei, striatum, parts of the cortex, superior colliculus, optic tract, interpeduncular nucleus, supramammillary nucleus, periaqueductal gray matter, nucleus of the solitary tract, and locus coeruleus (Merlo Pich et al. 1999). *C-FOS*–related antigens are C-FOS proteins that heterodimerize with C-JUN proteins to produce complexes of activator protein-1 and transcriptionally regulate large numbers of genes related to plasticity (Dobranzki et al. 1991; Merlo Pich et al. 1997).

Another protein researchers have studied extensively is the cyclic adenosine monophosphate–response element binding protein (CREB), because it is part of the signaling cascade for several receptors, including nAChRs (Nestler 2001). Acute treatment with nicotine had no effect on levels of total CREB or phosphorylated CREB (p-CREB). However, 18 hours after withdrawal from long-term administration of nicotine, total concentrations of CREB and p-CREB decreased in the shell but not in the core of the nucleus accumbens (Pluzarev and Pandey 2004) and in the medial and basolateral amygdala but not in the central amygdala (Pandey et al. 2001). The high Ca^{2+} permeability of nAChRs also leads to the stimulation of additional intracellular messenger systems such as calmodulin-dependent protein kinases, including Ca^{2+} calmodulin-dependent protein kinase II (CaMKII), which is the most abundant kinase in the brain (Schulman and Hanson 1993). Acute administration of nicotine in mice induced increases in CaMKII expression in the spinal cord that was involved in the antinociceptive effects of nicotine (Damaj 2000).

These are a few examples of the molecular changes observed after acute or long-term administration of nicotine and on withdrawal from long-term administration. These molecular changes demonstrate that nicotine induces changes in molecular mechanisms involved in long-term plasticity. Such molecular effects are likely to mediate several aspects of dependence on nicotine.

Clinical Imaging Studies

Clinical imaging studies have confirmed findings from basic research in rodents and have provided additional critical information about brain sites and processes involved in tobacco addiction in humans that cannot readily be investigated in animals (e.g., hedonic responses and craving). Some of the effects of nicotine in various regions of the brain have also been described elsewhere (see "Learning and Conditioning" earlier in this chapter). Similar to other drugs of abuse, nicotine decreases global glucose metabolism in the brain, as determined by PET with [18F]fluorodeoxyglucose (Stapleton et al. 2003). Long-term exposure to tobacco smoke also inhibits MAOA and MAOB activity (Volkow et al. 1999). Congruent with the suggested role of mesolimbic dopamine in the rewarding effects of nicotine in rodents, PET studies with [11C]raclopride indicate that cigarette smoking increased dopamine levels in the striatum of smokers (Brody et al. 2004b) and that the hedonic response of the smoker to cigarette smoking was proportional to the dopamine released in the striatum (Barrett et al. 2004). Other areas activated by nicotine or smoking are the prefrontal

cortex, ventral putamen, anterior cingulated cortex, superior parietal cortex, and thalamus (Kumari et al. 2003; Rose et al. 2003b; Brody et al. 2004b; Fallon et al. 2004; Jacobsen et al. 2004; Brody 2006). Smoking-associated images during inductions of craving that often lead to smoking increased the functional magnetic resonance imaging signal in reward circuits such as the right posterior amygdala, posterior hippocampus, VTA, and medial thalamus (Due et al. 2002). As mentioned previously, long-term administration of bupropion attenuated cue-induced craving and led to blunted activation of the perigenual and ventral anterior cingulate cortex (Brody et al. 2004a).

Functional magnetic resonance imaging was used in an interesting comparison of the effects of nicotine on the brains of patients with schizophrenia and the brains of control participants. Nicotine-induced activation of the anterior cingulate cortex and bilateral thalamus was greater in patients with schizophrenia than in control participants during performance of a cognitive task (Jacobsen et al. 2004). This finding suggests that nicotine may improve cognitive performance in patients with schizophrenia by enhancing the thalamocortical functional connectivity (Jacobsen et al. 2004) (see "Schizophrenia and Nicotine Dependence" later in this chapter). Relevant to the high prevalence of smoking among patients with depression, smokers showed cortical responses suggesting vulnerability to depression in a study that used tryptophan depletion to increase the depressed mood in smokers (Pergadia et al. 2004).

Psychiatric Comorbidity

Antidepressant and Antipsychotic Drugs and Nicotine Withdrawal

Another experimental approach used to identify systems that mediate nicotine withdrawal and dependence is a study of pharmacologic manipulations that reverse spontaneous nicotine withdrawal. Inferences can be made regarding the underlying abnormality associated with withdrawal through the mechanisms associated with the pharmacotherapy. On the basis of the phenomenological similarities among depression, the depression-like aspects of nicotine withdrawal, and the negative symptoms of schizophrenia, researchers hypothesize that overlapping neurobiologic substrates may mediate these depressive symptoms and that antidepressant and atypical antipsychotic treatments would alleviate the depression-like aspects of nicotine withdrawal (Markou et al. 1998; Markou and Kenny 2002).

Such common substrates mediating nicotine dependence and psychiatric disorders may explain the high prevalence of tobacco smoking among psychiatric populations. Compared with the percentage of smokers in the general population (20 to 30 percent), a higher percentage of mentally ill patients were smokers (26 to 88 percent, depending on the mental illness) (Lasser et al. 2000), particularly those with schizophrenia, depression, or addiction to alcohol or other drugs (Hughes et al. 1986; Glassman et al. 1990; Breslau 1995). For illustrative purposes, substrates that mediate depression, schizophrenia, and nicotine dependence are described in the following sections.

Depression and Nicotine Dependence

Although the estimates vary across age, population, and criteria for tobacco dependence, most estimates suggest that the incidence of major depressive disorder among smokers is approximately two to three times that among nonsmokers (Hughes et al. 1986; Glassman et al. 1988, 1990; Kandel et al. 2001; Fergusson et al. 2003). A history of major depression increased the risk for progression to daily smoking and nicotine dependence, and a history of daily smoking and nicotine dependence increased the risk for major depression (Breslau et al. 1993b, 1998). A depressed mood is one of the symptoms of tobacco withdrawal syndrome experienced by a significant proportion of persons who attempt to stop smoking (West et al. 1984; Hughes and Hatsukami 1992; APA 1994). Therefore, tobacco smoking may be self-medication for either the depression that preceded the drug use or the smoking-induced depression (Pomerleau et al. 1978; Waal-Manning and de Hamel 1978; Hughes et al. 1986; Glassman 1993; Markou et al. 1998).

In particular, 5HT and the 5HT1A receptors appear to be critically involved in the mode of action of several antidepressant drugs used clinically (Markou et al. 1998) and may play a role in nicotine withdrawal (Kenny and Markou 2001). Systemic administration of 5HT1A receptor agonists, such as 8-hydroxy-2-dipropylaminotetralin (8-OH-DPAT), exacerbated the increased startle response observed during nicotine withdrawal, whereas 5HT1A receptor antagonists (e.g., WAY-100635) alleviated this increased response (Rasmussen et al. 1997, 2000). In addition, the responsiveness of dorsal raphe nucleus neurons to 8-OH-DPAT increased during nicotine withdrawal (Rasmussen and Czachura 1997). Thus, nicotine withdrawal may increase the inhibitory influence of somatodendritic 5HT1A autoreceptors in the raphe nuclei, and thereby decrease the release of serotonin in the forebrain and limbic brain sites (Benwell and Balfour 1979, 1982; Ridley and Balfour 1997). This conclusion is supported by the observation that a serotonergic antidepressant treatment involving the coadministration of the selective serotonin

reuptake inhibitor fluoxetine and the 5HT1A receptor antagonist p-MPPI [4-(2'-methoxy-phenyl)-1-[2'-(n-2''-pyridinyl)-p-iodobenzamido]ethyl-piperazine] rapidly reversed the elevation in thresholds of brain-stimulation reward observed in rats with nicotine withdrawal, but the treatment did not block the somatic signs of withdrawal (Harrison et al. 2001). Consistent with this finding, the 5HT1A receptor partial agonist buspirone has shown limited efficacy in smoking cessation trials and may reduce the severity of withdrawal in persons attempting to stop smoking (West et al. 1991; Hilleman et al. 1992, 1994; Schneider et al. 1996). In conclusion, like depressions not induced by drugs, the depression-like aspects of nicotine withdrawal may be at least partly mediated by a decrease in monoaminergic transmission.

Consistent with the hypothesis that shared substrates mediate nicotine dependence and depression, clinical trials indicate that two of the antidepressant drug treatments are efficacious aids for smoking cessation. The atypical antidepressant bupropion, which primarily inhibits the reuptake of dopamine, was more effective than a placebo in clinical trials to achieve smoking cessation (Fiore et al. 2008), and bupropion has been approved for this use by the U.S. Food and Drug Administration (FDA). Preclinical research suggests that bupropion reverses both the depression-like and somatic aspects of nicotine withdrawal (Cryan et al. 2003), although its effects on the rewarding effects of nicotine are inconsistent (Bruijnzeel and Markou 2003). In addition, the tricyclic antidepressant nortriptyline, which primarily inhibits the reuptake of norepinephrine, is recommended by WHO and the U.S. Public Health Service (Fiore et al. 2008) as a smoking cessation aid. In conclusion, similar monoaminergic mechanisms appear to be involved in both depression and nicotine dependence.

Schizophrenia and Nicotine Dependence

More than 80 to 90 percent of patients with schizophrenia smoke compared with 20 to 30 percent of the general population (Masterson and O'Shea 1984; Goff et al. 1992; de Leon et al. 1995; Hughes 1996; Diwan et al. 1998). Persons with schizophrenia are commonly heavy smokers (>1.5 packs of cigarettes per day); smoke high-tar cigarettes, which are also high in nicotine content; and extract more nicotine from cigarettes than do smokers without schizophrenia (Masterson and O'Shea 1984; Hughes et al. 1986; Olincy et al. 1997).

The mesolimbic dopamine system and its efferent and afferent connections to other brain sites and systems, particularly dopamine-glutamate interactions, are strongly implicated in both the reinforcing effects of nicotine and schizophrenia (Snyder 1976; Carlsson 1977).

Abnormalities in these systems may render patients with schizophrenia more susceptible to the rewarding effects of nicotine (Chambers et al. 2001). Such patients may use nicotine to counteract the cognitive and/or depression-like aspects of schizophrenia that are not effectively treated with most antipsychotic drugs (Markou and Kenny 2002). Nicotine administration through tobacco smoking ameliorated visuospatial cognitive deficits of patients with schizophrenia (George et al. 2002) that involve the prefrontal cortex (Funahashi and Kubota 1994; Goldman-Rakic 1995; Callicott et al. 1998; Kikuchi-Yorioka and Sawaguchi 2000; Manoach et al. 2000).

Two forms of sensory-gating deficits (the inability to ignore or filter out irrelevant sensory information) that patients with schizophrenia exhibit may be influenced by actions on $\alpha7$ or other nAChRs (Freedman et al. 1997; Adler et al. 1998). The two deficits are (1) auditory P50 gating, a form of sensory blocking, and (2) prepulse inhibition of the startle response. Thus, smoking may be a form of self-medication to compensate for these gating deficits. In support of this hypothesis, one study found that acute nicotine treatment reversed disruptions in prepulse inhibition induced in mice by the administration of the *N*-methyl-D-aspartate receptor antagonist phencyclidine, which mimics human psychosis (Spielewoy and Markou 2003).

Nicotine administration may be a form of self-medication for the depression-like negative symptoms of schizophrenia. The atypical antipsychotic drug clozapine treats the negative symptoms of schizophrenia most effectively and has decreased tobacco smoking in some persons without any encouragement to reduce smoking (George et al. 1995). In addition, long-term pretreatment with clozapine attenuated the severity of the nicotine withdrawal syndrome in rats (Semenova and Markou 2003).

Summary and Future Directions

The VTA region of the brain and the dopamine neurotransmitter are primarily responsible for the positive reinforcing aspects of nicotine addiction. An increase in dopamine levels is mediated by nicotine directly stimulating nAChRs, primarily $\alpha4\beta2$ and $\alpha7$ homomeric nAChRs in the VTA. Nicotine stimulates nAChRs on glutamatergic terminals that release glutamate, an excitatory neurotransmitter, which results in increased dopamine release in the nucleus accumbens and the frontal cortex. Nicotine also excites nAChRs on GABA-releasing terminals. Thus, levels of GABA, an inhibitory neurotransmitter, are also increased by nicotine. However, the interplay between

the quick desensitization of nAChRs on the GABA neuron and the higher doses of nicotine required to desensitize nAChRs on the glutamate neuron results in a greater increase in dopamine levels. A critical role may also be played by nicotine-induced increases in norepinephrine transmission, although the role of this transmitter system in nicotine dependence has not been investigated as extensively as that of the dopamine, glutamate, and GABA systems. The role of endocannabinoids, serotonin, and endogenous opiates in nicotine addiction is less certain.

The neurophysiology associated with withdrawal symptoms may be based on the type of symptoms experienced (e.g., somatic versus affective). The nAChRs appear to be involved in both the somatic and affective components of nicotine withdrawal. Animal studies suggest that $\beta4$ plays an important role in the somatic symptoms of withdrawal, whereas $\beta2$ seems to play a role in the affective symptoms of withdrawal. The neuronal subunit $\alpha7$ may be involved only in some of the somatic (e.g., hyperalgesia) aspects of withdrawal. The role of $\alpha4$ is unclear, but it may influence both affective and somatic withdrawal effects. Decreased mesolimbic dopaminergic transmission seems to mediate various aspects of the withdrawal syndrome. Noradrenergic and serotonergic systems may also play a role in withdrawal. Decreased glutamate transmission appears to mediate the affective aspects of withdrawal, but GABA transmission does not appear to change with withdrawal. Although not discussed in this section, some studies also suggest that a dysregulation in the hypothalamic-pituitary axis occurs subsequent to withdrawal (al'Absi et al. 2004), and this dysregulation has been associated with relapse to smoking (al'Absi et al. 2005). In future research, the involvement of specific neuroreceptors and neurotransmitters relevant to the various aspects of addiction needs to be differentiated (see "Physiological Mechanisms and Indicators: Nicotine Tolerance, Withdrawal, and Reinforcement" earlier in this chapter).

Finally, understanding the pathophysiology of depression and schizophrenia, other psychiatric illnesses, and substance abuse disorders, as well as the effects of medications used to treat these disorders in smokers, may enhance understanding of the pathophysiology of nicotine addiction. Because of the high amount of overlap between prevalence of nicotine dependence and comorbid psychiatric disorders, the similar monoamines affected by these disorders, and the use of similar treatment medications, it is possible that common substrates mediate nicotine dependence and depression or schizophrenia, as well as other psychiatric disorders and can provide insight into effective treatments.

Genetics

There is strong evidence for a genetic influence on smoking behavior. Since the last Surgeon General's report on nicotine addiction (USDHHS 1988), knowledge has significantly increased in this area. For example, estimates of heritability have been determined for various phenotypes of smoking behavior. Studies of molecular genetic association and linkage studies were conducted to identify loci that influence these phenotypes. Furthermore, pharmacogenetic studies of smoking cessation were undertaken to increase understanding of interactions between genes and treatments. This research offers the possibility of interventions for smoking cessation that are tailored to individual genotypes.

Heritability of Smoking Behavior

Smoking behavior and nicotine addiction have generated far less research in behavioral genetics than have other addictive behaviors such as alcoholism. This is despite evidence from animal studies suggesting that key factors—such as the number and distribution of nicotinic receptors and the development of nicotine tolerance—are under a strong genetic influence (Stitzel et al. 2000). The evidence that does exist from studies of twins, adoption, and separated twins, however, has consistently suggested a strong genetic component in smoking behavior (Gilbert and Gilbert 1995). Behavioral genetics studies enable the contribution of genetic influences, environmental influence shared by persons such as twins or biologic relatives (shared environmental influences), and environmental influences unique to an individual (unique environmental influences) to be distinguished. The heritability coefficient itself reflects the genetic contribution. According to this evidence, inherited factors account for 28 to 85 percent of the observed variation in current smoking behavior in the population from which the data were drawn (Gilbert and Gilbert 1995). Researchers have suggested that the evidence for a genetic influence on smoking behavior is stronger than that for a genetic influence on alcoholism (Heath et al. 1995). Moreover, these studies have also indicated that these genetic factors relate to two aspects of smoking behavior: initiation and persistence.

Smoking Initiation

By comparing concordance rates for being a current or former smoker versus a lifetime nonsmoker, researchers can estimate the genetic contribution to smoking initiation. Such comparisons suggest that genetic

contributions to smoking initiation are substantial. For example, one study (Heath et al. 1995) reports heritability coefficients for smoking initiation of 0.44 in women and 0.51 in men in a sample of Swedish adults born between 1926 and 1958. This study also reports a strong influence of shared environmental factors on both smoking initiation and persistence, with little evidence of a role for unique environmental influences. Many additional studies have confirmed the heritability of smoking initiation, as well as smoking persistence and nicotine dependence (True et al. 1997; Kendler et al. 1999). Although the overall conclusion is robust, the specific heritability coefficients reported by individual studies are highly variable, ranging from less than 0.30 to more than 0.80 (Sullivan and Kendler 1999). This finding may be attributable to differences in the definitions of smoking initiation across studies. For example, current and former smokers are combined into a single "ever smoking" category in some studies, but not in others, and some studies require a threshold of exposure (e.g., 100 cigarettes smoked) and others do not have this requirement. Lack of critical attention to definition of phenotype may lead to inconsistencies across studies and to misleading conclusions.

The role of shared environmental influences on initiation of smoking and persistence in smoking is also inconsistent across populations, and some studies report minimal shared environmental influences (Heath et al. 1993). Differences in heritability coefficients by gender are generally not reported or are minimal, although one study (Hamilton et al. 2006) that tested differences by gender in the magnitude of genetic and environmental effects in a large cohort of twins indicated significantly higher heritability for smoking initiation in males than in females but no significant differences for smoking persistence. In that study, heritability for smoking initiation was defined as having smoked 100 or more cigarettes over their lifetime. In contrast, however, one meta-analysis (Li et al. 2003) reported higher heritability for smoking initiation in females than in males and higher heritability for smoking persistence in males than in females. Together, the evidence supports the importance of both genetic and shared environmental factors on smoking initiation. However, the relative importance of these factors is highly variable across populations. For example, one study reports different heritability coefficients for smoking behaviors in African Americans compared with White Americans (True et al. 1997). Nevertheless, evidence from non-Western cultures (Niu et al. 2000) suggests that the genetic influence on smoking behavior remains an important risk factor even in populations with much higher prevalence of smoking (e.g., in China). Reported heritability coefficients may vary with environmental factors such as the prevalence of smoking. For example, some of the highest heritability coefficients for smoking initiation are reported in studies on the population of twins during the Vietnam era, in which the participants were members of the U.S. Army at a time when smoking prevalence in the military was very high (True et al. 1997). This natural experiment, in which environmental variation in smoking initiation was minimized, may account for the high heritability coefficients in this study.

Smoking Persistence and Nicotine Dependence

Understanding smoking initiation is important to elucidate the etiology of nicotine addiction. However, smoking persistence is responsible for the adverse health consequences of smoking. The evidence for a genetic influence on smoking persistence (i.e., studies comparing current smokers with former smokers) is also strong. Several studies reported heritability coefficients of more than 0.50 for smoking persistence (Heath and Martin 1993) and nicotine dependence (Broms et al. 2007) in both men and women, and some studies (Sullivan and Kendler 1999; Vink et al. 2004) reported heritabilities of more than 0.70 for nicotine dependence. Studies of multiple indices of nicotine dependence (Lessov et al. 2004) indicate that salient behavioral indices are similar for women and men, with measures such as time to the first cigarette in the morning and the number of cigarettes smoked per day that may represent the most highly heritable symptoms of nicotine dependence for both women and men. Interpreting these results is complicated because genetic factors that influence smoking initiation may also influence smoking persistence and subsequent dependence. Some data (True et al. 1999) also suggest a common genetic vulnerability to nicotine and alcohol dependence in men. The balance of evidence suggests that the risk of smoking initiation is influenced by both genetic and environmental factors (True et al. 1997). However, the risk of smoking persistence is more strongly a function of genetic factors and some of the genetic influences on smoking behavior contribute to a risk for both smoking initiation and persistence (Kendler et al. 1999). Few studies have directly assessed the heritability of smoking cessation. However, one research study (Xian et al. 2003, 2005) indicated a heritability of 0.54 for failed smoking cessation, and another (Broms et al. 2006) suggests that genetic factors are related to the number of cigarettes smoked per day and to smoking cessation but are largely independent of smoking initiation. Another study (Pergadia et al. 2006) has

reported genetic influences specific to nicotine withdrawal, which may contribute both to smoking persistence and smoking cessation. However, because evidence from studies of twins and of adoption strongly indicates a genetic component in other aspects of smoking behavior, smoking cessation may also be strongly influenced by genetic factors.

Molecular Genetic Research on Smoking Behavior

Consistent evidence for the heritability of smoking behaviors led to molecular genetic studies designed to elucidate the specific genetic factors and biologic mechanisms involved in nicotine addiction. Two general scientific approaches to address this question include genetic linkage analysis and candidate gene studies. In linkage analysis, genetic variants or markers throughout the genome are tested within families (e.g., sibling pairs) and examined to identify markers that cosegregate with the trait of interest (e.g., nicotine dependence). This is a hypothesis-generating approach and does not require a priori knowledge about the biologic pathways involved. In contrast, studies of candidate genes, which are based on associations, use case-control methods to compare the prevalence of variants of candidate genes in two unrelated groups—for example, persons who are dependent on nicotine and those who are not dependent on nicotine. Although case-control studies have greater statistical power and are less costly than linkage analysis, such studies are not designed to identify novel genetic loci.

Cigarette smoking and nicotine dependence are complex traits arising from the interplay of multiple genetic and environmental influences. As mentioned previously (see "Definition of Nicotine Addiction" earlier in this chapter), definition of phenotype is a critical factor in genetic studies. Many genes are likely involved in smoking—for example, genes that influence the positive rewarding effects of nicotine, those that contribute to withdrawal symptoms and the negative reinforcing effects of nicotine (Pomerleau 1995), and those that determine general susceptibility to addiction (Nestler 2000). Interacting effects such as personality and environment are likely to also play an important role (Heath et al. 1995). Issues such as population heterogeneity (e.g., age, gender, and ethnicity) and bias (false positives results) introduced by ethnic admixture in study populations may also have a substantial impact on the outcome of association-based studies and may contribute to problems in replicating results (Munafò and Flint 2004).

Table 4.5   Genetic linkage studies of smoking behavior phenotypes

Study (country)	Population	Number of families	Number of markers	Primary phenotype	Markers of significant linkage	Chromosome number
Bergen et al. 1999 (United States)	Collaborative Study on the Genetics of Alcoholism	105 extended	296	Ever smoked vs. lifetime nonsmoking	D1S548 D2S379 D6S474 D9S64 D14S302 D17S968 D18S391 D21S120	1 2 6 9 14 17 18 21
Duggirala et al. 1999 (United States)	Collaborative Study on the Genetics of Alcoholism	105 extended	296	Pack-years[a] of smoking	D4S244 D5S1354 GATA193	4 5 17
Straub et al. 1999 (New Zealand and United States)	Convenience sample (Christchurch, New Zealand, and Richmond, Virginia)	130 and 91 nuclear, respectively	451	Nicotine dependence	D2S1326 D10S2469	2 10
Goode et al. 2003 (New Zealand and United States)	Framingham Heart Study	313 extended	401	Cigarettes/day (maximum)	ATA4F03 GATA151F03 GATA25A04 GATA47F05 321xd1	2 15 17 20 20
Li et al. 2003 (United States)	Framingham Heart Study	313 extended	401	Cigarettes/day	D9S257 D9S910 D11S1985 D11S2371 ATA78D02 D17S2196	9 9 11 11 17 17
Saccone et al. 2003 (United States)	Framingham Heart Study	313 extended	401	Cigarettes/day (maximum)	1648xb8 ATA59H06 GATA6B07 Mfd190 217xf4	5 9 13 14 22
Bierut et al. 2004 (United States)	Collaborative Study on the Genetics of Alcoholism	97 nuclear	366	Habitual vs. nonhabitual smoking	D5S815 D9S1120 D9A261 D9S904 D11S1354 D21S210	5 9 9 9 11 21
Sullivan et al. 2004 (New Zealand and United States)	Convenience sample (Christchurch, New Zealand)	130 nuclear	458	Nicotine dependence	D2S1326 D10S2469 CYP17	2 10 10

Table 4.5   Continued

Study (country)	Population	Number of families	Number of markers	Primary phenotype	Markers of significant linkage	Chromosome number
Vink et al. 2004 (The Netherlands)	Netherlands Twin Register	192 nuclear	379	Ever smoked vs. lifetime nonsmoking	D6S2410	6
					D6S1053	6
					Unk283	14
					D14S617	14
				Cigarettes/day	D3S3050	3
					D3S4545	3
				Both	D10S1412	10
					D10S1430	10
Wang et al. 2005 (United States)	Framingham Heart Study	430 nuclear	401	Cigarettes/day	ATA4E02	1
					GATA6G12	3
					GATA5B02	4
					GATA24D12	7
					GATA6B02	8
					GATA12C06	9
					GATA48E02	11
					290vc9	16
					GATA185H04	17
					ATA4E02	20
Gelernter et al. 2006 (United States)	Probands identified for panic disorder (Yale University, Connecticut)	12 extended	416	Habitual vs. nonhabitual smoking	D9S283	9
					D9S1677	9
					D11S4046	11

Note: Dominant ancestry for all studies was European.

[a]Pack-years = the number of years of smoking multiplied by the number of packs of cigarettes smoked per day.

Linkage Studies

Representative genetic linkage studies of smoking behavior phenotypes up to mid-2005 are shown in Table 4.5, although several of these report data from the same study samples (e.g., Collaborative Studies on the Genetics of Alcoholism and the Framingham Heart Study). Despite the success of linkage approaches in unraveling the genetic antecedents of disease (Menzel 2002), these initial findings about smoking behavior have not been consistent. Potential explanations include lack of refinement in phenotype definition and the relatively small sample sizes in some studies of smoking behavior. Subsequent studies have taken into account the complexity and heterogeneity of the nicotine dependence phenotype by using alternate measures, such as heavy smoking, severity of withdrawal, and history of smoking cessation (Li et al. 2006; Swan et

al. 2006). These data suggest that different genetic loci are linked to different measures and support a multidimensional concept of the nicotine dependence phenotype (Swan et al. 2006).

In addition to linkage studies, investigations using an approach of genomewide association can also reveal promising novel candidate genes for nicotine dependence (Bierut et al. 2007). With advancements in genotyping technology, phenotype definition, and analytic approaches, both case-control studies and linkage analysis will likely identify an increasing number of associations with novel variants important in nicotine dependence (Li 2006). Examples include *NTRK2* (Beuten et al. 2007), *GABARAP* (Lou et al. 2007), *CHRNA5* (Saccone et al. 2007), and *ANKK1* (Gelernter et al. 2006).

Candidate Gene Studies

A variety of plausible candidate genes have been examined for associations with smoking behavior. Most of these studies have focused on genetic variations in relevant neurotransmitter pathways, nicotine-metabolizing enzymes, or nAChRs. Genetic variants of relevant neurotransmitter pathways may have more generalized influences on addictive behaviors. Genes for nicotine-metabolizing enzymes and nAChRs may be specific for effects on nicotine dependence.

Nicotine Metabolism

To date, more than 20 published studies of candidate genes have investigated genes involved in the nicotine metabolism pathway (Table 4.6). Most of these studies investigated CYP2A6, for which researchers have identified functional genetic variants (Xu et al. 2002). Variants associated with *NULL activity (e.g., *2/*4) or reduced activity (*9/*12) are associated with reduced levels of the CYP2A6 enzyme and slower rates of nicotine metabolism, resulting in higher plasma nicotine levels from a given dose of nicotine (Malaiyandi et al. 2006). Thus, persons who carry these low activity alleles tend to have a lower risk of becoming smokers and, if they smoke, have slower rates of nicotine metabolism and tend toward reduced cigarette consumption compared with persons with a wild-type genotype (e.g., *1/*1). Furthermore, evidence from a meta-analysis that compared current versus former smokers suggests that the CYP2A6 alleles for reduced activity may increase the likelihood of smoking cessation (Munafò et al. 2004). However, the results are not consistent within or across all studies (Table 4.6). These inconsistencies may be attributable to relatively small sample sizes in some studies and differences in definition of phenotype and ethnic ancestry and genetic background.

Some studies investigated other cytochrome genes (CYP2D6 and CYP2E1), but evidence for a significant and reproducible role of these variants has not emerged, perhaps because the role of these enzymes in nicotine metabolism is limited.

Neuronal Nicotinic Receptors

Researchers have examined several genes for nAChR subunits to discover associations with smoking status (Table 4.7). The genes CHRNA4, CHRNA7, and CHRNB2 code for the α4, α7, and β2 subunits, respectively. However, because the functional relevance of variation in these genes is not known, these studies have explored associations of single nucleotide polymorphisms (SNPs) of unknown functional significance. To date, there is no evidence for associations of SNPs in the CHRNB2 gene with smoking behavior. However, two studies provide evidence for the role of CHRNA4 in nicotine dependence (Feng et al. 2004; Li et al. 2005). A small study of smokers with schizophrenia indicated that the CHRNA7 gene may be associated with smoking status. The relevance of this finding in the general population of smokers is unknown. However, studies have reported that these nAChR subtypes play a role in reinforcing the effects of nicotine and possibly withdrawal (see "Pathophysiology of Nicotine Addiction" earlier in this chapter). Moreover, because of the history of failure to replicate initial significant findings, these single studies require replication before the evidence can be considered to be confirmed.

Recently, genomewide scans have revealed an association of novel genes, such as NRXN1 and NRXN3, with nicotine dependence (Bierut et al. 2007). In addition, genomewide association and candidate gene studies have identified associations of smoking behavior and nicotine dependence with SNPs in the CHRNA5/CHRNA3/CHRNB4 gene cluster and in CHRNB3, which code for the nicotinic receptor subunits α5, α3, β4 and β3, respectively (Saccone et al. 2007; Berrettini et al. 2008; Bierut et al. 2008; Grucza et al. 2008; Sherva et al. 2008; Stevens et al. 2008; Thorgeirsson et al. 2008; Weiss et al. 2008; Caporaso et al. 2009; Chen et al. 2009).

Dopaminergic and Serotonergic Neurotransmitter and Receptor Systems

A large number of candidate gene studies have investigated genes involved in the dopamine pathway, and most have investigated the gene for the dopamine receptor D2 (DRD2) (Table 4.8). Most studies of the DRD2 *TAQ1A polymorphism have reported an association with smoking behavior, typically smoking status, but a substantial number have shown no association. Moreover, the functional significance of the *TAQ1A polymorphism remains unclear, although there is some reported evidence for an association with the density of D2 receptors in the brain. One study investigated the functional DRD2-141C *INS/*DEL polymorphism and reported a significant association with smoking status (Yoshida et al. 2001). A modest number of studies have investigated other genes for dopamine receptors (DRD1, DRD4, and DRD5), DAT, and genes involved in dopamine synthesis and metabolism, including tyrosine hydroxylase (an enzyme that converts amino acid L-tyrosine to dihydroxyphenylalanine, a precursor of dopamine), DβH (an enzyme that converts dopamine to norepinephrine), and COMT (an enzyme that degrades dopamine).

Table 4.6   Studies of candidate genes for nicotine metabolism and smoking behavior

Study (country)	Population — Study group	Population — Controls	Dominant ancestry	Gene
Cholerton et al. 1996 (United Kingdom)	100 current smokers	104 lifetime nonsmokers	NR	CYP2D6
Boustead et al. 1997 (United Kingdom)	100 current smokers	None	NR	CYP2D6
Pianezza et al. 1998 (Canada)	164 nicotine-dependent smokers 80 alcohol- and tobacco-dependent smokers	184 nonnicotine-dependent and former smokers	European	CYP2A6
London et al. 1999 (United States)	299 current or former smokers	161 lifetime nonsmokers	NR	CYP2A6
Gu et al. 2000 (United Kingdom)	142 current smokers	501 former smokers 389 lifetime nonsmokers	European	CYP2A6
Rao et al. 2000 (Canada)	292 current smokers	NA	European	CYP2A6
Saarikoski et al. 2000 (Finland)	85 current smokers	236 variable smokers 264 lifetime nonsmokers	European	CYP2A6
Tiihonen et al. 2000 (Finland)	285 current smokers	680 former smokers or lifetime nonsmokers	European	CYP2A6
Loriot et al. 2001 (United States)	65 current smokers	142 former smokers	European	CYP2A6
Schulz et al. 2001 (Germany)	130 current smokers	108 former smokers 109 lifetime nonsmokers	European	CYP2A6
Tan et al. 2001 (China)	380 persons who ever smoked	246 lifetime nonsmokers	East Asian	CYP2A6
Zhang et al. 2001 (Japan)	96 current smokers	141 nonsmokers	East Asian	CYP2A6
Ando et al. 2003 (Japan)	57 current smokers	44 former smokers 139 lifetime nonsmokers	East Asian	CYP2A6
Howard et al. 2003 (Canada)	1,512 smokers and nonsmokers	NA	Multiple (stratified)	CYP2E1
Minematsu et al. 2003 (Japan)	92 current smokers 111 former smokers	123 nonsmokers	East Asian	CYP2A6
Fujieda et al. 2004 (Japan)	1,705 smokers	NA	East Asian	CYP2A6
Iwahashi et al. 2004 (Japan)	103 smokers 101 nonsmokers	NA	East Asian	CYP2A6
O'Loughlin et al. 2004 (Canada)	228 adolescents who inhaled	NA	European	CYP2A6

Polymorphism	Primary phenotype	Main findings
*3, *4A, *5	Smoking status	No association with smoking status
*3, *4A, *5	Cigarettes/day Nicotine dependence	Association with nicotine dependence
*1, *2, *3	Nicotine dependence	Association with nicotine dependence (dependent vs. nondependent smokers) and amount smoked
*1, *2, *3	Smoking status Cigarettes/day	Marginal association with smoking status (lifetime nonsmokers vs. current and former smokers)
*1, *2, *NULL (allele not stated)	Smoking status Cigarettes/day	Association with smoking status (former vs. current smokers and lifetime nonsmokers)
*1, *2, *4, duplication	Cigarettes/day	Association with cigarettes/day
*1, *2, *3, *4B, *4C, *5, *10, *16	Smoking status	Association with smoking status (heavy vs. variable smokers and lifetime nonsmokers)
*NULL (allele not stated)	Smoking status Cigarettes/day	No association with smoking status or cigarettes/day
*1, *2, *4	Cigarettes/day	No association with cigarettes/day
*1, *2, *3	Smoking status Cigarettes/day	No association with smoking status or cigarettes/day
*1, *4	Smoking status Pack-years[a]	No association with smoking status or pack-years
*1, *DEL	Smoking status Cigarettes/day	No association with smoking status or cigarettes/day
*1A, *1B, *4C	Smoking status Cigarettes/day	No association with smoking status or cigarettes/day
*1C, *1D	Nicotine dependence Cotinine levels/cigarette Cigarettes/day	Association with nicotine dependence in those of East Asian ancestry and cotinine concentrations/cigarette in those of African ancestry
*1, *3, *DEL	Smoking status Pack-years	Association with pack-years among current and former smokers
*1A, *1B, *4, *7, *9, *10, *11	Cigarettes/day	Association with cigarettes/day
*1A, *1B, *4C	Smoking status	Association with smoking status
*1, *2, *4, *9, *12	Nicotine dependence Cigarettes/day	Association with increased risk of acquisition of nicotine dependence, but reduced cigarettes/day among those who become dependent

Table 4.6   Continued

Study (country)	Population		Dominant ancestry	Gene
	Study group	Controls		
Schoedel et al. 2004 (Canada)	375 current smokers	224 nonsmokers	European	CYP2A6
Vasconcelos et al. 2005 (Brazil)	144 current smokers 61 former smokers	207 nonsmokers	Mixed	CYP2A6

Note: **NA** = not applicable; **NR** = data not reported.
[a]Pack-years = the number of years of smoking multiplied by the number of packs of cigarettes smoked per day.

Table 4.7   Studies of candidate genes for neuronal nicotine receptors and smoking behavior

Study (country)	Population		Dominant ancestry	Gene
	Study group	Controls		
Silverman et al. 2000 (United States)	317 high- and 238 low-nicotine dependent smokers	317 nonsmokers	European	CHRNB2
Lueders et al. 2002 (United States)	184 current smokers	132 former smokers 427 lifetime nonsmokers	European	CHRNB2
De Luca et al. 2004 (Canada)	108 current smokers with schizophrenia	69 current nonsmokers with schizophrenia	European	CHRNA7
Feng et al. 2004 (China)	577 male smokers from 206 families	Family-based design	East Asian	CHRNA4
Li et al. 2005 (United States)	1,568 smokers from 602 families	Family-based design	European and African	CHRNA4 CHRNB2

Of the published studies of candidate genes involved in the serotonin pathway, eight investigated *5HTT*, and three investigated *TPH*, which is involved in serotonin synthesis (Table 4.9). All but one study of the functional *5HTTLPR* polymorphism found an association with smoking behavior. Three additional studies investigated the *MAOA* gene, which is involved in metabolism of both dopamine and serotonin and in norepinephrine pathways. Two of the three studies reported an association with smoking behavior that included both smoking status and cigarette consumption. Other studies of candidate genes are summarized in Table 4.10. Research is notably lacking on genes involved in glutamatergic and GABA-ergic mechanisms, despite basic research indicating the neurobiologic effects of nicotine on these systems. One study (Beuten et al. 2005) reports a significant association between a haplotype of SNPs in the $GABA_{B2}$ gene and nicotine dependence.

In summary, a few candidate genes appear to be associated with smoking behavior. Meta-analysis is a potentially powerful tool for assessing population-wide effects of candidate genes on complex behavioral phenotypes, such as smoking, although such meta-analysis requires that the phenotypes examined across studies are similar. It may also provide evidence for unrevealed diversity, such as heterogeneity in apparently similar populations (Munafò and Flint 2004). Despite the large number of studies reporting on the association between specific candidate genes and smoking behavior, one meta-analysis (Munafò et al. 2004) highlights the lack of depth of the research compared with the breadth that exists. The conclusion is that the "...evidence for a contribution of specific genes to smoking behavior remains modest" (p. 583). In this analysis, *5HTT* and *CYP2A6* were the only candidate genes for which there was evidence of an association with smoking behavior. Studies published

Polymorphism	Primary phenotype	Main findings
*1A, *1B, *2, *4, *5, *6, *7, *8, *9, *10, *12*	Smoking status Cigarettes/day	Association with smoking status and cigarettes/day
*1A, *1B, *2, *4, *9*	Smoking status	Association with smoking status (current and former smokers vs. nonsmokers) among those of European and mixed ancestry

Polymorphism	Primary phenotype	Main findings
Multiple	Smoking status Nicotine dependence	No association with smoking status or nicotine dependence
Haplotype	Smoking status Nicotine dependence	No association with smoking status or nicotine dependence
D15S1360	Smoking status	Association with smoking status (current smokers vs. nonsmokers)
Haplotype	Nicotine dependence	Association with nicotine dependence
Haplotype Haplotype	Nicotine dependence	Association of *CHRNA4* gene with nicotine dependence No association with *CHRNB2* gene

more recently strongly indicate that SNPs in the *CHRNA5/A3/B4* gene cluster are associated with smoking behavior and nicotine dependence (Berrettini et al. 2008; Bierut et al. 2008; Grucza et al. 2008; Sherva et al. 2008; Stevens et al. 2008; Thorgeirsson et al. 2008; Weiss et al. 2008; Caporaso et al. 2009; Chen et al. 2009; Saccone et al. 2009). Nonetheless, the relatively small effects and evidence for substantial heterogeneity between studies suggest that extreme care is necessary in the design of case-control studies of genetic association.

Pharmacogenetic Approaches

The basic premise of the pharmacogenetic approach is that inherited differences in drug metabolism and drug targets have important influence on the toxic effects and the efficacy of treatment (Evans and Relling 1999; Poolsup

et al. 2000). Advantages of a pharmacogenetic approach to the study of smoking cessation treatments include (1) use of more refined phenotypes for genetic analyses, which is facilitated by prospective assessment of withdrawal symptoms, side effects of treatment, and measures of the level of reward from nicotine; (2) use of various treatment conditions to aid smoking cessation; and (3) use of experimental designs that control the dosing and timing of the therapy (Lerman and Niaura 2002; Munafò et al. 2005b; Caporaso et al. 2009).

Nicotine Replacement Therapy

To date, two pharmacogenetic trials of NRT have been conducted. One placebo-controlled trial using the nicotine patch by a large group of general practice physicians in the United Kingdom (Johnstone et al. 2004b; Yudkin et al. 2004) focused on variations in the dopamine pathway, including the *DβH* and *DRD2* genes. The

Table 4.8   Studies of candidate genes for dopamine and smoking behavior

Study (country)	Population		Dominant ancestry	Gene
	Study group	Controls		
Noble et al. 1994 (United States)	57 current smokers	115 former smokers 182 lifetime nonsmokers	European	*DRD2*
Comings et al. 1996 (United States)	312 current smokers	714 lifetime nonsmokers	European	*DRD2*
Comings et al. 1997 (United States)	371 current smokers	126 lifetime nonsmokers	European	*DRD1* *DRD2*
Lerman et al. 1997 (United States)	315 current smokers	232 lifetime nonsmokers	European	*TH*
Shields et al. 1998 (United States)	283 current smokers	192 lifetime nonsmokers	European and African	*DRD4*
Singleton et al. 1998 (United Kingdom)	104 current smokers	117 lifetime nonsmokers	NR	*DRD2*
Spitz et al. 1998 (United States)	46 current smokers	67 former smokers 13 lifetime nonsmokers	European	*DRD2*
Lerman et al. 1999 (United States)	289 current smokers	233 lifetime nonsmokers	European and African	*DRD2* *DAT*
Sabol et al. 1999 (United States)	283 current smokers	231 former smokers 593 lifetime nonsmokers	European	*DAT*
Batra et al. 2000 (Germany)	110 nicotine-dependent smokers	60 nonnicotine-dependent or light smokers	NR	*DRD2*
Bierut et al. 2000 (United States)	388 habitual smokers 566 nonhabitual smokers	Family-based study	European	*DRD2*
Costa-Mallen et al. 2000 (United States)	152 newly diagnosed Parkinson's disease patients	231 with no history of Parkinson's or other neurodegenerative disease	European	*DRD2*
Jorm et al. 2000 (Australia)	198 current smokers	211 former smokers 452 lifetime nonsmokers	European	*DAT*
McKinney et al. 2000 (United Kingdom)	225 current smokers	No controls	European	*DβH* *MAOA* *COMT*
Wu et al. 2000 (United States)	73 current smokers	61 former smokers 88 lifetime nonsmokers	European and African	*DRD2*
Sullivan et al. 2001 (United States)	595 current smokers	338 lifetime nonsmokers	European	*DRD5*
Yoshida et al. 2001 (Japan)	77 current smokers	57 former smokers 198 lifetime nonsmokers	East Asian	*DRD2*
David et al. 2002 (United Kingdom)	266 current smokers	270 former smokers 265 lifetime nonsmokers	NR	*COMT*
Hamajima et al. 2002 (Japan)	226 current smokers	133 former smokers 434 lifetime nonsmokers	East Asian	*DRD2*

Polymorphism	Primary phenotype	Main findings
TAQ1A	Smoking status	Association with smoking status (current and former smokers vs. lifetime nonsmokers)
TAQ1A	Smoking status	Association with smoking status
DDE1 *TAQ1A*	Smoking status Packs/day	Association of DRD1 and DRD2 genes with smoking status and packs/day
VNTR	Smoking status	No association with smoking status
VNTR	Smoking status Cigarettes/day	Association with smoking status in participants of African ancestry
TAQ1A	Smoking status Nicotine dependence	No association with smoking status or nicotine dependence
TAQ1A *TAQ1B*	Smoking status Age at smoking initiation	No association with smoking status Association of both polymorphisms with age at smoking initiation
TAQ1A VNTR	Smoking status	Association of DAT and DRD2 genes with smoking status in participants of European ancestry
VNTR	Smoking status	Association with smoking status (current vs. former smokers)
FOK1 *TAQ1A*	Smoking status	Association of FOK1 polymorphism with smoking status (nicotine-dependent vs. nonnicotine-dependent or light smokers)
TAQ1A *INTRON 2*	Smoking status	No association with smoking status
TAQ1A *TAQ1B*	Smoking status	No association with smoking status
VNTR	Smoking status	No association with smoking status
G1368A C1460T A1947G (*VAL/*MET)	Cigarettes/day	Association of DβH and MAOA genes with cigarettes/day
TAQ1A *TAQ1B*	Smoking status Cigarettes/day	Association of both polymorphisms with smoking status (current vs. former smokers and lifetime nonsmokers) and cigarettes/day
Haplotype	Smoking status Nicotine dependence	No association with smoking status Association with nicotine dependence, although marginal
TAQ1A -141C *INS/*DEL	Smoking status	Association of TAQ1A polymorphism only with smoking status (current vs. former smokers and lifetime nonsmokers)
A1947G (*VAL/*MET)	Smoking status	No association with smoking status
MBO1 *TAQ1A*	Smoking status	Association of TAQ1A polymorphism only with smoking status in men (current vs. former smokers and lifetime nonsmokers)

Table 4.8   Continued

Study (country)	Population		Dominant ancestry	Gene
	Study group	Controls		
Johnstone et al. 2002 (United Kingdom)	1,524 current smokers	NA	European	*DβH* *MAOA*
Qi et al. 2002 (China)	174 current smokers	152 former smokers and lifetime nonsmokers	East Asian	*DRD2*
Vandenbergh et al. 2002 (United States)	98 current smokers	153 former smokers 114 nonsmokers 214 lifetime nonsmokers	European	*DAT*
Ito et al. 2003 (Japan)	147 current smokers	99 former smokers 258 lifetime nonsmokers	East Asian	*MAOA* *MAOB*
Lee et al. 2003 (South Korea)	94 current smokers	93 lifetime nonsmokers	East Asian	*DRD2*
Anney et al. 2004 (Australia)	51 nicotine-dependent smokers	186 nonnicotine-dependent smokers	European	*TH*
Audrain-McGovern et al. 2004a (United States)	292 adolescents who ever smoked	NA	European	*DRD2* *DAT*
Johnstone et al. 2004b (United Kingdom)	732 current smokers	243 lifetime nonsmokers	European	*DRD2*
Ling et al. 2004 (China)	668 current smokers	Family-based study	East Asian	*DAT*
Luciano et al. 2004 (Australia)	769 current smokers and nonsmokers	Family-based study	European	*DRD4*
Olsson et al. 2004 (Australia)	77 nicotine-dependent smokers	39 nonnicotine-dependent smokers	European	*TH*
Colilla et al. 2005 (United States)	277 female current smokers	505 female former smokers	European and African	*COMT*
Costa-Mallen et al. 2005 (United States)	232 persons who ever smoked	158 lifetime nonsmokers	European	*DRD2* *MAOB*
Elovainio et al. 2005 (Finland)	37 current smokers	113 nonsmokers	European	*DRD4*
Freire et al. 2006 (Brazil)	220 alcoholic and nonalcoholic smokers	112 nonsmokers	European	*DRD2* *DβH*
Laucht et al. 2005 (Germany)	184 adolescents who ever smoked	119 adolescent lifetime nonsmokers	European	*DRD4*
Zetteler et al. 2005 (United Kingdom)	141 current smokers	NA	European	*DβH*

Note: **NA** = not applicable; **NR** = data not reported.

Polymorphism	Primary phenotype	Main findings
G1368A *C1460T*	Cigarettes/day	No association with cigarettes/day
*TAQ1A **TAQ1B*	Smoking status Cigarettes/day	Association of **TAQ1A* polymorphism only with cigarette use No association with smoking status
VNTR	Smoking status	Association with smoking status (lifetime nonsmokers vs. former and current smokers)
VNTR *A644G*	Smoking status Nicotine dependence	Association of *MAOA* gene with smoking status among women and nicotine dependence among men
*TAQ1A	Smoking status	Association with smoking status Evidence of heterosis in women
VNTR	Nicotine dependence	Association with nicotine dependence
*TAQ1A *VNTR*	Smoking status Smoking progression	Association of *DRD2* gene with smoking progression in those exposed to nicotine
*TAQ1A	Smoking status Cigarettes/day	No association with smoking status or cigarettes/day
*RS27072	Nicotine dependence Age at smoking initiation	No association with nicotine dependence Association with age at smoking initiation among nicotine-dependent smokers only
VNTR	Smoking status Cigarettes/day	No association with smoking status or cigarettes/day
VNTR	Nicotine dependence	Association with nicotine dependence
A1947G (*VAL/*MET)	Smoking status	Association with smoking status
*TAQ1B *A644G*	Smoking status	No association with smoking status, although there was interactive effect between *DRD2* and *MAOB* genes in men
VNTR	Smoking status	Association with smoking status
*TAQ1A *C1021T*	Smoking status	Association of *DRD2* gene with smoking status Marginal association of *DβH* gene with smoking status
VNTR	Smoking status Daily smoking	Association with smoking status and daily smoking in men
G1368A	Nicotine dependence	Association with nicotine dependence

Table 4.9   Studies of candidate genes for serotonin and smoking behavior

Study (country)	Population		Dominant ancestry
	Study group	Controls	
Lerman et al. 1998 (United States)	268 current smokers	230 lifetime nonsmokers	European and African
Ishikawa et al. 1999 (Japan)	202 current smokers	103 former smokers 82 lifetime nonsmokers	East Asian
Hu et al. 2000 (United States)	177 current smokers	124 former smokers 458 lifetime nonsmokers	European
Lerman et al. 2000 (United States)	185 current smokers	None	European and African
McKinney et al. 2000 (United Kingdom)	225 current smokers	None	European
Lerman et al. 2001 (United States)	249 current smokers	202 lifetime nonsmokers	European
Johnstone et al. 2002 (United Kingdom)	1,524 current smokers	None	European
Ito et al. 2003 (Japan)	147 current smokers	99 former smokers 258 lifetime nonsmokers	East Asian
Mizuno et al. 2004 (Japan)	233 current smokers	135 former smokers 667 lifetime nonsmokers	East Asian
Brody et al. 2005 (United States)	110 current smokers 100 former smokers	275 lifetime nonsmokers	European and African
Gerra et al. 2005 (Italy)	107 adolescents who ever smoked	103 adolescent lifetime nonsmokers	European
Kremer et al. 2005 (Israel)	244 persons who ever smoked	486 lifetime nonsmokers	Other
Munafò et al. 2005a (United Kingdom)	141 current smokers	None	European
Reuter and Hennig 2005 (Germany)	108 current smokers	144 nonsmokers	European

Gene	Polymorphism	Primary phenotype	Main findings
5HTT	*LPR*	Smoking status	No association with smoking status
5HTT	*LPR*	Smoking status	Association with smoking status (current vs. former smokers and lifetime nonsmokers)
5HTT	*LPR*	Smoking status	Association with smoking status (current vs. former smokers and lifetime nonsmokers) among participants with high levels of neuroticism
5HTT	*LPR*	Nicotine dependence	Association of neuroticism with nicotine dependence among those with short allele
MAOA	*C1460T*	Cigarettes/day	Association with cigarettes/day
TPH	*A779C*	Smoking status Nicotine dependence	No association with smoking status or nicotine dependence Association with age at smoking initiation
MAOA	*C1460T*	Cigarettes/day	No association with cigarettes/day
MAOA *MAOB*	*VNTR* *A644G*	Smoking status Nicotine dependence	Association of *MAOA* gene with smoking status among women and with nicotine dependence among men
TPH	*C218A*	Smoking status	No association with smoking status
5HTT	*LPR*	Smoking status Nicotine dependence	No association with smoking status or nicotine dependence
5HTT	*LPR*	Smoking status	Association with smoking status
5HTT	*LPR* *VNTR*	Smoking status Nicotine dependence	Association with smoking status (persons who ever smoked vs. lifetime nonsmokers) No association with nicotine dependence
5HTT	*LPR*	Nicotine dependence	Association with nicotine dependence
TPH	*A779C*	Smoking status Nicotine dependence	Association with nicotine dependence (nonsmokers scored as having zero nicotine dependence)

Table 4.10   Other studies of candidate genes for smoking behavior

| Study (country) | Population | | Dominant ancestry |
	Study group	Controls	
Garciá-Closas et al. 1997 (United States)	315 current smokers	None	European
Comings et al. 2001 (United States)	12 current smokers 326 nicotine-dependent smokers	59 former smokers 120 lifetime nonsmokers 399 nondependent controls	European
Hamajima et al. 2001 (Japan)	126 current smokers	837 nonsmokers	East Asian
Pitha et al. 2002 (Czech Republic)	75 current and former smokers	60 lifetime nonsmokers	European
Uno et al. 2002 (Japan)	124 current smokers	131 former smokers 690 lifetime nonsmokers	East Asian
Füst et al. 2004 (Hungary)	171 persons who ever smoked	140 lifetime nonsmokers	European
Smits et al. 2004 (The Netherlands)	20,938 persons, including current and former smokers and lifetime nonsmokers	NA	European
Beuten et al. 2005 (United States)	990 current smokers 286 nonsmokers	Family-based study	European and African
Liu et al. 2005 (Japan)	213 current smokers	71 former smokers 55 lifetime nonsmokers	East Asian
Ma et al. 2005 (United States)	1,568 current smokers 469 nonsmokers	Family-based study	European and African
Takimoto et al. 2005 (Japan)	109 current smokers	162 nonsmokers	East Asian

Note: **NA** = not applicable.
[a]Pack-years = the number of years of smoking multiplied by the number of packs of cigarettes smoked per day.

dopamine pathway is widely considered to be central in the development of nicotine dependence (see "Pathophysiology of Nicotine Addiction" earlier in this chapter). Releasing dopamine after nicotine administration activates postsynaptic dopamine receptors, including the D2 receptor, whereas DβH is involved in the synthesis of noradrenalin from dopamine (Koob and Le Moal 2001).

The *$TAQ1A$ ($C^{32806}T$) allele of the *DRD2* gene is associated with reduced numbers of dopamine D2 receptors in the corpus striatum (Thompson et al. 1997), but the functional significance of this variant remains unclear. The *$1368A$ allele of the *DβH* gene is associated with smoking status (McKinney et al. 2000), although this polymorphism is not considered functional. The nicotine patch was significantly more effective for smoking cessation than was a placebo for carriers of the *$A1$ allele of the *DRD2* gene but not among those who were homozygous for the more common *$A2$ allele (Johnstone et al. 2004b). The difference in the effects of treatment in the genotype groups was significant after the first week of

Gene	Polymorphism	Primary phenotype	Main findings
CYP1A1 GSTM1 *NULL	*MSP1	Pack-years[a]	No association with pack-years
CCK	C-45T	Smoking status Nicotine dependence	Association with smoking status (current vs. former smokers vs. lifetime nonsmokers) and nicotine dependence (nicotine-dependent smokers vs. nondependent controls)
IL-1β	C-31T	Smoking status	No association with smoking status
CD14	C-159T	Smoking status	Association with smoking status (current and former smokers vs. lifetime nonsmokers)
IL-1β	C-31T	Smoking status	No association with smoking status
TNF2 C4A C4B	Haplotype Haplotype Haplotype	Smoking status Cigarettes/day	Association of TNF2 gene with smoking status (persons who ever smoked vs. lifetime nonsmokers)
CYP1A1 GSTM1 GSTT1 GSTP1 NAT2	*MSP1 *DEL *DEL *ILE/*VAL *4	Smoking status	No association with smoking status
GABA_{B2}	Haplotype	Nicotine dependence	Association with nicotine dependence
Various	Various	Smoking status	Association of OGG1, 5HTT, EPHX1, ESR1, and CYP17A1 genes with smoking status
DDC	Haplotype	Nicotine dependence	Association with nicotine dependence
CCK CCKAR	C-45T T779C 365 *VAL/*ILE	Smoking status	Association of CCK gene with smoking status

treatment but not at the end of 12 weeks of treatment. The nicotine patch was highly effective among smokers with both the *DRD2 *A1* allele and the *DβH *A* allele, but it was less effective for smokers with other genotypes. This genetic association with treatment response was significant at both 1 and 12 weeks of treatment, which suggests that the short-term efficacy of the nicotine patch may be modulated by *DRD2* and *DβH* genes. Longer follow-up in this analysis supported the association of the *DRD2* variant with abstinence from smoking at 6- and 12-month follow-ups, although this effect was observed only among women and the results for the *DβH* gene were not reported (Yudkin et al. 2004).

The second pharmacogenetic trial of NRT was an open-label trial of the nicotine patch versus nicotine nasal spray. This trial examined the role of the gene for the μ-opioid receptor (*OPRM1*) (Lerman et al. 2004). The opioid receptor is the primary site of action for the rewarding effects of the endogenous opioid peptide β-endorphin (Zadina et al. 1997), which is released in response to nicotine (Davenport et al. 1990; Boyadjieva and Sarkar 1997). Exon 1 of the human *OPRM1* gene includes a common A118G (*ASN40ASP*) missense SNP. The *ASP40* variant has been associated with reduced messenger RNA (mRNA) and lower protein levels for the receptor (Zhang et al. 2005). Smokers carrying the *OPRM1 *ASP40* variant were significantly more likely than those who were homozygous for the *ASN40* variant to be abstinent from smoking at the end of the treatment phase (Lerman et al. 2004). The differential treatment response among smokers was most pronounced for the nicotine patch, modest and nonsignificant for nicotine nasal spray, and nonsignificant for a placebo, in the bupropion clinical trial described in the next section. A longitudinal analysis in the nicotine patch group revealed a dose-response effect of the nicotine patch. The effect of the genotype in the *ASP40* group was greatest during the nicotine patch treatment of 21 milligrams (mg), but the effect was reduced as the treatment was tapered and disappeared after discontinuation. In addition, smokers who carried the *ASP40* variant gained less weight during the treatment period and reported greater reductions in symptoms of negative mood than did those who were not carriers of the variant. These findings suggest that smokers carrying the *ASP40* variant may be candidates for maintenance therapy with the 21-mg nicotine patch.

Additional investigations provided evidence for an association of the *COMT VAL158 MET* polymorphism with prospective smoking cessation in an NRT open-label trial. Female smokers treated with either the nicotine patch or nicotine nasal spray who carried the low-activity allele, which is associated with a slower degradation of dopamine, were significantly more likely than were those who did not carry this allele to stop smoking independent of the treatment. These findings are consistent with those reported in a retrospective comparison of female current versus female former smokers in a case-control study (Table 4.8) (Colilla et al. 2005).

Bupropion

The first pharmacogenetic analysis of treatment for tobacco dependence was conducted as part of a placebo-controlled clinical trial of bupropion for smoking cessation (Lerman et al. 2002) that focused on *CYP2B6*. Smokers who carried the *CYP2B6* variant, which, to some extent, is associated with slower nicotine metabolism, reported greater increases in craving for cigarettes after the target date for smoking cessation and had significantly higher rates of relapse to smoking than did those without the variant. These effects were modified by a significant interaction among gender, genotype, and treatment,

which suggests that bupropion attenuated the effects of genotype among female smokers.

A second report from this clinical trial (Lerman et al. 2006) examined two SNPs that may influence the expression of the DRD2 receptor. These SNPs included an insertion/deletion variant in the promoter region of the *DRD2* gene (*DRD2 -141C *INS/*DEL*). The transcriptional efficiency of the more common *-141C INS C* allele is greater than that of the variant with the *-141C DEL C* allele (Arinami et al. 1997), and a functional synonymous SNP in the *DRD2* (*C957T*) gene decreases mRNA stability and protein synthesis (Duan et al. 2003). At the end of the treatment phase, a statistically significant interaction between the *DRD2 -141C *INS/*DEL* genotype and the treatment indicated a more favorable response to bupropion among smokers homozygous for the *INS C* allele than that for smokers carrying a *DEL C* allele.

One study investigated whether the *TAQ1A* polymorphism in the *DRD2* gene is associated with smoking cessation outcomes after treatment with a combination of bupropion and behavioral counseling in smokers enrolled in an open-label randomized trial of effectiveness (Swan et al. 2005). Compared with women who were homozygous for the *A2* allele, women with at least one *A1* allele were significantly more likely to stop taking bupropion because of side effects from the medication and at 12 months were somewhat more likely to report smoking. However, relapse to smoking by 12 months after treatment was not statistically significant and constituted only a trend. Significant associations or trends were not observed in men.

In addition, another study reported data on 239 smokers who were offered bupropion in a group of general practice physicians in the United Kingdom (Johnstone et al. 2004a). Only 54 of these smokers made an active attempt to stop smoking. Allele frequencies for polymorphisms in the *DRD2*, *DAT*, *DβH*, and *MAOA* genes were reported. However, the sample size was insufficient for formal analysis of the effects of these polymorphisms on smoking cessation.

Varenicline

Varenicline, a partial agonist at the α4β2 nAChR, was approved by FDA as a treatment for smoking cessation in 2006 (USFDA 2006). Several large trials provide evidence that varenicline was more effective than bupropion or placebo as an aid to smoking cessation (Gonzales et al. 2006; Jorenby et al. 2006; Tonstad et al. 2006). Because of the efficacy and relative target selectivity (e.g., targeting a specific receptor subtype) of this compound, pharmacogenetic studies of varenicline are warranted.

Summary and Future Directions

Research on genetic influences on smoking behavior has yielded important insights about the biobehavioral basis of nicotine dependence. There is strong and consistent evidence from studies of twins that smoking initiation and nicotine dependence are influenced by heritable factors. Support for the role of functional genetic variation in nicotine-metabolizing enzymes (e.g., CYP2A6) and genetic variation in nAChR subunit genes (e.g., *CHRNA5*) is largely consistent, although the extent of their contribution to nicotine dependence is unclear. Additional but inconsistent evidence supports the roles of genetic variants in the dopamine pathways. Although the pharmacogenetic approach to smoking cessation holds early promise, larger studies in more diverse populations are required (Lerman et al. 2007). Designs for case-control studies of genetic association are limited, partly by the use of crude measures of smoking behavior phenotypes. This finding supports the importance of future studies to explore associations of candidate genes with endophenotypes, which are intermediate phenotypes of smoking behavior. Some phenotypes are biologically more proximal to their genetic antecedents than are complex behavioral phenotypes, because biologic proximity affords a more homogeneous phenotype and a stronger genetic signal. Endophenotypes that may be relevant to nicotine dependence encompass acoustic startle response, including prepulse inhibition and affective modulation of the acoustic startle (Hutchison et al. 2000); measures of the reinforcing value of nicotine in a paradigm of behavioral choice (Blendy et al. 2005; Ray et al. 2006); various paradigms of craving related to reactivity to cues (Tiffany et al. 2000); measures of attentional bias, such as the modified Stroop task (Munafò et al. 2003) and the dot-probe task (Waters et al. 2003a); and patterns of withdrawal after smoking cessation (David et al. 2003). The list of candidate endophenotypes is growing rapidly, and these may offer powerful measures for genetic analysis, although the role of these putative endophenotypes remains speculative in some cases.

Also deserving of attention is the study of the interaction between genetic variants, nicotine dependence, and disorders comorbid with nicotine dependence (e.g., depression and anxiety). Two studies suggest that smoking behaviors and nicotine dependence are influenced by an interaction between the *5HTT* gene and anxiety-related traits (Hu et al. 2000; Lerman et al. 2000). In one study, however, this association was not replicated (Munafò et al. 2005a). A better understanding of genetic influences on nicotine dependence in different psychiatric populations would be valuable for the development of targeted medications.

Pharmacogenetic investigations of smoking cessation treatments have provided promising initial evidence that genetic variations in drug targets, such as the dopamine system or nAChRs, may predict responses to treatments. Only a few such studies have been conducted, and these have focused on the two FDA-approved approaches for smoking cessation pharmacotherapy: bupropion and NRT. Several additional pharmacotherapies have been tested for efficacy in smoking cessation (Lerman et al. 2005). Although the overall effects of alternate pharmacotherapies, such as fluoxetine and naltrexone, have been modest, it is possible that subgroups of smokers who benefit from such treatments can be identified by genotype. Although pharmacogenetic research on smoking cessation treatments is in the early stages, this research may ultimately be used to tailor pharmacotherapies to smokers most likely to benefit, thereby improving the efficacy. Emerging health policy and ethical issues related to genetically tailored smoking cessation treatments are important to consider (Shields et al. 2004), as are barriers to and facilitators of the integration of genetic tests into smoking cessation in clinical practice (Shields et al. 2004; Munafò et al. 2005b).

Recent studies have begun to provide compelling support for association of some common genetic variants with smoking behavior and related disease phenotypes, such as SNPs within the *CHRNA5/A3/B4* gene cluster (Amos et al. 2008; Hung et al. 2008; Liu et al. 2008; Thorgeirsson 2009); however, the effect sizes described in these studies are very small, and it has been suggested that efforts may need to be directed elsewhere if the genetic architecture of complex traits is to be fully elucidated (Goldstein 2009; Hardy and Singleton 2009; Hirschhorn 2009). In particular, the hypothesis that common phenotypes, such as nicotine dependence, will be explained by common genetic variants has been questioned because the effect sizes observed to date suggest an unrealistically large number of alleles to explain the known heritability of a given phenotype (Goldstein 2009).

A complementary approach may be to seek out less common genetic variations that may have a more profound effect on phenotypes of interest. For example, recent studies have identified a possible role for copy number variants and de novo mutations in the etiology of psychiatric phenotypes such as schizophrenia (Xu et al. 2008) and autism (Sebat et al. 2007). Although no studies have yet investigated the role of copy number variants in smoking behavior, such studies are likely to emerge in the near future. As our understanding of the functional biology of genetic variation continues to develop, so too will the technologies and methods available to dissect the genetic architecture of complex phenotypes such as nicotine dependence.

Prevalence and Trajectory Toward Nicotine Dependence

Genes appear to predispose persons to smoking initiation and persistence and possibly are related to the extent of difficulty a person has in smoking cessation. Genetic transmission may include inheritance of polymorphisms of specific genes that affect responses of the body and the brain to nicotine. These responses include the rate of metabolism of nicotine, receptor sensitivity to nicotine and to certain neurotransmitters, and the levels of neurotransmitters available at neural synapses. These individual differences in response to nicotine are likely to affect the trajectory toward the development of nicotine dependence. Characterization of differences in trajectories has primarily focused on the adolescent population, because most smokers begin smoking cigarettes during this period of life. The next section describes the prevalence of adolescent smoking to increase understanding of the scope for potential development of dependence, differences in trajectory patterns toward dependence, and determinants for developing nicotine addiction. Epidemiologic, laboratory, and clinical studies are described to elucidate the emerging science in this area.

Epidemiology of Adolescent Smoking

A large body of epidemiologic literature has examined the prevalence of smoking, its initiation in adolescence, and the progression among adolescents from experimentation to regular use of cigarettes. This literature includes research on national samples in both school-based studies (University of Michigan 2007) and household studies (Substance Abuse and Mental Health Services Administration 2004). However, compared with an extensive amount of literature that examines adolescent smoking, work on adolescent nicotine dependence is more recent, so there are fewer empirical studies on early antecedents of nicotine addiction than on the antecedents of adolescent smoking (Colby et al. 2000a). Thus, in reviewing existing data, it is important to separate cigarette smoking and nicotine addiction as distinct outcomes (Hughes 2001). In addition, because most studies have focused on adolescent cigarette smoking rather than other forms of tobacco use, this review is restricted to studies of cigarette smoking.

Subsequent data suggest that approximately one in five high school students report "current" smoking, defined as any smoking in the past month (CDC 2008b). Smoking prevalence increases with age throughout adolescence. For example, data from the Monitoring the Future study (Johnston et al. 2007) show that current smoking is reported by 8.7 percent of 8th graders, 14.5 percent of 10th graders, and 21.0 percent of 12th graders. In addition to age, the prevalence of adolescent smoking varies with race and ethnicity. The highest rates were reported by American Indian and Alaska Natives, followed by non-Hispanic Whites, Hispanics, African Americans, and Asians (National Institute on Drug Abuse 2003). Few characteristics of adolescent smoking differed by gender, but adolescents with less-educated parents, lower aspirations for higher education, and rural residence are more likely to smoke cigarettes (Johnston et al. 2007). Finally, some adolescents smoke at high levels of frequency and quantity. For example, daily smoking is reported by 4.0 percent of 8th graders, 7.6 percent of 10th graders, and 12.2 percent of 12th graders; and 1.5 percent of 8th graders, 3.3 percent of 10th graders, and 5.9 percent of 12th graders smoke one-half pack or more of cigarettes per day (Johnston et al. 2007).

Measuring Nicotine Dependence in Adolescents

Colby and colleagues (2000b) summarized the literature on methods of measuring adolescent nicotine dependence. These researchers note that the two major approaches to measurement were formal diagnostic measures, such as interviews based on the *DSM-IV* criteria (APA 1994) and brief self-report measures that were most often modifications of the FTQ (Fagerström 1978). A brief self-report measure, Hooked on Nicotine Checklist (HONC), has been developed and used in longitudinal studies of the early acquisition of nicotine dependence (DiFranza et al. 2002a; O'Loughlin et al. 2003). This measure defines the onset of nicotine dependence as the point of experiencing loss of autonomy over tobacco use (DiFranza et al. 2002a). Although multiple measures have proved useful in predicting aspects of smoking behavior, as previously noted in this chapter, there is no gold standard for assessing nicotine dependence, either in adolescents or adults (Colby et al. 2000a,b; O'Loughlin et al. 2002).

The complexity of assessing adolescent nicotine dependence is evident from the modest correlation found between two of the most common methods for measuring dependence—*DSM*-based diagnoses and FTQ-derived self-report measures—and the fact that these measures do not identify the same adolescents as nicotine dependent (Kandel et al. 2005). This finding has also been reported for adult smokers (Moolchan et al. 2002). Kandel and colleagues (2005) found a low agreement between *DSM*-based and FTQ-derived measures, except with high cigarette consumption (≥16 cigarettes per day). The *DSM*-based measure identified a higher prevalence of adolescent dependence because smokers met diagnostic criteria at much lower quantities of cigarettes than with the FTQ-derived measure (e.g., 60 versus 19 percent among those adolescent smokers smoking two to five cigarettes per day). Furthermore, for adolescent smokers who smoked a low number of cigarettes per day (e.g., 2.5 cigarettes), increasing depressive symptoms were associated with higher risk for *DSM*-diagnosed dependence (Kandel et al. 2005). This association between *DSM* diagnoses of tobacco dependence and depression has also been reported in adults (Breslau and Johnson 2000) (see "Epidemiology of Tobacco Use and Nicotine Dependence in Adults" later in this chapter). These findings led the investigators to believe that the *DSM* criteria identify a psychological component or behavioral symptoms common to both dependence and depression, which are not found in the FTQ-derived measure. Finally, Kandel and colleagues (2005) examined ethnic differences in dependence and found that non-Hispanic Whites had higher prevalence of dependence than other racial or ethnic groups, but this difference was accounted for by higher prevalence of smoking among this population. Once adjustment was made for differences in prevalence of smoking, differences by ethnicity were attenuated or eliminated. Thus, extensiveness of smoking must be considered when measuring dependence in youth.

Prevalence of Symptoms and Diagnoses in Adolescence

Studies suggest that adolescents report symptoms of dependence even at low levels of cigarette consumption (Colby et al. 2000a,b; Hughes 2001; DiFranza et al. 2002b; Panday et al. 2007). The difference in sensitivity to nicotine in adolescents and adults is also reported in animal models (Slotkin 2002; Adriani et al. 2003; Torres et al. 2008). For example, Levin and colleagues (2003) found that when rats were first exposed to nicotine in adolescence, they self-administered more nicotine than did rats exposed in adulthood. These differences in self-administration by age at first exposure persisted into adulthood. Similarly, Beluzzi and colleagues (2004) found that a single nicotine injection during early adolescence was sufficient to establish conditioned place preference in rats, whereas such injections in late adolescence or adulthood were not sufficient. Thus, paradigms for both self-administration and conditioned place preference in rats

suggest that adolescence may be a developmental stage of particular vulnerability to the effects of tobacco exposure. Furthermore, a study by Torres and colleagues (2008), using a conditioned place preference paradigm, showed that adolescent rats not only found lower doses more reinforcing but also found higher doses less aversive compared with adult rats. If so, adolescents may be particularly vulnerable to developing tobacco dependence. DiFranza and colleagues (2002b) concluded that, on average, the onset of an initial symptom of tobacco dependence occurred when adolescents smoked only two cigarettes once a week. Even adolescents who smoked only once or twice in their lives reported an average of 1.3 symptoms on the HONC (1.0 for males and 1.4 for females) (O'Loughlin et al. 2003). As a cautionary note, the interpretation of the results relies on whether the HONC reflects valid symptoms of dependence.

Kandel and Chen (2000) examined a proxy measure of *DSM* diagnosis of nicotine dependence in data from the National Household Survey on Drug Abuse (now the National Survey on Drug Use & Health). They reported that, compared with adults, adolescents met the criteria for dependence at lower levels of cigarette consumption. Some researchers have suggested that these age differences reflect a greater sensitivity to nicotine among adolescents than among adults (Kandel and Chen 2000). However, researchers have also noted that these age differences can reflect cohort effects (Breslau et al. 2001; Hughes 2001). That is, given the national reductions in smoking prevalence are accompanied by greater social proscriptions against smoking, smoking among more recent (younger) cohorts may represent more "hard core" smoking with greater levels of dependence (Breslau et al. 2001), although other researchers have questioned whether a "hardening of smokers" has actually occurred (O'Connor et al. 2006).

Reported prevalence of nicotine dependence among current adolescent smokers varies depending on whether heavy or light smokers are considered. In one study, 19.4 percent of adolescents who smoked weekly were considered to be dependent on the basis of an analog measure from the *ICD* criteria (O'Loughlin et al. 2003). Even less-than-weekly tobacco use may result in progression toward nicotine dependence. A later study found that the most susceptible youth lose autonomy over tobacco within one or two days of first inhaling from a cigarette. The appearance of tobacco withdrawal symptoms and failed attempts to stop smoking can precede daily smoking dependence, as defined by *ICD-10*, and typically appears before consumption reaches two cigarettes per day (DiFranza et al. 2007). One study using data from the National Survey on Drug Use & Health reports a 28-percent prevalence of last-year nicotine dependence (based on symptoms approximating *DSM-IV* dependence criteria) among adolescents aged 12 through 17 years who smoked during the last month, which was only slightly lower than the prevalence for adults (e.g., 30 to 32 percent among those aged 18 through 49 years) (Kandel and Chen 2000). The majority of adolescent daily smokers meet criteria for nicotine dependence. For example, Kandel and colleagues (2005) found that 87 percent of adolescent daily smokers met *DSM* criteria and 63 percent met the modified FTQ criteria (score >3). Similarly, O'Loughlin and colleagues (2003) found that 65.9 percent of seventh graders who smoked daily met *ICD* criteria.

There has also been interest in whether adolescents experience withdrawal symptoms on the discontinuation of smoking, either as part of an attempt to stop smoking or during periods when they cannot smoke. Colby and colleagues (2000a) summarized six retrospective studies in which adolescent smokers recalled their experiences during periods of nonsmoking. Most adolescents reported at least one symptom of withdrawal. Craving was the most commonly reported symptom upon abstinence. Fernando and colleagues (2006) analyzed data from the National Youth Tobacco Survey and reported that 63 percent of adolescents who smoked five or fewer cigarettes per day reported at least one withdrawal symptom. Hanson and colleagues (2003) examined the effects of the nicotine patch on adolescent-reported withdrawal symptoms. Compared with the placebo group, the nicotine patch group had lower scores for withdrawal symptoms.

Killen and colleagues (2001) recruited adolescents from alternative high schools and from a homeless shelter who smoked at least 10 cigarettes per day. There were two assessment sessions. Participants were randomly assigned to the nicotine patch or the placebo patch for the second assessment. The researchers found a decrease in heart rate across sessions only for the placebo condition. However, they found significant increases in self-reported withdrawal symptoms for both the nicotine patch and the placebo patch conditions. The most intense withdrawal symptoms were craving and anxiety, which were not relieved by the nicotine patch. Finally, some adolescents who believed they had worn a nicotine patch had expectancy effects; they reported less craving and frustration and a greater ability to concentrate. Together, these results suggest that adolescent smokers experience withdrawal symptoms but that expectancy effects also influence findings. Prokhorov and colleagues (2005) suggest caution about interpreting nonspecific symptoms such as irritability, depression, insomnia, and trouble concentrating, which can have multiple causes besides tobacco withdrawal.

Some animal data suggest that adolescents experience a dampened withdrawal response compared with that in adults (O'Dell et al. 2004, 2006). O'Dell and colleagues (2004) precipitated withdrawal with mecamylamine in rats receiving long-term administration of nicotine versus saline and found mecamylamine-induced withdrawal in adult rats but not in adolescent rats. These findings in animal studies, combined with limited clinical data, indicate the need for further studies of differences in withdrawal symptoms by age.

Trajectories of Smoking from Adolescence to Adulthood

Cigarette smoking shows age-related trends with typical initiation of smoking occurring in early adolescence. Retrospective data from the 1999 National Survey on Drug Use & Health (Kopstein 2001) suggest that the average age at first use of cigarettes is 15.4 years and the average age at initiation of daily smoking is 18 years. Data from both retrospective and longitudinal studies suggest that smoking prevalence or incidence of daily smoking in adolescents increases over time, peaks in young adulthood, and then declines (Chen and Kandel 1995; Breslau et al. 2001). However, these data are limited in that they describe a single "average" trajectory of age-related changes in smoking behavior, which obscures substantial heterogeneity among smokers. For example, there is variation in age at smoking initiation (Breslau et al. 1993a; Chassin et al. 2000) in the time it takes to progress to daily smoking, and in the time to develop dependence symptoms (DiFranza et al. 2002b).

Advances in mixture modeling (Nagin 1999; Muthén and Muthén 2000) have enabled longitudinal studies to identify multiple age-related trajectories of smoking behavior. Some of these studies conducted follow-up on participants through adolescence (Colder et al. 2001; Audrain-McGovern et al. 2004b; Abroms et al. 2005). Wills and colleagues (2004) performed cluster analysis rather than mixture modeling. These studies have all identified multiple trajectory groups, which typically include a group with early-onset (7th grade) regular smoking (smoking at least a few times a week); a group with experimental smoking (smoking occasionally each year); nonsmokers; and a group with intermediate- (regular smoking in 9th grade) and late-onset (regular smoking in 10th grade) regular smoking. These studies do not assess tobacco dependence, and even the late-onset groups were younger than age 18 years. Karp and colleagues (2005) studied only adolescents who had started to smoke. Most of their participants remained at low levels of smoking, but there was heterogeneity in the speed at which the others escalated their cigarette use, and youth across all rates of escalation were more likely to show symptoms of nicotine dependence than those individuals who maintained low levels of cigarette use. Soldz and Cui (2002) conducted follow-up on participants through 12th grade. They identified the following groups: nonsmokers, experimental smokers, smokers with early or late escalation of smoking, and stable continuing smokers. Their findings are noteworthy for identifying a group who stopped smoking, which was absent in other studies.

Several studies had follow-up from adolescence to adulthood. White and colleagues (2002b) recruited 374 adolescents in New Jersey through random telephone sampling. The participants were interviewed five times from age 12 years to age 30 or 31 years. The investigators identified three trajectory groups: (1) nonsmokers and experimental smokers; (2) occasional smokers and smokers whose smoking peaked at 18 years of age and then declined; and (3) heavy smokers and regular smokers. Predictor variables distinguished between nonsmoking and smoking trajectories but could not predict heavy smoking among smokers. Predictor variables were disinhibition items from the Zuckerman Sensation Seeking Scale, low school grades, and use of other drugs. Chassin and colleagues (2000) recruited 8,556 adolescents in 6th through 12th grades in a midwestern county school system and surveyed them annually in 1980 through 1983. Additional follow-ups were conducted in 1987 and 1993 and identified a greater number of groups reflecting smoking trajectory. The groups included nonsmokers, experimental smokers, persons with early smoking initiation who became stable smokers, persons with late smoking initiation who became stable smokers, and persons who stopped smoking. On average, persons with early smoking initiation who became stable smokers were smoking daily by 15 years of age and averaged more than one-half pack of cigarettes per day by 18 years of age. In contrast, persons with late smoking initiation who became stable smokers averaged weekly smoking at age 18 years but less than one-half pack per day. Thus, the stable group with early initiation was also at particular risk for heavy smoking. This group was characterized by (1) a high frequency of parental smoking, perhaps reflecting both genetic and environmental risk factors; (2) less parental support; and (3) greater attitudinal tolerance for deviant behavior ("deviance proneness").

Orlando and colleagues (2004) identified similar groups: nonsmokers; triers (never exceeding one or two cigarettes per year, increasing slightly in early adolescence, then decreasing to very low levels in young adulthood); late-onset increasers (started at a low smoking rate, but increased smoking steadily with the sharpest increase occurring between 18 and 23 years); decreasers (smoked a few times per month at age 13 years but decreased to once or twice a year by age 23 years); and early increasers (started out at low level of smoking at age 12 years but rose sharply to weekly smoking by age 14 years with continuing increases in smoking). These researchers also identified a group of heavy smokers throughout the age range of 13 through 23 years. The studies by Chassin and associates (2000) and Orlando and colleagues (2004) both found that the group with late initiation seemed to be protected in adolescence by family factors, including (across the two studies) less familial smoking, more parental support, intact families, and higher levels of parental education. However, Orlando and colleagues (2004) found that the trajectory groups of the stable heavy smokers, the persons with early initiation who increased cigarette consumption, and those with late initiation who increased cigarette consumption all converged to a similar point of heavy smoking by 23 years of age. Thus, these studies identify a group of persons with early initiation and sharply escalating cigarette consumption who are at high risk for heavy smoking. However, late initiation of smoking does not necessarily imply protection against heavy smoking. Divergence among these groups may occur at ages older than 23 years, which were not represented in the study by Orlando and colleagues (2004).

Several studies focused on African Americans. Juon and colleagues (2002) conducted follow-up on inner-city participants who had low socioeconomic status (SES) and divided them into nonsmokers, former smokers, smokers with late initiation (after age 18 years), and smokers with early initiation. The group with early initiation was more aggressive in childhood, more likely to have lax parental supervision, and had more drug problems. White and colleagues (2004) modeled trajectories of the number of cigarettes smoked each day. They identified nonsmokers, light smokers, and heavy smokers and found that African Americans started smoking later and had lower cigarette consumption than did White participants. Similarly, Blitstein and colleagues (2003) found that progression of smoking was more likely to be slow among African Americans. Finally, Brook and colleagues (2006) modeled trajectories for African American and Puerto Rican adolescents from age 14 to 26 years and identified the following groups: nonsmokers, persons whose smoking peaked at 18 years of age and then declined, smokers with late initiation, and smokers with early initiation. Although there are few studies, these findings suggest that the age at smoking initiation and the speed of progression in cigarette consumption may differ by ethnicity. This hypothesis should be considered in describing smoking trajectories from adolescence to adulthood.

Another important consideration is that none of these longitudinal studies spanning adolescence and adulthood directly assessed nicotine dependence. Therefore, the extent to which predictors of early progression to heavy smoking are predictors of nicotine dependence is unknown. However, Storr and colleagues (2004) performed a latent class analysis of nicotine dependence symptoms by using data from the National Survey on Drug Use & Health. The findings indicated that early smoking initiation leads to a higher probability of experiencing nicotine dependence features within two years of smoking onset compared with those smokers who initiated smoking after age 20 years.

Determinants of Nicotine Addiction

Researchers have described the progression of cigarette smoking as a process of multiple stages, including precontemplation, contemplation or preparation, initial trying, experimental or irregular smoking, and established daily smoking (Mayhew et al. 2000). Researchers have also suggested that movement across these stages is determined by different factors (Flay et al. 1983). For example, social factors such as peer modeling and opportunities to experiment may have a greater influence on initial experimentation with smoking, whereas factors such as genetic risk, negative affect, and propensity to develop tolerance to nicotine have been hypothesized to play a greater role in determining movement across later stages of smoking (Flay et al. 1983). However, the empirical evidence for such stage-specific predictors is weak. Mayhew and colleagues (2000) reviewed this literature and found that few studies tested for stage-specific predictors. Rather, most studies aggregated data across stages, predicting any progression in smoking or predicting broad categories such as "regular" smoking, which ranges from smoking a single cigarette a month to daily heavy smoking. Moreover, much of the research on adolescent smoking initiation is motivated by an interest in smoking prevention. Therefore, many studies focus on the initiation of smoking or experimental smoking. Few studies have examined predictors of nicotine dependence or daily heavy smoking. For these reasons, little is known about stage-specific predictors of nicotine dependence.

Some studies have used genetically informed designs to examine the extent to which adolescent tobacco dependence is related to additive genetic influences, shared environmental influences that make siblings more alike, and unshared environmental influences that make siblings different (Boomsma et al. 2002). From the extensive literature on the genetics of adolescent smoking, several studies are selected for review, because they focus on heavy smoking or nicotine dependence in adolescence. McGue and colleagues (2000) report that 44 percent of the variance in nicotine dependence among 17-year-old twins was associated with additive genetic influence. However, shared environment also played an important role, accounting for 37 percent of the variance

in nicotine dependence. Similarly, a study that focused on high frequency of smoking rather than nicotine dependence reports that both additive genetic and shared environmental influences were important (Rende et al. 2005). One study reported differences by gender in heritability for "problem" tobacco use (Rhee et al. 2003). Heritability was a stronger influence, and shared environmental factors were a weaker influence for female than for male adolescents. Thus, studies of behavioral genetics in relation to adolescent heavy smoking or nicotine dependence suggest the importance of both genetic and environmental influences, although in an adult study population, tobacco dependence seems to be more strongly influenced by genetics (see "Genetics" earlier in this chapter).

Researchers have also associated maternal smoking during pregnancy with the later development of tobacco dependence in offspring. Buka and colleagues (2003) examined a sample (aged 17 to 39 years) from the Providence (Rhode Island) cohort of the National Collaborative Perinatal Project. They found an elevated risk for tobacco dependence when the mother smoked more than one pack of cigarettes per day during pregnancy. However, the investigators note that these results could also be explained by genetic influences. Moreover, because postnatal maternal smoking was not considered, social environmental mechanisms of intergenerational transmission of nicotine dependence (e.g., role modeling) could also influence findings. For example, Cornelius and colleagues (2005) found that the relationship between prenatal exposure and adolescent smoking was not significant after adjustment for factors such as the mother's current smoking and the smoking of friends.

Studies have also associated child and adolescent psychopathology with nicotine dependence and heavy smoking. Using data from the Yale Longitudinal High-Risk Study, Dierker and colleagues (2001) found a significant association of nicotine dependence with anxiety disorder, affective disorder, conduct disorder, oppositional defiant disorder, substance dependence, and parental substance dependence. The investigators reported that affective disorders and drug use disorders remained unique predictors of nicotine dependence after adjustment for confounding comorbidities. These relationships were found only for nicotine dependence and not for distinguishing between nonsmoking and experimentation or between regular smoking and a combined group of earlier stages of smoking progression. Clark and Cornelius (2004) also examined adolescents with or without parental substance use disorder. They found that substance use disorders and daily smoking in parents, as well as conduct disorder, oppositional defiant disorder, and attention-deficit/hyperactivity disorder in offspring predicted progression to daily smoking. However, these researchers found no significant relationship between anxiety or depressive disorders in adolescents and progression to daily smoking.

In a longitudinal study of a large sample of adolescents recruited from high schools, Rohde and colleagues (2004) report a finding similar to that of Clark and Cornelius (2004). Externalizing disorders (e.g., attention-deficit/hyperactivity disorder, disruptive behavior disorders, and alcohol and drug use disorders) are more strongly and consistently associated with smoking cigarettes than are internalizing disorders (e.g., mood and anxiety disorders). In a multivariate analysis that included familial psychopathology, familial smoking, and composite variables of internalizing and externalizing disorders, only the externalizing disorders predicted both progression to daily smoking and to nicotine dependence among daily smokers. Thus, these studies show a consistent support for externalizing disorders, but less consistent support for internalizing disorders, as predictors of frequent smoking or nicotine dependence. The inconsistent effects of internalizing disorders may reflect variation in study samples and methods and, particularly, differences in the choice of which variables are statistically controlled in models of multiple predictors. Inconsistent results may also reflect the presence of moderating variables. For example, Patton and colleagues (1998) found that depression and anxiety were significant predictors of transition to daily smoking only when there were high levels of peer smoking.

Finally, Lloyd-Richardson and colleagues (2002) used data from a cross-sectional study—the National Longitudinal Study of Adolescent Health—to compare adolescents who were at different smoking stages. The smoking stages compared were persons who never smoked; experimental smokers, who tried a cigarette but had not smoked in the past 30 days and had never smoked daily; intermittent smokers, who reported some smoking but no daily smoking in the past 30 days; and regular smokers, who smoked daily for the past 30 days. The investigators examined whether predictor variables had different effects at different smoking stages. For example, a variable might be particularly important at early stages of smoking and thus would differentiate persons who never smoked from those who experimented with smoking but would not significantly differentiate among the other groups. The results showed some stage specificity of predictors. Peer smoking and low level of school connectedness more strongly differentiated between regular smokers and persons who never smoked, experimental smokers, and intermittent smokers than differentiated among persons who never smoked, experimental smokers, and intermittent smokers. Thus, according to the investigators, peer smoking and low school connectedness were more influential in later stages of smoking than in early stages. Alcohol use showed

the opposite pattern and so was thought to be more influential in the early stages of smoking. However, there was also evidence that predictors were not stage specific. For example, depression, delinquency, parental smoking, and family connectedness significantly differentiated among all the smoking groups, and thus these variables were not found to be stage-specific predictors.

Summary and Future Directions

The literature on adolescent nicotine addiction is relatively recent and less extensive than that resulting from the years of research that has been conducted on adolescent smoking. Some data suggest that compared with adults, adolescents display nicotine addiction at lower levels of cigarette consumption and so may be particularly vulnerable to addiction when exposed to tobacco. To both replicate and explain this phenomenon, there is a critical need for systematic assessment of how adolescents differ in their experience of different aspects of addiction—development of tolerance, withdrawal, reinforcing effects, associative learning—which makes this population more vulnerable to addiction compared with adults. The developing brain may be especially susceptible and receptive to acute or repeated doses of nicotine (Adriani et al. 2003; Schochet et al. 2005) and potentially other tobacco-related constituents and to associative learning processes.

Multiple trajectories of smoking from adolescence to adulthood have been identified, with one subgroup showing early initiation and a steep escalation of smoking associated with familial smoking and lack of parental support and with risk for chronic heavy smoking in adulthood. Further studies are needed to identify the genetic and environmental contributions to such trajectories, as well as the endophenotypes underlying the genetic contributions. Epidemiologic studies are particularly useful in providing an understanding of the critical environmental influences that may interact with specific genes to enhance the risk for developing nicotine dependence.

Another risk factor for nicotine addiction may be the diagnosis or symptoms of externalizing disorders. Previous research has been focused on the common neurosubstrates associated with nicotine addiction and depression (see "Psychiatric Comorbidity" earlier in this chapter). However, a better understanding of the relationship and the neurophysiology that links smoking to externalizing disorders is needed. In summary, future research needs to focus on the complex interactions among genes, environment, social and neurodevelopmental phases, and their influence on the trajectory toward nicotine dependence.

Epidemiology of Tobacco Use and Nicotine Dependence in Adults

Prevalence of Cigarette Smoking and Nicotine Dependence

According to one study, the prevalence of current smoking among adults (aged ≥18 years), as assessed by the National Health Interview Survey, was approximately 19.8 percent, or 43.4 million U.S. adults (CDC 2008a). According to the survey, 77.8 percent of current smokers smoked every day and 22.2 percent smoked on some days. (Current smokers are defined as those who smoked ≥100 times during their lifetime and who are smoking every day or on some days.) This high prevalence of daily smokers indicates the highly addictive nature of cigarettes. More men (22.3 percent) than women (17.4 percent) reported current smoking. For the racial and ethnic groups, the lowest prevalence of smoking was among Asians (9.6 percent), and the highest prevalence was among American Indians and Alaska Natives (36.4 percent). Across educational levels and SES, the highest prevalence of smoking was among persons with low levels of education—44.0 percent of those with a General Educational Development diploma and 33.3 percent of those with 9 to 11 years of education, versus 6.2 percent of those with graduate degrees—and persons with the lowest levels of income—28.8 percent of adults living below the poverty level and 20.3 percent of those living at or above the poverty level. The prevalence of smoking was lowest among persons aged 65 years or older (10.2 percent) and highest among those aged 18 through 24 years (23.9 percent).

In adults, the diagnosis of nicotine dependence or addiction in population surveys has largely been based on *DSM* 3rd ed. (rev) (*DSM-III-R*), *DSM-IV* (APA 1987, 1994, 2000), and *ICD-10* (WHO 1992) diagnostic criteria. The adult survey instruments used to make the diagnosis have included the National Institute of Mental Health Diagnostic Interview Survey and the Composite International Diagnostic Interview-Substance Abuse Module (Colby et al. 2000b). Researchers also have used data from other population surveys, such as the National Survey on Drug Use & Health to assess symptoms of tobacco dependence. That survey includes terms or phrases such as (1) "reported daily use of the product for two weeks or longer," (2) "have tried to cut down on smoking," (3) "unable to cut down or quit or experienced difficulty quitting," (4) "felt a need for more tobacco for the same effect," (5) "felt dependent," or (6) "felt sick or experienced withdrawal symptoms when stopping smoking." Results have been reported on the percentage of smokers who indicated one or more of these symptoms of dependence or experienced at least one of the withdrawal symptoms, psychoactive effects (e.g., "it relaxes or calms me"), or difficulty with smoking cessation, as a sign of potential tobacco dependence (CDC 1994, 1995a,b). Researchers have also used the presence of a specified number of these symptoms as a proxy measure for *DSM-IV* criteria for nicotine dependence (Kandel et al. 1997).

The prevalence of nicotine dependence based on these measures in population- or community-based samples from studies conducted in the United States are shown in Table 4.11. The variability in the prevalence of nicotine dependence can be mostly attributed to the characteristics of the population surveyed and the diagnostic tools used. The lifetime prevalence of *DSM-III-R* diagnosis of nicotine dependence in the general U.S. population ranges from 20 to 24 percent, and past-year prevalence of *DSM-IV* diagnosis of nicotine dependence is 9 to 13 percent. By virtually any measure, the prevalence of lifetime nicotine dependence is higher for cigarette smoking than for any other category of substance abuse (Anthony et al. 1994; Giovino et al. 1995). The results from Table 4.11 also illustrate that almost one-third of persons who have ever tried smoking cigarettes became dependent on nicotine.

Examination of self-reports of specific symptoms by adult daily or dependent smokers (Table 4.12) shows that in the majority of studies that assessed these symptoms, the least frequently reported symptoms include tolerance, withdrawal, and giving up activities as a result of tobacco use. The most frequently reported symptoms include efforts to reduce smoking and the inability to reduce smoking; feeling dependent; using more cigarettes than intended; and perhaps, continuing to smoke cigarettes despite experiencing problems. Therefore, the symptoms of nicotine dependence most likely to be reported among adults tend to be behavioral or a loss of control over smoking, and the least reported items appear to be physiological (e.g., symptoms of tolerance and withdrawal). In a study by Kandel and Chen (2000), a higher proportion of adolescents reported experiencing symptoms of tolerance (22.2 percent) and/or physical and psychological problems (27.0 percent) resulting from tobacco use, compared with the proportion of adults aged 18 through 49 years (14.4 and 20.3 percent, respectively) and adults aged 50 years or older (9.9 and 11.0 percent, respectively). These results may reflect either the cohort effect or the effect described previously as higher sensitivity in adolescents than that in adults to the effects of nicotine on physiological symptoms of dependence.

Table 4.11   Lifetime and current prevalence of nicotine dependence in population studies in the United States

Study	Design/sample	Diagnostic measure	Prevalence (%)	Population characteristics
Hughes et al. 1987	1,006 middle-aged male smokers from Multiple Risk Factor Intervention Trial screening 1980	*DSM-III* FTQ score ≥7	90.0 36.0	Smokers (82% smoked ≥15 cigarettes/day, mean cigarettes/day ± standard deviation = 28.0 ± 12.8)
Breslau et al. 1991, 1993a	Random sample aged 21–30 years Large health maintenance organization N = 1,007 of 1,200 1989–1990 (follow-up)	NIMH-DIS *DSM-III-R*[a]	20.0 27.0 51.0	Total sample Ever smoked Ever smoked daily for 1 month Lifetime prevalence
Anthony et al. 1994	Population survey of noninstitutionalized persons aged 15–54 years National Comorbidity Survey N = 4,414 1990–1992	CIDI *DSM-III-R*[b]	24.1 31.9	General population Ever smoked[c] Lifetime prevalence
Centers for Disease Control and Prevention 1995b	NHSDA population survey of noninstitutionalized civilians aged ≥12 years N = 61,426 1991 and 1992	NHSDA (≥1 indicator of dependence) *DSM-IV*[d]	75.2 90.9	Smoked ≥1 time in past 30 days Daily smokers Smoked daily for ≥2 consecutive weeks in past 12 months
Cottler et al. 1995	Field trial using random-digit telephone dialing methods for general population sample N = 260 daily smokers 1990–1991	CIDI-SAM *DSM-III-R*[b] *ICD-10* *DSM-IV*[d]	71.0 77.0 66.0	Daily smoking for 1 month Lifetime prevalence
Kandel et al. 1997, 2001; Kandel and Chen 2000	NHSDA population survey of noninstitutionalized civilians aged ≥12 years N = 87,915: 1991–1993 N = 39,994: 1994–1996	NHSDA *DSM-IV*[d]	8.6–10.5 28.0 28.5	General population Used tobacco product in past year Smoked last month Prevalence in past year
Breslau and Johnson 2000	Random sample aged 21–30 years Large health maintenance organization N = 238 daily smokers 1989–1990 (follow-up)	NIMH-DIS *DSM-III-R*[a] FTND score ≥4	66.4 75.0 55.5 57.1	Daily smokers Daily smokers with FTND score ≥4 Daily smokers with FTND score <4 Daily smokers Lifetime prevalence
Breslau et al. 2001, 2004a	4,414 respondents to National Comorbidity Survey, Tobacco Supplement Aged 15–54 years 1990–1992	CIDI *DSM-III-R*[b]	24.0 48.0	Total population Daily smokers Lifetime prevalence

Table 4.11   Continued

Study	Design/sample	Diagnostic measure	Prevalence (%)	Population characteristics
Grant et al. 2004	NESARC population survey of noninstitutionalized civilians aged ≥18 years N = 43,093 2001–2002	NIAAA Alcohol Use Disorder and Associated Disabilities Interview Schedule *DSM-IV*[e]	12.8	Total sample Prevalence in past year

Note: **CIDI** = World Health Organization's Composite International Diagnostic Interview; **CIDI-SAM** = CIDI Substance Abuse Module; **DSM-III** = *Diagnostic and Statistical Manual of Mental Disorders,* 3rd ed.; **DSM-III-R** = *DSM,* 3rd ed. (rev); **DSM-IV** = *DSM,* 4th ed.; **FTND** = Fagerström Test for Nicotine Dependence; **FTQ** = Fagerström Tolerance Questionnaire; **ICD-10** = *International Classification of Diseases, Tenth Revision*; **NESARC** = National Epidemiology Survey on Alcohol and Related Conditions; **NHSDA** = National Survey on Drug Use & Health; **NIAAA** = National Institute on Alcohol Abuse and Alcoholism; **NIMH-DIS** = National Institute of Mental Health Diagnostic Interview Schedule.

[a]NIMH-DIS included ever smoking daily for ≥1 month plus *DSM-III-R* criteria for dependence with ≥3 of the following symptoms persisting for ≥1 month: greater use than intended; unsuccessful efforts to control use; important activities given up; continued use despite social, psychological, or health problems; tolerance; withdrawal symptoms; and use to avoid withdrawal symptoms. Excluded 2 symptoms listed in the general *DSM-III-R* criteria for psychoactive substance use disorders: (1) great deal of time spent in activities necessary to acquire substance or recover from effects and (2) frequent intoxication or withdrawal symptoms when expected to fulfill major role obligations.

[b]CIDI criteria included daily smoking for ≥1 month plus *DSM-III-R* criteria for dependence with ≥3 of criteria with symptoms persisting for ≥1 month.

[c]Data on persons who ever smoked estimated from synthesis with NHSDA data.

[d]*DSM-IV* criteria for dependence with ≥3 of the following symptoms within a 12-month period: tolerance; withdrawal; using larger amounts or longer than intended (assessed as needed or if smoker felt dependent on nicotine); unsuccessful efforts to cut down; negative social, occupational, and physical consequences; and persistent physical and psychological problems. Excluded spending significant amount of time to obtain substance; instead, quantity (smoking ≥2 packs daily in past 30 days) was examined in relation to dependence.

[e]NIAAA used *DSM-IV* criteria modified as follows: use of nicotine to relieve or avoid withdrawal as operationalized by using the following four symptom items: (1) use of nicotine on awakening, (2) use of nicotine after situation in which use was restricted, (3) use of nicotine to avoid nicotine withdrawal symptoms, and (4) waking up in middle of the night to use tobacco. "Giving up activities in favor of nicotine use" was assessed as (1) giving up or cutting down on important activities, such as associating with friends or relatives or attending social activities, because tobacco use was not permitted at activity and (2) giving up or cutting down on activities that were of interest or that gave pleasure because tobacco use was not permitted. The "great deal of time spent using tobacco" criterion was assessed by single symptom item, chain-smoking. The "using tobacco more than intended" criterion was operationalized as having a period when tobacco was used more than intended. Nicotine dependence was assessed for any tobacco product, including cigarettes, cigars, pipes, chewing tobacco, and snuff.

However, on the basis of animal studies, withdrawal symptoms would be presumed to be fewer in adolescents than in adults (O'Dell et al. 2004, 2006), yet more adolescents are endorsing physical problems than do adults. As pointed out previously, factors other than withdrawal may be associated with higher endorsement of withdrawal symptoms among adolescents. Another possibility is that questions on physical dependence, particularly on tolerance, are not asked in a manner that is understood by or relevant to adult smokers.

The symptoms most frequently reported by adults appear to be less specific to the diagnosis of nicotine dependence. For example, Breslau and colleagues (1994) observed that (1) 88.6 percent of dependent smokers reported the symptom of dependence described as "smoking more than intended" (p. 747) and (2) 93.6 percent reported "unsuccessful attempts to quit" (p. 747). However, these items were also reported by a substantial percentage of nondependent smokers (47.9 and 25.2 percent, respectively) who smoked daily for a month or more during their lifetime but never met criteria for nicotine dependence. However, 87 percent of dependent smokers as opposed to only 12 percent of nondependent smokers reported one or more of the three physiological indicators of dependence (tolerance, withdrawal symptoms, and/or cigarette use to avoid withdrawal symptoms).

With regard to the onset of nicotine dependence relative to daily smoking, one study of data from the

National Comorbidity Survey showed that the highest rates of becoming nicotine dependent, as defined by *DSM-III-R*, occurred in the first 16 years from the year after progression to daily smoking, whereas in the subsequent 10 years the progression to nicotine dependence declined and continued at a slower rate (Figure 4.5) (Breslau et al. 2001). Thus, nicotine dependence generally followed daily smoking, although 5.4 percent of nicotine dependence began before or in the same year as progression to daily smoking. In most cases, the onset of nicotine dependence occurred one or more years after the initiation of daily smoking. These results appear somewhat contrary to results described in "Prevalence of Symptoms and Diagnoses in Adolescence" earlier in this chapter, which indicates that dependence symptoms may occur even earlier in a person's history of smoking. The discrepancies in results may be a function of how nicotine dependence was diagnosed or defined, that is, whether one was examining symptoms or a diagnosis of dependence or cohort effects.

Prevalence by Dose, Duration, and Subpopulations

The results from Table 4.11 also show that the more a person smokes, the greater is the likelihood of a diagnosis of nicotine dependence (CDC 1995b). Kandel and Chen (2000) observed a linear dose-response relationship between the number of cigarettes smoked in the past month and the percentage of smokers with nicotine dependence in the last year. This finding was based on self-reporting of symptoms approximating *DSM-IV* criteria for dependence and was confirmed in other studies (Kawakami et al. 1998). The percentage of male and female smokers with a diagnosis of dependence rose sharply and significantly as the amount of smoking increased from less than one cigarette per day, to one to five cigarettes per day, and to one-half pack per day. Thereafter, the increase in the percentage of smokers with a diagnosis of dependence tended to rise minimally; however, at

Figure 4.5   Cumulative incidence curves of daily smoking and nicotine dependence in the National Comorbidity Survey

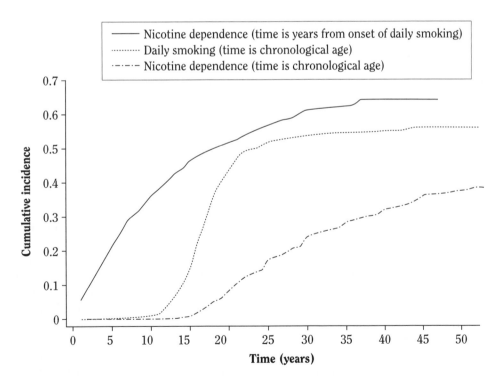

Source: Breslau et al. 2001. Reprinted with permission from American Medical Association, © 2001.
Note: Participants included 4,144 daily cigarette smokers and 2,136 smokers who were nicotine dependent.

Table 4.12   Prevalence of selected symptoms of nicotine dependence reported in selected studies

Study	Population	Used daily for ≥2 weeks	Tried to cut down	Unable to cut down/ unsuccessful attempts to control use (%)	Felt need for more/ tolerance (%)
Henningfield et al. 1990	NHSDA				
	Used at least once (N = 5,105)	51.1	54.2		11.7
	≥1 pack/day (N = 1,010)	91.2	84.3		23.9
Breslau et al. 1994	Random sample Health maintenance organization Aged 21–30 years (N = 1,200)				
	All smokers[a] (N = 394)			60.4	27.4
	Dependent[b] (N = 202)			93.6	45.5
	Nondependent[c] (N = 194)			25.2	8.3
Centers for Disease Control and Prevention 1995b	NHSDA 1991–1992 Aged ≥12 years				
	All responders (N = 14,688)	78.4	64.4	76.6	14.0
	Daily users in past year (N = 10,343)	NA	74.9	79.6	17.5
Kawakami et al. 1999[d]	Current male smokers Volunteers (N = 58)			64.2	
	Smoking cessation patients (N = 151)			65.5	
	Health Risk Assessment survey sample (N = 194)			59.3	
Storr et al. 2004	NHSDA 1995–1998 Recently initiated			21.7	16.0

Note: **NA** = data not available; **NHSDA** = National Survey on Drug Use & Health.
[a]Smoked daily for ≥1 month in their lifetime.
[b]*Diagnostic and Statistical Manual of Mental Disorders,* 3rd ed. (rev) *(DSM-III-R)* criteria for nicotine dependence.
[c]Has never met *DSM-III-R* criteria for nicotine dependence.
[d]Conducted in Japan.

numbers higher than one and one-half packs of cigarettes per day, females showed a higher prevalence of dependence than did males. The duration of cigarette smoking has also been related to the prevalence of nicotine dependence (Kandel and Chen 2000).

Kandel and Chen (2000) also found that among persons who smoked in the last month, the prevalence of nicotine dependence in middle-aged adults was similar to that in adolescents. After adjustment for the quantity of cigarettes smoked, the prevalence of dependence was generally higher among adolescents than among adults, particularly at lower levels of cigarette consumption. Several reasons that may account for this finding (i.e., cohort effects) have been discussed previously (see "Prevalence of Cigarette Smoking and Nicotine Dependence" earlier in this chapter). The lowest rates of nicotine dependence were in adults aged 50 years or older; this

finding was attributed to lower sensitivity to increased quantity of nicotine intake. The investigators also found that the prevalence of nicotine dependence was higher among females than among males, even after adjustment for the number of cigarettes smoked. However, this difference was observed only among persons 18 through 49 years of age. The prevalence of dependence was also higher among Whites than among Blacks, and this difference was particularly evident at the lower levels of cigarette consumption.

Other studies have found no differences by gender in the prevalence of nicotine dependence (Breslau et al. 1991; Anthony et al. 1994) but have confirmed differences by race when *DSM* criteria were used to diagnose nicotine dependence (Breslau et al. 1994, 2001). However, when time to the first cigarette was used as an indicator of dependence, more Blacks than Whites reported smoking

Felt dependent (%)	Felt sick when stopped/ withdrawal symptoms (%)	Greater use than intended (%)	Use despite problems (%)	Use to avoid/ relieve withdrawal (%)	Activities given up (%)	Salience (drug involvement) (%)
37.9	16.5					
79.2	33.3					
	30.5	68.8	44.4	26.6	6.6	
	58.9	88.6	72.3	49.0	12.9	
	0.3	47.9	15.1	3.1	0.0	
68.9	34.9					
85.0	37.4					
55.2	67.2	84.5	65.5	60.3	10.3	
54.7	73.0	73.0	56.1	63.5	17.6	
36.1	58.2	67.5	42.8	49.0	8.2	
	17.9	4.7–5.3		4.9	20.1	

within 10 minutes of awakening even though Blacks had lower or similar levels of cigarette consumption (Royce et al. 1993). In another study, Blacks also reported shorter time to the first cigarette than did Whites (Ahijevych and Gillespie 1997). Differences in nicotine metabolism and blood concentrations of cotinine may contribute to differences in the prevalence of dependence among Blacks and Whites (Benowitz et al. 1999). Among smokers who ever smoked daily, nonnicotine-dependent Blacks were 2.5 times more likely to persist in smoking than were nondependent Whites (Breslau et al. 2001). These findings suggest a weakness in diagnostic systems categorized by differences in ethnic and racial groups, differences in sensitivity to nicotine across groups, or differences in sociocultural factors (e.g., extent of cigarette promotion or smoking restrictions) that contribute to persistence in smoking across groups.

Nicotine Dependence and Psychiatric Comorbidity

As described in the previous sections, studies have found a strong association between nicotine dependence and comorbid disorders that warrants further discussion. It is estimated that nearly one-half of all cigarettes sold in the United States (44 percent) are consumed by people with mental illnesses or substance abuse disorders. In addition, the prevalence of tobacco use among those with either addictions and/or mental illness is between 38 to 98 percent, as opposed to 19.8 percent for the general population (Schroeder 2009). Breslau and colleagues (1991) have conducted several studies. One earlier population-based study in Michigan observed that young adults with a diagnosis of nicotine dependence reported higher prevalence of alcohol and drug dependence and major depression and anxiety disorders than did persons who had never experienced nicotine dependence (Breslau et al. 1991). The relationships between each disorder and nicotine dependence were observed even when adjustments were made for confounding comorbidities. These findings are similar to those observed for adolescent smokers described earlier (Dierker et al. 2001) (see "Determinants of Nicotine Addiction" earlier in this chapter). However, the results were contrary to other findings among adolescents (Clark and Cornelius 2004; Rohde et al. 2004). Other population-based research and clinical studies have also pointed to the strong relationship between daily smokers or nicotine-dependent smokers (as opposed to lifetime nonsmokers or nondependent smokers) and substance use disorders, anxiety disorders, and depression, with higher prevalence of comorbid psychiatric disorders among nicotine-dependent smokers and higher prevalence of nicotine-dependent smokers among persons with comorbid disorders. For example, in a U.S. population-based survey, Grant and colleagues (2004) observed that the prevalence of alcohol use disorders, current mood disorders, or current anxiety disorders among adult respondents with diagnoses of nicotine dependence during the past year ranged from 21 to 23 percent compared with 9 to 11 percent in the general population. Conversely, other studies have shown the percentage of persons with nicotine dependence among respondents with these comorbid disorders ranging from 25 to 35 percent and as high as 52 percent among respondents with drug use disorders compared with 12.8 percent in the general population (Glassman et al. 1990; Breslau et al. 1994, 2004b; Lasser et al. 2000; Degenhardt and Hall 2001; Kandel et al. 2001; Isensee et al. 2003; Schmitz et al. 2003; Grant et al. 2004; John et al. 2004).

Furthermore, studies have shown that the more severe the nicotine dependence, the more likely was the association with comorbid disorders. For example, John and colleagues (2004) found that the greater the number of nicotine-dependent symptoms or nicotine withdrawal symptoms and the higher the total FTND scores, the higher the odds ratios for psychiatric disorders. Nonetheless, even nonnicotine-dependent smokers, compared with nonsmokers, had significantly higher prevalence of alcohol and drug dependencies, but not of major depression or anxiety disorders (Breslau et al. 1991, 1994, 1996). This result suggests that smoking may either physiologically or perhaps more critically, socially, lower the threshold for substance abuse disorders. Conversely, the greater the number of psychiatric disorders experienced by the individual, the higher the prevalence or odds of smoking, particularly daily or heavy smoking (Lasser et al. 2000; Breslau et al. 2004b) and of diagnosis of nicotine dependence (Breslau et al. 2004b; John et al. 2004).

The relationship of major depression or anxiety disorders with nicotine dependence is complex and not extensively explored. Breslau and colleagues (1993b) examined the relationship between depression and nicotine dependence in a prospective investigation of 14 months. The investigators found that major depressive disorder increases the risk of progression to nicotine dependence and more severe levels of dependence. These results were confirmed in a subsequent analysis of cross-sectional data from the National Comorbidity Survey in which preexisting major depressive disorders, several anxiety disorders (e.g., phobias, generalized anxiety disorders, and posttraumatic stress disorders), and substance use disorders had resulted in an increased risk for progression to daily smoking or onset of nicotine dependence among daily smokers (Breslau et al. 2004b). Of the anxiety disorders assessed, neither preexisting agoraphobia nor panic disorder predicted a subsequent progression to daily smoking, and panic disorder did not increase the relative risk of transition to nicotine dependence. Similar findings had also been observed in earlier epidemiologic cross-sectional studies of adults (Breslau and Klein 1999) and in longitudinal studies with follow-up of adolescents into young adulthood (Johnson et al. 2000; Isensee et al. 2003).

Conversely, Breslau and colleagues (1993b) also observed that a history of nicotine dependence increased the risk for a subsequent first incident or recurrence of major depressive disorder. Daily smoking or nicotine dependence increased the risk of a subsequent onset of drug use, anxiety disorders, major depression, or dysthymia both in epidemiologic studies (Breslau et al. 1998, 2004a; Breslau and Klein 1999) and in population-based longitudinal studies (Kendler et al. 1993; Isensee et al. 2003). In a population-based longitudinal cohort study, adolescents who smoked one or more packs of cigarettes per day had higher odds of the onset of anxiety disorders (e.g., generalized anxiety disorders, panic disorder, and agoraphobia) in adulthood than did adolescents who smoked less than one pack a day (Johnson et al. 2000). Analysis of cross-sectional data from the National Comorbidity Survey found no differences between nicotine-dependent and nondependent daily smokers in the likelihood of a subsequent first onset of a psychiatric disorder (Breslau et al. 2004a). Therefore, daily smoking appears to be just as important a risk factor as a diagnosis of nicotine dependence. This finding may reflect the limitations of the criteria for a diagnosis of nicotine dependence.

This bidirectional finding in relation to cigarette smoking and some of the mood and substance use disorders can be considered either causal or a reflection of an underlying factor that is common to the predisposition to both disorders. For example, psychiatric disorders may lead to self-medication with nicotine, which targets the neurosystems that have mood-altering effects, or long-term exposure to nicotine may alter neurobiologic substrates, leading to the development of psychiatric comorbidities. Another possibility is that psychiatric disorder and nicotine addiction share genetic or environmental vulnerabilities or risk factors.

Few studies have been directed toward providing evidence for whether these factors are responsible for the relationships between smoking and psychiatric disorders. Support for self-medication of psychiatric disorders would come from three findings that show (1) smokers with psychiatric disorders have rates of smoking cessation lower than those for smokers who do not have these disorders; (2) remission of disorders is less likely to predict progression to daily smoking, because there is no need for self-medication, but preexisting active disorders are associated with increased risk for smoking and/or nicotine dependence; and (3) prevalence of smoking is higher among persons with remission of disorders than among those who continue to experience psychiatric symptoms because smoking reduced the psychiatric symptoms.

To date, the data show that the impact of psychiatric disorders on smoking cessation is equivocal (see "Trajectory of Recovery or Relapse" later in this chapter). However, these studies are limited to the disorders of major depression and alcohol abuse or dependence. Major depressive disorder is the only psychiatric disorder to meet the first two characteristics associating cigarette smoking with self-medication (findings 1 and 2) (Romans et al. 1993; Breslau et al. 2004a) (see "Trajectory of Recovery or Relapse" later in this chapter).

If the development of psychiatric disorders were caused by the effects of cigarette smoking or nicotine exposure, then findings to support this hypothesis would show that (1) a longer and higher exposure increases a smoker's odds of developing a psychiatric disorder; (2) longer abstinence from smoking leads to reduced risk for psychiatric disorder, unless the effects are irreversible; and (3) current but not former smoking is associated with higher risk for psychiatric disorder. The only disorders that appear to meet these characteristics are panic disorders and agoraphobia (Breslau and Klein 1999; Johnson et al. 2000; Isensee et al. 2003; Breslau et al. 2004a).

Support for common factors, hereditary or acquired, would be based on findings that show (1) both current and former daily smoking increase the risk for psychiatric disorders, (2) both active disorders and disorders in remission or only disorders in remission predict daily smoking or a progression to nicotine dependence, and (3) familial or genetic vulnerability is shared across nicotine dependence or smoking and psychiatric disorders. The greatest support for shared common factors is for substance abuse disorders and smoking.

Remission of substance abuse disorders has been a predictor of daily smoking and progression to nicotine dependence (Breslau et al. 2004b). Results of studies on families and twins support a shared familial and genetic vulnerability across substance use disorders (Bierut et al. 1998; Merikangas et al. 1998; Tsuang et al. 1998). The data on common factors for major depressive disorders and smoking are conflicting, showing both support (Breslau et al. 1994; Kendler and Gardner 2001; Johnson et al. 2004) and lack of support (Dierker et al. 2002; McCaffery et al. 2003). Researchers have attributed inconsistency in these results to differences in levels of cigarette consumption, definitions of depression, study methods, and analytic approaches (Johnson et al. 2004). The use of antidepressant treatments for both depression and smoking cessation, regardless of a history of depression, would support the concept of shared substrates that mediate nicotine dependence and depression (see "Pathophysiology of Nicotine Addiction" earlier in this chapter).

As a caveat, the strong relationship between nicotine dependence and some psychiatric disorders may be a function of the method used to diagnose nicotine dependence. For example, in another study conducted by Breslau and Johnson (2000), nicotine dependence, as defined by the FTND score, was not related to major depression. These researchers attributed the strong relationship between the *DSM-III-R* definition of nicotine dependence and major depression to the numerous behavioral symptoms associated with the diagnosis of nicotine dependence.

Summary and Future Directions

The effects of dose, age, race, and gender may be related to the prevalence of nicotine dependence. The number of cigarettes smoked per day and the duration of smoking are positively related to the percentage with diagnosis of nicotine dependence. Prevalence of nicotine dependence among adolescent smokers may be higher than that among adult smokers, particularly for those who smoke fewer cigarettes per day. Conflicting study results suggest that prevalence of nicotine dependence, as defined by *DSM* criteria, is higher among Whites than among Blacks but that prevalence is lower in Whites when time to the first cigarette of the day is the criterion for dependence. It is unclear whether the prevalence of nicotine dependence differs by gender. These results suggest the need for further research to explore reasons for the inconsistent findings across subgroups of smokers. A significant association also exists between psychiatric disorders and smoking, but the nature of this association is unclear. Depending on the disorder, the relationship may be causal; for example, smoking may increase the odds of panic disorder and major depressive disorder and may lead to self-medication with tobacco use. On the other hand, this association may result from common underlying factors that involve fundamental psychological or physiological processes, such as intolerance to states of negative affect or neurotransmitter dysfunction in a common pathway, which lead to nicotine dependence, substance abuse, and possibly depression. To date, understanding the causal relationships has relied predominantly on cross-sectional data sets. Prospective studies have been limited and have examined only a few psychiatric disorders, but this type of study is necessary to lend stronger evidence for any bidirectional causality or for common underlying causes

of cigarette smoking and nicotine dependence with specific psychiatric disorders. A clearer understanding of these relationships will result in a deeper understanding of the pathophysiology of nicotine addiction. Moreover, the studies of adults are limited in that the focus has been primarily on internalizing rather than externalizing disorders. In studies of adolescents, externalizing disorders may play an even greater role than do internalizing disorders in the development of nicotine addiction (see "Determinants of Nicotine Addiction" earlier in this chapter). Therefore, studies encompassing a broader range of diagnoses are warranted.

Trajectory of Recovery or Relapse

Studying recovery from smoking can provide valuable information on the nature of tobacco addiction and the factors affecting it. Every year about 45 percent of daily smokers in the United States stop smoking for 24 hours, but only 5 percent or less achieve long-lasting abstinence (CDC 2002, 2004). Thus, relapse is the principal limiting factor in the transition from smoking to nonsmoking status. This finding underscores the need to understand the nature of relapse and the factors affecting it.

Relapse: Definitions and Limitations of the Literature

Integration of information about relapse is difficult because definitions of critical events differ among studies. For instance, it seems useful to distinguish a lapse from a relapse. A lapse refers to an occurrence of smoking or tobacco use that takes place after an attempt to stop smoking but is not part of an ongoing pattern of consistent use (Brandon et al. 1986). Relapse refers to the point after an attempt to stop smoking when tobacco use becomes ongoing and persistent (Brandon et al. 1986). Although standards have been offered for defining "relapse" (Hughes et al. 2003), many reported results are based on idiosyncratic standards. In addition, there is no formally accepted definition of a "lapse." For instance, some studies define a lapse as only the first use of tobacco after an attempt to stop smoking, and other studies use broader definitions. Because of this diversity, this review reports results according to the definitions used by the investigators in each study. In addition, some investigators distinguish between relapse and failure of smoking

cessation, with relapse occurring only after a period of abstinence (e.g., after 48 hours) (Hughes et al. 2003). Again, few studies make such a distinction. Therefore, to render the bulk of the evidence comparable, this review uses the concept of return to smoking after a cessation attempt as an index of vulnerability to relapse, regardless of the duration of abstinence. In general, no distinction is made between cessation failure and relapse. Finally, some of the reviewed studies predict the likelihood of relapse while others predict relapse latency. In this review, either prediction is taken to reflect a higher level of vulnerability to relapse.

Natural History of Relapse

Prevalence

Two key characteristics of relapse are its high prevalence and its rapidity. Past reviews have consistently reported that persons who decide to stop smoking on their own and those who receive placebos in clinical trials achieve 6- to 12-month abstinence rates of only 3 to 5 percent (Cohen et al. 1989; Hughes et al. 2004c). Thus, within one year of an attempt to stop smoking, about 95 percent of persons who try to stop without a pharmacologic aid continue to smoke or resume smoking. Reviews of efficacious treatments reveal that 20 to 25 percent of those who tried to stop smoking succeeded for six months (Fiore et al. 2008). This finding means that about 75 percent of persons who try to stop smoking by using evidence-based treatments return to smoking within six months. The risk of relapse, however, does not end 6 to 12 months after the attempt at smoking cessation. Findings in studies of long-term outcome suggest that relapse ultimately claims 30 to 40 percent of smokers who stop smoking for one year (Eisinger 1971; Gilpin et al. 1997; Krall et al. 2002). For instance, Yudkin and colleagues (2003) found that about one-half of the smokers who had stopped smoking for one year relapse to smoking within the subsequent seven years. However, roughly 50 percent of those who have ever smoked eventually become long-term former smokers (Husten 2005) because many make repeated attempts to stop smoking until they are successful.

Rapidity

Most smokers who ultimately relapse resume smoking early after their attempt to stop. This pattern of early lapsing has been reported in persons receiving treatment (Kenford et al. 1994), as well as in those who decide on their own to stop smoking and in smokers who receive placebos (Hughes et al. 2004c). For example, Kenford and colleagues (1994) found that 80 to 90 percent of those who were smoking at six months after trying to stop had resumed smoking in the first two weeks of the attempt to stop. Other studies report similarly high rates of early lapsing in populations of treated and untreated smokers (Garvey et al. 1992; Gulliver et al. 1995; Westman et al. 1997; Hughes et al. 2004a). Women who stop smoking during pregnancy, however, tend not to relapse early in the attempt to stop, but rather tend to relapse after delivery, which is often weeks or months after initial cessation (Fingerhut et al. 1990; USDHHS 1990; Floyd et al. 1993; Stotts et al. 2000; Colman and Joyce 2003).

Lapse-Relapse Relationship

The odds of an eventual relapse are especially high among those who lapse or engage in initially isolated smoking episodes after the cessation date. Data suggest that lapsing is the single best predictor of an ultimate relapse (Brandon et al. 1990; Hughes et al. 1992; Kenford et al. 1994; Nides et al. 1995). Moreover, the risk of an ultimate relapse appears to increase with the number of lapse events (Wileyto et al. 2004). Nevertheless, even multiple lapses do not inevitably lead to a relapse (Nides et al. 1995). This finding attests to the wide variation in the course of both relapse and successful cessation in a population of smokers attempting to stop smoking.

The pattern of a return to regular smoking varies considerably across individuals and typically occurs over days and weeks rather than hours. On average, smokers have a second lapse three or four days after the first lapse (Shiffman et al. 1996b). Almost one-half of smokers have the second lapse within 24 hours of the first lapse (Brandon et al. 1990). On average, the latency between the first lapse to a relapse is three to five weeks (Brandon et

al. 1990; Shiffman et al. 1996a,b; Gwaltney et al. 2005a), which suggests that there is time after an initial lapse to engage in additional treatment to prevent progression to full relapse.

Risk Factors

To promote more precise thinking about the time courses and interactive and cumulative effects of different types of influences on relapse, several reviews recommend an organizational framework for categorizing forces that influence a relapse (Shiffman et al. 1986; Shiffman 1989a; Piasecki et al. 2002). In general, such recommendations have proposed three factors as important influences on relapse: person factors, emergent processes, and situational instigators. Person factors are stable characteristics that preexist the attempt to stop smoking and endure (e.g., gender and history of or proneness to depression). Emergent processes are dynamic factors that unfold over time and emerge sometime during the postcessation period. Such processes tend not to be bound to context. For example, although these processes may arise in response to an episodic event such as stress, they can persist for days or weeks. Withdrawal is an example of a dynamic variable that arises gradually in response to falling blood concentrations of nicotine (Hughes et al. 1990b; Piasecki et al. 2003a). Although situational factors may affect withdrawal symptoms (McCarthy et al. 2006), the symptoms persist well beyond the situational influences and are not wholly explained by them. Situational instigators are factors such as cues, contexts, or events that give rise to short-lived (phasic) reactions lasting from seconds to hours. Such reactions might comprise affective reactions to a stressor, such as an argument, or to exposure to smoking cues, such as seeing someone smoke.

Thus, this organizational scheme reflects the instigator of the process, such as a contextual cue, as well as the time course of vulnerability associated with relapse. Such categorization is complex, because the distinction among the time courses of influences is somewhat arbitrary and various influences may interact (Piasecki et al. 2002; Gwaltney et al. 2005b). These influences are not mutually exclusive or independent, which adds to the complexity of this organizational method. For example, person factors may affect situational reactions or emergent patterns of symptoms. The categorization scheme described here is only one approach to conceptualizing the causes of relapse. This approach has, however, allowed researchers to identify factors that consistently predict relapse and is consistent with a greater body of research and theory showing that person factors, phasic reactions, and contexts powerfully affect behavior (Mischel 2004).

Person Factors

Cognitive and Attitudinal Influences

There is evidence that relatively stable attitudinal variables affect the vulnerability to relapse of smokers. For example, precessation assessments of expectations that smoking will alleviate distress (e.g., negative moods and stress) predict the subsequent likelihood of a relapse (Wetter et al. 1994; Brandon et al. 1999). In addition, multiple studies conclude that baseline measures of confidence in the ability to stop smoking can also predict outcomes (Condiotte and Lichtenstein 1981; Baer et al. 1986; Shiffman et al. 2000). Other findings indicate that confidence before attempts to stop smoking and positive expectations may interact to predict risk of relapse to smoking. Smokers with low confidence and high expectations for smoking reinforcement are especially likely to relapse (Shadel and Mermelstein 1993; Dijkstra and Brosschot 2003). Finally, high levels of motivation, based on health concerns (Nides et al. 1995; Dijkstra and Brosschot 2003) or other reasons (Turner and Mermelstein 2004), may foster cessation and protect against relapse. However, motivation tends to be less effective than other factors, such as level of tobacco dependence or self-efficacy, that is, self-confidence in the ability to stop smoking cigarettes (Hyland et al. 2004; University of Michigan 2006).

Other cognitive variables are less consistently related to lapse and relapse. For instance, expectations about the negative effects of smoking (e.g., risk of disease) appear to predict the motivation or intention to stop smoking but not the likelihood of a relapse (Wetter et al. 1994; Brandon et al. 1999). Also, one study found that a strong commitment to continuing abstinence from smoking was related to reduced rates of relapse, but this finding was obtained in a population that comprised persons who abused opiates and alcohol in addition to smokers, and this condition made the relevance to smoking per se unclear (Hall et al. 1990).

Finally, cognitive dimensions such as expectations or motivation are sometimes hard to classify. For example, motivational structures and attitudes may affect behavior over many years (Etter et al. 2003b; Beltman and Volet 2007). However, motivational phenomena change over time and can be affected by contextual factors (Beltman and Volet 2007; McCaul et al. 2007; Sanderson et al. 2008; Weiss-Gerlach et al. 2008). Therefore, cognitive and motivational factors are discussed both as person factors and emergent processes, with the distinction reflecting the time course of their emergence.

Other data show that the attentional salience of smoking cues also predicts vulnerability to relapse. Using the Stroop paradigm, researchers presented smoking-related and neutral words to 158 volunteers for a smoking cessation program (Waters et al. 2003b). Results show that if words related to smoking attracted the attention of smokers, an early relapse was more likely within a three-month follow-up interval. In theory, the attention-grabbing properties of words related to smoking reflect the motivational potency of smoking that could then account for the greater likelihood of a relapse.

Tobacco Dependence

Measures of tobacco dependence predict the likelihood that a smoker will achieve long-term abstinence from tobacco use. For instance, self-report measures of dependence tend to predict cessation and relapse (Breslau and Johnson 2000; Piper et al. 2004; Shiffman et al. 2004a). However, the various self-report measures of dependence often do not show good agreement with one another (Breslau and Johnson 2000; Moolchan et al. 2002). This finding is consistent with emerging evidence that nicotine dependence is multifactorial (Hudmon et al. 2003; Piper et al. 2004; Shiffman et al. 2004b). More recent evidence suggests that some dependence factors are more predictive of dependence than are others. In particular, self-report measures of tobacco dependence that assess heavy automatic smoking that is not discriminated on time or context are most consistently associated with heightened risk of relapse (Transdisciplinary Tobacco Use Research Center 2007; Piper et al. 2008). This finding is consistent with the observation that objective measures of a high rate of smoking, such as expired carbon monoxide levels and serum concentrations of cotinine, are often related to the likelihood of a relapse (Nørregaard et al. 1993; Faue et al. 1997; Kenford et al. 2002). Even in the best circumstances, however, measures of tobacco dependence account for only modest amounts of variation in risk of relapse. This finding is consistent with the notion that relapse is a function of multiple person factors, emerging processes, and contextual factors.

In addition to dependence, the sensitivity of a smoker to a nicotine reinforcement predicts a shorter latency to relapse (Perkins et al. 2002a). In contrast, formal laboratory measures of tolerance to the effects of nicotine do not appear to be significantly related to relapse (Perkins et al. 2002a).

Demographic and Lifestyle Variables

Studies have related numerous variables of demographic factors and lifestyle to vulnerability to relapse. For example, researchers have related an increased likelihood of relapse to younger age (Nides et al. 1995; Ockene et al. 2000; Hyland et al. 2004), a low SES or a low level of education (Nides et al. 1995; Ockene et al. 2000; Wetter et al. 2005b), being unmarried (Nides et al. 1995; Ockene et al. 2000), higher levels of tonic stress, and more stressors or the perception of a higher stress level (Swan et al. 1988; Wewers 1988; Cohen and Lichtenstein 1990; McKee et al. 2003). Of these factors, low SES and low educational status appear to be especially strong and consistent predictors of ability to abstain from smoking on a continuing basis (Mullen 2004; Wetter et al. 2005a; Fernández et al. 2006; Lee and Kahende 2007; Letourneau et al. 2007). In addition, some data from clinical trials and population samples indicate that women may be less likely than men to maintain abstinence from tobacco use (Hubert et al. 1987; Bjornson et al. 1995; Community Intervention Trial for Smoking Cessation 1995; Wetter et al. 1999; Smith et al. 2003; Hyland et al. 2004). However, such relationships are not consistently found across different data sets. For instance, as noted above, numerous data sets reveal that females are more likely to relapse to tobacco use than are males. However, a substantial number of studies fail to find such a relationship (Gritz et al. 1998; Killen et al. 2002; Westmaas and Langsam 2005; Velicer et al. 2007; Walsh et al. 2007). Besides the issue of consistency, additional topics deserve greater research attention. These topics include exploration of how the various person factors "work together" to affect the success or failure of smoking cessation. In addition, it is important to determine whether the different person factors are associated with different sorts of relapse mechanisms or processes; that is, regardless of the likelihood of relapse in different smoker groups, it is important to determine whether relapse processes "unfold" differently in such groups.

Research suggests that men and women may differ in sensitivity to environmental events. There is evidence, for instance, that environmental or conditioned cues related to use of nicotine, such as seeing information about nicotine dose, seeing others smoking, or receiving cues previously paired with nicotine, tend to elicit stronger motivational response to use the drug in women than in men (Pomerleau et al. 2005; Perkins et al. 2006; Leventhal et al. 2007; Walsh et al. 2007). These data agree with animal research data showing that nicotine-paired environmental cues are more effective in eliciting self-administration of nicotine in female rats than in male rats (Chaudhri et al. 2005). Complementary data suggest that men are more likely to be responsive to actual nicotine dose and other pharmacologic properties than are women (Perkins et al. 2006). If men are indeed more sensitive to nicotine's pharmacologic properties than are women, this could explain why men who use NRT sometimes achieve higher levels of success with smoking cessation than do women who use NRT (Wetter et al. 1999; Perkins 2001; Cepeda-Benito et al. 2004) and why this finding did not

hold for use of psychosocial interventions (Velicer et al. 2007).

Other studies show additional differences by gender. Data from study of a community-based population sample suggest that financial stressors may be more likely to inhibit smoking cessation in women than in men and that negative health events are more likely to prompt cessation in men (McKee et al. 2003). Other research shows that male smokers tend to be more reactive to relatively minor stressful events (i.e., hassles) than are women (Wetter et al. 1999; Delfino et al. 2001; Todd 2004). Although there is mounting evidence of differences by gender in reaction to nicotine or environmental cues (Perkins et al. 1999), and in motivation to use tobacco or nicotine, these differences have not been definitively linked with either relapse or differences by gender in relapse. Even less is known about the relationship of factors such as low SES or educational attainment to likelihood of smoking cessation (Wetter et al. 2005a).

One innovative approach to unraveling the complex interrelationships among the multiple person factors and relapse is to conduct classification or decision-tree analyses. These analyses have been used to determine whether categories of person factors (e.g., male versus female) comprise smoker subgroups that can be distinguished on the basis of their risk profiles for cessation failure. One example of this approach generated six subgroups of women smokers (Swan et al. 2004). For some subgroups, cessation failure appeared to be related to educational attainment and the number of previous attempts to stop smoking; for others, failure was more strongly related to body mass index and family history of depression (Swan et al. 2004). In contrast, male smokers comprised subgroups more highly distinguished by variables related to nicotine dependence, such as FTND score (Heatherton et al. 1991) and the number of years of smoking. In addition, male subgroups were distinguished on the basis of previous NRT and a history of depression. This type of classification or decision-tree analysis is useful because it has the potential to reveal factors that are highly predictive of cessation outcome in a subgroup of smokers, even if a factor is not important over an entire sample (Swan et al. 1997, 1999). Further research is needed to assess the replicability of such findings.

Psychiatric and Affective Dimensions

Some researchers have reported that the vulnerability to failure of smoking cessation or relapse to smoking is positively related to a history of depression, alcohol intake, a tendency toward negative affect, and an intolerance of psychological distress. As with most other individual differences, these relationships are either small in magnitude, inconsistent, or both. For example, both studies of population samples and clinical trials indicate that a history of depression or depressive symptoms predicts a greater likelihood of a relapse or a failure to stop smoking (Anda et al. 1990; Romans et al. 1993; Ferguson et al. 2003; Smith et al. 2003; Japuntich et al. 2007). However, one meta-analysis of data from 15 clinical trials failed to find such an effect (Hitsman et al. 2003). Studies in this meta-analysis generally excluded participants who were currently depressed or taking antidepressant medication.

One hypothesis is that if depression is correlated with vulnerability to relapse, the correlation may be attributable to the presence of two specific subpopulations of persons who have depression. Hitsman and colleagues (2003) observed that several studies have found a relationship between recurrent (multiple episode) depression and heightened risk of failure to stop smoking (Glassman et al. 1993; Covey et al. 1999; Brown et al. 2001). Haas and colleagues (2004) also found that a high rate of failure to stop smoking was associated with a history of multiple, but not single, episodes of depression. There also is evidence that current depression is more strongly associated with relapse than is past depression (Niaura et al. 2001; Japuntich et al. 2007; Turner et al. 2008). These results suggest that associations between depression and relapse may be attributable to subpopulations with depression, that is, those who are either currently depressed or who are prone to recurrent depression. These types of depression may be linked to risk of relapse because both were associated with recurrent or chronic negative mood (Niaura et al. 2001; Haas et al. 2004; Japuntich et al. 2007), and negative mood has repeatedly been linked with increased likelihood of relapse to smoking among persons with depression (Kahler et al 2002; Leventhal et al. 2008). However, it is possible that the heightened risk of relapse presented by current or recurrent depression is caused by other factors, such as poor coping skills or low self-efficacy.

There is also mixed evidence as to whether a history of alcohol abuse or dependence increases vulnerability to relapse to smoking. Some studies show an elevated risk of relapse (Hughes 1993; Breslau et al. 1996), but in others risk is not elevated (Covey et al. 1993; Hurt et al. 1995). Perhaps the best characterization of the evidence is the finding that active abuse of or dependence on alcohol constitutes a risk factor for relapse to smoking (Hurt et al. 1994; Kalman et al. 2001, 2002). However, there may be little or no risk if problems with alcohol are in remission (Hughes and Callas 2003). Evidence also shows that an active consumption of alcohol enhances the risk of relapse to smoking (Krall et al. 2002; McKee et al. 2003). Thus, the risk of relapse posed by alcohol use is not attributable to alcohol being a marker for a trait-like vulnerability to relapse but rather is attributable to the immediate

(situational) effects of intoxication. However, there is modest evidence that another syndrome of disinhibition, attention-deficit/hyperactivity disorder, is associated with elevated risk of relapse to smoking (Humfleet et al. 2005).

An additional affective dimension that has been studied and may contribute to a heightened risk for relapse is the ability of a person to tolerate distress or to persist in a distressing task. Hence, several studies have associated measures of distress tolerance among smokers with the likelihood of or latency to relapse. In these studies, smokers with low vulnerability to relapse showed a greater persistence in tasks such as breathholding and mental arithmetic than did smokers with high vulnerability to relapse (Hajek et al. 1987; Brown et al. 2002). This finding provides evidence that characteristics such as an inability or unwillingness to tolerate distress is linked to a vulnerability to relapse. An inability to tolerate negative affect may be especially related to early relapse to smoking (Zvolensky et al. 2004; Brown et al. 2008).

In summary, the person factors that yield the strongest or most consistent prediction of relapse are measures of tobacco dependence and cognitive and attitudinal variables such as expectation of smoking reinforcement. In addition, measures of low SES and low educational attainment are also fairly consistently related to risk of relapse. Other relatively stable person factors are more modestly or inconsistently related to smoking relapse. Predictors of relapse vary from study to study, probably reflecting differences in the populations studied, different mixes of predictors included in the studies, and diverse methods and measures of the same target constructs. In addition, much of the variation in vulnerability to relapse is no doubt caused by other factors not measured in most studies—for example, exposure to episodic events and reactions to smoking cessation (Shiffman et al. 1996a,c; Kenford et al. 2002; Gwaltney et al. 2005a,b; McCarthy et al. 2006). Also, other variables may account for apparent direct associations between person factors and relapse. For instance, persons who drink heavily may be especially likely to socialize with other smokers, and an exposure to smokers may cause heightened risk of relapse.

Emergent Processes

Emergent processes are reflected in rapid changes in symptoms or behaviors that occur within several days before a lapse or relapse. Researchers have typically studied emergent processes across two temporal windows: one that begins at the time of smoking cessation and therefore captures initial responses to the event and a second that starts close in time to a lapse in cessation and captures changes in behaviors or symptoms leading up to the event. Both types of analyses provide evidence that emergent processes set the stage for smoking lapses and relapses. In general, emergent processes do not depend on the sort of treatment or cessation strategy used—for example, they occur in smokers receiving active or placebo pharmacotherapy.

Tobacco Withdrawal and Affective Symptoms

Perhaps the strongest evidence that emergent processes affect vulnerability to relapse comes from research on the tobacco withdrawal syndrome. Until recently, major reviews concluded there was little evidence that withdrawal symptoms were consistently related to the likelihood of a relapse (Hughes et al. 1990b; Patten and Martin 1996). However, in the decade ending in 2004, research has shed light on the nature of withdrawal, as well as its relationship to a relapse (Hughes 2007). First, in many smokers, perhaps most of those attempting to stop smoking, withdrawal symptoms are persistent and often remain elevated for months after an attempt to stop smoking (Gilbert et al. 1998, 2002; Piasecki et al. 1998, 2000). Second, withdrawal results (1) in great heterogeneity of symptoms, both in and across smokers, and (2) in volatile changes in affect and craving (see Figure 4.6 for

craving pattern) (Piasecki et al. 2003a; McCarthy et al. 2006). Third, withdrawal results in vulnerability to more severe symptoms in reaction to environmental events than those that occur before smoking cessation (Figure 4.7) (McCarthy et al. 2006). In addition, research shows that some of these symptomatic effects of tobacco withdrawal are associated with an increased vulnerability to relapse. In general, smokers are more likely to relapse if withdrawal symptoms after smoking cessation are severe, increase in severity over time, or are highly variable (Piasecki et al. 1998, 2000, 2003b; McCarthy et al. 2006). Research also shows that withdrawal symptoms indicate vulnerability to relapse, as the result of either immediate increases in symptoms in response to abstinence from smoking or emergent changes in symptoms that occur across the days preceding a lapse in smoking cessation (Figure 4.8) (Piasecki et al. 2003b; McCarthy et al. 2006).

Withdrawal measures tap a variety of symptoms, but research suggests that self-reported craving and negative affect are the symptoms most predictive of relapse (West et al. 1989; Killen et al. 1991; Swan et al. 1996; Killen and Fortmann 1997; Piasecki et al. 1998; McCarthy et al.

Figure 4.6   Individual estimated slopes in craving ratings over three weeks prequit, from just before to just after midnight on the quit date, and over three weeks postquit

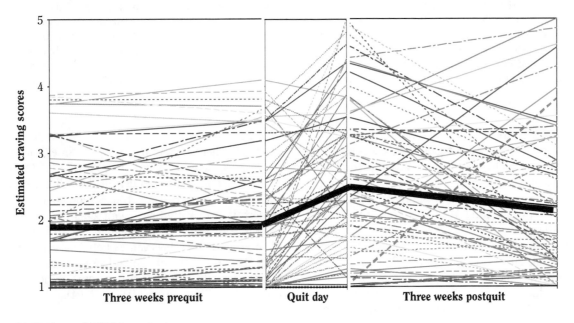

Source: McCarthy et al. 2006.
Note: The synthesized trajectories are based on multiple daily ratings made in real time with electronic diaries. The heavy black line represents the mean trend in craving ratings across all individuals. All other lines represent the slopes or trajectories of craving ratings for individual smokers and show how variable withdrawal symptoms can be across smokers across time.

Figure 4.7   Reactions for the three-week period before the quit date and the three-week period after the quit date

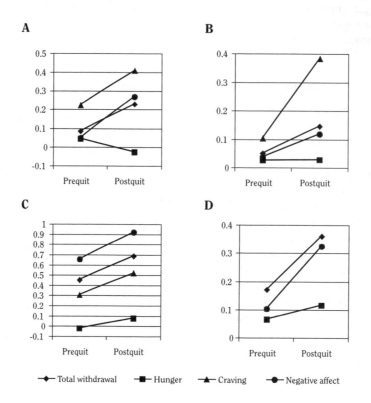

Source: McCarthy et al. 2006.
Note: Data are from 70 smokers making a quit attempt. The *y*-axis depicts the magnitude of the average standardized coefficient derived from multivariate, multilevel models. Episodic event coefficients were estimated separately in the prequit and postquit periods. The beta weights shown reflect the degree of symptom change (in overall withdrawal, hunger, craving, and negative affect) associated with the presence versus absence of an episodic event. (A) Symptom coefficients associated with smoking in the past 15 minutes in models of overall withdrawal. (B) Symptom coefficients associated with recent exposure to smoking behavior. (C) Symptom coefficients associated with exposure to recent stressful events. (D) Symptom coefficients associated with recent strong urges and temptations. Results suggest greater symptomatic reactivity to events after quitting than before quitting.

2006). Other elements of the withdrawal syndrome, such as sleep disturbances or weight gain, are less consistent indices of a vulnerability to relapse (Wetter et al. 1995; Borrelli et al. 2001).

One piece of evidence that supports the role of withdrawal in precipitating relapse is research showing that withdrawal suppression appears to mediate the effects of pharmacologic treatments for smoking cessation (McCarthy et al. 2006; Shiffman et al. 2006). Statistical tests suggest that nicotine replacement and bupropion treatments reduce relapse risk to the extent that they suppress withdrawal symptoms. These studies suggest only partial mediation, however, consistent with the notion that other factors also influence relapse.

Although it is clear that emergent trends can set the stage for lapses and relapses to smoking, much remains to

be learned about these associations. The time course by which emergent symptoms anticipate lapses, for example, needs more focused examination, because a gradual emergence of symptoms would permit the delivery of preventive interventions. Several studies show that craving and exacerbation of withdrawal symptoms precede lapses by several days (Piasecki et al. 2003b; McCarthy et al. 2006; Allen et al. 2008). However, as noted earlier in this section, other research shows that lapse-provoking increases in negative affect unfold within hours rather than days (Figure 4.9) (Shiffman and Waters 2004).

Cognitive and Attitudinal Influences

Emergent cognitive and attitudinal processes may also enhance vulnerability to relapse. For instance, one study used real-time data recording to show that low

Figure 4.8   Withdrawal severity and lapse behavior among smokers who abstained for the first five days of a quit attempt

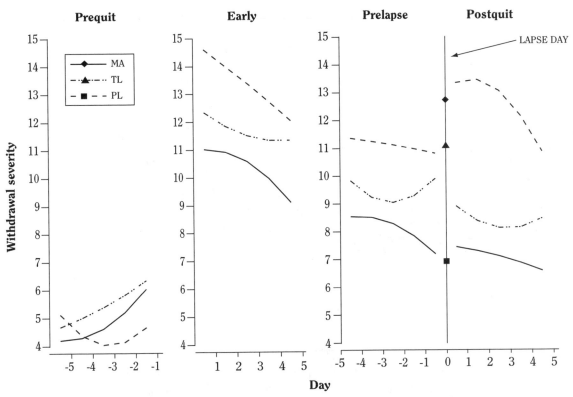

Source: Piasecki et al. 2003b.
Note: Matched abstainers (MAs; n = 152) had never smoked during the follow-up period. Transient lapsers (TLs; n = 124) had lapsed but did not immediately resume regular smoking. Protracted lapsers (PLs; n = 28) had immediately returned to regular smoking upon lapsing. The figure shows predicted withdrawal severity growth functions for these three groups over several periods: baseline (prequit: prior to day 0 in the first panel), the first five days of the quit attempt, the five days preceding and following the lapse dates of the lapsers (TL and PL participants); and last five days of the quit attempt (when TL and PL participants were smoking and MA participants were abstinent). Each lapsed participant was paired with an MA to produce temporal equivalence across the prelapse and postlapse windows. To compare the symptoms of lapsers with those of nonlapsers, the investigators randomly matched each lapser with a person who did not lapse, then compared the predicted symptom trajectories of these individuals over the same postquit periods of time defined by when a lapse actually occurred.

abstinence and self-efficacy estimates, along with high expectations of smoking reinforcement, predicted a lapse to smoking that occurred on the following day (Gwaltney et al. 2005a). These effects were independent of scores for these measures on the day of smoking cessation, suggesting that the effects reflect emergent processes and not trait differences. Other research shows that persons who lapse to smoking appear to experience a marked dip in motivation during the week leading up to a lapse (Hedeker and Mermelstein 1996).

Timing and Motivational Significance of Emergent Processes

As previously noted, both symptomatic and attitudinal changes emerge across the period after smoking cessation and predict a relapse. Such changes may occur in the first few hours after cessation or in the hours or days just before a lapse to smoking (Figures 4.8 and 4.9) (Hedeker and Mermelstein 1996; Gwaltney et al. 2005a). Emergent symptoms may occur at any time during the postcessation period. However, research shows that symptoms that occur early in this period (e.g., in the first 24 hours) may

Figure 4.9 Negative affect in the days and hours preceding the first lapse for smokers who attributed their first lapse to a stressor or bad mood (stress trigger) or to some other type of event (other trigger)

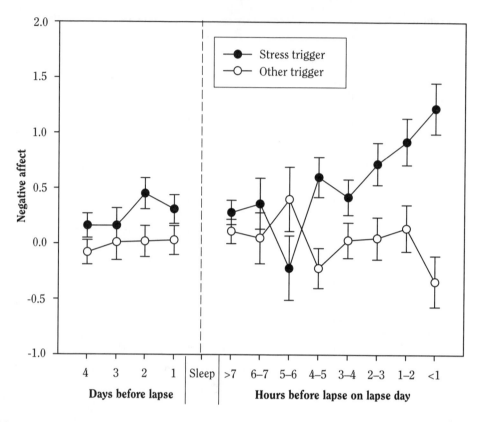

Source: Adapted from Shiffman and Waters 2004 with permission.
Note: Stress trigger, n = 29; other trigger, n = 61. These data suggest that increasing negative affect is a risk factor for lapsing for some smokers. Error bars show one standard error.

be more tightly linked to outcomes than are later symptoms. For instance, in the Killen and Fortmann (1997) research, 2,600 smokers were entered into three studies through population-based recruitment. Across all three studies, craving ratings gathered early in the attempt to stop smoking (e.g., 24 hours postcessation) predicted relapses across the first year after cessation. Smokers with ratings in the highest quartile for craving were twice as likely to relapse as were smokers in the lowest quartile (31 versus 16 percent, respectively, averaged across all three studies). This research agrees with a wealth of other evidence that appearance of symptoms early in the attempt to stop smoking is negatively related to an ability to remain abstinent and to avoid a relapse (Killen et al. 1991; Doherty et al. 1995; McCarthy et al. 2006).

These data supported a large amount of evidence showing that various types of self-reports become markedly more predictive of ultimate outcomes as soon as

persons have some experience in the attempt to stop smoking (Kenford et al. 2002; Gwaltney et al. 2005a). This evidence suggests that even though smokers have experience with abstinence from smoking and have memories of previous attempts to stop smoking, many are still unprepared for the forces unleashed by abstinence, which ultimately lead to a relapse.

Situational Instigators

A large body of research shows that lapses and relapse are associated with a limited set of contextual or situational features. Studies that use remote data collection techniques, in which data are gathered long after the lapse or relapse occurred, show that the contexts of lapses are characterized by features such as negative affect, urges to smoke, alcohol consumption, and cues to smoke (O'Connell and Martin 1987; Brandon et al. 1990).

Research using real-time data acquisition shows that situations in which lapses occur (lapse situations) can be distinguished from temptations, that is, instances in which smoking did not actually occur, and from random occasions on the basis of the negative moods that occur in relation to lapses (Shiffman et al. 1996c). Negative moods are significantly more likely to co-occur with lapses than with temptations without smoking or to occur alone at randomly determined times. These negative moods tend to be strongly associated with reports of interpersonal stress such as arguments.

Shiffman and colleagues (1996c) also found that lapse situations can be distinguished from temptation situations and random occasions in that lapses are more likely to be accompanied by alcohol intake and strong urges to smoke that occur later in the day. Considerable additional evidence demonstrates that alcohol intake sets the stage for lapses (Borland 1990; Brandon et al. 1990). Also, both lapses and temptation situations tend to co-occur in the presence of other persons who are smoking. Thus, the availability of cigarettes and the modeling of smoking are associated with an increased desire to smoke. However, such cues do not reliably distinguish between the desire to smoke and the occurrence of smoking. Finally, the smoker is not a passive party in the progression to relapse. The data show that the execution of a coping response is more characteristic of temptation than of lapse occasions, suggesting that coping detoxifies temptation situations (Shiffman et al. 1996c).

Attesting to the powerful influence of contextual factors, recent research shows that smoking policies or the numbers of smokers in the person's environment reliably predict likelihood of relapse or success in cessation (Letourneau et al. 2007). For instance, risk of relapse or rapidity of relapse is heightened by the number of smokers in a person's social network, whether the person's partner smokes (Mullen 2004; Letourneau et al. 2007; Macy et al. 2007; Solomon et al. 2007), and whether there are smoking restrictions at the person's place of work or at home (Gilpin et al. 1999; Lee and Kahende 2007; Macy et al. 2007). However, some data suggest that bans in social contexts or restaurants may not be related to the success of cessation (Albers et al. 2007).

In general, research on situational indicators suggests that temptations to smoke and smoking lapses are contingent on internal symptoms of withdrawal (e.g., urges to smoke), alcohol use, and environmental signals of smoking, including the availability of cigarettes and the status of smoking restrictions. These findings are consistent with theories that drug availability and distress both constitute potent prods to motivation for drug use (Niaura et al. 1988; Skjei and Markou 2003; Baker et al. 2004).

Integration Across Relapse Influences

Person factors, situational cues, and emergent processes all influence risk of relapse. Moreover, research suggests that relapse risk reflects an interaction among these types of influences (Shiffman 1989a; Piasecki et al. 2002). For example, the intensity of the urge to smoke during temptation events predicts the likelihood of a lapse (Shiffman et al. 1997). However, this relationship depends on the level of urges to smoke reported on the day of smoking cessation. Thus, situational ratings are related to trait characteristics, such as tobacco dependence or emergent trends (e.g., withdrawal) that affect ratings for the urge to smoke on the day of smoking cessation. The relationship between the type of lapse situation and an emergent negative affect are shown in Figure 4.9. Data also show that the intensity of the urge to smoke during temptation episodes grows in the days leading up to a lapse (Shiffman et al. 1997). These data provide further evidence for the role of emergent processes in affecting situational reactions that, in turn, are related to lapse events. Finally, this same research shows that the level of the urge to smoke reported by persons on awakening predicted the likelihood of a lapse later on the same day. For some reason, urges to smoke in the morning, as opposed to urges reported at other times, tended to provide the most powerful predictions of lapses. In sum, research on the urge to smoke shows that the likelihood of a lapse reflects the interaction of trait factors, emergent processes, and situational cues.

Other data suggest interactive influences on the likelihood of a lapse. For example, Gwaltney and colleagues (2005b) found that persons who have low levels of trait-like self-efficacy at baseline show marked declines in self-efficacy in situations that produce strong urges or negative affect. Hence, trait measures capture a person's vulnerability to succumb to situational challenges. A chief goal of future research is to elucidate how various types of influences on relapse interact to produce a relapse in a particular person at a particular time.

Transition from Lapse to Relapse or Recovery

Exploration of the factors that transform lapses into relapses is vital, because initial incidents of tobacco use routinely usher in a return to regular smoking (Baer et al. 1989; Garvey et al. 1992; Kenford et al. 1994). Study of the factors that influence the lapse-relapse progression is also important, because it seems that factors affecting this progression differ from factors that affect the occurrence of the lapse itself. For instance, Wileyto and colleagues

(2005) found that the likelihood of lapse in a smoker was relatively unaffected by his or her dependence level (FTND score) or symptoms of depression. However, both of these factors were associated with greater difficulty in recovering from a lapse—that is, reestablishing abstinence for at least 24 hours.

Researchers have found that the probability or the latency of a relapse after a lapse can be predicted by nicotine dependence (Shiffman et al. 1996b, 1997) and by features of the lapse situation, such as the failure to make a coping response, feelings of hopelessness, and stronger urges to smoke during the lapse (Shiffman et al. 1996b). In addition, postlapse declines in self-efficacy of abstinence indicate a greater likelihood of or a faster progression to a relapse (Gwaltney et al. 2005b). Thus, it appears that individual capitulation in the cessation attempt and high levels of nicotine dependence foster the progression to a relapse.

Lapses appear to play a causal role in precipitating a relapse. This finding is indicated by the report that smokers randomly assigned to experimental lapse events resume smoking more rapidly than do smokers not assigned to such lapse experiences (Chornock et al. 1992).

Summary and Future Directions

The data suggest that factors contributing to a relapse are multidimensional and involve many processes associated with addiction, including personal traits, past experiences with nicotine, associative learning and conditioning, and the manifestation of withdrawal symptoms. Development of treatments to prevent lapses (occasional smoking) is important, because these events so frequently lead to a relapse. In addition, this review suggests that treatments should target specific phenomena that may motivate lapses and relapses: (1) increases in withdrawal symptoms, especially urges to smoke and negative affect that occur in the first 48 hours of smoking cessation (Figures 4.6 and 4.8); (2) emergent increases or spikes in negative affect and urges that occur at any point after smoking cessation (Figures 4.8 and 4.9); (3) the drop in self-confidence or the increase in urges engendered by a lapse; (4) urges that occur shortly after awakening that may or may not reflect conditioned withdrawal effect (Figure 4.6); (5) a trait-like intolerance of distress; (6) increased urges to smoke and withdrawal symptoms prompted by smoking-related cues or stressful events (Figure 4.7); and (7) alcohol consumption and its effects on cognitive and motivational processes. Although relapse has also been associated with relatively stable demographic factors such as SES and educational status, it is unclear why these factors are associated with failure of smoking cessation and which treatment strategies could be used to counter them. Future research should be focused on further refining types for relapse and recovery, understanding genetic and neurobiologic underpinnings, and developing effective treatments for these types.

Evidence Summary

The 1988 Surgeon General's Report, *The Health Consequences of Nicotine Addiction,* concluded that "nicotine is the drug in tobacco that causes addiction" (USDHHS 1988, p. 9). Studies show that animals self-administer or prefer nicotine over saline and that many people smoke to regulate blood concentrations of nicotine. For example, if smokers are given cigarettes with lower nicotine yields than their usual brands, they tend to smoke more intensely or to cover the filter ventilation holes to increase their nicotine intake. The VTA region of the brain and the mesocorticolimbic dopamine neurons originating in this brain site are primarily responsible for the positive reinforcing aspects of nicotine. An increase in levels of dopamine is mediated by nicotine directly stimulating nAChRs, primarily $\alpha 7$ homomeric and $\alpha 4\beta 2$-containing nAChRs within the VTA, thus increasing activity of VTA neurons projecting to the nucleus accumbens and the frontal cortex. Nicotine stimulates $\alpha 7$ nAChRs on glutamatergic terminals that release glutamate, an excitatory neurotransmitter, which results in increased release of dopamine in the nucleus accumbens, amygdala, and frontal cortex. Nicotine also excites nAChRs on GABA-releasing terminals. Thus, levels of GABA, an inhibitory neurotransmitter, are also increased by nicotine. However, the interplay between the quick desensitization of nAChRs on the GABA neuron and the higher doses of nicotine required to desensitize nAChRs on the glutamate neuron result in a greater increase in dopamine levels.

The neurophysiology associated with withdrawal symptoms may be based on the type of symptoms experienced (e.g., somatic versus affective). It appears that nAChRs differ in their involvement in both the somatic and affective components of nicotine withdrawal and dependence. As seen in animal studies, $\beta 4$ nAChRs play an important role in the somatic signs of withdrawal, whereas $\beta 2$ nAChRs play an important role in the affective, but not somatic, aspects of withdrawal. The role of α4 nAChRs is unclear, but these receptors may play a role in both the affective and somatic withdrawal effects of nicotine addiction. The α7 nAChRs appear to be involved only in some of the somatic signs of nicotine withdrawal.

The amount and speed of nicotine delivery also plays a critical role in the potential for abuse of tobacco products. The speed and amount of nicotine delivered to the brain depend on the amount of nicotine in the product, the alkalinity of the product, and the route of administration. Nicotine, 3-(1-methyl-2-pyrrolidinyl)pyridine, is a volatile alkaloid in the tobacco plant, and its absorption and renal secretion is highly dependent on pH. Products with higher alkalinity are associated with greater amounts of nicotine in the nonionized or free base state, which can vaporize more easily into the gas phase, can be deposited directly on the lung tissues, and crosses cell membranes more rapidly than ionized nicotine. Tobacco products can contain constituents such as ammonia to increase the conversion of nicotine to the nonionized or free base state. Physical design features such as filter-tip ventilation also increase the free base fraction of nicotine (see Chapter 3, "Chemistry and Toxicology of Cigarette Smoke and Biomarkers of Exposure and Harm"). The fastest rate of nicotine delivery is through smoking cigarettes. Nicotine, when inhaled, enters the lungs, which present a large surface area of small airways and alveoli, undergoes dissolution in pulmonary fluid at a high pH, is transported to the heart, and then immediately passes to the brain. This rapid and bolus delivery of nicotine through cigarettes leads to greater control over the amount of nicotine delivered to the brain and results in higher abuse potential than do other tobacco- or nicotine-containing products.

Nicotine in the tobacco product and its kinetic profile are not the only factors that might contribute to a tobacco product's potential for addiction. Other constituents may also serve as reinforcers or may enhance blood levels of nicotine or its effects. For example, animal studies have shown that nornicotine, a secondary tobacco alkaloid, functions as a reinforcer, but at less potency than nicotine. The effect of nornicotine in humans is unclear. Acetaldehyde, another constituent in tobacco smoke, which results from burning sugars and other materials in the tobacco leaf, may play a role in increasing the reinforcing effects of nicotine. In animal studies, acetaldehyde enhanced the acquisition of nicotine self-administration among adolescent rats but not adult rats. Extracts from flue-cured tobacco that appear to inhibit MAO activity in the brain may be another contributory factor to the reinforcing effects of cigarettes. Increased MAO inhibition results in increased levels of catecholamines. Current smokers have lower levels of MAO than do nonsmokers or former smokers.

Tobacco product design and ingredients contribute to the risk of addiction by reducing noxious effects such as the unpleasant taste of nicotine and unpleasant sensory effects (see Chapter 2, "The Changing Cigarette"). Such designs include ventilation to cool the smoke and ingredients such as menthol and chocolate that make nicotine inhalation more pleasant. Other nonnicotine factors can also contribute to addiction potential. These factors include the associative learning processes (internal and environmental cues linked with nicotine administration) that develop with repeated tobacco use. This associative learning can be as powerful as the direct effects of nicotine. For example, presenting smokers with sensory aspects of smoking without nicotine has resulted in a decrease in craving for cigarettes, a decreased subset of withdrawal symptoms, and short-term reinforcing efficacy similar to that of cigarettes containing nicotine (see Chapter 3, "Chemistry and Toxicology of Cigarette Smoke and Biomarkers of Exposure and Harm").

Typically, smoking initiation occurs during adolescence. Research shows that adolescent smokers report some symptoms of dependence even at low levels of cigarette consumption, and animal studies show that sensitivity to nicotine in adolescents differs from that in adults. For example, results from the paradigms of self-administration and conditioned place preference in rats demonstrate that adolescence may be at a stage of development with higher sensitivity to nicotine exposure than that in adults. Using mixture modeling, longitudinal studies have identified multiple age-related trajectories of smoking behavior. These trajectories typically include smokers with early initiation of smoking and steep acceleration of smoking, persons who engage in experimental or light smoking, smokers with late initiation and accelerated progression of smoking, persons who stopped smoking, and those who never smoked. The group with early initiation and steeply escalating and persistent smoking has been associated with familial smoking, which reflects genetic and/or environmental risk factors, less parental support, and a risk for chronic heavy smoking in adulthood. Ethnic differences have also been observed for the age at initiation of smoking and the speed of progression in smoking. These studies showed that African Americans were more likely to have slower progression of smoking and a lower number of cigarettes smoked than do Whites. Studies that have looked at predictors for developing nicotine addiction or heavy smoking suggest the importance of both genes and environmental influences. Parental smoking, parental substance abuse disorders, and externalizing disorders (attention-deficit/hyperactivity, disruptive behavior, and alcohol and drug abuse) have been found to be predictive of nicotine dependence and/or daily smoking.

Initiation and persistence of smoking and nicotine dependence show strong heritability. Most coefficients of reported heritability range from less than 0.3 to more than 0.8 and vary on the basis of the smoking behavior phenotype examined and the social or environmental factors such as prevalence of smoking. The balance of evidence suggests that the risk of smoking initiation is influenced by both genetic and environmental factors, whereas the risk of smoking persistence may have a stronger genetic component. Although some genetic influences on smoking initiation and persistence are common, there are also separate and unique genetic influences for initiation and for persistence. Studies also suggest that the ability to stop smoking is under a strong genetic influence, and some consider this phenotype to be the key behavioral phenotype for nicotine dependence. Molecular genetic studies have been conducted to examine the specific genetic factors and biologic mechanisms involved in nicotine addiction. Most of the candidate gene studies have focused on genetic variation in nAChRs, relevant neurotransmitter pathways, or genes for nicotine-metabolizing enzymes. Candidate gene studies are association-based studies comparing prevalence of candidate gene variants in two unrelated groups—for example, nicotine-dependent versus nondependent persons. Examples of candidate gene variants that have been examined include nAChR subunits, such as *CHRNA4* and *CHRNA5*; dopamine receptors D2 and D4 (*DRD2* and *DRD4*) and dopamine transporter (*DAT*) genes; tryptophan hydroxylase, which is associated with serotonin biosynthesis; serotonin transporter *5HTTLPR*, which is associated with genes that code for serotonin reuptake; *MAOA* and *DβH* genes, which affect norepinephrine pathways; genes in the endogenous opioid pathway (e.g., *OPRM1*); and genes involved in the metabolism of nicotine (e.g., *CYP2A6*).

To date, the only candidate genes with consistent evidence of an association with smoking behavior or nicotine dependence are *CYP2A6* and *5HTT* and SNPs in the *CHRNA5/A3/B4* gene cluster. More research has been conducted on the effects of *CYP2A6*. Variants of P-450 *CYP2A6* associated with *NULL* or reduced activity are associated with reduced levels of the CYP2A6 enzyme and slower rates of nicotine metabolism, leading to higher plasma levels of nicotine for a given dose of nicotine. Persons who carry these variants with *NULL* or reduced activity tend to have lower risk for becoming smokers, reduced cigarette consumption, and possibly higher likelihood of successful smoking cessation than that for persons with wild-type genotypes and higher rates of nicotine

metabolism. Research in this area will be greatly enhanced when there is agreement in the field on phenotypes for smoking initiation, trajectory toward nicotine dependence, and nicotine dependence. One area of research that has provided promising initial evidence is the pharmacogenetics of treatment to aid in smoking cessation, which included examining genetic variations in drug-metabolizing enzymes and variations in drug targets to predict responses to treatment. It is important to recognize that although genes may play an important role in the various aspects of smoking behavior, the risk for smoking exists in persons without the gene variants, and it is predominantly exposure, rather than the host, that leads to smoking-related illnesses.

Studying recovery from smoking can provide valuable information on the nature of tobacco addiction and the factors that affect it. Relapse to smoking occurs at a high rate, and most smokers who ultimately relapse resume smoking early after the attempt to stop smoking. The risk for relapse is particularly high among those who lapse or engage in a single episode of smoking after their first day of cessation. The pattern of return to smoking varies across individuals. However, on average, a second lapse occurs within 24 hours of the first lapse, and lapse to relapse occurs three to five weeks after the cessation attempt. Several multidimensional factors may be associated with relapse. These factors include the expectations that the effects from smoking will be rewarding, confidence in the ability to stop smoking, educational status, and degree of tobacco dependence. Situational indicators suggest that temptations to smoke and smoking lapse and relapse are associated with alcohol use and environmental signals such as the sight of others smoking and the availability of cigarettes.

Evidence supports the relationship of tobacco withdrawal syndrome with vulnerability to relapse. Studies show three important findings for many smokers: (1) withdrawal symptoms are persistent and often severe for several months after an attempt to stop smoking, (2) the heterogeneity in withdrawal symptoms is great, and (3) features such as the severity, variability, and the course of withdrawal symptoms confer increased risk for relapse. Craving and negative affect are the withdrawal symptoms most predictive of relapse, including urges to smoke that are experienced immediately after awakening in the morning. Research suggests complex interrelationships within and across the different types of influences. Future research is needed to elucidate these interactions.

Conclusions

1. Nicotine is the key chemical compound that causes and sustains the powerful addicting effects of commercial tobacco products.

2. The powerful addicting effects of commercial tobacco products are mediated by diverse actions of nicotine at multiple types of nicotinic receptors in the brain.

3. Evidence is suggestive that there may be psychosocial, biologic, and genetic determinants associated with different trajectories observed among population subgroups as they move from experimentation to heavy smoking.

4. Inherited genetic variation in genes such as *CYP2A6* contributes to the differing patterns of smoking behavior and smoking cessation.

5. Evidence is consistent that individual differences in smoking histories and severity of withdrawal symptoms are related to successful recovery from nicotine addiction.

References

Abood LG, Grassi S, Junig J, Crane A, Costanzo M. Specific binding and metabolism of (-)- and (+)-[3H]-nicotine in isolated rat hepatocytes and hepatocyte membranes. *Archives Internationales Pharmacodynamie et de Thérapie* 1985;273(1):62–73.

Abood LG, Reynolds DT, Booth H, Bidlack JM. Sites and mechanisms for nicotine's action in the brain. *Neuroscience and Biobehavioral Reviews* 1981;5(4):479–86.

Abroms L, Simons-Morton B, Haynie DL, Chen R. Psychosocial predictors of smoking trajectories during middle and high school. *Addiction* 2005;100(6):852–61.

Addolorato G, Caputo F, Capristo E, Colombo G, Gessa GL, Gasbarrini G. Ability of baclofen in reducing alcohol craving and intake. II: preliminary clinical evidence. *Alcoholism, Clinical and Experimental Research* 2000; 24(1):67–71.

Addolorato G, Caputo F, Capristo E, Domenicali M, Bernardi M, Janiri L, Agabio R, Colombo G, Gessa GL, Gasbarrini G. Baclofen efficacy in reducing alcohol craving and intake: a preliminary double-blind randomized controlled study. *Alcohol and Alcoholism* 2002a; 37(5):504–8.

Addolorato G, Caputo F, Capristo E, Janiri L, Bernardi M, Agabio R, Colombo G, Gessa GL, Gasbarrini G. Rapid suppression of alcohol withdrawal syndrome by baclofen. *American Journal of Medicine* 2002b;112(3):226–9.

Adler LE, Olincy A, Waldo M, Harris JG, Griffith J, Stevens K, Flach K, Nagamoto H, Bickford P, Leonard S, et al. Schizophrenia, sensory gating, and nicotinic receptors. *Schizophrenia Bulletin* 1998;24(2):189–202.

Adriani W, Macrì S, Pacifici R, Laviola G. Peculiar vulnerability to nicotine oral self-administration in mice during early adolescence. *Neuropsychopharmacology* 2002;27(2):212–24.

Adriani W, Spijker S, Deroche-Gamonet V, Laviola G, Le Moal M, Smit AB, Piazza PV. Evidence for enhanced neurobehavioral vulnerability to nicotine during periadolescence in rats. *Journal of Neuroscience* 2003;23(11):4712–6.

Ahijevych K, Gillespie J. Nicotine dependence and smoking topography among black and white women. *Research in Nursing Health* 1997;20(6):505–14.

al'Absi M, Hatsukami D, Davis GL. Attenuated adrenocorticotropic responses to psychological stress are associated with early smoking relapse. *Psychopharmacology* 2005;181(1):107–17.

al'Absi M, Hatsukami D, Davis GL, Wittmers LE. Prospective examination of effects of smoking abstinence on cortisol and withdrawal symptoms as predictors of early smoking relapse. *Drug and Alcohol Dependence* 2004;73(3):267–78.

Albers AB, Siegel M, Cheng DM, Biener L, Rigotti NA. Effect of smoking regulations in local restaurants on smokers' anti-smoking attitudes and quitting behaviours. *Tobacco Control* 2007;16(2):101–6.

Albuquerque EX, Alkondon M, Pereira EFR, Castro NG, Schrattenholz A, Barbosa CTF, Bonfante-Cabarcas R, Aracava Y, Eisenberg HM, Maelicke A. Properties of neuronal nicotinic acetylcholine receptors: pharmacological characterization and modulation of synaptic function. *Journal of Pharmacology and Experimental Therapeutics* 1997;280(3):1117–36.

Alkondon M, Pereira EFR, Barbosa CTF, Albuquerque EX. Neuronal nicotinic acetylcholine receptor activation modulates γ-aminobutyric acid release from CA1 neurons of rat hippocampal slices. *Journal of Pharmacology and Experimental Therapeutics* 1997;283(3): 1396–411.

Allen SS, Bade T, Hatsukami D, Center B. Craving, withdrawal, and smoking urges on days immediately prior to smoking relapse. *Nicotine & Tobacco Research* 2008; 10(1):35–45.

Allen SS, Hatsukami D, Christianson D, Nelson D. Symptomatology and energy intake during the menstrual cycle in smoking women. *Journal of Substance Abuse* 1996;8(3):303–19.

American Psychiatric Association. *Diagnostic and Statistical Manual of Mental Disorders,* 3rd ed. (rev). Washington: American Psychiatric Association, 1987:165–8.

American Psychiatric Association. *Diagnostic and Statistical Manual of Mental Disorders,* 4th ed. Washington: American Psychiatric Association, 1994.

American Psychiatric Association. *Diagnostic and Statistical Manual of Mental Disorders,* 4th ed. (text rev.). Arlington (VA): American Psychiatric Association, 2000.

Amos CI, Wu X, Broderick P, Gorlov IP, Gu J, Eisen T, Dong Q, Zhang Q, Gu X, Vijayakrishnan J, et al. Genome-wide association scan of tag SNPs identifies a susceptibility locus for lung cancer at 15q25.1. *Nature Genetics* 2008;40(5):616–22.

Anda RF, Williamson DF, Escobedo LG, Mast EE, Giovino GA, Remington PL. Depression and the dynamics of smoking: a national perspective. *JAMA: the Journal of the American Medical Association* 1990;264(12): 1541–5.

Ando M, Hamajima N, Ariyoshi N, Kamataki T, Matsuo K, Ohno Y. Association of *CYP2A6* gene deletion with cigarette smoking status in Japanese adults. *Journal of Epidemiology* 2003;13(3):176–81.

Anney RJL, Olsson CA, Lotfi-Miri M, Patton GC, Williamson R. Nicotine dependence in a prospective population-based study of adolescents: the protective role of a functional tyrosine hydroxylase polymorphism. *Pharmacogenetics* 2004;14(2):73–81.

Anthony JC, Warner LA, Kessler RC. Comparative epidemiology of dependence on tobacco, alcohol, controlled substances, and inhalants: basic findings from the National Comorbidity Survey. *Experimental and Clinical Psychopharmacology* 1994;2(3):244–68.

Araujo DM, Lapchak PA, Collier B, Quirion R. Characterization of N-[^{3}H]methylcarbamylcholine binding sites and effect of N-methylcarbamylcholine on acetylcholine release in rat brain. *Journal of Neurochemistry* 1988;51(1):292–9.

Arinami T, Gao M, Hamaguchi H, Toru M. A functional polymorphism in the promoter region of the dopamine D2 receptor gene is associated with schizophrenia. *Human Molecular Genetics* 1997;6(4):577–82.

Arneric SP, Sullivan JP, Williams M. Neuronal nicotinic acetylcholine receptors: novel targets for central nervous system therapeutics. In: Bloom FE, Kupfer DJ, editors. *Psychopharmacology: The Fourth Generation of Progress*. New York: Raven Press, 1995:95–110.

Audrain-McGovern J, Lerman C, Wileyto EP, Rodriguez D, Shields PG. Interacting effects of genetic predisposition and depression on adolescent smoking progression. *American Journal of Psychiatry* 2004a;161(7):1224–30.

Audrain-McGovern J, Rodriguez D, Tercyak KP, Cuevas J, Rodgers K, Patterson F. Identifying and characterizing adolescent smoking trajectories. *Cancer Epidemiology, Biomarkers & Prevention* 2004b;13(12):2023–34.

Baer JS, Holt CS, Lichtenstein E. Self-efficacy and smoking reexamined: construct validity and clinical utility. *Journal of Consulting and Clinical Psychology* 1986;54(6):846–52.

Baer JS, Kamarck T, Lichtenstein E, Ransom CC Jr. Prediction of smoking relapse: analyses of temptations and transgressions after initial cessation. *Journal of Consulting and Clinical Psychology* 1989;57(5):623–7.

Baker TB, Piper ME, McCarthy DE, Majeskie MR, Fiore MC. Addiction motivation reformulated: an affective processing model of negative reinforcement. *Psychological Review* 2004;111(1):33–51.

Balfour DJK. The neurobiology of tobacco dependence: a preclinical perspective on the role of the dopamine projections to the nucleus accumbens. *Nicotine & Tobacco Research* 2004;6(6):899–912.

Balfour DJK, Ridley DL. The effects of nicotine on neural pathways implicated in depression: a factor in nicotine addiction? *Pharmacology, Biochemistry, and Behavior* 2000;66(1):79–85.

Balfour DJK, Wright AE, Benwell MEM, Birrell CE. The putative role of extra-synaptic mesolimbic dopamine in the neurobiology of nicotine dependence. *Behavioural Brain Research* 2000;113(1–2):73–83.

Bancroft A, Levin ED. Ventral hippocampal $\alpha 4\beta 2$ nicotinic receptors and chronic nicotine effects on memory. *Neuropharmacology* 2000;39(13):2770–8.

Bardo MT, Bevins RA, Klebaur JE, Crooks PA, Dwoskin LP. (–)-Nornicotine partially substitutes for (+)-amphetamine in a drug discrimination paradigm in rats. *Pharmacology, Biochemistry, and Behavior* 1997;58(4):1083–7.

Bardo MT, Green TA, Crooks PA, Dwoskin LP. Nornicotine is self-administered intravenously by rats. *Psychopharmacology* 1999;146(3):290–6.

Barr RS, Pizzagalli DA, Culhane MA, Goff DC, Evins AE. A single dose of nicotine enhances reward responsiveness in nonsmokers: implications for development of dependence. *Biological Psychiatry* 2008;63(11):1061–5.

Barrett SP, Boileau I, Okker J, Pihl RO, Dagher A. The hedonic response to cigarette smoking is proportional to dopamine release in the human striatum as measured by positron emission tomography and [^{11}C]raclopride. *Synapse* 2004;54(2):65–71.

Batra A, Gelfort G, Bartels M, Smoltczyk H, Buchkremer G, Riess O, Schöls L. The dopamine D2 receptor (DRD2) gene—a genetic risk factor in heavy smoking? *Addiction Biology* 2000;5(4):429–36.

Belluzzi JD, Lee AG, Oliff HS, Leslie FM. Age-dependent effects of nicotine on locomotor activity and conditioned place preference in rats. *Psychopharmacology* 2004;174(3):389–95.

Belluzzi JD, Wang R, Leslie FM. Acetaldehyde enhances acquisition of nicotine self-administration in adolescent rats. *Neuropsychopharmacology* 2005;30(4):705–12.

Beltman S, Volet S. Exploring the complex and dynamic nature of sustained motivation. *European Psychologist* 2007;12(4):314–23.

Benowitz NL. Drug therapy: pharmacologic aspects of cigarette smoking and nicotine addiction. *New England Journal of Medicine* 1988;319(20):1318–30.

Benowitz NL. Nicotine addiction. *Primary Care* 1999;26(3):611–31.

Benowitz NL. Clinical pharmacology of inhaled drugs of abuse: implications in understanding nicotine dependence. In: Chang CN, Hawks RL, editors. *Research Findings on Smoking of Abused Substances*. NIDA Research Monograph 99. Rockville (MD): U.S. Department of Health and Human Services, Public Health

Service, Alcohol, Drug Abuse, and Mental Health Administration, National Institute on Drug Abuse, 1990:12–29. DHHS Publication No. (ADM) 90-1690.

Benowitz NL, Hatsukami D. Gender differences in the pharmacology of nicotine addiction. *Addiction Biology* 1998;3(4):383–404.

Benowitz NL, Jacob P III. Nicotine and cotinine elimination pharmacokinetics in smokers and nonsmokers. *Clinical Pharmacology and Therapeutics* 1993;53(3): 316–23.

Benowitz NL, Jacob P III. Metabolism of nicotine to cotinine studied by a dual stable isotope method. *Clinical Pharmacology and Therapeutics* 1994;56(5):483–93.

Benowitz NL, Perez-Stable EJ, Fong I, Modin G, Herrera B, Jacob P III. Ethnic differences in *N*-glucuronidation of nicotine and cotinine. *Journal of Pharmacology and Experimental Therapeutics* 1999;291(3):1196–203.

Benowitz NL, Pomerleau OF, Pomerleau CS, Jacob P III. Nicotine metabolite ratio as a predictor of cigarette consumption. *Nicotine & Tobacco Research* 2003; 5(5):621–4.

Benowitz NL, Porchet H, Sheiner L, Jacob P III. Nicotine absorption and cardiovascular effects with smokeless tobacco use: comparison with cigarettes and nicotine gum. *Clinical Pharmacology and Therapeutics* 1988;44(1):23–8.

Benwell MEM, Balfour DJK. Effects of nicotine administration and its withdrawal on plasma corticosterone and brain 5-hydroxyindoles. *Psychopharmacology* 1979; 63(1):7–11.

Benwell MEM, Balfour DJK. The effects of nicotine administration on 5-HT uptake and biosynthesis in rat brain. *European Journal of Pharmacology* 1982;84(1–2): 71–7.

Benwell MEM, Balfour DJK. The effects of acute and repeated nicotine treatment on nucleus accumbens dopamine and locomotor activity. *British Journal of Pharmacology* 1992;105(4):849–56.

Benwell MEM, Balfour DJK. Regional variation in the effects of nicotine on catecholamine overflow in rat brain. *European Journal of Pharmacology* 1997; 325(1):13–20.

Bergen AW, Korczak JF, Weissbecker KA, Goldstein AM. A genome-wide search for loci contributing to smoking and alcoholism. *Genetic Epidemiology* 1999;17(Suppl 1): S55–S60.

Berrendero F, Kieffer BL, Maldonado R. Attenuation of nicotine-induced antinociception, rewarding effects, and dependence in μ-opioid receptor knock-out mice. *Journal of Neuroscience* 2002;22(24):10935–40.

Berrendero F, Mendizábal V, Robledo P, Galeote L, Bilkei-Gorzo A, Zimmer A, Maldonado R. Nicotine-induced antinociception, rewarding effects, and physical dependence are decreased in mice lacking the preproenkephalin gene. *Journal of Neuroscience* 2005;25(5):1103–12.

Berrettini W, Yuan X, Tozzi F, Song K, Francks C, Chilcoat H, Waterworth D, Muglia P, Mooser V. α5/α3 nicotinic receptor subunit alleles increase risk for heavy smoking. *Molecular Psychiatry* 2008;13(4):368–73.

Berridge KC, Robinson TE. Parsing reward. *Trends in Neurosciences* 2003;26(9):507–13.

Beuten J, Ma JZ, Payne TJ, Dupont RT, Crews KM, Somes G, Williams NJ, Elston RC, Li MD. Single- and multilocus allelic variants within the GABA$_B$ receptor subunit 2 (*GABAB2*) gene are significantly associated with nicotine dependence. *American Journal of Human Genetics* 2005;76(5):859–64.

Beuten J, Ma JZ, Payne TJ, Dupont RT, Lou X-Y, Crews KM, Elston RC, Li MD. Association of specific haplotypes of neurotrophic tyrosine kinase receptor 2 gene (*NTRK2*) with vulnerability to nicotine dependence in African-Americans and European-Americans. *Biological Psychiatry* 2007;61(1):48–55.

Bevins RA, Palmatier MI. Extending the role of associative learning processes in nicotine addiction. *Behavioral and Cognitive Neuroscience Reviews* 2004;3(3):143–58.

Bierut LJ, Dinwiddie SH, Begleiter H, Crowe RR, Hesselbrock V, Nurnberger JI Jr, Porjesz B, Schuckit MA, Reich T. Familial transmission of substance dependence: alcohol, marijuana, cocaine, and habitual smoking: a report from the Collaborative Study on the Genetics of Alcoholism. *Archives of General Psychiatry* 1998;55(11):982–8.

Bierut LJ, Madden PA, Breslau N, Johnson EO, Hatsukami D, Pomerleau OF, Swan GE, Rutter J, Bertelsen S, Fox L, et al. Novel genes identified in a high-density genome wide association study for nicotine dependence. *Human Molecular Genetics* 2007;16(1):24–35.

Bierut LJ, Rice JP, Edenberg HJ, Goate A, Foroud T, Cloninger CR, Begleiter H, Conneally PM, Crowe RR, Hesselbrock V, et al. Family-based study of the association of the dopamine D2 receptor gene (*DRD2*) with habitual smoking. *American Journal of Medical Genetics* 2000;90(4):299–302.

Bierut LJ, Rice JP, Goate A, Hinrichs AL, Saccone NL, Foroud T, Edenberg HJ, Cloninger CR, Begleiter H, Conneally PM, et al. A genomic scan for habitual smoking in families of alcoholics: common and specific genetic factors in substance dependence. *American Journal of Medical Genetics* 2004;124(1):19–27.

Bierut LJ, Stitzel JA, Wang JC, Hinrichs AL, Grucza RA, Xuei X, Saccone NL, Saccone SF, Bertelsen S, Fox L, et al. Variants in nicotinic receptors and risk for nicotine dependence. *American Journal of Psychiatry* 2008;165(9):1163–71.

Bjornson W, Rand C, Connett JE, Lindgren P, Nides M, Pope F, Buist AS, Hoppe-Ryan C, O'Hara P. Gender differences in smoking cessation after 3 years in the Lung Health Study. *American Journal of Public Health* 1995;85(2):223–30.

Blendy JA, Strasser A, Walters CL, Perkins KA, Patterson F, Berkowitz R, Lerman C. Reduced nicotine reward in obesity: cross-comparison in human and mouse. *Psychopharmacology* 2005;180(2):306–15.

Blitstein JL, Robinson LA, Murray DM, Klesges RC, Zbikowski SM. Rapid progression to regular cigarette smoking among nonsmoking adolescents: interactions with gender and ethnicity. *Preventive Medicine* 2003;36(4):455–63.

Boomsma D, Busjahn A, Peltonen L. Classical twin studies and beyond. *Nature Reviews Genetics* 2002;3(11):872–82.

Borland R. Slip-ups and relapse in attempts to quit smoking. *Addictive Behaviors* 1990;15(3):235–45.

Borrelli B, Spring B, Niaura R, Hitsman B, Papandonatos G. Influences of gender and weight gain on short-term relapse to smoking in a cessation trial. *Journal of Consulting and Clinical Psychology* 2001;69(3):511–5.

Boustead C, Taber H, Idle JR, Cholerton S. *CYP2D6* genotype and smoking behaviour in cigarette smokers. *Pharmacogenetics* 1997;7(5):411–4.

Boyadjieva NI, Sarkar DK. The secretory response of hypothalamic β-endorphin neurons to acute and chronic nicotine treatments and following nicotine withdrawal. *Life Sciences* 1997;61(6):PL59–PL66.

Brandon TH, Juliano LM, Copeland AL. Expectancies for tobacco smoking. In: Kirsch I, editor. *How Expectancies Shape Experience*. Washington: American Psychological Association, 1999:263–99.

Brandon TH, Tiffany ST, Baker TB. The process of smoking relapse. In: Tims FM, Leukefeld CG, editors. *Relapse and Recovery in Drug Abuse*. NIDA Research Monograph 72. Rockville (MD): U.S. Department of Health and Human Services, Public Health Service, Alcohol, Drug Abuse, and Mental Health Administration, National Institute on Drug Abuse, 1986:104–17. DHHS Publication No. (ADM) 90-1473.

Brandon TH, Tiffany ST, Obremski KM, Baker TB. Postcessation cigarette use: the process of relapse. *Addictive Behaviors* 1990;15(2):105–14.

Brazell MP, Mitchell SN, Gray JA. Effect of acute administration of nicotine on *in vivo* release of noradrenaline in the hippocampus of freely moving rats: a dose–response and antagonist study. *Neuropharmacology* 1991;30(8):823–33.

Brebner K, Childress AR, Roberts DC. A potential role for GABA_B agonists in the treatment of psychostimulant addiction. *Alcohol and Alcoholism* 2002;37(5):478–84.

Breslau N. Psychiatric comorbidity of smoking and nicotine dependence. *Behavior Genetics* 1995;25(2):95–101.

Breslau N, Fenn N, Peterson EL. Early smoking initiation and nicotine dependence in a cohort of young adults. *Drug and Alcohol Dependence* 1993a;33(2):129–37.

Breslau N, Johnson EO. Predicting smoking cessation and major depression in nicotine-dependent smokers. *American Journal of Public Health* 2000;90(7):1122–7.

Breslau N, Johnson EO, Hiripi E, Kessler R. Nicotine dependence in the United States: prevalence, trends, and smoking persistence. *Archives of General Psychiatry* 2001;58(9):810–6.

Breslau N, Kilbey MM, Andreski P. Nicotine dependence, major depression, and anxiety in young adults. *Archives of General Psychiatry* 1991;48(12):1069–74.

Breslau N, Kilbey MM, Andreski P. Nicotine dependence and major depression: new evidence from a prospective investigation. *Archives of General Psychiatry* 1993b;50(1):31–5.

Breslau N, Kilbey MM, Andreski P. DSM-III-R nicotine dependence in young adults: prevalence, correlates and associated psychiatric disorders. *Addiction* 1994;89(6):743–54.

Breslau N, Klein DF. Smoking and panic attacks: an epidemiologic investigation. *Archives of General Psychiatry* 1999;56(12):1141–7.

Breslau N, Novak SP, Kessler RC. Daily smoking and the subsequent onset of psychiatric disorders. *Psychological Medicine* 2004a;34(2):323–33.

Breslau N, Novak SP, Kessler RC. Psychiatric disorders and stages of smoking. *Biological Psychiatry* 2004b;55(1):69–76.

Breslau N, Peterson E, Schultz L, Andreski P, Chilcoat H. Are smokers with alcohol disorders less likely to quit? *American Journal of Public Health* 1996;86(7):985–90.

Breslau N, Peterson EL, Schultz LR, Chilcoat HD, Andreski P. Major depression and stages of smoking: a longitudinal investigation. *Archives of General Psychiatry* 1998;55(2):161–6.

Breteler MHM, Hilberink SR, Zeeman G, Lammers SMM. Compulsive smoking: the development of a Rasch homogeneous scale of nicotine dependence. *Addictive Behaviors* 2004;29(1):199–205.

Brody AL. Functional brain imaging of tobacco use and dependence. *Journal of Psychiatric Research* 2006;40(5):404–18.

Brody AL, Mandelkern MA, Lee G, Smith E, Sadeghi M, Saxena S, Jarvik ME, London ED. Attenuation of cue-induced cigarette craving and anterior cingulate cortex activation in bupropion-treated smokers: a preliminary study. *Psychiatry Research* 2004a;130(3):269–81.

Brody AL, Olmstead RE, London ED, Farahi J, Meyer JH, Grossman P, Lee GS, Huang J, Hahn EL, Mandelkern MA. Smoking-induced ventral striatum dopamine release. *American Journal of Psychiatry* 2004b;161(7):1211–8.

Brody CL, Hamer DH, Haaga DAF. Depression vulnerability, cigarette smoking, and the serotonin transporter gene. *Addictive Behaviors* 2005;30(3):557–66.

Broms U, Madden PAF, Heath AC, Pergadia ML, Shiffman S, Kaprio J. The Nicotine Dependence Syndrome Scale in Finnish smokers. *Drug and Alcohol Dependence* 2007;89(1):42–51.

Broms U, Silventoinen K, Madden PAF, Heath AC, Kaprio J. Genetic architecture of smoking behavior: a study of Finnish adult twins. *Twin Research and Human Genetics* 2006;9(1):64–72.

Brook JS, Pahl K, Ning Y. Peer and parental influences on longitudinal trajectories of smoking among African Americans and Puerto Ricans. *Nicotine & Tobacco Research* 2006;8(5):639–51.

Brown RA, Kahler CW, Niaura R, Abrams DB, Sales SD, Ramsey SE, Goldstein MG, Burgess ES, Miller IW. Cognitive-behavioral treatment for depression in smoking cessation. *Journal of Consulting and Clinical Psychology* 2001;69(3):471–80.

Brown RA, Lejuez CW, Kahler CW, Strong DR. Distress tolerance and duration of past smoking cessation attempts. *Journal of Abnormal Psychology* 2002;111(1):180–5.

Brown RA, Lejuez CW, Kahler CW, Strong DR, Zvolensky MJ. Distress tolerance and early smoking lapse. *Clinical Psychology Review* 2005;25(6):713–33.

Brown RA, Palm KM, Strong DR, Lejuez CW, Kahler CW, Zvolensky MJ, Hayes SC, Wilson JG, Gifford EV. Distress tolerance treatment for early-lapse smokers: rationale, program description, and preliminary findings. *Behavior Modification* 2008;32(3):302–32.

Browne CL. *The Design of Cigarettes*. 3rd ed. Charlotte (NC): Hoechst Celanese Corporation, 1990.

Bruijnzeel AW, Markou A. Characterization of the effects of bupropion on the reinforcing properties of nicotine and food in rats. *Synapse* 2003;50(1):20–8.

Bruijnzeel AW, Markou A. Adaptations in cholinergic transmission in the ventral tegmental area associated with the affective signs of nicotine withdrawal in rats. *Neuropharmacology* 2004;47(4):572–9.

Buka SL, Shenassa ED, Niaura R. Elevated risk of tobacco dependence among offspring of mothers who smoked during pregnancy: a 30-year prospective study. *American Journal of Psychiatry* 2003;160(11):1978–84.

Caggiula AR, Donny EC, Chaudhri N, Perkins KA, Evans-Martin FF, Sved AF. Importance of nonpharmacological factors in nicotine self-administration. *Physiology and Behavior* 2002a;77(4–5):683–7.

Caggiula AR, Donny EC, White AR, Chaudhri N, Booth S, Gharib MA, Hoffman A, Perkins KA, Sved AF. Cue dependency of nicotine self-administration and smoking. *Pharmacology, Biochemistry, and Behavior* 2001;70(4):515–30.

Caggiula AR, Donny EC, White AR, Chaudhri N, Booth S, Gharib MA, Hoffman A, Perkins KA, Sved AF. Environmental stimuli promote the acquisition of nicotine self-administration in rats. *Psychopharmacology* 2002b;163(2):230–7.

Callicott JH, Ramsey NF, Tallent K, Bertolino A, Knable MB, Coppola R, Goldberg T, van Gelderen P, Mattay VS, Frank JA, et al. Functional magnetic resonance imaging brain mapping in psychiatry: methodological issues illustrated in a study of working memory in schizophrenia. *Neuropsychopharmacology* 1998;18(3):186–96.

Caporaso N, Gu F, Chatterjee N, Sheng-Chih J, Yu K, Yeager M, Chen C, Jacobs K, Wheeler W, Landi MT, et al. Genome-wide and candidate gene association study of cigarette smoking behaviors. *PLoS ONE* 2009;4(2):e4653. doi:10.1371/journal.pone.0004653.

Carboni E, Bortone L, Giua C, Di Chiara G. Dissociation of physical abstinence signs from changes in extracellular dopamine in the nucleus accumbens and in the prefrontal cortex of nicotine dependent rats. *Drug and Alcohol Dependence* 2000;58(1–2):93–102.

Carlsson A. Does dopamine play a role in schizophrenia? *Psychological Medicine* 1977;7(4):583–97.

Carr LA, Basham JK. Effects of tobacco smoke constituents on MPTP-induced toxicity and monoamine oxidase activity in the mouse brain. *Life Sciences* 1991;48(12):1173–7.

Carroll ME, Lac ST, Asencio M, Keenan RM. Nicotine dependence in rats. *Life Sciences* 1989;45(15):1381–8.

Carter BL, Tiffany ST. Meta-analysis of cue-reactivity in addiction research. *Addiction* 1999;94(3):327–40.

Cartmell J, Schoepp DD. Regulation of neurotransmitter release by metabotropic glutamate receptors. *Journal of Neurochemistry* 2000;75(3):889–907.

Castañe A, Valjent E, Ledent C, Parmentier M, Maldonado R, Valverde O. Lack of CB1 cannabinoid receptors modifies nicotine behavioural responses, but not nicotine abstinence. *Neuropharmacology* 2002;43(5):857–67.

Centers for Disease Control and Prevention. Reasons for tobacco use and symptoms of nicotine withdrawal among adolescent and young adult tobacco users—United States, 1993. *Morbidity and Mortality Weekly Report* 1994;43(41):745–50.

Centers for Disease Control and Prevention. Indicators of nicotine addiction among women—United States, 1991–1992. *Morbidity and Mortality Weekly Report* 1995a;44(6):102–5.

Centers for Disease Control and Prevention. Symptoms of substance dependence associated with use of cigarettes, alcohol, and illicit drugs—United States, 1991–1992. *Morbidity and Mortality Weekly Report* 1995b;44(44):830–1, 837–9.

Centers for Disease Control and Prevention. Cigarette smoking among adults—United States, 2000. *Morbidity and Mortality Weekly Report* 2002;51(29):642–5.

Centers for Disease Control and Prevention. Cigarette smoking among adults—United States, 2002. *Morbidity and Mortality Weekly Report* 2004;53(20):427–31.

Centers for Disease Control and Prevention. Cigarette smoking among adults—United States, 2004. *Morbidity and Mortality Weekly Report* 2005;54(44):1121–4.

Centers for Disease Control and Prevention. Cigarette smoking among adults—United States, 2007. *Morbidity and Mortality Weekly Report* 2008a;57(45):1221–6.

Centers for Disease Control and Prevention. Cigarette smoking among high school students—United States, 1991–2007. *Morbidity and Mortality Weekly Report* 2008b;57(25):689–91.

Cepeda-Benito A, Reynoso JT, Erath S. Meta-analysis of the efficacy of nicotine replacement therapy for smoking cessation: differences between men and women. *Journal of Consulting and Clinical Psychology* 2004;72(4):712–22.

Chambers RA, Krystal JH, Self DW. A neurobiological basis for substance abuse comorbidity in schizophrenia. *Biological Psychiatry* 2001;50(2):71–83.

Chassin L, Presson CC, Pitts SC, Sherman SJ. The natural history of cigarette smoking from adolescence to adulthood in a midwestern community sample: multiple trajectories and their psychosocial correlates. *Health Psychology* 2000;19(3):223–31.

Chaudhri N, Caggiula AR, Donny EC, Booth S, Gharib MA, Craven LA, Allen SS, Sved AF, Perkins KA. Sex differences in the contribution of nicotine and nonpharmacological stimuli to nicotine self-administration in rats. *Psychopharmacology* 2005;180(2):258–66.

Chaudhri N, Caggiula AR, Donny EC, Palmatier MI, Liu X, Sved AF. Complex interactions between nicotine and nonpharmacological stimuli reveal multiple roles for nicotine in reinforcement. *Psychopharmacology* 2006;184(3–4):353–66.

Cheeta S, Tucci S, File SE. Antagonism of the anxiolytic effect of nicotine in the dorsal raphé nucleus by dihydro-β-erythroidine. *Pharmacology, Biochemistry, and Behavior* 2001;70(4):491–6.

Chen D, Dang H, Patrick JW. Contributions of N-linked glycosylation to the expression of a functional α7-nicotinic receptor in *Xenopus* oocytes. *Journal of Neurochemistry* 1998;70(1):349–57.

Chen K, Kandel DB. The natural history of drug use from adolescence to the mid-thirties in a general population sample. *American Journal of Public Health* 1995; 85(1):41–7.

Chen X, Chen J, Williamson VS, An SS, Hettema JM, Aggen SH, Neale MC, Kendler KS. Variants in nicotinic acetylcholine receptors alpha5 and alpha3 increase risks to nicotine dependence. *American Journal of Medical Genetics Part B, Neuropsychiatric Genetics* 2009;150B(7):926–33.

Chiamulera C. Cue reactivity in nicotine and tobacco dependence: a "multiple-action" model of nicotine as a primary reinforcement and as an enhancer of the effects of smoking-associated stimuli. *Brain Research Brain Research Reviews* 2005;48(1):74–97.

Cholerton S, Boustead C, Taber H, Arpanahi A, Idle JR. *CYP2D6* genotypes in cigarette smokers and non-tobacco users. *Pharmacogenetics* 1996;6(3):261–3.

Chornock WM, Stitzer ML, Gross J, Leischow S. Experimental models of smoking re-exposure: effects on relapse. *Psychopharmacology* 1992;108(4):495–500.

Churchill L, Dilts RP, Kalivas PW. Autoradiographic localization of γ-aminobutyric acid$_A$ receptors within the ventral tegmental area. *Neurochemical Research* 1992;17(1):101–6.

Cinciripini PM, Aubin H-J, Dale LC, Niaura R, Anthenelli RM, STRATUS Group. Pooled analysis of three short-term, randomized, double-blind, placebo controlled trials with Rimonabant 20 mg/day in smoking cessation. Poster presented at the 8th Annual Conference of the SNRT Europe; September 23–26, 2006; Kusadasi, Turkey.

Clark DB, Cornelius J. Childhood psychopathology and adolescent cigarette smoking: a prospective survival analysis in children at high risk for substance use disorders. *Addictive Behaviors* 2004;29(4):837–41.

Clarke PBS. The fall and rise of neuronal α-bungarotoxin binding proteins. *Trends in Pharmacological Sciences* 1992;13(11):407–13.

Clarke PBS, Reuben M. Release of [^{3}H]-noradrenaline from rat hippocampal synaptosomes by nicotine: mediation by different nicotinic receptor subtypes from striatal [^{3}H]-dopamine release. *British Journal of Pharmacology* 1996;117(4):595–606.

Cohen C, Kodas E, Griebel G. CB1 receptor antagonists for the treatment of nicotine addiction. *Pharmacology, Biochemistry, and Behavior* 2005;81(2):387–95.

Cohen C, Perrault G, Voltz C, Steinberg R, Soubrie P. SR141716, a central cannabinoid (CB$_1$) receptor antagonist, blocks the motivational and dopamine-releasing effects of nicotine in rats. *Behavioural Pharmacology* 2002;13(5–6):451–63.

Cohen S, Lichtenstein E. Perceived stress, quitting smoking, and smoking relapse. *Health Psychology* 1990; 9(4):466–78.

Cohen S, Lichtenstein E, Prochaska JO, Rossi JS, Gritz ER, Carr CR, Orleans CT, Schoenbach VJ, Biener L, Abrams D, et al. Debunking myths about self-quitting: evidence from 10 prospective studies of persons who attempt to quit smoking by themselves. *American Psychologist* 1989;44(11):1355–65.

Colby SM, Tiffany ST, Shiffman S, Niaura RS. Are adolescent smokers dependent on nicotine: a review of the evidence. *Drug and Alcohol Dependence* 2000a; 59(Suppl 1):S83–S95.

Colby SM, Tiffany ST, Shiffman S, Niaura RS. Measuring nicotine dependence among youth: a review of available approaches and instruments. *Drug and Alcohol Dependence* 2000b;59(Suppl 1):S23–S39.

Colder CR, Mehta P, Balanda K, Campbell RR, Mayhew KP, Stanton WR, Pentz MA, Flay BR. Identifying trajectories of adolescent smoking: an application of latent growth mixture modeling. *Health Psychology* 2001;20(2):127–35.

Colilla S, Lerman C, Shields PG, Jepson C, Rukstalis M, Berlin J, Demichele A, Bunin G, Strom BL, Rebbeck TR. Association of catechol-*O*-methyltransferase with smoking cessation in two independent studies of women. *Pharmacogenetics and Genomics* 2005;15(6): 393–8.

Colman GJ, Joyce T. Trends in smoking before, during, and after pregnancy in ten states. *American Journal of Preventive Medicine* 2003;24(1):29–35.

Colquhoun LM, Patrick JW. α3, β2, and β4 form heterotrimeric neuronal nicotinic acetylcholine receptors in *Xenopus* oocytes. *Journal of Neurochemistry* 1997; 69(6):2355–62.

Comings DE, Ferry L, Bradshaw-Robinson S, Burchette R, Chiu C, Muhleman D. The dopamine D_2 receptor (*DRD2*) gene: a genetic risk factor in smoking. *Pharmacogenetics* 1996;6(1):73–9.

Comings DE, Gade R, Wu S, Chiu C, Dietz G, Muhleman D, Saucier G, Ferry L, Rosenthal RJ, Lesieur HR, et al. Studies of the potential role of the dopamine D_1 receptor gene in addictive behaviors. *Molecular Psychiatry* 1997;2(1):44–56.

Comings DE, Wu S, Gonzalez N, Iacono WG, McGue M, Peters WW, MacMurray JP. Cholecystokinin (*CCK*) gene as a possible risk factor for smoking: a replication in two independent samples. *Molecular Genetics and Metabolism* 2001;73(4):349–53.

COMMIT Research Group. Community Intervention Trial for Smoking Cessation (COMMIT). I: cohort results from a four-year community intervention. *American Journal of Public Health* 1995;85(2):183–92.

Condiotte MM, Lichtenstein E. Self-efficacy and relapse in smoking cessation programs. *Journal of Consulting and Clinical Psychology* 1981;49(5):648–58.

Conklin CA, Perkins KA. Subjective and reinforcing effects of smoking during negative mood induction. *Journal of Abnormal Psychology* 2005;114(1):153–64.

Conklin CA, Tiffany ST. Cue-exposure treatment: time for change [letter]. *Addiction* 2002;97(9):1219–21.

Conroy WG, Berg DK. Neurons can maintain multiple classes of nicotinic acetylcholine receptors distinguished by different subunit compositions. *Journal of Biological Chemistry* 1995;270(9):4424–31.

Cooper BR, Wang CM, Cox RF, Norton R, Shea V, Ferris RM. Evidence that the acute behavioral and electrophysiological effects of bupropion (Wellbutrin) are mediated by a noradrenergic mechanism. *Neuropsychopharmacology* 1994;11(2):133–41.

Cornelius MD, Leech SL, Goldschmidt L, Day NL. Is prenatal tobacco exposure a risk factor for early adolescent smoking: a follow-up study. *Neurotoxicology and Teratology* 2005;27(4):667–76.

Corrigall WA, Coen KM. Opiate antagonists reduce cocaine but not nicotine self-administration. *Psychopharmacology* 1991a;104(2):167–70.

Corrigall WA, Coen KM. Selective dopamine antagonists reduce nicotine self-administration. *Psychopharmacology* 1991b;104(2):171–6.

Corrigall WA, Coen KM, Adamson KL. Self-administered nicotine activates the mesolimbic dopamine system through the ventral tegmental area. *Brain Research* 1994;653(1–2):278–84.

Corrigall WA, Coen KM, Adamson KL, Chow BLC, Zhang J. Response of nicotine self-administration in the rat to manipulations of mu-opioid and γ-aminobutyric acid receptors in the ventral tegmental area. *Psychopharmacology* 2000;149(2):107–14.

Corrigall WA, Coen KM, Zhang J, Adamson KL. GABA mechanisms in the pedunculopontine tegmental nucleus influence particular aspects of nicotine self-administration selectively in the rat. *Psychopharmacology* 2001;158(2):190–7.

Corrigall WA, Franklin KBJ, Coen KM, Clarke PBS. The mesolimbic dopaminergic system is implicated in the reinforcing effects of nicotine. *Psychopharmacology* 1992;107(2–3):285–9.

Cossu G, Ledent C, Fattore L, Imperato A, Bohme GA, Parmentier M, Fratta W. Cannabinoid CB_1 receptor knockout mice fail to self-administer morphine but not other drugs of abuse. *Behavioural Brain Research* 2001;118(1):61–5.

Costa-Mallen P, Costa LG, Checkoway H. Genotype combinations for monoamine oxidase-B intron 13 polymorphism and dopamine D2 receptor TaqIB polymorphism are associated with ever-smoking status among men. *Neuroscience Letters* 2005;385(2):158–62.

Costa-Mallen P, Costa LG, Smith-Weller T, Franklin GM, Swanson PD, Checkoway H. Genetic polymorphism of dopamine D2 receptors in Parkinson's disease and interactions with cigarette smoking and MAOB intron 13 polymorphism. *Journal of Neurology, Neurosurgery, and Psychiatry* 2000;69(4):535–7.

Cottler LB, Schuckit MA, Helzer JE, Crowley T, Woody G, Nathan P, Hughes J. The DSM-IV field trial for substance use disorders: major results. *Drug and Alcohol Dependence* 1995;38(1):59–69, 71–83.

Cousins MS, Stamat HM, de Wit H. Effects of a single dose of baclofen on self-reported subjective effects and tobacco smoking. *Nicotine & Tobacco Research* 2001;3(2):123–9.

Covey LS, Glassman AH. A meta-analysis of double-blind placebo-controlled trials of clonidine for smoking cessation. *British Journal of Addiction* 1991;86(8):991–8.

Covey LS, Glassman AH, Stetner F. Naltrexone effects on short-term and long-term smoking cessation. *Journal of Addictive Diseases* 1999;18(1):31–40.

Covey LS, Glassman AH, Stetner F, Becker J. Effect of history of alcoholism or major depression on smoking cessation. *American Journal of Psychiatry* 1993;150(10):1546–7.

Crooks PA, Dwoskin LP. Contribution of CNS nicotine metabolites to the neuropharmacological effects of nicotine and tobacco smoking. *Biochemical Pharmacology* 1997;54(7):743–53.

Cryan JF, Bruijnzeel AW, Skjei KL, Markou A. Bupropion enhances brain reward function and reverses the affective and somatic aspects of nicotine withdrawal in the rat. *Psychopharmacology* 2003;168(3):347–58.

Dale LC, Glover ED, Sachs DP, Schroeder DR, Offord KP, Croghan IT, Hurt RD. Bupropion for smoking cessation: predictors of successful outcome. *Chest* 2001; 119(5):1357–64.

Damaj MI. The involvement of spinal Ca^{2+}/calmodulin-protein kinase II in nicotine-induced antinociception in mice. *European Journal of Pharmacology* 2000; 404(1–2):103–10.

Damsma G, Day J, Fibiger HC. Lack of tolerance to nicotine-induced dopamine release in the nucleus accumbens. *European Journal of Pharmacology* 1989; 168(3):363–8.

Dani JA. Properties underlying the influence of nicotinic receptors on neuronal excitability and epilepsy. *Epilepsia* 2000;41(8):1063–5.

Davenport KE, Houdi AA, Van Loon GR. Nicotine protects against μ-opioid receptor antagonism by β-funaltrexamine: evidence for nicotine-induced release of endogenous opioids in brain. *Neuroscience Letters* 1990;113(1):40–6.

David S, Lancaster T, Stead LF. Opioid antagonists for smoking cessation. *Cochrane Database of Systematic Reviews* 2006 Issue 4. Art. No.: CD003086. DOI: 10.1002/14651858.CD003086.pub2.

David SP, Johnstone E, Griffiths SE, Murphy M, Yudkin P, Mant D, Walton R. No association between functional catechol *O*-methyl transferase 1947A to G polymorphism and smoking initiation, persistent smoking or smoking cessation. *Pharmacogenetics* 2002;12(3): 265–8.

David SP, Munafò MR, Johansen-Berg H, Smith SM, Rogers RD, Matthews PM, Walton RT. Ventral striatum/nucleus accumbens activation to smoking-related pictorial cues in smokers and nonsmokers: a functional magnetic resonance imaging study. *Biological Psychiatry* 2005;58(6):488–94.

David SP, Niaura R, Papandonatos GD, Shadel WG, Burkholder GJ, Britt DM, Day A, Stumpff J, Hutchison K, Murphy M, et al. Does the *DRD2-Taq1 A* polymorphism influence treatment response to bupropion hydrochloride for reduction of the nicotine withdrawal syndrome? *Nicotine & Tobacco Research* 2003;5(6):935–42.

De Clercq M, Truhaut R. Recherches sur le métabolisme du tryptophane chez des rats intoxiqués d'une façon aiguë, par la cotinine: etude de l elimination urinaire et dosage dans le cerveau et les intestines de certains derives indoliques. (Research on tryptophan metabolism in the rat subjected to chronic cotinine poisoning: study of urinary elimination and determination of certain indole derivatives in the brain and intestines) [French]. *Bulletin de la Societe de Chimie Biologique (Paris)* 1963;45(9–10):995–1001.

de Leon J, Dadvand M, Canuso C, White AO, Stanilla JK, Simpson GM. Schizophrenia and smoking: an epidemiological survey in a state hospital. *American Journal of Psychiatry* 1995;152(3):453–5.

De Luca V, Wang H, Squassina A, Wong GWH, Yeomans J, Kennedy JL. Linkage of M5 muscarinic and α7-nicotinic receptor genes on 15q13 to schizophrenia. *Neuropsychobiology* 2004;50(2):124–7.

De Vries TJ, de Vries W, Janssen MC, Schoffelmeer AN. Suppression of conditioned nicotine and sucrose seeking by the cannabinoid-1 receptor antagonist SR141716A. *Behavioural Brain Research* 2005;161(1):164–8.

Degenhardt L, Hall W. The relationship between tobacco use, substance-use disorders and mental health: results from the National Survey of Mental Health and Wellbeing. *Nicotine & Tobacco Research* 2001;3(3):225–34.

Delfino RJ, Jamner LD, Whalen CK. Temporal analysis of the relationship of smoking behavior and urges to mood states in men versus women. *Nicotine & Tobacco Research* 2001;3(3):235–48.

Deneris ES, Connolly J, Rogers SW, Duvoisin R. Pharmacological and functional diversity of neuronal nicotinic acetylcholine receptors. *Trends in Pharmacological Sciences* 1991;12(1):34–40.

DeNoble VJ, Mele PC. Behavioral pharmacology annual report. 1983. Philip Morris Collection. Bates No. 1003060364/0441. <http://legacy.library.ucsf.edu/tid/wot74e00>.

Dewey SL, Brodie JD, Gerasimov M, Horan B, Gardner EL, Ashby CR Jr. A pharmacologic strategy for the treatment of nicotine addiction. *Synapse* 1999;31(1):76–86.

Dewey SL, Morgan AE, Ashby CR Jr, Horan B, Kushner SA, Logan J, Volkow ND, Fowler JS, Gardner EL, Brodie JD. A novel strategy for the treatment of cocaine addiction. *Synapse* 1998;30(2):119–29.

Dewey SL, Smith GS, Logan J, Brodie JD, Yu DW, Ferrieri RA, King PT, MacGregor RR, Martin TP, Wolf AP, et al. GABAergic inhibition of endogenous dopamine release measured *in vivo* with ^{11}C-raclopride and positron emission tomography. *Journal of Neuroscience* 1992;12(10):3773–80.

deWit H, Zacny J. Abuse potential of nicotine replacement therapies. *CNS Drugs* 1995;4(6):456–68.

Di Chiara G. Behavioural pharmacology and neurobiology of nicotine reward and dependence. In: Clementi F, Fornasari D, Gotti C, editors. *Neuronal Nicotinic Receptors*. Handbook of Experimental Pharmacology, vol. 144. New York: Springer-Verlag, 2000:603–750.

Di Matteo V, Pierucci M, Esposito E. Selective stimulation of serotonin$_{2c}$ receptors blocks the enhancement of striatal and accumbal dopamine release induced by nicotine administration. *Journal of Neurochemistry* 2004;89(2):418–29.

Dierker LC, Avenevoli S, Merikangas KR, Flaherty BP, Stolar M. Association between psychiatric disorders and the progression of tobacco use behaviors. *Journal of the American Academy of Child and Adolescent Psychiatry* 2001;40(10):1159–67.

Dierker LC, Avenevoli S, Stolar M, Merikangas KR. Smoking and depression: an examination of mechanisms of comorbidity. *American Journal of Psychiatry* 2002;159(6):947–53.

DiFranza JR, Savageau JA, Fletcher K, Ockene JK, Rigotti NA, McNeill AD, Coleman M, Wood C. Measuring the loss of autonomy over nicotine use in adolescents: the DANDY (Development and Assessment of Nicotine Dependence in Youths) study. *Archives of Pediatrics & Adolescent Medicine* 2002a;156(4):397–403.

DiFranza JR, Savageau JA, Fletcher K, Pbert L, O'Loughlin J, McNeill AD, Ockene JK, Friedman K, Hazelton J, Wood C, Dussault G, Wellman RJ. Susceptibility to nicotine dependence: the Development and Assessment of Nicotine Dependence in Youth 2 study. *Pediatrics* 2007;120(4):e974–e983.

DiFranza JR, Savageau JA, Rigotti NA, Fletcher K, Ockene JK, McNeill AD, Coleman M, Wood C. Development of symptoms of tobacco dependence in youths: 30 month follow up data from the DANDY study. *Tobacco Control* 2002b;11(3):228–35.

Dijkstra A, Brosschot J. Worry about health in smoking behaviour change. *Behaviour Research and Therapy* 2003;41(9):1081–92.

Diwan A, Castine M, Pomerleau CS, Meador-Woodruff JH, Dalack GW. Differential prevalence of cigarette smoking in patients with schizophrenic vs mood disorders. *Schizophrenia Research* 1998;33(1–2):113–8.

Dobrzanzki P, Noguchi T, Kovary K, Rizzo CA, Lazo PS, Bravo R. Both products of the *fosB* gene, FosB and its short form, FosB/SF, are transcriptional activators in fibroblasts. *Molecular and Cellular Biology* 1991;11(11):5470–8.

Doherty K, Kinnunen T, Militello FS, Garvey AJ. Urges to smoke during the first month of abstinence: relationship to relapse and predictors. *Psychopharmacology* 1995;119(2):171–8.

Duan J, Wainwright MS, Comeron JM, Saitou N, Sanders AR, Gelernter J, Gejman PV. Synonymous mutations in the human *dopamine receptor D2 (DRD2)* affect mRNA stability and synthesis of the receptor. *Human Molecular Genetics* 2003;12(3):205–16.

Due DL, Huettel SA, Hall WG, Rubin DC. Activation in mesolimbic and visuospatial neural circuits elicited by smoking cues: evidence from functional magnetic resonance imaging. *American Journal of Psychiatry* 2002;159(6):954–60.

Duggirala R, Almasy L, Blangero J. Smoking behavior is under the influence of a major quantitative trait locus on human chromosome 5q. *Genetic Epidemiology* 1999;17(Suppl 1):S139–S144.

Dwoskin LP, Crooks PA, Teng L, Green TA, Bardo MT. Acute and chronic effects of nornicotine on locomotor activity in rats: altered response to nicotine. *Psychopharmacology* 1999a;145(4):442–51.

Dwoskin LP, Teng LH, Buxton ST, Crooks PA. (*S*)-(–)-cotinine, the major brain metabolite of nicotine, stimulates nicotinic receptors to evoke [^{3}H]dopamine release from rat striatal slices in a Ca^{2+}-dependent manner. *Journal of Pharmacology and Experimental Therapeutics* 1999b;288(2):905–11.

Dwoskin LP, Teng LH, Crooks PA. Nornicotine, a nicotine metabolite and tobacco alkaloid: desensitization of nicotinic receptor-stimulated dopamine release from rat striatum. *European Journal of Pharmacology* 2001;428(1):69–79.

Eisinger RA. Psychosocial predictors of smoking recidivism. *Journal of Health and Social Behavior* 1971; 12(4):355–62.

Eissenberg T. Measuring the emergence of tobacco dependence: the contribution of negative reinforcement models. *Addiction* 2004;99(Suppl 1):5–29.

Elgoyhen AB, Vetter DE, Katz E, Rothlin CV, Heinemann SF, Boulter J. α10: a determinant of nicotinic cholinergic receptor function in mammalian vestibular and cochlear mechanosensory hair cells. *Proceedings of the National Academy of Sciences of the United States of America* 2001;98(6):3501–6.

Elovainio M, Kivimäki M, Viikari J, Ekelund K, Keltikangas-Järvinen L. The mediating role of novelty seeking in the association between the type 4 dopamine receptor gene polymorphism and cigarette-smoking behavior. *Personality and Individual Differences* 2005;38(3):639–45.

Engberg G, Kling-Petersen T, Nissbrandt H. GABA_B-receptor activation alters the firing pattern of dopamine neurons in the rat substantia nigra. *Synapse* 1993; 15(3):229–38.

Epping-Jordan MP, Watkins SS, Koob GF, Markou A. Dramatic decreases in brain reward function during nicotine withdrawal. *Nature* 1998;393(6680):76–9.

Epstein AM, King AC. Naltrexone attenuates acute cigarette smoking behavior. *Pharmacology, Biochemistry, and Behavior* 2004;77(1):29–37.

Erenmemisoglu A, Tekol Y. Do nicotine metabolites have an effect on pain perception: antinociceptive effect of cotinine in mice. *Die Pharmazie* 1994;49(5):374–5.

Essman WB. Nicotine-related neurochemical changes: some implications for motivational mechanisms and differences. In: Dunn WL Jr, editor. *Smoking Behaviour: Motives and Incentives*. Washington: VH Winston and Sons, 1973:51–65.

Etter J-F. A comparison of the content-, construct- and predictive validity of the cigarette dependence scale and the Fagerström test for nicotine dependence. *Drug and Alcohol Dependence* 2005;77(3):259–68.

Etter J-F, Duc TV, Perneger TV. Validity of the Fagerström test for nicotine dependence and of the Heaviness of Smoking Index among relatively light smokers. *Addiction* 1999;94(2):269–81.

Etter J-F, Le Houezec J, Perneger TV. A self-administered questionnaire to measure dependence on cigarettes: the cigarette dependence scale. *Neuropsychopharmacology* 2003a;28(2):359–70.

Etter J-F, Pélissolo A, Pomerleau C, De Saint-Hilaire Z. Associations between smoking and heritable temperament traits. *Nicotine & Tobacco Research* 2003b; 5(3):401–9.

Evans WE, Relling MV. Pharmacogenomics: translating functional genomics into rational therapeutics. *Science* 1999;286(5439):487–91.

Everitt, BJ, Robbins, TW. Neural systems of reinforcement for drug addiction: from actions to habits to compulsion. *Nature Neuroscience* 2005;8(11):1481–9.

Fagerström KO. Measuring degree of physical dependence to tobacco smoking with reference to individualization of treatment. *Addictive Behaviors* 1978;3(3–4):235–41.

Fagerström KO. Nicotine-replacement therapies. In: Ference R, Slade J, Room R, Pope M, editors. *Nicotine and Public Health*. Washington: American Public Health Association, 2000:199–207.

Fagerström KO, Hughes JR. Nicotine concentrations with concurrent use of cigarettes and nicotine replacement: a review. *Nicotine & Tobacco Research* 2002; 4(Suppl 2):S73–S79.

Fagerström KO, Schneider NG. Measuring nicotine dependence: a review of the Fagerström Tolerance Questionnaire. *Journal of Behavioral Medicine* 1989; 12(2):159–82.

Fallon JH, Keator DB, Mbogori J, Turner J, Potkin SG. Hostility differentiates the brain metabolic effects of nicotine. *Brain Research Cognitive Brain Research* 2004;18(2):142–8.

Fant RV, Henningfield JE, Nelson RA, Pickworth WB. Pharmacokinetics and pharmacodynamics of moist snuff in humans. *Tobacco Control* 1999a;8(4):387–92.

Fant RV, Owen LL, Henningfield JE. Nicotine replacement therapy. *Primary Care* 1999b;26(3):633–52.

Fattore L, Cossu G, Martellotta MC, Fratta W. Baclofen antagonizes intravenous self-administration of nicotine in mice and rats. *Alcohol and Alcoholism* 2002;37(5): 495–8.

Faue M, Folen RA, James LC, Needels T. The Tripler Tobacco-Cessation Program: predictors for success and improved efficacy. *Military Medicine* 1997;162(7): 445–9.

Feng Y, Niu T, Xing H, Xu X, Chen C, Peng S, Wang L, Laird N, Xu X. A common haplotype of the nicotine acetylcholine receptor α4 subunit gene is associated with vulnerability to nicotine addiction in men. *American Journal of Human Genetics* 2004;75(1):112–21.

Ferguson JA, Patten CA, Schroeder DR, Offord KP, Eberman KM, Hurt RD. Predictors of 6-month tobacco abstinence among 1224 cigarette smokers treated for nicotine dependence. *Addictive Behaviors* 2003; 28(7):1203–18.

Fernández E, Schiaffino A, Borrell C, Benach J, Ariza C, Ramon JM, Twose J, Nebot M, Kunst A. Social class, education, and smoking cessation: long-term follow-up of patients treated at a smoking cessation unit. *Nicotine & Tobacco Research* 2006;8(1):29–36.

Fernando WW, Wellman RJ, DiFranza JR. The relationship between level of cigarette consumption and latency to the onset of retrospectively reported withdrawal symptoms. *Psychopharmacology* 2006;188(3):335–42.

Ferris RM, Cooper BR, Maxwell RA. Studies of bupropion's mechanism of antidepressant activity. *Journal of Clinical Psychiatry* 1983;44(5 Pt 2):74–8.

Fingerhut LA, Kleinman JC, Kendrick JS. Smoking before, during, and after pregnancy. *American Journal of Public Health* 1990;80(5):541–4.

Fiore MC, Jaén CR, Baker TB, Bailey WC, Benowitz NL, Curry SJ, Dorfman SF, Froelicher ES, Goldstein MG, Healton CG, et al. *Treating Tobacco Use and Dependence: 2008 Update*. Clinical Practice Guideline. Rockville (MD): U.S. Department of Health and Human Services, Public Health Service, 2008.

Flay BR, d'Avernas JR, Best JA, Kersell MW, Ryan KB. Cigarette smoking: why young people do it and ways of preventing it. In: McGrath PJ, Firestone P, editors. *Pediatric and Adolescent Behavioral Medicine: Issues in Treatment*. New York: Springer, 1983:132–83.

Flores CM, Rogers SW, Pabreza LA, Wolfe BB, Kellar KJ. A subtype of nicotinic cholinergic receptor in rat brain is composed of α4 and β2 subunits and is up-regulated by chronic nicotine treatment. *Molecular Pharmacology* 1992;41(1):31–7.

Floyd RL, Rimer BK, Giovino GA, Mullen PD, Sullivan SE. A review of smoking in pregnancy: effects of pregnancy outcomes and cessation efforts. *Annual Review of Public Health* 1993;14:379–411.

Fowler JS, Logan J, Wang G-J, Volkow ND. Monoamine oxidase and cigarette smoking. *Neurotoxicology* 2003;24(1):75–82.

Fowler JS, Wang G-J, Volkow ND, Franceschi D, Logan J, Pappas N, Shea C, MacGregor RR, Garza V. Maintenance of brain monoamine oxidase B inhibition in smokers after overnight cigarette abstinence. *American Journal of Psychiatry* 2000;157(11):1864–6.

Freedman R, Coon H, Myles-Worsley M, Orr-Urtreger A, Olincy A, Davis A, Polymeropoulos M, Holik J, Hopkins J, Hoff M, et al. Linkage of a neurophysiological deficit in schizophrenia to a chromosome 15 locus. *Proceedings of the National Academy of Sciences of the United States of America* 1997;94(2):587–92.

Freire MTMV, Marques FZC, Hutz MH, Bau CHD. Polymorphisms in the DBH and DRD2 gene regions and smoking behavior. *European Archives of Psychiatry and Clinical Neuroscience* 2006;256(2):93–7.

Fu Y, Matta SG, Brower VG, Sharp BM. Norepinephrine secretion in the hypothalamic paraventricular nucleus of rats during unlimited access to self-administered nicotine: an *in vivo* microdialysis study. *Journal of Neuroscience* 2001;21(22):8979–89.

Fu Y, Matta SG, Gao W, Brower VG, Sharp BM. Systemic nicotine stimulates dopamine release in nucleus accumbens: re-evaluation of the role of N-methyl-D-aspartate receptors in the ventral tegmental area. *Journal of Pharmacology and Experimental Therapeutics* 2000;294(2):458–65.

Fu Y, Matta SG, Kane VB, Sharp BM. Norepinephrine release in amygdala of rats during chronic nicotine self-administration: an in vivo microdialysis study. *Neuropharmacology* 2003;45(4):514–23.

Fu Y, Matta SG, Sharp BM. Local α-bungarotoxin-sensitive nicotinic receptors modulate hippocampal norepinephrine release by systemic nicotine. *Journal of Pharmacology and Experimental Therapeutics* 1999;289(1):133–9.

Fujieda M, Yamazaki H, Saito T, Kiyotani K, Gyamfi MA, Sakurai M, Dosaka-Akita H, Sawamura Y, Yokota J, Kunitoh H, et al. Evaluation of *CYP2A6* genetic polymorphisms as determinants of smoking behavior and tobacco-related lung cancer risk in male Japanese smokers. *Carcinogenesis* 2004;25(12):2451–8.

Funahashi S, Kubota K. Working memory and prefrontal cortex. *Neuroscience Research* 1994;21(1):1–11.

Fung YK, Schmid MJ, Anderson TM, Lau Y-S. Effects of nicotine withdrawal on central dopaminergic systems. *Pharmacology, Biochemistry, and Behavior* 1996;53(3):635–40.

Füst G, Arason GJ, Kramer J, Szalai C, Duba J, Yang Y, Chung EK, Zhou B, Blanchong CA, Lokki M-L, et al. Genetic basis of tobacco smoking: strong association of a specific major histocompatibility complex haplotype on chromosome 6 with smoking behavior. *International Immunology* 2004;16(10):1507–14.

Fuxe K, Everitt BJ, Hökfelt T. On the action of nicotine and cotinine on central 5-hydroxytryptamine neurons. *Pharmacology, Biochemistry, and Behavior* 1979;10(5):671–7.

Gallardo KA, Leslie FM. Nicotine-stimulated release of [3H]norepinephrine from fetal rat locus coeruleus cells in culture. *Journal of Neurochemistry* 1998;70(2):663–70.

García-Closas M, Kelsey KT, Wiencke JK, Xu X, Wain JC, Christiani DC. A case-control study of cytochrome *P450 1A1*, glutathione S-transferase M1, cigarette smoking and lung cancer susceptibility (Massachusetts, United States). *Cancer Causes & Control* 1997;8(4):544–53.

Garvey AJ, Bliss RE, Hitchcock JL, Heinold JW, Rosner B. Predictors of smoking relapse among self-quitters: a report from the Normative Aging Study. *Addictive Behaviors* 1992;17(4):367–77.

Gelernter J, Yu Y, Weiss R, Brady K, Panhuysen C, Yang B-Z, Kranzler HR, Farrer L. Haplotype spanning *TTC12* and *ANNKK1*, flanked by the *DRD2* and *NCAM1* loci, is strongly associated to nicotine dependence in two distinct American populations. *Human Molecular Genetics* 2006;15(24):3498–507.

George TP, Sernyak MJ, Ziedonis DM, Woods SW. Effects of clozapine on smoking in chronic schizophrenic outpatients. *Journal of Clinical Psychiatry* 1995;56(8):344–6.

George TP, Vessicchio JC, Termine A, Sahady DM, Head CA, Pepper WT, Kosten TR, Wexler BE. Effects of smoking abstinence on visuospatial working memory function in schizophrenia. *Neuropsychopharmacology* 2002;26(1):75–85.

Gerra G, Garofano L, Zaimovic A, Moi G, Branchi B, Bussandri M, Brambilla F, Donnini C. Association of the serotonin transporter promoter polymorphism with smoking behavior among adolescents. *American Journal of Medical Genetics Part B, Neuropsychiatric Genetics* 2005;135B(1):73–8.

Gilbert DG, Gilbert BO. Personality, psychopathology, and nicotine response as mediators of the genetics of smoking. *Behavior Genetics* 1995;25(2):133–47.

Gilbert DG, McClernon FJ, Rabinovich NE, Plath LC, Jensen RA, Meliska CJ. Effects of smoking abstinence on mood and craving in men: influences of negative-affect-related personality traits, habitual nicotine intake and repeated measurements. *Personality & Individual Differences* 1998;25(3):399–423.

Gilbert DG, McClernon FJ, Rabinovich NE, Plath LC, Masson CL, Anderson AE, Sly KF. Mood disturbance fails to resolve across 31 days of cigarette abstinence in women. *Journal of Consulting and Clinical Psychology* 2002;70(1):142–52.

Gilpin EA, Pierce JP, Farkas AJ. Duration of smoking abstinence and success in quitting. *Journal of the National Cancer Institute* 1997;89(8):572–6.

Gilpin EA, White MM, Farkas AJ, Pierce JP. Home smoking restrictions: which smokers have them and how they are associated with smoking behavior. *Nicotine & Tobacco Research* 1999;1(2):153–62.

Gioanni Y, Rougeot C, Clarke PBS, Lepousé C, Thierry AM, Vidal C. Nicotinic receptors in the rat prefrontal cortex: increase in glutamate release and facilitation of mediodorsal thalamo-cortical transmission. *European Journal of Neuroscience* 1999;11(1):18–30.

Giovino GA, Henningfield JE, Tomar SL, Escobedo LG, Slade J. Epidemiology of tobacco use and dependence. *Epidemiologic Reviews* 1995;17(1):48–65.

Glassman AH. Cigarette smoking: implications for psychiatric illness. *American Journal of Psychiatry* 1993;150(4):546–53.

Glassman AH, Covey LS, Dalack GW, Stetner F, Rivelli SK, Fleiss J, Cooper TB. Smoking cessation, clonidine, and vulnerability to nicotine among dependent smokers. *Clinical Pharmacology and Therapeutics* 1993;54(6):670–9.

Glassman AH, Helzer JE, Covey LS, Cottler LB, Stetner F, Tipp JE, Johnson J. Smoking, smoking cessation, and major depression. *JAMA: the Journal of the American Medical Association* 1990;264(12):1546–9.

Glassman AH, Stetner F, Walsh BT, Raizman PS, Fleiss JL, Cooper TB, Covey LS. Heavy smokers, smoking cessation, and clonidine: results of a double-blind, randomized trial. *JAMA: the Journal of the American Medical Association* 1988;259(19):2863–6.

Glautier S. Measures and models of nicotine dependence: positive reinforcement. *Addiction* 2004;99(Suppl 1):30–50.

Glick SD, Maisonneuve IM, Kitchen BA. Modulation of nicotine self-administration in rats by combination therapy with agents blocking $\alpha 3\beta 4$ nicotinic receptors. *European Journal of Pharmacology* 2002;448(2–3):185–91.

Goff DC, Henderson DC, Amico E. Cigarette smoking in schizophrenia: relationship to psychopathology and medication side effects. *American Journal of Psychiatry* 1992;149(9):1189–94.

Goldberg SR, Risner ME, Stolerman IP, Reavill C, Garcha HS. Nicotine and some related compounds: effects on schedule-controlled behaviour and discriminative properties in rats. *Psychopharmacology* 1989;97(3):295–302.

Goldman-Rakic PS. Cellular basis of working memory. *Neuron* 1995;14(3):477–85.

Goldstein, DB. Common genetic variation and human traits. *New England Journal of Medicine* 2009;360(17):1696–8.

Gonzales D, Rennard SI, Nides M, Oncken C, Azoulay S, Billing CB, Watsky EJ, Gong J, Williams KE, Reeves KR, et al. Varenicline, an $\alpha 4\beta 2$ nicotinic acetylcholine receptor partial agonist, vs sustained-release bupropion and placebo for smoking cessation: a randomized controlled trial. *JAMA: the Journal of the American Medical Association* 2006;296(1):47–55.

Goode EL, Badzioch MD, Kim H, Gagnon F, Rozek LS, Edwards KL, Jarvik GP. Multiple genome-wide analyses of smoking behavior in the Framingham Heart Study. *BMC Genetics* 2003;4(Suppl 1):S012.

Gordon J. AR-R17779: A high affinity, subtype-selective full agonist of the alpha-7 nicotinic acetylcholine receptor. Paper presented at the 2nd International Symposium on Nicotinic Acetylcholine Receptors. Series AR-R17779: A high affinity, subtype-selective full agonist of the alpha-7 nicotinic acetylcholine receptor. Annapolis (MD): 1999.

Gotti C, Zoli M, Clementi F. Brain nicotinic acetylcholine receptors: native subtypes and their relevance. *Trends in Pharmacological Sciences* 2006;27(9):482–91.

Gourlay SG, Benowitz NL. Arteriovenous differences in plasma concentration of nicotine and catecholamines and related cardiovascular effects after smoking, nicotine nasal spray, and intravenous nicotine. *Clinical Pharmacology and Therapeutics* 1997;62(4):453–63.

Grady SR, Meinerz NM, Cao J, Reynolds AM, Picciotto MR, Changeux J-P, McIntosh JM, Marks MJ, Collins AC. Nicotinic agonists stimulate acetylcholine release from mouse interpeduncular nucleus: a function mediated by a different nAChR than dopamine release from striatum. *Journal of Neurochemistry* 2001;76(1):258–68.

Grant BF, Hasin DS, Chou SP, Stinson FS, Dawson DA. Nicotine dependence and psychiatric disorders in the United States: results from the National Epidemiologic Survey on Alcohol and Related Conditions. *Archives of General Psychiatry* 2004;61(11):1107–15.

Gray R, Rajan AS, Radcliffe KA, Yakehiro M, Dani JA. Hippocampal synaptic transmission enhanced by low concentrations of nicotine. *Nature* 1996;383(6602):713–6.

Green TA, Phillips SB, Crooks PA, Dwoskin LP, Bardo MT. Nornicotine pretreatment decreases intravenous nicotine self-administration in rats. *Psychopharmacology* 2000;152(3):289–94.

Grenhoff J, Aston-Jones G, Svensson TH. Nicotinic effects on the firing pattern of midbrain dopamine neurons. *Acta Physiologica Scandinavica* 1986;128(3):351–8.

Griffiths RR, Henningfield JE, Bigelow GE. Human cigarette smoking: manipulation of number of puffs per bout, interbout interval and nicotine dose. *Journal of Pharmacology and Experimental Therapeutics* 1982; 220(2):256–65.

Grillner P, Svensson TH. Nicotine-induced excitation of midbrain dopamine neurons in vitro involves ionotropic glutamate receptor activation. *Synapse* 2000; 38(1):1–9.

Gritz ER, Thompson B, Emmons K, Ockene JK, McLerran DF, Nielsen IR. Gender differences among smokers and quitters in the Working Well Trial. *Preventive Medicine* 1998;27(4):553–61.

Grottick AJ, Trube G, Corrigall WA, Huwyler J, Malherbe P, Wyler R, Higgins GA. Evidence that nicotinic $\alpha7$ receptors are not involved in the hyperlocomotor and rewarding effects of nicotine. *Journal of Pharmacology and Experimental Therapeutics* 2000;294(3):1112–9.

Grucza RA, Wang JC, Stitzel JA, Hinrichs AL, Saccone SF, Saccone NL, Bucholz KK, Cloninger CR, Neuman RJ, Budde JP, et al. A risk allele for nicotine dependence in *CHRNA5* is a protective allele for cocaine dependence. *Biological Psychiatry* 2008;64(11):922–9.

Gu DF, Hinks LJ, Morton NE, Day INM. The use of long PCR to confirm three common alleles at the *CYP2A6* locus and the relationship between genotype and smoking habit. *Annals of Human Genetics* 2000; 64(Pt 5):383–90.

Gulliver SB, Hughes JR, Solomon LJ, Dey AN. An investigation of self-efficacy, partner support and daily stresses as predictors of relapse to smoking in self-quitters. *Addiction* 1995;90(6):767–72.

Gwaltney CJ, Shiffman S, Balabanis MH, Paty JA. Dynamic self-efficacy and outcome expectancies: prediction of smoking lapse and relapse. *Journal of Abnormal Psychology* 2005a;114(4):661–75.

Gwaltney CJ, Shiffman S, Sayette MA. Situational correlates of abstinence self-efficacy. *Journal of Abnormal Psychology* 2005b;114(4):649–60.

Haas AL, Muñoz RF, Humfleet GL, Reus VI, Hall SM. Influences of mood, depression history, and treatment modality on outcomes in smoking cessation. *Journal of Consulting and Clinical Psychology* 2004;72(4): 563–70.

Haddock CK, Lando H, Klesges RC, Talcott GW, Renaud EA. A study of the psychometric and predictive properties of the Fagerström Test for Nicotine Dependence in a population of young smokers. *Nicotine & Tobacco Research* 1999;1(1):59–66.

Hajek P, Belcher M, Stapleton J. Breath-holding endurance as a predictor of success in smoking cessation. *Addictive Behaviors* 1987;12(3):285–8.

Hall SM, Havassy BE, Wasserman DA. Commitment to abstinence and acute stress in relapse to alcohol, opiates, and nicotine. *Journal of Consulting and Clinical Psychology* 1990;58(2):175–81.

Hall SM, Reus VI, Muñoz RF, Sees KL, Humfleet G, Hartz DT, Frederick S, Triffleman E. Nortriptyline and cognitive-behavioral therapy in the treatment of cigarette smoking. *Archives of General Psychiatry* 1998;55(8):683–90.

Hamajima N, Ito H, Matsuo K, Saito T, Tajima K, Ando M, Yoshida K, Takahashi T. Association between smoking habits and *dopamine receptor D2 taqI A A2* allele in Japanese males: a confirmatory study. *Journal of Epidemiology* 2002;12(4):297–304.

Hamajima N, Katsuda N, Matsuo K, Saito T, Ito LS, Ando M, Inoue M, Takezaki T, Tajima K. Smoking habit and interleukin lB C-31T polymorphism. *Journal of Epidemiology* 2001;11(3):120–5.

Hamilton AS, Lessov-Schlaggar CN, Cockburn MG, Unger JB, Cozen W, Mack TM. Gender differences in determinants of smoking initiation and persistence in

California twins. *Cancer Epidemiology, Biomarkers & Prevention* 2006;15(6):1189–97.

Hanson K, Allen S, Jensen S, Hatsukami D. Treatment of adolescent smokers with the nicotine patch. *Nicotine & Tobacco Research* 2003;5(4):515–26.

Hardy J, Singleton A. Genomewide association studies and human disease. *New England Journal of Medicine* 2009;360(17):1759–68.

Harrison AA, Liem YTB, Markou A. Fluoxetine combined with a serotonin-1A receptor antagonist reversed reward deficits observed during nicotine and amphetamine withdrawal in rats. *Neuropsychopharmacology* 2001;25(1):55–71.

Harvey DM, Yasar S, Heishman SJ, Panlilio LV, Henningfield JE, Goldberg SR. Nicotine serves as an effective reinforcer of intravenous drug-taking behavior in human cigarette smokers. *Psychopharmacology* 2004; 175(2):134–42.

Harvey SC, Luetje CW. Determinants of competitive antagonist sensitivity on neuronal nicotinic receptor β subunits. *Journal of Neuroscience* 1996;16(12): 3798–806.

Hasin D, Paykin A, Meydan J, Grant B. Withdrawal and tolerance: prognostic significance in DSM-IV alcohol dependence. *Journal of Studies on Alcohol* 2000;61(3): 431–8.

Hatsukami D, Lexau B, Nelson D, Pentel PR, Sofuoglu M, Goldman A. Effects of cotinine on cigarette self-administration. *Psychopharmacology* 1998a;138(2):184–9.

Hatsukami D, Pentel PR, Jensen J, Nelson D, Allen SS, Goldman A, Rafael D. Cotinine: effects with and without nicotine. *Psychopharmacology* 1998b;135(2):141–50.

Hatsukami DK, Grillo M, Pentel PR, Oncken C, Bliss R. Safety of cotinine in humans: physiologic, subjective, and cognitive effects. *Pharmacology, Biochemistry, and Behavior* 1997;57(4):643–50.

Hauptmann N, Shih JC. 2-Naphthylamine, a compound found in cigarette smoke, decreases both monoamine oxidase A and B catalytic activity. *Life Sciences* 2001;68(11):1231–41.

Heath AC, Cates R, Martin NG, Meyer J, Hewitt JK, Neale MC, Eaves LJ. Genetic contribution to risk of smoking initiation: comparisons across birth cohorts and across cultures. *Journal of Substance Abuse* 1993;5(3): 221–46.

Heath AC, Madden PAF, Slutske WS, Martin NG. Personality and the inheritance of smoking behavior: a genetic perspective. *Behavior Genetics* 1995;25(2):103–17.

Heath AC, Martin NG. Genetic models for the natural history of smoking: evidence for a genetic influence on smoking persistence. *Addictive Behaviors* 1993;18(1):19–34.

Heatherton TF, Koslowski LT, Frecker RC, Fagerström K-O. The Fagerström Test for Nicotine Dependence: a revision of the Fagerström Tolerance Questionnaire. *British Journal of Addiction* 1991;86(9):1119–27.

Heatherton TF, Kozlowski LT, Frecker RC, Rickert W, Robinson J. Measuring the heaviness of smoking: using self-reported time to the first cigarette of the day and number of cigarettes smoked per day. *British Journal of Addiction* 1989;84(7):791–800.

Hecht SS, Murphy SE, Carmella SG, Zimmerman CL, Losey L, Kramarczuk I, Roe MR, Puumala SS, Li YS, Le C, et al. Effects of reduced cigarette smoking on the uptake of a tobacco-specific lung carcinogen. *Journal of the National Cancer Institute* 2004;96(2):107–15.

Hedeker D, Mermelstein RJ. Application of random-effects regression models in relapse research. *Addiction* 1996;91(12 Suppl):S211–S229.

Heimer L, Alheid GF. Piecing together the puzzle of basal forebrain anatomy. *Advances in Experimental Medicine and Biology* 1991;295:1–42.

Heishman SJ, Taylor RC, Henningfield JE. Nicotine and smoking: a review of effects on human performance. *Experimental and Clinical Psychopharmacology* 1994; 2(4):345–95.

Helton DR, Modlin DL, Tizzano JP, Rasmussen K. Nicotine withdrawal: a behavioral assessment using schedule controlled responding, locomotor activity, and sensorimotor reactivity. *Psychopharmacology* 1993; 113(2):205–10.

Henningfield JE, Clayton R, Pollin W. Involvement of tobacco in alcoholism and illicit drug use. *British Journal of Addiction* 1990;85(2):279–92.

Henningfield JE, Goldberg SR. Nicotine as a reinforcer in human subjects and laboratory animals. *Pharmacology, Biochemistry, and Behavior* 1983;19(6):989–92.

Henningfield JE, Keenan RM. Nicotine delivery kinetics and abuse liability. *Journal of Consulting and Clinical Psychology* 1993;61(5):743–50.

Henningfield JE, Keenan RM, Clarke PBS. Nicotine. In: Schuster CR, Kuhar M, editors. *Pharmacological Aspects of Drug Dependence: Toward an Integrated Neurobehavioral Approach*. Handbook of Experimental Pharmacology, vol. 118. New York: Springer, 1996: 271–314.

Henningfield JE, Stapleton JM, Benowitz NL, Grayson RF, London ED. Higher levels of nicotine in arterial than in venous blood after cigarette smoking. *Drug and Alcohol Dependence* 1993;33(1):23–9.

Hildebrand BE, Nomikos GG, Hertel P, Schilström B, Svensson TH. Reduced dopamine output in the nucleus accumbens but not in the medial prefrontal cortex in rats displaying a mecamylamine-precipitated nicotine withdrawal syndrome. *Brain Research* 1998;779(1–2): 214–25.

Hildebrand BE, Panagis G, Svensson TH, Nomikos GG. Behavioral and biochemical manifestations of mecamylamine-precipitated nicotine withdrawal in the rat: role of nicotinic receptors in the ventral tegmental area. *Neuropsychopharmacology* 1999;21(4):560–74.

Hilleman DE, Mohiuddin SM, DelCore MG, Sketch MH Sr. Effect of buspirone on withdrawal symptoms associated with smoking cessation. *Archives of Internal Medicine* 1992;152(2):350–2.

Hilleman DE, Mohiuddin SM, DelCore MG. Comparison of fixed-dose transdermal nicotine, tapered-dose transdermal nicotine, and buspirone in smoking cessation. *Journal of Clinical Pharmacology* 1994;34(3):222–4.

Hirschhorn JN. Genomewide association studies—illuminating biologic pathways. *New England Journal of Medicine* 2009;360(17):1699–1701.

Hitsman B, Borrelli B, McChargue DE, Spring B, Niaura R. History of depression and smoking cessation outcome: a meta-analysis. *Journal of Consulting and Clinical Psychology* 2003;71(4):657–63.

Hogarth L, Duka T. Human nicotine conditioning requires explicit contingency knowledge: is addictive behavior cognitively mediated? *Psychopharmacology* 2006;184(3–4):553–66.

Holladay MW, Dart MJ, Lynch JK. Neuronal nicotinic acetylcholine receptors as targets for drug discovery. *Journal of Medicinal Chemistry* 1997;40(26):4169–94.

Holm H, Jarvis MJ, Russell MAH, Feyerabend C. Nicotine intake and dependence in Swedish snuff takers. *Psychopharmacology* 1992;108(4):507–11.

Howard LA, Ahluwalia JS, Lin S-K, Sellers EM, Tyndale RF. *CYP2E1*1D* regulatory polymorphism: association with alcohol and nicotine dependence. *Pharmacogenetics* 2003;13(6):321–8.

Hu S, Brody CL, Fisher C, Gunzerath L, Nelson ML, Sabol SZ, Sirota LA, Marcus SE, Greenberg BD, Murphy DL, et al. Interaction between the serotonin transporter gene and neuroticism in cigarette smoking behavior. *Molecular Psychiatry* 2000;5(2):181–8.

Hubert HB, Eaker ED, Garrison RJ, Castelli WP. Lifestyle correlates of risk factor change in young adults: an eight-year study of coronary heart disease risk factors in the Framingham offspring. *American Journal of Epidemiology* 1987;125(5):812–31.

Hudmon KS, Marks JL, Pomerleau CS, Bolt DM, Brigham J, Swan GE. A multidimensional model for characterizing tobacco dependence. *Nicotine & Tobacco Research* 2003;5(5):655–64.

Hughes JR. Tobacco withdrawal in self-quitters. *Journal of Consulting and Clinical Psychology* 1992;60(5): 689–97.

Hughes JR. Treatment of smoking cessation in smokers with past alcohol/drug problems. *Journal of Substance Abuse Treatment* 1993;10(2):181–7.

Hughes JR. The future of smoking cessation therapy in the United States. *Addiction* 1996;91(12):1797–802.

Hughes JR. Distinguishing nicotine dependence from smoking: why it matters to tobacco control and psychiatry. *Archives of General Psychiatry* 2001;58(9):817–8.

Hughes JR. Effects of abstinence from tobacco: valid symptoms and time course. *Nicotine & Tobacco Research* 2007;9(3):315–27.

Hughes JR, Callas PW. Past alcohol problems do not predict worse smoking cessation outcomes. *Drug and Alcohol Dependence* 2003;71(3):269–73.

Hughes JR, Gulliver SB, Fenwick JW, Valliere WA, Cruser K, Pepper S, Shea P, Solomon LJ, Flynn BS. Smoking cessation among self-quitters. *Health Psychology* 1992;11(5):331–4.

Hughes JR, Gust SW, Keenan RM, Fenwick JW. Effect of dose on nicotine's reinforcing, withdrawal-suppression and self-reported effects. *Journal of Pharmacology and Experimental Therapeutics* 1990a;252(3):1175–83.

Hughes JR, Gust SW, Pechacek TF. Prevalence of tobacco dependence and withdrawal. *American Journal of Psychiatry* 1987;144(2):205–8.

Hughes JR, Hatsukami DK. The nicotine withdrawal syndrome: a brief review and update. *International Journal of Smoking Cessation* 1992;1(2):21–6.

Hughes JR, Hatsukami DK, Mitchell JE, Dahlgren LA. Prevalence of smoking among psychiatric outpatients. *American Journal of Psychiatry* 1986;143(8):993–7.

Hughes JR, Higgins ST, Hatsukami D. Effects of abstinence from tobacco: a critical review. In: Kozlowski LT, Annis H, Cappell HD, Glaser FB, Goodstadt MS, Israel Y, Kalant H, Sellers EM, Vingilis ER, editors. *Research Advances in Alcohol and Drug Problems*. Vol. 10. New York: Plenum Press, 1990b:317–98.

Hughes JR, Keely J, Naud S. Shape of the relapse curve and long-term abstinence among untreated smokers. *Addiction* 2004a;99(1):29–38.

Hughes JR, Keely JP, Niaura RS, Ossip-Klein DJ, Richmond RL, Swan GE. Measures of abstinence in clinical trials: issues and recommendations. *Nicotine & Tobacco Research* 2003;5(1):13–25.

Hughes JR, Oliveto AH, Riggs R, Kenny M, Liguori A, Pillitteri JL, MacLaughlin MA. Concordance of different measures of nicotine dependence: two pilot studies. *Addictive Behaviors* 2004b;29(8):1527–39.

Hughes JR, Rose GL, Callas PW. Nicotine is more reinforcing in smokers with a past history of alcoholism than in smokers without this history. *Alcoholism, Clinical and Experimental Research* 2000;24(11):1633–8.

Hughes JR, Stead LF, Lancaster T. Antidepressants for smoking cessation. *Cochrane Database of Systematic Reviews* 2004c, Issue 4. Art. No.: CD000031. DOI: 10.1002/14651858.CD000031.pub2.

Humfleet GL, Prochaska JJ, Mengis M, Cullen J, Muñoz R, Reus V, Hall SM. Preliminary evidence of the association between the history of childhood attention-deficit/hyperactivity disorder and smoking treatment failure. *Nicotine & Tobacco Research* 2005;7(3):453–60.

Hung RJ, McKay JD, Gaborieau V, Boffetta P, Hashibe M, Zaridze D, Mukeria A, Szeszenia-Dabrowska N, Lissowska J, Rudnai P, et al. A susceptibility locus for lung cancer maps to nicotinic acetylcholine receptor subunit genes on 15q25. *Nature* 2008;452(7187):633–7.

Hurt RD, Dale LC, Offord KP, Croghan IT, Hays JT, Gomez-Dahl L. Nicotine patch therapy for smoking cessation in recovering alcoholics. *Addiction* 1995;90(11):1541–6.

Hurt RD, Eberman KM, Croghan IT, Offord KP, Davis LJ Jr, Morse RM, Palmen MA, Bruce BK. Nicotine dependence treatment during inpatient treatment for other addictions: a prospective intervention trial. *Alcoholism, Clinical and Experimental Research* 1994;18(4):867–72.

Hurt RD, Robertson CR. Prying open the door to the tobacco industry's secrets about nicotine: the Minnesota Tobacco Trial. *JAMA: the Journal of the American Medical Association* 1998;280(13):1173–81.

Husten C. Eliminating tobacco-related death and disease. *Chronic Disease Notes & Reports* 2005;18(1); <http://www.cdc.gov/nccdphp/publications/CDNR/pdf/CDNRDec05/pdf>; accessed: July 16, 2008.

Hutchison KE, Monti PM, Rohsenow DJ, Swift RM, Colby SM, Gnys M, Niaura RS, Sirota AD. Effects of naltrexone with nicotine replacement on smoking cue reactivity: preliminary results. *Psychopharmacology* 1999a;142(2):139–43.

Hutchison KE, Niaura R, Swift R. Smoking cues decrease prepulse inhibition of the startle response and increase subjective craving in humans. *Experimental and Clinical Psychopharmacology* 1999b;7(3):250–6.

Hutchison KE, Niaura R, Swift R. The effects of smoking high nicotine cigarettes on prepulse inhibition, startle latency, and subjective responses. *Psychopharmacology* 2000;150(3):244–52.

Hutchison KE, Rutter M-C, Niaura R, Swift RM, Pickworth WB, Sobik L. Olanzapine attenuates cue-elicited craving for tobacco. *Psychopharmacology* 2004;175(4):407–13.

Hyland A, Li Q, Bauer JE, Giovino GA, Steger C, Cummings KM. Predictors of cessation in a cohort of current and former smokers followed over 13 years. *Nicotine & Tobacco Research* 2004;6(Suppl 3):S363–S369.

Hyman SE. Addiction: a disease of learning and memory. *American Journal of Psychiatry* 2005;162(8):1414–22.

Imperato A, Mulas A, Di Chiara G. Nicotine preferentially stimulates dopamine release in the limbic system of freely moving rats. *European Journal of Pharmacology* 1986;132(2–3):337–8.

Isensee B, Wittchen H-U, Stein MB, Höfler M, Lieb R. Smoking increases the risk of panic. *Archives of General Psychiatry* 2003;60(7):692–700.

Ishikawa H, Ohtsuki T, Ishiguro H, Yamakawa-Kobayashi K, Endo K, Lin Y-L, Yanagi H, Tsuchiya S, Kawata K, Hamaguchi H, et al. Association between serotonin transporter gene polymorphism and smoking among Japanese males. *Cancer Epidemiology, Biomarkers & Prevention* 1999;8(9):831–3.

Isola R, Vogelsberg V, Wemlinger TA, Neff NH, Hadjiconstantinou M. Nicotine abstinence in the mouse. *Brain Research* 1999;850(1–2):189–96.

Ito H, Hamajima N, Matsuo K, Okuma K, Sato S, Ueda R, Tajima K. *Monoamine oxidase* polymorphisms and smoking behaviour in Japanese. *Pharmacogenetics* 2003;13(2):73–9.

Iwahashi K, Waga C, Takimoto T. Whole deletion of CYP2A6 gene (*CYP2A6*4C*) and smoking behavior. *Neuropsychobiology* 2004;49(2):101–4.

Jackson KJ, Martin BR, Changeux JP, Damaj MI. Differential role of nicotinic acetylcholine receptor subunits in physical and affective nicotine withdrawal signs. *Journal of Pharmacology and Experimental Therapeutics* 2008;325(1):302–12.

Jacobsen LK, D'Souza DC, Mencl WE, Pugh KR, Skudlarski P, Krystal JH. Nicotine effects on brain function and functional connectivity in schizophrenia. *Biological Psychiatry* 2004;55(8):850–8.

Japuntich SJ, Smith SS, Jorenby DE, Piper ME, Fiore MC, Baker TB. Depression predicts smoking early but not late in a quit attempt. *Nicotine & Tobacco Research* 2007;9(6):677–86.

John U, Meyer C, Rumpf H-J, Hapke U. Smoking, nicotine dependence and psychiatric comorbidity—a population-based study including smoking cessation after three years. *Drug and Alcohol Dependence* 2004;76(3):287–95.

Johnson EO, Rhee SH, Chase GA, Breslau N. Comorbidity of depression with levels of smoking: an exploration of the shared familial risk hypothesis. *Nicotine & Tobacco Research* 2004;6(6):1029–38.

Johnson JG, Cohen P, Pine DS, Klein DF, Kasen S, Brook JS. Association between cigarette smoking and anxiety disorders during adolescence and early adulthood. *JAMA: the Journal of the American Medical Association* 2000;284(18):2348–51.

Johnson MW, Bickel WK. The behavioral economics of cigarette smoking: the concurrent presence of a substitute and independent reinforcer. *Behavioural Pharmacology* 2003;14(2):137–44.

Johnston LD, O'Malley PM, Bachman JG, Schulenberg JE. *Monitoring the Future: National Survey Results on Drug Use, 1975–2006. Volume I: Secondary School Students*. Bethesda (MD): U.S. Department of Health and Human Services, National Institutes of Health, National Institute on Drug Abuse, 2007. NIH Publication No. 07-6205.

Johnstone E, Benowitz N, Cargill A, Jacob R, Hinks L, Day I, Murphy M, Walton R. Determinants of the rate of nicotine metabolism and effects on smoking behavior. *Clinical Pharmacology and Therapeutics* 2006;80(4):319–30.

Johnstone E, Hey K, Drury M, Roberts S, Welch S, Walton R, Murphy M. Zyban for smoking cessation in a general practice setting: the response to an invitation to make a quit attempt. *Addiction Biology* 2004a;9(3–4):227–32.

Johnstone EC, Clark TG, Griffiths S-E, Murphy MFG, Walton RT. Polymorphisms in dopamine metabolic enzymes and tobacco consumption in smokers: seeking confirmation of the association in a follow-up study. *Pharmacogenetics* 2002;12(7):585–7.

Johnstone EC, Yudkin PL, Hey K, Roberts SJ, Welch SJ, Murphy MF, Griffiths SE, Walton RT. Genetic variation in dopaminergic pathways and short-term effectiveness of the nicotine patch. *Pharmacogenetics* 2004b;14(2):83–90.

Jorenby DE, Hays JT, Rigotti, NA, Azoulay S, Watsky EJ, Williams KE, Billing CB, Gong J, Reeves KR, Varenicline Phase 3 Study Group. Efficacy of varenicline, an alpha4beta2 nicotinic acetylcholine receptor partial agonist, vs placebo or sustained-release bupropion for smoking cessation. *JAMA: the Journal of the American Medical Association* 2006;296(1):56–63.

Jorm AF, Henderson AS, Jacomb PA, Christensen H, Korten AE, Rodgers B, Tan X, Easteal S. Association of smoking and personality with a polymorphism of the dopamine transporter gene: results from a community survey. *American Journal of Medical Genetics Part B: Neuropsychiatric Genetics* 2000;96(3):331–4.

Jung MJ, Lippert B, Metcalf BW, Böhlen P, Schechter PJ. γ-Vinyl GABA (4-amino-hex-5-enoic acid), a new selective irreversible inhibitor of GABA-T: effects on brain GABA metabolism in mice. *Journal of Neurochemistry* 1977;29(5):797–802.

Juon H-S, Ensminger ME, Sydnor KD. A longitudinal study of developmental trajectories to young adult cigarette smoking. *Drug and Alcohol Dependence* 2002;66(3):303–14.

Kahler CW, Brown RA, Ramsey SE, Niaura R, Abrams DB, Goldstein MG, Mueller TI, Miller IW. Negative mood, depressive symptoms, and major depression after smoking cessation treatment in smokers with a history of major depressive disorder. *Journal of Abnormal Psychology* 2002;111(4):670–5.

Kaiser SA, Soliakov L, Harvey SC, Luetje CW, Wonnacott S. Differential inhibition by α-conotoxin-MII of the nicotinic stimulation of [³H]dopamine release from rat striatal synaptosomes and slices. *Journal of Neurochemistry* 1998;70(3):1069–76.

Kalant H, LeBlanc AE, Gibbins RJ. Tolerance to, and dependence on, some non-opiate psychotropic drugs. *Pharmacological Reviews* 1971;23(3):135–91.

Kalivas PW, Striplin CD, Steketee JD, Klitenick MA, Duffy P. Cellular mechanisms of behavioral sensitization to drugs of abuse. *Annals of the New York Academy of Sciences* 1992;654:128–35.

Kalman D, Hayes K, Colby SM, Eaton CA, Rohsenow DJ, Monti PM. Concurrent versus delayed smoking cessation treatment for persons in early alcohol recovery: a pilot study. *Journal of Substance Abuse Treatment* 2001;20(3):233–8.

Kalman D, Tirch D, Penk W, Denison H. An investigation of predictors of nicotine abstinence in a smoking cessation treatment study of smokers with a past history of alcohol dependence. *Psychology of Addictive Behaviors* 2002;16(4):346–9.

Kandel D, Chen K, Warner LA, Kessler RC, Grant B. Prevalence and demographic correlates of symptoms of last year dependence on alcohol, nicotine, marijuana and cocaine in the U.S. population. *Drug and Alcohol Dependence* 1997;44(1):11–29.

Kandel D, Schaffran C, Griesler P, Samuolis J, Davies M, Galanti R. On the measurement of nicotine dependence in adolescence: comparisons of the mFTQ and a DSM-IV-based scale. *Journal of Pediatric Psychology* 2005;30(4):319–32.

Kandel DB, Chen K. Extent of smoking and nicotine dependence in the United States: 1991–1993. *Nicotine & Tobacco Research* 2000;2(3):263–74.

Kandel DB, Hu MC, Schaffran C, Udry JR, Benowitz NL. Urine nicotine metabolites and smoking behavior in a multiracial/multiethnic national sample of young adults. *American Journal of Epidemiology* 2007; 165(8):901–10.

Kandel DB, Huang F-Y, Davies M. Comorbidity between patterns of substance use dependence and psychiatric syndromes. *Drug and Alcohol Dependence* 2001; 64(2):233–41.

Karp I, O'Loughlin J, Paradis G, Hanley J, DiFranza J. Smoking trajectories of adolescent novice smokers in a longitudinal study of tobacco use. *Annals of Epidemiology* 2005;15(6):445–52.

Kassel JD, Stroud LR, Paronis CA. Smoking, stress, and negative affect: correlation, causation, and context across stages of smoking. *Psychological Bulletin* 2003;129(2):270–304.

Kawakami N, Takatsuka N, Inaba S, Shimizu H. Development of a screening questionnaire for tobacco/nicotine dependence according to *ICD-10*, *DSM-III-R*, and *DSM-IV*. *Addictive Behaviors* 1999;24(2):155–66.

Kawakami N, Takatsuka N, Shimizu H, Takai A. Lifetime prevalence and risk factors of tobacco/nicotine dependence in male ever-smokers in Japan. *Addiction* 1998;93(7):1023–32.

Keenan RM, Hatsukami DK, Pentel PR, Thompson TN, Grillo MA. Pharmacodynamic effects of cotinine in abstinent cigarette smokers. *Clinical Pharmacology and Therapeutics* 1994;55(5):581–90.

Keenan RM, Hatsukami DK, Pickens RW, Gust SW, Strelow LJ. The relationship between chronic ethanol exposure and cigarette smoking in the laboratory and the natural environment. *Psychopharmacology* 1990;100(1):77–83.

Kendler KS, Gardner CO. Monozygotic twins discordant for major depression: a preliminary exploration of the role of environmental experiences in the aetiology and course of illness. *Psychological Medicine* 2001;31(3):411–23.

Kendler KS, Neale MC, MacLean CJ, Heath AC, Eaves LJ, Kessler RC. Smoking and major depression: a causal analysis. *Archives of General Psychiatry* 1993;50(1):36–43.

Kendler KS, Neale MC, Sullivan P, Corey LA, Gardner CO, Prescott CA. A population-based twin study in women of smoking initiation and nicotine dependence. *Psychological Medicine* 1999;29(2):299–308.

Kenford SL, Fiore MC, Jorenby DE, Smith SS, Wetter D, Baker TB. Predicting smoking cessation: who will quit with and without the nicotine patch. *JAMA: the Journal of the American Medical Association* 1994;271(8):589–94.

Kenford SL, Smith SS, Wetter DW, Jorenby DE, Fiore MC, Baker TB. Predicting relapse back to smoking: contrasting affective and physical models of dependence. *Journal of Consulting and Clinical Psychology* 2002;70(1):216–27.

Kenny PJ, File SE, Neal MJ. Evidence for a complex influence of nicotinic acetylcholine receptors on hippocampal serotonin release. *Journal of Neurochemistry* 2000;75(6):2409–14.

Kenny PJ, Gasparini F, Markou A. Group II metabotropic and α-amino-3-hydroxy-5-methyl-4-isoxazole propionate (AMPA)/kainate glutamate receptors regulate the deficit in brain reward function associated with nicotine withdrawal in rats. *Journal of Pharmacology and Experimental Therapeutics* 2003;306(3):1068–76.

Kenny PJ, Markou A. Neurobiology of the nicotine withdrawal syndrome. *Pharmacology, Biochemistry, and Behavior* 2001;70(4):531–49.

Kenny PJ, Markou A. The ups and downs of addiction: role of metabotropic glutamate receptors. *Trends in Pharmacological Sciences* 2004;25(5):265–72.

Kenny PJ, Markou A. Conditioned nicotine withdrawal profoundly decreases the activity of brain reward systems. *Journal of Neuroscience* 2005;25(26):6208–12.

Khalil AA, Steyn S, Castagnoli N Jr. Isolation and characterization of a monoamine oxidase inhibitor from tobacco leaves. *Chemical Research in Toxicology* 2000;13(1):31–5.

Kikuchi-Yorioka Y, Sawaguchi T. Parallel visuospatial and audiospatial working memory processes in the monkey dorsolateral prefrontal cortex. *Nature Neuroscience* 2000;3(11):1075–6.

Killen JD, Ammerman S, Rojas N, Varady J, Haydel F, Robinson TN. Do adolescent smokers experience withdrawal effects when deprived of nicotine? *Experimental and Clinical Psychopharmacology* 2001;9(2):176–82.

Killen JD, Fortmann SP. Craving is associated with smoking relapse: findings from three prospective studies. *Experimental and Clinical Psychopharmacology* 1997;5(2):137–42.

Killen JD, Fortmann SP, Newman B, Varady A. Evaluation of a treatment approach combining nicotine gum with self-guided behavioral treatments for smoking relapse prevention. *Journal of Consulting and Clinical Psychology* 1990;58(1):85–92.

Killen JD, Fortmann SP, Newman B, Varady A. Prospective study of factors influencing the development of craving associated with smoking cessation. *Psychopharmacology* 1991;105(2):191–6.

Killen JD, Fortmann SP, Varady A, Kraemer HC. Do men outperform women in smoking cessation trials: maybe, but not by much. *Experimental and Clinical Psychopharmacology* 2002;10(3):295–301.

King A, de Wit H, Riley RC, Cao D, Niaura R, Hatsukami D. Efficacy of naltrexone in smoking cessation: a preliminary study and an examination of sex differences. *Nicotine & Tobacco Research* 2006;8(5):671–82.

Klitenick MA, DeWitte P, Kalivas PW. Regulation of somatodendritic dopamine release in the ventral tegmental area by opioids and GABA: an *in vivo* microdialysis study. *Journal of Neuroscience* 1992;12(7):2623–32.

Kokkinidis L, Zacharko RM, Predy PA. Post-amphetamine depression of self-stimulation responding from the substantia nigra: reversal by tricyclic antidepressants.

Pharmacology, Biochemistry, and Behavior 1980; 13(3):379–83.

Koob GF. Neurobiology of addiction. In: Galanter M, Kleber HD, editors. *The American Psychiatric Publishing Textbook of Substance Abuse Treatment. 4th Edition.* Arlington (VA): American Psychiatric Publishing, 2008:3–16.

Koob GF, Le Moal M. Drug addiction, dysregulation of reward, and allostasis. *Neuropsychopharmacology* 2001;24(2):97–129.

Koob GF, Markou A, Weiss F, Schultheis G. Opponent process and drug dependence: neurobiological mechanisms. *Seminars in Neuroscience* 1993;5(3):351–8.

Kopstein A. *Tobacco Use in America: Findings from the 1999 National Household Survey on Drug Abuse.* Rockville (MD): U.S. Department of Health and Human Services, Substance Abuse and Mental Health Services Administration, Office of the Assistant Secretary, 2001. Analytic Series: A-15, DHHS Publication No. SMA02-3622.

Kotlyar M, Mendoza-Baumgart MI, Li Z, Pentel PR, Barnett BC, Feuer RM, Smith EA, Hatsukami DK. Nicotine pharmacokinetics and subjective effects of three potential reduced exposure products, moist snuff and nicotine lozenge. *Tobacco Control* 2007;16(2):138–42.

Krall EA, Garvey AJ, Garcia RI. Smoking relapse after 2 years of abstinence: findings from the VA Normative Aging Study. *Nicotine & Tobacco Research* 2002;4(1): 95–100.

Kremer I, Bachner-Melman R, Reshef A, Broude L, Nemanov L, Gritsenko I, Heresco-Levy U, Elizur Y, Ebstein RP. Association of the serotonin transporter gene with smoking behavior. *American Journal of Psychiatry* 2005;162(5):924–30.

Kumari V, Gray JA, ffytche DH, Mitterschiffthaler MT, Das M, Zachariah E, Vythelingum GN, Williams SCR, Simmons A, Sharma T. Cognitive effects of nicotine in humans: an fMRI study. *Neuroimage* 2003;19(3): 1002–13.

LaBar KS, LeDoux JE. Coping with danger: the neural basis of defensive behavior and fearful feelings. In: McEwen BS, Goodman HM, editors. *Handbook of Physiology, Section 7: The Endocrine System.* Coping with the Environment: Neural and Endocrine Mechanisms. Vol. IV. New York: Oxford University Press, 2001:139–54.

Lança AJ, Adamson KL, Coen KM, Chow BLC, Corrigall WA. The pedunculopontine tegmental nucleus and the role of cholinergic neurons in nicotine self-administration in the rat: a correlative neuroanatomical and behavioral study. *Neuroscience* 2000;96(4):735–42.

Lane JD, Rose JE. Effects of daily caffeine intake on smoking behavior in the natural environment. *Experimental and Clinical Psychopharmacology* 1995;3(1):49–55.

Lasser K, Boyd JW, Woolhandler S, Himmelstein DU, McCormick D, Bor DH. Smoking and mental illness: a population-based prevalence study. *JAMA: the Journal of the American Medical Association* 2000;284(20): 2606–10.

Laucht M, Becker K, El-Faddagh M, Hohm E, Schmidt MH. Association of the DRD4 exon III polymorphism with smoking in fifteen-year-olds: a mediating role for novelty seeking? *Journal of the American Academy of Child and Adolescent Psychiatry* 2005;44(5):477–84.

Le Foll B, Diaz J, Sokoloff P. Increased dopamine D_3 receptor expression accompanying behavioral sensitization to nicotine in rats. *Synapse* 2003;47(3):176–83.

Le Foll B, Goldberg SR. Control of the reinforcing effects of nicotine by associated environmental stimuli in animals and humans. *Trends in Pharmacological Sciences* 2005;26(6):287–93.

Lee CW, Kahende J. Factors associated with successful smoking cessation in the United States. *American Journal of Public Health* 2007;97(8):1503–9.

Lee EM, Malson JL, Waters AJ, Moolchan ET, Pickworth WB. Smoking topography: reliability and validity in dependent smokers. *Nicotine & Tobacco Research* 2003;5(5):673–9.

Léna C, Changeux J-P. Allosteric nicotinic receptors, human pathologies. *Journal of Physiology Paris* 1998; 92(2):63–74.

Léna C, Changeux J-P. The role of β2-subunit-containing nicotinic acetylcholine receptors in the brain explored with a mutant mouse. *Annals of the New York Academy of Sciences* 1999;868:611–6.

Léna C, de Kerchove d'Exaerde A, Cordero-Erausquin M, Le Novère N, del Mar Arroyo-Jimenez M, Changeux J-P. Diversity and distribution of nicotinic acetylcholine receptors in the *locus ceruleus* neurons. *Proceedings of the National Academy of Sciences of the United States of America* 1999;96(21):12126–31.

Lerman C, Caporaso NE, Audrain J, Main D, Bowman ED, Lockshin B, Boyd NR, Shields PG. Evidence suggesting the role of specific genetic factors in cigarette smoking. *Health Psychology* 1999;18(1):14–20.

Lerman C, Caporaso NE, Audrain J, Main D, Boyd NR, Shields PG. Interacting effects of the serotonin transporter gene and neuroticism in smoking practices and nicotine dependence. *Molecular Psychiatry* 2000; 5(2):189–92.

Lerman C, Caporaso NE, Bush A, Zheng Y-L, Audrain J, Main D, Shields PG. Tryptophan hydroxylase gene variant and smoking behavior. *American Journal of Medical Genetics* 2001;105(6):518–20.

Lerman C, Jepson C, Wileyto EP, Epstein LH, Rukstalis M, Patterson F, Kaufmann V, Restine S, Hawk L, Niaura R, et al. Role of functional genetic variation in the dopamine D2 receptor (*DRD2*) in response to bupropion and nicotine replacement therapy for tobacco dependence: results of two randomized clinical trials. *Neuropsychopharmacology* 2006;31(1):231–42.

Lerman C, Niaura R. Applying genetic approaches to the treatment of nicotine dependence. *Oncogene* 2002; 21(48):7412–20.

Lerman C, Patterson F, Berrettini W. Treating tobacco dependence: state of the science and new directions. *Journal of Clinical Oncology* 2005;23(2):311–23.

Lerman C, Shields PG, Audrain J, Main D, Cobb B, Boyd NR, Caporaso N. The role of the serotonin transporter gene in cigarette smoking. *Cancer Epidemiology, Biomarkers & Prevention* 1998;7(3):253–5.

Lerman C, Shields PG, Main D, Audrain J, Roth J, Boyd NR, Caporaso NE. Lack of association of tyrosine hydroxylase genetic polymorphism with cigarette smoking. *Pharmacogenetics* 1997;7(6):521–4.

Lerman C, Shields PG, Wileyto EP, Audrain J, Pinto A, Hawk L, Krishnan S, Niaura R, Epstein L. Pharmacogenetic investigation of smoking cessation treatment. *Pharmacogenetics* 2002;12(8):627–34.

Lerman C, Wileyto EP, Patterson F, Rukstalis M, Audrain-McGovern J, Restine S, Shields PG, Kaufmann V, Redden D, Benowitz N, et al. The functional mu opioid receptor (OPRM1) Asn40Asp variant predicts short-term response to nicotine replacement therapy in a clinical trial. *Pharmacogenomics Journal* 2004;4(3):184–92.

Lerman CE, Schnoll RA, Munafò MR. Genetics and smoking cessation improving outcomes in smokers at risk. *American Journal of Preventive Medicine* 2007; 33(6 Suppl 1):S398–S405.

Lessov CN, Martin NG, Statham DJ, Todorov AA, Slutske WS, Bucholz KK, Heath AC, Madden PAF. Defining nicotine dependence for genetic research: evidence from Australian twins. *Psychological Medicine* 2004;34(5):865–79.

Letourneau AR, Batten S, Mazure CM, O'Malley SS, Dziura J, Colson ER. Timing and predictors of postpartum return to smoking in a group of inner-city women: an exploratory pilot study. *Birth* 2007;34(3):245–52.

Leventhal AM, Ramsey SE, Brown RA, LaChance HR, Kahler CW. Dimensions of depressive symptoms and smoking cessation. *Nicotine & Tobacco Research* 2008; 10(3):507–17.

Leventhal AM, Waters AJ, Boyd S, Moolchan ET, Lerman C, Pickword WB. Gender differences in acute tobacco withdrawal: effects on subjective, cognitive, and physiological measures. *Experimental and Clinical Psychopharmacology* 2007;15(1):21–36.

Levin ED, Bettegowda C, Blosser J, Gordon J. AR-R17779, and α7 nicotinic agonist, improves learning

and memory in rats. *Behavioral Pharmacology* 1999; 10(6–7):675–80.

Levin ED, Rezvani AH, Montoya D, Rose JE, Swartzwelder HS. Adolescent-onset nicotine self-administration modeled in female rats. *Psychopharmacology* 2003; 169(2):141–9.

Levine DG. "Needle freaks": compulsive self-injection by drug users. *American Journal of Psychiatry* 1974; 131(3):297–300.

Li MD. The genetics of nicotine dependence. *Current Psychiatry Reports* 2006;8(2):158–64.

Li MD, Beuten J, Ma JZ, Payne TJ, Lou X-Y, Garcia V, Duenes AS, Crews KM, Elston RC. Ethnic- and gender-specific association of the nicotinic acetylcholine receptor α4 subunit gene (*CHRNA4*) with nicotine dependence. *Human Molecular Genetics* 2005;14(9):1211–9.

Li MD, Ma JZ, Cheng R, Dupont RT, Williams NJ, Crews KM, Payne TJ, Elston RC. A genome-wide scan to identify loci for smoking rate in the Framingham Heart Study population. *BMC Genetics* 2003;4(Suppl 1):S103.

Li MD, Payne TJ, Ma JZ, Lou XY, Zhang D, Dupont RT, Crews KM, Somes G, Williams NJ, Elston RC. A genomewide search finds major susceptibility loci for nicotine dependence on chromosome 10 in African Americans. *American Journal of Human Genetics* 2006;79(4):745–51.

Li SX-M, Perry KW, Wong DT. Influence of fluoxetine on the ability of bupropion to modulate extracellular dopamine and norepinephrine concentrations in three mesocorticolimbic areas of rats. *Neuropharmacology* 2002;42(2):181–90.

Lindstrom J, Anand R, Gerzanich V, Peng X, Wang F, Wells G. Structure and function of neuronal nicotinic acetylcholine receptors. *Progress in Brain Research* 1996;109:125–37.

Ling D, Niu T, Feng Y, Xing H, Xu X. Association between polymorphism of the dopamine transporter gene and early smoking onset: an interaction risk on nicotine dependence. *Journal of Human Genetics* 2004;49(1): 35–9.

Ling W, Shoptaw S, Majewska D. Baclofen as a cocaine anti-craving medication: a preliminary clinical study. *Neuropsychopharmacology* 1998;18(5):403–4.

Lippert B, Metcalf BW, Jung MJ, Casara P. 4-Amino-hex-5-enoic acid, a selective catalytic inhibitor of 4-aminobutyric-acid aminotransferase in mammalian brain. *European Journal of Biochemistry* 1977;74(3):441–5.

Liu P, Vikis HG, Wang D, Lu Y, Wang Y, Schwartz AG, Pinney SM, Yang P, de Andrade M, Petersen GM, et al. Familial aggregation of common sequence variants on 15q24-25.1 in lung cancer. *Journal of the National Cancer Institute* 2008;100(18):1326–30.

Liu Y, Yoshimura K, Hanaoka T, Ohnami S, Ohnami S, Kohno T, Yoshida T, Sakamoto H, Sobue T, Tsugane S. Association of habitual smoking and drinking with single nucleotide polymorphism (SNP) in 40 candidate genes: data from random population-based Japanese samples. *Journal of Human Genetics* 2005;50(2):62–8.

Lloyd-Richardson EE, Papandonatos G, Kazura A, Stanton C, Niaura R. Differentiating stages of smoking intensity among adolescents: stage-specific psychological and social influences. *Journal of Consulting and Clinical Psychology* 2002;70(4):998–1009.

London SJ, Idle JR, Daly AK, Coetzee GA. Genetic variation of *CYP2A6*, smoking, and risk of cancer. *Lancet* 1999;353(9156):898–9.

Loriot M-A, Rebuissou S, Oscarson M, Cenée S, Miyamoto M, Ariyoshi N, Kamataki T, Hémon D, Beaune P, Stücker I. Genetic polymorphisms of cytochrome P450 2A6 in a case–control study on lung cancer in a French population. *Pharmacogenetics* 2001;11(1):39–44.

Lou X-Y, Ma JZ, Sun D, Payne TJ, Li MD. Fine mapping of a linkage region on chromosome 17p13 reveals that *GABARAP* and *DLG4* are associated with vulnerability to nicotine dependence in European-Americans. *Human Molecular Genetics* 2007;16(2):142–53.

Luciano M, Zhu G, Kirk KM, Whitfield JB, Butler R, Heath AC, Madden PAF, Martin NG. Effects of dopamine receptor D4 variation on alcohol and tobacco use and on novelty seeking: multivariate linkage and association analysis. *American Journal of Medical Genetics Part B, Neuropsychiatric Genetics* 2004;124(1):113–23.

Ludwig AM. Pavlov's "bells" and alcohol craving. *Addictive Behaviors* 1986;11(2):87–91.

Lueders KK, Hu S, McHugh L, Myakishev MV, Sirota LA, Hamer DH. Genetic and functional analysis of single nucleotide polymorphisms in the β2-neuronal nicotinic acetylcholine receptor gene (CHRNB2). *Nicotine & Tobacco Research* 2002;4(1):115–25.

Luo S, Kulak JM, Cartier GE, Jacobsen RB, Yoshikami D, Olivera BM, McIntosh JM. α-conotoxin AuIB selectively blocks α3β4 nicotinic acetylcholine receptors and nicotine-evoked norepinephrine release. *Journal of Neuroscience* 1998;18(21):8571–9.

Ma JZ, Beuten J, Payne TJ, Dupont RT, Elston RC, Li MD. Haplotype analysis indicates an association between the DOPA decarboxylase (*DDC*) gene and nicotine dependence. *Human Molecular Genetics* 2005;14(12):1691–8.

Macy JT, Seo D-C, Chassin L, Presson CC, Sherman SJ. Prospective predictors of long-term abstinence versus relapse among smokers who quit as young adults. *American Journal of Public Health* 2007;97(8):1470–5.

Malaiyandi V, Lerman C, Benowitz NL, Jepson C, Patterson F, Tyndale RF. Impact of *CYP2A6* genotype on pretreatment smoking behaviour and nicotine levels from and usage of nicotine replacement therapy. *Molecular Psychiatry* 2006;11(4):400–9.

Malin DH. Nicotine dependence: studies with a laboratory model. *Pharmacology, Biochemistry, and Behavior* 2001;70(4):551–9.

Malin DH, Lake JR, Carter VA, Cunningham JS, Wilson OB. Naloxone precipitates nicotine abstinence syndrome in the rat. *Psychopharmacology* 1993;112(2–3):339–42.

Malin DH, Lake JR, Newlin-Maultsby P, Roberts LK, Lanier JG, Carter VA, Cunningham JS, Wilson OB. Rodent model of nicotine abstinence syndrome. *Pharmacology, Biochemistry, and Behavior* 1992;43(3):779–84.

Manoach DS, Gollub RL, Benson ES, Searl MM, Goff DC, Halpern E, Saper CB, Rauch SL. Schizophrenic subjects show aberrant fMRI activation of dorsolateral prefrontal cortex and basal ganglia during working memory performance. *Biological Psychiatry* 2000;48(2):99–109.

Mansvelder HD, Keath JR, McGehee DS. Synaptic mechanisms underlie nicotine-induced excitability of brain reward areas. *Neuron* 2002;33(6):905–19.

Mansvelder HD, McGehee DS. Long-term potentiation of excitatory inputs to brain reward areas by nicotine. *Neuron* 2000;27(2):349–57.

Markou A. Pathways and systems involved in nicotine dependence. In: Bock G, Goode J, editors. *Understanding Nicotine and Tobacco Addiction*. Novartis Foundation Symposium 275. Hoboken (NJ): John Wiley & Sons, 2006:132–52.

Markou A, Kenny PJ. Neuroadaptations to chronic exposure to drugs of abuse: relevance to depressive symptomatology seen across psychiatric diagnostic categories. *Neurotoxicity Research* 2002;4(4):297–313.

Markou A, Koob GF. Postcocaine anhedonia: an animal model of cocaine withdrawal. *Neuropsychopharmacology* 1991;4(1):17–26.

Markou A, Kosten TR, Koob GF. Neurobiological similarities in depression and drug dependence: a self-medication hypothesis. *Neuropsychopharmacology* 1998;18(3):135–74.

Markou A, Paterson NE. The nicotinic antagonist methyllycaconitine has differential effects on nicotine self-administration and nicotine withdrawal in the rat. *Nicotine & Tobacco Research* 2001;3(4):361–73.

Markou A, Weiss F, Gold LH, Caine SB, Schultheis G, Koob GF. Animal models of drug craving. *Psychopharmacology* 1993;112(2–3):163–82.

Marlatt GA, Gordon JR, editors. *Relapse Prevention: Maintenance Strategies in the Treatment of Addictive Behaviors*. New York: Guilford Press, 1985.

Masterson E, O'Shea B. Smoking and malignancy in schizophrenia. *British Journal of Psychiatry* 1984; 145:429–32.

Mayhew KP, Flay BR, Mott JA. Stages in the development of adolescent smoking. *Drug and Alcohol Dependence* 2000;59(Suppl 1):S61–S81.

McCaffery JM, Niaura R, Swan GE, Carmelli D. A study of depressive symptoms and smoking behavior in adult male twins from the NHLBI twin study. *Nicotine & Tobacco Research* 2003;5(1):77–83.

McCarthy DE, Piasecki TM, Fiore MC, Baker TB. Life before and after quitting smoking: an electronic diary study. *Journal of Abnormal Psychology* 2006;115(3):454–66.

McCaul KD, Mullens AB, Romanek KM, Erickson SC, Gatheridge BJ. The motivational effects of thinking and worrying about the effects of smoking cigarettes. *Cognition & Emotion* 2007;21(8):1780–98.

McClernon FJ, Gilbert DG. Human functional neuroimaging in nicotine and tobacco research: basics, background, and beyond. *Nicotine & Tobacco Research* 2004;6(6):941–59.

McGehee DS, Role LW. Physiological diversity of nicotinic acetylcholine receptors expressed by vertebrate neurons. *Annual Review of Physiology* 1995;57:521–46.

McGehee DS, Role LW. Presynaptic ionotropic receptors. *Current Opinion in Neurobiology* 1996;6(3):342–9.

McGue M, Elkins I, Iacono WG. Genetic and environmental influences on adolescent substance use and abuse. *American Journal of Medical Genetics* 2000;96(5): 671–7.

McKee SA, Maciejewski PK, Falba T, Mazure CM. Sex differences in the effects of stressful life events on changes in smoking status. *Addiction* 2003;98(6):847–55.

McKinney EF, Walton RT, Yudkin P, Fuller A, Haldar NA, Mant D, Murphy M, Welsh KI, Marshall SE. Association between polymorphisms in dopamine metabolic enzymes and tobacco consumption in smokers. *Pharmacogenetics* 2000;10(6):483–91.

Medical Economics Company. *Physicians' Desk Reference*. Montvale (NJ): Medical Economics Company, 2000.

Menzel S. Genetic and molecular analyses of complex metabolic disorders: genetic linkage. *Annals of the New York Academy of Sciences* 2002;967:249–57.

Merikangas KR, Stolar M, Stevens DE, Goulet J, Preisig MA, Fenton B, Zhang H, O'Malley SS, Rounsaville BJ. Familial transmission of substance use disorders. *Archives of General Psychiatry* 1998;55(11):973–9.

Merlo Pich E, Chiamulera C, Carboni L. Molecular mechanisms of the positive reinforcing effect of nicotine. *Behavioural Pharmacology* 1999;10(6–7):587–96.

Merlo Pich E, Pagliusi SR, Tessari M, Talabot-Ayer D, Hooft van Huijsduijnen R, Chiamulera C. Common neural substrates for the addictive properties of nicotine and cocaine. *Science* 1997;275(5296):83–6.

Mifsud J-C, Hernandez L, Hoebel BG. Nicotine infused into the nucleus accumbens increases synaptic dopamine as measured by in vivo microdialysis. *Brain Research* 1989;478(2):365–7.

Miller DK, Wong EHF, Chesnut MD, Dwoskin LP. Reboxetine: functional inhibition of monoamine transporters and nicotinic acetylcholine receptors. *Journal of Pharmacology and Experimental Therapeutics* 2002; 302(2):687–95.

Minematsu N, Nakamura H, Iwata M, Tateno H, Nakajima T, Takahashi S, Fujishima S, Yamaguchi K. Association of *CYP2A6* deletion polymorphism with smoking habit and development of pulmonary emphysema. *Thorax* 2003;58(7):623–8.

Mischel W. Toward an integrative science of the person. *Annual Review of Psychology* 2004;55:1–22.

Mitchell SH, de Wit H, Zacny JP. Effects of varying ethanol dose on cigarette consumption in healthy normal volunteers. *Behavioural Pharmacology* 1995;6(4):359–65.

Mitchell SN, Smith KM, Joseph MH, Gray JA. Increases in tyrosine hydroxylase messenger RNA in the locus coeruleus after a single dose of nicotine are followed by time-dependent increases in enzyme activity and noradrenaline release. *Neuroscience* 1993;56(4):989–97.

Mizuno S, Ito H, Hamajima N, Tamakoshi A, Hirose K, Tajima K. Association between smoking habits and tryptophan hydroxylase gene C218A polymorphism among the Japanese population. *Journal of Epidemiology* 2004;14(3):94–9.

Mogg K, Bradley BP. Selective processing of smoking-related cues in smokers: manipulation of deprivation level and comparison of three measures of processing bias. *Journal of Psychopharmacology* 2002;16(4): 385–92.

Moolchan ET, Radzius A, Epstein DH, Uhl G, Gorelick DA, Cadet JL, Henningfield JE. The Fagerström Test for Nicotine Dependence and the Diagnostic Interview Schedule: do they diagnose the same smokers? *Addictive Behaviors* 2002;27(1):101–13.

Mullen PD. How can more smoking suspension during pregnancy become lifelong abstinence? Lessons learned about predictors, interventions, and gaps in our accumulated knowledge. *Nicotine & Tobacco Research* 2004;6(Suppl 2):S217–S238.

Munafò M, Mogg K, Roberts S, Bradley BP, Murphy M. Selective processing of smoking-related cues in current smokers, ex-smokers and never-smokers on the modified Stroop task. *Journal of Psychopharmacology* 2003;17(3):310–6.

Munafò MR, Clark TG, Johnstone EC, Murphy MFG, Walton RT. The genetic basis for smoking behavior: a systematic review and meta-analysis. *Nicotine & Tobacco Research* 2004;6(4):583–98.

Munafò MR, Flint J. Meta-analysis of genetic association studies. *Trends in Genetics* 2004;20(9):439–44.

Munafò MR, Roberts K, Johnstone EC, Walton RT, Yudkin PL. Association of serotonin transporter gene polymorphism with nicotine dependence: no evidence for interaction with trait neuroticism. *Personality and Individual Differences* 2005a;38(4):843–50.

Munafò MR, Shields AE, Berrettini WH, Patterson F, Lerman C. Pharmacogenetics and nicotine addiction treatment. *Pharmacogenomics* 2005b;6(3):211–23.

Muthén B, Muthén LK. Integrating person-centered and variable-centered analyses: growth mixture modeling with latent trajectory classes. *Alcoholism, Clinical and Experimental Research* 2000;24(6):882–91.

Nagin DS. Analyzing developmental trajectories: a semiparametric, group-based approach. *Psychological Methods* 1999;4(2):139–57.

National Cancer Institute. *The FTC Cigarette Test Method for Determining Tar, Nicotine, and Carbon Monoxide Yields of U.S. Cigarettes: Report of the NCI Expert Committee*. Smoking and Tobacco Control Monograph No. 7. Bethesda (MD): U.S. Department of Health and Human Services, Public Health Service, National Institutes of Health, National Cancer Institute, 1996. NIH Publication No. 96-4028.

National Cancer Institute. *Risks Associated with Smoking Cigarettes with Low Machine-Measured Yields of Tar and Nicotine*. Smoking and Tobacco Control Monograph No. 13. Bethesda (MD): U.S. Department of Health and Human Services, Public Health Service, National Institutes of Health, National Cancer Institute, 2001. NIH Publication No. 02-5047.

National Cancer Institute. *Phenotypes and Endophenotypes: Foundations for Genetic Studies of Nicotine Use and Dependence*. Smoking and Tobacco Control Monograph No. 20. Bethesda (MD): U.S. Department of Health and Human Services, National Institutes of Health, National Cancer Institute, 2009. NIH Publication No. 08-6366.

National Institute on Drug Abuse. *Drug Use Among Racial/Ethnic Minorities*. Revised. Bethesda (MD): National Institute on Drug Abuse, 2003. NIH Publication No. 03-3888.

Nestler EJ. Genes and addiction. *Nature Genetics* 2000;26(3):277–81.

Nestler EJ. Molecular basis of long-term plasticity underlying addiction. *Nature Reviews Neuroscience* 2001;2(3):119–28.

Niaura R. Cognitive social learning and related perspectives on drug craving. *Addiction* 2000;95(Suppl 2):S155–S163.

Niaura R. Does 'unlearning' ever really occur: comment on Conklin & Tiffany [letter]. *Addiction* 2002;97(3):357.

Niaura R, Abrams DB, Monti PM, Pedraza M. Reactivity to high risk situations and smoking cessation outcome. *Journal of Substance Abuse* 1989;1(4):393–405.

Niaura R, Britt DM, Shadel WG, Goldstein M, Abrams D, Brown R. Symptoms of depression and survival experience among three samples of smokers trying to quit. *Psychology of Addictive Behaviors* 2001;15(1):13–7.

Niaura R, Sayette M, Shiffman S, Glover ED, Nides M, Shelanski M, Shadel W, Koslo R, Robbins B, Sorrentino J. Comparative efficacy of rapid-release nicotine gum versus nicotine polacrilex gum in relieving smoking cue-provoked craving. *Addiction* 2005;100(11):1720–30.

Niaura RS, Rohsenow DJ, Binkoff JA, Monti PM, Pedraza M, Abrams DB. Relevance of cue reactivity to understanding alcohol and smoking relapse. *Journal of Abnormal Psychology* 1988;97(2):133–52.

Nides MA, Rakos RF, Gonzales D, Murray RP, Tashkin DP, Bjornson-Benson WM, Lindgren P, Connett JE. Predictors of initial smoking cessation and relapse through the first 2 years of the Lung Health Study. *Journal of Consulting and Clinical Psychology* 1995;63(1):60–9.

Nil R, Buzzi R, Bättig K. Effects of single doses of alcohol and caffeine on cigarette smoke puffing behavior. *Pharmacology, Biochemistry, and Behavior* 1984;20(4):583–90.

Nisell M, Marcus M, Nomikos GG, Svensson TH. Differential effects of acute and chronic nicotine on dopamine output in the core and shell of the rat nucleus accumbens. *Journal of Neural Transmission* 1997;104(1):1–10.

Nisell M, Nomikos GG, Svensson TH. Infusion of nicotine in the ventral tegmental area or the nucleus accumbens of the rat differentially affects accumbal dopamine release. *Pharmacology and Toxicology* 1994a;75(6):348–52.

Nisell M, Nomikos GG, Svensson TH. Systemic nicotine-induced dopamine release in the rat nucleus accumbens is regulated by nicotinic receptors in the ventral tegmental area. *Synapse* 1994b;16(1):36–44.

Niu T, Chen C, Ni J, Wang B, Fang Z, Shao H, Xu X. Nicotine dependence and its familial aggregation in Chinese. *International Journal of Epidemiology* 2000;29(2):248–52.

Noble EP, St Jeor ST, Ritchie T, Syndulko K, St Jeor SC, Fitch RJ, Brunner RL, Sparkes RS. D2 dopamine receptor gene and cigarette smoking: a reward gene? *Medical Hypotheses* 1994;42(4):257–60.

Nomikos GG, Damsma G, Wenkstern D, Fibiger HC. Acute effects of bupropion on extracellular dopamine concentrations in rat striatum and nucleus accumbens studied by in vivo microdialysis. *Neuropsychopharmacology* 1989;2(4):273–9.

Nomikos GG, Damsma G, Wenkstern D, Fibiger HC. Effects of chronic bupropion on interstitial concentrations of dopamine in rat nucleus accumbens and striatum. *Neuropsychopharmacology* 1992;7(1):7–14.

Nørregaard J, Tønnesen P, Petersen L. Predictors and reasons for relapse in smoking cessation with nicotine and placebo patches. *Preventive Medicine* 1993;22(2): 261–71.

O'Brien CP, Childress AR, McLellan T, Ehrman R. Integrating systematic cue exposure with standard treatment in recovering drug dependent patients. *Addictive Behaviors* 1990;15(4):355–65.

Ockene JK, Emmons KM, Mermelstein RJ, Perkins KA, Bonollo DS, Voorhees CC, Hollis JF. Relapse and maintenance issues for smoking cessation. *Health Psychology* 2000;19(1 Suppl):17–31.

O'Connell KA, Martin EJ. Highly tempting situations associated with abstinence, temporary lapse, and relapse among participants in smoking cessation programs. *Journal of Consulting and Clinical Psychology* 1987;55(3):367–71.

O'Connor RJ, Giovino GA, Kozlowski LT, Shiffman S, Hyland A, Bernert JT, Caraballo RS, Cummings KM. Changes in nicotine intake and cigarette use over time in two nationally representative cross-sectional samples of smokers. *American Journal of Epidemiology* 2006;164(8):750–9.

O'Dell LE, Bruijnzeel AW, Ghozland S, Markou A, Koob GB. Nicotine withdrawal in adolescent and adult rats. *Annals of the New York Academy of Sciences* 2004;1021:167–74.

O'Dell LE, Bruijnzeel AW, Smith RT, Parsons LH, Merves ML, Goldberger BA, Richardson HN, Koob GF, Markou A. Diminished nicotine withdrawal in adolescent rats: implications for vulnerability to addiction. *Psychopharmacology* 2006;186(4):612–9.

O'Dell LE, Torres OV, Natividad LA, Tejeda HA. Adolescent nicotine exposure produces less affective measures of withdrawal relative to adult nicotine exposure in male rats. *Neurotoxicology and Teratology* 2007;29(1): 17–22.

Olausson P, Åkesson P, Engel JA, Söderpalm B. Effects of 5-HT$_{1A}$ and 5-HT$_2$ receptor agonists on the behavioral and neurochemical consequences of repeated nicotine treatment. *European Journal of Pharmacology* 2001;420(1):45–54.

Olincy A, Young DA, Freedman R. Increased levels of the nicotine metabolite cotinine in schizophrenic smokers compared to other smokers. *Biological Psychiatry* 1997;42(1):1–5.

O'Loughlin J, DiFranza J, Tarasuk J, Meshefedjian G, McMillan-Davey E, Paradis G, Tyndale RF, Clarke P, Hanley J. Assessment of nicotine dependence symptoms in adolescents: a comparison of five indicators. *Tobacco Control* 2002;11(4):354–60.

O'Loughlin J, DiFranza J, Tyndale RF, Meshefedjian G, McMillan-Davey E, Clarke PBS, Hanley J, Paradis G. Nicotine-dependence symptoms are associated with smoking frequency in adolescents. *American Journal of Preventive Medicine* 2003;25(3):219–25.

O'Loughlin J, Paradis G, Kim W, DiFranza J, Meshefedjian G, McMillan-Davey E, Wong S, Hanley J, Tyndale RF. Genetically decreased *CYP2A6* and the risk of tobacco dependence: a prospective study of novice smokers. *Tobacco Control* 2004;13(4):422–8.

O'Loughlin J, Tarasuk J, DiFranza J, Paradis G. Reliability of selected measures of nicotine dependence among adolescents. *Annals of Epidemiology* 2002;12(5): 353–62.

Olsson C, Anney R, Forrest S, Patton G, Coffey C, Cameron T, Hassett A, Williamson R. Association between dependent smoking and a polymorphism in the tyrosine hydroxylase gene in a prospective population-based study of adolescent health. *Behavior Genetics* 2004; 34(1):85–91.

O'Malley SS, Cooney JL, Krishnan-Sarin S, Dubin JA, McKee SA, Cooney NL, Blakeslee A, Meandzija B, Romano-Dahlgard D, Wu R, et al. A controlled trial of naltrexone augmentation of nicotine replacement therapy for smoking cessation. *Archives of Internal Medicine* 2006;166(6):667–74.

O'Neill SE, Sher KJ. Physiological alcohol dependence symptoms in early adulthood: a longitudinal perspective. *Experimental and Clinical Psychopharmacology* 2000;8(4):493–508.

Orlando M, Tucker JS, Ellickson PL, Klein DJ. Developmental trajectories of cigarette smoking and their correlates from early adolescence to young adulthood. *Journal of Consulting and Clinical Psychology* 2004;72(3):400–10.

Palmatier MI, Liu X, Matteson GL, Donny EC, Caggiula AR, Sved AF. Conditioned reinforcement in rats established with self-administered nicotine and enhanced by noncontingent nicotine. *Psychopharmacology* 2007; 195(2):235–43.

Panagis G, Hildebrand BE, Svensson TH, Nomikos GG. Selective *c-fos* induction and decreased dopamine release in the central nucleus of amygdala in rats displaying a mecamylamine-precipitated nicotine withdrawal syndrome. *Synapse* 2000;35(1):15–25.

Panday S, Reddy SP, Ruiter RAC, Bergstrom E, DeVries H. Nicotine dependence and withdrawal symptoms among occasional smokers. *Journal of Adolescent Health* 2007;40(2):144–50.

Pandey SC, Roy A, Xu T, Mittal N. Effects of protracted nicotine exposure and withdrawal on the expression and phosphorylation of the CREB gene transcription factor in rat brain. *Journal of Neurochemistry* 2001; 77(3):943–52.

Paterson D, Norberg A. Neuronal nicotinic receptors in the human brain. *Progress in Neurobiology* 2000;61(1): 75–111.

Paterson NE, Bruijnzeel AW, Kenny PJ, Wright CD, Froestl W, Markou A. Prolonged nicotine exposure does not alter GABA$_B$ receptor-mediated regulation of brain reward function. *Neuropharmacology* 2005a;49(7): 953–62.

Paterson NE, Froestl W, Markou A. The GABA$_B$ receptor agonists baclofen and CGP44532 decreased nicotine self-administration in the rat. *Psychopharmacology* 2004;172(2):179–86.

Paterson NE, Froestl W, Markou A. Repeated administration of the GABA$_B$ receptor agonist CGP44532 decreased nicotine self-administration, and acute administration decreased cue-induced reinstatement of nicotine-seeking in rats. *Neuropsychopharmacology* 2005b;30(1):119–28.

Paterson NE, Markou A. Increased GABA neurotransmission via administration of gamma-vinyl GABA decreased nicotine self-administration in the rat. *Synapse* 2002;44(4):252–3.

Paterson NE, Markou A. The metabotropic glutamate receptor 5 antagonist MPEP decreased break points for nicotine, cocaine and food in rats. *Psychopharmacology* 2005;179(1):255–61.

Paterson NE, Markou A. Animal models and treatments for addiction and depression co-morbidity. *Neurotoxicity Research* 2007;11(1):1–32.

Paterson NE, Myers C, Markou A. Effects of repeated withdrawal from continuous amphetamine administration on brain reward function in rats. *Psychopharmacology* 2000;152(4):440–6.

Paterson NE, Semenova S, Gasparini F, Markou A. The mGluR5 antagonist MPEP decreased nicotine self-administration in rats and mice. *Psychopharmacology* 2003;167(3):257–64.

Patten CA, Martin JE. Does nicotine withdrawal affect smoking cessation: clinical and theoretical issues. *Annals of Behavioral Medicine* 1996;18(3):190–200.

Patton GC, Carlin JB, Coffey C, Wolfe R, Hibbert M, Bowes G. Depression, anxiety, and smoking initiation: a prospective study over 3 years. *American Journal of Public Health* 1998;88(10):1518–22.

Pergadia M, Spring B, Konopka LM, Twardowska B, Shirazi P, Crayton JW. Double-blind trial of the effects of tryptophan depletion on depression and cerebral blood flow in smokers. *Addictive Behaviors* 2004;29(4): 665–71.

Pergadia ML, Heath AC, Martin NG, Madden PAF. Genetic analyses of DSM-IV nicotine withdrawal in adult twins. *Psychological Medicine* 2006;36(7):963–72.

Perkins KA. Weight gain following smoking cessation. *Journal of Consulting and Clinical Psychology* 1993; 61(5):768–77.

Perkins KA. Smoking cessation in women. Special considerations. *CNS Drugs.* 2001;15(5):391–411.

Perkins KA. Chronic tolerance to nicotine in humans and its relationship to tobacco dependence. *Nicotine & Tobacco Research* 2002;4(4):405–22.

Perkins KA, Broge M, Gerlach D, Sanders M, Grobe JE, Cherry C, Wilson AS. Acute nicotine reinforcement, but not chronic tolerance, predicts withdrawal and relapse after quitting smoking. *Health Psychology* 2002a;21(4):332–9.

Perkins KA, Donny E, Caggiula AR. Sex differences in nicotine effects and self-administration: review of human and animal evidence. *Nicotine & Tobacco Research* 1999;1(4):301–15.

Perkins KA, Doyle T, Ciccocioppo M, Conklin C, Sayette M, Caggiula A. Sex differences in the influence of nicotine dose instructions on the reinforcing and self-reported rewarding effects of smoking. *Psychopharmacology* 2006;184(3–4):600–7.

Perkins KA, Epstein LH, Grobe J, Fonte C. Tobacco abstinence, smoking cues, and the reinforcing value of smoking. *Pharmacology, Biochemistry, and Behavior* 1994;47(1):107–12.

Perkins KA, Gerlach D, Broge M, Fonte C, Wilson A. Reinforcing effects of nicotine as a function of smoking status. *Experimental and Clinical Psychopharmacology*, 2001a;9(3):243–50.

Perkins KA, Gerlach D, Broge M, Grobe JE, Sanders M, Fonte C, Vender J, Cherry C, Wilson A. Dissociation of nicotine tolerance from tobacco dependence in humans. *Journal of Pharmacology and Experimental Therapeutics* 2001b;296(3):849–56.

Perkins KA, Gerlach D, Broge M, Sanders M, Grobe J, Fonte C, Cherry C, Wilson A, Jacob R. Quitting cigarette smoking produces minimal loss of chronic tolerance to nicotine. *Psychopharmacology* 2001c;158(1):7–17.

Perkins KA, Gerlach D, Vender J, Grobe J, Meeker J, Hutchison S. Sex differences in the subjective and reinforcing effects of visual and olfactory cigarette smoke stimuli. *Nicotine & Tobacco Research* 2001d; 3(2):141–50.

Perkins KA, Grobe JE, Caggiula A, Wilson AS, Stiller RL. Acute reinforcing effects of low-dose nicotine nasal spray in humans. *Pharmacology, Biochemistry, and Behavior* 1997;56(2):235–41.

Perkins KA, Grobe JE, D'Amico D, Fonte C, Wilson AS, Stiller RL. Low-dose nicotine nasal spray use and effects during initial smoking cessation. *Experimental and Clinical Psychopharmacology* 1996a;4(2):157–65.

Perkins KA, Grobe JE, Mitchell SL, Goettler J, Caggiula A, Stiller RL, Scierka A. Acute tolerance to nicotine in smokers: lack of dissipation within two hours. *Psychopharmacology* 1995;118(2):164–70.

Perkins KA, Grobe JE, Weiss D, Fonte C, Caggiula A. Nicotine preference in smokers as a function of smoking abstinence. *Pharmacology, Biochemistry, and Behavior* 1996b;55(2):257–63.

Perkins KA, Jacobs L, Sanders M, Caggiula AR. Sex differences in the subjective and reinforcing effects of cigarette nicotine dose. *Psychopharmacology* 2002b;163(2): 194–201.

Perkins KA, Levine M, Marcus M, Shiffman S, D'Amico D, Miller A, Keins A, Ashcom J, Broge M. Tobacco withdrawal in women and menstrual cycle phase. *Journal of Consulting and Clinical Psychology* 2000;68(1): 176–80.

Pianezza ML, Sellers EM, Tyndale RF. Nicotine metabolism defect reduces smoking [letter]. *Nature* 1998; 393(6687):750.

Piasecki TM. Relapse to smoking. *Clinical Psychology Review* 2006;26(2):196–215.

Piasecki TM, Fiore MC, Baker TB. Profiles in discouragement: two studies of variability in the time course of smoking withdrawal symptoms. *Journal of Abnormal Psychology* 1998;107(2):238–51.

Piasecki TM, Fiore MC, McCarthy DE, Baker TB. Have we lost our way: the need for dynamic formulations of smoking relapse proneness. *Addiction* 2002;97(9):1093–108.

Piasecki TM, Jorenby DE, Smith SS, Fiore MC, Baker TB. Smoking withdrawal dynamics. I: abstinence distress in lapsers and abstainers. *Journal of Abnormal Psychology* 2003a;112(1):3–13.

Piasecki TM, Jorenby DE, Smith SS, Fiore MC, Baker TB. Smoking withdrawal dynamics. II: improved tests of withdrawal–relapse relations. *Journal of Abnormal Psychology* 2003b;112(1):14–27.

Piasecki TM, Niaura R, Shadel WG, Abrams D, Goldstein M, Fiore MC, Baker TB. Smoking withdrawal dynamics in unaided quitters. *Journal of Abnormal Psychology* 2000;109(1):74–86.

Picciotto MR, Corrigall WA. Neuronal systems underlying behaviors related to nicotine addiction: neural circuits and molecular genetics. *Journal of Neuroscience* 2002;22(9):3338–41.

Picciotto MR, Zoli M, Léna C, Bessis A, Lallemand Y, LeNovère N, Vincent P, Pich EM, Brûlet P, Changeux J-P. Abnormal avoidance learning in mice lacking functional high-affinity nicotine receptor in the brain. *Nature* 1995;374(6517):65–7.

Picciotto MR, Zoli M, Rimondini R, Léna C, Marubio LM, Pich EM, Fuxe K, Changeux J-P. Acetylcholine receptors containing the β2 subunit are involved in the reinforcing properties of nicotine [letter]. *Nature* 1998;391(6663):173–7.

Pidoplichko VI, DeBiasi M, Williams JT, Dani JA. Nicotine activates and desensitizes midbrain dopamine neurons [letter]. *Nature* 1997;390(6658):401–4.

Pinto RP, Abrams DB, Monti PM, Jacobus SI. Nicotine dependence and likelihood of quitting smoking. *Addictive Behaviors* 1987;12(4):371–4.

Piper ME, Bolt DM, Kim S-Y, Japuntich SJ, Smith SS, Niederdeppe J, Cannon DS, Baker TB. Refining the tobacco dependence phenotype using the Wisconsin Inventory of Smoking Dependence Motives. *Journal of Abnormal Psychology* 2008;117(4):747–61.

Piper ME, McCarthy DE, Baker TB. Assessing tobacco dependence: a guide to measure evaluation and selection. *Nicotine and Tobacco Research* 2006;8(3):339–51.

Piper ME, Piasecki TM, Federman EB, Bolt DM, Smith SS, Fiore MC, Baker TB. A multiple motives approach to tobacco dependence: the Wisconsin Inventory of Smoking Dependence Motives (WISDM-68). *Journal of Consulting and Clinical Psychology* 2004;72(2):139–54.

Pitha J, Hubacek JA, Skodova Z, Poledne R. Is the CD14 receptor gene a marker for smoking dependence? *Medical Science Monitor* 2002;8(5):BR172–BR174.

Pluzarev O, Pandey SC. Modulation of CREB expression and phosphorylation in the rat nucleus accumbens during nicotine exposure and withdrawal. *Journal of Neuroscience Research* 2004;77(6):884–91.

Pomerleau OF. Individual differences in sensitivity to nicotine: implications for genetic research on nicotine dependence. *Behavior Genetics* 1995;25(2):161–77.

Pomerleau CS, Carton SM, Lutzke ML, Flessland KA, Pomerleau OF. Reliability of the Fagerström Tolerance Questionnaire and the Fagerström Test for Nicotine Dependence. *Addictive Behaviors* 1994;19(1):33–9.

Pomerleau CS, Pomerleau OF, Majchrazak MJ, Kloska DD, Mulakati R. Relationship between nicotine tolerance questionnaire scores and plasma cotinine. *Addictive Behaviors* 1990;15(1):73–80.

Pomerleau O, Adkins D, Pertschuk M. Predictors of outcome and recidivism in smoking cessation treatment. *Addictive Behaviors* 1978;3(2):65–70.

Pomerleau OF, Pomerleau CS, Mehringer AM, Snedecor SM, Ninowski R, Sen A. Nicotine dependence, depression, and gender: characterizing phenotypes based on withdrawal discomfort, response to smoking, and ability to abstain. *Nicotine & Tobacco Research* 2005; 7(1):91–102.

Pomerleau OF, Pomerleau CS, Snedecor SM, Gaulrapp S, Brouwer RN, Cameron OG. Depression, smoking abstinence and HPA function in women smokers. *Human Psychopharmacology* 2004;19(7):467–76.

Pontieri FE, Tanda G, Orzi F, Di Chiara G. Effects of nicotine on the nucleus accumbens and similarity to those of addictive drugs [letter]. *Nature* 1996;382(6588): 255–7.

Poolsup N, Li Wan Po A, Knight TL. Pharmacogenetics and psychopharmacotherapy. *Journal of Clinical Pharmacy and Therapeutics* 2000;25(3):197–220.

Prokhorov AV, De Moor C, Pallonen UE, Hudmon KS, Koehly L, Hu S. Validation of the modified Fagerström Tolerance Questionnaire with salivary cotinine among adolescents. *Addictive Behaviors* 2000;25(3):429–33.

Prokhorov AV, Hudmon KS, Cinciripini PM, Marani S. "Withdrawal symptoms" in adolescents: a comparison of former smokers and never-smokers. *Nicotine & Tobacco Research* 2005;7(6):909–13.

Prokhorov AV, Pallonen UE, Fava JL, Ding L, Niaura R. Measuring nicotine dependence among high-risk adolescent smokers. *Addictive Behaviors* 1996;21(1): 117–27.

Qi J, Tan W, Xing D, Miao X, Lin D. Study on the association between smoking behavior and dopamine receptor D2 gene polymorphisms among lung cancer cases. *Zhonghua Liu Xing Bing Xue Za Zhi* 2002;23(5):370–3.

Radzius A, Gallo JJ, Gorelick DA, Cadet JL, Uhl G, Henningfield JE, Moolchan ET. Nicotine dependence criteria of the DIS and *DSM-III-R*: a factor analysis. *Nicotine & Tobacco Research* 2004;6(2):303–8.

Rahman S, Zhang J, Engleman EA, Corrigall WA. Neuroadaptive changes in the mesoaccumbens dopamine system after chronic nicotine self-administration: a microdialysis study. *Neuroscience* 2004;129(2):415–24.

Ramos EJB, Meguid MM, Zhang L, Miyata G, Fetissov SO, Chen C, Suzuki S, Laviano A. Nicotine infusion into rat ventromedial nuclei and effects on monoaminergic system. *Neuroreport* 2004;15(14):2293–7.

Rao TS, Correa LD, Adams P, Santori EM, Sacaan AI. Pharmacological characterization of dopamine, norepinephrine and serotonin release in the rat prefrontal cortex by neuronal nicotinic acetylcholine receptor agonists. *Brain Research* 2003;990(1–2):203–8.

Rao Y, Hoffmann E, Zia M, Bodin L, Zeman M, Sellers EM, Tyndale RF. Duplications and defects in the *CYP2A6* gene: identification, genotyping, and in vivo effects on smoking. *Molecular Pharmacology* 2000;58(4):747–55.

Rasmussen K, Calligaro DO, Czachura JF, Dreshfield-Ahmad LJ, Evans DC, Hemrick-Luecke SK, Kallman MJ, Kendrick WT, Leander JD, Nelson DL, et al. The novel 5-hydroxytryptamine$_{1A}$ antagonist LY426965: effects on nicotine withdrawal and interactions with fluoxetine. *Journal of Pharmacology and Experimental Therapeutics* 2000;294(2):688–700.

Rasmussen K, Czachura JF. Nicotine withdrawal leads to increased sensitivity of serotonergic neurons to the 5-HT$_{1A}$ agonist 8-OH-DPAT. *Psychopharmacology* 1997; 133(4):343–6.

Rasmussen K, Kallman MJ, Helton DR. Serotonin-1A antagonists attenuate the effects of nicotine withdrawal on the auditory startle response. *Synapse* 1997; 27(2):145–52.

Rauhut AS, Mullins SN, Dwoskin LP, Bardo MT. Reboxetine: attenuation of intravenous nicotine self-administration in rats. *Journal of Pharmacology and Experimental Therapeutics* 2002;303(2):664–72.

Ray R, Jepson C, Patterson F, Strasser A, Rukstalis M, Perkins K, Lynch KG, O'Malley S, Berrettini WH, Lerman C, et al. Association of *OPRM1* A118G variant with the relative reinforcing value of nicotine. *Psychopharmacology* 2006;188(3):355–63.

Razavi D, Vandecasteele H, Primo C, Bodo M, Debrier F, Verbist H, Pethica D, Eerdekens M, Kaufman L. Maintaining abstinence from cigarette smoking: effectiveness of group counselling and factors predicting outcome. *European Journal of Cancer* 1999;35(8):1238–47.

Reid MS, Fox L, Ho LB, Berger SP. Nicotine stimulation of extracellular glutamate levels in the nucleus accumbens: neuropharmacological characterization. *Synapse* 2000;35(2):129–36.

Rende R, Slomkowski C, McCaffery J, Lloyd-Richardson EE, Niaura R. A twin-sibling study of tobacco use in adolescence: etiology of individual differences and extreme scores. *Nicotine & Tobacco Research* 2005;7(3):413–9.

Reuter M, Hennig J. Pleiotropic effect of the TPH A779C polymorphism on nicotine dependence and personality. *American Journal of Medical Genetics Part B, Neuropsychiatric Genetics* 2005;134(1):20–4.

Rhee SH, Hewitt JK, Young SE, Corley RP, Crowley TJ, Stallings MC. Genetic and environmental influences on substance initiation, use, and problem use in adolescents. *Archives of General Psychiatry* 2003;60(12): 1256–64.

Ribeiro EB, Bettiker RL, Bogdanov M, Wurtman RJ. Effects of systemic nicotine on serotonin release in rat brain. *Brain Research* 1993;621(2):311–8.

Richter KP, Ahluwalia HK, Mosier MC, Nazir N, Ahluwalia JS. A population-based study of cigarette smoking among illicit drug users in the United States. *Addiction* 2002;97(7):861–9.

Ridley DL, Balfour DJK. The influence of nicotine on 5-HT overflow in the dorsal hippocampus of the rat. *British Journal of Pharmacology* 1997;112(Suppl):301P.

Risner ME, Goldberg SR, Prada JA, Cone EJ. Effects of nicotine, cocaine and some of their metabolites on schedule-controlled responding by beagle dogs and squirrel monkeys. *Journal of Pharmacology and Experimental Therapeutics* 1985;234(1):113–9.

Robins LN, Cottler LB, Babor T. The WHO/ADAMHA Composite International Diagnostic Interview-Substance Abuse Module (SAM). In: *The WHO/ADAMHA Composite International Diagnostic Interview-Substance Abuse Module* (SAM). St. Louis: Department of Psychiatry, Washington University School of Medicine, 1990.

Robinson TE, Berridge KC. The neural basis of drug craving: an incentive-sensitization theory of addiction. *Brain Research Brain Research Reviews* 1993;18(3):247–91.

Robinson TE, Berridge KC. Incentive-sensitization and addiction. *Addiction* 2001;96(1):103–14.

Rohde P, Kahler CW, Lewinsohn PM, Brown RA. Psychiatric disorders, familial factors, and cigarette smoking. II: associations with progression to daily smoking. *Nicotine & Tobacco Research* 2004;6(1):119–32.

Rojas NL, Killen JD, Haydel KF, Robinson TN. Nicotine dependence among adolescent smokers. *Archives of Pediatric & Adolescent Medicine* 1998;152(2):151–6.

Role LW, Berg DK. Nicotinic receptors in the development and modulation of CNS synapses. *Neuron* 1996;16(6):1077–85.

Roll JM, Higgins ST, Tidey J. Cocaine use can increase cigarette smoking: evidence from laboratory and naturalistic settings. *Experimental and Clinical Psychopharmacology* 1997;5(3):263–8.

Romans SE, McNoe BM, Herbison GP, Walton VA, Mullen PE. Cigarette smoking and psychiatric morbidity in women. *Australian and New Zealand Journal of Psychiatry* 1993;27(3):399–404.

Rose JE. Nicotine and nonnicotine factors in cigarette addiction. *Psychopharmacology* 2006;184(3–4):274–85.

Rose JE, Behm FM. Extinguishing the rewarding value of smoke cues: pharmacological and behavioral treatments. *Nicotine & Tobacco Research* 2004;6(3):523–32

Rose JE, Behm FM, Levin ED. Role of nicotine dose and sensory cues in the regulation of smoke intake. *Pharmacology, Biochemistry, and Behavior* 1993;44(4):891–900.

Rose JE, Behm FM, Ramsey C, Ritchie JC Jr. Platelet monoamine oxidase, smoking cessation, and tobacco withdrawal symptoms. *Nicotine & Tobacco Research* 2001a;3(4):383–90.

Rose JE, Behm FM, Westman EC. Acute effects of nicotine and mecamylamine on tobacco withdrawal symptoms, cigarette reward, and ad lib smoking. *Pharmacology, Biochemistry, and Behavior* 2001b;68(2):187–97.

Rose JE, Behm FM, Westman EC, Bates JE. Mecamylamine acutely increases human intravenous nicotine self-administration. *Pharmacology, Biochemistry, and Behavior* 2003a;76(2):307–13.

Rose JE, Behm FM, Westman EC, Coleman RE. Arterial nicotine kinetics during cigarette smoking and intravenous nicotine administration: implications for addiction. *Drug and Alcohol Dependence* 1999;56(2):99–107.

Rose JE, Behm FM, Westman EC, Mathew RJ, London ED, Hawk TC, Turkington TG, Coleman RE. PET studies of the influences of nicotine on neural systems in cigarette smokers. *American Journal of Psychiatry* 2003b;160(2):323–33.

Rose JE, Corrigall WA. Nicotine self-administration in animals and humans: similarities and differences. *Psychopharmacology* 1997;130(1):28–40.

Rosecrans JA, Chance WT. Cholinergic and non-cholinergic aspects of the discriminative stimulus properties of nicotine. In: Lal H, editor. *Discriminative Stimulus Properties of Drugs*. New York: Plenum Press, 1977:155–85.

Rossetti ZL, Hmaidan Y, Gessa GL. Marked inhibition of mesolimbic dopamine release: a common feature of ethanol, morphine, cocaine, and amphetamine abstinence in rats. *European Journal of Pharmacology* 1992;221(2–3):227–34.

Royal College of Physicians of London. *Nicotine Addiction in Britain: A Report of the Tobacco Advisory Group of the Royal College of Physicians*. London: Royal College of Physicians of London, 2000.

Royce JM, Hymowitz N, Corbett K, Hartwell TD, Orlandi MA. Smoking cessation among African Americans and whites. COMMIT Research Group. *American Journal of Public Health* 1993;83(2):220–6.

Rukstalis M, Jepson C, Strasser A, Lynch KG, Perkins K, Patterson F, Lerman C. Naltrexone reduces the relative reinforcing value of nicotine in a cigarette smoking choice paradigm. *Psychopharmacology* 2005;180(1):41–8.

Rush CR, Higgins ST, Vansickel AR, Stoops WW, Lile JA, Glaser PEA. Methylphenidate increases cigarette smoking. *Psychopharmacology* 2005;181(4):781–9.

Saarikoski ST, Sata F, Husgafvel-Pursiainen K, Rautalahti M, Haukka J, Impivaara O, Järvisalo J, Vainio H, Hirvonen A. CYP2D6 ultrarapid metabolizer genotype as a potential modifier of smoking behaviour. *Pharmacogenetics* 2000;10(1):5–10.

Sabol SZ, Nelson ML, Fisher C, Gunzerath L, Brody CL, Hu S, Sirota LA, Marcus SE, Greenberg BD, Lucas FR, et al. A genetic association for cigarette smoking behavior. *Health Psychology* 1999;18(1):7–13.

Saccone NL, Neuman RJ, Saccone SF, Rice JP. Genetic analysis of maximum cigarette-use phenotypes. *BMC Genetics* 2003;4(Suppl 1):S105.

Saccone NL, Saccone SF, Hinrichs AL, Stitzel JA, Duan W, Pergadia ML, Agrawal A, Breslau N, Grucza RA, Hatsukami D, et al. Multiple distinct risk loci for nicotine dependence identified by dense coverage of the complete family of nicotinic receptor subunit [*CHRN*] genes. *American Journal of Medical Genetics Part B, Neuropsychiatric Genetics* 2009;150B(4):453–66.

Saccone SF, Hinrichs AL, Saccone NL, Chase GA, Konvicka K, Madden PA, Breslau N, Johnson EO, Hatsukami D, Pomerleau O, et al. Cholinergic nicotinic receptor genes implicated in a nicotine dependence association study targeting 348 candidate genes with 3713 SNPs. *Human Molecular Genetics* 2007;16(1):36–49.

Salas R, Pieri F, De Biasi M. Decreased signs of nicotine withdrawal in mice null for the β4 nicotinic acetylcholine receptor subunit. *Journal of Neuroscience* 2004;24(45):10035–9.

Samaha AN, Yau WYW, Yang P, Robinson TE. Rapid delivery of nicotine promotes behavioral sensitization and alters its neurobiological impact. *Biological Psychiatry* 2005;57(4):351–60.

Sanderson SC, Humphries SE, Hubbart C, Hughes E, Jarvis MJ, Wardle J. Psychological and behavioural impact of genetic testing smokers for lung cancer risk: a phase II exploratory trial. *Journal of Health Psychology* 2008;13(4):481–94.

Sargent PB. The diversity of neuronal nicotinic acetylcholine receptors. *Annual Review of Neuroscience* 1993;16:403–43.

Sayette MA, Hufford MR. Effects of cue exposure and deprivation on cognitive resources in smokers. *Journal of Abnormal Psychology* 1994;103(4):812–8.

Scherer G. Smoking behaviour and compensation: a review of the literature. *Psychopharmacology* 1999; 145(1):1–20.

Schiffer WK, Gerasimov MR, Marsteller DA, Geiger J, Barnett C, Alexoff DL, Dewey SL. Topiramate selectively attenuates nicotine-induced increases in monoamine release. *Synapse* 2001;42(3):196–8.

Schilström B, Nomikos GG, Nisell M, Hertel P, Svensson TH. N-methyl-D-aspartate receptor antagonism in the ventral tegmental area diminishes the systemic nicotine-induced dopamine release in the nucleus accumbens. *Neuroscience* 1998a;82(3):781–9.

Schilström B, Svensson HM, Svensson TH, Nomikos GG. Nicotine and food induced dopamine release in the nucleus accumbens of the rat: putative role of α7 nicotinic receptors in the ventral tegmental area. *Neuroscience* 1998b;85(4):1005–9.

Schmitz N, Kruse J, Kugler J. Disabilities, quality of life, and mental disorders associated with smoking and nicotine dependence. *American Journal of Psychiatry* 2003;160(9):1670–6.

Schneider NG, Olmstead RE, Steinberg C, Sloan K, Daims RM, Brown HV. Efficacy of buspirone in smoking cessation: a placebo-controlled trial. *Clinical Pharmacology and Therapeutics* 1996;60(5):568–75.

Schochet TL, Kelley AE, Landry CF. Differential expression of *arc* mRNA and other plasticity-related genes induced by nicotine in adolescent rat forebrain. *Neuroscience* 2005;135(1):285–97

Schoedel KA, Hoffmann EB, Rao Y, Sellers EM, Tyndale RF. Ethnic variation in *CYP2A6* and association of genetically slow nicotine metabolism and smoking in adult Caucasians. *Pharmacogenetics* 2004;14(9):615–26.

Schroeder SA. How to mainstream behavioral health into national health policy. PowerPoint presentation at the NASMHPD Summer 2009 Commissioners Meeting; July 19, 2009; St. Louis.

Schuckit MA, Daeppen J-B, Danko GP, Tripp ML, Smith TL, Li T-K, Hesselbrock VM, Bucholz KK. Clinical implications for four drugs of the DSM-IV distinction between substance dependence with and without a physiological component. *American Journal of Psychiatry* 1999;156(1):41–9.

Schulman H, Hanson PI. Multifunctional Ca^{2+}/calmodulin-dependent protein kinase. *Neurochemistry Research* 1993;18(1):65–77.

Schulteis G, Markou A, Cole M, Koob GF. Decreased brain reward produced by ethanol withdrawal. *Proceedings of the National Academy of Sciences of the United States of America* 1995;92(13):5880–4.

Schulteis G, Markou A, Gold LH, Stinus L, Koob GF. Relative sensitivity to naloxone of multiple indices of opiate withdrawal: a quantitative dose-response analysis. *Journal of Pharmacology and Experimental Therapeutics* 1994;271(3):1391–8.

Schulz DW, Loring RH, Aizenman E, Zigmond RE. Autoradiographic localization of putative nicotinic receptors in the rat brain using ^{125}I-neuronal bungarotoxin. *Journal of Neuroscience* 1991;11(1):287–97.

Schulz TG, Ruhnau P, Hallier E. Lack of correlation between CYP2A6 genotype and smoking habits. *Advances in Experimental Medicine and Biology* 2001; 500:213–5.

Sebat J, Lakshmi B, Malhotra D, Troge J, Lese-Martin C, Walsh T, Yamrom B, Yoon S, Krasnitz A, Kendall J, et al. Strong association of de novo copy number mutations with autism. *Science* 2007;316(5823):445–9.

Semenova S, Bespalov A, Markou A. Decreased prepulse inhibition during nicotine withdrawal in DBA/2J mice is reversed by nicotine self-administration. *European Journal of Pharmacology* 2003;472(1–2):99–110.

Semenova S, Markou A. Clozapine treatment attenuated somatic and affective signs of nicotine and amphetamine withdrawal in subsets of rats exhibited hyposensitivity to the initial effects of clozapine. *Biological Psychiatry* 2003;54(11):1249–64.

Sershen H, Balla A, Lajtha A, Vizi ES. Characterization of nicotinic receptors involved in the release of noradrenaline from the hippocampus. *Neuroscience* 1997; 77(1):121–30.

Shadel WG, Mermelstein RJ. Cigarette smoking under stress: the role of coping expectancies among smokers in a clinic-based smoking cessation program. *Health Psychology* 1993;12(6):443–50.

Shahan TA, Bickel WK, Madden GJ, Badger GJ. Comparing the reinforcing efficacy of nicotine containing and de-nicotinized cigarettes: a behavioral economic analysis. *Psychopharmacology* 1999;147(2):210–6.

Sharples CGV, Kaiser S, Soliakov L, Marks MJ, Collins AC, Washburn M, Wright E, Spencer JA, Gallagher T, Whiteaker P, et al. UB-165: a novel nicotinic agonist with subtype selectivity implicates the α4β2 subtype in the modulation of dopamine release from rat striatal synaptosomes. *Journal of Neuroscience* 2000;20(8):2783–91.

Sheffield EB, Quick MW, Lester RAJ. Nicotinic acetylcholine receptor subunit mRNA expression and channel function in medial habenula neurons. *Neuropharmacology* 2000;39(13):2591–603.

Sherva R, Wilhelmsen K, Pomerleau CS, Chasse SA, Rice JP, Snedecor SM, Bierut LJ, Neuman RJ, Pomerleau OF. Association of a single nucleotide polymorphism in neuronal acetylcholine receptor subunit alpha 5 (CHRNA5) with smoking status and with 'pleasurable buzz' during early experimentation with smoking. *Addiction* 2008;103(9):1544–52.

Shields AE, Lerman C, Sullivan PF. Translating emerging research on the genetics of smoking into clinical practice: ethical and social considerations. *Nicotine & Tobacco Research* 2004;6(4):675–88.

Shields PG, Lerman C, Audrain J, Bowman ED, Main D, Boyd NR, Caporaso NE. Dopamine D4 receptors and the risk of cigarette smoking in African-Americans and Caucasians. *Cancer Epidemiology, Biomarkers & Prevention* 1998;7(6):453–8.

Shiffman S. Relapse following smoking cessation: a situational analysis. *Journal of Consulting and Clinical Psychology* 1982;50(1):71–86.

Shiffman S. Conceptual issues in the study of relapse. In: Gossop M, editor. *Relapse and Addictive Behaviour*. New York: Tavistock/Routledge, 1989a:149–79.

Shiffman S. Tobacco "chippers"–individual differences in tobacco dependence. *Psychopharmacology* 1989b; 97(4):539–47.

Shiffman S, Balabanis MH, Paty JA, Engberg J, Gwaltney CJ, Liu KS, Gnys M, Hickcox M, Paton SM. Dynamic effects of self-efficacy on smoking lapse and relapse. *Health Psychology* 2000;19(4):315–23.

Shiffman S, Engberg JB, Paty JA, Perz WG, Gnys M, Kassel JD, Hickox M. A day at a time: predicting smoking lapse from daily urge. *Journal of Abnormal Psychology* 1997;106(1):104–16.

Shiffman S, Gnys M, Richards TJ, Paty JA, Hickcox M, Kassel JD. Temptations to smoke after quitting: a comparison of lapsers and maintainers. *Health Psychology* 1996a;15(6):455–61.

Shiffman S, Hickcox M, Paty JA, Gnys M, Kassel JD, Richards TJ. Progression from a smoking lapse to relapse: prediction from abstinence violation effects, nicotine dependence, and lapse characteristics. *Journal of Consulting and Clinical Psychology* 1996b;64(5):933–1002.

Shiffman S, Paton SM. Individual differences in smoking: gender and nicotine addiction. *Nicotine & Tobacco Research* 1999;1(Suppl 2):S153–S137.

Shiffman S, Paty J. Smoking patterns and dependence: contrasting chippers and heavy smokers. *Journal of Abnormal Psychology* 2006;115(3):509–23.

Shiffman S, Paty JA, Gnys M, Kassel JA, Hickcox M. First lapses to smoking: within-subjects analysis of real-time reports. *Journal of Consulting and Clinical Psychology* 1996c;64(2):366–79.

Shiffman S, Sayette MA. Validation of the nicotine dependence syndrome scale (NDSS): a criterion-group design contrasting chippers and regular smokers. *Drug and Alcohol Dependence* 2005;79(1):45–52.

Shiffman S, Scharf DM, Shadel WG, Gwaltney CJ, Dang Q, Paton SM, Clark DB. Analyzing milestones in smoking cessation: illustration in a nicotine patch trial in adult smokers. *Journal of Consulting and Clinical Psychology* 2006;74(2):276-85.

Shiffman S, Shadel WG, Niaura R, Khayrallah MA, Jorenby DE, Ryan CF, Ferguson CL. Efficacy of acute administration of nicotine gum in relief of cue-provoked cigarette craving. *Psychopharmacology* 2003;166(4): 343–50.

Shiffman S, Shumaker SA, Abrams DB, Cohen S, Garvey A, Grunberg NE, Swan GE. Models of smoking relapse. *Health Psychology* 1986;5(Suppl):13–27.

Shiffman S, Waters AJ. Negative affect and smoking lapses: a prospective analysis. *Journal of Consulting and Clinical Psychology* 2004;72(2):192–201.

Shiffman S, Waters AJ, Hickcox M. The Nicotine Dependence Syndrome Scale: a multidimensional measure of nicotine dependence. *Nicotine & Tobacco Research* 2004a;6(2):327–48.

Shiffman S, West RJ, Gilbert DG, SRNT Work Group. Recommendation for the assessment of tobacco craving and withdrawal in smoking cessation trials. *Nicotine & Tobacco Research* 2004b;6(4):599–614.

Shiffman S, Zettler-Segal M, Kassel J, Paty J, Benowitz NL, O'Brien G. Nicotine elimination and tolerance in nondependent cigarette smokers. *Psychopharmacology* 1992;109(4):449–56.

Shoaib M, Benwell MEM, Akbar MT, Stolerman IP, Balfour DJK. Behavioural and neurochemical adaptations to nicotine in rats: influence of NMDA antagonists. *British Journal of Pharmacology* 1994;111(4):1073–80.

Shoaib M, Sidhpura N, Shafait S. Investigating the actions of bupropion on dependence-related effects of nicotine in rats. *Psychopharmacology* 2003;165(4):405–12.

Shoaib M, Stolerman IP. MK801 attenuates behavioural adaptation to chronic nicotine administration in rats. *British Journal of Pharmacology* 1992;105(3):514–5.

Shoaib M, Swanner LS, Beyer CE, Goldberg SR, Schindler CW. The GABA$_B$ agonist baclofen modifies cocaine self-administration in rats. *Behavioural Pharmacology* 1998;9(3):195–206.

Silagy C, Lancaster T, Stead L, Mant D, Fowler G. Nicotine replacement therapy for smoking cessation. *Cochrane Database of Systematic Reviews* 2004, Issue 3. Art. No.: CD000146. DOI: 10.1002/14651858.CD000146.pub2.

Silagy C, Mant D, Fowler G, Lodge M. The effectiveness of nicotine replacement therapies in smoking cessation. *Online Journal of Current Clinical Trials* 1994; Doc. No. 113.

Silverman MA, Neale MC, Sullivan PF, Harris-Kerr C, Wormley B, Sadek H, Ma Y, Kendler KS, Straub RE. Haplotypes of four novel single nucleotide polymorphisms in the nicotinic acetylcholine receptor β2-subunit (CHRNB2) gene show no association with smoking initiation or nicotine dependence. *American Journal of Medical Genetics Part B, Neuropsychiatric Genetics* 2000;96(5):646–53.

Singer S, Rossi S, Verzosa S, Hashim A, Lonow R, Cooper T, Sershen H, Lajtha A. Nicotine-induced changes in neurotransmitter levels in brain areas associated with cognitive function. *Neurochemical Research* 2004; 29(9):1779–92.

Singleton AB, Thomson JH, Morris CM, Court JA, Lloyd S, Cholerton S. Lack of association between the dopamine D2 receptor gene allele *DRD2*A1* and cigarette smoking in a United Kingdom population. *Pharmacogenetics* 1998;8(2):125–8.

Skjei KL, Markou A. Effects of repeated withdrawal episodes, nicotine dose, and duration of nicotine exposure on the severity and duration of nicotine withdrawal in rats. *Psychopharmacology* 2003;168(3):280–92.

Slade J, Bero LA, Hanauer P, Barnes DE, Glantz SA. Nicotine and addiction: the Brown & Williamson documents. *JAMA: the Journal of the American Medical Association* 1995;274(3):225–33.

Slotkin TA. Nicotine and the adolescent brain: insights from an animal model. *Neurotoxicology and Teratology* 2002;24(3):369–84.

Smith SS, Jorenby DE, Leischow SJ, Nides MA, Rennard SI, Johnston JA, Jamerson B, Fiore MC, Baker TB. Targeting smokers at increased risk for relapse: treating women and those with a history of depression. *Nicotine & Tobacco Research* 2003;5(1):99–109.

Smits KM, Benhamou S, Garte S, Weijenberg MP, Alamanos Y, Ambrosone C, Autrup H, Autrup JL, Baranova H, Bathum L, et al. Association of metabolic gene polymorphisms with tobacco consumption in healthy controls. *International Journal of Cancer* 2004;110(2):266–70.

Snyder SH. Dopamine and schizophrenia. *Psychiatric Annals* 1976;6(1):53–65.

Soldz S, Cui X. Pathways through adolescent smoking: a 7-year longitudinal grouping analysis. *Health Psychology* 2002;21(5):495–504.

Solomon LJ, Higgins ST, Heil SH, Badger GJ, Thomas CS, Bernstein IM. Predictors of postpartum relapse to smoking. *Drug and Alcohol Dependence* 2007; 90(2–3):224–7.

Spielewoy C, Markou A. Withdrawal from chronic phencyclidine treatment induces long-lasting depression in brain reward function. *Neuropsychopharmacology* 2003;28(6):1106–16.

Spitz MR, Shi H, Yang F, Hudmon KS, Jiang H, Chamberlain RM, Amos CI, Wan Y, Cinciripini P, Hong WK, et al. Case–control study of the D2 dopamine receptor gene and smoking status in lung cancer patients. *Journal of the National Cancer Institute* 1998;90(5):358–63.

Stapleton JM, Gilson SF, Wong DF, Villemagne VL, Dannals RF, Grayson RF, Henningield JE, London ED. Intravenous nicotine reduces cerebral glucose metabolism: a preliminary study. *Neuropsychopharmacology* 2003;28(4):765–72.

Stevens VL, Bierut LJ, Talbot JT, Wang JC, Sun J, Hinrichs AL, Thun MJ, Goate A, Calle EE. Nicotinic receptor gene variants influence susceptibility to heavy smoking. *Cancer Epidemiology, Biomarkers & Prevention* 2008;17(12):3517–25.

Stewart J, de Wit H, Eikelboom R. Role of unconditioned and conditioned drug effects in the self-administration of opiates and stimulants. *Psychological Review* 1984;91(2):251–68.

Stitzel JA, Lu Y, Jimenez M, Tritto T, Collins AC. Genetic and pharmacological strategies identify a behavioral function of neuronal nicotinic receptors. *Behavioural Brain Research* 2000;113(1–2):57–64.

Stitzer ML, de Wit H. Abuse liability of nicotine. In: Benowitz NL, editor. *Nicotine Safety and Toxicity*. New York: Oxford University Press, 1998:119–31.

Stolerman IP, Jarvis MJ. The scientific case that nicotine is addictive. *Psychopharmacology* 1995;117(1):2–10.

Storr CL, Zhou H, Liang K-Y, Anthony JC. Empirically derived latent classes of tobacco dependence syndromes observed in recent-onset tobacco smokers: epidemiological evidence from a national probability sample survey. *Nicotine & Tobacco Research* 2004;6(3):533–45.

Stotts AL, DiClemente CC, Carbonari JP, Mullen PD. Postpartum return to smoking: staging a "suspended" behavior. *Health Psychology* 2000;19(4):324–32.

Stratton K, Shetty P, Wallace R, Bonderant S, editors. *Clearing the Smoke: Assessing the Science Base for Tobacco Harm Reduction*. Washington: National Academy Press, 2001.

Straub RE, Sullivan PF, Ma Y, Myakishev MV, Harris-Kerr C, Wormley B, Kadambi B, Sadek H, Silverman MA, Webb BT, et al. Susceptibility genes for nicotine dependence: a genome scan and followup in an independent sample suggest that regions on chromosomes 2, 4, 10, 16, 17 and 18 merit further study. *Molecular Psychiatry* 1999;4(2):129–44.

Substance Abuse and Mental Health Services Administration. *Results from the 2003 National Survey on Drug Use and Health: National Findings*. NSDUH Series H-25. Rockville (MD): U.S. Department of Health and Human Services, Substance Abuse and Mental Health Services Administration, Office of Applied Studies, 2004. DHHS Publication No. SMA 04-3964.

Sugita S, Johnson SW, North RA. Synaptic inputs to $GABA_A$ and $GABA_B$ receptors originate from discrete afferent neurons. *Neuroscience Letters* 1992;134(2):207–11.

Sullivan PF, Kendler KS. The genetic epidemiology of smoking. *Nicotine & Tobacco Research* 1999;1(Suppl 2):S51–S57.

Sullivan PF, Neale BM, van den Oord E, Miles MF, Neale MC, Bulik CM, Joyce PR, Straub RE, Kendler KS. Candidate genes for nicotine dependence via linkage, epistasis, and bioinformatics. *American Journal of Medical Genetics Part B, Neuropsychiatric Genetics* 2004;126(1):23–36.

Sullivan PF, Neale MC, Silverman MA, Harris-Kerr C, Myakishev MV, Wormley B, Webb BT, Ma Y, Kendler KS, Straub RE. An association study of DRD5 with smoking initiation and progression to nicotine dependence. *American Journal of Medical Genetics* 2001;105(3):259–65.

Summers KL, Giacobini E. Effects of local and repeated systemic administration of (–)nicotine on extracellular levels of acetylcholine, norepinephrine, dopamine, and serotonin in rat cortex. *Neurochemical Research* 1995;20(6):753–9.

Swan GE, Denk CE, Parker SD, Carmelli D, Furze CT, Rosenman RH. Risk factors for late relapse in male and female ex-smokers. *Addictive Behaviors* 1988; 13(3):253–66.

Swan GE, Hops H, Wilhelmsen KC, Lessov-Schlaggar CN, Cheng LS, Hudmon KS, Amos CI, Feiler HS, Ring HZ, Andrews JA, Tildesley E, Benowitz N. A genome-wide screen for nicotine dependence susceptibility loci. *American Journal of Medical Genetics Part B, Neuropsychiatric Genetics* 2006;141(4):354–60.

Swan GE, Jack LM, Niaura R, Borrelli B, Spring B. Subgroups of smokers with different success rates after treatment with fluoxetine for smoking cessation [abstract]. *Nicotine & Tobacco Research* 1999;1(3):281.

Swan GE, Jack LM, Ward MM. Subgroups of smokers with different success rates after use of transdermal nicotine. *Addiction* 1997;92(2):207–17.

Swan GE, Javitz HS, Jack LM, Curry SJ, McAfee T. Heterogeneity in 12-month outcome among female and male smokers. *Addiction* 2004;99(2):237–50.

Swan GE, Valdes AM, Ring HZ, Khroyan TV, Jack LM, Ton CC, Curry SJ, McAfee T. Dopamine receptor *DRD2* genotype and smoking cessation outcome following treatment with bupropion SR. *Pharmacogenomics Journal* 2005;5(1):21–9.

Swan GE, Ward MM, Jack LM. Abstinence effects as predictors of 28-day relapse in smokers. *Addictive Behaviors* 1996;21(4):481–90.

Swedberg MDB, Henningfield JE, Goldberg SR. Nicotine dependency: animal studies. In: Wonnacott S, Russell MAH, Stolerman IP, editors. *Nicotine Psychopharmacology: Molecular, Cellular and Behavioural Aspects*. New York: Oxford University Press, 1990:38–76.

Takada K, Swedberg MD, Goldberg SR, Katz JL. Discriminative stimulus effects of intravenous *l*-nicotine and nicotine analogs or metabolites in squirrel monkeys. *Psychopharmacology* 1989;99(2):208–12.

Takada Y, Urano T, Ihara H, Takada A. Changes in the central and peripheral serotonergic system in rats exposed to water-immersion restrained stress and nicotine administration. *Neuroscience Research* 1995;23(3):305–11.

Takimoto T, Terayama H, Waga C, Okayama T, Ikeda K, Fukunishi I, Iwahashi K. Cholecystokinin (CCK) and the CCKA receptor gene polymorphism, and smoking behavior. *Psychiatry Research* 2005;133(2–3):123–8.

Tan W, Chen G-F, Xing D-Y, Song C-Y, Kadlubar FF, Lin D-X. Frequency of *CYP2A6* gene deletion and its relation to risk of lung and esophageal cancer in the Chinese population. *International Journal of Cancer* 2001;95(2):96–101.

Tapper AR, McKinney SL, Nashmi R, Schwarz J, Deshpande P, Labarca C, Whiteaker P, Marks MJ, Collins AC, Lester HA. Nicotine activation of α4* receptors: sufficient for reward, tolerance, and sensitization. *Science* 2004;306(5698):1029–32.

Teng L, Crooks PA, Buxton ST, Dwoskin LP. Nicotinic-receptor mediation of S(-)nornicotine-evoked [³H] overflow from rat striatal slices preloaded with [³H]dopamine. *Journal of Pharmacology and Experimental Therapeutics* 1997;283(2):778–87.

Thompson J, Thomas N, Singleton A, Piggott M, Lloyd S, Perry EK, Morris CM, Perry RH, Ferrier IN, Court JA. D2 dopamine receptor gene (*DRD2*) *Taq*1 A polymorphism: reduced dopamine D2 receptor binding in the human striatum associated with the A1 allele. *Pharmacogenetics* 1997;7(6):479–84.

Thorgeirsson TE, Geller F, Sulem P, Rafnar T, Wiste A, Magnusson KP, Manolescu A, Thorleifsson G, Stefansson H, Ingason A, et al. A variant associated with nicotine dependence, lung cancer and peripheral arterial disease. *Nature* 2008;452(7187):638–42.

Tidey JW, O'Neill SC, Higgins ST. d-Amphetamine increases choice of cigarette smoking over monetary reinforcement. *Psychopharmacology* 2000;153(1):85–92.

Tiffany ST, Conklin CA, Shiffman S, Clayton RR. What can dependence theories tell us about assessing the emergence of tobacco dependence? *Addiction* 2004;99 (Suppl 1):78–86.

Tiffany ST, Cox LS, Elash CA. Effects of transdermal nicotine patches on abstinence-induced and cue-elicited craving in cigarette smokers. *Journal of Consulting and Clinical Psychology* 2000;68(2):233–40.

Tiihonen J, Pesonen U, Kauhanen J, Koulu M, Hallikainen T, Leskinen L, Salonen JT. CYP2A6 genotype and smoking [letter]. *Molecular Psychiatry* 2000;5(4):347–8.

Todd M. Daily processes in stress and smoking: effects of negative events, nicotine dependence, and gender. *Psychology of Addictive Behaviors* 2004;18(1):31–9.

Toide K, Arima T. Effects of cholinergic drugs on extracellular levels of acetylcholine and choline in rat cortex, hippocampus and striatum studied by brain dialysis. *European Journal of Pharmacology* 1989;173(2–3): 133–41.

Tonstad S, Tønnesen P, Hajek P, Williams KE, Billing CB, Reeves KR, Varenicline Phase 3 Study Group. Effect of maintenance therapy with varenicline on smoking cessation: a randomized controlled trial. *JAMA: the Journal of the American Medical Association* 2006;296(1):64–71.

Torres OV, Tejeda HA, Natividad LA, O'Dell LE. Enhanced vulnerability to the rewarding effects of nicotine during the adolescent period of development. *Pharmacology, Biochemistry, and Behavior* 2008;90(4):658–63.

Toth E, Sershen H, Hashim A, Vizi ES, Lajtha A. Effect of nicotine on extracellular levels of neurotransmitters assessed by microdialysis in various brain regions: role of glutamic acid. *Neurochemical Research* 1992;17(3):265–71.

Transdisciplinary Tobacco Use Research Center, Tobacco Dependence Phenotype Workgroup, Baker TB, Piper ME, McCarthy DE, Bolt DM, Smith SS, Kim S-Y, Colby S, Conti D, et al. Time to first cigarette in the morning as an index of ability to quit smoking: implications for nicotine dependence. *Nicotine & Tobacco Research* 2007;9(Suppl 4):S555–S570.

True WR, Heath AC, Scherrer JF, Waterman B, Goldberg J, Lin N, Eisen SA, Lyons MJ, Tsuang MT. Genetic and environmental contributions to smoking. *Addiction* 1997;92(10):1277–87.

True WR, Xian H, Scherrer JF, Madden PA, Bucholz KK, Heath AC, Eisen SA, Lyons MJ, Goldberg J, Tsuang M. Common genetic vulnerability for nicotine and alcohol dependence in men. *Archives of General Psychiatry* 1999;56(7):655–61.

Tsuang MT, Lyons MJ, Meyer JM, Doyle T, Eisen SA, Goldberg J, True W, Lin N, Toomey R, Eaves L. Co-occurrence of abuse of different drugs in men: the role of drug-specific and shared vulnerabilities. *Archives of General Psychiatry* 1998;55(11):967–72.

Turner LR, Mermelstein R. Motivation and reasons to quit: predictive validity among adolescent smokers. *American Journal of Health Behavior* 2004;28(6):542–50.

Turner LR, Mermelstein R, Hitsman B, Warnecke RB. Social support as a moderator of the relationship between recent history of depression and smoking cessation among lower-educated women. *Nicotine & Tobacco Research* 2008;10(1):201–12.

U.S. Department of Health and Human Services. *The Health Consequences of Smoking: Nicotine Addiction. A Report of the Surgeon General*. Atlanta: U.S. Department of Health and Human Services, Public Health Service, Centers for Disease Control, National Center for Chronic Disease Prevention and Health Promotion, Office on Smoking and Health, 1988. DHHS Publication No. (CDC) 88-8406.

U.S. Department of Health and Human Services. *The Health Benefits of Smoking Cessation. A Report of the Surgeon General*. Atlanta: U.S. Department of Health and Human Services, Public Health Service, Centers for Disease Control, National Center for Chronic Disease Prevention and Health Promotion, Office on

Smoking and Health, 1990. DHHS Publication No. (CDC) 90-8416.

U.S. Department of Health and Human Services. *Preventing Tobacco Use Among Young People. A Report of the Surgeon General*. Atlanta: U.S. Department of Health and Human Services, Public Health Service, Centers for Disease Control and Prevention, National Center for Chronic Disease Prevention and Health Promotion, Office on Smoking and Health, 1994.

U.S. Food and Drug Administration. FDA Approves Novel Medication for Smoking Cessation [press release]. Rockville (MD): U.S. Food and Drug Administration, May 11, 2006.

University of Michigan. Decline in daily smoking by younger teens has ended. Ann Arbor (MI): University of Michigan News Service, December 21, 2006.

University of Michigan. Monitoring the Future, 2007; <http://www.monitoringthefuture.org/>; accessed: October 9, 2007.

Uno M, Ito LS, Oba SM, Marie SKN, Shinjo SK, Saito T, Tajima K, Hamajima N. Why is the impact of genetic polymorphisms on the smoking habit not consistent: possibly diluted association with the *Interleukin-1B* C-31T polymorphism in Japanese Brazilians. *Asian Pacific Journal of Cancer Prevention* 2002;3(2):173–5.

Vandenbergh DJ, Bennett CJ, Grant MD, Strasser AA, O'Connor R, Stauffer RL, Vogler GP, Kozlowski LT. Smoking status and the human dopamine transporter variable number of tandem repeats (VNTR) polymorphism: failure to replicate and finding that never-smokers may be different. *Nicotine & Tobacco Research* 2002;4(3):333–40.

Vasconcelos GM, Struchiner CJ, Suarez-Kurtz G. *CYP2A6* genetic polymorphisms and correlation with smoking status in Brazilians. *Pharmacogenomics Journal* 2005;5(1):42–8.

Velicer WF, Redding CA, Sun X, Prochaska JO. Demographic variables, smoking variables, and outcome across five studies. *Health Psychology* 2007;26(3): 278–87.

Vidal C. Nicotinic receptors in the brain: molecular biology, function, and therapeutics. *Molecular and Chemical Neuropathology* 1996;28(1–3):3–11.

Vink JM, Beem AL, Posthuma D, Neale MC, Willemsen G, Kendler KS, Slagboom PE, Boomsma DI. Linkage analysis of smoking initiation and quantity in Dutch sibling pairs. *Pharmacogenomics Journal* 2004;4(4):274–82.

Volkow ND, Fowler JS, Ding Y-S, Wang G-J, Gatley SJ. Imaging the neurochemistry of nicotine actions: studies with positron emission tomography. *Nicotine & Tobacco Research* 1999;1(Suppl 2):S127–S132.

Waal-Manning HJ, de Hamel FA. Smoking habit and psychometric scores: a community study. *New Zealand Medical Journal* 1978;88(619):188–91.

Walaas I, Fonnum F. The distribution and origin of glutamate decarboxylase and choline acetyltransferase in ventral pallidum and other basal forebrain regions. *Brain Research* 1979;177(2):325–36.

Walaas I, Fonnum F. Biochemical evidence for γ-aminobutyrate containing fibres from the nucleus accumbens to the substantia nigra and ventral tegmental area in the rat. *Neuroscience* 1980;5(1):63–72.

Walsh PM, Carrillo P, Flores G, Masuet C, Morchon S, Ramon JM. Effects of partner smoking status and gender on long term abstinence rates of patients receiving smoking cessation treatment. *Addictive Behaviors* 2007;32(1):128–36.

Wang D, Ma JZ, Li MD. Mapping and verification of susceptibility loci for smoking quantity using permutation linkage analysis. *Pharmacogenomics Journal* 2005;5(3):166–72.

Wang F, Chen H, Steketee JD, Sharp BM. Upregulation of ionotropic glutamate receptor subunits within specific mesocorticolimbic regions during chronic nicotine self-administration. *Psychopharmacology* 2007;32(1): 103–9.

Waters AJ, Shiffman S, Bradley BP, Mogg K. Attentional shifts to smoking cues in smokers. *Addiction* 2003a;98(10):1409–17.

Waters AJ, Shiffman S, Sayette MA, Paty JA, Gwaltney C, Balabanis M. Cue-provoked craving and nicotine replacement therapy in smoking cessation. *Journal of Consulting and Clinical Psychology* 2004;72(6): 1136–43.

Waters AJ, Shiffman S, Sayette MA, Paty JA, Gwaltney CJ, Balabanis MH. Attentional bias predicts outcome in smoking cessation. *Health Psychology* 2003b; 22(4):378–87.

Watkins SS, Epping-Jordan MP, Koob GF, Markou A. Blockade of nicotine self-administration with nicotinic antagonists in rats. *Pharmacology, Biochemistry, and Behavior* 1999;62(4):743–51.

Watkins SS, Stinus L, Koob GF, Markou A. Reward and somatic changes during precipitated nicotine withdrawal in rats: centrally and peripherally mediated effects. *Journal of Pharmacology and Experimental Therapeutics* 2000;292(3):1053–64.

Wayne GF, Connolly GN, Henningfield JE. Assessing internal tobacco industry knowledge of the neurobiology of tobacco dependence. *Nicotine & Tobacco Research* 2004;6(6):927–40.

Weiss RB, Baker TB, Cannon DS, von Niederhausern A, Dunn DM, Matsunami N, Singh NA, Baird L, Coon H, McMahon WM, et al. A candidate gene approach identifies the *CHRNA5-A3-B4* region as a risk factor for age-dependent nicotine addiction. *PLoS Genetics* 2008;4(7):e1000125. doi:10.1371/journal.pgen. 1000125.

Weiss-Gerlach E, Franck M, Neuner B, Gentilello LM, Neumann T, Tønnesen H, Kolbeck S, Cammann H, Perka C, MacGuill M, et al. Motivation of trauma patients to stop smoking after admission to the emergency department. *Addictive Behaviors* 2008;33(7):906–18.

West R, Hajek P, McNeill A. Effect of buspirone on cigarette withdrawal symptoms and short-term abstinence rates in a smokers clinic. *Psychopharmacology* 1991;104(1):91–6.

West RJ, Hajek P, Belcher M. Severity of withdrawal symptoms as a predictor of outcome of an attempt to quit smoking. *Psychological Medicine* 1989;19(4):981–5.

West RJ, Jarvis MJ, Russell MAH, Carruthers ME, Feyerabend C. Effect of nicotine replacement on the cigarette withdrawal syndrome. *British Journal of Addiction* 1984;79(2):215–9.

Westmaas JL, Langsam K. Unaided smoking cessation and predictors of failure to quit in a community sample: effects of gender. *Addictive Behaviors* 2005;30(7): 1405–24.

Westman EC, Behm FM, Simel DL, Rose JE. Smoking behavior on the first day of a quit attempt predicts long-term abstinence. *Archives of Internal Medicine* 1997;157(3):335–40.

Wetter DW, Cofta-Gunn L, Fouladi RT, Irvin JE, Daza P, Mazas C, Wright K, Cinciripini PM, Gritz ER. Understanding the associations among education, employment characteristics, and smoking. *Addictive Behaviors* 2005a;30(5):905–14.

Wetter DW, Cofta-Gunn L, Irvin JE, Fouladi RT, Wright K, Daza P, Mazas C, Cinciripini PM, Gritz ER. What accounts for the association of education and smoking cessation? *Preventive Medicine* 2005b;40(4):452–60.

Wetter DW, Fiore MC, Baker TB, Young TB. Tobacco withdrawal and nicotine replacement influence objective measures of sleep. *Journal of Consulting and Clinical Psychology* 1995;63(4):658–67.

Wetter DW, Kenford SL, Smith SS, Fiore MC, Jorenby DE, Baker TB. Gender differences in smoking cessation. *Journal of Consulting and Clinical Psychology* 1999;67(4):555–62.

Wetter DW, Smith SS, Kenford SL, Jorenby DE, Fiore MC, Hurt RD, Offord KP, Baker TB. Smoking outcome expectancies: factor structure, predictive validity, and discriminant validity. *Journal of Abnormal Psychology* 1994;103(4):801–11.

Wewers ME. The role of postcessation factors in tobacco abstinence: stressful events and coping responses. *Addictive Behaviors* 1988;13(3):297–302.

White HR, Nagin D, Replogle E, Stouthamer-Loeber M. Racial differences in trajectories of cigarette use. *Drug and Alcohol Dependence* 2004;76(3):219–27.

White HR, Pandina RJ, Chen PH. Developmental trajectories of cigarette use from early adolescence into young adulthood. *Drug and Alcohol Dependence* 2002b;65(2):167–78.

Wikler A. Dynamics of drug dependence: implications of a conditioning theory for research and treatment. *Archives of General Psychiatry* 1973;28(5):611–6.

Wileyto EP, Patterson F, Niaura R, Epstein LH, Brown RA, Audrain-McGovern J, Hawk LW Jr, Lerman C. Do small lapses predict relapse to smoking behavior under bupropion treatment? *Nicotine & Tobacco Research* 2004;6(2):357–67.

Wileyto EP, Patterson F, Niaura R, Epstein LH, Brown RA, Audrain-McGovern J, Hawk LW Jr, Lerman C. Recurrent event analysis of lapse and recovery in a smoking cessation clinical trial using bupropion. *Nicotine & Tobacco Research* 2005;7(2):257–68.

Wilkie GI, Hutson P, Sullivan JP, Wonnacott S. Pharmacological characterization of a nicotinic autoreceptor in rat hippocampal synaptosomes. *Neurochemical Research* 1996;21(9):1141–8.

Williams M, Robinson JL. Binding of the nicotinic cholinergic antagonist, dihydro-β-erythroidine, to rat brain tissue. *Journal of Neuroscience* 1984;4(12):2906–11.

Wills TA, Resko JA, Ainette MG, Mendoza D. Smoking onset in adolescence: a person-centered analysis with time-varying predictors. *Health Psychology* 2004; 23(2):158–67.

Wilson SJ, Sayette MA, Fiez JA. Prefrontal responses to drug cues: a neurocognitive analysis. *Nature Neuroscience* 2004;7(3):211–4.

Wonnacott S. Presynaptic nicotinic ACh receptors. *Trends in Neurosciences* 1997;20(2):92–8.

Wonnacott S, Sidhpura N, Balfour DJK. Nicotine: from molecular mechanisms to behaviour. *Current Opinion in Pharmacology* 2005;5(1):53–9.

World Health Organization. *International Statistical Classification of Diseases and Related Health Problems, Tenth Revision*. Geneva: World Health Organization, 1992.

Wu X, Hudmon KS, Detry MA, Chamberlain RM, Spitz MR. D_2 dopamine receptor gene polymorphisms among African-Americans and Mexican-Americans: a lung cancer case-control study. *Cancer Epidemiology, Biomarkers & Prevention* 2000;9(10):1021–6.

Xian H, Scherrer JF, Madden PAF, Lyons MJ, Tsuang M, True WR, Eisen SA. The heritability of failed smoking cessation and nicotine withdrawal in twins who smoked and attempted to quit. *Nicotine & Tobacco Research* 2003;5(2):245–54.

Xian H, Scherrer JF, Madden PA, Lyons MJ, Tsuang M, True WR, Eisen SA. Latent class typology of nicotine withdrawal: genetic contributions and association with failed smoking cessation and psychiatric disorders. *Psychological Medicine* 2005;35(3):409–19.

Xu B, Roos JL, Levy S, van Rensburg EJ, Gogos JA, Karayiorgou M. Strong association of *de novo* copy number mutations with sporadic schizophrenia. *Nature Genetics* 2008;40(7):880–5.

Xu C, Rao YS, Xu B, Hoffmann E, Jones J, Sellers EM, Tyndale RF. An *in vivo* pilot study characterizing the new *CYP2A6*7, *8*, and *10* alleles. *Biochemical and Biophysical Research Communications* 2002;290(1): 318–24.

Yamamoto K-I, Domino EF. Nicotine-induced EEG and behavioral arousal. *International Journal of Neuropharmacology* 1965;4(6):359–73.

Yang Z-J, Blaha V, Meguid MM, Oler A, Miyata G. Infusion of nicotine into the LHA enhances dopamine and 5-HT release and suppresses food intake. *Pharmacology, Biochemistry, and Behavior* 1999;64(1):155–9.

Yim CY, Mogenson GJ. Electrophysiological studies of neurons in the ventral tegmental area of Tsai. *Brain Research* 1980;181(2):301–13.

Yoshida K, Hamajima N, Kozaki K, Saito H, Maeno K, Sugiura T, Ookuma K, Takahashi T. Association between the dopamine D2 receptor A2/A2 genotype and smoking behavior in the Japanese. *Cancer Epidemiology, Biomarkers & Prevention* 2001;10(4):403–5.

Yu PH, Boulton AA. Irreversible inhibition of monoamine oxidase by some components of cigarette smoke. *Life Sciences* 1987;41(6):675–82.

Yudkin P, Hey K, Roberts S, Welch S, Murphy M, Walton R. Abstinence from smoking eight years after participation in randomised controlled trial of nicotine patch. *BMJ (British Medical Journal)* 2003;327(7405):28–9.

Yudkin P, Munafò M, Hey K, Roberts S, Welch S, Johnstone E, Murphy M, Griffiths S, Walton R. Effectiveness of nicotine patches in relation to genotype in women versus men: randomised controlled trial. *BMJ (British Medical Journal)* 2004;328(7446):989–90.

Zacny JP, Stitzer ML. Cigarette brand-switching: effects on smoke exposure and smoking behavior. *Journal of Pharmacology and Experimental Therapeutics* 1988;246(2):619–27.

Zadina JE, Hackler L, Ge L-J, Kastin AJ. A potent and selective endogenous agonist for the μ-opiate receptor [letter]. *Nature* 1997;386(6624):499–502.

Zetteler JI, Clark TG, Johnstone EC, Munafò MR. Association of the dopamine-β-hydroxylase gene with nicotine dependence: no evidence for mediation by personality. *Personality and Individual Differences* 2005;39(6):1113–22.

Zhang X, Amemo K, Ameno S, Iwahashi K, Kinoshita H, Kubota T, Mostofa J, Ijiri I. Lack of association between smoking and CYP2A6 gene polymorphisms in a Japanese population. *Japanese Journal of Alcohol Studies and Drug Dependence* 2001;36(5):486–90.

Zhang Y, Wang D, Johnson AD, Papp AC, Sadée W. Allelic expression imbalance of human mu opioid receptor (OPRM1) caused by variant *A118G*. *Journal of Biological Chemistry* 2005;280(38):32618–24.

Zvolensky MJ, Baker KM, Leen-Feldner E, Bonn-Miller MO, Feldner MT, Brown RA. Anxiety sensitivity: association with intensity of retrospectively-rated smoking-related withdrawal symptoms and motivation to quit. *Cognitive Behaviour Therapy* 2004;33(3):114–25.

Chapter 5
Cancer

Introduction

The 2004 Surgeon General's report, *The Health Consequences of Smoking: A Report of the Surgeon General* (U.S. Department of Health and Human Services [USDHHS] 2004), concluded that the evidence is sufficient to infer a causal relationship between smoking and cancers of the lung, larynx, oral cavity, pharynx, esophagus, pancreas, bladder, kidney, cervix, and stomach, and acute myeloid leukemia. In addition, the report found that evidence suggests a causal relationship between smoking and colorectal and liver cancers. This chapter examines the mechanisms by which cigarette smoking induces cancer. Literature citations for this section's discussion appear in subsequent sections of this chapter, as appropriate. A schematic overview of the pertinent mechanisms discussed in this chapter is presented in Figure 5.1. The figure depicts the major established pathways of cancer causation by cigarette smoking: (1) the exposure to carcinogens (cancer-causing substances), (2) the formation of covalent bonds between the carcinogens and DNA (DNA adduct formation), and (3) the resulting accumulation of permanent somatic mutations in critical genes (genes appear in italics). Somatic mutations lead to clonal outgrowth and, through accumulation of additional mutations, to development of cancer.

Each puff of each cigarette contains a mixture of thousands of compounds, including more than 60 well-established carcinogens. The carcinogens in cigarette smoke belong to multiple chemical classes, including polycyclic aromatic hydrocarbons (PAHs), *N*-nitrosamines, aromatic amines, aldehydes, volatile organic hydrocarbons, and metals. In addition to these well-established carcinogens, others have been less thoroughly investigated. These include alkylated PAHs, oxidants, free radicals, and ethylating agents. Considerable evidence indicates that in human cancers caused by cigarette smoking, PAHs, *N*-nitrosamines, aromatic amines, and certain volatile organic agents play a major role. Extensive data in the literature demonstrate the uptake of these carcinogens by smokers. The data confirm the expected presence of metabolites of these substances in the urine of smokers at higher levels than those in nonsmokers.

Most carcinogens in cigarette smoke require a metabolic activation process, generally catalyzed by cytochrome P-450 enzymes (P-450s), to convert the carcinogens to forms that can covalently bind to DNA and form DNA adducts. P-450s 1A1 and 1B1, which are inducible by cigarette smoke through interactions with the aryl hydrocarbon receptor, are particularly important in the metabolic activation of PAHs. The inducibility of these P-450s may be a critical aspect of cancer susceptibility in smokers. P-450s 1A2, 2A6, 2A13, and 2E1 are also important in the activation of cigarette smoke carcinogens. Competing with the activation process is metabolic detoxification, which excretes carcinogen metabolites in generally harmless forms and is catalyzed by a variety of enzymes, including glutathione-*S*-transferases (GSTs), uridine-5'-disphosphate-glucuronosyltransferases (UGTs), epoxide hydrolases, and sulfatases. The balance between metabolic activation and detoxification of carcinogens varies among persons and likely affects cancer susceptibility. Persons with a higher activation and lower detoxification capacity are at the highest risk for smoking-related cancers. This finding is supported by considerable evidence from molecular epidemiologic studies of the polymorphisms (variants) in these enzymes.

The metabolic activation of carcinogens results in the formation of DNA adducts, which are absolutely central to the carcinogenic process. However, some carcinogens can directly form DNA adducts without metabolic activation. Since the mid-1980s, extensive studies have examined the presence of DNA adducts in human tissues. Studies that used nonspecific methods, such as ^{32}P-postlabeling and immunoassays, to measure adducts concluded that adduct levels in the lung and in other tissues are higher in smokers than in nonsmokers. Some epidemiologic data link higher adduct levels with a higher probability of developing cancer.

There are ample cellular repair systems that can remove DNA adducts and maintain a normal DNA structure. These systems include direct repair of DNA bases by alkyltransferases, the excision of DNA damage by base and nucleotide excision repair, mismatch repair, and double-strand break repair. If repair enzymes are overwhelmed by DNA damage or for other reasons cannot function efficiently, DNA adducts may persist and increase the likelihood of developing somatic mutations. Inherited polymorphic variants in some DNA repair enzymes are also associated with decreased DNA repair activity and a potentially higher probability of developing cancer.

Persistent DNA adducts can cause miscoding (e.g., insertion of the wrong base) during replication of DNA when DNA polymerase enzymes process the adducts incorrectly. Considerable specificity exists in the relationship between specific DNA adducts caused by carcinogens in cigarette smoke and the types of observed somatic mutations; for example, an O^6-methylguanine adduct causes G→A transitions. These types of mutations are frequently observed in the *KRAS* oncogene in lung

Figure 5.1   Link between cigarette smoking and cancer through carcinogens in tobacco smoke

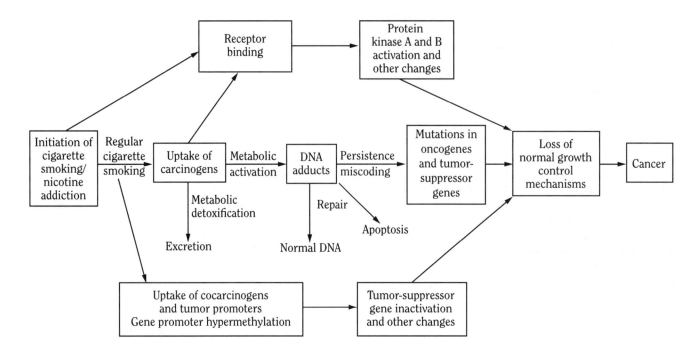

cancer and in the *TP53* gene in a variety of cancers induced by cigarette smoke. The *KRAS* and *TP53* mutations observed in lung cancer in smokers appear to reflect DNA damage caused by metabolically activated PAHs. However, a number of other carcinogens or toxicants, such as *N*-nitrosamines and aldehydes, as well as oxidative damage, are also likely to be involved. Animal studies have firmly established the cancer-causing role of mutations in these genes.

Gene mutations can cause the loss of normal functions in control of cellular growth, ultimately resulting in cellular proliferation and cancer. Studies have strongly linked chromosome damage in cells throughout the aerodigestive tract to exposure to cigarette smoke. The protective process of programmed cell death (apoptosis) can counterbalance these mutational events by removing cells with DNA damage. The balance between mechanisms leading to apoptosis and those suppressing apoptosis has a major impact on tumor growth. In addition, researchers have observed numerous cytogenetic changes in lung cancer.

The central track of Figure 5.1 that proceeds through genetic damage is clearly established as a major pathway by which carcinogens in cigarette smoke can cause cancer.

However, the top and bottom tracks of Figure 5.1 indicate that other pathways also contribute to carcinogenesis. Nicotine and tobacco-specific nitrosamines bind to nicotinic receptors and other cellular receptors. This binding then leads to the activation of protein kinase B (AKT, also known as PKB), protein kinase A (PKA), and other key biologic pathways for cytogenetic changes. Cigarette smoke activates EGFR and COX-2, both known to be important in cell proliferation and transformation. Furthermore, the occurrence of cocarcinogens and tumor promoters in cigarette smoke is well established. Although these compounds are not carcinogenic, they clearly enhance the carcinogenicity of cigarette smoke carcinogens through mechanisms that usually lead to stimulation of cell proliferation. The reversibility of cancer risk after smoking cessation supports the role of tumor promoters and other epigenetic factors in tobacco carcinogenesis. However, the specifics of these effects have not been fully elucidated. An important epigenetic pathway is the enzymatic hypermethylation of promoter regions of genes, which can result in gene silencing. If this occurs in tumor-suppressor genes, the result can be unregulated cellular proliferation.

Carcinogen Exposure, Metabolism, and DNA Adducts

Carcinogens in Cigarette Smoke

Carcinogens in cigarette smoke that were evaluated by the International Agency for Research on Cancer (IARC 2004) are listed in Table 5.1. All are carcinogenic in laboratory animals, and 15 are rated as carcinogenic in humans (group 1 carcinogens). Similar evaluations have been published by the USDHHS (2005). The total exposure of smokers to these compounds is approximately 1.4 to 2.2 milligrams (mg) per cigarette (Table 5.1). This estimate is based on machine measurements and may underestimate actual exposure. Some of the strongest of these carcinogens are PAHs, *N*-nitrosamines, and aromatic amines, which occur in the lowest amounts, and some of the weaker carcinogens, such as acetaldehyde and isoprene, occur in the highest amounts. Thus, a simple addition of the amounts of carcinogenic agents could be misleading. For other carcinogens in cigarette smoke that IARC has not evaluated (e.g., broad spectra of PAHs and aromatic amines), data on frequency of occurrence, levels, and carcinogenic activities are incomplete (IARC 1986).

PAHs are incomplete combustion products first identified as carcinogenic constituents of coal tar (Phillips 1983). These products occur as mixtures in tar, soot, broiled foods, automobile engine exhaust, and other materials generated by incomplete combustion (IARC 1983). Generally, PAHs are carcinogens that act locally. Some PAHs, such as benzo[*a*]pyrene (B[*a*]P), have powerful carcinogenic activity. Studies have typically evaluated PAH carcinogenicity by application to mouse skin, but PAHs also induce tumors of the lung, trachea, and mammary gland, depending on the route of administration and the animal model used (Dipple et al. 1984).

Heterocyclic compounds include analogs of PAHs containing nitrogen, as well as simpler compounds such as furan, which is a liver carcinogen. *N*-nitrosamines are a large class of carcinogens with demonstrated activity in at least 30 animal species (Preussmann and Stewart 1984). They are potent and systemic carcinogens that affect different tissues depending on their structure. Two of the most important *N*-nitrosamines in cigarette smoke are the tobacco-specific 4-(methylnitrosamino)-1-(3-pyridyl)-1-butanone (NNK) and *N'*-nitrosonornicotine (NNN) (Hecht and Hoffmann 1988). NNK caused lung tumors in all species tested, and activity in rats was particularly high. Studies using animal models have demonstrated that NNK also induces tumors of the pancreas, nasal cavity, and liver. In addition, NNN produces esophageal and nasal tumors in rats and respiratory tract tumors in mice and hamsters (Hecht 1998).

Aromatic amines in cigarette smoke are combustion products that include the well-known human bladder carcinogens 2-naphthylamine and 4-aminobiphenyl (4-ABP), which were first characterized as human carcinogens attributable to industrial exposures in the dye industry (Luch 2005). Heterocyclic aromatic amines are also combustion products and are best known for their occurrence in broiled foods (Sugimura 1995), but they also occur in cigarette smoke.

Aldehydes such as formaldehyde and acetaldehyde occur widely in the human environment and are endogenous metabolites found in human blood (IARC 1995c, 1999; Gao et al. 2002). The phenolic compounds catechol and caffeic acid are common dietary constituents. High doses of catechol cause glandular stomach tumors when administered in the diet. Catechol can also act as a cocarcinogen, enhancing the activity of carcinogens such as B[*a*]P (IARC 1999). Dietary caffeic acid caused renal cell tumors in female mice (IARC 1993). The volatile hydrocarbons include 1,3-butadiene, a powerful multiorgan carcinogen in mice that was shown to have weaker activity in rats, and benzene, a known human leukemogen (IARC 1982, 1999). 1,3-butadiene and benzene are arguably the two most prevalent potent carcinogens in cigarette smoke, on the basis of toxicologic criteria (Fowles and Dybing 2003).

Other carcinogenic organic compounds in cigarette smoke include the human carcinogens vinyl chloride in low amounts and ethylene oxide in substantial quantities (IARC 1979). Ethylene oxide is associated with malignancies of the lymphatic and hematopoietic systems in both humans and laboratory animals (IARC 1994). Diverse metals such as the human carcinogen cadmium are also present in cigarette smoke, as is the radioisotope polonium 210, which is carcinogenic to humans.

Cigarette smoke also contains oxidants such as nitric oxide (about 600 micrograms [μg] per cigarette) and related species (Hecht 1999). Free radicals have been detected by electron spin resonance and spin trapping (Hecht 1999). Researchers postulate that the major species of free radicals are a quinone-hydroquinone complex. Other compounds may also be involved in the oxidative damage produced by cigarette smoke. In addition, several studies demonstrate the presence in cigarette smoke of an uncharacterized ethylating agent, which ethylates both DNA and hemoglobin (Hb) (Carmella et al. 2002a; Singh et al. 2005).

Table 5.1   IARC evaluations of carcinogens in mainstream cigarette smoke

Carcinogen[a]	Quantity (per cigarette)	IARC evaluations of evidence of carcinogenicity in humans			IARC Monograph[c] (volume, year)
		In animals	In humans	IARC group[b]	
Polycyclic aromatic hydrocarbons					
Benz[*a*]anthracene	20–70 ng	Sufficient		2A	*32*, 1983; *S7*, 1987
Benzo[*b*]fluoranthene	4–22 ng	Sufficient		2B	*32*, 1983; *S7*, 1987
Benzo[*j*]fluoranthene	6–21 ng	Sufficient		2B	*32*, 1983; *S7*, 1987
Benzo[*k*]fluoranthene	6–12 ng	Sufficient		2B	*32*, 1983; *S7*, 1987
Benzo[*a*]pyrene	8.5–17.6 ng	Sufficient	Limited	1	*32*, 1983; *S7*, 1987; *92*, in press
Dibenz[*a,h*]anthracene	4 ng	Sufficient		2A	*32*, 1983; *S7*, 1987
Dibenzo[*a,i*]pyrene	1.7–3.2 ng	Sufficient		2B	*32*, 1983; *S7*, 1987
Dibenzo[*a,e*]pyrene	Present	Sufficient		2B	*32*, 1983; *S7*, 1987
Indeno[*1,2,3-cd*]pyrene	4–20 ng	Sufficient		2B	*32*, 1983; *S7*, 1987
5-methylchrysene	ND–0.6 ng	Sufficient		2B	*32*, 1983; *S7*, 1987
Heterocyclic compounds					
Furan	20–40 µg	Sufficient		2B	*63*, 1995a
Dibenz[*a,h*]acridine	ND–0.1 ng	Sufficient		2B	*32*, 1983; *S7*, 1987
Dibenz[*a,j*]acridine	ND–10 ng	Sufficient		2B	*32*, 1983; *S7*, 1987
Dibenzo[*c,g*]carbazole	ND–0.7 ng	Sufficient		2B	*32*, 1983; *S7*, 1987
Benzo[*b*]furan	Present	Sufficient		2B	*63*, 1995a
N-nitrosamines					
N-nitrosodimethylamine	0.1–180 ng	Sufficient		2A	*17*, 1978; *S7*, 1987
N-nitrosoethylmethylamine	ND–13 ng	Sufficient		2B	*17*, 1978; *S7*, 1987
N-nitrosodiethylamine	ND–25 ng	Sufficient		2A	*17*, 1978; *S7*, 1987
N-nitrosopyrrolidine	1.5–110 ng	Sufficient		2B	*17*, 1978; *S7*, 1987
N-nitrosopiperidine	ND–9 ng	Sufficient		2B	*17*, 1978; *S7*, 1987
N-nitrosodiethanolamine	ND–36 ng	Sufficient		2B	*17*, 1978; *77*, 2000
N'-nitrosonornicotine	154–196 ng	Sufficient	Limited	1	*37*, 1985; *S7*, 1987; *89*, in press
4-(methylnitrosamino)-1-(3-pyridyl)-1-butanone	110–133 ng	Sufficient	Limited	1	*37*, 1985; *S7*, 1987; *89*, in press
Aromatic amines					
2-toluidine	30–200 ng	Sufficient	Limited	2A	*S7*, 1987; *77*, 2000
2,6-dimethylaniline	4–50 ng	Sufficient		2B	*57*, 1993
2-naphthylamine	1–22 ng	Sufficient	Sufficient	1	*4*, 1974; *S7*, 1987
4-aminobiphenyl	2–5 ng	Sufficient	Sufficient	1	*1*, 1972; *S7*, 1987
Heterocyclic aromatic amines					
2-amino-9*H*-pyrido[2,3-*b*]indole	25–260 ng	Sufficient		2B	*40*, 1986; *S7*, 1987
2-amino-3-methyl-9*H*-pyrido[2,3-*b*]indole	2–37 ng	Sufficient		2B	*40*, 1986; *S7*, 1987
2-amino-3-methylimidazo[4,5-*f*]quinoline	0.3 ng	Sufficient		2A	*S7*, 1987; *56*, 1993
3-amino-1,4-dimethyl-5*H*-pyrido[4,3-*b*]indole	0.3–0.5 ng	Sufficient		2B	*31*, 1983; *S7*, 1987
3-amino-1-methyl-5*H*-pyrido[4,3-*b*]indole	0.8–1.1 ng	Sufficient		2B	*31*, 1983; *S7*, 1987
2-amino-6-methylpyrido[1,2-*a*:3′,2′-*d*]imidazole	0.37–0.89 ng	Sufficient		2B	*40*, 1986; *S7*, 1987
2-aminodipyrido[1,2-*a*:3′,2′-*d*]imidazole	0.25–0.88 ng	Sufficient		2B	*40*, 1986; *S7*, 1987
2-amino-1-methyl-6-phenylimidazo[4,5-*b*]pyridine	11–23 ng	Sufficient		2B	*56*, 1993

Table 5.1   Continued

Carcinogen[a]	Quantity (per cigarette)	IARC evaluations of evidence of carcinogenicity in humans			IARC Monograph[c] (volume, year)
		In animals	In humans	IARC group[b]	
Aldehydes					
Formaldehyde	10.3–25 µg	Sufficient	Sufficient	1	*S7*, 1987; *62*, 1995b
Acetaldehyde	770–864 µg	Sufficient		2B	*S7*, 1987; *71*, 1999
Phenolic compounds					
Catechol	59–81 µg	Sufficient		2B	*S7*, 1987; *71*, 1999
Caffeic acid	<3 µg	Sufficient		2B	*56*, 1993
Volatile hydrocarbons					
1,3-butadiene	20–40 µg	Sufficient	Limited	2A	*S7*, 1987; *71*, 1999
Isoprene	450–1,000 µg	Sufficient		2B	*60*, 1994; *71*, 1999
Benzene	12–50 µg	Sufficient	Sufficient	1	*29*, 1982; *S7*, 1987
Nitrohydrocarbons					
Nitromethane	0.5–0.6 µg	Sufficient		2B	*77*, 2000
2-nitropropane	0.7–1.2 ng	Sufficient		2B	*S7*, 1987; *71*, 1999
Nitrobenzene	25 µg	Sufficient		2B	*65*, 1996
Miscellaneous organic compounds					
Acetamide	38–56 µg	Sufficient		2B	*S7*, 1987; *71*, 1999
Acrylamide	Present	Sufficient		2A	*S7*, 1987; *60*, 1994
Acrylonitrile	3–15 µg	Sufficient		2B	*S7*, 1987; *71*, 1999
Vinyl chloride	11–15 ng	Sufficient	Sufficient	1	*19*, 1979; *S7*, 1987
1,1-dimethylhydrazine	Present	Sufficient		2B	*4*, 1974; *71*, 1999
Ethylene oxide	7 µg	Sufficient	Limited	1	*60*, 1994; *S7*, 1987
Propylene oxide	0–100 ng	Sufficient		2B	*60*, 1994; *S7*, 1987
Urethane	20–38 ng	Sufficient		2B	*7*, 1974; *S7*, 1987
Metals and inorganic compounds					
Arsenic	40–120 ng	Sufficient	Sufficient	1	*84*, 2004
Beryllium	0.5 ng	Sufficient	Sufficient	1	*S7*, 1987; *58*, 1993
Nickel	ND–600 ng	Sufficient	Sufficient	1	*S7*, 1987; *49*, 1990
Chromium (hexavalent)	4–70 ng	Sufficient	Sufficient	1	*S7*, 1987; *49*, 1990
Cadmium	41–62 ng	Sufficient	Sufficient	1	*S7*, 1987; *58*, 1993
Cobalt	0.13–0.20 ng	Sufficient		2B	*52*, 1991
Lead (inorganic)	34–85 ng	Sufficient	Limited	2A	*23*, 1980; *S7*, 1987; *87*, in press
Hydrazine	24–43 ng	Sufficient		2B	*S7*, 1987; *71*, 1999
Radioisotope polonium-210	0.03–1.0 picocurie	Sufficient		1	*78*, 2001

Source: Adapted from Hoffmann et al. 2001 and International Agency for Research on Cancer 2004 with permission from American Chemical Society, © 2001 and International Agency for Research on Cancer, © 2004.

Note: **IARC** = International Agency for Research on Cancer; **ND** = not detected; **ng** = nanograms; ***S7*** = Supplement 7; **µg** = micrograms.

[a]Virtually all these compounds are known carcinogens in experimental animals, and IARC found sufficient evidence for carcinogenicity in animals for all the compounds.

[b]Using data on cancer in humans and, in some cases, other data, IARC established classifications for compounds as group 1 (carcinogenic to humans), group 2A (probably carcinogenic to humans), and group 2B (possibly carcinogenic to humans).

[c]If more than two IARC evaluations were performed, only the two most recent monographs are listed.

In summary, cigarette smoke contains diverse carcinogens. PAH, *N*-nitrosamines, aromatic amines, 1,3-butadiene, benzene, aldehydes, and ethylene oxide are probably the most important carcinogens because of their carcinogenic potency and levels in cigarette smoke.

Biomarkers of Carcinogens in Smokers

Measurements of carcinogens or their metabolites in urine, blood, and breath can provide convenient and reliable quantitative information on human exposure to carcinogens. The information provided by these measurements, which are biomarkers of exposure, is critical to objective evaluation of carcinogen doses in smokers.

Urinary Biomarkers

Urinary biomarkers are the most widely applied biomarkers of carcinogen exposure in smokers (Hecht 2002b). Urine is relatively simple to obtain in large quantities, and obtaining study participants' consent and specimens for testing is almost never a difficulty. Carcinogens in cigarette smoke and/or their metabolites are frequently present in substantial quantities in urine. Therefore, reliable quantitation is generally feasible. This section provides an overview of some of the urinary biomarkers most commonly used to estimate carcinogen doses in smokers. The chemical structures of all compounds discussed in this section are illustrated in Figure 5.2.

Polycyclic Aromatic Hydrocarbons

Phenanthrene metabolites. Phenanthrene is the simplest PAH with a bay region (the region of a molecule between positions 4 and 5), a feature closely associated with the carcinogenic activity of PAHs (Figure 5.2). Phenanthrene, however, is inactive as a carcinogen (LaVoie and Rice 1988). Concentrations of phenanthrene in mainstream smoke range from 85 to 620 nanograms (ng) per cigarette (IARC 1986). Studies have quantified the phenanthrene metabolites phenanthrols, phenanthrene dihydrodiols, and *r*-1,*t*-2,3,*c*-4-tetrahydroxy-1,2,3,4-tetrahydrophenanthrene (*trans, anti*-PheT) in human urine (Hecht 2002b). Levels of phenanthrols in human urine differed between smokers and nonsmokers in some studies but not in others (reviewed in Carmella et al. 2004a). There are sources of phenanthrene exposure other than cigarette smoke, and all people have phenanthrene metabolites in their urine. This finding is well documented in environmental and occupational settings with high exposures to PAH (Grimmer et al. 1993, 1997; Angerer et

al. 1997). One metabolite of phenanthrene, *trans, anti*-PheT, results from the diol epoxide metabolic activation pathway common to many carcinogenic PAHs. This metabolite is a promising new biomarker for PAH uptake and metabolic activation and can be readily quantified by gas chromatography (GC)–negative ion chemical ionization–mass spectrometry (MS) (Hecht et al. 2003). Levels of *trans, anti*-PheT are higher in smokers than in nonsmokers (Hecht et al. 2003).

1-hydroxypyrene. Pyrene is a noncarcinogenic component in all PAH mixtures; levels in mainstream cigarette smoke were 50 to 270 ng per cigarette (IARC 1986). The major metabolite of pyrene is 1-hydroxypyrene (1-HOP) glucuronide, which can be measured in urine (Jongeneelen et al. 1985). To quantify 1-HOP in urine, enzymatic hydrolysis is used to release 1-HOP, which is then enriched by reverse-phase chromatography and quantified by high-performance liquid chromatography (HPLC) with fluorescence detection. Studies have described variations of this method (Carmella et al. 2004b). Hundreds of studies of occupational and environmental PAH exposure have measured 1-HOP as a surrogate marker for total PAH exposure. In reviews of the data on the effects of smoking (Jongeneelen 1994, 2001; Van Rooij et al. 1994; Levin 1995; Heudorf and Angerer 2001; Hecht 2002b), most of the studies noted that 1-HOP levels in the urine of smokers were about twice as high as those in the urine of nonsmokers, although some studies have reported greater differences. Levels of 1-HOP may be influenced by genetic polymorphisms in carcinogen-metabolizing enzymes (Alexandrie et al. 2000; Nerurkar et al. 2000; Nan et al. 2001; van Delft et al. 2001).

Other metabolites of polycyclic aromatic hydrocarbons. Studies examining urine biomarkers have measured phenolic metabolites of naphthalene and a variety of PAHs, which show promise as urinary biomarkers of PAH uptake from cigarette smoke (Hecht 2002b; Smith et al. 2002a,b; Serdar et al. 2003). Studies have quantified B[*a*]P metabolites in urine, but the levels are generally low, limiting their routine application in large studies (Hecht 2002b).

Aromatic Amines and Heterocyclic Aromatic Amines

Researchers have quantified aromatic amines, but not their metabolites, in human urine. In one study, levels of 2-toluidine excreted by smokers were 6.3 ± 3.7 (standard deviation [SD]) μg/24 hours and levels excreted by nonsmokers were 4.1 ± 3.2 (SD) μg/24 hours. The difference was not significant (El-Bayoumy et al. 1986). Another investigation reported urine levels of 2-toluidine that were higher in smokers than in nonsmokers (Riffelmann et al.

Figure 5.2   Chemical structures of biomarkers of carcinogen exposure

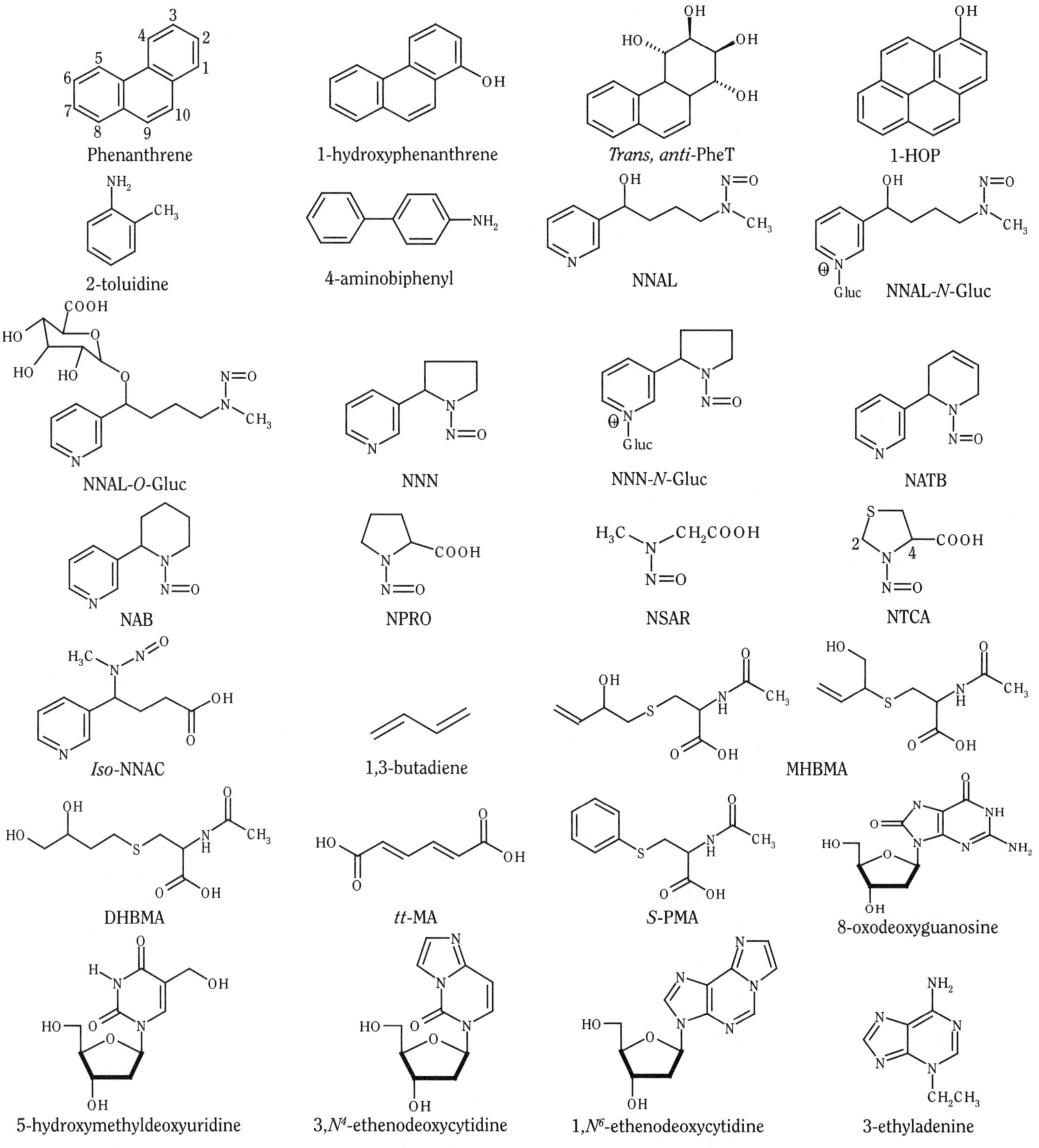

Phenanthrene

1-hydroxyphenanthrene

Trans, anti-PheT

1-HOP

2-toluidine

4-aminobiphenyl

NNAL

NNAL-*N*-Gluc

NNAL-*O*-Gluc

NNN

NNN-*N*-Gluc

NATB

NAB

NPRO

NSAR

NTCA

Iso-NNAC

1,3-butadiene

MHBMA

DHBMA

tt-MA

S-PMA

8-oxodeoxyguanosine

5-hydroxymethyldeoxyuridine

3,*N*⁴-ethenodeoxycytidine

1,*N*⁶-ethenodeoxycytidine

3-ethyladenine

Note: **1-HOP** = 1-hydroxypyrene; **DHBMA** = dihydroxybutylmercapturic acid; ***iso*-NNAC** = 4-(methylnitrosamino)-4-(3-pyridyl)butyric acid; **MHBMA** = monohydroxybutenylmercapturic acid; **NAB** = *N'*-nitrosoanabasine; **NATB** = *N'*-nitrosoanatabine; **NNAL** = 4-(methylnitrosamino)-1-(3-pyridyl)-1-butanol; **NNAL-*N*-Gluc** = 4-(methylnitrosamino)-1-(3-pyridyl)-1-butanol-*N*-glucuronide; **NNAL-*O*-Gluc** = 4-(methylnitrosamino)-1-(3-pyridyl)-1-butanol-*O*-glucuronide; **NNN** = *N'*-nitrosonornicotine; **NNN-*N*-Gluc** = *N'*-nitrosonornicotine-*N*-glucuronide; **NPRO** = *N*-nitrosoproline; **NSAR** = *N*-nitrososarcosine; **NTCA** = *N*-nitrosothiazolidine 4-carboxylic acid; **S-PMA** = *S*-phenylmercapturic acid; ***trans, anti*-PheT** = *r*-1,*t*-2,3,*c*-4-tetrahydroxy-1,2,3,4-tetrahydrophenanthrene; ***tt*-MA** = *trans,trans*-muconic acid.

1995). There appear to be significant sources of human uptake of 2-toluidine in addition to cigarette smoke. Although these sources are not fully characterized, diet is one likely source. Amounts of 4-ABP excreted by smokers (78.6 ± 85.2 [SD] ng/24 hours) were similar to those excreted by nonsmokers (68.1 ± 91.5 ng/24 hours), and amounts of 2-naphthylamine excreted by smokers (84.5 ± 102.7 ng/24 hours) were similar to those excreted by nonsmokers (120.8 ± 279.2 ng/24 hours) (Grimmer et al. 2000). In another study, Hb adducts appeared to be better biomarkers of exposure to aromatic amines from tobacco smoke than were urinary levels of metabolites (Skipper and Tannenbaum 1990).

Researchers have measured urinary biomarkers of heterocyclic aromatic amines mainly in studies of dietary exposure. Little information is available on the contributions of cigarette smoke to urinary levels of heterocyclic aromatic amines (Hecht 2002b).

N-*Nitrosamines*

4-(methylnitrosamino)-1-(3-pyridyl)-1-butanol and its glucuronides. In rodents and humans, 4-(methylnitrosamino)-1-(3-pyridyl)-1-butanol (NNAL) and its glucuronides are quantitatively significant metabolites of NNK (Hecht 1998). Both NNAL and NNK are pulmonary carcinogens with particularly strong activity in rats; NNAL also induces pancreatic tumors (Hecht 1998). Glucuronidation of NNAL at the pyridine nitrogen gives NNAL-*N*-glucuronide, and conjugation at the carbinol oxygen yields NNAL-*O*-glucuronide. Both NNAL-*N*-glucuronide and NNAL-*O*-glucuronide exist as a mixture of two diastereomers, and each diastereomer is a mixture of *E*- and *Z*-rotamers (Upadhyaya et al. 2001). The NNAL-*N*-glucuronide and NNAL-*O*-glucuronide isomers are collectively referred to as NNAL glucuronides. (*R*)-NNAL-*O*-glucuronide does not induce tumors in mice (Upadhyaya et al. 1999). The (*S*) isomer has not been tested, but glucuronidation generally deactivates a carcinogenic metabolite in any event.

NNAL and NNAL glucuronides can be readily determined in urine by using GC with nitrosamine-selective detection (Carmella et al. 1993, 1995; Hecht et al. 1999) and by MS methods (Carmella et al. 1993, 1999; Parsons et al. 1998; Lackmann et al. 1999; Hecht et al. 2001; Byrd and Ogden 2003). Typical levels are about 1 nanomole (nmol) of NNAL in 24 hours and 2.2 nmol of NNAL glucuronides in 24 hours, with no detection of unchanged NNK. NNAL and NNAL glucuronides are absolutely specific to exposure to tobacco and have not been detected in the urine of nontobacco users unless they were exposed to secondhand smoke. Because NNAL is not present in cigarette

smoke, the origin of NNAL and NNAL glucuronides found in urine is the metabolism of NNK. Most investigations demonstrate a correlation between NNAL plus NNAL glucuronides and cotinine in urine. This finding indicates that NNAL and NNAL glucuronides are a biomarker of uptake of the lung carcinogen NNK and that cotinine is a biomarker of nicotine uptake. Ratios of NNAL glucuronides to NNAL vary at least 10-fold in smokers. This ratio could be a potential indicator of cancer risk, because NNAL glucuronides are detoxification products, whereas NNAL is carcinogenic (Carmella et al. 1995; Richie et al. 1997). In human urine, (*S*)-NNAL-*O*-glucuronide is the predominant diastereomer of NNAL-*O*-glucuronide, and the level of (*S*)-NNAL is slightly higher than that of (*R*)-NNAL (Carmella et al. 1999). (*S*)-NNAL is the more tumorigenic enantiomer of NNAL in the A/J mouse lung (Upadhyaya et al. 1999). NNAL and NNAL glucuronides are released slowly from the human body only after smoking cessation. This finding has been linked to a particularly strong retention of (*S*)-NNAL, possibly at a receptor site (Hecht et al. 1999; Zimmerman et al. 2004). Recent studies indicate that levels of NNAL plus NNAL-glucuronides are not only biomarkers of NNK exposure but also are biomarkers of risk for lung cancer in smokers (Church et al. 2009; Yuan et al. 2009)

N'-nitrosonornicotine, N'-nitrosoanatabine, N'-nitrosoanabasine, and their pyridine-N-glucuronides. Researchers developed a method to analyze NNN, *N'*-nitrosoanatabine (NATB), *N'*-nitrosoanabasine (NAB), and their pyridine *N*-glucuronides (e.g., NNN-*N*-glucuronide) in human urine. NATB and NAB are tobacco-specific nitrosamines that like NNN and NNK are formed by the nitrosation of tobacco alkaloids (Hecht and Hoffmann 1988). Studies show that NATB is not carcinogenic but that NAB is a weak esophageal carcinogen in rats (Hecht 1998). Mean levels of total NNN, NATB, and NAB in the urine of 14 smokers were 0.18 ± 0.22 SD, 0.19 ± 0.20, and 0.040 ± 0.039 picomoles/mg of creatinine, respectively. These compounds have not been detected in the urine of nonsmokers with no exposure to secondhand smoke.

Nitrosamino acids. Researchers have used the *N*-nitrosoproline (NPRO) test to compare endogenous nitrosation in smokers and nonsmokers (Bartsch et al. 1989). The results of clinical studies indicate that the frequency of endogenous formation of NPRO is higher in smokers than in nonsmokers and that it may be enhanced by thiocyanate catalysis (Bartsch et al. 1989; Tsuda and Kurashima 1991; Tricker 1997). However, some population-based studies document similar levels of NPRO in smokers and nonsmokers, because this precursor biomarker for nitrosamine formation is primarily from dietary sources (Tricker 1997).

The major nitrosamino acids present in human urine are *N*-nitrososarcosine, *N*-nitrosothiazolidine 4-carboxylic acid (NTCA), and *trans-* and *cis-*isomers of *N*-nitroso-2-methylthiazolidine 4-carboxylic acid (NMTCA) (Bartsch et al. 1989; Tsuda and Kurashima 1991). NTCA and NMTCA are formed by reactions of formaldehyde or acetaldehyde with cysteine, followed by nitrosation. Some studies demonstrate increased levels of urinary NTCA and NMTCA in smokers (Tsuda and Kurashima 1991). Although some studies show a correlation between total nitrosamino acids and urinary nicotine plus cotinine among smokers (Malaveille et al. 1989), other studies show mixed results (Tricker 1997). Collectively, the available data support the concept that nitrosamines can be formed endogenously in smokers under some conditions.

Studies suggest that 4-(methylnitrosamino)-4-(3-pyridyl)butyric acid is a potential monitor of endogenous nitrosation of nicotine (Djordjevic et al. 1991). However, researchers could not find any evidence for its formation after oral administration of nicotine or cotinine to persons abstaining from smoking (Tricker et al. 1993).

1,3-butadiene. The major urinary metabolites of 1,3-butadiene are monohydroxybutenyl-mercapturic acids (MHBMAs) and dihydroxybutyl-mercapturic acid (DHBMA). Levels of MHBMA were 86.4 ± 14.0 (SD) µg/24 hours in smokers and 12.5 ± 1.0 µg/24 hours in nonsmokers—a significant difference (Urban et al. 2003). Corresponding levels of DHBMA were 644 ± 90 (SD) µg/24 hours in smokers and 459 ± 72 µg/24 hours in nonsmokers, which were not significantly different (Urban et al. 2003). DHBMA does not appear to be specific to exposure to 1,3-butadiene and is probably not a useful biomarker. Hb adducts have also proven useful as markers of long-term exposure to 1,3-butadiene. The long half-lives of these adducts result in an average measurement that is more time weighted than that for some other metabolites (e.g., urinary meta-bolites) (Swenberg et al. 2001; Boysen et al. 2007).

Benzene. One path of benzene metabolism proceeds by ring oxidation, ultimately by ring cleavage to *trans,trans*-muconaldehyde, and finally to *trans,trans*-muconic acid (*tt*-MA), a metabolite widely used as a biomarker of benzene uptake (Scherer et al. 1998). Most studies have found significantly elevated levels of *tt*-MA in the urine of smokers (Scherer et al. 1998; Cocco et al. 2003; Lee et al. 2005). Levels of *tt*-MA were 1.4 to 4.8 times higher in smokers than in nonsmokers, and the additional amount of *tt*-MA excreted by smokers ranged from 0.022 to 0.20 mg/gram of creatinine (Scherer et al. 1998). However, sorbic acid, a food constituent that can be transformed metabolically into *tt*-MA, can contribute to urinary levels of *tt*-MA and thereby decrease its specificity as a biomarker for benzene uptake (Scherer et al. 1998; Pezzagno et al. 1999).

S-phenylmercapturic acid (*S*-PMA) is formed by the metabolism of the glutathione conjugate of benzene oxide and has the potential to be specific for benzene uptake (Stommel et al. 1989; van Sittert et al. 1993; Boogaard and van Sittert 1995, 1996; Qu et al. 2000). In one study, *S*-PMA levels were significantly higher in smokers (1.71 micromoles [µmol]/mole of creatinine) than those in nonsmokers (0.94 µmol/mole of creatinine), whereas *tt*-MA levels were not significantly different (Boogaard and van Sittert 1996). Researchers believe that *S*-PMA and *tt*-MA are the most sensitive biomarkers for low levels of exposure to benzene (Qu et al. 2000, 2003).

Phenol, hydroquinone, catechol, and 1,2,4-trihydroxybenzene are also urinary metabolites of benzene. Studies relating urinary levels of these metabolites to occupational exposure to benzene have mixed results, because background levels of the metabolites are high (Inoue et al. 1988, 1989; Ong et al. 1995, 1996; Qu et al. 2000). Urinary catechol levels did not differ significantly between smokers and nonsmokers (Carmella et al. 1982), and diet has been shown to be a major source of urinary catechol (Carmella et al. 1982).

Products of oxidative damage. The presence of free radicals and oxidants in cigarette smoke can lead to oxidative DNA damage and the subsequent formation of products such as 8-oxodeoxyguanosine, thymine glycol, thymidine glycol, and 5-hydroxymethyluracil. Repair of these modified DNA constituents ultimately leads to their excretion in urine. Researchers have frequently quantified 8-oxodeoxyguanosine in urine of smokers and nonsmokers (Loft and Poulsen 1998; Prieme et al. 1998; Renner et al. 2000). Cigarette smoking usually results in levels of 8-oxodeoxyguanosine in urine that modestly increase to 16 to 50 percent higher than those in nonsmokers, but studies have also reported negative results (Nia et al. 2001; Harman et al. 2003; Mukherjee et al. 2004). Smoking cessation caused a 21-percent decrease in the excretion of 8-oxodeoxyguanosine (Prieme et al. 1998). Longitudinal studies have not shown convincing increases in urinary 8-oxodeoxyguanosine that were attributable to smoking, and a complex pattern of factors may affect background levels of this biomarker in urine (Kasai et al. 2001; Pilger et al. 2001; Mukherjee et al. 2004). Studies on the effects of smoking on urinary levels of 5-hydroxymethyluracil or 5-hydroxymethyldeoxyuridine have obtained mixed results (Pourcelot et al. 1999; Harman et al. 2003). One study showed a correlation between smoking and urinary excretion of 3,N^4-ethenodeoxycytidine, which may result from endogenous lipid peroxidation (Chen et al. 2004a). Studies have also detected 1,N^6-ethenodeoxyadenosine in human urine, but no differences were observed between levels in smokers and those in nonsmokers (Hillestrøm et al. 2004).

Products of alkylating agents. The reaction of alkylating agents with DNA forms alkyladenines, alkylguanines, and other products (Singer and Grunberger 1983). Alkylation at the 3-position of deoxyadenosine or at the 7-position of deoxyguanosine results in products with an unstable glycosidic bond. These products are readily removed from DNA, either spontaneously or by glycosylases, which results in the urinary excretion of 3-alkyladenines and 7-alkylguanines. Studies have more extensively investigated 3-alkyladenines as biomarkers of exposure to alkylating agents, because researchers expected the background levels of 3-alkyladenines in urine to be lower than those of 7-alkylguanines. However, substantial amounts of 3-methyladenine occur in the diet (Prevost et al. 1993; Fay et al. 1997). Nevertheless, two controlled studies demonstrated an increase in the urinary excretion of 3-methyladenine among smokers (Kopplin et al. 1995; Prevost and Shuker 1996). Another study found lower background levels of 3-ethyladenine than those of 3-methyladenine (Prevost et al. 1993). Two studies demonstrated convincing increases in urinary levels of 3-ethyladenine in smokers, indicating the presence in cigarette smoke of an unidentified ethylating agent (Kopplin et al. 1995; Prevost and Shuker 1996). There was no effect from smoking on urinary levels of 3-(2-hydroxyethyl)adenine (Prevost and Shuker 1996). A population-based study found higher levels of both 3-methyladenine and 7-methylguanine in smokers than in nonsmokers, and a second study found no difference in the 3-methyladenine levels (Shuker et al. 1991; Stillwell et al. 1991).

Metals. Studies of urinary cadmium have most consistently demonstrated differences between smokers and nonsmokers. Large studies in Germany and the United States showed increases in urinary cadmium levels with age and smoking (IARC 2004). These results were consistent with those of other studies.

Breath and Blood Biomarkers

Benzene, 1,3-butadiene, and a variety of volatile organic compounds including xylenes, styrene, isoprene, 2,5-dimethylfuran, ethane, and octane were measured in expired air; levels were generally higher in smokers than in nonsmokers (Gordon et al. 2002; Perbellini et al. 2003; IARC 2004). Levels of benzene and 1,3-butadiene in the breath of smokers were 360 and 522 µg/cubic meter (m^3), respectively (Gordon et al. 2002). In another study, mean benzene levels ranged from 58.1 to 81.3 µg/m^3, depending on the cigarette brand (IARC 2004).

Studies have quantified volatile organic compounds, including benzene and styrene, in the blood of smokers; levels were generally higher than those in the blood of nonsmokers. Benzene levels in blood were significantly associated with the number of cigarettes smoked (IARC 2004). Cadmium levels were also higher in the blood of smokers. Measurements of NNAL in blood demonstrated a mean level of 42 femtomoles/milliliter of plasma in smokers; NNAL was not detected in nonsmokers (Carmella et al. 2005). Cigarette smoke induces oxidative damage as determined by elevated blood protein carbonyls (Reznick et al. 1992) and blood protein-bound glutathione (Muscat et al. 2004). F_2-isoprostane levels, which are biomarkers of oxidative damage, were higher in the plasma of smokers than in the plasma of nonsmokers and decreased with vitamin C treatments (Morrow et al. 1995; Dietrich et al. 2002). Hb adducts and DNA adducts in white blood cells are discussed in the next section.

Summary

Quantitative analysis of carcinogens or their metabolites in urine, breath, and blood provides a convenient and reliable method of comparing carcinogen exposure among smokers and between smokers and nonsmokers. The most extensive measurements have been made in urine. Urinary biomarkers of several major types of carcinogens in cigarette smoke are reliable indicators of exposure. These biomarkers include *trans, anti*-PheT and 1-HOP for PAH; total NNAL (NNAL plus NNAL glucuronides) for NNK; MHBMA for 1,3-butadiene; and *tt*-MA and *S*-PMA for benzene. The measurements provide good estimates of minimum doses of relevant carcinogens in smokers and allow comparisons with those in nonsmokers. The total carcinogen dose is generally difficult to calculate because the extent of conversion of a given carcinogen to the measured metabolite is usually unknown and can vary widely among individuals. Nevertheless, the results of these studies are illuminating. They show, for example, that levels of metabolites of benzene (about 1,100 nmol/24 hours of *tt*-MA and 8 nmol/24 hours of *S*-PMA) and 1,3-butadiene (about 340 nmol/24 hours of MHBMA) exceed levels of other biomarkers (e.g., about 3 nmol/24 hours of NNAL plus NNAL glucuronides and 2 nmol/24 hours of 1-HOP). These results are consistent with the levels of benzene and 1,3-butadiene in cigarette smoke, which were higher than those of NNK and PAH.

However, metabolites of benzene and a metabolite of 1,3-butadiene (DHBMA) are also found in nonsmokers in considerable quantities. Comparisons of smokers and nonsmokers demonstrate that total NNAL is the most discriminatory carcinogen biomarker because the only source of the parent carcinogen NNK is tobacco products. Total NNAL is not detected in nonsmokers unless they have been exposed to secondhand tobacco smoke. Therefore, this biomarker is particularly useful for comparing carcinogen uptake in smokers who, for example, use different tobacco products, because the measurements are not confounded by other exposures such as diet, occupation, or the general environment.

Metabolic Activation and Detoxification of Carcinogens

Most of the carcinogens listed in Table 5.1 require metabolic activation to become intermediate agents, generally electrophiles, which react with nucleophilic sites in DNA to form DNA adducts. All PAHs, heterocyclic compounds, N-nitrosamines, aromatic amines, and heterocyclic aromatic amines in cigarette smoke require metabolic activation. Other compounds in Table 5.1 that require metabolic activation are 1,3-butadiene, isoprene, benzene, nitromethane, 2-nitropropane, nitrobenzene, acrylamide, vinyl chloride, and urethane. Detoxification reactions in most cases compete with metabolic activation and also affect the disposition of compounds that do not require metabolic activation, such as ethylene oxide.

An overview of the metabolism of six carcinogens in tobacco smoke that are implicated in the formation of DNA adducts identified in human tissues is presented in Figure 5.3. The six carcinogens are B[a]P, NNK, N-nitrosodimethylamine (NDMA), NNN, ethylene oxide, and 4-ABP.

The major metabolic activation pathway of B[a]P that results in DNA adducts identified in human tissues is the conversion to the highly mutagenic B[a]P-7,8-diol-9,10-epoxides (BPDEs). The formation of BPDE occurs in three steps: the metabolism of B[a]P to B[a]P-7,8-epoxide; hydration of B[a]P-7,8-epoxide to give the dihydrodiol B[a]P-7,8-diol; and further epoxidation to produce BPDE. One of the four enantiomers is strongly carcinogenic and reacts with DNA to form adducts at N^2 of deoxyguanosine (BPDE-N^2-deoxyguanosine) (Cooper et al. 1983; IARC 1983; Thakker et al. 1985). This adduct was also observed in animals treated with B[a]P.

Two other proposed metabolic activation pathways of B[a]P exist, but the evidence for their involvement in DNA adduct formation in laboratory animals and humans is not as strong as that for BPDE. One pathway involves the conversion of B[a]P-7,8-diol to the corresponding catechol metabolite catalyzed by dihydrodiol dehydrogenase. The catechol can undergo redox cycling to produce a quinone reactive with DNA, and the redox cycling process can produce oxidative damage to DNA (Penning et al. 1999; Yu et al. 2002). Another metabolic activation process occurs when one electron oxidation of B[a]P produces unstable depurinating DNA adducts that can lead to apurinic sites and miscoding (Casale et al. 2001). A common mechanism

of metabolic activation for a number of PAHs is the formation of diol epoxides in which the epoxide ring is in the bay region of the PAH molecule, similar to that in BPDE (Conney 1982; Thakker et al. 1985; Baird and Ralston 1997). Competing with B[a]P metabolic activation processes are detoxification pathways leading to (1) phenols through direct hydroxylation or rearrangement of initially formed epoxides, (2) dihydrodiols through hydration of epoxides catalyzed by epoxide hydrolase, and (3) formation of glutathione, glucuronide, and sulfate conjugates. Researchers have also observed the formation of quinone metabolites from initial hydroxylation at the 6-position, followed by further oxidation (Cooper et al. 1983).

Metabolic activation of NDMA occurs by α-hydroxylation and leads to an unstable α-hydroxymethyl metabolite. This compound spontaneously loses formaldehyde and forms methanediazohydroxide, the same intermediate agent produced in the α-methylene hydroxylation of NNK. Researchers also observed the consequent formation of methyl DNA adducts such as 7-methylguanine, O^6-methylguanine, and O^4-methylthymidine. Denitrosation produces nitrite and methylamine and is a detoxification pathway (Preussmann and Stewart 1984; Hecht and Samet 2007). The metabolism of NNK and NDMA forms aldehydes, whose roles in carcinogenesis are unclear, but studies show that formaldehyde reacts with DNA and protein to form cross-links and other products (Chaw et al. 1980; Beland et al. 1984; Hecht and Samet 2007).

α-hydroxylation of NNN adjacent to the pyridine ring produces the same intermediate agent formed by methyl hydroxylation of NNK, which leads to pyridyloxobutyl (POB)-DNA adducts (Hecht 1998). α-hydroxylation distal from the pyridine ring also produces a reactive diazohydroxide, but its reactions with DNA have not been fully characterized. The acetate esters of the α-hydroxy-NNN metabolites are mutagenic (Hecht 1998; Hecht and Samet 2007). β-hydroxylation of NNN, a minor pathway, and pyridine-N-oxidation are detoxification reactions. NNN is also detoxified by denitrosation and oxidation to produce norcotinine, and by glucuronidation of the pyridine ring (Hecht 1998; Stepanov and Hecht 2005; Hecht and Samet 2007).

Ethylene oxide reacts directly with DNA to form 7-(2-hydroxyethyl)guanine and other adducts (IARC 1994; Hecht and Samet 2007). Competing detoxification pathways involve glutathione conjugation and excretion of mercapturic acids (IARC 1994).

4-ABP is metabolically activated by N-hydroxylation (Kadlubar and Beland 1985; Hecht and Samet 2007). Conjugation of the resulting hydroxylamine with acetate or other groups, such as sulfate, ultimately produces nitrenium ions, which react with DNA and form adducts

Figure 5.3   Metabolism of six carcinogens in tobacco smoke that produce DNA adducts identified in the lungs of smokers

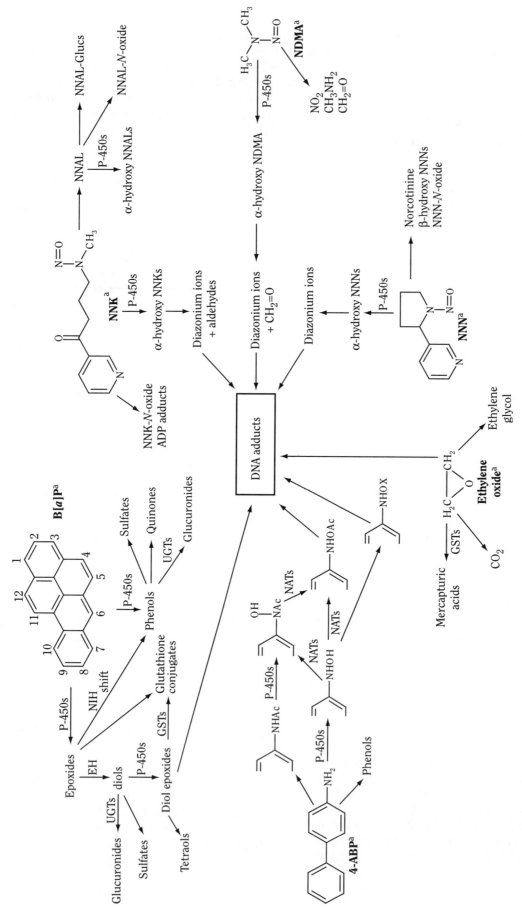

Source: Adapted from Cooper et al. 1983; Preussmann and Stewart 1984; Kadlubar and Beland 1985; International Agency for Research on Cancer 1994; and Hecht 1998, 1999.
Note: In 4-ABP scheme, X represents conjugates such as glucuronide or sulfate. **4-ABP** = 4-aminobiphenyl; **Ac** = acetyl; **ADP** = adenosine diphosphate; **B[a]P** = benzo[a]pyrene; **EH** = epoxide hydrolase; **Glucs** = glucuronides; **GSTs** = glutathione-S-transferases; **NATs** = N-acetyltransferases; **NDMA** = N-nitrosodimethylamine; **NIH shift** = National Institutes of Health phenomenon of hydroxylation-induced intramolecular migration; **NNAL** = 4-(methylnitrosamino)-1-(3-pyridyl)-1-butanol; **NNK** = 4-(methylnitrosamino)-1-(3-pyridyl)-1-butanone; **NNN** = N'-nitrosonornicotine; **P-450s** = cytochrome P-450 enzymes; **UGTs** = uridine-5'-diphosphate-glucuronosyltransferases.
[a]Carcinogens in tobacco smoke.

mainly at C-8 of guanine. Other aromatic amines, as well as heterocyclic aromatic amines, are predominantly activated metabolically in similar ways. Acetylation of 4-ABP can be a detoxification pathway if it is not followed by N-hydroxylation. Ring hydroxylation and conjugation of the phenols result in detoxification.

Two other important carcinogens from cigarette smoke that require metabolic activation are benzene and 1,3-butadiene. DNA adducts of these compounds have not been detected in human samples. However, there is considerable information on their conversion to intermediate agents that react with DNA.

Benzene is metabolized to benzene epoxide, which is in equilibrium with its 7-member ring tautomer oxepin (Scherer et al. 2001; Hecht and Samet 2007). Researchers have observed the reaction of benzene epoxide with DNA to produce 7-phenylguanine. Further metabolism of benzene epoxide-oxepin can occur in a variety of ways. One way is nonenzymatic rearrangement to phenol, which can be further hydroxylated to hydroquinone, catechol, and 1,2,4-trihydroxybenzene. These metabolites can then be conjugated as glucuronides or sulfates. Hydroquinone can be further oxidized to benzoquinone, which can bind to DNA, or hydration catalyzed by epoxide hydrolase can produce benzene dihydrodiol, which can then be converted to catechol or *tt*-MA. Another possibility involves conjugation with glutathione that ultimately produces S-PMA. Other pathways of benzene metabolism result in the formation of biphenyl and benzene dioxetane, which can also lead to *tt*-MA (Scherer et al. 2001; Hecht and Samet 2007). Studies have detected nitrobenzene, nitrobiphenyl, and nitrophenol isomers in the bone marrow of mice treated with benzene; these isomers presumably formed from reactions of benzene with endogenously generated nitric oxide (Chen et al. 2004b; Hecht and Samet 2007).

1,3-butadiene is metabolically activated by epoxidation to give a monoepoxide that can be further metabolized to a diepoxide and a dihydrodiol epoxide (van Sittert et al. 2000; Hecht and Samet 2007), which all form DNA adducts. The dihydrodiol epoxide also produces cross-links in DNA and may be the most important of these intermediate agents (Park and Tretyakova 2004; Hecht and Samet 2007). The epoxides can be hydrated to dihydrodiols and conjugated by reactions with glutathione. 1,3-butadiene metabolism can also lead to epoxidation and formation of N-terminal Hb adducts, providing a longer-term, "time-weighted" measurement of exposure (Swenberg et al. 2001).

Although details remain to be determined, the major pathways of metabolic activation and detoxification of some of the principal carcinogens in cigarette smoke are well established. Reactive intermediate agents that are critical in forming DNA adducts include diol epoxides of PAH, diazonium ions generated by α-hydroxylation of nitrosamines, nitrenium ions formed from esters of N-hydroxylated aromatic amines, and epoxides such as ethylene oxide. Glutathione and glucuronide conjugation play major roles in the detoxification of carcinogens in cigarette smoke.

Enzymology of Carcinogen Metabolism

Introduction

A number of enzyme families are important in both the activation and detoxification of carcinogens in cigarette smoke, including P-450s, GSTs, UGTs, N-acetyltransferases (NATs), epoxide hydrolases, and sulfotransferases. The importance of each enzyme to the activation or detoxification of a particular carcinogen depends on characteristics of both the carcinogen (size, polarity, and lipophilicity) and the enzyme (structure, tissue distribution, and regulation of expression). The large number of carcinogens in cigarette smoke and the wide variety of enzymes involved in metabolizing these carcinogens preclude a comprehensive discussion of current understanding of the contribution of each enzyme to every pathway. Therefore, the goals of this presentation are to introduce the families of enzymes involved and to highlight some of the activation and detoxification reactions for specific enzymes and carcinogens.

Cytochrome P-450 Enzymes

P-450s, encoded by *CYP* genes, are microsomal enzymes that catalyze the oxidation of myriad chemicals, including many of the carcinogens in cigarette smoke. Sequencing the human genome has identified 57 *CYP* genes, about 15 of which are considered important in the metabolism of xenobiotics (Nelson 2003; Guengerich 2004). Among the P-450s encoded by these genes, a reasonable argument can be made for the role of six (1A1, 1B1, 1A2, 2A6, 2A13, and 2E1) as important catalysts for the metabolic activation of carcinogens in cigarette smoke. PAHs are metabolized by P-450s 1A1 and 1B1 (Shimada and Fujii-Kuriyama 2004), aromatic amines by P-450 1A2 (Kim and Guengerich 2005), and N-nitrosamines by P-450s 2A6, 2A13, and 2E1 (Yoo et al. 1988; Guengerich et al. 1991; Yamazaki et al. 1992; Jalas et al. 2005; Wong et al. 2005a). P-450 2E1 also catalyzes the epoxidation of benzene and 1,3-butadiene (Guengerich et al. 1991; Bolt et al. 2003).

P-450s 1A1 and 1B1 are expressed in a wide range of extrahepatic tissues and catalyze both the activation and detoxification reactions of PAH metabolism (Shimada and Fujii-Kuriyama 2004). In addition, both enzymes are inducible by the PAHs in cigarette smoke (Nebert et al. 2004). Induction of these two enzymes is generally mediated by the aryl hydrocarbon receptor, but differences may exist in the mode of induction for each enzyme. Historically, researchers believed that P-450 1A1 was the predominant P-450 catalyst for the metabolism of PAHs, particularly in the lung. However, the discovery of P-450 1B1 (Sutter et al. 1994) clarified the equal or more predominant role P-450 1B1 may play in the activation of PAHs compared with that of P-450 1A1 (Shimada et al. 1996). Studies show that P-450 1B1, which is heterologously expressed, activates the proximate carcinogen of many PAHs and that in several cases, P-450 1B1 was more efficient than P-450 1A1 (Shimada et al. 1996). For example, (+)-B[*a*]P-7,8-diol was activated to a genotoxic species to a greater extent by P-450 1B1 than by P-450 1A1 (Shimada et al. 1996). In addition, the ratio of the maximum velocity (V_{max}) of an enzyme-catalyzed reaction to the concentration of a substrate that leads to half-maximal velocity (K_m) for the formation of B[*a*]P-7,8-diol was 3.5-fold greater for P-450 1B1 than for P-450 1A1 (Shimada et al. 1999). (The V_{max} to K_m ratio measures an enzyme's efficiency.) In contrast, P-450 1A1 was a better catalyst of B[*a*]P 3-hydroxylation, which is a detoxification pathway (Shimada et al. 1997). Taken together, these data indicate that P-450 1B1 activity, but not P-450 1A1 activity, may contribute to individual susceptibility to B[*a*]P-induced carcinogenesis. However, cigarette smoke has many different PAH carcinogens, and either P-450 1B1 or 1A1 individually or together may be important in their metabolic activation.

As noted previously (see "Cytochrome P-450 Enzymes" earlier in this chapter), both P-450 1A1 and 1B1 are inducible by PAHs. Studies have reported that levels of messenger RNA (mRNA) and protein of both P-450s were higher in the lungs of smokers than in the lungs of lifetime nonsmokers (Willey et al. 1997; Kim et al. 2004a; Port et al. 2004). The levels of P-450 1A1 and 1B1 proteins were correlated in lung microsomes from all participants who smoked. However, the absolute amount of P-450 1A1 in each person was, on average, more than 10-fold greater than the amount of P-450 1B1 (Kim et al. 2004a). Despite the ability of P-450 1B1 to more efficiently mediate the activation of some PAHs, the higher P-450 1A1 levels may result in each enzyme contributing similarly to the total metabolism of PAHs. An equally important factor in determining the role of these P-450s in the activation of PAHs in cigarette smoke is the variability in the induction of P-450s across individuals. Researchers do not know whether the responsible mechanism is common to both P-450s 1A1 and 1B1.

Studies have characterized P-450 1A2 as the best catalyst for aromatic amine *N*-oxidation, which is the first step in the activation of these bladder carcinogens (Butler et al. 1989; Landi et al. 1999; Kim and Guengerich 2005). P-450 1A2 is both constitutively expressed and inducible in the liver. The induction of P-450 1A2 is mediated by the aryl hydrocarbon receptor, and hepatic levels vary more than 60-fold from person to person (Nebert et al. 2004). Cigarette smoking induces the levels of this enzyme in the liver. Researchers have also reported that P-450s 1A1 and 1B1 metabolically activate a number of aromatic amines, including 4-ABP, and may play a role in extrahepatic metabolism (Shimada et al. 1996).

Although hepatic P-450 2A6 catalyzes the metabolic activation of NNK (Yamazaki et al. 1992; Jalas et al. 2005), P-450 2A6 is not a particularly efficient catalyst. The extrahepatic P-450 2A13 might be a more important catalyst of the activation of this carcinogen (Jalas et al. 2005). P-450 2A13 is expressed in the lung (Su et al. 2000) and catalyzes the α-hydroxylation of NNK significantly more efficiently than does P-450 2A6. P-450 2A13 is an excellent catalyst of NNK α-hydroxylation, with a low K_m and a high V_{max}. P-450 2A13 is the sole catalyst of NNK α-hydroxylation in human fetal nasal tissue and is considered equally important in the lung (Wong et al. 2005b). P-450 2E1 has also catalyzed the activation of both NNN and NNK (Yamazaki et al. 1992). However, the catalytic efficiencies of these reactions are poor (Hecht 1998; Jalas et al. 2005). Studies have identified P-450 2E1 as the best catalyst of NDMA metabolism (Yoo et al. 1988; Guengerich et al. 1991) and as an excellent catalyst of the epoxidation and activation of benzene and 1,3-butadiene (Guengerich et al. 1991; Bolt et al. 2003).

Epoxide Hydrolases

Several carcinogens of tobacco smoke, including PAH, 1,3-butadiene, and benzene, are metabolized to epoxides. These epoxide metabolites are substrates for MEH (also known as EPHX1), an enzyme that catalyzes their hydrolysis (Wood et al. 1976; Snyder et al. 1993; Krause and Elfarra 1997; Fretland and Omiecinski 2000). In mammals, at least five epoxide hydrolases were identified. However, four of these predominantly or exclusively catalyze the hydrolysis of endogenous substrates (Fretland and Omiecinski 2000). The fifth, MEH, plays a role in both the detoxification and activation of xenobiotics. Specifically, MEH is involved in the formation of the reactive diol epoxide metabolites of PAHs, and its activity is therefore critical to the carcinogenicity of these compounds (Conney 1982). For example, MEH catalyzes the hydrolysis of

B[*a*]P-7,8-epoxide to B[*a*]P-7,8-diol, which is then oxidized to the ultimate carcinogen BPDE (Levin et al. 1976; Gautier et al. 1996). The importance of this enzyme to PAH carcinogenicity is supported by the observation that MEH-null mice are highly resistant to carcinogenesis induced by 7,12-dimethylbenz[*a*]anthracene (Miyata et al. 1999).

In contrast to its role in the activation of PAHs, MEH detoxifies the epoxides of 1,3-butadiene (Krause and Elfarra 1997; Wickliffe et al. 2003). Studies have reported that several polymorphisms in MEH result in an increased sensitivity to the genotoxic effects of 1,3-butadiene (Abdel-Rahman et al. 2003, 2005). Benzene oxide is also a substrate for MEH (Snyder et al. 1993). However, male mice deficient in MEH are not susceptible to toxic effects induced by benzene (Bauer et al. 2003). The role of benzene oxide in carcinogenesis is unclear.

Glutathione-*S*-Transferases

Another mechanism that may detoxify carcinogenic epoxides is conjugation with glutathione. This reaction can be catalyzed by cytosolic GSTs (Sheehan et al. 2001; Hayes et al. 2005), which are dimeric. Seven classes (alpha, mu, pi, sigma, theta, omega, and zeta) exist in mammalian species (Sheehan et al. 2001), and at least 16 GST subunits exist in humans. However, only four homodimeric enzymes to date have been characterized as catalysts of glutathione conjugation of tobacco smoke carcinogens (Cheng et al. 1995; Norppa et al. 1995; Wiencke et al. 1995; Jernstrom et al. 1996; Sundberg et al. 1998, 2002; Landi 2000; Verdina et al. 2001; Fustinoni et al. 2002; Sørensen et al. 2004a; Hayes et al. 2005). These enzymes are members of four GST classes: alpha (GSTA1-1), mu (GSTM1-1), pi (GSTP1-1), and theta (GSTT1-1). The protein levels of each GST vary significantly from person to person, as well as across tissues within an individual (Rowe et al. 1997; Sherratt et al. 1997; Mulder et al. 1999). Researchers have identified several polymorphisms in the genes encoding these subunits (Hayes et al. 2005). Of particular note with regard to cancer risk in smokers are the *NULL* alleles for *GSTM1* and *GSTT1*, which have decreased detoxification capacity and elevated DNA damage. *GSTA1*, *GSTM1*, and *GSTT1* are expressed in the liver of persons who are not homozygous for either null phenotype; little GSTP1 is present in the liver (Rowe et al. 1997; Sherratt et al. 1997; Mulder et al. 1999). In contrast, the lung expresses higher levels of GSTP1 than those expressed by the other three subunits (Rowe et al. 1997; Sherratt et al. 1997).

GSTA1-1, GSTM1-1, and GSTP1-1 each catalyze the glutathione conjugation of a number of PAH diol epoxides (Jernstrom et al. 1996; Sundberg et al. 1998, 2002). However, the efficiencies and stereoselectivity of each of these enzymes vary with the diol epoxide substrate. For example, GSTM1-1 is a more efficient catalyst of glutathione conjugation of (+)-*anti*-BPDE than is either GSTA1-1 or GSTP1-1 (Sundberg et al. 1997). The GSTA1-1 and GSTP1-1 enzymes have overall K_{cat}/K_m values for catalytic rate or turnover number that are about 3-fold lower than the value for GSTM1-1, but GSTM1-1 is almost 30-fold better as a catalyst for the conjugation of (-)-*anti*-BPDE (Sundberg et al. 1997). The contribution of each GST enzyme to the detoxification of PAH diol epoxides varies with the substrate and across different tissues on the basis of their expression levels. In lung tissue from smokers, levels of (+)-*anti*-BPDE–DNA adducts were dependent on the *GSTM1* genotype (Alexandrov et al. 2002). Persons with the *GSTM1* null genotype had significantly higher adduct levels than did those with the *GST* wild-type genotype. These data support the importance of GSTM1-1 activity in BPDE detoxification in the lung, but they do not exclude a role for GSTA1-1 and GSTP1-1 in the detoxification of this or other PAHs.

GSTM1-1 and GSTT1-1 enzymes play a key role in the conjugation of two 1,3-butadiene epoxide metabolites: 3,4-epoxybutene (EB) and diepoxybutane (DEB) (Norppa et al. 1995; Wiencke et al. 1995; Thier et al. 1996; Bernardini et al. 1998; Landi 2000; Fustinoni et al. 2002; Schlade-Bartusiak et al. 2004). The direct measurement of either GSTM1-1 or GSTT1-1 activity with these epoxide substrates has not been reported. However, several studies of sister chromatid exchange (SCE) in human lymphocyte cultures from persons with the *GSTT1* null genotype support the role of GSTT1-1 in the detoxification of DEB (Norppa et al. 1995; Wiencke et al. 1995; Bernardini et al. 1998; Landi 2000; Schlade-Bartusiak et al. 2004). In conflict with these data, one study reports the increased mutagenicity of DEB in *Salmonella typhimurium* TA1535 expressing *GSTT1-1*, suggesting that the conjugation of this diepoxide is an activation pathway (Thier et al. 1996). The role of both GSTM1-1 and GSTT1-1 in the detoxification of EB is supported by a higher induction of SCE by EB in lymphocyte cultures from persons with either the *GSTM1-1* or the *GSTT1-1* null genotype (Uusküla et al. 1995; Bernardini et al. 1998). Although GSTs play a role in the metabolism of 1,3-butadiene, it remains unclear whether polymorphisms in GSTs modulate the carcinogenic effects of 1,3-butadiene in humans (Fustinoni et al. 2002).

One major excreted metabolite of benzene is *S*-PMA, which is formed from the glutathione conjugate of benzene oxide (Snyder and Hedli 1996). This glutathione conjugate may be generated both enzymatically and nonenzymatically, and it is not clear which pathway predominates. However, a number of studies on benzene exposure and toxicity have suggested a role for either GSTM1-1 or

GSTT1-1 in the conjugation of benzene oxide (Hsieh et al. 1999; Verdina et al. 2001; Wan et al. 2002; Kim et al. 2004b). Researchers have not directly measured which enzyme is the better catalyst of glutathione conjugation of benzene oxide. The in vivo role of GSTT1-1 in benzene oxide detoxification is supported by a report that *S*-PMA levels excreted by persons exposed to benzene who carried the wild-type *GSTT1** allele were higher than those of persons homozygous for the *GSTT1* NULL* allele (Sørensen et al. 2004b).

Ethylene oxide is also detoxified by glutathione conjugation (Brown et al. 1996). Although studies have not directly evaluated the role of specific human GSTs, evidence supports the role of GSTT1-1 as a catalyst of this reaction (Hallier et al. 1993; Fennell et al. 2000). On exposure to ethylene oxide, lymphocytes from persons with the *GSTT1-1* NULL* allele had higher levels of SCE than did those from persons with the wild-type allele (Hallier et al. 1993). In addition, levels of 2-hydroxyethylvaline Hb adducts were higher in smokers than in nonsmokers, because of exposure to ethylene and ethylene oxide in cigarette smoke, and were higher in smokers with the *GSTT1*NULL* allele than in those with the wild-type allele (Fennell et al. 2000).

Uridine-5′-Diphosphate-Glucuronosyltransferases

Conjugation with glucuronic acid is an important metabolic pathway for a number of carcinogens in tobacco smoke (Bock 1991; Hecht 2002a; Nagar and Remmel 2006). (Conjugation is the addition of a polar moiety to a metabolite to facilitate excretion.) The microsomal enzymes, UGTs, catalyze these conjugation reactions. Researchers have identified 18 human UGTs that are members of two families (UGT1 and UGT2) (Tukey and Strassburg 2000; Burchell 2003; Nagar and Remmel 2006). The UGT1A proteins are encoded by a single gene cluster, and expression of the nine members of this subfamily occurs through exon sharing. Exon 1 is unique for each *UGT1A*, whereas exon 2 to exon 5 are shared by all *UGT1As* (Tukey and Strassburg 2000). Thus, all UGT1A proteins are identical in the 245 amino acids of the carboxyl terminus encoded by exon 2 to exon 5 (Tukey and Strassburg 2000; Finel et al. 2005). In contrast, proteins from the UGT2 family are all unique gene products (Riedy et al. 2000; Tukey and Strassburg 2000). The expression of UGTs is tissue specific, and there are large differences in expression among tissues (Gregory et al. 2000, 2004; Tukey and Strassburg 2000; Wells et al. 2004). For example, UGTs 1A1, 1A3, 1A4, 1A6, and 1A9 are highly expressed in the liver; UGTs 1A7, 1A8, and 1A10 are mainly expressed in extrahepatic tissues (Tukey and Strassburg 2000; Gregory et al. 2004; Wells et al. 2004).

Aromatic amines and their *N*-hydroxy metabolites are glucuronidated to facilitate excretion (Bock 1991; Tukey and Strassburg 2000; Zenser et al. 2002). Glucuronidation is a detoxification reaction. Therefore, variations in the expression and catalytic efficiency of the enzymes that catalyze this reaction may influence the carcinogenicity of particular aromatic amines. In general, researchers have suggested that members of the UGT1A family contribute to the glucuronidation of these carcinogens (Orzechowski et al. 1994; Green and Tephly 1998; Tukey and Strassburg 2000; Zenser et al. 2002). However, UGT2B7 also catalyzes their glucuronidation (Zenser et al. 2002). In most cases, data support UGT1A9 as the best catalyst. For the tobacco smoke carcinogen 4-ABP, the relative catalytic efficiency of *N*-glucuronidation is UGT1A9>UGT1A4>UGT1A7>UGT2B7>UGT1A6, but the catalytic efficiency of all these proteins is approximately equal to that of UGT1A1 (Zenser et al. 2002).

The phenol and diol metabolites of PAHs are primarily eliminated as glucuronide conjugates. Researchers have studied the role of specific UGTs in the metabolism of B[*a*]P (Bock 1991; Guillemette et al. 2000; Fang et al. 2002; Dellinger et al. 2006). Studies with UGT1A-deficient rats have implicated UGT1A enzymes in the detoxification of B[*a*]P (Wells et al. 2004). The glucuronidation of B[*a*]P-7,8-diol and 3-hydroxy-, 7-hydroxy-, and 9-hydroxy-B[*a*]P by heterologously expressed human UGTs has been characterized for a number of UGT1A and UGT2B enzymes (Fang et al. 2002; Dellinger et al. 2006). Among the phenols, UGT1A10 was the most efficient UGT1A catalyst of glucuronidation. UGTs 2B7, 2B15, and 2B17 all catalyzed conjugation of the three B[*a*]P phenols. However, the K_m of the reaction for UGT2B enzymes was 2- to 250-fold higher than that for UGT1A10 (Dellinger et al. 2006). For the carcinogenic (-)-B[*a*]P-7,8-diol, UGT1A10 was a better catalyst of glucuronidation than was UGT1A9, and UGT2B7 did not catalyze detectable levels of glucuronidation (Fang et al. 2002), but UGT2B7 did catalyze the glucuronidation of (+)-B[*a*]P-7,8-diol.

In smokers, glucuronidation also plays an important role in the excretion of the NNK metabolite NNAL (Carmella et al. 2002b; Hecht 2002a). Both *O*-linked and *N*-linked NNAL glucuronide conjugates are formed (Carmella et al. 2002b). In addition, the direct detoxification of the hydroxymethyl metabolite of NNK occurs by glucuronidation in rats (Murphy et al. 1995). However, the contribution of this pathway to NNK detoxification in smokers has not been identified. In vitro studies with fibroblasts both from UGT1A-deficient and control rats have confirmed a role for UGT1A enzymes in the protection of these cells from NNK-induced micronuclei formation (Kim and Wells 1996). Human UGT1A9, UGT2B7, and UGT2B17 catalyze NNAL-*O*-glucuronidation, with UGT2B17 being the most active, and UGT1A4 catalyzes NNAL-*N*-glucuronidation (Ren et al. 2000; Wiener et al. 2004b; Lazarus et al. 2005). The rate of NNAL *O*- and *N*-glucuronidation by human liver microsomes varies significantly among persons; researchers have suggested that polymorphisms in *UGT2B7* and *UGT1A4* contribute to this variability (Wiener et al. 2004a).

Glucuronidation may also contribute to the detoxification of benzene (Bock 1991). In hepatocytes from rats treated with 3-methylcholanthrene to induce UGTs, phenol glucuronidation increases compared with sulfation. Glucuronide conjugates are more stable than the corresponding sulfates, and researchers have suggested the glucuronidation of phenol as a detoxification pathway (Bock 1991). However, to date, the role of glucuronidation in benzene-induced carcinogenesis has not been characterized and is poorly understood.

N-Acetyltransferases

NATs are cytosolic enzymes that catalyze the transfer of the acetyl group from acetylcoenzyme A to an acceptor molecule (Hein et al. 2000b). This transfer occurs through an enzyme intermediate in which cysteine 68 is acetylated and then deacetylated during the course of the reaction. Humans express two unique enzymes, NAT1 and NAT2, which catalyze both *N*- and *O*-acetylation reactions. Researchers have recognized the polymorphic nature of *NAT2* for more than 40 years and, more recently, have identified more than 35 alleles (Hein et al. 2000b; Hein 2002). *NAT1* is less well studied but is also polymorphic, and more than 25 alleles have been identified (Hein 2002; University of Louisville School of Medicine 2006). Researchers suggest that polymorphisms in both *NAT1* and *NAT2* influence the activation and detoxification of carcinogenic aromatic amines in tobacco smoke (Hein 2002).

The *N*-acetylation of aromatic amines, such as 4-ABP, is a detoxification reaction (Hein 2002). In contrast, *O*-acetylation of the *N*-hydroxy metabolites of arylamines generated by P-450 (e.g., *N*-hydroxy-4-ABP) is an activation reaction leading to DNA adduct formation (Hein et al. 1993, 1995; Hein 2002). NAT1 and NAT2 both catalyze each of these reactions (Hein et al. 1993). However, NAT2 is generally considered the more important catalyst of detoxification, and NAT1 is the more important catalyst of activation (Badawi et al. 1995; Hein 2002). This assumption is based on differences in the catalytic efficiency of the enzymes and their tissue distribution in humans as well as on studies with animal models (Hein et al. 1993; Hein 2002).

Studies with recombinant human *NAT1* and *NAT2* have described differences in the *N*-acetylation of 4-ABP. The apparent affinity of 4-ABP for NAT2 is significantly greater than that for NAT1, and ratios of NAT1 activity to NAT2 activity and clearance calculations support a greater role for NAT2 than for NAT1 in the *N*-acetylation of arylamines (Hein et al. 1993). The characterization of NAT1 as the key catalyst of the *O*-acetylation (i.e., activation) of aromatic amines is more speculative and is primarily driven by the tissue distribution of NAT1 (see the discussion below). No data in the literature report differences between the efficiencies of NAT1- and NAT2-catalyzed *O*-acetylation of aromatic amines. However, more recent studies that engineered *S. typhimurium* strains to overexpress either *NAT1* or *NAT2* reported that NAT1, but not NAT2, catalyzed the genotoxic activation of *N*-hydroxy-4-ABP (Oda 2004). These data provide support for NAT1 as an important catalyst in the activation of this aromatic amine.

The organ and tissue distribution of NAT1 and NAT2 differ markedly (Dupret and Rodrigues-Lima 2005). The NAT2 protein is mainly expressed in the gut and liver; the NAT1 protein is expressed in the liver and a number of other tissues, including the colon and bladder. Researchers believe that aromatic amines in tobacco smoke contribute to smoking-related bladder cancer. Therefore, the potential activation of these compounds in the bladder is important in understanding the etiology of bladder cancer. Researchers have detected NAT1 activity, but not NAT2 activity, in samples of bladder tissue from smokers (Badwawi et al. 1995). In addition, DNA adduct levels measured by ^{32}P-postlabeling correlated with NAT1 activity. These data are thus consistent with a role for NAT1 in the activation of arylamines in tobacco smoke.

Epidemiologic studies that demonstrate a modest increase in risk of bladder cancer in persons phenotypically and genotypically identified as having slow acetylation catalyzed by NAT2 further support the role of NAT2 in the detoxification of aromatic amines (Green et al. 2000; Hein et al. 2000a; Gu et al. 2005) (see "Molecular Epidemiology of Polymorphisms in Carcinogen-Metabolizing Genes" later in this chapter). A number of the *NAT2* variant alleles identified in persons with slow acetylation were expressed heterologously and demonstrated a decrease in activity for both the *N*-acetylation of 4-ABP and *O*-acetylation of *N*-hydroxy-4-ABP, primarily because of the instability of the variant enzymes (Hein et al. 1995; Zhu et al. 2002). Both activation and detoxification would be diminished in persons expressing variant NAT2 activity, but NAT1 activity would be maintained. Studies that have characterized NAT1 proteins from a number of variants of this gene have also reported a decrease in enzyme activity (Fretland et al. 2002).

DNA Adducts and Biomarkers

Introduction

Although formation of carcinogen-DNA adducts is a well-characterized phenomenon in laboratory animals, there were no reports of analyses of DNA adducts in smokers before the mid-1980s. In the past 20 years, a large body of literature on DNA adducts in human tissues has emerged with the development of sensitive methods such as HPLC fluorescence, GC–MS, liquid chromatography (LC)–MS, electrochemical detection, ^{32}P-postlabeling, and immunoassay. Researchers have applied all of these methods to analyze DNA adducts, producing data on these biomarkers in molecular epidemiologic studies of cancer susceptibility. Thus, a discussion of DNA adducts in human tissues also includes biomarkers of DNA adduct formation in smokers.

Characterized Adducts in the Human Lung

Available data on characterized DNA adducts in human lung tissue, the tissue most extensively investigated to date, are summarized in Table 5.2. The small number of studies reflects several difficulties in this research. First, DNA from human lung tissue is difficult to obtain. The amounts of DNA available from routine procedures, such as bronchoscopy, are generally too small for analysis of specific DNA adducts. Second, the levels of DNA adducts are generally low: between 1 in 10 million and 1 in 100 million normal DNA bases. Analyzing such small amounts of material is challenging. Nevertheless, methods such as those listed previously and in Table 5.2 were successfully applied. However, because of the limitations noted, the number of participants in most of the studies is small.

The major DNA adduct of B[*a*]P observed in laboratory animals is BPDE-N^2-deoxyguanosine. Acid hydrolysis of DNA containing this adduct releases B[*a*]P-7,8,9,10-tetraol, which can be analyzed by HPLC with fluorescence detection (Rojas et al. 1998). Other BPDE-derived DNA adducts may be hydrolyzed simultaneously. This assay has been applied to lung tissue obtained during surgery (Alexandrov et al. 2002; Boysen and Hecht 2003). Compared with nonsmokers, smokers with the *GSTM1* null genotype displayed higher levels of BPDE-DNA adducts in lung tissue, although this finding is based on a small number of cases (Rojas et al. 1998, 2004). BPDE-DNA adducts were detectable in 40 percent of the smokers with whole lung analyses (Boysen and Hecht 2003) and in all samples with analyses of bronchial epithelial cells (Rojas et al. 2004). When the adduct localization in genes was determined by in vitro studies, one target was seen to be at mutational hot spots in the *P53* tumor-suppressor gene

and the *KRAS* oncogene in cells (Tang et al. 1999; Feng et al. 2002).

Several studies have quantified 7-methyldeoxyguanosine in human lung tissue. The source of this adduct in smokers could be NDMA, NNK, or perhaps other methylating agents. Studies have reported mixed results: some show higher adduct levels in smokers than in nonsmokers (Hecht and Tricker 1999; Lewis et al. 2004). One study examined O^6-methyldeoxyguanosine in human lung tissue but was too small to draw conclusions about the effect of smoking (Wilson et al. 1989).

Three small studies provided evidence for ethyl DNA adducts in human lung tissue (Wilson et al. 1989; Blömeke et al. 1996; Godschalk et al. 2002). Levels of both O^6-ethyldeoxyguanosine and O^4-ethylthymidine were higher in smokers than in nonsmokers. Although one source of these adducts could be *N*-nitrosodiethylamine, its level in cigarette smoke is low. As discussed previously, cigarette smoke contains a direct-acting, but chemically uncharacterized, ethylating agent that may be responsible for the presence of these adducts (see "Carcinogens in Cigarette Smoke" earlier in this chapter).

NNK and NNN are metabolically activated to intermediate agents that pyridyloxobutylate DNA. The resulting POB-DNA adducts can be hydrolyzed with acid to yield 4-hydroxy-1-(3-pyridyl)-1-butanone, which can be detected by GC–MS. Application of this method demonstrated higher levels of POB-DNA adducts in lung tissue of smokers than in that of nonsmokers in a small study (Foiles et al. 1991). One study detected 7-(2-hydroxyethyl) deoxyguanosine in human lung tissue (Zhao et al. 1999), and ethylene oxide is the likely source of this adduct. Studies have detected 4-ABP–DNA adducts in human lungs but show no clear effect of smoking on adduct levels (Wilson et al. 1989; Lin et al. 1994).

Researchers have quantified 1,N^6-ethenodeoxyadenosine and 3,N^4-ethenodeoxycytidine in human lungs by ^{32}P-postlabeling (Godschalk et al. 2002). These adducts may result from lipid peroxidation or from metabolic activation of vinyl chloride or ethyl carbamate. No differences were reported between smokers and nonsmokers. Studies of the oxidative-damage product 8-oxodeoxyguanosine in the human lung obtained mixed results regarding a relationship between detection of this product and smoking status (Asami et al. 1997; Lee et al. 1999a).

In summary, data on the quantitation of specific DNA adducts in the human lung are limited. However, some studies document clear evidence for elevated levels of adducts resulting from exposure to specific carcinogens such as B[*a*]P, NNK, or NNN. Several methods used in these studies—HPLC fluorescence, GC–MS, LC–MS, and ^{32}P-postlabeling with modifications for specific adducts—have the potential for application to molecular

Table 5.2   DNA adducts in human lung tissue

Study	Carcinogen	DNA base	Adduct structures[a]	Type of evidence[b]
Rojas et al. 1998, 2004 Boysen and Hecht 2003	Benzo[a]pyrene	dG		1
Wilson et al. 1989 Mustonen et al. 1993 Kato et al. 1995 Blömeke et al. 1996 Petruzzelli et al. 1996	N-nitrosodimethylamine NNK Others	dG	$7—CH_3$ $O^6—CH_3$	2 2
Wilson et al. 1989 Blömeke et al. 1996 Godschalk et al. 2002	N-nitrosodiethylamine Others	dG T	$7—CH_3CH_2$ $O^6—CH_3CH_2$ $O^4—CH_3CH_2$	2 2 2
Foiles et al. 1991	NNK N'-nitrosonornicotine	dG, T, dC		1
Eide et al. 1999	Ethylene oxide	dG	$7—HOCH_2CH_2$	2
Wilson et al. 1989 Lin et al. 1994	4-aminobiphenyl	dG		2
Godschalk et al. 2002	Vinyl chloride Ethyl carbamate Oxidants	Deoxyadenosine dC		2 2
Asami et al. 1997 Lee et al. 1999a	Oxidants	dG	8—oxo	3

Note: **dC** = deoxycytidine; **dG** = deoxyguanosine; **NNK** = 4-(methylnitrosamino)-1-(3-pyridyl)-1-butanone; **T** = thymidine.
[a]Adduct structures show position of attachment to the base (e.g., N^2-, O^6-, or 7- of dG) and the organic moiety derived from the carcinogen.
[b]1 = detection of a released adducted moiety by a specific method; 2 = detection of a nucleoside or base by a relatively nonspecific method (e.g., ^{32}P-postlabeling or immunoassay); 3 = detection of a nucleoside or base by a specific method (e.g., mass spectrometry, high-performance liquid chromatography [HPLC]-fluorescence, or HPLC-electrochemical detection).

epidemiologic studies that relate specific DNA adduct levels to tobacco exposure and cancer risk.

Uncharacterized Adducts in Human Lung Tissue

Studies have extensively applied two main nonspecific methods—^{32}P-postlabeling and immunoassay—to analyze DNA adducts in human lung tissue, as well as in other tissues. Researchers have discussed the advantages and disadvantages of these methods (Kriek et al. 1998; Wild and Pisani 1998; Poirier et al. 2000; Phillips 2002). Major advantages include high sensitivity for analyzing small amounts of DNA, simplicity of analysis, and no need for extremely expensive equipment. Disadvantages include a lack of chemical specificity, particularly in ^{32}P-postlabeling analyses, and difficulty in quantitation. Studies have extensively reviewed the application of these methods to tissues obtained from smokers (Phillips 2002; Wiencke 2002; IARC 2004).

The output of assays using ^{32}P-postlabeling is often a "diagonal radioactive zone" (DRZ), which consists of uncharacterized radioactive components referred to in the literature as hydrophobic or aromatic DNA adducts. In most cases, little if any evidence supports the true chemical characteristics of these adducts. Nevertheless, the intensity of the DRZ is consistently elevated in samples from smokers. Immunoassays have used various methods of detection, including the fluorescent staining of tissue specimens that allows for the location of adducts. Cross-reactivity is a common problem of immunoassays. For example, antibodies raised against protein conjugates of B[*a*]P–DNA adducts cross-react with adducts generated from other PAHs.

Many studies using ^{32}P-postlabeling methods examined DNA adduct levels in the peripheral lung, bronchial epithelium, or cells obtained by bronchial lavage of smokers. Most of the studies found that adduct levels were higher in smokers compared with nonsmokers (Győrffy et al. 2004; IARC 2004). Investigations that attempted to draw quantitative relationships between the extent of smoking and adduct levels had inconsistent results (IARC 2004).

Adducts in Other Tissues

Numerous studies have evaluated DNA adduct formation in fetuses and in various tissues and fluids of smokers, including samples from the larynx, oral and nasal mucosa, bladder, cervix, breast, pancreas, stomach, placenta, and cardiovascular system, and samples of sputum, sperm, and blood cells. Researchers have comprehensively reviewed these studies (Phillips 2002; Weincke 2002; IARC 2004), most of which used ^{32}P-postlabeling and immunoassay techniques.

Levels of 7-alkyl-deoxyguanosines determined by ^{32}P-postlabeling in laryngeal DNA were higher in smokers than in nonsmokers (Szyfter et al. 1996), and they correlated with the DRZ in these samples. Studies used immunoassay also to detect 4-ABP–DNA adducts in laryngeal tissue (Flamini et al. 1998). Other studies examined the DRZ by ^{32}P-postlabeling (IARC 2004).

Researchers have detected 1,N^2-propanodeoxyguanosine (PdG) adducts derived from acrolein and crotonaldehyde in the DNA of gingival tissue of smokers and nonsmokers; adduct levels were higher in smokers (Nath et al. 1998). Adducts detected by ^{32}P-postlabeling in oral and nasal tissue were also higher in smokers than in nonsmokers. Use of immunoassay techniques revealed that levels of BPDE-DNA, 4-ABP–DNA, and malondialdehyde-DNA adducts in human oral mucosal cells of smokers were higher than those for nonsmokers (IARC 2004).

Using ^{32}P-postlabeling, researchers found 4-ABP–DNA (C-8 deoxyguanosine) adducts in exfoliated urothelial cells and bladder biopsy samples (IARC 2004). In studies using antibodies to 4-ABP–DNA, levels detected in biopsy specimens from the bladder of smokers were higher than those for nonsmokers (IARC 2004). Studies using ^{32}P-postlabeling of bladder DNA from smokers and nonsmokers yielded mixed results; some studies showed higher adduct levels in smokers (IARC 2004).

Using GC–MS, Melikian and colleagues (1999) documented that BPDE-DNA adducts were higher in cervical epithelial cells of smokers than in those of nonsmokers. An immunohistochemical analysis using antibodies to BPDE-DNA adduct in human cervical cells also showed higher adduct levels in smokers than in nonsmokers (Mancini et al. 1999). ^{32}P-postlabeling consistently showed higher adduct levels in cervical tissues of smokers than in those of nonsmokers (IARC 2004).

The ^{32}P-postlabeling of DNA from breast tissue yields the characteristic DRZ from smokers. Researchers also investigated adduct levels by using antibodies against BPDE-DNA; results were generally mixed with respect to smoking status (IARC 2004). Studies that used ^{32}P-postlabeling to measure adduct levels in pancreatic and stomach tissues reported a correlation with smoking status (IARC 2004).

Some studies indicate the presence of smoking-related DNA adducts in human placenta, but the overall relationship of placental DNA adducts to smoking is weak (IARC 2004). Analyses of sperm DNA also reported mixed results with respect to smoking status (IARC 2004).

Many studies have examined DNA adducts in blood cells (IARC 2004). The common use of blood cells in these studies is obviously related to the ease of clinically obtaining these samples. From this viewpoint, blood cell DNA is advantageous for biomarker studies. A disadvantage of using blood cells is that adduct levels in blood cells are not necessarily directly related to levels of DNA adducts in the tissues in which smoking-related cancers occur. The collective results of the studies are somewhat inconsistent with respect to the effects of smoking on levels of DNA adducts. This inconsistency probably results in part from competing sources of adduct formation such as diet, occupation, and the general environment. Another factor is the lifetime of the blood cells investigated; longer-lived cells appear to provide more consistent results with respect to smoking (IARC 2004). Studies comparing levels of blood cell–DNA adducts in smokers with or without cancer had mixed results (IARC 2004).

A meta-analysis of the relationship of DNA adduct levels in smokers to cancer, determined by ^{32}P-postlabeling, used data from case-control studies of lung cancer (five studies), oral cancer (one study), and bladder cancer (one study). Six studies measured adducts in white blood cells, and one study used normal lung tissue. Among current smokers, adduct levels for case patients were significantly higher than those for control participants (Veglia et al. 2003).

Protein Adducts as Surrogates for DNA Adducts

Researchers have proposed that levels of carcinogen-Hb adducts and carcinogen-albumin adducts be used as surrogates for the measurements of DNA adducts discussed in the preceding section (Osterman-Golkar et al. 1976; Ehrenberg and Osterman-Golkar 1980). Although these proteins are not considered targets for carcinogenesis, all carcinogens that react with DNA are also thought to react with protein to some extent. Advantages of Hb adducts as surrogates include the ready availability of Hb in blood and the long lifetime of the erythrocyte in humans (approximately 120 days), which provides an opportunity for adducts to accumulate. Other researchers have comprehensively reviewed studies on protein adducts in smokers (Phillips 2002; IARC 2004).

The Hb adducts of aromatic amines have emerged as highly informative carcinogen biomarkers. Levels of these adducts are consistently higher in smokers than in nonsmokers, particularly for 3-ABP–Hb and 4-ABP–Hb adducts. Adduct levels decrease with smoking cessation and are related to the number of cigarettes smoked (Maclure et al. 1990; Skipper and Tannenbaum 1990; Castelao et al. 2001). Adducts that form with the amino terminal valine of Hb are also informative. Important examples include adducts derived from ethylene oxide, butadiene, acrylonitrile, and acrylamide (Bergmark 1997; Fennell et al. 2000; Swenberg et al. 2001). Ethylated N-terminal valine of Hb is also higher in smokers than in nonsmokers (Carmella et al. 2002a).

Summary

Overwhelming evidence indicates that DNA adduct levels are higher in most tissues of smokers than in corresponding tissues of nonsmokers. This observation provides bedrock support for the major pathway of cancer induction in smokers that proceeds through DNA adduct formation and genetic damage. DNA adducts studied can generally be divided into two classes: nonspecific adducts, which are detected by ^{32}P-postlabeling and immunoassay, and specific adducts, which are detected by structure-specific methods. Studies of nonspecific DNA adducts are far more common than studies of specific DNA adducts, which are still scarce and are limited mainly to human lung tissue. Strong evidence exists for the presence of a variety of specific adducts in the human lung, and in several cases, adduct levels are higher in smokers than in nonsmokers. Measuring levels of Hb adducts by MS provides a simple and perhaps more practical approach for assessing carcinogen exposure of the cell. In several instances, levels of specific adducts are substantially higher in smokers than in nonsmokers. Collectively, the results of these biomarker studies demonstrate the potential for genetic damage in smokers from the persistence of DNA adducts. The propagation of this genetic damage during clonal outgrowth is consistent with the accumulation of multiple genetic changes observed in lung cancer progression.

Molecular Epidemiology of Polymorphisms in Carcinogen-Metabolizing Genes

Introduction

Genetic polymorphisms may play a role in tobacco-related neoplasms. Researchers have established cigarette smoking as a major cause of lung cancer: more than 85 percent of lung cancers are attributable to smoking (Ries et al. 2004). However, not all smokers develop lung cancer, and lung cancer can arise in lifetime nonsmokers. This variation in disease has stimulated interest in molecular epidemiologic investigations of genetic polymorphisms, including carcinogen-metabolizing enzymes that may lead to variations in susceptibility to the carcinogens in tobacco smoke (Table 5.3). Considerable data exist on genetic polymorphisms in cancers other than lung cancer, but the discussion here focuses only on lung cancer and bladder cancer, two of the most heavily investigated cancers.

Table 5.3 Selected gene polymorphisms evaluated by molecular epidemiology investigations for relationship to lung cancer through variation in susceptibility to carcinogens in tobacco smoke

Metabolic genes	Nucleotide change	Amino acid change	Enzymatic activity
CYP1A1	T→C (*MSPI*)	NA	Increased
	A→G	Ile462Val	Increased
CYP2E1	T→A (*DRAI*)	NA	Increased
	G→C (*RSAI*)	NA	Increased
CYP2A13	C→T	Arg257Cys	Decreased
GSTM1	Deletion	NA	None
GSTP1	A→G	Ile105Val	Decreased
GSTT1	Deletion	NA	None
NAT2	T→C	Ile114Thr	Decreased
	C→T	Lys161Lys	Decreased
	A→G	Lys268Arg	Decreased
	G→A	Arg197Gln	Decreased
	C→T	Tyr94Tyr	Decreased
	G→A	Gly286Glu	Decreased
MEH	T→C	Tyr113His	Decreased
	A→G	His139Arg	Increased

Note: **NA** = not applicable.

Studies have identified polymorphisms in phase I and II enzymes. Phase I enzymes, such as P-450s, generally add an oxygen atom to a carcinogen, and phase II enzymes, such as GSTs or UGTs, modify the carcinogen by making it highly water soluble for more facile excretion. These enzymes are involved in the activation and detoxification of carcinogens and may be associated with a differential ability to process carcinogens. Researchers have hypothesized that the accumulation of active carcinogen metabolites and hence increased DNA adduct formation add to lung cancer risk. Studies of cases with autopsy of cancer-free lung tissue indicate that polymorphisms in *CYP1A1* and *GSTM1* genes may be associated with higher DNA adduct levels, suggesting that variations in metabolic pathways can play a role in individual response to carcinogen exposure (Kato et al. 1995). Numerous studies have extended this line of analysis to investigate whether this differential ability to metabolize carcinogens leads to differential lung cancer risk. Overall, data from the study of these polymorphisms have generated inconsistent results. These inconsistencies may be explained in part by the combination of a small sample size and variable frequencies of the polymorphic alleles within different ethnic populations. A summary of some of the specific gene polymorphisms investigated is provided in Table 5.3. A recent

review summarizes the effects of genetic polymorphisms on lung cancer (Schwartz et al. 2007), and specific examples are discussed here.

CYP1A1 Gene

Researchers hypothesize that interindividual variations in the ability to activate carcinogens such as PAH through the *CYP1A1* gene may lead to differential carcinogenic effects. Studies describe at least two variant polymorphisms in the *CYP1A1* gene. The first is a T3801C base change in intron 6, which results in a new *MSPI* restriction site (Kawajiri et al. 1990). (A restriction site is a site in the gene that is cleaved by a specific restriction enzyme.) The second polymorphism is an A2455G base change in exon 7, which results in an Ile to Val amino acid change (Hayashi et al. 1991). Although these polymorphisms appear to be linked, study results are inconsistent, and wide disparities exist among populations.

Studies of Japanese and Chinese populations associate both of the *CYP1A1* variant polymorphisms with an increase in lung cancer risk. Nakachi and colleagues (1991) were the first to report an association of the **MSPI* polymorphism with lung cancer risk. For patients with lung cancer, the frequency of harboring the homozygous variant genotype was more than two times higher than that for control participants. Among patients with squamous cell carcinoma (SCC), the homozygous variant genotype was associated with an increased risk of developing lung cancer, especially in those with a lower cumulative dose of cigarette smoke. At low levels of exposure to cigarette smoke, the odds ratio (OR) for developing lung cancer among persons with the homozygous variant genotype was 7.31 (95 percent confidence interval [CI], 2.13–25.12). This increased risk was persistent, but of a lesser magnitude, at higher levels of exposure to cigarette smoke (Nakachi et al. 1991). Okada and colleagues (1994) reported similar findings.

Studies have also associated the *ILE462VAL* polymorphism of *CYP1A1* with lung cancer risk in Japanese and Chinese populations. Again, the homozygous variant *VAL/*VAL* genotype was associated with lung cancer at lower cumulative doses of cigarette smoke (Nakachi et al. 1993; Yang et al. 2004; Ng et al. 2005). One explanation posited for this relationship with the dose level in smokers has been that the relevant enzyme is saturated at high doses but not at low doses of cigarette smoke (Vineis et al. 1997). The effects of genetic variability and differential enzymatic activity are more apparent at low doses, when saturation has not been reached.

Results have been inconsistent outside Asian populations. Individual studies often lack statistical power to detect an association (Shields and Harris 2000). Also, *CYP1A1* polymorphisms are common in Asian populations (30 percent of the population) (Nakachi et al. 1993), but are far less common among Europeans and North Americans (<10 percent of the population) (Warren and Shields 1997). A study of African Americans and Mexican Americans showed a twofold increase in the risk of lung cancer among light smokers with the *MSPI* variant genotype (Ishibe et al. 1997). However, a Brazilian study showed an increase in risk with the *ILE/*VAL* polymorphism but not with the *MSPI* polymorphism (Hamada et al. 1995). A more recent study suggested that in Latinos, the *MSPI* variant genotype was associated with an overall inverse OR of 0.51 (95 percent CI, 0.32–0.81), which reflected the inverse interaction with smoking (Wrensch et al. 2005). Reports from Finland, Norway, and Sweden show a lack of association between either of the *CYP1A1* polymorphisms and lung cancer risk (Tefre et al. 1991; Hirvonen et al. 1992; Alexandrie et al. 2004). A meta-analysis provides little support for this association (Houlston 2000).

Because of the small sample sizes in these studies, Vineis and colleagues (2003) conducted an analysis of pooled data from the International Collaborative Study on Genetic Susceptibility to Environmental Carcinogens, which included raw data from 22 case-control studies totaling 2,451 cases and 3,358 controls. This data set thus

comprised approximately one-half of the case-control studies published at that time. Researchers found an association in Whites between the *CYP1A1* homozygous *MSPI* variant and lung cancer risk after adjustment of values for age and gender (OR = 2.36; 95 percent CI, 1.16–4.81). The association held for both SCC and adenocarcinomas (Vineis et al. 2003). However, this association failed to reach statistical significance among Asians in this analysis. Moreover, studies such as the research conducted by Nakachi and colleagues (1991, 1993) discussed previously in this section were not included, making the Asian data difficult to interpret.

CYP2E1 Gene

The *CYP2E1* gene is involved in the metabolic activation of NDMA, as well as several other tobacco smoke carcinogens. Le Marchand and colleagues (1998) performed a population-based, case-control study with 341 lung cancer cases and 456 controls. These researchers found that *CYP2E1* polymorphisms were associated with a decrease in risk of lung adenocarcinoma. A Chinese study (Wang et al. 2003c) confirmed this finding. However, the presence of at least one variant *CYP1A1 *MSPI* allele was associated with an increased risk of SCC, both alone (2.4-fold increase in risk) and in combination with *GSTM1* deletion (3.1-fold increase in risk) (Le Marchand et al. 1998). These researchers suggest that the associations between *CYP1A1* and *CYP2E1* polymorphisms and subsets of lung cancer indicate a specificity of PAHs to induce SCC and of nitrosamines to induce adenocarcinomas.

CYP2A13 Gene

The *CYP2A13* gene is expressed primarily in the respiratory tract and participates in the metabolic activation of *N*-nitrosamines such as NNK. Researchers have identified a polymorphism in *CYP2A13* in which a C→T transition leads to an Arg→Cys substitution at position 257. The variant 257CYS protein, the product of this gene, has one-half to one-third the capacity of the 257ARG protein to activate NNK (Su et al. 2000; Zhang et al. 2002). In a study of 724 lung cancer patients and 791 control participants, Wang and colleagues (2003a) demonstrated that the variant *CYP2A13* genotype (*C/*T* or *T/*T*) was associated with a reduced risk for lung cancer, particularly for adenocarcinomas (OR = 0.41; 95 percent CI, 0.23–0.71). The reduction in risk did not reach statistical significance for SCC or other histologies of lung cancer. The reduced risk for adenocarcinomas was apparent only in smokers, and in light smokers rather than in heavy smokers (Wang et al. 2003a). This finding again indicates that genetic polymorphisms may play a greater role when the carcinogen dose is low and does not saturate enzymatic capacity.

GSTM1 Gene

Study reports have noted large variations in enzymatic activity for several GSTs. About 50 percent of the White population is homozygous for a deletion in the *GSTM1* gene that leads to null expression (Seidegard et al. 1988). The GSTM1 enzyme is important in detoxifying carcinogens, and numerous studies have investigated the possible association of the *GSTM1* null genotype with lung cancer risk.

Some studies have found an association between the *GSTM1* null mutation and lung cancer across many populations. In a Japanese population, the *GSTM1* null genotype was positively correlated with SCC of the lung but not with adenocarcinomas (Kihara et al. 1993). A similar analysis in a Finnish population also correlated the *GSTM1* null genotype with SCC (Hirvonen et al. 1993). Analyses of Scottish (Zhong et al. 1991), Norwegian (Ryberg et al. 1997), and Turkish populations (Pinarbasi et al. 2003) had similar findings. A U.S. study also suggested that the *GSTM1* null genotype was associated with a modest elevation in lung cancer risk, which increased among heavy smokers (Nazar-Stewart et al. 2003). However, some studies have not shown a significant association between the *GSTM1* null genotype and lung cancer risk for SCC or overall for lung cancer (London et al. 1995; Rebbeck 1997). A meta-analysis of data from 12 case-control studies comprising 1,593 cases and 2,135 controls showed a moderate increase in the risk of lung cancer across all histologies with the *GSTM1* null genotype (OR = 1.41; 95 percent CI, 1.23–1.61) (McWilliams et al. 1995). A more recent meta-analysis of 43 studies including more than 18,000 persons showed a smaller but statistically significant OR of 1.17 (95 percent CI, 1.07–1.27) (Benhamou et al. 2002).

Kihara and colleagues (1994) analyzed data on 178 Japanese patients with lung cancer and 201 healthy control participants and found that the *GSTM1* null genotype was associated with an overall increase in lung cancer risk (OR = 1.87; 95 percent CI, 1.21–2.87). The strongest association was for SCC (OR = 2.13; 95 percent CI, 1.11–4.07). With stratification by the amount of smoking, the proportion of *GSTM1* null genotype increased progressively in the SCC group from 50 percent in light smokers to 72 percent in heavy smokers (Kihara et al. 1994). One study suggested that higher intakes of cruciferous vegetables reduced lung cancer risk among persons with the *GSTM1* genotype (highest versus lowest tertile for amount of smoking; OR = 0.61; 95 percent CI, 0.39–0.95) but not among persons with the *GSTM1* null genotype (highest versus lowest tertile; OR = 1.15; 95 percent CI, 0.78–1.68) (Wang et al. 2004b). However, several other studies have shown a greater protective effect in persons with the *GSTM1* null genotype who consumed cruciferous vegetables (London et al. 2000; Spitz et al. 2000). One hypothesis is that these participants were less able to eliminate protective isothiocyanates by conjugation with glutathione. In a case-control study, Cheng and colleagues (1999) analyzed data from 162 patients with SCC of the head and neck and 315 healthy control participants. They found that 53.1 percent of the case patients and 42.9 percent of the control participants were null for *GSTM1* (p <0.05), whereas 32.7 percent of case patients and 17.5 percent of control participants were null for *GSTT1* (p <0.001).

Thus, the effect of *GSTM1* alone may not be dramatic. However, it appears to be magnified by gene-environment and gene-diet interactions, and the effects were significantly greater as exposure to cigarette smoke increased. In addition, the high frequency of *GSTM1* polymorphisms observed across all ethnicities may contribute to the importance of this variant as a risk factor for developing lung cancer (Brennan et al. 2005).

CYP1A1 and GSTM1 in Combination

Studies of the effect of combined *CYP1A1* and *GSTM1* variant genotypes hypothesized that increased PAH activation and decreased PAH detoxification in tobacco smokers might lead to an increase in lung cancer risk. Numerous studies have explored this association. Perhaps the studies with the strongest support for this association come from Japan, although they are generally limited by small sample sizes.

Combination of the *CYP1A1* variant genotype and the *GSTM1* null genotype enhanced the risk of smoking-related lung cancers in a Japanese population. Hayashi and colleagues (1992) demonstrated this finding with the *ILE/*VAL polymorphism. These investigators found an increased frequency of the homozygous *VAL/*VAL genotype combined with the *GSTM1* null genotype in lung cancer patients compared with control participants (8.5 percent versus 2.2 percent, respectively). Nakachi and colleagues (1991) reported similar results with both the *MSPI and *ILE/*VAL polymorphisms and the *GSTM1* null genotype. The case-control study found that for light smokers, either of the two *CYP1A1* susceptible genotypes combined synergistically with the deficient *GSTM1* genotype to create a high risk for lung cancer (OR = 16; 95 percent CI, 3.76–68.02 for *MSPI, and OR = 41; 95 percent CI, 8.68–193.61 for *ILE/*VAL). Eighty-seven percent of the light smokers who developed lung cancer had at least one of the three homozygous variant genotypes. The investigators suggested that particularly when the cigarette dose is low, *CYP1A1* and *GSTM1* may be an important determinant of susceptibility to lung cancer (Nakachi et al. 1991).

Kihara and colleagues (1994) also demonstrated a synergistic effect. Persons with these variant genotypes in both *CYP1A1* and *GSTM1* had a much higher risk of lung cancer than did those with the variant *CYP1A1* and wild-type *GSTM1* (OR = 21.9; 95 percent CI, 4.68–112.7 versus OR = 3.2; 95 percent CI, 0.37–24.0). Studies in Scandinavian populations (Alexandrie et al. 1994; Anttila et al. 1994), as well as U.S. populations (García-Closas et al. 1997), support an increase in the risk of lung cancer with the combination of variant *CYP1A1* and *GSTM1* genotypes. Using data from the International Collaborative Study on Genetic Susceptibility to Environmental Carcinogens database, Vineis and colleagues (2004) found a statistically significant effect of the *MSPI* variant on lung cancer risk in Whites (OR = 2.6; 95 percent CI, 1.2–5.7) with evidence for an interaction between the *MSPI* and *GSTM1* null genotypes (OR = 2.8; 95 percent CI, 0.9–8.4).

GSTP1 Gene

Studies have reported polymorphisms in the *GSTP1* gene family of phase II enzymes with high expression in the lung. One *GSTP1* polymorphism includes an A→G base change that leads to an isoleucine→valine substitution, which results in lower enzymatic activity toward 1-chloro-2,4-dinitrobenzene (Watson et al. 1998) but higher activity toward PAH diol epoxides (Sundberg et al. 1998). Several studies showed no statistically significant association between *GSTP1* polymorphisms and lung cancer risk (Harris et al. 1998; Katoh et al. 1999; To-Figueras et al. 1999; Nazar-Stewart et al. 2003). However, in the study with the largest sample size of 1,042 cases and 1,161 controls, the *GSTP1* homozygous variant genotype was associated with a higher lung cancer risk at any level of exposure to smoke than was the wild-type genotype (Miller et al. 2003).

The combination of the *GSTM1* null genotype and the *GSTP1* *G/*G genotype may increase lung cancer risk (Ryberg et al. 1997; Kihara et al. 1999; Perera et al. 2002). In a study of 1,694 cases and 1,694 controls, double variants in *GSTM1* and *GSTP1*, as well as in *GSTP1* and *TP53*, were associated with an increase in lung cancer risk among persons aged 55 years or younger (adjusted OR [AOR] = 4.03; 95 percent CI, 1.47–11.1 for the M1-P1 double variant, and AOR = 5.10; 95 percent CI, 1.42–18.30 for the P1-P53 double variant) (Miller et al. 2002). Another study included 350 persons younger than age 50 years with a diagnosis of lung cancer who were identified from the metropolitan Detroit Surveillance, Epidemiology, and End Results program. The study compared these patients with 410 control participants matched by age, race, and gender. The results indicated that African Americans carrying at least one *G allele at the *GSTP1* locus

were 2.9 times more likely to develop lung cancer than were African Americans without a *G allele (95 percent CI, 1.29–6.20). African Americans with either one or two genotypes that carry risk at the *GSTM1* and *GSTP1* loci were at higher risk of developing lung cancer than were African Americans who had fully functional *GSTM1* and *GSTP1* genes (OR = 2.8; 95 percent CI, 1.1–7.2 for *GSTM1*, and OR = 4.0; 95 percent CI, 1.3–12.2 for *GSTP1*). No significant single-gene associations were observed between *GSTM1*, *GSTT1*, or *GSTP1* and early-onset lung cancer in Whites (Cote et al. 2005).

GSTT1 Gene

Previous results have not supported an association of the *GSTT1* gene with lung cancer risk (To-Figueras et al. 1997; Malats et al. 2000; Stücker et al. 2002; Ruano-Ravina et al. 2003; Wang et al. 2003b). In a study of Chinese living in Hong Kong, the *GSTT1* null genotype was associated with a higher risk of lung cancer than was the functional *GSTT1* genotype (AOR = 1.69; 95 percent CI, 1.12–2.56) only in nonsmokers (Chan-Yeung et al. 2004). A study from Denmark also suggested that the *GSTT1* null genotype is associated with a higher risk of lung cancer (Sørensen et al. 2004a).

NAT2 Gene

Several widely studied polymorphisms for the *NAT2* gene are associated with decreased activity or reduced stability of the enzyme. Phenotypically, these polymorphisms result in slow or fast acetylation. Study results on the association of the *NAT2* gene with lung cancer risk are conflicting. Most studies report no overall increase in risk with the genotype for either slow or fast acetylation (Philip et al. 1988; Martinez et al. 1995; Bouchardy et al. 1998; Saarikoski et al. 2000). However, a few studies report an increase in risk with the genotype for either slow acetylation (Oyama et al. 1997; Seow et al. 1999) or fast acetylation (Cascorbi et al. 1996). In the largest study, of 1,115 lung cancer patients and 1,250 control participants, no association between the *NAT2* genotype and lung cancer risk was observed. However, the study noted a significant interaction with smoking. Among nonsmokers, the genotype for rapid acetylation decreased lung cancer risk more than did the genotype for slow acetylation. This relationship was reversed among smokers, and persons with the genotype for rapid acetylation had a higher risk. The authors hypothesized that for nonsmokers, the NAT2 protein may provide a means for *N*-acetylation, thereby detoxifying aromatic amines and protecting a person against cancer. However, cigarette smoke markedly induces CYP oxidation and could increase the production of reactive intermediate agents in smokers. In this setting, NAT2 may instead *O*-acetylate these metabolites and thereby produce more reactive metabolites, thus augmenting the cancer risk (Zhou et al. 2002b). A study from Denmark confirmed the associations of the *NAT2* gene with smoking status (Sørensen et al. 2005). However, a study from Taiwan suggested that the *NAT2* genotype for fast acetylation is associated with an increased risk of lung cancer among women who were lifetime nonsmokers (Chiou et al. 2005).

The NAT2 protein plays an important role in the bioactivation and detoxification of the aromatic amines associated with bladder cancer induced by cigarette smoke. In the phenotypic studies, persons with slow acetylation had increased risk of bladder cancer, particularly when they had occupational exposure to arylamines or were cigarette smokers (Green et al. 2000; Johns and Houlston 2000). In the genotype analysis, more than 20 independent studies, many with small sample size have assessed the association of *NAT2* polymorphisms with the risk of bladder cancer. A meta-analysis of published case-control studies conducted in the general population (22 studies, 2,496 cases, and 3,340 controls) examined the relationship of acetylation status (phenotype and genotype) to bladder cancer risk. Persons with slow acetylation had a 40-percent increase in risk compared with risk for persons with rapid acetylation (OR = 1.4; 95 percent CI, 1.2–1.6) (Marcus et al. 2000b). However, studies conducted in Asia generated a summary OR of 2.1 (95 percent CI, 1.2–3.8), studies in Europe generated a summary OR of 1.4 (95 percent CI, 1.2–1.6), and studies in the United States generated a summary OR of 0.9 (95 percent CI, 0.7–1.3).

In addition, a case series meta-analysis of data from a case series of 16 studies of bladder cancer, conducted in the general population and involving 1,999 cases, showed a weak interaction between smoking status and *NAT2* slow acetylation (OR = 1.3; 95 percent CI, 1.0–1.6). The interaction was stronger when analyses were restricted to studies conducted in Europe (OR = 1.5; 95 percent CI, 1.1–1.9) (Marcus et al. 2000a). In a pooled analysis of data from 1,530 cases and 731 controls from four case-control studies plus two case series conducted in Whites in European countries, a significant association was reported between *NAT2* slow acetylation and bladder cancer (OR = 1.42; 95 percent CI, 1.14–1.77) (Vineis et al. 2001). The risk of cancer was elevated in smokers and in persons with occupational exposure to cigarette smoke, and the highest risk was for persons with slow acetylation (Vineis et al. 2001).

In a hospital-based, case-control study of 201 men in northern Italy and a case-control study with 507 White patients with bladder cancer in the United States, findings

also suggested that the *NAT2* genotype for slow acetylation was associated with an increased risk of bladder cancer, especially with the joint effects of cigarette smoking and occupational exposure to aromatic amines (Hung et al. 2004; Gu et al. 2005). In a case-control study of bladder cancer in females, exclusive use of permanent hair dye was associated with a 2.9-fold increased risk of bladder cancer among persons with the *NAT2* genotype and slow acetylation but not in those with the *NAT2* genotype and rapid acetylation (Gago-Dominguez et al. 2003). All of these results confirmed that the genotype for *NAT2* slow acetylation is a risk factor for bladder cancer through interaction with smoking or occupational exposure. However, several studies that included populations of Chinese (Ma et al. 2004), northern Indians (Mittal et al. 2004), and Poles (Jaskula-Sztul et al. 2001) reported no association between the *NAT2* genotype and bladder cancer risk.

Microsomal Epoxide Hydrolase

Like NAT2, MEH can act as both an activator and a detoxifier of carcinogens. As a detoxifier, MEH catalyzes the hydrolysis of highly reactive epoxide intermediate agents to less reactive dihydrodiols that are excretable. As an activator, MEH is involved in further metabolism of PAH epoxides. Several identified polymorphisms include a T→C base change in exon 3 leading to a tyrosine→histidine substitution at residue 113, which is associated with a decrease in enzymatic activity, and an A→G base change in exon 4, leading to a histidine→arginine substitution at residue 139, which leads to an increase in enzymatic activity (Hassett et al. 1994). Several reports of studies have noted an increased risk of lung cancer among persons carrying polymorphisms associated with an increase in enzymatic activity. A study of Mexican Americans and African Americans found a greater risk of lung cancer among young Mexican Americans with the exon 4 polymorphism, but not among those with the exon 3 polymorphism. No association was observed among African Americans (Wu et al. 2001). The homozygous variant genotype at exon 4 confers increased enzymatic activity and was again associated with an increase in lung cancer risk in a study in Texas (Cajas-Salazar et al. 2003). A study from Austria suggested an association between the exon 3 polymorphism of the *MEH* gene and a significantly decreased risk of lung cancer (Gsur et al. 2003). The combination of exon 3 and exon 4 polymorphisms that conferred high enzymatic activity also significantly increased the risk (Cajas-Salazar et al. 2003; Park et al. 2005). In a Chinese population in Taiwan, high MEH activity, defined by the corresponding combination of exon 3 and exon 4 polymorphisms, was associated with an increased risk for SCC (Lin et al. 2000). In a French population, high MEH activity was similarly associated with lung cancer risk (Benhamou et al. 1998).

A study of 974 White patients with lung cancer and 1,142 control participants found no relationship between *MEH* polymorphisms and lung cancer risk overall. However, evidence of gene-environment interactions was observed. Low-activity *MEH* genotypes were a risk factor for lung cancer among nonsmokers (OR = 1.89; 95 percent CI, 1.08–3.28) but were protective among heavy smokers (OR = 0.65; 95 percent CI, 0.42–1.00) (Zhou et al. 2001b). This effect was stronger in SCC than in adenocarcinoma. The researchers hypothesized that this difference may be explained by the dual actions of MEH. In nonsmokers, the presence of low MEH activity may lead to a decreased ability to detoxify environmental pollutants, thus increasing lung cancer risk. In smokers, MEH may participate in activating the PAHs in cigarette smoke. Therefore, low activity is protective for heavy smokers. Similar results were reported in a Slovak study (Habalová et al. 2004).

In a meta-analysis of data from seven published studies that included 2,078 case patients with lung cancer and 3,081 control participants, investigators found no consistent overall association for either the exon 3 or exon 4 polymorphisms with lung cancer risk (Lee et al. 2002c). However, in an analysis of pooled data from eight studies (four published and four unpublished at that time) with 986 case patients and 1,633 control participants, researchers observed a significant decrease in lung cancer risk (OR = 0.70; 95 percent CI, 0.51–0.96) for the exon 3 *HIS/*HIS genotype. The protective effect of the exon 3 polymorphism seems stronger for adenocarcinomas of the lung than for other histologic types. Researchers found no overall association between MEH activity and lung cancer risk and no consistent modification of the carcinogenic effect of smoking according to the *MEH* polymorphism. However, the risk of lung cancer decreased among lifetime nonsmokers with high MEH activity and among heavy smokers with the exon 3 *HIS/*HIS genotype (Lee et al. 2002c).

Genes in the Pathway for Metabolism of Reactive Oxygen Species

Studies have identified an alanine→valine substitution at codon 16 of manganese superoxide dismutase (SOD), which may be associated with a less efficient enzyme transport into mitochondria. The *VAL/*VAL genotype is associated with risk of lung cancer higher than that for the wild-type genotype (AOR = 1.67; 95 percent CI, 1.27–2.20) (Wang et al. 2001a). Other studies also associate the heterozygous variant genotype with an increased risk of lung cancer (AOR = 1.34; 95 percent CI, 1.05–1.70) (Wang et al. 2001a, 2004c). Studies have identified a G→A polymorphism in the promoter region of myeloperoxidase (MPO) that decreases *A allele transcription. A study of bronchoalveolar lavage fluid and cells from 106 White smokers who had lung cancer showed an association of the variant genotypes with reduced MPO activity in the fluid and reduced levels of smoking-related DNA adducts in bronchoalveolar cells (Van Schooten et al. 2004). The association was stronger in persons having two variant alleles (homozygous variants) than it was in persons having one normal and one variant allele (heterozygous variants).

Findings on lung cancer risk are conflicting. Most studies performed since 1999 suggested that the variant *MPO* genotypes are associated with a decreased risk of lung cancer (Le Marchand et al. 2000; Dally et al. 2002; Feyler et al. 2002; Kantarci et al. 2002; Lu et al. 2002; Schabath et al. 2002). In contrast, two studies found no association between either the heterozygous or homozygous variant genotypes and lung cancer risk (Xu et al. 2002; Chevrier et al. 2003). Another study suggested that the *MPO-G463A* polymorphism associated with a novel estrogen-receptor-binding site modifies the association between the *SOD ALA16VAL* polymorphism and risk of non-small-cell lung cancer (NSCLC) differently by gender. For women carrying *MPO* variant genotypes, the AOR of the *SOD* polymorphism (*VAL/*VAL versus *ALA/*ALA) was 3.26 (95 percent CI, 1.55–6.83). No associations were found in men or women who carried the *MPO *G/*G wild-type genotype (Liu et al. 2004).

Summary

Studies to date suggest a role for genetic polymorphisms in the risk of lung and bladder cancer in smokers and support a possible association between specific genes and smoking status. Investigations continue on the role of multiple genetic variants that occur simultaneously and the interactions between metabolic gene variants and other kinds of heritable variations, such as DNA repair, cell-cycle control, tumor-suppressor genes, and oncogene activity.

DNA Repair and Conversion of Adducts to Mutations

Repair of DNA Adducts

Introduction

Tobacco products and smoke contain many chemicals that can damage DNA. Multiple repair pathways protect a human cell against the mutagenic and carcinogenic activities of these DNA-damaging agents. Pathways involved in the repair of tobacco-related DNA damage include direct base repair by alkyltransferases, excision of DNA damage by base excision repair (BER), or nucleotide excision repair (NER), mismatch repair (MMR), and double-strand break repair (DSBR). The inadequate removal of DNA damage results in increased rates of mutagenesis and, as a consequence, the increased likelihood of a person developing cancer.

O^6-Alkylguanine–DNA Alkyltransferase

Overview

O^6-alkylguanine adducts are repaired by the repair protein O^6-alkylguanine–DNA alkyltransferase (AGT) in a reaction involving transfer of the methyl group from the O^6 position of guanine to a cysteinyl residue on the protein (Pegg 2000). This transfer reaction results in an error-proof repair as it regenerates an unmodified guanine residue in DNA. However, the repair protein is inactivated as the alkylated protein undergoes a conformational change (Daniels et al. 2000) and is degraded (Srivenugopal et al. 1996; Xu-Welliver and Pegg 2002). As a consequence of this repair mechanism, the constitutive levels of AGT determine the initial repair capacity of a cell by this mechanism. Overall capacity of the O^6-alkylguanine repair is determined by the rate of protein synthesis and the amount of alkylation at the O^6 position of guanine.

Substrate Specificity

Mammalian AGT specifically repairs O^6-alkylguanine adducts, and it repairs the larger O^6-alkylguanine residues more readily than does the bacterial protein. In rodents, AGT repairs O^6-methylguanine, O^6-butylguanine, and O^6-[4-oxo-4-(3-pyridyl)butyl]guanine at comparable rates, whereas human AGT repairs the bulky adducts more slowly (Mijal et al. 2004). This ability of the rodent protein to accommodate such large structural differences likely results from the additional amino acid residue (Gly166) in the binding pocket of the rodent proteins (Loktionova

and Pegg 2002). Therefore, the steric constraints of an active AGT site determine whether it can efficiently repair a bulky O^6-alkylguanine adduct such as those more commonly resulting from exposure to smoke.

Protecting Against Mutagenicity of Tobacco Carcinogens

Tobacco smoke contains a number of alkylating agents, such as tobacco-specific nitrosamines, which are capable of forming O^6-alkylguanine adducts (Wang et al. 1997; Hecht 1998). AGT protects against the mutagenic and carcinogenic properties of alkylating agents.

In vitro studies. Increased expression of AGT protects against the mutagenic effects of O^6-alkylguanine (Ellison et al. 1989) and alkylating agents (Kaina et al. 1991; Wu et al. 1992; Ferrezuelo et al. 1998a,b). Consistently, alkylating agents are more toxic and mutagenic when coadministered with AGT inactivators such as O^6-benzylguanine or related compounds (Dolan et al. 1990, 1991; Bronstein et al. 1992). The mutagenic activity of O^6-methylguanine or O^6-[4-oxo-4-(3-pyridyl)butyl]guanine is enhanced when cells are pretreated with O^6-benzylguanine (Pauly et al. 1995, 2002). This finding indicated that AGT is important in protecting against the mutagenic activity of these adducts derived from tobacco constituents.

In vivo studies. AGT is depleted in tissues from NNK-treated rats, and AGT levels are depleted in Clara cells (Belinsky et al. 1988). NNK also reduces AGT levels in the lungs and liver of A/J mice (Peterson et al. 2001). Although the liver function recovers to control values within 96 hours after exposure, AGT activity remains depressed in the lung. Consistently, O^6-methylguanine is efficiently repaired in the liver of NNK-treated mice, but it persists for at least two weeks in lung DNA (Peterson and Hecht 1991; Peterson et al. 2001). Notably, levels of O^6-methylguanine in lung DNA are highly correlated with pulmonary tumorigenic activity in A/J mice (Peterson and Hecht 1991; Peterson et al. 2001). These observations strongly suggest that the inefficient repair of O^6-methylguanine, presumably by AGT, is linked to the tumorigenic activity of NNK. This conclusion is supported by the observation from another study that high AGT levels protect against NNK-induced lung tumorigenesis and that NNK is a less potent lung carcinogen in transgenic mice containing the human *AGT* transgene (Liu et al. 1999).

Base Excision Repair

Overview

BER is a major pathway for the repair of small DNA damage, primarily to alkylated and oxidized DNA bases, as well as the repair of apurinic/apyrimidinic (AP) sites and single-stranded breaks (Fortini et al. 2003; Fromme et al. 2004). BER is initiated by a recognition of the damaged DNA by specific DNA glycosylases. Studies have characterized 12 human glycosylases (Table 5.4) (Christmann et al. 2003; Fortini et al. 2003). Each enzyme has different

but sometimes overlapping substrate specificities that are subgrouped into type I and type II glycosylases, depending on their mode of action (Christmann et al. 2003). Type I glycosylases catalyze the cleavage of the *N*-glycosidic bond, leaving an AP site. Type II glycosylases remove the damaged base in a similar manner. They contain 3′-endonuclease activity that cleaves the AP site, which generates a single-strand break with a 3′-terminal deoxyribose phosphate. Spontaneous hydrolysis of a glycosidic bond can also directly generate AP sites. AP sites are substrates for DNA AP endonuclease, which cuts the phosphodiester

Table 5.4   Human DNA glycosylases

Study	Glycosylase	Specificity	Subgroup
Chakravarti et al. 1991 O'Connor and Laval 1991 Samson et al. 1991	Alkylpurine DNA glycosylase or methylpurine DNA glycosylase	3-methyladenine, 7-methylguanine, 3-methylguanine, ethenoadenine, hypoxanthine	Type I
Hendrich and Bird 1998 Hendrich et al. 1999	Methyl-CpG binding endonuclease 1	U or T opposite G, preferentially in CpG sites	Type I
Slupska et al. 1996, 1999 Fortini et al. 2003	Adenine DNA glycosylase	A opposite 8-oxoguanine	Type I
Hazra et al. 2002a,b	Nei-like DNA glycosylase 1	Formamidopyrimidines, oxidized pyrimidines, 8-oxoguanine opposite C, G, or T	Type II
Hazra et al. 2002a,b	Nei-like DNA glycosylase 2	5-hydroxyuracil, 5-hydroxycytosine	Type II
Takao et al. 2002	Nei-like DNA glycosylase 3	Fragmented and oxidized pyrimidines	NR
Aspinwall et al. 1997 Hilbert et al. 1997 Miyabe et al. 2002 Fortini et al. 2003	Thymine glycol DNA glycosylase 1	Ring-saturated, oxidized, and fragmented pyrimidines	Type II
Bjørås et al. 1997 Radicella et al. 1997 Rosenquist et al. 1997 Fortini et al. 2003	8-oxoguanine DNA glycosylase 1	8-oxoguanine opposite C, T, or G	Type II
Hazra et al. 1998	8-oxoguanine DNA glycosylase 2	8-oxoguanine opposite A or G	NR
Haushalter et al. 1999 Nilsen et al. 2001	Mismatch-specific uracil DNA glycosylase 1	Uracil opposite G	Type I
Neddermann and Jiricny 1993, 1994 Neddermann et al. 1996	Thymidine DNA glycosylase	Uracil, T, or ethenoC opposite G; T opposite G, C, or T	Type I
Olsen et al. 1989 Muller and Caradonna 1991 Fortini et al. 2003	Uracil DNA glycosylase	Uracil	Type I

Source: Adapted from Christmann et al. 2003 with permission from Elsevier, © 2003.
Note: **NR** = data not reported.

bond and causes the formation of a strand break with a 5'-terminal deoxyribose phosphate (Barzilay et al. 1995).

Once the phosphodiester bond is cleaved, BER can proceed through two pathways: short-patch or long-patch (Figure 5.4). The balance of the two pathways can depend on tissue type (Sancar et al. 2004). In general, short-patch BER dominates when BER is initiated by glycosylases. Long-patch BER is the preferred pathway when BER is initiated with the formation of AP sites through spontaneous hydrolysis or oxidative base loss (Sancar et al. 2004).

In short-patch BER, DNA polymerase β (polβ) inserts a new nucleotide at the lesion site and catalyzes the release of 5'-terminal deoxyribose phosphates by β-elimination (Matsumoto and Kim 1995; Sobol et al. 1996; Prasad et al. 1998). This step is followed by ligation of the remaining break by the ligase III x-ray repair cross-complementation group 1 (XRCC1) complex (Kubota et al. 1996).

Long-patch BER occurs in oxidized or reduced AP sites, 3'-unsaturated aldehydes, or 3'-phosphates, because these modifications are resistant to β-elimination by polβ. Therefore, this damage is further processed by long-patch repair dependent on the proliferating cell nuclear antigen (PCNA) after the insertion of a nucleotide at the lesion site by polβ (Christmann et al. 2003; Fortini et al. 2003). This mechanism displaces the damaged strand, which is followed by DNA synthesis of an oligonucleotide (up to 10 nucleotides) by polδ or polε in concert with PCNA and replication factor C (Stucki et al. 1998). The flap endonuclease 1 (FEN1) recognizes and cleaves off the damaged oligonucleotide flap structure (Klungland and Lindahl 1997). Ligase I catalyzes the final ligation step (Prasad et al. 1996; Srivastava et al. 1998).

Substrate Specificity

Tobacco smoke is rich in reactive oxygen species that can oxidize DNA bases. BER is an important pathway for the repair of oxidized DNA bases, such as 8-oxoguanine and oxidized pyrimidines, and for the repair of single-strand breaks. Tobacco smoke contains *N*-nitrosamines capable of generating small alkylguanine damage that is repaired by this pathway. The small chemical alterations frequently miscode if they are not repaired by BER. Therefore, this pathway is particularly important in preventing mutagenesis.

Protecting Against Mutagenicity and Carcinogenicity of Tobacco Carcinogens

Single-gene knockouts of glycosylases in mice are well tolerated, with only modest increases in rates of spontaneous mutagenesis (Fortini et al. 2003). This observation likely results from an overlapping specificity of the various glycosylases and repair pathways. However, mutagenicity of methyl methanesulfonate (MMS) in lymphocytes from alkylpurine-DNA-*N*-glycosylase–null mice was three to four times higher than that in lymphocytes from wild-type control mice (Elder et al. 1998). Most of the mutations were AT→TA transversions. In addition, 8-oxoguanine DNA glycosylase 1 (OGG1) knockout mice that are aging eventually develop lung cancer (Sakumi et al. 2003). However, in another study, knockout of proteins involved in the steps after removal of the base caused the knockout mice to die at a very young age (Fortini et al. 2003).

Imbalances in the proteins involved in this pathway could have negative consequences. Chinese hamster ovary cells that overexpress alkylpurine DNA glycosylase are more sensitive to both the toxic and mutagenic effects of MMS and have higher numbers of mutations at AT base pairs than do normal Chinese hamster ovary cells (Calléja et al. 1999). This result suggests that an enhanced repair of 3-methyladenine leads to an accumulation of unprocessed AP sites that are also mutagenic. Findings in another study indicate that imbalances and/or polymorphisms in the proteins involved in BER may cause an increase in cancer susceptibility (Fortini et al. 2003).

Nucleotide Excision Repair

Overview

NER repairs a wide class of helix-distorting lesions that interfere with base pairing, blocking transcription and normal replication (Petit and Sancar 1999; Sancar et al. 2004). NER is the primary repair mechanism for bulky DNA damage caused by chemicals or ultraviolet (UV) radiation or as a result of protein-DNA cross-links (Sancar et al. 2004). Two NER pathways exist (Figure 5.5): global genomic NER (GGR), which surveys the whole genome for DNA damage, and transcription-coupled repair (TCR), which primarily repairs damage that interferes with transcription. Both pathways involve recognition of DNA damage and excision of the damaged DNA, followed by the synthesis and ligation of new DNA.

Global genomic nucleotide excision repair. Researchers think that GGR is largely transcription independent, occurring throughout the genome because no gene or strand preference for this repair pathway exists (Hanawalt et al. 2003). Proteins involved in this pathway are presented in Table 5.5. The initial step involves recognition of DNA damage (Figure 5.5). The complex of repair factors in the xeroderma pigmentosum group C (XPC) and the homologous recombinational repair group 23B (HR23B) can directly recognize some DNA damage (Hey et al. 2002). However, in some cases, DNA-binding pro-

Figure 5.4   Mechanism of base excision repair

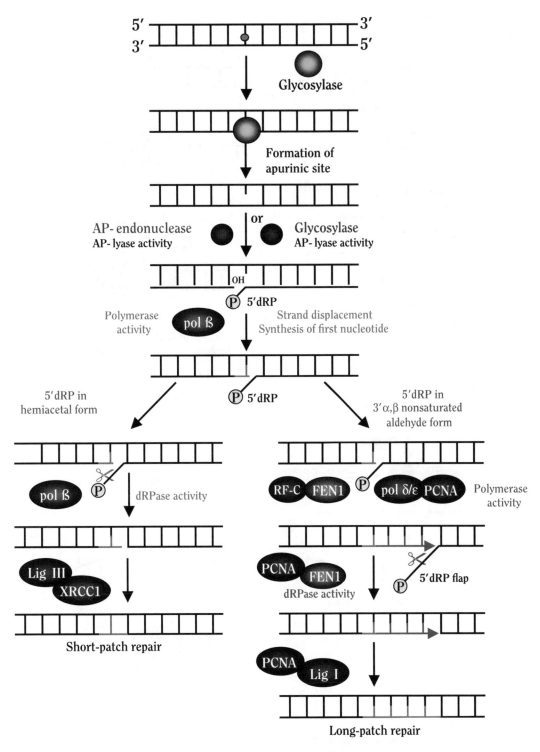

Source: Adapted from Christmann et al. 2003 with permission from Elsevier, © 2003.
Note: **5′dRP** = 5′-deoxyribose phosphate; **AP** = apurinic/apyrimidinic; **dRPase** = DNA deoxyribophosphodiesterase; **FEN1** = flap endonuclease 1; **Lig** = ligase; **OH** = hydroxide; **P** = phosphate; **PCNA** = proliferating cell nuclear antigen; **pol** = polymerase; **RF-C** = replication factor C; **XRCC1** = x-ray repair cross-complementation group 1.

Figure 5.5 **Mechanism of nucleotide excision repair: (A) global genomic repair; (B) transcription-coupled repair**

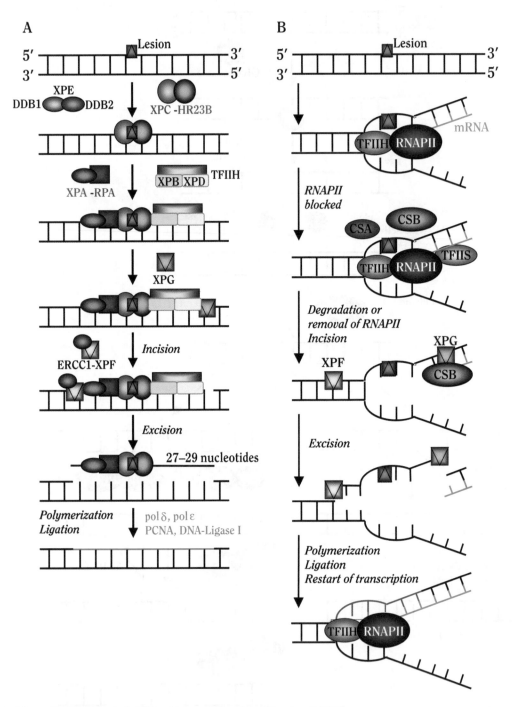

Source: Adapted from Christmann et al. 2003 with permission from Elsevier, © 2003.

Note: **CSA** = Cockayne syndrome complementation group A; **CSB** = Cockayne syndrome complementation group B; **DDB** = DNA binding protein; **ERCC1** = excision repair cross-complementation group 1; **HR23B** = homologous recombinational repair group 23B; **mRNA** = messenger RNA; **PCNA** = proliferating cell nuclear antigen; **pol** = polymerase; **RNAPII** = RNA polymerase II; **RPA** = replication protein A; **TFIIH** = transcription initiation factor IIH; **TFIIS** = transcription initiation factor IIS; **XP** = xeroderma pigmentosum (groups A–G).

Table 5.5   Factors involved in nucleotide excision repair activity in humans

Factor	Proteins	Factor activity	Role in repair
XPA	XPA	DNA binding	Damage recognition
RPA	P70	XPA binding	Damage recognition
	P34	DNA binding	NR
	P11	NR	NR
TFIIH	XPB	DNA-dependent ATPase	Formation of preincision complexes
	XPD	Helicase	NR
	P62	GTP	NR
	P52	NR	NR
	P44	CAK	NR
	CDK7	NR	NR
	CYCH	NR	NR
	P34	NR	NR
XPC	XPC	DNA binding	Molecular matchmaker
	HR23B	NR	Stabilization of preincision complex 1
XPG	XPG	NR	3′ incision
XPF	XPF	NR	5′ incision
	ERCC1	NR	NR

Source: Adapted from Petit and Sancar 1999 with permission from Elsevier, © 1999.
Note: **ATPase** = adenosine triphosphatase; **CAK** = cyclin-dependent kinase-activating kinase; **CDK7** = cyclin-dependent kinase 7; **CYCH** = cytochrome *c*-type biogenesis protein; **ERCC1** = excision repair cross-complementation group 1; **GTP** = guanosine triphosphate; **HR23B** = homologous recombinational repair group 23; **NR** = data not reported; **RPA** = replication protein A; **TFIIH** = transcription initiation factor IIH; **XP** = xeroderma pigmentosum (groups A–G).

tein is required to enhance the DNA distortion before the recruitment of XPC-HR23B (Tan and Chu 2002; Hanawalt et al. 2003). Repair factors XPA and replication protein A are then recruited to the complex to verify that the alteration in the DNA structure results from a lesion, as opposed to a natural variation in DNA structure (Hanawalt et al. 2003).

The DNA is then unwound at the site of the lesion. This step occurs on recruitment of the basal transcription initiation factor IIH (TFIIH) multiprotein complex (Christmann et al. 2003). This complex is likely involved in a further verification of damage and detection of the damaged strand. The helicase subunits of TFIIH, XPB, and XPD then unwind the DNA around the lesion.

Once the DNA has unwound, the lesion is excised at defined sites on either side of the damage (Evans et al. 1997). The 3′-incision is catalyzed by XPG (Habraken et al. 1994; O'Donovan et al. 1994), and the 5′-incision is catalyzed by the excision repair cross-complementation group 1 (ERCC1) XPF complex (Sijbers et al. 1996). The resulting DNA gap is filled in by the PCNA-dependent polymerases: polδ and polε (Aboussekhra et al. 1995; Araújo et al. 2000). The final ligation is performed by DNA ligase I and

associated proteins (Aboussekhra et al. 1995; Mu et al. 1995; Araújo et al. 2000). Findings from in vivo studies suggest that the NER machinery is assembled in a stepwise manner from the individual components at the lesion site. After the repair of a DNA lesion, the entire complex is believed by researchers to disassemble (Houtsmuller et al. 1999; Hoeijmakers 2001).

GGR appears to be inducible in humans (Hanawalt et al. 2003). The proteins that recognize DNA damage in GGR are maintained at low levels under normal physiological conditions. However, as a result of genomic stress, the efficiency of GGR is increased through the activation of the *P53* tumor-suppressor gene (Hanawalt et al. 2003). Consequently, the levels of XPC and XPE increase. Repair of PAH adducts depends on the presence of the P53 protein (Hanawalt et al. 2003). These adducts are not repaired in human fibroblasts that lack a functional P53 protein or other gene product (Lloyd and Hanawalt 2000, 2002; Wani et al. 2000).

Transcription-coupled repair. TCR occurs when DNA damage blocks elongating RNA polymerases (Tornaletti and Hanawalt 1999). The transcription-coupled, repair-specific factors belong to two Cockayne syndrome complementation groups (A and B) and are involved in the displacement of the stalled polymerase (Christmann et al. 2003). At this point, TFIIH is recruited to the lesion, and the subsequent steps in TCR proceed in a manner apparently similar to the steps for GGR. Because of the mechanism of DNA damage recognition, TCR is specific to a DNA strand.

Substrate Specificity

The substrate specificity of NER ranges from small to large distortions in DNA structure. The bulky DNA damage generated by PAHs and aromatic amines in tobacco smoke is repaired primarily by NER (Friedberg 2001). The finding that human NER repairs 8-oxoguanine in vitro more efficiently than thymine dimers or thymine glycol (Reardon et al. 1997) suggests that this pathway may be important for the repair of this mutagenic adduct. In addition, human NER repairs O^6-methylguanine and N^6-methyladenine, as well as A:G and G:G mismatches (Huang et al. 1994).

Protecting Against Mutagenicity and Carcinogenicity of Tobacco Carcinogens

Consistent with the primary role of NER in the repair of bulky DNA damage from PAHs and aromatic amines, cells deficient in NER are more susceptible to the mutagenic and toxic effects of PAHs (Quan et al. 1994, 1995; Lloyd and Hanawalt 2000, 2002; Wani et al. 2000).

Mismatch Repair

Overview

MMR corrects replication errors (base-base or insertion-deletion mismatches) resulting from DNA polymerase errors. This repair pathway is also involved in the repair of alkylation DNA damage, such as repair of O^6-methylguanine (Duckett et al. 1996), cisplatin-derived 1,2-intrastrand cross-links (Duckett et al. 1996), and adducts derived from B[*a*]P (Wu et al. 1999), 2-aminofluorene, and *N*-acetyl-2-aminofluorene (Li et al. 1996). This pathway can also repair 8-oxoguanine (Colussi et al. 2002).

An overview of MMR is displayed in Figure 5.6. Recognition of DNA damage occurs primarily by the mutSα complex (Christmann et al. 2003). This complex is composed of the mutS homologous proteins MSH2 (Fishel et al. 1993; Leach et al. 1993) and MSH6 (Palombo et al. 1995). Once the heterodimer is bound to the mismatch, it undergoes an adenosine-triphosphate (ATP)-dependent conformational change (Stojic et al. 2004). This complex is involved in determining which strand is the newly

Figure 5.6   Mechanism of mismatch repair

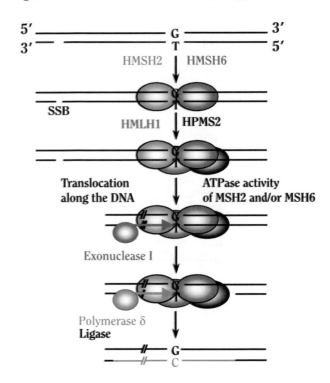

Source: Adapted from Christmann et al. 2003 with permission from Elsevier, © 2003.
Note: For two steps dependent on adenosine triphosphatase (ATPase), see text. **C** = cytosine; **G** = guanine; **HMLH1** = human mutL homolog 1 protein; **HMSH2** = human mutS homolog 2 protein; **HMSH6** = human mutS homolog 6 protein; **HPMS2** = human postmeiotic segregation increased 2 protein; **SSB** = single-stranded DNA binding protein; **T** = thymine.

synthesized DNA (Christmann et al. 2003). A second heterodimer (mutLα) composed of mutL homologs MLH1 and PMS2 then binds to the mutSα-DNA complex in another ATP-dependent step (Nicolaides et al. 1994; Papadopoulos et al. 1994; Li and Modrich 1995; Stojic et al. 2004). Exonuclease I then excises the DNA strand containing the mispaired base (Genschel et al. 2002), followed by the resynthesis of new DNA by polδ (Longley et al. 1997).

MSH2 can also complex with MSH3 to form mutSβ (Acharya et al. 1996; Palombo et al. 1996). The substrate specificity of this alternate complex is different from that of mutSα (Christmann et al. 2003). The mutSα complex recognizes base-base mismatches, as well as insertion-deletion mismatches (Umar et al. 1994), whereas mutSβ binds only to insertion-deletion mismatches (Palombo et al. 1996; Genschel et al. 1998).

Protecting Against Mutagenicity and Carcinogenicity of Tobacco Carcinogens

Persistent adducts that escape repair by AGT, BER, or NER may be processed by MMR. Because MMR occurs after DNA replication (Stojic et al. 2004), this is the last opportunity for DNA damage repair before cell division. Consequently, a defective MMR results in an increase in mutagenesis (Schofield and Hsieh 2003). The overall effect of a defective MMR is the likelihood that cells with persistent DNA damage survive with a miscoded DNA. This combination results in a higher cancer risk.

The role of MMR in the toxicity and mutagenicity of alkylating agents is well documented for methylating agents (Karran 2001; Stojic et al. 2004). Cells lacking functional MMR are more resistant to the toxic effects of methylating agents (Koi et al. 1994; Risinger et al. 1995; Umar et al. 1997; de Wind et al. 1999; Karran 2001; Stojic et al. 2004). However, these cells are sensitive to the mutagenic effects of these compounds (Umar et al. 1997; Zhu et al. 1998). These effects are linked to the ineffective MMR of O^6-methylguanine. As a result, a defective MMR is associated with increases in mutagenesis and carcinogenesis mediated by O^6-methylguanine (Hickman and Samson 1999; Pauly and Moschel 2001). Similar effects were reported for ethylating agents (Claij et al. 2003).

Double-Strand Break Repair

Overview

Two pathways exist for DSBRs: homologous recombination and nonhomologous end-joining. Homologous recombination occurs during DNA replication in the S and G_2 phases, whereas nonhomologous end-joining occurs during G_0 and G_1 phases. Homologous recombination uses the sister chromatid as the template for aligning the breaks in the proper orientation and is consequently error free (Hoeijmakers 2001). However, nonhomologous end-joining does not require sequence homology between the two breaks to ligate them and is therefore prone to errors (Hoeijmakers 2001).

Homologous Recombination

The meiotic recombination 11 (MRE11)-RAD50-NBS1 protein complex initiates DSBR by catalyzing the degradation of the DNA in the 5′ to 3′ direction, generating 3′ single-stranded DNA (Figure 5.7). This single-stranded DNA is protected from degradation by a heptameric ring complex of RAD52 proteins (Stasiak et al. 2000). Replication factor A facilitates the assembly of a RAD51 nucleoprotein filament, which consists of RAD51B, RAD51C, and RAD51D, as well as XRCC2 and XRCC3 (Christmann et al. 2003). RAD51 is able to exchange the single strand with the same sequence from the sister chromatid DNA. This double-stranded copy is then used as a template to correctly repair with DNA synthesis machinery. The resulting Holliday structures are subsequently resolved to generate the repaired DNA (Constantinou et al. 2001).

Nonhomologous End-Joining

Nonhomologous end-joining merely links the ends of a DSB together in the absence of a template (Figure 5.8). The break is initially recognized by a heterodimer consisting of the proteins KU70 (Reeves and Sthoeger 1989) and KU80 (Jeggo et al. 1992). This binding protects the DNA from digestion and associates it with the protein kinase catalytic subunit DNA-PK_{cs}, which is dependent on DNA. This complex, in turn, activates XRCC4-ligase IV, which connects the broken DNA pieces together once the MRE11-RAD50-NBS1 complex has processed the break (Maser et al. 1997; Nelms et al. 1998). Researchers think that FEN1 and Artemis also play a role in the processing of DSBs (Christmann et al. 2003).

Protecting Against Mutagenicity and Carcinogenicity of Tobacco Carcinogens

Scientists think that DSBs trigger large chromosomal aberrations such as chromosomal breaks and exchanges (Pfeiffer et al. 2000). Studies link an increase in chromosomal aberrations to tobacco exposure (DeMarini 2004). These aberrations are more common in pulmonary lung tumors from smokers than in those from nonsmokers (Sanchez-Cespedes et al. 2001). DSBs are also important in triggering cell death (Rich et al. 2000; Lips and Kaina 2001).

Molecular Epidemiology of DNA Repair

Studies support the substantial interindividual variations in DNA repair capacity (DRC). Researchers hypothesize that common variants in the genes that regulate these protein expressions may modulate repair and influence susceptibility to tobacco carcinogenesis. Two complementary approaches to studying DNA repair as a risk factor for tobacco carcinogenesis are applying functional assays and genotyping variants in gene pathways for DNA repair. Table 5.6 summarizes some relevant genes and their variants in pathways involved in repairing tobacco-induced DNA damage.

Figure 5.7   Proposed mechanism of homologous recombination

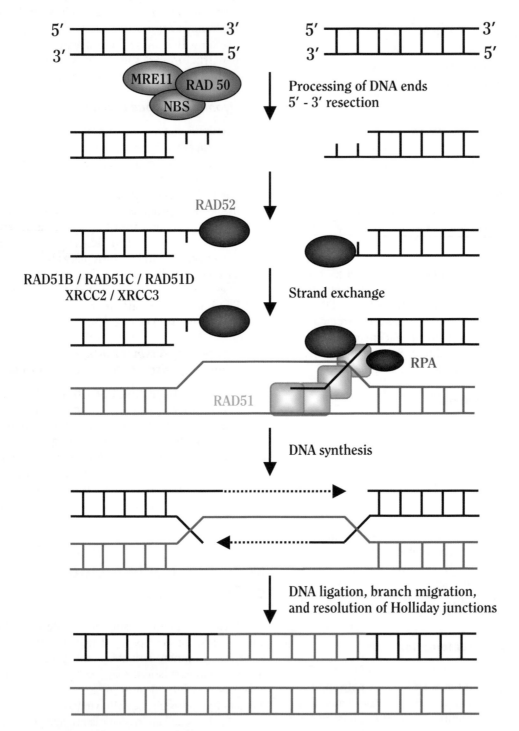

Source: Adapted from Christmann et al. 2003 with permission from Elsevier, © 2003.
Note: **MRE11** = meiotic recombination 11; **RAD** = *S. cerevisiae* DNA damage recognition and repair protein; **RPA** = replication protein A; **XRCC2/XRCC3** = x-ray repair cross-complementation groups 2 and 3.

Functional Assays of DNA Damage and Repair to Tobacco Carcinogens

Berwick and Vineis (2000) extensively reviewed the types of functional assays. The review included assays that use a chemical or physical mutagen challenge such as mutagen sensitivity, single-cell microgel electrophoresis (comet assay), and assays of induced adducts and unscheduled DNA synthesis. The review also included the host-cell reactivation (HCR) assay, which measures cellular ability to remove adducts from plasmids transfected into lymphocyte cultures in vitro by the expression of damaged reporter genes.

Host-Cell Reactivation Assay

The HCR assay measures the expression level of damaged reporter genes, which are involved in reactivation of the host cell. The assay uses undamaged host lymphocytes, is fast, and objectively measures intrinsic cellular repair (Athas et al. 1991). In the assay, lymphocytes are transfected with a damaged, nonreplicating recombinant plasmid harboring a chloramphenicol acetyltransferase (CAT) reporter gene (*PCMVCAT*). To study tobacco-related cancers, the mutagen challenge is B[a]P (Gelboin 1980). Experimental conditions produce at least one BPDE-DNA adduct per plasmid, completely blocking transcription of the *PCMVCAT* gene without inducing conformational changes in the DNA. This finding is important because conformational change of the plasmid could reduce the transfection rate. Because even a single unrepaired DNA adduct can effectively block *PCMVCAT* transcription (Koch et al. 1993), any measurable *PCMV-CAT* activity reflects the ability of the transfected cells to remove BPDE-induced adducts from the plasmids (Athas et al. 1991).

Both lymphocytes and skin fibroblasts from patients with basal cell carcinoma, but not with XP, were found to have lower excision repair rates than those from persons without cancer (Wei et al. 1993). Consequently, the repair capacity of lymphocytes may reflect the overall repair capacity of a person. Spitz and colleagues (2003) showed that case patients with lung cancer had a significantly lower DRC than did control participants and that case patients aged 63 years or younger and lifetime nonsmokers had a lower DRC than that of matched control participants. DRC appears to be highest among case patients and control participants who were current smokers than among those who were former smokers and lifetime nonsmokers. Heavy smokers among both case patients and control participants tended to have more proficient DRC than did light smokers. This finding indicated that cigarette smoking may stimulate DRC in response to the DNA damage caused by carcinogens in tobacco.

Figure 5.8   Proposed mechanism of nonhomologous end-joining

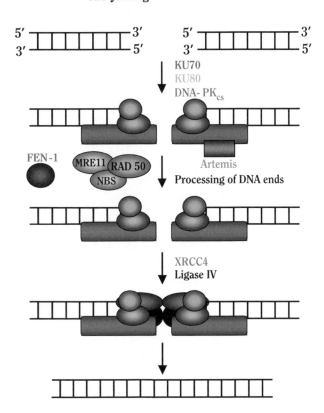

Source: Adapted from Christmann et al. 2003 with permission from Elsevier, © 2003.

Note: **FEN1** = flap endonuclease 1; **MRE11** = meiotic recombination 11; **PK$_{cs}$** = protein kinase catalytic subunit; **XRCC4** = x-ray repair cross-complementation group 4.

Such an adaptation would be consistent with a baseline DRC that can be mobilized on an increased demand for repair (Eller et al. 1997; Cheng et al. 1998). This adaptation of DRC to smoking, if it exists, appears to be long term rather than transient, because the effect was still present in former smokers but was not stronger in those who had smoked in the 24 hours before the blood sample was drawn (Wei et al. 2000). The finding that long-term heavy smokers with lung cancer had an efficient DRC may also indicate that heavy exposure overwhelms even relatively resistant phenotypes.

Luciferase Host-Cell Reactivation Assay

Researchers have modified the HCR assay by replacing CAT with luciferase (LUC). The cell-extraction procedure is far more simplified for the LUC assay. A luminometer measures LUC optical density, and the laboratory

Table 5.6   Select candidate genes and polymorphisms implicated in repair of tobacco-induced DNA damage

Gene	Nucleotide position	Nucleotide change	Amino acid change	Allele frequency
Alkyltransferases				
AGT, MGMT			Ile143Val	0.05–0.2
Base excision repair				
MBD4	13390	T/C	Ser342Pro	0.05
	13402	G/A	Glu346Lys	0.07
TDG	27090	G/A	Gly199Ser	0.09
MUTYH	18556	G/C	Gly335His	0.44
OGG1	18069	C/G	Ser326Cys	0.25
APEX1	11865	T/G	Glu148Asp	0.25
XRCC1	32584	C/T	Arg194Trp	0.08
	33746	G/A	Arg280His	0.05
	34432	G/A	Arg399Gln	0.31
ADPRT	75787	T/C	Val761Ala	0.38
	77525	C/T	Pro882Leu	0.20
POLD1	24569	G/A	Arg19His	0.12
	27479	A/G	His119Arg	0.16
	27715	A/G	Ser173Asn	0.06
Nucleotide excision repair				
XPC	30197	C/T	Ala499Val	0.24
	42635	A/C	Lys939Gln	0.38
XPD	16232	G/A	Asp312Asn	0.40
	28572	A/C	Lys751Gln	0.33
XPF	34637	T/C	Ser662Pro	0.06
RAD23B	48769	C/T	Ala249Val	0.18
CCNH	23563	C/T	Val270Ala	0.10
XPG	39583	G/C	His1104Asp	0.32
LIG1	29008	A/C	Ala170Ala	0.39
	61130	C/T	Asp802Asp	0.21
	62525	C/G	Ala814Ala	0.30
Double-strand break repair				
Homologous recombination				
RAD51	692 (cDNA)	G/T	Ala143Ser	0.33
XRCC3	26044	T/C	Thr241Met	0.22
RAD52	45137	C/A	Ser346Ter	0.05
RAD54L	1222 (cDNA)	G/C	Arg374Ser	0.11
BRCA2	27113	T/G	His372Asn	0.23
	93268	G/A	Ile3412Val	0.05
RAD50	3374 (cDNA)	G/T	Arg1111Ile	0.25
NBS1	137331	C/G	Gln185Glu	0.46
Nonhomologous end-joining				
KU70	336 (cDNA)	G/A	Glu107Lys	0.06
	454 (cDNA)	T/C	Val146Ala	0.11
	1825 (cDNA)	T/C	Leu603Pro	0.10
KU80	1487 (cDNA)	C/T	Pro485Leu	0.14
LIG4	8 (cDNA)	C/T	Ala3Val	0.07
	27 (cDNA)	C/T	Thr9Ile	0.14
XRCC4	21965	G/T	Ala247Ser	0.08

Note: **cDNA** = complementary DNA.

procedures are shorter. The results for the DRC phenotype from the independent CAT and LUC assays in parallel are highly correlated, with a correlation coefficient of 0.65 (p <0.0001) (Qiao et al. 2002a). This finding suggests that these two assays are comparable.

8-Oxoguanine DNA Glycosylase Activity Assay

The OGG test is another functional repair assay that measures the specific activity of the enzyme 8-oxoguanine DNA *N*-glycosylase in protein extracts prepared from peripheral blood mononuclear cells (Paz-Elizur et al. 2003). The OGG1 enzyme removes 8-oxoguanine from DNA and leaves behind an abasic site that is rapidly cleaved by the AP lyase of OGG1. OGG activity (in units per μg of protein extract) is the amount of fragment cleaved by 1 μg of extract in one hour under standard reaction conditions (Paz-Elizur et al. 2003). In a pilot case-control study of NSCLC, the mean value of OGG activity in the case patients was significantly lower than that in the control participants and was independent of tumor histology, gender, and smoking status (Paz-Elizur et al. 2003). In addition, OGG activity in protein extracts from peripheral blood mononuclear cells correlated well with that from lung tissue in the same patients (p = 0.003).

Mutagen Sensitivity Assays

Researchers use cytogenetic assays extensively to measure human exposure and response to genotoxic agents. These assays are based on the unproven hypothesis that the extent of genetic damage in the lymphocytes may reflect critical events in carcinogenesis in the affected tissues. The assays can only indirectly indicate DRC from the cellular damage that remains after mutagenic exposure and recovery and therefore probably reflect nonspecific impairment of the DNA repair machinery (Berwick and Vineis 2000).

Hsu and colleagues (1989) developed the in vitro mutagen challenge assay to demonstrate interindividual differences in susceptibility to carcinogenic agents. This assay counts the frequency of bleomycin-induced breaks in short-term lymphocyte cultures, as a measure of cancer susceptibility. Bleomycin is a clastogenic agent that mimics the effects of radiation by generating free oxygen radicals capable of producing DNA single-strand breaks and DSBs after forming a complex with DNA, ferrous ions, and oxygen that releases oxygen radicals (Burger et al. 1981). Most of the breaks are repaired by BER. Repair is rapid, with a half-life of only a few minutes (López-Larraza et al. 1990).

Mutagen sensitivity is an independent risk factor for lung cancer that has a dose-response relationship with the number of induced chromosomal breaks (Spitz et al. 1995,

2003; Strom et al. 1995; Wu et al. 1995, 1998a; Zheng et al. 2003). The risks associated with mutagen sensitivity, stratified by smoking status, are elevated in all smoking strata but are highest in current smokers and in the heaviest smokers. For studying tobacco-related cancers, a more appropriate mutagen to trigger DNA damage is BPDE; BPDE-induced sensitivity is a risk factor for lung cancer (Wei et al. 1996; Wu et al. 1998a,b).

Comet Assay

The comet assay (single-cell microgel electrophoresis) is applicable to any cell line or tissue from which a single-cell suspension can be obtained (Ross et al. 1995). Singh and associates (1988) have described the methods in detail. For this assay, a cell culture is mixed with agarose gel and attached to a microscope slide. The cells are lysed by submerging the slides in freshly prepared lysis buffer to remove all cellular proteins. To allow for DNA denaturation, unwinding, and expression of the alkali-labile sites, the slides are then placed in an alkali buffer (pH = 12.0). To separate the damaged DNA from the intact nuclei, a constant electric current is applied, and the slides are neutralized, fixed, and stored in the dark at room temperature until ready for analysis. During electrophoresis, damaged DNA migrates from the nucleus toward the anode as a result of the constant electric current, which forms the typical "comet" cell. A predetermined number of cells are manually selected, and comet cells are automatically quantified with appropriate imaging software.

Case patients with lung and bladder cancer had significantly higher levels of induced DNA damage after exposure to both BPDE and γ-radiation, which were assessed by the mean "tail moment" in lymphocytes. (The tail moment is the product of lymphocyte tail length and the fraction of the total DNA in the tail.) Higher levels of DNA damage were positively associated with increased risk of bladder and lung cancer (Schabath et al. 2003; Wu et al. 2005). Schmezer and colleagues (2001) showed that case patients with lung cancer were significantly more sensitive to bleomycin and had a reduced DRC (68 percent in case patients and 81 percent in control participants [p <0.001]). Rajee-Behbahani and colleagues (2001) reported a similar DRC finding of 67 percent in 160 case patients with lung cancer and 79.3 percent in 180 control participants. When the data from the cases and controls were considered together, only 18 percent of the case patients were below the median level of sensitivity to bleomycin for all control participants, and 82 percent were in the hypersensitive range.

Mohrenweiser and Jones (1998) have pointed out several lines of evidence documenting that differences in DRC reflect genetic differences. DRC in lymphocyte subpopulations from an individual exhibited similar repair capacities. Furthermore, intraindividual variations in repair capacity among subpopulations of lymphocytes are significantly smaller than are interindividual variations (Crompton and Ozsahin 1997). The phenotype of reduced repair capacity in the NER pathway is independent of the phenotype for DSBR (Wu et al. 1998a).

Researchers have performed extensive resequencing of DNA repair genes to identify variations that may be associated with a reduced function of their encoded proteins rather than an absence of function. Such polymorphisms could explain interindividual differences in DRC (Spitz et al. 2001; Qiao et al. 2002b; Wu et al. 2003). Although the variant alleles are likely to be associated with only a modest cancer risk, because they exist at a polymorphic frequency, the attributable risks can become substantial. As Berwick and Vineis (2000) noted, studies that compare genetic polymorphisms with results of functional assays will likely be the most valuable type of investigations to clarify the role of a defect in DRC with the development of cancer.

Polymorphisms in O^6-Alkylguanine–DNA Alkyltransferase

The ability of a cell to withstand alkyl damage is related to the number of AGT molecules in the cell and the rate of de novo synthesis of AGT. AGT levels differed among persons, and protein levels in the liver, colon, and peripheral blood varied 4-, 10-, and 20-fold, respectively (Myrnes et al. 1983; Strauss et al. 1989; Povey et al. 2000). Environmental and genetic factors, but not age, affect expression levels of AGT (Margison et al. 2003). AGT levels are higher in normal lung, colorectal, and placental tissues from smokers than in those from nonsmokers, although these findings are controversial (Slupphaug et al. 1992; Drin et al. 1994; Povey et al. 2000). Exposure to AGT inhibitory aldehydes, such as formaldehyde from occupational exposure, can deplete AGT activity (Hayes et al. 1997). Expression of AGT is higher in NSCLC tumor tissues from smokers than in those from nonsmokers (Mattern et al. 1998). However, small-scale studies examining AGT activity in peripheral lymphocytes have not observed significant differences between smokers and nonsmokers (Vähäkangas et al. 1991; Oesch and Klein 1992; Hall et al. 1993) or between case patients with cancer and control participants (Boffetta et al. 2002). It is not clear how well AGT activity in lymphocytes predicts levels in lung tissue.

The *AGT* gene contains multiple polymorphisms in the 5′ upstream region, which comprises the promoter and enhancer regions, as well as exon 1 (Egyházi et al. 2002; Krzesniak et al. 2004). These genetic variations may account for some of the interindividual variations in expression levels. Eight allelic variants in this region occur at a frequency of at least 0.01. One-half of these variants have a prevalence of 0.1 to 0.6, and this finding suggests a contribution to the variability in AGT expression within populations (Krzesniak et al. 2004). The prevalence of the best-studied enhancer polymorphism, *C1099T*, is 0.09 to 0.12 and is associated with an increase in promoter-enhancer activity in the LUC assay (Krzesniak et al. 2004). However, heterozygotes for this enhancer polymorphism do not appear to be at a markedly lower risk of developing lung cancer (OR = 0.82; 95 percent CI, 0.41–1.67) (Krzesniak et al. 2004). None of the other enhancer-promoter polymorphisms have been examined for their relationship with AGT or cancer risk.

Mutations at or near the cysteine acceptor site can affect AGT activity (Crone et al. 1994). Two polymorphisms have been identified in this region of the protein: codon 143 *ILE/*VAL* and codon 160 *GLY/*ARG*. The variant isoform codon 160 *GLY/*ARG* has exhibited activity to repair bulky alkylated DNA adducts that is significantly less than that of the *GLY* wild-type phenotype (Edara et al. 1996; Mijal et al. 2004). The estimated prevalence of the 143 variant is 0.07 in Whites, 0.03 in African Americans (Kaur et al. 2000), and as high as 0.24 in Swedish populations (Ma et al. 2003). The codon 160 variant allele is likely a mutant, because it was found at a frequency less than 0.01 (Kaur et al. 2000). These researchers reported a marginally significant increase in the risk of lung cancer associated with the codon 143 *ILE/*VAL* genotype (OR = 2.1; 95 percent CI, 1.01–4.7), and no interaction of genotype and smoking dose was seen. More recently, Cohet and colleagues (2004) reported an OR of 2.05 (95 percent CI, 1.03–4.07) for lung cancer among lifetime carriers of the codon 143 and 160 variant alleles who were nonsmokers. The authors suggested that the strongest risk was associated with exposure to secondhand tobacco smoke.

Polymorphisms in the Pathway for Repair of Base Excision

Cross-Complementation Group 1 for Excision Repair

The *XRCC1* gene encodes a protein that functions in BER and involves the excision of the damaged region, followed by repair synthesis that uses the opposite strand as the template. The XRCC1 protein forms scaffolding with DNA ligase III, polβ, and poly (adenosine diphosphate–ribose) polymerase (PARP) to rejoin DNA strand breaks and repair gaps left during BER. Of the estimated 17 variants, 1 is a polymorphism at the *XRCC1* 28152 site

(G→A transition) of codon 399 in exon 10 that results in a nonconservative amino acid substitution of arginine for glutamine. Goode and colleagues (2002) extensively reviewed the conflicting results for lung cancer studies. For example, Divine and colleagues (2001) reported a more than twofold risk for lung adenocarcinoma associated with the *GLN/*GLN genotype. Zhou and colleagues (2003) found an association that was largely restricted to nonsmokers and light smokers. Some studies failed to find any association between the *GLN/*GLN genotype and lung cancer risk (Butkiewicz et al. 2001; Ratnasinghe et al. 2001; Popanda et al. 2004; Zhang et al. 2005b). However, Matullo and colleagues (2001a) did find an association for bladder cancer. David-Beabes and London (2001) reported a decreased risk of lung cancer for both African American and White patients. Other studies also report conflicting findings regarding an increased risk associated with the exon 10 *ARG/*ARG genotype (Lee et al. 2001; Stern et al. 2001).

Another polymorphism at the *XRCC1* 26304 site (C→T transversion) of codon 194 in exon 6 results in a nonconservative amino acid substitution of arginine. Most studies suggest a reduced risk of cancer associated with the 399*ARG variant allele (Goode et al. 2002). Studies of lung, bladder, head and neck, and gastric cancers all showed inverse associations with the variant allele; some studies included evidence of an interaction with smoking (Sturgis et al. 1999; David-Beabes and London 2001; Ratnasinghe et al. 2001; Stern et al. 2001). Two studies noted no association for esophageal and lung cancers (Butkiewicz et al. 2001; Lee et al. 2001).

A few earlier studies evaluated the functional significance of these polymorphisms. Lunn and colleagues (1999) noted that persons with the 399*GLN allele were at a significantly higher risk (OR = 2.4) for exhibiting detectable aflatoxin B_1 adducts and a higher frequency of the glycophorin A variant than were carriers of the 399*ARG/*ARG allele. This study also reported a dose-response relationship between smoking status and presence of the polymorphism for detecting the adducts and the glycophorin A variant (Lunn et al. 1999). However, no significant effects were noted for other *XRCC1* polymorphisms. Duell and colleagues (2000) found elevated SCE frequencies and polyphenol DNA adducts with 399*GLN/*GLN homozygous genotypes. Abdel-Rahman and El-Zein (2000) noted that persons carrying the *GLN allele had significantly higher numbers of SCEs in response to NNK treatment than did *ARG/*ARG genotype carriers. No differences were detected in persons with the codon 194 genotype.

Matullo and colleagues (2001b) found higher DNA adduct levels among lifetime nonsmokers who were healthy and were homozygous for the 399*GLN allele than among those with the wild-type genotype (15.6 versus 6.78, p = 0.007). Wang and colleagues (2003a) showed that persons with the variant 194*TRP allele had fewer bleomycin- and BPDE-induced breaks per cell than did those with the wild-type genotype. The *XRCC1* codon 399 is within the BRCT domain (amino acids 301 to 402) that interacts with PARP and is in many proteins with activity involving response to DNA damage and cell-cycle checkpoints. This region also has homology with yeast *RAD4* repair-related genes. Because the role of *XRCC1* in BER brings together DNA polβ, DNA ligase III, and PARP at the site of DNA damage, repair activity of the exon 10 variant may be altered. The codon 194 polymorphism is in the linker region of the *XRCC1* N-terminal domain separating the helix 3 and polβ involved in binding a single-nucleotide gap DNA substrate (Marintchev et al. 1999). Therefore, this polymorphism is less likely to cause a significant change in repair function.

OGG1 *Gene*

The product of the *OGG1* gene catalyzes the excision of a modified base, 8-oxoguanine, which may be formed by exposure to reactive oxygen species. The reduced ability to excise 8-oxoguanine may lead to an accumulation of oxidation-induced mutations. Studies have identified several polymorphisms at the *OGG1* locus. The most frequently studied polymorphism is a common C→G transversion in exon 7 that results in an amino acid alteration at codon 326 (Ser→Cys). The HOGG1 protein encoded by the wild-type 326*SER allele exhibited substantially higher DNA repair activity than did the 326*CYS variant in an in vitro *Escherichia coli* complementation activity assay (Kohno et al. 1998).

Researchers have observed fairly consistent increased risks of *OGG1* polymorphisms (Goode et al. 2002). The largest study was a U.S.-population-based, multiethnic study of lung cancer that identified a significantly increased risk associated with the *CYS/*CYS genotype (*CYS/*CYS versus *SER/*SER; OR = 2.1; 95 percent CI, 1.2–3.7) (Le Marchand et al. 2002). A small, hospital-based study of lung cancer in Japan supported these results (Sugimura et al. 1999). Findings in a third study of lung cancer that also suggested an increased risk had similar findings for comparison of the two homozygote groups (OR = 2.2; 95 percent CI, 0.4–11.8) (Wikman et al. 2000). Analyses of esophageal cancer also showed an increased risk associated with the *CYS/*CYS genotype (OR = 1.9; 95 percent CI, 1.3–2.6) (Xing et al. 2001). However, overall findings regarding an interaction with smoking were inconsistent.

Polymorphisms in the Pathway for Nucleotide Excision Repair

Xeroderma Pigmentosum A

XPA is an essential DNA-binding protein in the NER pathway that aids in correctly positioning the repair machinery around the damaged areas and in maintaining contact with core repair factors during the repair process. XPA interacts with other proteins, such as replication protein A, TFIIH, and XRCC1/XPF (Volker et al. 2001). Studies have identified an A→G transversion variant in the 5' noncoding region (Butkiewicz et al. 2000). Researchers investigating this polymorphism in lung cancer reported similar results in two studies. Wu and colleagues (2003) reported that the presence of one or two copies of the *G allele instead of the *A allele was associated with a reduced lung cancer risk for all ethnic groups. Furthermore, control participants with one or two copies of the *G allele demonstrated more efficient DRC, as measured by the HCR assay, than did control participants with the homozygous A genotype. In a study in Korea, Park and colleagues (2002) reported that the *G/*G genotype was also associated with a significantly decreased lung cancer risk when the combined *A/*A and *A/*G genotype was used as the reference group. Butkiewicz and colleagues (2004) reported similarly increased risks that had borderline statistical significance for the *A/*A genotype in all participants and for SCC and adenocarcinomas. For heavy smokers, the risk estimate was 2.52 (95 percent CI, 1.2–5.4). Popanda and colleagues (2004) reported a nonsignificant risk of 1.53 for the *A/*A genotype compared with the *G/*G genotype. Thus, all studies confirm the protective effect of the *G/*G genotype and the enhanced risk for the *A/*A genotype.

Xeroderma Pigmentosum C

XPC is the step-limiting factor in NER. Researchers have found two single nucleotide polymorphisms (SNPs) in the coding region. ALA499VAL is a single *C/*T nucleotide polymorphism that codes for an amino acid substitution (Ala/Val) at codon 499. Another SNP, LYS939GLN, is a single *A/*C nucleotide polymorphism that codes for an amino acid substitution (Lys/Gln) at codon 939. This variant allele is associated with an increased risk of bladder cancer (Sanyal et al. 2004). There is also a bi-allelic poly AT insertion/deletion polymorphism (PAT) in intron 9 of XPC. The *PAT allele has been associated with risk of head and neck cancer (Shen et al. 2001).

Cross-Complementation Group 1 for Excision Repair

The XRCC1 gene codes for a 5' incision subunit of the NER complex (Mohrenweiser et al. 1989). The XRCC1 and XPF proteins form a stable complex in vivo and in vitro (de Laat et al. 1999). Although studies have reported no defect in the human XRCC1 gene, cells from XRCC1-deficient mice have an increase in genomic instability and a repair-deficient phenotype (Melton et al. 1998). Five known polymorphisms of the XRCC1 gene do not cause an amino acid change and are validated in the SNP500Cancer Database of the National Cancer Institute. However, researchers think that a polymorphism with A→C transversion at nucleotide 8092 in the 3' untranslated region affects mRNA stability (Shen et al. 1998). Studies have implicated the XRCC1 polymorphism in the risk of adult-onset glioma (Chen et al. 2000) but not in head and neck cancer (Sturgis et al. 2002). Zhou and colleagues (2005) found no overall effect on lung cancer risk, but they did find a lower lung cancer risk in heavy smokers and a significantly higher risk in lifetime nonsmokers (OR = 2.11; 95 percent CI, 1.03–4.31).

Xeroderma Pigmentosum Complementation Group D

XPD (XRCC2) is one of the seven genetic complementation groups that encode for proteins in the NER pathway. The XPD protein has a role in both NER and basal transcription. XPD functions as an evolutionary conserved ATP-dependent helicase within the multisubunit transcription repair factor complex TFIIH. Of the three polymorphisms identified in XPD, two are in exons and the third is silent. The G→A transition in exon 10 at codon 312 results in an amino acid change (Asp→Asn). The transition A→C at codon 751 in exon 23 produces a Lys→Gln change. The amino acid substitution Lys751Gln in exon 23 does not reside in a known helicase/adenosine triphosphatase domain, but it is an amino acid residue identical in human, mouse, hamster, and fish XPD. This finding suggests a functional relevance for such a highly evolutionary conserved sequence (Shen et al. 1998). Goode and colleagues (2002) extensively reviewed numerous reports from case-control studies of lung cancer that have conflicting results. The largest study included 1,092 lung cancer case patients and 1,240 control participants who were spouses or friends (Zhou et al. 2002a). The overall AOR was 1.47 (95 percent CI, 1.1–2.0) for the ASP312ASN polymorphism (*ASN/*ASN versus

*ASP/*ASP), but there was no association for the LYS-751GLN polymorphism (*GLN/*GLN versus *LYS/*LYS). Analyses of the interactions between genes and smoking revealed that the adjusted ORs for each of the two polymorphisms decreased significantly as pack-years[1] increased. The interaction between the ASP312ASN polymorphism and smoking status was stronger than that between the LYS751GLN polymorphism and smoking. The researchers concluded that cumulative cigarette smoking modified the association between XPD polymorphisms and lung cancer risk. Spitz and colleagues (2001) reported AORs for the variant LYS751GLN and ASP312ASN genotypes of 1.36 and 1.51, respectively, although neither estimate was statistically significant. For persons homozygous for the variant genotype at either locus, the AOR was 1.84 (95 percent CI, 1.11–3.04; p = 0.018 for trend).

A recent review and meta-analysis of nine international case-control studies that included 2,886 lung cancer cases and 3,085 controls for codon 312 (*LYS751GLN*) and 3,374 lung cancer cases and 3,880 controls for codon 751 (*ASP312ASN*) did not demonstrate significant associations with either variant genotype (Benhamou and Sarasin 2005). However, for U.S. studies alone, both variants were associated with a significantly increased risk for lung cancer (ORs = 1.43 and 1.25, respectively). Hu and colleagues (2004) conducted another meta-analysis. The combined case-control studies reported a 21-percent higher risk for the *751*C/*C* genotype (OR = 1.21; 95 percent CI, 1.02–1.43) and a 27-percent higher risk for the *XPD 312*A/*A* genotype (OR = 1.27; 95 percent CI, 1.04–1.56) among cases than among controls. Among studies of persons of Asian versus White descent, only the studies of Whites found a significantly higher risk for the *XPD 751*C/*C* genotype (OR = 1.23; 95 percent CI, 1.03–1.47). For the *XPD 312*A/*A* genotype, the risk among Whites compared with other races had borderline statistical significance (OR = 1.22; 95 percent CI, 0.99–1.49) among cases compared with controls. TFIIH transcriptional activity may be tolerant to amino acid changes in the XPD protein, and mutations may destroy or alter the repair function without affecting transcriptional activity. As Lunn and colleagues (2000) suggested, the effects of the *LYS* allele may differ in different repair pathways, as assessed by different repair assays. The overall effect of conservative mutations in *XPD* may be subtle, because they do not alter XPB and XPD helicase activity, and multiple alterations might be needed before any effect is noted.

XPF/ERCC1 *Gene Complex*

ERCC1 forms a complex with *XPF* when it makes a dual incision at the single-strand to double-strand transition at the 5′ end of the damaged DNA strand (Shen et al. 1998). This complex is required to repair interstrand cross-links. A T→C transition at codon 662 results in a serine→proline substitution. Fan and colleagues (1999) reported six SNPs, five in coding regions. Three of the SNPs resulted in nonconserved amino acid differences.

XPG/ERCC5 *Gene Complex*

This complex shows homology with yeast RAD2 and carries out incision at the 3′ end of the lesion in the DNA strand (Harada et al. 1995; Hyytinen et al. 1999). Only two of the seven validated SNPs appear with significant frequency. In one polymorphism, a single nucleotide substitution (G→C) causes an amino acid change (His1104Asp) at codon 1104. In the other polymorphism, a C→G substitution produces an amino acid change from cysteine to serine at codon 529. Sanyal and colleagues (2004) showed that the variant *C/*C* genotype was significantly less frequent in cases of bladder cancer than in controls. Jeon and colleagues (2003) reported similar findings for 310 lung cancer cases, in which the frequency of the variant genotype was less than that for the other two genotypes combined (AOR = 0.54; 95 percent CI, 0.37–0.80). This protective effect was attenuated in heavy smokers. Jeon and colleagues (2003) pointed out that because this SNP is in the C-terminus, it might alter binding to other proteins in the incision complex, thereby affecting DRC.

RAD23B *Gene*

The *RAD23B* gene is an evolutionary, well-conserved gene with 10 exons. The protein complexes with XPC to bind to different types of lesions and recruit the necessary factors for NER. Of the six validated SNPs, four are seen with considerable frequency. One of the most frequently observed polymorphisms is a substitution (C→T) resulting in an amino acid change at codon 249 (Ala249Val).

Genotype-Phenotype Correlations

Amino acid differences, especially at conserved sites in these enzymes, could result in changes in repair proficiency. The next logical step is the challenging task of evaluating the functional relevance of these polymorphisms. A variety of factors that modulate the path from genotype to

---

[1]Pack-years = the number of years of smoking multiplied by the number of packs of cigarettes smoked per day.

phenotype include protein-protein interaction, posttranslational modification, gene silencing, epigenetic regulation, and environmental factors. Furthermore, proteins involved in DNA repair pathways are often multifunctional, resulting in a variety of phenotypes.

Both of the common genotypes *LYS/*LYS 751 and 312 *ASP/*ASP XPD were associated with a DRC more efficient than that for heterozygotes and with a significantly higher DRC than that for the homozygote mutants (Spitz et al. 2001). These results were confirmed in a different study population with a different mutagen challenge: a UV exposure of 800 joules per square meter that like BPDE invoked NER (Qiao et al. 2002b). Additional validation came from a correlative study that used the comet assay to assess DNA damage and repair (Schabath et al. 2003). These data are consistent with some of the published small-scale studies of these types of genotype-phenotype correlations. Hou and colleagues (2002) noted a significant increase in DNA adduct levels, as measured by ^{32}P-postlabeling, with an increased number of variant alleles in exon 10 (p = 0.02) and exon 23 (p = 0.001). In addition, persons with the combined exon 10 *A/*A and exon 23 *C/*C genotype showed significantly higher levels of adducts than those for persons carrying any of the other genotypes (p = 0.02). Lunn and colleagues (2000) reported that possessing the common XPD genotype, *LYS/*LYS 751, was associated with an increased risk of suboptimal DRC, which was reflected in the number of x-ray–induced lymphocyte chromatid aberrations. No association with the *ASN312 allele was found.

However, Møller and colleagues (1998) reported no relationship between the LYS751GLN polymorphism and DRC, as measured by HCR or comet assay in 80 participants, including 20 healthy persons. Another study with a small sample of 76 healthy persons found no association between either SCE frequencies or the presence of DNA adducts by LYS751GLN genotype (Duell et al. 2000).

For a complex disease such as cancer, multiple genes—each with a small effect—probably act independently or interact with other genes to influence the disease phenotype. Although these data suggest that the polymorphisms have a functional relevance, biochemical and biologic characterizations of the variants are needed to validate these findings.

Polymorphisms in the Pathway for Double-Strand Break Repair

The XRCC3 gene encodes a protein that acts in the pathway for DSB/homologous recombination repair (DSB/REC repair) and repairs chromosomal damage such as breaks, translocations, and deletions. XRCC3 is a protein related to RAD51, which is a critical component of DSB/REC. Shen and colleagues (1998) identified a C→T substitution in exon 7 at position 18067 of XRCC3, a polymorphism that results in a threonine→methionine amino acid substitution at codon 241. David-Beabes and colleagues (2001) found no significant association between the XRCC3241 polymorphism and lung cancer. This finding was consistent with a smaller study of NSCLC that also found no association after adjustments for age and smoking (Butkiewicz et al. 2001). Wang and colleagues (2003c) reported an elevated but not statistically significant risk of lung cancer associated with polymorphisms of the XRCC3 *T allele in African Americans and Mexican Americans, which was evident largely in heavy smokers. Other studies have associated this XRCC3 polymorphism with an increased risk for melanoma skin cancer (Winsey et al. 2000) and bladder carcinoma (Matullo et al. 2001a). The THR241MET genetic variant may also contribute to increases in DNA adducts and bladder cancer risk (Stern et al. 2002).

Summary

The association between common variants in DNA repair genes and the risk for tobacco-induced cancers is the focus of considerable interest, but the results to date are inconsistent. Complementary functional studies are likely to be valuable in addressing these inconsistencies. Molecular epidemiologists now have better access to high-throughput genotyping platforms and an enhanced ability to focus on analyses based on pathways. Haplotype analyses also increase the power to detect relevant associations. In addition, computational algorithms such as PolyPhen and Scale-Invariant Feature Transform correlate with risk estimates, and new analytic tools are being developed.

Conversion of DNA Adducts to Mutations

DNA replication plays a major role in inducing point mutations—substitutions of one base pair for another and small mutations due to insertion or deletion of bases. DNA adducts per se are not mutations and can be removed by various DNA repair mechanisms in cells (Friedberg et al. 1995). When repair is not completed before a replication complex encounters the DNA adducts or other lesions, various events are induced, which are sensed by cell-cycle checkpoint mechanisms that halt cell-cycle progression (Sancar et al. 2004). When the lesion is a strand break, replication causes a DSB that is repaired by homologous recombination or by the erroneous nonhomologous end-joining mechanism. When the lesion is an interstrand cross-link, the stall of a replication complex triggers the unhooking of the cross-link by endonucleolytic incisions on both sides of the cross-link in one strand. When the lesion is a modified base or the loss of a base, a DNA polymerase often inserts a nucleotide, either correctly or incorrectly, opposite the lesion and extends the DNA strand beyond the site. The modification of a template nucleotide generally impairs its ability to serve as a template in efficiency and fidelity. Therefore, DNA synthesis slows down or is blocked at the site of the adducted template.

Translesion DNA synthesis occurs when a DNA polymerase succeeds in DNA synthesis over the modified template. The synthesis reaction sometimes results in the insertion of an incorrect nucleotide opposite a lesion. This insertion leads to base-substitution mutations, the skipping of the lesion nucleotide template, or the realignment of a growing primer strand on the template strand at the adducted region, which produces frameshift mutations. This step results in the introduction of mutations, and the subsequent replication of the mutated strand establishes the mutation in the genome. This section describes the mechanism of mutation induction by translesion DNA synthesis.

Molecular Analysis of Conversion to Mutations

The strategy for studying the conversion of adducts to mutations is to incorporate a chemically characterized DNA adduct or lesion into a specific sequence (Basu and Essigmann 1988). A DNA adduct can be incorporated into an oligonucleotide sequence by total chemical synthesis. However, a modified oligonucleotide may be prepared by direct reaction with a mutagen, followed by HPLC and/or gel electrophoresis purification. The modified oligonucleotide is then used as a substrate for in vitro and in vivo studies of translesion DNA synthesis, repair, and structure. This experimental approach generally demonstrates a clear relationship between cause and effect. The advantage of this approach is the ability to analyze in detail events in translesion synthesis such as (1) quantification of the effects of blocking DNA synthesis, (2) miscoding frequency, and (3) miscoding specificity.

In vitro studies of translesion synthesis that use purified DNA polymerases complement the in vivo studies. As described in the following section, cells have various types of DNA polymerases and some of them are responsible for translesion synthesis. Therefore, the characterization of in vitro translesion synthesis could help to identify the polymerase responsible for translesion synthesis in cells. In vitro studies can be divided into two phases: insertion and extension steps. The insertion step determines which nucleotide is most efficiently inserted opposite a lesion by a given polymerase. The extension step determines which

nucleotide terminus is most efficiently extended opposite a lesion. These experiments characterize the efficiency and fidelity of translesion synthesis by a given polymerase. The results of the in vitro experiments may be reflected in translesion synthesis in cells if the polymerase is involved in the synthesis. The involvement of a candidate polymerase is examined by studying translesion synthesis in a host cell lacking the polymerase of interest. Finally, the involvement is confirmed by a complementation experiment in mutant cells that express the exogenous gene for the polymerase of interest. Thus, translesion synthesis across a given DNA lesion is studied in detail. One limitation of this site-specific experiment is the inability to study the effects on chromosomal aberrations. In addition, the results may not apply to other sequence contexts. Nevertheless, this approach has provided a tremendous amount of information on the mechanism of DNA adduct conversion to mutations.

Translesion Synthesis in Mammalian Cells

DNA polymerases are key players in mutation induction. They introduce mutations during replication and determine the types of mutations generated. Great progress has been made in DNA polymerase studies in the last several years. Many novel DNA polymerases were discovered in prokaryotes and eukaryotes (Hübscher et al. 2002). These DNA polymerases play important roles in various aspects of DNA metabolism. The Y family polymerases (Ohmori et al. 2001) include eukaryotic polη, polκ, and polι, as well as REV1 and *E. coli* polIV and polV. In addition, polζ is a member of the B family. Researchers think these Y family polymerases are specialized for translesion synthesis (Prakash and Prakash 2002). These discoveries have led to the general idea that these polymerases are responsible for overcoming the blocking effects of DNA adducts and constitute an important mechanism for tolerating unrepaired DNA lesions.

The role of the polη polymerase is most clearly understood. This polymerase is coded by the *XPV* gene, which is defective in persons with XP variant cells (Johnson et al. 1999; Masutani et al. 1999). Although these cells possess NER capability, they carry a predisposition to skin cancer on exposure to sunlight. The discovery that polη is able to bypass the *cis-syn* thymine-thymine dimer efficiently and accurately (Masutani et al. 1999) indicates that this polymerase plays a very important role in protection from the deleterious effects of unrepaired UV photoproducts. In its absence, the unrepaired lesions are bypassed by one or more other polymerases in an error-prone manner leading to skin cancer (Gibbs et al. 1998, 2000). X-ray crystallographic studies reveal that Y family polymerases have loose catalytic pockets enabling them to accommodate

Table 5.7   Translesion-specialized DNA polymerases (pol) and activities on various DNA lesions

DNA adduct	polη	polκ	polζ	polη + polζ	polι + polζ	polδ + polζ	REV1 + polζ
cis-syn TT	+ (a)	– (b)	– (c)		– (c)		
(6-4) TT	– (a)	– (b)	– (c)	+ (d)	+ (c)		
Abasic site	+ (a)	+ (b)	– (c)	+ (e)	+ (c)	+ (f)	+ (f)
Acetylaminofluorene C8-dG adduct	+ (a)	+ (b)					
Cisplatin intrastrand dG-dG adduct	+ (a)	– (b)					
1,N^6-ethenodeoxyadenosine	+ (g)	+ (g)					
8-oxodeoxyguanosine	+ (h)	+ (i)					
(+) BPDE-N^2-dG	+ (j)	+ (i)					
(–) BPDE-N^2-dG		+ (i)					

Note: (a) Masutani et al. 2000; (b) Ohashi et al. 2000; (c) Johnson et al. 2000; (d) Johnson et al. 2001b; (e) Yuan et al. 2000; (f) Haracska et al. 2001; (g) Levine et al. 2001; (h) Haracska et al. 2000; (i) Zhang et al. 2000a; (j) Zhang et al. 2000b.
BPDE-N^2-dG = *trans-anti*-benzo[*a*]pyrene-N^2-deoxyguanosine; **dG** = deoxyguanosine; **TT** = thymine-thymine dimer.

Figure 5.9   Model of mechanism for mammalian translesion synthesis

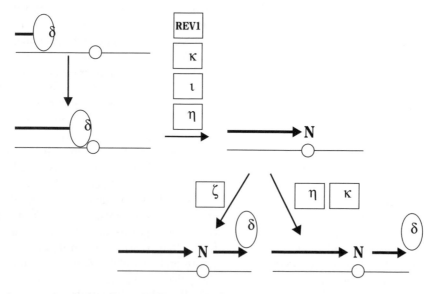

Note: Replicative polymerase δ encounters DNA lesion (open circle) in template, progression of DNA synthesis is blocked, and δ temporarily disengages. Y family polymerases (η, κ, ι, and REV1) are recruited to the sites, and 1 or more polymerases catalyze the insertion of a nucleotide opposite a lesion and the extension from the newly generated terminus. With some DNA lesions, the Y family polymerases can insert a nucleotide (N), but further extension is inhibited. Then, the second translesion polymerase, ζ, catalyzes the extension step. After translesion synthesis, δ resumes replication.

unusual base pairs (Trincao et al. 2001). This structural feature could explain the low fidelity of DNA synthesis on a normal DNA template.

In vitro experiments on translesion synthesis using purified polymerases reveal that each polymerase catalyzes bypass synthesis across various lesions with a different efficiency and fidelity (Table 5.7). The current model of the mechanism for mammalian translesion synthesis is illustrated in Figure 5.9. When a replicative DNA polymerase is inhibited by a lesion, translesion synthesis can be completed by the action of one polymerase or by the cooperation of two polymerases (Prakash and Prakash 2002). Among these polymerases, polζ is unique because it has low ability to insert a nucleotide opposite a lesion but is efficient at extending from unmatched terminal pairs (Johnson et al. 2000). Therefore, researchers think that this polymerase plays a role mainly in extending from a terminus opposite a lesion where another polymerase has inserted a nucleotide and the further extension is blocked.

Factors in Outcome of Translesion Synthesis

Many studies reveal that the efficiency and fidelity of translesion synthesis depend on the host (Moriya et al. 1994, 1996). Some DNA adducts miscode in one host (human cells) but not in another (*E. coli*), and the reverse also occurs (Moriya et al. 1994; Pandya and Moriya 1996). This finding underscores the importance of evaluating translesion events in the appropriate host: human cells. The discrepancy most likely reflects the difference in the activity of the translesion polymerases involved.

Sequence context also plays an important role in determining the outcome of translesion synthesis. Generally, a DNA adduct in iterated sequences, such as monotonous repeats (e.g., GGGGG) and dinucleotide repeats (e.g., GCGCGC), tends to cause frameshift mutations because these sequences misalign easily (Benamira et al. 1992). However, the same adduct induces base-substitution mutations in a different sequence context (Moriya et

Table 5.8   Mutational specificity of selected DNA adducts derived from tobacco smoke

Study	DNA adduct	Mutation specificity
Loechler et al. 1984 Dosanjh et al. 1991 Pauly and Moschel 2001	O^6-methyldeoxyguanosine	G→A
Pauly et al. 2002	O^6-[4-oxo-4-(3-pyridyl)butyl]-deoxyguanosine	G→A
Dosanjh et al. 1991 Pauly and Moschel 2001	O^4-methylthymidine	T→C
Wood et al. 1990 Moriya 1993	8-oxodeoxyguanosine	G→T
Kanuri et al. 2002 Yang et al. 2002	1,N^2-propanodeoxyguanosine from acrolein	G→T
Moriya et al. 1994	3,N^4-ethenodeoxycytidine	C→A, T
Pandya and Moriya 1996	1,N^6-ethenodeoxyadenosine	A→G, T
Lawrence et al. 1990 Cabral Neto et al. 1994 Gibbs and Lawrence 1995	Apurinic/apyrimidinic sites	AP→T, A, G
Moriya et al. 1996 Page et al. 1998	Benzo[*a*]pyrene-7,8-diol-9,10-epoxide-N^2-deoxyguanosine	G→T, A, C
Page et al. 1999	Benzo[*a*]pyrene-7,8-diol-9,10-epoxide-N^6-deoxyadenosine	A→T
Verghis et al. 1997	4-aminobiphenyl-*C*8-deoxyguanosine	G→C

al. 1994). Sequence context influences base-substitution events (Moriya et al. 1996; Page et al. 1998) and translesion efficiency (Latham et al. 1993) (see "Benzo[*a*] pyrene-7,8-Diol-9,10-Epoxide-N^2-Deoxyguanosine stereoisomers" later in this chapter).

Thus, translesion events are determined by the interplay between a DNA adduct, its sequence environment, and the DNA polymerase involved. This finding underscores the importance of conducting experiments with use of a proper sequence context and host.

Conversion of Cigarette-Smoke-Induced DNA Adducts to Mutations

Conversion of DNA adducts induced by cigarette smoke to mutations is summarized in Table 5.8. The discussion that follows provides additional details.

O^6-Pyridyloxobutyl-Deoxyguanosine

O^6-POB-deoxyguanosine is formed by a pyridyloxobutylating metabolite of the tobacco-specific *N*-nitrosamines NNK and NNN and is removed by AGT. Therefore, in the presence of this repair enzyme, the adduct induced only a moderate miscoding frequency. The resulting mutations were G→A transitions. In the absence of AGT, the miscoding frequency markedly increased to more than 90 percent (Pauly et al. 2002). The results were similar in *E. coli* and human cells. These results indicate that the frequency of miscoding for this adduct is high. The DNA polymerase involved almost exclusively inserts deoxythymidine monophosphate opposite the adduct, leading to G→A transitions. Thus, repair by the alkyltransferase is extremely critical to the avoidance of mutation induction by this adduct. The biologic characteristics of this adduct are similar to those of O^6-methyldeoxyguanosine (Pauly and Moschel 2001). The DNA polymerase that catalyzes the translesion synthesis and the bypass efficiency of this synthesis remain to be determined.

O^6-Methyldeoxyguanosine and O^4-Methylthymidine

The O^6-methyldeoxyguanosine and O^4-methylthymidine adducts induce mutations by stable pairing to thymidine (Dosanjh et al. 1993) and deoxyguanosine (Toorchen and Topal 1983), respectively. Accordingly, their miscoding potentials are high (Dosanjh et al. 1991; Pauly and Moschel 2001) and are similar to those of O^6-POB-deoxyguanosine. MMR acts on base pairs containing O^6-methyldeoxyguanosine after replication (Branch et al. 1993) and leads to cell death as a result of a futile MMR. Therefore, MMR mutants are more resistant to methylating agents (Branch et al. 1993) and are more prone to

mutation after exposure to these agents (Pauly and Moschel 2001).

8-Oxodeoxyguanosine

8-oxodeoxyguanosine is a representative adduct formed by oxidative damage to DNA, and researchers have extensively studied its mutagenic properties and repair mechanisms (Grollman and Moriya 1993). The miscoding property of this adduct derives from its propensity to assume a *syn* conformation and to pair easily with deoxyadenosine (*anti*), which leads to G→T transversions. To avoid this mutation induction, cells have developed an elaborate postreplication BER mechanism that specifically removes misinserted deoxyadenosine by the action of the DNA glycosylase, adenine-DNA-glycosylase (Parker and Eshleman 2003). Subsequently, when deoxycytidine monophosphat) is inserted opposite the adduct, 8-oxodeoxyguanosine is removed by another BER initiated by OGG1, and a G:C pair is restored.

This adduct is also formed in the nucleotide pool. When 8-oxodeoxyguanosine-triphosphate is inserted opposite a deoxyadenosine template, the misinsertion leads to an A→C transition. To avoid this event, the cellular enzyme MTH1 converts 8-oxodeoxyguanosine triphosphate to 8-oxodeoxyguanosine monophosphate, which is no longer a substrate for DNA synthesis. Thus, cells have developed several layers of defense mechanisms against 8-oxodeoxyguanosine. Therefore, the apparent frequency of mutation induction by this adduct is low in normal cells. However, when *MYH* is inactivated, the frequency of G→T transversions increases drastically (Moriya and Grollman 1993; Hashimoto and Moriya, unpublished data) and mutations in this gene lead to a high incidence of spontaneous human colon cancer (Al-Tassan et al. 2002).

1,N²-Propanodeoxyguanosine

Various unsaturated α,β-aldehydes, such as acrolein and crotonaldehyde, produce the DNA adduct PdG. Acrolein produces two positional isomers: 8-(γ-) and 6-(α-) xy hydroxyl PdG. When positioned in double-stranded DNA, the α adduct is more genotoxic than the γ adduct. The α adduct has significantly more blocking effects, and the γ adduct, but not the α adduct, miscodes with G→T transversions at a frequency of approximately 10 percent (Yang et al. 2002). Most of the miscoding events were induced by polη (Yang et al. 2003). Structural studies reveal that the exocyclic ring of the γ adduct, but not the α adduct, opens in a manner similar to that of the malondialdehyde-induced deoxyguanosine adduct (Mao et al. 1999) when paired to deoxycytidine (de los Santos et al. 2001). This finding may account for the weaker blocking effect and the lack of miscoding, because the ring-opened γ adduct pairs nicely to deoxycytidine with the Watson-Crick type of (*anti-anti*) conformation. When the γ adduct is inserted in single-stranded DNA and replicates in mammalian cells, the resulting structure miscodes by inducing G→T transversions (Kanuri et al. 2002). In addition, the ring-opened deoxyguanosine adduct forms interstrand G-G cross-links in the sequence 5′CpG (Kozekov et al. 2003), which may also contribute to the genotoxicity of acrolein.

Exocyclic Etheno Adducts

Although the etheno adduct 1,N^6-ethenodeoxyadenosine miscodes efficiently in simian kidney cells, it does not miscode in *E. coli* (Pandya and Moriya 1996). This finding emphasizes the importance of the host. The finding is probably attributable to the difference in the fidelity of the DNA polymerase involved in translesion synthesis. The etheno adduct 3,N^4-ethenodeoxycytidine miscodes efficiently in both hosts (Moriya et al. 1994).

Apurinic/Apyrimidinic Sites

AP sites are generated by the cleavage of a glycosidic bond between a base and a sugar in DNA for various reasons such as (1) the action of a DNA glycosylase and (2) modifications to a base that destabilize the glycosidic bond. These sites do not convey any coding information. Deoxyadenosine is often inserted opposite these sites in *E. coli* (Lawrence et al. 1990), which is known as "the A rule" (Strauss 1991). However, this rule does not appear to be applicable in mammalian cells: various bases are inserted opposite these sites in those cells (Cabral Neto et al. 1994; Gibbs and Lawrence 1995).

Benzo[a]pyrene-7,8-Diol-9,10-Epoxide-N^2-Deoxyguanosine Stereoisomers

Studies have extensively characterized the genotoxicity of different stereoisomers of BPDE-N^2-deoxyguanosine (Moriya et al. 1996; Fernandes et al. 1998). A prominent feature is that both the surrounding DNA sequence and the host markedly influence miscoding frequency (Moriya et al. 1996; Fernandes et al. 1998; Page et al. 1998) and miscoding specificity (Kozack et al. 2000). The major adduct, (+)-BPDE-N^2-deoxyguanosine, induces mainly G→T and G→A transversions in 5′-TGC and 5′-AGA sequence contexts, respectively, which researchers hypothesize is attributable to differences in adduct conformations in different sequence contexts (Kozack et al. 2000). The deoxyadenosine adduct (BPDE-N^6-deoxyadenosine) also miscodes with A→T transversions (Page et al. 1999).

4-Aminobiphenyl-C8-Deoxyguanosine

The adduct 4-ABP-C8-deoxyguanosine barely miscodes in *E. coli* by inducing G→C transversions (Verghis et al. 1997). Because researchers observed G→T, G→A, and G→C mutations in an experiment that used a randomly modified single-strand DNA (Verghis et al. 1997), the possibilities of the effects from the sequence context and the involvement of other deoxyguanosine adducts, such as those at N^2, remain to be explored. Furthermore, it appears that a 4-ABP-deoxyadenosine adduct induces A→T transversions (Lasko et al. 1988; Hatcher and Swaminathan 1995).

Assessment of Genotoxicity of DNA Adducts

Genotoxic properties of a DNA lesion can be characterized by using chemically defined substrates. The genotoxicity of a DNA lesion is determined by factors such as the efficiency and fidelity of translesion synthesis and repair. For point mutations, however, the "genotoxic potency" of a DNA adduct can be determined by assessing the bypass efficiency and the miscoding potency. According to this formula, a DNA lesion that is easily bypassed with a high frequency of miscoding events is defined as a highly genotoxic DNA adduct. Furthermore, when the genotoxicity of a DNA lesion is assessed, the information on its abundance in the genome, which reflects the balance between formation and removal, should also be considered. Therefore, conceptually, the total genotoxicity of a DNA adduct could be estimated by determining its genotoxic potency and its abundance in DNA.

According to these criteria, the genotoxicity of the 8-oxodeoxyguanosine adduct, which is a unique case, would be high because it exists in high levels in genomic DNA and is easily bypassed by a DNA polymerase with a high miscoding frequency. However, the apparent genotoxicity is low because of the postreplication repair that is catalyzed by MYH. Therefore, when the postreplication repair is inactivated, this adduct can become a significant genotoxic adduct (Al-Tassan et al. 2002).

Data for the genotoxic effects of DNA lesions derived from tobacco smoke are scarce, and a systematic study is needed. Together with information on the abundance of each lesion, the genotoxicity of tobacco-related DNA adducts might be ranked by using site-specific modified plasmids, introducing them with the use of host cells, and subsequently recovering them for sequence analysis.

Gene Mutations in Tobacco-Induced Cancer

Chromosome Instability and Loss

Lung Cancer

The detection of numerous cytogenetic changes provided the first link to the molecular pathogenesis of lung cancer. Mapping chromosomal sites for rearrangement, breakpoints, and losses revealed both common and distinct changes in both SCLC and NSCLC. In SCLC, breakpoints are commonly seen in chromosomes 1, 3, 5, and 17, although researchers have observed losses of the short arm (p) of chromosomes 3 and 17 and of the long arm (q) of chromosome 5 (Balsara and Testa 2002). Subsequent studies using comparative genomic hybridization showed that deletions on chromosomes 3p, 4q, 5q, 10q, 13q, and 17p were common in SCLC (Petersen et al. 1997). In NSCLC, multiple numeric and structural changes were seen across many chromosomes. The most frequent sites (60 to 80 percent) for chromosome loss were found on chromosomes 3p, 6q, 8p, 9p, 9q, 17p, 18q, 19p, 21q, and 22q (Balsara and Testa 2002). Some of the most common sites for chromosome loss included 3p, 9p, 13q, and 17p. These sites were also detected in nonmalignant bronchial epithelium of current and former smokers and were absent in lifetime nonsmokers (Mao et al. 1997; Witsuba et al. 1997). These findings strongly link tobacco exposure to the development of chromosome damage throughout the aerodigestive tract.

Identification of Tumor-Suppressor Genes

The commonality for specific regions in the genome to lose alleles suggested the presence of tumor-suppressor genes within these loci. The RB gene was the first tumor-suppressor gene linked to lung cancer (Harbour et al. 1988). A loss of function of this gene through either deletion or point mutation occurs in 90 percent of SCLCs, whereas few NSCLCs harbor changes in this tumor-suppressor gene (Table 5.9) (Shimizu et al. 1994). The most frequently inactivated tumor-suppressor gene in lung cancer is *TP53*. *TP53* mutations are found in 70 percent of SCLCs, 65 percent of SCCs, and 33 percent of adenocarcinomas (Greenblatt et al. 1994). (For discussion of specific mutations and their potential relationship to carcinogens in cigarette smoke, see "Relationship of *TP53* Mutations to Smoking and Carcinogens" later in this chapter.)

A frequent deletion within chromosome 3p14 led to the identification of the *FHIT* gene (Zabarovsky et al. 2002). The most common fragile site of the human genome *FRA3B* maps in the *FHIT* gene and may contribute to the susceptibility of this locus to gene rearrangement induced by carcinogens in cigarette smoke. Researchers have observed a loss of the FHIT protein in 50 percent of lung cancers, but somatic mutations are uncommon in the *FHIT* gene. The epigenetic inactivation by methylation of the 5'CpG island located in the promoter region of *FHIT* represents another mechanism for inactivating this gene in lung cancer (see "Gene Promoter Hypermethylation in Cancer Induced by Tobacco Smoke" later in this chapter).

The importance of the inactivation of tumor-suppressor genes *FHIT*, *RB*, and *TP53* in lung cancer is evident from their functions. The binding of hypophosphorylated *RB* to cyclin-dependent kinase (CDK) 4 or 6 blocks transit of the RB protein through the G_1/S boundary of the cell cycle. Inactivating mutations result in the loss of a functional hypophosphorylated protein associated with a shortening of the G_1 phase of the cell cycle and the enhancement of cell proliferation, a hallmark of the cancer cell (Nevins 1992). The *TP53* gene is central to several critical processes needed to control the response of the cell to exogenous stress from exposure to cigarette smoke. This gene functions as a transcription factor within several pathways and as a sensor of DNA damage (Robles et al. 2002). Thus, the *TP53* gene has an important role in cell-cycle checkpoints, DNA repair, apoptosis, and senescence. A loss of *TP53* function is also an early event

Table 5.9   Frequency of mutation or deletion of tumor-suppressor genes in lung cancer

Gene	Chromosomal location	Frequency (%)	
		Small-cell lung cancer	Non-small-cell lung cancer
RB	13q14	90	15
TP53	17p13	70	50
CHFR	12q24	ND	6
MYO18B	22q12	ND	13
PTEN	10q23	9	17
LKB1/STK11	19p13	ND	35

Note: **ND** = not determined.

in the genesis of SCC that occurs in bronchial dysplasia (Sozzi et al. 1992; Bennett et al. 1993). Studies have also detected *TP53* mutations in peripheral lung tissue from patients with lung cancer, a finding that supports a role for this gene in the early development of adenocarcinomas (Hussain et al. 2001). The *FHIT* gene induces apoptosis mediated by CASPASE-8 and independent of mitochondrial mediators and inhibits cell growth through interactions with the SRC protein kinase (Pekarsky et al. 2004; Roz et al. 2004). A loss of function of the *FHIT*, *RB*, and *TP53*, genes leads to the immortalization of bronchial epithelial cells, a key step in neoplastic transformation (Reddel et al. 1988) (see "Signal Transduction" later in this chapter).

Tumor-Suppressor Genes Inactivated in Lung Cancer

The search for tumor-suppressor genes inactivated through the two-hit mechanism of the loss of one allele and the mutation of the remaining allele has not recently identified any genes with a frequency of inactivation approaching that seen for the *RB* and *TP53* genes. The discussion that follows describes the involvement of several genes and their functions in subsets of lung cancer (Table 5.9). The mitotic checkpoint gene *CHFR*, which functions in early prophase to regulate chromosome condensation, was mutated in 3 of 53 lung carcinomas (Mariatos et al. 2003). Studies found three somatic mutations in the proapoptotic gene *CASPASE-8* in 2 of 30 lung tumors (Hosomi et al. 2003). *MYO18B* is a candidate tumor-suppressor gene at chromosome 22q12. Of 46 primary NSCLCs, 6 contained somatic mutations within this gene. Restoring *MYO18B* function in cell lines inhibited anchorage-independent growth, thus supporting its function as a tumor-suppressor gene in lung cancer (Nishioka et al. 2002).

The *PTEN* gene is located on chromosome 10. Its gene product is phosphatidylinositol 3'-phosphatase, a protein tyrosine phosphatase that uses the phosphoinositide second messenger, phosphatidylinositol 3,4,5-triphosphate (PIP3), as a physiological substrate (Maehama et al. 2001). Researchers have identified point mutations of the *PTEN* gene in cell lines from 3 of 35 SCLCs and 3 of 18 NSCLCs; there were two homozygous deletions in primary SCLCs (Forgacs et al. 1998). Mutations that impair *PTEN* function result in a marked increase in PIP3 levels and in the constitutive activation of AKT survival, thus signaling pathways that in turn promote hyperplasia and tumor formation. Thus, although it is not common in lung cancer, a *PTEN* mutation or deletion profoundly affects an important signaling pathway in the cell.

Two additional genes with poorly characterized functions and localized to chromosome 3p are altered in lung cancer through deletion or mutation. A specific ATG→AGG mutation in codon 50 of the *ARP* gene was seen in 8 of 20 lung cancers. In addition, researchers observed either exon deletion or intron insertion in the *DLC1* gene in 11 of 30 NSCLCs (Zabarovsky et al. 2002). Frequent deletion involving the short arm of chromosome 19 occurs in lung adenocarcinomas (Sanchez-Cespedes et al. 2001). One gene mapped to this chromosome region is *STK11*, in which germline mutations are causal for Peutz-Jeghers syndrome. This syndrome is characterized by a series of anomalies and increased risk for gastrointestinal and extraintestinal malignancies (Giardiello et al. 1987). Inactivating mutations and/or deletion of the LKB1/STK11 protein were described in about one-third of primary adenocarcinomas (Sanchez-Cespedes et al. 2002; Ji et al. 2007), and these abnormalities were closely associated with mutation of the *KRAS* oncogene in the same tumors (Ji et al. 2007; Matsumoto et al. 2007). The *STK11* gene may function as a growth-inhibiting gene that is activated through phosphorylation by the *ATM* gene, which senses DNA damage (Sapkota et al. 2002), and acts through pathways dependent or independent of the P53 protein to suppress invasion and metastasis (Karuman et al. 2001; Upadhyay et al. 2006; Ji et al. 2007). In addition to inactivating by mutation, epigenetic silencing by promoter hypermethylation has emerged as a major mechanism for inactivating many genes in lung cancer, some of which are described here (e.g., *MYO18B*). (For a detailed discussion, see "Gene Promoter Hypermethylation in Cancer Induced by Tobacco Smoke" later in this chapter.)

Activation of Oncogenes in Lung Cancer

Oncogenes encode proteins that influence cell cycling and promote cancer. They are usually "gain-of-function" mutations of normal genes. Researchers see *KRAS* gene mutations in approximately 30 to 40 percent of adenocarcinomas but rarely in SCCs, SCLCs, or lung tumors from nonsmokers (Slebos et al. 1990; Westra et al. 1996; Ahrendt et al. 2003). Mutations are localized to codons 12, 13, and 61. More than 85 percent occur within codon 12. Nearly 70 percent of the mutations are G→T transversions within codon 12 that change a glycine codon (GGT) to valine (GTT) or cysteine (TGT). Mouse lung tumors induced by B[*a*]P and other PAHs show exclusively G→T transversions in codon 12 of the *Kras* gene. These findings support the hypothesis that activation of this oncogene in lung tumors results from DNA damage leading to base mispairing of these deoxyguanosines. In vitro studies have demonstrated that DNA adducts formed from the metabolism of B[*a*]P, NNK, and reactive oxygen species can all lead to G→T transversions (Table 5.8) (You et al. 1989; Belinsky et al. 1992). Thus, the activation of carcinogens in tobacco smoke and the pulmonary inflammation that ensues from exposure to particulate matter together can lead to activation of the *KRAS* oncogene. Studies detected *KRAS* gene mutations in 39 percent of atypical alveolar hyperplasia, a putative precursor to adenocarcinoma (Slebos et al. 1996). A similarity in the percentage of precursor lesions and tumors containing *KRAS* mutations supports the importance of this gene in tumor progression in a subset of adenocarcinomas.

The sequence of events leading to activation of the RAS signal transduction pathway is well characterized (Lechner and Fugaro 2000). When the RAS protein is activated through mutations in codon 12, 13, or 61, it binds irreversibly to guanosine triphosphate (GTP) in the cell, which initiates a cascade of protein activations, beginning with v-raf-murine leukemia viral oncogene 1 (*RAF-1*), that transmits a signal from the cell membrane to the nuclear transcription machinery. Ultimately, these signals culminate in the activation of transcription factors including MYC, FOS, and JUN, which in turn influence many cellular activities such as transcription, translation, cytoskeletal organization, and cell-cell interactions. This signal remains active until GTPase (guanosine triphosphatase) dephosphorylates GTP to guanosine diphosphate.

Thus, a *RAS* oncogene mutation leads to the disruption of many cellular pathways and provides a strong oncogenic signal for neoplastic transformation (see "Signal Transduction" later in this chapter).

The *MYC* family of genes (*C-MYC*, *N-MYC*, and *L-MYC*) plays a prominent role in the growth of the developing and mature adult lung. Extensive studies have evaluated the expression and amplification of these genes in NSCLC and SCLC (Jänne and Johnson 2000). Most lung cancers express one or more of the *MYC* family of genes, whereas gene amplification is seen in a minority of primary tumors (Table 5.10). Gene rearrangements involving different exons are associated with amplification detected in cell lines but are uncommon in primary tumors (Kinzler et al. 1986; Mäkelä et al. 1991; Sekido et al. 1992). Mechanisms responsible for the increased expression of the *MYC* genes in the absence of gene amplification are not well understood. Increased expression could occur through increased activity in the RAS signaling pathway through either *KRAS* oncogene mutations or effects on the activity of genes in this pathway, such as the activity of mitogen-activated protein kinase (MAPK) (Jull et al. 2001).

Increased gene expression is common in lung cancer but often is not associated with gene amplification. Two genes studied extensively are *EGFR* and *NEU* (*HER-2/NEU* [*ERBB2*]). EGFR is the receptor for the epidermal

Table 5.10   Frequency of gene amplification and increased expression of genes in lung cancer

Gene	Tumor histology	Frequency (%)	
		Amplification	Expression
C-MYC	Small-cell lung cancer	5	25
N-MYC	Small-cell lung cancer	7	3
L-MYC	Small-cell lung cancer	12	33
EGFR	Small-cell lung cancer	0	0
HER-2/NEU	Small-cell lung cancer	<1	0–7
C-MYC	Non-small-cell lung cancer	8	33
N-MYC	Non-small-cell lung cancer	0	ND
L-MYC	Non-small-cell lung cancer	3	ND
EGFR	Non-small-cell lung cancer	9–25	34–62
HER-2/NEU	Non-small-cell lung cancer	2–4	23–58

Note: **ND** = not determined.

growth factor and the HER-2/NEU protein, and the binding of these growth factors to this receptor is associated with increased DNA synthesis, cell proliferation, and differentiation. An increased expression of the *EGFR* gene was not seen in SCLCs but occurred in 34 to 62 percent of NSCLCs (Hirsch et al. 2003b; Suzuki et al. 2005). In addition, an increased expression of this gene was more common in SCC than in adenocarcinoma—82 versus 44 percent (Hirsch et al. 2003b). In contrast, gene amplification was detected in 9 to 25 percent of tumors (Hirsch et al. 2003b; Suzuki et al. 2005). Expression of the *HER-2/NEU* gene was seen in 23 to 58 percent of NSCLCs and in 0 to 7 percent of SCLCs (Shi et al. 1992; Junker et al. 2005; Pelosi et al. 2005). Similar to *EGFR*, *HER-2/NEU* was more commonly expressed in SCC than in adenocarcinoma, and gene amplification was rare in all tumors (<5 percent).

Observation of *EGFR* expression in 34 to 62 percent of NSCLCs led to the development of small molecule inhibitors of the tyrosine kinase domain of the wild-type EGFR protein (Fukuoka et al. 2003; Herbst and Bunn 2003; Lynch et al. 2004; Amann et al. 2005; Baselga and Arteaga 2005). The clinical response of approximately 10 percent of European patients and 30 percent of patients from Japan to treatment with the EGFR inhibitors gefitinib or erlotinib led to a search for the mechanism responsible (Kris et al. 2003; Pérez-Soler et al. 2004). The outcome of these studies was the identification of somatic mutations in the tyrosine kinase domain of the *EGFR* gene in most patients who had demonstrated a clinical response to the drugs (Lynch et al. 2004; Amann et al. 2005). In addition, recent studies suggest that the *EGFR* copy number and *KRAS* mutation may also be involved in determining a response to gefitinib and erlotinib. Subsequent studies have sequenced the *EGFR* gene in thousands of NSCLCs from patients in Asia, Europe, and the United States. These studies found that most mutations were due to either a deletion involving exon 19 or a missense mutation in exon 21. In addition, mutations were two to three times more likely in women than in men and three to five times more likely in nonsmokers than in current or former smokers (Johnson and Jänne 2005). Finally, the prevalence of mutations was 10 percent in tumors of patients from Europe and the United States compared with 30 percent in tumors from persons of Asian background residing in Japan and Taiwan.

The *BRAF* gene encodes a RAS-regulated kinase that can mediate cell growth. *BRAF* mutations were found in 5 of 179 NSCLCs and are almost exclusively confined to adenocarcinomas (Brose et al. 2002; Naoki et al. 2002). Although the mutation is relatively uncommon in lung cancer, its location in either exon 11 or exon 15 altered the

phosphorylation of *BRAF* by AKT (Guan et al. 2000). The disruption of AKT-induced *BRAF* inhibition could contribute to malignant transformation.

Oncogene Activation, Tumor-Suppressor Gene Inactivation, and Lung Cancer Survival

Researchers have studied the prognostic impact of commonly altered genes in lung cancer. The effect of an activated *KRAS* oncogene on survival was assessed in 69 patients, including 48 with stage I adenocarcinoma that was completely resected (Slebos et al. 1990). Twelve of 19 patients with a *KRAS* mutation died within the follow-up period (median, 47 months) compared with 22 of 50 patients with a tumor negative for the *KRAS* oncogene. This significant difference in survival was observed even though patients with a *KRAS* mutation had a less advanced disease than those with no mutation. All seven patients with stage III disease were negative for mutations. Rosell and colleagues (1993) conducted a similar study of largely stage I resected adenocarcinomas that again revealed a reduced survival rate independent of lymph node status for patients whose tumor contained a mutated *KRAS* gene. In contrast, a larger study of 127 adenocarcinomas found no difference in survival by *KRAS* mutation status (Keohavong et al. 1996). Overall, data are conflicting with respect to *KRAS* mutations as prognostic factors and further research is needed (Aviel-Ronen et al. 2006).

Studies have examined the effect of *TP53* gene mutations on prognosis in both early- and late-stage lung cancers. After four years of follow-up, the hazard ratio for 106 patients with stage I resected NSCLC with a *TP53* mutation was 2.8 for death, compared with patients who had a wild-type gene (Ahrendt et al. 2003). Four years after surgery, 78 percent of patients with no *TP53* mutation and 52 percent with a *TP53* mutation were alive. A previous study by Tomizawa and colleagues (1999) found a similar survival benefit for patients with stage I NSCLC and no *TP53* mutations, which also confer a poor clinical outcome for those with advanced NSCLC. Independent of chemotherapy or supportive care, median survival duration for patients with stage III or IV NSCLC with or without a *TP53* mutation was 17 versus 39 weeks, respectively (Murakami et al. 2000). Recently, a study of 420 patients with primary head and neck cancer (Poeta et al. 2007) showed that disruptive *TP53* mutations in tumor DNA are associated with reduced survival after surgical treatment of SCC of the head and neck (hazard ratio, 1.7; 95 percent CI, 1.2–2.4; p = 0.003).

Together, it is apparent that the inactivation of the *TP53* tumor-suppressor gene and the activation of the *KRAS* oncogene in NSCLCs and other tumors are correlated with exposure to cigarette smoke and contribute to a phenotype that reduces survival in both early and advanced stages of the disease.

Relationship of *TP53* Mutations to Smoking and Carcinogens

TP53 Mutations in Smoking-Associated Lung Cancers

TP53 gene mutations are found in approximately 40 percent of human lung cancers; *TP53* is the most commonly mutated tumor-suppressor gene in lung cancer (see "Identification of Tumor-Suppressor Genes" earlier in this chapter). These mutations are generally more common in smokers than in nonsmokers (Greenblatt et al.

1994; Hernandez-Boussard and Hainaut 1998; Pfeifer et al. 2002). One study shows that the relative risk of having a *TP53* mutation in lung cancer was up to 13 times higher in lifetime heavy smokers than in lifetime nonsmokers (Le Calvez et al. 2005). G→T transversions are commonly observed in smoking-associated lung cancers (Greenblatt et al. 1994; Hainaut and Hollstein 2000; Hainaut and Pfeifer 2001). The frequency of G→T transversions in lung cancers from smokers is higher than that for lung cancers and most other cancers in nonsmokers (Greenblatt et al. 1994; Husgafvel-Pursiainen and Kannio 1996; Hernandez-Boussard and Hainaut 1998; Bennett et al. 1999; Hainaut and Pfeifer 2001). Mutational patterns for lung cancers from smokers and nonsmokers are shown in Figure 5.10. The difference between 28.9 percent G→T transversion mutations in "designated smokers" (i.e., smoking status

Figure 5.10   Patterns of *TP53* gene mutations and percentage of G→T transversion mutations in human lung cancers

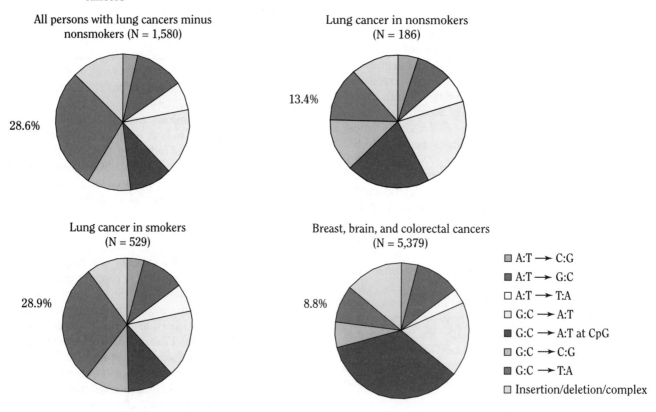

Source: Data are from the R9 version (July 2004) of the International Agency for Research on Cancer *TP53* mutation database (IARC 2006).

Note: Cell lines and metastatic cancers were excluded, as well as cancers with defined exposures other than tobacco (e.g., asbestos, radon, mustard gas, and air pollution) (see database Web site for specifications of exposure data). Nonsmokers included a series of 21 mutations (Le Calvez et al. 2005) not included in the database, in addition to 165 database entries. Data from Gao et al. 1997 were excluded (see Hainaut and Pfeifer 2001 for detailed selection criteria). **N** = total number of mutations.

indicated in literature) and 13.4 percent G→T mutations in nonsmokers has high statistical significance (p <0.001, χ^2 test). The frequency of G→T transversions is higher in lung cancer tumors than in other tumors, except for liver cancers associated with geographic areas with evidence of food contamination from aflatoxins (Greenblatt et al. 1994).

In most internal cancers not strongly linked to smoking, such as breast, brain, and colorectal, the frequency of G→T mutations is 8 to 10 percent (Figure 5.10). Nonsmokers have a higher percentage of G→A transitions (42.5 percent) than do smokers (27.9 percent), a difference that is also statistically significant. Figure 5.10 includes categories of both designated smokers and "all lung cancer cases minus nonsmokers." This category is based on the knowledge that, overall, 90 percent of these lung cancers occur in smokers (Proctor 2001). The proportion of G→T transversions, as well as the overall mutation pattern for all persons with lung cancers, except nonsmokers, is similar to observations of researchers for designated smokers (Figure 5.10). The difference in G→T transversions in smokers versus nonsmokers may be attributable to bias in the database used, which pools data from studies that differ in aims, size, and methods for ascertaining smoking status. However, in a more recent study of a series of 21 mutations that was designed to address this possibility, *TP53* gene mutations were found in 27.5 percent of current smokers, 15.8 percent of former smokers, and 4.8 percent of lifetime nonsmokers (Le Calvez et al. 2005). These observations suggest that the difference in G→T transversions in smokers versus nonsmokers may be larger than that indicated in the database, perhaps due to the misclassification in the database of long-term former smokers as nonsmokers.

To address the issue of whether the major histologic types of lung cancer show differences in *TP53* mutational patterns, researchers analyzed the IARC *TP53* mutation database separately for these tumors (Figure 5.11). The frequencies of G→T transversions in the *TP53* database were 31.4 percent in adenocarcinomas, 27.1 percent in SCCs, 27.5 percent in SCLCs, and 34.7 percent in large-cell carcinomas. Furthermore, the global mutation patterns were similar in the two main histologic types: adenocarcinoma and SCC. Thus, the different types of lung cancer in smokers all show an excess of G→T transversions compared with cancers unrelated to exposure to tobacco smoke.

TP53 mutations do not occur at random along the coding sequence. They are typically clustered at mutation "hot spots," which are within the DNA binding domain of the TP53 protein and span codons 120 to 300. Figure 5.12 shows the concordance of codon distribution of G→T transversions (upper panel) along the *TP53* gene in lung cancer with the distribution of adducts in this gene in bronchial epithelial cells treated with BPDE. Hot spots of G→T mutations in cancers of the brain, breast, and colon differ from those in lung cancers (Pfeifer et al. 2002). The codons containing mutation hot spots are important because they may allow determination of which carcinogen caused the mutation. However, hot spot codons may exist solely as a consequence of phenotypic selection in tumors. To address this issue, studies have compared the mutational events in different types of cancers at a number of common hot spot codons. The major lung cancer mutation hot spots at codons 158, 245, 248, and 273 are commonly G→T transversions in lung cancer but are generally other mutation types (almost exclusively G→A) in other internal tumors not associated with smoking (Pfeifer et al. 2002).

G→T Transversions in Lung Cancer

The major product of the diol epoxide BPDE reaction with DNA is BPDE-N^2-deoxyguanosine, which induces mainly G→T transversions, depending on the sequence context, after a DNA polymerase carries out error-prone translesion synthesis past this adduct (Eisenstadt et al. 1982; Chen et al. 1990; Ruggeri et al. 1993; Yoon et al. 2001) (see "Conversion of DNA Adducts to Mutations" earlier in this chapter). Using the UvrABC incision method in combination with a ligation-mediated polymerase chain reaction (LMPCR), scientists mapped the distribution of BPDE and other PAH diol epoxide adducts at the nucleotide level along exons of the *TP53* gene in normal human bronchial epithelial cells treated with diol epoxide (Denissenko et al. 1996; Smith et al. 2000). Frequent adduct formation occurred at guanine positions in codons 156, 157, 158, 245, 248, and 273. These positions of preferential formation of PAH adducts are major mutational hot spots in human lung cancers (Figure 5.12). The only exception is codon 156, where G→T substitution commonly results in a phenotypically silent mutation and is therefore not selected during tumorigenesis.

Researchers analyzed the distribution of BPDE-N^2-deoxyguanosine within *TP53* exons by using stable isotope labeling LC-electrospray ionization tandem MS (Tretyakova et al. 2002; Matter et al. 2004). In this approach, specific guanine nucleobases within *TP53* gene sequences were labeled with ^{15}N so the BPDE adducts originating from these positions could be distinguished from the lesions formed at other sites. Researchers observed an excellent agreement with the data from the UvrABC-LMPCR method (Denissenko et al. 1996). All four diastereomers of BPDE-N^2-deoxyguanosine were formed preferentially at the frequently mutated *TP53* codons 157, 158, 245, 248, and 273. The contributions of individual

Figure 5.11 Patterns of *TP53* gene mutations and percentage of G→T transversion mutations in different histologic types of lung cancer

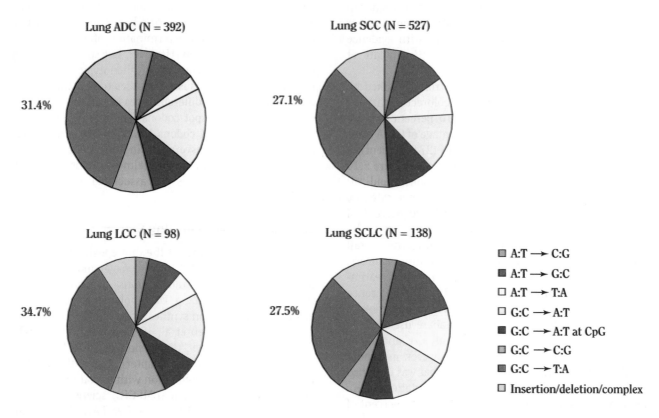

Source: Data are from the R9 version (July 2004) of the International Agency for Research on Cancer *TP53* mutation database (IARC 2006).

Note: Cancers were classified according to *International Classification of Diseases, Tenth Revision* (*ICD-10*), World Health Organization 1994. The data set excluded lung cancers from nonsmokers. Cell lines and cancers metastatic to the lung were excluded, as well as all cancers with defined exposures other than tobacco (e.g., asbestos, radon, mustard gas, and air pollution). **ADC** = adenocarcinoma (*ICD* C34-8140/3); **LCC** = large-cell carcinoma (*ICD* C34-8012/3); **N** = total number of mutations; **SCC** = squamous cell carcinoma (*ICD* C34-8070/3); **SCLC** = small-cell lung carcinoma (*ICD* C34-8041/3).

diastereomers to the total adducts at a given site varied but were highest (70.8 to 92.9 percent) for (+)-*trans*-BPDE-N^2-deoxyguanosine (Matter et al. 2004).

A mechanistic basis for the selectivity of formation of diol epoxide–DNA adducts in the *TP53* gene is the enhancement of adduct formation by 5-methylcytosine bases present at CpG dinucleotide sequences (Denissenko et al. 1997; Chen et al. 1998; Weisenberger and Romano 1999; Tretyakova et al. 2002; Matter et al. 2004). All CpG sequences in *TP53* coding exon 5 through exon 9 were completely methylated in all of the tissues examined, including the lung (Tornaletti and Pfeifer 1995). In the *TP53* gene of lung cancers, the five major G→T mutational hot spots at codons 157, 158, 245, 248, and 273 (Figure 5.12) consisted of methylated CpGs (Yoon et al.

2001). Methylation at CpG sites may increase the binding of planar carcinogenic compounds at the intercalation step through the hydrophobic effect of the methyl group that can stabilize intercalated adduct conformations (Zhang et al. 2005a). However, the precise mechanism by which cytosine methylation at CpG sites enhances carcinogen binding and mutagenesis still needs to be determined. In contrast, the presence of 5'-neighboring 5-methylcytosine inhibited formation of guanine adducts by NNK metabolites (Rajesh et al. 2005).

Studies show that the preferential formation of BPDE adducts at methylated CpG sites is reflected in the strongly enhanced mutagenesis at CpG sequences after cells were treated with BPDE. This finding was demonstrated with three different mutated reporter genes, including two chromosomal genes with methylated CpG sequences (Yoon et al. 2001).

Methylated CpG sites are preferentially modified by several carcinogens, including aromatic amines and aflatoxins (Chen et al. 1998). However, the exact range of compounds that target methylated CpGs is not known. In one study, researchers did not observe a preferential mutagenesis at methylated CpGs by the aromatic amine 4-ABP (Besaratinia et al. 2002). G→T transversions resulting from 8-oxodeoxyguanosine are not specifically targeted to methylated CpG sequences (Lee et al. 2002a). A more recent study demonstrated that the DNA

adduction profile of acrolein in the *P53* gene was similar to that of BPDE and other PAH diol epoxides, indicating that this α,β-unsaturated aldehyde reacts at methylated CpG sites and, because of its high concentration in cigarette smoke compared with that of PAHs, could contribute to the *TP53* mutations observed in lung tumors from smokers (Feng et al. 2006).

Hussain and colleagues (2001) have shown that exposing bronchial epithelial cells to BPDE produces G→T transversions in the *TP53* gene at lung cancer hot spot codons 157, 248, and 249. Nontumorous lung tissues from smokers with lung cancer carried a high *TP53* mutational

Figure 5.12   Concordance between codon distribution of G→T transversions along *TP53* gene in lung cancers (top) and distribution of adducts of benzo[*a*]pyrene-7,8-diol-9,10-epoxide (BPDE)–DNA adducts in bronchial epithelial cells (bottom)

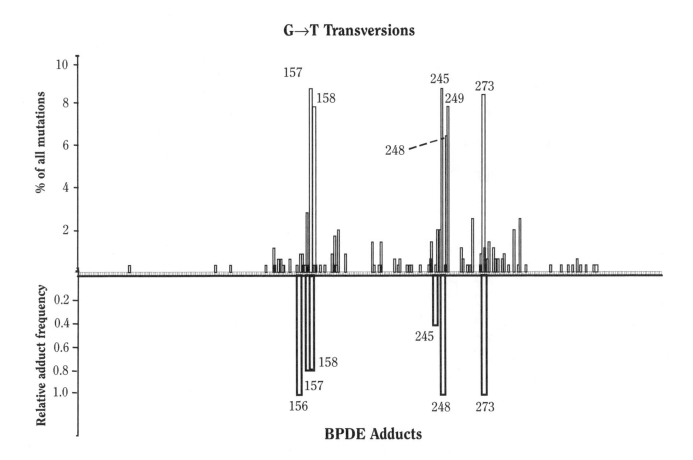

Source: Adduct data were quantitated from Denissenko et al. 1996 and Smith et al. 2000.

Note: Distribution of G→T mutations is shown along the *TP53* coding sequence, and "hot spot" codons for major mutations are indicated. Mutation data from the International Agency for Research on Cancer *TP53* mutation database were used. Cell lines and cancers metastatic to the lung were excluded, as well as all cancers with defined exposures other than tobacco (e.g., asbestos, radon, mustard gas, and air pollution). Length of bars indicates relative adduct frequency at major hot spots for adducts. For adducts of BPDE, the strongest binding site has a value of 1. Sites with values less than 0.2 are not shown. Numbers correspond to *TP53* codon numbers.

Figure 5.13 **Patterns of *TP53* gene mutations and percentage of G→T transversions in smoking-associated cancers other than lung cancer**

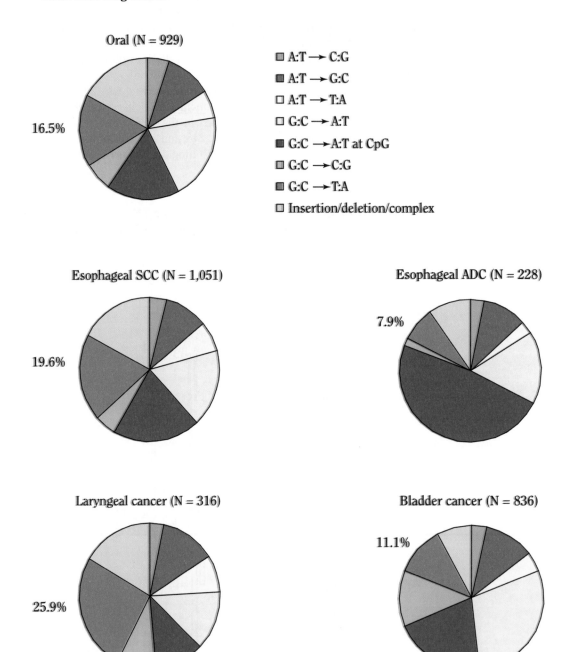

Source: Data are from R9 version (July 2004) of International Agency for Research on Cancer *TP53* mutation database (IARC 2006).
Note: Oral cancers include cancers of oropharynx, hypopharynx, gum, palate, floor of mouth, and tongue. Cases with defined exposures other than tobacco (e.g., asbestos, radon, mustard gas, and air pollution) were excluded. **ADC** = adenocarcinoma; **N** = total number of mutations; **SCC** = squamous cell carcinoma.

load at these codons, even when another *TP53* mutation was present in the tumor itself. DeMarini and colleagues (2001) studied *TP53* and *KRAS* mutations in lung tumors from Chinese women who were nonsmokers and whose tumors were associated with exposure to smoky coal containing high levels of PAHs and probably other compounds such as acrolein. The tumors showed a high percentage of mutations that were G→T transversions in the *KRAS* oncogene (86 percent) or the *TP53* gene (76 percent). In the *TP53* gene, the mutations clustered at the CpG-rich codons 153 through 158 and at codons 249 and 273.

The site specificity of mutagenesis by PAH diol epoxides implies that targeted adduct formation, in addition to phenotypic selection, is responsible for shaping the *TP53* mutational spectrum in lung tumors. According to the IARC *TP53* mutation database, more than 80 percent of G→T transversions in lung cancers are targeted to guanines on the nontranscribed DNA strand. This observation suggests that a preferential repair of DNA lesions occurs on the transcribed strand. DNA repair experiments analyzing BPDE adducts in the *TP53* gene showed that the nontranscribed strand is repaired more slowly than is the transcribed strand (Denissenko et al. 1998). These findings support the proposal that both the initial DNA adduct levels and a bias in repair of DNA strands may contribute to the mutational spectrum of the human *TP53* gene in lung cancer.

TP53 Gene Mutations in Other Smoking-Associated Cancers

Of four cancer types analyzed, only SCC of the larynx showed a strong similarity with lung cancers. Prevalence of G→T transversions was high (25.9 percent), and many occurred at PAH-target codons 157 and 245. A gradient in the upper respiratory tract reflects the prevalence of *TP53* G→T transversions in cancers of smokers. This prevalence ranges from low in the oral cavity, to intermediate in the larynx, and high in various histologic types of lung cancers. The gradient may reflect the existence of an underlying, parallel gradient in the extent of exposure of respiratory tract cells to carcinogens in tobacco smoke. In oral cancers, studies show that the *TP53* mutation load is proportional to the extent of smoking, with an almost fourfold increase in the prevalence of mutations among

heavy smokers compared with nonsmokers (Brennan et al. 1995). In one study of oral and esophageal SCC, however, the frequency of G→T transversions is only slightly higher (16.5 and 19.6 percent, respectively) than those in cancers not strongly related to exposure to tobacco smoke (e.g., breast, colorectal, and brain cancers). The patterns of mutations in both oral and esophageal SCC are similar, perhaps reflecting the importance of common risk factors, such as the combined use of tobacco and alcohol, infections by human papilloma virus (Gillison and Shah 2003), and various lifestyle behaviors such as tobacco chewing or consuming scalding hot beverages, as well as similar histology in oral and esophageal tissues. In contrast, the mutation pattern is different in esophageal adenocarcinomas, with a high prevalence of G→T transversions at CpG sites (Figure 5.13) and a type of mutation that could be associated with the overproduction of reactive nitrogen species due to inflammation (Ambs et al. 1999).

For bladder cancer, the mutation pattern shows an unusually high prevalence of G→A transitions at non-CpG sites. These mutations are not distributed at random, and bladder-specific mutation hot spots can be seen at codons 280 and 285, according to the IARC *TP53* database. Both codons occur within the same primary sequence context (5'AGAG), which raises the possibility that this sequence may be a preferential target site for a carcinogen involved in bladder carcinogenesis. However, aromatic amines, a potent class of bladder carcinogens in tobacco smoke, produce mainly G→T mutations (Besaratinia et al. 2002).

Limitations to the Study of *TP53* Mutations and Smoking-Induced Cancer

Although the study of mutations in the *TP53* gene provides potentially useful leads for understanding mechanisms of tobacco carcinogenesis, this approach also has limitations. As already mentioned, various carcinogen-DNA adducts can produce G→T transversions and even similar spectra of mutations. In addition, most of this research is not population based, and the studies may be biased with respect to the stage of lung cancer represented. Finally, lack of a mutation in the *TP53* gene does not necessarily mean that the tumor is not related to smoking, because other uncharacterized changes could have occurred.

Loss of Mechanisms for Growth Control

Signal Transduction

Introduction

Normally, cell signaling is very tightly regulated and begins with the transduction of the signal through a membrane receptor. The signal is conveyed through a series of intracellular proteins, and the result is the regulation of cellular processes including proliferation and apoptosis. In lung cancer cells, the processes governing these events are frequently deregulated by DNA-damaging mutations induced by cigarette smoke or other alterations in the molecules of numerous signaling pathways. The balance between mechanisms leading to apoptosis (proapoptotic) and those suppressing apoptosis (antiapoptotic) or suppressing increased proliferation will have a major impact on lung tumor growth. Identifying and targeting signaling pathways that lead to therapeutic resistance could help to neutralize a patient's resistance to standard therapies.

Apoptosis

Apoptosis was first described in 1972 (Kerr et al. 1972). The term "apoptosis" is from the Greek word for "falling off." Apoptosis is a natural process that consists of a well-orchestrated cascade of distinct biologic and histologic events (Kerr et al. 1972). These events are critical for eliminating injured or genomically unstable cells while minimizing damage to surrounding normal cells (Martin 2002). The induction of apoptosis prevents the malignant growth of cancer cells (Rich et al. 2000). The deregulation of the mechanisms governing apoptosis is a distinctive characteristic of most cancer cells (Hanahan and Weinberg 2000).

Apoptosis is characterized by morphologic features including membrane blebbing, cell shrinking, and chromosomal condensation. Apoptosis is generally believed to occur through two "effector" mechanisms: extrinsic (death receptor mediated) and intrinsic (mitochondrial mediated) (Hengartner 2000). The extrinsic pathway is regulated by binding a "death receptor molecule" to the cancer cell's membrane receptor (i.e., death receptor). The intrinsic pathway is mediated by rendering the mitochondrial membrane permeable, a phenomenon directly influenced by the ratio of the interaction of proapoptotic and antiapoptotic proteins. In general, researchers believe that the inactivation of apoptosis through the intrinsic pathway is the primary mechanism through which DNA-damaging agents from tobacco smoke act to enhance the survival of lung cancer cells, which is the focus of this section.

Key Apoptotic Regulators

One or more pathways may lead to apoptosis. Stress signals stimulate a pathway that activates proteins to respond to DNA damage. These proteins subsequently phosphorylate, activate, and stabilize the P53 protein. The activated P53 protein drives the transcription of genes associated with cell-cycle arrest, DNA repair, and apoptosis. These genes include the BCL-2 family of proteins, which consists of both proapoptotic and antiapoptotic members. The BCL-2 family of proteins interacts with the outer mitochondrial membrane to regulate the release of cytochrome *c*, which results in the activation of aspartyl and cysteine proteases (caspases) (Igney and Krammer 2002). The caspases are crucial executioners of apoptosis (Meier et al. 2000; Reed 2000). Once stimulated, the caspases activate endonucleases that subsequently cleave the DNA of the targeted cell into nucleosome-sized fragments, which is a common characteristic of apoptosis.

A multitude of signaling molecules mediate the mechanisms that govern apoptosis. An imbalance in proapoptotic and antiapoptotic signaling events contributes to the development and progression of lung cancer. The mechanisms for the deregulation of apoptosis can be categorized into (1) the decrease of signaling associated directly with the induction of apoptosis and (2) the increase of signaling leading to the suppression of apoptosis. This decrease may include mutations induced by cigarette smoke or other smoke-related mechanisms that activate oncogenes or inactivate tumor-suppressor proteins or other proapoptotic proteins. The increase may include mutations induced by cigarette smoke, certain kinases, other antiapoptotic proteins or transcription factors, or overexpression or constitutive activation of growth factors. The end result of this deregulation usually includes a profound resistance to apoptosis.

Regulation of Tumor Suppressors and Proapoptotic Proteins

Decrease of important proapoptotic proteins of the BCL-2 family and tumor suppressors such as the P53 and RB proteins is a characteristic in many types of cancers, including lung cancer. This decrease provides lung cancer cells with a strong ability to resist apoptosis, which leads to a distinct advantage for cell survival (Figure 5.14).

Figure 5.14   Tobacco-associated suppression of proapoptotic proteins and tumor-suppressor proteins

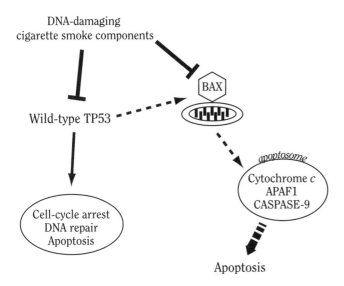

Note: Tobacco-associated suppression of proapoptotic proteins and tumor-suppressor proteins increases cell proliferation and resistance to apoptosis. Two major signaling pathways that are downregulated by DNA-damaging tobacco agents are the TP53 protein and the proapoptotic family of BCL-2 proteins.
APAF1 = apoptotic-releasing factor 1; **BAX** = BCL-2 associated X protein; **CASPASE-9** = cysteine-aspartic acid protease-9.

BCL-2 Family Proteins

In normal cells, stresses initiate apoptosis through the mitochrondrial or intrinsic pathway, and the BCL-2 family proteins are important mediators of the apoptotic response. These proteins are characterized by the presence of one to four conserved BCL-2 homology (BH) domains. The BCL-2 family can be divided into antiapoptotic members: BCL-2, BCL-X$_L$, and myeloid cell leukemia-1. The proapoptotic BCL-2 proteins are subdivided into two groups: the multidomain BAX subfamily (BAK, BAX, and BOK) and the BH3-only proteins (BAD, BID, and BIM) (Korsmeyer 1995; Hale et al. 1996; Adams and Cory 1998; Huang and Strasser 2000; Cory et al. 2003). The BCL-2 family of proteins appears to directly influence the permeability of the mitochrondrial membrane to regulate apoptosis.

The interaction of BAX with the mitochrondrial membrane causes the release of cytochrome *c* into the cytosol, where it binds to apoptotic-releasing factor 1. The binding of cytochrome *c* and apoptotic-releasing factor 1 results in the activation of cysteine-aspartic acid

protease-9 (CASPASE-9), which is required to form the "apoptosome" complex that initiates apoptosis. The apoptotic response is critically dependent on the ratio of the expression of proapoptotic and antiapoptotic BCL-2 members (Zha et al. 1997; Korsmeyer 1999; Kroemer 1999; Reed 1999; Huang and Strasser 2000; Lutz 2000; Cheng et al. 2001; Ruvolo et al. 2001). A lack of BAX (Zhang et al. 2000a; Schmitt and Lowe 2002) or an increase of BCL-2 or BCL-X$_L$ (Schott et al. 1995; Walczak et al. 2000; Chipuk et al. 2001) suppresses apoptosis, whereas a decrease of BCL-X$_L$ or BCL-2 enhances apoptosis (Hayward et al. 2003). Dimers containing BAX and BCL-2 inactivate BAX and therefore inhibit apoptosis. In addition, phosphorylation of the BAD protein results in its inactivation, because only the nonphosphorylated form of BAD can antagonize the antiapoptotic BCL-2 or BCL-X$_L$ at the mitochondrial membrane (Hermeking 2003).

Nicotine suppresses the death of lung cancer cells by phosphorylation mediated by the extracellular signal-regulated kinase (ERK) of BCL-2 (Heusch and Maneckjee 1998; Mai et al. 2003). Conversely, NNK inactivates BAD through β-adrenergic receptors and protein kinase C (PKC), which promotes survival of NSCLC cells (Lahn et al. 2004; Jin et al. 2005). Nicotine also stimulates cell survival through the phosphorylation and inhibition of BAD activated by β-adrenergic-receptor–mediated AKT-, PKA-, and/or ERK-dependent pathways (Jin et al. 2004a). These studies show that BCL-2 family members are critical effectors of signaling pathways that promote cancer cell survival in response to components of cigarette smoke—in these cases, through direct receptor binding rather than DNA damage.

P53 Protein

The P53 pathway is clearly involved in cellular life or death. The P53 tumor-suppressor protein can induce the expression of BAX and additional proapoptotic members of the BCL-2 family (Miyashita and Reed 1995; Yin et al. 1997; Oda et al. 2000a,b; Nakano and Vousden 2001). In addition to having direct effects on BCL-2 family proteins, the P53 protein also increases activity of the *APAF1* gene (Robles et al. 2001), which as indicated earlier, is a member of the apoptosome complex and is critical for the activation of CASPASE-9 to initiate apoptosis (Soengas et al. 1999) (see "BCL-2 Family Proteins" earlier in this chapter). Although it is primarily a nuclear protein, P53 may function outside the nucleus by translocating to the mitochondria, where it interacts directly with antiapoptotic proteins such as BCL-2 and BCL-X$_L$ to induce apoptosis (Mihara et al. 2003). The aberrant inactivation of P53 leads to a deregulation of cell-cycle control and a suppression of many crucial proapoptotic pathways (Ford and Hanawalt 1995; Wang et al. 1995a,b; Offer et al. 1999; Vogelstein et al. 2000; Zhou et al. 2001a). The loss of P53 function markedly decreases the sensitivity of lung cancer cells to apoptosis induced by exposure to tobacco smoke or other stresses (Lowe et al. 1994).

Retinoblastoma Protein

Inactivation of the RB protein results in the release and activation of the transcription factor E2F (Flemington et al. 1993; Helin et al. 1993). Some E2F family members induce expression of the genes important in apoptosis, such as the *P14ARF* gene (DeGregori et al. 1997; Bates et al. 1998). The P14ARF protein is a negative regulator of murine double minute 2 (MDM2), a P53 binding protein.

The inhibition of MDM2 leads to elevated P53 levels and apoptosis. The E2F protein can also activate proapoptotic BCL-2 family members and caspases (Nahle et al. 2002; Hershko and Ginsberg 2004).

Regulation of Antiapoptotic Proteins and Effects

Studies document that many genes and signaling proteins are overexpressed or display gain-of-function mutations in lung cancers. These include the *EGFR* gene, signal transduction and activator of transcription, PKC, RAS/MAPK, phosphatidylinositol-3 kinase (PI-3K)/AKT, PTEN, nuclear factor-kappa B (NF-κB), and COX (Figure 5.15).

Figure 5.15   Protein-signaling pathways deregulated in lung cancer

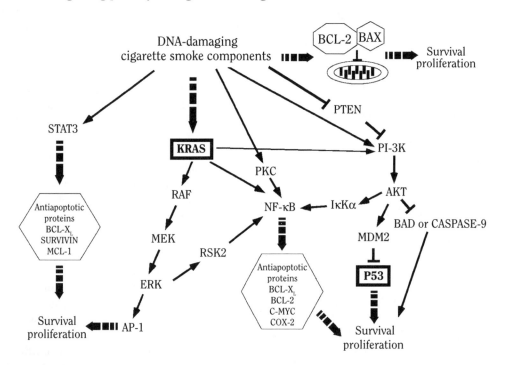

Note: Many protein-signaling pathways deregulated in lung cancer represent a dense interactive network with a range of potential survival-enhancing effects. Tobacco- or cigarette smoke-associated activation of antiapoptotic proteins provides lung cancer cells with a distinct growth advantage. Major protein survival-signaling pathways activated by tobacco carcinogens are illustrated. KRAS and P53 are boxed to emphasize that *KRAS* and *TP53* are the most commonly mutated genes. Mutationally activated KRAS is locked in its active form, resistant to the inactivating effects of GTPase-activating proteins, and cannot hydrolyze guanosine triphosphate to guanosine diphosphate. Similarly, mutated P53 cannot carry out many of its normal protective functions with respect to cell cycle control and apoptosis. **AKT** = protein kinase B; **AP-1** = activator protein-1; **BAD** = BCL-associated death protein; **BAX** = BCL-2 associated X protein; **CASPASE-9** = cysteine-aspartic acid protease-9; **ERK** = extracellular signal-regulated kinase; **IκKα** = I kappa-B kinase alpha; **MDM2** = murine double minute 2 protein; **MEK** = mitogen-activated protein kinase kinase; **NF-κB** = nuclear factor-kappa beta; **PI-3K** = phosphatidylinositol 3-kinase; **PKC** = protein kinase C signaling pathway; **PTEN** = phosphatase and tensin homolog; **RAF** = v-raf murine leukemia viral oncogene; **RSK2** = P90 ribosomal protein S6 kinase; **STAT3** = signal transducer and activator of transcription 3.

Epidermal Growth Factor Receptor

Exposure of oral cells to cigarette smoke caused an increase in EGFR tyrosine kinase activity (Moraitis et al. 2005). Signaling through EGFR can lead to survival signals that suppress dependent (downstream) apoptotic pathways or stimulate cell proliferation. Some evidence suggests that EGFR signaling can influence the levels and activities of antiapoptotic BCL-2 family members (Kari et al. 2003). The *EGFR* gene is overexpressed and thus constitutively activated in lung cancer cells (Sridhar et al. 2003) and bronchial preneoplastic lesions (Rusch et al. 1995; Kurie et al. 1996; Piyathilake et al. 2002). In addition, a truncated form of the EGFR protein (EGFRvIII) is constitutively active in NSCLC cells (Okamoto et al. 2003). The expression of this mutant form of *EGFR* is associated with an increase in cell transformation and with the constitutive activation of important downstream signaling pathways for survival, including the PI-3K/AKT pathway (Antonyak et al. 1998; Moscatello et al. 1998; Tang et al. 2000).

RAS/Mitogen-Activated Protein Kinase

Activation of the RAS pathway sends a strong antiapoptotic signal, and the constitutive activation of RAS can transform normal cells. Oncogenic RAS protein has a primary role in the development of lung cancer (Johnson et al. 2001a). RAS activates several pathways, including RAF/mitogen-activated protein kinase kinase (MEK)/ERK, PKC, PI-3K/AKT, and NF-κB (Kauffmann-Zeh et al. 1997; Kennedy et al. 1997; Peeper et al. 1997; Baldwin 2001). These pathways are commonly deregulated by RAS in lung cancers (Adjei 2001a,b). RAF/MEK/ERK pathway activation can lead to changes in downstream gene expression through the activation of activator protein-1 (AP-1). AP-1 is a well-characterized transcription factor composed of homodimers and/or heterodimers of the *JUN* and *FOS* gene families (Angel and Karin 1991). AP-1 regulates the transcription of various genes. Many stimuli, including tumor promoters, mediate AP-1 binding to the DNA of genes that govern cellular processes such as inflammation, proliferation, and apoptosis (Angel and Karin 1991).

Phosphatidylinositol-3 Kinase, Phosphatidylinositol 3'-Phosphatase, and Protein Kinase B

PI-3K consists of a family of heterodimeric complexes, each composed of a p110 catalytic subunit and a regulatory subunit that exists primarily as a p85 form (Tolias et al. 1995; Vanhaesebroeck et al. 1997; Wymann and Pirola 1998). This family of proteins is involved in the regulation of proliferation, viability, adhesion, and motility migration in numerous cell types (Carpenter and Cantley 1996; Khwaja 1999; Rameh and Cantley 1999; Blume-Jensen and Hunter 2001; Roymans and Slegers 2001). Cell survival and oncogenic transformation require PI-3K activation (Datta et al. 1999; Stambolic et al. 1999). PI-3K–dependent kinases include 3-phosphoinositide–dependent protein kinase-1 (PDK1) and AKT (PKB). The PI-3K pathway can also be activated by the EGFR protein and by an activated RAS protein (Rodriguez-Viciana et al. 1997). One of the first steps in PI-3K signaling is the activation of PDK1, which phosphorylates and activates AKT (Coffer et al. 1998; Belham et al. 1999). AKT phosphorylates and inactivates several proapoptotic proteins, including BAD and CASPASE-9. Other targets of AKT important in the regulation of apoptosis include glycogen-synthase-kinase-3 (Pap and Cooper 1998), the Forkhead transcription factor FKHRL1 (Brunet et al. 1999), and the mammalian target of rapamycin/p70S6 kinase (McCormick 2004). Furthermore, AKT inactivates P53 by phosphorylating MDM2, which increases the ability of MDM2 to bind to and promote P53 degradation (Ogawara et al. 2002). AKT also suppresses apoptosis by activating NF-κB through AKT phosphorylation of I kappa-B kinase alpha (Ozes et al. 1999; Romashkova and Makarov 1999).

Most NSCLC cells display an increase in PI-3K activity that results in highly active AKT and other downstream mediators (Moore et al. 1998; Brognard et al. 2001). AKT is important in the survival of lung cancer cells and is constitutively activated in most NSCLC cell lines to promote the survival of NSCLC cells under stressful conditions (Brognard et al. 2001). Studies have also found AKT expression in SCLC tumor samples (Lee et al. 2002b; Mukohara et al. 2003), SCLC cell lines (Moore et al. 1998), SCLC tumors (Blackhall et al. 2003), mouse tumors induced by tobacco carcinogens (West et al. 2003), and human bronchial dysplastic lesions (Tsao et al. 2003). (For additional details on AKT activation by components of cigarette smoke through receptor interactions, see "Activation of Cytoplasmic Kinase by Tobacco Smoke" later in this chapter.)

Nuclear Factor-Kappa B

NF-κB is a rapidly induced transcription factor responsive to stress that functions to intensify the transcription of a variety of genes, including those encoding cytokines, growth factors, and acute response proteins (Baldwin 1996). Nicotinic activation of nicotinic acetylcholine receptors (nAChRs) stimulates NF-κB activity downstream of ERK and AKT, which promotes tumor growth and angiogenesis through the vascular endothelial growth factor (VEGF) in vivo (Heeschen et al. 2001, 2002). Moreover, NF-κB activation by exposure to cigarette smoke in lung cancer cells induces the expression of COX-2 (Anto et al. 2002; Shishodia and Aggarwal 2004). Recent results suggest that nicotine, but not NNK, activates NF-κB–dependent survival of lung cancer cells in addition to their proliferation. These studies illustrate that the activation of NF-κB by nicotine or by cigarette smoke in its entirety through receptor binding can promote tumorigenesis in the lung through many mechanisms, including increased levels of VEGF and COX-2.

Cyclooxygenase

COX-1 and COX-2 were shown to catalyze synthesis of prostaglandins from arachidonic acid. Researchers observed that COX-1 was constitutively expressed in most tissues, whereas COX-2 was inducible and found at elevated levels in various cancers (Koki et al. 2002; Dannenberg and Subbaramaiah 2003; Dubinett et al. 2003). In lung cancers, researchers have found COX-2 expression at most stages of tumor progression (Hida et al. 1998; Huang et al. 1998; Wolff et al. 1998; Hosomi et al. 2000; Anderson et al. 2002; Fang et al. 2003). Others reported high levels of COX-2 in NSCLC and premalignant lesions, but COX-2 expression is less consistent in SCLC (Wolff et al. 1998; Hosomi et al. 2000). Studies show that NNK induces a high expression of COX-2 in rats (El-Bayoumy et al. 1999). Levels of COX-2 mRNA are about four times higher in the oral mucosa of smokers than in that of lifetime nonsmokers (Moraitis et al. 2005). Researchers believe that at least one role of COX-2 in cancer is associated with cell resistance to apoptosis and an increase in metastatic potential (Gupta and Dubois 2001). The supporting evidence shows that COX-2 overexpression coincides with an increased BCL-2 expression (Tsujii and DuBois 1995) and an increased stabilization of the antiapoptotic protein survivin (Li et al. 1998a; Krysan et al. 2004). Lung cancer cells that were induced to express COX-2 demonstrated an increase in survival time (Lin et al. 2001b), and COX-2 inhibitors stimulated apoptosis in lung carcinoma cells (Hida et al. 2000; Yao et al. 2000; Chang and Weng 2001).

Summary

Apoptosis is commonly suppressed in lung cancer, which correlates with increases in cancer cell survival and proliferation. Deregulation of the many pathways for growth control (Figure 5.15) in lung cancer is attributable partly to interactions of carcinogens in cigarette smoke with the *KRAS* oncogene, the *P53* tumor-suppressor gene, and other genes. These pathways represent a dense interactive network with a range of potential effects on cell survival. Mechanisms associated with cigarette smoke that increase resistance to apoptosis include activation of antiapoptotic proteins and/or suppression of proapoptotic and tumor-suppressor proteins.

Cigarette Smoke and Activation of Cell-Surface Receptors in Cancer

Airway Epithelial Cells

Nicotinic Acetylcholine Receptors

Neuronal nAChRs are large membrane-associated proteins that are the first line of contact between cells and components of cigarette smoke such as nicotine and NNK. These proteins were originally described as receptors for acetylcholine (ACh). Their function in the brain has been studied in detail because of their ability to mediate the addictive effects of nicotine. Each receptor is made up of five subunits arranged in a barrel-like structure, creating a pore that allows calcium to enter the cell in response to ligand binding. Nine alpha subunits (α2 through α10) and three beta subunits (β2 through β4) combine with each other to form heteropentamers (combinations of α2 through α6 with β2 through β4) or homopentamers (α7 through α10). Each nAChR consists of 5 subunits, and researchers have identified at least 12 subunits; thus, many functional nAChRs exist. Different ligands, including nicotine, NNK, and ACh, have varying affinities for different nAChRs. Despite this complexity, the primary receptors that mediate the addictive effects of nicotine are α4β2 nAChRs, whereas α7 nAChRs are high-affinity receptors for NNK (Lindstrom 1997, 2003). Moreover, the discovery that mutations in the α4 nAChR subunit lower the threshold for addiction raises the possibility that genetic variations in these receptors could increase susceptibility to nicotine dependence and exposure to carcinogens through smoking (Tapper et al. 2004).

Although nAChRs were originally thought to be limited to neuronal cells, studies have identified functional nAChRs in tissues outside the nervous system. This finding raises the possibility that these receptors may mediate some of the systemic effects of smoking. In lung tissues, researchers have discovered nAChRs in human bronchial epithelial cells, vascular endothelial cells, pulmonary neuroendocrine cells, neuroepithelial bodies, NSCLC cells, and SCLC cells (Tarroni et al. 1992; Maneckjee and Minna 1994; Macklin et al. 1998; Maus et al. 1998; Schuller and Orloff 1998; Wang et al. 2001b; Fu et al. 2003; Schuller et al. 2003; Song et al. 2003a,b; Tsurutani et al. 2005).

The stimulation of nAChRs by components of cigarette smoke has biologic effects on cells that are important for the initiation, progression, and maintenance of cancer.

The activation of nAChRs in lung epithelial cells by nicotine or NNK promotes the survival and proliferation of human mesothelioma and lung cancer cells (Maneckjee and Minna 1994; Schuller and Orloff 1998; West et al. 2002; Schuller et al. 2003; Trombino et al. 2004; Tsurutani et al. 2005). In normal cells, nicotine can stimulate properties consistent with cell transformation and the early stages of cancer formation, such as increased cell proliferation, decreased cellular dependence on the extracellular matrix for survival, and decreased contact inhibition, which is the natural process of arresting cell growth when two or more cells come in contact with each other (West et al. 2003). Furthermore, nicotine stimulation of endothelial nAChRs promotes angiogenesis, another property of cancer (Heeschen et al. 2001, 2002; Zhu et al. 2003). Thus, the induced activation of nAChRs in lung tissues by components of cigarette smoke can promote processes required for development of cancer.

In addition to stimulating nAChRs directly, components of cigarette smoke can indirectly stimulate nAChRs by promoting the growth of tobacco-related cancers that express and secrete ACh, the endogenous ligand for these receptors. SCLC and NSCLC cells synthesize, transport, and release ACh in vitro, which stimulates proliferation of cancer cells through the autocrine activation of nAChRs (Song et al. 2003a; Proskocil et al. 2004). This finding suggests that there are many mechanisms for activation of nAChRs in lung cancer and further emphasizes the importance of these receptors in the biology of tobacco-related cancer.

β-Adrenergic Receptors

The β-adrenergic receptors are neuronal receptors that may play a role in mediating effects of cigarette smoke related to signal transduction. NNK is structurally similar to epinephrine, the endogenous ligand for the β-adrenergic receptor, suggesting that in addition to binding nAChRs, NNK may bind to these receptors. Once bound to β-adrenergic receptors, NNK can stimulate the release of arachidonic acid (Schuller et al. 1999; Weddle et al. 2001). The enzyme COX-2 converts arachidonic acid to prostaglandin E_2, which mediates inflammation and promotes cell survival and proliferation in cancer. This finding is important because cell lines from human lung cancer overexpress the β-adrenergic receptor (Schuller et al. 2001), and several studies suggest that the presence or expression of arachidonic acid is a risk factor for pulmonary adenocarcinomas (Alavanja et al. 1993, 2001). Thus, these studies indicate that the β-adrenergic receptor may be an important mediator of signal transduction pathways associated with exposure to cigarette smoke.

Other Receptors

The ERBB family is another group of EGFRs that indirectly mediate signal transduction associated with cigarette smoke. The four types of ERBB receptors are EGFR (HER-1), HER-2, HER-3, and HER-4. These receptors act in pairs to stimulate downstream signaling pathways that mediate the survival and proliferation of both normal cells and cancer cells. Ligands that bind to ERBB family members include the epidermal growth factor TGFα and amphiregulin. In addition, receptors can be activated in the absence of a ligand through overexpression of the receptors themselves. Both of these mechanisms play a role in activation of these receptors mediated by cigarette smoke.

The hypothesis that ERBB receptors mediate the effects of cigarette smoke on airway epithelial cells emerged from correlative clinical data and mechanisms defined in vitro. Clinical data include many reports of EGFR and HER-2 overexpression in lung cancer (Hendler and Ozanne 1984; Cerny et al. 1986; Veale et al. 1987; Hirsch et al. 2003a; Tan et al. 2003). In addition, some studies have shown that EGFR overexpression and activation in human lung cancers correlate with shorter survival times, suggesting that they play an important role in development of cancer (Kern et al. 1990; Kanematsu et al. 2003; Selvaggi et al. 2004).

Clinical data also support the hypothesis that ERBB expression and activation change with exposure to cigarette smoke or its components. Studies have demonstrated the overexpression of EGFR and ERBB3 in the bronchial epithelium of smokers (Yoneda 1994; O'Donnell et al. 2004). Results of mechanistic in vitro studies, such as the demonstration that NNK-induced transformation of lung epithelial cells is associated with an increase in EGFR expression, support these observations (Lonardo et al. 2002). Moreover, exposure to nicotine alone can increase the expression of EGFR in cervical cancer cell lines (Mathur et al. 2000). Studies also demonstrate that exposure to tobacco smoke increases the activity of EGFR, and metabolites of B[a]P induce activation of EGFR and downstream signaling pathways that promote proliferation (Burdick et al. 2003; Moraitis et al. 2005). These studies support the idea that components of cigarette smoke modulate the expression and activation of the ERBB family of receptors.

In addition to increasing the expression of ERBB family members, components of tobacco smoke stimulate cells to produce ligands that activate the receptors. In clinical specimens, studies have described the coexpression of EGFR and its ligand TGFα in human NSCLC. In one study, both EGFR and TGFα were expressed in 38 percent of the cases of NSCLC examined (Rusch et al. 1993). In a second study, 72 percent of SCCs and 34 percent of adenocarcinomas expressed both EGFR and TGFα (Hsieh et al. 2000). This finding may be clinically important because a retrospective analysis showed that the coexpression of EGFR and TGFα is an indicator of a poor prognosis (Tateishi et al. 1990). These studies suggest that the stimulation of ERBB ligands induced by cigarette smoke may be an important mechanism of signal transduction.

Consistent with the clinical data, in vitro studies show that condensate from cigarette smoke stimulates the release of amphiregulin and TGFα from the cell membrane, which leads to the autocrine activation of EGFR and cell proliferation (Richter et al. 2002; Lemjabbar et al. 2003; Moraitis et al. 2005). Several studies demonstrate that cigarette smoke condensate activates matrix metalloproteinases (MMPs), which are enzymes on the extracellular surface of cells that cleave these ligands from the extracellular matrix. Support for these in vitro observations comes from the demonstration that MMP activity is higher in lung tissues from smokers than in those from nonsmokers (Kang et al. 2003; Kangavari et al. 2004).

In addition to stimulating downstream kinases, EGFR activation by cigarette smoke may provide a mechanistic link to the increased inflammation characteristic of smokers by increasing COX-2 activity (see "Activation of Cytoplasmic Kinase by Tobacco Smoke" later in this chapter). In vitro data suggest that autocrine activation of EGFR, by the expression of the *TGFα* and *AREG* genes induced by tobacco smoke, stimulates COX-2 expression (Moraitis et al. 2005). Cigarette smoke also increases COX-2 expression by lung fibroblasts in vitro, and B[*a*]P increases COX-2 expression by oral epithelial cells (Kelley et al. 1997; Martey et al. 2004). Thus, many in vitro studies demonstrate that EGFR activation by components of cigarette smoke can contribute to inflammation through the increased expression and activation of COX-2.

Clinical data support the validity of these in vitro observations. For example, studies document increased levels of COX-2 in the oral mucosa of smokers (Moraitis et al. 2005) and in urothelial tissues from smokers with bladder cancer (Badawi et al. 2002). Moreover, COX-2 is expressed only in neoplastic epithelial cells, not in normal bronchial epithelial cells (Hastürk et al. 2002). COX-2 overexpression in lung cancer is associated with tumor angiogenesis and survival and proliferation of tumor cells (Riedl et al. 2004) and with a poor prognosis in NSCLC (Achiwa et al. 1999; Yuan et al. 2005). Thus, the stimulation of EGFR that leads to COX-2 activity by exposure to cigarette smoke is another mechanism mediated by a growth factor receptor to promote cell survival and proliferation in carcinogenesis.

Activation of Cytoplasmic Kinase by Tobacco Smoke

Activation of cell-surface receptors by components of tobacco smoke stimulates downstream kinases that mediate cancer cell survival, proliferation, and resistance to chemotherapy. The best-described kinases activated by smoking are AKT, ERK, PKC, and PKA. All of these kinases can be activated by cigarette smoke components through nAChRs, but ERBB family members also mediate AKT and ERK activation by cigarette smoke components. In addition, β-adrenergic receptor activation by cigarette smoke components can activate PKA and PKC. Thus, these proteins can be activated by tobacco smoke components through multiple receptor-mediated mechanisms, suggesting that the proteins are important mediators of smoking-induced signal transduction.

Protein Kinase B

The serine/threonine kinase AKT may be the critical effector of signaling induced by cigarette smoke, because AKT is stimulated in response to the activation of nAChRs, β-adrenergic receptors, and the ERBB family of receptors. Moreover, AKT controls many cellular processes that promote cell survival, proliferation, and the resistance of cancer cells to chemotherapy. Clinical data also suggest that AKT activation indicates a poor prognosis in many tobacco-related cancers. Thus, activation of this kinase by components of tobacco smoke can affect many cellular processes important for the initiation, growth, and progression of tumors.

AKT might be important for the initiation as well as the maintenance of tobacco-related cancers. Nicotine and NNK cause rapid AKT activation through different nAChRs (West et al. 2003; Tsurutani et al. 2005). B[*a*]P metabolites activate AKT in breast epithelial cells, although the cellular receptor responsible for the effect has not been identified (Burdick et al. 2003). Furthermore, nicotine-induced AKT activation in normal human bronchial cells or in small airway epithelial cells promotes cell survival, proliferation, and anchorage-independent growth, all of which are properties of transformed cells (West et al. 2003). These studies are important because they suggest that AKT activation by tobacco smoke components may precede the formation of DNA mutations that cause cancer. Thus, AKT activation could serve as a biochemical gatekeeper for lung carcinogenesis by promoting the survival of cells that would normally die from DNA damage.

In addition to promoting AKT-dependent growth and survival of normal epithelial cells, tobacco smoke components have similar effects on cells throughout the phenotypic spectrum of transformation. In a mouse model of NNK-induced lung tumorigenesis, an increase in AKT activation was associated with an increase in the progression of NNK-induced lung lesions (West et al. 2004b). In human lung cancer cells, nicotine or NNK activated the AKT pathway and stimulated AKT-dependent proliferation through nAChRs (Tsurutani et al. 2005). Moreover, these researchers showed that nicotinic activation of AKT increased survival of lung cancer cells after treatment with chemotherapeutic agents or radiation (Tsurutani et al. 2005). The fact that tobacco smoke components activate AKT and promote the survival of cancer cells is important, and it is supported by the finding that cancer patients who continue to smoke during chemotherapy have a worse prognosis than those who stop smoking (Johnston-Early et al. 1980; Browman et al. 1993; Videtic et al. 2003).

Clinical data and preclinical models support the hypothesis that AKT activation is an early event in carcinogenesis. AKT is activated in preneoplastic lung lesions induced by exposure to NNK (West et al. 2004a) and in dysplastic lung lesions from smokers (Massion et al. 2004). In addition, AKT activation is associated with poor survival in patients with tobacco-related cancers, including lung cancer and pancreatic cancer (David et al. 2004; Hirami et al. 2004; Yamamoto et al. 2004; Tsurutani et al. 2005). Together, these clinical studies support the idea that AKT plays an important role in the formation and maintenance of tobacco-related cancers.

Extracellular Signal-Regulated Kinases

In addition to AKT, ERK may play an important role in smoking-related cancers because it can be activated in response to components of tobacco smoke through both nAChR and ERBB receptors. In normal cells, ERK is activated in response to many extracellular signals and stimulates cell proliferation. In SCLC and pulmonary neuroendocrine cells, NNK-induced activation of nAChR leads to the activation of RAF-1 and its downstream effector ERK (Jull et al. 2001; Schuller et al. 2003). In addition, B[a]P metabolites activate ERK (Burdick et al. 2003), and nicotine activates ERK and promotes cell survival (Heusch and Maneckjee 1998). Thus, like AKT, ERK can be activated as an acute response to tobacco smoke components. Because ERK and AKT can promote cell survival and proliferation, early activation of both kinases may contribute to the initiation, promotion, and progression of cancer.

Researchers have also described ERK activation in tobacco-related cancers, thus validating the mechanisms defined in vitro. ERK activation is associated with poor survival in SCLC, which occurs almost exclusively in smokers (Blackhall et al. 2003). The overexpression of *C-MYC*, an oncogene activated by ERK, has been described in lung cancer and promotes proliferation as well as

resistance to cell death (Zajac-Kaye 2001). Thus, tobacco smoke components stimulate ERK, which promotes cell proliferation and contributes to the poor prognosis of lung cancer patients with this biochemical alteration.

Protein Kinase C

The PKC kinases also mediate cellular responses to exposure to tobacco smoke. Several isoforms of PKC can promote cell survival, most notably PKCα. Nicotine- and NNK-induced activation of PKCα through the β-adrenergic receptor promotes the survival of lung cancer cells (Schuller et al. 2003). In addition, nicotinic activation of nAChRs activates PKC in human bronchial epithelial cells, as well as in lung cancer cells (Maneckjee and Minna 1994; Carlisle et al. 2004). In SCLC, NNK-induced activation of nAChRs causes PKC activation associated with cell proliferation (Jull et al. 2001). Another PKC isoform, PKCδ, seems to act atypically in NSCLC cells. Activation of PKCδ in NSCLC promotes cell survival and resistance to chemotherapeutic agents (Clark et al. 2003), and nicotine can prevent chemotherapy from inhibiting PKC (Heusch and Maneckjee 1998). Like AKT, nicotinic activation of PKC has ramifications for smokers by contributing to chemotherapeutic resistance. This finding is consistent with the finding that patients with lung cancer who continue to smoke during chemotherapy have a worse prognosis than those who stop smoking.

A clinical study also demonstrates the importance of PKC in tobacco-related cancers. Lahn and colleagues (2004) found that PKCα is overexpressed in a subset of NSCLC. Collectively, the results suggest that the activation of prosurvival PKC isoforms by cigarette smoke is an important mechanism of cell proliferation mediated by nAChRs and β-adrenergic receptors in carcinogenesis.

Protein Kinase A

Another cytoplasmic kinase activated by components of tobacco smoke is PKA. Under normal physiological conditions, PKA is stimulated through the production of cyclic adenosine monophosphate by activated G protein–coupled receptors. Nicotinic activation of PKA occurs through both nAChRs and β-adrenergic receptors (Dajas-Bailador et al. 2002; Jin et al. 2004a). The primary effect of nAChR-mediated PKA activation was an increase in cell proliferation. Nicotinic activation of PKA through β-adrenergic receptors, however, promoted cell survival. Although the data on PKA are limited, they suggest that PKA might be an important mediator of signal transduction, mediating cell survival and proliferation in response to activation by nAChRs and β-adrenergic receptors.

Downstream Targets of Signaling Cascades Mediated by Tobacco Smoke

Activation of cell-surface receptors induced by components of tobacco smoke and the subsequent activation of cytoplasmic kinases stimulate other proteins that dictate cellular responses, such as cell survival and proliferation. Although activated kinases have many downstream targets, the two most studied are the transcription factor NF-κB and proteins in the BCL-2 family. Activation of these proteins by tobacco smoke components through signaling cascades promotes processes involved in initiation, progression, and maintenance of cancers (see "Signal Transduction" earlier in this chapter).

Gene Promoter Hypermethylation in Cancer Induced by Tobacco Smoke

Alternative to Mutation

Gene promoter hypermethylation is an epigenetic change of a gene involving extensive methylation at the 5' position of C in CpG islands within the promoter region and often extending into exon 1 of regulatory genes (Jones and Baylin 2002; Herman and Baylin 2003). "Epigenetic" refers to alteration in gene expression resulting from changes other than DNA sequence. The end result of this process can be loss of gene transcription and therefore the silencing of gene function.

Inactivation of the *P16* Gene in Lung Cancer

One region on chromosome 9p contains the *CDKN2A* (*P16*) tumor-suppressor gene (Kamb et al. 1994; Merlo et al. 1994). Mutations within the *P16* coding sequence are uncommon in lung cancer (Kamb et al. 1994). In contrast, this gene is inactivated by hypermethylation at prevalences up to 60 percent and 70 percent in adenocarcinomas and SCC of the lung, respectively (Merlo et al. 1995; Belinsky et al. 1998; Kim et al. 2001; Zöchbaur-Müller et al. 2001; Divine et al. 2005). This discovery of inactivation of a tumor-suppressor gene by hypermethylation in lung cancer and identification of such inactivation of the *P16* gene launched an area of research to uncover other genes inactivated by this mechanism. The targeting of *P16* for inactivation is likely attributable to the critical function of this gene in the cell, which is to inhibit CDKs that bind cyclin D1 and phosphorylate the *RB* gene product (Lukas et al. 1995; Weinberg 1995).

This regulation is lost if either the *P16* or the *RB* gene is inactivated. The reciprocal relationship between *RB* alterations in SCLC and *P16* alterations in NSCLC supports the premise that dysfunction within the *RB* pathway is a major target in research on the genesis of lung cancer (Swafford et al. 1997).

Critical Pathways Inactivated in Non-Small-Cell and Small-Cell Lung Cancer

More than 50 genes are inactivated by gene promoter hypermethylation in lung cancer, and new genes are still being identified through genomewide screening approaches (Suzuki et al. 2002; Palmisano et al. 2003). The pathways and genes involved are summarized in Table 5.11.

Of particular importance is the DNA repair gene *AGT*, which protects cells from the carcinogenic effects of alkylating agents by removing adducts from the O^6 position of deoxyguanosine (see "Repair of DNA Adducts" earlier in this chapter). Failure to repair this DNA adduct could lead to mutations in genes such as *KRAS* and *TP53*. *AGT* is inactivated by gene promoter methylation in 24 to 48 percent of adenocarcinomas (Esteller et al. 1999; Zöchbaur-Müller et al. 2001; Pulling et al. 2003). SCLC studies conducted for methylation of this gene are limited. Studies have reported an association between *AGT* promoter hypermethylation and a G→A transition mutation at CpG sites within the *TP53* gene in NSCLC (Wolf et al. 2001). In contrast, no association was found between *AGT* gene methylation and a transition mutation in codon 12 of the *KRAS* gene from adenocarcinomas (Pulling et al. 2003).

The RAS superfamily of GTP-binding proteins plays an important role in signal transduction pathways that control cell proliferation, differentiation, and death (Campbell et al. 1998; Downward 2001) (see "Activation of Oncogenes in Lung Cancer" earlier in this chapter). Researchers identified a new family of genes that encode RAS-binding proteins. One of these genes, *RASSF1A*, is located at chromosome 3p21 and inactivated in 30 percent of NSCLCs and in 100 percent of SCLCs (Dammann et al. 2000; Burbee et al. 2001). Attempts to determine the function of this gene are continuing (Agathanggelou et al. 2003). RASSF1A protein forms a heterodimer with NORE1A, which allows it to bind with the proapoptotic protein MST1 (Khokhlatchev et al. 2002). Binding RAS to this complex may mediate RAS-dependent apoptosis. *NORE1A* is also silenced by methylation in NSCLC but not in SCLC (Hesson et al. 2003). Therefore, silencing either *RASSF1A* or *NORE1A* could effectively block apoptosis mediated by RAS activation. Two other RASSF

Table 5.11   Pathways altered through gene silencing by promoter methylation

Pathway	Gene	Methylation prevalence (%)	
		Non-small-cell lung cancer	Small-cell lung cancer
Cell cycle	P16	26–70	0
	PAX5α	64–74	ND
	PAX5β	52–61	ND
	CHFR	10–19	ND
DNA repair	AGT	27–47	0–19
Apoptosis	DAPK	24–48	33
	CASPASE-8	0	35–52
	FAS	ND	40
	TRAIL-R1	ND	40
	FHIT	38–45	ND
RAS signaling	RASSF1A	30	100
	RASSF4	20	20
	NORE1A	24	0
Invasion	E-CADHERIN	16–19	ND
	H-CADHERIN	43	ND
	TIMP3	19–24	ND
	LAMA3	27–58	65
	LAMB3	20–32	77
	LAMC2	13–32	58
	MYO18B	31	45

Source: Belinsky 2004. Reprinted with permission from Macmillan Publishers Ltd., © 2004.
Note: **ND** = not determined.

family members appear to be involved in lung cancer development. Studies show that RASSF2 binds directly to the *KRAS* gene in a GTP-dependent manner and appears to promote both cell-cycle arrest and apoptosis through this interaction (Vos et al. 2003). The expression of this gene is markedly reduced in some lung cancer cell lines, thus suggesting silencing by gene promoter hypermethylation. There is support for this mechanism of inactivation in studies on colon cancer that document hypermethylation of this gene in 70 percent of tumors (Hesson et al. 2005). A third member of this gene family, *RASSF4*, shares 25 percent homology with *RASSF1A* and 40 percent with *RASSF2* and is methylated in approximately 20 percent of NSCLCs and SCLCs (Eckfeld et al. 2004). Thus, the loss of function among members of the *RASSF* gene family is important to the development of lung cancer.

Gene Silencing in Lung Cancer

The most extensively studied gene with respect to timing of methylation in NSCLC is *P16*. Examination of biopsy specimens from premalignant lesions obtained from people without SCLC or from different airways or at different bronchial generations revealed a progressive increase in the prevalence of *P16* methylation as the disease developed. The frequency of *P16* methylation was 17 percent in basal cell hyperplasia, and the frequency increased incrementally over the histologic stages to 60 percent in SCCs (Belinsky et al. 1998). Further studies examined bronchial epithelial cells obtained by bronchoscopy from cancer-free smokers and found that inactivation of the *P16* gene is likely one of the earliest events in lung cancer (Belinsky et al. 2002). Researchers detected *P16* methylation in specimens from 25 of 137 biopsy procedures (18 percent) classified as histologically normal, metaplasia, or mild dysplasia. In contrast, no *P16* methylation was found in biopsy specimens obtained from lifetime nonsmokers. Researchers used an animal model to determine the timing of *P16* methylation in adenocarcinomas. In rats, 94 percent of adenocarcinomas induced by NNK were hypermethylated at the *P16* promoter; this change was frequently detected in precursor lesions to the tumors: adenomas and hyperplastic lesions (Belinsky et al. 1998).

Inactivation of the *AGT* gene appears to be a later event in lung cancer than is the inactivation of *P16*. Only 3 of 40 biopsy specimens (8 percent) from heavy smokers with histologies including normal, hyperplasia, metaplasia, and dysplasia showed methylation of the *AGT* gene (Pulling et al. 2003). In addition, the prevalence of *AGT* methylation increased between stage I adenocarcinoma and stages II to IV. Finally, of the 137 bronchial biopsy specimens studied, 3 percent of the *DAPK* gene and none of the *RASSF1A* genes showed methylation, which suggests that the silencing of these genes likely occurs after *P16* inactivation in SCC (Pulling et al. 2003). In contrast, the inactivation of *DAPK* by methylation in alveolar hyperplasias in a murine model of lung adenocarcinomas suggests a role for this gene in the early development of adenocarcinomas (Pulling et al. 2004).

Gene Promoter Hypermethylation, Prognosis, and Clinical Risk Factors

Numerous studies have evaluated relationships between gene promoter methylation and established clinical risk factors such as smoking dose and tumor stage. In addition, researchers have examined in detail the effect of gene-specific methylation on the survival of patients with a diagnosis of early-stage lung cancer. Results from investigations of the most commonly studied genes in lung cancer are highlighted here.

P16 methylation was significantly associated with pack-years of smoking and with an independent risk factor that predicts a shorter survival for patients who had resection of a stage I adenocarcinoma (Kim et al. 2001). Several other studies also support *P16* methylation as a prognostic factor for survival of patients who had resection of a stage I adenocarcinoma (Suzuki et al. 2002; Wang et al. 2004a). In contrast, *RASSF1A* methylation in stage III NSCLC was a stronger predictor of poor survival than was *P16* methylation (Wang et al. 2004a). These two genes may differ in that the silencing of *P16* is an early event involved in initiation of tumorigenesis, whereas *RASSF1A* methylation is a later event more likely involved in progression of tumorigenesis. Thus, the methylation of *RASSF1A* may lead to a more aggressive tumor phenotype. This hypothesis is supported by the more frequent involvement of *RASSF1A* methylation in tumors with a vascular invasion, pleural involvement, and a poorly differentiated histology (Tomizawa et al. 2002). Persons who started smoking before 19 years of age were 4.2 times more likely to have methylation of the *RASSF1A* gene than were those who started smoking after 19 years of age (Kim et al. 2003). This research also suggests that for patients with stage I or stage II NSCLC at diagnosis, methylation of this gene is associated with a poorer prognosis (Kim et al. 2003).

Other Tobacco-Related Cancers

In addition to the studies on lung cancer described here, other studies have shown association of cigarette smoking with gene promoter hypermethylation in other tobacco-related cancers, such as the head and neck and bladder. Aberrant promoter methylation is common in head and neck cancer and has been detected by using saliva samples (Rosas et al. 2001). Promoter methylation of the *P16*, *DAPK*, *E-CADHERIN*, and *RASSF1A* genes was associated with smoking and commonly found in head and neck cancer (Hasegawa et al. 2002). *P16* promoter hypermethylation and the loss of P16 protein expression were detected in head and neck SCC; loss of expression correlated significantly with a history of alcohol consumption or tobacco use (Ai et al. 2003). The prevalence of *P15* methylation in the healthy epithelium of patients with head and neck SCC who had long-term smoking and drinking behaviors was significantly higher than that in nonsmokers (Wong et al. 2003). Another study suggested that *P15* gene methylation could be induced by chronic smoking and drinking and could play a role in the early stages of head and neck SCC (Chang et al. 2004).

Cigarette smoking was also associated with an increased risk of promoter methylation of the *P16* gene in bladder cancer (Marsit et al. 2006).

Molecular Epidemiology of Cell-Cycle Control and Tobacco-Induced Cancer

Introduction

Cell-cycle checkpoints delay cell-cycle progression, thereby affording adequate time for DNA repair to occur. Such checkpoint signaling also activates pathways leading to apoptosis if the damage cannot be repaired. The introduction of new techniques of profiling gene expression has enabled researchers to comprehensively evaluate activity of proteins in regulating the cell cycle (Singhal et al. 2003). A hallmark of the neoplastic cell is the ability to disrupt the tightly regulated cell-cycle control and enable the cell to bypass checkpoints, especially at the G_1/S and G_2/M boundaries (Hanahan and Weinberg 2000). Persons with defects in cell-cycle checkpoints (acquired or inherited) could therefore exhibit chromosome damage, genomic instability, and increased susceptibility to tobacco carcinogenesis.

In vitro studies show an association between exposure to tobacco carcinogens and the disruption of cell-cycle control (Khan et al. 1999). Furthermore, Jin and colleagues (2004b) provide data showing that NNK promotes cell survival and proliferation through phosphorylation of the proteins BCL-2 and C-MYC. Studies implicate tobacco carcinogens in genetic alterations in the P16-RB and P14^{ARF}-P53 pathways, mainly through the formation of DNA adducts. Variations in cell-cycle checkpoints might also be attributed to functional polymorphisms in cell-cycle control genes. The SNP500Cancer Database reports that 27 genes related to the cell cycle are polymorphic, and these include genes that control checkpoints for both the G_1/S and G_2 phases of the cell cycle. However, only a few genes, including *CCND1*, *TP53*, *P21*, and *P73*, have been studied in tobacco-related cancers.

CCND1 Gene

The *CCND1* gene, together with *CDK4*, *P16*, and the tumor-suppressor gene *RB*, comprise a linked system governing the passage of the cell through the cell cycle (Betticher et al. 1997). A common finding in a variety of cancers is the amplification or overexpression of *CCND1*, which contributes to tumor initiation, progression, and outcome, such as death. A G→A polymorphism at codon 242 in the conserved splice donor region of exon 4 increases alternate splicing (Betticher et al. 1995). The alternate transcript appears to encode for a protein-missing sequence involved in protein turnover, and therefore, the encoded protein may have a longer half-life. This extended half-life, in turn, would facilitate passage of damaged cells through the checkpoint for the G_1/S phase and promote proliferation rather than apoptosis. Researchers have studied the association between the *CCND1* genotype and cancer risk in several tobacco-related cancers. Qiuling and colleagues (2003) reported that the *CCND1 *A/*A* genotype was associated with a significantly increased risk of lung cancer (OR = 1.87; 95 percent CI, 1.01–3.45) compared with that for the **G/*G* genotype. The risk was even higher in young persons and men. A similar finding was reported in cancer of the head and neck (Zheng et al. 2001). These investigators demonstrated that carriers of the **A/*A* genotype, on average, had diagnoses of cancer 3.5 years earlier than did carriers of the **G/*G* genotype. Wang and colleagues (2002) reported that the **A/*A* genotype was associated with a significantly higher risk of transitional cell carcinoma of the bladder than that for the **A/*G* plus **G/*G* genotypes (OR = 1.76; 95 percent CI, 1.09–2.84). However, neither Cortessis and colleagues (2003) nor Yu and colleagues (2003) reported significant associations with either bladder cancer or esophageal SCC, respectively. Spitz and colleagues (2005) demonstrated an increased risk for lung cancer associated with this polymorphism. The risk estimate was 1.35 (95 percent CI, 1.05–1.73) for the **A/*A* and **A/*G* genotypes compared with the **G/*G* genotypes.

P21 Protein

Cell-cycle inhibitor protein P21 (WAF1/CIP1) acts as a checkpoint regulator for the G_1/S and G_2/M phases. Markwick and colleagues (2002) showed a significant increase in P21 mRNA expression in alveolar epithelial cells after exposure to condensate from cigarette smoke and concluded that oxidative stress induced by cigarette smoke modulates the expression of P21.

Three studies of lung cancer have examined the association of cancer risk with a polymorphism of *P21* at codon 31 (*SER31ARG*), but the findings were inconsistent. Själander and colleagues (1996) reported an increased frequency of the variant allele (**ARG*) among patients with lung cancer (p <0.004). Two other studies failed to replicate this finding (Shih et al. 2000; Su et al. 2003). However, Chen and colleagues (2002) reported that the variant allele (**ARG*) was associated with increased risk of bladder cancer.

TP53 Gene

Studies have reported 14 polymorphisms in the *TP53* gene, 3 of which have been widely studied: a G→C polymorphism at codon 72 (proline/arginine), a 16bp insertion in intron 3, and a G→A transition in intron 6. Polymorphisms in codons 21, 36, and 213 are silent. The polymorphism in codon 47 involves a rare allele with a frequency less than 5 percent. The codon 72 polymorphism on exon 4 produces variant proteins with an arginine (CGC) or proline (CCC) at the site. Thomas and colleagues (1999) reported differences between the two variants in their ability to interact with basic elements of the transcriptional machinery and to induce apoptosis. Weston and colleagues (1992) reported an increased frequency of the proline allele in lung adenocarcinoma, which was consistent with findings in a Japanese study of lung cancer (Kawajiri et al. 1993). Jin and colleagues (1995) reported significantly higher risks for the **PRO/*PRO* genotype among patients with lung cancer who were younger than 55 years of age and among patients reporting fewer than 30 pack-years of smoking. In a study of NSCLC, Nelson and coworkers (2005) found that mutation on the **PRO* allele was associated with a significantly worse outcome than that for patients with no mutation or with mutation on the **ARG* allele.

Mutations in intron sequences may initiate aberrant pre-mRNA splicing that results in a defective protein (Hillebrandt et al. 1997) or that may influence mutations in the coding region. Either result would increase the likelihood of a deleterious phenotype (Malkinson and You 1994). Biroš and colleagues (2001) reported a higher percentage of the intron 6 variant allele in patients with lung cancer than in control participants. However, Birgander and colleagues (1995) found no association of the allele with lung cancer. Several studies estimated the pairwise haplotype frequencies for the polymorphisms in exon 4 and introns 3 and 6. The researchers proposed that the *P53* haplotypes were associated with a higher risk for lung cancer (Birgander et al. 1995; Biroš et al. 2001). In one study of 635 pairs of lung cancer patients and control participants, variant alleles of *TP53* exon 4, introns 3 and 6, and their variant haplotypes were associated with an increased risk of lung cancer (Wu et al. 2002). In a meta-analysis of *TP53* polymorphisms and lung cancer risk that included data from 16 case-control studies, Matakidou and colleagues (2003) concluded that persons with the *P53* exon 4 **PRO/*PRO* genotype had a 1.18-fold increase in lung cancer risk (OR = 1.18; 95 percent CI, 0.99–1.41). Other researchers have observed a similar association with polymorphisms of *P53* introns 3 and 6. However, evidence of these associations has not been consistent (Wang et al. 1999; Mabrouk et al. 2003).

P73 Gene

The *P73* gene activates the promoters of several genes that are responsive to the *TP53* gene and participate in cell-cycle control, DNA repair, and apoptosis and inhibit cell growth in a P53-like manner by inducing apoptosis or cell-cycle arrest in the G_1 phase (Nomoto et al. 1998; Cai et al. 2000). Loss of heterozygosity at the *P73* locus is relatively common. Studies have identified an estimated 17 polymorphisms. Two common SNPs at positions 4 (G→A) and 14 (C→T) in the uncoding region of exon 2 of the *P73* gene are in complete linkage disequilibrium and may affect *P73* function by altering the efficiency of translation initiation (Kaghad et al. 1997).

Studies have reported the role of the *P73* G4C14→A4T14 polymorphism in the risk of smoking-related cancer (Ryan et al. 2001; Hamajima et al. 2002; Hiraki et al. 2003; Huang et al. 2003). In NSCLC, the most significant effect observed was among male smokers (OR = 1.87; 95 percent CI, 1.25–2.80) with SCLC, suggesting that this *P73* polymorphism may have an impact on the repair of tobacco-associated DNA damage. A study of 1,054 patients with lung cancer and 1,139 control participants found a dose-response relationship between the frequency of heterozygous or homozygous variant alleles and risk of lung cancer (trend test, p <0.001). ORs were 1.32 (95 percent CI, 1.10–1.59) for the frequency of heterozygous alleles and 1.54 (95 percent CI, 1.05–2.26) for the frequency of homozygous alleles (Li et al. 2004b). The risk of lung cancer was more pronounced in persons younger than 50 years of age, men, light smokers, and patients with SCLC. The variant genotypes were also associated with an increased risk for SCCs of the head and neck that was statistically significant (OR = 1.33) and an even higher risk among current smokers (OR = 1.77) (Li et al. 2004a).

Other Aspects

Carcinogenic Effects of Whole Mixture and Fractions of Tobacco Smoke

Researchers have conducted inhalation studies of cigarette smoke in hamsters, rats, mice, rabbits, dogs, and nonhuman primates. The model systems used in these studies had various problems, including the inability of any study to accurately duplicate human smoking behaviors. Nevertheless, comprehensive reviews of these studies have found a large amount of useful information (IARC 1986, 2004; Coggins 1998; Witschi 2000). Researchers observed the most consistent results on cancer induction in Syrian golden hamsters; whole cigarette smoke and its particulate phase induced malignant tumors and other lesions in the larynx. Tumors were not induced by the gas phase of cigarette smoke.

Findings of studies that induced malignant tumors by inhalation of cigarette smoke and its particulate phase are consistent with those in the substantial amount of literature demonstrating that condensate from cigarette smoke, which lacks volatile constituents of the gas phase, causes benign and malignant tumors when applied to mouse skin and rabbit ears or instilled in rat lungs by intrapulmonary administration (Hoffmann et al. 1978; IARC 1986, 2004). Collectively, these results clearly show that major carcinogenic fractions of cigarette smoke reside in the particulate phase.

Extensive fractionation studies were conducted with cigarette smoke condensate (Hoffmann et al. 1978). Bioassays of the resulting fractions applied to the skin of mice demonstrated that the neutral portion of the condensate has carcinogenic activity and the acidic portion has tumor-promoting and cocarcinogenic activity. The recombined neutral and acidic portions accounted for about 80 percent of the carcinogenic activity of the condensate. Subfractionation of the neutral portion revealed that certain PAHs were the major tumor initiators in this fraction. However, these PAHs alone, in the levels at which they occur, were insufficient to induce tumors. Moreover, when these PAHs were added to the condensate, the tumor yield was higher than with the condensate alone. These results indicate that the combination of PAHs acting as tumor initiators, together with cocarcinogens in the condensate, accounted for the tumorigenicity of the condensate on mouse skin. Researchers identified catechol and alkyl catechols as major cocarcinogens in the condensate, and the weakly acidic portion of the condensate demonstrated tumor-promoting activity (Van Duuren and Goldschmidt 1976; Hecht et al. 1981). Other cocarcinogens in cigarette smoke include undecane, pyrene, fluoranthene, and B[*a*]P (Van Duuren and Goldschmidt 1976). The identity of tumor promoters in cigarette smoke is largely unknown, although simple phenols may contribute weakly (Hecht et al. 1975). Researchers have also observed tumor-promoting activity of cigarette smoke in inhalation experiments with hamsters (IARC 1986). PAH-enriched fractions of cigarette smoke condensate instilled in the rat lung also resulted in tumor formation (IARC 1986).

These results clearly demonstrate the carcinogenic, tumor-promoting, and cocarcinogenic activity of the particulate phase of cigarette smoke. However, some data indicate that constituents of the gas phase also contribute to tumor induction. Early studies in Snell's mice demonstrated an increase in pulmonary adenocarcinomas in animals exposed to the gas phase alone (IARC 2004). In an exposure model using 89 percent sidestream smoke and 11 percent mainstream smoke, increased multiplicity of lung adenomas was consistently observed in A/J mice exposed to the smoke for five months, followed by a four-month resting period. Tumor response in this model was clearly attributable to the gas phase, because filtration had no effect on multiplicity of lung adenomas (Witschi 2000; IARC 2004). The results of these studies indicate that a volatile carcinogen in cigarette smoke—possibly 1,3-butadiene—produced a tumorigenic response in the A/J mouse lung.

Two other studies not included in the reviews previously cited here demonstrate convincingly that cigarette smoke administered to rats or mice by whole-body exposure for extended periods induces benign and malignant tumors of the respiratory tract (Mauderly et al. 2004; Hutt et al. 2005). When male and female F-344 rats were exposed to smoke from 1R3 research cigarettes or to clean air for six hours per day, five days per week for up to 30 months, the exposure significantly increased the incidence of nonneoplastic and neoplastic proliferative lung lesions in females. The combined incidence of bronchoalveolar adenomas and carcinomas was 14 percent in the high-exposure group (250 mg of particulates per m^3 of air), 6 percent in the low-exposure group (100 mg/m^3), and none in the controls. Mutations in codon 12 of the *KRAS* gene occurred in 4 of 23 tumors. Both males and females had significant increases in neoplasia of the nasal cavity (Mauderly et al. 2004). Female B6C3F1 mice were exposed to smoke for 6 hours per day, 5 days per week, for 925 days (250 mg/m^3) or were sham exposed. The incidence of lung adenoma (28 percent) and lung adenocarcinoma (20 percent) in the mice exposed to smoke were significant (Hutt et al. 2005).

Synergistic Interactions in Tobacco Carcinogenesis

Alcohol

There is persuasive epidemiologic evidence that alcohol consumption and smoking synergistically increase the risk for cancers of the oral cavity, pharynx, larynx, and esophagus (IARC 2004). No single mechanism clearly explains these observations, but several have been proposed and there is reasonable support for some. The most consistent body of evidence relates to the effects of alcohol on the distribution of carcinogenic nitrosamines. Swann and colleagues (1984) demonstrated that alcohol could inhibit the hepatic metabolism and clearance of NDMA, a carcinogen in tobacco smoke. This inhibition occurs because ethanol competitively inhibits hepatic cytochrome P-450 2E1, the main hepatic enzyme responsible for metabolism of NDMA. Consequently, more NDMA reaches extrahepatic tissues where it can be metabolically activated and has the potential to cause cancer. Anderson and coworkers (1992, 1996) demonstrated that coadministration of ethanol and NDMA to A/J mice resulted in an incidence of lung tumors higher than that in mice treated with NDMA alone and that this increase was a consequence of inhibition of hepatic metabolism and not of tumor promotion. Furthermore, administration of ethanol to patas monkeys before they received NDMA resulted in a 14.6-fold increase in O^6-methylguanine in esophageal DNA and other extrahepatic tissues (Anderson et al. 1996).

Another potential mechanism also involves the effects of ethanol on P-450 2E1, but as an inducer of this enzyme. Chronic ethanol consumption is known to induce production of hepatic P-450 2E1, and researchers hypothesized that this induction could lead to increased metabolic activation of carcinogens in tobacco smoke (McCoy et al. 1979). Some *N*-nitrosamines in tobacco smoke—NDMA, *N*-nitrosodiethylamine, and *N*-nitrosopyrrolidine—are all substrates for P-450 2E1. McCoy and colleagues (1981) demonstrated that chronic ethanol consumption in hamsters increased the metabolism of *N*-nitrosopyrrolidine in hepatic and target tissue (e.g., trachea), as well as the carcinogenicity of this nitrosamine, which increases the occurrence of tumors in the nasal cavity and trachea. The carcinogenicity of *N*-nitrosodiethylamine in the rat esophagus was also increased by simultaneous administration of ethanol (Gibel 1967). Overall, however, the effects of ethanol consumption on *N*-nitrosamine carcinogenesis have been mixed, and they appear to depend on the *N*-nitrosamine studied and the protocol used. For example, long-term ethanol consumption had no effect on the carcinogenicity of NNN in the hamster and only modest or no effect in the rat (McCoy et al. 1981; Trushin et al. 1984).

Other mechanisms for the enhancing effect of alcohol consumption on tobacco carcinogenesis have been discussed (Pöschl and Seitz 2004). Persons who abuse alcohol generally have nutritional deficiencies, which could exacerbate the effects of smoking. They commonly have folate deficiency that could contribute to an inhibition of transmethylation, which is important in gene regulation. Zinc deficiency is known to result in enhanced carcinogenesis in the rat esophagus (Fong et al. 2001). Reduced serum and hepatic levels of vitamin A in persons with long-term alcohol abuse may affect carcinogenesis. Alcohol could also act as a solvent, increasing absorption of tobacco carcinogens (Squier et al. 1986).

Asbestos

Smoking and exposure to asbestos interact synergistically to increase the risk for lung cancer (IARC 2004). The mechanism for this synergy is unknown. Researchers have investigated a number of possibilities, however, and these have been summarized (Nelson and Kelsey 2002). It has been proposed that asbestos fibers serve as a vehicle to deliver tobacco carcinogens to the cell nucleus. Surfactant phospholipids may help to solubilize carcinogenic PAH, increasing their concentrations in the lung epithelium. Studies have also demonstrated that asbestos fibers can induce chromosomal aberrations and extensive deletions, potentially adding to the DNA damage produced by carcinogens in tobacco smoke. Furthermore, asbestos may cause oxidative damage that could be related to inflammation and cell death related to pulmonary fibrosis associated with exposure to asbestos. It seems likely that asbestos fibers could cause proliferation that may increase the probability of mutations attributable to DNA damage by tobacco smoke carcinogens.

Carcinogens as Causes of Specific Cancers

Data from carcinogenicity studies, product analyses, and findings from studies using biochemistry and molecular biology support a significant role for certain carcinogens in tobacco-induced cancer (Table 5.12).

Considerable evidence favors PAHs and NNK as major factors in development of lung cancer. PAHs are strong carcinogens acting locally; thus, fractions of tobacco smoke enriched in these compounds are carcinogenic (Hoffmann et al. 1978; Deutsch-Wenzel et al. 1983; IARC 1983) (see "Carcinogens in Cigarette Smoke" earlier in this chapter). Researchers have detected PAH-DNA adducts in human lungs, and the spectrum of mutations in the *TP53* gene isolated from lung tumors was similar to the pattern of DNA damage produced in vitro by PAH diol epoxide metabolites and in cell cultures by B[*a*]P (Pfeifer et al. 2002; Phillips 2002; Boysen and Hecht 2003; Liu et al. 2005) (see "DNA Adducts and Biomarkers" earlier in this chapter).

NNK is a strong systemic carcinogen in lungs of rodents that induces lung tumors independent of the route of administration (Hecht 1998). NNK was found to

be particularly potent in the rat. Significant incidence of lung tumors was induced by total doses as low as 6 mg/kilogram (kg) of body weight or by 1.8 mg/kg as part of a dose-response trend. These doses are comparable to an estimated NNK dose of 1.1 mg/kg in persons who have smoked for 40 years (Hecht 1998). DNA adducts derived from NNK or from the related tobacco-specific nitrosamine, NNN, are present in lung tissue from smokers, and metabolites of NNK are found in the urine of smokers (Hecht 2002b). Epidemiologic data indicate that a systemic carcinogen causes lung cancer in cigar smokers who do not inhale the smoke; this finding is consistent with the tumorigenic properties of NNK (Boffetta et al. 1999; Shapiro et al. 2000).

The changing histology of lung cancer is also consistent with the role of NNK: adenocarcinoma has now overtaken SCC as the most common lung cancer type. This nitrosamine in tobacco smoke produces primarily adenocarcinomas in rodents. However, this outcome has also been attributed to differing inhalation patterns of current cigarette smokers (Travis et al. 1995; Hecht 1998). As nitrate concentrations in tobacco increased from 1959 to 1997, NNK concentrations in mainstream smoke increased and those of B[*a*]P decreased. Researchers attributed these changes to tobacco blends with higher levels of air-cured tobacco, the use of reconstituted tobacco, and other factors (Hoffmann et al. 2001). Other compounds that could be involved in lung cancer include 1,3-butadiene, isoprene, ethylene oxide, ethyl carbamate, aldehydes, benzene, metals, and oxidants, but the collective evidence for each of these substances is not as strong as the evidence for PAHs and NNK (Hecht 1999).

The particulate phase of cigarette smoke causes tumors of the larynx in hamsters, which could be attributed to PAHs (IARC 1986). *TP53* gene mutations identified in tumors of the human larynx support a role for PAHs in the development of this cancer (Pfeifer et al. 2002). *N*-nitrosamines, as well as acetaldehyde and formaldehyde, induce nasal tumors in rodents and are likely candidates for causing nasal tumors associated with smoking (Preussmann and Stewart 1984; IARC 1995c, 1999). On the basis of animal studies, PAH, NNK, and NNN are the most likely causes of oral cancer in smokers (Hoffmann and Hecht 1990). *N*-nitrosamines are the most effective esophageal carcinogens known. NNN causes tumors of the esophagus in rats and is the most prevalent *N*-nitrosamine carcinogen in cigarette smoke (Hecht and Hoffmann 1989; Lijinsky 1992).

NNK and several other *N*-nitrosamines and furan in cigarette smoke are effective hepatocarcinogens in rats (Preussmann and Stewart 1984; IARC 1995b). NNK and its major metabolite NNAL are the only known pancreatic carcinogens in tobacco products. Biochemical data from

Table 5.12   Carcinogens and tobacco-induced cancers

Study	Cancer type	Likely carcinogen involvement[a]
Hoffmann and Hecht 1990 Hecht et al. 1994 Törnqvist and Ehrenberg 1994 Hecht 1999 Hoffmann et al. 2001 Pfeifer et al. 2002	Lung	PAHs, NNK (major), 1,3-butadiene, isoprene, ethylene oxide, ethyl carbamate, aldehydes, benzene, metals
IARC 1986 Hoffmann et al. 2001 Pfeifer et al. 2002	Larynx	PAHs
Preussmann and Stewart 1984 IARC 1995c, 1999 Hecht 1998	Nasal	NNK, NNN, other nitrosamines, aldehydes
Hecht et al. 1986 Hoffmann et al. 1987, 1995, 2001 Hecht and Hoffmann 1988, 1989 Hoffmann and Hecht 1990 Hecht 1998 Vainio and Weiderpass 2003	Oral cavity	PAHs, NNK, NNN
Hecht and Hoffmann 1989 Lijinsky 1992 Hecht 1998 Hoffmann et al. 2001	Esophagus	NNN, other nitrosamines
Preussmann and Stewart 1984 IARC 1995a Hecht 1998	Liver	NNK, other nitrosamines, furan
Rivenson et al. 1988 Hecht 1998 Hoffmann et al. 2001 Prokopczyk et al. 2002	Pancreas	NNK, NNAL
Melikian et al. 1999 Prokopczyk et al. 2001 Phillips 2002	Cervix	PAHs, NNK
IARC 1974 Hoffmann and Hecht 1990 Skipper and Tannenbaum 1990 Skipper et al. 1994 Landi et al. 1996 Probst-Hensch et al. 2000 Hoffmann et al. 2001	Bladder	4-aminobiphenyl, other aromatic amines
IARC 1982	Leukemia	Benzene

Source: Adapted from Hecht 2003 with permission.
Note: **IARC** = International Agency for Research on Cancer; **NNAL** = 4-(methylnitrosamino)-1-(3-pyridyl)-1-butanol; **NNK** = 4-(methylnitrosamino)-1-(3-pyridyl)-1-butanone; **NNN** = *N'*-nitrosonornicotine; **PAHs** = polycyclic aromatic hydrocarbons.
[a]Based on carcinogenicity studies in laboratory animals, biochemical evidence from human tissues and fluids, and epidemiologic data when available.

studies of human tissue provide some support for the role of these carcinogens in smoking-related pancreatic cancer, although the studies did not detect DNA adducts (Rivenson et al. 1988; Prokopczyk et al. 2002, 2005). Biochemical studies demonstrate that both NNK and PAHs can reach the cervix in humans and are metabolically activated in these tissues (Melikian et al. 1999; Prokopczyk et al. 2001). Researchers have detected DNA adducts derived from B[*a*]P and other hydrophobic compounds in cervical tissue from smokers (Melikian et al. 1999; Phillips 2002). Therefore, in combination with the human papilloma virus, these compounds may contribute to development of cervical cancer in smokers (IARC 1995a). 4-ABP and 2-naphthylamine are known human bladder carcinogens, and considerable data from human studies support the role of aromatic amines as the major cause of bladder cancer in smokers (IARC 1974; Skipper and Tannenbaum 1990; Skipper et al. 1994; Landi et al. 1996; Probst-Hensch et al. 2000; Castelao et al. 2001). The most probable cause of leukemia in smokers is exposure to benzene, which occurs in large quantities in cigarette smoke and is a known cause of acute myelogenous leukemia in humans (IARC 1982).

Cigarette smoke causes oxidative damage probably because it contains free radicals, such as nitric oxide, and contains mixtures of hydroquinones, semiquinones, and quinones that can induce reduction and oxidation (redox cycling) (Pryor et al. 1998; Hecht 1999). Smokers have lower levels of ascorbic acid in plasma and, sometimes, higher levels of oxidized DNA bases in white blood cells than do nonsmokers. However, the role of oxidative damage as a cause of specific tobacco-induced cancers remains unclear (Hecht 1999).

Tobacco Carcinogens, Immune System, and Cancer

Cigarette smoke alters a range of immunological functions including innate and adaptive immune responses (Sopori 2002). These effects, acting as tumor-promoting or cocarcinogenic stimuli, could affect tobacco-related carcinogenesis. Cigarette smoking increases the number of alveolar macrophages in the lung, possibly leading to higher levels of oxygen radicals and MPO activity, which are hypothesized to be important in tumor promotion. Investigators examined the effects of smoking on the function of natural killer (NK) cells—a lymphoid cell type involved in surveillance of tumor growth (Lu et al. 2007). They obtained strong evidence that suppression of NK cell activation was related to increased lung metastases in mice exposed to cigarette

smoke. Other studies demonstrated that nicotine is immunosuppressive and thus might be responsible for some of the effects of cigarette smoke (Sopori 2002).

Epidemiology of Family History and Lung Cancer

Studies of familial aggregation of lung cancer provide indirect evidence supporting the possibility of an inherited component to tobacco carcinogenesis. A number of published studies showed that significantly more lung cancers were reported in first-degree relatives of probands with lung cancer than were reported in first-degree relatives of healthy control participants. Assuming that the family structure does not differ between cases and controls, this pattern could be explained by shared genes among the family members, shared smoking patterns, or a combination of both factors. By incorporating smoking histories of the probands and the first-degree relatives into a study of familial aggregation, researchers can begin to assess the level of familial risk of cancer while adjusting for tobacco use. However, few studies of familial aggregation incorporate history of involuntary exposure of family members to tobacco smoke. Estimates of the overall proportion of patients with lung cancer who have family history of lung cancer in a first-degree relative range from 6 (Li and Hemminki 2004) to 16 percent (Sellers et al. 1992).

Forty years ago, Tokuhata and Lilienfeld (1963) observed that the number of deaths from lung cancer was higher among relatives of lung cancer case patients than it was among relatives of control participants. These researchers also reported a fourfold excess of lung cancer mortality in nonsmoking relatives of 270 lung cancer probands. The effect among relatives who smoked was less pronounced (twofold). These findings suggest that the risk was not solely attributable to shared smoking patterns in the relatives. Other studies have since demonstrated a familial component of risk for lung cancer. The ORs associated with family history ranged from 1.3 to 7.2 (Ooi et al. 1986; Samet et al. 1986; Wu et al. 1988, 1996; Osann 1991; Shaw et al. 1991; Schwartz et al. 1996; Mayne et al. 1999). For example, in a comparison of 336 lung cancer probands with relatives of control spouses, Ooi and colleagues (1986) reported an association between a family history of lung cancer and a threefold excess risk (OR = 3.09; 95 percent CI, 1.9–5.0). Shaw and associates (1991) found an OR of 2.8 (95 percent CI, 1.2–6.6) for risk of lung cancer among two or more relatives of case patients. Brownson and colleagues (1997) reported a trend for increasing risk associated with the number of first-degree relatives with lung cancer. The risk was more than twofold for persons with five affected family members.

One approach that evaluates familial aggregation while controlling for the impact of smoking focused on lifetime nonsmokers. Wu and colleagues (2004) evaluated 216 lung cancer probands who were female non-smokers and reported that family history of lung cancer was associated with a 5.7-fold (OR = 5.7; 95 percent CI, 1.9–16.9) increase in lung cancer risk. Wu and colleagues (1988) noted, after adjustment for exposure to second-hand smoke, a 30-percent increase in risk that was not statistically significant for history of cancers of the respiratory tract. This association was especially evident in mothers and sisters. The risk was also slightly elevated for lung cancer (OR = 1.3; 95 percent CI, 1.0–1.6). Mayne and colleagues (1999) also focused on familial risk in a population-based, case-control study of 437 lifetime nonsmokers and former smokers who had lung cancer and 437 matched control participants. The investigators observed increased risk of cancers of the aerodigestive tract among parents of case patients (OR = 2.78; 95 percent CI, 1.30–5.95) and increased risk of lung cancer among siblings and offspring of case patients (OR = 4.14; 95 percent CI, 0.88–19.46; p = 0.07). They also reported approximately twofold increases in risk of breast cancer among mothers (OR = 2.52; 95 percent CI, 1.21–5.24) and sisters (OR = 2.07; 95 percent CI, 0.99–4.31) of lung cancer patients who were nonsmokers. On the other hand, Kreuzer and colleagues (2002) reported no evidence of familial risk in 234 lung cancer probands who were female nonsmokers.

Other investigators have reported familial aggregation of lung cancer among relatives of case patients who were nonsmokers with early-onset of lung cancer (at ≤60 years of age). Schwartz and colleagues (1996) noted that family members of these case patients (aged 40 to 59 years) had a sixfold increase in risk of lung cancer after adjustments for the age, gender, and race of each relative. In a subsequent study involving 118 population-based probands, Schwartz and colleagues (1999) also showed that family members of case patients younger than 40 years of age who had lung cancer were at increased risk for other cancers. Kreuzer and colleagues (1998) concluded that lung cancer in a first-degree relative was associated with a 2.6-fold increase in risk of lung cancer among young case patients younger than 46 years of age. Elevated risk was not detected in older case patients. A study in Germany of 945 lung cancer cases and 983 controls reported increased risk of lung cancer among first-degree relatives (RR = 1.7; 95 percent CI, 1.1–2.5) and a 4.75-fold increase in risk among relatives of probands younger than 50 years of age who had a diagnosis of lung cancer (Bromen et al. 2000). Radzikowska and colleagues (2001) also noted stronger evidence from a study in Poland for aggregation of cancers among 757 patients with lung cancer who were younger than 50 years of age.

On the other hand, Etzel and colleagues (2003) observed the familial aggregation of lung cancer and smoking-related cancers in late-onset lung cancers in persons older than 55 years of age, but not in early-onset lung cancers. An advantage of this study was the ability to adjust for the smoking status of the relatives. The study noted an excess of cancer among relatives of probands who were current smokers but not among relatives of lifetime nonsmokers. More recently, Li and Hemminki (2004) evaluated familial risks by using data from the Swedish Family Cancer Database and demonstrated that the histologic type of lung cancer in relatives was generally random. These researchers also estimated that 25 percent of familial lung cancers were diagnosed before 50 years of age, which represented about 1.6 percent of all lung cancers before 68 years of age.

However, a cohort study of lung cancer mortality among male twins showed no role for genetic predisposition (Braun et al. 1994). Li and colleagues (1998b) used a parametric likelihood approach and adjustment for shared covariates to study familial association in the age at onset that they hypothesized to be attributable to genetic factors. The analysis indicated that a history of smoking, exposure to secondhand smoke, and chronic obstructive airway disease were all associated with lung cancer risk. After adjustments were made for these factors, there was little evidence of familial aggregation.

In a recent series with high-risk multiplex families, Bailey-Wilson and colleagues (2004) mapped a major susceptibility locus of lung cancer through a genome-wide linkage analysis to chromosome 6q23–25 near the *PARKIN* gene, which carries predisposition for a significantly increased hereditary risk of lung cancer. A study of this locus also indicated presence of gene-environment interaction, and even light smoking by carriers of this gene significantly increased the risk for lung cancer compared with that among heavy smokers. Carriers who did not smoke had much lower risk, comparable to risk for noncarriers. This finding indicated existence of a sensitive group of persons for whom any amount of smoking is deleterious.

Studies have also presented evidence of Mendelian inheritance in lung cancer. Sellers and colleagues (1990) found that the pattern of occurrence of lung cancer was compatible with the Mendelian codominant inheritance of a rare and major autosomal gene. However, a similar study of families with lung cancer probands who did not smoke revealed no evidence for a major gene model and reported that an environmental model best explained the segregation pattern in the data (Yang et al. 1997).

Gauderman and Morrison (2000) determined that when the same data were analyzed but missing data for smoking behaviors were produced from modeling techniques, a single autosomal dominant locus provided a slightly better fit than the codominant model suggested by Sellers and colleagues (1990). In addition to possible etiologic heterogeneity, the inconsistency of these findings may be partly due to the insufficient power for the statistical analysis of limited sample sizes. A reanalysis by Yang and colleagues (1999) found evidence of a major gene with the Mendelian codominant model in the families of probands of nonsmokers younger than 60 years of age. This analysis rejected both the codominant and environmental models and suggested that multiple genetic and/or environmental factors contribute to the age at onset of lung cancer. Therefore, researchers need more complex genetic models for the distribution of age at onset.

Xu and colleagues (2005) completed a segregation analysis on 14,378 persons from 1,561 case families with aggregation of lung cancer. In their modeling, these researchers adjusted for the effects of smoking, gender, and age. This work provided evidence for a model involving multiple gene loci and interactions that contribute to the age at onset of lung cancer.

One caveat that applies to all of these studies is the validity of data on family history, an issue indirectly addressed in an evaluation of family histories of cancer in participants in the Prostate, Lung, Colorectal and Ovarian Cancer Screening Trial (Pinsky et al. 2003). The data showed that in the ratios of reported-to-expected rates of cancer in family members, there were important differences in rates of reporting family history of cancer according to the gender, race, ethnicity, and age of the respondents. These differences were mostly due to underreporting with respect to these covariates. Ziogas and Anton-Culver (2003) found that family histories of cancer reported by probands were more accurate for first-degree relatives and that probands referred through clinics had lower false-positive rates for reporting of family history than did population-based probands. Bondy and colleagues (1994) evaluated the accuracy of cancer diagnosis reported by probands among family members by comparing reported cancer information with documentation available through medical records and death certificates. The study noted high levels of accuracy for cancers of first-degree relatives, as evidenced by agreement between reporting by probands and information in records. Thus, these findings of familial aggregation suggest a role for the inherited susceptibility of lung cancer beyond that associated with familial clustering of smoking behaviors, taking into account family size and structure.

A genomewide association study in 2008 identified a region of strong linkage disequilibrium on the long arm of chromosome 15 as a susceptibility locus for lung cancer (Amos et al. 2008). Studies replicating this association have focused attention on the most likely candidate genes in this region, *CHRNA3* and *CHRNA5*, which encode subunits of the nAChR (Hung et al. 2008). Le Marchand and colleagues (2008) found that carriers of the lung-cancer-associated variants in these genes extract more nicotine and are thus exposed to a higher internal dose of carcinogenic nicotine-derived nitrosamines. SNPs in the same region have also been associated with nicotine dependence and smoking intensity (Caporaso et al. 2009).

Evidence Summary

Although cigarette smoke contains diverse carcinogens, PAH, *N*-nitrosamines, aromatic amines, 1,3-butadiene, benzene, aldehydes, and ethylene oxide are among the most important carcinogens because of their carcinogenic potency and levels in cigarette smoke. Moreover, the major pathways of metabolic activation and detoxification of some of the principal carcinogens in cigarette smoke are well established. Reactive intermediate agents critical in forming DNA adducts include diol epoxides of PAH, diazonium ions generated by α-hydroxylation of nitrosamines, nitrenium ions formed from esters of *N*-hydroxylated aromatic amines, and epoxides such as ethylene oxide. Glutathione and glucuronide conjugation play major roles in detoxification of carcinogens in cigarette smoke.

Familial predisposition and genetic polymorphisms may play a role in tobacco-related neoplasms. Researchers have established cigarette smoking as a major cause of lung cancer; more than 85 percent of lung cancers are attributable to smoking. However, not all smokers develop lung cancer, and lung cancer can arise in lifetime nonsmokers. This variation in disease has stimulated interest in molecular epidemiology of genetic polymorphisms, including genes that regulate the cell cycle and genes for carcinogen-metabolizing enzymes that may lead to variations in susceptibility to the carcinogens in tobacco smoke. Studies to date suggest a role for these genetic polymorphisms in the risk of lung and bladder cancer in smokers, and they support the possibility of interactions between genes and smoking status.

Quantitative analysis of carcinogens or their metabolites in urine, breath, and blood provides a convenient and reliable method of comparing exposure to carcinogens among smokers and between smokers and nonsmokers. Urinary biomarkers of several major types of carcinogens in cigarette smoke are reliable indicators of exposure, and the measurements provide good estimates of minimum doses of relevant carcinogens in smokers and allow comparisons with nonsmokers. The total carcinogen dose is generally difficult to calculate because the extent of conversion of a given carcinogen to the measured metabolite is usually unknown. However, relative carcinogen levels in cigarettes generally correlate with metabolite levels in urine. Comparisons of smokers and nonsmokers demonstrate that total NNAL is the most discriminatory biomarker in that tobacco products are the only source of the parent carcinogen NNK.

Evidence is overwhelming that DNA adduct levels are higher in most tissues of smokers than in corresponding tissues of nonsmokers. This observation provides bedrock support for the major pathway of cancer induction in smokers that proceeds through formation of DNA adducts and genetic damage. Studies of specific adducts are still scarce and are limited mainly to human lung tissue. Strong evidence supports the presence of a variety of specific adducts in the human lung, and in several studies, adduct levels are higher in smokers than in nonsmokers. Collectively, the results of these biomarker studies clearly demonstrate the potential for genetic damage in smokers from the persistence of DNA adducts.

Adducts lead to mutations that drive the process of tumor formation and progression through additional genetic alterations. Chromosomal losses are more common in tumors from smokers. Furthermore, inactivating mutations of the *TP53* tumor-suppressor gene and activating mutations of the *KRAS* oncogene in NSCLCs and other tumors are correlated with exposure to cigarette smoke, and they contribute to a phenotype that reduces survival time in both early and advanced stages of the disease. Different types of lung cancer in smokers all show an excess of G→T transversions compared with cancers that are not related to exposure to tobacco smoke. The site specificity of mutagenesis by PAH diol epoxides implies that targeted adduct formation, in addition to phenotypic selection, is responsible for shaping the *TP53* mutational spectrum in lung tumors. Propagation of these genetic alterations during clonal outgrowth is consistent with accumulation of multiple genetic changes observed in progression of lung cancer.

Gene promoter hypermethylation is an epigenetic change involving extensive methylation at the 5-position of C in CpG islands within the promoter region and often extending into exon 1 of regulatory genes. The end result of this process can be loss of gene transcription and therefore the silencing of gene function. Promoter methylation of several genes including *P16* occurs early in tumor formation. *P16* methylation was significantly associated with pack-years of smoking and was an independent risk factor for shorter survival in patients with early resectable adenocarcinomas. Other genes such as *RASSF1A* may be more frequently methylated in various tumor types from smokers. Methylation of genes, such as *AGT* promoter hypermethylation, may increase G→A transition mutations at CpG sites within the *TP53* gene in NSCLC.

The activation of nAChRs in lung epithelial cells by nicotine or NNK promotes survival and proliferation of cancer cells and also leads to increased angiogenesis. Activation of cell-surface receptors induced by components of tobacco smoke and subsequent activation of cytoplasmic kinases stimulate other proteins that dictate cellular responses, such as cell survival and proliferation. Although activated kinases have many downstream targets, the two most studied are the transcription factor NF-κB and proteins in the BCL-2 family. Activation of key intracellular proteins by tobacco smoke components through signaling cascades promotes processes that are important for initiation, progression, and maintenance of cancer. Apoptosis, the normal mechanism of endogenous cell elimination, is also commonly suppressed in lung cancer by these components. Thus, key genetic and epigenetic events that lead to cancer causation, as well as critical cellular pathways that further growth and development of transformed cells, are directly targeted by components of cigarette smoke individually and in combination as a potent carcinogenic mixture.

Conclusions

1. The doses of cigarette smoke carcinogens resulting from inhalation of tobacco smoke are reflected in levels of these carcinogens or their metabolites in the urine of smokers. Certain biomarkers are associated with exposure to specific cigarette smoke carcinogens, such as urinary metabolites of the tobacco-specific nitrosamine 4-(methylnitrosamino)-1-(3-pyridyl)-1-butanone and hemoglobin adducts of aromatic amines.

2. The metabolic activation of cigarette smoke carcinogens by cytochrome P-450 enzymes has a direct effect on the formation of DNA adducts.

3. There is consistent evidence that a combination of polymorphisms in the *CYP1A1* and *GSTM1* genes leads to higher DNA adduct levels in smokers and higher relative risks for lung cancer than in those smokers without this genetic profile.

4. Carcinogen exposure and resulting DNA damage observed in smokers results directly in the numerous cytogenetic changes present in lung cancer.

5. Smoking increases the frequency of DNA adducts of cigarette smoke carcinogens such as benzo[*a*]pyrene and tobacco-specific nitrosamines in the lung and other organs.

6. Exposure to cigarette smoke carcinogens leads to DNA damage and subsequent mutations in *TP53* and *KRAS* in lung cancer.

7. There is consistent evidence that smoking leads to the presence of promoter methylation of key tumor suppressor genes such as *P16* in lung cancer and other smoking-caused cancers.

8. There is consistent evidence that smoke constituents such as nicotine and 4-(methylnitrosamino)-1-(3-pyridyl)-1-butanone can activate signal transduction pathways directly through receptor-mediated events, allowing the survival of damaged epithelial cells that would normally die.

9. There is consistent evidence for an inherited susceptibility of lung cancer with some less common genotypes unrelated to a familial clustering of smoking behaviors.

10. Smoking cessation remains the only proven strategy for reducing the pathogenic processes leading to cancer in that the specific contribution of many tobacco carcinogens, alone or in combination, to the development of cancer has not been identified.

References

Abdel-Rahman SZ, Ammenheuser MM, Omiecinski CJ, Wickliffe JK, Rosenblatt JI, Ward JB Jr. Variability in human sensitivity to 1,3-butadiene: influence of polymorphisms in the 5′-flanking region of the microsomal epoxide hydrolase gene (EPHX1). *Toxicological Sciences* 2005;85(1):624–31.

Abdel-Rahman SZ, El-Zein RA. The *399Gln* polymorphism in the DNA repair gene *XRCC1* modulates the genotoxic response induced in human lymphocytes by the tobacco-specific nitrosamine NNK. *Cancer Letters* 2000;159(1):63–71.

Abdel-Rahman SZ, El-Zein RA, Ammenheuser MM, Yang Z, Stock TH, Morandi M, Ward JB Jr. Variability in human sensitivity to 1,3-butadiene: influence of the allelic variants of the microsomal epoxide hydrolase gene. *Environmental and Molecular Mutagenesis* 2003;41(2):140–6.

Aboussekhra A, Biggerstaff M, Shivji MK, Vilpo JA, Moncollin V, Podust VN, Protic M, Hubscher U, Egly JM, Wood RD. Mammalian DNA nucleotide excision repair reconstituted with purified protein components. *Cell* 1995;80(6):859–68.

Acharya S, Wilson T, Gradia S, Kane MF, Guerrette S, Marsischky GT, Kolodner R, Fishel R. hMSH2 forms specific mispair-binding complexes with hMSH3 and hMSH6. *Proceedings of the National Academy of Sciences of the United States of America* 1996;93(24):13629–34.

Achiwa H, Yatabe Y, Hida T, Kuroishi T, Kozaki K, Nakamura S, Ogawa M, Sugiura T, Mitsudomi T, Takahashi T. Prognostic significance of elevated cyclooxygenase 2 expression in primary, resected lung adenocarcinomas. *Clinical Cancer Research* 1999;5(5):1001–5.

Adams JM, Cory S. The Bcl-2 protein family: arbiters of cell survival. *Science* 1998;281(5381):1322–6.

Adjei AA. Blocking oncogenic Ras signaling for cancer therapy. *Journal of the National Cancer Institute* 2001a;93(14):1062–74.

Adjei AA. Ras signaling pathway proteins as therapeutic targets. *Current Pharmaceutical Design* 2001b;7(16):1581–94.

Agathanggelou A, Bièche I, Ahmed-Choudhury J, Nicke B, Dammann R, Baksh S, Gao B, Minna JD, Downward J, Maher ER, et al. Identification of novel gene expression targets for the Ras association domain family 1 (*RASSF1A*) tumor suppressor gene in non-small cell lung cancer and neuroblastoma. *Cancer Research* 2003;63(17):5344–51.

Ahrendt SA, Hu Y, Buta M, McDermott MP, Benoit N, Yang SC, Wu L, Sidransky D. p53 Mutations and survival in stage I non-small-cell lung cancer: results of a prospective study. *Journal of the National Cancer Institute* 2003;95(13):961–70.

Ai L, Stephenson KK, Ling W, Zuo C, Mukunyadzi P, Suen JY, Hanna E, Fan CY. The p16 (CDKN2a/INK4a) tumor-suppressor gene in head and neck squamous cell carcinoma: a promoter methylation and protein expression study in 100 cases. *Modern Pathology* 2003;16(9):944–50.

Alavanja MC, Brown CC, Swanson C, Brownson RC. Saturated fat intake and lung cancer risk among nonsmoking women in Missouri. *Journal of the National Cancer Institute* 1993;85(23):1906–16.

Alavanja MC, Field RW, Sinha R, Brus CP, Shavers VL, Fisher EL, Curtain J, Lynch CF. Lung cancer risk and red meat consumption among Iowa women. *Lung Cancer* 2001;34(1):37–46.

Alexandrie A-K, Nyberg F, Warholm M, Rannug A. Influence of *CYP1A1*, *GSTM1*, *GSTT1*, and *NQO1* genotypes and cumulative smoking dose on lung cancer risk in a Swedish population. *Cancer Epidemiology, Biomarkers & Prevention* 2004;13(6):908–14.

Alexandrie A-K, Sundberg MI, Seidegård J, Tornling G, Rannug A. Genetic susceptibility to lung cancer with special emphasis on *CYP1A1* and *GSTM1*: a study on host factors in relation to age at onset, gender and histological cancer types. *Carcinogenesis* 1994;15(9):1785–90.

Alexandrie A-K, Warholm M, Carstensen U, Axmon A, Hagmar L, Levin JO, Östman C, Rannug A. *CYP1A1* and *GSTM1* polymorphisms affect urinary 1-hydroxypyrene levels after PAH exposure. *Carcinogenesis* 2000;21(4):669–76.

Alexandrov K, Cascorbi I, Rojas M, Bouvier G, Kriek E, Bartsch H. *CYP1A1* and *GSTM1* genotypes affect benzo[a]pyrene DNA adducts in smokers' lung: comparison with aromatic/hydrophobic adduct formation. *Carcinogenesis* 2002;23(12):1969–77.

Al-Tassan N, Chmiel NH, Maynard J, Fleming N, Livingston AL, Williams GT, Hodges AK, Davies DR, David SS, Sampson JR, et al. Inherited variants of *MYH* associated with somatic G:C→T:A mutations in colorectal tumors. *Nature Genetics* 2002;30(2):227–32.

Amann J, Kalyankrishna S, Massion PP, Ohm JE, Girard L, Shigematsu H, Peyton M, Juroske D, Huang Y, Stuart Salmon J, et al. Aberrant epidermal growth factor receptor signaling and enhanced sensitivity to EGFR inhibitors in lung cancer. *Cancer Research* 2005;65(1):226–35.

Ambs S, Bennett WP, Merriam WG, Ogunfusika MO, Oser SM, Harrington AM, Shields PG, Felley-Bosco E, Hussain P, Harris CC. Relationship between p53 mutations and inducible nitric oxide synthase expression in human colorectal cancer. *Journal of the National Cancer Institute* 1999;91(1):86–8.

Amos CI, Wu X, Broderick P, Gorlov IP, Gu J, Eisen T, Dong Q, Zhang Q, Gu X, Vijayakrishnan J, et al. Genome-wide association scan of tag SNPs identifies a susceptibility locus for lung cancer at 15q25.1. *Nature Genetics* 2008;40(5):616–22.

Anderson LM, Carter JP, Logsdon DL, Driver CL, Kovatch RM. Characterization of ethanol's enhancement of tumorigenesis by *N*-nitrosodimethylamine in mice. *Carcinogenesis* 1992;13(11):2107–11.

Anderson LM, Souliotis VL, Chhabra SK, Moskal TJ, Harbaugh SD, Kyrtopoulos SA. *N*-nitrosodimethylamine-derived O^6-methylguanosine in DNA of monkey gastrointestinal and urogenital organs and enhancement by ethanol. *International Journal of Cancer* 1996;66(1):130–4.

Anderson WF, Umar A, Viner JL, Hawk ET. The role of cyclooxygenase inhibitors in cancer prevention. *Current Pharmaceutical Design* 2002;8(12):1035–62.

Angel P, Karin M. The role of Jun, Fos and the AP-1 complex in cell-proliferation and transformation. *Biochimica et Biophysica Acta* 1991;1072(2–3):129–57.

Angerer J, Mannschreck C, Gündel J. Biological monitoring and biochemical effect monitoring of exposure to polycyclic aromatic hydrocarbons. *International Archives of Occupational and Environmental Health* 1997;70(6):365–77.

Anto RJ, Mukhopadhyay A, Shishodia S, Gairola CG, Aggarwal BB. Cigarette smoke condensate activates nuclear transcription factor-κB through phosphorylation and degradation of IκBα: correlation with induction of cyclooxygenase-2. *Carcinogenesis* 2002;23(9):1511–8.

Antonyak MA, Moscatello DK, Wong AJ. Constitutive activation of c-Jun N-terminal kinase by a mutant epidermal growth factor receptor. *Journal of Biological Chemistry* 1998;273(5):2817–22.

Anttila S, Hirvonen A, Husgafvel-Pursiainen K, Karjalainen A, Nurminen T, Vainio H. Combined effect of *CYP1A1* inducibility and *GSTM1* polymorphism on histologic type of lung cancer. *Carcinogenesis* 1994;15(6):1133–5.

Araújo SJ, Tirode F, Coin F, Pospiech H, Syväoja JE, Stucki M, Hübscher U, Egly J-M, Wood RD. Nucleotide excision repair of DNA with recombinant human proteins: definition of the minimal set of factors, active forms of TFIIH, and modulation by CAK. *Genes & Development* 2000;14(3):349–59.

Asami S, Manabe H, Miyake J, Tsurudome Y, Hirano T, Yamaguchi R, Itoh H, Kasai H. Cigarette smoking induces an increase in oxidative DNA damage, 8-hydroxydeoxyguanosine, in a central site of the human lung. *Carcinogenesis* 1997;18(9):1763–6.

Aspinwall R, Rothwell DG, Roldan-Arjona T, Anselmino C, Ward CJ, Cheadle JP, Sampson JR, Lindahl T, Harris PC, Hickson ID. Cloning and characterization of a functional human homolog of *Escherichia coli* endonuclease III. *Proceedings of the National Academy of Sciences of the United States of America* 1997;94(1):109–14.

Athas WF, Hedayati MA, Matanoski GM, Farmer ER, Grossman L. Development and field-test validation of an assay for DNA repair in circulating human lymphocytes. *Cancer Research* 1991;51(21):5786–93.

Aviel-Ronen S, Blackhall FH, Shepherd FA, Tsao MS. *K-ras* mutations in non-small-cell lung carcinoma: a review. *Clinical Lung Cancer* 2006;8(1):30–8.

Badawi AF, Habib SL, Mohammed MA, Abadi AA, Michael MS. Influence of cigarette smoking on prostaglandin synthesis and cyclooxygenase-2 gene expression in human urinary bladder cancer. *Cancer Investigation* 2002;20(5–6):651–6.

Badawi AF, Hirvonen A, Bell DA, Lang NP, Kadlubar FF. Role of aromatic amine acetyltransferases, NAT1 and NAT2, in carcinogen-DNA adduct formation in the human urinary bladder. *Cancer Research* 1995;55(22):5230–7.

Bailey-Wilson JE, Amos CI, Pinney SM, Petersen GM, de Andrade M, Wiest JS, Fain P, Schwartz AG, You M, Franklin W, et al. A major lung cancer susceptibility locus maps to chromosome 6q23–25. *American Journal of Human Genetics* 2004;75(3):460–74.

Baird WM, Ralston SL. Carcinogenic polycyclic aromatic hydrocarbons. In: Bowden GT, Fischer SM, editors. *Comprehensive Toxicology: Chemical Carcinogens and Anticarcinogens*. Vol. 12. New York: Elsevier Science, 1997:171–200.

Baldwin AS. Control of oncogenesis and cancer therapy resistance by the transcription factor NF-κB. *Journal of Clinical Investigation* 2001;107(3):241–6.

Baldwin AS Jr. The NF-κB and IκB proteins: new discoveries and insights. *Annual Review of Immunology* 1996;14:649–81.

Balsara BR, Testa JR. Chromosomal imbalances in human lung cancer. *Oncogene* 2002;21(45):6877–83.

Bartsch H, Ohshima H, Pignatelli B, Calmels S. Human exposure to endogenous N-nitroso compounds: quantitative estimates in subjects at high risk for cancer of the oral cavity, oesophagus, stomach and urinary bladder. *Cancer Surveys* 1989;8(2):335–62.

Barzilay G, Walker LJ, Robson CN, Hickson ID. Site-directed mutagenesis of the human DNA repair enzyme HAP1: identification of residues important for AP endonuclease and RNase H activity. *Nucleic Acids Research* 1995;23(9):1544–50.

Baselga J, Arteaga CL. Critical update and emerging trends in epidermal growth factor receptor targeting in cancer. *Journal of Clinical Oncology* 2005;23(11):2445–59.

Basu AK, Essigmann JM. Site-specifically modified oligodeoxynucleotides as probes for the structural and biological effects of DNA-damaging agents. *Chemical Research in Toxicology* 1988;1(1):1–18.

Bates S, Phillips AC, Clark PA, Stott F, Peters G, Ludwig RL, Vousden KH. p14^{ARF} links the tumour suppressors RB and p53. *Nature* 1998;395(6698):124–5.

Bauer AK, Faiola B, Abernethy DJ, Marchan R, Pluta LJ, Wong VA, Gonzalez FJ, Butterworth BE, Borghoff SJ, Everitt JI, et al. Male mice deficient in microsomal epoxide hydrolase are not susceptible to benzene-induced toxicity. *Toxicological Sciences* 2003;72(2): 201–9.

Beland FA, Fullerton NF, Heflich RH. Rapid isolation, hydrolysis and chromatography of formaldehyde-modified DNA. *Journal of Chromatography A* 1984;308: 121–31.

Belham C, Wu S, Avruch J. Intracellular signalling: PDK1 - a kinase at the hub of things. *Current Biology* 1999; 9(3):R93–R96.

Belinsky SA. Gene-promoter hypermethylation as a biomarker in lung cancer. *Nature Reviews Cancer* 2004; 4(9):707–17.

Belinsky SA, Devereux, TR, Foley JF, Maronpot RR, Anderson MW. Role of the alveolar type II cell in the development and progression of pulmonary tumors induced by 4-(methylnitrosamino)-1-(3-pyridyl)-1-butanone in the A/J mouse. *Cancer Research* 1992;52(11):3164–73.

Belinsky SA, Dolan ME, White CM, Maronpot RR, Pegg AE, Anderson MW. Cell specific differences in O^6-methylguanine-DNA methyltransferase activity and removal of O^6-methylguanine in rat pulmonary cells. *Carcinogenesis* 1988;9(11):2053–8.

Belinsky SA, Nikula KJ, Palmisano WA, Michels R, Saccomanno G, Gabrielson E, Baylin SB, Herman JG. Aberrant methylation of *p16^{INK4a}* is an early event in lung cancer and a potential biomarker for early diagnosis. *Proceedings of the National Academy of Sciences of the United States of America* 1998;95(20):11891–6.

Belinsky SA, Palmisano WA, Gilliland FD, Crooks LA, Divine KK, Winters SA, Grimes MJ, Harms HJ, Tellez CS, Smith TM, et al. Aberrant promoter methylation in bronchial epithelium and sputum from current and former smokers. *Cancer Research* 2002;62(8):2370–7.

Benamira M, Singh U, Marnett LJ. Site-specific frameshift mutagenesis by a propanodeoxyguanosine adduct positioned in the (CpG)$_4$ hot-spot of *Salmonella typhimurium hisD3052* carried on an M13 vector. *Journal of Biological Chemistry* 1992;267(31):22392–400.

Benhamou S, Lee WJ, Alexandrie A-K, Boffetta P, Bouchardy C, Butkiewicz D, Brockmöller J, Clapper ML, Daly A, Dolzan V, et al. Meta- and pooled analyses of the effects of glutathione-*S*-transferase M1 polymorphisms and smoking on lung cancer risk. *Carcinogenesis* 2002;23(8):1343–50.

Benhamou S, Reinikainen M, Bouchardy C, Dayer P, Hirvonen A. Association between lung cancer and microsomal epoxide hydrolase genotypes. *Cancer Research* 1998;58(23):5291–3.

Benhamou S, Sarasin A. *ERCC2/XPD* gene polymorphisms and lung cancer: a HuGE review. *American Journal of Epidemiology* 2005;161(1):1–14.

Bennett WP, Colby TV, Travis WD, Borkowski A, Jones RT, Lane DP, Metcalf RA, Samet JM, Takeshima Y, Gu JR, et al. p53 Protein accumulates frequently in early bronchial neoplasia. *Cancer Research* 1993;53(20):4817–22.

Bennett WP, Hussain SP, Vahakangas KH, Khan MA, Shields PG, Harris CC. Molecular epidemiology of human cancer risk: gene-environment interactions and *p53* mutation spectrum in human lung cancer. *Journal of Pathology* 1999;187(1):8–18.

Bergmark E. Hemoglobin adducts of acrylamide and acrylonitrile in laboratory workers, smokers and nonsmokers. *Chemical Research in Toxicology* 1997; 10(1):78–84.

Bernardini S, Hirvonen A, Pelin K, Norppa H. Induction of sister chromatid exchange by 1,2-epoxy-3-butene in cultured human lymphocytes: influence of GSTT1 genotype. *Carcinogenesis* 1998;19(2):377–80.

Berwick M, Vineis P. Markers of DNA repair and susceptibility to cancer in humans: an epidemiologic review. *Journal of the National Cancer Institute* 2000; 92(11):874–97.

Besaratinia A, Bates SE, Pfeifer GP. Mutational signature of the proximate bladder carcinogen *N*-hydroxy-4-acetylaminobiphenyl: inconsistency with the *p53* mutational spectrum in bladder cancer. *Cancer Research* 2002;62(15):4331–8.

Betticher DC, Thatcher N, Altermatt HJ, Hoban P, Ryder WDJ, Heighway J. Alternate splicing produces a novel cyclin D1 transcript. *Oncogene* 1995;11(5):1005–11.

Betticher DC, White GRM, Vonlanthen S, Liu X, Kappeler A, Altermatt HJ, Thatcher N, Heighway J. G$_1$ control gene status is frequently altered in resectable non-small cell lung cancer. *International Journal of Cancer* 1997;74(5):556–62.

Birgander R, Själander A, Rannug A, Alexandrie A-K, Sundberg MI, Seidegård J, Tornling G, Beckman G, Beckman L. P53 polymorphisms and haplotypes in lung cancer. *Carcinogenesis* 1995;16(9):2233–6.

Biroš E, Kalina I, Kohút A, Štubňa J, Šalagovič J. Germ line polymorphisms of the tumor suppressor gene p53 and lung cancer. *Lung Cancer* 2001;31(2–3):157–62.

Bjørås M, Luna L, Johnsen B, Hoff E, Haug T, Rognes T, Seeberg E. Opposite base-dependent reactions of a human base excision repair enzyme on DNA containing 7,8-dihydro-8-oxoguanine and abasic sites. *EMBO Journal* 1997;16(20):6314–22.

Blackhall FH, Pintilie M, Michael M, Leighl N, Feld R, Tsao M-S, Shepherd FA. Expression and prognostic significance of kit, protein kinase B, and mitogen-activated protein kinase in patients with small cell lung cancer. *Clinical Cancer Research* 2003;9(6):2241–7.

Blömeke B, Greenblatt MJ, Doan VD, Bowman ED, Murphy SE, Chen CC, Kato S, Shields PG. Distribution of 7-alkyl-2′-deoxyguanosine adduct levels in human lung. *Carcinogenesis* 1996;17(4):741–8.

Blume-Jensen P, Hunter T. Oncogenic kinase signalling. *Nature* 2001;411(6835):355–65.

Bock KW. Roles of UDP-glucuronosyltransferases in chemical carcinogenesis. *Critical Reviews in Biochemistry and Molecular Biology* 1991;26(2):129–50.

Boffetta P, Nyberg F, Mukeria A, Benhamou S, Constantinescu V, Batura-Gabryel H, Brüske-Hohlfeld I, Schmid G, Simonato L, Pelkonen P, et al. O^6-alkylguanine-DNA-alkyltransferase activity in peripheral leukocytes, smoking and risk of lung cancer. *Cancer Letters* 2002;180(1):33–9.

Boffetta P, Pershagen G, Jöckel K-H, Forastiere F, Gaborieau V, Heinrich J, Jahn I, Kreuzer M, Merletti F, Nyberg F, et al. Cigar and pipe smoking and lung cancer risk: a multicenter study from Europe. *Journal of the National Cancer Institute* 1999;91(8):697–701.

Bolt HM, Roos PH, Thier R. The cytochrome P-450 isoenzyme CYP2E1 in the biological processing of industrial chemicals: consequences for occupational and environmental medicine. *International Archives of Occupational and Environmental Health* 2003;76(3):174–85.

Bondy ML, Strom SS, Colopy MW, Brown BW, Strong LC. Accuracy of family history of cancer obtained through interviews with relatives of patients with childhood sarcoma. *Journal of Clinical Epidemiology* 1994;47(1):89–96.

Boogaard PJ, van Sittert NJ. Biological monitoring of exposure to benzene: a comparison between *S*-phenylmercapturic acid, trans,trans-muconic acid, and phenol. *Occupational and Environmental Medicine* 1995;52(9):611–20.

Boogaard PJ, van Sittert NJ. Suitability of *S*-phenyl mercapturic acid and trans-trans-muconic acid as biomarkers for exposure to low concentrations of benzene. *Environmental Health Perspectives* 1996;104(Suppl 6):1151–7.

Bouchardy C, Mitrunen K, Wikman H, Husgafvel-Pursiainen K, Dayer P, Benhamou S, Hirvonen A. N-acetyltransferase NAT1 and NAT2 genotypes and lung cancer risk. *Pharmacogenetics* 1998;8(4):291–8.

Boysen G, Georgieva NI, Upton PB, Walker VE, Swenberg JA. N-terminal globin adducts as biomarkers for formation of butadiene derived epoxides. *Chemico-Biological Interactions* 2007;166(1–3):84–92.

Boysen G, Hecht SS. Analysis of DNA and protein adducts of benzo[*a*]pyrene in human tissues using structure-specific methods. *Mutation Research* 2003;543(1):17–30.

Branch P, Aquilina G, Bignami M, Karran P. Defective mismatch binding and a mutator phenotype in cells tolerant to DNA damage. *Nature* 1993;362(6421):652–4.

Braun MM, Caporaso NE, Page WF, Hoover RN. Genetic component of lung cancer: cohort study of twins. *Lancet* 1994;344(8920):440–3.

Brennan JA, Boyle JO, Koch WM, Goodman SN, Hruban RH, Eby YJ, Couch MJ, Forastiere AA, Sidransky D. Association between cigarette smoking and mutation of the p53 gene in squamous-cell carcinoma of the head and neck. *New England Journal of Medicine* 1995;332(11):712–7.

Brennan P, Hsu CC, Moullan N, Szeszenia-Dabrowska N, Lissowska J, Zaridze D, Rudnai P, Fabianova E, Mates D, Bencko V, et al. Effect of cruciferous vegetables on lung cancer in patients stratified by genetic status: a mendelian randomisation approach. *Lancet* 2005;366(9496):1558–60.

Brognard J, Clark AS, Ni Y, Dennis PA. Akt/protein kinase B is constitutively active in non-small cell lung cancer cells and promotes cellular survival and resistance to chemotherapy and radiation. *Cancer Research* 2001;61(10):3986–97.

Bromen K, Pohlabeln H, Ingeborg J, Ahrens W, Jöckel K-H. Aggregation of lung cancer in families: results from a population-based case-control study in Germany. *American Journal of Epidemiology* 2000;152(6):497–505.

Bronstein SM, Hooth MJ, Swenberg JA, Skopek TR. Modulation of ethylnitrosourea-induced toxicity and mutagenicity in human cells by O^6-benzylguanine. *Cancer Research* 1992;52(14):3851–6.

Brose MS, Volpe P, Feldman M, Kumar M, Rishi I, Gerrero R, Einhorn E, Herlyn M, Minna J, Nicholson A, et al. *BRAF* and *RAS* mutations in human lung cancer and melanoma. *Cancer Research* 2002;62(23):6997–7000.

Browman GP, Wong G, Hodson I, Sathya J, Russell R, McAlpine L, Skingley P, Levine MN. Influence of cigarette smoking on the efficacy of radiation therapy in head and neck cancer. *New England Journal of Medicine* 1993;328(3):159–63.

Brown CD, Wong BA, Fennell TR. *In vivo* and *in vitro* kinetics of ethylene oxide metabolism in rats and mice. *Toxicology and Applied Pharmacology* 1996;136(1):8–19.

Brownson RC, Alavanja MCR, Caporaso N, Berger E, Chang JC. Family history of cancer and risk of lung cancer in lifetime non-smokers and long-term ex-smokers. *International Journal of Epidemiology* 1997;26(2):256–63.

Brunet A, Bonni A, Zigmond MJ, Lin MZ, Juo P, Hu LS, Anderson MJ, Arden KC, Blenis J, Greenberg ME. Akt promotes cell survival by phosphorylating and inhibiting a Forkhead transcription factor. *Cell* 1999; 96(6):857–68.

Burbee DG, Forgacs E, Zöchbauer-Müeler S, Shivaku-mar L, Fong K, Gao B, Randle D, Kondo M, Virmani A, Bader S, et al. Epigenetic inactivation of RASSF1A in lung and breast cancers and malignant phenotype suppression. *Journal of the National Cancer Institute* 2001;93(9):691–9.

Burchell B. Genetic variation of human UDP-glucuro-nosyltransferase: implications in disease and drug glucuronidation. *American Journal of Pharmacoge-nomics* 2003;3(1):37–52.

Burdick AD, Davis JW II, Liu KJ, Hudson LG, Shi H, Monske ML, Burchiel SW. Benzo(*a*)pyrene quinones increase cell proliferation, generate reactive oxygen species, and transactivate the epidermal growth fac-tor receptor in breast epithelial cells. *Cancer Research* 2003;63(22):7825–33.

Burger RM, Peisach J, Horwitz SB. Mechanism of bleo-mycin action: *in vitro* studies. *Life Sciences* 1981; 28(7):715–27.

Butkiewicz D, Popanda O, Risch A, Edler L, Dienemann H, Schulz V, Kayser K, Drings P, Bartsch H, Schme-zer P. Association between the risk for lung adenocar-cinoma and a (–4) G-to-A polymorphism in the *XPA* gene. *Cancer Epidemiology, Biomarkers & Prevention* 2004;13(12):2242–6.

Butkiewicz D, Rusin M, Enewold L, Shields PG, Chorazy M, Harris CC. Genetic polymorphisms in DNA repair genes and risk of lung cancer. *Carcinogenesis* 2001; 22(4):593–7.

Butkiewicz D, Rusin M, Harris CC, Chorazy M. Identifica-tion of four single nucleotide polymorphisms in DNA repair genes: *XPA* and *XPB* (*ERCC3*) in Polish popula-tion. *Human Mutation* 2000;15(6):577–8.

Butler MA, Iwasaki M, Guengerich FP, Kadlubar FF. Human cytochrome P-450$_{PA}$ (P-450IA2), the phenace-tin *O*-deethylase, is primarily responsible for the hepatic 3-demethylation of caffeine and N-oxidation of carcino-genic arylamines. *Proceedings of the National Acad-emy of Sciences of the United States of America* 1989; 86(20):7696–700.

Byrd GD, Ogden MW. Liquid chromatographic/tandem mass spectrometric method for the determination of the tobacco-specific nitrosamine metabolite NNAL in smokers' urine. *Journal of Mass Spectrometry* 2003; 38(1):98–107.

Cabral Neto JB, Caseira Cabral RE, Margot A, Le Page F, Sarasin A, Gentil A. Coding properties of a unique apu-rinic/apyrimidinic site replicated in mammalian cells. *Journal of Molecular Biology* 1994;240(5):416–20.

Cai YC, Yang G-Y, Nie Y, Wang L-D, Zhao X, Song Y-L, Seril DN, Liao J, Xing EP, Yang CS. Molecular altera-tions of *p73* in human esophageal squamous cell carci-nomas: loss of heterozygosity occurs frequently; loss of imprinting and elevation of *p73* expression may be related to defective p53. *Carcinogenesis* 2000;21(4): 683–9.

Cajas-Salazar N, Au WW, Zwischenberger JB, Sierra-Torres CH, Salama SA, Alpard SK, Tyring SK. Effect of epoxide hydrolase polymorphisms on chromosome aberrations and risk for lung cancer. *Cancer Genetics and Cytoge-netics* 2003;145(2):97–102.

Calléja F, Jansen JG, Vrieling H, Laval F, van Zeeland AA. Modulation of the toxic and mutagenic effects induced by methyl methanesulfonate in Chinese hamster ovary cells by overexpression of the rat *N*-alkylpurine-DNA glycosylase. *Mutation Research* 1999;425(2):185–94.

Campbell SL, Khosravi-Far R, Rossman KL, Clark GJ, Der CJ. Increasing complexity of Ras signaling. *Oncogene* 1998;17(11):1395–413.

Caporaso N, Gu F, Chatterjee N, Sheng-Chih J, Yu K, Yeager M, Chen C, Jacobs K, Wheeler W, Landi MT, et al. Genome-wide and candidate gene association study of cigarette smoking behaviors. *PLoS ONE* 2009;4(2):e4653.doi:10.1371/journal.pone.0004653.

Carlisle DL, Hopkins TM, Gaither-Davis A, Silhanek MJ, Luketich JD, Christie NA, Siegfried JM. Nicotine sig-nals through muscle-type and neuronal nicotinic acetylcholine receptors in both human bronchial epithelial cells and airway fibroblasts. *Respiratory Research* 2004;5(1):27.

Carmella SG, Akerkar S, Hecht SS. Metabolites of the tobacco-specific nitrosamine 4-(methylnitrosamino)-1-(3-pyridyl)-1-butanone in smokers' urine. *Cancer Research* 1993;53(4):721–4.

Carmella SG, Akerkar S, Richie JP Jr, Hecht SS. Intraindividual and interindividual differences in metabolites of the tobacco-specific lung carcinogen 4-(methylnitrosamino)-1-(3-pyridyl)-1-butanone (NNK) in smokers' urine. *Cancer Epidemiology, Bio-markers & Prevention* 1995;4(6):635–42.

Carmella SG, Chen M, Villalta PW, Gurney JG, Hatsu-kami DK, Hecht SS. Ethylation and methylation of hemoglobin in smokers and nonsmokers. *Carcinogen-esis* 2002a;23(11):1903–10.

Carmella SG, Chen M, Yagi H, Jerina DM, Hecht SS. Analysis of phenanthrols in human urine by gas chromatography-mass spectrometry: potential use in carcinogen metabolite phenotyping. *Cancer Epi-demiology, Biomarkers & Prevention* 2004a;13(12): 2167–74.

Carmella SG, Han S, Villalta PW, Hecht SS. Analysis of total 4-(methylnitrosamino)-1-(3-pyridyl)-1-butanol in smokers' blood. *Cancer Epidemiology, Biomarkers & Prevention* 2005;14(11):2669–72.

Carmella SG, LaVoie EJ, Hecht SS. Quantitative analysis of catechol and 4-methylcatechol in human urine. *Food and Chemical Toxicology* 1982;20(5):587–90.

Carmella SG, Le K-A, Hecht SS. Improved method for determination of 1-hydroxypyrene in human urine. *Cancer Epidemiology, Biomarkers & Prevention* 2004b;13(7):1261–4.

Carmella SG, Le K-A, Upadhyaya P, Hecht SS. Analysis of *N*- and *O*-glucuronides of 4-(methylnitrosamino)-1-(3-pyridyl)-1-butanol (NNAL) in human urine. *Chemical Research in Toxicology* 2002b;15(4):545–50.

Carmella SG, Ye M, Upadhyaya P, Hecht SS. Stereochemistry of metabolites of a tobacco-specific lung carcinogen in smokers' urine. *Cancer Research* 1999;59(15):3602–5.

Carpenter CL, Cantley LC. Phosphoinositide kinases. *Current Opinion in Cell Biology* 1996;8(2):153–8.

Casale GP, Singhal M, Bhattacharya S, Ramanathan R, Roberts KP, Barbacci DC, Zhao J, Jankowiak R, Gross ML, Cavalieri EL, et al. Detection and quantification of depurinated benzo[*a*]pyrene-adducted DNA bases in the urine of cigarette smokers and women exposed to household coal smoke. *Chemical Research in Toxicology* 2001;14(2):192–201.

Cascorbi I, Brockmoller J, Mrozikiewicz PM, Bauer S, Loddenkemper R, Roots I. Homozygous rapid arylamine N-acetyltransferase (NAT2) genotype as a susceptibility factor for lung cancer. *Cancer Research* 1996;56(17):3961–6.

Castelao JE, Yuan J-M, Skipper PL, Tannenbaum SR, Gago-Dominguez M, Crowder JS, Ross RK, Yu MC. Gender- and smoking-related bladder cancer risk. *Journal of the National Cancer Institute* 2001;93(7):538–45.

Cerny T, Barnes DM, Hasleton P, Barber PV, Healy K, Gullick W, Thatcher N. Expression of epidermal growth factor receptor (EGF-R) in human lung tumours. *British Journal of Cancer* 1986;54(2):265–9.

Chakravarti D, Ibeanu GC, Tano K, Mitra S. Cloning and expression in *Escherichia coli* of a human cDNA encoding the DNA repair protein *N*-methylpurine-DNA glycosylase. *Journal of Biological Chemistry* 1991;266(24):15710–5.

Chang H-C, Weng C-F. Cyclooxygenase-2 level and culture conditions influence NS398-induced apoptosis and caspase activation in lung cancer cells. *Oncology Reports* 2001;8(6):1321–5.

Chang HW, Ling GS, Wei WI, Yuen AP-W. Smoking and drinking can induce *p15* methylation in the upper aerodigestive tract of healthy individuals and patients with head and neck squamous cell carcinoma. *Cancer* 2004;101(1):125–32.

Chan-Yeung M, Tan-Un KC, Ip MSM, Tsang KWT, Ho SP, Ho JCM, Chan H, Lam WK. Lung cancer susceptibility and polymorphisms of glutathione-S-transferase genes in Hong Kong. *Lung Cancer* 2004;45(2):155–60.

Chaw YF, Crane LE, Lange P, Shapiro R. Isolation and identification of cross-links from formaldehyde-treated nucleic acids. *Biochemistry* 1980;19(24):5525–31.

Chen H-JC, Wu C-F, Hong C-L, Chang C-M. Urinary excretion of 3,N^4-etheno-2'-deoxycytidine in humans as a biomarker of oxidative stress: association with cigarette smoking. *Chemical Research in Toxicology* 2004a;17(7):896–903.

Chen JX, Zheng Y, West M, Tang MS. Carcinogens preferentially bind at methylated CpG in the p53 mutational hotspots. *Cancer Research* 1998;58(10):2070–5.

Chen K-M, El-Bayoumy K, Cunningham J, Aliaga C, Li H, Melikian AA. Detection of nitrated benzene metabolites in bone marrow of B6C3F$_1$ mice treated with benzene. *Chemical Research in Toxicology* 2004b;17(3):370–7.

Chen P, Wiencke J, Aldape K, Kesler-Diaz A, Miike R, Kelsey K, Lee M, Liu J, Wrensch W. Association of an *ERCC1* polymorphism with adult-onset glioma. *Cancer Epidemiology, Biomarkers & Prevention* 2000;9(8):843–7.

Chen R-H, Maher VM, McCormick JJ. Effect of excision repair by diploid human fibroblasts on the kinds and locations of mutations induced by (±)-7β,8α-dihydroxy-9α,10α-epoxy-7,8,9,10-tetrahydrobenzo[*a*]pyrene in the coding region of the *HPRT* gene. *Proceedings of the National Academy of Sciences of the United States of America* 1990;87(21):8680–4.

Chen W-C, Wu H-C, Hsu C-D, Chen H-Y, Tsai F-J. p21 Gene codon 31 polymorphism is associated with bladder cancer. *Urologic Oncology* 2002;7(2):63–6.

Cheng EH, Wei MC, Weiler S, Flavell RA, Mak TW, Lindsten T, Korsmeyer SJ. BCL-2, BCL-X$_L$ sequester BH3 domain-only molecules preventing BAX- and BAK-mediated mitochondrial apoptosis. *Molecular Cell* 2001;8(3):705–11.

Cheng L, Eicher SA, Guo Z, Hong WK, Spitz MR, Wei Q. Reduced DNA repair capacity in head and neck cancer patients. *Cancer Epidemiology, Biomarkers & Prevention* 1998;7(6):465–8.

Cheng L, Sturgis EM, Eicher SA, Char D, Spitz MR, Wei Q. Glutathione-*S*-transferase polymorphisms and risk of squamous-cell carcinoma of the head and neck. *International Journal of Cancer* 1999;84(3):220–4.

Cheng T-J, Christiani DC, Xu X, Wain JC, Wiencke JK, Kelsey KT. Glutathione S-transferase μ genotype, diet, and smoking as determinants of sister chromatid exchange frequency in lymphocytes. *Cancer Epidemiology, Biomarkers & Prevention* 1995;4(5):535–42.

Chevrier I, Stücker I, Houllier A-M, Cenee S, Beaune P, Laurent-Puig P, Loriot M-A. Myeloperoxidase: new polymorphisms and relation with lung cancer risk. *Pharmacogenetics and Genomics* 2003;13(12):729–39.

Chiou H-L, Wu M-F, Chien W-P, Cheng Y-W, Wong R-H, Chen C-Y, Lin T-S, Lee H. NAT2 fast acetylator genotype is associated with an increased risk of lung cancer among never-smoking women in Taiwan. *Cancer Letters* 2005;223(1):93–101.

Chipuk JE, Bhat M, Hsing AY, Ma J, Danielpour D. Bcl-xL blocks transforming growth factor-β1-induced apoptosis by inhibiting cytochrome *c* release and not by directly antagonizing Apaf-1-dependent caspase activation in prostate epithelial cells. *Journal of Biological Chemistry* 2001;276(28):26614–21.

Christmann M, Tomicic MT, Roos WP, Kaina B. Mechanisms of human DNA repair: an update. *Toxicology* 2003;193(1–2):3–34.

Church TR, Anderson KE, Caporaso NE, Geisser MS, Le CT, Zhang Y, Benoit AR, Carmella SG, Hecht SS. A prospectively measured serum biomarker for a tobacco-specific carcinogen and lung cancer in smokers. *Cancer Epidemiology, Biomarkers & Prevention* 2009;18(1):260–6.

Claij N, van der Wal WA, Dekker M, Jansen L, te Riele H. DNA mismatch repair deficiency stimulates *N*-ethyl-*N*-nitrosourea-induced mutagenesis and lymphomagenesis. *Cancer Research* 2003;63(9):2062–6.

Clark AS, West KA, Blumberg PM, Dennis PA. Altered protein kinase C (PKC) isoforms in non-small cell lung cancer cells: PKCδ promotes cellular survival and chemotherapeutic resistance. *Cancer Research* 2003; 63(4):780–6.

Cocco P, Tocco MG, Ibba A, Scano L, Ennas MG, Flore C, Randaccio FS. *trans,trans*-Muconic acid excretion in relation to environmental exposure to benzene. *International Archives of Occupational and Environmental Health* 2003;76(6):456–60.

Coffer PJ, Jin J, Woodgett JR. Protein kinase B (c-Akt): a multifunctional mediator of phosphatidylinositol 3-kinase activation. *Biochemical Journal* 1998;335 (Pt 1):1–13.

Coggins CR. A review of chronic inhalation studies with mainstream cigarette smoke in rats and mice. *Toxicologic Pathology* 1998;26(3):307–14.

Cohet C, Borel S, Nyberg F, Mukeria A, Brüske-Hohlfeld I, Constantinescu V, Benhamou S, Brennan P, Hall J, Boffetta P. Exon 5 polymorphisms in the O^6-alkylguanine DNA alkyltransferase gene and lung cancer risk in non–smokers exposed to second-hand smoke. *Cancer Epidemiology, Biomarkers & Prevention* 2004;13(2):320–3.

Colussi C, Parlanti E, Degan P, Aquilina G, Barnes D, Macpherson P, Karran P, Crescenzi M, Dogliotti E, Bignami M. The mammalian mismatch repair pathway removes DNA 8-oxodGMP incorporated from the oxidized dNTP pool. *Current Biology* 2002;12(11):912–8.

Conney AH. Induction of microsomal enzymes by foreign chemicals and carcinogenesis by polycyclic aromatic hydrocarbons: G.H.A. Clowes Memorial Lecture. *Cancer Research* 1982;42(12):4875–917.

Constantinou A, Davies AA, West SC. Branch migration and Holliday junction resolution catalyzed by activities from mammalian cells. *Cell* 2001;104(2):259–68.

Cooper CS, Grover PL, Sims P. The metabolism and activation of benzo[*a*]pyrene. In: Bridges JW, Chasseaud LF, editors. *Progress in Drug Metabolism*. Vol. 7. New York: John Wiley & Sons, 1983:295–396.

Cortessis VK, Siegmund K, Xue S, Ross RK, Yu MC. A case-control study of cyclin D1 *CCND1* 870A → G polymorphism and bladder cancer. *Carcinogenesis* 2003; 24(10):1645–50.

Cory S, Huang DCS, Adams JM. The Bcl-2 family: roles in cell survival and oncogenesis. *Oncogene* 2003; 22(53):8590–607.

Cote ML, Kardia SLR, Wenzlaff AS, Land SJ, Schwartz AG. Combinations of glutathione *S*-transferase genotypes and risk of early-onset lung cancer in Caucasians and African Americans: a population-based study. *Carcinogenesis* 2005;26(4):811–9.

Crompton NEA, Ozsahin M. A versatile and rapid assay of radiosensitivity of peripheral blood leukocytes based on DNA and surface-marker assessment of cytotoxicity. *Radiation Research* 1997;147(1):55–60.

Crone TM, Goodtzova K, Edara S, Pegg AE. Mutations in human O^6-alkylguanine-DNA alkyltransferase imparting resistance to O^6-benzylguanine. *Cancer Research* 1994;54(23):6221–7.

Dajas-Bailador FA, Soliakov L, Wonnacott S. Nicotine activates the extracellular signal-regulated kinase 1/2 via the α7 nicotinic acetylcholine receptor and protein kinase A, in SH-SY5Y cells and hippocampal neurones. *Journal of Neurochemistry* 2002;80(3):520–30.

Dally H, Gassner K, Jäger B, Schmezer P, Spiegelhalder B, Edler L, Drings P, Dienemann H, Schulz V, Kayser K, et al. Myeloperoxidase (*MPO*) genotype and lung cancer histologic types: the *MPO -463 A* allele is associated with reduced risk for small cell lung cancer in smokers. *International Journal of Cancer* 2002;102(5):530–5.

Dammann R, Li C, Yoon J-H, Chin PL, Bates S, Pfeifer GP. Epigenetic inactivation of a RAS association domain family protein from the lung tumour suppressor locus 3p21.3. *Nature Genetics* 2000;25(3):315–9.

Daniels DS, Mol CD, Arvai AS, Kanugula S, Pegg AE, Tainer JA. Active and alkylated human AGT structures: a novel zinc site, inhibitor and extrahelical base binding. *EMBO Journal* 2000;19(7):1719–30.

Dannenberg AJ, Subbaramaiah K. Targeting cyclooxygenase-2 in human neoplasia: rationale and promise. *Cancer Cell* 2003;4(6):431–6.

Datta SR, Brunet A, Greenberg ME. Cellular survival: a play in three Akts. *Genes & Development* 1999;13(22):2905–27.

David O, Jett J, LeBeau H, Dy G, Hughes J, Friedman M, Brody AR. Phospho-Akt overexpression in non–small cell lung cancer confers significant stage-independent survival disadvantage. *Clinical Cancer Research* 2004;10(20):6865–71.

David-Beabes GL, London SJ. Genetic polymorphism of *XRCC1* and lung cancer risk among African–Americans and Caucasians. *Lung Cancer* 2001;34(3):333–9.

David-Beabes GL, Lunn RM, London SJ. No association between the *XPD* (Lys751Gln) polymorphism or the *XRCC3* (Thr241Met) polymorphism and lung cancer risk. *Cancer Epidemiology, Biomarkers & Prevention* 2001;10(8):911–2.

de Laat WL, Jaspers NGJ, Hoeijmakers JHJ. Molecular mechanism of nucleotide excision repair. *Genes & Development* 1999;13(7):768–85.

de los Santos C, Zaliznyak T, Johnson F. NMR characterization of a DNA duplex containing the major acrolein-derived deoxyguanosine adduct γ-OH-1,N^2-propano-2'-deoxyguanosine. *Journal of Biological Chemistry* 2001;276(12):9077–82.

de Wind N, Dekker M, Claij N, Jansen L, van Klink Y, Radman M, Riggins G, van der Valk M, van't Wout K, te Riele H. HNPCC-like cancer predisposition in mice through simultaneous loss of Msh3 and Msh6 mismatch-repair protein functions. *Nature Genetics* 1999;23(3):359–62.

DeGregori J, Leone G, Miron A, Jakoi L, Nevins JR. Distinct roles for E2F proteins in cell growth control and apoptosis. *Proceedings of the National Academy of Sciences of the United States of America* 1997;94(14):7245–50.

Dellinger RW, Fang J-L, Chen G, Weinberg R, Lazarus P. Importance of UDP-glucuronosyltransferase 1A10 (UGT1A10) in the detoxification of polycyclic aromatic hydrocarbons: decreased glucuronidative activity of the UGT1A10[139LYS] isoform. *Drug Metabolism and Disposition* 2006;34(6):943–9.

DeMarini DM. Genotoxicity of tobacco smoke and tobacco smoke condensate: a review. *Mutation Research* 2004;567(2–3):447–74.

DeMarini DM, Landi S, Tian D, Hanley NM, Li X, Hu F, Roop BC, Mass MJ, Keohavong P, Gao W, et al. Lung tumor *KRAS* and *TP53* mutations in nonsmokers reflect exposure to PAH-rich coal combustion emissions. *Cancer Research* 2001;61(18):6679–81.

Denissenko MF, Chen JX, Tang M, Pfeifer GP. Cytosine methylation determines hot spots of DNA damage in the human *P53* gene. *Proceedings of the National Academy of Sciences of the United States of America* 1997;94(8):3893–8.

Denissenko MF, Pao A, Pfeifer GP, Tang M. Slow repair of bulky DNA adducts along the nontranscribed strand of the human *p53* gene may explain the strand bias of transversion mutations in cancers. *Oncogene* 1998;16(10):1241–7.

Denissenko MF, Pao A, Tang M-S, Pfeifer GP. Preferential formation of benzo[*a*]pyrene adducts at lung cancer mutational hotspots in *P53*. *Science* 1996;274(5286):430–2.

Deutsch-Wenzel RP, Brune H, Grimmer G, Dettbarn G, Misfeld J. Experimental studies in rat lungs on the carcinogenicity and dose-response relationships of eight frequently occurring environmental polycyclic aromatic hydrocarbons. *Journal of the National Cancer Institute* 1983;71(3):539–44.

Dietrich M, Block G, Hudes M, Morrow JD, Norkus EP, Traber MG, Cross CE, Packer L. Antioxidant supplementation decreases lipid peroxidation biomarker F_2-isoprostanes in plasma of smokers. *Cancer Epidemiology, Biomarkers & Prevention* 2002;11(1):7–13.

Dipple A, Moschel RC, Bigger CAH. Polynuclear aromatic hydrocarbons. In: Searle CE, editor. *Chemical Carcinogens*. ACS Monograph 182, 2nd ed., vol. 1. Washington: American Chemical Society, 1984:41–163.

Divine KK, Gilliland FD, Crowell RE, Stidley CA, Bocklage TJ, Cook DL, Belinsky SA. The *XRCC1* 399 glutamine allele is a risk factor for adenocarcinoma of the lung. *Mutation Research* 2001;461(4):273–8.

Divine KK, Pulling LC, Marron-Terada PG, Liechty KC, Kang T, Schwartz AG, Bocklage TJ, Coons TA, Gilliland FD, Belinsky SA. Multiplicity of abnormal promoter methylation in lung adenocarcinomas from smokers and never smokers. *International Journal of Cancer* 2005;114(3):400–5.

Djordjevic MV, Sigountos CW, Brunnemann KD, Hoffmann D. Formation of 4-(methylnitrosamino)-4-(3-pyridyl)butyric acid in vitro and in mainstream cigarette smoke. *Journal of Agricultural and Food Chemistry* 1991;39(1):209–13.

Dolan ME, Mitchell RB, Mummert C, Moschel RC, Pegg AE. Effect of O^6-benzylguanine analogues on sensitivity of human tumor cells to the cytotoxic effects of alkylating agents. *Cancer Research* 1991;51(13):3367–72.

Dolan ME, Moschel RC, Pegg AE. Depletion of mammalian O^6-alkylguanine-DNA alkyltransferase activity by O^6-benzylguanine provides a means to evaluate the role of this protein in protection against carcinogenic and therapeutic alkylating agents. *Proceedings of the National Academy of Sciences of the United States of America* 1990;87(14):5368–72.

Dosanjh MK, Menichini P, Eritja R, Singer B. Both O^4-methylthymine and O^4-ethylthymine preferentially form alkyl TG pairs that do not block in vitro replication in a defined sequence. *Carcinogenesis* 1993; 14(9):1915–9.

Dosanjh MK, Singer B, Essigmann JM. Comparative mutagenesis of O^6-methylguanine and O^4-methylthymine in *Escherichia coli. Biochemistry* 1991;30(28):7027–33.

Downward J. The ins and outs of signalling. *Nature* 2001;411(6839):759–62.

Drin I, Schoket B, Kostic S, Vincze I. Smoking-related increase in O^6-alkylguanine-DNA alkyltransferase activity in human lung tissue. *Carcinogenesis* 1994; 15(8):1535–9.

Dubinett SM, Sharma S, Huang M, Dohadwala M, Pold M, Mao JT. Cyclooxygenase-2 in lung cancer. *Progress in Experimental Tumor Research* 2003;37:138–62.

Duckett DR, Drummond JT, Murchie AIH, Reardon JT, Sancar A, Lilley DMJ, Modrich P. Human MutSα recognizes damaged DNA base pairs containing O^6-methylguanine, O^4-methylthymine, or the cis-platin-d(GpG) adduct. *Proceedings of the National Academy of Sciences of the United States of America* 1996;93(13):6443–7.

Duell EJ, Wiencke JK, Cheng T-J, Varkonyi A, Zuo ZF, Ashok TDS, Mark EJ, Wain JC, Christiani DC, Kelsey KT. Polymorphisms in the DNA repair genes *XRCC1* and *ERCC2* and biomarkers of DNA damage in human blood mononuclear cells. *Carcinogenesis* 2000;21(5):965–71.

Dupret J-M, Rodrigues-Lima F. Structure and regulation of the drug-metabolizing enzymes arylamine N-acetyltransferases. *Current Medicinal Chemistry* 2005;12(3):311–8.

Eckfeld K, Hesson L, Vos MD, Bieche I, Latif F, Clark GJ. RASSF4/AD037 is a potential Ras effector/rumor suppressor of the RASSF family. *Cancer Research* 2004;64(23):8688–93.

Edara S, Kanugula S, Goodtzova K, Pegg AE. Resistance of the human O^6-alkylguanine-DNA alkyltransferase containing arginine at codon 160 to inactivation by O^6-benzylguanine. *Cancer Research* 1996;56(24): 5571–5.

Egyházi S, Ma S, Smoczynski K, Hansson J, Platz A, Ringborg U. Novel O^6-methylguanine-DNA methyltransferase SNPs: a frequency comparison of patients with familial melanoma and healthy individuals in Sweden. *Human Mutation* 2002;20(5):408–9.

Ehrenberg L, Osterman-Golkar S. Alkylation of macromolecules for detecting mutagenic agents. *Teratogenesis, Carcinogenesis, and Mutagenesis* 1980;1(1):105–27.

Eide I, Zhao C, Kumar R, Hemminki K, Wu K, Swenberg JA. Comparison of ^{32}P-postlabeling and high-resolution GC/MS in quantifying N7-(-hydroxyethyl)

guanine adducts. *Chemical Research in Toxicology* 1999;12(10):979–84.

Eisenstadt E, Warren AJ, Porter J, Atkins D, Miller JH. Carcinogenic epoxides of benzo[*a*]pyrene and cyclopenta[*cd*]pyrene induce base substitutions via specific transversions. *Proceedings of the National Academy of Sciences of the United States of America* 1982; 79(6):1945–9.

El-Bayoumy K, Donahue JM, Hecht SS, Hoffmann D. Identification and quantitative determination of aniline and toluidines in human urine. *Cancer Research* 1986;46(12 Pt 1):6064–7.

El-Bayoumy K, Iatropoulos M, Amin S, Hoffmann D, Wynder EL. Increased expression of cyclooxygenase-2 in rat lung tumors induced by the tobacco-specific nitrosamine 4-(methylnitrosamino)-4-(3-pyridyl)-1-butanone: the impact of a high-fat diet. *Cancer Research* 1999;59(7):1400–3.

Elder RH, Jansen JG, Weeks RJ, Willington MA, Deans B, Watson AJ, Mynett KJ, Bailey JA, Cooper DP, Rafferty JA, et al. Alkylpurine-DNA-*N*-glycosylase knockout mice show increased susceptibility to induction of mutations by methyl methanesulfonate. *Molecular and Cellular Biology* 1998;18(10):5828–37.

Eller MS, Maeda T, Magnoni C, Atwal D, Gilchrest BA. Enhancement of DNA repair in human skin cells by thymidine dinucleotides: evidence for a p53-mediated mammalian SOS response. *Proceedings of the National Academy of Sciences of the United States of America* 1997;94(23):12627–32.

Ellison KS, Dogliotti E, Connors TD, Basu AK, Essigmann JM. Site-specific mutagenesis by O^6-alkylguanines located in the chromosomes of mammalian cells: influence of the mammalian O^6-alkylguanine-DNA alkyltransferase. *Proceedings of the National Academy of Sciences of the United States of America* 1989;86(22):8620–4.

Esteller M, Hamilton SR, Burger PC, Baylin SB Herman JG. Inactivation of the DNA repair gene O^6-*methylguanine-DNA methyltransferase* by promoter hypermethylation is a common event in primary human neoplasia. *Cancer Research* 1999;59(4):793–7.

Etzel CJ, Amos CI, Spitz MR. Risk for smoking-related cancer among relatives of lung cancer patients. *Cancer Research* 2003;63(23):8531–5.

Evans E, Moggs JG, Hwang JR, Egly JM, Wood RD. Mechanism of open complex and dual incision formation by human nucleotide excision repair factors. *EMBO Journal* 1997;16(21):6559–73.

Fan F, Liu C, Tavaré S, Arnheim N. Polymorphisms in the human DNA repair gene XPF. *Mutation Research* 1999;406(2–4):115–20.

Fang HY, Lin T-S, Lin J-P, Wu YC, Chow K-C, Wang L-S. Cyclooxygenase-2 in human non-small cell lung cancer. *European Journal of Surgical Oncology* 2003; 29(2):171–7.

Fang J-L, Beland FA, Doerge DR, Wiener D, Guillemette C, Marques MM, Lazarus P. Characterization of benzo(*a*) pyrene-*trans*-7,8-dihydrodiol glucuronidation by human tissue microsomes and overexpressed UDP-glucuronosyltransferase enzymes. *Cancer Research* 2002;62(7):1978–86.

Fay LB, Leaf CD, Gremaud E, Aeschlimann JM, Steen C, Shuker DE, Turesky RJ. Urinary excretion of 3-methyladenine after consumption of fish containing high levels of dimethylamine. *Carcinogenesis* 1997;18(5):1039–44.

Feng Z, Hu W, Chen JX, Pao A, Li H, Rom W, Hung M-C, Tang M. Preferential DNA damage and poor repair determine ras gene mutational hotspot in human cancer. *Journal of the National Cancer Institute* 2002;94(20):1527–36.

Feng Z, Hu W, Hu Y, Tang M-S. Acrolein is a major cigarette-related lung cancer agent: preferential biding at *p53* mutational hotspots and inhibition of DNA repair. *Proceedings of the National Academy of Sciences of the United States of America* 2006;103(42):15404–9.

Fennell TR, MacNeela JP, Morris RW, Watson M, Thompson CL, Bell DA. Hemoglobin adducts from acrylonitrile and ethylene oxide in cigarette smokers: effects of *glutathione S-transferase T1*-null and *M1*-null genotypes. *Cancer Epidemiology, Biomarkers & Prevention* 2000;9(7):705–12.

Fernandes A, Liu T, Amin S, Geacintov NE, Grollman AP, Moriya M. Mutagenic potential of stereoisomeric bay region (+)- and (–)-*cis-anti*-benzo[*a*]pyrene diol epoxide-N^2-2'-deoxyguanosine adducts in *Escherichia coli* and simian kidney cells. *Biochemistry* 1998;37(28): 10164–72.

Ferrezuelo F, Prieto-Álamo M-J, Jurado J, Pueyo C. Influence of DNA repair by (A)BC excinuclease and Ogt alkyltransferase on the distribution of mutations induced by *n*-propyl-*N*-nitrosourea in *Escherichia coli*. *Environmental and Molecular Mutagenesis* 1998a;31(1):82–91.

Ferrezuelo F, Prieto-Álamo M-J, Jurado J, Pueyo C. Role of DNA repair by (A)BC excinuclease and *Ogt* alkyltransferase in the final distribution of LacI^{-d} mutations induced by *N*-butyl-*N*-nitrosourea in *Esherichia coli*. *Mutagenesis* 1998b;13(5):507–14.

Feyler A, Voho A, Bouchardy C, Kuokkanen K, Dayer P, Hirvonen A, Benhamou S. Point: myeloperoxidase $^{-463}$G → A polymorphism and lung cancer risk. *Cancer Epidemiology, Biomarkers & Prevention* 2002; 11(12):1550–4.

Finel M, Li X, Gardner-Stephen D, Bratton S, Mackenzie PI, Radominska-Pandya A. Human UDP-glucuronosyl-transferase 1A5: identification, expression, and activity. *Journal of Pharmacology and Experimental Therapeutics* 2005;315(3):1143–9.

Fishel R, Lescoe MK, Rao MR, Copeland NG, Jenkins NA, Garber J, Kane M, Kolodner R. The human mutator gene homolog MSH2 and its association with hereditary nonpolyposis colon cancer. *Cell* 1993;7(1): 1027–38.

Flamini G, Romano G, Curigliano G, Chiominto A, Capelli G, Boninsegna A, Signorelli C, Ventura L, Santella RM, Sgambato A, et al. 4-Aminobiphenyl-DNA adducts in laryngeal tissue and smoking habits: an immunohistochemical study. *Carcinogenesis* 1998;19(2):353–7.

Flemington EK, Speck SH, Kaelin WG Jr. E2F-1-mediated transactivation is inhibited by complex formation with the retinoblastoma susceptibility gene product. *Proceedings of the National Academy of Sciences of the United States of America* 1993;90(15):6914–8.

Foiles PG, Akerkar SA, Carmella SG, Kagan M, Stoner GD, Resau JH, Hecht SS. Mass spectrometric analysis of tobacco-specific nitrosamine-DNA adducts in smokers and nonsmokers. *Chemical Research in Toxicology* 1991;4(3):364–8.

Fong LYY, Nguyen VT, Farber JL. Esophageal cancer prevention in zinc-deficient rats: rapid induction of apoptosis by replenishing zinc. *Journal of the National Cancer Institute* 2001;93(20):1525–33.

Ford JM, Hanawalt PC. Li-Fraumeni syndrome fibroblasts homozygous for p53 mutations are deficient in global DNA repair but exhibit normal transcription-coupled repair and enhanced UV resistance. *Proceedings of the National Academy of Sciences of the United States of America* 1995;92(19):8876–80.

Forgacs E, Biesterveld EJ, Sekido Y, Fong K, Muneer S, Wistuba II, Milchgrub S, Brezinschek R, Virmani A, Gazdar AF, et al. Mutation analysis of the *PTEN/MMAC1* gene in lung cancer. *Oncogene* 1998;17(12):1557–65.

Fortini P, Pascucci B, Parlanti E, D'Errico M, Simonelli V, Dogliotti E. The base excision repair: mechanisms and its relevance for cancer susceptibility. *Biochimie* 2003;85(11):1053–71.

Fowles J, Dybing E. Application of toxicological risk assessment principles to the chemical constituents of cigarette smoke. *Tobacco Control* 2003;12(4):424–30.

Fretland AJ, Doll MA, Zhu Y, Smith L, Leff MA, Hein DW. Effect of nucleotide substitutions in *N*-acetyltransferase-1 on *N*-acetylation (deactivation) and *O*-acetylation (activation) of arylamine carcinogens: implications for cancer predisposition. *Cancer Detection and Prevention* 2002;26(1):10–4.

Fretland AJ, Omiecinski CJ. Epoxide hydrolases: biochemistry and molecular biology. *Chemico-Biological Interactions* 2000;129(1–2):41–59.

Friedberg EC. How nucleotide excision repair protects against cancer. *Nature Reviews Cancer* 2001;1(1): 22–33.

Friedberg EC, Walker GC, Siede W, editors. *DNA Repair and Mutagenesis*. Washington: ASM Press, 1995.

Fromme JC, Banerjee A, Verdine GL. DNA glycosylase recognition and catalysis. *Current Opinion in Structural Biology* 2004;14(1):43–9.

Fu XW, Nurse CA, Farragher SM, Cutz E. Expression of functional nicotinic acetylcholine receptors in neuroepithelial bodies of neonatal hamster lung. *American Journal of Physiology – Lung Cellular and Molecular Physiology* 2003;285(6):L1203–L1212.

Fukuoka M, Yano S, Giaccone G, Tamura T, Nakagawa K, Douillard J-Y, Nishiwaki Y, Vansteenkiste J, Kudoh S, Rischin D, et al. Multi-institutional randomized phase II trial of gefitinib for previously treated patients with advanced non–small-cell lung cancer. *Journal of Clinical Oncology* 2003;21(12):2237–46.

Fustinoni S, Soleo L, Warholm M, Begemann P, Rannug A, Neumann H-G, Swenberg JA, Vimercati L, Foà V, Colombi A. Influence of metabolic genotypes on biomarkers of exposure to 1,3-butadiene in humans. *Cancer Epidemiology, Biomarkers & Prevention* 2002; 11(10):1082–90.

Gago-Dominguez M, Bell DA, Watson MA, Yuan J-M, Castelao JE, Hein DW, Chan KK, Coetzee GA, Ross RK, Yu MC. Permanent hair dyes and bladder cancer: risk modification by cytochrome P4501A2 and *N*-acetyltransferases 1 and 2. *Carcinogenesis* 2003;24(3):483–9.

Gao C, Takezaki T, Wu J, Li Z, Wang J, Ding J, Liu Y, Hu X, Xu T, Tajima K, et al. Interaction between cytochrome P-450 2E1 polymorphisms and environmental factors with risk of esophageal and stomach cancers in Chinese. *Cancer Epidemiology, Biomarkers & Prevention* 2002;11(1):29–34.

García-Closas M, Kelsey KT, Wiencke JK, Xu X, Wain JC, Christiani DC. A case-control study of cytochrome *P450 1A1*, glutathione S-transferase M1, cigarette smoking and lung cancer susceptibility (Massachusetts, United States). *Cancer Causes & Control* 1997;8(4):544–53.

Gauderman WJ, Morrison JL. Evidence for age-specific genetic relative risks in lung cancer. *American Journal of Epidemiology* 2000;151(1):41–9.

Gautier J-C, Urban P, Beaune P, Pompon D. Simulation of human benzo[*a*]pyrene metabolism deduced from the analysis of individual kinetic steps in recombinant yeast. *Chemical Research in Toxicology* 1996;9(2): 418–25.

Gelboin HV. Benzo[*a*]pyrene metabolism, activation, and carcinogenesis: role and regulation of mixed function oxidases and related enzymes. *Physiological Reviews* 1980;60(4):1107–66.

Genschel J, Bazemore LR, Modrich P. Human exonuclease I is required for 5′ and 3′ mismatch repair. *Journal of Biological Chemistry* 2002;277(15):13302–11.

Genschel J, Littman SJ, Drummond JT, Modrich P. Isolation of MutSβ from human cells and comparison of the mismatch repair specificities of MutSβ and MutSα. *Journal of Biological Chemistry* 1998;273(31): 19895–901.

Giardiello FM, Welsh SB, Hamilton SR, Offerhaus GJ, Gittelsohn AM, Booker SV, Krush AJ, Yardley JH, Luk GD. Increased risk of cancer in the Peutz-Jeghers syndrome. *New England Journal of Medicine* 1987;316(24): 1511–14.

Gibbs PEM, Lawrence CW. Novel mutagenic properties of abasic sites in *Saccharomyces cerevisiae*. *Journal of Molecular Biology* 1995;251(2):229–36.

Gibbs PEM, McGregor WG, Maher VM, Nisson P, Lawrence CW. A human homolog of the *Saccharomyces cerevisiae REV3* gene, which encodes the catalytic subunit of DNA polymerase ζ. *Proceedings of the National Academy of Sciences of the United States of America* 1998;95(12):6876–80.

Gibbs PEM, Wang X-D, Li Z, McManus TP, McGregor WG, Lawrence CW, Maher VM. The function of the human homolog of *Saccharomyces cerevisiae REV1* is required for mutagenesis induced by UV light. *Proceedings of the National Academy of Sciences of the United States of America* 2000;97(8):4186–91.

Gibel VW. Experimentelle untersuchung zur synkarzinogenese beim ösophaguskarzinom (Experimental studies on syncarcinogenesis in esophageal carcinoma) [German]. *Archiv für Geschwulstforschung* 1967; 30(3):181–9.

Gillison ML, Shah KV. Chapter 9: role of human papillomavirus in nongenital cancers. *Journal of the National Cancer Institute Monographs* 2003;(31):57–65.

Godschalk R, Nair J, van Schooten FJ, Risch A, Drings P, Kayser K, Dienemann H, Bartsch H. Comparison of multiple DNA adduct types in tumor adjacent human lung tissue: effect of cigarette smoking. *Carcinogenesis* 2002;23(12):2081–6.

Goode EL, Ulrich CM, Potter JD. Polymorphisms in DNA repair genes and associations with cancer risk. *Cancer Epidemiology, Biomarkers & Prevention* 2002; 11(12):1513–30.

Gordon SM, Wallace LA, Brinkman MC, Callahan PJ, Kenny DV. Volatile organic compounds as breath biomarkers for active and passive smoking. *Environmental Health Perspectives* 2002;110(7):689–98.

Green J, Banks E, Berrington A, Darby S, Deo H, Newton R. *N*-acetyltransferase 2 and bladder cancer: an overview and consideration of the evidence for gene-environment interaction. *British Journal of Cancer* 2000;83(3):412–7.

Green MD, Tephly TR. Glucuronidation of amine substrates by purified and expressed UDP- glucuronosyltransferase proteins. *Drug Metabolism and Disposition* 1998;26(9):860–7.

Greenblatt MS, Bennett WP, Hollstein M, Harris CC. Mutations in the p53 tumor suppressor gene: clues to cancer etiology and molecular pathogenesis. *Cancer Research* 1994;54(18):4855–78.

Gregory PA, Hansen AJ, Mackenzie PI. Tissue specific differences in the regulation of the UDP glucuronosyltransferase 2B17 gene promoter. *Pharmacogenetics* 2000;10(9):809–20.

Gregory PA, Lewinsky RH, Gardner-Stephen DA, Mackenzie PI. Regulation of UDP glucuronosyltransferases in the gastrointestinal tract. *Toxicology and Applied Pharmacology* 2004;199(3):354–63.

Grimmer G, Dettbarn G, Jacob J. Biomonitoring of polycyclic aromatic hydrocarbons in highly exposed coke plant workers by measurement of urinary phenanthrene and pyrene metabolites (phenols and dihydrodiols). *International Archives of Occupational and Environmental Health* 1993;65(3):189–99.

Grimmer G, Dettbarn G, Seidel A, Jacob J. Detection of carcinogenic aromatic amines in the urine of nonsmokers. *Science of the Total Environment* 2000;247(1):81–90.

Grimmer G, Jacob J, Dettbarn G, Naujack KW. Determination of urinary metabolites of polycyclic aromatic hydrocarbons (PAH) for the risk assessment of PAH-exposed workers. *International Archives of Occupational and Environmental Health* 1997;69(4):231–9.

Grollman AP, Moriya M. Mutagenesis by 8-oxoguanine: an enemy within. *Trends in Genetics* 1993;9(7):246–9.

Gsur A, Zidek T, Schnattinger K, Feik E, Haidinger G, Hollaus P, Mohn-Staudner A, Armbruster C, Madersbacher S, Schatzl G, et al. Association of microsomal epoxide hydrolase polymorphisms and lung cancer risk. *British Journal of Cancer* 2003;89(4):702–6.

Gu J, Liang D, Wang Y, Lu C, Wu X. Effects of *N*-acetyl transferase 1 and 2 polymorphisms on bladder cancer risk in Caucasians. *Mutation Research* 2005;581(1–2): 97–104.

Guan K-L, Figueroa C, Brtva TR, Zhu T, Taylor J, Barber TD, Vojtek AB. Negative regulation of the serine/threonine kinase B-Raf by Akt. *Journal of Biological Chemistry* 2000;275(35):27354–9.

Guengerich FP. Cytochrome P450: what have we learned and what are the future issues? *Drug Metabolism Reviews* 2004;36(2):159–97.

Guengerich FP, Kim DH, Iwasaki M. Role of human cytochrome P-450 IIE1 in the oxidation of many low molecular weight cancer suspects. *Chemical Research in Toxicology* 1991;4(2):168–79.

Guillemette C, Ritter JK, Auyeung DJ, Kessler FK, Housman DE. Structural heterogeneity at the UDP-glucuronosyltransferase 1 locus: functional consequences of three novel missense mutations in the human UGT1A7 gene. *Pharmacogenetics* 2000;10(7):629–44.

Gupta RA, Dubois RN. Colorectal cancer prevention and treatment by inhibition of cyclooxygenase-2. *Nature Reviews Cancer* 2001;1(1):11–21.

Győrffy E, Anna L, Győri Z, Segesdi J, Minárovits J, Soltész I, Kostič S, Csekeő A, Poirier MC, Schoket B. DNA adducts in tumour, normal peripheral lung and bronchus, and peripheral blood lymphocytes from smoking and non-smoking lung cancer patients: correlations between tissues and detection by ^{32}P-postlabelling and immunoassay. *Carcinogenesis* 2004;25(7):1201–9.

Habalová V, Šalagovič J, Kalina I, Štubňa J. Combined analysis of polymorphisms in glutathione S-transferase M1 and microsomal epoxide hydrolase in lung cancer patients. *Neoplasma* 2004;51(5):352–7.

Habraken Y, Sung P, Prakash L, Prakash S. A conserved 5′ to 3′ exonuclease activity in the yeast and human nucleotide excision repair proteins RAD2 and XPG. *Journal of Biological Chemistry* 1994;269(16): 31342–5.

Hainaut P, Hollstein M. p53 and human cancer: the first ten thousand mutations. *Advances in Cancer Research* 2000;77:81–137.

Hainaut P, Pfeifer GP. Patterns of p53 G $\rightarrow$ T transversions in lung cancers reflect the primary mutagenic signature of DNA-damage by tobacco smoke. *Carcinogenesis* 2001;22(3):367–74.

Hale AJ, Smith CA, Sutherland LC, Stoneman VEA, Longthorne VL, Culhane AC, Williams GT. Apoptosis: molecular regulation of cell death. *European Journal of Biochemistry* 1996;236(1):1–26.

Hall J, Brésil H, Donato F, Wild CP, Loktionova NA, Kazanova OI, Komyakov IP, Lemekhov VG, Likhachev AJ, Montesano R. Alkylation and oxidation-DNA damage repair activity in blood leukocytes of smokers and nonsmokers. *International Journal of Cancer* 1993;54(5):728–33.

Hallier E, Langhof T, Dannappel D, Leutbecher M, Schroder K, Goergens HW, Muller A, Bolt HM. Polymorphism of glutathione conjugation of methyl bromide, ethylene oxide and dichloromethane in human blood: influence on the induction of sister chromatid exchanges (SCE) in lymphocytes. *Archives of Toxicology* 1993;67(3):173–8.

Hamada GS, Sugimura H, Suzuki I, Nagura K, Kiyokawa E, Iwase T, Tanaka M, Takahashi T, Watanabe S, Kino J, et al. The heme-binding region polymorphism of cytochrome P450IA1 (*CypIA1*) rather than the *Rsal* polymorphisms of *IIE1* (*CypIIE1*), is associated with lung cancer in Rio de Janeiro. *Cancer Epidemiology, Biomarkers & Prevention* 1995;4(1):63–7.

Hamajima N, Matsuo K, Suzuki T, Nakamura T, Matsuura A, Hatooka S, Shinoda M, Kodera Y, Yamamura Y, Hirai T, et al. No associations of *p73* G4C14-to-A4T14 at exon 2 and *p53* Arg72Pro polymorphisms with the risk of digestive tract cancers in Japanese. *Cancer Letters* 2002;181(1):81–5.

Hanahan D, Weinberg RA. The hallmarks of cancer. *Cell* 2000;100(1):57–70.

Hanawalt PC, Ford JM, Lloyd DR. Functional characterization of global genomic DNA repair and its implications for cancer. *Mutation Research* 2003;544(2–3):107–14.

Haracska L, Unk I, Johnson RE, Johansson E, Burgers PMJ, Prakash S, Prakash L. Roles of yeast DNA polymerase δ and ζ and of Rev1 in the bypass of abasic sites. *Genes & Development* 2001;15(8):945–54.

Haracska L, Yu S-L, Johnson RE, Prakash L, Prakash S. Efficient and accurate replication in the presence of 7,8-dihydro-8-oxoguanine by DNA polymerase η. *Nature Genetics* 2000;25(4):458–61.

Harada YN, Matsuda Y, Shiomi N, Shiomi T. Complementary DNA sequence and chromosomal localization of *xpg*, the mouse counterpart of human repair gene XPG/ERCC5. *Genomics* 1995;28(1):59–65.

Harbour JW, Lai SL, Whang-Peng J, Gazdar AF, Minna JD, Kaye FJ. Abnormalities in structure and expression of the human retinoblastoma gene in SCLC. *Science* 1988;241(4863):353–7.

Harman SM, Liang L, Tsitouras PD, Gucciardo F, Heward CB, Reaven PD, Ping W, Ahmed A, Cutler RG. Urinary excretion of three nucleic acid oxidation adducts and isoprostane $F_2\alpha$ measured by liquid chromatography-mass spectrometry in smokers, ex-smokers, and nonsmokers. *Free Radical Biology & Medicine* 2003;35(10):1301–9.

Harris MJ, Coggan M, Langton L, Wilson SR, Board PG. Polymorphism of the Pi class glutathione-*S*-transferase in normal populations and cancer patients. *Pharmacogenetics* 1998;8(1):27–31.

Hasegawa M, Nelson HH, Peters E, Ringstrom E, Posner M, Kelsey KT. Patterns of gene promoter methylation in squamous cell cancer of the head and neck. *Oncogene* 2002;21(27):4231–6.

Hassett C, Aicher L, Sidhu JS, Omiecinski CJ. Human microsomal epoxide hydrolase: genetic polymorphism and functional expression in vitro of amino acid variants. *Human Molecular Genetics* 1994;3(3):421–8.

Hastürk S, Kemp B, Kalapurakal SK, Kurie JM, Hong WK, Lee JS. Expression of cyclooxygenase-1 and cyclooxygenase-2 in bronchial epithelium and nonsmall cell lung carcinoma. *Cancer* 2002;94(4):1023–31.

Hatcher JF, Swaminathan S. Detection of deoxyadenosine-4-aminobiphenyl adduct in DNA of human uroepithelial cells treated with *N*-hydroxy-4-aminobiphenyl following nuclease P1 enrichment and ^{32}P-postlabeling analysis. *Carcinogenesis* 1995;16(2):295–301.

Haushalter KA, Todd Stukenberg MW, Kirschner MW, Verdine GL. Identification of a new uracil-DNA glycosylase family by expression cloning using synthetic inhibitors. *Current Biology* 1999;9(4):174–85.

Hayashi S, Watanabe J, Kawajiri K. High susceptibility to lung cancer analyzed in terms of combined genotypes of P4501A1 and μ-class glutathione *S*-transferase genes. *Japanese Journal of Cancer Research* 1992;83(8):866–70.

Hayashi S, Watanabe J, Nakachi K, Kawajiri K. Genetic linkage of lung cancer-associated *MspI* polymorphisms with amino acid replacement in the heme binding region of the human cytochrome P450IA1 gene. *Journal of Biochemistry* 1991;110(3):407–11.

Hayes JD, Flanagan JU, Jowsey IR. Glutathione transferases. *Annual Review of Pharmacology and Toxicology* 2005;45:51–88.

Hayes RB, Klein S, Suruda A, Schulte P, Boeniger M, Stewart P, Livingston GK, Oesch F. O^6-alkylguanine DNA alkyltransferase activity in student embalmers. *American Journal of Industrial Medicine* 1997;31(3):361–5.

Hayward RL, Macpherson JS, Cummings J, Monia BP, Smyth JF, Jodrell DI. Antisense Bcl-xl down-regulation switches the response to topoisomerase I inhibition from senescence to apoptosis in colorectal cancer cells, enhancing global cytotoxicity. *Clinical Cancer Research* 2003;9(7):2856–65.

Hazra TK, Izumi T, Boldogh I, Imhoff B, Kow YW, Jaruga P, Dizdaroglu M, Mitra S. Identification and characterization of a human DNA glycosylase for repair of modified bases in oxidatively damaged DNA. *Proceedings of the National Academy of Sciences of the United States of America* 2002a;99(6):3523–8.

Hazra TK, Izumi T, Maidt L, Floyd RA, Mitra S. The presence of two distinct 8-oxoguanine repair enzymes in human cells: their potential complementary roles in preventing mutation. *Nucleic Acids Research* 1998;26(22):5116–22.

Hazra TK, Kow YW, Hatahet Z, Imhoff B, Boldogh I, Mokkapati SK, Mitra S, Izumi T. Identification and characterization of a novel human DNA glycosylase for repair of cytosine-derived lesions. *Journal of Biological Chemistry* 2002b;277(34):30417–20.

Hecht SS. Biochemistry, biology, and carcinogenicity of tobacco-specific *N*-nitrosamines. *Chemical Research in Toxicology* 1998;11(6):559–603.

Hecht SS. Tobacco smoke carcinogens and lung cancer. *Journal of the National Cancer Institute* 1999;91(14):1194–210.

Hecht SS. Cigarette smoking and lung cancer: chemical mechanisms and approaches to prevention. *Lancet Oncology* 2002a;3(8):461–9.

Hecht SS. Human urinary carcinogen metabolites: biomarkers for investigating tobacco and cancer. *Carcinogenesis* 2002b;23(6):907–22.

Hecht SS. Tobacco carcinogens, their biomarkers and tobacco-induced cancer. *Nature Reviews* 2003;3(10): 733–44.

Hecht SS, Carmella SG, Chen M, Koch JFD, Miller AT, Murphy SE, Jensen JA, Zimmerman CL, Hatsukami DK. Quantitation of urinary metabolites of a tobacco-specific lung carcinogen after smoking cessation. *Cancer Research* 1999;59(3):590–6.

Hecht SS, Carmella S, Mori H, Hoffmann D. Role of catechol as a major cocarcinogen in the weakly acidic fraction of smoke condensate. *Journal of the National Cancer Institute* 1981;66(1):163–9.

Hecht SS, Chen M, Yagi H, Jerina DM, Carmella SG. *r-1,t-*2,3,*c*-4-Tetrahydroxy-1,2,3,4-tetrahydrophenanthrene in human urine: a potential biomarker for assessing polycyclic aromatic hydrocarbon metabolic activation. *Cancer Epidemiology, Biomarkers & Prevention* 2003;12(12):1501–8.

Hecht SS, Hoffmann D. Tobacco-specific nitrosamines, an important group of carcinogens in tobacco and tobacco smoke. *Carcinogenesis* 1988;9(6):875–84.

Hecht SS, Hoffmann D. The relevance of tobacco-specific nitrosamines to human cancer. *Cancer Surveys* 1989; 8(2):273–94.

Hecht SS, Isaacs S, Trushin N. Lung tumor induction in A/J mice by the tobacco smoke carcinogens 4-(methylnitrosamino)-1-(3-pyridyl)-1-butanone and benzo[*a*]pyrene: a potentially useful model for evaluation of chemopreventive agents. *Carcinogenesis* 1994; 15(12):2721–5.

Hecht SS, Rivenson A, Braley J, DiBello J, Adams JD, Hoffmann D. Induction of oral cavity tumors in F344 rats by tobacco-specific nitrosamines and snuff. *Cancer Research* 1986;46(8):4162–6.

Hecht SS, Samet JM. Cigarette smoking. In: Rom WN, Markowitz SB, editors. *Environmental and Occupational Medicine.* 4th ed. Philadelphia: Lippincott Williams & Wilkins, 2007:1521–51.

Hecht SS, Thorne RL, Maronpot RR, Hoffmann D. A study of tobacco carcinogenesis. XIII: tumor-promoting subfractions of the weakly acidic fraction. *Journal of the National Cancer Institute* 1975;55(6):1329–36.

Hecht SS, Tricker AR. Nitrosamines derived from nicotine and other tobacco alkaloids. In: Gorrod JW, Jacob P III, editors. *Analytical Determination of Nicotine and Related Compounds and Their Metabolites.* New York: Elsevier Science, 1999:421–88.

Hecht SS, Ye M, Carmella SG, Fredrickson A, Adgate JL, Greaves IA, Church TR, Ryan AD, Mongin SJ, Sexton K. Metabolites of a tobacco-specific lung carcinogen in the urine of elementary school-aged children. *Cancer Epidemiology, Biomarkers & Prevention* 2001; 10(11):1109–16.

Heeschen C, Jang JJ, Weis M, Pathak A, Kaji S, Hu RS, Tsao PS, Johnson FL, Cooke JP. Nicotine stimulates angiogenesis and promotes tumor growth and atherosclerosis. *Nature Medicine* 2001;7(7):833–9.

Heeschen C, Weis M, Aicher A, Dimmeler S, Cooke JP. A novel angiogenic pathway mediated by non-neuronal nicotinic acetylcholine receptors. *Journal of Clinical Investigation* 2002;110(4):527–36.

Hein DW. Molecular genetics and function of NAT1 and NAT2: role in aromatic amine metabolism and carcinogenesis. *Mutation Research* 2002;506–507:65–77.

Hein DW, Doll MA, Fretland AJ, Leff MA, Webb SJ, Xiao GH, Devanaboyina U-S, Nangju NA, Feng Y. Molecular genetics and epidemiology of the *NAT1* and *NAT2* acetylation polymorphisms. *Cancer Epidemiology, Biomarkers & Prevention* 2000a;9(1):29–42.

Hein DW, Doll MA, Rustan TD, Ferguson RJ. Metabolic activation of N-hydroxyarylamines and N-hydroxyarylamides by 16 recombinant human NAT2 allozymes: effects of 7 specific NAT2 nucleic acid substitutions. *Cancer Research* 1995;55(16):3531–6.

Hein DW, Doll MA, Rustan TD, Gray K, Feng Y, Ferguson RJ, Grant DM. Metabolic activation and deactivation of arylamine carcinogens by recombinant human NAT1 and polymorphic NAT2 acetyltransferases. *Carcinogenesis* 1993;14(8):1633–8.

Hein DW, McQueen CA, Grant DM, Goodfellow GH, Kadlubar FF, Weber WW. Pharmacogenetics of the arylamine *N*-acetyltransferases: a symposium in honor of Wendell W. Weber. *Drug Metabolism and Disposition* 2000b;28(12):1425–32.

Helin K, Harlow E, Fattaey A. Inhibition of E2F-1 transactivation by direct binding of the retinoblastoma protein. *Molecular and Cellular Biology* 1993;13(10):6501–8.

Hendler FJ, Ozanne BW. Human squamous cell lung cancers express increased epidermal growth factor receptors. *Journal of Clinical Investigation* 1984; 74(2):647–51.

Hendrich B, Bird A. Identification and characterization of a family of mammalian methyl-CpG binding proteins. *Molecular and Cellular Biology* 1998;18(11):6538–47.

Hendrich B, Hardeland U, Ng H-H, Jiricny J, Bird A. The thymine glycosylase MBD4 can bind to the product of deamination at methylated CpG sites. *Nature* 1999;401(6777):301–4.

Hengartner MO. The biochemistry of apoptosis. *Nature* 2000;407(6805):770–6.

Herbst RS, Bunn PA Jr. Targeting the epidermal growth factor receptor in non-small cell lung cancer. *Clinical Cancer Research* 2003;9(16 Pt 1):5813–24.

Herman JG, Baylin SB. Gene silencing in cancer in association with promoter hypermethylation. *New England Journal of Medicine* 2003;349(21):2042–54.

Hermeking H. The 14-3-3 cancer connection. *Nature Reviews Cancer* 2003;3(12):931–43.

Hernandez-Boussard TM, Hainaut P. A specific spectrum of *p53* mutations in lung cancer from smokers: review of mutations compiled in the IARC *p53* database. *Environmental Health Perspectives* 1998;106(7): 385–91.

Hershko T, Ginsberg D. Up-regulation of Bcl-2 homology 3 (BH3)-only proteins by E2F1 mediates apoptosis. *Journal of Biological Chemistry* 2004;279(10):8627–34.

Hesson L, Dallol A, Minna JD, Maher ER, Latif F. *NORE1A*, a homologue of *RASSF1A* tumour suppressor gene is inactivated in human cancers. *Oncogene* 2003; 22(6):947–54.

Hesson LB, Wilson R, Morton D, Adams C, Walker M, Maher ER, Latif F. CpG island promoter hypermethylation of a novel Ras-effector gene *RASSF2A* is an early event in colon carcinogenesis and correlates inversely with K-ras mutations. *Oncogene* 2005;24(24):3987–94.

Heudorf U, Angerer J. Urinary monohydroxylated phenanthrenes and hydroxypyrene - the effects of smoking habits and changes induced by smoking on monooxygenase-mediated metabolism. *International Archives of Occupational and Environmental Health* 2001; 74(3):177–83.

Heusch WL, Maneckjee R. Signalling pathways involved in nicotine regulation of apoptosis of human lung cancer cells. *Carcinogenesis* 1998;19(4):551–6.

Hey T, Lipps G, Sugasawa K, Iwai S, Hanaoka F, Krauss G. The XPC-HR23B complex displays high affinity and specificity for damaged DNA in a true-equilibrium fluorescence assay. *Biochemistry* 2002;41(21):6583–7.

Hickman MJ, Samson LD. Role of DNA mismatch repair and p53 in signaling induction of apoptosis by alkylating agents. *Proceedings of the National Academy of Sciences of the United States of America* 1999; 96(19):10764–9.

Hida T, Kozaki K, Muramatsu H, Masuda A, Shimizu S, Mitsudomi T, Sugiura T, Ogawa M, Takahashi T. Cyclooxygenase-2 inhibitor induces apoptosis and enhances cytotoxicity of various anticancer agents in non-small cell lung cancer cell lines. *Clinical Cancer Research* 2000;6(5):2006–11.

Hida T, Yatabe Y, Achiwa H, Muramatsu H, Kozaki K, Nakamura S, Ogawa M, Mitsudomi T, Sugiura T, Takahashi T. Increased expression of cyclooxygenase 2 occurs frequently in human lung cancers, specifically in adenocarcinomas. *Cancer Research* 1998;58(17): 3761–4.

Hilbert TP, Chaung W, Boorstein RJ, Cunningham RP, Teebor GW. Cloning and expression of the cDNA encoding the human homologue of the DNA repair enzyme, *Escherichia coli* endonuclease III. *Journal of Biological Chemistry* 1997;272(10):6733–40.

Hillebrandt S, Streffer C, Demidchik EP, Biko J, Reiners C. Polymorphisms in the p53 gene in thyroid tumours and blood samples of children from areas in Belarus. *Mutation Research* 1997;381(2):201–7.

Hillestrøm PR, Hoberg A-M, Weimann A, Poulsen HE. Quantification of 1,N^6-etheno-2'-deoxyadenosine in human urine by column-switching LC/APCI-MS/MS. *Free Radical Biology & Medicine* 2004;36(11):1383–92.

Hiraki A, Matsuo K, Hamajima N, Ito H, Hatooka S, Suyama M, Mitsudomi T, Tajima K. Different risk relations with smoking for non-small-cell lung cancer: comparison of *TP53* and *TP73* genotypes. *Asian Pacific Journal of Cancer Prevention* 2003;4(2):107–12.

Hirami Y, Aoe M, Tsukuda K, Hara F, Otani Y, Koshimune R, Hanabata T, Nagahiro I, Sano Y, Date H, et al. Relation of epidermal growth factor receptor, phosphorylated-Akt, and hypoxia-inducible factor-1α in non-small cell lung cancers. *Cancer Letters* 2004;214(2):157–64.

Hirsch FR, Scagliotti GV, Langer CJ, Varella-Garcia M, Franklin WA. Epidermal growth factor family of receptors in preneoplasia and lung cancer: perspectives for targeted therapies. *Lung Cancer* 2003a;41(Suppl 1): S29–S42.

Hirsch FR, Varella-Garcia M, Bunn PA Jr, Di Maria MV, Veve R, Bremmes RM. Epidermal growth factor receptor in non–small-cell lung carcinomas: correlation between gene copy number and protein expression and impact on prognosis. *Journal of Clinical Oncology* 2003b;21(20):3798–807.

Hirvonen A, Husgafvel-Pursiainen K, Anttila S, Vainio H. The GSTM1 null genotype as a potential risk modifier for squamous cell carcinoma of the lung. *Carcinogenesis* 1993;14(7):1479–81.

Hirvonen A, Husgafvel-Pursiainen K, Karjalainen A, Anttila S, Vainio H. Point mutational Msp and Ile-Val polymorphisms closely linked in the CYP1A1 gene: lack of association with susceptibility to lung cancer in a Finnish study population. *Cancer Epidemiology, Biomarkers & Prevention* 1992;1(6):485–9.

Hoeijmakers JH. Genome maintenance mechanisms for preventing cancer. *Nature* 2001;411(6835):366–74.

Hoffmann D, Adams JD, Lisk D, Fisenne I, Brunnemann KD. Toxic and carcinogenic agents in dry and moist snuff. *Journal of the National Cancer Institute* 1987; 79(6):1281–6.

Hoffmann D, Djordjevic MV, Fan J, Zang E, Glynn T, Connolly GN. Five leading U.S. commercial brands of moist snuff in 1994: assessment of carcinogenic *N*-nitrosamines. *Journal of the National Cancer Institute* 1995;87(24):1862–9.

Hoffmann D, Hecht SS. Advances in tobacco carcinogenesis. In: Cooper CS, Grover PL, editors. *Handbook of Experimental Pharmacology*. Vol. 94/I. Heidelberg (Germany): Springer-Verlag, 1990:63–102.

Hoffmann D, Hoffmann I, El Bayoumy K. The less harmful cigarette: a controversial issue. A tribute to Ernst L. Wynder. *Chemical Research in Toxicology* 2001; 14(7):767–90.

Hoffmann D, Schmeltz I, Hecht SS, Wynder EL. Tobacco carcinogenesis. In: Gelboin H, Ts'o POP, editors. *Polycyclic Hydrocarbons and Cancer*. 1st ed. New York: Academic Press, 1978:85–117.

Hosomi Y, Gemma A, Hosoya Y, Nara M, Okano T, Takenaka K, Yoshimura A, Koizumi K, Shimizu K, Kudoh S. Somatic mutation of the Caspase-5 gene in human lung cancer. *International Journal of Molecular Medicine* 2003;12(4):443–6.

Hosomi Y, Yokose T, Hirose Y, Nakajima R, Nagai K, Nishiwaki Y, Ochiai A. Increased cyclooxygenase 2 (COX-2) expression occurs frequently in precursor lesions of human adenocarcinoma of the lung. *Lung Cancer* 2000;30(2):73–81.

Hou S-M, Fält S, Angelini S, Yang K, Nyberg F, Lambert B, Hemminki K. The *XPD* variant alleles are associated with increased aromatic DNA adduct level and lung cancer risk. *Carcinogenesis* 2002;23(4):599–603.

Houlston RS. CYP1A1 polymorphisms and lung cancer risk: a meta-analysis. *Pharmacogenetics* 2000;10(2):105–14.

Houtsmuller AB, Rademakers S, Nigg AL, Hoogstraten D, Hoeijmakers JHJ, Vermeulen W. Action of DNA repair endonuclease ERCC1/XPF in living cells. *Science* 1999;284(5416):958–61.

Hsieh ETK, Shepherd FA, Tsao M-S. Co-expression of epidermal growth factor receptor and transforming growth factor-α is independent of *ras* mutations in lung adenocarcinoma. *Lung Cancer* 2000;29(2):151–7.

Hsieh L-L, Liou S-H, Chiu L-L, Chen Y-H. Glutathione *S*-transferase (GST) M1 and GST T1 genotypes and hematopoietic effects of benzene exposure. *Archives of Toxicology* 1999;73(2):80–2.

Hsu TC, Johnston DA, Cherry LM, Ramkissoon D, Schantz SP, Jessup JM, Winn RJ, Shirley L, Furlong C. Sensitivity to genotoxic effects of bleomycin in humans: possible relationship to environmental carcinogenesis. *International Journal of Cancer* 1989;43(3):403–9.

Hu Z, Wei Q, Wang X, Shen H. DNA repair gene XPD polymorphism and lung cancer risk: a meta-analysis. *Lung Cancer* 2004;46(1):1–10.

Huang DCS, Strasser A. BH3-only proteins—essential initiators of apoptotic cell death. *Cell* 2000;103(6):839–42.

Huang JC, Hsu DS, Kazantsev A, Sancar A. Substrate spectrum of human excinuclease: repair of abasic sites, methylated bases, mismatches, and bulky adducts. *Proceedings of the National Academy of Sciences of the United States of America* 1994;91(25):12213–7.

Huang M, Stolina M, Sharma S, Mao JT, Zhu L, Miller PW, Wollman J, Herschman H, Dubinett SM. Non-small cell lung cancer cyclooxygenase-2-dependent regulation of cytokine balance in lymphocytes and macrophages: up-regulation of interleukin 10 and down-regulation of interleukin 12 production. *Cancer Research* 1998;58(6):1208–16.

Huang X-E, Hamajima N, Katsuda N, Matsuo K, Hirose K, Mizutani M, Iwata H, Miura S, Xiang J, Tokudome S, et al. Association of *p53* codon Arg72Pro and *p73* G4C14-to-A4T14 at exon 2 genetic polymorphisms with the risk of Japanese breast cancer. *Breast Cancer* 2003;10(4):307–11.

Hübscher U, Maga G, Spadari S. Eukaryotic DNA polymerases. *Annual Review of Biochemistry* 2002;71:133–63.

Hung RJ, Boffetta P, Brennan P, Malaveille C, Hautefeuille A, Donato F, Gelatti U, Spaliviero M, Placidi D, Carta A, et al. GST, NAT, SULT1A1, CYP1B1 genetic polymorphisms, interactions with environmental exposures and bladder cancer risk in a high-risk population. *International Journal of Cancer* 2004;110(4):598–604.

Hung RJ, McKay JD, Gaborieau V, Boffetta P, Hashibe M, Zaridze D, Mukeria A, Szeszenia-Dabrowska N, Lissowska J, Rudnai P, et al. A susceptibility locus for lung cancer maps to nicotinic acetylcholine receptor subunit genes on 15q25. *Nature* 2008;452(7187):633–7.

Husgafvel-Pursiainen K, Kannio A. Cigarette smoking and p53 mutations in lung cancer and bladder cancer. *Environmental Health Perspectives* 1996;104 (Suppl 3):553–6.

Hussain SP, Amstad P, Raja K, Sawyer M, Hofseth L, Shields PG, Hewer A, Phillips DH, Ryberg D, Haugen A, et al. Mutability of p53 hotspot codons to benzo(*a*) pyrene diol epoxide (BPDE) and the frequency of p53 mutations in nontumorous human lung. *Cancer Research* 2001;61(17):6350–5.

Hutt JA, Vuillemenot BR, Barr EB, Grimes MJ, Hahn FF, Hobbs CH, March TH, Gigliotti AP, Seilkop SK, Finch GL, et al. Life-span inhalation exposure to mainstream cigarette smoke induces lung cancer in B6C3F1 mice through genetic and epigenetic pathways. *Carcinogenesis* 2005;26(11):1999–2009.

Hyytinen ER, Frierson HF Jr, Sipe TW, Li CL, Degeorges A, Sikes RA, Chung LW, Dong JT. Loss of heterozygosity and lack of mutations of the *XPG/ERCC5* DNA repair gene at 13q33 in prostate cancer. *Prostate* 1999; 41(3):190–5.

Igney FH, Krammer PH. Death and anti-death: tumour resistance to apoptosis. *Nature Reviews Cancer* 2002; 2(4):277–88.

Inoue O, Seiji K, Kasahara M, Nakatsuka H, Watanabe T, Yin SG, Li GL, Cai SX, Jin C, Ikeda M. Determination of catechol and quinol in the urine of workers exposed to benzene. *British Journal of Industrial Medicine* 1988;45(7):487–92.

Inoue O, Seiji K, Nakatsuka H, Watanabe T, Yin S, Li GL, Cai SX, Jin C, Ikeda M. Excretion of 1,2,4-benzenetriol in the urine of workers exposed to benzene. *British Journal of Industrial Medicine* 1989;46(8):559–65.

International Agency for Research on Cancer. *IARC Monographs on the Evaluation of Carcinogenic Risks to Humans: Some Aromatic Amines, Hydrazine and Related Substances, N-Nitroso Compounds and Miscellaneous Alkylating Agents.* Vol. 4. Lyon (France): International Agency for Research on Cancer, 1974: 127–36.

International Agency for Research on Cancer. *IARC Monographs on the Evaluation of Carcinogenic Risks to Humans: Some Monomers, Plastics and Synthetic Elastomers, and Acrolein.* Vol. 19. Lyon (France): International Agency for Research on Cancer, 1979: 377–438.

International Agency for Research on Cancer. *IARC Monographs on the Evaluation of Carcinogenic Risks to Humans: Some Industrial Chemicals and Dyestuffs.* Vol. 29. Lyon (France): International Agency for Research on Cancer, 1982:93–148.

International Agency for Research on Cancer. *IARC Monographs on the Evaluation of Carcinogenic Risks to Humans: Polynuclear Aromatic Compounds, Part 1: Chemical, Environmental and Experimental Data.* Vol. 32. Lyon (France): International Agency for Research on Cancer, 1983:33–451.

International Agency for Research on Cancer. *IARC Monographs on the Evaluation of Carcinogenic Risks to Humans: Tobacco Smoking.* Vol. 38. Lyon (France): International Agency for Research on Cancer, 1986.

International Agency for Research on Cancer. *IARC Monographs on the Evaluation of Carcinogenic Risks to Humans: Some Naturally Occurring Substances: Food Items and Constituents, Heterocyclic Aromatic Amines and Mycotoxins.* Vol. 56. Lyon (France): International Agency for Research on Cancer, 1993.

International Agency for Research on Cancer. *IARC Monographs on the Evaluation of Carcinogenic Risks to Humans: Some Industrial Chemicals.* Vol. 60. Lyon (France): International Agency for Research on Cancer, 1994.

International Agency for Research on Cancer. *IARC Monographs on the Evaluation of Carcinogenic Risks to Humans: Dry Cleaning, Some Chlorinated Solvents and Other Industrial Chemicals.* Vol. 63. Lyon (France): International Agency for Research on Cancer, 1995a: 393–407.

International Agency for Research on Cancer. *IARC Monographs on the Evaluation of Carcinogenic Risks to Humans: Human Papillomaviruses.* Vol. 64. Lyon (France): International Agency for Research on Cancer, 1995b:35–378.

International Agency for Research on Cancer. *IARC Monographs on the Evaluation of Carcinogenic Risks to Humans: Wood Dust and Formaldehyde.* Vol. 62. Lyon (France): International Agency for Research on Cancer, 1995c:217–362.

International Agency for Research on Cancer. *IARC Monographs on the Evaluation of Carcinogenic Risks to Humans: Re-evaluation of Some Organic Chemicals, Hydrazine and Hydrogen Peroxide.* Vol. 71. Lyon (France): International Agency for Research on Cancer, 1999.

International Agency for Research on Cancer. *IARC Monographs on the Evaluation of Carcinogenic Risks to Humans: Tobacco Smoke and Involuntary Smoking.* Vol. 83. Lyon (France): International Agency for Research on Cancer, 2004.

International Agency for Research on Cancer. IARC TP53 Mutation Database, October 2006; <http://www-p53.iarc.fr/>; accessed: November 8, 2006.

International Agency for Research on Cancer. *IARC Monographs on the Evaluation of Carcinogenic Risks to Humans: Smokeless Tobacco and Tobacco-Specific Nitrosamines.* Vol. 89. Lyon (France): International Agency for Research on Cancer, 2007.

International Agency for Research on Cancer. *IARC Monographs on the Evaluation of Carcinogenic Risks to Humans: Air Pollution, Part 1, Some Non-heterocyclic Polycyclic Aromatic Hydrocarbons and Some Related Industrial Exposures.* Vol. 92. Lyon (France): International Agency for Research on Cancer, in press.

Ishibe N, Wiencke JK, Zuo ZF, McMillan A, Spitz M, Kelsey KT. Susceptibility to lung cancer in light smokers associated with CYP1A1 polymorphisms in Mexican- and African-Americans. *Cancer Epidemiology, Biomarkers & Prevention* 1997;6(12):1075–80.

Jalas JR, Hecht SS, Murphy SE. Cytochrome P450 enzymes as catalysts of metabolism of 4-(methylnitrosamino)-1-(3-pyridyl)-1-butanone, a tobacco-specific carcinogen. *Chemical Research in Toxicology* 2005;18(2):95–110.

Jänne PA, Johnson BE. The role of *MYC, JUN,* and *FOS* oncogenes. In: Pass HI, Mitchell JB, Johnson DH, Turrisi ATM, Minna JD, editors. *Lung Cancer: Principles and Practice.* 2nd ed. Philadelphia: Lippincott Williams & Wilkins, 2000:98–119.

Jaskula-Sztul R, Sokolowski W, Gajecka M, Szyfter K. Association of arylamine N-acetyltransferase (NAT1 and NAT2) genotypes with urinary bladder cancer risk. *Journal of Applied Genetics* 2001;42(2):223–31.

Jeggo PA, Hafezparast M, Thompson AF, Broughton BC, Kaur GP, Zdzienicka MZ, Athwal RS. Localization of a DNA repair gene (XRCC5) involved in double-strand-break rejoining to human chromosome 2. *Proceedings of the National Academy of Sciences of the United States of America* 1992;89(14):6423–7.

Jeon H-S, Kim KM, Park SH, Lee SY, Choi JE, Lee GY, Kam S, Park RW, Kim I-S, Kim CH, et al. Relationship between XPG codon 1104 polymorphism and risk of primary lung cancer. *Carcinogenesis* 2003;24(10):1677–81.

Jernstrom B, Funk M, Frank H, Mannervik B, Seidel A. Glutathione S-transferase A1-1-catalysed conjugation of bay and fjord region diol epoxides or polycyclic aromatic hydrocarbons with glutathione. *Carcinogenesis* 1996;17(7):1491–8.

Ji H, Ramsey MR, Hayes DN, Fan C, McNamara K, Kozlowski P, Torrice C, Wu MC, Shimamura T, Perera SA, et al. LKB1 modulates lung cancer differentiation and metastasis. *Nature* 2007;448(7155):801–10.

Jin X, Wu X, Roth JA, Amos CI, King TM, Branch C, Honn SE, Spitz MR. Higher lung cancer risk for younger African-Americans with the Pro/Pro *p53* genotype. *Carcinogenesis* 1995;16(9):2205–8.

Jin Z, Gao F, Flagg T, Deng X. Nicotine induces multisite phosphorylation of Bad in association with suppression of apoptosis. *Journal of Biological Chemistry* 2004a;279(22):23837–44.

Jin Z, Gao F, Flagg T, Deng X. Tobacco-specific nitrosamine 4-(methylnitrosamino)-1-(3-pyridyl)-1-butanone promotes functional cooperation of Bcl2 and c-Myc through phosphorylation in regulating cell survival and proliferation. *Journal of Biological Chemistry* 2004b;279(38):40209–19.

Jin Z, Xin M, Deng X. Survival function of protein kinase Cι as a novel nitrosamine 4-(methylnitrosamino)-1-(3-pyridyl)-1-butanone-activated Bad kinase. *Journal of Biological Chemistry* 2005;280(16):16045–52.

Johns LE, Houlston RS. *N*-acetyl transferase-2 and bladder cancer risk: a meta-analysis. *Environmental and Molecular Mutagenesis* 2000;36(3):221–7.

Johnson BE, Jänne PA. Epidermal growth factor receptor mutations in patients with non-small cell lung cancer. *Cancer Research* 2005;65(17):7525–9.

Johnson L, Mercer K, Greenbaum D, Bronson RT, Crowley D, Tuveson DA, Jacks T. Somatic activation of the *K-ras* oncogene causes early onset lung cancer in mice. *Nature* 2001a;410(6832):1111–6.

Johnson RE, Haracska L, Prakash S, Prakash L. Role of DNA polymerase η in the bypass of a (6-4) TT photoproduct. *Molecular and Cellular Biology* 2001b;21(10):3558–63.

Johnson RE, Kondratick CM, Prakash S, Prakash L. *hRAD30* Mutations in the variant form of xeroderma pigmentosum. *Science* 1999;285(5425):263–5.

Johnson RE, Washington MT, Haracska L, Prakash S, Prakash L. Eukaryotic polymerases ι and ζ act sequentially to bypass DNA lesions. *Nature* 2000;406(6799):1015–9.

Johnston-Early A, Cohen MH, Minna JD, Paxton LM, Fossieck BE Jr, Ihde DC, Bunn PA Jr, Matthews MJ, Makuch R. Smoking abstinence and small cell lung cancer survival. An association. *JAMA: the Journal of the American Medical Association* 1980;244(19):2175–9.

Jones PA, Baylin SB. The fundamental role of epigenetic events in cancer. *Nature Reviews Genetics* 2002;3(6):415–28.

Jongeneelen FJ. Biological monitoring of environmental exposure to polycyclic aromatic hydrocarbons; 1-hydroxypyrene in urine of people. *Toxicology Letters* 1994;72(1–3):205–11.

Jongeneelen FJ. Benchmark guideline for urinary 1-hydroxypyrene as biomarker of occupational exposure to polycyclic aromatic hydrocarbons. *Annals of Occupational Hygiene* 2001;45(1):3–13.

Jongeneelen FJ, Anzion RB, Leijdekkers CM, Bos RP, Henderson PT. 1-Hydroxypyrene in human urine after exposure to coal tar and a coal tar derived product. *International Archives of Occupational and Environmental Health* 1985;57(1):47–55.

Jull BA, Plummer HK III, Schuller HM. Nicotinic receptor-mediated activation by the tobacco-specific nitrosamine NNK of a Raf-1/MAP kinase pathway, resulting in phosphorylation of c-myc in human small cell lung carcinoma cells and pulmonary neuroendocrine cells. *Journal of Cancer Research and Clinical Oncology* 2001;127(12):707–17.

Junker K, Stachetzki U, Rademacher D, Linder A, Macha H-N, Heinecke A, Müller K-M, Thomas M. HER2/neu expression and amplification in non-small cell lung cancer prior to and after neoadjuvant therapy. *Lung Cancer* 2005;48(1):59–67.

Kadlubar FF, Beland FA. Chemical properties of ultimate carcinogenic metabolites of arylamines and arylamides. In: Harvey RG, editor. *Polycyclic Hydrocarbons and Carcinogenesis*. ACS Symposium Series 283. Washington: American Chemical Society, 1985:341–70.

Kaghad M, Bonnet H, Yang A, Creancier L, Biscan J-C, Valent A, Minty A, Chalon P, Lelias J-M, Dumont X, et al. Monoallelically expressed gene related to p53 at 1p36, a region frequently deleted in neuroblastoma and other human cancers. *Cell* 1997;90(4):809–19.

Kaina B, Fritz G, Mitra S, Coquerelle T. Transfection and expression of human O^6-methylguanine-DNA methyltransferase (MGMT) cDNA in Chinese hamster cells: the role of MGMT in protection against the genotoxic effects of alkylating agents. *Carcinogenesis* 1991;12(10):1857–67.

Kamb A, Gruis NA, Weaver-Feldhaus J, Liu Q, Harshman K, Tavtigian SV, Stockert E, Day RS III, Johnson BE, Skolnick MH. A cell cycle regulator potentially involved in genesis of many tumor types. *Science* 1994;264(5157):436–40.

Kanematsu T, Yano S, Uehara H, Bando Y, Sone S. Phosphorylation, but not overexpression, of epidermal growth factor receptor is associated with poor prognosis of non-small cell lung cancer patients. *Oncology Research* 2003;13(5):289–98.

Kang MJ, Oh Y-M, Lee JC, Kim DG, Park MJ, Lee MG, Hyun IG, Han SK, Shim Y-S, Jung K-S. Lung matrix metalloproteinase-9 correlates with cigarette smoking and obstruction of airflow. *Journal of Korean Medical Science* 2003;18(6):821–7.

Kangavari S, Matetzky S, Shah PK, Yano J, Chyu K-Y, Fishbein MC, Cercek B. Smoking increases inflammation and metalloproteinase expression in human carotid atherosclerotic plaques. *Journal of Cardiovascular Pharmacology and Therapeutics* 2004;9(4):291–8.

Kantarci OH, Lesnick TG, Yang P, Meyer RL, Hebrink DD, McMurray CT, Weinshenker BG. Myeloperoxidase –463 (G → A) polymorphism associated with lower risk of lung cancer. *Mayo Clinic Proceedings* 2002;77(1):17–22.

Kanuri M, Minko IG, Nechev LV, Harris TM, Harris CM, Lloyd RS. Error prone translesion synthesis past γ-hydroxypropano deoxyguanosine, the primary acrolein-derived adduct in mammalian cells. *Journal of Biological Chemistry* 2002;277(21):18257–65.

Kari C, Chan TO, Rocha de Quadros M, Rodeck U. Targeting the epidermal growth factor receptor in cancer: apoptosis takes center stage. *Cancer Research* 2003;63(1):1–5.

Karran P. Mechanisms of tolerance to DNA damaging therapeutic drugs. *Carcinogenesis* 2001;22(12):1931–7.

Karuman P, Gozani O, Odze RD, Zhou XC, Zhu H, Shaw R, Brien TP, Bozzuto CD, Ooi D, Cantley LC, et al. The Peutz-Jegher gene product LKB1 is a mediator of p53-dependent cell death. *Molecular Cell* 2001;7(6):1307–19.

Kasai H, Iwamoto-Tanaka N, Miyamoto T, Kawanami K, Kawanami S, Kido R, Ikeda M. Life style and urinary 8-hydroxydeoxyguanosine, a marker of oxidative DNA damage: effects of exercise, working conditions, meat intake, body mass index, and smoking. *Japanese Journal of Cancer Research* 2001;92(1):9–15.

Kato S, Bowman EF, Harrington A, Blomeke B, Shields PG. Human lung carcinogen-DNA adduct levels mediated by genetic polymorphisms in vivo. *Journal of the National Cancer Institute* 1995;87(12):902–7.

Katoh T, Kaneko S, Takasawa S, Nagata N, Inatomi H, Ikemura K, Itoh H, Matsumoto T, Kawamoto T, Bell DA. Human glutathione-*S*-transferase P1 polymorphism and susceptibility to smoking related epithelial cancer; oral, lung, gastric, colorectal and urothelial cancer. *Pharmacogenetics* 1999;9(2):165–9.

Kauffmann-Zeh A, Rodriguez-Viciana P, Ulrich E, Gilbert C, Coffer P, Downward J, Evan G. Suppression of c-Myc-induced apoptosis by Ras signalling through PI(3)K and PKB. *Nature* 1997;385(6616):544–8.

Kaur TB, Travaline JM, Gaughan JP, Richie JP Jr, Stellman SD, Lazarus P. Role of polymorphisms in codons 143 and 160 of the O^6-alkylguanine DNA alkyltransferase gene in lung cancer risk. *Cancer Epidemiology, Biomarkers & Prevention* 2000;9(3):339–42.

Kawajiri K, Nakachi K, Imai K, Watanabe J, Hayashi S-I. Germ line polymorphisms of p53 and CYP1A1 genes involved in human lung cancer. *Carcinogenesis* 1993;14(6):1085–9.

Kawajiri K, Nakachi K, Imai K, Yoshii A, Shinoda N, Watanabe J. Identification of genetically high risk individuals to lung cancer by DNA polymorphisms of the cytochrome P450 0IA1 gene. *FEBS Letters* 1990;263(1):131–3.

Kelley DJ, Mestre JR, Subbaramaiah K, Sacks PG, Schantz SP, Tanabe T, Inoue H, Ramonetti JT, Dannenberg AJ. Benzo[*a*]pyrene up-regulates cyclooxygenase-2 gene expression in oral epithelial cells. *Carcinogenesis* 1997;18(4):795–9.

Kennedy SG, Wagner AJ, Conzen SD, Jordan J, Bellacosa A, Tsichlis PN, Hay N. The PI 3-kinase/Akt signaling pathway delivers an anti-apoptotic signal. *Genes & Development* 1997;11(6):701–13.

Keohavong P, DeMichele MAA, Melacrinos AC, Landreneau RJ, Weyant RJ, Siegfried JM. Detection of K-*ras* mutations in lung carcinomas: relationship to prognosis. *Clinical Cancer Research* 1996;2(2):411–8.

Kern JA, Schwartz DA, Nordberg JE, Weiner DB, Greene MI, Torney L, Robinson RA. p185[neu] Expression in human lung adenocarcinomas predicts shortened survival. *Cancer Research* 1990;50(16):5184–7.

Kerr JFR, Wyllie AH, Currie AR. Apoptosis: a basic biological phenomenon with wide-ranging implications in tissue kinetics. *British Journal of Cancer* 1972;26(4):239–57.

Khan QA, Vousden KH, Dipple A. Lack of p53-mediated G1 arrest in response to an environmental carcinogen. *Oncology* 1999;57(3):258–64.

Khokhlatchev A, Rabizadeh S, Xavier R, Nedwidek M, Chen T, Zhang X, Seed B, Ayruch J. Identification of a novel ras-regulated proapoptotic pathway. *Current Biology* 2002;12(4):253–65.

Khwaja A. Akt is more than just a Bad kinase. *Nature* 1999;401(6748):33–4.

Kihara M, Kihara M, Noda K. Lung cancer risk of GSTM1 null genotype is dependent on the extent of tobacco smoke exposure. *Carcinogenesis* 1994;15(2):415–8.

Kihara M, Kihara M, Noda K. Lung cancer risk of the *GSTM1* null genotype is enhanced in the presence of the *GSTP1* mutated genotype in male Japanese smokers. *Cancer Letters* 1999;137(1):53–60.

Kihara M, Kihara M, Noda K, Okamoto N. Increased risk for lung cancer in Japanese smokers with mu class glutathione-*S*-transferase gene deficiency. *Cancer Letters* 1993;71(1–3):151–5.

Kim D, Guengerich FP. Cytochrome P450 activation of arylamines and heterocyclic amines. *Annual Review of Pharmacology and Toxicology* 2005;45:27–49.

Kim D-H, Kim JS, Ji Y-I, Shim YM, Kim H, Han J, Park J. Hypermethylation of *RASSF1A* promoter is associated with the age at starting smoking and a poor prognosis in primary non-small cell lung cancer. *Cancer Research* 2003;63(13):3743–6.

Kim D-H, Nelson HH, Wiencke JK, Christiani DC, Wain JC, Mark EJ, Kelsey KT. Promoter methylation of DAP-kinase: association with advanced stage in non-small cell lung cancer. *Oncogene* 2001;20(14):1765–70.

Kim JH, Sherman ME, Curriero FC, Guengerich FP, Strickland PT, Sutter TR. Expression of cytochromes P450 1A1 and 1B1 in human lung from smokers, non-smokers, and ex-smokers. *Toxicology and Applied Pharmacology* 2004a;199(3):210–9.

Kim PM, Wells PG. Genoprotection by UDP-glucuronosyltransferases in peroxidase-dependent, reactive oxygen species-mediated micronucleus initiation by the carcinogens 4-(methylnitrosamino)-1-(3-pyridyl)-1-butanone and benzo[*a*]pyrene. *Cancer Research* 1996;56(7):1526–32.

Kim SY, Choi JK, Cho YH, Chung EJ, Paek D, Chung HW. Chromosomal aberrations in workers exposed to low levels of benzene: association with genetic polymorphisms. *Pharmacogenetics* 2004b;14(7):453–63.

Kinzler KW, Zehnbauer BA, Brodeur GM, Seeger RC, Trent JM, Meltzer PS, Vogelstein B. Amplification units containing human N-*myc* and c-*myc* genes. *Proceedings of the National Academy of Sciences of the United States of America* 1986;83(4):1031–5.

Klungland A, Lindahl T. Second pathway for completion of human DNA base excision-repair: reconstitution with purified proteins and requirement for DNase IV (FEN1). *EMBO Journal* 1997;16(11):3341–8.

Koch KS, Fletcher RG, Grond MP, Inyang AI, Lu XP, Brenner DA, Leffert HL. Inactivation of plasmid reporter gene expression by one benzo(*a*)pyrene diol-epoxide DNA adduct in adult rat hepatocytes. *Cancer Research* 1993;53(10 Suppl):2279–86.

Kohno T, Shinmura K, Tosaka M, Tani M, Kim S-R, Sugimura H, Nohmi T, Kasai H, Yokota J. Genetic polymorphisms and alternative splicing of the *hOGG1* gene, that is involved in the repair of 8-hydroxyguanine in damaged DNA. *Oncogene* 1998;16(25):3219–25.

Koi M, Umar A, Chauhan DP, Cherian SP, Carethers JM, Kunkel TA, Boland CR. Human chromosome 3 corrects mismatch repair deficiency and microsatellite instability and reduces *N*-methyl-*N*'-nitro-*N*-nitrosoguanidine tolerance in colon tumor cells with homozygous hMLH1 mutation. *Cancer Research* 1994;54(16):4308–12.

Koki A, Khan NK, Woerner BM, Dannenberg AJ, Olson L, Seibert K, Edwards D, Hardy M, Isakson P, Masferrer JL. Cyclooxygenase-2 in human pathological disease. *Advances in Experimental Medicine and Biology* 2002;507:177–84.

Kopplin A, Eberle-Adamkiewicz G, Glüsenkamp KH, Nehls P, Kirstein U. Urinary excretion of 3-methyladenine and 3-ethyladenine after controlled exposure to tobacco smoke. *Carcinogenesis* 1995;16(11):2637–41.

Korsmeyer SJ. Regulators of cell death. *Trends in Genetics* 1995;11(3):101–5.

Korsmeyer SJ. *BCL-2* gene family and the regulation of programmed cell death. *Cancer Research* 1999;59(7 Suppl):1693s–1700s.

Kozack R, Seo K-Y, Jelinsky SA, Loechler EL. Toward an understanding of the role of DNA adduct conformation in defining mutagenic mechanism based on studies of the major adduct (formed at N^2-dG) of the potent environmental carcinogen, benzo[*a*]pyrene. *Mutation Research* 2000;450(1–2):41–59.

Kozekov ID, Nechev LV, Moseley MS, Harris CM, Rizzo CJ, Stone MP, Harris TM. DNA interchain cross-links formed by acrolein and crotonaldehyde. *Journal of the American Chemical Society* 2003;125(1):50–61.

Krause RJ, Elfarra AA. Oxidation of butadiene monoxide to *meso*- and (±)-diepoxybutane by cDNA-expressed human cytochrome P450s and by mouse, rat, and human liver microsomes: evidence for preferential hydration of *meso*-diepoxybutane in rat and human liver microsomes. *Archives of Biochemistry and Biophysics* 1997;337(2):176–84.

Kreuzer M, Heinrich J, Kreienbrock L, Rosario AS, Gerken M, Wichmann HE. Risk factors for lung cancer among nonsmoking women. *International Journal of Cancer* 2002;100(6):706–13.

Kreuzer M, Kreienbrock L, Gerken M, Heinrich J, Bruske-Hohlfeld I, Muller K-M, Wichmann HE. Risk factors for lung cancer in young adults. *American Journal of Epidemiology* 1998;147(11):1028–37.

Kriek E, Rojas M, Alexandrov K, Bartsch H. Polycyclic aromatic hydrocarbon-DNA adducts in humans: relevance as biomarkers for exposure and cancer risk. *Mutation Research* 1998;400(1–2):215–31.

Kris MG, Natale RB, Herbst RS, Lynch TJ Jr, Prager D, Belani CP, Schiller JH, Kelly K, Spiridonidis H, Sandler A, et al. Efficacy of gefitinib, an inhibitor of the epidermal growth factor receptor tyrosine kinase, in symptomatic patients with non–small cell lung cancer: a randomized trial. *JAMA: The Journal of the American Medical Association* 2003;290(16):2149–58.

Kroemer G. Mitochondrial control of apoptosis: an overview. *Biochemical Society Symposium* 1999;66:1–15.

Krysan K, Merchant FH, Zhu L, Dohadwala M, Luo J, Ling Y, Heuze-Vourc'h N, Põld M, Seligson D, Chia D, et al. COX-2-dependent stabilization of survivin in non-small cell lung cancer. *FASEB Journal* 2004;18(1):206–8.

Krzesniak M, Butkiewicz D, Samojedny A, Choraży M, Rusin M. Polymorphisms in *TDG* and *MGMT* genes–epidemiological and functional study in lung cancer patients from Poland. *Annals of Human Genetics* 2004; 68(4):300–12.

Kubota Y, Nash RA, Klungland A, Schar P, Barnes DE, Lindahl T. Reconstitution of DNA base excision-repair with purified human proteins: interaction between DNA polymerase beta and the XRCC1 protein. *EMBO Journal* 1996;15(23):6662–70.

Kurie JM, Shin HJ, Lee JS, Morice RC, Ro JY, Lippman SM, Hittelman WN, Yu R, Lee JJ, Hong WK. Increased epidermal growth factor receptor expression in metaplastic bronchial epithelium. *Clinical Cancer Research* 1996;2(10):1787–93.

Lackmann GM, Salzberger U, Töllner U, Chen M, Carmella SG, Hecht SS. Metabolites of a tobacco-specific carcinogen in the urine from newborns. *Journal of the National Cancer Institute* 1999;91(5):459–65.

Lahn M, Su C, Li S, Chedid M, Hanna KR, Graff JR, Sandusky GE, Ma D, Nikikiza C, Sundell KL, et al. Expression levels of protein kinase C-α in non-small-cell lung cancer. *Clinical Lung Cancer* 2004;6(3):184–9.

Landi S. Mammalian class theta GST and differential susceptibility to carcinogens: a review. *Mutation Research* 2000;463(3):247–83.

Landi MT, Sinha R, Lang NP, Kadlubar FF. Human cytochrome P4501A2. *IARC Scientific Publications* 1999; (148):173–95.

Landi MT, Zocchetti C, Bernucci I, Kadlubar FF, Tannenbaum S, Skipper P, Bartsch H, Malaveille C, Shields P, Caporaso NE, et al. Cytochrome P4501A2: enzyme induction and genetic control in determining 4-aminobiphenyl-hemoglobin adduct levels. *Cancer Epidemiology, Biomarkers & Prevention* 1996;5(9):693–8.

Lasko DD, Harvey SC, Malaikal SB, Kadlubar FF, Essigmann JM. Specificity of mutagenesis by 4-aminobiphenyl: a possible role for *N*-(deoxyadenosin-8-yl)-4-aminobiphenyl as a premutational lesion. *Journal of Biological Chemistry* 1988;263(30):15429–35.

Latham GJ, Zhou L, Harris CM, Harris TM, Lloyd RS. The replication fate of *R*- and *S*-styrene oxide adducts on adenine N^6 is dependent on both the chirality of the lesion and the local sequence context. *Journal of Biological Chemistry* 1993;268(31):23427–34.

LaVoie EJ, Rice JE. Structure-activity relationships among tricyclic polynuclear aromatic hydrocarbons. In: Yang SK, Silverman BD, editors. *Polycyclic Aromatic Hydrocarbon Carcinogenesis: Structure-Activity Relationships*. Vol. 1. Boca Raton (FL): CRC Press, 1988:151–75.

Lawrence CW, Borden A, Banerjee SK, LeClerc JE. Mutation frequency and spectrum resulting from a single abasic site in a single–stranded vector. *Nucleic Acids Research* 1990;18(8):2153–7.

Lazarus P, Zheng Y, Runkle EA, Muscat JE, Wiener D. Genotype-phenotype correlation between the polymorphic *UGT2B17* gene deletion and NNAL glucuronidation activities in human liver microsomes. *Pharmacogenetics and Genomics* 2005;15(11):769–78.

Le Calvez F, Mukeria A, Hunt JD, Kelm O, Hung RJ, Tanière P, Brennan P, Boffetta P, Zaridze DG, Hainut P. *TP53* and *KRAS* mutation load and types in lung cancers in relation to tobacco smoke: distinct patterns in never, former, and current smokers. *Cancer Research* 2005;65(12):5076–83.

Le Marchand L, Derby KS, Murphy SE, Hecht SS, Hatsukami D, Carmella SG, Tiirikainen M, Wang H. Smokers with the *CHRNA* lung cancer-associated variants are exposed to higher levels of nicotine equivalents and a carcinogenic tobacco-specific nitrosamine. *Cancer Research* 2008;68(22):9137–40.

Le Marchand L, Donlon T, Lum-Jones A, Seifried A, Wilkens LR. Association of the *hOGG1* Ser326Cys polymorphism with lung cancer risk. *Cancer Epidemiology, Biomarkers & Prevention* 2002;11(4):409–12.

Le Marchand L, Seifried A, Lum A, Wilkens LR. Association of the myeloperoxidase $^{-463}$G→A polymorphism with lung cancer risk. *Cancer Epidemiology, Biomarkers & Prevention* 2000;9(2):181–4.

Le Marchand L, Sivaraman L, Pierce L, Seifried A, Lum A, Wilkens LR, Lau AF. Associations of CYP1A1, GSTM1, and CYP2E1 polymorphisms with lung cancer suggest cell type specificities to tobacco carcinogens. *Cancer Research* 1998;58(21):4858–63.

Leach FS, Nicolaides NC, Papadopoulos N, Liu B, Jen J, Parsons R, Peltomaki P, Sistonen P, Aaltonen LA, Nystrom-Lahti M. Mutations of a *mutS* homolog in hereditary nonpolyposis colorectal cancer. *Cell* 1993; 75(6):1215–25.

Lechner JF, Fugaro JM. *RAS* and *ERBB 2*. In: Pass HI, Mitchell JB, Johnson DH, Turrisi AT, Minna JD, editors. *Lung Cancer Principles and Practice,* 2nd ed. Philadelphia: Lippincott Williams & Wilkins, 2000:89–97.

Lee BL, Ong HY, Ong YB, Ong CN. A sensitive liquid chromatographic method for the spectrophotometric determination of urinary *trans,trans*-muconic acid. *Journal of Chromatography B* 2005;818(2):277–83.

Lee D-H, O'Connor TR, Pfeifer GP. Oxidative DNA damage induced by copper and hydrogen peroxide promotes CG→TT tandem mutations at methylated CpG dinucleotides in nucleotide excision repair-deficient cells. *Nucleic Acids Research* 2002a;30(16):3566–73.

Lee H-C, Lim MLR, Lu C-Y, Liu VWS, Fahn H-J, Zhang C, Nagley P, Wei Y-H. Concurrent increase of oxidative DNA damage and lipid peroxidation together with mitochondrial DNA mutation in human lung tissues during aging—smoking enhances oxidative stress on the aged tissues. *Archives of Biochemistry and Biophysics* 1999a;362(2):309–16.

Lee J-M, Lee Y-C, Yang S-Y, Yang P-W, Luh S-P, Lee C-J, Chen C-J, Wu M-T. Genetic polymorphisms of *XRCC1* and risk of the esophageal cancer. *International Journal of Cancer* 2001;95(4):240–6.

Lee SH, Kim HS, Park WS, Kim SY, Lee KY, Kim SH, Lee JY, Yoo NJ. Non-small cell lung cancers frequently express phosphorylated Akt; an immunohistochemical study. *APMIS* 2002b;110(7–8):587–92.

Lee WJ, Brennan P, Boffetta P, London SJ, Benhamou S, Rannug A, To-Figueras J, Ingelman-Sundberg M, Shields P, Gaspari L, et al. Microsomal epoxide hydrolase polymorphisms and lung cancer risk: a quantitative review. *Biomarkers* 2002c;7(3):230–41.

Lemjabbar H, Li D, Gallup M, Sidhu S, Drori E, Basbaum C. Tobacco smoke-induced lung cell proliferation mediated by tumor necrosis factor α-converting enzyme and amphiregulin. *Journal of Biological Chemistry* 2003;278(28):26202–7.

Levin JO. First international workshop on hydroxypyrene as a biomarker for PAH exposure in man—summary and conclusions. *Science of the Total Environment* 1995;163(1–3):165–8.

Levin W, Wood AW, Yagi H, Dansette PM, Jerina DM, Conney AH. Carcinogenicity of benzo[*a*]pyrene 4,5-, 7,8-, and 9,10-oxides on mouse skin. *Proceedings of the National Academy of Sciences of the United States of America* 1976;73(1):243–7.

Levine RL, Miller H, Grollman A, Ohashi E, Ohmori H, Masutani C, Hanaoka F, Moriya M. Translesion DNA synthesis catalyzed by human pol η and pol κ across $1,N^6$-ethenodeoxyadenosine. *Journal of Biological Chemistry* 2001;276(22):18717–21.

Lewis SJ, Cherry NM, Niven RM, Barber PV, Povey AC. Associations between smoking, GST genotypes and N7-methylguanine levels in DNA extracted from bronchial lavage cells. *Mutation Research* 2004;559(1–2):11–8.

Li F, Ambrosini G, Chu EY, Plescia J, Tognin S, Marchisio PC, Altieri DC. Control of apoptosis and mitotic spindle checkpoint by survivin. *Nature* 1998a;396(6711):580–4.

Li G, Sturgis EM, Wang L-E, Chamberlain RM, Amos C, Spitz MR, El-Naggar A, Hong WK, Wei Q. Association of a *p73* exon 2 G4C14-to-A4T14 polymorphism with risk of squamous cell carcinoma of the head and neck. *Carcinogenesis* 2004a;25(7):1–7.

Li G, Wang L-E, Chamberlain RM, Amos CI, Spitz MR, Wei Q. *p73* G4C14-to-A4T14 polymorphism and risk of lung cancer. *Cancer Research* 2004b;64(19):6863–6.

Li GM, Modrich P. Restoration of mismatch repair to nuclear extracts of H6 colorectal tumor cells by a heterodimer of human MutL homologs. *Proceedings of the National Academy of Sciences of the United States of America* 1995;92(6):1950–4.

Li GM, Wang H, Romano LJ. Human MutSα specifically binds to DNA containing aminofluorene and acetylaminofluorene adducts. *Journal of Biological Chemistry* 1996;271(39):24084–8.

Li H, Yang P, Schwartz AG. Analysis of age of onset data from case–control family studies. *Biometrics* 1998b;54(3)1030–9.

Li X, Hemminki K. Inherited predisposition to early onset lung cancer according to histological type. *International Journal of Cancer* 2004;112(3):451–7.

Lijinsky W. *Chemistry and Biology of N-Nitroso Compounds*. New York: Cambridge University Press, 1992.

Lin D, Lay JO Jr, Bryant MS, Malaveille C, Friesen M, Bartsch H, Lang NP, Kadlubar FF. Analysis of 4-aminobiphenyl-DNA adducts in human urinary bladder and lung by alkaline hydrolysis and negative ion gas chromatography-mass spectrometry. *Environmental Health Perspectives* 1994;102(Suppl 6):11–6.

Lin P, Wang S-L, Wang H-J, Chen K-W, Lee H-S, Tsai K-J, Chen C-Y, Lee H. Association of *CYP1A1* and microsomal epoxide hydrolase polymorphisms with lung squamous cell carcinoma. *British Journal of Cancer* 2000;82(4):852–7.

Lin X, Böhle AS, Dohrmann P, Leuschner I, Schulz A, Kremer B, Fändrich F. Overexpression of phosphatidylinositol 3-kinase in human lung cancer. *Langenbeck's Archives of Surgery* 2001b;386(4):293–301.

Lindstrom J. Nicotinic acetylcholine receptors in health and disease. *Molecular Neurobiology* 1997;15(2):193–222.

Lindstrom JM. Nicotinic acetylcholine receptors of muscles and nerves: comparison of their structures, functional roles, and vulnerability to pathology. *Annals of the New York Academy of Sciences* 2003;998:41–52.

Lips J, Kaina B. DNA double-strand breaks trigger apoptosis in p53-deficient fibroblasts. *Carcinogenesis* 2001;22(4):579–85.

Liu G, Zhou W, Wang LI, Park S, Miller DP, Xu L-L, Wain JC, Lynch TJ, Su L, Christiani DC. *MPO* and *SOD2* polymorphisms, gender, and the risk of non-small cell lung carcinoma. *Cancer Letters* 2004;214(1):69–79.

Liu L, Qin X, Gerson SL. Reduced lung tumorigenesis in human methylguanine DNA—methyltransferase transgenic mice achieved by expression of transgene within the target cell. *Carcinogenesis* 1999;20(2):279–84.

Liu Z, Muehlbauer K-R, Schmeiser HH, Hergenhahn M, Belharazem D, Hollstein MC. p53 Mutations in benzo(*a*)pyrene-exposed human p53 knock-in murine fibroblasts correlate with p53 mutations in human lung tumors. *Cancer Research* 2005;65(7):2583–7.

Lloyd DR, Hanawalt PC. p53-dependent global genomic repair of benzo[*a*]pyrene-7,8-diol-9,10-epoxide adducts in human cells. *Cancer Research* 2000;60(3):517–21.

Lloyd DR, Hanawalt PC. p53 controls global nucleotide excision repair of low levels of structurally diverse benzo(*g*)chrysene-DNA adducts in human fibroblasts. *Cancer Research* 2002;62(18):5288–94.

Loechler EL, Green CL, Essigmann JM. *In vivo* mutagenesis by O^6-methylguanine built into a unique site in a viral genome. *Proceedings of the National Academy of Sciences of the United States of America* 1984;81(20):6271–5.

Loft S, Poulsen HE. Estimation of oxidative DNA damage in man from urinary excretion of repair products. *Acta Biochimica Polonica* 1998;45(1):133–44.

Loktionova NA, Pegg AE. Interaction of mammalian O^6-alkylguanine-DNA alkyltransferases with O^6-benzylguanine. *Biochemical Pharmacology* 2002;63(8):1431–42.

Lonardo F, Dragnev KH, Freemantle SJ, Ma Y, Memoli N, Sekula D, Knauth EA, Beebe JS, Dmitrovsky E. Evidence for the epidermal growth factor receptor as a target for lung cancer prevention. *Clinical Cancer Research* 2002;8(1):54–60.

London SJ, Daly AK, Cooper J, Navidi WC, Carpenter CL, Idle JR. Polymorphism of glutathione-*S*-transferase *M1* and lung cancer risk among African-Americans and Caucasians in Los Angeles County, California. *Journal of the National Cancer Institute* 1995;87(16):1246–53.

London SJ, Yuan JM, Chung FL, Gao YT, Coetzee GA, Ross RK, Yu MC. Isothiocyanates, glutathione *S*-transferase M1 and T1 polymorphisms, and lung-cancer risk: a prospective study of men in Shanghai, China. *Lancet* 2000;356(9231):724–9.

Longley MJ, Pierce AJ, Modrich P. DNA polymerase δ is required for human mismatch repair *in vitro*. *Journal of Biological Chemistry* 1997;272(16):10917–21.

López-Larraza D, De Luca JC, Bianchi NO. The kinetics of DNA damage by bleomycin in mammalian cells. *Mutation Research* 1990;232(1):57–61.

Lowe SW, Bodis S, McClatchey A, Remington L, Ruley HE, Fisher DE, Housman DE, Jacks T. p53 status and

the efficacy of cancer therapy in vivo. *Science* 1994; 266(5186):807–10.

Lu L-M, Zavitz CCJ, Chen B, Kianpour S, Wan Y, Stampfli MR. Cigarette smoke impairs NK cell-dependent tumor immune surveillance. *Journal of Immunology* 2007;178(2):936–43.

Lu W, Xing D, Qi J, Tan W, Miao X, Lin D. Genetic polymorphism in myeloperoxidase but not *GSTM1* is associated with risk of lung squamous cell carcinoma in a Chinese population. *International Journal of Cancer* 2002;102(3):275–9.

Luch A. Nature and nurture – lessons from chemical carcinogenesis. *Nature Reviews Cancer* 2005;5(2):113–25.

Lukas J, Parry D Aagaard L, Mann DJ, Bartkova J, Strauss M, Peters G, Bartek J. Retinoblastoma-protein-dependent cell-cycle inhibition by the tumor suppressor p16. *Nature* 1995;375(6531):503–6.

Lunn RM, Helzlsouer KJ, Parshad R, Umbach DM, Harris EL, Sanford KK, Bell DA. XPD polymorphisms: effects on DNA repair proficiency. *Carcinogenesis* 2000; 21(4):551–5.

Lunn RM, Langlois RG, Hsieh LL, Thompson CL, Bell DA. XRCC1 polymorphisms: effects on aflatoxin B_1–DNA adducts and glycophorin A variant frequency. *Cancer Research* 1999;59(11):2557–61.

Lutz RJ. Role of the BH3 (Bcl-2 homology 3) domain in the regulation of apoptosis and Bcl-2-related proteins. *Biochemical Society Transactions* 2000;28(2):51–6.

Lynch TJ, Bell DW, Sordella R, Gurubhagavatula S, Okimoto RA, Brannigan BW, Harris PL, Haserlat SM, Supko JG, Haluska FG, et al. Activating mutations in the epidermal growth factor receptor underlying responsiveness of non–small-cell lung cancer to gefitinib. *New England Journal of Medicine* 2004;350(21):2129–39.

Ma QW, Lin GF, Chen JG, Xiang CQ, Guo WC, Golka K, Shen JH. Polymorphism of N-acetyltransferase 2 (NAT2) gene polymorphism in Shanghai population: occupational and non-occupational bladder cancer patient groups. *Biomedical and Environmental Sciences* 2004;17(3):291–8.

Ma S, Egyházi S, Ueno T, Lindholm C, Kreklau EL, Stierner U, Ringborg U, Hansson J. O^6-methylguanine-DNA-methyltransferase expression and gene polymorphisms in relation to chemotherapeutic response in metastatic melanoma. *British Journal of Cancer* 2003;89(8): 1517–23.

Mabrouk I, Baccouche S, El-Abed R, Mokdad-Gargouri R, Mosbah A, Said S, Daoud J, Frikha M, Jlidi R, Gargouri A. No evidence of correlation between p53 codon 72 polymorphism and risk of bladder or breast carcinoma in Tunisian patients. *Annals of the New York Academy of Sciences* 2003;1010:764–70.

Macklin KD, Maus ADJ, Pereira EFR, Albuquerque EX, Conti-Fine BM. Human vascular endothelial cells express functional nicotinic acetylcholine receptors. *Journal of Pharmacology and Experimental Therapeutics* 1998;287(1):435–9.

Maclure M, Bryant MS, Skipper PL, Tannenbaum SR. Decline of the hemoglobin adduct of 4-minobiphenyl during withdrawal from smoking. *Cancer Research* 1990;50(1):181–4.

Maehama T, Taylor GS, Dixon JE. PTEN and myotubularin: novel phosphoinositide phosphatases. *Annual Review of Biochemistry* 2001;70:247–79.

Mai H, May WS, Gao F, Jin Z, Deng X. A functional role for nicotine in Bcl2 phosphorylation and suppression of apoptosis. *Journal of Biological Chemistry* 2003;278(3):1886–91.

Mäkelä TP, Kere J, Winqvist R, Alitalo K. Intrachromosomal rearrangements fusing L-myc and rlf in smallcell lung cancer. *Molecular and Cellular Biology* 1991;11(8):4015–21.

Malats N, Camus-Radon A-M, Nyberg F, Ahrens W, Constantinescu V, Mukeria A, Benhamou S, Batura-Gabryel H, Bruske-Hohfeld I, Simonato L, et al. Lung cancer risk in nonsmokers and *GSTM1* and *GSTT1* genetic polymorphism. *Cancer Epidemiology, Biomarkers & Prevention* 2000;9(8):827–33.

Malaveille C, Vineis P, Esteve J, Ohshima H, Brun G, Hautefeuille A, Gallet P, Ronco G, Terracini B, Bartsch H. Levels of mutagens in the urine of smokers of black and blond tobacco correlate with their risk of bladder cancer. *Carcinogenesis* 1989;10(3):577–86.

Malkinson AM, You M. The intronic structure of cancer-related genes regulates susceptibility to cancer. *Molecular Carcinogenesis* 1994;10(2):61–5.

Mancini R, Romano G, Sgambato A, Flamini G, Giovagnoli MR, Boninsegna A, Carraro C, Vecchione A, Cittadini A. Polycyclic aromatic hydrocarbon-DNA adducts in cervical smears of smokers and nonsmokers. *Gynecologic Oncology* 1999;75(1):68–71.

Maneckjee R, Minna JD. Opioids induce while nicotine suppresses apoptosis in human lung cancer cells. *Cell Growth & Differentiation* 1994;5(10):1033–40.

Mao H, Schnetz-Boutaud NC, Weisenseel JP, Marnett LJ, Stone MP. Duplex DNA catalyzes the chemical rearrangement of a malondialdehyde deoxyguanosine adduct. *Proceedings of the National Academy of Sciences of the United States of America* 1999;96(12):6615–20.

Mao L, Lee JS, Kurie JM, Fan YH, Lippman SM, Lee JJ, Ro JY, Broxson A, Yu R, Morice RC, et al. Clonal genetic alterations in the lungs of current and former smokers. *Journal of the National Cancer Institute* 1997;89(12):857–62.

Marcus PM, Hayes RB, Vineis P, García-Closas M, Caporaso NE, Autrup H, Branch RA, Brockmöller J, Ishizaki T, Karakaya AE, et al. Cigarette smoking, *N*-acetyltransferase 2 acetylation status, and bladder cancer risk: a case-series meta-analysis of a gene-environment interaction. *Cancer Epidemiology, Biomarkers & Prevention* 2000a;9(5):461–7.

Marcus PM, Vineis P, Rothman N. NAT2 slow acetylation and bladder cancer risk: a meta-analysis of 22 case-control studies conducted in the general population. *Pharmacogenetics* 2000b;10(2):115–22.

Margison GP, Povey AC, Kaina B, Santibáñez Koref MF. Variability and regulation of O^6-alkylguanine-DNA alkyltransferase. *Carcinogenesis* 2003;24(4):625–35.

Mariatos G, Bothos J, Zacharatos P, Summers MK, Scolnick DM, Kittas C, Halazonetis TD, Gorgoulis VG. Inactivating mutations targeting the *chfr* mitotic checkpoint gene in human lung cancer. *Cancer Research* 2003;63(21):7185–9.

Marintchev A, Mullen MA, Maciejewski MW, Pan B, Gryk MR, Mullen GP. Solution structure of the single-strand break repair protein XRCC1 N-terminal domain. *Nature Structural Biology* 1999;6(9):884–93.

Marsit CJ, Karagas MR, Danaee H, Liu M, Andrew A, Schned A, Nelson HH, Kelsey KT. Carcinogen exposure and gene promoter hypermethylation in bladder cancer. *Carcinogenesis* 2006;27(1):112–6.

Martey CA, Pollock SJ, Turner CK, O'Reilly KMA, Baglole CJ, Phipps RP, Sime PJ. Cigarette smoke induces cyclooxygenase-2 and microsomal prostaglandin E_2 synthase in human lung fibroblasts: implications for lung inflammation and cancer. *American Journal of Physiology – Lung Cellular and Molecular Physiology* 2004;287(5):L981–L991.

Martin SJ. Destabilizing influences in apoptosis: sowing the seeds of IAP destruction. *Cell* 2002;109(7):793–6.

Martinez C, Agundez JAG, Olivera M, Martin R, Ladero JM, Benitez J. Lung cancer and mutations at the polymorphic NAT2 locus. *Pharmacogenetics* 1995;5(4):207–14.

Marwick JA, Kirkham P, Gilmour PS, Donaldson K, MacNee W, Rahman I. Cigarette smoke-induced oxidative stress and TGF-β1 increase $p21^{wafl/cip1}$ expression in alveolar epithelial cells. *Annals of the New York Academy of Sciences* 2002;973:278–83.

Maser RS, Monsen KJ, Nelms BE, Petrini JH. hMre11 and hRad50 nuclear foci are induced during the normal cellular response to DNA double-strand breaks. *Molecular and Cellular Biology* 1997;17(10):6087–96.

Massion PP, Taflan PM, Shyr Y, Rahman SMJ, Yildiz P, Shakthour B, Edgerton ME, Ninan M, Andersen JJ, Gonzalez AL. Early involvement of the phosphatidylinositol 3-kinase/Akt pathway in lung cancer progression. *American Journal of Respiratory and Critical Care Medicine* 2004;170(10):1088–94.

Masutani C, Kusumoto R, Iwai S, Hanaoka F. Mechanisms of accurate translesion synthesis by human DNA polymerase η. *EMBO Journal* 2000;19(12):3100–9.

Masutani C, Kusumoto R, Yamada A, Dohmae N, Yokio M, Yuasa M, Araki M, Iwai S, Takio K, Hanaoka F. The *XPV* (xeroderma pigmentosum variant) gene encodes human DNA polymerase η. *Nature* 1999;399(6737): 700–4.

Matakidou A, Eisen T, Houlston RS. *TP53* polymorphisms and lung cancer risk: a systematic review and meta-analysis. *Mutagenesis* 2003;18(4):377–85.

Mathur RS, Mathur SP, Young RC. Up-regulation of epidermal growth factor-receptors (EGF-R) by nicotine in cervical cancer cell lines: this effect may be mediated by EGF. *American Journal of Reproductive Immunology* 2000;44(2):114–20.

Matsumoto S, Iwakawa R, Takahashi K, Kohno T, Nakanishi Y, Matsuno Y, Suzuki K, Nakamoto M, Shimizu E, Minna JD, et al. Prevalence and specificity of *LKB1* genetic alterations in lung cancers. *Oncogene* 2007;26(40):5911–8.

Matsumoto Y, Kim K. Excision of deoxyribose phosphate residues by DNA polymerase beta during DNA repair. *Science* 1995;269(5224):699–702.

Matter B, Wang G, Jones R, Tretyakova N. Formation of diastereomeric benzo[*a*]pyrene diol epoxide-guanine adducts in *p53* gene-derived DNA sequences. *Chemical Research in Toxicology* 2004;17(6):731–41.

Mattern J, Koomägi R, Volm M. Smoking-related increase in O^6-methylguanine-DNA methyltransferase expression in human lung carcinomas. *Carcinogenesis* 1998;19(7):1247–50.

Matullo G, Guarrera S, Carturan S, Peluso M, Malaveille C, Davico L, Piazza A, Vineis P. DNA repair gene polymorphisms, bulky DNA adducts in white blood cells and bladder cancer in a case-control study. *International Journal of Cancer* 2001a;92(4):562–7.

Matullo G, Palli D, Peluso M, Guarrera S, Carturan S, Celentano E, Krogh V, Munnia A, Tumino R, Polidoro S, et al. *XRCC1, XRCC3, XPD* gene polymorphisms, smoking and ^{32}P-DNA adducts in a sample of healthy subjects. *Carcinogenesis* 2001b;22(9):1437–45.

Mauderly JL, Gigliotti AP, Barr EB, Bechtold WE, Belinsky SA, Hahn FF, Hobbs CA, March TH, Seilkop SK, Finch GL. Chronic inhalation exposure to mainstream cigarette smoke increases lung and nasal tumor incidence in rats. *Toxicological Sciences* 2004;81(2):280–92.

Maus AD, Pereira EFR, Karachunski PI, Horton RM, Navaneetham D, Macklin K, Cortes WS, Albuquerque EX, Conti-Fine BM. Human and rodent bronchial epithelial cells express functional nicotinic acetylcholine receptors. *Molecular Pharmacology* 1998;54(5): 779–88.

Mayne ST, Buenconsejo J, Janerich DT. Familial cancer history and lung cancer risk in United States nonsmoking men and women. *Cancer Epidemiology, Biomarkers & Prevention* 1999;8(12):1065–9.

McCormick F. Cancer: survival pathways meet their end. *Nature* 2004;428(6980):267–9.

McCoy GD, Chen C-H, Hecht SS, McCoy EC. Enhanced metabolism and mutagenesis of nitrosopyrrolidine in liver fractions isolated from chronic ethanol-consuming hamsters. *Cancer Research* 1979;39(3):793–6.

McCoy GD, Hecht SS, Katayama S, Wynder EL. Differential effect of chronic ethanol consumption on the carcinogenicity of *N*-nitrosopyrrolidine and *N'*-nitrosonornicotine in male Syrian golden hamsters. *Cancer Research* 1981;41(7):2849–54.

McWilliams JE, Sanderson BJS, Harris EL, Richert-Boe KE, Henner WD. Glutathione-S-transferase M1 (GSTM1) deficiency and lung cancer risk. *Cancer Epidemiology, Biomarkers & Prevention* 1995;4(6): 589–94.

Meier P, Finch A, Evan G. Apoptosis in development. *Nature* 2000;407(6805):796–801.

Melikian AA, Sun P, Prokopczyk B, El-Bayoumy K, Hoffmann D, Wang X, Waggoner S. Identification of benzo[*a*]pyrene metabolites in cervical mucus and DNA adducts in cervical tissues in humans by gas chromatography-mass spectrometry. *Cancer Letters* 1999;146(2):127–34.

Melton DW, Ketchen A-M, Nuñez F, Bonatti-Abbondandolo S, Abbondandolo A, Squires S, Johnson RT. Cells from *ERCC1*-deficient mice show increased genome instability and a reduced frequency of S-phase-dependent illegitimate chromosome exchange but a normal frequency of homologous recombination. *Journal of Cell Science* 1998;111(Pt 3):395–404.

Merlo A, Gabrielson E, Askin F, Sidransky D. Frequent loss of chromosome 9 in human primary non-small cell lung cancer. *Cancer Research* 1994;54(3):640–42.

Merlo A, Herman JG, Mao L, Lee DJ, Gabrielson E, Burger PC, Baylin SB, Sidransky D. 5'CpG island methylation is associated with transcriptional silencing of the tumour suppressor *p16/CDKN2/MTS1* in human cancers. *Nature Medicine* 1995;1(7):686–92.

Mihara M, Erster S, Zaika A, Petrenko O, Chittenden T, Pancoska P, Moll UM. p53 has a direct apoptogenic role at the mitochondria. *Molecular Cell* 2003;11(3): 577–90.

Mijal RS, Thomson NM, Fleischer NL, Pauly GT, Moschel RC, Kanugula S, Fang Q, Pegg AE, Peterson LA. The repair of the tobacco specific nitrosamine derived adduct O^6-[4-oxo-4-(3-pyridyl)butyl]guanine by O^6-alkylguanine-DNA alkyltransferase variants. *Chemical Research in Toxicology* 2004;17(3):424–34.

Miller DP, Liu G, De Vivo I, Lynch TJ, Wain JC, Su L, Christiani DC. Combinations of the variant genotypes of *GSTP1, GSTM1*, and *p53* are associated with an increased lung cancer risk. *Cancer Research* 2002; 62(10):2819–23.

Miller DP, Neuberg D, De Vivo I, Wain JC, Lynch TJ, Su L, Christiani DC. Smoking and the risk of lung cancer: *susceptibility with* GSTP1 *polymorphisms*. *Epidemiology* 2003;14(5):545–51.

Mittal RD, Srivastava DS, Mandhani A. NAT2 gene polymorphism in bladder cancer: a study from North India. *International Brazilian Journal of Urology* 2004;30(4):279–88.

Miyabe I, Zhang Q-M, Kino K, Sugiyama H, Takao M, Yasui A, Yonei S. Identification of 5-formyluracil DNA glycosylase activity of human hNTH1 protein. *Nucleic Acids Research* 2002;30(15):3443–8.

Miyashita T, Reed JC. Tumor suppressor p53 is a direct transcriptional activator of the human *bax* gene. *Cell* 1995;80(2):293–9.

Miyata M, Kudo G, Lee Y-H, Yang TJ, Gelboin HV, Fernandez-Salguero P, Kimura S, Gonzalez FJ. Targeted disruption of the microsomal epoxide hydrolase gene: microsomal epoxide hydrolase is required for the carcinogenic activity of 7,12-dimethylbenz[*a*]anthracene. *Journal of Biological Chemistry* 1999;274(34): 23963–8.

Mohrenweiser HW, Carrano AV, Fertitta A, Perry B, Thompson LH, Tucker JD, Weber CA. Refined mapping of the three DNA repair genes, ERCC1, ERCC2, and XRCC1, on human chromosome 19. *Cytogenetics and Cell Genetics* 1989;52(1–2):11–14.

Mohrenweiser HW, Jones IM. Variation in DNA repair is a factor in cancer susceptibility: a paradigm for the promises and perils of individual and population risk estimation? *Mutation Research* 1998;400(1–2):15–24.

Møller P, Knudsen LE, Frentz G, Dybdahl M, Wallin H, Nexø BA. Seasonal variation of DNA damage and repair in patients with non-melanoma skin cancer and referents with and without psoriasis. *Mutation Research* 1998;407(1):25–34.

Moore SM, Rintoul RC, Walker TR, Chilvers ER, Haslett C, Sethi T. The presence of a constitutively active phosphoinositide 3-kinase in small cell lung cancer cells mediates anchorage-independent proliferation via a protein kinase B and p70s6k-dependent pathway. *Cancer Research* 1998;58(22):5239–47.

Moraitis D, Du B, De Lorenzo MS, Boyle JO, Weksler BB, Cohen EG, Carew JF, Altorki NK, Lopelovitch L, Subbaramaiah K, et al. Levels of cyclooxygenase-2 are increased in the oral mucosa of smokers: evidence for the role of epidermal growth factor receptor and its ligands. *Cancer Research* 2005;65(2):664–70.

Moriya M, Grollman AP. Mutations in the *mutY* gene of *Escherichia coli* enhance the frequency of targeted G:C→T:A transversions induced by a single 8-oxoguanine residue in single-stranded DNA. *Molecular and General Genetics* 1993;239(1–2):72–6.

Moriya M, Spiegel S, Fernandes A, Amin S, Liu T, Geacintov N, Grollman AP. Fidelity of translesional synthesis past benzo[*a*]pyrene diol epoxide—2′-deoxyguanosine DNA adducts: marked effects of host cell, sequence context, and chirality. *Biochemistry* 1996;35(51):16646–51.

Moriya M, Zhang W, Johnson F, Grollman AP. Mutagenic potency of exocyclic DNA adducts: marked differences between *Escherichia coli* and simian kidney cells. *Proceedings of the National Academy of Sciences of the United States of America* 1994;91(25):11899–903.

Morrow JD, Frei B, Longmire AW, Gaziano JM, Lynch SM, Shyr Y, Strauss WE, Oates JA, Roberts LJ II. Increase in circulating products of lipid peroxidation (F$_2$-isoprostanes) in smokers: smoking as a cause of oxidative damage. *New England Journal of Medicine* 1995;332(18):1198–203.

Moscatello DK, Holgado-Madruga M, Emlet DR, Montgomery RB, Wong AJ. Constitutive activation of phosphatidylinositol 3-kinase by a naturally occurring mutant epidermal growth factor receptor. *Journal of Biological Chemistry* 1998;273(1):200–6.

Mu D, Park C-H, Matsunaga T, Hsu DS, Reardon JT, Sancar A. Reconstitution of human DNA repair excision nuclease in a highly defined system. *Journal of Biological Chemistry* 1995;270(6):2415–8.

Mukherjee S, Palmer LJ, Kim JY, Aeschliman DB, Houk RS, Woodin MA, Christiani DC. Smoking status and occupational exposure affects oxidative DNA injury in boilermakers exposed to metal fume and residual oil fly ash. *Cancer Epidemiology, Biomarkers & Prevention* 2004;13(3):454–60.

Mukohara T, Kudoh S, Yamauchi S, Kimura T, Yoshimura N, Kanazawa H, Hirata K, Wanibuchi H, Fukushima S, Inoue K, et al. Expression of epidermal growth factor receptor (EGFR) and downstream-activated peptides in surgically excised non-small-cell lung cancer (NSCLC). *Lung Cancer* 2003;41(2):123–30.

Mulder TPJ, Court DA, Peters WHM. Variability of glutathione *S*-transferase α in human liver and plasma. *Clinical Chemistry* 1999;45(3):355–9.

Muller SJ, Caradonna S. Isolation and characterization of a human cDNA encoding uracil-DNA glycosylase. *Biochimica et Biophysica Acta* 1991;1088(2):197–207.

Murakami I, Hiyama K, Ishioka S, Yamakido M, Kasagi F, Yokosaki Y. p53 gene mutations are associated with shortened survival in patients with advanced non-small cell lung cancer: an analysis of medically managed patients. *Clinical Cancer Research* 2000;6(2):526–30.

Murphy SE, Spina DA, Nunes MG, Pullo DA. Glucuronidation of 4-(hydroxymethyl)nitrosamino)-1-(3-pyridyl)-1-butanone, a metabolically activated form of 4-(methylnitrosamino)-1-(3-pyridyl)-1-butanone, by phenobarbital-treated rats. *Chemical Research in Toxicology* 1995;8(5):772–9.

Muscat JE, Kleinman W, Colosimo S, Muir A, Lazarus P, Park J, Richie JP Jr. Enhanced protein glutathiolation and oxidative stress in cigarette smokers. *Free Radical Biology & Medicine* 2004;36(4):464–70.

Mustonen R, Schoket B, Hemminki K. Smoking-related DNA adducts: ^{32}P-postlabeling analysis of 7-methyl-guanine in human bronchial and lymphocyte DNA. *Carcinogenesis* 1993;14(1):151–4.

Myrnes B, Giercksky KE, Krokan H. Interindividual variation in the activity of O^6-methyl-guanine-DNA methyltransferase and uracil-DNA glycosylase in human organs. *Carcinogenesis* 1983;4(12):1565–8.

Nagar S, Remmel RP. Uridine diphosphoglucuronosyltransferase pharmacogenetics and cancer. *Oncogene* 2006;25(11):1659–72.

Nahle Z, Polakoff J, Davuluri RV, McCurrach ME, Jacobson MD, Narita M, Zhang MQ, Lazebnik Y, Bar-Sagi D, Lowe SW. Direct coupling of the cell cycle and cell death machinery by E2F. *Nature Cell Biology* 2002;4(11):859–64.

Nakachi K, Imai K, Hayashi S, Kawajiri K. Polymorphisms of the CYP1A1 and glutathione-S-transferase genes associated with susceptibility to lung cancer in relation to cigarette dose in a Japanese population. *Cancer Research* 1993;53(13):2994–9.

Nakachi K, Imai K, Hayashi S, Watanabe J, Kawajiri K. Genetic susceptibility to squamous cell carcinoma of the lung in relation to cigarette smoking dose. *Cancer Research* 1991;51(19):5177–80.

Nakano K, Vousden KH. *PUMA*, a novel proapoptotic gene, is induced by p53. *Molecular Cell* 2001;7(3):683–94.

Nan H-M, Kim H, Lim H-S, Choi JK, Kawamoto T, Kang J-W, Lee C-H, Kim Y-D, Kwon EH. Effects of occupation, lifestyle and genetic polymorphisms of CYP1A1, CYP2E1, GSTM1 and GSTT1 on urinary 1-hydroxypyrene and 2-naphthol concentrations. *Carcinogenesis* 2001;22(5):787–93.

Naoki K, Chen T-H, Richard WG, Sugarbaker DJ, Meyerson M. Missense mutations of the *BRAF* gene in human lung adenocarcinomas. *Cancer Research* 2002;62(23):7001–3.

Nath RG, Ocando JE, Guttenplan JB, Chung FL. 1,N^2-propanodeoxyguanosine adducts: potential new biomarkers of smoking-induced DNA damage in human oral tissue. *Cancer Research* 1998;58(4):581–4.

Nazar-Stewart V, Vaughan TL, Stapleton P, Van Loo J, Nicol-Blades B, Eaton DL. A population-based study of glutathione *S*-transferase M1, T1 and P1 genotypes and risk for lung cancer. *Lung Cancer* 2003;40(3):247–58.

Nebert DW, Dalton TP, Okey AB, Gonzalez FJ. Role of aryl hydrocarbon receptor-mediated induction of the CYP1 enzymes in environmental toxicity and cancer. *Journal of Biological Chemistry* 2004;279(23):23847–50.

Neddermann P, Gallinari P, Lettieri T, Schmid D, Truong O, Hsuan JJ, Wiebauer K, Jiricny J. Cloning and expression of human G/T mismatch-specific thymine-DNA glycosylase. *Journal of Biological Chemistry* 1996;271(22):12767–74.

Neddermann P, Jiricny J. The purification of a mismatch-specific thymine-DNA glycosylase from HeLa cells. *Journal of Biological Chemistry* 1993;268(28):21218–24.

Neddermann P, Jiricny J. Efficient removal of uracil from *G/U* mispairs by the mismatch-specific thymine DNA glycosylase from HeLa cells. *Proceedings of the National Academy of Sciences of the United States of America* 1994;91(5):1642–6.

Nelms BE, Maser RS, MacKay JF, Lagally MG, Petrini JHJ. In situ visualization of DNA double-strand break repair in human fibroblasts. *Science* 1998;280(5363):590–2.

Nelson DR. Comparison of P450s from human and fugu: 420 million years of vertebrate P450 evolution. *Archives of Biochemistry and Biophysics* 2003;409(1):18–24.

Nelson HH, Kelsey KT. The molecular epidemiology of asbestos and tobacco in lung cancer. *Oncogene* 2002;21(48):7284–8.

Nelson HH, Wilkojmen M, Marsit CJ, Kelsey KT. *TP53* mutation, allelism and survival in non-small cell lung cancer. *Carcinogenesis* 2005;26(10):1770–3.

Nerurkar PV, Okinaka L, Aoki C, Seifried A, Lum-Jones A, Wilkens LR, Le Marchand L. *CYP1A1*, *GSTM1*, and *GSTP1* genetic polymorphisms and urinary 1-hydroxypyrene excretion in non-occupationally exposed individuals. *Cancer Epidemiology, Biomarkers & Prevention* 2000;9(10):1119–22.

Nevins JR. E2F: a link between the Rb tumor suppressor protein and viral oncoproteins. *Science* 1992;258(5081):424–9.

Ng D-P, Tan K-W, Zhao B, Seow A. *CYP1A1* polymorphisms and risk of lung cancer in non-smoking Chinese women: influence of environmental tobacco smoke exposure and *GSTM1/T1* genetic variation. *Cancer Causes & Control* 2005;16(4):399–405.

Nia AB, van Schooten FJ, Schilderman PAEL, De Kok TMCM, Haenen GR, Van Herwijnen MHM, van Agen E, Pachen D, Kleinjans JCS. A multi-biomarker approach to study the effects of smoking on oxidative DNA damage and repair and antioxidative defense mechanisms. *Carcinogenesis* 2001;22(3):395–401.

Nicolaides NC, Papadopoulos N, Liu B, Wei YF, Carter KC, Ruben SM, Rosen CA, Haseltine WA, Fleischmann RD, Fraser CM, et al. Mutations of two PMS homologues in hereditary nonpolyposis colon cancer. *Nature* 1994;371(6492):75–80.

Nilsen H, Haushalter KA, Robins P, Barnes DE, Verdine GL, Lindahl T. Excision of deaminated cytosine from the vertebrate genome: role of the SMUG1 uracil–DNA glycosylase. *EMBO Journal* 2001;20(15):4278–86.

Nishioka M, Kohno T, Tani M, Yanaihara N, Tomizawa Y, Otsuka A, Sasaki S, Kobayashi K, Niki T, Maeshima A, et al. *MYO18B*, a candidate tumor suppressor gene at chromosome 22q12.1, deleted, mutated, and methylated in human lung cancer. *Proceedings of the National Academy of Sciences of the United States of America* 2002;99(19):12269–74.

Nomoto S, Haruki N, Kondo M, Konishi H, Takahashi T, Takahashi T, Takahashi T. Search for mutations and examination of allelic expression imbalance of the *p73* gene at 1p36.33 in human lung cancers. *Cancer Research* 1998;58(7):1380–3.

Norppa H, Hirvonen A, Jarventaus H, Uuskula M, Tasa G, Ojajarvi A, Sorsa,M. Role of *GSTT1* and *GSTM1* genotypes in determining individual sensitivity to sister chromatid exchange induction by diepoxybutane in cultured human lymphocytes. *Carcinogenesis* 1995;16(6):1261–4.

O'Connor TR, Laval J. Human cDNA expressing a functional DNA glycosylase excising 3-methyladenine and 7-methylguanine. *Biochemical and Biophysical Research Communications* 1991;176(3):1170–7.

Oda Y. Analysis of the involvement of human *N*-acetyltransferase 1 in the genotoxic activation of bladder carcinogenic arylamines using a SOS/*umu* assay system. *Mutation Research* 2004;554(1–2):399–406.

Oda E, Ohki R, Murasawa H, Nemoto J, Shibue T, Yamashita T, Tokino T, Taniguchi T, Tanaka N. Noxa, a BH3-only member of the Bcl-2 family and candidate mediator of p53-induced apoptosis. *Science* 2000a;288(5468):1053–8.

Oda K, Arakawa H, Tanaka T, Matsuda K, Tanikawa C, Mori T, Nishimori H, Tamai K, Tokino T, Nakamura Y, Taya Y. *p53AIP1*, a potential mediator of p53-dependent apoptosis, and its regulation by Ser-46-phosphorylated p53. *Cell* 2000b;102(6):849–62.

O'Donnell RA, Richter A, Ward J, Angco G, Mehta A, Rousseau K, Swallow DM, Holgate ST, Dujukanovic R, Davies DE, et al. Expression of ErbB receptors and mucins in the airways of long term current smokers. *Thorax* 2004;59(12):1032–40.

O'Donovan A, Davies AA, Moggs JG, West SC, Wood RD. XPG endonuclease makes the 3′ incision in human DNA nucleotide excision repair. *Nature* 1994;371(6496): 432–5.

Oesch F, Klein S. Relevance of environmental alkylating agents to repair protein O^6-alkylguanine-DNA alkyltransferase: determination of individual and collective repair capacities of O^6-methylguanine. *Cancer Research* 1992;52(7):1801–3.

Offer H, Wolkowicz R, Matas D, Blumenstein S, Livneh Z, Rotter V. Direct involvement of p53 in the base excision repair pathway of the DNA repair machinery. *FEBS Letters* 1999;450(3):197–204.

Ogawara Y, Kishishita S, Obata T, Isazawa Y, Suzuki T, Tanaka K, Masuyama N, Gotoh Y. Akt enhances Mdm2-mediated ubiquitination and degradation of p53. *Journal of Biological Chemistry* 2002;277(24):21843–50.

Ohashi E, Ogi T, Kusumoto R, Iwai S, Masutani C, Hanaoka F, Ohmori H. Error-prone bypass of certain DNA lesions by the human DNA polymerase κ. *Genes & Development* 2000;14(13):1589–94.

Ohmori H, Friedberg EC, Fuchs RP, Goodman MF, Hanaoka F, Hinkle D, Kunkel TA, Lawrence CW, Livneh Z, Nohmi T, et al. The Y-family of DNA polymerases [letter]. *Molecular Cell* 2001;8(1):7–8.

Okada T, Kawashima K, Fukushi S, Minakuchi T, Nishimura S. Association between a cytochrome P450 CYPIA1 genotype and incidence of lung cancer. *Pharmacogenetics* 1994;4(6):333–40.

Okamoto I, Kenyon LC, Emlet DR, Mori T, Sasaki J, Hirosako S, Ichikawa Y, Kishi H, Godwin AK, Yoshioka M, et al. Expression of constitutively activated EGFRvIII in non-small cell lung cancer. *Cancer Science* 2003;94(1):50–6.

Olsen LC, Aasland R, Wittwer CU, Krokan HE, Helland DE. Molecular cloning of human uracil-DNA glycosylase, a highly conserved DNA repair enzyme. *EMBO Journal* 1989;8(10):3121–5.

Ong CN, Kok PW, Lee BL, Shi CY, Ong HY, Chia KS, Lee CS, Luo XW. Evaluation of biomarkers for occupational exposure to benzene. *Occupational and Environmental Medicine* 1995;52(8):528–33.

Ong CN, Kok PW, Ong HY, Shi CY, Lee BL, Phoon WH, Tan KT. Biomarkers of exposure to low concentrations of benzene: a field assessment. *Occupational and Environmental Medicine* 1996;53(5):328–33.

Ooi WL, Elston RC, Chen VW, Bailey-Wilson JE, Rothschild H. Increased familial risk for lung cancer. *Journal of the National Cancer Institute* 1986;76(2):217–22.

Orzechowski A, Schrenk D, Bock-Hennig BS, Bock KW. Glucuronidation of carcinogenic arylamines and their N-hydroxy derivatives by rat and human phenol UDP-glucuronosyltransferase of the UGT1 gene complex. *Carcinogenesis* 1994;15(8):1549–53.

Osann KE. Lung cancer in women: the importance of smoking, family history of cancer, and medical history of respiratory diseases. *Cancer Research* 1991; 51(18):4893–7.

Osterman-Golkar S, Ehrenberg L, Segerback D, Hallstrom I. Evaluation of genetic risks of alkylating agents. II: haemoglobin as a dose monitor. *Mutation Research* 1976;34(1):1–10.

Oyama T, Kawamoto T, Mizoue T, Yasumoto K, Kodama Y, Mitsudomi T. N-acetylation polymorphism in patients with lung cancer and its association with p53 gene mutation. *Anticancer Research* 1997;17(1B):577–81.

Ozes ON, Mayo LD, Gustin JA, Pfeffer SR, Pfeffer LM, Donner DB. NF-κB activation by tumour necrosis factor requires the Akt serine-threonine kinase [letter]. *Nature* 1999;401(6748):82–5.

Page JE, Pilcher AS, Yagi H, Sayer JM, Jerina DM, Dipple A. Mutational consequences of replication of M13mp7L2 constructs containing cis-opened benzo[*a*]pyrene 7,8-diol 9,10-epoxide–deoxyadenosine adducts. *Chemical Research in Toxicology* 1999;12(3):258–63.

Page JE, Zajc B, Oh-hara T, Lakshman MK, Sayer JM, Jerina DM, Dipple A. Sequence context profoundly influences the mutagenic potency of trans-opened benzo[*a*]pyrene 7,8-diol 9,10-epoxide–purine nucleoside adducts in site-specific mutation studies. *Biochemistry* 1998;37(25):9127–37.

Palmisano WA, Crume KP, Grimes MJ, Winters SA, Toyota M, Esteller M, Joste N, Baylin SB, Belinsky SA. Aberrant promoter methylation of the transcription factor genes PAX5 α and β in human cancers. *Cancer Research* 2003;63(15):4620–5.

Palombo F, Gallinari P, Iaccarino I, Lettieri T, Hughes M, D'Arrigo A, Truong O, Hsuan JJ, Jiricny J. GTBP, a 160-kilodalton protein essential for mismatch-binding activity in human cells. *Science* 1995;268(5219):1912–4.

Palombo F, Iaccarino I, Nakajima E, Ikejima M, Shimada T, Jiricny J. hMutSβ, a heterodimer of hMSH2 and hMSH3, binds to insertion/deletion loops in DNA. *Current Biology* 1996;6(9):1181–4.

Pandya G, Moriya M. 1,N^6-ethenodeoxyadenosine, a DNA adduct highly mutagenic in mammalian cells. *Biochemistry* 1996;35(35):11487–92.

Pap M, Cooper GM. Role of glycogen synthase kinase-3 in the phosphatidylinositol 3-kinase/Akt cell survival pathway. *Journal of Biological Chemistry* 1998;273(32):19929–32.

Papadopoulos N, Nicolaides NC, Wei YF, Ruben SM, Carter KC, Rosen CA, Haseltine WA, Fleischmann RD, Fraser CM, Adams MD, et al. Mutation of a mutL homolog in hereditary colon cancer. *Science* 1994;263(5153):1625–9.

Park JY, Chen L, Elahi A, Lazarus P, Tockman MS. Genetic analysis of microsomal epoxide hydrolase gene and its association with lung cancer risk. *European Journal of Cancer Prevention* 2005;14(3):223–30.

Park JY, Park SH, Choi JE, Lee SY, Jeon H-S, Cha SI, Kim CH, Park J-H, Kam S, Park RW, et al. Polymorphisms of the DNA repair gene *Xeroderma pigmentosum group A* and risk of primary lung cancer. *Cancer Epidemiology, Biomarkers & Prevention* 2002;11(10 Pt 1):993–7.

Park S, Tretyakova N. Structural characterization of the major DNA-DNA cross-link of 1,2,3,4-diepoxybutane. *Chemical Research in Toxicology* 2004;17(2):129–36.

Parker AR, Eshleman JR. Human MutY: gene structure, protein functions and interactions, and role in carcinogenesis. *Cellular and Molecular Life Sciences* 2003;60(10):2064–83.

Parsons WD, Carmella SG, Akerkar S, Bonilla LE, Hecht SS. A metabolite of the tobacco-specific lung carcinogen 4-(methylnitrosamino)-1-(3-pyridyl)-1-butanone (NNK) in the urine of hospital workers exposed to environmental tobacco smoke. *Cancer Epidemiology, Biomarkers & Prevention* 1998;7(3):257–60.

Pauly GT, Hughes SH, Moschel RC. Mutagenesis in *Escherichia coli* by three O^6-substituted guanines in double-stranded or gapped plasmids. *Biochemistry* 1995;34(27):8924–30.

Pauly GT, Moschel RC. Mutagenesis by O^6-methyl-, O^6-ethyl- and O^6-benzylguanine and O^4-methylthymine in human cells: effects of O^6-alkylguanine-DNA alkyltransferase and mismatch repair. *Chemical Research in Toxicology* 2001;14(7):894–900.

Pauly GT, Peterson LA, Moschel RC. Mutagenesis by O^6-[4-oxo-4-(3-pyridyl)butyl]guanine in *Escherichia coli* and human cells. *Chemical Research in Toxicology* 2002;15(2):165–9.

Paz-Elizur T, Krupsky M, Blumenstein S, Elinger D, Schechtman E, Livneh Z. DNA repair activity for oxidative damage and risk of lung cancer. *Journal of the National Cancer Institute* 2003;95(17):1312–9.

Peeper DS, Upton TM, Ladha MH, Neuman E, Zalvide J, Bernards R, DeCaprio JA, Ewen ME. Ras signalling linked to the cell-cycle machinery by the retinoblastoma protein [letter]. *Nature* 1997;386(6621):177–81.

Pegg AE. Repair of O^6-alkylguanine by alkyltransferases. *Mutation Research* 2000;462(2–3):83–100.

Pekarsky Y, Garrison PN, Palamarchuk A, Zanesi N, Aqeilan RI, Huebner K, Barnes LD, Croce CM. Fhit is a physiological target of the protein kinase Src. *Proceedings of the National Academy of Sciences of the United States of America* 2004;101(11):3775–9.

Pelosi G, Del Curto B, Dell'Orto P, Pasini F, Veronesi G, Spaggiari L, Maisonneuve P, Iannucci A, Terzi A, Lonardoni A, et al. Lack of prognostic implications of HER-2/*neu* abnormalities in 345 stage I nonsmall cell carcinomas (NSCLC) and 207 stage I-III neuroendocrine tumours (NET) of the lung. *International Journal of Cancer* 2005;113(1):101–8.

Penning TM, Burczynski ME, Hung C-F, McCoull KD, Palackal NT, Tsuruda LS. Dihydrodiol dehydrogenases and polycyclic aromatic hydrocarbon activation: generation of reactive and redox active o-quinones. *Chemical Research in Toxicology* 1999;12(1):1–18.

Perbellini L, Princivalle A, Cerpelloni M, Pasini F, Brugnone F. Comparison of breath, blood and urine concentrations in the biomonitoring of environmental exposure to 1,3-butadiene, 2,5-dimethylfuran, and benzene. *International Archives of Occupational and Environmental Health* 2003;76(6):461–6.

Perera FP, Mooney LA, Stampfer M, Phillips DH, Bell DA, Rundle A, Cho S, Tsai W-Y, Ma J, Blackwood A, et al. Associations between carcinogen–DNA damage, glutathione *S*-transferase genotypes, and risk of lung cancer in the prospective Physicians' Health Cohort Study. *Carcinogenesis* 2002;23(10):1641–46.

Pérez-Soler R, Chachoua A, Hammond LA, Rowinsky EK, Huberman M, Karp D, Rigas J, Clark GM, Santabárbara P, Bonomi P. Determinants of tumor response and survival with erlotinib in patients with non–small-cell lung cancer. *Journal of Clinical Oncology* 2004;22(16):3238–47.

Petersen I, Langreck H, Wolf G, Schwendel A, Psille R, Vogt P, Reichel MB, Ried T, Dietel M. Small-cell lung cancer is characterized by a high incidence of deletions on chromosomes 3p, 4q, 5q, 10q, 13q and 17p. *British Journal of Cancer* 1997;75(1):79–86.

Peterson LA, Hecht SS. O^6-methylguanine is a critical determinant of 4-(methylnitrosamino)-1-(3-pyridyl)-1-butanone tumorigenesis in A/J mouse lung. *Cancer Research* 1991;51(20):5557–64.

Peterson LA, Thomson NM, Crankshaw DL, Donaldson EE, Kenney PJ. Interactions between methylating and pyridyloxobutylating agents in A/J mouse lungs: implications for 4-(methylnitrosamino)-1-(3-pyridyl)-1-butanone-induced lung tumorigenesis. *Cancer Research* 2001;61(15):5757–63.

Petit C, Sancar A. Nucleotide excision repair: from *E. coli* to man. *Biochimie* 1999;81(1–2):15–25.

Petruzzelli S, Tavanti LM, Celi A, Giuntini C. Detection of N7-methyldeoxyguanosine adducts in human pulmonary alveolar cells. *American Journal of Respiratory Cell and Molecular Biology* 1996;15(2):216–23.

Pezzagno G, Maestri L, Fiorentino ML. Trans,trans-muconic acid, a biological indicator to low levels of environmental benzene: some aspects of its specificity. *American Journal of Industrial Medicine* 1999;35(5):511–8.

Pfeifer GP, Denissenko MF, Olivier M, Tretyakova N, Hecht SS, Hainaut P. Tobacco smoke carcinogens, DNA damage and p53 mutations in smoking-associated cancers. *Oncogene* 2002;21(48):7435–51.

Pfeiffer P, Goedecke W, Obe G. Mechanisms of DNA double-strand break repair and their potential to induce chromosomal aberrations. *Mutagenesis* 2000; 15(4):289–302.

Philip PA, Fitzgerald DL, Cartwright RA, Peake MD, Rogers HJ. Polymorphic *N*-acetylation capacity in lung cancer. *Carcinogenesis* 1988;9(3):491–3.

Phillips DH. Fifty years of benzo[*a*]pyrene. *Nature* 1983; 303(5917):468–72.

Phillips DH. Smoking-related DNA and protein adducts in human tissues. *Carcinogenesis* 2002;23(12):1979–2004.

Pilger A, Germadnik D, Riedel K, Meger-Kossien I, Scherer G, Rudiger HW. Longitudinal study of urinary 8-hydroxy-2′-deoxyguanosine excretion in healthy adults. *Free Radical Research* 2001;35(3):273–80.

Pinarbasi H, Silig Y, Cetinkaya O, Seyfikli Z, Pinarbasi E. Strong association between the GSTM1-null genotype and lung cancer in a Turkish population. *Cancer Genetics and Cytogenetics* 2003;146(2):125–9.

Pinsky PF, Kramer BS, Reding D, Buys S. Reported family history of cancer in the prostate, lung, colorectal, and ovarian cancer screening trial. *American Journal of Epidemiology* 2003;157(9):792–9.

Piyathilake CJ, Frost AR, Manne U, Weiss H, Bell WC, Heimburger DC, Grizzle WE. Differential expression of growth factors in squamous cell carcinoma and precancerous lesions of the lung. *Clinical Cancer Research* 2002;8(3):734–44.

Poeta ML, Manola J, Goldwasser MA, Forastiere A, Benoit N, Califano JA, Ridge JA, Goodwin J, Kenady D, Saunders J, et al. TP53 mutations and survival in squamous-cell carcinoma of the head and neck. *New England Journal of Medicine* 2007;357(25):2552–61.

Poirier MC, Santella RM, Weston A. Carcinogen macromolecular adducts and their measurement. *Carcinogenesis* 2000;21(3):353–9.

Popanda O, Schattenberg T, Phong CT, Butkiewicz D, Risch A, Edler L, Kayser K, Dienemann H, Schulz V, Drings P, et al. Specific combinations of DNA repair gene variants and increased risk for non-small cell lung cancer. *Carcinogenesis* 2004;25(12):2433–41.

Port JL, Yamaguchi K, Du B, De Lorenzo M, Chang M, Heerdt PM, Kopelovich L, Marcus CB, Altorki NK, Subbaramaiah K, et al. Tobacco smoke induces CYP1B1 in the aerodigestive tract. *Carcinogenesis* 2004; 25(11):2275–81.

Pöschl G, Seitz HK. Alcohol and cancer. *Alcohol and Alcoholism* 2004;39(3):155–65.

Pourcelot S, Faure H, Firoozi F, Ducros V, Tripier M, Hee J, Cadet J, Favier A. Urinary 8-oxo-7,8-dihydro-2′-deoxyguanosine and 5-(hydroxymethyl)uracil in smokers. *Free Radical Research* 1999;30(3):173–80.

Povey AC, Hall CN, Cooper DP, O'Connor PJ, Margison GP. Determinants of O^6-alkylguanine-DNA alkyltransferase activity in normal and tumour tissue from human colon and rectum. *International Journal of Cancer* 2000;85(1):68–72.

Prakash S, Prakash L. Translesion DNA synthesis in eukaryotes: a one- or two-polymerase affair. *Genes & Development* 2002;16(15):1872–83.

Prasad R, Beard WA, Strauss PR, Wilson SH. Human DNA polymeraseβ deoxyribose phosphate lyase: substrate specificity and catalytic mechanism. *Journal of Biological Chemistry* 1998;273(24):15263–70.

Prasad R, Singhal RK, Srivastava DK, Molina JT, Tomkinson AE, Wilson SH. Specific interaction of DNA polymeraseβ and DNA ligase I in a multiprotein base excision repair complex from bovine testis. *Journal of Biological Chemistry* 1996;271(27):16000–7.

Preussmann R, Stewart BW. *N*-Nitroso carcinogens. In: Searle CE, editor. *Chemical Carcinogens, Second Edition.* ACS Monograph 182. Vol. 2. Washington: American Chemical Society, 1984:643–828.

Prevost V, Shuker DE, Friesen MD, Eberle G, Rajewsky MF, Bartsch H. Immunoaffinity purification and gas chromatography-mass spectrometric quantification of 3-alkyladenines in urine: metabolism studies and basal excretion levels in man. *Carcinogenesis* 1993;14(11):199–204.

Prevost V, Shuker DEG. Cigarette smoking and urinary 3-alkyladenine excretion in man. *Chemical Research in Toxicology* 1996;9(2):439–44.

Prieme H, Loft S, Klarlund M, Gronbaek K, Tonnesen P, Poulsen HE. Effect of smoking cessation on oxidative DNA modification estimated by 8-oxo-7,8-dihydro-2′-deoxyguanosine excretion. *Carcinogenesis* 1998;19(2):347–51.

Probst-Hensch NM, Bell DA, Watson MA, Skipper PL, Tannenbaum SR, Chan KK, Ross RK, Yu MC. *N*-Acetyltransferase 2 phenotype but not *NAT1*10* genotype affects aminobiphenyl-hemoglobin adduct levels. *Cancer Epidemiology, Biomarkers & Prevention* 2000;9(6):619–23.

Proctor RN. Tobacco and the global lung cancer epidemic. *Nature Reviews Cancer* 2001;1(1):82–6.

Prokopczyk B, Hoffmann D, Bologna M, Cunningham AJ, Trushin N, Akerkar S, Boyiri T, Amin S, Desai D, Colosimo S, et al. Identification of tobacco-derived compounds in human pancreatic juice. *Chemical Research in Toxicology* 2002;15(5):677–85.

Prokopczyk B, Leder G, Trushin N, Cunningham AJ, Akerkar S, Pittman B, Ramadani M, Straeter J, Beger HG, Henne-Bruns D, et al. 4-Hydroxy-1-(3-pyridyl)-1-butanone, an indicator for 4-(methylnitrosamino)-1-(3-pyridyl)-1-butanone–induced DNA damage, is not detected in human pancreatic tissue. *Cancer Epidemiology, Biomarkers & Prevention* 2005;14(2):540–1.

Prokopczyk B, Trushin N, Leszczynska J, Waggoner SE, El-Bayoumy K. Human cervical tissue metabolizes the tobacco-specific nitrosamine, 4-(methylnitrosamino)-1-(3-pyridyl)-1-butanone, via α-hydroxylation and carbonyl reduction pathways. *Carcinogenesis* 2001; 22(1):107–14.

Proskocil BJ, Sekhon HS, Jia Y, Savchenko V, Blakely RD, Lindstrom J, Spindel ER. Acetylcholine is an autocrine or paracrine hormone synthesized and secreted by airway bronchial epithelial cells. *Endocrinology* 2004;145(5):2498–506.

Pryor WA, Stone K, Zang L-Y, Bermúdez E. Fractionation of aqueous cigarette tar extracts: fractions that contain the tar radical cause DNA damage. *Chemical Research in Toxicology* 1998;11(5):441–8.

Pulling LC, Divine KK, Klinge DM, Gilliland FD, Kang T, Schwartz AG, Bocklage TJ, Belinsky SA. Promoter hypermethylation of the O^6-methylguanine-DNA methyltransferase gene: more common in lung adenocarcinomas from never-smokers than smokers and associated with tumor progression. *Cancer Research* 2003;63(16):4842–8.

Pulling LC, Vuillemenot BR, Hutt JA, Devereux TR, Belinsky SA. Aberrant promoter hypermethylation of the *death-associated protein kinase* gene is early and frequent in murine lung tumors induced by cigarette smoke and tobacco carcinogens. *Cancer Research* 2004; 64(11):3844–8.

Qiao Y, Spitz MR, Guo Z, Hadeyati M, Grossman L, Kraemer KH, Wei Q. Rapid assessment of repair of ultraviolet DNA damage with a modified host-cell reactivation assay using a luciferase reporter gene and correlation with polymorphisms of DNA repair genes in normal human lymphocytes. *Mutation Research* 2002a;509 (1–2):165–74.

Qiao Y, Spitz MR, Shen H, Guo Z, Shete S, Hedayati M, Grossman L, Mohrenweiser H, Wei Q. Modulation of repair of ultraviolet damage in the host-cell reactivation assay by polymorphic *XPC* and *XPD/ERCC2* genotypes. *Carcinogenesis* 2002b;23(2):295–9.

Qiuling S, Yuxin Z, Suhua Z, Cheng X, Shuguang L, Fengsheng H. Cyclin D1 polymorphism and susceptibility to lung cancer in a Chinese population. *Carcinogenesis* 2003;24(9):1499–1503.

Qu Q, Cohen BS, Shore R, Chen LC, Li G, Jin X, Melikian AA, Yin S, Yan H, Xu B, et al. Benzene exposure measurement in shoe and glue manufacturing: a study to validate biomarkers. *Applied Occupational and Environmental Hygiene* 2003;18(12):988–98.

Qu Q, Melikian AA, Li G, Shore R, Chen L, Cohen B, Yin S, Kagan MR, Li H, Meng M, et al. Validation of biomarkers in humans exposed to benzene: urine metabolites. *American Journal of Industrial Medicine* 2000; 37(5):522–31.

Quan T, Reiners JJ Jr, Bell AO, Hong N, States JC. Cytotoxicity and genotoxicity of (+/-)-benzo[a]pyrene-trans-7,8-dihydrodiol in CYP1A1-expressing human fibroblasts quantitatively correlate with CYP1A1 expression level. *Carcinogenesis* 1994;15(9):1827–32.

Quan T, Reiners JJ Jr, Culp SJ, Richter P, States JC. Differential mutagenicity and cytotoxicity of (+/-)-benzo[*a*]pyrene-trans-7,8-dihydrodiol and (+/-)-anti-benzo[*a*]pyrene-trans-7,8-dihydrodiol-9,10-epoxide in genetically engineered human fibroblasts. *Molecular Carcinogenesis* 1995;12(2):91–102.

Radicella JP, Dherin C, Desmaze C, Fox MS, Boiteux S. Cloning and characterization of *hOGG1*, a human homolog of the *OGG1* gene of *Saccharomyces cerevisiae*. *Proceedings of the National Academy of Sciences of the United States of America* 1997;94(15):8010–5.

Radzikowska E, Roszkowski K, Głaz P. Lung cancer in patients under 50 years old. *Lung Cancer* 2001;33(2–3):203–11.

Rajee-Behbahani N, Schmezer P, Risch A, Rittgen W, Kayser KW, Dienemann H, Schulz V, Drings P, Thiel S, Bartsch H. Altered DNA repair capacity and bleomycin sensitivity as risk markers for non-small cell lung cancer. *International Journal of Cancer* 2001;95(2):86–91.

Rajesh M, Wang G, Jones R, Tretyakova N. Stable isotope labeling-mass spectrometry analysis of methyl- and pyridyloxobutyl-guanine adducts of 4-(methylnitrosamino)-1-(3-pyridyl)-1-butanone in *p53*-derived DNA sequences. *Biochemistry* 2005;44(6):2197–207.

Rameh LE, Cantley LC. The role of phosphoinositide 3-kinase lipid products in cell function. *Journal of Biological Chemistry* 1999;274(13):8347–50.

Ratnasinghe D, Yao S-X, Tangrea JA, Qiao Y-L, Andersen MR, Barrett MJ, Giffen CA, Erozan Y, Tockman MS, Taylor PR. Polymorphisms of the DNA repair gene *XRCC1* and lung cancer risk. *Cancer Epidemiology, Biomarkers & Prevention* 2001;10(2):119–23.

Reardon JT, Bessho T, Kung HC, Bolton PH, Sancar A. *In vitro* repair of oxidative DNA damage by human nucleotide excision repair system: possible explanation for neurodegeneration in xeroderma pigmentosum patients. *Proceedings of the National Academy of Sciences of the United States of America* 1997;94(17):9463–8.

Rebbeck TR. Molecular epidemiology of the human glutathione *S*-transferase genotypes *GSTM1* and *GSTT1* in cancer susceptibility. *Cancer Epidemiology, Biomarkers & Prevention* 1997;6(9):733–43.

Reddell RR, Ke Y, Gerwin BI, McMenamin MG, Lechner JF, Su RT, Brash DE, Park JB, Rhim JS, Harris CC. Transformation of human bronchial epithelial cells by infection with SV40 or adenovirus-12 SV40 hybrid virus, or transfection via strontium phosphate coprecipitation with a plasmid containing the SV40 early region genes. *Cancer Research* 1988;48(7):1904–9.

Reed JC. Dysregulation of apoptosis in cancer. *Journal of Clinical Oncology* 1999;17(9):2941–53.

Reed JC. Mechanisms of apoptosis. *American Journal of Pathology* 2000;157(5):1415–30.

Reeves WH, Sthoeger ZM. Molecular cloning of cDNA encoding the p70 (Ku) lupus autoantigen. *Journal of Biological Chemistry* 1989;264(9):5047–52.

Ren Q, Murphy SE, Zheng Z, Lazarus P. *O*-Glucuronidation of the lung carcinogen 4-(methylnitrosamino)-1-(3-pyridyl)-1-butanol (NNAL) by human UDP-glucuronosyltransferases 2B7 and 1A9. *Drug Metabolism and Disposition* 2000;28(11):1352–60.

Renner T, Fechner T, Scherer G. Fast quantification of the urinary marker of oxidative stress 8-hydroxy-2′-deoxyguanosine using solid-phase extraction and high-performance liquid chromatography with triple-stage quadrupole mass detection. *Journal of Chromatography B: Biomedical Sciences and Applications* 2000;738(2):311–7.

Reznick AZ, Cross CE, Hu ML, Suzuki YJ, Khwaja S, Safadi A, Motchnik PA, Packer L, Halliwell B. Modification of plasma proteins by cigarette smoke as measured by protein carbonyl formation. *Biochemical Journal* 1992;286(Pt 2):607–11.

Rich T, Allen RL, Wyllie AH. Defying death after DNA damage. *Nature* 2000;407(6805):777–83.

Richie JP Jr, Carmella SG, Muscat JE, Scott DG, Akerkar SA, Hecht SS. Differences in the urinary metabolites of the tobacco-specific lung carcinogen 4-(methylnitrosamino)-1-(3-pyridyl)-1-butanone in black and white smokers. *Cancer Epidemiology, Biomarkers & Prevention* 1997;6(10):783–90.

Richter A, O'Donnell RA, Powell RM, Sanders MW, Holgate ST, Djukanović R, Davies DE. Autocrine ligands for the epidermal growth factor receptor mediate interleukin-8 release from bronchial epithelial cells in response to cigarette smoke. *American Journal of Respiratory Cell and Molecular Biology* 2002;27(1):85–90.

Riedl K, Krysan K, Põld M, Dalwadi H, Heuze-Vourc'h N, Dohadwala M, Liu M, Cui X, Figlin R, Mao JT, et al. Multifaceted roles of cyclooxygenase-2 in lung cancer. *Drug Resistance Updates* 2004;7(3):169–84.

Riedy M, Wang J-Y, Miller AP, Buckler A, Hall J, Guida M. Genomic organization of the UGT2b gene cluster on human chromosome 4q13. *Pharmacogenetics* 2000;10(3):251–60.

Ries LAG, Eisner MP, Kosary CL, Hankey BF, Miller BA, Clegg L, Mariotto A, Feuer EJ, Edwards BK, editors. *SEER Cancer Statistics Review, 1975–2001*. Bethesda (MD): National Cancer Institute, 2004.

Riffelmann M, Muller G, Schmieding W, Popp W, Norpoth K. Biomonitoring of urinary aromatic amines and arylamine hemoglobin adducts in exposed workers and nonexposed control persons. *International Archives of Occupational and Environmental Health* 1995;68(1):36–43.

Risinger JI, Umar A, Barrett JC, Kunkel TA. A *hPMS2* mutant cell line is defective in strand-specific mismatch repair. *Journal of Biological Chemistry* 1995; 270(31):18183–6.

Rivenson A, Hoffmann D, Prokopczyk B, Amin S, Hecht SS. Induction of lung and exocrine pancreas tumors in F344 rats by tobacco-specific and *Areca*-derived N-nitrosamines. *Cancer Research* 1988;48(23):6912–7.

Robles AI, Bemmels NA, Foraker AB, Harris CC. *APAF-1* is a transcriptional target of p53 in DNA damage-induced apoptosis. *Cancer Research* 2001;61(18): 6660–4.

Robles AI, Linke SP, Harris CC. The p53 network in lung carcinogenesis. *Oncogene* 2002;21(45):6898–907.

Rodriguez-Viciana P, Warne PH, Khwaja A, Marte BM, Pappin D, Das P, Waterfield MD, Ridley A, Downward J. Role of phosphoinositide 3-OH kinase in cell transformation and control of the actin cytoskeleton by Ras. *Cell* 1997;89(3):457–67.

Rojas M, Alexandrov K, Cascorbi I, Brockmoller J, Likhachev A, Pozharisski K, Bouvier G, Auburtin G, Mayer L, Koop-Schneider A, et al. High benzo[*a*]pyrene diolepoxide DNA adduct levels in lung and blood cells from individuals with combined CYP1A1 MspI/Msp-GSTM1*0/*0 genotypes. *Pharmacogenetics* 1998;8(2): 109–18.

Rojas M, Marie B, Vignaud JM, Martinet N, Siat J, Grosdidier G, Cascorbi I, Alexandrov K. High DNA damage by benzo[*a*]pyrene 7,8-diol-9,10-epoxide in bronchial epithelial cells from patients with lung cancer: comparison with lung parenchyma. *Cancer Letters* 2004; 207(2):157–63.

Romashkova JA, Makarov SS. NF-κB is a target of AKT in anti-apoptotic PDGF signaling [letter]. *Nature* 1999;401(6748):86–90.

Rosas SLB, Koch W, da Costa Carvalho MG, Wu L, Califano J, Westra W, Jen J, Sidransky D. Promoter hypermethylation patterns of *p16*, *O6-methylguanine-DNA-methyltransferase*, and *death-associated protein kinase* in tumors and saliva of head and neck cancer patients. *Cancer Research* 2001;61(3):939–42.

Rosell R, Li S, Skacel Z, Mate JL, Maestre J, Canela M, Tolosa E, Armengol P, Barnadas A, Ariza A. Prognostic impact of mutated K-ras gene in surgically resected non-small cell lung cancer patients. *Oncogene* 1993;8(9):2407–12.

Rosenquist TA, Zharkov DO, Grollman AP. Cloning and characterization of a mammalian 8-oxoguanine DNA glycosylase. *Proceedings of the National Academy of Sciences of the United States of America* 1997;94(14): 7429–34.

Ross GM, McMillan TJ, Wilcox P, Collins AR. The single cell microgel electrophoresis assay (comet assay): technical aspects and applications. *Mutation Research* 1995;337(1):57–60.

Rowe JD, Nieves E, Listowsky I. Subunit diversity and tissue distribution of human glutathione *S*-transferases: interpretations based on electrospray ionization-MS and peptide sequence-specific antisera. *Biochemical Journal* 1997;325(Pt 2):481–6.

Roymans D, Slegers H. Phosphatidylinositol 3-kinases in tumor progression. *European Journal of Biochemistry* 2001;268(3):487–98.

Roz L, Andriana F, Ferreira CG, Giaccone G, Sozzi G. The apoptotic pathway triggered by the Fhit protein in lung cancer cell lines is not affected by Bcl-2 or Bcl-x(L) overexpression. *Oncogene* 2004;23(56):9102–10.

Ruano-Ravina A, Figueiras A, Loidi L, Barros-Dios JM. GSTM1 and GSTT1 polymorphisms, tobacco and risk of lung cancer: a case-control study from Galicia, Spain. *Anticancer Research* 2003;23(56):4333–7.

Ruggeri B, DiRado M, Zhang SY, Bauer B, Goodrow T, Klein-Szanto AJP. Benzo[*a*]pyrene-induced murine skin tumors exhibit frequent and characteristic G to T mutations in the p53 gene. *Proceedings of the National Academy of Sciences of the United States of America* 1993;90(3):1013–7.

Rusch V, Baselga J, Cordon-Cardo C, Orazem J, Zaman M, Hoda S, McIntosh J, Kurie J, Dmitrovsky E. Differential expression of the epidermal growth factor receptor and its ligands in primary non-small cell lung cancers and adjacent benign lung. *Cancer Research* 1993;53(10 Suppl):2379–85.

Rusch V, Klimstra D, Linkov I, Dmitrovsky E. Aberrant expression of p53 or the epidermal growth factor receptor is frequent in early bronchial neoplasia and coexpression precedes squamous cell carcinoma development. *Cancer Research* 1995;55(6):1365–72.

Ruvolo PP, Deng X, May WS. Phosphorylation of Bcl2 and regulation of apoptosis. *Leukemia* 2001;15(4):515–22.

Ryan BM, McManus R, Daly JS, Carton E, Keeling PWN, Reynolds JV, Kelleher D. A common *p73* polymorphism is associated with a reduced incidence of oesophageal carcinoma. *British Journal of Cancer* 2001; 85(10):1499–503.

Ryberg D, Skaug V, Hewer A, Phillips DH, Harries LW, Wolf CR, Ogreid D, Ulvik A, Vu P, Haugen A. Genotypes of glutathione transferase M1 and P1 and their significance for lung DNA adduct levels and cancer risk. *Carcinogenesis* 1997;18(7):1285–9.

Saarikoski ST, Reinikainen M, Antilla S, Karjalainen A, Vainio H, Husgafvel-Pursiainen K, Hirvonen A. Role of NAT2 deficiency in susceptibility to lung cancer among asbestos-exposed individuals. *Pharmacogenetics* 2000;10(2):183–5.

Sakumi K, Tominaga Y, Furuichi M, Xu P, Tsuzuki T, Sekiguchi M, Nakabeppu Y. *Ogg1* knockout-associated lung tumorigenesis and its suppression by *Mth1* gene disruption. *Cancer Research* 2003;63(5):902–5.

Samet JM, Humble CG, Pathak DR. Personal and family history of respiratory disease and lung cancer risk. *American Review of Respiratory Disease* 1986;134(3):466–70.

Samson L, Derfler B, Boosalis M, Call K. Cloning and characterization of a 3-methyladenine DNA glycosylase cDNA from human cells whose gene maps to chromosome 16. *Proceedings of the National Academy of Sciences of the United States of America* 1991; 88(20):9127–31.

Sancar A, Lindsey-Boltz LA, Ünsal-Kaçmaz K, Linn S. Molecular mechanisms of mammalian DNA repair and the DNA damage checkpoints. *Annual Review of Biochemistry* 2004;73:39–85.

Sanchez-Cespedes M, Ahrendt SA, Piantadosi S, Rosell R, Monzo M, Wu L, Westra WH, Yang SC, Jen J, Sidransky D. Chromosomal alterations in lung adenocarcinoma from smokers and nonsmokers. *Cancer Research* 2001; 61(4):1309–13.

Sanchez-Cespedes M, Parrella P, Esteller M, Nomoto S, Trink B, Engles JM, Westra WH, Herman JG, Sidransky D. Inactivation of LKB1/STK11 is a common event in adenocarcinomas of the lung. *Cancer Research* 2002;62(13):3659–62.

Sanyal S, Festa F, Sakano S, Zhang Z, Steineck G, Norming U, Wijström H, Larsson P, Kumar R, Hemminki K. Polymorphisms in DNA repair and metabolic genes in bladder cancer. *Carcinogenesis* 2004;25(5):729–34.

Sapkota GP, Deak M, Kieloch A, Morrice N, Goodarzi AA, Smythe C, Shiloh Y, Lees-Miller SP, Alessi DR. Ionizing radiation induces ataxia telangiectasia mutated kinase (ATM)-mediated phosphorylation of LKB1/STK11 at Thr-366. *Biochemical Journal* 2002;68(Pt 2):507–16.

Schabath MB, Spitz MR, Grossman HB, Zhang K, Dinney CP, Zheng P-J, Wu X. Genetic instability in bladder cancer assessed by the comet assay. *Journal of the National Cancer Institute* 2003;95(7):540–7.

Schabath MB, Spitz MR, Hong WK, Delclos GL, Reynolds WF, Gunn GB, Whitehead LW, Wu X. A myeloperoxidase polymorphism associated with reduced risk of lung cancer. *Lung Cancer* 2002;37(1):35–40.

Scherer G, Meger M, Meger-Kossien I, Pachinger A. Biological monitoring of the tobacco-smoke related exposure to benzene. *Proceedings of the American Association for Cancer Research* 2001;42:150.

Scherer G, Renner T, Meger M. Analysis and evaluation of *trans,trans*-muconic acid as a biomarker for benzene exposure. *Journal of Chromatography B: Biomedical Sciences and Applications* 1998;717(1–2):179–99.

Schlade-Bartusiak K, Rozik K, Laczmanska I, Ramsey D, Sasiadek M. Influence of GSTT1, mEH, CYP2E1 and RAD51 polymorphisms on diepoxybutane-induced SCE frequency in cultured human lymphocytes. *Mutation Research* 2004;558(1–2):121–30.

Schmezer P, Rajaee-Behbahani N, Risch A, Thiel S, Rittgen W, Drings P, Dienemann H, Kayser KW, Schulz V, Bartsch H. Rapid screening assay for mutagen sensitivity and DNA repair capacity in human peripheral blood lymphocytes. *Mutagenesis* 2001;16(1):25–30.

Schmitt CA, Lowe SW. Apoptosis and chemoresistance in transgenic cancer models. *Journal of Molecular Medicine* 2002;80(3):137–46.

Schofield MJ, Hsieh P. DNA mismatch repair: molecular mechanisms and biological function. *Annual Review of Microbiology* 2003;57:579–608.

Schott AF, Apel IJ, Nuñez G, Clarke MF. Bcl-X$_L$ protects cancer cells from p53-mediated apoptosis. *Oncogene* 1995;11(7):1389–94.

Schuller HM, Orloff M. Tobacco-specific carcinogenic nitrosamines: ligands for nicotinic acetylcholine receptors in human lung cancer cells. *Biochemical Pharmacology* 1998;55(9):1377–84.

Schuller HM, Plummer HK III, Bochsler PN, Dudric P, Bell JL, Harris RE. Co-expression of β-adrenergic receptors and cyclooxygenase-2 in pulmonary adenocarcinoma. *International Journal of Oncology* 2001;19(3):445–9.

Schuller HM, Plummer HK III, Jull BA. Receptor-mediated effects of nicotine and its nitrosated derivative NNK on pulmonary neuroendocrine cells. *Anatomical Record Part A, Discoveries in Molecular, Cellular, and Evolutionary Biology* 2003;270(1):51–8.

Schuller HM, Tithof PK, Williams M, Plummer H III. The tobacco-specific carcinogen 4-(methylnitrosamino)-1-(3-pyridyl)-1-butanone is a β-adrenergic agonist and stimulates DNA synthesis in lung adenocarcinoma via β-adrenergic receptor-mediated release of arachidonic acid. *Cancer Research* 1999;59(18):4510–5.

Schwartz AG, Prysak GM, Bock CH, Cote ML. The molecular epidemiology of lung cancer. *Carcinogenesis* 2007;28(3):507–18.

Schwartz AG, Siegfried JM, Weiss L. Familial aggregation of breast cancer with early onset lung cancer. *Genetic Epidemiology* 1999;17(1):274–84.

Schwartz AG, Yang P, Swanson GM. Familial risk of lung cancer among nonsmokers and their relatives. *American Journal of Epidemiology* 1996;144(6):554–62.

Seidegard J, Vorachek WR, Pero RW, Pearson WR. Hereditary differences in the expression of the human glutathione transferase active in trans-stilbene oxide are due to a gene deletion. *Proceedings of the National Academy of Sciences of the United States of America* 1988;85(19):7293–7.

Sekido Y, Takahashi T, Mäkelä TP, Obata Y, Ueda R, Hida T, Hibi K, Shimokata K, Alitalo K, Takahashi T. Complex intrachromosomal rearrangement in the process of amplification of the L-myc gene in small-cell lung cancer. *Molecular and Cellular Biology* 1992;12(4): 1747–54.

Sellers TA, Bailey-Wilson JE, Elston RC, Wilson AF, Elston GZ, Ooi WL, Rothschild H. Evidence for mendelian inheritance in the pathogenesis of lung cancer. *Journal of the National Cancer Institute* 1990;82(15):1272–9.

Sellers TA, Elston RC, Atwood LD, Rothschild H. Lung cancer histologic type and family history of cancer. *Cancer* 1992;69(1):86–91.

Selvaggi G, Novello S, Torri V, Leonardo E, De Giuli P, Borasio P, Mossetti C, Ardissone F, Lausi P, Scagliotti GV. Epidermal growth factor receptor overexpression correlates with a poor prognosis in completely resected non-small-cell lung cancer. *Annals of Oncology* 2004;15(1):28–32.

Seow A, Zhao B, Poh W-T, Teh M, Eng P, Wang Y-T, Tan W-C, Lee EJD, Lee H-P. NAT2 slow acetylator genotype is associated with increased risk of lung cancer among non-smoking Chinese women in Singapore. *Carcinogenesis* 1999;20(9):1877–81.

Serdar B, Waidyanatha S, Zheng Y, Rappaport SM. Simultaneous determination of urinary 1- and 2-naphthols, 3- and 9-phenanthrols, and 1-pyrenol in coke oven workers. *Biomarkers* 2003;8(2):93–109.

Shapiro JA, Jacobs EJ, Thun MJ. Cigar smoking in men and risk of death from tobacco-related cancers. *Journal of the National Cancer Institute* 2000;92(4):333–7.

Shaw GL, Falk RT, Pickle LW, Mason TJ, Buffler PA. Lung cancer risk associated with cancer in relatives. *Journal of Clinical Epidemiology* 1991;44(4–5):429–37.

Sheehan D, Meade G, Foley VM, Dowd CA. Structure, function and evolution of glutathione transferases: implications for classification of non-mammalian members of an ancient enzyme superfamily. *Biochemical Journal* 2001;360(Pt 1):1–16.

Shen H, Sturgis EM, Khan SG, Qiao Y, Shahlavi T, Eicher SA, Xu Y, Wang X, Strom SS, Spitz MR, et al. An intronic poly (AT) polymorphism of the DNA repair gene *XPC* and risk of squamous cell carcinoma of the head and neck: a case-control study. *Cancer Research* 2001;61(8):3321–5.

Shen MR, Jones IM, Mohrenweiser H. Nonconservative amino acid substitution variants exist at polymorphic frequency in DNA repair genes in healthy humans. *Cancer Research* 1998;58(4):604–8.

Sherratt PJ, Pulford DJ, Harrison DJ, Green T, Hayes JD. Evidence that human class Theta glutathione S-transferase T1-1 can catalyse the activation of dichloromethane, a liver and lung carcinogen in the mouse: comparison of the tissue distribution of GST T1-1 with that of classes Alpha, Mu and Pi GST in human. *Biochemical Journal* 1997;326(Pt 3):837–46.

Shi D, He G, Cao S, Pan W, Zhang HZ, Yu D, Hung MC. Overexpression of the c-erbB-2/neu-encoded p185 protein in primary lung cancer. *Molecular Carcinogenesis* 1992;5(3):213–8.

Shields PG, Harris CG. Cancer risk and low-penetrance susceptibility genes in gene-environment interactions. *Journal of Clinical Oncology* 2000;18(11):2309–15.

Shih C-M, Lin P-T, Wang H-C, Huang W-C, Wang Y-C. Lack of evidence of association of p21$^{WAF1/CP1}$ polymorphism with lung cancer susceptibility and prognosis in Taiwan. *Japanese Journal of Cancer Research* 2000;91(1):9–15.

Shimada T, Fujii-Kuriyama Y. Metabolic activation of polycyclic aromatic hydrocarbons to carcinogens by cytochromes P450 1A1 and 1B1. *Cancer Science* 2004; 95(1):1–6.

Shimada T, Gillam EMJ, Oda Y, Tsumura F, Sutter TR, Guengerich FP, Inoue K. Metabolism of benzo[*a*] pyrene to *trans*-7,8-dihydroxy-7, 8-dihydrobenzo[*a*] pyrene by recombinant human cytochrome P450 1B1 and purified liver epoxide hydrolase. *Chemical Research in Toxicology* 1999;12(7):623–9.

Shimada T, Gillam EMJ, Sutter TR, Strickland PT, Guengerich FP, Yamazaki H. Oxidation of xenobiotics by recombinant human cytochrome P450 1B1. *Drug Metabolism and Disposition* 1997;25(5):617–22.

Shimada T, Hayes CL, Yamazaki H, Amin S, Hecht SS, Guengerich FP, Sutter TR. Activation of chemically diverse procarcinogens by human cytochrome P450 1B1. *Cancer Research* 1996;56(13):2979–84.

Shimizu E, Coxon A, Otterson GA, Steinberg SM, Kratzke RA, Kim YW, Fedorko J, Oie H, Johnson BE, Mulshine JL, et al. RB protein status and clinical correlation from 171 cell lines representing lung cancer, extrapulmonary small cell carcinoma, and mesothelioma: a predictive evidence for conformational change to influence mitochondrial transport and a study of allelic association in Parkinson's disease. *Oncogene* 1994;9(9):2441–8.

Shishodia S, Aggarwal BB. Cyclooxygenase (COX)-2 inhibitor celecoxib abrogates activation of cigarette smoke-induced nuclear factor (NF)-κB by suppressing activation of IκBα kinase in human non-small cell lung carcinoma: correlation with suppression of cyclin D1, COX-2, and matrix metalloproteinase-9. *Cancer Research* 2004;64(14):5004–12.

Shuker DE, Friesen MD, Garren L, Prevost V. A rapid gas chromatography-mass spectrometry method for the determination of urinary 3-methyladenine: application in human subjects. *IARC Scientific Publications* 1991;(105):102–6.

Sijbers AM, de Laat WL, Ariza RR, Biggerstaff M, Wei Y-F, Moggs JG, Carter KC, Shell BK, Evans E, de Jong MC, et al. Xeroderma pigmentosum group F caused by a defect in a structure-specific DNA repair endonuclease. *Cell* 1996;86(5):811–22.

Singer B, Grunberger D. *Molecular Biology of Mutagens and Carcinogens*. New York: Plenum Press, 1983: 45–94.

Singh NP, McCoy MT, Tice RR, Schneider EL. A simple technique for quantitation of low levels of DNA damage in individual cells. *Experimental Cell Research* 1988;175(1):184–91.

Singh R, Kaur B, Farmer PB. Detection of DNA damage derived from a direct acting ethylating agent present in cigarette smoke by use of liquid chromatography-tandem mass spectrometry. *Chemical Research in Toxicology* 2005;18(2):249–56.

Singhal S, Amin KM, Kruklitis R, DeLong P, Friscia ME, Litzky LA, Putt ME, Kaiser LR, Albelda SM. Alterations in cell cycle genes in early stage lung adenocarcinoma identified by expression profiling. *Cancer Biology & Therapy* 2003;2(3):291–8.

Själander A, Birgander R, Rannug A, Alexandrie A-K, Tornling G, Beckman G. Association between the p21 codon 31 A1 (arg) allele and lung cancer. *Human Heredity* 1996;46(4):221–5.

Skipper PL, Peng X, Soohoo CK, Tannenbaum SR. Protein adducts as biomarkers of human carcinogen exposure. *Drug Metabolism Reviews* 1994;26(1–2):111–24.

Skipper PL, Tannenbaum SR. Protein adducts in the molecular dosimetry of chemical carcinogens. *Carcinogenesis* 1990;11(4):507–18.

Slebos RJ, Kibbelaar RE, Dalesio O, Kooistra A, Stam J, Meijer CJ, Wagenaar SS, Vanderschueren RG, van Zandwijk N, Mooi WJ, et al. K-ras oncogene activation as a prognostic marker in adenocarcinoma of the lung. *New England Journal of Medicine* 1990;323(9):561–5.

Slupphaug G, Lettrem I, Myrnes B, Krokan HE. Expression of O^6-methylguanine-DNA methyltransferase and uracil-DNA glycolase in human placentae from smokers and nonsmokers. *Carcinogenesis* 1992;13(10): 1769–73.

Slupska MM, Baikalov C, Luther WM, Chiang JH, Wei YF, Miller JH. Cloning and sequencing a human homolog (*hMYH*) of the *Escherichia coli mutY* gene whose function is required for the repair of oxidative DNA damage. *Journal of Bacteriology* 1996;178(13):3885–92.

Slupska MM, Luther WM, Chiang JH, Yang H, Miller JH. Functional expression of hMYH, a human homolog of the *Escherichia coli* MutY protein. *Journal of Bacteriology* 1999;181(19):6210–3.

Smith CJ, Huang W, Walcott CJ, Turner W, Grainger J, Patterson DG Jr. Quantification of monohydroxy-PAH metabolites in urine by solid-phase extraction with isotope dilution-GC-MS. *Analytical and Bioanalytical Chemistry* 2002a;372(1):216–20.

Smith CJ, Walcott CJ, Huang W, Maggio V, Grainger J, Patterson DG Jr. Determination of selected monohydroxy metabolites of 2-, 3- and 4-ring polycyclic aromatic hydrocarbons in urine by solid-phase microextraction and isotope dilution gas chromatography—mass spectrometry. *Journal of Chromatography B* 2002b;778 (1–2):157–64.

Smith LE, Denissenko MF, Bennett WP, Li H, Amin S, Tang M-S, Pfeifer GP. Targeting of lung cancer mutational hotspots by polycyclic aromatic hydrocarbons. *Journal of the National Cancer Institute* 2000;92(10):803–11.

Snyder R, Chepiga T, Yang CS, Thomas H, Platt K, Oesch, F. Benzene metabolism by reconstituted cytochromes P450 2B1 and 2E1 and its modulation by cytochrome b_5, microsomal epoxide hydrolase, and glutathione transferases: evidence for an important role of microsomal epoxide hydrolase in the formation of hydroquinone. *Toxicology and Applied Pharmacology* 1993;122(2):172–81.

Snyder R, Hedli CC. An overview of benzene metabolism. *Environmental Health Perspectives* 1996;104(Suppl 6): 1165–71.

Sobol RW, Horton JK, Kuhn R, Gu H, Singhal RK, Prasad R, Rajewsky K, Wilson SH. Requirement of mammalian DNA polymerase-β in base-excision repair. *Nature* 1996;379(6561):183–6.

Soengas MS, Alarcón RM, Yoshida H, Giaccia AJ, Hakem R, Mak TW, Lowe SW. Apaf-1 and caspase-9 in p53-dependent apoptosis and tumor inhibition. *Science* 1999;284(5411):156–9.

Song P, Sekhon HS, Jia Y, Keller JA, Blusztajn JK, Mark GP, Spindel ER. Acetylcholine is synthesized by and acts as an autocrine growth factor for small cell lung carcinoma. *Cancer Research* 2003a;63(1):214–21.

Song P, Sekhon HS, Proskocil B, Blusztajn JK, Mark GP, Spindel ER. Synthesis of acetylcholine by lung cancer. *Life Sciences* 2003b;72(18–19):2159–68.

Sopori M. Effects of cigarette smoke on the immune system. *Nature Reviews Immunology* 2002;2(5):372–7.

Sørensen M, Autrup H, Tjønneland A, Overvad K, Raaschou-Nielsen O. Glutathione *S*-transferase T1 null-genotype is associated with an increased risk of lung cancer. *International Journal of Cancer* 2004a;110(2): 219–24.

Sørensen M, Autrup H, Tjønneland A, Overvad K, Raaschou-Nielsen O. Genetic polymorphisms in *CYP1B1*, *GSTA1*, *NQO1* and *NAT2* and the risk of lung cancer. *Cancer Letters* 2005;221(2):185–90.

Sørensen M, Poole J, Autrup H, Muzyka V, Jensen A, Loft S, Knudsen LE. Benzene exposure assessed by metabolite excretion in Estonian oil shale mineworkers: influence of glutathione *S*-transferase polymorphisms. *Cancer Epidemiology, Biomarkers & Prevention* 2004b;13(11):1729–35.

Sozzi G, Miozzo M, Donghi R, Pilotti S, Cariani CT, Pastorino U, Della Porta G, Pierotti MA. Deletions of 17p and p53 mutations in preneoplastic lesions of the lung. *Cancer Research* 1992;52(21):6079–82.

Spitz MR, Duphorne CM, Detry MA, Pillow PC, Amos CI, Lei L, de Andrade M, Gu X, Hong WK, Wu X. Dietary intake of isothiocyanates: evidence of a joint effect with glutathione *S*-transferase polymorphisms in lung cancer risk. *Cancer Epidemiology, Biomarkers & Prevention* 2000;9(10):1017–20.

Spitz MR, Hsu TC, Wu X, Fueger JJ, Amos CI, Roth JA. Mutagen sensitivity as a biologic marker of lung cancer risk in African Americans. *Cancer Epidemiology, Biomarkers & Prevention* 1995;4(2):99–103.

Spitz MR, Wei Q, Dong Q, Amos CI, Wu X. Genetic susceptibility to lung cancer: the role of DNA damage and repair. *Cancer Epidemiology, Biomarkers & Prevention* 2003;12(8):689–98.

Spitz MR, Wu X, Mills G. Integrative epidemiology: from risk assessment to outcome prediction. *Journal of Clinical Oncology* 2005;23(2):267–75.

Spitz MR, Wu X, Wang Y, Wang L-E, Shete S, Amos CI, Guo Z, Lei L, Mohrenweiser H, Wei Q. Modulation of nucleotide excision repair capacity by XPD polymorphisms in lung cancer patients. *Cancer Research* 2001;61(4):1354–7.

Squier CA, Cox P, Hall BK. Enhanced penetration of nitrosonornicotine across oral mucosa in the presence of ethanol. *Journal of Oral Pathology* 1986;15(5):276–9.

Sridhar SS, Seymour L, Shepherd FA. Inhibitors of epidermal-growth-factor receptors: a review of clinical research with a focus on non-small-cell lung cancer. *Lancet Oncology* 2003;4(7):397–406.

Srivastava DK, Vande Berg BJ, Prasad R, Molina JT, Beard WA, Tomkinson AE, Wilson SH. Mammalian abasic site base excision repair: identification of the reaction sequence and rate-determining steps. *Journal of Biological Chemistry* 1998;273(33):21203–9.

Srivenugopal KS, Yuan X-H, Friedman HS, Ali-Osman F. Ubiquitination-dependent proteolysis of O^6-methylguanine-DNA methyltransferase in human and murine tumor cells following inactivation with O^6-benzylguanine or 1,3-*bis*(2-chloroethyl)-1-nitrosourea. *Biochemistry* 1996;35(4):1328–34.

Stambolic V, Mak TW, Woodgett JR. Modulation of cellular apoptotic potential: contributions to oncogenesis. *Oncogene* 1999;18(45):6094–103.

Stasiak AZ, Larquet E, Stasiak A, Müller S, Engel A, Van Dyck E, West SC, Egelman EH. The human Rad52 protein exists as a heptameric ring. *Current Biology* 2000;10(6):337–40.

Stepanov I, Hecht SS. Tobacco-specific nitrosamines and their pyridine-*N*-glucuronides in the urine of smokers and smokeless tobacco users. *Cancer Epidemiology, Biomarkers & Prevention* 2005;14(4):885–91.

Stern MC, Umbach DM, Lunn RM, Taylor JA. DNA repair gene *XRCC3* codon 241 polymorphism, its interaction with smoking and *XRCC1* polymorphisms, and bladder cancer risk. *Cancer Epidemiology, Biomarkers & Prevention* 2002;11(9):939–43.

Stern MC, Umbach DM, van Gils CH, Lunn RM, Taylor JA. DNA repair gene *XRCC1* polymorphisms, smoking, and bladder cancer risk. *Cancer Epidemiology, Biomarkers & Prevention* 2001;10(2):125–31.

Stillwell WG, Glogowski J, Xu HX, Wishnok JS, Zavala D, Montes G, Correa P, Tannenbaum SR. Urinary excretion of nitrate, *N*-nitrosoproline, 3-methyladenine, and 7-methylguanine in a Colombian population at high risk for stomach cancer. *Cancer Research* 1991;51(1):190–4.

Stojic L, Brun R, Jiricny J. Mismatch repair and DNA damage signalling. *DNA Repair* 2004;3(8–9):1091–101.

Stommel P, Müller G, Stücker W, Verkoyen C, Schöbel S, Norpoth K. Determination of S-phenylmercapturic acid in the urine—an improvement in the biological monitoring of benzene exposure. *Carcinogenesis* 1989;10(2):279–82.

Strauss BS. The 'A rule' of mutagen specificity: a consequence of DNA polymerase bypass of non-instructional lesions? *BioEssays* 1991;13(2):79–84.

Strauss B, Sagher D, Schwartz J, Karrison T, Larson R. Heterogeneity in the O^6-alkyl-guanine DNA alkyltransferase (AGT) activity of human peripheral blood lymphocytes (PBL's). In: Lambert MW, Laval J, editors. *DNA Repair Mechanisms and Their Biological Implications in Mammalian Cells*. New York: Plenum Press, 1989:618.

Strom SS, Wu X, Sigurdson AJ, Hsu TC, Fueger JJ, Lopez J, Tee PG, Spitz MR. Lung cancer, smoking patterns, and mutagen sensitivity in Mexican-Americans. *Journal of the National Cancer Institute Monographs* 1995;18:29–33.

Stücker I, Hirvonen A, de Waziers I, Cabelguenne A, Mitrunen K, Cénée S, Koun-Besson E, Hémon D, Beaune P, Loriot M-A. Genetic polymorphisms of glutathione-S-transferases as modulators of lung cancer susceptibility. *Carcinogenesis* 2002;23(9):1475–81.

Stucki M, Pascucci B, Parlanti E, Fortini P, Wilson SH, Hübscher U, Dogliotti E. Mammalian base excision repair by DNA polymerases δ and ε. *Oncogene* 1998;17(7):835–43.

Sturgis EM, Castillo EJ, Li L, Zheng R, Eicher SA, Clayman GL, Strom SS, Spitz MR, Wei Q. Polymorphisms of DNA repair gene *XRCC1* in squamous cell carcinoma of the head and neck. *Carcinogenesis* 1999;20(11):2125–9.

Sturgis EM, Dahlstrom KR, Spitz MR, Wei Q. DNA repair gene *ERCC1* and *ERCC2/XPD* polymorphisms and risk of squamous cell carcinoma of the head and neck. *Archives of Otolaryngology—Head & Neck Surgery* 2002;128(9):1084–8.

Su L, Liu G, Zhou W, Xu LL, Miller DP, Park S, Lynch TJ, Wain JC, Christiani DC. No association between the *p21 codon 31 serine-arginine* polymorphism and lung cancer risk. *Cancer Epidemiology, Biomarkers & Prevention* 2003;12(2):174–5.

Su T, Bao Z, Zhang Q-Y, Smith TJ, Hong J-Y, Ding X. Human cytochrome P 450 CYP2A13: predominant expression in the respiratory tract and in high efficiency metabolic activation of a tobacco-specific carcinogen, 4-(methylnitrosamino)-1-(3-pyridyl)-1-butanone. *Cancer Research* 2000;60(18):5074–9.

Sugimura T. History, present and future, of heterocyclic amines, cooked food mutagens. *Princess Takamatsu Symposia* 1995;23:214–31.

Sugimura H, Kohno T, Wakai K, Nagura K, Genka K, Igarashi H, Morris BJ, Baba S, Ohno Y, Gao CM, et al. *hOGG1* Ser326Cys polymorphism and lung cancer susceptibility. *Cancer Epidemiology, Biomarkers & Prevention* 1999;8(8):669–74.

Sundberg K, Dreij K, Seidel A, Jernström B. Glutathione conjugation and DNA adduct formation of dibenzo[*a,l*]pyrene and benzo[*a*]pyrene diol epoxides in V79 cells stably expressing different human glutathione transferases. *Chemical Research in Toxicology* 2002;15(2):170–9.

Sundberg K, Johansson A-S, Stenberg G, Widersten M, Seidel A, Mannervik B, Jernström B. Differences in the catalytic efficiencies of allelic variants of glutathione transferase P1-1 towards carcinogenic diol epoxides of polycyclic aromatic hydrocarbons. *Carcinogenesis* 1998;19(3):433–6.

Sundberg K, Widersten M, Seidel A, Mannervik B, Jernström B. Glutathione conjugation of bay- and fjord-region diol epoxides of polycyclic aromatic hydrocarbons by glutathione transferases M1-1 and P1-1. *Chemical Research in Toxicology* 1997;10(11):1221–7.

Sutter TR, Tang YM, Hayes CL, Wo YY, Jabs EW, Li X, Yin H, Cody CW, Greenlee WF. Complete cDNA sequence of a human dioxin-inducible mRNA identifies a new gene subfamily of cytochrome P450 that maps to chromosome 2. *Journal of Biological Chemistry* 1994;269(18):13092–9.

Suzuki H, Gabrielson E, Chen W, Anbazhagan R, van Engeland M, Weijenber MP, Herman JG, Baylin SB. A genomic screen for genes upregulated by demethylation and histone deacetylase inhibition in human colorectal cancer. *Nature Genetics* 2002;31(2):141–9.

Suzuki S, Dobashi Y, Sakurai H, Nishikawa K, Hanawa M, Ooi A. Protein overexpression and gene amplification of epidermal growth factor receptor in non-small cell lung carcinomas: an immunohistochemical and fluorescence in situ hybridization study. *Cancer* 2005;103(6):1265–73.

Swafford DS, Middleton SK, Palmisano WA, Nikula KJ, Tesfaigzi J, Baylin SB, Herman JG, Belinsky SA. Frequent aberrant methylation of *p16^{INK4a}* in primary rat lung tumors. *Molecular and Cellular Biology* 1997;17(3):1366–74.

Swann PF, Coe AM, Mace R. Ethanol and dimethylnitrosamine and diethylnitrosamine metabolism and disposition in the rat: possible relevance to the influence of ethanol on human cancer incidence. *Carcinogenesis* 1984;5(10):1337–43.

Swenberg JA, Koc H, Upton PB, Georguieva N, Ranasinghe A, Walker VE, Henderson R. Using DNA and hemoglobin adducts to improve the risk assessment of butadiene. *Chemico-Biological Interactions* 2001;135–136:387–403.

Szyfter K, Hemminki K, Szyfter W, Szmeja Z, Banaszewski J, Pabiszczak M. Tobacco smoke-associated N7-alkylguanine in DNA of larynx tissue and leucocytes. *Carcinogenesis* 1996;17(3):501–6.

Takao M, Kanno S, Kobayashi K, Zhang Q-M, Yonei S, van der Horst GTJ, Yasui A. A back-up glycosylase in *Nth1* knock-out mice is a functional Nei (endonuclease VIII) homologue. *Journal of Biological Chemistry* 2002;277(44):42205–13.

Tan D, Deeb G, Wang J, Slocum HK, Winston J, Wiseman S, Beck A, Sait S, Anderson T, Nwogu C, et al. HER-2/*neu* protein expression and gene alteration in stage I-IIIA non–small-cell lung cancer: a study of 140 cases using a combination of high throughput tissue microarray, immunohistochemistry, and fluorescent in situ hybridization. *Diagnostic Molecular Pathology* 2003;12(4):201–11.

Tan T, Chu G. p53 binds and activates the xeroderma pigmentosum *DDB2* gene in humans but not mice. *Molecular and Cellular Biology* 2002;22(10):3247–54.

Tang CK, Gong X-Q, Moscatello DK, Wong AJ, Lippman ME. Epidermal growth factor receptor vIII enhances tumorigenicity in human breast cancer. *Cancer Research* 2000;60(11):3081–7.

Tang M-S, Zheng JB, Denissenko MF, Pfeifer GP, Zheng Y. Use of UvrABC nuclease to quantify benzo[*a*]pyrene diol epoxide–DNA adduct formation at methylated versus unmethylated CpG sites in the p53 gene. *Carcinogenesis* 1999;20(6):1085–9.

Tapper AR, McKinney SL, Nashmi R, Schwarz J, Deshpande P, Labarca C, Whiteaker P, Marks MJ, Collins AC, Lester HA. Nicotine activation of α4* receptors:

sufficient for reward, tolerance, and sensitization. *Science* 2004;306(5698):1029–32.

Tarroni P, Rubboli F, Chini B, Zwart R, Oortgiesen M, Sher E, Clementi F. Neuronal-type nicotinic receptors in human neuroblastoma and small-cell lung carcinoma cell lines. *FEBS Letters* 1992;312(1):66–70.

Tateishi M, Ishida T, Mitsudomi T, Kaneko S, Sugimachi K. Immunohistochemical evidence of autocrine growth factors in adenocarcinoma of the human lung. *Cancer Research* 1990;50(21):7077–80.

Tefre T, Rybert D, Haugen A, Nebert DW, Skaug V, Brogger A, Borresen AL. Human CYP1A1 gene: lack of association between the Msp I restriction fragment length polymorphism and incidence of lung cancer in a Norwegian population. *Pharmacogenetics* 1991;1(1):20–5.

Terakawa N, Kanamori Y, Yoshida S. Loss of PTEN expression followed by Akt phosphorylation is a poor prognostic factor for patients with endometrial cancer. *Endocrine-Related Cancer* 2003;10(2):203–8.

Thakker DR, Yagi H, Levin W, Wood AW, Conney AH, Jerina DM. Polycyclic aromatic hydrocarbons: metabolic activation to ultimate carcinogens. In: Anders MW, editor. *Bioactivation of Foreign Compounds*. New York: Academic Press, 1985:177–242.

Thier R, Pemble SE, Kramer H, Taylor JB, Guengerich FP, Ketterer B. Human glutathione *S*-transferase T1-1 enhances mutagenicity of 1,2-dibromoethane, dibromomethane and 1,2,3,4-diepoxybutane in *Salmonella typhimurium*. *Carcinogenesis* 1996;17(1):163–6.

Thomas M, Kalita A, Labrecque S, Pim D, Banks L, Matlashewski G. Two polymorphic variants of wild-type p53 differ biochemically and biologically. *Molecular and Cellular Biology* 1999;19(2):1092–100.

To-Figueras J, Gené M, Gómez-Catalán J, Galán MC, Fuentes M, Ramón JM, Rodamilans M, Huguet E, Corbella J. Glutathione-S-transferase M1 (GSTM1) and T1 (GSTT1) polymorphism and lung cancer risk among northwestern Mediterraneans. *Carcinogenesis* 1997;18(8):1529–33.

To-Figueras J, Gené M, Gómez-Catalán J, Piqué E, Borrego N, Carrasco JL, Rámon J, Corbella J. Genetic polymorphism of glutathione-S-transferase P1 gene and lung cancer risk. *Cancer Causes & Control* 1999;10(1):65–70.

Tokuhata GK, Lilienfeld AM. Familial aggregation of lung cancer in humans. *Journal of the National Cancer Institute* 1963;30(2):289–312.

Tolias KF, Cantley LC, Carpenter CL. Rho family GTPases bind to phosphoinositide kinases. *Journal of Biological Chemistry* 1995;270(30):17656–9.

Tomizawa Y, Kohno T, Fujita T, Kiyama M, Saito R, Noguchi M, Matsuno Y, Hirohashi S, Yamaguchi N, Nakajima T, et al. Correlation between the status of the *p53* gene and survival in patients with stage I non-small cell lung carcinoma. *Oncogene* 1999;18(4):1007–14.

Tomizawa Y, Kohno T, Kondo H, Otsuka A, Nishioka M, Niki T, Yamada T, Maeshima A, Yoshimura K, Saito R, et al. Clinicopathological significance of epigenetic inactivation of *RASSF1A* at 3p21.3 in stage I lung adenocarcinoma. *Clinical Cancer Research* 2002;8(7):2362–8.

Toorchen D, Topal MD. Mechanisms of chemical mutagenesis and carcinogenesis: effects on DNA replication of methylation at the O^6-guanine position of dGTP. *Carcinogenesis* 1983;4(12):1591–7.

Tornaletti S, Hanawalt PC. Effect of DNA lesions on transcription elongation. *Biochimie* 1999;81(1–2):139–46.

Tornaletti S, Pfeifer GP. Complete and tissue-independent methylation of CpG sites in the p53 gene: implications for mutations in human cancers. *Oncogene* 1995;10(8):1493–9.

Törnqvist M, Ehrenberg L. On cancer risk estimation of urban air pollution. *Environmental Health Perspectives* 1994;102(Suppl 4):173–82.

Travis WD, Travis LB, Devesa SS. Lung cancer. *Cancer* 1995;75(1 Suppl):191–202.

Tretyakova N, Matter B, Jones R, Shallop A. Formation of benzo[*a*]pyrene diol epoxide–DNA adducts at specific guanines within *K-ras* and *p53* gene sequences: stable isotope-labeling mass spectrometry approach. *Biochemistry* 2002;41(30):9535–44.

Tricker AR. N-nitroso compounds and man: sources of exposure, endogenous formation and occurrence in body fluids. *European Journal of Cancer Prevention* 1997;6(3):226–68.

Tricker AR, Scherer G, Conze C, Adlkofer F, Pachinger A, Klus H. Evaluation of 4-(*N*-methylnitrosamino)-4-(3-pyridyl)butyric acid as a potential monitor of endogenous nitrosation of nicotine and its metabolites. *Carcinogenesis* 1993;14(7):1409–14.

Trincao J, Johnson RE, Escalante CR, Prakash S, Prakash L, Aggarwal AK. Structure of the catalytic core of *S. cerevisiae* DNA polymerase η: implications for translesion DNA synthesis. *Molecular Cell* 2001;8(2):417–26.

Trombino S, Cesario A, Margaritora S, Granone PL, Motta G, Falugi C, Russo P. α7-Nicotinic acetylcholine receptors affect growth regulation of human mesothelioma cells: role of mitogen-activated protein kinase pathway. *Cancer Research* 2004;64(1):135–45.

Trushin N, Castonguay A, Rivenson A, Hecht SS. Effects of ethanol consumption on the metabolism and carcinogenicity of *N′*-Nitrosonornicotine in F344 rats. *Annals of the New York Academy of Sciences* 1984;435(1):214–8.

Tsao AS, McDonnell T, Lam S, Putnam JB, Bekele N, Hong WK, Kurie JM. Increased phospho-AKT (Ser[473]) expression in bronchial dysplasia: implications for lung cancer prevention studies. *Cancer Epidemiology, Biomarkers & Prevention* 2003;12(7):660–4.

Tsuda M, Kurashima Y. Tobacco smoking, chewing, and snuff dipping: factors contributing to the endogenous formation of N-nitroso compounds. *Critical Reviews in Toxicology* 1991;21(4):243–53.

Tsujii M, DuBois RN. Alterations in cellular adhesion and apoptosis in epithelial cells overexpressing prostaglandin endoperoxide synthase 2. *Cell* 1995;83(3):493–501.

Tsurutani J, Castillo SS, Brognard J, Granville CA, Zhang C, Gills JJ, Sayyah J, Dennis PA. Tobacco components stimulate Akt-dependent proliferation and NFκB-dependent survival in lung cancer cells. *Carcinogenesis* 2005;26(7):1182–95.

Tukey RH, Strassburg CP. Human UDP-glucuronosyltransferases: metabolism, expression, and disease. *Annual Review of Pharmacology and Toxicology* 2000; 40:581–616.

Umar A, Boyer JC, Kunkel TA. DNA loop repair by human cell extracts. *Science* 1994;266(5186):814–6.

Umar A, Koi M, Risinger JI, Glaab WE, Tindall KR, Kolodner RD, Boland CR, Barrett JC, Kunkel TA. Correction of hypermutability, N-methyl-N'-nitro-N-nitrosoguanidine resistance, and defective DNA mismatch repair by introducing chromosome 2 into human tumor cells with mutations in MSH2 and MSH6. *Cancer Research* 1997;57(18):3949–55.

U.S. Department of Health and Human Services. *The Health Consequences of Smoking: A Report of the Surgeon General*. Atlanta: U.S. Department of Health and Human Services, Centers for Disease Control and Prevention, National Center for Chronic Disease Prevention and Health Promotion, Office on Smoking and Health, 2004.

U.S. Department of Health and Human Services. *11th Report on Carcinogens*. Research Triangle Park (NC): U.S. Department of Health and Human Services, Public Health Service, National Toxicology Program, 2005.

University of Louisville School of Medicine. Arylamine *N*-Acetyltransferase (NAT) Nomenclature, October 24, 2006; <http://www.louisville.edu/medschool/pharmacology/NAT.html>; accessed: November 3, 2006.

Upadhyaya P, Kenney PMJ, Hochalter JB, Wang M, Hecht SS. Tumorigenicity and metabolism of 4-(methylnitrosamino)-1-(3-pyridyl)-1-butanol (NNAL) enantiomers and metabolites in the A/J mouse. *Carcinogenesis* 1999;20(8):1577–82.

Upadhyaya P, McIntee EJ, Hecht SS. Preparation of pyridine-*N*-glucuronides of tobacco-specific nitrosamines. *Chemical Research in Toxicology* 2001;14(5):555–61.

Upadhyay S, Liu C, Chatterjee A, Hoque MO, Kim MS, Engles J, Westra W, Trink B, Ratovitski E, Sidransky D. LKB1/STK11 suppresses cyclooxygenase-2 induction and cellular invasion through PEA3 in lung cancer. *Cancer Research* 2006;66(16):7870–9.

Urban M, Gilch G, Schepers G, van Miert E, Scherer G. Determination of the major mercapturic acids of 1,3-butadiene in human and rat urine using liquid chromatography with tandem mass spectrometry. *Journal of Chromatography B* 2003;796(1):131–40.

Uusküla M, Järventaus H, Hirvonen A, Sorsa M, Norppa H. Influence of *GSTM1* genotype on sister chromatid exchange induction by styrene-7,8-oxide and 1,2-epoxy-3-butene in cultured human lymphocytes. *Carcinogenesis* 1995;16(4):947–50.

Vähäkangas K, Trivers GE, Plummer S, Hayes RB, Krokan H, Rowe M, Swartz RP, Yeager H Jr, Harris CC. O^6-methylguanine-DNA methyltransferase and uracil DNA glycosylase in human broncho-alveolar lavage cells and peripheral blood mononuclear cells from tobacco smokers and nonsmokers. *Carcinogenesis* 1991; 12(8):1389–94

Vainio H, Weiderpass E. Smokeless tobacco: harm reduction or nicotine overload? *European Journal of Cancer Prevention* 2003;12(2):89–92.

van Delft JH, Steenwinkel M-JST, van Asten JG, de Vogel N, Bruijntjes-Rozier TCDM, Schouten T, Cramers P, Maas L, Van Herwijnen MH, van Schooten F-J, et al. Biological monitoring the exposure to polycyclic aromatic hydrocarbons of coke oven workers in relation to smoking and genetic polymorphisms for *GSTM1* and *GSTT1*. *Annals of Occupational Hygiene* 2001;45(5):395–408.

Van Duuren BL, Goldschmidt BM. Cocarcinogenic and tumor-promoting agents in tobacco carcinogenesis. *Journal of the National Cancer Institute* 1976; 56(6):1237–42.

Van Rooij JGM, Veeger MMS, Bodelier-Bade MMJ, Scheepers PTJ, Jongeneelen FJ. Smoking and dietary intake of polycyclic aromatic hydrocarbons as sources of interindividual variability in the baseline excretion of 1- hydroxypyrene in urine. *International Archives of Occupational and Environmental Health* 1994;66(1):55–65.

Van Schooten FJ, Boots AW, Knaapen AM, Godschalk RWL, Maas LM, Borm PJ, Drent M, Jacobs JA. Myeloperoxidase *(MPO) –463G→A* reduces MPO activity and DNA adduct levels in bronchoalveolar lavages of smokers. *Cancer Epidemiology, Biomarkers & Prevention* 2004;13(5):828–33.

van Sittert NJ, Boogaard PJ, Beulink GD. Application of the urinary S-phenylmercapturic acid test as a biomarker for low levels of exposure to benzene in industry. *British Journal of Industrial Medicine* 1993;50(5):460–9.

van Sittert NJ, Megens HJ, Watson WP, Boogaard PJ. Biomarkers of exposure to 1,3-butadiene as a basis for cancer risk assessment. *Toxicological Sciences* 2000; 56(1):189–202.

Vanhaesebroeck B, Leevers SJ, Panayotou G, Waterfield MD. Phosphoinositide 3-kinases: a conserved family of signal transducers. *Trends in Biochemical Sciences* 1997;22(7):267–72.

Veale D, Ashcroft T, Marsh C, Gibson GJ, Harris AL. Epidermal growth factor receptors in non-small cell lung cancer. *British Journal of Cancer* 1987;55(5):513–6.

Veglia F, Matullo G, Vineis P. Bulky DNA adducts and risk of cancer: a meta-analysis. *Cancer Epidemiology, Biomarkers & Prevention* 2003;12(2):157–60.

Verdina A, Galati R, Falasca G, Ghittori S, Imbriani M, Tomei F, Marcellini L, Zijno A, Vecchio VD. Metabolic polymorphisms and urinary biomarkers in subjects with low benzene exposure. *Journal of Toxicology and Environmental Health A* 2001;64(8):607–18.

Verghis SBM, Essigmann JM, Kadlubar FF, Morningstar ML, Lasko DD. Specificity of mutagenesis by 4-aminobiphenyl: mutations at G residues in bacteriophage M13 DNA and G→C transversions at a unique dG$^{8\text{-}ABP}$ lesion in single-stranded DNA. *Carcinogenesis* 1997;18(12):2403–14.

Videtic GMM, Stitt LW, Dar AR, Kocha WI, Tomiak AT, Truong PT, Vincent MD, Yu EW. Continued cigarette smoking by patients receiving concurrent chemoradiotherapy for limited-stage small-cell lung cancer is associated with decreased survival. *Journal of Clinical Oncology* 2003;21(8):1544–9.

Vineis P. Molecular epidemiology: low-dose carcinogens and genetic susceptibility. *International Journal of Cancer* 1997;71(1):1–3.

Vineis P, Fabrizio V, Benhamou S, Butkiewicz D, Cascorbi I, Clapper ML, Dolzan V, Haugen A, Hirvonen A, Ingelman-Sundberg M, et al. CYP1A1 T^{3801} C polymorphism and lung cancer: a pooled analysis of 2,451 cases and 3,358 controls. *International Journal of Cancer* 2003;104(5):650–7.

Vineis P, Marinelli D, Autrup H, Brockmöller J, Cascorbi I, Daly AK, Golka K, Okkels H, Risch A, Rothman N, et al. Current smoking, occupation, *N*-acetyltransferase-2 and bladder cancer: a pooled analysis of genotype-based studies. *Cancer Epidemiology, Biomarkers & Prevention* 2001;10(12):1249–52.

Vineis P, Veglia F, Anttila S, Benhamou S, Clapper ML, Dolzan V, Ryberg D, Hirvonen A, Kremers P, Le Marchand L, et al. CYP1A1, GSTM1 and GSTT1 polymorphisms and lung cancer: a pooled analysis of gene-gene interactions. *Biomarkers* 2004;9(3):298–305.

Vogelstein B, Lane D, Levine AJ. Surfing the p53 network. *Nature* 2000;408(6810):307–10.

Volker M, Moné MJ, Karmakar P, van Hoffen A, Schul W, Vermeulen W, Hoeijmakers JHJ, van Driel R, van Zeeland AA, Mullenders LHF. Sequential assembly of the nucleotide excision repair factors in vivo. *Molecular Cell* 2001;8(1):213–24.

Vos MD, Ellis CA, Elam C, Ülkü AS, Taylor BJ. RASSF2 is a novel K-Ras-specific effector and potential tumor suppressor. *Journal of Biological Chemistry* 2003;278(30):28045–51.

Walczak H, Bouchon A, Stahl H, Krammer PH. Tumor necrosis factor-related apoptosis-inducing ligand retains its apoptosis-inducing capacity on Bcl-2- or Bcl-x$_L$-overexpressing chemotherapy-resistant tumor cells. *Cancer Research* 2000;60(11):3051–7.

Wan J, Shi J, Hui L, Wu D, Jin X, Zhao N, Huang W, Xia Z, Hu G. Association of genetic polymorphisms in *CYP2E1, MPO, NQO1, GSTM1,* and *GSTT1* genes with benzene poisoning. *Environmental Health Perspectives* 2002;110(12):1213–8.

Wang H, Tan W, Hao B, Miao X, Zhou G, He F, Lin D. Substantial reduction in risk of lung adenocarcinoma associated with genetic polymorphism in CYP2A13, the most active cytochrome P450 for the metabolic activation of tobacco-specific carcinogen NNK. *Cancer Research* 2003a;63(22):8057–61.

Wang J, Deng Y, Cheng J, Ding J, Tokudome S. GST genetic polymorphisms and lung adenocarcinoma susceptibility in a Chinese population. *Cancer Letters* 2003b;201(2):185–93.

Wang J, Deng Y, Li L, Kuriki K, Ding J, Pan X, Zhuge X, Jiang J, Luo C, Lin P, Tokudome S. Association of GSTM1, CYP1A1 and CYP2E1 genetic polymorphisms with susceptibility to lung adenocarcinoma: a case-control study in Chinese population. *Cancer Science* 2003c;94(5):448–52.

Wang J, Lee JJ, Wang L, Liu DD, Lu C, Fan Y-H, Hong WK, Mao L. Value of *p16^{INK4a}* and *RASSF1A* promoter hypermethylation in prognosis of patients with resectable non–small cell lung cancer. *Clinical Cancer Research* 2004a;10(18 Pt 1):6119–25.

Wang L, Habuchi T, Takahashi T, Mitsumori K, Kamato T, Kakehi Y, Kakinuma H, Sato K, Nakamura A, Ogawa O, et al. Cyclin D1 gene polymorphism is associated with an increased risk of urinary bladder cancer. *Carcinogenesis* 2002;23(2):257–64.

Wang L, Spratt TE, Liu X-K, Hecht SS, Pegg AE, Peterson LA. Pyridyloxobutyl adduct O^6-[4-oxo-4-(3-pyridyl) butyl]guanine is present in 4-(acetoxymethylnitrosamino)-1-(3-pyridyl)-1-butanone-treated DNA and is a substrate for O^6-alkylguanine-DNA alkyltransferase. *Chemical Research in Toxicology* 1997;10(5):562–7.

Wang LI, Giovannucci EL, Hunter D, Neuberg D, Su L, Christiani DC. Dietary intake of cruciferous vegetables, *glutathione S-transferase* (*GST*) polymorphisms and lung cancer risk in a Caucasian population. *Cancer Causes & Control* 2004b;15(10):977–85.

Wang LI, Miller DP, Sai Y, Liu G, Su L, Wain JC, Lynch TJ, Christiani DC. Manganese superoxide dismutase alanine-to-valine polymorphism at codon 16 and lung cancer risk. *Journal of the National Cancer Institute* 2001a;93(23):1818–21.

Wang LI, Neuberg D, Christiani DC. Asbestos exposure, *manganese superoxide dismutase (MnSOD)* genotype, and lung cancer risk. *Journal of Occupational and Environmental Medicine* 2004c;46(6):556–64.

Wang X, Christiani DC, Wiencke JK, Fischbein M, Xu X, Cheng TJ, Mark E, Wain JC, Kelsey KT. Mutations in the *p53* gene in lung cancer are associated with cigarette smoking and asbestos exposure. *Cancer Epidemiology, Biomarkers & Prevention* 1995a;4(5):543–8.

Wang XW, Yeh H, Schaeffer L, Roy R, Moncollin V, Egly J-M, Wang Z, Freidberg EC, Evans MK, Taffe BG, et al. p53 Modulation of TFIIH–associated nucleotide excision repair activity. *Nature Genetics* 1995b;10(2):188–95.

Wang Y, Pereira EFR, Maus ADJ, Ostlie NS, Navaneetham D, Lei S, Albuquerque EX, Conti-Fine BM. Human bronchial epithelial and endothelial cells express α7 nicotinic acetylcholine receptors. *Molecular Pharmacology* 2001b;60(6):1201–9.

Wang Y-C, Lee H-S, Chen S-K, Chang Y-Y, Chen C-Y. Prognostic significance of *p53* codon 72 polymorphism in lung carcinomas. *European Journal of Cancer* 1999;35(2):226–30.

Wani MA, Zhu Q, El-Mahdy M, Venkatachalam S, Wani AA. Enhanced sensitivity to *anti*-benzo(*a*)pyrene-diol-epoxide DNA damage correlates with decreased global genomic repair attributable to abrogated p53 function in human cells. *Cancer Research* 2000;60(8):2273–80.

Warren AJ, Shields PG. Molecular epidemiology: carcinogen-DNA adducts and genetic susceptibility. *Proceedings of the Society for Experimental Biology and Medicine* 1997;216(2):172–80.

Watson MA, Stewart RK, Smith GB, Massey TE, Bell DA. Human glutathione-*S*-transferase P1 polymorphisms: relationship to lung tissue enzyme activity and population frequency distribution. *Carcinogenesis* 1998;19(2):275–80.

Weddle DL, Tithoff P, Williams M, Schuller HM. β-Adrenergic growth regulation of human cancer cell lines derived from pancreatic ductal carcinomas. *Carcinogenesis* 2001;22(3):473–9.

Wei Q, Cheng L, Amos CI, Wang L-E, Guo Z, Hong WK, Spitz MR. Repair of tobacco carcinogen-induced DNA adducts and lung cancer risk: a molecular epidemiological study. *Journal of the National Cancer Institute* 2000;92(21):1764–72.

Wei Q, Gu J, Cheng L, Bondy ML, Jiang H, Hong WK, Spitz MR. Benzo(*a*)pyrene diol epoxide-induced chromosomal aberrations and risk of lung cancer. *Cancer Research* 1996;56(17):3975–9.

Wei Q, Matanoski GM, Farmer ER, Hedayati MA, Grossman L. DNA repair and aging in basal cell carcinoma: a molecular epidemiology study. *Proceedings of the National Academy of Sciences of the United States of America* 1993;90(4):1614–8.

Weinberg RA. The retinoblastoma protein and cell cycle control. *Cell* 1995;81(3):323–30.

Weisenberger DJ, Romano LJ. Cytosine methylation in a CpG sequence leads to enhanced reactivity with benzo[*a*]pyrene diol epoxide that correlates with a conformational change. *Journal of Biological Chemistry* 1999;274(34):23948–55.

Wells PG, Mackenzie PI, Chowdhury JR, Guillemette C, Gregory PA, Ishii Y, Hansen AJ, Kessler FK, Kim PM, Chowdhury NR, et al. Glucuronidation and the UDP-glucuronosyltransferases in health and disease. *Drug Metabolism and Disposition* 2004;32(3):281–90.

West KA, Brognard J, Clark AS, Linnoila IR, Yang X, Swain SM, Harris C, Belinsky S, Dennis PA. Rapid Akt activation by nicotine and a tobacco carcinogen modulates the phenotype of normal human airway epithelial cells. *Journal of Clinical Investigation* 2003;111(1):81–90.

West KA, Castillo SS, Dennis PA. Activation of the PI3K/Akt pathway and chemotherapeutic resistance. *Drug Resistance Updates* 2002;5(6):234–48.

West KA, Linnoila IR, Belinsky SA, Harris CC, Dennis PA. Tobacco carcinogen-induced cellular transformation increases activation of the phosphatidylinositol 3′-kinase/Akt pathway *in vitro* and *in vivo*. *Cancer Research* 2004a;64(2):446–51.

West KA, Linnoila IR, Brognard J, Belinsky S, Harris C, Dennis PA. Tobacco carcinogen-induced cellular transformation increases Akt activation *in vitro* and *in vivo*. *Chest* 2004b;125(5 Suppl):101S–102S.

Weston A, Perrin LS, Forrester K, Hoover RN, Trump BF, Harris CC, Caporaso NE. Allelic frequency of a *p53* polymorphism in human lung cancer. *Cancer Epidemiology, Biomarkers & Prevention* 1992;1(6):481–3.

Westra WH, Baas IO, Hruban RH, Askin FB, Wilson K, Offerhaus GJA, Slebos RJC. K-*ras* oncogene activation in atypical alveolar hyperplasias of the human lung. *Cancer Research* 1996;56(9):2224–8.

Wickliffe JK, Ammenheuser MM, Salazar JJ, Abdel-Rahman SZ, Hastings-Smith DA, Postlethwait EM, Lloyd RS, Ward JB Jr. A model of sensitivity: 1,3-butadiene increases mutant frequencies and genomic damage in mice lacking a functional microsomal epoxide hydrolase gene. *Environmental and Molecular Mutagenesis* 2003;42(2):106–10.

Wiencke JK. DNA adduct burden and tobacco carcinogenesis. *Oncogene* 2002;21(48):7376–91.

Wiencke JK, Pemble S, Ketterer B, Kelsey KT. Gene deletion of glutathione S-transferase θ: correlation with induced genetic damage and potential role in endogenous mutagenesis. *Cancer Epidemiology, Biomarkers & Prevention* 1995;4(3):253–9.

Wiener D, Doerge DR, Fang J-L, Upadhyaya P, Lazarus P. Characterization of *N*-glucuronidation of the lung carcinogen 4-(methylnitrosamino)-1-(3-pyridyl)-1-butanol (NNAL) in human liver: importance of UDP-glucuronosyltransferase 1A4. *Drug Metabolism and Disposition* 2004a;32(1):72–9.

Wiener D, Fang J-L, Dossett N, Lazarus P. Correlation between *UDP-glucuronosyltransferase* genotypes and 4-(methylnitrosamino)-1-(3-pyridyl)-1-butanone glucuronidation phenotype in human liver microsomes. *Cancer Research* 2004b;64(3):1190–6.

Wikman H, Risch A, Klimek F, Schmezer P, Spiegelhalder B, Dienemann H, Kayser K, Schulz V, Drings P, Bartsch H. *hOGG1* polymorphism and loss of heterozygosity (LOH): significance for lung cancer susceptibility in a Caucasian population. *International Journal of Cancer* 2000;88(6):932–7.

Wild CP, Pisani P. Carcinogen DNA and protein adducts as biomarkers of human exposure in environmental cancer epidemiology. *Cancer Detection and Prevention* 1998;22(4):273–83.

Willey JC, Coy EL, Frampton MW, Torres A, Apostolakos MJ, Hoehn G, Schuermann WH, Thilly WG, Olson DE, Hammersley JR, et al. Quantitative RT-PCR measurement of cytochromes p450 1A1, 1B1, and 2B7, microsomal epoxide hydrolase, and NADPH oxidoreductase expression in lung cells of smokers and nonsmokers. *American Journal of Respiratory Cell and Molecular Biology* 1997;17(1):114–24.

Wilson VL, Weston A, Manchester DK, Trivers GE, Roberts DW, Kadlubar FF, Wild CP, Montesano R, Willey JC, Mann DL, Harris CC, et al. Alkyl and aryl carcinogen adducts detected in human peripheral lung. *Carcinogenesis* 1989;10(11):2149–53.

Winsey SL, Haldar NA, Marsh HP, Bunce M, Marshall SE, Harris AL, Wojnarowska F, Welsh KI. A variant within the DNA repair gene *XRCC3* is associated with the development of melanoma skin cancer. *Cancer Research* 2000;60(20):5612–6.

Wistuba II, Lam S, Behrens C, Virmani AK, Fong KM, LeRiche J, Samet JM, Srivastava S, Minna JD, Gazdar AF. Molecular damage in the bronchial epithelium of current and former smokers. *Journal of the National Cancer Institute* 1997;89(18):1366–73.

Witschi H. Successful and not so successful chemoprevention of tobacco smoke-induced lung tumors. *Experimental Lung Research* 2000;26(8):743–55.

Wolf P, Hu YC, Doffek K, Sidransky D, Ahrendt SA. O^6-Methylguanine-DNA methyltransferase promoter hypermethylation shifts the *p53* mutational spectrum in non-small cell lung cancer. *Cancer Research* 2001; 61(22):8113–7.

Wolff H, Saukkonen K, Anttila S, Karjalainen A, Vainio H, Ristimäki A. Expression of cyclooxygenase-2 in human lung carcinoma. *Cancer Research* 1998;58(22): 4997–5001.

Wong HL, Murphy SE, Hecht SS. Cytochrome P450 2A-catalyzed metabolic activation of structurally similar carcinogenic nitrosamines: *N'*-nitrosonornicotine enantiomers, *N*-nitrosopiperidine, and *N*-nitrosopyrrolidine. *Chemical Research in Toxicology* 2005a; 18(1):61–9.

Wong HL, Zhang X, Zhang Q-Y, Gu J, Ding X, Hecht SS, Murphy SE. Metabolic activation of the tobacco carcinogen 4-(methylnitrosamino)-(3-pyridyl)-1-butanone by cytochrome p450 2A13 in human fetal nasal microsomes. *Chemical Research in Toxicology* 2005b;18(6):913–8.

Wong T-S, Man MW-L, Lam AK-Y, Wei WI, Kwong Y-L, Yuen AP-W. The study of *p16* and *p15* gene methylation in head and neck squamous cell carcinoma and their quantitative evaluation in plasma by real-time PCR. *European Journal of Cancer* 2003;39(13):1881–7.

Wood AW, Levin W, Lu AY, Yagi H, Hernandez O, Jerina DM, Conney AH. Metabolism of benzo(a)pyrene and benzo(a)pyrene derivatives to mutagenic products by highly purified hepatic microsomal enzymes. *Journal of Biological Chemistry* 1976;251(16):4882–90.

Wood ML, Dizdaroglu M, Gajewski E, Essigmann JM. Mechanistic studies of ionizing radiation and oxidative mutagenesis: genetic effects of a single 8-hydroxyguanine (7-hydro-8-oxoguanine) residue inserted at a unique site in a viral genome. *Biochemistry* 1990; 29(30):7024–32.

World Health Organization. *The International Classification of Diseases, Tenth Revision*. Geneva: World Health Organization, 1994.

Wrensch MR, Miike R, Sison JD, Kelsey KT, Liu M, McMillan A, Quesenberry C, Wiencke J. K. *CYP1A1* variants and smoking-related lung cancer in San Francisco Bay area Latinos and African Americans. *International Journal of Cancer* 2005;113(1):141–7.

Wu AH, Fontham ETH, Reynolds P, Greenberg RS, Buffler P, Liff J, Boyd P, Correa P. Family history of cancer and risk of lung cancer among lifetime nonsmoking women in the United States. *American Journal of Epidemiology* 1996;143(6):535–42.

Wu AH, Yu MC, Thomas DC, Pike MC, Henderson BE. Personal and family history of lung disease as risk factors for adenocarcinoma of the lung. *Cancer Research* 1988;48(24 Pt 1):7279–84.

Wu J, Gu L, Wang H, Geacintov NE, Li G-M. Mismatch repair processing of carcinogen-DNA adducts triggers apoptosis. *Molecular and Cellular Biology* 1999;19(12):8292–301.

Wu P-F, Lee C-H, Wang M-J, Goggins WB, Chiang T-A, Huang M-S, Ko Y-C. Cancer aggregation and complex segregation analysis of families with female non-smoking lung cancer probands in Taiwan. *European Journal of Cancer* 2004;40(2):260–6.

Wu X, Delclos GL, Annegers FJ, Bondy ML, Honn SE, Henry B, Hsu TC, Spitz MR. A case-control study of wood dust exposure, mutagen sensitivity, and lung cancer risk. *Cancer Epidemiology, Biomarkers & Prevention* 1995;4(6):583–8.

Wu X, Gu J, Amos CI, Jiang H, Hong WK, Spitz MR. A parallel study of in vitro sensitivity to benzo[a]pyrene diol epoxide and bleomycin in lung carcinoma cases and controls. *Cancer* 1998a;83(6):1118–27.

Wu X, Gwyn K, Lamos C, Makan N, Hong WK, Spitz MR. The association of microsomal epoxide hydrolase polymorphisms and lung cancer risk in African–Americans and Mexican–Americans. *Carcinogenesis* 2001;22(6):923–8.

Wu X, Roth JA, Zhao H, Luo S, Zheng Y-L, Chiang S, Spitz MR. Cell cycle checkpoints, DNA damage/repair and lung cancer risk. *Cancer Research* 2005;65(1):349–57.

Wu X, Zhao H, Amos CI, Shete S, Makan N, Hong WK, Kadlubar FF, Spitz MR. p53 Genotypes and haplotypes associated with lung cancer susceptibility and ethnicity. *Journal of the National Cancer Institute* 2002;94(9):681–90.

Wu X, Zhao H, Honn SE, Tomlinson GE, Minna JD, Hong WK, Spitz MR. Benzo[a]pyrene diol epoxide-induced 3p21.3 aberrations and genetic predisposition to lung cancer. *Cancer Research* 1998b;58(8):1605–8.

Wu X, Zhao H, Wei Q, Amos CI, Zhang K, Guo Z, Qiao Y, Hong WK, Spitz MR. XPA polymorphism associated with reduced lung cancer risk and a modulating effect on nucleotide excision repair capacity. *Carcinogenesis* 2003;24(3):505–9.

Wu ZN, Chan CL, Eastman A, Bresnick E. Expression of human O^6-methylguanine-DNA methyltransferase in a DNA excision repair-deficient Chinese hamster ovary cell line and its response to certain alkylating agents. *Cancer Research* 1992;52(1):32–5.

Wymann MP, Pirola L. Structure and function of phosphoinositide 3-kinases. *Biochimica et Biophysica Acta* 1998;1436(1–2):127–50.

Xing D-Y, Tan W, Song N, Lin D-X. Ser326Cys polymorphism in *hOGG1* gene and risk of esophageal cancer in a Chinese population. *International Journal of Cancer* 2001;95(3):140–3.

Xu H, Spitz MR, Amos CI, Shete S. Complex segregation analysis reveals a multigene model for lung cancer. *Human Genetics* 2005;116(1–2):121–7.

Xu L-L, Liu G, Miller DP, Zhou W, Lynch TJ, Wain WC, Su L, Christiani DC. Counterpoint: the myeloperoxidase $^{-463}$G→A polymorphism does not decrease lung cancer susceptibility in Caucasians. *Cancer Epidemiology, Biomarkers & Prevention* 2002;11(12):1555–9.

Xu-Welliver M, Pegg AE. Degradation of the alkylated form of the DNA repair protein, O^6-alkylguanine-DNA alkyltransferase. *Carcinogenesis* 2002;23(5):823–30.

Yamamoto S, Tomita Y, Hoshida Y, Morooka T, Nagano H, Dono K, Umeshita K, Sakon M, Ishikawa K, Ohigashi H, et al. Prognostic significance of activated Akt expression in pancreatic ductal adenocarcinoma. *Clinical Cancer Research* 2004;10(8):2846–50.

Yamazaki H, Inui Y, Yun CH, Guengerich FP, Shimada T. Cytochrome P450 2E1 and 2A6 enzymes as major catalysts for metabolic activation of *N*-nitrosodialkylamines and tobacco-related nitrosamines in human liver microsomes. *Carcinogenesis* 1992;13(10):1789–94.

Yang I-Y, Chan G, Miller H, Huang Y, Torres MC, Johnson F, Moriya M. Mutagenesis by acrolein-derived propanodeoxyguanosine adducts in human cells. *Biochemistry* 2002;41(46):13826–32.

Yang I-Y, Miller H, Wang Z, Frank E, Ohmori H, Hanaoka F, Moriya M. Mammalian translesion DNA synthesis across an acrolein-derived deoxyguanosine adduct: participation of pol η in error-prone synthesis in human cells. *Journal of Biological Chemistry* 2003;278(16):13989–94.

Yang P, Schwartz AG, McAllister AE, Aston CE, Swanson GM. Genetic analysis of families with nonsmoking lung cancer probands. *Genetic Epidemiology* 1997;14(2):181–97.

Yang P, Schwartz AG, McAllister AE, Swanson GM, Aston CE. Lung cancer risk in families of nonsmoking probands: heterogeneity by age at diagnosis. *Genetic Epidemiology* 1999;17(4):253–73.

Yang XR, Wacholder S, Xu Z, Dean M, Clark V, Gold B, Brown LM, Stone BJ, Fraumeni JF Jr, Caporaso NE. CYP1A1 and GSTM1 polymorphisms in relation to lung cancer risk in Chinese women. *Cancer Letters* 2004;214(2):197–204.

Yao R, Rioux N, Castonguay A, You M. Inhibition of COX-2 and induction of apoptosis: two determinants of nonsteroidal anti-inflammatory drugs' chemopreventive efficacies in mouse lung tumorigenesis. *Experimental Lung Research* 2000;26(8):731–42.

Yin C, Knudson CM, Korsmeyer SJ, Van Dyke T. *Bax* suppresses tumorigenesis and stimulates apoptosis *in vivo*. *Nature* 1997;385(6617):637–40.

Yoneda K. Distribution of proliferating-cell nuclear antigen and epidermal growth factor receptor in intraepithelial squamous cell lesions of human bronchus. *Modern Pathology* 1994;7(4):480–6.

Yoo JS, Guengerich FP, Yang CS. Metabolism of N-nitrosodialkylamines by human liver microsomes. *Cancer Research* 1988;48(6):1499–504.

Yoon J-H, Smith LE, Feng Z, Tang M-S, Lee C-S, Pfeifer GP. Methylated CpG dinucleotides are the preferential targets for G-to-T transversion mutations induced by benzo[a]pyrene diol epoxide in mammalian cells: similarities with the p53 mutation spectrum in smoking-associated lung cancers. *Cancer Research* 2001;61(19):7110–7.

You M, Candrian U, Maronpot RR, Stoner GD, Anderson MW. Activation of the Ki-*ras* protooncogene in spontaneously occurring and chemically induced lung tumors of the strain A mouse. *Proceedings of the National Academy of Sciences of the United States of America* 1989;86(9):3070–4.

Yu C, Lu W, Tan W, Xing D, Liang G, Miao X, Lin D. Lack of association between *CCND1* G870A polymorphism and risk of esophageal squamous cell carcinoma. *Cancer Epidemiology, Biomarkers & Prevention* 2003; 12(2):176.

Yu D, Berlin JA, Penning TM, Field J. Reactive oxygen species generated by PAH *o*-quinones cause change-in-function mutations in *p53*. *Chemical Research in Toxicology* 2002;15(6):832–42.

Yuan A, Yu C-J, Shun C-T, Luh K-T, Kuo S-H, Lee Y-C, Yang P-C. Total cyclooxygenase-2 mRNA levels correlate with vascular endothelial growth factor mRNA levels, tumor angiogenesis and prognosis in non-small cell lung cancer patients. *International Journal of Cancer* 2005;115(4):545–55.

Yuan F, Zhang Y, Rajpal DK, Wu X, Guo D, Wang M, Taylor J-S, Wang Z. Specificity of DNA lesion bypass by the yeast DNA polymerase η. *Journal of Biological Chemistry* 2000;275(11):8233–9.

Yuan JM, Koh WP, Murphy SE, Fan Y, Wang R, Carmella SG, Han S, Wickham K, Gao YT, Yu MC, Hecht SS. Urinary levels of tobacco-specific nitrosamine metabolites in relation to lung cancer development in two prospective cohorts of cigarette smokers. *Cancer Research* 2009;69(7):2990–5.

Zabarovsky ER, Lerman MI, Minna JD. Tumor suppressor genes on chromosome 3p involved in the pathogenesis of lung and other cancers. *Oncogene* 2002;21(45): 6915–35.

Zajac-Kaye M. Myc oncogene: a key component in cell cycle regulation and its implication for lung cancer. *Lung Cancer* 2001;34(Suppl 2):S43–S46.

Zenser TV, Lakshmi VM, Hsu FF, Davis BB. Metabolism of N-acetylbenzidine and initiation of bladder cancer. *Mutation Research* 2002;506–507:29–40.

Zha J, Harada H, Osipov K, Jockel J, Waksman G, Korsmeyer SJ. BH3 domain of BAD is required for heterodimerization with BCL-X_L and pro-apoptotic activity. *Journal of Biological Chemistry* 1997;272(39): 24101–4.

Zhang L, Yu J, Park BH, Kinzler KW, Vogelstein B. Role of *BAX* in the apoptotic response to anticancer agents. *Science* 2000a;290(5493):989–92.

Zhang N, Lin C, Huang X, Kolbanovskiy A, Hingerty BE, Amin S, Broyde S, Geacintov NE, Patel DJ. Methylation of cytosine at C5 in a CpG sequence context causes a conformational switch of a benzo[a]pyrene diol epoxide-N^2-guanine adduct in DNA from a minor groove alignment to intercalation with base displacement. *Journal of Molecular Biology* 2005a;346(4):951–65.

Zhang X, Miao X, Liang G, Hao B, Wang Y, Tan W, Li Y, Guo Y, He F, Wei Q, et al. Polymorphisms in DNA base excision repair genes *ADPRT* and *XRCC1* and risk of lung cancer. *Cancer Research* 2005b;65(3):722–6.

Zhang X, Su T, Zhang Q-Y, Gu J, Caggana M, Li H, Ding X. Genetic polymorphisms of the human *CYP2A13* gene: identification of single-nucleotide polymorphisms and functional characterization of the Arg257Cys variant. *Journal of Pharmacology and Experimental Therapeutics* 2002;302(2):416–23.

Zhang Y, Yuan F, Wu X, Rechkoblit O, Taylor J-S, Geacintov NE, Wang Z. Error-prone lesion bypass by human DNA polymerase η. *Nucleic Acids Research* 2000b; 28(23):4717–24.

Zhao C, Tyndyk M, Eide I, Hemminki K. Endogenous and background DNA adducts by methylating and 2-hydroxyethylating agents. *Mutation Research* 1999; 424(1–2):117–25.

Zheng Y, Shen H, Sturgis EM, Wang L-E, Eicher SA, Strom SS, Frazier ML, Spitz MR, Wei Q. Cyclin D1 polymorphism and risk for squamous cell carcinoma of the head and neck: a case-control study. *Carcinogenesis* 2001;22(8):1195–9.

Zheng Y-L, Loffredo CA, Yu Z, Jones RT, Krasna MJ, Alberg AJ, Yung R, Perlmutter D, Enewold L, Harris CC, et al. Bleomycin-induced chromosome breaks as a risk marker for lung cancer: a case-control study with population and hospital controls. *Carcinogenesis* 2003;24(2):269–74.

Zhong S, Howie AF, Ketterer B, Taylor J, Hayes JD, Beckett GJ, Wathen CG, Wolf CR, Spurr NK. Glutathione S-transferase mu locus: use of genotyping and phenotyping assays to assess association with lung cancer susceptibility. *Carcinogenesis* 1991;12(9):1533–7.

Zhou J, Ahn J, Wilson SH, Prives C. A role for p53 in base excision repair. *EMBO Journal* 2001a;20(4):914–23.

Zhou W, Liu G, Miller DP, Thurston SW, Xu LL, Wain JC, Lynch TJ, Su L, Christiani DC. Gene-environment interaction for the *ERCC2* polymorphisms and cumulative cigarette smoking exposure in lung cancer. *Cancer Research* 2002a;62(5):1377–81.

Zhou W, Liu G, Miller DP, Thurston SW, Xu LL, Wain JC, Lynch TJ, Su L, Christiani DC. Polymorphisms in the DNA repair genes *XRCC1* and *ERCC2*, smoking, and lung cancer risk. *Cancer Epidemiology, Biomarkers & Prevention* 2003;12(4):359–65.

Zhou W, Liu G, Park S, Wang Z, Wain JC, Lynch TJ, Su L, Christiani DC. Gene-smoking interaction associations for the *ERCC1* polymorphisms in the risk of lung cancer. *Cancer Epidemiology, Biomarkers & Prevention* 2005;14(2):491–6.

Zhou W, Liu G, Thurston SW, Xu LL, Miller DP, Wain JC, Lynch TJ, Su L, Christiani DC. Genetic polymorphisms in *N*-acetyltransferase-2 and microsomal epoxide hydrolase, cumulative cigarette smoking, and lung cancer. *Cancer Epidemiology, Biomarkers & Prevention* 2002b;11(1):15–21.

Zhou W, Thurston SW, Liu G, Xu LL, Miller DP, Wain JC, Lynch TJ, Su L, Christiani DC. The interaction between microsomal epoxide hydrolase polymorphisms and cumulative cigarette smoking in different histological subtypes of lung cancer. *Cancer Epidemiology, Biomarkers & Prevention* 2001b;10(5):461–6.

Zhu BQ, Heeschen C, Sievers RE, Karliner JS, Parmley WW, Glantz SA, Cooke JP. Second hand smoke stimulates tumor angiogenesis and growth. *Cancer Cell* 2003; 4(3):191–6.

Zhu W, Yamasaki H, Mironov N. Frequency of *HPRT* gene mutations induced by *N*-methyl-*N'*-nitro-*N*-nitrosoguanidine corresponds to replication error phenotypes of cell lines. *Mutation Research* 1998; 398(1–2):93–9.

Zhu Y, Doll MA, Hein DW. Functional genomics of C190T single nucleotide polymorphism in human N-acetyltransferase 2. *Biological Chemistry* 2002;383(6):983–7.

Zimmerman CL, Wu Z, Upadhyaya P, Hecht SS. Stereoselective metabolism and tissue retention in rats of the individual enantiomers of 4-(methylnitrosamino)-1-(3-pyridyl)-1-butanol (NNAL), metabolites of the tobacco-specific nitrosamine, 4-(methylnitrosamino)-1-(3-pyridyl)-1-butanone (NNK). *Carcinogenesis* 2004; 25(7):1237–42.

Ziogas A, Anton-Culver H. Validation of family history data in cancer family registries. *American Journal of Preventive Medicine* 2003;24(2):190–8.

Zöchbauer-Müller S, Fong KM, Virmani AK, Geradts J, Gazdar AF, Minna JD. Aberrant promoter methylation of multiple genes in non-small cell lung cancers. *Cancer Research* 2001;61(1):249–55.

Chapter 6
Cardiovascular Diseases

Introduction

This chapter reviews the epidemiology of smoking-induced cardiovascular disease (CVD) and the mechanisms by which tobacco smoke is thought to cause CVD. The discussion includes use of biomarkers to diagnose smoking-induced CVD and treatment implications of the pathophysiology of the disease. The link between

secondhand smoke and CVD has been reviewed in the 2006 report of the Surgeon General, *The Health Consequences of Involuntary Exposure to Tobacco Smoke* (U.S. Department of Health and Human Services [USDHHS] 2006), so discussion of secondhand smoke in this report is limited.

Tobacco Use and Cardiovascular Disease

Cigarette smoking is a major cause of CVD, and past reports of the Surgeon General extensively reviewed the relevant evidence (U.S. Department of Health, Education, and Welfare [USDHEW] 1971, 1979; USDHHS 1983, 2001, 2004). Cigarette smoking has been responsible for approximately 140,000 premature deaths annually from CVD (USDHHS 2004). More than 1 in 10 deaths worldwide from CVD in 2000 were attributed to smoking (Ezzati et al. 2005). In the United States, smoking accounted for 33 percent of all deaths from CVD and 20 percent of deaths from ischemic heart disease in persons older than 35 years of age (Centers for Disease Control and Prevention 2008). Cigarette smoking also influences other cardiovascular risk factors, such as glucose intolerance and low serum levels of high-density lipoprotein cholesterol (HDLc). However, studies have reported that smoking increases the risk of CVD beyond the effects of smoking on other risk factors. In other words, the risk attributable to smoking persisted even when adjustments were made for differences between persons who smoke and nonsmokers in levels of these other risk factors (Friedman et al. 1979; USDHHS 1983, 2001, 2004; Shaper et al. 1985; Criqui et al. 1987; Ragland and Brand 1988; Shaten et al. 1991; Neaton and Wentworth 1992; Freund et al. 1993; Cremer et al. 1997; Gartside et al. 1998; Wannamethee et al. 1998; Jacobs et al. 1999a). For example, in one study, the effect of cigarette smoking on the risk of coronary heart disease (CHD) was evident even among persons with low serum levels of cholesterol (Blanco-Cedres et al. 2002).

Beyond its status as an independent risk factor, smoking appears to have a multiplicative interaction with the other major risk factors for CHD—high serum levels of lipids, untreated hypertension, and diabetes mellitus (USDHHS 1983). For instance, if the presence of smoking alone doubles the level of risk, the simultaneous presence of another major risk factor is estimated to quadruple the risk (2×2). The presence of two other risk factors with

smoking results in approximately eight times the risk ($2 \times 2 \times 2$) of persons with no risk factors. Cigarette smoking also is a cause of peripheral arterial disease (PAD), aortic aneurysm, CHD, and cerebrovascular disease, but the relative risk (RR) of disease varies with the vascular bed (USDHEW 1971, 1979; USDHHS 1983, 2001, 2004). The highest RRs are observed for diseases of peripheral arteries in the lower extremities, and the lowest are for stroke; RRs are intermediate for CHD and aortic aneurysm.

The general mechanisms by which smoking results in cardiovascular events include development of atherosclerotic changes with narrowing of the vascular lumen and induction of a hypercoagulable state, which create risk of acute thrombosis (USDHHS 1983, 2004). The rapid decline in risk of a recurrent myocardial infarction (MI) after smoking cessation (USDHHS 1990) supports the role of smoking in thrombosis. In addition, abundant evidence demonstrates that smoking contributes to development of atherosclerotic plaque (Strong and Richards 1976; Auerbach and Garfinkel 1980; Solberg and Strong 1983; USDHHS 1983, 2004).

Estimation of Risk

The risk of CHD from cigarette smoking can be described in terms of RR and excess risk (Thun et al. 1997). The RR is the ratio of CHD rates for populations of smokers to rates for lifetime nonsmokers. Excess risk is the difference between the rates of disease for smokers and nonsmokers.

These two estimates of risk can lead to conflicting impressions of the changes in smoking-related CHD risks with advancing age. The RRs and excess death rates for CHD are shown by age group in data from Cancer Prevention Study II (CPS-II) (Thun et al. 1997), sponsored by the American Cancer Society (see Figure 6.1 for data on men).

Figure 6.1   Relative risk and excess death rate for coronary heart disease among men, by age group

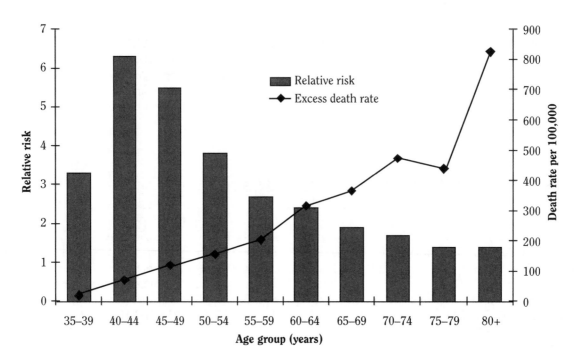

Source: Burns 2003. Adapted from Thun et al. 1997 with permission from Elsevier, © 2003.
Note: Data are from the American Cancer Society's Cancer Prevention Study II.

The RRs were highest at younger ages (35 to 54 years) and declined steeply with advancing age. This finding leaves the false impression that the disease burden of CHD from smoking declined with age or was low among older smokers. However, excess CHD death rates for smokers by age group presented different evidence. The high RR for CHD at younger ages can be explained in part because mortality rates are low for death from CHD at those ages and because coronary events in young people occur primarily among smokers. Even though RR declined with increasing age, because the absolute rate of deaths from CHD increased markedly, the magnitude of the CHD burden produced by smoking increased with advancing age.

The age at onset of substantial excess risk differs by disease. For smokers, age-specific excess death rates attributable to CHD, lung cancer, cerebrovascular disease, and chronic obstructive pulmonary disease (COPD) are illustrated by data from CPS-II (Figure 6.2 shows data for men) (Thun et al. 1997). For persons younger than age 45 years, CHD was the dominant cause of increased mortality attributable to cigarette smoking. Excess rates for death from lung cancer increased steeply after age 50 years, and excess death rates from COPD were largely confined to the seventh and eighth decades of life. Late in life, excess deaths from COPD matched and those from lung cancer exceeded the excess death rates attributable to CHD. The RR for death from a cerebrovascular disease among smokers was substantially elevated among younger smokers (RR = 4 to 5; data not shown). However, the absolute rate of stroke at these younger ages was low, and this finding resulted in a low excess mortality rate. At older ages, the death rate from stroke in the general population increased and the RR among smokers declined, thus moderating the excess death rate attributable to smoking.

Coronary Heart Disease

Cigarettes Smoked per Day

Studies showed increased risk of having CHD at all levels of cigarette smoking, and increased risks were evident even for persons who smoked fewer than five cigarettes per day (Rosengren et al. 1992; Prescott et al. 2002; Bjartveit and Tverdal 2005). Prospective mortality studies conducted in the 1960s and 1970s showed a clear increase in CHD mortality with an increase in the number of cigarettes smoked per day, regardless of the actual number

(Doll and Peto 1976; USDHHS 1983). Other studies suggested that risk increased up to at least 40 cigarettes per day (Miettinen et al. 1976; Willett et al. 1987). However, more recent data appeared to show an increase in CHD risk with more cigarettes smoked per day only up to about 25 cigarettes; the risk increased relatively little even with further increases in cigarette consumption (Neaton and Wentworth 1992; Rosengren et al. 1992; Thun et al. 1997).

Law and Wald (2003), who conducted a meta-analysis of five large studies of smoking and CHD, demonstrated a nonlinear dose-response relationship between the number of cigarettes smoked per day and the RR of disease (Figure 6.3). The researchers suggested that the effect of cigarette smoking on risk of CHD may have a low threshold and that the dose-response characteristics of the risk relationship are less steep at higher doses. This hypothesis was used to explain the seeming anomaly of a high RR of CHD associated with relatively low exposure to secondhand smoke. By using serum levels of cotinine (a metabolite of nicotine) as biomarkers of exposure, Whincup and colleagues (2004) explored the dose response relationship between exposure to cigarette smoke and CHD in persons involuntarily exposed to cigarette smoke. More than 2,000 men who said they did not smoke had blood levels of cotinine measured in 1978–1980 and then had follow-up for 20 years. Nicotine exposure was examined by quartiles of blood cotinine as follows: less than or equal to 0.7 nanograms per milliliter (ng/mL), 0 to 1.4, 1.5 to 2.7, and 2.8 to 14.0. Hazard ratios for CHD, which included deaths and non-fatal MIs, were significantly increased at all upper quartiles (hazard ratios, 1.43 to 1.57) compared with the lowest exposure quartile, after adjustment for established CHD risk factors. Hazard ratios were also higher at the first and second five-year follow-ups (3.73 to 10.58 and 1.95 to 2.48, respectively) than those at later follow-ups. The

Figure 6.2   Age-specific excess death rates among male smokers for coronary heart disease, lung cancer, chronic obstructive pulmonary disease (COPD), and cerebrovascular disease

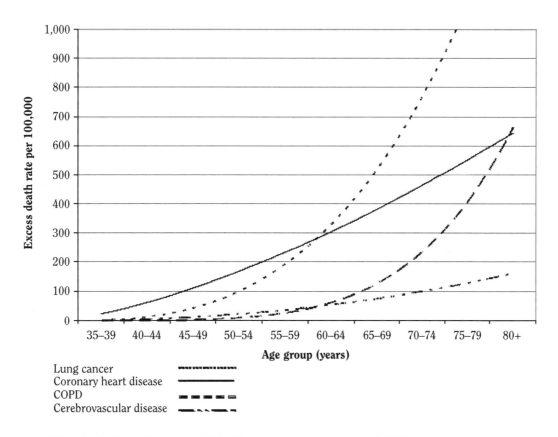

Source: Burns 2003. Adapted from Thun et al. 1997 with permission from Elsevier, © 2003.
Note: Data are from the American Cancer Society's Cancer Prevention Study II.

Figure 6.3   Dose-response relationship between number of cigarettes smoked per day and relative risk of ischemic heart disease

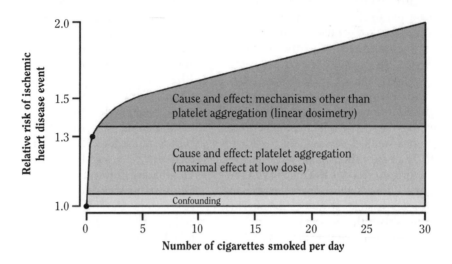

Source: Law and Wald 2003. Reprinted with permission from Elsevier, © 2003.
Note: The dose-response relationship between exposure to tobacco smoke and ischemic heart disease events is compartmentalized into separate associations attributable to confounding (difference between smokers and nonsmokers in blood pressure, body weight, blood lipids, and diet), cause and effect maximal at low dose, and cause and effect with linear dosimetry.

substantial cardiovascular risk attributable to involuntary exposure to cigarette smoke (USDHHS 2006) and the practice in most CVD studies of not excluding from the control group persons who had secondhand smoke exposure have resulted in underestimation, in many research reports, of the effects of active smoking compared with no exposure to cigarette smoke.

The data on secondhand smoke and CHD risk indicate that the dose-response relationship between exposure to smoke and cardiovascular effects is nonlinear. Another consideration is that the number of cigarettes smoked per day may not provide a linear measure of exposure to tobacco smoke. When carboxyhemoglobin or serum cotinine levels were used as measures of the smoke taken in, persons who smoked more cigarettes per day had higher levels of these biologic substances (Benowitz 1996). Even so, the carboxyhemoglobin and cotinine levels were substantially lower than those predicted by linear extrapolation from data on persons who reported smoking 1 to 20 cigarettes per day (Law et al. 1997). Among smokers of 40 or more cigarettes per day, the levels of these biomarkers were 35 percent lower than those predicted by linear extrapolation from data on persons who reported smoking fewer than 20 cigarettes per day.

At the same reported number of cigarettes per day, cotinine levels varied substantially (Benowitz 1996).

Smokers titrate cigarette smoke to achieve a consistent intake of nicotine by altering the number of cigarettes smoked per day or by changing the puffing pattern—that is, by taking deeper, faster, more, or longer puffs (National Cancer Institute [NCI] 2001). When these smoking behaviors fail to restore the level of nicotine intake, as they may with cigarettes that have very low machine-measured yields, smokers may increase the number of cigarettes per day to maintain the same level of nicotine intake.

These observations suggest that the number of cigarettes smoked per day may have become a less precise measure of exposure to tobacco smoke with the introduction of cigarettes with low machine-measured yields of tar and nicotine. This diminished precision of cigarettes smoked per day as a measure of exposure may account for some of the discordance between studies that define increased risk by an increase of more than one pack per day in the number of cigarettes smoked. By using serum cotinine as an indicator of nicotine intake and exposure to tobacco smoke in the population demonstrates a linear increase for 10 to 15 cigarettes per day. However, as use exceeds 10 to 15 cigarettes per day, a progressively smaller increment in serum cotinine for each increment in the number of cigarettes smoked per day is observed (Caraballo et al. 1998; O'Connor et al. 2006). This flattening of the relationship between exposure and cigarettes smoked per day was similar to flattening of the relationship between the RR of CHD and the number of cigarettes smoked per day. Thus, researchers should be cautious about defining the absence of a continuing increase in risk among smokers of more than 20 cigarettes per day as evidence that increases in actual exposure are not accompanied by increases in risk.

Duration of Smoking

Researchers have not always demonstrated a significant relationship between duration of cigarette smoking and CHD risk when adjustment was made for other risk factors and the number of cigarettes smoked per day (Kuller et al. 1991; Tverdal 1999). Variation in the number of cigarettes smoked per day and in the products smoked during the lifetime of a smoker is often substantial, but this variable is not well captured in epidemiologic studies.

Age is colinear with duration of smoking, because the two variables grow in tandem after a person starts to smoke and the RRs for smoking and CHD decline with advancing age. Furthermore, most smokers begin to smoke during adolescence, which promotes the colinearity. These realities make it difficult to estimate the independent contributions of age and duration of smoking to risk of CHD in multivariate models. However, the two studies of the American Cancer Society are a good source of data, because each study consists of more than 1 million men and women (Burns et al. 1997; Thun et al. 1997). Analyses of these data stratified by age and the number of cigarettes smoked per day showed steady increases in CHD mortality rates with increasing duration of smoking for persons younger than age 70 years. Using data from

CPS-I, investigators calculated the risk of developing CHD by age and duration of smoking (see Table 6.1 for data on White men) (Burns et al. 1997). For almost all age groups younger than age 70 years, RRs increased with increasing duration of smoking. Data from CPS-II on men (Thun et al. 1997) also demonstrated a pattern of increasing RR with age-specific mortality due to CHD and increasing duration of smoking for each level of cigarettes smoked per day (Table 6.2). Even though data in these analyses were not adjusted for potential differences in other cardiovascular risk factors, the findings presented a convincing picture of increasing risk of CHD with longer duration of smoking.

Smoking Cessation

The risks of MI and death from CHD are lower among former smokers than among continuing smokers in many studies, including those with data adjusted for levels of other risk factors (Gordon et al. 1974; Åberg et al. 1983; USDHHS 1990; Kuller et al. 1991; Frost et al. 1996). The risk fell rapidly, decreasing about one-half in one year (Lightwood and Glantz 1997). Risks appear to remain slightly elevated for more than a decade after persons stopped smoking, but in some studies this increased risk was not statistically significant (Dagenais et al. 1990; Omenn et al. 1990; Kawachi et al. 1993a, 1994; Jacobs et al. 1999a; Qiao et al. 2000). Among smokers who had MI or angiographically documented CHD, persons who stopped smoking had a substantially lower rate of reinfarction than did those who continued to smoke. Reduction in risk was evident within the first year after MI. Risk continued to be lower among former smokers than among continuing

Table 6.1   Rate ratios for coronary heart disease among White men, by age and duration of cigarette smoking[a]

Age (years)	Duration of smoking (years)							
	20–24	25–29	30–34	35–39	40–44	45–49	50–54	55–59
40–44	1.95	2.47	4.23	NR	NR	NR	NR	NR
45–49	1.79	2.5	2.66	2.64	4.39	NR	NR	NR
50–54	2.06	2.25	2.22	2.74	2.82	3.4	NR	NR
55–59	1.71	1.66	2.13	2.03	2.43	2.99	2.17	NR
60–64	1.83	1.44	1.86	1.75	1.92	2.12	2.45	4.06
65–69	1.34	1.56	1.52	1.61	1.49	1.6	2.09	2.25
70–74	1.17	1.14	1.23	1.08	1.55	1.26	1.53	1.78
75–79	1.09	1.2	1.31	1.12	1.55	1.46	0.94	1.36

Source: Adapted from Burns et al. 1997.

Note: **NR** = data not reported.

[a]From Cancer Prevention Study I, American Cancer Society.

Table 6.2   Death rates and rate ratios for death from coronary heart disease among men, by age and duration of smoking by number of cigarettes smoked per day[a]

Number of cigarettes/day	Death rates (per 100,000)[b]					Rate ratios[c]				
	Age (years)	Number of years of smoking				Age (years)	Number of years of smoking			
		20–29	30–39	40–49	≥50		20–29	30–39	40–49	≥50
1–19	50–59	241.1	276	277.9	NR	50–59	2.7	3.1	3.2	NR
	60–69	340.6	560.3	643.5	866.5	60–69	1.1	1.8	2.1	2.8
20	50–59	213.9	272.6	493.4	956.4	50–59	2.4	3.1	5.6	NR
	60–69	299.9	509	729.5	1,088.9	60–69	1	1.6	2.4	3.5
21–39	50–59	195.8	237.4	367.2	NR	50–59	2.2	2.7	4.2	NR
	60–69	232.2	350.8	607.2	1,113.4	60–69	NR	1.1	2	3.6
40	50–59	144.9	281.6	321.4	664.5	50–59	1.6	3.2	3.7	NR
	60–69	470.8	458.3	607.6	988.3	60–69	1.5	1.5	2	3.2

Source: Adapted from Thun et al. 1997.
Note: **NR** = data not reported.
[a]From Cancer Prevention Study II, American Cancer Society (CPS-II).
[b]CPS-II data, Appendix Table 10, Thun et al. 1997.
[c]CPS-II data, Appendix Table 12, Thun et al. 1997.

smokers for prolonged periods after the first MI (Daly et al. 1983; Omenn et al. 1990). Studies also demonstrated rapid reduction in risk after persons stopped smoking among populations at high risk for CHD (Ockene et al. 1990) and among women (Kawachi et al. 1993a, 1994).

Patients with angiographically documented CHD who stopped smoking at the diagnosis of CHD (Vlietstra et al. 1986) or before diagnosis (Hermanson et al. 1988) had lower death rates from MI or CHD than did continuing smokers. In addition, the benefit of stopping smoking did not decline with advancing age.

In the 16-year follow-up of the Multiple Risk Factor Intervention Trial Research Group (1990, 1996), mortality from CHD was 11.4 percent lower in the "special intervention" group than in the "usual care" group. This result may illustrate the benefit of stopping smoking, because one of the interventions targeted smoking cessation. A trial of advice to civil servants in London, England, to stop smoking demonstrated an 18-percent reduction in mortality from CHD in the intervention group versus the control group after 10 years of follow-up (Rose et al. 1982). Suskin and colleagues (2001) reported that in addition to benefits for CHD, stopping smoking also reduces morbidity and mortality in patients with left ventricular dysfunction. In this study, the benefits of stopping smoking on mortality and recurrent congestive heart failure requiring hospitalization were similar to the benefits from treatments with

angiotensin-converting-enzyme (ACE) inhibiting drugs, β-blockers, or spironolactone, which are mainstays for the treatment of heart failure.

Women

Women have lower absolute rates of CHD than do men. However, cigarette smoking has been associated with higher RR of MI (Njølstad et al. 1996) and higher CHD mortality (Kawachi et al. 1994; Thun et al. 1997) among women than among men. The absolute increase in risk of CHD from smoking is similar for men and women (USDHHS 1983, 2001).

A prospective evaluation of fatal and nonfatal CVD events among women in the Nurses' Health Study (Willett et al. 1987) found that smoking was an independent cause of CVD. Age-adjusted risks of disease increased progressively with more cigarettes smoked per day up to 45 or more per day. Even when the combined risks of fatal CHD and nonfatal MI were adjusted for levels of other risk factors, risks increased with increasing numbers of cigarettes per day.

Researchers have demonstrated a rapid decline in excess risk of CHD in women after they stopped smoking cigarettes. Even so, 10 to 14 years of nonsmoking are required before risks approach those of lifetime nonsmokers (Kawachi et al. 1993a, 1994).

Race and Ethnicity

In 2004, heart disease mortality was higher among African Americans than among Whites (National Heart, Lung, and Blood Institute [NHLBI] 2007). From 1999 through 2004, the prevalence of acute MI was higher for African Americans than for Whites aged 35 through 54 years; however, for ages 55 years and older, the prevalence of acute MI was higher among Whites (NHLBI 2007).

The INTERHEART study is a case-control investigation of acute MI in 52 countries in Africa, Asia, Australia, the Middle East Crescent, and North and South America (Teo et al. 2006). The odds ratio (OR) for acute MI in smokers was 2.95 for this large multiethnic population compared with lifetime nonsmokers. In addition, the risk of MI was higher among persons who smoked bidis than among nonsmokers in countries where use of this form of tobacco is common.

Researchers also identified cigarette smoking as a significant risk factor for CHD among Hispanic populations (Mendelson et al. 1998) and Asian populations (Kiyohara et al. 1990; Miyake et al. 2000; Lam et al. 2002).

Sudden Death

Most sudden death is due to CVD. In many epidemiologic studies, RRs for sudden cardiac death were higher than RRs for CHD or MI among persons who smoked. The RRs for sudden death among current smokers, compared with lifetime nonsmokers, often exceeded 3.0 (USDHEW 1971, 1979; Dawber 1980; Kannel and Thomas 1982; USDHHS 1983; Wannamethee et al. 1995; Sexton et al. 1997). In multivariate analyses of the combined data from the Framingham Heart Study and the Albany Study, which examined sudden cardiac death in men aged 45 through 64 years, cigarette smoking was the risk factor with the highest statistical significance (Kannel et al. 1975). In a study of data from the 1986 National Mortality Followback Survey among persons with no history of CHD, cigarette smoking was the only modifiable risk factor associated with sudden coronary death and it was one factor associated with increased risk of sudden coronary death among persons with known CHD (Escobedo and Zack 1996; Escobedo and Caspersen 1997). Cigarette smoking was also associated with risk of sudden cardiac death in the 18-year follow-up of the Honolulu Heart Program (Kagan et al. 1989) and the 28-year follow-up of the Framingham Heart Study (Cupples et al. 1992).

Peters and colleagues (1995) found an association between smoking cessation and reduction in death from cardiac arrhythmia for patients with left ventricular dysfunction after MI. Finally, the risk of recurrent cardiac arrest among smokers surviving out-of-hospital cardiac arrest was lower among persons who then stopped smoking than among those who continued to smoke (Hallstrom et al. 1986).

Stroke

After adjustment of data for other risk factors, cigarette smokers have higher risk of stroke and higher mortality from cerebrovascular disease than do lifetime nonsmokers, and a dose-response relationship is evident (USDHHS 1983, 2001, 2004; Neaton et al. 1984; Colditz et al. 1988; Wolf et al. 1988; Kannel and Higgins 1990; Kuller et al. 1991; Freund et al. 1993; Hames et al. 1993; Håheim et al. 1996; Tanne et al. 1998; Jacobs et al. 1999a; Sharrett et al. 1999; Djoussé et al. 2002). In addition, in the 20-year follow-up of a prospective study of mortality that controlled for other cardiovascular risk factors, cigarette smoking increased the risk of death from stroke and mortality rates grew the number of cigarettes smoked increased (Hart et al. 1999).

In a meta-analysis of data from 32 studies, the overall RR for stroke associated with cigarette smoking was 1.5 (95 percent confidence interval [CI], 1.4–1.6) (Shinton and Beevers 1989). The RRs varied with the stroke subtypes: 1.9 for cerebral infarction, 0.7 for cerebral hemorrhage, and 2.9 for subarachnoid hemorrhage. The researchers reported a dose-response relationship between the number of cigarettes smoked per day and the RR. The data suggested a sustained higher risk of stroke among former smokers younger than age 75 years than the risk for nonsmokers in the same age group. For all ages combined, RR for former smokers was 1.2.

During the 26-year follow-up of the cohort in the Framingham Heart Study, cigarette smoking was a significant risk factor for stroke (Wolf et al. 1988). The risk declined, however, among smokers who had stopped smoking for two years and was similar to that of lifetime nonsmokers after five years of abstinence from smoking. In the 12-year follow-up of the Nurses' Health Study (Kawachi et al. 1993b), RR for stroke among current smokers was 2.58 compared with nonsmokers, but it was 1.34 among former smokers compared with nonsmokers. Once those who stopped smoking had abstained for two to four years, their risk for stroke could not be distinguished from that of lifetime nonsmokers. In addition, the pattern of decline in total risk for stroke after stopping smoking remained the same after adjustments for other risk factors.

Aortic Aneurysm

Mortality studies consistently demonstrated higher risk of death from abdominal aortic aneurysm among cigarette smokers than among nonsmokers (Hammond and Horn 1958; Weir and Dunn 1970; USDHHS 1983, 2004; Strachan 1991; Nilsson et al. 2001). In addition, the risk rose with an increasing number of cigarettes smoked per day (Kahn 1966; Hammond and Garfinkel 1969; Burns et al. 1997; Blanchard et al. 2000; Vardulaki et al. 2000).

Studies have demonstrated an association of cigarette smoking with prevalence of aortic aneurysm or aortic dilation, as determined by ultrasonography in cohorts of men and women, even after adjustment for a large number of known risk factors (Alcorn et al. 1996; Lee et al. 1997; Wilmink et al. 1999; Jamrozik et al. 2000; Lederle et al. 2001). The U.S. Preventive Services Task Force (2005) recommended a one-time screening by ultrasonography for abdominal aortic aneurysm among men aged 65 to 75 years who had ever smoked. Cigarette smoking has been associated with increased growth of abdominal aortic aneurysms (Brady et al. 2004). This finding suggests that more frequent monitoring of smokers for this condition is necessary. With increasing duration of abstinence from smoking, the risk of developing an abdominal aneurysm appears to slowly decline (Wilmink et al. 1999).

Peripheral Arterial Disease

Cigarette smoking and diabetes are well established as the major risk factors for PAD, and a strong dose-response relationship for smoking was observed even after adjustment for other CVD risk factors (Weiss 1972; Kannel and Shurtleff 1973; USDHHS 1983; Wilt et al. 1996; Price et al. 1999; Meijer et al. 2000; Ness et al. 2000). Data from the Framingham Heart Study demonstrated increased risk of PAD among both young and older male and female cigarette smokers after adjustment for other cardiovascular risk factors. In addition, this risk increased with the increase in the number of cigarettes smoked per day, and this result was statistically significant (Freund et al. 1993). The Framingham Offspring Study reported a similar finding (Murabito et al. 2002). Finally, researchers have observed a significantly higher rate of late arterial occlusion in patients who continued to smoke after peripheral vascular surgery than in those who stopped smoking (Wray et al. 1971; Ameli et al. 1989; Wiseman et al. 1989). Among smokers with claudication, progression to critical limb ischemia is reduced in those who stopped smoking (Jonason and Bergström 1987).

Pipes, Cigars, and Low-Tar Cigarettes

"Low-tar" or "light" cigarettes were designed to produce low machine-measured yields of tar and nicotine (NCI 2001). Design characteristics of low-tar cigarettes include increased ventilation and more rapid cigarette burn rate. By changing the way they smoke or the number of cigarettes smoked, persons who smoke these products can obtain as much nicotine as from "regular" or "full-flavored" cigarettes, thereby satisfying their addiction (USDHEW 1979; NCI 2001). Comprehensive reviews of this issue concluded that use of low-tar cigarettes has not resulted in meaningful reduction in the risk of CVD (NCI 2001; Stratton et al. 2001; Scientific Advisory Committee on Tobacco Product Regulation 2002; USDHHS 2004).

Compared with persons who smoke cigarettes, smokers who exclusively smoke pipes or cigars have lower risk for many smoking-related diseases (NCI 1998). Smoke from pipes and cigars contains the same toxic substances as cigarette smoke, but those who use a pipe or cigar usually smoke at lower intensity; observation indicates that they tend not to inhale the smoke, thus reducing their exposure to its toxic substances (USDHEW 1979; NCI 1998; Shanks et al. 1998). Most current cigar users are young males who often smoke less than one cigar daily (NCI 1998); no data on risk for this population are available. For older adults who regularly use cigars, particularly those who smoke more than one cigar per day or inhale the smoke, risk of CHD is modestly higher than that for nonsmokers (NCI 1998; Iribarren et al. 1999; Jacobs et al. 1999b; Baker et al. 2000). Studies have reported similar increases in risks for CHD and cerebrovascular disease for persons who smoke a pipe exclusively (Henley et al. 2004).

Summary

Cigarette smoking and involuntary exposure to cigarette smoke are major causes of CHD, stroke, aortic aneurysm, and PAD. The risk is seen both as an increased risk of acute thrombosis of narrowed vessels and as an increased degree of atherosclerosis in the blood vessels involved. The cardiovascular risks attributable to cigarette smoking increase with the number of cigarettes smoked and with the duration of smoking. However, risk is substantially increased even by exposure to low levels of cigarette smoke as with exposure to secondhand smoke or smoking a few cigarettes per day. Risks are not reduced by smoking cigarettes with lower machine-measured yields of tar and nicotine. Smokers of only pipes or cigars seem to have lower risks of CVD than do cigarette smokers. However, cigarette smokers who switch to pipes or cigars often inhale the tobacco smoke and may not experience the lower CVD risk of persons who primarily smoke a pipe or cigar. Stopping cigarette smoking and eliminating exposure to secondhand smoke rapidly and substantially reduce risks of various CVDs.

Secondhand Tobacco Smoke and Cardiovascular Disease

The 2006 Surgeon General's report on involuntary exposure to tobacco smoke (USDHHS 2006) and Barnoya and Glantz (2005) extensively reviewed risks of CVD among nonsmokers exposed to secondhand tobacco smoke. They found a causal relationship among both men and women between exposure to secondhand smoke and increased risks of CHD morbidity and mortality. Pooled RRs from meta-analyses indicated a 25- to 30-percent increase in risk of CHD from exposure to secondhand smoke. The study by Whincup and associates (2004), which was based on blood levels of cotinine in men, suggested a 50- to 60-percent increase in risk of CHD from exposure to secondhand smoke. The risk of acute MI appeared to decline rapidly after cessation of exposure to secondhand smoke, as evidenced by a decline in hospital admissions for MI after smoke-free laws were put in place (Dinno and Glantz 2007; Lightwood and Glantz 2009; Meyers et al. 2009). As for stroke, the evidence was insufficient to infer a causal relationship between increased risk of CHD morbidity and mortality and exposure to secondhand smoke. Studies of the effects of secondhand smoke on subclinical vascular disease, particularly thickening of the walls of the carotid arteries, also suggest a causal relationship between exposure to secondhand smoke and atherosclerosis. As mentioned previously, the substantial CVD risk associated with involuntary exposure to cigarette smoke indicates that the risks estimated in most studies of active smoking are biased downward because the control groups generally included large numbers of persons with exposure to secondhand smoke.

Pathophysiology

This section on pathophysiology focuses primarily on mechanisms by which cigarette smoking may increase risk of CVD.

Cigarette Smoke Constituents and Cardiovascular Disease

Three constituents of cigarette smoke have received the greatest attention as potential contributors to CVD: nicotine, carbon monoxide (CO), and oxidant gases. Some research also investigated the contributions of polycyclic aromatic hydrocarbons (PAHs), particulate matter, and other constituents of tobacco smoke to the pathophysiology of CVD including atherogenesis (Brook et al. 2004; Vermylen et al. 2005; Bhatnagar 2006).

Nicotine, which is absorbed rapidly from cigarette smoke, was found in arterial blood levels of 40 to 100 ng/mL after each cigarette was smoked (Henningfield et al. 1993). The typical dose of nicotine systematically absorbed from each cigarette is 1 to 2 milligrams (mg). Although plasma nicotine levels peaked sharply after each cigarette, trough values also rose during the first six to eight hours of regular smoking during the day (Benowitz et al. 1982a). This accumulation pattern was consistent with an elimination half-life for nicotine of two hours (Benowitz et al. 1982a). In persons who smoke regularly, venous plasma levels of nicotine reached a plateau in early afternoon and remained at that level until bedtime (Figure 6.4). Significant levels of nicotine were in the smoker's venous blood even on waking in the morning. Thus, these findings indicate that the regular smoker is exposed to significant levels of nicotine 24 hours per day.

Nicotine is a sympathomimetic drug that releases catecholamines both locally from neurons and systemically from the adrenal gland. In studies of the pharmacodynamics of nicotine, the intensity of its maximal effect was greater with more rapid delivery (Porchet et al. 1987). Pharmacodynamic studies also indicated that although tolerance to the effects of nicotine developed rapidly, tolerance was incomplete (Porchet et al. 1987). In one study, a constant intravenous infusion of nicotine increased the

Figure 6.4   Plasma nicotine and carboxyhemoglobin concentrations throughout a day of cigarette smoking

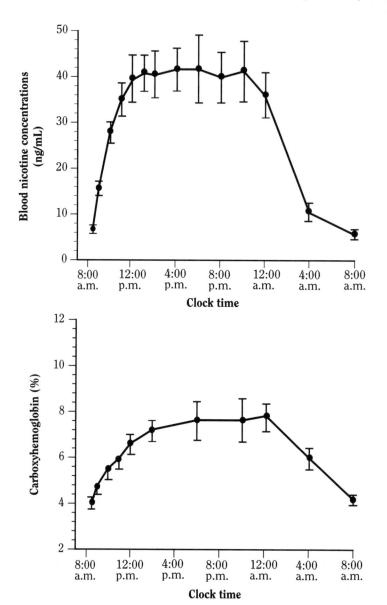

Source: Benowitz 2003. Adapted from Benowitz et al. 1982b with permission from Elsevier, © 2003.
Note: Mean (± standard error of measurement) blood nicotine and carboxyhemoglobin concentrations in cigarette smokers.
Participants smoked cigarettes every half-hour from 8:30 a.m. to 11:00 p.m., for a total of 30 cigarettes per day. **ng/mL** = nanograms
per milliliter.

heart rate even though nicotine levels in the blood were relatively low. As the infusion continued, the heart rate reached a plateau despite a progressive rise in blood levels of nicotine (Benowitz et al. 1982a). The same phenomenon was observed in comparisons of acceleration of heart rate with level of blood nicotine during regular cigarette smoking throughout the day (Benowitz et al. 1984).

In another study, heart rate measured by ambulatory monitoring was higher throughout the day when persons were smoking than when they were not smoking (Benowitz et al. 1984). The extent of elevation was independent of the blood level of nicotine absorbed from the cigarettes. The researchers concluded that the elevated heart rate reflected persistent stimulation of the sympathetic nervous system, a possible contributing factor to CVD. Nicotine may also contribute to endothelial dysfunction, lipid abnormalities, and insulin resistance (Benowitz 2003).

CO is a major constituent of cigarette smoke. In regular smokers, carboxyhemoglobin levels average about 5 percent, compared with 10 percent or higher in heavy smokers (Benowitz et al. 1982b). These values compare with levels of 0.5 to 2 percent in nonsmokers, depending on exposure to automobile exhaust. Like nicotine levels, elevated carboxyhemoglobin levels persist for 24 hours a day in smokers (Figure 6.4).

CO exposure can aggravate ischemia and worsen symptoms in persons with vascular disease, although it is not clear that CO contributes directly to atherosclerosis (Benowitz 2003). CO binds avidly to hemoglobin, reducing the amount of hemoglobin available to carry oxygen and impeding release of oxygen by hemoglobin. In some studies, inhalation of CO at levels comparable to those in cigarette smokers reduced exercise tolerance in patients with angina pectoris, intermittent claudication, or COPD (Calverley et al. 1981; Allred et al. 1989). Another study reported that CO exposure in persons with obstructive coronary disease resulted in a greater degree of exercise-induced ventricular dysfunction and an increase in the number and complexity of ventricular arrhythmias during exercise (Sheps et al. 1990). Inhaling CO reduced the threshold for ventricular fibrillation in animals (DeBias et al. 1976).

Long-term CO exposure in smokers resulted in greater red blood cell mass and reduced the oxygen-carrying capacity of red blood cells, resulting in relative hypoxemia (Benowitz 2003). In response to hypoxemia, red blood cell masses increased to maintain the amount of oxygen needed by organs in the body. The increase in red blood cell mass increased blood viscosity and may contribute to hypercoagulation in smokers.

Cigarette smoke delivers a high level of oxidizing chemicals to smokers, including oxides of nitrogen and many free radicals from both the gas and tar phases of cigarette smoke (Church and Pryor 1985). Exposure to oxidant chemicals in smoke was associated with depletion of endogenous levels of antioxidants, manifested as lower blood levels of vitamin C in smokers than in nonsmokers (Lykkesfeldt et al. 2000). Cigarette smoking also was reported to increase levels of lipid peroxidation products in the plasma and urine of smokers (Morrow et al. 1995). Study results also indicated that oxidant stress contributes to several potential mechanisms of CVD, including inflammation, endothelial dysfunction, lipid abnormalities such as oxidation of low-density lipoprotein (LDL), and platelet activation (Burke and FitzGerald 2003).

Acrolein, a reactive aldehyde produced by endogenous lipid peroxidation, is present at high levels in cigarette smoke. Acrolein binds covalently to form protein adducts, and acrolein-induced modification of proteins has been implicated in atherogenesis. Acrolein modifies apolipoprotein A-I (APO A-I), the major protein in HDL (Shao et al. 2005). HDL protects against atherosclerosis. Acrolein-protein adducts co-localize with APO A-I in macrophages in the intima of human atheromatous blood vessels (Szadkowski and Myers 2008).

Acrolein also oxidized thioredoxins 1 and 2 in endothelial cells. Thioredoxins are prominent antioxidant proteins that regulate the oxidation-reduction balance critical for normal cell function. These results suggest that oxidation of thioredoxins can result in dysfunction and death of endothelial cells, contributing to atherosclerosis. In addition, acrolein induces production of the enzyme cyclooxygenase-2 (COX-2) in human endothelial cells in vitro (Park et al. 2007). This finding is relevant because COX-2 is expressed in atherosclerotic lesions and may participate in atherogenesis. Acrolein may contribute to thrombogenicity in smokers by inhibiting antithrombin activity (Gugliucci 2007). Finally, acrolein induces hypercontraction in isolated human arteries and could contribute to smoking-induced coronary vasospasm (Conklin et al. 2006).

Cigarette smoke contains a number of metals, including aluminum, cadmium, copper, lead, mercury, nickel, and zinc. Metals in cigarette smoke catalyze the oxidation of cellular proteins (Bernhard et al. 2005). This reaction may lead to structural damage, endothelial dysfunction, and detachment of endothelial cells from the walls of blood vessels. Mixtures of metals and oxidants may be particularly damaging to endothelial cells. Cadmium levels are higher in serum of smokers, and cadmium accumulates in the aortic walls of smokers (Abu-Hayyeh et al. 2001). Epidemiologic evidence indicates an association between serum levels of cadmium and lead and CVD, including hypertension and MI (Abu-Hayyeh et al. 2001).

PAHs found in the tar fraction of cigarette smoke reportedly accelerated atherosclerosis in experimental animals. Weekly injections of benzo[a]pyrene and 7,12-dimethylbenz[a]anthracene, at doses below those that produce tumors, increased development of atherosclerotic plaque in the aortas of cockerels (Penn and Snyder 1988). Similarly, inhaled butadiene, a component of the vapor phase of cigarette smoke, increased the amount of atherosclerotic plaque in the same animal model (Penn and Snyder 1996). The researchers speculated that one mechanism of atherogenesis is a mutation, followed by hyperproliferation of smooth muscle or other cells that may contribute to growth of atherosclerotic plaque.

Figure 6.5   Overview of mechanisms by which cigarette smoking causes an acute cardiovascular event

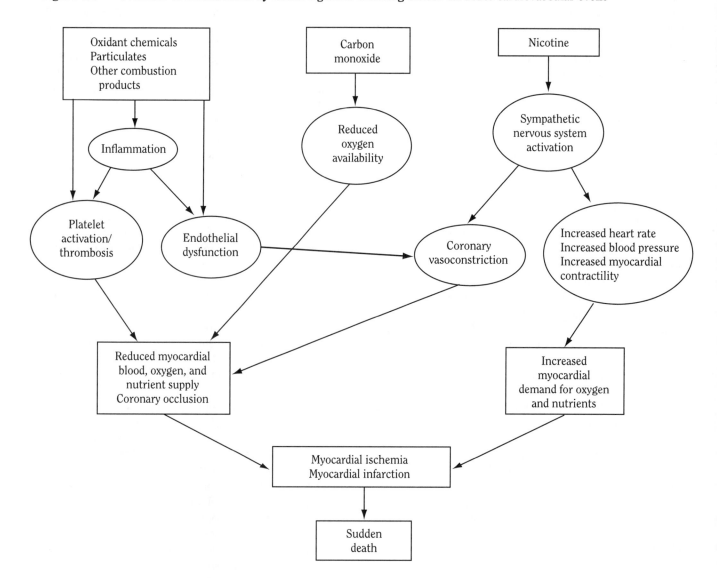

Source: Benowitz 2003. Reprinted with permission from Elsevier, © 2003.

Studies of the cardiovascular effects of smokeless tobacco may be informative for understanding the pathophysiology of smoking-induced CVD. Oral and nasal smokeless tobacco products have been used for centuries around the world (International Agency for Research on Cancer [IARC] 2007). Traditional smokeless tobacco products vary widely among countries; however, similar to Sweden, forms of oral snuff are the most common types of products used in the United States (Substance Abuse and Mental Health Services Administration 2009). These products contain a large array of chemicals, including nicotine, nitrosamines, nitrosamine acids, PAHs, aldehydes, and metals (IARC 2007). A recent systematic review reported that studies from both the United States and Sweden showed an increased risk of death from MI and stroke related to the frequency and duration of use of smokeless tobacco products (Boffetta and Straif 2009). This review relied heavily (85–89 percent of the weight) on results of a large U.S. cohort study conducted in two waves between 1959–1971 and 1982–1988 and may not represent risk associated with products currently marketed in the United States and Europe. As in cigarettes, nicotine is the principal alkaloid in smokeless tobacco products, and the concentrations of nicotine (mg/gram [g] tobacco) are similar between cigarettes and the types of oral snuff sold in the United States (Djordjevic and Doran 2009). An analysis comparing the effects of using oral snuff with those of smoking cigarettes provided insights into the role of nicotine versus the effects of other toxins from tobacco smoke on CVD and cardiovascular risk factors (Benowitz et al. 1988, 1989). In addition clinical trials of nicotine patches in patients with known CVD have not shown that transdermal nicotine increased cardiovascular risk (Working Group for the Study of Transdermal Nicotine in Patients with Coronary Artery Disease 1994; Joseph et al. 1996). In the study of 3,094 middle-aged smokers with chronic obstructive lung disease, the U.S. Lung Health Study found no evidence of increased cardiovascular risk in subjects who quit smoking by using nicotine gum versus those who quit without use of nicotine gum (Murray et al. 1996). These studies and related evidence suggest that chemicals other than nicotine may contribute to the elevated risk of death from MI and stroke. In the INTERHEART study, the OR of acute MI was 2.23 among those who used only smokeless tobacco compared with those who used no tobacco. The OR was comparable to that of current cigarette smokers (OR = 2.95) compared with those who used no tobacco (Teo et al. 2006). In addition, the risk of acute MI among smokers who also used smokeless tobacco was the highest risk related to tobacco use (OR = 4.09), suggesting that some of the toxicants involved in the elevated cardiovascular risk could be contained in both tobacco smoke and smokeless products. Smokeless tobacco products have been found to have significant amounts of numerous other toxicants and carcinogens, particularly tobacco-specific nitrosamines as well as volatile aldehydes and PAHs (Stepanov et al. 2008). Additional research on these and other toxicants in smokeless tobacco, such as heavy metals like cadmium, is needed to understand the observed cardiovascular risks among users of smokeless tobacco products.

Mechanisms

Cigarette smoking produces acute myocardial ischemia by adversely affecting the balance of demand for myocardial oxygen and nutrients with myocardial blood supply (Figure 6.5). The increase in demand for oxygen in the myocardium is a consequence of nicotine stimulation of the sympathetic nervous system and the heart. Cigarette smoking acutely increases levels of plasma norepinephrine and epinephrine and enhanced 24-hour urinary excretion of these catecholamines (review by Benowitz and Gourlay 1997). Regular smoking increases the heart rate both in the short term (up to 20 beats per minute) and throughout the day (average increase, 7 beats per minute), as measured during ambulatory monitoring. Nicotine also increases heart rate, blood pressure, and myocardial contractility. These hemodynamic changes result in increases in myocardial work that in turn require increased myocardial blood flow.

In healthy persons, cigarette smoking increases coronary blood flow in response to increases in myocardial work. In smokers, the response in coronary blood flow to increased myocardial demand was impaired (i.e., reduced coronary vasodilatory reserve) (Czernin and Waldherr 2003). Cigarette smoking played a direct role by constricting coronary arteries through nicotine-mediated action on α-adrenergic receptors and by induction of endothelial dysfunction by nicotine and oxidizing chemicals (Nicod et al. 1984; Puranik and Celermajer 2003). In addition, oxidant chemicals contribute to platelet activation and thrombogenesis (Burke and FitzGerald 2003).

Exposure to CO may also contribute to the adverse hemodynamic effects of cigarette smoking. By producing functional anemia, CO increases the need for coronary blood flow, especially during physical exertion. An in-adequate vasodilatory flow reserve produced by cigarette smoking, in the face of need for increased coronary blood flow mediated by carbon dioxide, could contribute to myocardial ischemia with exercise in smokers.

In addition to the mechanisms described in Figure 6.5, cigarette smoking has effects on inflammation, insulin sensitivity, and lipid abnormalities that most likely contribute to smoking-induced CVD.

Hemodynamic Effects

Blood Pressure and Heart Rate

In 1907, Erich Hesse published "The Influence of Smoking on the Circulation," which documents his observations on the effects of smoking on heart rate and blood pressure (Hesse 1907). In most study participants, both heart rate and blood pressure increased immediately after smoking. Hesse observed a greater response in blood pressure after smoking in persons who smoked than in nonsmokers. Speculating that the increases in blood pressure and heart rate reflected stimulation of the heart or nervous system, he instituted a rule prohibiting patients with a "heart weakness" from smoking, to avoid unnecessary strain and stress for the heart muscle. Many investigators confirmed Hesse's observations on the hemodynamic effects of cigarette smoking (Deanfield et al. 1986; Czernin et al. 1995; Barutcu et al. 2004).

The positive chronotropic, inotropic, and blood pressure effects of smoking are explained by nicotine-induced activation of the sympathetic nervous system (review by Benowitz 2003). Nicotine promotes the release of epinephrine and norepinephrine from the adrenal medulla and terminal nerve endings, resulting in increased heart rate and greater contractility through stimulation of myocardial β_1 receptors. Peripheral vascular resistance increases through α-receptor mediated vasoconstriction that in turn increases blood pressure. Coronary β_2 and α_2 receptors are also stimulated: stimulation of β_2 receptors promoted vasodilation, and stimulation of α_2 receptors promoted vasoconstriction (Cryer et al. 1976; Benowitz 2003).

Cryer and colleagues (1976) elucidated the mechanisms behind observed hemodynamic changes during smoking. They observed more than a 150-percent increase in plasma epinephrine levels (from 44 to 113 picograms [pg]/mL) at 10 minutes after participants started to smoke a cigarette. Norepinephrine values increased to a smaller degree (from 227 to 315 pg/mL) at 12.5 minutes after the start of smoking. These increases were associated with significant increases in heart rate and blood pressure. Pretreatment with α-receptor blockers and β-receptor blockers had little effect on the increase in plasma levels of catecholamines, but increases in blood pressure and heart rate were eliminated. This study confirmed that smoking-induced increases in blood pressure and heart rate are attributable to adrenergic mechanisms.

The hemodynamic effects of cigarette smoking are mediated primarily by nicotine, although oxidizing chemicals in tobacco smoke also affect vascular function.

Intravenous nicotine, nicotine nasal spray, and nicotine chewing gum all increased the heart rate up to 10 to 15 beats per minute and raised systolic blood pressure by up to 5 to 10 millimeters of mercury (mm Hg), responses similar to the effects of cigarette smoking (Gourlay and Benowitz 1997). Nicotine increased cardiac output by increasing both heart rate and myocardial contractility. Different vascular beds express different types and ratios of adrenergic receptors. Therefore, not all vascular responses to nicotine or tobacco smoke are the same. For example, nicotine constricts some vascular beds, such as the skin, and cutaneous vasoconstriction explains the reduced temperature of the fingertip observed with administration of nicotine (Benowitz et al. 1982a). Conversely, nicotine appears to dilate other vascular beds, such as skeletal muscle (Diana et al. 1990). Vasodilation of skeletal muscle may partly result from the increase in cardiac output, although the release of epinephrine from nerve terminals may also contribute. The net result of increases in heart rate, blood pressure, and myocardial contractility is an increase in myocardial work, followed by increased myocardial blood flow.

Coronary Blood Flow

An important hemodynamic consequence of cigarette smoking is its effect on blood flow in the coronary arteries. Cigarette smoking acutely increased coronary blood flow by up to 40 percent, apparently a response to the increase in myocardial work (review by Czernin and Waldherr 2003).

In anesthetized dogs, coronary blood flow showed a biphasic response to nicotine. Initially, researchers hypothesized that increases in coronary blood flow—in the large coronary vessels as well as the smaller vessels—resulted from an increase in myocardial metabolic demand.

Cigarette smoking impairs the response of coronary blood flow to an increase in myocardial demand for oxygen; that is, it reduces the coronary vasodilatory flow reserve. Thus, the increase in coronary blood flow based on the level of myocardial work is less than would be expected in the absence of exposure to tobacco smoke. Considerable evidence indicates that cigarette smoking causes dysfunction of the coronary arterial endothelium (see "Endothelial Injury or Dysfunction" later in this chapter).

Cigarette smoking may also be associated with coronary vasoconstriction. Although cigarette smoking increases coronary blood flow in a person who does not have CHD, it may decrease coronary blood flow in the presence of coronary disease. Regan and colleagues (1960) measured coronary sinus blood flow in seven male volunteers with documented CHD before and after they smoked two cigarettes during a period of about 25 minutes; cardiac work increased by about 30 percent during smoking. Even so, in response to smoking, coronary blood flow fell in three patients, did not change in three patients, and increased in one patient. Similar paradoxical responses were observed after long-term smokers were exposed to cold by testing with cold pressors (Campisi et al. 1998). In the testing, the hand is immersed in ice water for one to two minutes. This painful procedure evokes a mixed adrenergic response involving coronary receptors α_1 and α_2 (vasoconstriction), β_2 (vasodilation), and myocardial β_1 (indirect coronary vasodilation). Endothelial α_2 receptors that promote indirect coronary vasodilation may also be involved. In healthy volunteers, cold-induced increases of about 30 percent in the product of heart rate and blood pressure were associated with appropriate and similar increases in blood flow. In contrast, smokers showed no measurable increases in blood flow in response to the cold. Campisi and colleagues (1998) ascribed this observation to coronary endothelial dysfunction.

Kaufmann and colleagues (2000) provided additional evidence for the association between smoking and endothelial dysfunction. Using quantitative positron emission tomography, they found that coronary microvascular function was abnormal in smokers but could be restored by infusion of vitamin C. Earlier, Zeiher and colleagues (1995) used quantitative coronary angiography to measure the effects of long-term smoking on the diameter of the coronary artery at study entry, during flow-mediated coronary vasodilation, and after intracoronary administration of nitroglycerin. The study population consisted of patients with or without mild disease of the left anterior descending coronary artery and no other cardiac problems. Flow-mediated vasodilation was markedly blunted in long-term smokers. In a study of smokers with CHD, cigarette smoking increased coronary vascular resistance, an effect that can be blocked by α-adrenergic blockers. This finding indicates that the mechanism of increased coronary artery resistance is at least partly due to stimulation of the sympathetic nervous system by nicotine.

Intracoronary measurements by Doppler ultrasonography demonstrated that cigarette smoking constricts epicardial arteries and increases total coronary vascular resistance. This result indicates that impairment of coronary blood flow by cigarette smoking results from constriction of both epicardial and resistance blood vessels.

In one study, after pretreatment with calcium-channel-blocking agents or nitroglycerin, cigarette smoking increased coronary blood flow in patients with CHD who had manifested no increase after cigarette smoking alone (Winniford et al. 1987). This finding that coronary vasodilator drugs, which block chemically mediated vasoconstriction, permit the usual increase in coronary blood flow in response to increased myocardial work supports the hypothesis that cigarette smoking directly produces coronary vasoconstriction. In another study, chewing 4 mg of nicotine gum by healthy nonsmokers blunted the increase in coronary blood flow that occurs with increased heart rate produced by cardiac pacing (Kaijser and Berglund 1985). This result confirmed that even low doses of nicotine can directly constrict coronary arteries in humans.

Another study found that nicotine worsened myocardial dysfunction in "regionally stunned" ischemic myocardium of anesthetized dogs (Przyklenk 1994). In a placebo-controlled experiment, transient ischemia was induced in dogs by clamping the left anterior descending coronary artery for 15 minutes. Segmental shortening of the myocardium recovered to only 29 percent of the preischemic baseline values in dogs pretreated with nicotine, compared with 54 percent in saline-treated control dogs. The doses of nicotine administered to the animals did not alter heart rate, blood pressure, or blood flow or cause myocyte necrosis.

In patients with vasospastic angina, cigarette smoking is associated with increased occurrence of the condition and a poorer response to medication compared with the response in nonsmokers (Caralis et al. 1992). The researchers observed that cigarette smoking during coronary angiography (cardiac catheterization) produced an acute coronary vasospasm.

Schelbert and colleagues (1979) extensively studied the relationship of coronary vasomotion, endothelial function, and myocardial blood flow to potential reversibility of coronary vasomotor abnormalities. They adopted a noninvasive approach by measuring blood flow with positron emission tomography using ^{13}N ammonia: (1) at rest during testing with cold pressors to probe endothelium-dependent coronary vasomotion and (2) during dipyridamole-induced hyperemia to assess endothelium-independent coronary vasomotion. Using this protocol, Czernin and associates (1995) investigated the effects of short- and long-term smoking on myocardial blood flow and flow reserve in smokers. The investigators sought to determine whether abnormalities in coronary vasomotion in response to cold could be reversed in response to L-arginine infusion (Campisi et al. 1998, 1999). The findings indicated that short-term and long-term smokers had normal coronary vasodilatory capacity. Short-term smoking, however, reduced flow reserve in both short- and long-term smokers. Also, exposure of long-term smokers to cold resulted in abnormal blood flow. The smoking-associated abnormalities in vasomotion were restored by intravenous L-arginine, and this result further implicates the endothelium as the target of toxic substances contained in cigarette smoke. Campisi and colleagues (1999) quantified myocardial blood flow during exposure to cold while L-arginine, the substrate of ENOS, was infused intravenously for 45 minutes at a dose of 30 g as 10 percent arginine hydrochloride. This infusion produced significant improvement in responses of myocardial blood flow to cold. In addition to active smoking, exposure to secondhand smoke for 30 minutes abruptly reduces coronary blood flow velocity in nonsmokers, as assessed by echocardiography (Otsuka et al. 2001).

Summary

Cigarette smoking impairs the vascular endothelial function and activates the sympathetic nervous system. These effects can result in inappropriate reduction in or failure to increase coronary blood flow in response to increases in myocardial demand. Together with long-term atherosclerotic damage from smoking, these effects contribute to ischemic cardiac events. Coronary endothelial dysfunction clearly increases the risk for cardiovascular events. The smoking-induced alterations in vasomotor function appear to be substantially reversible, which underscores the importance of smoking cessation programs and policies to promote a smoke-free environment.

Smoking and the Endothelium

Endothelial Injury or Dysfunction

Endothelial injury and dysfunction are thought to contribute to the initiation of atherogenesis and to have a major role in acute cardiovascular events. Cigarette smoking produces endothelial injury and dysfunction in both peripheral and coronary arteries. Other cardiovascular risk factors such as hypercholesterolemia, diabetes, and hypertension also produce endothelial dysfunction.

The healthy endothelium is a diaphanous film of tissue that invests the luminal surface of all blood and lymphatic vessels. In larger-conduit vessels, the endothelium forms a monolayer between the circulating blood and the vessel wall. The tissue capillaries, which are the smallest conduits for blood and lymphatic flow, are composed exclusively of endothelial cells. Because of the ubiquity of endothelial cells, the surface area of the endothelium in a human weighing 70 kilograms (kg) is 1,000 to 4,000 square meters—equivalent to two to four tennis courts—with a weight of approximately 1 kg (Wolinsky 1980). The endothelium produces a variety of paracrine factors that regulate vascular homeostasis, including proteins, lipids, and small molecules that (1) can relax or activate the underlying vascular smooth muscle, (2) regulate the interaction of the vessel wall with circulating blood elements, and (3) modulate vessel structure (Aird 2005). In healthy persons, the endothelium primarily exerts a vasodilator influence that reduces vascular resistance and maintains blood flow. The endothelium maintains the blood's fluidity by elaborating anticoagulant substances and generally resists adherence of platelets and infiltration of immune cells.

Regeneration of Endothelium

With aging, the normal functioning of the endothelium requires replacement of apoptotic or injured cells. Normally, the turnover of endothelial cells is low, on the order of 0.1 percent of the cells undergoing mitosis at any time (Wright 1972). The rate of endothelial turnover increases, however, in areas of disturbed flow (bends, branches, or bifurcations of blood vessels). The length of chromosome telomeres documents that endothelial aging occurs more rapidly in these areas (Chang and Harley 1995). Furthermore, the accelerated aging in these areas may lead to focal senescence, which is demonstrated by impaired endothelium-dependent vasodilation (McLenachan et al. 1990).

Persons who smoke may have impaired ability to regenerate the endothelium. The endothelial monolayer is regenerated in part from circulating endothelial progenitor cells derived from bone marrow, and the supply of these cells may be a key determinant of endothelial health. The number of circulating endothelial progenitor cells, which is estimated by ex vivo colony counts or by analysis using fluorescence-activated cell sorting, is directly associated with the ability of the endothelium to induce vasodilation (Hibbert et al. 2003; Hill et al. 2003). Smokers have reduced numbers of circulating endothelial progenitor cells and impaired endothelium-dependent vasodilation (Vasa et al. 2001, Hill et al. 2003). In addition, smoking cessation was associated with a rebound in the number of circulating endothelial progenitor cells and improvement in endothelium-dependent vasodilation (Moreno et al. 1998; Kondo et al. 2004).

Endothelial Dysfunctions

A variety of endothelial dysfunctions may contribute to disorders of vessel tone and structure that precede clinical vascular disease. Cardiovascular risk factors such as hypercholesterolemia, hypertension, diabetes, and use of tobacco cause endothelial aberrations long before clinical vascular disease becomes evident. Endothelial dysfunction is the first step in vascular disease, because it leads to vascular inflammation, cell proliferation, and thrombosis, which contribute to progression of vascular disease.

Endothelial generation of adhesion molecules increases in smokers, as evidenced by higher plasma levels of soluble adhesion molecules (Blann et al. 1997, 1998). These molecules include soluble forms of the vascular cell adhesion molecule (sVCAM) and the intercellular adhesion molecule (sICAM). The soluble adhesion molecules, which are shed from the endothelium, reflect the increased endothelial production of these adhesion molecules in the context of vascular inflammation. Endothelial adhesion molecules are required for adherence to blood leukocytes and their infiltration into the vessel wall (Gimbrone 1995). The increased elaboration of adhesion molecules is an endothelial dysfunction that promotes leukocyte infiltration, vascular inflammation, and progression of atherosclerosis. Studies have associated elevated levels of either sVCAM or sICAM with increased risk of cardiovascular events (Blankenberg et al. 2001).

Smoking also impairs the ability of the endothelium to resist thrombosis. Compared with nonsmokers, smokers have higher levels of von Willebrand factor protein (MacCallum 2005) and tissue factor (Matetzky et al. 2000; Sambola et al. 2003), which may be generated by the endothelium. Tissue factor activates the coagulation cascade, and von Willebrand factor protein mediates adherence of platelets to the vessel wall (MacCallum 2005). Furthermore, study findings indicate that smoking impairs capacity to lyse the thrombus that is formed. Plasma levels of tissue plasminogen activator (tPA), a thrombolytic protein produced by the endothelium, are reduced in smokers (Newby et al. 2001). In contrast, smoking increases levels of plasminogen activator inhibitor-1

(PAI-1) (Simpson et al. 1997). By interfering with the function of tPA, PAI-1 reduces thrombolytic capacity (MacCallum 2005). Imbalance in thrombolytic capacity attributable to higher PAI-1 values or reduction in tPA levels is associated with occurrence of adverse cardiovascular events.

The healthy endothelium elaborates vasodilator substances such as nitric oxide (NO), prostacyclin, atrial natriuretic peptide, endothelium-derived hyperpolarizing factor, and adrenomedullin (Chen and Burnett 1998; Busse and Fleming 2003; Brain and Grant 2004). In doing so, the healthy endothelium increases the diameter of the blood vessels and reduces resistance to blood flow. When the endothelium becomes diseased, synthesis and bioactivity of the vasodilators are reduced, and the balance tips in favor of endothelium-derived vasoconstrictors such as endothelin and thromboxane (Vanhoutte et al. 2005). This derangement in endothelial function has clinical consequences. Because vasodilator function is impaired, coronary vascular resistance increases, and ischemia can result. Furthermore, endothelial vasodilator dysfunction in the coronary arteries of humans is associated with reversible myocardial perfusion defects, which are associated with other vascular abnormalities (Hasdai et al. 1997b). These abnormalities include expression of adhesion molecules, adherence and infiltration of leukocytes, and proliferation of smooth muscle cells.

Most of the endothelium-derived vasodilators also oppose key processes involved in atherogenesis (cell adhesion, proliferation, and inflammation) (Cooke and Dzau 1997a,b). Thus, by reducing the generation or bioactivity of endothelial vasodilators, exposure to tobacco can accelerate atherosclerosis. This mechanistic explanation for tobacco-related CVD is supported by the finding that dysfunction of endothelial vasodilators is an independent predictor of vascular events (Schächinger et al. 2000; Suwaidi et al. 2000; Gokce et al. 2003). The role of these mechanisms involving NO is vascular protection, which is impaired by exposure to tobacco.

Nitric Oxide and Vascular Homeostasis

NO induces vasodilation by stimulating soluble guanylate cyclase to produce cyclic guanosine monophosphate (Ignarro et al. 1984). NO, which has a short half-life, avidly interacts with sulfhydryl-containing proteins, heme proteins, and oxygen-derived free radicals. By virtue of its ability to nitrosylate proteins, NO may change their activity or behavior (Hess et al. 2005). The significant increase in vascular resistance induced in animals and humans exposed to pharmacologic antagonists of ENOS reflects the physiological importance of this endothelium-derived vasodilator (Rees et al. 1989; Vallance et al. 1989).

Endothelium-derived NO also inhibits adherence of platelets and leukocytes to the vessel wall (Kubes et al. 1991; Tsao et al. 1994). This effect is mediated partly by activation of cyclic guanosine monophosphate and phosphorylation of intracellular signaling proteins such as vasodilator-stimulated phosphoprotein (Smolenski et al. 1998). In addition, NO suppresses expression of adhesion molecules and chemokines that regulate endothelial interactions with circulating blood elements (Tsao et al. 1996, 1997). These observations suggest that NO is an endogenous antiatherogenic molecule. Impairment of *ENOS* contributes to the pathologic alterations in vascular reactivity and structure observed in atherosclerosis (Cooke and Dzau 1997a,b). The pharmacologic inhibition or genetic deficiency of *ENOS* inhibits endothelium-dependent vasodilation, impairs blood flow in tissues, and raises blood pressure (Huang et al. 1995; Kielstein et al. 2004). Furthermore, NO deficiency promotes adherence to and intimal accumulation of mononuclear cells and accelerates formation of lesions in animal models of atherosclerosis (Kuhlencordt et al. 2001). In contrast, enhancing production of NO in the vessel wall slows or even reverses atherogenesis and restenosis (Cooke et al. 1992; von der Leyen et al. 1995; Candipan et al. 1996). NO is a survival factor for endothelial cells, and it induces apoptosis of macrophages and proliferation of vascular smooth muscle cells (Wang et al. 1999).

Certain polymorphisms of the *ENOS* gene predict development of CHD (Ichihara et al. 1998; Tsukada et al. 1998; Yoshimura et al. 1998). The *ENOS* gene *GLU298ASP* polymorphism is more prevalent in patients with variant angina, essential hypertension, and acute MI (Hibi et al. 1998; Miyamoto et al. 1998; Shimasaki et al. 1998; Yoshimura et al. 1998). Intriguingly, this polymorphism is associated with greater sensitivity to the effects of smoking on endothelial vasodilator function. Young men who are carriers of the *ENOS* *ASP298* allele have increased susceptibility to smoking-associated reduction in endothelial function (Leeson et al. 2002). Similarly, a quadruple repeat of a sequence of 27 base pairs in *intron 4 of the *ENOS* gene (allele *a) is associated with increased risk of CHD and acute MI (Ichihara et al. 1998). Smokers who are homozygous for the *ENOS* allele *a are at risk for more severe CHD than are those who are not homozygous (Wang et al. 1996).

Endothelium-Dependent Vasodilation

The effect of exposure to tobacco on endothelium-dependent vasodilation in humans was assessed by observing its effect on flow-mediated vasodilation. As blood flow through a vessel is increased, the vessel relaxes. In animal models, this flow-mediated vasodilation was abolished by removing the endothelium (Pohl et al. 1986). When a pharmacologic antagonist of ENOS was used, flow-mediated vasodilation in the rabbit iliac artery depended on the endothelial release of NO (Cooke et al. 1991). Celermajer and colleagues (1992) used duplex ultrasonography to record flow-mediated vasodilation of the brachial artery in response to hyperemic vasodilation of the forearm. The investigators induced vasodilation by using a blood pressure cuff inflated to suprasystolic pressures to transiently occlude blood flow in the forearm. Joannides and colleagues (1995) extended this finding by showing that flow-mediated vasodilation of the brachial artery could be abolished by pharmacologic antagonism of ENOS. Subsequently, numerous studies used this approach to document impairment of flow-mediated, endothelium-dependent vasodilation in smokers and in persons exposed to secondhand smoke (Celermajer et al. 1993, 1996; Barua et al. 2001). Researchers also observed that tobacco use impaired endothelium-dependent vasodilation in the coronary microcirculation. Intracoronary infusion of acetylcholine induced vasodilation that was partly attributable to release of NO, and this response was blunted in persons who smoked (Kugiyama et al. 1996).

Impairment of Endothelium-Dependent Vasodilation

Many factors contribute to the ability of tobacco to impair endothelial function. Tobacco use adversely affects the ENOS pathway. Exposure of cultured endothelial cells derived from human coronary arteries or umbilical veins to sera from smokers reduced expression and activity of ENOS (Barua et al. 2001, 2003). The researchers attributed this effect partly to the oxygen-derived free radicals in tobacco smoke. In addition, the half-life of NO was markedly shortened by oxidative stress (Rubanyi and Vanhoutte 1986).

Superoxide anion reacts avidly with NO to form a peroxynitrite ($ONOO^-$) anion, which itself is a highly reactive free radical (Beckman and Koppenol 1996). Other sources of free radicals that may inactivate NO and impair endothelial vasodilator function include activated leukocytes, xanthine oxidase, the mitochondrial electron-transport chain, and uncoupling of ENOS itself (Heitzer et al. 2000; Barua et al. 2003; Kayyali et al. 2003; Sydow and Münzel 2003; Guthikonda et al. 2003). Investigators postulated that this uncoupling occurs when amounts of the NOS cofactor tetrahydrobiopterin or the NO precursor L-arginine are insufficient. These conditions involve transfer of electrons from ENOS to oxygen and thus formation of a superoxide anion.

Oxidative stress also impairs the NOS pathway by increasing accumulation of asymmetric dimethylarginine (ADMA), an endogenous competitive inhibitor of ENOS produced by all cells during degradation of methylated nuclear proteins (Vallance et al. 1992; Tran et al. 2003). Most of the ADMA produced is degraded by the enzyme dimethylarginine dimethylaminohydrolase. Oxidative stress impairs the activity of this enzyme and leads to accumulation of ADMA and suppression of ENOS (Cooke 2004).

Blood levels of antioxidant vitamins are lower than normal in smokers, reflecting endogenous consumption of these vitamins in response to ongoing oxidant stress (Lykkesfeldt et al. 2000). Administration of vitamin C reverses the impairment of endothelium-mediated vasodilation in smokers, a finding consistent with an oxidant mechanism of endothelial dysfunction (Heitzer et al. 1996).

Nicotine itself may injure endothelial cells. Studies showed that in levels similar to those found in the blood of cigarette smokers, nicotine altered structural and functional characteristics of cultured vascular smooth muscle and endothelial cells (Csonka et al. 1985; Thyberg 1986). In one study, oral nicotine administered to rats to achieve blood levels comparable to those in human smokers produced myointimal thickening of the aorta after an experimental injury (denudation of the endothelium with a balloon catheter) (Krupski et al. 1987). The excessive myointimal thickening in nicotine-treated animals is consistent with persistent injury to endothelial cells. Studies reported increased numbers of circulating endothelial cells in the venous blood, reflecting endothelial injury, and decreased platelet aggregate ratios, reflecting platelet aggregation in persons who had never smoked but who, for experimental purposes, smoked cigarettes containing tobacco (Davis et al. 1985). These results were not observed in nonsmokers who smoked cigarettes that did not contain tobacco. These findings further support a role for nicotine in injury to endothelial cells.

Nicotine may influence endothelial function in other ways. In studies of cultured endothelial cells, nicotine enhanced release of the basic fibroblast growth factor

and inhibited production of transforming growth factor β_1 (Villablanca 1998; Cucina et al. 1999). Nicotine also increased DNA synthesis, mitogenic activity, and endothelial proliferation. Nicotine has been shown to induce endothelial dysfunction (Chalon et al. 2000; Sarabi and Lind 2000; Neunteufl et al. 2002).

Pathologic Angiogenesis

Another endothelial function influenced by exposure to tobacco is development of new blood vessels (angiogenesis). Angiogenesis requires activation of endothelial cells by an angiogenic cytokine, followed by endothelial cell proliferation and migration and the formation of tubes. Exposure to secondhand smoke promotes tumor angiogenesis and growth (Zhu et al. 2003). Human lung cancer cells implanted in a subcutaneous or orthotopic location grew more rapidly in mice when they were exposed to secondhand tobacco smoke. Furthermore, these mice had higher plasma levels of vascular endothelial growth factor, and capillary density in their tumor nodules was greater than that in control mice. Mecamylamine, an antagonist of the nicotinic acetylcholine receptor (nAChR), abolished the effects of exposure to secondhand smoke. These observations indicate that secondhand smoke increases tumor angiogenesis and growth, at least partly through a nicotine-mediated mechanism.

Researchers observed the effect of nicotine in promoting pathologic angiogenesis in numerous murine models of tobacco-related diseases, including lung cancer, atherosclerosis, and retinopathy (Heeschen et al. 2001, 2002; Natori et al. 2003; Shin et al. 2004; Suñer et al. 2004). Tumor angiogenesis was required for tumor growth, and correspondingly, promotion of tumor angiogenesis accelerated tumor growth (Folkman 2003). Conversely, antiangiogenic agents inhibit progression of cancer and are now approved as treatment for some advanced human malignant diseases (Jain 2005). The effect of nicotine on promotion of tumor angiogenesis may be attributable to a direct effect on endothelial cells. In clinically relevant levels, nicotine promoted endotheliaprocesses that may be involved in tumor angiogenesis. At these doses, nicotine promoted survival, proliferation, and migration of endothelial cells (Heeschen et al. 2001, 2002). Nicotine also induced elaboration and release of angiogenic factors, including NO, prostacyclin, vascular endothelial growth factor, and fibroblast growth factor (Carty et al. 1996; Heeschen et al. 2001a; Lane et al. 2005). These effects of nicotine were mediated by nAChRs on the endothelium (Heeschen et al. 2002). Conversely, pharmacologic inhibition or genetic deficiency of endothelial nAChRs reduced angiogenic response to nicotine. A variety of human lung cancer cells synthesized acetylcholine or expressed nAChRs. Nicotine increased growth of these cells in vitro, but this effect was inhibited by antagonists of the nAChRs (Schuller 2002).

The importance of pathologic angiogenesis in growth of tumors is well known. Less widely recognized, however, is the role of neovascularization in progression of atherosclerotic plaque. Large atherosclerotic plaques in human coronary arteries are well vascularized by microvessels originating from the vasa vasorum (Barger et al. 1984). In mice with hypercholesterolemia, growth of atheroma can be inhibited by antiangiogenic agents, and in the same murine models, nicotine promoted neovascularization of plaque and its progression in the aorta (Heeschen et al. 2001; Moulton et al. 2003). The effect of nicotine in increasing neovascularization and progression of plaque may partially explain increased risk of atherosclerotic disease in persons who smoke.

Similarly, in a model of age-related macular degeneration in mice, nicotine stimulated retinal neovascularization (Suñer et al. 2004). This effect was antagonized by hexamethonium, another antagonist of nAChRs. In a clinical study, the most virulent form of age-related maculopathy is associated with retinal neovascularization that contributes to visual deterioration, and tobacco smokers are at greater risk of age-related macular degeneration than are nonsmokers (Christen et al. 1996; Seddon et al. 1996). Thus, a variety of tobacco-related diseases are characterized by pathologic neovascularization, an effect that may be promoted by nicotine.

Notwithstanding nicotine's effect as a promoter of neovascularization, long-term exposure to tobacco may impair therapeutic angiogenesis. In a murine model of hindlimb ischemia, short-term exposure to nicotine paradoxically increased capillary density and improved regional blood flow in the ischemic hindlimb (Heeschen et al. 2001, 2003). However, long-term exposure to nicotine for 16 weeks (about one-third of the life span of a mouse)

before induction of ischemia obliterated angiogenic response to nicotine (Konishi et al. 2010).

The relevance of animal models for research on nicotine and angiogenesis to human smokers is not clear. It is important to differentiate studies that show effects of pure nicotine from those in which the exposure is to tobacco smoke. In mice, effects of nicotine on angiogenesis depended on release of NO, but the net effect of smoking in humans seems to be impaired release of NO. Also, most studies on angiogenesis involve short-term administration of nicotine, although tolerance to the effects of nicotine may develop with long-term use.

Inhibition of ACE normalized impaired bradykinin-mediated, endothelium-dependent venodilation in smokers (Chalon et al. 1999). Furthermore, coronary vasomotor responses to acetylcholine in patients with CHD improved in response to the ACE inhibitor quinapril to a much greater extent in smokers than in nonsmokers (Schlaifer et al. 1999). ACE inhibitors have an antioxidant activity, which could contribute to the clinical benefit in smokers.

Summary

The endothelium, a delicate monolayer of cells that invests all blood vessels, is a major regulator of vascular reactivity and structure. Healthy endothelium maintains vascular homeostasis by promoting fluidity of the blood, vasodilation, and relaxation of the underlying vascular smooth muscle. Endothelial dysfunction regularly accompanies and promotes vascular disease. Endothelial vasodilator dysfunction is an independent risk factor for major adverse cardiovascular events and mortality. Active smoking and involuntary exposure to cigarette smoke injure endothelial cells and impair endothelial vasodilation. Thus, each type of exposure to tobacco or tobacco smoke contributes to the development of CVD.

Thrombogenic Effects

This section on thrombogenic effects reviews the state of knowledge of mechanisms by which smoking or secondhand smoke exposure may predispose a person to thrombosis, a pathologic reaction that commonly results in smoking-related MI or stroke. Smoking-mediated thrombosis appears to be a major factor in the pathogenesis of acute cardiovascular events.

Epidemiologic evidence indicates that cigarette smoking increases risk of acute MI and sudden death more than it increases risk of angina pectoris. Researchers hypothesize that risk of acute MI and sudden death is mediated by thrombosis, whereas angina is mediated primarily by hemodynamic factors. Successful revascularization in patients with MI after treatment with thrombolysis is more likely in smokers than in non-smokers (Bowers et al. 1996). At the time of MI, smokers are younger and have fewer cardiac risk factors and less severe underlying coronary disease than do nonsmokers (Metz and Waters 2003). Enhanced thrombosis superimposed on less severely stenotic arteries best explains these observations. In men who died suddenly, a history of cigarette smoking was significantly more likely when pathologic examination showed acute thrombosis (75 percent of cases) than when the finding was plaque with no thrombosis (41 percent) (Burke et al. 1997). Conversely, stable plaque with no thrombosis was the more common finding in nonsmokers.

Thrombosis occurs when fibrinogen is converted to fibrin, a process involving interaction of platelets, blood-borne proteins, endothelial cells, and subendothelial vascular tissue. An endogenous antithrombotic mechanism involves these same components. Imbalance in these pathways results in predisposition to thrombosis. Virchow's triad, first described in 1856 and modified by Aschoff in 1924, provides a framework for risk factors for thrombosis that is still valid. These authorities described the cardinal risk factors as "alterations in blood coagulation," "alterations in blood flow," and "alterations in the blood vessel wall."

Alterations in Blood

Blood contains platelets, red blood cells, and leukocytes suspended in plasma. Plasma in turn contains a variety of coagulation proteins and lipids that also contribute to the clotting process. Smokers tend to develop MI at a lower burden of atheroma than do nonsmokers. This finding suggests a greater role for formed elements of blood or for cardiac electrical instability in cardiovascular events in smokers.

Platelets

Platelets, although only a minor component of the solid phase of blood, are critical to the coagulation process and are important mediators of the impact of smoking on cardiovascular outcomes (Figure 6.6).

Turnover and Activation

Studies have reported that sudden cardiac death is 2.5 times higher in smokers than in nonsmokers (Kannel et al. 1984; Goldenberg et al. 2003). Research findings broadly implicated activation of platelets and subsequent focal ischemia in sudden cardiac death among smokers. The turnover of platelets is accelerated in cigarette smokers (Fuster et al. 1981). Researchers related the

number of newly formed reticulated platelets, rather than absolute platelet count, to incidence of thrombotic events (Rinder et al. 1998).

Urinary excretion of thromboxane metabolites (TxMs), such as 2,3-dinor thromboxane B_2 (TxB$_2$) and 11-dehydro TxB$_2$, which are markers of platelet activation in vivo, increases in smokers in a dose-dependent manner (Murray et al. 1985). Studies demonstrated increases in levels of urinary TxM among smokers who were monozygotic twins but divergent for smoking behaviors (Lassila et al. 1988). These increases were also observed in young Swedish army recruits who smoked but had no apparent vascular disease (Wennmalm et al. 1991). Studies also showed that mainstream and sidestream smoke directly promoted platelet activation and enhanced activation induced by shear stress (Rubenstein et al. 2004).

Elevated levels of TxM observed in persons who smoke decreased substantially within days of smoking cessation, although they did not reach the levels found in nonsmokers (Rangemark et al. 1993; Saareks et al. 2001). In an ex vivo study, platelets from smokers showed greater aggregation than those from nonsmokers (Takajo et al. 2001). A decline in platelet aggregation during 14 days of abstinence from smoking was reversed rapidly after smoking was resumed (Morita et al. 2005). Ex vivo aggregability, however, is a crude index of in vivo platelet activation and aggregation. Some studies reported diminished ex vivo aggregability in smokers. This finding suggests that partial activation in vivo resulted in the harvest of a less responsive subset of platelets for study ex vivo. Increased levels of urinary TxMs in smokers may be attributable to activation of both platelets and macrophages. Low-dose aspirin, which inhibits COX activity in platelets, substantially depressed the increment of TxM in smokers, leading investigators to hypothesize that TxM was principally derived from the activity of platelet COX-1 rather than macrophage COX-2 (Nowak et al. 1987; McAdam et al. 2005).

Generation of Nitric Oxide

Platelets constitutively express ENOS. Although platelet-derived NO is a modest inhibitor of platelet activation in vitro, it may be critical to inhibit recruitment of platelets to a growing thrombus (Freedman et al. 1997). Aggregating platelets obtained from patients with acute coronary syndromes produced less NO than did those from patients with stable angina (Freedman et al. 1998). Such findings must be interpreted with caution, however, because results reflect in vivo platelet activity (see "Turnover and Activation" earlier in this chapter). In one study, levels of platelet-derived NO were lower in smokers than in nonsmokers (Takajo et al. 2001). This

Figure 6.6   Potential sites of actions and mechanisms of effects of smoking on platelets

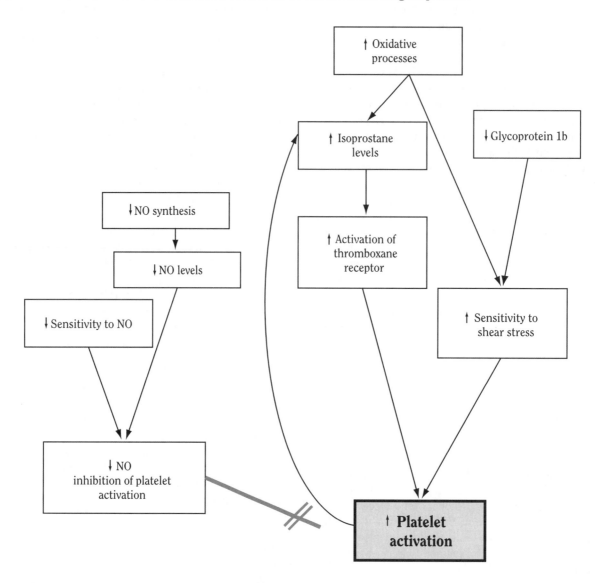

Note: Smoking decreases NO-mediated inhibition of platelet activation and increases platelet activation through oxidative stress and other mechanisms. **NO** = nitric oxide.

finding was associated with lower levels of intraplatelet-reduced glutathione—a marker of oxidative stress and increased platelet aggregation. In another study, both the platelet-derived release of NO and the glutathione levels recovered in a time-dependent manner after smoking cessation, but they rapidly decreased again when smoking was resumed (Morita et al. 2005). Abstinence from smoking was also associated with decreased agonist-induced platelet aggregation ex vivo. Furthermore, levels of intraplatelet nitrotyrosine and urinary 8-hydroxy-2′-deoxyguanosine, which are markers of oxidative stress, were also depressed after smoking cessation. One study showed that supplementation with vitamin C restored NO levels and platelet aggregation in current smokers to levels observed in non-smokers (Takajo et al. 2001). Another study demonstrated that the normal morning increase in platelet sensitivity to NO ex vivo was lost in smokers, leaving platelets potentially more susceptible to activation during early morning hours, when MIs are most common (Sawada et al. 2002). In yet another study, platelets from smokers were less sensitive to administration of nitroglycerin, a documented NO donor (Haramaki et al. 2001).

Oxidative Stress and Platelet Function

Cigarette smoke has been shown to be an abundant source of free radicals (Church and Pryor 1985). Levels of isoprostanes—quantitative indices of in vivo oxidative stress—are higher in smokers than in nonsmokers (Reilly et al. 1996; Chehne et al. 2001; Dietrich et al. 2002), and they decrease with smoking cessation (Reilly et al. 1996; Praticò et al. 1997). In addition to serving as biomarkers of oxidative stress, isoprostanes may serve as secondary messengers that exert biologic effects, at least in vitro.

Studies demonstrated elevated production of isoprostanes and decreased levels of reduced glutathione in the platelets of smokers (Takajo et al. 2001). Intraplatelet levels of nitrotyrosine, which is a marker of modification of proteins induced by oxidative stress, decreased with smoking abstinence but increased rapidly when smoking was resumed, together with return of increased sensitivity to agonist-induced platelet aggregation ex vivo (Morita et al. 2005). In another study, products from activated platelets induced oxidative stress in vascular smooth muscle cells, which is associated with increased expression of tissue factor, a highly thrombogenic protein (Görlach et al. 2000). Other investigators showed that administration of antioxidants to persons with diabetes, just as to smokers, decreased production of isoprostane and urinary TxM (Davì et al. 1999) and decreased platelet aggregation ex vivo (Salonen et al. 1991).

Isoprostanes and Platelet Function

In one study, platelets oxidized ex vivo demonstrated increased aggregation induced by shear stress, an effect that is only partly inhibited by administration of aspirin (Chung et al. 2002). In another study, oxidation of platelet membranes was associated with reduced expression of glycoprotein Ib, a receptor for the von Willebrand factor that is critical to platelet activation and aggregation under conditions of shear stress (Escolar and White 2000). The researchers postulated that decreased expression of glycoprotein Ib indicates a highly reactive status of platelets.

Some evidence indicates that isoprostanes may act as platelet and vascular agonists through ligation of the thromboxane A_2 receptor (TP) (Audoly et al. 2000). To date, no molecular evidence exists for a distinct isoprostane receptor (Praticò et al. 1996). One study reported that infusion of isoprostanes elevated blood pressure and activated platelets—effects that are lost in mice lacking TP. Binding of isoprostane $iPF_{2\alpha}$-III to TP promoted change in platelet shape and facilitated response to other proaggregatory stimuli (Praticò et al. 1996). In another study,

however, isoprostane alone did not induce platelet activation and partially blocked the proaggregatory effects of TP agonists and high-dose collagen (Cranshaw et al. 2001). Also, isoprostane $iPF_{2\alpha}$-III was reported to decrease the antiplatelet activity of NO (Minuz et al. 1998). Some researchers speculated that this isoprostane has a role in the resistance to low-dose aspirin observed in patients with CVD (Csiszar et al. 2002). It is not known, however, how these effects, which are demonstrable in vitro, relate to endogenous levels of isoprostanes attained locally in vivo under conditions of oxidative stress.

Summary

Thus, platelets from smokers demonstrate a dose-dependent increase in activity and adhesiveness that rapidly decreases with smoking abstinence. Findings suggest that the inhibitory NO pathway is impaired and responsiveness to other agonists is increased at least partially through the mediation of TP.

Red Blood Cells

Hematocrit in Adults

Smoking is associated with an increase in hematocrit or red blood cell mass attributable to increased levels of CO and carboxyhemoglobin. Hematocrit decreases with smoking cessation, but increased blood viscosity and deformability of red blood cells may persist (Haustein et al. 2004). Increases in hematocrit and blood viscosity are associated with increasing risk of CVD. It is unclear, however, whether these risk factors are independent of smoking and other conventional risk factors, particularly in women (Lowe et al. 1997; Irace et al. 2003; Woodward et al. 2003). When data are adjusted for smoking, hypertension, and high cholesterol, viscosity remains a significant risk factor for stroke and for PAD but not for ischemic heart disease. This finding suggests that the effect of high viscosity may be an independent risk factor for stroke or PAD (Lee et al. 1996; Lowe et al. 1997).

Hematocrit in Neonates

Researchers showed that the effects of smoking on hematocrit were transmitted to the fetus during pregnancy. Some studies reported a dose-dependent increase in hemoglobin levels in infants of mothers who smoked (al-Alawi and Jenkins 2000; Habek et al. 2002). Furthermore, infants born to mothers who smoked more than 20 cigarettes per day had higher rates of fetal hypoxia, polycythemia, and neurological complications than did infants of nonsmoking mothers.

Leukocytes

Polymorphonuclear Leukocytes

In one study, persons who smoked had higher numbers of circulating polymorphonuclear leukocytes than did nonsmokers (Sela et al. 2002). In other research, neutrophils from smokers had higher levels of myeloperoxidase (Bridges et al. 1985) and increased expression of integrins CD11b, CD15, and CD63, which are markers of leukocyte activation (Gustafsson et al. 2000). Furthermore, when stimulated, these leukocytes released superoxide at a faster rate than did leukocytes from nonsmokers (Sela et al. 2002), which further increased local oxidative stress. Studies documented a greater variety of circulating cellular adhesion molecules, including ICAM-1, VCAM, P-selectin, and E-selectin, in smokers than in nonsmokers (Mazzone et al. 2001; Bermudez et al. 2002). An increase in these cellular adhesion molecules (monocytes) may facilitate recruitment of inflammatory cells to sites of vascular injury (Figure 6.7).

Monocytes

Monocytes from smokers demonstrated increased expression of the integrins CD11b and CD18, which augment adhesiveness of monocytes to endothelial cells, at least in vitro (Weber et al. 1996). This process is thought to be mediated by activation of protein kinase C (Kalra et al. 1994) and is attenuated by supplementation with vitamin C (Weber et al. 1996). In one study, isoprostane iPF$_{2\alpha}$-III inhibited adhesion of monocytes to cultured dermal cells or renal endothelial cells in rats but paradoxically increased adhesion of monocytes to human endothelial cells in the umbilical vein (Leitinger et al. 2001; Kumar et al. 2005). Adhesion of monocytes to endothelial cells may increase their access into the subendothelium, where they differentiate into macrophages and promote atherogenesis (Ross 1999). Differentiation of monocytes into macrophages depends on production of intracellular reactive oxygen species induced by nicotinamide adenine dinucleotide phosphate, but no evidence exists for a role of cigarette smoking in this differentiation (Barbieri et al. 2003).

Summary

In summary, smoking induced changes in the numbers and activity of polymorphonuclear leukocytes and monocytes. In addition, it promoted expression of chemoattractant and adhesion molecules and integrins, which would be expected to increase recruitment of activated leukocytes to areas of oxidative stress, including sites of platelet deposition after vascular injury.

Circulating Proteins

In addition to its effects on the cellular elements of blood, smoking alters the proteins involved in the coagulation pathway by changing procoagulant factors in

Figure 6.7   Potential sites of effects of smoking on thrombosis through oxidative stress and other mechanisms

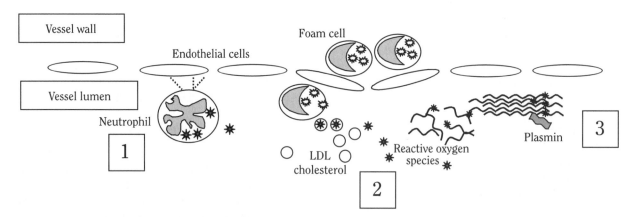

Note: 1. Increased numbers and activation of polymorphonuclear leukocytes; increased production of superoxide radicals; and increased expression of integrins and adhesion molecules on leukocytes and endothelial cells. 2. Increased oxidation of LDL cholesterol; oxidized LDL cholesterol taken up more easily into macrophages to produce foam cells; and increased adhesiveness of monocytes to endothelial cells. 3. Increased levels of fibrinogen; increased nitration of tyrosine residues on fibrinogen, rendering it more thrombogenic; impaired activity of plasmin; and decreased thrombolysis. **LDL** = low-density lipoprotein.

the circulation and anticoagulation factors derived from the endothelium.

Fibrinogen

Study findings indicate that circulating levels of fibrinogen increase in smokers and decrease with smoking cessation (Thomas et al. 1995; Hunter et al. 2001; Tuut and Hense 2001). Also, research suggests that elevated fibrinogen values are an independent risk factor for CHD (Paramo et al. 2004) and deep-vein thrombosis (Vayá et al. 2002). For CVD, the predictive effect was reportedly similar and additive to traditional cardiovascular risk factors (Woodward et al. 1998). The effect of fibrinogen on CVD is partly attributable to smoking and seems to be mediated through alterations in rates of synthesis by the liver. Use of snuff is not associated with increased fibrinogen levels (Eliasson et al. 1995).

Nitration of tyrosine residues, a marker of NO-dependent damage, is increased in smokers (Petruzzelli et al. 1997). Presence of these residues depends strictly on availability of nitrogen dioxide radicals that are in turn derived from ONOO$^-$ (Kirsch et al. 2002). Tyrosine nitration modifies a variety of proteins, including fibrinogen (Petruzzelli et al. 1997; Pignatelli et al. 2001). Nitrogenated fibrinogen is more reactive and thrombogenic than is native fibrinogen (Gole et al. 2000), a fact that seems attributable to accelerated formation of clots without modification in plasmin-induced thrombolysis (Vadseth et al. 2004). The antioxidants glutathione and vitamin C protect against formation of nitrogenated fibrinogen by interfering with interaction of nitrate radicals with tyrosine (Kirsch and de Groot 2000; Kirsch et al. 2001). ONOO$^-$ is likely to derive from interaction of NO from cigarette smoke with superoxide radicals from pulmonary macrophages (Deliconstantinos et al. 1994). In studies of both animal models and human volunteers, even brief exposure to tobacco smoke induced prolonged production (>30 minutes) of ONOO$^-$, apparently from pulmonary macrophages (Deliconstantinos et al. 1994).

Plasmin

Circulating plasminogen is activated to plasmin by fibrin, thrombin, and tPA. Plasminogen has fibrinolytic and collagenase activities. In vitro studies showed that levels of ONOO$^-$ increased in smokers and that ONOO$^-$ induced nitration of plasminogen in a concentration-dependent manner and reduced proteolytic activity of plasmin (Nowak et al. 2004). This effect is partially reduced by glutathione.

C-Reactive Protein

Chronic, low-level inflammation—reflected by elevated levels of C-reactive protein (CRP) and other biomarkers—is an important risk factor for atherosclerosis (Koenig et al. 1999). Investigators reported that levels of CRP, which likely contributes to both oxidative stress and mitogenic and fibrogenic characteristics of atherosclerotic plaque, are higher in smokers than in nonsmokers in a dose-dependent manner (Bakhru and Erlinger 2005). This increase persisted even after adjustment for diabetes, lipid profile, and CVD, as well as age, gender, and race. More important, five years after smoking cessation, CRP levels were decreased to levels similar to those in lifetime nonsmokers. This finding suggests vascular healing. The timeframe is consistent with that observed in the multinational monitoring of trends and determinants of CVD (MONICA) (Dobson et al. 1991) and in the Northwick Park Heart studies (Meade et al. 1987). In those studies, cardiovascular risk was reduced at two to five years after a person stopped smoking.

Oxidized Low-Density Lipoprotein Cholesterol

In vitro research on oxidative modification of LDL cholesterol (LDLc) by extracts from cigarette smoke showed a significant increase in atherogenicity (Chisolm and Steinberg 2000). In one study, LDL isolated after participants smoked six or seven cigarettes was more susceptible to ex vivo oxidation than was LDL isolated after 24 hours of abstinence from smoking (Harats et al. 1989). In another study, oxidizability of LDL ex vivo decreased with smoking cessation (Sasaki et al. 1997). Oxidized LDLc, but not native LDL, interacted with scavenger receptors on lipid-laden lung cells (foam cells) and was readily incorporated into atherosclerotic plaque. Findings in other studies suggest that oxidized LDL prompts migration and degranulation of neutrophils (Sedgwick et al. 2003) and increases expression of the Toll-like receptor, a transmembrane protein in macrophages, thus promoting their activation (Xu et al. 2001).

Clinical studies produced conflicting data on the ability of cigarette smoke to oxidize LDLc and on the role of cigarette smoke in the process in vivo. Findings in several studies (Scheffler et al. 1992; Mahfouz et al. 1995; Kagota et al. 1996; Gouaze et al. 1998; Yamaguchi et al. 2005), but not all studies (Princen et al. 1992; Siekmeier et al. 1996; Marangon et al. 1997; van den Berkmortel et al. 2000), suggest that smoking increases oxidation of LDLc. Studies of an animal model suggest a similar oxidative effect (Yamaguchi et al. 2002, 2004). In one study, modification of LDLc by cigarette smoke was diminished in a dose-dependent manner by administration of fluvastatin (Yamaguchi et al. 2002; Franzoni et al. 2003). Fluvastatin is a potent scavenger of the peroxyl radical. A similar clinical study showed no decrease in oxidized LDL with administration of atorvastatin, despite improvement in endothelial function (Beckman et al. 2004). It is unclear whether failure to demonstrate an association between improved endothelial function and oxidative stress in the study of atorvastatin reflects a true independence of these effects, a distinction from fluvastatin, or limitations attributable to the small sample size.

Thus, cigarette smoking may induce changes in both coagulation and fibrinolytic pathways to promote a prothrombotic state. In addition to its effects on inflammatory cells, smoking promotes production of inflammatory markers and acute-phase reactants.

Alterations in Blood Vessels

Nitric Oxide

Cigarette smoking has injurious effects on the vascular endothelium (see "Smoking and the Endothelium" earlier in this chapter). Abnormalities in the release of chemical mediators occur as a consequence of endothelial dysfunction and are likely to contribute to the prothrombotic condition of smokers. Examples include decreases in NO-mediated inhibition of interactions between platelets and the blood vessel wall, in platelet-induced NO, and in inhibition of platelet activation (see "Platelets" earlier in this chapter). Blood vessel tone is more sensitive to low NO levels than is platelet function (Loscalzo 2001). The importance of NO deficiency mediated by oxidative stress in thrombosis is suggested by familial childhood stroke resulting from deficiency in glutathione peroxidase. This condition decreases NO levels in association with both increased expression of P-selectin in platelets and platelet aggregation and activation (Kenet et al. 1999).

Prostacyclin Production

In vitro studies showed impaired production of prostacyclin by vascular cells exposed to cigarette smoke extracts. In vivo studies, however, showed increased biosynthesis of prostacyclin that is presumed to be reactive to accelerated interactions of platelets and neutrophils with vessel walls in smokers (Murray et al. 1990; Lassila and Laustiola 1992). Consistent with this concept, levels of markers of platelet and leukocyte activation were greater in smokers than in nonsmokers. Thus, the augmented

biosynthesis of prostacyclin is likely to reflect a compensatory reaction by the vascular endothelium.

von Willebrand Factor

Studies reported higher circulating levels of von Willebrand factor in smokers than in nonsmokers (Blann and McCollum 1993; Smith et al. 1993), and findings indicated that these levels may precede clinically overt atherosclerosis (Prisco et al. 1999). The von Willebrand factor is essential for initial adhesion of activated platelets to the vessel wall and for expansion of thrombi. It is unclear to what degree high levels of von Willebrand factor might contribute to the increased thrombosis and atherogenesis observed in smokers.

Tissue Factor

Tissue factor is a prothrombotic protein made by numerous cells in the blood vessel wall, predominantly macrophages but also vascular smooth muscle and endothelial cells. Tissue factor is released when the endothelium is injured and can start the clotting cascade. Studies assessing the effects of smoking on tissue factor yielded mixed results (Barua et al. 2002; Sambola et al. 2003). The immunoreactivity of tissue factor was higher in specimens of plaque obtained during endarterectomy from smokers than in those from nonsmokers (Matetzky et al. 2000). In mice with APO E deficiency that were fed high-cholesterol diets, exposure to cigarette smoke resulted in higher levels of tissue factor and VCAM-1 and higher macrophage counts in atherosclerotic plaques than in those of unexposed mice (Lykkesfeldt et al. 2000). Aspirin treatment of cigarette smokers and of mice exposed to smoke was associated with lower levels of tissue factor in plaque. This finding indicates that aspirin may have a protective role for smokers.

Tissue Plasminogen Activator

Vascular endothelial cells and other tissues secrete tPA. This protein has a central role in fibrinolysis, which limits expansion of clots during thrombosis and eventually dissolves the clot during thrombolysis. Evidence from the Physicians' Health Study indicates that high levels of tPA are an independent risk factor for stroke and suggests that activation of the endogenous fibrinolytic system occurs years before arterial vessels become occluded (Ridker et al. 1994). PAI-1, which is also secreted by vascular endothelial cells, opposes the actions of tPA.

Data on the effects of smoking on tPA and PAI-1 are conflicting (Blann et al. 2000; Enderle et al. 2000; Matetzky et al. 2000; Newby et al. 2001). Using an in vitro model, researchers showed that serum from smokers impaired tPA production by human umbilical vein endothelial cells but that PAI-1 production was unchanged (Barua et al. 2002). In an in vivo model, bradykinin (Newby et al. 1999; Pretorius et al. 2002) and substance P (Newby et al. 1999; Pretorius et al. 2002) stimulated the production of tPA, which had decreased in smokers, but there was no effect on the release of methacholine-induced tPA. Vitamin C failed to ameliorate this decrease (Pellegrini et al. 2004). Studies showed that levels of PAI-1 may decrease after smoking cessation (Simpson et al. 1997).

Thus, the evidence suggests that smoking decreases the production of tPA and perhaps also increases the amount of PAI-1 produced. These changes would be expected to impair fibrinolytic activity. Alternatively, a population-based study demonstrated increased levels of fibrinogen, but fibrinolytic activity in smokers did not differ from that in nonsmokers (Eliasson et al. 1995). Another study suggested that differences between smokers and nonsmokers in thrombolysis may be evident only in older adults (Ikarugi et al. 2003).

Summary

A variety of abnormalities can be observed in endothelial cell function among smokers compared with nonsmokers. These abnormalities affect the ability of the endothelium to modulate vascular tone, platelet function, thrombogenesis, and thrombolysis. Administration of antioxidants mitigates some but not all of these abnormalities. The relative importance of these abnormalities and their interactions in clinical settings remains to be elucidated.

Exposure to Secondhand Tobacco Smoke

In one study, levels of fibrinogen and coagulation factor VII were higher in nonsmoking adolescent offspring of smokers than in nonsmoking adolescent offspring of nonsmokers (Stavroulakis et al. 2000). This finding is in keeping with a prothrombotic state in smokers. In addition, levels of PAI-1 were lower in nonsmoking offspring of smokers. This result suggests decreased fibrinolysis, but there was no difference in tPA levels. Levels of thrombomodulin, which is produced by the vascular endothelium and has anticoagulant effects, were higher in nonsmoking offspring of smokers, but levels of von Willebrand factor were unchanged. Another study demonstrated that TxM levels increased in one exposure to secondhand smoke; after six hours of exposure, levels approached those observed in smokers (Schmid et al. 1996). In other

research, exposure to secondhand smoke decreased sensitivity of platelets to the inhibitory effects of prostacyclin in vitro (Burghuber et al. 1986).

Thus, many of the effects from active smoking can be observed in persons involuntarily exposed to cigarette smoke. The magnitude of the effect of secondhand smoke is relatively large considering the low systemic exposure to tobacco smoke for nonsmokers compared with that for active smokers and supports the finding of high cardiovascular risk at low levels of exposure to smoke.

Nicotine and Thrombosis

Nicotine replacement therapy (NRT) does not seem to increase the acute risk of thrombosis, even in patients with established cardiac disease (Joseph et al. 1996). However, investigators have not fully studied cardiovascular effects of extended administration of nicotine, which might be used as an adjunct for persons trying to stop smoking (Stratton et al. 2001). The high urinary excretion of TxM in smokers declines rapidly after smoking cessation. In one study, this decline did not occur in smokers who were using NRT, suggesting that nicotine may be contributing to platelet activation (Saareks et al. 2001). However, other studies in which smokers switched to nicotine patches found a decline in eicosanoid excretion and that long-term use of smokeless tobacco, which results in nicotine exposure similar to that of cigarette smokers, does not increase urinary excretion of TxM (Wennmalm et al. 1991; Benowitz et al. 1993). These findings suggest that nicotine per se does not activate platelets. When nicotine or cotinine was added to the platelet-rich plasma of nonsmokers, platelet-dependent formation of thrombin increased (Hioki et al. 2001). The magnitude of the effect was similar to that observed in smokers, even though the basal nicotine levels in smokers were higher than those in nonsmokers. When cultured endothelial cells from the human brain were exposed to nicotine, tPA levels were unchanged (Zidovetzki et al. 1999). Rather, PAI-1 messenger RNA and protein expression increased, favoring a prothrombotic state. Alternatively, when transdermal nicotine was administered to nonsmokers, the release of tPA induced by substance P was greater than that in nonsmokers who had received placebo patches (Pellegrini et al. 2001). This finding suggests a more favorable effect in vivo.

A study of cardiovascular biomarkers indicates that smokeless tobacco produced neither the inflammatory reaction found in smokers nor endothelial dysfunction, activation of platelets, or evidence of oxidant stress (Axelsson et al. 2001). Leukocyte counts; levels of CRP, fibrinogen, and antioxidant vitamins; and lipid profiles were similar in users of smokeless tobacco and in persons who did not use tobacco.

Summary

Multiple factors produced in the blood and released from the vasculature determine the likelihood of a clinically significant thrombosis. Cigarette smoke and components of the smoke stimulate formation or activity of factors that favor the development of thrombosis. It remains to be seen whether biomarkers of individual cardiovascular risk among smokers will emerge and which genetic variants might particularly influence these risks in smokers. The implications of the hypercoagulable state are observed both in the epidemiology of active and involuntary smoking-related cardiovascular events and in the rapid rate of decline in the major component of excess risk for those events after smoking cessation. A hypercoagulable state can result in acute MI in persons who have less severe underlying coronary disease, so smokers who stop smoking have a better prognosis than do nonsmokers after MI. A more gradual decline of residual risk may reflect resolution of smoking-induced vascular injury, which in turn stimulates platelet activation.

Inflammation

Studies demonstrate that cigarette smoking results in a chronic inflammatory state, evidenced by increased counts of circulating leukocytes, CRP, and acute-phase reactants such as fibrinogen (Tracy et al. 1997; Jensen et al. 1998; Tuut and Hense 2001). Cigarette smoking also activates monocytes and enhances recruitment and adhesion of leukocytes to blood vessel walls, an integral step in vascular inflammation (Lehr et al. 1994). Research indicates that inflammation contributes to atherogenesis, because high leukocyte counts and high levels of CRP and fibrinogen are all powerful predictors of future cardiovascular events (Libby et al. 2002).

However, the mechanisms by which cigarette smoking promotes inflammation are not completely elucidated. As discussed previously, oxidant stress appears to be a critical factor; oxidized LDL is a proinflammatory stimulus (see "Cigarette Smoke Constituents and Cardiovascular Disease" earlier in this chapter). Studies also show that the products of lipid peroxidation are proinflammatory, acting in part on the receptor for platelet-activating factor (PAF). In hamsters, the antioxidant vitamin C prevented adhesion of leukocytes to the endothelium and leukocyte-platelet aggregation (Lehr et al. 1994). In the same animal model, adhesion of leukocytes and formation of leukocyte-platelet aggregates were mediated by PAF-like agonists (Lehr et al. 1997). This PAF-like factor was derived from oxidative modification of phospholipids and was distinct from biosynthetic PAF. Treatment with vitamin C inhibited generation of PAF-like lipids. In contrast, oral L-arginine but not vitamin C reversed the effect of sera from smokers by promoting monocyte-endothelial cell adhesion, which is associated with higher levels of ICAM (Newby et al. 2001). The study findings suggest that smoking-related impairment of NO release is an important determinant of increased adhesion of monocytes to endothelial cells.

Nicotine may contribute to inflammation by acting as a chemotactic agent for migration of neutrophils (Nicod et al. 1984). One study indicates that nicotine enhanced leukocyte-endothelium interactions, resulting in greater leukocyte rolling and adhesion in the cerebral microcirculation of mice (Nitenberg et al. 1993). Nicotine reportedly acts on human monocyte-derived dendritic cells to stimulate an inflammatory response (Nowak et al. 1987). Dendritic cells, which were detected in the walls of arteries and in atherosclerotic lesions, present antigens and are thus required for the start of adaptive immunity. Studies showed that nicotine is a potent inducer of expression of a variety of co-stimulatory molecules and that it increases secretion of the proinflammatory cytokine interleukin-12 in cultured dendritic cells (Aicher et al. 2003). Nicotine augmented the capacity of dendritic cells to stimulate proliferation of T cells and cytokines. Finally, intravenous injection of nicotine increased the movement of dendritic cells into atherosclerotic lesions in vivo in mice deficient in APO E. This line of research suggests that nicotine could contribute to adaptive immunity, which may have a role in atherogenesis. However, switching from smoking to transdermal nicotine resulted in a significant decline in the leukocyte count (Benowitz et al. 1993). In addition, use of smokeless tobacco did not produce higher leukocyte counts or higher CRP levels than are seen in persons who do not use tobacco. These observations suggest that nicotine is not the main determinant of the inflammatory response in smokers.

Smoking and Diabetes

Cigarette smoking is widely known to increase the risks of CVD. Even so, this knowledge does not appear to influence smoking behaviors among patients with diabetes, who bear a higher risk of cardiovascular morbidity and mortality than those who do not have diabetes (Haffner et al. 1998). Surveys found that smoking patterns were similar in patients with diabetes and comparable populations without that disorder (Ford et al. 1994; Gill et al. 1996).

Numerous experimental studies demonstrated that smoking had negative effects on the metabolism of glucose and lipids in persons with or without diabetes. Investigators reported that cigarette smoking in patients with diabetes was associated with deterioration of metabolic control (Madsbad et al. 1980; Bott et al. 1994) and increased risk of microvascular and macrovascular complications and death (Chase et al. 1991; Morrish et al. 1991). Furthermore, cigarette smoking increases risk of type 2 diabetes in the general population (Will et al. 2001). This risk may be mediated through direct metabolic effects alone or in combination with a metabolically unfavorable lifestyle.

Risk

In several prospective studies, cigarette smoking was associated with increased risk of type 2 diabetes in both men and women (Willi et al. 2007). Generally, these prospective studies were large and population based. Most of the information was collected by mailing participants a questionnaire, which in some cases, was supplemented with information from medical records. Most of these studies included follow-up of more than 10 years. Results were generally presented after adjustments for possible covariates.

In the Health Professionals Follow-Up Study, the RR of developing diabetes among men who smoked 25 or more cigarettes per day was 1.94 (95 percent CI, 1.25–3.03) when nonsmokers were the reference group (Rimm et al. 1995). In a smaller British study, the risk of diabetes was 50 percent higher among smokers, but this finding was not independent of other risk factors, such as obesity and low levels of physical activity (Perry et al. 1995). Another British study demonstrated that RR for diabetes in men who smoked was approximately 1.7, after adjustments for the effects of age, body mass index, physical

activity, alcohol intake, social class, undiagnosed CHD, and treatment for hypertension (Wannamethee et al. 2001). Mean follow-up was almost 17 years. The increased risk of diabetes was lower 5 years after smoking cessation, and the risk normalized 20 years later. A Japanese study found similar results and also reported a positive correlation between use of tobacco products and risk of diabetes (Uchimoto et al. 1999).

Almost identical results were presented in the Physicians' Health Study (Manson et al. 2000). During 12 years (255,830 person-years[1]) of follow-up, the risk of diabetes in men who smoked more than 20 cigarettes per day was 70 percent higher than that in nonsmokers, after adjustment for multiple variables. The results also showed a significant positive association between the risk of developing diabetes and higher consumption of cigarettes (Manson et al. 2000). In addition, the Insulin Resistance Atherosclerosis Study monitored a cohort of 906 study participants for five years with equal representation of African Americans, Hispanics, and Whites (Foy et al. 2005). For all persons studied, current smoking was associated with development of diabetes: the adjusted OR was 2.66 (95 percent CI, 1.49–4.77). Among participants who had normal glucose tolerance at baseline, the OR was 5.27 (95 percent CI, 2.11–13.16).

At least three other studies of men confirmed the main results of these prospective studies (Feskens and Kromhout 1989; Kawakami et al. 1997; Ko et al. 2001). There have been fewer studies with women, but two major prospective surveys yielded similar results. In the Nurses' Health Study (114,247 women; 1,277,589 person-years of follow-up), RR for diabetes in heavy smokers was 1.42, after adjustments for other risk factors (Rimm et al. 1993).

In an analysis of data from the Nurses' Health Study after 16 years of follow-up, Hu and colleagues (2001) showed that the strongest predictors of diabetes were being overweight or obese. In addition, poor diet, smoking, abstinence from alcohol, and low levels of physical activity were all independently associated with the risk of developing diabetes. Adjusted RR for developing diabetes was approximately 1.4 for smokers compared with nonsmokers.

Data from CPS-I, a prospective cohort study conducted between 1959 and 1972, were used to analyze the correlation between tobacco use and risk of diabetes in both men and women (Will et al. 2001). In comparison

---

[1]Person-year = the sum of the number of years that each member of a population has been smoking.

with the risk of developing diabetes for nonsmokers, the risks were higher for men who smoked more than one pack of cigarettes per day (RR = 1.19) or two packs per day (RR = 1.45). Risks were also higher for women who smoked more than one pack per day (RR = 1.21) or two packs per day (RR = 1.74). After smoking cessation, the risk returned to normal after 5 years for women and after 10 years for men (Will et al. 2001).

Only a few studies, all from the 1970s or 1980s, failed to demonstrate a positive association between smoking and diabetes, likely due to inadequate study design or lack of power in the study to test this hypothesis (Medalie et al. 1975; Keen et al. 1982; Wilson et al. 1986).

It is generally accepted that risk increases more for type 2 diabetes than for type 1, because type 1 diabetes is relatively rare among the age groups in the studies. Risk for type 2 diabetes is also consistent with the adverse metabolic effects of smoking (see "Insulin Resistance" later in this chapter). Type 1 diabetes is insulin deficiency caused by autoimmune destruction of pancreatic beta cells; in type 2 diabetes, insulin resistance is combined with impaired secretion of insulin (Reaven 1988; Kahn 2001).

Metabolic Control

Some studies examined the effects of cigarette smoking on the body's requirement for insulin and metabolic control in patients with diabetes. In a cross-sectional study, Madsbad and colleagues (1980) investigated the relationship between insulin doses and related variables in patients treated with injections of insulin. Insulin doses and serum levels of triglycerides were significantly higher in the 114 persons who smoked than in the 163 who did not smoke, and these values increased in a dose-dependent manner in relation to the number of cigarettes smoked. Hemoglobin A_{1c} (HbA_{1c})—a marker of long-term glucose elevation—was not measured in this study, but blood and urine levels of glucose did not differ between the two groups. This finding suggests that in patients who smoke, a larger insulin dose is needed to achieve metabolic control similar to that in patients who do not smoke.

In a cross-sectional study of 192 patients with type 1 diabetes, smoking was more common in those with higher HbA_{1c} values (Lundman et al. 1990). Other differences between the smokers and nonsmokers were in attitudes toward diabetes, psychological well-being, and similar factors.

In a relatively large prospective study that examined the effects of intensified insulin treatment and of an educational program, smoking was the most consistent determinant of HbA_{1c} levels in relatively young articipants treated with insulin (Bott et al. 1994). The investigators performed a three-year follow-up on 697 patients with diabetes who had no debilitating late complications. HbA_{1c} levels were higher throughout the study in smokers but eventually improved to levels similar to those in nonsmokers, presumably because of the educational program.

Insulin Resistance

The metabolic effects of smoking have been generally studied in persons who did not have diabetes. Insulin sensitivity was usually determined by using the euglycemic hyperinsulinemic clamp technique (DeFronzo et al. 1979). This technique or a slightly modified version of it is considered to be the gold standard in metabolic studies.

In 1993, Attvall and colleagues showed that short-term smoking caused impaired insulin sensitivity in healthy young men. Separately, two cross-sectional studies of men compared uptake of insulin-mediated glucose (insulin sensitivity) in smokers and nonsmokers (Facchini et al. 1992; Eliasson et al. 1997a). Insulin sensitivity was significantly lower (by 10 to 40 percent) in smokers. The degree of insulin resistance was positively correlated with tobacco use, and in long-term users of nicotine gum, with serum cotinine values (Eliasson et al. 1994, 1996). Because cotinine is a metabolite of nicotine, serum and urine levels of cotinine reflect the amount of nicotine use. Insulin resistance in smokers normalized eight weeks after smoking cessation, despite a weight gain of 2.7 kg (Eliasson et al. 1997a).

Smokers in these two cross-sectional studies had signs of insulin-resistance syndrome, such as significantly high serum levels of free fatty acids (FFAs) and triglycerides and low levels of HDLc (Facchini et al. 1992; Eliasson et al. 1997b). In the study by Eliasson and colleagues (1997b), smokers had a high proportion of atherogenic small and dense LDL particles, high fibrinogen levels, and high PAI-1 activity compared with those of nonsmokers. PAI-1 activity among long-term users of nicotine gum was similar, but effects on lipids were not as pronounced as those in smokers (Eliasson et al. 1996).

One aspect of insulin-resistance syndrome that attracted attention was postprandial hypertriglyceridemia, a phenomenon associated with CVD and insulin resistance (Patsch et al. 1992; Jeppesen et al. 1995). This phenomenon is also observed in smokers (Axelsen et al. 1995; Eliasson et al. 1997b), but its cause is unknown. One possible explanation is the inability of smokers to adequately clear triglyceride-rich chylomicrons and their remnants from the body (Mero et al. 1997).

Other studies that did not use exact measurements of insulin sensitivity reported changes in glucose metabolism in smokers compared with nonsmokers. Compared with nonsmokers, smokers were hyperinsulinemic and relatively glucose intolerant (Eliasson et al. 1991; Zavaroni et al. 1994; Frati et al. 1996; Ronnemaa et al. 1996). A large cross-sectional study showed that after adjustments for confounding factors, smoking behaviors were clearly correlated with HbA_{1c} values in persons who did not have diabetes (Sargeant et al. 2001), but researchers have debated the importance of HbA_{1c} in persons who do not have diabetes. Even so, these findings add support to the hypothesis that use of tobacco exerts adverse effects on glucose homeostasis.

Results in a few studies did not support these findings. Godsland and Walton (1992) found no differences in insulin sensitivity between women smokers and nonsmokers, but this result may be attributable to lower levels of tobacco use. In addition, the results were from analysis of data obtained to test a different hypothesis. In a study of metabolic changes in patients with or without hypertension, no differences in insulin sensitivity between smokers and nonsmokers were detected (Nilsson et al. 1995). However, the study design likely did not enable discrimination between metabolic changes caused by hypertension and those caused by smoking.

In patients with type 1 diabetes, Helve and colleagues (1986) examined cross-sectional and short-term effects of smoking on insulin sensitivity. Despite elevated levels of circulating epinephrine, cortisol, growth hormone, and glucagon after smoking, no effect of smoking on insulin sensitivity was observed. The investigators concluded that fluctuations in blood glucose and metabolic control disguised the influence of smoking in these patients with diabetes. In a study of 28 smokers and 12 nonsmokers with type 2 diabetes, the researchers measured insulin sensitivity by using euglycemic clamps (Targher et al. 1997). Smokers had higher insulin resistance and glucose intolerance than did nonsmokers. The researchers concluded that smoking markedly and in a dose-dependent manner aggravated insulin resistance observed in patients with type 2 diabetes (Targher et al. 1997).

Axelsson and colleagues (2001) reported that nicotine administered intravenously to nonsmokers caused a marked reduction (about 30 percent) in insulin sensitivity in those with type 2 diabetes but not in healthy control participants. These results suggest that nicotine and possibly tobacco use or other environmental factors may have particularly adverse effects in persons susceptible to diabetes but not in those who are healthy (insulin sensitive).

Microvascular Complications

Microvascular complications in diabetes (retinopathy, nephropathy, and neuropathy) are linked to metabolic control in both type 1 and type 2 disease (*New England Journal of Medicine* 1993; *Lancet* 1998). The mechanisms for development of microvascular complications are not fully understood, although several pathogenetic pathways have been suggested (Brownlee et al. 1984; Tomlinson 1999; Cai and Boulton 2002). Hyperglycemia has a central role as a trigger for subsequent events, such as conversion of glucose to sorbitol by aldose reductase; nonenzymatic glycosylation of proteins and receptors in susceptible tissues; increased exposure to oxidative stress; and activation of protein kinase C and mitogen-activated protein kinases. Researchers have suggested that these pathogenetic pathways lead to the disturbances in morphology and function found in diabetic nephropathy, retinopathy, and neuropathy (Brownlee et al. 1984; Tomlinson 1999; Cai and Boulton 2002).

Nephropathy

Some studies showed that smoking increased risk of microvascular complications in diabetes. Several studies of patients with type 1 diabetes reported negative effects of tobacco use on albuminuria and renal function. Chase and colleagues (1991), for example, showed that the albumin excretion rate was 2.8 times higher in smokers than in nonsmokers, after statistical corrections for glycemic control, duration of diabetes, age, gender, and blood pressure. In addition, albuminuria progressed at a more rapid rate in smokers than in nonsmokers.

Smoking promoted progression of renal disease in persons with type 2 diabetes (Biesenbach et al. 1997; Chuahirun and Wesson 2002; Chuahirun et al. 2003). Biesenbach and colleagues (1997) studied only 36 patients, but follow-up lasted 13 years. At study entry, smokers and nonsmokers had similar clinical and laboratory characteristics, but progression of nephropathy and development of atherosclerotic disease progressed more rapidly in the smokers than in the nonsmokers. Multiple regression analysis showed that only tobacco use and blood pressure levels were independently associated with impairment in renal function. This finding underscored the roles of smoking and vascular disease in susceptibility to renal disease (Biesenbach et al. 1997). In two prospective studies by Chuahirun and colleagues (2002, 2003), the effects of cigarette smoking on acceleration of nephropathy in patients with type 2 diabetes were confirmed even in those who had optimal therapy for hypertension. Research presented further evidence of functional and structural changes in the glomeruli of patients with type 2 diabetes who smoke (Baggio et al. 2002). In a study of 96 patients who had biopsy of the kidney, electron and light microscopy demonstrated significant changes in glomeruli and basal membranes that corresponded to impaired glomerular filtration rates in the smokers.

Retinopathy

Generally, investigators have not considered smoking to be a substantial risk factor for diabetic retinopathy (Porta and Bandello 2002). Findings in fairly large studies with mixed populations showed no strong support for such an association, except in older adults with certain conditions (Walker et al. 1985; Moss et al. 1991). At least two studies of patients with type 1 diabetes, however, suggest that smoking does predispose these patients to retinopathy (Mulhauser et al. 1986, 1996). In addition, Chase and colleagues (1991) showed that retinopathy was more common in patients with type 1 diabetes who smoked than in those who did not smoke, but after adjustments for covariates, differences were not statistically significant. The study also reported accelerated progression of retinopathy in patients who smoked. Thus, smoking may be a risk factor for diabetic retinopathy, but only in certain subgroups.

Neuropathy

The role of tobacco in the development of diabetic neuropathy is relatively difficult to examine because of methodologic problems and the frequent prevalence of confounding factors (Westerman et al. 1992). Diabetic neuropathy usually develops during a long period, and it may affect different sensory, motor, and autonomic nerve fibers in varying degrees in individuals. This variation makes it difficult to standardize study methods. One case-control study reported that risk of neuropathy was three times higher in patients with type 1 diabetes who smoked than in those who did not smoke (Mitchell et al. 1990). Smoking was not related to neuropathy in patients with type 2 diabetes. In a study of young patients treated with insulin, independent risk factors for progression of distal sensory neuropathy, apart from poor glycemic control, were cigarette smoking, greater height, and female gender (Christen et al. 1999). Other studies in patients with type 1 diabetes confirmed the roles of glycemic control and smoking behaviors in development of clinical neuropathy (Maser et al. 1989; Reichard 1992).

Macrovascular Complications

The multiple effects of smoking on the vascular and hemostatic systems and on inflammation are reviewed elsewhere in this chapter (see "Hemodynamic Effects," "Smoking and the Endothelium," "Nicotine and Thrombosis," and "Inflammation" earlier in this chapter). Diabetes patients are particularly susceptible to some effects of smoking, because their risk of cardiovascular morbidity and mortality is elevated (Jarrett et al. 1982; Manson et al. 1991; Morrish et al. 1991).

In a study cohort in London, England, in the prospective Multinational Study of Vascular Disease in Diabetes, sponsored by the World Health Organization, smokers with type 1 or type 2 diabetes had significantly increased risk of CHD, but not stroke, during the eight-year follow-up (Morrish et al. 1991). In the Diabetes Control and Complications Trial (*New England Journal of Medicine* 1993), designed to study the role of intensive insulin treatment and optimized glycemic control in type 1 diabetes, smoking was not a significant risk factor for macrovascular complications. Because the participants were relatively young, this trial was not optimally designed to study the role of tobacco use. Other studies with slightly older participants who had type 1 diabetes reported that smoking increased risk of CHD (Moy et al. 1990; Sinha et al. 1997).

Among patients with type 2 diabetes in the United Kingdom Prospective Diabetes Study, cigarette smoking was a significant and independent risk factor for CHD (Turner et al. 1998), stroke (Kothari et al. 2002), and PAD (Adler et al. 2002). Also, an analysis of data from the Nurses' Health Study demonstrated that for women with type 2 diabetes, a dose-effect relationship existed between smoking behaviors and mortality (Al-Delaimy et al. 2001). Compared with nonsmokers, risk of mortality from all causes was 1.64 for women who smoked 15 to 34 cigarettes per day and 2.19 for women who smoked more than 34 cigarettes per day. Ten years after smoking cessation, risk of mortality had normalized. Researchers published similar data on smoking and CHD risk in the same cohort (Al-Delaimy et al. 2002).

A relatively large prospective study that analyzed the effects of smoking cessation on cardiovascular risk in persons with diabetes compared mortality risk for former smokers with that for lifetime nonsmokers (Chaturvedi et al. 1997). Compared with mortality risk for lifetime nonsmokers, risk of death from all causes was approximately 50 percent higher for patients who had stopped smoking during the past one to nine years and 25 percent higher for those who had not smoked for more than nine years. Smoking cessation reduced mortality risk among persons with diabetes, but risks remained high several years after smoking cessation and were highly dependent on the duration of smoking.

Pathophysiological Mechanisms

Having diabetes, even for nonsmokers, is associated with long-term exposure to oxidative stress, impaired endothelial function, and dyslipidemia (Brownlee et al. 1984; Turner et al. 1998; Dogra et al. 2001; Cai and Boulton 2002; Komatsu et al. 2002). The causes of type 2 diabetes are still not fully understood, although the main metabolic aberrations are well characterized. Research showed that type 2 diabetes is caused by insulin resistance in combination with relative impairment of insulin secretion (Reaven 1988; Kahn 2001). Published studies have not demonstrated a significant impairment in insulin secretion among cigarette smokers (Epifano et al. 1992; Facchini et al. 1992; Persson et al. 2000), but several studies documented a negative effect of smoking on insulin sensitivity (Facchini et al. 1992; Eliasson et al. 1997a,b).

Cigarette smoking and intake of nicotine increase the circulating levels of insulin-antagonistic hormones (i.e., catecholamines, cortisol, and growth hormone) (Kershbaum and Bellet 1966; Cryer et al. 1976; Wilkins et al. 1982; Kirschbaum et al. 1992). Smoking also activates the sympathetic nervous system (Niedermaier et al. 1993; Lucini et al. 1996). Nicotine likely impairs insulin

sensitivity directly or indirectly through these and possibly other mechanisms. An additional negative factor for insulin-mediated glucose uptake is high circulating levels of FFAs, secondary to increased lipolysis (Bergman and Ader 2000). Research has shown that smoking acutely elevates circulating FFA levels (Kershbaum and Bellet 1966).

Researchers have proposed, but not fully elucidated, the potential role of endothelial dysfunction or inflammation in development of insulin resistance and type 2 diabetes.

Summary

Many clinical and experimental studies have found significant associations between cigarette smoking and development of diabetes, impaired glycemic control, and diabetic complications (microvascular and macrovascular). A different lifestyle of smokers, in contrast to that maintained by nonsmokers, may also contribute to these effects. Most of the reviewed studies, however, either attempted to statistically adjust for confounding factors or were designed to examine short-term effects of tobacco and nicotine.

The development of type 2 diabetes is another harmful consequence of cigarette smoking, one that adds to the heightened risks of CVD. In diabetes care, smoking cessation is crucial to facilitating glycemic control and limiting development of complications.

Lipid Abnormalities

Cigarette smoking is associated with an atherogenic lipid profile likely to contribute to risk of CVD.

Epidemiologic Observations

Several observations are central to the relationship between cigarette smoking and lipids. Compared with nonsmokers, smokers have higher levels of triglycerides associated with very-low-density lipoprotein (VLDL), total triglycerides, and APO B, in addition to modest increases in LDLc and lower levels of plasma HDLc and APO A-I (Billimoria et al. 1975; Criqui et al. 1980; Wilson et al. 1983; Craig et al. 1989; Muscat et al. 1991; Freeman and Packard 1995; Villablanca et al. 2000). These findings are robust and are reported in numerous survey studies. Researchers observed a dose-response relationship

between the number of cigarettes smoked per day and plasma lipid levels (Muscat et al. 1991). In contrast, plasma lipid and lipoprotein levels in former smokers typically are similar to those in nonsmokers.

The ratio of LDLc to HDLc, which is used as a measure of atherogenic risk, is higher in smokers than in nonsmokers. Cigarette smoking is thought to raise the LDLc to HDLc ratio by 15 to 20 percent. Increased levels of plasma triglycerides are associated with lower HDLc levels, but reduction in HDLc from cigarette smoking persists even after corrections for levels of total triglycerides. Early epidemiologic studies, such as the Lipid Research Clinics Program Prevalence Study and the Framingham Heart Study (Criqui et al. 1980; Muscat et al. 1991; Freeman and Packard 1995), emphasized lower HDLc values as the primary effect of cigarette smoking.

Researchers have estimated, however, that these effects of cigarette smoking on plasma lipids and lipoproteins account for only 10 percent of the observed 70 percent increase in risk of vascular disease associated with cigarette smoking (Craig et al. 1989). In the Edinburgh Artery Study, for example, adjusting for known CHD risk factors reduced the RR of CHD in heavy smokers from 3.94 to 2.72 and the RR in moderate smokers from 2.72 to 1.70 (Price et al. 1999). However, cigarette smoking still accounted for 75 percent of the risk of developing PAD, after adjustment for other known risk factors, such as hyperlipidemia and type 2 diabetes (Lu and Creager 2004). Other researchers reported similar findings (Cullen et al. 1998). Cigarette smoking thus appears to have atherogenic effects that are not explained by traditional CHD risk factors, including abnormal levels of blood lipids.

Analyses of mechanisms related to lipid and lipoprotein metabolism may be required for understanding the atherogenicity of cigarette smoking. Such mechanisms include lipid oxidation; changes in composition of lipoproteins; alterations in plasma- and lipoprotein-associated lipid transfer enzymes; changes in metabolism of fatty acids; effects on levels of postprandial lipids; and changes in cholesterol fluxes, particularly reverse cholesterol transport (RCT). The following discussion reviews the effects of cigarette smoking on these potential underlying mechanisms.

Lipoprotein Composition and Apolipoprotein Levels

Cigarette smoking clearly reduces APO A-I and the ratio of A-I to A-II (Mero et al. 1998). APO A-I is a major component of HDL particles. The reduction in A-I levels observed in smokers is similar to, although perhaps somewhat lower than, the reduction in HDLc levels seen in this population. For example, Mero and colleagues (1998) documented that levels of plasma APO A-I were 4 to 6 percent lower and HDLc values were 6 to 9 percent lower in moderate-to-heavy smokers. The effects of cigarette smoking on APO B and other APOs are also well documented (Billimoria et al. 1975; Craig et al. 1989; Muscat et al. 1991; Villablanca et al. 2000).

Researchers have associated abnormalities in different subfractions of HDL with different risks of CHD. Cigarette smoking reduced different HDL subfractions in different studies (Billimoria et al. 1975; Craig et al. 1989; Muscat et al. 1991). Even so, the true atherogenicity of different HDL subfractions remains controversial. The role of altered HDL subfractions in arterial disease associated with cigarette smoking requires further study.

Plasma- and Lipoprotein-Associated Lipid Transfer Enzymes

Several enzymes in plasma—either free or associated with lipoproteins—are involved in transport and use of lipids. Lipoprotein lipase (LPL) activity is involved in clearance of total triglycerides from triglyceride-rich lipoproteins (TGRLs), particularly the chylomicra formed in persons after a meal containing fat. Cigarette smoking reportedly reduced plasma LPL activity after a mixed meal (Freeman et al. 1998). Reduced LPL activity may contribute to the reduced clearance of TGRLs reported for total triglycerides, APO B, and retinyl-ester components of TGRLs (Mero et al. 1998). In another study, the cholesterol ester transfer protein (CETP) received considerable attention as a therapeutic target for raising HDLc levels (Brousseau et al. 2004; Ruggeri 2005). CETP mediates transfer of cholesterol esters between HDL and other lipoproteins (VLDL and LDL). However, controversy exists as to whether CETP activity is beneficial or deleterious to the process of RCT. Moreover, the proatherogenic or antiatherogenic consequences of changing HDLc by the CETP mechanism remain uncertain (Ruggeri 2005). Studies have reported both increases and decreases in plasma CETP activity in smokers (Dullaart et al. 1994; Zaratin et al. 2004).

Some studies measured other enzymes in smokers. For example, cigarette smoking did not appear to markedly alter lecithin cholesterol acyltransferase activity (McCall et al. 1994).

Oxidized Lipoproteins

Many investigators hypothesized that oxidized LDL is highly atherogenic (Dullaart et al. 1994; Zaratin et al. 2004), and studies reported increased oxidative damage to LDL in smokers (Ambrose and Barua 2004). However, attribution of a precise atherogenic contribution from oxidative damage to LDL remains speculative. The inadequacy of the metrics of pro-oxidative and antioxidative status in vivo needs to be resolved before the role of oxidative damage to LDL can be adequately evaluated.

Postprandial Lipid Changes

Traditionally, plasma lipid and lipoprotein measurements used to evaluate CHD risks have, for largely technical reasons, been performed in the fasting (postabsorptive) state. Plasma levels of metabolites are more easily characterized in steady-state conditions than in a nonsteady state. From a pathophysiological perspective, however, events in the postprandial state may be critical in atherogenesis (Zilversmit 1979). Some studies explored effects of cigarette smoking on postprandial lipid metabolism (Mero et al. 1998). For example, total triglycerides increased to higher levels after a mixed meal in smokers than in nonsmokers. These researchers observed increases in plasma APO B level and reductions in levels of APO A-I, lipoprotein A-I, HDLc, and LDL-APO B after a meal. Other investigators postulated that the mechanisms underlying altered postprandial lipid changes in smokers include lower LPL activity (Freeman et al. 1998), but higher endogenous production of VLDL-total triglycerides by the liver has not been excluded. The postprandial effects of cigarette smoking in particular and their role in atherogenesis in general are not completely understood.

Metabolism of Free Fatty Acids

Changes in FFAs (nonesterified fatty acids) are attributed to an increase in adipocyte lipolysis, and they represent the most well-characterized mechanistic action of cigarette smoking in the context of alterations in lipids and lipoproteins. Many studies reported higher plasma levels of FFAs in smokers than in nonsmokers (Kershbaum et al. 1963; Bizzi et al. 1972; Walsh et al. 1977; Hellerstein et al. 1994; Neese et al. 1994).

Using stable (nonradioactive) isotopes to measure FFA kinetics, researchers demonstrated that cigarette smoking immediately and markedly increased influx of FFAs into the bloodstream and thereby raised plasma levels of FFA (Hellerstein et al. 1994; Neese et al. 1994). Plasma FFAs are primarily derived from adipose tissue by lipolytic breakdown of stored triglycerides. Catecholamines stimulate hormone-sensitive lipase activity in adipose tissue and oppose various antilipolytic actions of insulin. Increases in FFA levels and flux induced by smoking were temporally correlated with increases in plasma epinephrine levels (Watts 1960; Bizzi et al. 1972; Arcavi et al. 1994; Hellerstein et al. 1994; Neese et al. 1994). These increases are prevented by β-adrenergic blockers. Nicotine increases the adrenal medullary release of epinephrine in persons with nontolerance of nicotine (Arcavi et al. 1994). Therefore, the model implicated as the cause of increases in plasma FFA levels induced by cigarette smoking seems clear: cigarette smoking→nicotine→increased plasma epinephrine→increased lipolysis in adipose tissue→increased release of FFAs into plasma→increased plasma levels of FFA.

The fate of FFAs released into the bloodstream in response to cigarette smoking is also relevant. Cigarette smoking increases expenditure of energy through the activity of nicotine and catecholamines (Ilebekk et al.

1975; Perkins et al. 1989; Hellerstein et al. 1994; Neese et al. 1994). However, most of the FFAs released in response to cigarette smoking are not oxidized but taken up and reesterified to triglycerides in tissues, particularly the liver. This conclusion was partly based on kinetic studies that compared the rates at which plasma FFA appeared with whole-body rates of fat oxidation (Hellerstein et al. 1994; Neese et al. 1994). These studies demonstrated that the rate of FFA influx into plasma in response to cigarette smoking greatly exceeded changes in whole-body fat oxidation.

Accordingly, the catabolic effects of cigarette smoking on total adipose triglycerides do not directly promote oxidation of body fat (weight loss); instead, the primary result is overproduction of VLDL-total triglycerides (Hellerstein et al. 1994; Neese et al. 1994). This "futile cycle," a substrate cycle in which adipose triglycerides are converted to hepatic VLDL triglycerides, is modestly wasteful of energy. It accounts for about 5 percent of the thermogenic effects of long-term cigarette smoking—for example, fewer than 10 kilocalories (kcal)/day if cigarette smoking increases total energy expenditure by 200 kcal/day. This cycle, however, may be the central driving force behind the atherogenic dyslipidemia associated with cigarette smoking. Overproduction of VLDL-total triglycerides typically results in elevated plasma levels of VLDL-total triglycerides and APO B, as well as increased numbers of LDL particles (Sniderman et al. 2001). Furthermore, high VLDL-total triglycerides contribute to lowering of HDLc through CETP-mediated transfer of cholesterol-ester from HDL to VLDL particles (Brousseau et al. 2004; Ruggeri et al. 2005). Influx of FFAs into the liver for reesterification and secretion of total triglycerides is most likely a major reason for the low HDLc levels observed in smokers, but perhaps it does not represent the entire effect of smoking on HDLc (Criqui et al. 1980; Muscat et al. 1991; Freeman and Packard 1995).

If nicotine-stimulated release of catecholamine is responsible for the hypertriglyceridemia and low HDLc levels observed in smokers, NRT as an adjunct to smoking cessation should logically prevent improvements in plasma lipids and lipoproteins after smoking cessation. Moffatt and colleagues (2000) reported that nicotine-patch therapy prevented the normalization of HDLc levels observed with smoking cessation in the absence of the nicotine patch. The patch also prevented weight gain after smoking cessation (Allen et al. 2005), a finding consistent with the hypothesis that shared catecholamines are the basis for two important effects of cigarette smoking: weight reduction and dyslipidemia. Other studies, however, did not confirm that use of the nicotine patch as an agent for smoking cessation prevents improvements in HDL levels (Allen et al. 1994). In addition, lipid profiles are similar in persons who use smokeless tobacco and in those who do not use any form of tobacco. To the extent that dyslipidemia contributes to vascular disease associated with cigarette smoking, it is important to determine the full range of effects of NRT on lipid and lipoprotein metabolism.

Reverse Cholesterol Transport

RCT refers to the pathway by which cholesterol is mobilized from tissues, carried through the blood, and excreted from the body. HDL and its associated membrane receptors (e.g., $SR-B_1$, $ABC-A_1$, and $ABC-G_1$), plasma enzymes (e.g., CETP and phospholipid transfer protein), APOs (e.g., APO A-I), and hepatobiliary enzymes (e.g., cholesterol 7α-hydroxylase) constitute a system that mediates the complex process of RCT through pathways that are increasingly well characterized in molecular terms (Neese et al. 1994; Tall 1998). RCT is generally accepted as the leading explanation for the cardioprotective activity of HDL, although other actions of HDL (e.g., antioxidative and anti-inflammatory) may also be involved.

Flux through the RCT pathway and, thus, antiatherogenic activity cannot be predicted simply from plasma levels of HDL or APO A-I (Tall 1998). Thus, changes in levels of HDLc, VLDL-total triglycerides, and other lipoproteins may not fully capture the effects of cigarette smoking on pro-atherogenic or antiatherogenic fluxes such as RCT. Until more recently, however, there were no viable techniques for measuring RCT fluxes. Therefore, this question could be addressed only indirectly—for example, through changes in lipid transfer proteins in plasma that may influence the efficiency of RCT. Studies reported decreases in activity of CETP and phospholipid transfer protein in smokers after they had smoked a cigarette (Zaratin et al. 2004).

Reduced capacity for remodeling HDL particles in the vascular compartment could alter these fluxes in a manner not reflected by HDLc levels. This possibility will remain speculative, however, until RCT fluxes are measured in humans. The ability to directly measure effects of cigarette smoking on the cardioprotective process of RCT could provide a major tool for advancing understanding of the role of lipids in causing vascular disease associated with cigarette smoking.

Effects of Smoking Cessation

Research on smoking cessation largely confirmed the associations observed in smokers (Gordon et al. 1975;

Rabkin 1984; Stamford et al. 1986; Critchley and Capewell 2004). Many studies documented the return of normal levels of plasma lipids and lipoproteins after cessation of cigarette smoking.

Therapeutic Implications of Pathogenic Mechanisms

If stimulation of lipolysis underlies the atherogenic dyslipidemia associated with cigarette smoking, inhibition of lipolysis might be an effective therapeutic strategy to improve blood lipid profiles in smokers or persons receiving NRT. This strategy is an attractive approach in one sense because inhibition of lipolysis does not block the thermogenic actions of nicotine. The cycle of lipolysis and reesterification accounts for less than 5 percent of the increase in energy expenditure observed in cigarette smokers (Hellerstein et al. 1994; Neese et al. 1994). Another consideration is that if FFAs released by lipolysis are involved in the insulin resistance reportedly associated with cigarette smoking (Facchini et al. 1992), lipolysis inhibitors may have an additional therapeutic use.

Niacin, a hypolipidemic agent, is thought to act at least partly by inhibiting total triglyceride lipolysis in adipose tissue (Meyers et al. 2004). The use of niacin in smokers who are at high risk for CHD has not been fully investigated. The side effects of niacin, including cutaneous flushing and worsening of insulin resistance in some persons, perhaps from effects on pancreatic islet function, may discourage its clinical use. The impact of niacin and its analogs on lipolysis is complex. They induce a rebound overshoot of lipolysis after initial inhibition, but niacin does reduce production of VLDL-total triglycerides (Wang et al. 2001).

Other strategies for use of lipolysis inhibitors to prevent CHD related to cigarette smoking may require development of specific antilipolytic agents that are well tolerated. One possibility is the thiazolidinedione class of insulin-sensitizing drugs. In one study, such drugs reduced lipolysis in adipose tissue, perhaps by activating glyceroneogenesis and thereby promoting intra-adipocytic reesterification of FFAs (Chen et al. 2005). No studies are known to have tested the efficacy of thiazolidinediones in smokers to determine effects on lipid abnormalities or sensitivity to insulin. However, recent research indicates that rosiglitazone (a thiazolidinedione) increases CHD risk, although pioglitazone, another drug in the same class, does not increase this risk (Lincoff et al. 2007; Nissen and Wolski 2007). Thus, it is unclear whether the possible benefits of this class of drugs in smokers will be pursued.

Summary

Effects of cigarette smoking on standard measures of blood lipids and lipoproteins are well characterized. The most important effects are to lower levels of HDLc and increase levels of total triglycerides. The metabolic mechanisms underlying these changes are known to some extent, particularly the catecholamine-mediated increase in adipocyte lipolysis, changes in plasma levels of FFAs, and reesterification of FFAs by the liver. However, the predicted effect from changes in standard lipid risk factors for vascular disease associated with cigarette smoking appears to be modest. Future research will reveal whether this estimation of a modest effect is a true estimate of the pathogenic importance of smoking-induced changes in blood lipid levels or an inability to measure the full effects of cigarette smoking on atherogenesis.

Cardiovascular Biomarkers

Biomarkers of smoking-related CVD risk are useful for stratifying individual risk and, perhaps, for assessing product risk. Biomarkers for CVD risk can be divided into three categories: (1) constituents of cigarette smoke that contribute to CVD, (2) physiological changes involving potential mechanisms of CVD, and (3) chemical biomarkers of cardiovascular dysfunction and disease (Table 6.3). Studies showed that cigarette smoking altered many of the CVD biomarkers, as evidenced by comparisons of smokers with nonsmokers and former smokers. However, fewer studies prospectively examined reversal of such changes after smoking cessation. More important, to date, there are no data on how changes in smoking-related biomarkers predict risk of disease.

Three constituents of cigarette smoke received the greatest attention as potential contributors to CVD: CO measured as exhaled CO or as blood carboxyhemoglobin, nicotine, and oxidant chemicals (Benowitz 2003). These constituents are used as general biomarkers of exposure to tobacco or tobacco smoke. Apparently, no direct measures of levels of oxidizing chemicals in the body have been developed, but numerous measures of the biologic consequences of exposure to oxidizing chemicals exist. Exposure to particulate matter in cigarette smoke is likely to contribute to CVD in smokers (Brook et al. 2004; Vermylen et al. 2005; Bhatnagar 2006), but no direct biomarkers of particulate exposure are available. Particulate matter appears to affect oxidative stress, coagulability, and inflammation, for which biomarkers are available. A lesser body of research suggests that PAHs and other constituents of tobacco smoke may also contribute to atherogenesis (Penn and Snyder 1988, 1996). Urine levels of PAH metabolites can also be measured in smokers; 1-hydroxypyrene is most widely used for this purpose.

Cigarette smoke exposes the smoker to high levels of potentially oxidizing chemicals (Burke and FitzGerald 2003). In one study, cigarette smoking increased levels of lipid peroxidation products, such as F_2-isoprostanes, in the plasma and urine (Nowak et al. 1987). Other markers of oxidative stress in smokers included higher plasma levels of oxidized LDL and oxidized fibrinogen, higher urine levels of substances reactive with thiobarbituric acid, and reduced plasma levels of antioxidant vitamins such as E, C, and beta-carotene.

The hemodynamic effects of cigarette smoking can be observed while a person smokes a cigarette. These effects include elevation in heart rate, blood pressure, and cardiac output. Coronary blood flow, as assessed by coronary perfusion studies, may increase or decrease with smoking, depending on underlying atherosclerosis and endothelial function (Czernin and Waldherr 2003).

Researchers have proposed numerous biomarkers for measuring endothelial dysfunction, and many of these biomarkers are affected by cigarette smoking. The functional assessment most widely used is flow-mediated arterial vasodilation (Puranik and Celermajer 2003), a test that measures the diameter of the brachial artery in response to changes in forearm blood flow. The brachial artery is imaged by using Doppler ultrasonography before and after release of a blood pressure cuff that is inflated over the forearm to occlude arterial blood flow. With release of the cuff, the increase in blood flow triggers an increase in the diameter of the brachial artery that is mediated by release of NO and prostacyclin by endothelial cells. Many researchers demonstrated impairment of flow-mediated dilation in populations of active smokers and persons exposed involuntarily to cigarette smoke, but estimates of impairment in persons with no exposure to smoke overlapped considerably with those for the other two groups. Other potential markers of endothelial dysfunction that can be measured in the blood include ADMA, von Willebrand factor, tPA, E-selectin, and P-selectin. Prostacyclin metabolites can be measured in the urine (Cooke 2000). Selectins are adhesion molecules released by both endothelial cells and platelets (Ley 2003).

Table 6.3   Biomarkers of risk for cardiovascular disease from exposure to cigarette smoke

		Study			
Biomarker	**Measurement of:**	**Smokers vs. nonsmokers**	**Change with smoking cessation**	**Dose-response relationship**	**Change with reduced smoking**
		Chemical biomarkers			
Carbon monoxide	Delivery of potential chemical toxins	SRNT Subcommittee on Biochemical Verification 2002	SRNT Subcommittee on Biochemical Verification 2002	Benowitz and Jacob 1984	Hecht et al. 2004
Nicotine and cotinine	Delivery of potential chemical toxins	SRNT Subcommittee on Biochemical Verification 2002	SRNT Subcommittee on Biochemical Verification 2002	Benowitz and Jacob 1984	Benowitz et al. 1983
		Physiological and biochemical markers			
Blood pressure	Hemodynamic effects	Benowitz et al. 2002	Benowitz et al. 2002		
C-reactive protein	Inflammation	Bazzano et al. 2003	Bazzano et al. 2003	Bazzano et al. 2003	
Carotid and femoral artery intima-media thickness	Atherosclerosis	Wallenfeldt et al. 2001			
Circulating endothelial precursor cells	Endothelial function	Kondo et al. 2004	Kondo et al. 2004	Kondo et al. 2004	
E-selectin	Endothelial function	Bazzano et al. 2003	Bazzano et al. 2003		
Fibrinogen	Hypercoagulable state	Bazzano et al. 2003	Bazzano et al. 2003	Bazzano et al. 2003	
Flow-mediated dilation	Endothelial function	Czernin and Waldherr 2003	Czernin and Waldherr 2003	Czernin and Waldherr 2003	
Glucose-clamping studies	Insulin resistance	Eliasson et al. 1997a	Eliasson et al. 1997a	Eliasson et al. 1997a	
HDL cholesterol	Lipid marker	Stubbe et al. 1982	Stubbe et al. 1982		
Heart rate	Hemodynamic effects	Benowitz et al. 1984	Benowitz et al. 1984		
Hemoglobin A_{1c}	Insulin resistance	Sargeant et al. 2001			
Homocysteine	Hypercoagulable state	Bazzano et al. 2003	Bazzano et al. 2003	Bazzano et al. 2003	

Table 6.3   Continued

Biomarker	Measurement of:	Smokers vs. nonsmokers	Change with smoking cessation	Dose-response relationship	Change with reduced smoking
			Study		
Insulin/glucose ratio	Insulin resistance	Zavaroni et al. 1994			
Interleukin-6	Inflammation	Bermudez et al. 2002	Bermudez et al. 2002		
Nuclear coronary perfusion studies	Hemodynamic effects	Czernin and Waldherr 2003			Mahmarian et al. 1997
Oxidized LDL cholesterol	Oxidative stress/lipid marker	Panagiotakos et al. 2004	Panagiotakos et al. 2004		
P-selectin	Endothelial function	Bazzano et al. 2003	Bazzano et al. 2003		
Red blood cell mass	Hypercoagulable state	Blann et al. 1997	Blann et al. 1997		
Serum concentrations of vitamin C	Oxidative stress	Lykkesfeldt et al. 2000			
Serum triglycerides	Lipid marker	Axelsen et al. 1995			
Soluble intercellular adhesion molecule-1	Inflammation	Scott et al. 2000	Scott et al. 2000	Scott et al. 2000	
Thiobarbituric acid reactive substances	Oxidative stress				
Tissue plasminogen activator	Hypercoagulable state	Simpson et al. 1997			
Urine F_2-isoprostanes	Oxidative stress	Morrow et al. 1995	Pilz et al. 2000		
Urine thromboxane A_2 metabolite	Hypercoagulable state	Nowak et al. 1987	Saareks et al. 2001		
von Willebrand factor	Endothelial function	Blann et al. 1997	Blann et al. 1997		
White blood cell count	Inflammation	Jensen et al. 1998	Jensen et al. 1998	Jensen et al. 1998	

Note: **HDL** = high-density lipoprotein; **LDL** = low-density lipoprotein; **SRNT** = Society for Research on Nicotine and Tobacco.

Markers of the hypercoagulable state include increased urine levels of thromboxane A_2 metabolites. Thromboxane A_2 is released when platelets aggregate in vivo, and its metabolites in urine are a useful noninvasive measure of the point of activation (Nowak et al. 1987). Other relevant biomarkers of a hypercoagulable state include fibrinogen, red blood cell mass, blood viscosity, tPA, PAI-1, homocysteine, and P-selectin (Benowitz 2003).

Biomarkers used to assess an inflammatory state include total leukocyte and neutrophil counts and levels of CRP, fibrinogen, and interleukin-6 (Pearson et al. 2003). In addition, the counts of several cell-surface adhesion molecules increased in inflammatory states. These molecules included ICAM, sVCAM-1, and monocyte chemoattractant protein-1.

Another study found several markers to be useful for assessing insulin resistance (Eliasson 2003). For example, in persons with insulin resistance, levels of plasma glucose were likely to be elevated in fasting status and two hours after eating. HbA_{1c} levels, which reflect plasma glucose levels throughout the day, were elevated in persons in a hyperglycemic state. The ratio of insulin to glucose after glucose loading was useful as an index of insulin sensitivity. The most definitive investigations were glucose-clamping studies, in which insulin levels were measured when the glucose level was constant or vice versa.

Numerous standard markers of lipids may be altered in cigarette smokers. These markers include HDLc, LDLc, the ratio of total cholesterol to HDL, and serum triglyceride levels.

Nuclear coronary perfusion studies with or without physical exercise are among several functional studies for diagnosing cardiovascular dysfunction or disease. They indicate that cigarette smoking reduces cardiac perfusion in patients with coronary disease (Czernin and Waldherr 2003). Reserve in endothelial function can be assessed by studying flow-mediated dilation (see "Endothelium-Dependent Vasodilation" earlier in this chapter). Findings in another study indicate that vascular disease can be assessed by measuring intima-media thickness of the carotid and femoral arteries by ultrasonography, which provides a direct measure of early atherosclerotic changes in blood vessels (de Groot et al. 2004).

Numerous cardiovascular biomarkers that might be used to assess the effects of cigarette smoking and involuntary smoking and that are expected to increase the risk of CVD are discussed here. Many biomarkers, however, do not reflect causal pathways related to development of CVD. Instead, they reflect the pathophysiological effects of the constituents of cigarette smoke. In addition, many biomarkers are influenced by processes and risk factors that are independent of cigarette smoking. Many of the same abnormalities produced by smoking are also produced by diabetes, hypercholesterolemia, and hypertension. Thus, it is unclear which biomarkers are most specific to cigarette smoking. It is also unclear which biomarkers best predict the risk of CVD attributable to cigarette smoke. Also, a given biomarker profile can indicate any of several marked differences in a person's susceptibility to CVD.

The potential exists to develop improved biomarkers for CVD by using advances in high-throughput genomics and by examining the relationships of gene polymorphisms or alterations in protein expression or activity to smoking-induced disease (Zhang et al. 2001). Emerging genomic and proteomic technologies may cast light on the signaling pathways activated by smoking and the constituents of tobacco smoke that culminate in cardiovascular dysfunction. Such approaches may also contribute to an understanding of individual differences in susceptibility to the cardiovascular complications of smoking.

Numerous studies of clinical genetics examined differences in susceptibility to smoking-induced CVD as a function of different genetic variants (Wang et al. 2003). Such studies, combined with genomic and proteomic approaches, may provide mechanistic information on pathogenesis and, in combination with other biomarkers, may result in better predictions of cardiovascular risk in smokers.

Smoking Cessation and Cardiovascular Disease

Smoking cessation reduces the risk of cardiovascular morbidity and mortality for smokers with or without CVD (USDHHS 1990). Smoking directly accelerates atherogenesis, causes acute cardiovascular events, and contributes to and acts synergistically with other risk factors, such as hyperlipidemia and diabetes (see "Smoking and Diabetes" earlier in this chapter). Although cigarette smoking does not cause hypertension, smoking is associated with higher blood pressure in persons with hypertension and enhances the likelihood of complications, including progression of renal disease in patients with hypertension (Green et al. 1986; Mann et al. 1991; McNagny et al. 1997; Regalado et al. 2000). One study demonstrated that cigarette smoking was a substantial contributor to morbidity and mortality in patients with left ventricular dysfunction (Suskin et al. 2001). In such patients, the benefit of reducing the likelihood of death by smoking cessation is equal to or greater than the benefit of therapy with inhibitors of ACE, β-blockers, or spironolactone. Smoking cessation is particularly important in patients with diabetes. For these patients, smoking markedly increases cardiovascular risks, including the risk that diabetic nephropathy will progress. Smoking also increases insulin resistance and increases the difficulty of controlling diabetes. For these and other reasons, smoking cessation in patients with CVD is an essential therapeutic intervention.

The 1990 Surgeon General's report on smoking cessation (USDHHS 1990) outlines the evidence that stopping smoking helps to prevent CVD, and subsequent research has reinforced this concept (Hasdai et al. 1997a; van Domburg et al. 2000; Wilson et al. 2000). Estimates in case-control and cohort studies indicate that most risk reduction for mortality occurred in the first one to three years after smoking cessation, and approximately one-half of the risk of smokers for a nonfatal MI was eliminated in the first year after cessation. It takes about three to five years of abstinence from smoking for most of the excess CVD risk to be gone (USDHHS 1990; Lightwood and Glantz 1997).

Smoking cessation after MI reduces the risk of cardiovascular morbidity and mortality by 36 to 50 percent (USDHHS 1990; Kumanan et al. 2000; Wilson et al. 2000; Rea et al. 2002; Critchley and Capewell 2003). Smoking cessation is highly cost-effective (Krumholz et al. 1993; Lightwood 2003) and is recommended in professional guidelines for prevention of recurrent cardiovascular events in persons with known CVD (Smith et al. 2001). Evidence supports the central roles of smoking cessation and eliminating exposure to secondhand smoke in preventing development and progression of CVD (USDHHS 1990, 2006; Benowitz and Gourlay 1997; Hasdai et al. 1997a; van Domburg et al. 2000; Wilson et al. 2000; Goldenberg et al. 2003).

Methods

Tobacco use and dependence are determined by complex physiological and psychological factors. Use of nicotine causes tolerance, physical dependence, and a withdrawal syndrome when smoking is stopped (USDHHS 1988). Use of tobacco is a learned behavior that becomes part of the daily routine of a smoker and is often used to cope with stress, anxiety, anger, and depression (USDHHS 1988; Rigotti 2002).

Interventions to achieve smoking cessation target both the physiological and psychological factors that contribute to tobacco use. Evidence from randomized controlled clinical trials of cessation methods has been summarized in meta-analyses conducted independently by two groups—the U.S. Public Health Service (PHS) and the Cochrane Database of Systematic Reviews (the Cochrane Library). These reviews document the efficacy of both psychosocial counseling and pharmacologic agents for cessation (Fiore et al. 2000, 2008). Combination of the two methods is the most effective strategy. Interventions in psychosocial counseling range from brief counseling by the physician to intensive, cognitive-behavioral counseling interventions during several weeks. There is a dose-response relationship between behavioral treatment and smoking cessation; that is, the efficacy of counseling interventions increases with increased intensity and duration of the program (Fiore et al. 2000, 2008; USDHHS 2000). The U.S. Food and Drug Administration (FDA) has approved pharmacotherapy for tobacco dependence. The pharmacotherapy includes five types of NRT (gum, transdermal patch, nasal spray, vapor inhaler, and lozenge), sustained-release bupropion, and varenicline. PHS designated these medications as first-line therapies for smoking cessation in *Treating Tobacco Use and Dependence: Clinical Practice Guidelines* (Fiore et al. 2000). Two other drugs—nortriptyline and clonidine—were efficacious in randomized controlled trials and were shown to be effective in the Cochrane review and in meta-analyses conducted for development of the PHS guidelines (Fiore et al. 2000, 2008; Gourlay et al. 2004; Hughes et al. 2004b). These drugs have not been approved by FDA for use in smoking cessation, and in the PHS report, they are designated as second-line interventions. There is no evidence to support use of alternative therapies such as acupuncture and hypnosis for smoking cessation (Abbot et al. 1998; Fiore et al. 2000, 2008; White et al. 2002).

Interventions

Multiple randomized controlled clinical trials demonstrated the benefits of counseling patients with CVD on smoking cessation (Table 6.4) (Thomson and Rigotti 2003). In contrast, relatively few clinical trials tested the safety or efficacy of pharmacotherapy for treating smokers with CVD (Table 6.5). Researchers raised concerns about the safety of NRT and sustained-release bupropion in patients with CVD, because both agents can have sympathomimetic activity and can theoretically increase myocardial work, and NRT might also reduce the myocardial oxygen supply through coronary vasoconstriction by aggravating endothelial dysfunction (Benowitz and Gourlay 1997).

Table 6.4   **Randomized controlled trials of counseling for smokers hospitalized with cardiovascular disease**

Study	Population	In-hospital counselor, duration of counseling	Postdischarge counseling	Smoking cessation rates (%)	RR or OR (95% CI) p value
Taylor et al. 1990	Acute MI I vs. C: 86 vs. 87 5 hospitals San Francisco Bay, California	Nurse Average duration 3.5 hours for baseline and postdischarge counseling	TC: 1, 2, 3 weeks, then every month x 4 CV for relapse after smoking cessation	12 months I vs. C: 61 vs. 32	1.9 (1.3, 2.8) p <0.001
Ockene et al. 1992	Coronary angiogram I vs. C: 135 vs. 132 3 hospitals Massachusetts	Health educator 30 minutes	TC: 1, 3 weeks; 3 months for relapse after smoking cessation; 2 and 4 months for relapse after smoking cessation	12 months SR: 57 vs. 48 I vs. C: 35 vs. 28 3-vessel CAD I vs. C: 65 vs. 41	1.5 (0.9, 2.4) p = 0.06 1.4 (0.8, 2.4) p = 0.19 13.4 (3.1, 58.0)
DeBusk et al. 1994	Acute MI I vs. C: 131 vs. 121 5 hospitals San Francisco Bay, California	Nurse Duration not stated	TC: 2 days, 1 week, monthly x 6	12 months I vs. C: 70 vs. 53	p = 0.03
Rigotti et al. 1994	Coronary artery bypass graft I vs. C: 44 vs. 43 Massachusetts General Hospital, Boston	Nurse 60 minutes	TC: once per week x 3	12 months I vs. C: 61 vs. 54	p >0.52
Dornelas et al. 2000	Acute MI I vs. C: 54 vs. 46 Hartford Hospital Hartford, Connecticut	Psychologist Duration not stated	TC: <1, 4, 8, 12, 16, 20, and 26 weeks	6 months SR: 67 vs. 43 12 months SR: 55 vs. 34 FV: 66 vs. 37	p <0.05 p = 0.04 p <0.05
Hajek et al. 2002	Acute MI or cardiac bypass surgery I vs. C: 267 vs. 273 17 hospitals England	Nurse 20–30 minutes	None	12 months I vs. C: 37 vs. 41	p = 0.40
Quist-Paulsen and Gallefoss 2003	Acute MI, unstable angina, or cardiac bypass surgery I vs. C: 100 vs. 118 1 hospital Norway	Cardiac nurses (no training) Duration not stated	TC: 2 days, 1 week, 3 weeks, 3 months, 5 months CV: 6 weeks	12 months I vs. C: 50 vs. 37	Absolute risk reduction: 35% (0%, 26%)

Note: **CAD** = coronary artery disease; **CI** = confidence interval; **CV** = clinic visit; **FV** = validated by family; **I vs. C** = intervention versus control; **MI** = myocardial infarction; **OR** = odds ratio; **RR** = relative risk; **SR** = self-reported; **TC** = telephone call.

Table 6.5   Randomized controlled trials of pharmacologic interventions for smoking cessation in patients with cardiovascular disease

Study	Population	Treatment	Counseling (I & C)	Smoking cessation rates[a] (%)	RR or OR (95% CI), p value	Adverse events (I vs. C)
Transdermal nicotine						
Working Group for the Study of Transdermal Nicotine in Patients with Coronary Artery Disease 1994	Stable outpatients with CVD I vs. C: 77 vs. 79 General medical and cardiology clinics Media advertising 4 centers United States	14 mg could be increased to 21 mg after 1 week 5 weeks	Group counseling weekly x 5	5 weeks I vs. C: 36 vs. 22	p <0.05	No differences in episodes of angina or change in blood pressure, heart rate, or EKG readings
Joseph et al. 1996 Joseph and Antonnucio 1999	Stable outpatient veterans with CVD I vs. C: 288 vs. 287 10 Veterans Affairs medical centers United States	21 mg x 6 weeks 14 mg x 2 weeks 7 mg x 2 weeks	Behavioral counseling 15 minutes at study entry 10 minutes at 1 and 6 weeks	14 weeks I vs. C: 21 vs. 9 6 months I vs. C: 14 vs. 11 12 months I vs. C: 10 vs. 12	p = 0.001 p = 0.67 p = 0.41	No difference in primary endpoints (death, MI, cardiac arrest, or admission to hospital) or secondary endpoints (other CVD)
Tzivoni et al. 1998	Stable outpatients with CAD in smoking cessation program I vs. C: 52 vs. 54 2 centers Israel	21 mg (>20 cigarettes/day) or 14 mg (<20 cigarettes/day) 2 weeks	Smoking cessation program Group meetings weekly	2 weeks I vs. C: 73 vs. 52	p <0.05[b]	No differences in EKG changes, exercise testing, or heart rate and blood pressure
Bupropion-sustained release						
Tonstad et al. 2003	Stable outpatients with CVD I vs. C: 313 vs. 313 28 centers in 10 European countries	150 mg BID 7 weeks Target date for smoking cessation 7–14 days after starting drug	TC: 1 day before smoking cessation 3 days afterward Monthly x 12 CV: brief counseling at 3, 6, and 12 months	12 months I vs. C: 27 vs. 12 Continuous abstinence weeks 4–52 I vs. C: 22 vs. 9	p <0.001 p <0.001	Cardiovascular events I vs. C: 24 vs. 14 (p = NS)

Table 6.5   Continued

Study	Population	Treatment	Counseling (I & C)	Smoking cessation rates[a] (%)	RR or OR (95% CI), p value	Adverse events (I vs. C)
Rigotti et al. 2006	Acute MI, unstable angina, or other CVD hospital admission I vs. C: 124 vs. 124 5 academic medical centers New England	150 mg BID 12 weeks Started during hospitalization	Nurse counseling for 40 minutes in hospital TC: 48 hours, 1, 3, 8, and 12 weeks after discharge	12 weeks I vs. C: 37 vs. 27 12 months I vs. C: 25 vs. 21	1.61 (0.74, 2.76) p = 0.08 1.23 (0.68, 2.23) p = 0.49	No difference in CVD mortality (0% vs. 2%) or in CVD events at 12 weeks (16% vs. 14%, IRR 1.22 [0.61–2.48]) or 1 year (26% vs. 18%, IRR 1.56 [0.88, 2.82])

Note: **BID** = twice a day; **CAD** = coronary artery disease; **CI** = confidence interval; **CV** = clinic visit; **CVD** = cardiovascular disease; **EKG** = electrocardiogram; **I vs. C** = intervention versus control; **IRR** = incidence rate ratio; **mg** = milligrams; **MI** = myocardial infarction; **NS** = not significant; **OR** = odds ratio; **RR** = relative risk; **TC** = telephone call.

[a]Abstinence measured by point prevalence (no smoking in previous seven days) unless otherwise noted.

[b]p value calculated with χ^2 test.

Counseling

Several randomized controlled clinical trials demonstrated the efficacy of counseling for patients hospitalized with CVD (Table 6.4). The evidence for efficacy is strongest for patients who had acute MI (Pozen et al. 1977; Taylor et al. 1990; Ockene et al. 1992; DeBusk et al. 1994; Dornelas et al. 2000). In one study, an intensive, nurse-managed intervention to achieve smoking cessation for 173 smokers hospitalized with an acute MI doubled the cessation rates at one year (61 versus 32 percent, p <0.001) (Taylor et al. 1990). At the bedside, the nurse delivered a 30-minute cognitive-behavioral counseling session focused on self-efficacy and prevention of relapse. Additional counseling was delivered by telephone at one, two, and three weeks after discharge and then every month for four months. A second study of the same patients expanded the nurse-delivered counseling model to target multiple cardiac risk factors (DeBusk et al. 1994). This study also reported rates of smoking abstinence higher than those in the first study (Taylor et al. 1990). A third trial assigned 100 consecutive smokers admitted with MI to either minimal care or bedside counseling with seven follow-up telephone calls (Dornelas et al. 2000). Smoking cessation rates at one year were higher in the intervention group than in the minimal care group (55 versus 34 percent, p <0.05). A more recent study of 240 smokers admitted to the hospital for MI, unstable angina, or cardiac bypass surgery demonstrated that counseling by cardiac nurses untrained in counseling and then follow-up counseling during the next five

months reduced smoking rates at one year (50 versus 37 percent, absolute risk reduction, 13 percentage points [95 percent CI, 0 to 26 percentage points]) (Quist-Paulsen and Gallefoss 2003).

Other studies that lacked the same intensity of follow-up after hospital discharge produced less impressive results. One study examined a multicomponent behavioral smoking intervention delivered to 267 patients having coronary angiography (Ockene et al. 1992). Compared with patients who did not receive the intervention, those with angiography had higher rates of validated smoking abstinence at 6 months (45 versus 34 percent) and 12 months (35 versus 28 percent), but these differences were not statistically significant. Two randomized trials (Rigotti et al. 1994; Hajek et al. 2002) and one partially randomized trial (Bolman et al. 2002) examined the effects of inpatient counseling with minimal follow-up in cardiac patients. These studies showed no improvement in abstinence rates with the counseling intervention versus usual care.

The most successful counseling interventions for cardiac inpatients include high-intensity baseline counseling with sustained contacts after discharge for prevention of relapse. However, even with the most successful counseling interventions, at least 40 percent of smokers who have cardiac disease resume smoking within one year. Guidelines for smoking cessation recommend addition of pharmacotherapy to counseling (Fiore et al. 2000, 2008). Pharmacotherapy has the potential to improve smoking cessation rates in smokers with CVD (see "Nicotine Replacement Therapy" and "Bupropion" later in this chapter).

Nicotine Replacement Therapy

NRT helps smokers stop smoking and also reduces nicotine withdrawal symptoms, which begin a few hours after the last cigarette is smoked and can last up to four weeks (Hughes et al. 1992). The typical withdrawal syndrome is characterized by agitation, anxiety, depressed mood, difficulty concentrating, increased appetite, insomnia, irritability, restlessness, and an intense craving to smoke. Most smokers who stop smoking relapse to smoking within the first week, when withdrawal symptoms are strongest.

In multiple clinical trials, all the NRT products approximately doubled rates of smoking abstinence compared with rates for participants receiving a placebo (Fiore et al. 2000; Silagy et al. 2004). Meta-analyses conducted for PHS demonstrated ORs of 1.9 (95 percent CI, 1.7–2.2) for the nicotine patch and 1.5 (95 percent CI, 1.3–1.8) for nicotine gum. Meta-analyses from the Cochrane Library found similar results; ORs were 1.74 (95 percent CI, 1.57–1.93) for the patch and 1.66 (95 percent CI, 1.52–1.81) for the gum (Silagy et al. 2004). For smokers with greater dependence on nicotine, the 4-mg dose of nicotine gum was more effective than the 2-mg dose. Maximum effectiveness depended on correct chewing techniques. Similar ORs were reported after meta-analyses of data on the nicotine inhaler and nicotine nasal spray (Fiore et al. 2000). Only one study compared the efficacy of four forms of NRT (patch, gum, inhaler, and nasal spray); they demonstrated similar efficacy rates after 12 weeks of follow-up (Hajek et al. 1999).

Nicotine directly affects the cardiovascular system by multiple mechanisms (see "Cigarette Smoke Constituents and Cardiovascular Disease" earlier in this chapter). The various effects lead to increased heart rate, blood pressure, and myocardial contractility, and reduced coronary blood flow. Nicotine may also contribute to insulin resistance and development of a more atherogenic lipid profile. The nicotine dose in NRT products is usually lower than the dose from smoking, but there have been concerns about the safety of NRT in patients with CVD. Case reports in the medical literature described atrial fibrillation, MI, and stroke in patients receiving NRT (Joseph and Fu 2003). It is difficult to assess the cardiovascular risk from NRT on the basis of these reports, because of the inability to control for individual risk factors for these events, especially that these persons were smokers (Benowitz and Gourlay 1997; Joseph and Fu 2003).

To date, three randomized controlled trials of transdermal use of nicotine have been conducted in patients with stable CVD. The first study enrolled 156 patients with CHD and randomly assigned them to receive either 14-mg nicotine patches or a placebo for five weeks (Working Group for the Study of Transdermal Nicotine in Patients with Coronary Artery Disease 1994). The dose was increased to 21 mg if smoking persisted. Smoking abstinence was achieved at five weeks by 36 percent in the patch group and 22 percent in the placebo group (p <0.05). Patients recorded all episodes of angina, palpitations, and other cardiac symptoms in daily diaries and had a 12-lead electrocardiogram at three time points. The nicotine patch did not affect the frequency of angina, arrhythmias, or depression of the ST segment (isoelectric period) on electrocardiograms during the five weeks of treatment, even in patients who smoked intermittently.

A second randomized trial of transdermal nicotine included 584 outpatients with CVD from 10 Veterans Affairs hospitals (Joseph et al. 1996). The participants were randomly assigned to receive 21-mg patches or a placebo for 10 weeks. Primary cardiovascular endpoints during 14 weeks of follow-up included MI, cardiac arrest, death, and hospital admission for angina, dysrhythmia, or congestive heart failure. The two groups did not differ in the proportion of patients who reached at least one cardiovascular endpoint (5.4 versus 7.9 percent, p = 0.23). Concomitant use of the nicotine patch and smoking was not associated with an increase in adverse events. Although use of the patch was safe in this population, no improvement was observed in rates of short-term or long-term smoking abstinence in comparisons with the placebo group (Joseph et al. 1996; Joseph and Antonuccio 1999).

A third trial tested use of the nicotine patch in 106 smokers with CHD (Tzivoni et al. 1998). Patients were randomly assigned to receive nicotine patches or placebo patches for two weeks. All patients had ambulatory electrocardiogram monitoring and exercise testing at study entry, after the first application of the patch, and at two weeks. No difference was observed at any of the three time points, between the patch and placebo groups, in resting heart rate, blood pressure, the number or duration of ischemic episodes, frequency of arrhythmias, exercise duration, or time to 1-mm depression of the ST segment on an electrocardiogram. In a randomized study of 234 patients with both cardiovascular and respiratory diseases, no increase in adverse events was observed in patients assigned to the nicotine patch or the placebo (Campbell et al. 1996).

In a case-control study, Kimmel and colleagues (2001) found no increased risk of a first MI with use of the nicotine patch in persons who stopped smoking or those who continued to smoke. Using a computerized database for general practice in the United Kingdom, Hubbard and colleagues (2005) studied the relative incidence of MI and stroke in four two-week periods before and after the first prescription for NRT. They found a progressive increase in risk in the 56 days after the first NRT prescription but no evidence of increased cardiovascular events or mortality in the 56 days after the NRT prescription.

Meine and colleagues (2005) addressed the safety of transdermal nicotine in the setting of acute CHD. These investigators analyzed data in the Duke University Cardiovascular Databank for 9,991 smokers who had cardiac catheterization after hospital admission for unstable angina or non-ST-segment MI. This retrospective observational study compared outcomes of patients who did or did not receive transdermal nicotine during hospitalization. The study identified 194 patients who had been treated with transdermal nicotine during the hospital stay. The investigators used a "propensity score analysis" to compare patients receiving transdermal nicotine with matched patients from the database who did not receive the medication. Because patients were not randomly assigned to receive transdermal nicotine, selection bias could have confounded these results. In an attempt to reduce this bias, patients who did or did not receive transdermal nicotine were matched on demographic characteristics, diagnosis, cardiac risk factors, and mean cardiac ejection fraction. Rates of cardiac outcomes in the two groups were compared. No differences in 7-day, 30-day, or one-year mortality rates were observed. Patients receiving transdermal nicotine were not more likely to have coronary artery bypass grafting or percutaneous transluminal coronary angioplasty during hospitalization. It was not possible to control for the dose of medication received, the amount of smoking before hospital admission, or relapse to smoking after hospitalization. These results provide some evidence that NRT was safe in the setting of acute CVD, but randomized controlled trials are needed to establish the safety of NRT in patients who have unstable cardiac disease.

Other studies examined markers of exposure to tobacco smoke related to cardiovascular risk as surrogate endpoints for cardiovascular events in clinical trials. There was no evidence that NRT raised blood pressure in any of the efficacy trials, but these trials typically excluded patients with poor control of hypertension. In one small trial of 30 smokers with or without hypertension, NRT increased mean arterial pressure in smokers with normal blood pressure but not in smokers who had hypertension (Tanus-Santos et al. 2001).

To date, two studies have tested the effect of NRT on coronary circulation in smokers with CHD. One study examined the size of defects in myocardial perfusion in 36 patients with baseline CHD who were treated with nicotine patches (Mahmarian et al. 1997). Participants continued to smoke but at reduced levels. The researchers concluded that use of the patch, even with concomitant smoking and higher plasma levels of nicotine, resulted in reduction of exercise-induced ischemia in a comparison with baseline values. This finding suggested that components of tobacco smoke other than nicotine are responsible for impaired coronary blood flow. The second study investigated the effect of nicotine gum on coronary perfusion in former cigarette smokers having angiography (Nitenberg and Antony 1999). The findings demonstrated that the gum did not reduce the surface area of normal or diseased segments of the coronary artery. Other studies of the effects of smoking cessation on lipids and thrombosis reported improvements in these markers, even among smokers using NRT (Allen et al. 1994; Lúdvíksdóttir et al. 1999; Eliasson et al. 2001; Haustein et al. 2002).

In summary, despite anecdotal reports of cardiovascular events attributable to use of NRT, data from multiple clinical trials of smokers with or without CVD show no evidence for increased cardiovascular risk when NRT is used to treat tobacco dependence. However, the safety of NRT has not been tested in a more acute setting, such as during hospitalization for a cardiovascular event. Observational data suggest that use of the nicotine patch in patients with unstable cardiac disease is probably safe (Meine et al. 2005), but randomized trials are needed to confirm these findings. Current PHS guidelines recommend that NRT be used with caution in smokers with unstable angina, MI in the past two weeks, or serious arrhythmia (Fiore et al. 2000).

Bupropion

Bupropion is an aminoketone approved by FDA in 1989 for treatment of depression and in 1997 for smoking cessation. The drug is included in national guidelines as first-line therapy for smoking cessation (Fiore et al. 2000, 2008). Its mechanism of action is not fully understood, but researchers think it acts by inhibiting neuronal uptake of norepinephrine and dopamine. Bupropion may also block activity of nAChRs. The mechanism of action for smoking cessation appears to be unrelated to the antidepressant effects of bupropion. A preparation of the drug for sustained release provides a better safety profile and more convenient dosing than does the immediate-release form.

Evidence from several randomized controlled trials shows that bupropion doubled the smoking cessation rates obtained with a placebo. Meta-analyses of data on bupropion for smoking cessation conducted by PHS and the Cochrane Library yielded ORs of 2.1 (95 percent CI, 1.5–3.0) and 2.06 (95 percent CI, 1.77–2.40), respectively (Fiore et al. 2000; Hughes et al. 2004b). One trial compared use of bupropion, a nicotine patch, bupropion plus a patch, and a placebo among 893 participants (Jorenby et al. 1999). Smoking abstinence rates at one year were 15.6 percent in the placebo group, 16.4 percent in the nicotine-patch group, 30.3 percent in the bupropion group (p <0.0001 versus the placebo group), and 35.5 percent in the bupropion-plus-patch group (p <0.0001 versus the placebo group; p = 0.06 versus the bupropion-alone group).

The major risk of bupropion is that it lowers a person's seizure threshold. The risk of seizure from the sustained-release formulation is 0.1 percent, which is no different from that for other antidepressants (Hughes et al. 1999; Rigotti 2002). No seizures were reported in any of the clinical trials that tested sustained-release bupropion for smoking cessation.

As with NRT, early case reports of serious cardiovascular events with sustained-release bupropion raised questions about the safety of this agent in patients with CVD. These reports, which were mostly in Canada and England, included cardiac deaths, chest pain, MI, and myocarditis (Joseph and Fu 2003). Assessment of the contribution of bupropion to these events is difficult because evaluation of other cardiac risk factors in these patients was not possible.

To date, none of the efficacy trials of bupropion for smoking cessation has reported a significant increase in cardiovascular events. Two randomized controlled trials enrolled only smokers with CVD. The first trial enrolled 629 outpatients with stable CVD—that is, MI or an interventional cardiac procedure more than three months earlier and stable angina pectoris, PAD, or congestive heart failure (Tonstad et al. 2003). Patients were randomly assigned to receive bupropion or a placebo for seven weeks. This study found no differences in the number of deaths in the two groups—two in the bupropion group and two in the placebo group. Overall, 38 participants (6 percent) reported a single adverse cardiovascular event—24 in the bupropion group and 14 in the placebo group. The most common cardiovascular events were angina pectoris, hypertension, and palpitations; 13 events occurred in the bupropion group versus 8 events in the placebo group. No statistical tests were performed on the rates of adverse events. Patients who took bupropion were more likely to have stopped smoking at one year than were patients who took the placebo (27 versus 12 percent, p <0.001).

A second trial enrolled 248 smokers hospitalized with acute CVD, including acute MI, unstable angina, or other cardiovascular conditions (Rigotti et al. 2006). Patients were randomly assigned to receive sustained-release bupropion or a placebo for 12 weeks, and all patients received intensive counseling during hospitalization and follow-up. At the one-year follow-up, the difference between death rates in the bupropion group (no

deaths) and in the placebo group (two deaths) was not statistically significant. During the 12 weeks of drug treatment, the difference between the number of cardiovascular events in the bupropion group (20 events) and the placebo group (17 events) was also not significant. Cardiovascular events included death, nonfatal MI, unstable angina, congestive heart failure, stroke, and coronary revascularization procedure. At the one-year follow-up, the number of cardiovascular events in the bupropion group (32 events, 26 percent) exceeded the number in the placebo group (22 events, 18 percent), but this difference was not significant. In addition, at one year, the difference between the smoking abstinence rates for the bupropion group (25 percent) versus the placebo group (21 percent) was not significant. However, the results after 12 weeks of drug treatment suggested that bupropion had short-term efficacy (37 versus 27 percent, p = 0.08).

In summary, sustained-release bupropion is effective and safe for treating smokers with stable CVD. The drug appears to be less efficacious in smokers hospitalized with acute CVD than in other groups of patients. Bupropion is the only medication for treating tobacco dependence that has been tested in patients with acute CVD, and it appears to be safe for those with either stable or acute disease.

Other Pharmacotherapy

Varenicline, a partial agonist of the α4β2 nAChR, has been marketed for the treatment of tobacco dependence but its use in smokers with CVD has not yet been studied (Coe et al. 2005). The drug produces approximately 50 percent of the receptor stimulation provided by nicotine, but it blocks the effects of any nicotine taken in from cigarette smoking. Clinical trials have found it superior to bupropion in promoting smoking cessation, and prolonged administration has been shown to reduce relapse in smokers who had been abstinent 12 weeks after initial therapy (Gonzalez et al. 2006; Jorenby et al. 2006; Tonstad et al. 2006). Two other medications have been demonstrated to be effective for smoking cessation: nortriptyline, a tricyclic antidepressant, and clonidine, a central α-agonist antihypertension agent. However, neither drug has been approved by FDA for smoking cessation. Both agents have potential cardiovascular side effects, and the safety profile of these drugs should be considered carefully before use in smokers with CVD.

Meta-analyses of data on use of clonidine for treating smokers resulted in ORs for smoking abstinence of 2.1 (95 percent CI, 1.4–3.2) (Fiore et al. 2000) and 1.89 (95 percent CI, 1.30–2.74) (Gourlay et al. 2004). To date, no safety data for patients with CVD are available. However, clonidine is known to cause orthostatic hypotension, rebound hypertension from abrupt cessation of the drug, and rarely, atrioventricular nodal blockade. Nortriptyline is also effective in promoting smoking cessation; meta-analyses yielded ORs of 3.2 (95 percent CI, 1.8–5.7) (Fiore et al. 2000) and 2.79 (95 percent CI, 1.70–4.59) (Hughes et al. 2004b). Nortriptyline was designated a second-line drug for smoking cessation in PHS clinical guidelines because of a smaller evidence base of support and greater side effects than those of other medications for smoking cessation. In general, tricyclic antidepressants are avoided in patients with CVD because of concerns about increased risks for arrhythmias and depression of myocardial contractility (Joseph and Fu 2003).

Although the focus of the preceding section ("Methods") was on clinical interventions to reduce smoking, it is important to recognize that policy-based interventions, such as smoke-free environments and community and statewide tobacco control programs, are also important elements in a strategy to improve cardiovascular health. For example, smoke-free workplaces are a highly cost-effective approach to promoting smoking cessation with an impact on cardiovascular health (Ong and Glantz 2004). Decreases in admissions to hospitals have been observed after smoke-free laws have gone into effect (Dinno and Glantz 2007). The California Tobacco Control Program substantially accelerated the decline in the heart disease death rate in the state (Fichtenberg and Glantz 2000).

It should be noted that although long-term smoking quit rates after various interventions in cardiovascular patients may appear to be low (most less than 30 percent),

smoking cessation therapy has an important impact on CVD, and the cost per life saved is lower than that of many other therapeutic interventions for CHD that are considered to be the standard (such as treatment of hypertension and hyperlipidemia) (Lightwood 2003).

Summary

Smoking cessation is a key element in both primary and secondary prevention of CVD. Guidelines from PHS recommend counseling, NRT, sustained-release bupropion, and varenicline as first-line treatments to achieve smoking cessation. Studies show that NRT and bupropion are effective in patients with CVD, although not all trials demonstrated efficacy. Several studies have demonstrated the safety of NRT in patients with stable CVD, but randomized trials are needed to establish the safety of this treatment for patients hospitalized with acute disease. Bupropion appears to be safe in patients with stable or unstable CVD, but it is less effective in patients with acute disease. Varenicline is a partial agonist of the $\alpha4\beta2$ nAChR that is effective in treating tobacco dependence, but it has not yet been studied in smokers with CVD. The development of more effective pharmacotherapies to aid smoking cessation that are safe in persons with CVD is a high research priority.

Methods to Reduce Exposure

Evidence-based interventions for treating smokers include behavioral and pharmacological treatments, which significantly increase rates for long-term abstinence from smoking. Even so, absolute rates of abstinence are modest; they range from 8 to 25 percent, depending on the study population and the treatment. In addition, only a small proportion of smokers are interested in treatment at any given time. Interest in smoking cessation and success in achieving long-term abstinence are greater among patients with CVD than in the general population of smokers (Thomson and Rigotti 2003). Nevertheless, abstinence rates remain disappointingly low, particularly in light of the important health benefits for this population when they do stop smoking (USDHHS 1990; Burns 2003).

Suboptimal treatment outcomes prompted interest in testing interventions that might decrease the risk of smoking among those who continue to use tobacco.

These strategies are often termed "harm reduction" interventions, although data are limited as to whether harm is really lessened with reduced exposure to tobacco. To date, the effect of methods for reducing exposure on risk factors for CVD and on development of CVD has been evaluated in a limited number of clinical trials, prospective cohort studies, and epidemiologic studies.

Endpoints with respect to CVD that have been measured in studies of reduced exposure include measures of exposure to tobacco constituents (e.g., nicotine and CO); biomarkers of inflammation (e.g., CRP, leukocyte counts, and fibrinogen); thrombosis (e.g., fibrinogen and PAI-1); lipid abnormalities (e.g., levels of total cholesterol, HDLc, LDLc, triglycerides, APOs A-I and B, and HDLc to LDLc ratio); oxidative stress that reflects and may contribute to cardiovascular risk (e.g., F_2-isoprostanes); and clinical outcomes (blood pressure, heart rate, angina, exercise tolerance, MI, other adverse events, and death) (Table 6.3).

Reduced Smoking

Important methodologic considerations in evaluating studies of reduced smoking include the extent and duration of smoking reduction, use of nicotine replacement products, doses, and timing of endpoint measurements (Table 6.6). In addition, some studies report outcome data on the basis of intention to treat all participants, regardless of whether treatment was successful. Others report only on subgroups who achieve specific goals for smoking reduction.

Eliasson and colleagues (2001) tested the effect of nicotine nasal spray on achieving smoking reduction and abstinence among 58 healthy adult smokers in an open-label cohort study. The primary goal for the first eight weeks of the study was to reduce daily smoking by 50 percent; participants were asked to stop smoking after eight weeks. Cardiovascular risk factors were evaluated at baseline, at eight weeks, and after eight weeks of abstinence. The 33 study participants provided data at all three time points. After participants completed eight weeks of smoking reduction, mean cigarette use decreased by 50.2 percent, expired CO dropped 17 percent, and plasma thiocyanate decreased by 20.1 percent. Significant improvements included fibrinogen levels (from 2.9 g/liter [L] to 2.65 g/L, p = 0.011); hemoglobin values (from 13.8 to 13.3 g/L, p <0.001); leukocyte counts (from 7.0 to 6.2 x 10^9/L, p = 0.005); and HDLc to LDLc ratio (from 0.33 to 0.37, p <0.005). Eight weeks of abstinence from smoking was associated with further improvements in hemoglobin levels, leukocyte counts, and HDL and LDL levels, and significant reduction in PAI-1 activity. These researchers did not observe improvements in HDLc and LDLc levels with reduction in smoking.

Hurt and colleagues (2000) conducted a small, open-label cohort study to test the effect of a nicotine inhaler on biomarkers of exposure to cigarette smoke among 23 heavy smokers. Levels of blood thiocyanate, several urine carcinogens, and expired CO were measured at study entry and at 4, 8, 12, and 24 weeks. Despite an average reduction among participants from 40 or more to 10 cigarettes per day, expired CO decreased only from 30.4 to 26.0 parts per million (ppm), reflecting compensatory smoking or misreporting of reduction in smoking. This change was not statistically significant.

In the U.S. Lung Health Study, 5,887 male and female smokers were randomly assigned to one of three groups: intervention for smoking cessation, including nicotine gum, plus bronchodilator therapy; intervention plus a placebo; or usual care (Hughes et al. 2004a). Among 3,923 participants in the intervention at the one-year follow-up, 1,722 continued to smoke daily. Reduction in the number of cigarettes smoked was not an objective of the intervention, but 16 percent of those who continued to smoke daily smoked 1 to 24 percent fewer cigarettes than at baseline; another 27 percent reduced smoking by 25 to 49 percent; 19 percent, by 50 to 74 percent; and 11 percent, by 75 to 99 percent. The mean reduction in cigarettes smoked was 29 percent (from 32 to 22 cigarettes per day), and the mean reduction in CO levels was 24 percent (from 34 to 26 ppm). Thus, more than 80 percent of those who did not stop smoking achieved some level of reduction. However, the reduction in CO was not as large as the reduction in cigarettes per day. This finding again suggests compensatory smoking.

Hatsukami and colleagues (2005) examined the effect of smoking reduction on cardiovascular risk factors among 151 cigarette smokers interested in stopping smoking but not in reducing their smoking. Nicotine patches and gum were used to assist with reduction of smoking. The cardiovascular risk factors (CO and cholesterol levels, leukocyte counts, blood pressure, and heart rate) were measured for 12 weeks after study entry. Biomarkers did not change among persons who continued to smoke ad libitum, but the 61 persons who reduced smoking achieved significant improvements. Smokers who reduced the self-reported number of cigarettes smoked per day by 40 percent or more had significantly reduced leukocyte counts (from 7.39 to 6.98 x 10^9/L, p <0.001); higher HDLc levels (from 50.3 to 52.8 mg per deciliter [dL], p <0.0167); improved HDL to LDL ratios (from 0.47 to 0.49, p <0.0167); lower APO B levels (from 103.7 to 103.0 mg/dL, p <0.0167); lower systolic blood pressure (from 123.0 to 120.3 mm Hg, p <0.0167); and lower heart rate (from 75.7 to 70.2 beats per minute, p <0.001). Although some of these changes were statistically significant, they are modest, and the clinical importance is undetermined. Levels of triglycerides, total cholesterol, APO A-I, and diastolic blood pressure did not change, and LDLc levels increased from 122.1 to 124.4 mg/dL (p <0.0167).

To date, only one randomized controlled trial of an intervention for smoking reduction among persons with known CVD has been conducted (Joseph et al. 2005). Treatment included behavioral counseling and NRT with patches and gum. The goal of this study of 152 participants was at least a 50-percent reduction in cigarettes smoked per day; usual care was the standard for comparison. At study entry, participants smoked an average of 27.4 cigarettes per day. At six months, the intervention group had reduced cigarette use by 39 percent, versus a decline of 25 percent in the usual care group, but this difference was not statistically significant. Biomarkers for carcinogenesis and CVD were measured, as were clinical outcomes. No significant differences between the treatment groups were observed for levels of CO, fibrinogen, F_2-isoprostanes, or CRP, or for leukocyte counts. The groups did not differ in clinical

Table 6.6   Smoking reduction and cardiovascular disease endpoints: biomarkers and clinical outcomes

Study	Design	n	Follow-up	NRT	Reduction from baseline CPD	Nicotine	CO (ppm)
Hurt et al. 2000	Open-label cohort	23	24 weeks	Inhaler	≥40 to 10**	_[a]	NS
Eliasson et al. 2001	Open-label cohort	33	9 weeks	Nasal spray	21.5 to 10.8**; 50.2%	-	-
Godtfredsen et al. 2003	Prospective cohort study	643[c]	Mean 13.8 years	NA	≥50%[d]	Significant	13.2 vs. 8.7***
Hughes et al. 2004a	Reduction cohort in RCT	1,722	1 year	Gum	32 to 22; 29%	-	NS
Hatsukami et al. 2005	Reduction cohort in RCT	61	12 weeks	Patch and gum	24.16 to 6.93*; >40%	_[f]	19.9 to 6.77***
Joseph et al.[h] 2005	RCT	152	6 months	Patch and gum	27.7 to 16.8*	NS	NS

Note: **APO A-I** = apolipoprotein A-I; **APO B** = apolipoprotein B; **BP** = blood pressure; **CCSC** = Canadian Cardiovascular Society classification; **CO (ppm)** = carbon monoxide (parts per million); **CPD** = cigarettes/day; **Fibr** = fibrinogen concentrations; **g/L** = grams per liter; **Hb** = hemoglobin; **HDL** = high-density lipoprotein; **hs-CRP** = high-sensitivity C-reactive protein; **LDL** = low-density lipoprotein; **mg/dL** = milligrams per deciliter; **MI** = myocardial infarction; **n** = number in sample (or study) population; **NA** = not applicable; **NRT** = nicotine replacement therapy; **NS** = not significant; **PAI-1** = plasminogen activator inhibitor-1; **Plts** = platelets; **RCT** = reverse cholesterol transport; **SAEs** = serious adverse events; **Trigly** = triglycerides; **WBC** = white blood cells.

outcomes, including body weight, distance completed in a six-minute walking test, the proportion of participants completing that test, the prevalence and frequency of angina, the need for urgent cardiac care, and other serious adverse events. Because no significant differences between treatment groups were observed and because both groups achieved significant reductions in cigarette use from baseline, results for the entire cohort at six months were compared with the baseline data. There were no significant differences in biomarkers of cardiovascular risk, including leukocyte counts and levels of F_2-isoprostanes or CRP, but CO had decreased by 6.0 ppm (p = 0.007).

Godtfredsen and colleagues (2003) conducted a prospective cohort study in Denmark to examine changes in the incidence of MI after spontaneous reductions in cigarette use. This study included 10,956 men and 8,467 women who provided detailed information on smoking behavior during two examinations. Mortality registers and hospital registers were searched for an incident of hospital admission or a death attributable to MI. A sample consisting of pooled data from three population studies yielded 643 participants who were heavy smokers at study entry and were evaluated for the effects of reduced smoking.

These persons reported unassisted reductions in tobacco use by at least 50 percent and were compared

			Reduction from baseline			
Hb (g/L)	WBC × 10⁹/L	Fibr (g/L)	LDL (mg/dL)	HDL (mg/dL)	Other biomarkers	Clinical outcomes
-	-	-	-	-	-	-
13.8 to 13.3**	7.0 to 6.2**	2.9 to 2.6*	NS[b]	NS	Plts NS PAI-1 NS	-
-	-	-	-[e]	NS	-	Systolic BP NS Diastolic BP 80.7 vs. 78.8*** Risk of MI NS
-	-	-	-	-	-	-
14.49 to 14.40*	7.39 to 6.98***	-	122.14 to 124.36*[g]	50.27 to 52.82*	Trigly NS APO A-I NS APO B 103.74 to 103.0*	Systolic BP 122.97 to 122.29* Diastolic BP NS Heart rate 75.7 to 70.18***
NS	NS	NS	-	-	hs-CRP NS F_2-isoprostanes NS	6-minute walk, angina presences/ frequency, CCSC classification, cardiac or other SAEs NS

[a]Thiocyanate concentrations increased from 189 to 198 micromoles/L (p <0.05).
[b]HDL to LDL ratio increased from 0.33 to 0.37, p <0.005.
[c]Total cohort = 19,423.
[d]22.2 grams tobacco per day in continued heavy smokers versus 10.5 grams per day in reducers (p <0.001).
[e]Total cholesterol NS.
[f]Anatabine decreased from 4.69 to 3.02 nanograms per milligram of creatinine (statistically significant).
[g]HDL to LDL ratio increased from 0.47 to 0.49, p <0.0167.
[h]Reduction in CPD reported for smoking reduction intervention group, significance tests reported for smoking reduction versus control group.
*p <0.05, **p <0.01, ***p <0.001.

with 1,379 persons who reported abstinence from smoking. Outcomes were adjusted for baseline cardiovascular risk factors. Smoking cessation was associated with a hazard ratio for MI of 0.71 (95 percent CI, 0.59–0.85), but smoking reduction was not associated with a statistically significant reduction in risk of MI (hazard ratio, 1.15 [95 percent CI, 0.94–1.40]). A subgroup analysis demonstrated significant reductions in levels of expired CO among persons who reduced cigarette smoking. The investigators concluded that the results were consistent with a short-term thrombogenic effect of tobacco exposure rather than with a cumulative effect of exposure.

They speculated that an approximate 50-percent reduction (from 20 g to 10 g of tobacco smoked per day) was not sufficient to improve cardiovascular risk. These epidemiologic data make an important contribution because they are population based and come from a large cohort of smokers who reduced their smoking during a period longer than the usual timeframe for clinical trials.

In summary, these studies show that a significant reduction in cigarette use, even to levels as low as 10 cigarettes per day, results in reduction of exposure to CO from tobacco smoke that is smaller than expected. This finding most likely reflects compensatory smoking. Some but not all studies showed reduced exposure to nicotine, as well as improvements in values for hemoglobin, leukocyte counts, and fibrinogen and cholesterol levels. However, the improvements in values are relatively minor compared with those observed with abstinence from smoking. Many of these improvements occurred in study participants who were using NRT (see "Nicotine Replacement Therapy" below). None of the studies showed improvements in clinical outcomes of heart disease, consistent with evidence presented earlier that low levels of smoke exposure trigger many of the adverse cardiovascular effects of smoke (see "Exposure to Secondhand Tobacco Smoke" earlier in this chapter).

Nicotine Replacement Therapy

In addition to providing data on smoking reduction, the Lung Health Study of 3,094 persons offered a unique opportunity to examine the natural history and safety of prolonged use of nicotine gum among thousands of people during a five-year follow-up (Murray et al. 1996). Persistent smoking, but not use of nicotine gum, predicted fatal and nonfatal cardiovascular events and elevation of diastolic blood pressure.

In general, trials of smoking cessation and smoking reduction showed improvements in lipid profiles, even with NRT. Eliasson and colleagues (2001) observed that use of nicotine nasal spray for smoking reduction or cessation yielded significant improvements in HDLc to LDLc ratios at 9 weeks, with further improvements if smokers abstained from smoking for 17 weeks (see "Reduced Smoking" earlier in this chapter). In addition, significant improvements in fibrinogen levels and leukocyte counts were observed. A clinical trial of smoking cessation also reported significant decreases in hemoglobin values, leukocyte counts, and total and LDLc concentrations (Lúdvíksdóttir et al. 1999). In addition, HDLc to LDLc ratios improved among participants who abstained from smoking after three months of treatment with a nicotine nasal spray. Allen and colleagues (1994) also observed significantly increased HDLc levels in participants treated with the nicotine patch.

Investigators have noted improvements in markers of thrombogenesis among persons who abstained from smoking and were using medicinal nicotine. In one study, plasma fibrinogen levels were reduced among 164 men using a combination of a nicotine patch and gum for 12 weeks to stop smoking (Haustein et al. 2002). In another study, use of transdermal nicotine appeared to activate platelet aggregation less than smoking did (Benowitz et al. 1993).

Mahmarian and colleagues (1997) used single photon emission computed tomography to measure the combined effects of smoking and use of nicotine patches on myocardial perfusion. In 36 patients with known CHD who were treated with nicotine patches, the amount of heart muscle deprived of normal blood flow (size of perfusion defects) decreased despite increased serum nicotine levels. The baseline size of defects and changes in CO levels, but not in nicotine levels, predicted the size of perfusion defects. The researchers concluded that the reduction in the size of defects resulted from reduction in smoking that was facilitated by NRT and from decreased exposure to CO. They also concluded that nicotine patches were safe to use in smokers with heart disease.

Nitenberg and Antony (1999) used angiography to examine short-term effects of use of nicotine gum on perfusion of the coronary arteries in former cigarette smokers at study entry, after a test with immersion of the hand in cold water (cold pressor test) before and after administration of the gum. The gum did not augment the result of the cold pressor test, which constricted normal and diseased segments of the coronary artery, reducing their cross-sectional area, and it did not reduce the surface area of the arterial segments at rest or under conditions of sympathetic stimulation.

These results suggest that reduction of exposure to tobacco smoke through use of NRT or with abstinence from smoking is associated with improvements in biomarkers of cardiovascular risk.

Summary

Epidemiologic studies demonstrate a strong dose-response relationship between the number of cigarettes smoked per day and cardiovascular risk. The relationship is not linear, however, and even low levels of exposure to tobacco, such as a few cigarettes per day, occasional smoking, or exposure to secondhand tobacco smoke are sufficient to substantially increase risk of cardiac events. Some interventions have accomplished significant reductions in the number of cigarettes smoked per day, but the reductions in levels of biomarkers of exposure and biomarkers of cardiovascular risk factors are not proportional, probably because of compensatory smoking by study participants and the nonlinear dose-response relationship. The limited data on clinical outcome do not confirm reduction in cardiovascular events due to reduced smoking. Other methods for reducing exposure, including NRT with abstinence from smoking, are associated with more improvement in risk factors for CVD than is smoking reduction with or without pharmacologic support. Accordingly, these methods hold more potential for reducing risk.

Implications

These findings suggest that to lower cardiac risk, interventions would have to reduce exposure to tobacco smoke to extremely low levels or eliminate the exposure. Studies of smoking reduction to date suggest that goals would be difficult to accomplish. Reducing exposure by reducing smoking, therefore, appears to have limited promise for improving cardiac risk unless this method contributes to eventual smoking cessation (Hughes 2000). Because smoking cessation is associated with marked improvements in the risk of MI, sudden death, and stroke, it should be stressed as the goal for interventions dealing with dependence on tobacco. The safety and efficacy of long-term NRT use to reduce cardiovascular risk by maintaining smoking cessation have not been established.

Evidence Summary

Exposure to tobacco smoke is associated with accelerated atherosclerosis and an increased risk of acute MI, stroke, PAD, aortic aneurysm, and sudden death. Smoking appears to have both causal relationships and multiplicative interactions with other major risk factors for CHD, including hyperlipidemia, hypertension, and diabetes mellitus.

The cardiovascular risk attributable to cigarette smoking increases sharply at low levels of cigarette consumption and with exposure to secondhand smoke. The risk then tends to plateau at higher levels of smoking. This finding indicates a low threshold for effect and a nonlinear dose-response relationship. Some of the nonlinearity of the relationship between the number of cigarettes smoked per day and CVD risk may be due to impreciseness of this measure of actual exposure to smoke. However, the data on risk associated with exposure to secondhand smoke indicate a true nonlinear relationship between exposure and CVD risk. Cardiovascular risk is not reduced by smoking cigarettes of lower machine-delivered yields of nicotine or tar.

The constituents of tobacco smoke believed to be responsible for cardiovascular disease include oxidizing chemicals, nicotine, CO, and particulate matter. Oxidizing chemicals, including oxides of nitrogen and many free radicals, increase lipid peroxidation and contribute to several potential mechanisms of CVD, including inflammation, endothelial dysfunction, oxidation of LDL, and platelet activation.

Nicotine is a sympathomimetic drug that increases heart rate and cardiac contractility, transiently increasing blood pressure and constricting coronary arteries. Nicotine may also contribute to endothelial dysfunction, insulin resistance, and lipid abnormalities. However, international epidemiologic evidence and data from clinical trials of nicotine patches suggest that chemicals other than nicotine contribute to an elevated risk of death from MI and stroke. CO reduces the delivery of oxygen to the heart and other tissues and can aggravate angina pectoris or PAD and can lower the threshold for arrhythmias in the presence of CHD. Exposure to particulates is associated with oxidant stress and cardiovascular autonomic disturbances that potentially contribute to acute cardiovascular events.

Cigarette smoking causes acute cardiovascular events such as MI and sudden death by adversely affecting the balance of myocardial demand for oxygen and nutrients and coronary blood flow. Smoking results in increased myocardial work, reduced coronary blood flow, and enhanced thrombogenesis. Enhancement of thrombogenesis appears to be particularly important in that smokers with acute MI have less severe underlying coronary artery disease than do nonsmokers with MI, but smokers have a greater burden of thrombus.

Several potential mechanisms appear to contribute to the effects of smoking in accelerating atherosclerosis. These mechanisms include inflammation, endothelial dysfunction, impaired insulin sensitivity, and lipid abnormalities. Cigarette smoking is a risk factor for diabetes and aggravates insulin resistance in persons with diabetes. The mechanism appears to involve both the effects of oxidizing chemicals in the smoke and the sympathomimetic effects of nicotine.

Conclusions

1. There is a nonlinear dose response between exposure to tobacco smoke and cardiovascular risk, with a sharp increase at low levels of exposure (including exposures from secondhand smoke or infrequent cigarette smoking) and a shallower dose-response relationship as the number of cigarettes smoked per day increases.

2. Cigarette smoking leads to endothelial injury and dysfunction in both coronary and peripheral arteries. There is consistent evidence that oxidizing chemicals and nicotine are responsible for endothelial dysfunction.

3. Tobacco smoke exposure leads to an increased risk of thrombosis, a major factor in the pathogenesis of smoking-induced cardiovascular events.

4. Cigarette smoking produces a chronic inflammatory state that contributes to the atherogenic disease processes and elevates levels of biomarkers of inflammation, known powerful predictors of cardiovascular events.

5. Cigarette smoking produces an atherogenic lipid profile, primarily due to an increase in triglycerides and a decrease in high-density lipoprotein cholesterol.

6. Smoking cessation reduces the risk of cardiovascular morbidity and mortality for smokers with or without coronary heart disease.

7. The use of nicotine or other medications to facilitate smoking cessation in people with known cardiovascular disease produces far less risk than the risk of continued smoking.

8. The evidence to date does not establish that a reduction of cigarette consumption (that is, smoking fewer cigarettes per day) reduces the risks of cardiovascular disease.

9. Cigarette smoking produces insulin resistance and chronic inflammation, which can accelerate macrovascular and microvascular complications, including nephropathy.

References

Abbot NC, Stead LF, White AR, Barnes J. Hypnotherapy for smoking cessation. *Cochrane Database of Systematic Reviews* 1998, Issue 2. Art. No.: CD001008. DOI: 10.1002.14651858.CD001008.

Åberg A, Bergstrand R, Johansson S, Ulvenstam G, Vedin A, Wedel H, Wilhelmsson C, Wilhelmsen L. Cessation of smoking after myocardial infarction: effects on mortality after 10 years. *British Heart Journal* 1983;49(5):416–22.

Abu-Hayyeh S, Sian M, Jones KG, Manuel A, Powell JT. Cadmium accumulation in aortas of smokers. *Arteriosclerosis, Thrombosis, and Vascular Biology* 2001; 21(5):863–7.

Adler AI, Stevens RJ, Neil A, Stratton IM, Boulton AJM, Holman RR. UKPDS 59: hyperglycemia and other potentially modifiable risk factors for peripheral vascular disease in type 2 diabetes. *Diabetes Care* 2002; 25(5):894–9.

Aicher A, Heeschen C, Mohaupt M, Cooke JP, Zeiher AM, Dimmeler S. Nicotine strongly activates dendritic cell-mediated adaptive immunity: potential role for progression of atherosclerotic lesions. *Circulation* 2003; 107(4):604–11.

Aird WC. The endothelium as an organ. In: Aird WC, editor. *Endothelial Cells in Health and Disease.* Boca Raton (FL): Taylor and Francis Group, 2005:1–31.

al-Alawi E, Jenkins D. Does maternal smoking increase the risk of neonatal polycythaemia? *Irish Medical Journal* 2000;93(6):175–6.

Alcorn HG, Wolfson SK Jr, Sutton-Tyrrell K, Kuller LH, O'Leary D. Risk factors for abdominal aortic aneurysms in older adults enrolled in the Cardiovascular Health Study. *Arteriosclerosis, Thrombosis, and Vascular Biology* 1996;16(8):963–70.

Al-Delaimy WK, Manson JE, Solomon CG, Kawachi I, Stampfer MJ, Willett WC, Hu FB. Smoking and risk of coronary heart disease among women with type 2 diabetes mellitus. *Archives of Internal Medicine* 2002; 162(3):273–9.

Al-Delaimy WK, Willett WC, Manson JE, Speizer FE, Hu FB. Smoking and mortality among women with type 2 diabetes: the Nurses' Health Study cohort. *Diabetes Care* 2001;24(12):2043–8.

Allen SS, Hatsukami D, Brintnell DM, Bade T. Effect of nicotine replacement therapy on post-cessation weight gain and nutrient intake: a randomized controlled trial of postmenopausal female smokers. *Addictive Behaviors* 2005;30(7):1273–80.

Allen SS, Hatsukami D, Gorsline J, Transdermal Nicotine Study Group. Cholesterol changes in smoking cessation using the transdermal nicotine system. *Preventive Medicine* 1994;23(2):190–6.

Allred EN, Bleecker ER, Chaitman BR, Dahms TE, Gottlieb SO, Hackney JD, Pagano M, Selvester RH, Walden SM, Warren J. Short-term effects of carbon monoxide exposure on the exercise performance of subjects with coronary artery. *New England Journal of Medicine* 1989;321(21):1426–32.

Ambrose JA, Barua RS. The pathophysiology of cigarette smoking and cardiovascular disease: an update. *Journal of the American College of Cardiology* 2004; 43(10):1731–7.

Ameli FM, Stein M, Provan JL, Prosser R. The effect of postoperative smoking on femoropopliteal bypass grafts. *Annals of Vascular Surgery* 1989;3(1):20–5.

Arcavi L, Jacob P III, Hellerstein M, Benowitz NL. Divergent tolerance to metabolic and cardiovascular effects of nicotine in smokers with low and high levels of cigarette consumption. *Clinical Pharmacology and Therapeutics* 1994;56(1):55–64.

Attvall S, Fowelin J, Lager I, Von Schenck H, Smith U. Smoking induces insulin resistance—a potential link with the insulin resistance syndrome. *Journal of Internal Medicine* 1993;233(4):327–32.

Audoly LP, Rocca B, Fabre J-E, Koller BH, Thomas D, Loeb AL, Coffman TM, FitzGerald GA. Cardiovascular responses to the isoprostane iPF$_{2\alpha}$-III and iPE$_{2\alpha}$-III are mediated via the thromboxane A$_2$ receptor in vivo. *Circulation* 2000;101(24):2833–40.

Auerbach O, Garfinkel L. Atherosclerosis and aneurysm of aorta in relation to smoking habits and age. *Chest* 1980; 78(6):805–9.

Axelsen M, Eliasson B, Joheim E, Lenner RA, Taskinen MR, Smith U. Lipid intolerance in smokers. *Journal of Internal Medicine* 1995;237(5):449–55.

Axelsson T, Jansson P-A, Smith U, Eliasson B. Nicotine infusion acutely impairs insulin sensitivity in type 2 diabetic patients but not in healthy subjects. *Journal of Internal Medicine* 2001;249(6):539–44.

Baggio B, Budakovic A, Vestra MD, Saller A, Bruseghin M, Fioretto P. Effects of cigarette smoking on glomerular structure and function in type 2 diabetic patients. *Journal of the American Society of Nephrology* 2002;13(11):2730–6.

Baker F, Ainsworth SR, Dye JT, Crammer C, Thun MJ, Hoffmann D, Repace JL, Henningfield JE, Slade J, Pinney J, et al. Health risks associated with cigar smoking.

JAMA: the Journal of the American Medical Association 2000;284(6):735–40.

Bakhru A, Erlinger TP. Smoking cessation and cardiovascular disease risk factors: results from the Third National Health and Nutrition Examination Survey. *PLoS Medicine* 2005;2(6):e160; doi: 10.1371/journal.pmed.0020160.

Barbieri SS, Eligini S, Brambilla M, Tremoli E, Colli S. Reactive oxygen species mediate cyclooxygenase-2 induction during monocyte to macrophage differentiation: critical role of NADPH oxidase. *Cardiovascular Research* 2003;60(1):187–97.

Barger AC, Beeuwkes R 3rd, Lainey LL, Silverman KJ. Hypothesis: vasa vasorum and neovascularization of human coronary arteries: a possible role in the pathophysiology of atherosclerosis. *New England Journal of Medicine* 1984;310(3):175–7.

Barnoya J, Glantz S. Cardiovascular effects of secondhand smoke: nearly as large as smoking. *Circulation* 2005;111(20):2684–98.

Barua RS, Ambrose JA, Eales-Reynolds LJ, DeVoe MC, Zervas JG, Saha DC. Dysfunctional endothelial nitric oxide biosynthesis in healthy smokers with impaired endothelium-dependent vasodilatation. *Circulation* 2001;104(16):1905–10.

Barua RS, Ambrose JA, Saha DC, Eales-Reynolds LJ. Smoking is associated with altered endothelial-derived fibrinolytic and antithrombotic factors: an in vitro demonstration. *Circulation* 2002;106(8):905–8.

Barua RS, Ambrose JA, Srivastava S, DeVoe MC, Eales-Reynolds LJ. Reactive oxygen species are involved in smoking-induced dysfunction of nitric oxide biosynthesis and upregulation of endothelial nitric oxide synthase: an in vitro demonstration in human coronary artery endothelial cells. *Circulation* 2003;107(18):2342–7.

Barutcu I, Esen AM, Degirmenci B, Acar M, Kaya D, Turkmen M, Melek M, Onrat E, Esen OB, Kirma C. Acute cigarette smoking-induced hemodynamic alterations in the common carotid artery—a transcranial Doppler study. *Circulation Journal* 2004;68(12):1127–31.

Bazzano LA, He J, Muntner P, Vupputuri S, Whelton PK. Relationship between cigarette smoking and novel risk factors for cardiovascular disease in the United States. *Annals of Internal Medicine* 2003;138(11):891–7.

Beckman JA, Liao JK, Hurley S, Garrett LA, Chui D, Mitra D, Creager MA. Atorvastatin restores endothelial function in normocholesterolemic smokers independent of changes in low-density lipoprotein. *Circulation Research* 2004;95(2):217–23.

Beckman JS, Koppenol WH. Nitric oxide, superoxide, and peroxynitrite: the good, the bad, and ugly. *American Journal of Physiology – Cell Physiology* 1996;271(5 Pt 1): C1424–C1437.

Benowitz NL. Biomarkers of cigarette smoking. In: *The FTC Cigarette Test Method for Determining Tar, Nicotine, and Carbon Monoxide Yields of U.S. Cigarettes. Report of the NCI Expert Committee.* Smoking and Tobacco Control Monograph No. 7. Bethesda (MD): U.S. Department of Health and Human Services, Public Health Service, National Institutes of Health, National Cancer Institute, 1996:93–111. NIH Publication No. 96-4028.

Benowitz NL. Cigarette smoking and cardiovascular disease: pathophysiology and implications for treatment. *Progress in Cardiovascular Diseases* 2003;46(1): 91–111.

Benowitz NL, Fitzgerald GA, Wilson M, Zhang Q. Nicotine effects on eicosanoid formation and hemostatic function: comparison of transdermal nicotine and cigarette smoking. *Journal of the American College of Cardiology* 1993;22(4):1159–67.

Benowitz NL, Gourlay SG. Cardiovascular toxicity of nicotine: implications for nicotine replacement therapy. *Journal of the American College of Cardiology* 1997; 29(7):1422–31.

Benowitz NL, Hall SM, Herning RI, Jacob P III, Jones RT, Osman AL. Smokers of low-yield cigarettes do not consume less nicotine. *New England Journal of Medicine* 1983;309(3):139–42.

Benowitz NL, Hansson A, Jacob P III. Cardiovascular effects of nasal and transdermal nicotine and cigarette smoking. *Hypertension* 2002;39(6):1107–12.

Benowitz NL, Jacob P III. Daily intake of nicotine during cigarette smoking. *Clinical Pharmacology and Therapeutics* 1984;35(4):499–504.

Benowitz NL, Jacob P III, Jones RT, Rosenberg J. Interindividual variability in the metabolism and cardiovascular effects of nicotine in man. *Journal of Pharmacology and Experimental Therapeutics* 1982a;221(2):368–72.

Benowitz NL, Jacob P III, Yu L. Daily use of smokeless tobacco: systemic effects. *Annals of Internal Medicine* 1989; 111(2):112–6.

Benowitz NL, Kuyt F, Jacob P III. Circadian blood nicotine concentrations during cigarette smoking. *Clinical Pharmacology and Therapeutics* 1982b;32(6):758–64.

Benowitz NL, Kuyt F, Jacob P III. Influence of nicotine on cardiovascular and hormonal effects of cigarette smoking. *Clinical Pharmacology and Therapeutics* 1984; 36(1):74–81.

Benowitz NL, Porchet H, Sheiner L, Jacob P III. Nicotine absorption and cardiovascular effects with smokeless tobacco use: comparison with cigarettes and nicotine gum. *Clinical Pharmacology and Therapeutics* 1988; 44(1):23–8.

Bergman RN, Ader M. Free fatty acids and pathogenesis of type 2 diabetes mellitus. *Trends in Endocrinology and Metabolism* 2000;11(9):351–6.

Bermudez EA, Rifai N, Buring JE, Manson JE, Ridker PM. Relation between markers of systemic vascular inflammation and smoking in women. *American Journal of Cardiology* 2002;89(9):1117–9.

Bernhard D, Csordas A, Henderson B, Rossmann A, Kind M, Wick G. Cigarette smoke metal-catalyzed protein oxidation leads to vascular endothelial cell contraction by depolymerization of microtubules. *FASEB Journal* 2005;19(9):1096–107.

Bhatnagar A. Environmental cardiology: studying mechanistic links between pollution and heart disease. *Circulation Research* 2006;99(7):692–705.

Biesenbach G, Grafinger P, Janko O, Zazgornik J. Influence of cigarette-smoking on the progression of clinical diabetic nephropathy in type 2 diabetic patients. *Clinical Nephrology* 1997;48(3):146–50.

Billimoria JD, Pozner H, Metselaar B, Best FW, James DC. Effect of cigarette smoking on lipids, lipoproteins, blood coagulation, fibrinolysis and cellular components of human blood. *Atherosclerosis* 1975;21(1):61–76.

Bizzi A, Tacconi MT, Medea A, Garattini S. Some aspects of the effect of nicotine on plasma FFA and tissue triglycerides. *Pharmacology* 1972;7(4):216–24.

Bjartveit K, Tverdal A. Health consequences of smoking 1–4 cigarettes per day. *Tobacco Control* 2005;14(5):315–20.

Blanchard JF, Armenian HK, Friesen PP. Risk factors for abdominal aortic aneurysm: results of a case-control study. *American Journal of Epidemiology* 2000; 151(6):575–83.

Blanco-Cedres L, Daviglus ML, Garside DB, Liu K, Pirzada A, Stamler J, Greenland P. Relation of cigarette smoking to 25-year mortality in middle-aged men with low baseline serum cholesterol: the Chicago Heart Association Detection Project in Industry. *American Journal of Epidemiology* 2002;155(4):354–60.

Blankenberg S, Rupprecht HJ, Bickel C, Peetz D, Hafner G, Tiret L, Meyer J. Circulating cell adhesion molecules and death in patients with coronary artery disease. *Circulation* 2001;104(12):1336–42.

Blann AD, Amiral J, McCollum CN, Lip GYH. Differences in free and total tissue factor pathway inhibitor, and tissue factor in peripheral artery disease compared to healthy controls. *Atherosclerosis* 2000;152(1):29–34.

Blann AD, McCollum CN. Adverse influence of cigarette smoking on the endothelium. *Thrombosis and Haemostasis* 1993;70(4):707–11.

Blann AD, Seigneur M, Steiner M, Miller JP, McCollum CN. Circulating ICAM-1 and VCAM-1 in peripheral artery disease and hypercholesterolaemia: relationship to the location of atherosclerotic disease, smoking, and

in the prediction of adverse events. *Thrombosis and Haemostasis* 1998;79(6):1080–5.

Blann AD, Steele C, McCollum CN. The influence of smoking on soluble adhesion molecules and endothelial cell markers. *Thrombosis Research* 1997;85(5):433–8.

Boffetta P, Straif K. Use of smokeless tobacco and risk of myocardial infarction and stroke: systematic review with meta-analysis BMJ (British Medical Journal) 2009;339:b3060; doi: 10.1136/bmj.b3060.

Bolman C, de Vries H, van Breukelen G. A minimal-contact intervention for cardiac inpatients: long-term effects on smoking cessation. *Preventive Medicine* 2002; 35(2):181–92.

Bott U, Jorgens V, Grusser M, Bender R, Muhlhauser I, Berger M. Predictors of glycaemic control in type 1 diabetic patients after participation in an intensified treatment and teaching programme. *Diabetic Medicine* 1994;11(4):362–71.

Bowers TR, Terrien EF, O'Neill WW, Sachs D, Grines CL. Effect of reperfusion modality on outcome in non-smokers and smokers with acute myocardial infarction (a Primary Angioplasty in Myocardial Infarction [PAMI] substudy). PAMI Investigators. *American Journal of Cardiology* 1996;78(5):511–5.

Brady AR, Thompson SG, Fowkes FGR, Greenhalgh RM, Powell JT, UK Small Aneurysm Trial Participants. Abdominal aortic aneurysm expansion: risk factors and time intervals for surveillance. *Circulation* 2004; 110(1):16–21.

Brain SD, Grant AD. Vascular actions of calcitonin gene-related peptide and adrenomedullin. *Physiological Reviews* 2004;84(3):903–34.

Bridges RB, Fu MC, Rehm SR. Increased neutrophil myeloperoxidase activity associated with cigarette smoking. *European Journal of Respiratory Disease* 1985;67(2):84–93.

Brook RD, Franklin B, Cascio W, Hong Y, Howard G, Lipsett M, Luepker R, Mittleman M, Samet J, Smith SC Jr, et al. Air pollution and cardiovascular disease: a statement for healthcare professionals from the Expert Panel on Population and Prevention Science of the American Heart Association. *Circulation* 2004;109(21):2655–71.

Brousseau ME, Schaefer EJ, Wolfe ML, Bloedon LT, Digenio AG, Clark RW, Mancuso JP, Rader DJ. Effects of an inhibitor of cholesteryl ester transfer protein on HDL cholesterol. *New England Journal of Medicine* 2004;350(15):1505–15.

Brownlee M, Vlassara H, Cerami A. Nonenzymatic glycosylation and the pathogenesis of diabetic complications. *Annals of Internal Medicine* 1984;101(4):527–37.

Burghuber OC, Punzengruber C, Sinzinger H, Haber P, Silberbauer K. Platelet sensitivity to prostacyclin in smokers and non-smokers. *Chest* 1986;90(1):34–8.

Burke A, FitzGerald GA. Oxidative stress and smoking-induced vascular tissue injury. *Progress in Cardiovascular Diseases* 2003;46(1):79–90.

Burke AP, Farb A, Malcom GT, Liang YH, Smialek J, Virmani R. Coronary risk factors and plaque morphology in men with coronary disease who died suddenly. *New England Journal of Medicine* 1997;336(18):1276–82.

Burns DM. Epidemiology of smoking-induced cardiovascular disease. *Progress in Cardiovascular Diseases* 2003;46(1):11–29.

Burns DM, Shanks T, Choi W, Thun M, Heath C, Garfinkel L. The American Cancer Society Cancer Prevention Study I: 12-year followup of 1 million men and women. In: *Changes in Cigarette-Related Disease Risks and Their Implication for Prevention and Control.* Smoking and Tobacco Control Monograph No. 8. Bethesda (MD): U.S. Department of Health and Human Services, Public Health Service, National Institutes of Health, National Cancer Institute, 1997:113–304. NIH Publication No. 97-4213.

Busse R, Fleming I. Regulation of endothelium-derived vasoactive autacoid production by hemodynamic forces. *Trends in Pharmacological Sciences* 2003;24(1):24–9.

Cai J, Boulton M. The pathogenesis of diabetic retinopathy: old concepts and new questions. *Eye* 2002;16(3):242–60.

Calverley PM, Leggett RJ, Flenley DC. Carbon monoxide and exercise tolerance in chronic bronchitis and emphysema. *BMJ (British Medical Journal)* 1981;283(6296):878–80.

Campbell IA, Prescott RJ, Tjeder-Burton SM. Transdermal nicotine plus support in patients attending hospital with smoking-related diseases: a placebo-controlled study. *Respiratory Medicine* 1996;90(1):47–51.

Campisi R, Czernin J, Schöder H. Sayre JW, Marengo FD, Phelps ME, Schelbert HR. Effects of long-term smoking on myocardial blood flow, coronary vasomotion, and vasodilator capacity. *Circulation* 1998;98(2):119–25.

Campisi R, Czernin J, Schöder H, Sayre JW, Schelbert HR. L-arginine normalizes coronary vasomotion in long-term smokers. *Circulation* 1999;99(4):491–7.

Candipan RC, Wang B-Y, Buitrago R, Tsao PS, Cooke JP. Regression or progression: dependency on vascular nitric oxide. *Arteriosclerosis, Thrombosis, and Vascular Biology* 1996;16(1):44–50.

Caraballo RS, Giovino GA, Pechacek TF, Mowery PD, Richter PA, Strauss WJ, Sharp DJ, Eriksen MP, Pirkle JL, Maurer KR. Racial and ethnic differences in serum cotinine levels of cigarette smokers: Third National Health and Nutrition Examination Survey, 1988–1991. *JAMA: the Journal of the American Medical Association* 1998;280(2):135–9.

Caralis DG, Deligonul U, Kern MJ, Cohen JD. Smoking is a risk factor for coronary spasm in young women. *Circulation* 1992;85(3):905–9.

Carty CS, Soloway PD, Kayastha S, Bauer J, Marsan B, Ricotta JJ, Dryjski M. Nicotine and cotinine stimulate secretion of basic fibroblast growth factor and affect expression of matrix metalloproteinases in cultured human smooth muscle cells. *Journal of Vascular Surgery* 1996;24(6):927–34.

Celermajer DS, Adams MR, Clarkson P, Robinson J, McCredie R, Donald A, Deanfield JE. Passive smoking and impaired endothelium-dependent arterial dilatation in healthy young adults. *New England Journal of Medicine* 1996;334(3):150–4.

Celermajer DS, Sorensen KE, Georgakopoulos D, Bull C, Thomas O, Robinson J, Deanfield JE. Cigarette smoking is associated with dose-related and potentially reversible impairment of endothelium-dependent dilation in healthy young adults. *Circulation* 1993;88(5 Pt 1):2149–55.

Celermajer DS, Sorensen KE, Gooch VM, Spiegelhalter DJ, Miller OI, Sullivan ID, Lloyd JK, Deanfield JE. Non-invasive detection of endothelial dysfunction in children and adults at risk of atherosclerosis. *Lancet* 1992;340(8828):1111–5.

Centers for Disease Control and Prevention. Smoking-attributable mortality, years of potential life lost, and productivity losses—United States, 2000–2004. *Morbidity and Mortality Weekly Report* 2008;57(45):1226–8.

Chalon S, Moreno H Jr, Benowitz NL, Hoffman BB, Blaschke TF. Nicotine impairs endothelium-dependent dilatation in human veins in vivo. *Clinical Pharmacology and Therapeutics* 2000;67(4):391–7.

Chalon S, Moreno H Jr, Hoffman BB, Blaschke TF. Angiotensin-converting enzyme inhibition improves venous endothelial dysfunction in chronic smokers. *Clinical Pharmacology and Therapeutics* 1999;65(3):295–303.

Chang E, Harley CB. Telomere length and replicative aging in human vascular tissues. *Proceedings of the National Academy of Sciences of the United States of America* 1995;92(24):11190–4.

Chase HP, Garg SK, Marshall G, Berg CL, Harris S, Jackson WE, Hamman RE. Cigarette smoking increases the risk of albuminuria among subjects with type I diabetes. *JAMA: the Journal of the American Medical Association* 1991;265(5):614–7.

Chaturvedi N, Stevens L, Fuller JH. Which features of smoking determine mortality risk in former cigarette smokers with diabetes: the World Health Organization Multinational Study Group. *Diabetes Care* 1997;20(8):1266–72.

Chehne F, Oguogho A, Lupattelli G, Budinsky AC, Palumbo B, Sinzinger H. Increase of isoprostane 8-epi-PGF$_{2\alpha}$ after restarting smoking. *Prostaglandins, Leukotrienes, and Essential Fatty Acids* 2001;64(6):307–10.

Chen HH, Burnett JC Jr. C-type natriuretic peptide: the endothelial component of the natriuretic peptide system. *Journal of Cardiovascular Pharmacology* 1998; 32(Suppl 3):S22–S28.

Chen JL, Peacock E, Samady W, Turner SM, Neese RA, Hellerstein MK, Murphy EJ. Physiologic and pharmacologic factors influencing glyceroneogenic contribution to triacylglyceride glycerol measured by mass isotopomer distribution analysis. *Journal of Biological Chemistry* 2005;280(27):25396–402.

Chisolm GM, Steinberg D. The oxidative modification hypothesis of atherogenesis: an overview. *Free Radical Biology & Medicine* 2000;28(12):1815–26.

Christen WG, Glynn RJ, Manson JE, Ajani UA, Buring JE. A prospective study of cigarette smoking and risk of age-related macular degeneration in men. *JAMA: the Journal of the American Medical Association* 1996;276(14):1147–51.

Christen WG, Manson JE, Bubes V, Glynn RJ. Risk factors for progression of distal symmetric polyneuropathy in type 1 diabetes mellitus: Sorbinil Retinopathy Trial Research Group. *American Journal of Epidemiology* 1999;150(11):1142–51.

Chuahirun T, Khanna A, Kimball K, Wesson DE. Cigarette smoking and increased urine albumin excretion are interrelated predictors of nephropathy progression in type 2 diabetes. *American Journal of Kidney Diseases* 2003;41(1):13–21.

Chuahirun T, Wesson DE. Cigarette smoking predicts faster progression of type 2 established diabetic nephropathy despite ACE inhibition. *American Journal of Kidney Diseases* 2002;39(2):376–82.

Chung TW, Tyan YC, Hsieh JH, Wang SS, Chu SH. Shear stress-induced aggregation of oxidized platelets. *Thrombosis Research* 2002;105(4):325–9.

Church DF, Pryor WA. Free-radical chemistry of cigarette smoke and its toxicological implications. *Environmental Health Perspectives* 1985;64:111–26.

Coe JW, Brooks PR, Vetelino MG, Wirtz MC, Arnold EP, Huang J, Sands SB, Davis TI, Lebel LA, Fox CB, et al. Varenicline: an $\alpha4\beta2$ nicotinic receptor partial agonist for smoking cessation. *Journal of Medicinal Chemistry* 2005;48(10):3474–7.

Colditz GA, Bonita R, Stampfer MJ, Willett WC, Rosner B, Speizer FE, Hennekens CH. Cigarette smoking and risk of stroke in middle-aged women. *New England Journal of Medicine* 1988;318(15):937–41.

Conklin DJ, Bhatnagar A, Cowley HR, Johnson GH, Wiechmann RJ, Sayre LM, Trent MB, Boor PJ. Acrolein generation stimulates hypercontraction in isolated human blood vessels. *Toxicology and Applied Pharmacology* 2006;217(3):277–88.

Cooke JP. Does ADMA cause endothelial dysfunction? *Arteriosclerosis, Thrombosis, and Vascular Biology* 2000;20(9):2032–7.

Cooke JP. Asymmetrical dimethylarginine: the Uber marker? *Circulation* 2004;109(15):1813–8.

Cooke JP, Dzau VJ. Derangements of the nitric oxide synthase pathway, L-arginine, and cardiovascular diseases. *Circulation* 1997a;96(2):379–82.

Cooke JP, Dzau VJ. Nitric oxide synthase: role in the genesis of vascular disease. *Annual Review of Medicine* 1997b; 48:489–509.

Cooke JP, Rossitch E Jr, Andon NA, Loscalzo J, Dzau VJ. Flow activates an endothelial potassium channel to release an endogenous nitrovasodilator. *Journal of Clinical Investigation* 1991;88(5):1663–71.

Cooke JP, Singer AH, Tsao P, Zera P, Rowan RA, Billingham ME. Antiatherogenic effects of L-arginine in the hypercholesterolemic rabbit. *Journal of Clinical Investigation* 1992;90(3):1168–72.

Craig WY, Palomaki GE, Haddow JE. Cigarette smoking and serum lipid and lipoprotein concentrations: an analysis of published data. *BMJ (British Medical Journal)* 1989;298(6676):784–8.

Cranshaw JH, Evans TW, Mitchell JA. Characterization of the effects of isoprostanes on platelet aggregation in human whole blood. *British Journal of Pharmacology* 2001;132(8):1699–706.

Cremer P, Nagel D, Mann H, Labrot B, Müller-Berninger R, Elster H, Seidel D. Ten-year follow-up results from the Goettingen Risk, Incidence and Prevalence Study (GRIPS). I: risk factors for myocardial infarction in a cohort of 5790 men. *Atherosclerosis* 1997;129(2): 221–30.

Criqui MH, Cowan LD, Tyroler HA, Bangdiwala S, Heiss G, Wallace RB, Cohn R. Lipoproteins as mediators for the effects of alcohol consumption and cigarette smoking on cardiovascular mortality: results from the Lipid Research Clinics Follow-up Study. *American Journal of Epidemiology* 1987;126(4):629–37.

Criqui MH, Wallace RB, Heiss G, Mishkel M, Schonfeld G, Jones GT. Cigarette smoking and plasma high-density lipoprotein cholesterol: the Lipid Research Clinics Program Prevalence Study. *Circulation* 1980;62(4 Pt 2): IV70–IV76.

Critchley J, Capewell S. Smoking cessation for the secondary prevention of coronary heart disease. *Cochrane Database of Systematic Reviews* 2004, Issue 4. Art. No.: CD003041. DOI: 10.1002/114651858.CD003041.pub2.

Critchley JA, Capewell S. Mortality risk reduction associated with smoking cessation in patients with coronary heart disease: a systematic review. *JAMA: the Journal of the American Medical Association* 2003;290(1):86–97.

Cryer PE, Haymond MW, Santiago JV, Shah SD. Norepinephrine and epinephrine release and adrenergic mediation of smoking-associated hemodynamic and metabolic events. *New England Journal of Medicine* 1976;295(11):573–7.

Csiszar A, Stef G, Pacher P, Ungvari Z. Oxidative stress-induced isoprostane formation may contribute to aspirin resistance in platelets. *Prostaglandins, Leukotrienes, and Essential Fatty Acids* 2002;66(5–6):557–8.

Csonka E, Somogyi A, Augustin J, Haberbosch W, Schettler G, Jellinek H. The effect of nicotine on cultured cells of vascular origin. *Virchows Archiv A, Pathological Anatomy and Histopathology* 1985;407(4):441–7.

Cucina A, Corvino V, Sapienza P, Borrelli V, Lucarelli M, Scarpa S, Strom R, Santoro-D'Angelo L, Cavallaro A. Nicotine regulates basic fibroblastic growth factor and transforming growth factor β_1 production in endothelial cells. *Biochemical and Biophysical Research Communications* 1999;257(2):306–12.

Cullen P, Schulte H, Assmann G. Smoking, lipoproteins and coronary heart disease risk: data from the Munster Heart Study (PROCAM). *European Heart Journal* 1998;19(11):1632–41.

Cupples LA, Gagnon DR, Kannel WB. Long- and short-term risk of sudden coronary death. *Circulation* 1992; 85(1 Suppl):I11–I18.

Czernin J, Sun K, Brunken R, Böttcher M, Phelps M, Schelbert H. Effect of acute and long-term smoking on myocardial blood flow and flow reserve. *Circulation* 1995;91(12):2891–7.

Czernin J, Waldherr C. Cigarette smoking and coronary blood flow. *Progress in Cardiovascular Diseases* 2003; 45(5):395–404.

Dagenais GR, Robitaille NM, Lupien PJ, Christen A, Gingras S, Moorjani S, Meyer F, Rochon J. First coronary heart disease event rates in relation to major risk factors: Quebec Cardiovascular Study. *Canadian Journal of Cardiology* 1990;6(7):274–80.

Daly LE, Mulcahy R, Graham IM, Hickey N. Long term effect on mortality of stopping smoking after unstable angina and myocardial infarction. *BMJ (British Medical Journal)* 1983;287(6388):324–6.

Davì G, Ciabattoni G, Consoli A, Mezzetti A, Falco A, Santarone S, Pennese E, Vitacolonni E, Bucciarelli T, Constantini F, et al. In vivo formation of 8-iso-prostaglandin $F_{2\alpha}$ and platelet activation in diabetes mellitus: effects of improved metabolic control and vitamin E supplementation. *Circulation* 1999;99(2):224–9.

Davis JW, Shelton L, Eigenberg DA, Hignite CE, Watanabe IS. Effects of tobacco and non-tobacco cigarette smoking on endothelium and platelets. *Clinical Pharmacology and Therapeutics* 1985;37(5):529–33.

Dawber TR. *The Framingham Study: The Epidemiology of Atherosclerotic Disease*. Cambridge (MA): Harvard University Press, 1980.

de Groot E, Hovingh GK, Wiegman A, Duriez P, Smit AJ, Fruchart JC, Kastelein JJ. Measurement of arterial wall thickness as a surrogate marker for atherosclerosis. *Circulation* 2004;109(23 Suppl 1):III33–III38.

Deanfield JE, Shea MJ, Wilson RA, Horlock P, de Landsheere CM, Selwyn AP. Direct effects of smoking on the heart: silent ischemic disturbances of coronary flow. *American Journal of Cardiology* 1986;57(13):1005–9.

DeBias DA, Banerjee CM, Birkhead NC, Greene CH, Scott SD, Harrer WV. Effects of carbon monoxide inhalation on ventricular fibrillation. *Archives of Environmental Health* 1976;31(1):42–6.

DeBusk RF, Miller NH, Superko R, Dennis CA, Thomas RJ, Lew HT, Berger WE III, Heller RS, Rompf J, Gee D, et al. A case-management system for coronary risk factor modification after acute myocardial infarction. *Annals of Internal Medicine* 1994;120(9):721–9.

DeFronzo RA, Tobin JD, Andres R. Glucose clamp technique: a method for quantifying insulin secretion and resistance. *American Journal of Physiology – Endocrinology and Metabolism* 1979;237(3):E214–E223.

Deliconstantinos G, Villiotou V, Stavrides JC. Scavenging effects of hemoglobin and related heme containing compounds on nitric oxide, reactive oxidants and carcinogenic volatile nitrosocompounds of cigarette smoke: a new method for protection against the dangerous cigarette constituents. *Anticancer Research* 1994;14(6B):2717–26.

Diana JN, Qian SF, Heesch CM, Barron KW, Chien CY. Nicotine-induced skeletal muscle vasodilation is mediated by release of epinephrine from nerve terminals. *American Journal of Physiology* 1990;259 (6 Pt 2):H1718–H1729.

Dietrich M, Block G, Hudes M, Morrow JD, Norkus EP, Traber MG, Cross CE, Packer L. Antioxidant supplementation decreases lipid peroxidation biomarker F_2-isoprostanes in plasma of smokers. *Cancer Epidemiology, Biomarkers & Prevention* 2002;11(1):7–13.

Dinno A, Glantz S. Clean indoor air laws immediately reduce heart attacks. *Preventive Medicine* 2007;45(1): 9–11.

Djordjevic MV, Doran KA. Nicotine content and delivery across tobacco products. In Henningfield JE, London ED, Pogun S, editors. Nicotine Psychopharmacology. Handbook of Experimental Pharmacology, vol. 192. Berlin: Springer, 2009:61–92.

Djoussé L, Myers RH, Province MA, Hunt SC, Eckfeldt JH, Evans G, Peacock JM, Ellison RC. Influence of apolipoprotein E, smoking, and alcohol intake on carotid atherosclerosis: National Heart, Lung, and Blood Institute Family Heart Study. *Stroke* 2002;33(5):1357–61.

Dobson AJ, Alexander HM, Heller RF, Lloyd DM. How soon after quitting smoking does risk of heart attack decline? *Journal of Clinical Epidemiology* 1991;44(11):1247–53.

Dogra G, Rich L, Stanton K, Watts GF. Endothelium-dependent and independent vasodilation studies at normoglycaemia in type I diabetes mellitus with and without microalbuminuria. *Diabetologia* 2001; 44(5):593–601.

Doll R, Peto R. Mortality in relation to smoking: 20 years' observations on male British doctors. *BMJ (British Medical Journal)* 1976;2(6051):1525–36.

Dornelas EA, Sampson RA, Gray JF, Waters D, Thompson PD. A randomized controlled trial of smoking cessation counseling after myocardial infarction. *Preventive Medicine* 2000;30(4):261–8.

Dullaart RP, Hoogenberg K, Dikkeschei BD, van Tol A. Higher plasma lipid transfer protein activities and unfavorable lipoprotein changes in cigarette-smoking men. *Arteriosclerosis and Thrombosis* 1994;14(10):1581–5.

Eliasson B. Cigarette smoking and diabetes. *Progress in Cardiovascular Diseases* 2003;45(5):405–13.

Eliasson B, Attvall S, Taskinen MR, Smith U. The insulin resistance syndrome in smokers is related to smoking habits. *Arteriosclerosis and Thrombosis* 1994; 14(12):1946–50.

Eliasson B, Attvall S, Taskinen MR, Smith U. Smoking cessation improves insulin sensitivity in healthy middle-aged men. *European Journal of Clinical Investigation* 1997a;27(5):450–6.

Eliasson B, Hjalmarson A, Kruse E, Landfeldt B, Westin Å. Effect of smoking reduction and cessation on cardiovascular risk factors. *Nicotine & Tobacco Research* 2001;3(3):249–55.

Eliasson B, Mero N, Taskinen MR, Smith U. The insulin resistance syndrome and postprandial lipid intolerance in smokers. *Atherosclerosis* 1997b;129(1):79–88.

Eliasson B, Taskinen MR, Smith U. Long-term use of nicotine gum is associated with hyperinsulinemia and insulin resistance. *Circulation* 1996;94(5):878–81.

Eliasson M, Asplund K, Evrin PE, Lundblad D. Relationship of cigarette smoking and snuff dipping to plasma fibrinogen, fibrinolytic variables and serum insulin: the Northern Sweden MONICA Study. *Atherosclerosis* 1995;113(1):41–53.

Eliasson M, Lundblad D, Hagg E. Cardiovascular risk factors in young snuff-users and cigarette smokers. *Journal of Internal Medicine* 1991;230(1):17–22.

Enderle MD, Pfohl M, Kellermann N, Haering HU, Hoffmeister HM. Endothelial function, variables of fibrinolysis and coagulation in smokers and healthy controls. *Haemostasis* 2000;30(3):149–58.

Epifano L, Di Vincenzo A, Fanelli C, Porcellati F, Perriello G, De Feo P, Motolese M, Brunetti P, Bolli GB. Effect of cigarette smoking and of a transdermal nicotine delivery system on glucoregulation in type 2 diabetes mellitus. *European Journal of Clinical Pharmacology* 1992;43(3):257–63.

Escobedo LG, Caspersen CJ. Risk factors for sudden coronary death in the United States. *Epidemiology* 1997; 8(2):175–80.

Escobedo LG, Zack MM. Comparison of sudden and non-sudden coronary deaths in the United States. *Circulation* 1996;93(11):2033–6.

Escolar G, White JG. Changes in glycoprotein expression after platelet activation: differences between in vitro and in vivo studies. *Thrombosis and Haemostasis* 2000; 83(3):371–86.

Ezzati M, Henley SJ, Thun MJ, Lopez AD. Role of smoking in global and regional cardiovascular mortality. *Circulation* 2005;112(4):489–97.

Facchini FS, Hollenbeck CB, Jeppesen J, Chen YD, Reaven GM. Insulin resistance and cigarette smoking. *Lancet* 1992;339(8802):1128–30.

Feskens EJ, Kromhout D. Cardiovascular risk factors and the 25-year incidence of diabetes mellitus in middle-aged men: the Zutphen Study. *American Journal of Epidemiology* 1989;130(6):1101–8.

Fichtenberg CM, Glantz SA. Association of the California Tobacco Control Program with declines in cigarette consumption and mortality from heart disease. *New England Journal of Medicine* 2000;343(24):1772–7.

Fiore MC, Bailey WC, Cohen SJ, Dorfman SF, Goldstein MG, Gritz ER, Heyman RB, Jaén CR, Kottke TE, Lando HA, et al. *Treating Tobacco Use and Dependence*. Clinical Practice Guideline. Rockville (MD): U.S. Department of Health and Human Services, Public Health Service, 2000.

Fiore MC, Jaén CR, Baker TB, Bailey WC, Benowitz NL, Curry SJ, Dorfma SF, Froelicher ES, Goldstein MG, Heaton CG, et al. *Treating Tobacco Use and Dependence: 2008 Update*. Clinical Practice Guideline. Rockville (MD): U.S. Department of Health and Human Services, Public Health Service, 2008.

Folkman J. Fundamental concepts of the angiogenic process. *Current Molecular Medicine* 2003;3(7):643–51.

Ford ES, Malarcher AM, Herman WH, Aubert RE. Diabetes mellitus and cigarette smoking: findings from the 1989 National Health Interview Survey. *Diabetes Care* 1994;17(7):688–92.

Foy GC, Bell RA, Farmer DF, Goff DC Jr, Wagenknecht LE. Smoking and incidence of diabetes among U.S. adults: findings from the Insulin Resistance Atherosclerosis Study. *Diabetes Care* 2005;28(10):2501–7.

Franzoni F, Quiñones-Galvan A, Regoli F, Ferrannini E, Galetta F. A comparative study of the in vitro antioxidant activity of statins. *International Journal of Cardiology* 2003;90(2–3):317–21.

Frati AC, Iniestra F, Ariza CR. Acute effect of cigarette smoking on glucose tolerance and other cardiovascular risk factors. *Diabetes Care* 1996;19(2):112–8.

Freedman JE, Loscalzo J, Barnard MR, Alpert C, Keaney JF Jr, Michelson AD. Nitric oxide released from activated platelets inhibits platelet recruitment. *Journal of Clinical Investigation* 1997;100(2):350–6.

Freedman JE, Ting B, Hankin B, Loscalzo J, Keaney JF Jr, Vita JA. Impaired platelet production of nitric oxide predicts presence of acute coronary syndromes. *Circulation* 1998;98(15):1481–6.

Freeman DJ, Caslake MJ, Griffin BA, Hinnie J, Tan CE, Watson TD, Packard CJ, Shepherd J. The effect of smoking on post-heparin lipoprotein and hepatic lipase, cholesteryl ester transfer protein and lecithin: cholesterol acyl transferase activities in human plasma. *European Journal of Clinical Investigation* 1998;28(7):584–91.

Freeman DJ, Packard CJ. Smoking and plasma lipoprotein metabolism. *Clinical Science (London)* 1995;89(4):333–42.

Freund KM, Belanger AJ, D'Agostino RB, Kannel WB. The health risks of smoking. The Framingham Study: 34 years of follow-up. *Annals of Epidemiology* 1993;3(4):417–24.

Friedman GD, Dales LG, Ury HK. Mortality in middle-aged smokers and nonsmokers. *New England Journal of Medicine* 1979;300(5):213–7.

Frost PH, Davis BR, Burlando AJ, Curb JD, Guthrie GP Jr, Isaacsohn JL, Wassertheil-Smoller S, Wilson AC, Stamler J. Coronary heart disease risk factors in men and women aged 60 years and older: findings from the Systolic Hypertension in the Elderly Program. *Circulation* 1996;94(1):26–34.

Fuster V, Chesebro JH, Frye RL, Elveback LR. Platelet survival and the development of coronary artery disease in the young adult: effects of cigarette smoking, strong family history and medical therapy. *Circulation* 1981;63(3):546–51.

Gartside PS, Wang P, Glueck CJ. Prospective assessment of coronary heart disease risk factors: the NHANES I Epidemiologic Follow-up Study (NHEFS) 16-year follow-up. *Journal of the American College of Nutrition* 1998;17(3):263–9.

Gill GV, Rolfe M, MacFarlane IA, Huddle KR. Smoking habits of black South African patients with diabetes mellitus. *Diabetic Medicine* 1996;13(11):996–9.

Gimbrone MA Jr. Vascular endothelium: an integrator of pathophysiologic stimuli in atherosclerosis. *American Journal of Cardiology* 1995;75(6):67B–70B.

Godsland IF, Walton C. Insulin resistance and cigarette smoking [letter]. *Lancet* 1992;340(8819):607.

Godtfredsen NS, Osler M, Vestbo J, Andersen I, Prescott E. Smoking reduction, smoking cessation, and incidence of fatal and non-fatal myocardial infarction in Denmark 1976–1998: a pooled cohort study. *Journal of Epidemiology and Community Health* 2003;57(6):412–6.

Gokce N, Keaney JF Jr, Hunter LM, Watkins MT, Nedeljkovic ZS, Menzoian JO, Vita JA. Predictive value of noninvasively determined endothelial dysfunction for long-term cardiovascular events in patients with peripheral vascular disease. *Journal of the American College of Cardiology* 2003;41(10):1769–75.

Goldenberg I, Jonas M, Tenenbaum A, Boyko V, Matetzky S, Shotan A, Behar S, Reicher-Reiss H. Current smoking, smoking cessation, and the risk of sudden cardiac death in patients with coronary artery disease. *Archives of Internal Medicine* 2003;163(19):2301–5.

Gole MD, Souza JM, Choi I, Hertkorn C, Malcolm S, Foust RF III, Finkel B, Lanken PN, Ischiropoulos H. Plasma proteins modified by tyrosine nitration in acute respiratory distress syndrome. *American Journal of Physiology – Lung Cellular and Molecular Physiology* 2000;278(5):L961–L967.

Gonzales D, Rennard SI, Nides M, Oncken C, Azoulay S, Billing CB, Watsky EJ, Gong J, Williams KE, Reeves KR, et al. Varenicline, an α4β2 nicotinic acetylcholine receptor partial agonist, vs sustained-release bupropion and placebo for smoking cessation: a randomized controlled trial. *JAMA: the Journal of the American Medical Association* 2006;296(1):47–55.

Gordon T, Kannel WB, Dawber TR, McGee D. Changes associated with quitting cigarette smoking: the Framingham Study. *American Heart Journal* 1975;90(3):322–8.

Gordon T, Kannel WB, McGee D, Dawer TR. Death and coronary attacks in men after giving up cigarette smoking: a report from the Framingham Study. *Lancet* 1974;2(7893):1345–8.

Görlach A, Brandes RP, Bassus S, Kronemann N, Kirchmaier CM, Busse R, Schini-Kerth VB. Oxidative stress and expression of p22phox are involved in the up-regulation of tissue factor in vascular smooth muscle cells in response to activated platelets. *FASEB Journal* 2000;14(11):1518–28.

Gouaźe V, Dousset N, Dousset J-C, Valdiguié P. Effect of nicotine and cotinine on the susceptibility to in vitro oxidation of LDL in healthy non smokers and smokers. *Clinica Chimica Acta* 1998;277(1):25–37.

Gourlay SG, Benowitz NL. Arteriovenous differences in plasma concentration of nicotine and catecholamines and related cardiovascular effects after smoking, nicotine nasal spray, and intravenous nicotine. *Clinical Pharmacology and Therapeutics* 1997;62(4):453–63.

Gourlay SG, Stead LF, Benowitz NL. Clonidine for smoking cessation. *Cochrane Database of Systematic Reviews* 2004, Issue 3. Art. No.: CD000058. DOI: 10.1002/14651858.CD000058.pub2.

Green MS, Jucha E, Luz Y. Blood pressure in smokers and nonsmokers: epidemiologic findings. *American Heart Journal* 1986;111(5):932–40.

Gugliucci A. Antithrombin activity is inhibited by acrolein and homocysteine thiolactone: protection by cysteine. *Life Sciences* 2007;82(7–8):413–8.

Gustafsson A, Åsman B, Bergström K. Cigarette smoking as an aggravating factor in inflammatory tissue-destructive diseases: increase in tumor necrosis factor-alpha priming of peripheral neutrophils measured as generation of oxygen radicals. *International Journal of Clinical & Laboratory Research* 2000; 30(4):187–90.

Guthikonda S, Sinkey C, Barenz T, Haynes WG. Xanthine oxidase inhibition reverses endothelial dysfunction in heavy smokers. *Circulation* 2003;107(3):416–21.

Habek D, Habek JC, Ivanišević M, Djelmiš J. Fetal tobacco syndrome and perinatal outcome. *Fetal Diagnosis and Therapy* 2002;17(6):367–71.

Haffner SM, Lehto S, Rönnemaa T, Pyörälä K, Laakso M. Mortality from coronary heart disease in subjects with type 2 diabetes and in nondiabetic subjects with and without prior myocardial infarction. *New England Journal of Medicine* 1998;339(4):229–34.

Håheim LL, Holme I, Hjermann I, Leren P. Smoking habits and risk of fatal stroke: 18 years follow up of the Oslo Study. *Journal of Epidemiology and Community Health* 1996;50(6):621–4.

Hajek P, Taylor TZ, Mills P. Brief intervention during hospital admission to help patients to give up smoking after myocardial infarction and bypass surgery: randomized controlled trial. *BMJ (British Medical Journal)* 2002;324(7329):87–9.

Hajek P, West R, Foulds J, Nilsson F, Burrows S, Meadow A. Randomized comparative trial of nicotine polacrilex, a transdermal patch, nasal spray, and an inhaler. *Archives of Internal Medicine* 1999;159(17):2033–8.

Hallstrom AP, Cobb LA, Ray R. Smoking as a risk factor for recurrence of sudden cardiac arrest. *New England Journal of Medicine* 1986;314(5):271–5.

Hames CG, Rose K, Knowles M, Davis CE, Tyroler HA. Black-white comparisons of 20-year coronary heart disease mortality in the Evans County Heart Study. *Cardiology* 1993;82(2–3):122–36.

Hammond EC, Garfinkel L. Coronary heart disease, stroke, and aortic aneurysm: factors in the etiology. *Archives of Environmental Health* 1969;19(2):167–82.

Hammond EC, Horn D. Smoking and death rates: report on forty-four months of follow-up of 187,783 men. II: death rates by cause. *JAMA: the Journal of the American Medical Association* 1958;166(11):1294–308.

Haramaki N, Ikeda H, Takajo Y, Katoh A, Kanaya S, Shintani S, Haramaki R, Murohara T, Imaizumi T. Long-term smoking causes nitroglycerin resistance in platelets by depletion of intraplatelet glutathione. *Arteriosclerosis, Thrombosis, and Vascular Biology* 2001;21(11):1852–6.

Harats D, Ben-Naim M, Dabach Y, Hollander G, Stein O, Stein Y. Cigarette smoking renders LDL susceptible to peroxidative modification and enhanced metabolism by macrophages. *Atherosclerosis* 1989;79(2–3):245–52.

Hart CL, Hole DJ, Smith GD. Risk factors and 20-year stroke mortality in men and women in the Renfrew/Paisley Study in Scotland. *Stroke* 1999;30(10): 1999–2007.

Hasdai D, Garratt KN, Grill DE, Lerman A, Holmes DR Jr. Effect of smoking status on the long-term outcome after successful percutaneous coronary revascularization. *New England Journal of Medicine* 1997a;336(11): 755–61.

Hasdai D, Gibbons RJ, Holmes DR Jr, Higano ST, Lerman A. Coronary endothelial dysfunction in humans is associated with myocardial perfusion defects. *Circulation* 1997b;96(10):3390–5.

Hatsukami DK, Kotlyar M, Allen S, Jensen J, Li S, Le C, Murphy S. Effects of cigarette reduction on cardiovascular risk factors and subjective methods. *Chest* 2005; 128(4):2528–37.

Hatsukami DK, Slade J, Benowitz NL, Giovino GA, Gritz ER, Leischow S, Warner KE. Reducing tobacco harm: research challenges and issues. *Nicotine & Tobacco Research* 2002;4(Suppl 2):S89–S101.

Haustein K-O, Krause J, Haustein H, Rasmussen T, Cort N. Effects of cigarette smoking or nicotine replacement on cardiovascular risk factors and parameters of haemorheology. *Journal of Internal Medicine* 2002;252(2):130–9.

Haustein K-O, Krause J, Haustein H, Rasmussen T, Cort N. Changes in hemorheological and biochemical parameters following short-term and long-term smoking cessation induced by nicotine replacement therapy (NRT). *International Journal of Clinical Pharmacology, Therapy, and Toxicology* 2004;42(2):83–92.

Hecht SS, Murphy SE, Carmella SG, Zimmerman CL, Losey L, Kramarczuk I, Roe MR, Puumala SS, Li YS, Le C, et al. Effects of reduced cigarette smoking on uptake of a tobacco-specific lung carcinogen. *Journal of the National Cancer Institute* 2004;96(2):107–15.

Heeschen C, Jang JJ, Weis M, Pathak A, Kaji S, Hu RS, Tsao PS, Johnson FL, Cooke JP. Nicotine stimulates angiogenesis and promotes tumor growth and atherosclerosis. *Nature Medicine* 2001;7(7):833–9.

Heeschen C, Weis M, Aicher A, Dimmeler S, Cooke JP. A novel angiogenic pathway mediated by non-neuronal nicotinic acetylcholine receptors. *Journal of Clinical Investigation* 2002;110(4):527–36.

Heeschen C, Weis M, Cooke JP. Nicotine promotes arteriogenesis. *Journal of the American College of Cardiology* 2003;41(3):489–96.

Heitzer T, Brockhoff C, Mayer B, Warnholtz A, Mollnau H, Henne S, Meinertz T, Münzel T. Tetrahydrobiopterin improves endothelium-dependent vasodilation in chronic smokers: evidence for a dysfunctional nitric oxide synthase. *Circulation Research* 2000;86(2): E36–E41.

Heitzer T, Just H, Munzel T. Antioxidant vitamin C improves endothelial dysfunction in chronic smokers. *Circulation* 1996;94(1):6–9.

Hellerstein MK, Benowitz NL, Neese RA, Schwartz JM, Hoh R, Jacob P III, Hsieh J, Faix D. Effects of cigarette smoking and its cessation on lipid metabolism and energy expenditure in heavy smokers. *Journal of Clinical Investigation* 1994;93(1):265–72.

Helve E, Yki-Järvinen H, Koivisto VA. Smoking and insulin sensitivity in type I diabetic patients. *Metabolism* 1986;35(9):874–7.

Henley SJ, Thun MJ, Chao A, Calle EE. Association between exclusive pipe smoking and mortality from cancer and other diseases. *Journal of the National Cancer Institute* 2004;96(11):853–61.

Henningfield JE, Stapleton JM, Benowitz NL, Grayson RF, London ED. Higher levels of nicotine in arterial than in venous blood after cigarette smoking. *Drug and Alcohol Dependence* 1993;33(1):23–9.

Hermanson B, Omenn GS, Kronmal RA, Gersh BJ. Beneficial six-year outcome of smoking cessation in older men and women with coronary artery disease: results from the CASS registry. *New England Journal of Medicine* 1988;319(21):1365–9.

Hess DT, Matsumoto A, Kim S-O, Marshall HE, Stamler JS. Protein S-nitrosylation: purview and parameters. *Nature Reviews Molecular Cell Biology* 2005;6(2): 150–66.

Hesse E. Der einfluss des rauchens auf den kreislauf (The influence of smoking on the circulation) [German]. *Archiv fur Klinische Medizin* 1907;89:565–75.

Hibbert B, Olsen S, O'Brien E. Involvement of progenitor cells in vascular repair. *Trends in Cardiovascular Medicine* 2003;13(8):322–6.

Hibi K, Ishigami T, Tamura K, Mizushima S, Nyui N, Fujita T, Ochiai H, Kosuge M, Watanabe Y, Yoshii Y, et al. Endothelial nitric oxide synthase gene polymorphism and acute myocardial infarction. *Hypertension* 1998;32(3):521–6.

Hill JM, Zalos G, Halcox JPJ, Schenke WH, Waclawiw MA, Quyyumi AA, Finkel T. Circulating endothelial progenitor cells, vascular function, and cardiovascular risk. *New England Journal of Medicine* 2003;348(7): 593–600.

Hioki H, Aoki N, Kawano K, Homori M, Hasumura Y, Yasumura T, Maki A, Yoshino H, Yanagisawa A, Ishikawa K. Acute effects of cigarette smoking on platelet-dependent thrombin generation. *European Heart Journal* 2001; 22(1):56–61.

Hu FB, Manson JE, Stampfer MJ, Colditz G, Liu S, Solomon CG, Willett WC. Diet, lifestyle, and the risk of type 2 diabetes mellitus in women. *New England Journal of Medicine* 2001;345(11):790–7.

Huang PL, Huang Z, Mashimo H, Bloch KD, Moskowitz MA, Bevan JA, Fishman MC. Hypertension in mice lacking the gene for endothelial nitric oxide synthase. *Nature* 1995;377(6546):239–42.

Hubbard R, Lewis S, Smith C, Godfrey C, Smeeth L, Farrington P, Britton J. Use of nicotine replacement therapy and the risk of acute myocardial infarction, stroke, and death. *Tobacco Control* 2005;14(6):416–21.

Hughes JR. Reduced smoking: an introduction and review of the evidence. *Addiction* 2000;95(Suppl 1):S3–S7.

Hughes JR, Goldstein MG, Hurt RD, Shiffman S. Recent advances in the pharmacotherapy of smoking. *JAMA: the Journal of the American Medical Association* 1999; 281(1):72–6.

Hughes JR, Gulliver SB, Fenwick JW, Valliere WA, Cruser K, Pepper S, Shea P, Solomon L, Flynn BS. Smoking cessation among self-quitters. *Health Psychology* 1992;11(5):331–4.

Hughes JR, Lindgren PG, Connett JE, Nides MA. Smoking reduction in the Lung Health Study. *Nicotine & Tobacco Research* 2004a;6(2):275–80.

Hughes JR, Stead LF, Lancaster T. Antidepressants for smoking cessation. *Cochrane Database of Systematic Reviews* 2004b, Issue 4. Art. No.: CD000031. DOI: 10.1002/14651858.CD000031.pub2.

Hunter KA, Garlick PJ, Broom I, Anderson SE, McNurlan MA. Effects of smoking and abstention from smoking on fibrinogen synthesis in humans. *Clinical Science (London)* 2001;100(4):459–65.

Hurt RD, Croghan GA, Wolter TD, Croghan IT, Offord KP, Williams GM, Djordjevic MV, Richie JP Jr, Jeffrey AM. Does smoking reduction result in reduction of biomarkers associated with harm: a pilot study using a nicotine inhaler. *Nicotine & Tobacco Research* 2000;2(4):327–36.

Ichihara S, Yamada Y, Fujimura T, Nakashima N, Yokota M. Association of a polymorphism of the endothelial constitutive nitric oxide synthase gene with myocardial infarction in the Japanese population. *American Journal of Cardiology* 1998;81(1):83–6

Ignarro LJ, Burke TM, Wood KS, Wolin MS, Kadowitz PJ. Association between cyclic GMP accumulation and acetylcholine-elicited relaxation of bovine intrapulmonary artery. *Journal of Pharmacology and Experimental Therapeutics* 1984;228(3):682–90.

Ikarugi H, Yamashita T, Aoki R, Ishii H, Kanki K, Yamamoto J. Impaired spontaneous thrombolytic activity in elderly and in habitual smokers, as measured by a new global thrombosis test. *Blood Coagulation & Fibrinolysis* 2003;14(8):781–4.

Ilebekk A, Miller NE, Mjos OD. Effects of nicotine and inhalation of cigarette smoke on total body oxygen consumption in dogs. *Scandinavian Journal of Clinical and Laboratory Investigation* 1975;35(1):67–72.

International Agency for Research on Cancer. IARC Monographs on the Evaluation of Carcinogenic Risks to Humans: Smokeless Tobacco and Some Tobacco-specific N-Nitrosamines. Vol. 89. Lyon (France): International Agency for Research on Cancer, 2007.

Irace C, Ciamei M, Crivaro A, Fiaschi E, Madia A, Cortese C, Gnasso A. Hematocrit is associated with carotid atherosclerosis in men but not in women. *Coronary Artery Disease* 2003;14(4):279–84.

Iribarren C, Tekawa IS, Sidney S, Friedman GD. Effect of cigar smoking on the risk of cardiovascular disease, chronic obstructive pulmonary disease, and cancer in men. *New England Journal of Medicine* 1999; 340(23):1773–80.

Jacobs DR Jr, Adachi H, Mulder I, Kromhout D, Menotti A, Nissinen A, Blackburn H. Cigarette smoking and mortality risk: twenty-five-year follow-up of the Seven Countries Study. *Archives of Internal Medicine* 1999a;159(7):733–40.

Jacobs EJ, Thun MJ, Apicella LF. Cigar smoking and death from coronary heart disease in a prospective study of US men. *Archives of Internal Medicine* 1999b; 159(20):2413–8.

Jain RK. Normalization of tumor vasculature: an emerging concept in antiangiogenic therapy. *Science* 2005;307(5706):58–62.

Jamrozik K, Norman PE, Spencer CA, Parsons RW, Tuohy R, Lawrence-Brown MM, Dickinson JA. Screening for abdominal aortic aneurysm: lessons from a population-based study. *Medical Journal of Australia* 2000;173(7):345–50.

Jarrett RJ, McCartney P, Keen H. The Bedford survey: ten year mortality rates in newly diagnosed diabetics, borderline diabetics and normoglycaemic controls and risk indices for coronary heart disease in borderline diabetics. *Diabetologia* 1982;22(2):79–84.

Jensen EJ, Pedersen B, Frederiksen R, Dahl R. Prospective study on the effect of smoking and nicotine substitution on leucocyte blood counts and relation between blood leucocytes and lung function. *Thorax* 1998;53(9):784–9.

Jeppesen J, Hollenbeck CB, Zhou M-Y, Coulston AM, Jones C, Chen Y-DI, Reaven GM. Relation between insulin resistance, hyperinsulinemia, postheparin plasma lipoprotein lipase activity, and postprandial lipemia. *Arteriosclerosis, Thrombosis, and Vascular Biology* 1995;15(3):320–4.

Joannides R, Haefeli WE, Linder L, Richard V, Bakkali EH, Thuillez C, Luscher TF. Nitric oxide is responsible for flow-dependent dilatation of human peripheral conduit arteries in vivo. *Circulation* 1995;91(5):1314–9.

Jonason T, Bergström R. Cessation of smoking in patients with intermittent claudication: effects on the risk of peripheral vascular complications, myocardial infarction and mortality. *Acta Medica Scandinavica* 1987;221(3):253–60.

Jorenby DE, Hays JT, Rigotti NA, Azoulay S, Watsky EJ, Williams KE, Billing CB, Gong J, Reeves KR, Varenicline Phase 3 Study Group. Efficacy of varenicline, an α4β2 nicotinic acetylcholine receptor partial agonist, vs placebo or sustained-release bupropion for smoking cessation: a randomized controlled trial. *JAMA: the Journal of the American Medical Association* 2006; 296(1):56–63.

Jorenby DE, Leischow SJ, Nides MA, Rennard SI, Johnston JA, Hughes AR, Smith SS, Muramoto ML, Daughton DM, Doan K, et al. A controlled trial of sustained-release bupropion, a nicotine patch, or both for smoking cessation. *New England Journal of Medicine* 1999;340(9):685–91.

Joseph A, Hecht S, Murphy S, Gross M, Lando H, Bliss R, Le C, Hatsukami D. A randomized controlled trial of smoking reduction in heart disease patients. Abstract presented at the Society for Research on Nicotine and Tobacco's 11th Annual Meeting; March 20–23, 2005; Prague; <http://www.srnt.org/pubs/abstract.html>; accessed: October 30, 2006.

Joseph AM, Antonnucio DO. Lack of efficacy of transdermal nicotine in smoking cessation. *New England Journal of Medicine* 1999;341(15):1157–8.

Joseph AM, Fu SS. Safety issues in pharmacotherapy for smoking in patients with cardiovascular disease. *Progress in Cardiovascular Diseases* 2003;45(6):429–41.

Joseph AM, Norman SM, Ferry LH, Prochazka AV, Westman EC, Steele BG, Sherman SE, Cleveland M, Antonnucio DO, Hartman N, et al. The safety of transdermal nicotine as an aid to smoking cessation in patients with cardiac disease. *New England Journal of Medicine* 1996;335(24):1792–8.

Kagan A, Yano K, Reed DM, MacLean CJ. Predictors of sudden cardiac death among Hawaiian-Japanese men. *American Journal of Epidemiology* 1989;130(2):268–77.

Kagota S, Yamaguchi Y, Shinozuka K, Kwon YM, Kunitomo M. Cigarette smoke-modified low density lipoprotein impairs endothelium-dependent relaxation in isolated rabbit arteries. *General Pharmacology* 1996;27(3):447–81.

Kahn HA. The Dorn study of smoking and mortality among U.S. veterans: report on 8 and one-half years of observation. In: Haenszel W, editor. *Epidemiological Approaches to the Study of Cancer and Other Chronic Diseases*. National Cancer Institute Monograph No. 19. Bethesda (MD): U.S. Department of Health, Education, and Welfare, Public Health Service, National Institutes of Health, National Cancer Institute, 1966:1–125.

Kahn SE. Beta cell failure: causes and consequences. *International Journal of Clinical Practice Supplement* 2001;(123):13–8.

Kaijser L, Berglund B. Effect of nicotine on coronary blood-flow in man. *Clinical Physiology* 1985;5(6):541–52.

Kalra VK, Ying Y, Deemer K, Natarajan R, Nadler JL, Coates TD. Mechanism of cigarette smoke condensate induced adhesion of human monocytes to cultured endothelial cells. *Journal of Cellular Physiology* 1994;160(1):154–62.

Kannel WB, Doyle JT, McNamara PM, Quickenton P, Gordon T. Precursors of sudden coronary death: factors related to the incidence of sudden death. *Circulation* 1975;51(4):606–13.

Kannel WB, Higgins M. Smoking and hypertension as predictors of cardiovascular risk in population studies. *Journal of Hypertension Supplement* 1990;8(Suppl 5):S3–S8.

Kannel WB, McGee DL, Castelli WP. Latest perspectives on cigarette smoking and cardiovascular disease: the Framingham Study. *Journal of Cardiac Rehabilitation* 1984;4(7):267.

Kannel WB, Shurtleff D. The Framingham Study: cigarettes and the development of intermittent claudication. *Geriatrics* 1973;28(2):61–8.

Kannel WB, Thomas HE Jr. Sudden coronary death: the Framingham Study. *Annals of the New York Academy of Sciences* 1982;382:3–21.

Kaufmann PA, Gnecchi-Ruscone T, di Terlizzi M, Schäfers KP, Lüscher TF, Camici PG. Coronary heart disease in smokers: vitamin C restores coronary microcirculatory function. *Circulation* 2000;102(11):1233–8.

Kawachi I, Colditz GA, Stampfer MJ, Willett WC, Manson JE, Rosner B, Hunter DJ, Hennekens CH, Speizer FE. Smoking cessation in relation to total mortality rates in women: a prospective cohort study. *Annals of Internal Medicine* 1993a;119(10):992–1000.

Kawachi I, Colditz GA, Stampfer MJ, Willett WC, Manson JE, Rosner B, Speizer FE, Hennekens CH. Smoking cessation and decreased risk of stroke in women. *JAMA: the Journal of the American Medical Association* 1993b;269(2):232–6.

Kawachi I, Colditz GA, Stampfer MJ, Willett WC, Manson JE, Rosner B, Speizer FE, Hennekens CH. Smoking cessation and time course of decreased risks of coronary heart disease in middle-aged women. *Archives of Internal Medicine* 1994;154(2):169–75.

Kawakami N, Takatsuka N, Shimizu H, Ishibashi H. Effects of smoking on the incidence of non-insulin-dependent diabetes mellitus: replication and extension in a Japanese cohort of male employees. *Amercan Journal of Epidemiology* 1997;145(2):103–9.

Kayyali US, Budhiraja R, Pennella CM, Cooray S, Lanzillo JJ, Chalkley R, Hassoun PM. Upregulation of xanthine oxidase by tobacco smoke condensate in pulmonary endothelial cells. *Toxicology and Applied Pharmacology* 2003;188(1):59–68.

Keen H, Jarrett RJ, McCartney P. The ten-year follow-up of the Bedford survey (1962–1972): glucose tolerance and diabetes. *Diabetologia* 1982;22(2):73–8.

Kenet G, Freedman J, Shenkman B, Regina E, Brok-Simoni F, Holzman F, Vavva F, Brand N, Michelson A, Trolliet M, et al. Plasma glutathione peroxidase deficiency and platelet insensitivity to nitric oxide in children with familial stroke. *Arteriosclerosis, Thrombosis, and Vascular Biology* 1999;19(8):2017–23.

Kershbaum A, Bellet S. Smoking as a factor in atherosclerosis: a review of epidemiological, pathological, and experimental studies. *Geriatrics* 1966;21(12):155–70.

Kershbaum A, Khorsandian R, Caplan RF, Bellet S, Feinberg LJ. The role of catecholamines in the free fatty acid response to cigarette smoking. *Circulation* 1963;28(1):52–7.

Kielstein JT, Impraim B, Simmel S, Bode-Böger SM, Tsikas D, Frölich JC, Hoeper MM, Haller H, Fliser D. Cardiovascular effects of systemic nitric oxide synthase inhibition with asymmetrical dimethylarginine in humans. *Circulation* 2004;109(2):172–7.

Kimmel SE, Berlin JA, Miles C, Jaskowiak J, Carson JL, Strom BL. Risk of acute first myocardial infarction and use of nicotine patches in a general population. *Journal of the American College of Cardiology* 2001; 37(5):1297–302.

Kirsch M, de Groot H. Ascorbate is a potent antioxidant against peroxynitrite-induced oxidation reactions: evidence that ascorbate acts by re-reducing substrate radicals produced by peroxynitrite. *Journal of Biological Chemistry* 2000;275(22):16702–8.

Kirsch M, Korth HG, Sustmann R, de Groot H. The pathobiochemistry of nitrogen dioxide. *Biological Chemistry* 2002;383(3–4):389–99.

Kirsch M, Lehnig M, Korth H-G, Sustmann R, de Groot H. Inhibition of peroxynitrite-induced nitration of tyrosine by glutathione in the presence of carbon dioxide through both radical repair and peroxynitrate formation. *Chemistry* 2001;7(15):3313–20.

Kirschbaum C, Wust S, Strasburger CJ. 'Normal' cigarette smoking increases free cortisol in habitual smokers. *Life Sciences* 1992;50(6):435–42.

Kiyohara Y, Ueda K, Fujishima M. Smoking and cardiovascular disease in the general population in Japan. *Journal of Hypertension* 1990;8(Suppl 5):S9–S15.

Ko GTC, Chan JCN, Tsang LWW, Critchley JAJH, Cockram CS. Smoking and diabetes in Chinese men. *Postgraduate Medical Journal* 2001;77(906):240–3.

Koenig W, Sund M, Fröhlich M, Fischer H-G, Löwel H, Döring A, Hutchinson WL, Pepys MB. C-reactive protein, a sensitive marker of inflammation, predicts future risk of coronary heart disease in initially healthy middle-aged men: results from the MONICA (Monitoring Trends and Determinants in Cardiovascular Disease) Augsburg Cohort Study, 1984 to 1992. *Circulation* 1999;99(2):237–42.

Komatsu M, Kawagishi T, Emoto M, Shoji T, Yamada A, Sato K, Hosoi M, Nishizawa Y. ecNOS gene polymorphism is associated with endothelium-dependent vasodilation in type 2 diabetes. *Journal of Physiology - Heart and Circulatory Physiology* 2002;283(2): H557–H561.

Kondo T, Hayashi M, Takeshita K, Numaguchi Y, Kobayashi K, Iino S, Inden Y, Murohara T. Smoking cessation rapidly increases circulating progenitor cells in peripheral blood in chronic smokers. *Arteriosclerosis, Thrombosis, and Vascular Biology* 2004;24(8): 1442–7.

Konishi H, Wu J, Cooke JP. Chronic exposure to nicotine impairs cholinergic angiogenesis. *Vascular Medicine* 2010;15(1):47–54.

Kothari V, Stevens RJ, Adler AI, Stratton IM, Manley SE, Neil HA, Holman RR. UKPDS 60: risk of stroke in type 2 diabetes estimated by the UK Prospective Diabetes Study risk engine. *Stroke* 2002;33(7):1776–81.

Krumholz HM, Cohen BJ, Tsevat J, Pasternak RC, Weinstein MC. Cost-effectiveness of a smoking cessation program after myocardial infarction. *Journal of the American College of Cardiology* 1993;22(6):1697–702.

Krupski WC, Olive GC, Weber CA, Rapp JH. Comparative effects of hypertension and nicotine on injury-induced myointimal thickening. *Surgery* 1987;102(2):409–15.

Kubes P, Suzuki M, Granger DN. Nitric oxide: an endogenous modulator of leukocyte adhesion. *Proceedings of the National Academy of Sciences of the United States of America* 1991;88(11):4651–5.

Kugiyama K, Yasue H, Ohgushi M, Motoyama T, Kawano H, Inobe Y, Hirashima O, Sugiyama S. Deficiency in nitric oxide bioactivity in epicardial coronary arteries of cigarette smokers. *Journal of the American College of Cardiology* 1996;28(5):1161–7.

Kuhlencordt PJ, Cyurko R, Han F, Scherrer-Crosbie M, Aretz TH, Hajjar R, Picard MH, Huang PL. Accelerated atherosclerosis, aortic aneurysm formation, and ischemic heart disease in apolipoprotein E/endothelial nitric oxide synthase double-knockout mice. *Circulation* 2001;104(4):448–54.

Kuller LH, Ockene JK, Meilahn E, Wentworth DN, Svendsen KH, Neaton JD, Multiple Risk Factor Intervention Trial Research Group. Cigarette smoking and mortality. *Preventive Medicine* 1991;20(5):638–54

Kumanan W, Gibson N, Willan A, Cook D. Effect of smoking cessation on mortality after myocardial infarction: meta-analyses of cohort studies. *Archives of Internal Medicine* 2000;160(7):939–44.

Kumar A, Kingdon E, Norman J. The isoprostane 8-iso-$PGF_{2\alpha}$ suppresses monocyte adhesion to human microvascular endothelial cells via two independent mechanisms. *FASEB Journal* 2005;19(3):443–5.

Lam TH, He Y, Shi QL, Huang JY, Zhang F, Wan ZH, Sun CS, Li LS. Smoking, quitting, and mortality in a Chinese cohort of retired men. *Annals of Epidemiology* 2002;12(5):316–20.

Lancet. Intensive blood-glucose control with sulphonylureas or insulin compared with conventional treatment and risk of complications in patients with type 2 diabetes (UKPDS 33). *Lancet* 1998;352(9131):837–53.

Lane D, Gray EA, Mathur RS, Mathur SP. Up-regulation of vascular endothelial growth factor-C by nicotine in cervical cancer cell lines. *American Journal of Reproductive Immunology* 2005;53(3):153–8.

Lassila R, Laustiola KE. Cigarette smoking and platelet-vessel wall interactions. *Prostaglandins, Leukotrienes, and Essential Fatty Acids* 1992;46(2):81–6.

Lassila R, Seyberth HW, Haapanen A, Schweer H, Koskenvuo M, Laustiola KE. Vasoactive and atherogenic effects of cigarette smoking: a study of monozygotic twins discordant for smoking. *BMJ (British Medical Journal)* 1988;297(6654):955–7.

Law MR, Morris JK, Watt HC, Wald NJ. The dose-response relationship between cigarette consumption, biochemical markers and risk of lung cancer. *British Journal of Cancer* 1997;75(11):1690–3.

Law MR, Wald NJ. Environmental tobacco smoke and ischemic heart disease. *Progress in Cardiovascular Diseases* 2003;46(1):31–8.

Lederle FA, Johnson GR, Wilson SE. Abdominal aortic aneurysm in women. *Journal of Vascular Surgery* 2001; 34(1):122–6.

Lee AJ, Fowkes FG, Carson MN, Leng GC, Allan PL. Smoking, atherosclerosis and risk of abdominal aortic aneurysm. *European Heart Journal* 1997;18(4):671–6.

Lee AJ, Fowkes FG, Rattray A, Rumley A, Lowe GD. Haemostatic and rheological factors in intermittent claudication: the influence of smoking and extent of arterial disease. *British Journal of Haematology* 1996;92(1):226–30.

Leeson CPM, Hingorani AD, Mullen MJ, Jeerooburkhan N, Kattenhorn M, Cole TJ, Muller DPR, Lucas A, Humphries SE, Deanfield JE. Glu298Asp endothelial nitric oxide synthase gene polymorphism interacts with environmental and dietary factors to influence endothelial function. *Circulation Research* 2002; 90(11):1153–8.

Lehr H-A, Frei B, Arfors KE. Vitamin C prevents cigarette smoke-induced leukocyte aggregation and adhesion to endothelium in vivo. *Proceedings of the National Academy of Sciences of the United States of America* 1994;91(16):7688–92.

Lehr H-A, Weyrich AS, Saetzler RK, Jurek A, Arfors KE, Zimmerman GA, Prescott SM, McIntyre TM. Vitamin C blocks inflammatory platelet-activating factor mimetics created by cigarette smoking. *Journal of Clinical Investigation* 1997;99(10):2358–64.

Leitinger N, Huber J, Rizza C, Mechtcheriakova D, Bochkov V, Koshelnick Y, Berliner JA, Binder BR. The isoprostane 8-iso-PGF$_{2\alpha}$ stimulates endothelial cells to bind monocytes: differences from thromboxane-mediated endothelial activation. *FASEB Journal* 2001; 15(7):1254–6.

Ley K. The role of selectins in inflammation and disease. *Trends in Molecular Medicine* 2003;9(6):263–8.

Libby P, Ridker PM, Maseri A. Inflammation and atherosclerosis. *Circulation* 2002;105(9):1135–43.

Lightwood J. Economics of smoking and cardiovascular disease. *Progress in Cardiovascular Diseases* 2003; 46(1):39–78.

Lightwood JM, Glantz SA. Short-term economic and health benefits of smoking cessation: myocardial infarction and stroke. *Circulation* 1997;96(4):1089–96.

Lightwood JM, Glantz SA. Declines in acute myocardial infarction after smoke-free laws and individual risk attributable to secondhand smoke. *Circulation* 2009;120(14):1373–9.

Lincoff AM, Wolski K, Nicholls SJ, Nissen SE. Pioglitazone and risk of cardiovascular events in patients with type 2 diabetes mellitus: a meta-analysis of randomized trials. *JAMA: the Journal of the American Medical Association* 2007;298(10):1180–8.

Loscalzo J. Nitric oxide insufficiency, platelet activation, and arterial thrombosis. *Circulation Research* 2001; 88(8):756–62.

Lowe GD, Lee AJ, Rumley A, Price JF, Fowkes FG. Blood viscosity and risk of cardiovascular events: the Edinburgh Artery Study. *British Journal of Haematology* 1997;96(1):168–73.

Lu JT, Creager MA. The relationship of cigarette smoking to peripheral arterial disease. *Reviews in Cardiovascular Medicine* 2004;5(4):189–93.

Lucini D, Bertocchi F, Malliani A, Pagani M. A controlled study of the autonomic changes produced by habitual cigarette smoking in healthy subjects. *Cardiovascular Research* 1996;31(4):633–9.

Lúdvíksdóttir D, Blöndal T, Franxon M, Gudmundsson TV, Säwe U. Effects of nicotine nasal spray on atherogenic and thrombogenic factors during smoking cessation. *Journal of Internal Medicine* 1999;246(1):61–6.

Lundman BM, Asplund K, Norberg A. Smoking and metabolic control in patients with insulin-dependent diabetes mellitus. *Journal of Internal Medicine* 1990; 227(2):101–6.

Lykkesfeldt J, Christen S, Wallock LM, Chang HH, Jacob RA, Ames BN. Ascorbate is depleted by smoking and repleted by moderate supplementation: a study in male smokers and nonsmokers with matched dietary antioxidant intakes. *American Journal of Clinical Nutrition* 2000;71(2):530–6.

MacCallum PK. Markers of hemostasis and systemic inflammation in heart disease and atherosclerosis in smokers. *Proceedings of the American Thoracic Society* 2005;2(1):34–43.

Madsbad S, McNair P, Christensen MS, Christiansen C, Faber OK, Binder C, Transbol I. Influence of smoking on insulin requirement and metabolic status in diabetes mellitus. *Diabetes Care* 1980;3(1):41–3.

Mahfouz MM, Hulea SA, Kummerow FA. Cigarette smoke increases cholesterol oxidation and lipid peroxidation of human low-density lipoprotein and decreases its binding to the hepatic receptor in vitro. *Journal of Environmental Pathology, Toxicology and Oncology* 1995;14(3–4):181–92.

Mahmarian JJ, Moyé LA, Nasser GA, Nagueh SF, Bloom MF, Benowitz NL, Verani MS, Byrd WG, Pratt CM. Nicotine patch therapy in smoking cessation reduces the extent of exercise-induced myocardial ischemia. *Journal of American College of Cardiology* 1997;30(1):125–30.

Mann SJ, James GD, Wang RS, Pickering TG. Elevation of ambulatory systolic blood pressure in hypertensive smokers. *JAMA: the Journal of the American Medical Association* 1991;265(17):2226–8.

Manson JE, Ajani UA, Liu S, Nathan DM, Hennekens CH. A prospective study of cigarette smoking and the incidence of diabetes mellitus among US male physicians. *American Journal of Medicine* 2000;109(7):538–42.

Manson JE, Colditz GA, Stampfer MJ, Willett WC, Krolewski AS, Rosner B, Arky RA, Speizer FE, Hennekens CH. A prospective study of maturity-onset diabetes mellitus and risk of coronary heart disease and stroke in women. *Archives of Internal Medicine* 1991;151(6):1141–7.

Marangon K, Herbeth B, Artur Y, Esterbauer H, Siest G. Low and very low density lipoprotein composition and resistance to copper-induced oxidation are not notably modified in smokers. *Clinica Chimica Acta* 1997;265(1):1–12.

Maser RE, Steenkiste AR, Dorman JS, Nielsen VK, Bass EB, Manjoo Q, Drash AL, Becker DJ, Kuller LH, Greene DA. Epidemiological correlates of diabetic neuropathy: report from Pittsburgh Epidemiology of Diabetes Complications Study. *Diabetes* 1989;38(11):1456–61.

Matetzky S, Tani S, Kangavari S, Dimayuga P, Yano J, Xu H, Chyu K-Y, Fishbein MC, Shah PK, Cercek B. Smoking increases tissue factor expression in atherosclerotic plaques: implications for plaque thrombogenicity. *Circulation* 2000;102(6):602–4.

Mazzone A, Cusa C, Mazzucchelli I, Vezzoli M, Ottini E, Ghio S, Tossini G, Pacifici R, Zuccaro P. Cigarette smoking and hypertension influence nitric oxide release and plasma levels of adhesion molecules. *Clinical Chemistry and Laboratory Medicine* 2001;39(9):822–6.

McAdam BF, Byrne D, Morrow JD, Oates JA. Contribution of cyclooxygenase-2 to elevated biosynthesis of thromboxane A$_2$ and prostacyclin in cigarette smokers. *Circulation* 2005;112(7):1024–9.

McCall MR, van den Berg JJ, Kuypers FA, Tribble DL, Krauss RM, Knoff LJ, Forte TM. Modification of LCAT activity and HDL structure: new links between cigarette smoke and coronary heart disease risk. *Arteriosclerosis and Thrombosis* 1994;14(2):248–53.

McLenachan JM, Vita J, Fish DR, Treasure CB, Cox DA, Ganz P, Selwyn AP. Early evidence of endothelial vasodilator dysfunction at coronary branch points. *Circulation* 1990;82(4):1169–73.

McNagny SE, Ahluwalia JS, Clark WS, Resnicow KA. Cigarette smoking and severe uncontrolled hypertension in inner-city African Americans. *American Journal of Medicine* 1997;103(2):121–7.

Meade TW, Imeson J, Stirling Y. Effects of changes in smoking and other characteristics on clotting factors and the risk of ischaemic heart disease. *Lancet* 1987;2(8566):986–8.

Medalie JH, Papier CM, Goldbourt U, Herman JB. Major factors in the development of diabetes mellitus in 10,000 men. *Archives of Internal Medicine* 1975;135(6):811–7.

Meijer WT, Grobbee DE, Hunink MGM, Hofman A, Hoes AW. Determinants of peripheral arterial disease in the elderly: the Rotterdam Study. *Archives of Internal Medicine* 2000;160(19):2934–8.

Meine TJ, Patel MR, Washam JB, Pappas PA, Jollis JG. Safety and effectiveness of transdermal nicotine patch in smokers admitted with acute coronary syndromes. *American Journal of Cardiology* 2005;95(8):976–8.

Mendelson G, Aronow WS, Ahn C. Prevalence of coronary artery disease, atherothrombotic brain infarction, and peripheral arterial disease: associated risk factors in older Hispanics in an academic hospital-based geriatrics practice. *Journal of the American Geriatric Society* 1998;46(4):481–3.

Mero N, Syvänne M, Eliasson B, Smith U, Taskinen M-R. Postprandial elevation of ApoB-48-containing triglyceride-rich particles and retinyl esters in normolipemic males who smoke. *Arteriosclerosis, Thrombosis, and Vascular Biology* 1997;17(10):2096–102.

Mero N, Van Tol A, Scheek LM, Van Gent T, Labeur C, Rosseneu M, Taskinen M-R. Decreased postprandial high density lipoprotein cholesterol and apolipoproteins A-I and E in normolipidemic smoking men: relations with lipid transfer proteins and LCAT activities. *Journal of Lipid Research* 1998;39(7):1493–502.

Metz L, Waters DD. Implications of cigarette smoking for the management of patients with acute coronary syndromes. *Progress in Cardiovascular Diseases* 2003;46(1):1–9.

Meyers CD, Kamanna VS, Kashyap ML. Niacin therapy in atherosclerosis. *Current Opinion in Lipidology* 2004;15(6):659–65.

Meyers DG, Neuberger JS, He J. Cardiovascular effects of bans on smoking in public places: a systematic review and meta-analysis. *Journal of the American College of Cardiology* 2009;54(14):1249–55.

Miettinen OS, Neff RK, Jick H. Cigarette-smoking and nonfatal myocardial infarction: rate ratio in relation to age, sex and predisposing conditions. *American Journal of Epidemiology* 1976;103(1):30–6.

Minuz P, Andrioli G, Degan M, Gaino S, Ortolani R, Tommasoli R, Zuliani V, Lechi A, Lechi C. The F_2-isoprostane 8-epiprostaglandin $F_{2\alpha}$ increases platelet adhesion and reduces the antiadhesive and antiaggregatory effects of NO. *Arteriosclerosis, Thrombosis, and Vascular Biology* 1998;18(8):1248–56.

Mitchell BD, Hawthorne VM, Vinik AI. Cigarette smoking and neuropathy in diabetic patients. *Diabetes Care* 1990;13(4):434–7.

Miyake Y. Risk factors for non-fatal acute myocardial infarction in middle-aged and older Japanese: Fukuoka Heart Study Group. *Japanese Circulation Journal* 2000; 64(2):103–9.

Miyamoto Y, Saito Y, Kajiyama N, Yoshimura M, Shimasaki Y, Nakayama M, Kamitani S, Harada M, Ishikawa M, Kuwahara K, et al. Endothelial nitric oxide synthase gene is positively associated with essential hypertension. *Hypertension* 1998;32(1):3–8.

Moffatt RJ, Biggerstaff KD, Stamford BA. Effects of the transdermal nicotine patch on normalization of HDL-C and its subfractions. *Preventive Medicine* 2000; 31(2 Pt 1):148–52.

Moreno H Jr, Chalon S, Urae A, Tangphao O, Abiose AK, Hoffman BB, Blaschke TF. Endothelial dysfunction in human hand veins is rapidly reversible after smoking cessation. *American Journal of Physiology* 1998; 275(3 Pt 2):H1040–H1045.

Morita H, Ikeda H, Haramaki N, Eguchi H, Imaizumi T. Only two-week smoking cessation improves platelet aggregability and intraplatelet redox imbalance of long-term smokers. *Journal of the American College of Cardiology* 2005;45(4):589–94.

Morrish NJ, Stevens LK, Fuller JH, Jarrett RJ, Keen H. Risk factors for macrovascular disease in diabetes mellitus: the London follow-up to the WHO Multinational Study of Vascular Disease in Diabetics. *Diabetologia* 1991;34(8):590–4.

Morrow JD, Frei B, Longmire AW, Gaziano JM, Lynch SM, Shyr Y, Strauss WE, Oates JA, Roberts LJ II. Increase in circulating products of lipid peroxidation (F_2-isoprostanes) in smokers: smoking as a cause of oxidative damage. *New England Journal of Medicine* 1995; 332(18):1198–203.

Moss SE, Klein R, Klein BE. Association of cigarette smoking with diabetic retinopathy. *Diabetes Care* 1991; 14(2):119–26.

Moulton KS, Vakili K, Zurakowski D, Soliman M, Butterfield C, Sylvin E, Lo K-M, Gillies S, Javaherian K, Folkman J. Inhibition of plaque neovascularization reduces macrophage accumulation and progression of advanced atherosclerosis. *Proceedings of the National Academy of Sciences of the United States of America* 2003;100(8):4736–41.

Moy CS, LaPorte RE, Dorman JS, Songer TJ, Orchard TJ, Kuller LH, Becker DJ, Drash AL. Insulin-dependent diabetes mellitus mortality: the risk of cigarette smoking. *Circulation* 1990;82(1):37–43.

Muhlhauser I, Bender R, Bott U, Jorgens V, Grusser M, Wagener W, Overmann H, Berger M. Cigarette smoking and progression of retinopathy and nephropathy in type 1 diabetes. *Diabetic Medicine* 1996;13(6):536–43.

Muhlhauser I, Sawicki P, Berger M. Cigarette-smoking as a risk factor for macroproteinuria and proliferative retinopathy in type 1 (insulin-dependent) diabetes. *Diabetologia* 1986;29(8):500–2.

Multiple Risk Factor Intervention Trial Research Group. Mortality rates after 10.5 years for participants in the Multiple Risk Factor Intervention Trial: findings related to a priori hypotheses of the trial. *JAMA: the Journal of the American Medical Association* 1990;263(13): 1795–801.

Multiple Risk Factor Intervention Trial Research Group. Mortality after 16 years for participants randomized to the Multiple Risk Factor Intervention Trial. *Circulation* 1996;94(5):946–51.

Murabito JM, Evans JC, Nieto K, Larson MG, Levy D, Wilson PWF. Prevalence and clinical correlates of peripheral arterial disease in the Framingham Offspring Study. *American Heart Journal* 2002;143(6):961–5.

Murray JJ, Nowak J, Oates JA, FitzGerald GA. Biosynthesis of thromboxane A_2 and prostacyclin during chronic smoking and withdrawal in man [abstract]. *Clinical Research* 1985;33:521A.

Murray JJ, Nowak J, Oates JA, FitzGerald GA. Platelet-vessel wall interactions in individuals who smoke cigarettes. *Advances in Experimental Medicine and Biology* 1990;273:189–98.

Murray RP, Bailey WC, Daniels K, Bjornson WM, Kurnow K, Connett JE, Nides MA, Kiley JP. Safety of nicotine polacrilex gum used by 3,094 participants in the Lung Health Study Research Group. *Chest* 1996;109(2): 438–45.

Muscat JE, Harris RE, Haley NJ, Wynder EL. Cigarette smoking and plasma cholesterol. *American Heart Journal* 1991;121(1 Pt 1):141–7.

National Cancer Institute. *Cigar Smoking in the United States: Health Effects and Trends.* Smoking and Tobacco Control Monograph No. 9. Bethesda (MD):

U.S. Department of Health and Human Services, Public Health Service, National Institutes of Health, National Cancer Institute, 1998. NIH Publication No. 98-4302.

National Cancer Institute. *Risks Associated with Smoking Cigarettes with Low Machine-Measured Yields of Tar and Nicotine*. Smoking and Tobacco Control Monograph No.13. Bethesda (MD): U.S. Department of Health and Human Services, Public Health Service, National Institutes of Health, National Cancer Institute, 2001. NIH Publication No. 02-5047.

National Heart, Lung, and Blood Institute. *Morbidity & Mortality: 2007 Chart Book on Cardiovascular, Lung, and Blood Diseases*. Bethesda (MD): U.S. Department of Health and Human Services, Public Health Service, National Institutes of Health, National Heart, Lung, and Blood Institute, June 2007.

Natori T, Sata M, Washida M, Hirata Y, Nagai R, Makuuchi M. Nicotine enhances neovascularization and promotes tumor growth. *Molecules and Cells* 2003;16(2):143–6.

Neaton JD, Kuller LH, Wentworth D, Borhani NO. Total and cardiovascular mortality in relation to cigarette smoking, serum cholesterol concentration, and diastolic blood pressure among black and white males followed up for five years. *American Heart Journal* 1984;108(3 Pt 2):759–69.

Neaton JD, Wentworth D. Serum cholesterol, blood pressure, cigarette smoking, and death from coronary heart disease: overall findings and differences by age for 316,099 white men. Multiple Risk Factor Intervention Trial Research Group. *Archives of Internal Medicine* 1992;152(1):56–64.

Neese RA, Benowitz NL, Hoh R, Faix D, LaBua A, Pun K, Hellerstein MK. Metabolic interactions between surplus dietary energy intake and cigarette smoking or its cessation. *American Journal of Physiology – Endocrinology and Metabolism* 1994;267(6 Pt 1):E1023–E1034.

Ness J, Aronow WS, Ahn C. Risk factors for symptomatic peripheral arterial disease in older persons in an academic hospital-based geriatrics practice. *Journal of the American Geriatric Society* 2000;48(3):312–4.

Neunteufl T, Heher S, Kostner K, Mitulovic G, Lehr S, Khoschsorur G, Schmid RW, Maurer G, Stefenelli T. Contribution of nicotine to acute endothelial dysfunction in long-term smokers. *Journal of the American College of Cardiology* 2002;39(2):251–6.

New England Journal of Medicine. The effect of intensive treatment of diabetes on the development and progression of long-term complications in insulin-dependent diabetes mellitus. Diabetes Control and Complications Trial Research Group. *New England Journal of Medicine* 1993;329(14):977–86.

Newby DE, McLeod AL, Uren NG, Flint L, Ludlam CA, Webb DJ, Fox KA, Boon NA. Impaired coronary tissue plasminogen activator release is associated with coronary atherosclerosis and cigarette smoking: direct link between endothelial dysfunction and atherothrombosis. *Circulation* 2001;103(15):1936–41.

Newby DE, Wright RA, Labinjoh C, Ludlam CA, Fox KAA, Boon NA, Webb DJ. Endothelial dysfunction, impaired endogenous fibrinolysis, and cigarette smoking: a mechanism for arterial thrombosis and myocardial infarction. *Circulation* 1999;99(11):1411–5.

Nicod P, Rehr R, Winniford MD, Campbell WB, Firth BG, Hillis LD. Acute systemic and coronary hemodynamic and serologic responses to cigarette smoking in long-term smokers with atherosclerotic coronary artery disease. *Journal of the American College of Cardiology* 1984;4(5):964–71.

Niedermaier ON, Smith ML, Beightol LA, Zukowska-Grojec Z, Goldstein DS, Eckberg DL. Influence of cigarette smoking on human autonomic function. *Circulation* 1993;88(2):562–71.

Nilsson PM, Lind L, Pollare T, Berne C, Lithell HO. Increased level of hemoglobin A_{1c}, but not impaired insulin sensitivity, found in hypertensive and normotensive smokers. *Metabolism* 1995;44(5):557–61.

Nilsson S, Carstensen JM, Pershagen G. Mortality among male and female smokers in Sweden: a 33 year follow up. *Journal of Epidemiology and Community Health* 2001;55(11):825–30.

Nissen SE, Wolski K. Effect of rosiglitazone on the risk of myocardial infarction and death from cardiovascular causes. *New England Journal of Medicine* 2007; 356(24):2457–71.

Nitenberg A, Antony I. Effects of nicotine gum on coronary vasomotor responses during sympathetic stimulation in patients with coronary artery stenosis. *Journal of Cardiovascular Pharmacology* 1999;34(5):694–9.

Nitenberg A, Antony I, Foult J-M. Acetylcholine-induced coronary vasoconstriction in young, heavy smokers with normal coronary arteriographic findings. *American Journal of Medicine* 1993;95(1):71–7.

Njølstad I, Arnesen E, Lund-Larsen PG. Smoking, serum lipids, blood pressure, and sex differences in myocardial infarction: a 12-year follow-up of the Finnmark Study. *Circulation* 1996;93(3):450–6.

Nowak J, Murray JJ, Oates JA, FitzGerald GA. Biochemical evidence of a chronic abnormality in platelet and vascular function in healthy individuals who smoke cigarettes. *Circulation* 1987;76(1):6–14.

Nowak P, Kołodziejczyk J, Wachowicz B. Peroxynitrite and fibrinolytic system: the effect of peroxynitrite on plasmin activity. *Molecular and Cellular Biochemistry* 2004;267(1–2):141–6.

Ockene J, Kristeller JL, Goldberg R, Ockene I, Merriam P, Barrett S, Pekow P, Hosmer D, Gianelly R. Smoking cessation and severity of disease: the coronary artery smoking intervention study. *Health Psychology* 1992;11(2):119–26.

Ockene JK, Kuller LH, Svendsen KH, Meilahn E. The relationship of smoking cessation to coronary heart disease and lung cancer in the Multiple Risk Factor Intervention Trial (MRFIT). *American Journal of Public Health* 1990;80(8):954–8.

O'Connor RJ, Giovino GA, Kozlowski LT, Shiffman S, Hyland A, Bernert JT, Caraballo RS, Cummings KM. Changes in nicotine intake and cigarette use over time in two nationally representative cross-sectional samples of smokers. *American Journal of Epidemiology* 2006; 164(8):750–9.

Omenn GS, Anderson KW, Kronmal RA, Vlietstra RE. The temporal pattern of reduction of mortality risk after smoking cessation. *American Journal of Preventive Medicine* 1990;6(5):251–7.

Ong MK, Glantz SA. Cardiovascular health and economic effects of smoke-free workplaces. *American Journal of Medicine* 2004;117(1):32–8.

Otsuka R, Watanabe H, Hirata K, Tokai K, Muro T, Yoshiyama M, Takeuchi K, Yoshikawa J. Acute effects of passive smoking on the coronary circulation in healthy young adults. *JAMA: the Journal of the American Medical Association* 2001;286(4):436–41.

Panagiotakos DB, Pitsavos C, Chrysohoou C, Skoumas J, Masoura C, Toutouzas P, Stefanadis C. Effect of exposure to secondhand smoke on markers of inflammation: the ATTICA study. *American Journal of Medicine* 2004;116(3):145–50.

Paramo JA, Beloqui O, Roncal C, Benito A, Orbe J. Validation of plasma fibrinogen as a marker of carotid atherosclerosis in subjects free of clinical cardiovascular disease. *Haematologica* 2004;89(10):1226–31.

Park YS, Kim J, Misonou Y, Takamiya R, Takahashi M, Freeman MR, Taniguchi N. Acrolein induces cyclooxygenase-2 and prostaglandin production in human umbilical vein endothelial cells: roles of p38 MAP kinase. *Arteriosclerosis, Thrombosis, and Vascular Biology* 2007;27(6):1319–25.

Patsch JR, Miesenbock G, Hopferwieser T, Muhlberger V, Knapp E, Dunn JK, Gotto AM Jr, Patsch W. Relation of triglyceride metabolism and coronary artery disease: studies in the postprandial state. *Arteriosclerosis and Thrombosis* 1992;12(11):1336–45.

Pearson TA, Mensah GA, Alexander RW, Anderson JL, Cannon RO 3rd, Criqui M, Fadl YY, Fortmann SP, Hong Y, Myers GL, et al. Markers of inflammation and cardiovascular disease: application to clinical and public health practice: a statement for healthcare professionals from the Centers for Disease Control and Prevention and the American Heart Association. *Circulation* 2003;107(3):499–511.

Pellegrini MP, Newby DE, Johnston NR, Maxwell S, Webb DJ. Vitamin C has no effect on endothelium-dependent vasomotion and acute endogenous fibrinolysis in healthy smokers. *Journal of Cardiovascular Pharmacology* 2004;44(1):117–24.

Pellegrini MP, Newby DE, Maxwell S, Webb DJ. Short-term effects of transdermal nicotine on acute tissue plasminogen activator release in vivo in man. *Cardiovascular Research* 2001;52(2):321–7.

Penn A, Snyder C. Arteriosclerotic plaque development is 'promoted' by polynuclear aromatic hydrocarbons. *Carcinogenesis* 1988;9(12):2185–9.

Penn A, Snyder CA. 1,3 Butadiene, a vapor phase component of environmental tobacco smoke, accelerates arteriosclerotic plaque development. *Circulation* 1996; 93(3):552–7.

Perkins KA, Epstein LH, Marks BL, Stiller RL, Jacob RG. The effect of nicotine on energy expenditure during light physical activity. *New England Journal of Medicine* 1989;320(14):898–903.

Perry IJ, Wannamethee SG, Walker MK, Thomson AG, Whincup PH, Shaper AG. Prospective study of risk factors for development of non-insulin dependent diabetes in middle aged British men. *BMJ (British Medical Journal)* 1995;310(6979):560–4.

Persson P-G, Carlsson S, Svanström L, Östenson C-G, Efendic S, Grill V. Cigarette smoking, oral moist snuff use and glucose intolerance. *Journal of Internal Medicine* 2000;248(2):103–10.

Peters RW, Brooks MM, Todd L, Liebson PR, Wilhelmsen L. Smoking cessation and arrhythmic death: the CAST experience. *Journal of the American College of Cardiology* 1995;26(5):1287–92.

Petruzzelli S, Puntoni R, Mimotti P, Pulerá N, Baliva F, Fornai E, Giuntini C. Plasma 3-nitrotyrosine in cigarette smokers. *American Journal of Respiratory and Critical Care Medicine* 1997;156(6):1902–7.

Pignatelli B, Li C-Q, Boffetta P, Chen Q, Ahrens W, Nyberg F, Mukeria A, Bruske-Hohlfeld I, Fortes C, Constantinescu V, et al. Nitrated and oxidized plasma proteins in smokers and lung cancer patients. *Cancer Research* 2001;61(2):778–84.

Pilz H, Oguogho A, Chehne F, Lupattelli G, Palumbo B, Sinzinger H. Quitting cigarette smoking results in a fast improvement of in vivo oxidation injury (determined via plasma, serum and urinary isoprostane). *Thrombosis Research* 2000;99(3):209–21.

Pohl U, Holtz J, Busse R, Bassenge E. Crucial role of endothelium in the vasodilator response to increased flow in vivo. *Hypertension* 1986;8(1):37–44.

Porchet HC, Benowitz NL, Sheiner LB, Copeland JR. Apparent tolerance to the acute effect of nicotine results in part from distribution kinetics. *Journal of Clinical Investigation* 1987;80(5):1466–71.

Porta M, Bandello F. Diabetic retinopathy: a clinical update. *Diabetologia* 2002;45(12):1617–34.

Pozen MW, Stechmiller JA, Harris W, Smith S, Fried DD, Voigt GC. A nurse rehabilitator's impact on patients with myocardial infarction. *Medical Care* 1977;15(10):830–7.

Praticò D, Reilly M, Lawson JA, FitzGerald GA. Novel indices of oxidant stress in cardiovascular disease: specific analysis of F_2-isoprostanes. *Agents and Actions Supplements* 1997;48:25–41.

Praticò D, Smyth EM, Viola F, FitzGerald GA. Local amplification of platelet function by 8-epi prostaglandin $F_{2\alpha}$ is not mediated by thromboxane receptor isoforms. *Journal of Biological Chemistry* 1996; 271(25):14916–24.

Prescott E, Scharling H, Osler M, Schnohr P. Importance of light smoking and inhalation habits on risk of myocardial infarction and all cause mortality: a 22 year follow up of 12,149 men and women in the Copenhagen City Heart Study. *Journal of Epidemiology and Community Health* 2002;56(9):702–6.

Pretorius M, Rosenbaum DA, Lefebvre J, Vaughan DE, Brown NJ. Smoking impairs bradykinin-stimulated t-PA release. *Hypertension* 2002;39(3):767–71.

Price JF, Mowbray PI, Lee AJ, Rumley A, Lowe GDO, Fowkes FGR. Relationship between smoking and cardiovascular risk factors in the development of peripheral arterial disease and coronary artery disease: Edinburgh Artery Study. *European Heart Journal* 1999;20(5):344–53.

Princen HM, Van Poppel G, Vogelezang C, Buytenhek R, Kok FJ. Supplementation with vitamin E but not β-carotene in vivo protects low density lipoproteins from lipid peroxidation in vitro: effect of cigarette smoking. *Arteriosclerosis and Thrombosis* 1992;12(5): 554–62.

Prisco D, Fedi S, Brunelli T, Chiarugi L, Lombardi A, Gianni R, Santoro E, Cappelletti C, Pepe G, Gensini GF, et al. The influence of smoking on von Willebrand factor is already manifest in healthy adolescent females: the Floren-teen (Florence Teenager) Study. *International Journal of Clinical & Laboratory Research* 1999;29(4):150–4.

Przyklenk K. Nicotine exacerbates postischemic contractile dysfunction of 'stunned' myocardium in the canine model: possible role of free radicals. *Circulation* 1994;89(3):1272–81.

Puranik R, Celermajer DS. Smoking and endothelial function. *Progress in Cardiovascular Diseases* 2003;45(6):443–58.

Qiao Q, Tervahauta M, Nissinen A, Tuomilehto J. Mortality from all causes and from coronary heart disease related to smoking and changes in smoking during a 35-year follow-up of middle-aged Finnish men. *European Heart Journal* 2000;21(19):1621–6.

Quist-Paulsen P, Gallefoss F. Randomised controlled trial of smoking cessation intervention after admission for coronary heart disease. *BMJ (British Medical Journal)* 2003;327(7426):1254–7.

Rabkin SW. Effect of cigarette smoking cessation on risk factors for coronary atherosclerosis: a control clinical trial. *Atherosclerosis* 1984;53(2):173–84.

Ragland DR, Brand RJ. Coronary heart disease mortality in the Western Collaborative Group Study: follow-up experience of 22 years. *American Journal of Epidemiology* 1988;127(3):462–75.

Rangemark C, Ciabattoni G, Wennmalm A. Excretion of thromboxane metabolites in healthy women after cessation of smoking. *Arteriosclerosis and Thrombosis* 1993;13(6):777–82.

Rea TD, Heckbert SR, Kaplan RC, Smith NL, Lemaitre RN, Psaty BM. Smoking status and risk for recurrent coronary events after myocardial infarction. *Annals of Internal Medicine* 2002;137(6):494–500.

Reaven GM. Banting lecture 1988: role of insulin resistance in human disease. *Diabetes* 1988;37(12): 1595–607.

Rees DD, Palmer RM, Moncada S. Role of endothelium-derived nitric oxide in the regulation of blood pressure. *Proceedings of the National Academy of Sciences of the United States of America* 1989;86(9):3375–8.

Regalado M, Yang S, Wesson DE. Cigarette smoking is associated with augmented progression of renal insufficiency in severe essential hypertension. *American Journal of Kidney Diseases* 2000;35(4):687–94.

Regan TJ, Hellems HK, Bing RJ. Effect of cigarette smoking on coronary circulation and cardiac work in patients with arteriosclerotic coronary disease. *Annals of the New York Academy of Sciences* 1960;190:186–9.

Reichard P. Risk factors for progression of microvascular complications in the Stockholm Diabetes Intervention Study (SDIS). *Diabetes Research and Clinical Practice* 1992;16(2):151–6.

Reilly M, Delanty N, Lawson JA, FitzGerald GA. Modulation of oxidant stress in vivo in chronic cigarette smokers. *Circulation* 1996;94(1):19–25.

Ridker PM, Hennekens CH, Stampfer MJ, Manson JE, Vaughan DE. Prospective study of endogenous tissue plasminogen activator and risk of stroke. *Lancet* 1994;343(8903):940–3.

Rigotti NA. Treatment of tobacco use and dependence. *New England Journal of Medicine* 2002;346(7):506–12.

Rigotti NA, McKool KM, Shiffman S. Predictors of smoking cessation after coronary artery bypass graft surgery: results of a randomized trial with 5-year follow-up. *Annals of Internal Medicine* 1994;120(4):287–93.

Rigotti NA, Thorndike AN, Regan S, McKool K, Pasternak RC, Chang Y, Swartz S, Torres-Finnerty N, Emmons KM, Singer DE. Bupropion for smokers hospitalized with acute cardiovascular disease. *American Journal of Medicine* 2006;119(12):1080–7.

Rimm EB, Chan J, Stampfer MJ. Prospective study of cigarette smoking, alcohol use, and the risk of diabetes in men. *BMJ (British Medical Journal)* 1995; 310(6979):555–9.

Rimm EB, Manson JE, Stampfer MJ, Colditz GA, Willett WC, Rosner B, Hennekens CH, Speizer FE. Cigarette smoking and the risk of diabetes in women. *American Journal of Public Health* 1993;83(2):211–4.

Rinder HM, Schuster JE, Rinder CS, Wang C, Schweidler HJ, Smith BR. Correlation of thrombosis with increased platelet turnover in thrombocytosis. *Blood* 1998;91(4):1288–94.

Ronnemaa T, Ronnemaa EM, Puukka P, Pyorala K, Laakso M. Smoking is independently associated with high plasma insulin levels in nondiabetic men. *Diabetes Care* 1996;19(11):1229–32.

Rose G, Hamilton PJS, Colwell L, Shipley MJ. A randomised controlled trial of anti-smoking advice: 10-year results. *Journal of Epidemiology and Community Health* 1982;36(2):102–8.

Rosengren A, Wilhelmsen L, Wedel H. Coronary heart disease, cancer and mortality in male middle-aged light smokers. *Journal of Internal Medicine* 1992; 231(4):357–62.

Ross R. Atherosclerosis—an inflammatory disease. *New England Journal of Medicine* 1999;340(2):115–26.

Rubanyi GM, Vanhoutte PM. Superoxide anions and hyperoxia inactivate endothelium-derived relaxing factor. *American Journal of Physiology – Heart and Circulatory Physiology* 1986;250(5 Pt 2):H822–H827.

Rubenstein D, Jesty J, Bluestein D. Differences between mainstream and sidestream cigarette smoke extracts and nicotine in the activation of platelets under static and flow conditions. *Circulation* 2004;109(1):78–83.

Ruggeri RB. Cholesteryl ester transfer protein: pharmacological inhibition for the modulation of plasma cholesterol levels and promising target for the prevention of atherosclerosis. *Current Topics in Medicinal Chemistry* 2005;5(3):257–64.

Saareks V, Ylitalo P, Alanko J, Mucha I, Riutta A. Effects of smoking cessation and nicotine substitution on systemic eicosanoid production in man. *Naunyn-Schmiedeberg's Archives of Pharmacology* 2001;363(5): 556–61.

Salonen JT, Salonen R, Seppanen K, Rinta-Kiikka S, Kuukka M, Korpela H, Alfthan G, Kantola M, Schalch W. Effects of antioxidant supplementation on platelet function: a randomized pair-matched, placebo-controlled, double-blind trial in men with low antioxidant status. *American Journal of Clinical Nutrition* 1991;53(5):1222–9.

Sambola A, Osende J, Hathcock J, Degen M, Nemerson Y, Fuster V, Crandall J, Badimon JJ. Role of risk factors in the modulation of tissue factor activity and blood thrombogenicity. *Circulation* 2003;107(7):973–7.

Sarabi M, Lind L. Short-term effects of smoking and nicotine chewing gum on endothelium-dependent vasodilation in young healthy habitual smokers. *Journal of Cardiovascular Pharmacology* 2000;35(3):451–6.

Sargeant LA, Khaw K-T, Bingham S, Day NE, Luben RN, Oakes S, Welch A, Wareham NJ. Cigarette smoking and glycaemia: the EPIC-Norfolk Study. *International Journal of Epidemiology* 2001;30(3):547–54.

Sasaki A, Kondo K, Sakamoto Y, Kurata H, Itakua H, Ikeda Y. Smoking cessation increases the resistance of low-density lipoprotein to oxidation. *Atherosclerosis* 1997;130(1–2):109–11.

Sawada M, Kishi Y, Numano F, Isobe M. Smokers lack morning increase in platelet sensitivity to nitric oxide. *Journal of Cardiovascular Pharmacology* 2002; 40(4):571–6.

Schächinger V, Britten MB, Zeiher AM. Prognostic impact of coronary vasodilator dysfunction on adverse long-term outcome of coronary heart disease. *Circulation* 2000;101(16):1899–906.

Scheffler E, Wiest E, Woehrle J, Otto I, Schulz I, Huber L, Ziegler R, Dresel HA. Smoking influences the atherogenic potential of low-density lipoprotein. *Clinical Investigation* 1992;70(3–4):263–8.

Schelbert HR, Phelps ME, Hoffman EJ, Huang SC, Selin CE, Kuhl DE. Regional myocardial perfusion assessed with N-13 labeled ammonia and positron emission computerized axial tomography. *American Journal of Cardiology* 1979;43(2):209–18.

Schlaifer JD, Mancini GBJ, O'Neill BJ, Pitt B, Haber HE, Pepine CJ. Influence of smoking status on angiotensin-converting enzyme inhibition–related improvement in coronary endothelial function. *Cardiovascular Drugs and Therapy* 1999;13(3):201–9.

Schmid P, Karanikas G, Kritz H, Pirich C, Stamatopoulos Y, Peskar BA, Sinzinger H. Passive smoking and platelet thromboxane. *Thrombosis Research* 1996;81(4): 451–60.

Schuller HM. Mechanisms of smoking-related lung and pancreatic adenocarcinomas development. *Nature Reviews Cancer* 2002;2(6):455–63.

Scientific Advisory Committee on Tobacco Product Regulation. *Recommendation on Health Claims Derived from ISO/FTC Method to Measure Cigarette Yield.* Geneva: World Health Organization, 2002.

Scott DA, Stapleton JA, Wilson RF, Sutherland G, Palmer RM, Coward PY, Gustavsson G. Dramatic decline in circulating intercellular adhesion molecule-1 concentration on quitting tobacco smoking. *Blood Cells, Molecules & Diseases* 2000;26(3):255–8.

Seddon JM, Willett WC, Speizer FE, Hankinson SE. A prospective study of cigarette smoking and age-related macular degeneration in women. *JAMA: the Journal of the American Medical Association* 1996;276(14): 1141–6.

Sedgwick JB, Hwang YS, Gerbyshak HA, Kita H, Busse WW. Oxidized low-density lipoprotein activates migration and degranulation of human granulocytes. *American Journal of Respiratory Cell and Molecular Biology* 2003;29(6):702–9.

Sela S, Shurtz-Swirski R, Awad J, Shapiro G, Nasser L, Shasha SM, Kristal B. The involvement of peripheral polymorphonuclear leukocytes in the oxidative stress and inflammation among cigarette smokers. *Israel Medical Association Journal* 2002;4(11):1015–9.

Sexton PT, Walsh J, Jamrozik K, Parsons R. Risk factors for sudden unexpected cardiac death in Tasmanian men. *Australian and New Zealand Journal of Medicine* 1997;27(1):45–50.

Shanks TG, Burns DM. Disease consequences of cigar smoking. In: *Cigars: Health Effects and Trends.* Smoking and Tobacco Control Monograph No. 9. Bethesda (MD): U.S. Department of Health and Human Services, Public Health Service, National Institutes of Health, National Cancer Institute, 1998:105–58. NIH Publication No. 98-4302.

Shao B, Fu X, McDonald TO, Green PS, Uchida K, O'Brien KD, Oram JF, Heinecke JW. Acrolein impairs ATP binding cassette transporter A1-dependent cholesterol export from cells through site-specific modification of apolipoprotein A-I. *Journal of Biological Chemistry* 2005;280(43):36386–96.

Shaper AG, Pocock SJ, Walker M, Phillips AN, Whitehead TP, Macfarlane PW. Risk factors for ischaemic heart disease: the prospective phase of the British Regional Heart Study. *Journal of Epidemiology and Community Health* 1985;39(3):197–209.

Sharrett AR, Sorlie PD, Chambless LE, Folsom AR, Hutchinson RG, Heiss G, Szklo M. Relative importance of various risk factors for asymptomatic carotid atherosclerosis versus coronary heart disease incidence: the Atherosclerosis Risk in Communities Study. *American Journal of Epidemiology* 1999;149(9):843–52.

Shaten BJ, Kuller LH, Neaton JD. Association between baseline risk factors, cigarette smoking, and CHD mortality after 10.5 years. *Preventive Medicine* 1991; 20(5):655–9.

Sheps DS, Herbst MC, Hinderliter AL, Adams KF, Ekelund LG, O'Neil JJ, Goldstein GM, Bromberg PA, Dalton JL, Ballenger MN, et al. Production of arrhythmias by elevated carboxyhemoglobin in patients with coronary artery disease. *Annals of Internal Medicine* 1990;113(5):343–51.

Shimasaki Y, Yasue H, Yoshimura M, Nakayama M, Kugiyama K, Ogawa H, Harada E, Masuda T, Koyama W, Saito Y, et al. Association of the missense Glu298Asp variant of the endothelial nitric oxide synthase gene with myocardial infarction. *Journal of the American College of Cardiology* 1998;31(7):1506–10.

Shin VY, Wu WK, Ye YN, So WH, Koo MW, Liu ES, Luo JC, Cho CH. Nicotine promotes gastric tumor growth and neovascularization by activating extracellular signal-regulated kinase and cyclooxygenase-2. *Carcinogenesis* 2004;25(12):2487–95.

Shinton R, Beevers G. Meta-analysis of relation between cigarette smoking and stroke. *BMJ (British Medical Journal)* 1989;298(6676):789–94.

Siekmeier R, Wulfroth P, Wieland H, Gross W, Marz W. Low-density lipoprotein susceptibility to in vitro oxidation in healthy smokers and non-smokers. *Clinical Chemistry* 1996;42(4):524–30.

Silagy C, Lancaster T, Stead L, Mant D, Fowler G. Nicotine replacement therapy for smoking cessation. *Cochrane Database of Systematic Reviews* 2004, Issue 3. Art. No.: CD000146. DOI: 10.1002/14651858.CD000146.pub2.

Simpson AJ, Gray RS, Moore NR, Booth NA. The effects of chronic smoking on the fibrinolytic potential of plasma and platelets. *British Journal of Haematology* 1997;97(1):208–13.

Sinha RN, Patrick AW, Richardson L, Wallymahmed M, MacFarlane IA. A six-year follow-up study of smoking habits and microvascular complications in young adults with type 1 diabetes. *Postgraduate Medical Journal* 1997;73(859):293–4.

Smith FB, Lowe GD, Fowkes FG, Rumley A, Rumley AG, Donnan PT, Housley E. Smoking, haemostatic factors and lipid peroxides in a population case control study of peripheral arterial disease. *Atherosclerosis* 1993;102(2):155–62.

Smith SC, Blair SN, Bonow RO, Brass LM, Cerqueira MD, Dracup K, Fuster V, Gotto A, Grundy SM, Miller NH, et al. AHA/ACC guidelines for preventing heart attack and death in patients with atherosclerotic cardiovascular disease: 2001 update. A statement for healthcare professionals from the American Heart Association and the American College of Cardiology. *Circulation* 2001;104(13):1577–9.

Smolenski A, Burkhardt AM, Eigenthaler M, Butt E, Gambaryan S, Lohmann SM, Walter U. Functional analysis of cGMP-dependent protein kinases I and II as mediators of NO/cGMP effects. *Naunyn-Schmiedeberg's Archives of Pharmacology* 1998;358(1):134–9.

Sniderman AD, Scantlebury T, Cianflone K. Hypertriglyceridemic hyperapoB: the unappreciated atherogenic dyslipoproteinemia in type 2 diabetes mellitus. *Annals of Internal Medicine* 2001;135(6):447–59.

Solberg LA, Strong JP. Risk factors and atherosclerotic lesions: a review of autopsy studies. *Arteriosclerosis* 1983;3(3):187–98.

SRNT Subcommittee on Biochemical Verification. Biochemical verification of tobacco use and cessation. *Nicotine & Tobacco Research* 2002;4(2):149–59.

Stamford BA, Matter S, Fell RD, Papanek P. Effects of smoking cessation on weight gain, metabolic rate, caloric consumption, and blood lipids. *American Journal of Clinical Nutrition* 1986;43(4):486–94.

Stavroulakis GA, Makris TK, Hatzizacharias AN, Tsoukala C, Kyriakidis MK. Passive smoking adversely affects the haemostasis/fibrinolytic parameters in healthy nonsmoker offspring of healthy smokers. *Thrombosis & Haemostasis* 2000;84(5):923–4.

Stepanov I, Jensen J, Hatsukami D, Hecht SS. New and traditional smokeless tobacco: comparison of toxicant and carcinogen levels. Nicotine & Tobacco Research 2008;10(12):1773–82.

Strachan DP. Predictors of death from aortic aneurysm among middle-aged men: the Whitehall Study. *British Journal of Surgery* 1991;78(4):401–4.

Stratton K, Shetty P, Wallace R, Bondurant S, editors. *Clearing the Smoke: Assessing the Science Base for Tobacco Harm Reduction*. Washington: National Academy Press, 2001.

Strong JP, Richards ML. Cigarette smoking and atherosclerosis in autopsied men. *Atherosclerosis* 1976; 23(3):451–76.

Stubbe I, Eskilsson J, Nilsson-Ehle P. High-density lipoprotein concentrations increase after stopping smoking. *BMJ (British Medical Journal)* 1982;284(6328):1511–3.

Substance Abuse and Mental Health Services Administration. Results from the 2008 National Survey on Drug Use & Health: National Findings. NSDUH Series H-36. Rockville (MD): U.S. Department of Health and Human Services, Substance Abuse and Mental Health Services Administration, Office of Applied Studies, 2009. HHS Publication No. SMA 09-4434.

Suñer IJ, Espinosa-Heidmann DG, Marin-Castano ME, Hernandez EP, Pereira-Simon S, Cousins SW. Nicotine increases size and severity of experimental choroidal neovascularization. *Investigative Ophthalmology & Visual Science* 2004;45(1):311–7.

Suskin N, Sheth T, Negassa A, Yusuf S. Relationship of current and past smoking to mortality and morbidity in patients with left ventricular dysfunction. *Journal of the American College of Cardiology* 2001;37(6): 1677–82.

Suwaidi JA, Hamasaki S, Higano ST, Nishimura RA, Holmes DR Jr, Lerman A. Long-term follow-up of patients with mild coronary artery disease and endothelial dysfunction. *Circulation* 2000;101(9):948–54.

Sydow K, Münzel T. ADMA and oxidative stress. *Atherosclerosis Supplements* 2003(4):41–51.

Szadkowski A, Myers CR. Acrolein oxidizes the cytosolic and mitochondrial thioredoxins in human endothelial cells. *Toxicology* 2008;243(1–2):164–76).

Takajo Y, Ikeda H, Haramaki N, Murohara T, Imaizumi T. Augmented oxidative stress of platelets in chronic smokers: mechanisms of impaired platelet-derived nitric oxide bioactivity and augmented platelet aggregability. *Journal of American College of Cardiology* 2001; 38(5):1320–7.

Tall AR. An overview of reverse cholesterol transport. *European Heart Journal* 1998;19(Suppl A):A31–A35.

Tanne D, Yaari S, Goldbourt U. Risk profile and prediction of long-term ischemic stroke mortality: a 21-year follow-up in the Israeli Ischemic Heart Disease (IIHD) Project. *Circulation* 1998;98(14):1365–71.

Tanus-Santos JE, Toledo JCY, Cittadino M, Sabha M, Rocha JC, Moreno H Jr. Cardiovascular effects of transdermal nicotine in mildly hypertensive smokers. *American Journal of Hypertension* 2001;14(7 Pt 1):610–4.

Targher G, Alberiche M, Zenere MB, Bonadonna RC, Muggeo M, Bonora E. Cigarette smoking and insulin resistance in patients with noninsulin-dependent diabetes mellitus. *Journal of Clinical Endocrinology and Metabolism* 1997;82(11):3619–24.

Taylor CB, Houston-Miller N, Killen JD, DeBusk RF. Smoking cessation after acute myocardial infarction: effects of a nurse-managed intervention. *Annals of Internal Medicine* 1990;113(2):118–23.

Teo KK, Ounpuu S, Hawken S, Pandey MR. Valentin V, Hunt D, Diaz R, Rashed W, Freeman R, Jiang L, et al. Tobacco use and risk of myocardial infarction in 52 countries in the INTERHEART study: a case-control study. *Lancet* 2006;368(9536):647–58.

Thomas AE, Green FR, Lamlum H, Humphries SE. The association of combined alpha and beta fibrinogen genotype on plasma fibrinogen levels in smokers and non-smokers. *Journal of Medical Genetics* 1995;32(8): 585–9.

Thomson CC, Rigotti NA. Hospital and clinic-based smoking cessation interventions for smokers with cardiovascular disease. *Progress in Cardiovascular Diseases* 2003;45(6):459–79.

Thun MJ, Myers DG, Day-Lally C, Namboodin MM, Calle EE, Flanders WD, Adams SL, Heath CW Jr. Age and the exposure-response relationships between cigarette smoking and premature death in Cancer Prevention Study II. In: *Changes in Cigarette-Related Disease Risks and Their Implications for Prevention and Control*. Smoking and Tobacco Control Monograph No. 8. Bethesda (MD): U.S. Department of Health and Human Services, Public Health Service, National Institutes of Health, National Cancer Institute, 1997:383–475. NIH Publication No. 97-4213.

Thyberg J. Effects of nicotine on phenotypic modulation and initiation of DNA synthesis in cultured arterial smooth muscle cells. *Virchows Archiv B, Cell Pathology Including Molecular Pathology* 1986;52(1):25–32.

Tomlinson DR. Mitogen-activated protein kinases as glucose transducers for diabetic complications. *Diabetologia* 1999;42(11):1271–81.

Tonstad S, Farsang C, Klaene G, Lewis K, Manolis A, Perruchoud AP, Silagy C, van Spiegel PI, Astbury C, Hider A, et al. Bupropion SR for smoking cessation in smokers with cardiovascular disease: a multicenter randomized study. *European Heart Journal* 2003;24(10): 946–55.

Tonstad S, Tønnesen P, Hajek P, Williams KE, Billing CB, Reeves KR, Varenicline Phase 3 Study Group. Effect of maintenance therapy with varenicline on smoking cessation: a randomized controlled trial. *JAMA: the Journal of the American Medical Association* 2006; 296(1):64–71.

Tracy RP, Psaty BM, Macy E, Bovill EG, Cushman M, Cornell ES, Kuller LH. Lifetime smoking exposure affects the association of C-reactive protein with cardiovascular disease risk factors and subclinical disease in healthy elderly subjects. *Arteriosclerosis, Thrombosis, and Vascular Biology* 1997;17(10):2167–76.

Tran CTL, Leiper JM, Vallance P. The DDAH/ADMA/NOS pathway. *Atherosclerosis Supplements* 2003;4(4): 33–40.

Tsao PS, Buitrago R, Chan JR, Cooke JP. Fluid flow inhibits endothelial adhesiveness: nitric oxide and transcriptional regulation of VCAM-1. *Circulation* 1996; 94(7):1682–9.

Tsao PS, McEvoy LM, Drexler H, Butcher EC, Cooke JP. Enhanced endothelial adhesiveness in hypercholesterolemia is attenuated by L-arginine. *Circulation* 1994; 89(5):2176–82.

Tsao PS, Wang BY, Buitrago R, Shyy JY-J, Cooke JP. Nitric oxide regulates monocyte chemotactic protein-1. *Circulation* 1997;96(3):934–40.

Tsukada T, Yokoyama K, Arai T, Takemoto F, Hara S, Yamada A, Kawaguchi Y, Hosoya T, Igari J. Evidence of association of the ecNOS gene polymorphism with plasma NO metabolite levels in humans. *Biochemical and Biophysical Research Communication* 1998;245(1):190–3.

Turner RC, Millns H, Neil HAW, Stratton IM, Manley SE, Matthews DR, Holman RR. Risk factors for coronary artery disease in non-insulin dependent diabetes mellitus: United Kingdom Prospective Diabetes Study (UKPDS: 23). *BMJ (British Medical Journal)* 1998;316(7134):823–8.

Tuut M, Hense H-W. Smoking, other risk factors and fibrinogen levels: evidence of effect modification. *Annals of Epidemiology* 2001;11(4):232–8.

Tverdal A. Calculation of risk for the development of acute myocardial infarction in the normal population based on long-term follow-up studies: smokers compared with non-smokers. *Journal of Cardiovascular Risk* 1999; 6(5):287–91.

Tzivoni D, Keren A, Meyler S, Khoury Z, Lerer T, Brunel P. Cardiovascular safety of transdermal nicotine patches in patients with coronary artery disease who try to quit smoking. *Cardiovascular Drugs and Therapy* 1998;12(3):239–44.

Uchimoto S, Tsumura K, Hayashi T, Suematsu C, Endo G, Fujii S, Okada K. Impact of cigarette smoking on the incidence of type 2 diabetes mellitus in middle-aged Japanese men: the Osaka Health Survey. *Diabetic Medicine* 1999;16(11):951–5.

U.S. Department of Health and Human Services. *The Health Consequences of Smoking: Cardiovascular Disease. A Report of the Surgeon General*. Rockville (MD): U.S. Department of Health and Human Services, Public Health Service, Office on Smoking and Health, 1983. DHHS Publication No. (PHS) 84-50204.

U.S. Department of Health and Human Services. *The Health Consequences of Smoking: Nicotine Addiction. A Report of the Surgeon General*. Atlanta: U.S. Department of Health and Human Services, Public Health Service, Centers for Disease Control, National Center for Chronic Disease Prevention and Health Promotion, Office on Smoking and Health, 1988. DHHS Publication No. (CDC) 88-8406.

U.S. Department of Health and Human Services. *The Health Benefits of Smoking Cessation. A Report of the*

Surgeon General. Atlanta: U.S. Department of Health and Human Services, Public Health Service, Centers for Disease Control, National Center for Chronic Disease Prevention and Health Promotion, Office on Smoking and Health, 1990. DHHS Publication No. (CDC) 90-8416.

U.S. Department of Health and Human Services. *Reducing Tobacco Use. A Report of the Surgeon General*. Atlanta: U.S. Department of Health and Human Services, Centers for Disease Control and Prevention, National Center for Chronic Disease Prevention and Health Promotion, Office on Smoking and Health, 2000.

U.S. Department of Health and Human Services. *Women and Smoking: A Report of the Surgeon General*. Rockville (MD): U.S. Department of Health and Human Services, Public Health Service, Office of the Surgeon General, 2001:272–307.

U.S. Department of Health and Human Services. *The Health Consequences of Smoking: A Report of the Surgeon General*. Atlanta: U.S. Department of Health and Human Services, Centers for Disease Control and Prevention, National Center for Chronic Disease Prevention and Health Promotion, Office on Smoking and Health, 2004.

U.S. Department of Health and Human Services. *The Health Consequences of Involuntary Exposure to Tobacco Smoke: A Report of the Surgeon General*. Atlanta: U.S. Department of Health and Human Services, Centers for Disease Control and Prevention, Coordinating Center for Health Promotion, National Center for Chronic Disease Prevention and Health Promotion, Office on Smoking and Health, 2006.

U.S. Department of Health, Education, and Welfare. *The Health Consequences of Smoking: A Report of the Surgeon General: 1971*. Washington: U.S. Department of Health, Education, and Welfare, Public Health Service, Health Services and Mental Health Administration, 1971. DHEW Publication No. (HSM) 71–7513.

U.S. Department of Health, Education, and Welfare. *Smoking and Health. A Report of the Surgeon General*. Washington: U.S. Department of Health, Education, and Welfare, Public Health Service, Office of the Assistant Secretary for Health, Office on Smoking and Health, 1979. DHEW Publication No. (PHS) 79-50066.

U.S. Preventive Services Task Force. Screening for abdominal aortic aneurysm: recommendation statement. *Annals of Internal Medicine* 2005;142(3):198–202.

Vadseth C, Souza JM, Thomson L, Seagraves A, Nagaswami C, Scheiner T, Torbet J, Vilaire G, Bennett JS, Murciano J-C, et al. Pro-thrombotic state induced by post-translational modification of fibrinogen by reactive nitrogen species. *Journal of Biological Chemistry* 2004;279(10):8820–6.

Vallance P, Collier J, Moncada S. Effects of endothelium-derived nitric oxide on peripheral arteriolar tone in man. *Lancet* 1989;2(8670):997–1000.

Vallance P, Leone A, Calver A, Collier J, Moncada S. Accumulation of an endogenous inhibitor of nitric oxide synthesis in chronic renal failure. *Lancet* 1992;339(8793):572–5.

van den Berkmortel FWJP, Demacker PNM, Wollersheim H, Thien T, Stalenhoef AFH. Smoking or its cessation does not alter the susceptibility to *in vitro* LDL oxidation. *European Journal of Clinical Investigation* 2000;30(11):972–9.

van Domburg RT, Meeter K, van Berkel DFM, Veldkamp RF, van Herwerden LA, Bogers AJJC. Smoking cessation reduces mortality after coronary artery bypass surgery: a 20-year follow-up study. *Journal of the American College of Cardiology* 2000;36(3):878–83.

Vanhoutte PM, Feletou M, Taddei S. Endothelium-dependent contractions in hypertension. *British Journal of Pharmacology* 2005;144(4):449–58.

Vardulaki KA, Walker NM, Day NE, Duffy SW, Ashton HA, Scott RA. Quantifying the risks of hypertension, age, sex and smoking in patients with abdominal aortic aneurysm. *British Journal of Surgery* 2000;87(2):195–200.

Vasa M, Fichtlscherer S, Aicher A, Adler K, Urbich C, Martin H, Zeiher AM, Dimmeler S. Number and migratory activity of circulating endothelial progenitor cells inversely correlate with risk factors for coronary artery disease. *Circulation Research* 2001;89(1):E1–E7.

Vayá A, Mira Y, Martínez M, Villa P, Ferrando F, Estellés A, Corella D, Aznar J. Biological risk factors for deep vein thrombosis. *Clinical Hemorheology and Microcirculation* 2002;26(1):41–53.

Vermylen J, Nemmar A, Nemery B, Hoylaerts MF. Ambient air pollution and acute myocardial infarction. *Journal of Thrombosis and Haemostasis* 2005;3(9):1955–61.

Villablanca AC. Nicotine stimulates DNA synthesis and proliferation in vascular endothelial cells in vitro. *Journal of Applied Physiology* 1998;84(6):2089–98.

Villablanca AC, McDonald JM, Rutledge JC. Smoking and cardiovascular disease. *Clinics in Chest Medicine* 2000;21(1):159–72.

Vlietstra RE, Kronmal RA, Oberman A, Frye RL, Killip T III. Effect of cigarette smoking on survival of patients with angiographically documented coronary artery disease: report from the CASS registry. *JAMA: the Journal of the American Medical Association* 1986;255(8):1023–7.

von der Leyen HE, Gibbons GH, Morishita R, Lewis NP, Zhang L, Nakajima M, Kaneda Y, Cooke JP, Dzau VJ. Gene therapy inhibiting neointimal vascular lesion: in vivo transfer of endothelial cell nitric oxide synthase gene. *Proceedings of the National Academy of Sciences of the United States of America* 1995;92(4):1137–41.

Walker JM, Cove DH, Beevers DG, Dodson PM, Leatherdale BA, Fletcher RF, Wright AD. Cigarette smoking, blood pressure and the control of blood glucose in the development of diabetic retinopathy. *Diabetes Research (Edinburgh, Scotland)* 1985;2(4):183–6.

Wallenfeldt K, Hulthe J, Bokemark L, Wikstrand J, Fagerberg B. Carotid and femoral atherosclerosis, cardiovascular risk factors and C-reactive protein in relation to smokeless tobacco use or smoking in 58-year-old men. *Journal of Internal Medicine* 2001;250(6):492–501.

Walsh CH, Wright AD, Allbutt E, Pollock A. The effect of cigarette smoking on blood sugar, serum insulin and non esterified fatty acids in diabetic and non diabetic subjects. *Diabetologia* 1977;13(5):491–4.

Wang B-Y, Ho H-K, Lin PS, Schwarzacher SP, Pollman MJ, Gibbons GH, Tsao PS, Cooke JP. Regression of atherosclerosis: role of nitric oxide and apoptosis. *Circulation* 1999;99(9):1236–41.

Wang W, Basinger A, Neese RA, Shane B, Myong S-A, Christiansen M, Hellerstein MK. Effect of nicotinic acid administration on hepatic very low density lipoprotein-triglyceride production. *American Journal of Physiology – Endocrinology and Metabolism* 2001;280(3):E540–E547.

Wang XL, Raveendran M, Wang J. Genetic influence on cigarette-induced cardiovascular disease. *Progress in Cardiovascular Diseases* 2003;45(5):361–82.

Wang XL, Sim AS, Badenhop RF, McCredie RM, Wilcken DE. A smoking-dependent risk of coronary artery disease associated with a polymorphism of the endothelial nitric oxide synthase gene. *Nature Medicine* 1996;2(1):41–5.

Wannamethee G, Shaper AG, Macfarlane PW, Walker M. Risk factors for sudden cardiac death in middle-aged British men. *Circulation* 1995;91(6):1749–56.

Wannamethee SG, Shaper AG, Perry IJ. Smoking as a modifiable risk factor for type 2 diabetes in middle-aged men. *Diabetes Care* 2001;24(9):1590–5.

Wannamethee SG, Shaper AG, Walker M, Ebrahim S. Lifestyle and 15-year survival free of heart attack, stroke, and diabetes in middle-aged British men. *Archives of Internal Medicine* 1998;158(22):2433–40.

Watts DT. The effect of nicotine and smoking on the secretion of epinephrine. *Annals of the New York Academy of Sciences* 1960;90:74–80.

Weber C, Erl W, Weber K, Weber PC. Increased adhesiveness of isolated monocytes to endothelium is prevented by vitamin C intake in smokers. *Circulation* 1996;93(8):1488–92.

Weir JM, Dunn JE Jr. Smoking and mortality: a prospective study. *Cancer* 1970;25(1):105–12.

Weiss NS. The value of roentgenographic abdominal aortic calcification in predicting site of occlusion in arteriosclerosis obliterans. *Angiology* 1972;23(3):136–9.

Wennmalm Å, Benthin G, Granström EF, Persson L, Petersson AS, Winell S. Relation between tobacco use and urinary excretion of thromboxane A_2 and prostacyclin metabolites in young men. *Circulation* 1991;83(5):1698–704.

Westerman RA, Lindblad LE, Wajnblum D, Roberts RG, Delaney CA. Confounding factors in non-invasive tests of neurovascular function in diabetes mellitus. *Clinical and Experimental Neurology* 1992;29:149–60.

Whincup PH, Gilg JA, Emberson JR, Jarvis MJ, Feyerabend C, Bryant A, Walker M, Cook DG. Passive smoking and risk of coronary heart disease and stroke: prospective study with cotinine measurement. *BMJ (British Medical Journal)* 2004;329(7459):200–5.

White AR, Rampes H, Ernst E. Acupuncture for smoking cessation. *Cochrane Database of Systematic Reviews* 2002, Issue 2. Art. No.: CD000009. DOI: 10.1002/14651858.CD000009.

Wilkins JN, Carlson HE, Van Vunakis H, Hill MA, Gritz E, Jarvik ME. Nicotine from cigarette smoking increases circulating levels of cortisol, growth hormone, and prolactin in male chronic smokers. *Psychopharmacology* 1982;78(4):305–8.

Will JC, Galuska DA, Ford ES, Mokdad A, Calle EE. Cigarette smoking and diabetes mellitus: evidence of a positive association from a large prospective cohort study. *International Journal of Epidemiology* 2001;30(3):540–6.

Willett WC, Green A, Stampfer MJ, Speizer FE, Colditz GA, Rosner B, Monson RR, Stason W, Hennekens CH. Relative and absolute excess risks of coronary heart disease among women who smoke cigarettes. *New England Journal of Medicine* 1987;317(21):1303–9.

Willi C, Bodenmann P, Ghali WA, Faris PD, Cornuz J. Active smoking and the risk of type 2 diabetes: a systematic review and meta-analysis. *JAMA: the Journal of the American Medical Association* 2007;298(22):2654–64.

Wilmink TBM, Quick CRG, Day NE. The association between cigarette smoking and abdominal aortic aneurysms. *Journal of Vascular Surgery* 1999;30(6):1099–105.

Wilson K, Gibson N, Willan A, Cook D. Effect of smoking cessation on mortality after myocardial infarction:

meta-analysis of cohort studies. *Archives of Internal Medicine* 2000;160(7):939–44.

Wilson PW, Anderson KM, Kannel WB. Epidemiology of diabetes mellitus in the elderly: the Framingham Study. *American Journal of Medicine* 1986;80(5A):3–9.

Wilson PW, Garrison RJ, Abbott RD, Castelli WP. Factors associated with lipoprotein cholesterol levels: the Framingham Study. *Arteriosclerosis* 1983;3(3):273–81

Wilt TJ, Davis BR, Meyers DG, Rouleau J-L, Sacks FM. Prevalence and correlates of symptomatic peripheral atherosclerosis in individuals with coronary heart disease and cholesterol levels less than 240 mg/dL: baseline results from the Cholesterol and Recurrent Events (CARE) Study. *Angiology* 1996;47(6):533–41.

Winniford MD, Jansen DE, Reynolds GA, Apprill P, Black WH, Hillis LD. Cigarette smoking-induced coronary vasoconstriction in atherosclerotic coronary artery disease and prevention by calcium antagonists and nitroglycerin. *American Journal of Cardiology* 1987; 59(4):203–7.

Wiseman S, Kenchington G, Dain R, Marshall CE, McCollum CN, Greenhalgh RM, Powell JT. Influence of smoking and plasma factors on patency of femoropopliteal vein grafts. *BMJ (British Medical Journal)* 1989; 299(6700):643–6.

Wolf PA, D'Agostino RB, Kannel WB, Bonita R, Belanger AJ. Cigarette smoking as a risk factor for stroke: the Framingham Study. *JAMA: the Journal of the American Medical Association* 1988;259(7):1025–9.

Wolinsky H. A proposal linking clearance of circulating lipoproteins to tissue metabolic activity as a basis for understanding atherogenesis. *Circulation Research* 1980;47(3):301–11.

Woodward M, Lowe GDO, Rumley A, Tunstall-Pedoe H. Fibrinogen as a risk factor for coronary heart disease and mortality in middle-aged men and women: the Scottish Heart Health Study. *European Heart Journal* 1998;19(1):55–62.

Woodward M, Rumley A, Tunstall-Pedoe H, Lowe GD. Does sticky blood predict a sticky end: associations of blood viscosity, haematocrit and fibrinogen with mortality in the West of Scotland. *British Journal of Haematology* 2003;122(4):645–50.

Working Group for the Study of Transdermal Nicotine in Patients with Coronary Artery Disease. Nicotine replacement therapy for patients with coronary artery disease. *Archives of Internal Medicine* 1994;154(9):989–95.

Wray R, DePalma RG, Hubay CH. Late occlusion of aortofemoral bypass grafts: influence of cigarette smoking. *Surgery* 1971;70(6):969–73.

Wright HP. Mitosis patterns in aortic endothelium. *Atherosclerosis* 1972;15(1):93–100.

Xu XH, Shah PK, Faure E, Equils O, Thomas L, Fishbein MC, Luthringer D, Xu X-P, Rajavashisth TB, Yano J, et al. Toll-like receptor-4 is expressed by macrophages in murine and human lipid-rich atherosclerotic plaques and upregulated by oxidized LDL. *Circulation* 2001; 104(25):3103–8.

Yamaguchi Y, Haginaka J, Morimoto S, Fujioka Y, Kunitomo M. Facilitated nitration and oxidation of LDL in cigarette smokers. *European Journal of Clinical Investigation* 2005;35(3):186–93.

Yamaguchi Y, Matsuno S, Kagota S, Haginaka J, Kunitomo M. Fluvastatin reduces modification of low-density lipoprotein in hyperlipidemic rabbit loaded with oxidative stress. *European Journal of Pharmacology* 2002;436(1–2):97–105.

Yamaguchi Y, Matsuno S, Kagota S, Haginaka J, Kunitomo M. Peroxynitrite-mediated oxidative modification of low-density lipoprotein by aqueous extracts of cigarette smoke and the preventive effect of fluvastatin. *Atherosclerosis* 2004;172(2):259–65.

Yoshimura M, Yasue H, Nakayama M, Shimasaki Y, Sumida H, Sugiyama S, Kugiyama K, Ogawa H, Ogawa Y, Saito Y, et al. A missense Glu298Asp variant in the endothelial nitric oxide synthase gene is associated with coronary spasm in the Japanese. *Human Genetics* 1998;103(1):65–9.

Zaratin ÁCM, Quintão ECR, Sposito AC, Nunes VS, Lottenberg AM, Morton RE, de Faria EC. Smoking prevents the intravascular remodeling of high-density lipoprotein particles: implications for reverse cholesterol transport. *Metabolism* 2004;53(7):858–62

Zavaroni I, Bonini L, Gasparini P, Dall'Aglio E, Passeri M, Reaven GM. Cigarette smokers are relatively glucose intolerant, hyperinsulinemic and dyslipidemic. *American Journal of Cardiology* 1994;73(12):904–5.

Zeiher AM, Schächinger V, Minners J. Long-term cigarette smoking impairs endothelium-dependent coronary arterial vasodilator function. *Circulation* 1995; 92(5):1094–100.

Zhang S, Day I, Ye S. Nicotine induced changes in gene expression by human coronary artery endothelial cells. *Atherosclerosis* 2001;154(2):277–83.

Zhu BQ, Heeschen C, Sievers RE, Karliner JS, Parmley WW, Glantz SA, Cooke JP. Second hand smoke stimulates tumor angiogenesis and growth. *Cancer Cell* 2003;4(3):191–6.

Zidovetzki R, Chen P, Fisher M, Hofman FM. Nicotine increases plasminogen activator inhibitor-1 production by human brain endothelial cells via protein kinase C–associated pathway. *Stroke* 1999;30(3):651–5.

Zilversmit DB. Atherogenesis: a postprandial phenomenon. *Circulation* 1979;60(3):473–85.

Chapter 7
Pulmonary Diseases

Introduction

The respiratory system extends from the nose and upper airway to the alveolar surface of the lungs, where gas exchange occurs. Inhaled tobacco smoke moves from the mouth through the upper airway, ultimately reaching the alveoli. As the smoke moves more deeply into the respiratory tract, more soluble gases are adsorbed and particles are deposited in the airways and alveoli. The substantial doses of carcinogens and toxins delivered to these sites place smokers at risk for malignant and nonmalignant diseases involving all components of the respiratory tract including the mouth.

Consider, for example, the lungs of a 60-year-old person with a 40-pack-year[1] smoking history starting at age 20 years. By age 60 years, this person will have inhaled the smoke from approximately 290,000 cigarettes and will bear a substantial risk for chronic obstructive pulmonary disease (COPD) and lung cancer. The dose of inhaled toxic particles and gases received from each of these cigarettes varies depending on the nature of the tobacco, the volume and number of puffs of smoke drawn from the cigarette, the amount of air drawn in through ventilation holes as the smoke is inhaled, and local characteristics within the lung that determine the diffusion of toxic gases and the deposition of particles. Because of this repetitive and sustained injurious stimulus, the repair and remodel process that heals the damaged lung tissue takes place at the same time the lung's defenses continue to deal with this unrelenting inhalation injury.

This chapter addresses the mechanisms by which tobacco smoke causes diseases other than cancer in the lower respiratory tract: the trachea, bronchi, and lungs. Beginning with the first Surgeon General's report in 1964 (U.S. Department of Health, Education, and Welfare [USDHEW] 1964), cigarette smoking has been causally linked to multiple diseases and to other adverse effects on the respiratory system (Table 7.1). In addition to causing lung cancer and COPD, smoking increases the risk of death from pneumonia and causes chronic bronchitis (U.S. Department of Health and Human Services [USDHHS] 2004). Typically, the lungs of smokers show evidence of diffuse changes affecting the lining of the airways, the epithelium, and the structure of the bronchioles, which are the smaller air-conducting tubes.

Previous reports of the Surgeon General have also addressed the effects of smoking on the respiratory tract. In discussing the plausibility of associations of cigarette smoke with chronic bronchitis and emphysema, the 1964 report gave full consideration to the nature of tobacco smoke and its effects on the respiratory tract (USDHEW 1964). That report concluded that cigarette smoking "… is the most important of the causes of chronic bronchitis in the United States…" (p. 302) and that "a relationship exists between pulmonary emphysema and cigarette smoking, but it has not been established that the relationship is causal" (p. 302). The 1984 report, which focused on COPD, covered mechanisms by which smoking affects the lung's structure and function and the deposition and toxicity of cigarette smoke in the lung (USDHHS 1984). The report concluded that "cigarette smoking is the major cause of chronic obstructive lung disease in the United States…" (p. vii). The mechanisms of lung injury were considered further in the 1990, 2004, and 2006 reports (USDHHS 1990, 2004, 2006).

The principal nonmalignant respiratory diseases caused by cigarette smoking—COPD, emphysema, chronic bronchitis, and asthma—are defined in Table 7.2. The definitions indicate that chronic bronchitis is a specific set of symptoms, whereas emphysema refers to a particular pattern of lung damage. COPD comprises a clinical syndrome characterized by limitation in airflow; persons with COPD often have chronic bronchitis as well, and their lungs typically display emphysema. Other nonmalignant respiratory diseases that have been linked to smoking include asthma and idiopathic pulmonary fibrosis (USDHHS 2004), but the evidence has not reached a level of certainty sufficient to warrant a conclusion of cause and effect.

The nonmalignant respiratory diseases caused by smoking contribute substantially to the burden of morbidity and mortality attributable to smoking in the United States (Table 7.1). In 2005, the Centers for Disease Control and Prevention (CDC) estimated that an average of 123,836 deaths per year could be attributed to lung cancer caused by smoking for the period 1997–2001 (CDC 2005). CDC estimated an additional 90,582 deaths from COPD and 10,872 from pneumonia and influenza annually.

Great advances have been made in our understanding of how smoking causes these diseases. Research has been facilitated by methods that directly assess changes in the lungs. Methods for obtaining biologic material from human lungs include bronchoalveolar lavage (BAL), a technique that allows recovery of cellular and

---

[1]Pack-years = the number of years of smoking multiplied by the number of packs of cigarettes smoked per day.

Table 7.1   Causal conclusions on smoking and diseases of the respiratory tract other than lung cancer: the 2004 and 2006 reports of the Surgeon General

Active Smoking

The evidence is sufficient to infer a **causal conclusion** between smoking and

- Acute respiratory illnesses, including pneumonia, in persons without underlying smoking-related chronic obstructive lung disease
- Impaired lung growth during childhood and adolescence
- Early onset of decline in lung function (during late adolescence and early adulthood)
- A premature onset of and an accelerated age-related decline in respiratory symptoms related to lung function in children and adolescents, including coughing, phlegm, wheezing, and dyspnea
- Asthma-related symptoms (i.e., wheezing) in childhood and adolescence
- All major respiratory symptoms among adults, including coughing, phlegm, wheezing, and dyspnea
- Poor asthma control
- Chronic obstructive pulmonary disease morbidity and mortality
- A reduction of lung function in infants of mothers who smoked during pregnancy

Involuntary Exposure to Tobacco Smoke

The evidence is sufficient to infer a **causal conclusion** between secondhand smoke exposure

From parental smoking and

- Lower respiratory illnesses in infants and children
- Middle ear disease in children, including acute and recurrent otitis media and chronic middle ear effusion
- Cough, phlegm, wheeze, and breathlessness among children of school age
- Ever having asthma among children of school age
- Onset of wheeze illnesses in early childhood

From maternal smoking during pregnancy and

- Persistent adverse effects on lung function across childhood

After birth and

- Lower level of lung function during childhood

And

- Odor annoyance
- Nasal irritation

Source: U.S. Department of Health and Human Services 2004, 2006.

noncellular components of the epithelial surface of the lower respiratory tract (Cantrell et al. 1973; Hunninghake et al. 1979; Reynolds 1987). BAL is of value in the study of immune and inflammatory mechanisms in the lower airways, because most of the cells recovered are believed to be derived from both air spaces and lung interstitium. Lung tissue obtained by biopsy or autopsy procedures can be used for cellular, protein, and nucleic acid assays. Exhaled breath condensate provides information about the composition of epithelial lining fluid (ELF) that can be used to detect inflammation and redox disturbance (Paredi et al. 2002). Blood samples may be used to assess systemic inflammatory responses, and blood cells serve as a source of nucleic acids.

Characteristics of Tobacco Smoke

Tobacco smoke, which comprises an aerosol (a mixture of solid and liquid particles) and gases, has thousands of chemical components, including many well-characterized toxins and carcinogens (International Agency for Research on Cancer [IARC] 2004). Many of these components are in the gas phase, and others are components of the particles. Nicotine, for example, is bound to particles in mainstream smoke. The chemical components in tobacco smoke were covered comprehensively in IARC Monograph 83 (IARC 2004) and described in previous reports of the Surgeon General. Numerous components of the smoke have the potential to injure the airways and alveoli.

Table 7.2 **Definitions for principal nonmalignant respiratory diseases caused by cigarette smoking**

Chronic obstructive pulmonary disease (COPD)	A preventable and treatable disease characterized by airflow limitation that is not fully reversible. The limitation is usually progressive and is associated with an abnormal inflammatory response of the lungs to noxious particles or gases, primarily caused by cigarette smoking. Although COPD affects the lungs, it also produces significant systemic consequences.
Emphysema	Permanent enlargement of the airspaces distal to the terminal bronchioles, accompanied by destruction of their walls and without obvious fibrosis. In patients with COPD, either condition may be present. However, the relative contribution of each to the disease process is often difficult to discern.
Chronic bronchitis	Chronic productive cough for 3 months in each of 2 successive years in a patient in whom other causes of productive chronic cough have been excluded.
Asthma	A chronic inflammatory disease of the airways in which many cell types play a role—in particular, mast cells, eosinophils, and T lymphocytes. In susceptible persons, the inflammation causes recurrent episodes of wheezing, breathlessness, chest tightness, and cough, particularly at night and/or in the early morning. These symptoms are usually associated with widespread and variable airflow obstruction that is at least partly reversible either spontaneously or with treatment. The inflammation also causes an associated increase in airway responsiveness to a variety of stimuli.

Source: American Thoracic Society 2000 and American Thoracic Society/European Respiratory Society Task Force 2005.

Components of tobacco smoke with the potential to injure the lungs through a variety of mechanisms are listed in Table 7.3. Some components adversely affect host defenses; others act through specific or nonspecific mechanisms. Notably, cigarette smoking has very strong oxidant potential in that both the gas and tar phases contain high concentrations of free radicals (Repine et al. 1997). Many of the components of cigarette smoke are the targets of regulations because of their toxic effects: these include nitrogen dioxide, carbon monoxide, and various metals. For information on the toxic effects of components, see reports of the U.S. Environmental Protection Agency (EPA) and other agencies (USEPA 1993, 2000; USDHHS 2000) and standard resources in toxicology (Gardner et al. 2000; Klaassen 2001).

Assessment of toxic effects of cigarette smoke in the respiratory tract requires consideration of the complexity of the mixture inhaled and the possibility of synergistic interactions among its many components. Although it is little studied, the possibility of numerous interactions has great plausibility because of the myriad components of cigarette smoke and the interlocking pathways of lung injury.

Dosimetry of Tobacco Smoke in the Respiratory System

To protect the lungs from injury, the respiratory tract has an elegant set of mechanisms for handling the

Table 7.3 **Selected components of cigarette smoke and potential mechanisms of injury**

Component	Mechanism
Acrolein	Cilia toxic; impairs lung defenses
Formaldehyde	Cilia toxic; irritant
Nitrogen oxides	Oxidant activity
Cadmium	Oxidative injury; promotion of emphysema
Hydrogen cyanide	Oxidative metabolism of cells affected

particles and gases in inhaled air (Figure 7.1). These defenses include physical barriers, reflexes and the cough response, the sorptive capacity of the epithelial lining, the mucociliary apparatus, alveolar macrophages, and immune responses of the lung (Schulz et al. 2000). These defenses are critical because of the substantial volume of air inhaled daily: about 10,000 liters per day are inhaled by an adult. Even harmful substances present at low concentrations may eventually achieve a toxic dose after sustained exposure. In addition, high-level exposures, particularly when sustained, may overwhelm the lung's defenses, and some agents have the potential to reduce the efficacy of these defenses. Cigarette smoke, for example,

Figure 7.1 Lung defenses

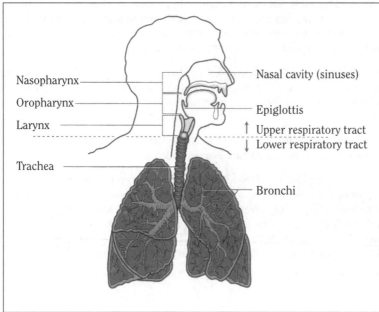

Host Defenses

Nasal hair

Convoluted
passages of
sinuses

Coughing,
sneezing,
swallowing

Mucociliary cells

Normal flora

Inflammatory
cells

Alveolar
macrophages

Labels: Nasopharynx, Oropharynx, Larynx, Trachea, Nasal cavity (sinuses), Epiglottis, ↑ Upper respiratory tract, ↓ Lower respiratory tract, Bronchi

Source: Cook 2000. Reprinted with permission from Elsevier Health, © 2000.

contains components that impair mucociliary clearance (Table 7.3).

The size of particles in the smoke inhaled directly from a cigarette (mainstream smoke) has been studied in a variety of systems. These studies indicate that the mass median aerodynamic diameter of particles is 0.3 to 0.4 micrometers (μm) (Martonen 1992; Bernstein 2004). Particles of this size penetrate to and are deposited in the deep lung.

The handling of particles by the lung's defense mechanisms depends on their size (Figure 7.2). Large particles (e.g., many pollens and road dust) are removed in the upper airway, largely by impaction (USDHHS 1984). Small particles, with a mean aerodynamic diameter less than about 2.5 μm, reach the lungs, where they deposit in airways and alveoli by impaction, sedimentation, or diffusion. About 60 percent of the particles inhaled in mainstream smoke are deposited. Although these particles are subject to handling by the mucociliary apparatus and alveolar macrophages, removal is not complete because of their very high numbers in the lungs of long-term smokers, which show evidence of a substantial burden of retained particles. Similarly, evidence shows that smokers clear these particles at a reduced rate (Cohen et al. 1979; USDHHS 1984; Kreyling and Scheuch 2000).

The removal of gases in the respiratory tract is accomplished through sorption by the liquid that lines the epithelial layer (Kreyling and Scheuch 2000). Both the site and the efficacy of removal of gases depend on the solubility of the gas. Highly soluble gases are removed high in the respiratory tract, but insoluble gases (e.g., carbon monoxide) may reach the alveoli and diffuse across the alveolar-capillary membrane. These dosimetric considerations indicate a high potential for lung injury in active smokers, who inhale a rich mixture of gases and particles that penetrates throughout the lungs, with deposit of particles and sorption of gases in the two anatomic sites most critical to respiration, the airways and alveoli.

Major Pulmonary Diseases Caused by Smoking

This section provides a brief overview of the principal diseases of the lung that are caused by smoking. A brief description of pathophysiology and pathogenesis is provided as background for the more comprehensive discussions of mechanisms. These topics are covered in great detail elsewhere (Mason et al. 2005) and were addressed in the 1984 and 2004 Surgeon General's reports (USDHHS 1984, 2004).

Figure 7.2   Fractional deposition of inhaled particles in the human respiratory tract

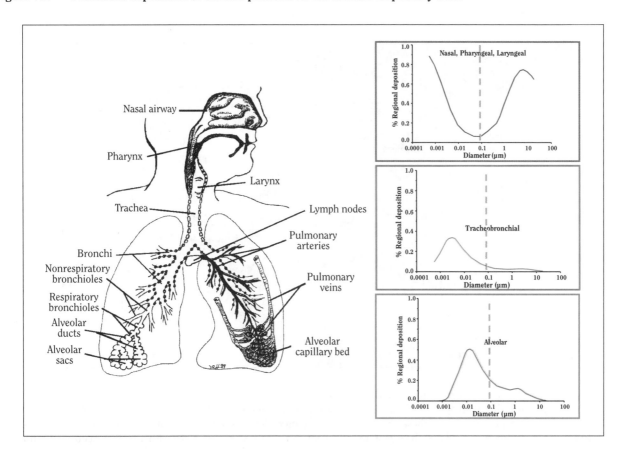

Source: Oberdörster et al. 2005. Reprinted with permission from *Environmental Health Perspectives,* © 2005. Figure based on data from the International Commission on Radiological Protection 1994. Drawing courtesy of Dr. Jack R. Harkema, Michigan State University.
Note: **μm** = micrometers.

Chronic Bronchitis

The symptom complex of chronic bronchitis has been investigated for decades. In the 1950s, the British Medical Research Council suggested that a diagnosis of chronic bronchitis was warranted when the symptoms of chronic cough and production of sputum were present on most days of the month for at least three months in two consecutive years without any other explanation (*BMJ* 1965). This proposal is reflected in the current definition of chronic bronchitis (Table 7.2). Earlier, Reid (1960) had used the size of the mucous gland layer as a predictor for the postmortem diagnosis of this condition but did not implicate the inflammatory process in the pathogenesis of either enlargement of the gland or the production of excess mucus. Subsequent studies of lung tissue surgically removed from cancer patients (Figure 7.3) have shown that the symptoms of chronic bronchitis are associated with an inflammatory response involving the mucosal surface, submucosal glands, and gland ducts, particularly in the small bronchi that are 2 to 4 millimeters (mm) in diameter (Mullen et al. 1985; Saetta et al. 1997). In addition, longitudinal studies of chronic bronchitis in persons with normal lung function have clarified that its presence does not predict future progression to more severe obstructive lung disease (Fletcher et al. 1976; Saetta et al. 1997). Presence of chronic bronchitis in persons who already have limited airflow, however, is predictive of a more rapid decline in lung function and a higher risk of hospitalization than are seen with a similar limitation of airflow but no chronic bronchitis (Saetta et al. 1997).

The inflammatory immune cells that infiltrate the epithelium, subepithelium, and glandular tissue in chronic bronchitis include the polymorphonuclear neutrophils (PMNs), macrophages, CD8-positive (CD8+) and

Figure 7.3   Comparison of normal bronchial gland (A) with enlarged bronchial glands (B and C) from a patient with chronic bronchitis

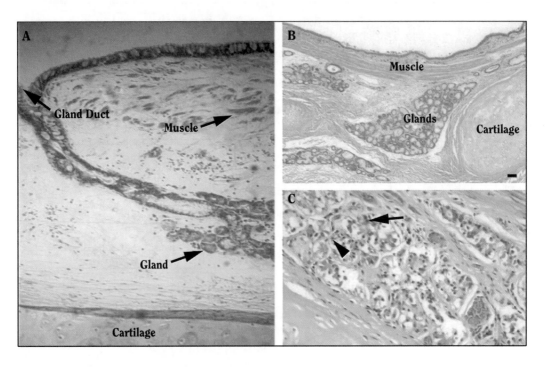

Source: Hogg 2004. Reprinted with permission from Elsevier, © 2004.
Note: (A) Histology of bronchus with epithelial lining that extends from lumen into gland duct and gland. (B) Enlarged glands from a patient with chronic bronchitis. (C) One of these glands at higher magnification showing inflammatory cells (arrow and arrowhead). Several studies of human lungs showed that the symptoms of chronic bronchitis were associated with an inflammatory response involving the mucosal surface, submucosal glands, and gland ducts, particularly in the smaller bronchi 2–4 millimeters in diameter.

CD4-positive (CD4+) T lymphocytes, and B cells that are part of the adaptive inflammatory immune process (Di Stefano et al. 1996; O'Shaughnessy et al. 1997; Saetta et al. 1997). This chronic inflammation, consisting of enlargement of the mucous glands and remodeling of the walls of both large and small bronchi reflects a deregulated healing process in tissue persistently damaged by the inhalation of tobacco smoke (Hogg 2004). The consequences of this process include both the development of a chronic cough and the accumulation of excess mucus in the airway's lumen. However, this inflammatory process has little influence on airflow limitation unless it extends to the small conducting airways that account for much of the increase in airway resistance in COPD.

Studies reported from the laboratory of Snider and associates in Israel (Breuer et al. 1993) were the first to show that elastase from PMNs was an important agent for the secretion of mucus by epithelial goblet cells. Later, Nadel (2001) and other investigators (Takeyama et al. 1999, 2000, 2001a,b; Burgel et al. 2000; Lee et al. 2000;

Kohri et al. 2002) extended these observations by linking the PMN-induced production of mucin to stimulation of EGFR. They showed that PMN elastase triggered the cleavage of membrane-tethered transforming growth factor alpha (TGFα), allowing it to attach to the external binding site of EGFR. This step is followed by phosphorylation of the intracellular component of this receptor and stimulation of downstream signaling pathways that activate the expression of the *MUC5AC* gene and lead to the production of mucus (Takeyama et al. 1999). This type of experiment established that EGFR and its ligands provide a regulatory axis for the production of mucin that involves several membrane-bound ligands of EGFR, such as TGFα and heparin-binding EGF. Nadel (2001) has also shown that reactive oxygen species (ROS) can bypass the extracellular sphere of influence of this regulatory axis. Other studies have shown that ROS can directly activate EGFR's intracellular domain (Burgel et al. 2000; Takeyama et al. 2000; Kohri et al. 2002).

More recent work in transgenic mice has found that overexpression of epithelial sodium ion channels resulted in excess reabsorption of epithelial sodium and volume depletion of periciliary fluid (Mall et al. 2004). The depletion of the periciliary fluid layer interferes with the frequency of ciliary beats and results in decreased clearance and adherence of mucus to the airway surface. Results of this study showed that depletion of the periciliary fluid in animals is associated with the accumulation of mucus in the lumen of both large and small airways, leading to greater susceptibility to infection of the lower respiratory tract and early death.

Chronic Obstructive Pulmonary Disease

The hallmark of COPD is chronic airflow obstruction demonstrated with spirometry and the accompanying dyspnea and limitation of activity. Maximum expiratory flow is determined by the product of the resistance to flow in the small conducting airways (centimeters of water $[H_2O]$ per liter per second) and the elastic recoil of the lung parenchyma that drives expiratory flow (liters per centimeter of H_2O). The product of these two variables, the time constant, characterizes the rapidity with which the lung fills and empties during respiration. Surprisingly, the time constant of the lung remains stable over a wide range of breathing frequencies in healthy lungs, but if disease increases either the compliance as in emphysema or the resistance as in obstruction of small airways, the time required to empty the lung is prolonged (Otis et al. 1956). The presence of a fixed limitation in airflow can be diagnosed by using a spirometer to measure the volume of air that can be forcibly expired from the lungs in one second (forced expiratory volume $[FEV_1]$) and then determining its ratio to forced vital capacity (FEV_1/FVC) after the administration of a bronchodilator.

The classic cohort study of the natural history of chronic bronchitis and emphysema performed by Fletcher and colleagues (*Lancet* 1965; Fletcher 1976) used this type of measurement to test the hypothesis of a sequence beginning with tobacco smoking and then moving to symptoms of chronic bronchitis or recurrent chest infections and, finally, chronic limitation of airflow. The natural history of the decline in FEV developed by Fletcher and colleagues (1976) to summarize findings of a six-year longitudinal study of men working in West London is illustrated in Figure 7.4. Subsequent studies have confirmed these findings (USDHHS 1984). The horizontal lines added to the Fletcher diagram indicate the boundaries of the five-stage classification of the severity of COPD by the Global Initiative for Chronic Obstructive Lung Disease (GOLD). The measurements used were FEV_1 and FEV_1/FVC (Pauwels et al. 2001; GOLD 2006). According to this classification, GOLD stage 0 defines persons with a normal FEV_1 and FEV_1/FVC who have symptoms attributable to significant exposure to tobacco smoke as being at risk for developing COPD. Those with mild, moderate, severe, or very severe COPD are placed in GOLD stages 1 through 4, respectively (Takeyama 2001b).

Fletcher and colleagues (1976) observed that only 15 to 25 percent of the smokers in the study developed airflow limitation, and they showed that smoking cessation slowed the rate of decline in FEV_1 in those who stopped smoking permanently. In subsequent studies of various populations, only a minority of smokers developed COPD. This repeated finding indicates a role for genetic factors that may determine susceptibility to cigarette smoke. These investigators rejected the hypothesis of a pathogenetic continuum from smoking to obstructive bronchitis. Most persons who developed airflow limitation during the study had no evidence of chronic bronchitis, a finding that was not consistent with the hypothesis of a continuum from smoking to bronchitis to obstruction. Subsequent studies have confirmed that the presence of chronic bronchitis in persons with normal lung function (GOLD stage 0) does not predict progression of disease (Vestbo and Lange 2002). Using data from the Copenhagen City Heart Study, however, Vestbo and colleagues (1996) found that the symptoms of chronic bronchitis were associated with an accelerated decline in FEV_1.

Acute exacerbations, a concern in treatment of COPD, are attributed to viral infections (Monto et al. 1975; Smith et al. 1980; Seemungal et al. 2001), bacterial infections, and occupational and environmental air pollution; an important residual of cases had no obvious cause (Pauwels et al. 2001; Rabe et al. 2007). Some unexplained exacerbations of COPD might be attributable to latent viral infection, because such infections can deregulate the expression of adhesion proteins that might initiate this response (Gonzáles et al. 1996; Keicho et al. 1997). Although Fletcher and colleagues (1976) found that these exacerbations had no effect on the rate of decline of FEV_1 in the working men in West London, the U.S. Lung Health Study showed that such exacerbations were associated with a more rapid decline in persons with mild disease who continued to smoke (Kanner et al. 2001). Subsequently, other investigators found that frequent exacerbations in patients with more severe COPD, especially those resulting from a higher bacterial load, were associated with more accelerated decline in FEV_1 (Donaldson et al. 2002; Wilkinson et al. 2003). Collectively, these data suggest that when lung defenses become compromised in the later stages of COPD, chronic infection might play a role in the pathogenesis of the airflow limitation.

Figure 7.4   Natural history of decline in forced expiratory volume with aging measured in a group of working men in West London over about six years

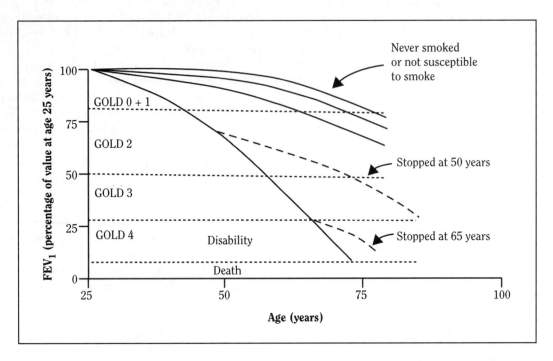

Source: Hogg 2004. Reprinted with permission from Elsevier, © 2004.
Note: Adapted from Fletcher et al. 1976. Horizontal lines have been added to their diagram to indicate the boundaries of the classification of severity of chronic obstructive pulmonary disease by the Global Initiative for Chronic Obstructive Lung Disease (GOLD).

Obstruction of Small Airways

Although spirometric measurement of FEV$_1$ and the FEV$_1$/FVC provides a reliable method for diagnosing airflow limitation and classifying its severity, spirometry cannot distinguish the contributions of either the obstruction of small airways or emphysematous destruction to the airflow limitation in COPD. Direct measurements of pressures and flows within the lung have shown that the small bronchi and bronchioles (<2 mm in diameter) are the major sites of airway obstruction in COPD (Hogg et al. 1968; van Brabandt et al. 1983; Yanai et al. 1992). This obstruction is related to an inflammatory process that thickens the airway wall, fills the lumen with exudates containing mucus, and narrows the airway by depositing connective tissue in the airway wall (Figure 7.5). McLean (1956) and Leopold and Gough (1957) recognized that an inflammatory process was present in the small bronchi and bronchioles of lungs affected by centrilobular emphysema. Leopold and Gough (1957) hypothesized that

centrilobular emphysema resulted from an extension of this process from the small conducting airways into the respiratory bronchioles. Later, Matsuba and Thurlbeck (1972) demonstrated an excess deposition of connective tissue in the adventitia of the small conducting airways in advanced emphysema and suggested that peribronchiolar fibrosis narrowed the airway lumen. In addition, cross-sectional studies of the pathology of COPD have shown that the peripheral inflammatory immune process found in the lungs of all smokers is amplified in severe (GOLD stage 3) and very severe (GOLD stage 4) COPD (Fletcher et al. 1976; Hogg et al. 2004). More recent evidence indicates that at these levels of disease severity, these changes are associated with an increase in the adaptive immune response. These findings may reflect the response to an antigenic stimulus from a limited number of antigens that might be microbial or possibly from autoantigens that develop within the damaged lung tissue (Agustí et al. 2003; Voelkel and Taraseviciene-Stewart 2005).

Figure 7.5   Nature of an obstruction in the small conducting airways (<2 millimeters in diameter)

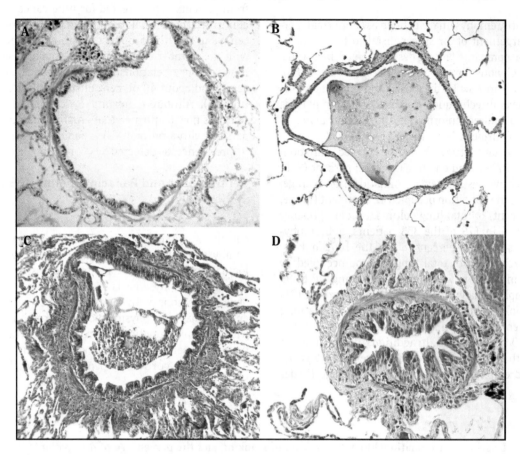

Source: Hogg 2004. Reprinted with permission from Elsevier, © 2004.
Note: A normal airway (A) is compared with another airway (B) in which the lumen is partially filled with a bland mucous plug containing a few epithelial cells. (C) An airway in which the wall contains an active inflammatory process that partially fills the lumen with inflammatory exudates containing mucus. (D) Airway narrowed by collagen deposition in the peribronchiolar space.

Emphysema

Emphysema was first described by René Laënnec in 1834 on the basis of observations made on the cut surface of postmortem human lungs that had been air-dried in inflation (Laënnec 1834), but the concept that emphysematous destruction produced airflow limitation by decreasing the elastic recoil forces required to drive air out of the lung was not fully developed until 1967 (Mead et al. 1967). The earliest concept regarding the pathogenesis of emphysema postulated that overinflation compressed the lung capillaries, leading to atrophy of lung tissue; this concept was mentioned in major textbooks of pathology as late as 1940 (McCallum 1940). As mentioned previously (see "Obstruction of Small Airways" earlier in this chapter), McLean (1956) and Leopold and Gough (1957) were the first to implicate the inflammatory response in the pathogenesis of alveolar destruction in their early descriptions of centrilobular emphysema, but skepticism about this association persisted because of the possibility that preterminal bronchopneumonia may have been responsible for the inflammation observed in the postmortem studies. The subsequent demonstration that emphysema could be produced experimentally by depositing the enzyme papain in the lung (Gross et al. 1964), combined with observational studies showing the association between emphysema and deficiency of α1-antitrypsin (AAT) (Laurell and Eriksson 1963), led naturally to the hypothesis that the pathogenesis of emphysema was based on a functional proteolytic imbalance within the inflammatory response induced by tobacco smoke (Gadek et al. 1979).

Currently, emphysema is defined as "abnormal, permanent enlargement of air spaces distal to the terminal bronchiole, accompanied by the destruction of their walls, and without obvious fibrosis" (Snider et al. 1985, p. 183). The condition can now be diagnosed and quantified during life by several techniques. Postmortem examinations have provided indirect information on the prevalence of emphysema (Thurlbeck 1963; Ryder et al. 1971).

An important study from the United Kingdom (Ryder et al. 1971) found emphysema in 62 percent (219) of 353 consecutive postmortem examinations. On average, when present, the condition occupied 12.6 percent (range, 0.5 to 95 percent) of total lung volume. Smoking history was established in 179 of the 353 patients, and emphysema was present in 75 percent (80) of the 106 smokers. The mean proportion of total lung volume occupied by emphysema in smokers was 10.8 percent (range, 0 to 90 percent). Emphysema was also present in 28 percent (21) of 73 nonsmokers, but the mean proportion of the lung taken up by emphysema in nonsmokers was only 1.7 percent (range, 0 to 40 percent). In addition, the nonsmokers lived longer than the smokers (aged 64.8 versus 60.2 years; p <0.05) and emphysema appeared at a later age (Ryder et al. 1971).

A laboratory study of more than 400 lungs removed from patients being treated for lung cancer (Hogg 2004) confirmed that a small proportion of smokers had emphysema and that the proportion with emphysema increases with the number of pack-years of smoking. However, the dose-response relationship plateaus at 50 to 100 pack-years, and about 40 percent of smokers are affected (Figure 7.6). Although imaging by computed tomography (CT) has now confirmed that emphysema can be found in persons with a normal FEV_1, population-based studies of its prevalence, as detected by CT, have not been attempted.

Centrilobular and Panacinar Forms of Emphysema

Pathologically, emphysema is characterized by its location as centrilobular or panlobular; the radiographic correlates are centriacinar emphysema and panacinar emphysema, respectively (Friedlander et al. 2007). Centrilobular emphysema is characteristic of smokers, whereas panacinar emphysema is found with AAT deficiency. In general, persons with a predominance of centrilobular emphysema have physiological abnormalities consistent with abnormal function of small airways, whereas panlobular emphysema is associated with high lung compliance. A substantial portion of people with emphysema have both types.

Figure 7.6   Dose-response relationship between level of smoking and the percentage of 408 patients in the St. Paul's Lung Study with morphologic evidence of significant emphysema in their lungs[a]

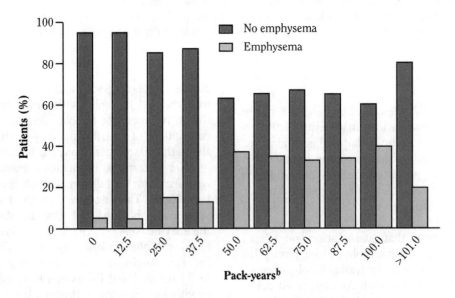

Source: Hogg 2004. Reprinted with permission from Elsevier, © 2004.

[a]The relationship plateaued with about 40 percent of the heavy smokers having emphysema.

[b]Pack-years = the number of years of smoking multiplied by the number of packs of cigarettes smoked per day.

Figure 7.7   Postmortem bronchogram performed on the lungs of a person with centrilobular emphysema

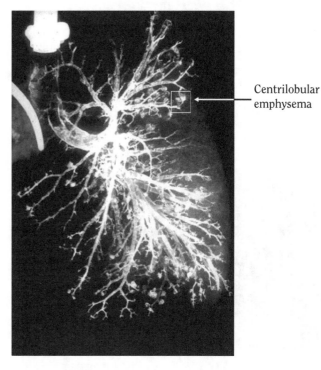

Centrilobular emphysema

Source: Hogg 2007. Reprinted with permission from Informa Healthcare, © 2007.
Note: The lesions hang from the distal airways like "Christmas tree balls" (arrow).

A postmortem bronchogram from a patient with lesions of centrilobular emphysema visible at a microscopic low power is shown in Figure 7.7. The nature of these lesions is shown to better advantage in Figure 7.8. Several normal terminal bronchioles within a secondary lung lobule (A) and the histology of a normal acinus beyond a single terminal bronchiole (B) can be compared with a line drawing from Leopold and Gough's (1957) original description of centrilobular emphysema (C) and a postmortem radiograph showing the destruction of the respiratory bronchioles (D). These centrilobular lesions affect the upper regions of the lung more commonly than the lower regions (Figure 7.9) and are also larger and more numerous in the upper lung (Gadek et al. 1979). Heppleston and Leopold (1961) used the term "focal emphysema" to describe a less severe form of centrilobular emphysema, but Dunnill (1982) argued that this distinction was not helpful and that the two conditions probably had a similar origin, with focal emphysema being more widely distributed and less severe than the classic

centrilobular form. Dunnill also preferred the term "centriacinar" to "centrilobular." "Centriacinar" seems more suitable in that each secondary lobule contains several acini (Figure 7.8A) and not all are involved in emphysematous destruction.

Wyatt and colleagues (1962) provided the first detailed account of the panacinar form of emphysema, in which more uniform destruction of the entire acinus takes place. Thurlbeck (1963) showed that it can be difficult to distinguish normal lung from lung with mild forms of panacinar emphysema, unless fully inflated specimens are carefully examined under a dissecting microscope. In contrast to centrilobular emphysema, the panacinar form tends to be more severe in the lower lobes than in the upper lobes (Figure 7.9), but this difference is substantial only in severe disease (Thurlbeck 1963). Panacinar emphysema is commonly associated with AAT deficiency but is also found in cases with no identified genetic abnormality (Thurlbeck 1963).

Other Forms of Emphysema

"Distal acinar," "mantle," and "paraseptal" emphysema describe lesions in the periphery of the lobule. These types of lesions are found along the lobular septa, particularly in the subpleural region (Hogg and Senior 2002). They also occur in isolation and have been associated with spontaneous pneumothorax in young adults (Ohata and Suzuki 1980) and bullous lung disease in older adults, whose lung function improved after the removal of large cysts (Morgan 1995). Less frequent forms of emphysema include the unilateral form (McLeod syndrome) that occurs as a complication of severe childhood infection by rubella or adenovirus; the congenital lobar form, a developmental abnormality in newborns; and paracicatricial emphysema, which forms around scars and lacks any special distribution within the acinus or lobule (Thurlbeck 1963; Dunnill 1982).

Pulmonary Hypertension

The invasive nature of right-heart catheterization in older adults with comorbid disease has made it difficult to study the prevalence of pulmonary hypertension in patients with COPD. In one six-year study of 131 patients (Kessler et al. 2001), COPD ranged from moderate (GOLD stage 2) to very severe (GOLD stage 4). At baseline, none of the patients had pulmonary hypertension, but after six years, it was present in 25 percent of the patients at rest and in more than 50 percent during exercise. These data suggest that the prevalence of pulmonary hypertension increases steadily with progression of COPD, appearing first during exercise and later at rest.

Figure 7.8   Details of centrilobular emphysema lesions

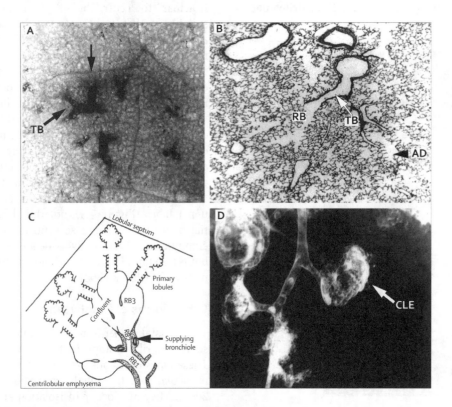

Source: Hogg 2004. Reprinted with permission from Elsevier, © 2004.
Note: (A) Several normal terminal bronchioles within a secondary lung lobule defined by its surrounding connective tissue septa (solid arrow) are shown for comparison with (B) the histology of a normal acinus beyond a single terminal bronchiole. (C) Line drawing from Leopold and Gough's original (1957) description of centrilobular emphysema showing the destruction of the respiratory bronchioles, and (D) a postmortem radiograph of the dilatation and destruction of the respiratory bronchioles. **AD** = alveolar duct; **CLE** = centrilobular emphysema; **RB** = respiratory bronchioles; **TB** = terminal bronchioles.

When pulmonary hypertension is absent at rest, but present during exercise, some of the increase in pulmonary vascular pressures can be attributed to the mechanical events associated with dynamic hyperinflation of the lung in persons with airflow limitation (Horsfield et al. 1968; Jezek et al. 1973; Weitzenblum et al. 1981; Wright et al. 1983a). When the time required to exhale becomes longer than the time between breaths, lung volume tends to increase, first as the breathing rate increases during exercise and later as it does so at rest. This increase in lung volume increases intrathoracic pressure, an increase that is transmitted to all the vessels within the thorax. As a result, both pulmonary artery and left atrial pressures are higher than atmospheric pressure but not higher than intrathoracic pressure. Treatment with oxygen at this stage of the disease lowers both pulmonary artery and left atrial pressure by slowing the breathing rate, thereby relieving the dynamic hyperinflation and lowering intrathoracic pressure. However, when lung emptying is more severely prolonged and alveolar pressure rises above intrathoracic pressure, there is a true increase in pulmonary artery pressure (Weitzenblum et al. 1981). Hypoxic vasoconstriction of the muscular pulmonary arteries and emphysematous destruction of the pulmonary vascular bed are more likely to contribute to pulmonary hypertension in severe (GOLD stage 3) and very severe (GOLD stage 4) COPD. At these more advanced stages, affected persons commonly experience chronic hypoxia and extensive destruction of the pulmonary capillary bed.

Studies of the microvessels of the lung in mild (GOLD stage 1) and moderate (GOLD stage 2) COPD show consistent changes in the intima. In more severe (GOLD

Figure 7.9   Cut surface of lungs removed from two patients with different forms of emphysema before receiving a lung transplant

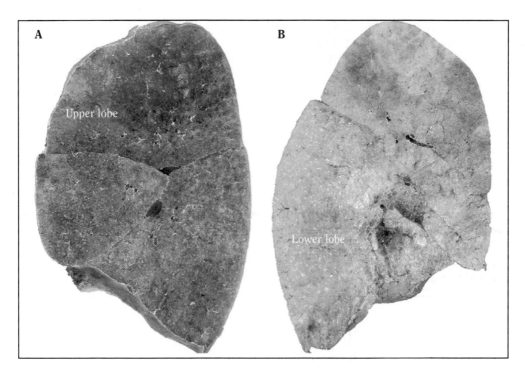

Source: From Dr. Joel Cooper in Hogg 2004. Reprinted with permission from Elsevier, © 2004.
Note: (A) The lung on the left is affected by centrilobular emphysema, which affected the upper lobe more severely than the lower lobe. (B) The lung on the right is from a patient who had α1-antitrypsin deficiency, which involved the lower lobe to a greater degree than the upper lobe.

stage 3) and very severe (GOLD stage 4) COPD, the vessel wall is commonly altered by fibroelastic thickening—the proliferation of smooth muscle and extension of the muscle into small vessels that do not normally contain muscle. However, the contribution of smooth muscle to thickness of the vessel wall is also reported to be greater in smokers with normal lung function than in nonsmokers and still greater in smokers whose lung function is impaired (Horsfield et al. 1968). In patients who have very severe emphysema, the overall wall thicknesses of vessels with external diameters of 100 to 200 μm correlate with both the rise in pulmonary arterial pressure during exercise and the difference between the pulmonary artery pressures measured during rest and during exercise (Hale et al. 1984; Kubo et al. 2000). The increase in muscle in the pulmonary arteries, which is variable, probably depends on the severity of the COPD. A greater amount of muscle

has been observed in the pulmonary vessels of smokers than in those of nonsmokers (Horsfield et al. 1968), but in mild COPD, little if any increase in muscle has been observed (Weitzenblum et al. 1981; Haniuda et al. 2003). Muscular medial thickening (Barberà et al. 2003), as opposed to overall wall thickening (Hale et al. 1984; Kubo et al. 2000), does not appear to be related to the severity of the pulmonary hypertension or the vascular response to oxygen in patients with COPD (Wright et al. 1992).

Reports from Barberà and associates (2003) from Spain indicate that this vascular remodeling process is also associated with, and possibly preceded by, an inflammatory process in which the vessels become infiltrated with a population of cells similar to those found around the small airways. The precise meaning of this finding and its role in the pathogenesis of the peripheral lung lesions observed in COPD is under investigation.

Smoking and Respiratory Defense Mechanisms

The innate defense system of the lung includes the apparatus for producing and clearing mucus, the epithelial cell barrier, and infiltrating inflammatory immune cells (Figure 7.10) (Abbas et al. 2000c; Knowles and Boucher 2002). The pulmonary epithelium plays a critical role in the host defense by recognizing insults and initiating innate responses (Greene and McElvaney 2005; Martin and Frevert 2005; Mayer and Dalpke 2007; Sabroe et al. 2007; Torrelles et al. 2008). The inhalation of tobacco smoke interferes with these defenses, resulting in both increased production of mucus and decreased effectiveness of the clearance process in the airway's lumen (Hogg 2008). Impairment of these defenses increases the potential for infection (Knowles and Boucher 2002; Drannik et al. 2004). Tobacco smoke also disrupts the tight junctions that form the epithelial barrier (Jones et al. 1980; Hulbert et al. 1981) and initiates the infiltration of the damaged tissue by a variety of inflammatory

Figure 7.10   Innate and adaptive immune system of the lung, including the mucous production and clearance apparatus, the epithelial barrier, and the inflammatory immune response

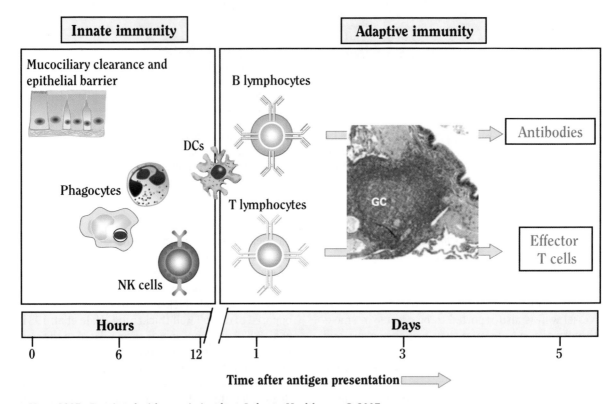

Source: Hogg 2007. Reprinted with permission from Informa Healthcare, © 2007.
Note: Chronic stimulation of this system by the tobacco-smoking habit results in both increased production and decreased clearance of mucus from the airway's lumen, disruption of the tight junctions that form the epithelial barrier and infiltration of the damaged tissue by polymorphonuclear and mononuclear phagocytes as well as natural killer cells and CD4+ and CD8+ T cells, and B-cell lymphocytes. The adaptive immune response requires antigen presentation primarily by dendritic cells and the organization of the lymphocytes into follicles with germinal centers. This type of response is rarely found in healthy nonsmokers but has been documented in about 5 percent of peripheral lung units of smokers with normal lung function, increasing to about 20 to 30 percent of airways in the later stages of chronic obstructive pulmonary disease. The source of antigen that drives this sharp increase in the adaptive immune response is unknown and may be related to either the colonization or infection of the lower airways by a variety of microbes in the later disease stages or to autoantigens that develop in the damaged tissue. **DCs** = dendritic cells; **GC** = germinal center; **NK** = natural killer.

immune cells, including polymorphonuclear and mononuclear phagocytes, natural killer cells, CD4+ and CD8+ T cells, and B lymphocytes (Nagaishi 1972; Niewoehner et al. 1974; Bosken et al. 1992; Richmond et al. 1993; Di Stefano et al. 1996; O'Shaughnessy et al. 1997; Ekberg-Jansson et al. 2001; Retamales et al. 2001; Cosio et al. 2002; Aoshiba et al. 2004; Hogg et al. 2004; Buzatu et al. 2005). The lymphocytes become organized into lymphoid follicles with germinal centers to mount an effective adaptive immune response. Lymphoid collections with these characteristics have been demonstrated in about 5 percent of the smaller airways of smokers (Hogg et al. 2004), and their frequency increases to about 20 to 30 percent of airways in the later stages of COPD (Nagaishi 1972; Richmond et al. 1993; Hogg et al. 2004). The source of antigen that drives this sharp increase in the adaptive immune response is unknown and may be related to either the colonization or infection of the lower airways by a variety of microbes in the later stages of the disease or to autoantigens that develop in the damaged tissue. This inflammatory immune process persists after cessation of smoking (Wright et al. 1983b; Rutgers et al. 2000). Smoking cessation slows the rate of decline in lung function and delays death (Fletcher et al. 1976; Anthonisen et al. 2005).

This section of the chapter briefly reviews both the inflammatory immune process in relation to the repair and remodeling of the tissue damaged by tobacco smoke and discusses the roles of these processes in the pathogenesis of the lesions that define COPD. This section of the chapter briefly reviews the inflammatory immune process in relation to the repair and remodeling of the tissue damaged by tobacco smoke and discusses its contribution to the pathogenesis of the lesions that define COPD. Both of these aspects of the pathogenesis of COPD are the focus of substantial research at present.

Infiltration of Innate Inflammatory Immune Cells

The epithelial cells covering the lung surface and the alveolar macrophages protecting that surface are key in defending the lung against inhaled gases and particles. Both of these cell types produce a broad array of proinflammatory chemokines and cytokines. When these signaling molecules are stimulated by tobacco smoke, they can be measured in induced sputum (Traves et al. 2002), in BAL fluid from patients with COPD (Morrison et al. 1998b), and in supernates of cultured cells exposed to particles and gases under controlled in vitro conditions (Becker et al.1996; Quay et al. 1998; Mukae et al. 2000; Fujii et al. 2001, 2002; van Eeden et al. 2001). More than

50 types of chemokine ligands (L) in four families were identified by the position of the cysteine residue; they were designated as CC, CXC, C, and CX_3C (Proudfoot 2002; Lukacs et al. 2005). These ligands interact with more than 20 chemokine receptors (R) to direct leukocyte traffic in the inflammatory immune response. Many chemokines, such as interleukin-8 (IL-8, or CXCL8), interact with more than one receptor (CXCR1 and CXCR2) to control the infiltration of PMN into damaged lung tissue (Keatings et al. 1996; Yamamoto et al. 1997). IL-8 is markedly increased in the sputum of patients with COPD (Keatings et al. 1996; Yamamoto et al. 1997) and can readily be measured in the supernates of cultured human bronchial epithelial cells (HBECs) as they take up toxic particles (Fujii et al. 2001, 2002). CXCL1 is also secreted by airway epithelial cells and alveolar macrophages and activates PMNs, monocytes, basophils, and T lymphocytes through CXCR2 (Proudfoot 2002; Lukacs et al. 2005). The migration of T lymphocytes is controlled by the chemokine receptor CXCR3 that is expressed in human peripheral airways (Saetta et al. 2002) and interacts with other chemokines, including CXCL9, CXCL10, and CXCL11 (Clark-Lewis et al. 2003). Increasingly, evidence indicates that safe and effective inhibitors of proinflammatory chemokines and cytokines may benefit persons who have COPD (Proudfoot 2002; Lukacs et al. 2005).

In studies involving the coculture of alveolar macrophages and HBECs, paracrine stimulation between these cell types enhances their production of chemokines and cytokines capable of controlling the recruitment and activation of leukocytes (TNFα, IL-1β, IL-8, and macrophage inflammatory protein 1α), enhancing phagocytosis (interferon-gamma), stimulating natural killer cell and T-cell function (IL-12), and initiating the repair process (granulocyte-macrophage colony-stimulating factor) (Mukae et al. 2001; Goto et al. 2004). Furthermore, instillation of the supernatants from alveolar macrophages and/or HBECs challenged with particles in vitro produces a systemic response similar to that achieved by instilling the same number of particles directly into the lungs of animals (Goto et al. 2004). The magnitude of the systemic response correlates with the number of particles phagocytosed by the macrophages (Mukae et al. 2001). More limited studies of living persons indicate that cytokines produced in the lungs (TNFα, IL-1β, and IL-6) enter the blood after smoke inhalation during natural forest fires and stimulate the liver to produce acute phase proteins and the bone marrow to increase production of leukocytes and release them into the circulation (Tan et al. 2000; van Eeden and Hogg 2000). Other studies in humans have shown a relationship among the count of circulating leukocytes, decline in lung function, and risk for early death from COPD (Chan-Yeung et al. 1988; Weiss et al. 1995).

These and other reports indicate that the inhalation of toxic particles and gases causes a local innate inflammatory immune response in the lung, initiating an adaptive immune response.

Adaptive Immune Response

The transition from the innate response to the more sophisticated adaptive immune response takes place in lymphoid follicles with germinal centers (Figure 7.10), found either in regional lymph nodes or in lymphoid collections within lung tissue (Figure 7.11). Those in the lung tissue are similar to those in the lymphoid collections observed in tonsils and adenoids in the nasopharynx and to Peyer's patches in the small bowel and the appendix of the large bowel (Nagaishi 1972; Pabst and Gehrke 1990; Richmond et al. 1993; Hogg et al. 2004). All of these structures are part of the mucosal immune system and differ from true lymph nodes in having no capsule and not receiving afferent lymphatic vessels (Nagaishi 1972; Hogg et al. 2004). The epithelium that covers the follicles in lung tissue contains specialized M cells (Figure 7.11) that transport antigens from the lumen to the lamina propria but do not function as antigen-presenting cells. Dendritic cells located in the epithelium and lamina propria pick up the antigen, which either penetrates the epithelial barrier or is transported by the M cells, and

Figure 7.11 Lymphoid collections within lung tissue

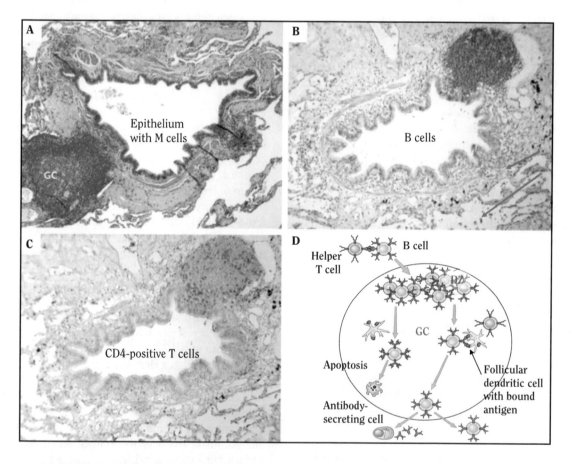

Source: Adapted from Hogg et al. 2007 with permission from Massachusetts Medical Society, © 2007.
Note: (A) Collection of bronchial lymphoid tissue with a lymphoid follicle containing a germinal center (GC) surrounded by a rim of darker-staining lymphocytes extending to the epithelium of both the small airway and alveolar surface (Movat's stain, x6). (B) Follicle in which GC stains strongly for B cells (x6). (C) Serial section of the same airway stained for CD4-positive T cells, which are scattered around the edge of the follicle and in the airway wall (x6.5). (D) Diagram of immune process triggered by antigens.

carry it to either the mucosal lymphatic collections or the regional lymph nodes (Buzatu et al. 2005). Lymphocytes enter these collections from the blood by attaching to specialized high endothelial cells lining the microvessels that supply mucosal lymphoid follicles (Abbas et al. 2000a,b).

The B cells concentrate in germinal centers rich in B lymphocytes, and the CD4+ and CD8+ T cells concentrate at the edge of the follicles and in the spaces between them (Hogg et al. 2004). This separation and concentration of B and T lymphocytes (Figure 7.11) greatly increases the opportunity for the migrating dendritic cells to present antigen to immature T and B lymphocytes as they make their way through the lymphoid collections to the efferent lymph. The T and B cells activated by the presented antigen migrate to the outer edge (dark zone) surrounding the germinal center (Figure 7.11) and enrich this zone with CD4+ helper T cells and B and T lymphocytes that have recognized similar antigens. This aggregation greatly increases the opportunity for CD4+ helper T cells, B cells, and T cells that have recognized the same antigen to interact to initiate an adaptive response.

The primary stimulus for production of antibodies is provided by the interaction between CD4+ helper T-cell receptors and the major histocompatibility complex class II antigen complex on the B cell (Abbas et al. 2000b). Secondary costimulatory signals delivered by interactions between B-7 on the dendritic cell and its ligand CD28 on the B cell and between CD40 on CD4+ helper T cells and its ligand on B cells stimulate clonal proliferation of the B cell and the production of antibodies (Abbas et al. 2000a,b).

The rich diversity of antigen receptors expressed on mature T and B lymphocytes is made possible by a somatic recombination of a limited number of gene segments encoded in spatially segregated regions of the germ line. The specificity of the antibodies produced is further enhanced by an affinity maturation process that depends on the presentation of the antigen to maturing B cells by a network of follicular dendritic cells in the germinal center (Abbas et al. 2000b). The B cells expressing high-affinity antibody to the antigen presented to them bind tightly to it and receive signals that allow them to survive and develop into either memory cells or antibody-producing plasma cells (Figure 7.11). Those B cells producing low-affinity antibody fail to make this tight connection and are removed through apoptosis (Abbas et al. 2000b).

The antigens that drive the production of antibodies in the lungs of cigarette smokers in either the early or late stages of COPD are poorly understood. The marked increase in the adaptive immune response that occurs in the later stages of the disease has been attributed to antigens introduced by colonization and infection of the lung with microorganisms (Sethi et al. 2002; Hogg et al. 2004;

Murphy et al. 2005) and to autoantigens arising from within damaged lung tissue (Agustí et al. 2003; Voelkel and Taraseviciene-Stewart 2005).

The persistent innate and adaptive immune inflammatory response described here is present in the lungs of all long-term smokers and appears to be amplified in those smokers who develop severe COPD (Figure 7.12) (Keatings et al.1996; Retamales et al. 2001; Hogg et al. 2004). Hogg and colleagues (2004), who examined predictors of FEV_1 obtained from quantitative analysis of lung specimens, measured inflammation, as well as the amount of tissue remodeling of airway walls. The various tissue indicators were compared across strata of GOLD stages for COPD. The extent of the immune response increased from the least to the most severe stage, although the total accumulated volume of cells increased only for B cells and CD8+ cells. In a multivariate analysis, these investigators found that the index of the remodeling of the wall tissue of small airways had the strongest association with the level of FEV_1, greater than the association with infiltration of the tissue by inflammatory cells (Hogg et al. 2004). Ongoing research should provide greater insight into the roles of innate and adaptive immune responses (Curtis et al. 2007).

Tissue Remodeling

Tissue remodeling in general is an intrinsic property of the wound-healing process most carefully studied in tissue damaged by an isolated injury (Clark 1996; Kumar et al. 2005). Observations of changes in small airways in lungs that represent the full range of COPD severity indicate the importance of a repair or remodeling process that thickens small airway walls (Hogg 2004). This type of injury initiates an acute inflammatory response lasting about three days (Figure 7.13). The increase in microvascular permeability that is part of this inflammatory process allows large molecules, such as fibrinogen, to leak from the vessels and initiate the formation of primitive granulation tissue. This tissue is subsequently organized by the processes of angiogenesis and fibrogenesis, which lead to the formation of a mature scar (Kumar et al. 2005). Studies of the details of these processes in the lungs of smokers have been reported (Hogg 2004).

Angiogenesis is the formation of new blood vessels within the granulation tissue by both budding from existing vessels at the edge of the wound and deposition of angioblasts derived from bone marrow, such as endothelial progenitor cells (EPCs) in the provisional matrix (Rafii et al. 2002; Reyes et al. 2002; Hill et al. 2003; Kubo and Alitalo 2003). Studies by Conway and associates (2001) and

Figure 7.12   Persistent innate and adaptive immune inflammatory response in alveolar tissue

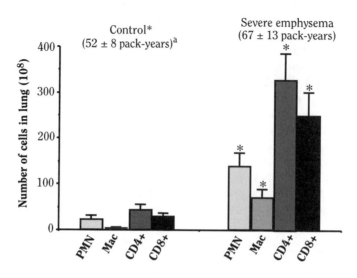

Source: Data from Table 3 in Retamales et al. 2001.
Note: Adaptive immune inflammatory response is present in the lungs of long-term smokers with normal lung function, is amplified in smokers who develop severe chronic obstructive pulmonary disease, and persists many years after smoking cessation.
CD4+ = CD4-positive T cells; **CD8+** = CD8-positive T cells; **Mac** = macrophages; **PMN** = polymorphonuclear neutrophils.
[a]Pack-years = the number of years of smoking multiplied by the number of packs of cigarettes smoked per day.
*p <0.05.

Kumar and colleagues (2005) laid a foundation for understanding the process of angiogenesis. Vascular endothelial growth factor (VEGF) and one of its receptors (VEGFR-2) enhance vascular permeability, encourage the proliferation of EPCs in the bone marrow and at the injury site, and control differentiation of EPCs in the granulation tissue as they form the fragile endothelial tubes. These early vascular structures are stabilized by the interaction of angiopoietin 1 with tyrosine kinase receptors on endothelial cells. Platelet-derived growth factor and TGFβ control the recruitment of smooth muscle to their outer surface and enhance production of the extracellular matrix that stabilizes these newly formed vessels. The migration of endothelial cells formed from EPCs is controlled by integrins, especially $\alpha_v\beta_3$ and matricellular proteins. These integrins, which participate in angiogenesis, include tenascin-C and thrombospondin, a secreted acidic protein rich in cysteine (Conway et al. 2001; Kumar et al. 2005).

The fibrogenic process is initiated by the activation of resting interstitial fibroblasts that migrate into the primitive granulation tissue (Kumar et al. 2005). These resting fibroblasts have a stellate shape with octopus-like projections that form a network connecting the epithelial to the endothelial boundaries of the interstitial compartment (Walker et al. 1995; Behzad et al. 1996; Burns et al. 2003).

The fibroblasts' projections send small, short extensions through tiny preformed holes in both the endothelial and epithelial basement membranes. The investigators also used three-dimensional reconstructions of serial electron micrographs of the interstitial space of the alveolar wall to demonstrate that the migrating inflammatory immune cells use both the preformed holes in the basement membrane and the surface of the fibroblast to navigate through the interstitial space. They found (Figure 7.14) that by seeking corners where three endothelial cells meet, the migrating inflammatory cells exit the microvessels in the alveolar wall without disrupting the tight junctions. After exiting, the migrating cells come into contact with the endothelial basement membrane and follow its surface until they contact one of the preformed holes that normally accommodate a fibroblast extension; the cells then crawl through the holes to enter the interstitial space. There, they contact the surface of a fibroblast that guides their movement through the interstitial compartment to bring them to the preformed holes in the epithelial basement membrane, where they exit. The cells then seek the junctions between alveolar type 1 and 2 epithelial cells to reach the alveolar surface (Walker et al. 1995; Burns et al. 2003). Pathways that are similar but not as well studied are used by migrating inflammatory cells to move

Figure 7.13   Remodeling process after a single clean surgical wound

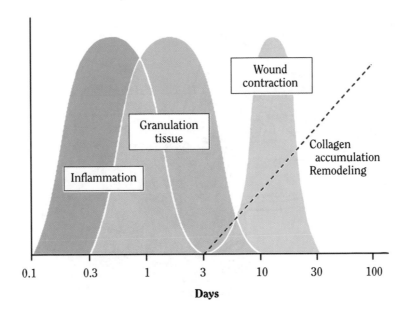

Source: Kumar et al. 2005. Adapted from Clark 1996 with permission from Springer Science and Business Media, © 1996.
Note: A clean surgical wound initiates an acute inflammatory response that lasts for about 3 days and is associated with an increase in microvascular permeability that allows large molecules such as fibrinogen to leak from the vessels and participate in the formation of primitive granulation tissue. This tissue is subsequently organized by the processes of angiogenesis and fibrogenesis leading to the formation of a mature scar. A major difference between this process and that observed in the lung tissue of tobacco smokers is persistent stimulation of the tissue by tobacco smoke as it heals, resulting in a persistent inflammatory immune response.

from the bronchial microvasculature to the conducting airways' surface.

Activation of the resting fibroblasts at the edge of a wound starts their migration into the primitive granulation tissue to initiate fibrogenesis (Cross and Mustoe 2003; Werner and Grose 2003). This process begins with differentiation of the fibroblasts into proto-myofibroblasts that contain bundles of microfilaments termed stress fibers and these proto-myofibroblasts then mature into myofibroblasts containing both stress fibers and α-SM actin (Kumar et al. 2005). The myofibroblasts generate contractile force within the granulation tissue in response to agonists such as endothelin; the increase in force they generate correlates with the level of expression of α-SM actin (Tomasek et al. 2002; Cross and Mustoe 2003; Kumar et al. 2005). Together with the reorganization of the extracellular matrix secreted by these cells, the forces generated by the myofibroblast reduce the size of the damaged tissue. Other reports indicate presence in the lung of myofibroblast precursors with a mesenchymal stem cell phenotype that has potential for differentiation along different pathways and for direction of specific types of tissue repair (Sabatini et al. 2005).

The inflammatory immune cells infiltrating the damaged tissue disappear within a few days of an uncomplicated single wound (Figure 7.13) but persist in the face of the relentless tissue damage caused by sustained smoking (Kumar et al. 2005). This persistent infiltration of inflammatory cells is associated with deregulation of the process of repair and remodeling that leads to the formation of a healthy scar. In a healthy scar, the balance between cellular and matrix synthesis and degradation controls the deposition of collagen that forms the scar (fibrosis). Synthesis is regulated by a wide variety of cytokines and growth factors, and degradation is controlled by the secretion and activation of proteolytic enzymes, including both matrix metalloproteinases (MMPs) and serine proteases. These processes are deregulated by the persistent injury that occurs in numerous chronic diseases, including diseases of the joint tissues such as rheumatoid arthritis, of the liver (hepatic cirrhosis), and of the lungs (pulmonary fibrosis). Deregulated healing may also underlie the pathogenesis of the lesions that develop in the lungs of smokers with COPD.

The more specific aspects of lung remodeling are a focus of research. Lung remodeling is central in the

Figure 7.14   Diagram based on three-dimensional reconstructions of serial electron micrographs illustrating how inflammatory immune cells navigate through interstitial space of alveolar wall

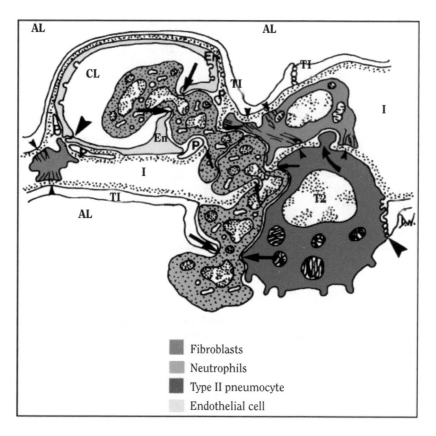

Source: Walker et al. 2005. Reprinted with permission from Elsevier, © 2005.
Note: Migrating inflammatory cells exit the microvessels in the alveolar wall without disrupting the tight junctions by seeking corners where 3 endothelial cells meet (arrows). They contact the endothelial basement membrane and follow it to preformed holes that allow them to enter the interstitial space and contact the surface of a fibroblast. They use the fibroblast surface to guide their movement across the interstitial compartment to the epithelial basement membrane where they find similar preformed holes and enter the epithelial compartment. They exit this compartment between the type 1 and type 2 alveolar epithelial cells. **AL** = alveolar airspace; **CL** = capillary lumen; **En** = endothelium; **F** = fibroblast; **I** = interstitial space; **P** = pericytes; **T1** = type 1; **T2** = type 2.

process that leads to airway fibrosis and narrowing in small airway obstruction, emphysema, and pulmonary hypertension (Postma and Timens 2006). Both the innate and adaptive immune responses are involved in these processes (Hogg 2008). Inflammation caused by smoking is central in driving these processes, but the heterogeneity of phenotypes among persons with COPD remains unexplained (Kim et al. 2008).

Summary

The healing of wounds inflicted by stimuli that persist as the healing takes place provides a model to study

the pathogenesis of a wide variety of chronic inflammatory lesions. This model provides useful insights into the pathogenesis of the lesions found in the lungs of long-term smokers because the damage to lung tissue induced by the smoking habit must heal in the presence of a chronic stimulus. As a result, the normal tissue remodeling process essential to repair lung tissue damaged by inhaled smoke takes place in the presence of a chronic immune inflammatory process. Evidence is growing that this chronic process deregulates the normal healing process in which the deposition of collagen to form a mature scar is determined by a combination of both deposition and degradation of collagen. Deregulation of the chemokines, cytokines, and growth factors that determine collagen deposition and the MMPs and serine proteases that control its degradation could account for both the thickening of the airway walls and the emphysematous destruction of the peripheral lung in COPD. An important feature of this hypothesis is that the application of what is known about the healing of chronic wounds to the pathogenesis of the pulmonary problems associated with smoking tobacco might lead to a better understanding of pathogenesis and new and better insights into targets for the development of new treatments for COPD.

Oxidative Stress

Rahman and MacNee (1998) elucidated the mechanisms by which oxidative stress is considered to play a central role in the lung injury caused by inhaling tobacco smoke. The lungs are directly exposed to the oxygen in inhaled air, and because the respiratory tract has direct contact with the environment through the large volume of inhaled air, it is subject to oxidative injury from inhaled oxidants generated exogenously. These exogenous oxidants come from cigarette smoke, ozone, nitrogen oxides, sulfur oxides, and other airborne pollutants. Endogenous oxidants are also generated from phagocytes and other lung cells. Consequently, the lungs have evolved an efficient antioxidant system to protect the airways and alveoli against both exogenous and endogenous oxidants. The lungs are protected against oxidative challenges by well-developed enzymatic and nonenzymatic antioxidant systems. If the balance between oxidant and antioxidant shifts unfavorably because of either an excess of oxidants or a depletion of antioxidants, oxidative stress occurs. Oxidative stress not only produces direct injurious effects in the lungs but also activates molecular mechanisms that initiate lung inflammation.

Generation of Reactive Oxygen Species

Oxygen, which constitutes 21 percent of the air inhaled, is a key element in the oxidation of organic compounds, the process by which mammalian cells produce the energy needed to sustain life (Davies 1995). One-ninth of all inhaled oxygen undergoes tetravalent reduction to produce H_2O in a reaction catalyzed by cytochrome oxidase in the mitochondrial electron-transport chain. Oxygen is also reduced in a nonenzymatic pathway in four reductions of single electrons:

$$O_2 + 4H^+ + 4e^- \rightarrow 2H_2O \text{ (Davies 1995)} \qquad (1)$$

The terminal electron acceptor in the respiratory chain is cytochrome oxidase, which must donate its reducing equivalents to oxygen to sustain electron transport for the production of adenosine triphosphate. The sequential tetravalent reduction of oxygen by the mitochondrial electron-transport chain is the process of aerobic energy production, but it can lead to the production of ROS (Davies 1995).

Free radicals are molecules with at least one unpaired electron (Davies 1995). The superoxide anion $(O_2 \bullet^-)$, the hydroxyl radical $(\bullet OH)$, and nitric oxide (NO) are examples of free radicals, whereas hydrogen peroxide (H_2O_2) is not a free radical, because all of its electrons are paired. Together, the free radicals are termed ROS. The addition of one electron to oxygen produces $O_2 \bullet^-$; adding a second electron leads to formation of H_2O_2, and a third electron results in the formation of $\bullet OH$ (Figure 7.15). Addition of a fourth electron to oxygen results in its full reduction to H_2O.

The mitochondria are a major intracellular locus for the generation of $O_2 \bullet^-$ (Davies 1995). A further source for generating $O_2 \bullet^-$ is the reduced nicotinamide adenine dinucleotide phosphate (NADPH) oxidase enzymatic system (Davies 1995; Conner and Grisham 1996). $O_2 \bullet^-$ is also generated by other mechanisms, including xanthine, sulfite, and aldehyde oxidases and metabolism of arachidonic acid. This anion, which is relatively unstable, has a half-life of milliseconds. Because of its charge, $O_2 \bullet^-$ does not cross cell membranes easily, but it will react with proteins that contain transition metal groups, such as heme moieties or clusters of iron sulfur. These reactions may result in damage to amino acids or loss of protein or enzyme function. The majority of $O_2 \bullet^-$ generated in vivo undergoes reactions that are nonenzymatic or are catalyzed by superoxide dismutase (SOD) and produce H_2O_2.

H_2O_2 is also produced directly by several oxidase enzymes, including xanthine oxidase, monoamine oxidase, and amino acid oxidase (Davies 1995):

$$O_2 \bullet^- + O_2 \bullet^- + 2H^+ \rightarrow H_2O_2 + O_2 \qquad (2)$$

Figure 7.15   Formation of reactive oxygen species

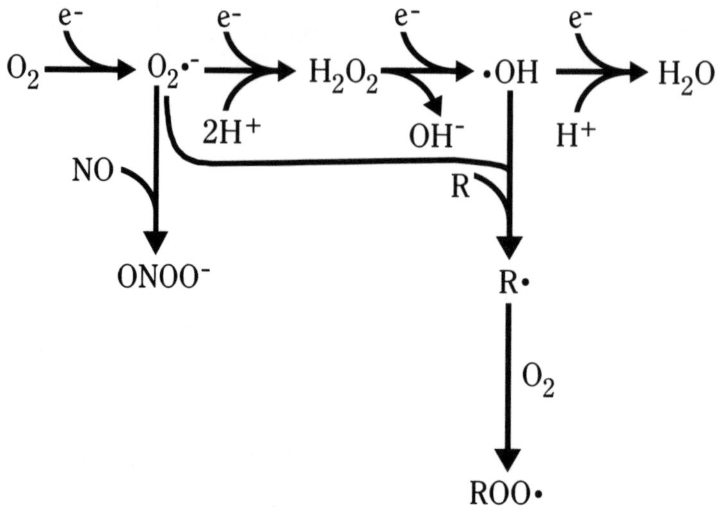

Source: Bowler et al. 2004. Reprinted with permission from Taylor & Francis Group, © 2004. http://www.informaworld.com.
Note: Sequential reduction of oxygen by the addition of electrons (e⁻) results in the formation of reactive oxygen species: superoxide anion ($O_2\bullet^-$), hydrogen peroxide (H_2O_2), and the hydroxyl radical ($\bullet OH$). $O_2\bullet^-$ can combine with nitric oxide (NO) to form peroxynitrite ($ONOO^-$). $O_2\bullet^-$ and the hydroxide radical OH^- can initiate lipid peroxidation to form lipid peroxides ($ROO\bullet$) that propagate free radical chain reactions. R and R represent lipid substituent groups. H^+ is a cationic hydrogen, and $2H^+$ represents 2 cationic hydrogens.

H_2O_2 can undergo oxidation by eosinophil-specific peroxidase (EPO) and neutrophil-specific myeloperoxidase (MPO), a reaction that uses halides (X^-) as a cosubstrate to form hypohalous acids (HOX), which are potent oxidants, and other reactive halogenating species:

$$H_2O_2 + X^- + H^+ \rightarrow HOX + H_2O \qquad (3)$$

where X = bromide and chloride (Davies 1995).

In a series of reactions catalyzed by transition metal irons, $O_2\bullet^-$ and H_2O_2 react in vivo to produce $\bullet OH$ (Halliwell and Gutteridge 1990). One such reaction is the iron-catalyzed Haber-Weiss reaction in which the ferric ion (Fe^{3+}) is reduced to the ferrous ion (Fe^{2+}). The Fenton reaction follows, as Fe^{2+} catalyzes the transformation of H_2O_2 into $\bullet OH$:

$$O_2\bullet^- + Fe^{3+} \rightarrow Fe^{2+} + O_2$$
$$H_2O_2 + Fe^{2+} \rightarrow Fe^{3+} + OH^- + \bullet OH \qquad (4)$$

$\bullet OH$ can also be formed in vivo by reactions involving MPO and EPO (Halliwell and Gutteridge 1990). In conditions with physiological concentrations of halides, MPO produces hypochlorous acid and EPO produces hypobromous acid. Hypochlorous acid can generate $\bullet OH$ after reacting with $O_2\bullet^-$:

$$O_2\bullet^- + HOX \rightarrow \bullet OH + X^+ + O_2 \qquad (5)$$

$\bullet OH$ is the most reactive of all the radicals produced, reacting immediately with organic molecules at its site of production (Halliwell and Gutteridge 1995).

NO, which is produced endogenously throughout the human body, has a variety of roles. NO is produced from its amino acid substrate L-arginine by the reaction of NO synthases (NOSs) (Figure 7.16). Several forms of NOS have been characterized (Lowenstein and Snyder 1992) and are classified as either constitutive or inducible (Nathan and Xie 1994; Wink et al. 1996). The constitutive forms (NOS I and III) are cytosolic and were originally described and cloned from neuronal and endothelial cells, respectively (Nathan and Xie 1994). They are dependent on calcium and calmodulin and release relatively small amounts of NO for short periods in response to receptor and physical stimulation. The inducible form of NOS (NOS II) is independent of the calcium ion, and it generates NO in large amounts for long periods (Wink et al. 1996). NO contains an odd number of electrons and is therefore a radical and highly reactive in nature.

Figure 7.16 Synthesis of nitric oxide (NO) and related products

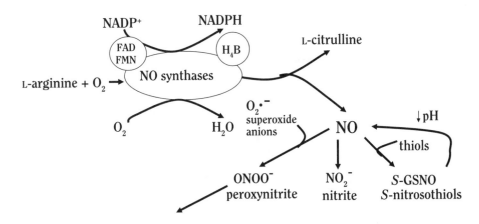

Note: **FAD** = flavin adenine dinucleotide; **FMN** = flavin mononucleotide; **H₄B** = tetrahydrobiopterin; **H₂O** = water; **NADP⁺** = glutamate dehydrogenase; **NADPH** = reduced nicotinamide adenine dinucleotide phosphate; **O₂** = oxygen; **S-GSNO** = *S*-nitrocysteine.

The reaction of NO with O_2 results in the formation of nitrite (NO_2^-) (Beckman and Koppenol 1996). Physiological concentrations of NO and O_2 may be too low for this reaction, but this result may have little importance in vivo. NO_2^- is also a substrate for MPO and EPO, which catalyze peroxidase-mediated oxidation and chlorination of biologic targets (Weiss et al. 1986). Peroxidase-catalyzed oxidation of NO_2^- results in the formation of a nitrogen dioxide radical ($NO_2\bullet$). NO_2^- is a major end product of NO that does not accumulate in vivo, because it is rapidly oxidized to nitrate (NO_3^-) (Wink et al. 1996). NO also reacts rapidly with free radicals to form reactive nitrogen species (RNS) (Parks et al. 1981; Singh and Evans 1997). One such reaction is that of NO with $O_2\bullet^-$ to form the potent oxidant peroxynitrite (ONOO-). ONOO- is relatively stable, but it can be protonated to yield peroxynitrous acid (ONOOH), which then rapidly decomposes to NO_3^- (Conner and Grisham 1996). ONOOH is highly reactive, unstable, and capable of both oxidizing and nitrating reactions. The amino acid tyrosine is particularly susceptible to nitration with the formation of free or protein-associated 3-nitrotyrosine, which has been used as a marker for the generation of RNS in vivo (Ramezanian et al. 1996; van der Vliet et al. 1999).

NO also reacts with compounds containing thiol groups, resulting in the formation of *S*-nitrosothiols (SNOs). This reaction is considered to be the mechanism by which NO groups are transported and targeted to specific effector sites acting as signaling molecules (Patel et al. 1999). SNOs such as *S*-nitroso-L-glutathione may inhibit enzymes that respond to oxidative stress, such as glutathione peroxidase (GPX), glutathione reductase (GRX), glutathione-*S*-transferase (GST), and glutamate cysteine ligase (GCL) (Clark and Debnam 1988; Becker et al. 1995; Han et al. 1996).

Antioxidants in Lungs

Although ROS and RNS have physiological functions, they also have the potential to cause tissue injury. The balance between these physiological functions and the potential to cause injury or damage is determined by their relative rates of formation and removal (Gutteridge 1994). Normally, ROS and RNS are removed rapidly, before they produce cellular dysfunction and eventually cell death. An antioxidant is defined as a substrate that, when present at lower concentrations than those of an oxidizable substrate, significantly delays or inhibits oxidation of that substrate. Antioxidants can be classified as either enzymatic or nonenzymatic (Figure 7.17). The enzyme antioxidants include SOD and catalase (Kinnula and Crapo 2003), the glutathione (GSH) redox system (Rahman and MacNee 2000), and the thioredoxin system (Arnér and Holmgren 2000).

Enzyme Antioxidants

The SOD family of enzymes is made up of ubiquitous antioxidant enzymes that catalyze the dismutation of $O_2\bullet^-$ into H_2O_2 and oxygen. Three SOD enzymes have been identified in mammals: manganese SOD (MNSOD),

Figure 7.17   Oxidant and antioxidant systems in the lungs

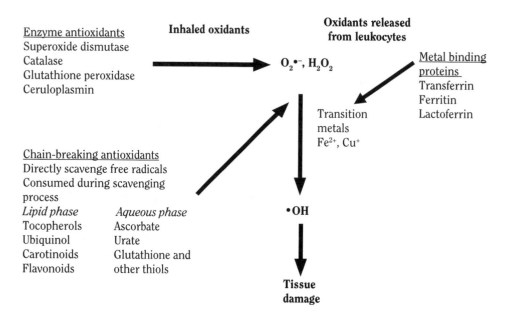

Note: **Cu⁺** = copper ion; **Fe²⁺** = iron ion; **H₂O₂** = hydrogen peroxide; **O₂•⁻** = superoxide anion; **•OH** = hydroxyl radical.

copper zinc SOD (CUZNSOD), and extracellular SOD (ECSOD) (McCord and Fridovich 1970; Marklund 1984; Oury et al. 1996). All three enzymes are expressed widely in human lungs (Kinnula and Crapo 2003). CUZNSOD, the major intracellular SOD, is present in both the cytosol and the nucleus of lysosomes (Slot et al. 1986) of human lungs. It is highly expressed in bronchial epithelium and is the most abundant SOD in the lungs (Lakari et al. 1998). MNSOD, which is localized in the mitochondria, is highly expressed in alveolar macrophages and type II alveolar epithelial cells in human lungs (Lakari et al. 1998, 2000).

ECSOD, the major extracellular SOD, is localized to the extracellular matrix and is particularly abundant in the blood vessels of the lungs, but it has also been found in bronchial and alveolar epithelium and in alveolar macrophages (Kinnula and Crapo 2003). CUZNSOD and MNSOD are generally considered to be the major scavengers of O₂•⁻. ECSOD is present at relatively high concentrations in the lungs, and its localization to the extracellular matrix suggests that it may provide an important protective mechanism in the lung matrix. Marklund (1984) showed that concentrations of ECSOD in the lungs were 2 to 10 times higher than those in other solid organs. SODs can also be induced by cytokines and oxidants (Kinnula and Crapo 2003).

Catalase is a tetrameric hemoprotein that undergoes oxidation and reduction at its active site in the presence of H₂O₂ (Chance et al. 1979). Accordingly, it has reductive activity for small molecules, such as H₂O₂ and methyl or ethyl hydroperoxide (Pietarinen et al. 1995; Carter et al. 2004). Catalase does not metabolize the peroxides with larger molecules, such as hydroperoxide products of lipid peroxidation. It is expressed intracellularly, mainly in alveolar macrophages and neutrophils.

The most important and abundant intracellular thiol antioxidant, GSH, has a critical function in maintaining the redox status within cells, and it is involved in the detoxification of compounds by conjugation reactions through GST (Meister and Anderson 1983). The enzymes associated with reduced GSH metabolism include GPXs, GCL, and GSH synthase.

The GSH peroxidases are a selenium-containing family of enzymes that play a central role in reducing H₂O₂, but they can also reduce lipid peroxides. There are five *GPX* gene products, one of which (GPX3) can be detected in the ELF of the human lung (Comhair et al. 2001). GPX requires GSH to serve as an electron donor. The oxidized GSH that results from this reaction (oxidized glutathione [GSSG]) is subsequently reduced back to GSH by GRX, a reaction generated by NADPH from the hexose monophosphate shunt as an electron donor (Meister and Anderson 1983; Deneke and Fanburg 1989).

In healthy nonstressed cells, the intracellular ratio of GSH to GSSG is high, which ensures the availability of GSH and thereby promotes active reduction of H_2O_2 through the GSH system (Doelman and Bast 1990; Bast et al. 1991). GSH can also function as a water-soluble anti-oxidant interacting directly with reactive oxygen intermediates in nonenzymatic catalyzed reactions. Scavenging of $O_2\bullet^-$ by GSH leads to the formation of thiol radicals (GS•) and H_2O_2. Thus, a substance that is generally thought of as an antioxidant may possess pro-oxidant activity under certain conditions.

GSH is synthesized by GCL and GS (Slot et al. 1986; Soini et al. 2001). The rate-limiting enzyme in GSH synthesis is GCL, which therefore plays a fundamental role in the regulation of GSH homeostasis in the lungs. GCL is a heterodimer with two subunits: a catalytic active heavy subunit and a light subunit that regulates the affinity of the heavy subunit for substrates and inhibitors. Both subunits of GCL are localized in the cytosol of cells and are particularly expressed in human bronchial epithelium and to a lesser extent in alveolar macrophages.

The fluid lining the alveolar epithelium has particularly high GSH levels. Cantin and colleagues (1987) estimated GSH levels in ELF specimens obtained by BAL. Total GSH levels in ELF, including reduced GSH and oxidized GSSG, were 140 times higher than those in plasma. Most of the GSH was present in the reduced form. GSH levels were higher for smokers than for nonsmokers.

The thioredoxin (TRX) system consists of the thioredoxin proteins TRX-1 and TRX-2; thioredoxin-like proteins (e.g., TLX-1 and 2; SPTRX-1 and 2); thioredoxin reductases (e.g., TRXR-1 and 2); peroxiredoxins (PRXs, thioredoxin peroxidases); and glutaredoxins (Rhee et al. 1999; Holmgren 2000; Powis et al. 2000; Gromer et al. 2004). These enzymes are important in reducing protein disulfides and may have additional antioxidant properties. They protect cells against high oxygen tensions and participate in the proliferation and survival of cells. TRX and TRXR are expressed in bronchial and alveolar epithelium and macrophages (Tiitto et al. 2003). Human lung expresses PRXs in bronchial epithelium, alveolar epithelium, and macrophages (Kinnula et al. 2002).

Nonenzymatic Antioxidants

Nonenzymatic antioxidant compounds may act directly with oxidizing agents and are therefore said to be "scavengers." Vitamin E (α-tocopherol) is a membrane-bound antioxidant that terminates the chain reaction of lipid peroxidases by scavenging lipid peroxyl radicals (LOO•) (Bast et al. 1991; van Acker et al. 1993; Davies 1995), thus producing the vitamin E radical, which is much less reactive than LOO•. At high concentrations,

however, the radical form of vitamin E may be pro-oxidant (Bast et al. 1991). Vitamin C can also directly scavenge $O_2\bullet^-$ and •OH to form a semidehydroascorbate free radical subsequently reduced by GSH (McCay 1985). Vitamin C is not considered a major antioxidant because it also has peroxide properties. Whether the pro-oxidant or antioxidant properties of vitamin C predominate in a particular tissue is determined by the available iron stores; iron overload favors excess generation of oxidants (Rowley and Halliwell 1983; Bast et al. 1991).

Other nonenzymatic antioxidants include beta-carotene, which scavenges $O_2\bullet^-$ and peroxyl radicals, and uric acid, which scavenges •OH, $O_2\bullet^-$, and peroxyl radicals. In addition, glucose can scavenge •OH, bilirubin scavenges LOO•, taurine quenches hypochlorous acid, albumin binds transition metals, and cysteine and cysteamine donate sulfhydryl groups (Bast et al. 1991).

Mucin is a glycoprotein with a core rich in serine and threonine to which sulfhydryls are attached. The antioxidant properties of mucus are derived from the abundance of sulfhydryl moieties in its structure (Gum 1992), which actively scavenge oxidants such as •OH (Cross et al. 1984, 1997). Alveolar ELF contains high concentrations of GSH (100-fold higher than in plasma), 90 percent of which is in the reduced form (Cantin et al. 1987). ELF also contains catalase, SOD, and GPX (Cantin and Crystal 1985). Other antioxidants in ELF include ceruloplasmin, transferrin, ascorbate, vitamin E, ferritin, albumin, and small molecules such as bilirubin (Heffner and Repine 1989).

The GSTs and multidrug-resistance proteins (MRPs) are a group of detoxifying enzymes that require intracellular GSH for catalytic activity. Researchers have identified three mammalian GST families (cytosolic, mitochondrial, and microsomal) (Hayes et al. 2005) and nine related MRPs (Kruh and Belinsky 2003). Both of these classes of detoxification enzymes are expressed in healthy lungs, predominantly in the airways (Anttila et al. 1993). They function to protect cells against oxidant-generating compounds, drugs, and other end products of oxidative metabolism.

γ-glutamyltranspeptidase (γGT), an enzyme in plasma membrane is expressed in lung epithelial cells and induced by oxidative stress (Kugelman et al. 1994). GSH is not freely diffusible into cells because it must first be broken down into its amino acids. γGT breaks down the γ-glutamyl bond of GSH. Heme oxygenase-1 is a stress response protein with important functions in cell protection and homeostasis; this enzyme can also be induced by oxidants and cytokines (Choi and Alam 1996).

Oxidants and Cigarette Smoke

Cigarette smoke is a complex mixture of more than 4,700 chemical compounds, including free radicals and other oxidants at high concentrations (Church and Pryor 1985; Pryor and Stone 1993). Among the reported consequences of oxidants in cigarette smoke are direct damage to lipids, nucleic acids, and proteins; depletion of antioxidants; and enhancement of the respiratory burst in phagocytic cells (Bowler et al. 2004; MacNee 2005a). Inactivation of proteases and enhancement of molecular mechanisms involved in the expression of proinflammatory mediator genes are other oxidant-induced effects.

Cigarette smoke is often separated into two phases (tar and gas), which both contain free radicals. The gas phase is less stable and contains approximately 10^{15} radicals per puff; and the more stable tar phase has been estimated to contain more than 10^{17} free radicals per gram (Zang et al. 1995). Short-lived oxidants, such as $O_2\bullet^-$ and NO, are predominantly found in the gas phase (Pryor and Stone 1993). NO and $O_2\bullet^-$ immediately react to form the highly reactive $ONOO^-$ molecule. NO is present in cigarette smoke at concentrations of 500 to 1,000 parts per million. Free radicals in the tar phase of cigarette smoke, such as the long-lived semiquinone radical ($Q\bullet^-$), are organic and can react with $O_2\bullet^-$ to form $\bullet OH$ and H_2O_2 (Nakayama et al. 1989). $Q\bullet^-$ is an example of a radical in the tar phase of cigarette smoke that can reduce oxygen to produce superoxide, the $\bullet OH$, and H_2O_2. The aqueous phase of cigarette smoke condensate may undergo redox recycling for a considerable time in ELF of smokers (Nakayama et al. 1989; Zang et al. 1995). The tar phase of cigarette smoke is also an effective metal chelator and can bind iron to produce tar-semiquinone + tar-Fe^{2+}, which can generate H_2O_2 continuously.

Quinone (Q), hydroquinone (QH_2), and $Q\bullet^-$ in the tar phase are present in equilibrium (Pryor and Stone 1993):

$$Q + QH_2 \rightarrow 2H^+ + Q\bullet^- \qquad (6)$$

Aqueous extracts of cigarette tar contain $Q\bullet^-$. This radical can reduce oxygen to form $O_2\bullet^-$, which may dismutate to form H_2O_2:

$$Q\bullet^- + O_2 \rightarrow Q + O_2\bullet^- \qquad (7)$$
$$2\ O_2\bullet^- + 2H^+ \rightarrow O_2 + H_2O_2 \qquad (8)$$

In addition, cigarette tar and lung ELF contain metal ions such as iron. In these circumstances, the Fenton reaction results in the production of $\bullet OH$. Cigarette smokers deposit up to 20 mg of tar per day (≤ 1 gram per day) in their lungs per cigarette smoked.

Cell-Derived Oxidants

In smokers, inflammation is a characteristic feature of the lungs and other organs (Saetta et al. 2002; Bowler et al. 2004; Di Stefano et al. 2004). This inflammation generates additional oxidants that contribute to oxidative stress. Alveolar macrophages obtained by BAL from the lungs of smokers are more activated than those obtained from the lungs of nonsmokers (Schaberg et al. 1992). One consequence of this activation is the release of higher levels of ROS, such as $O_2\bullet^-$ and H_2O_2, thereby further increasing the oxidative burden produced directly by inhaling cigarette smoke. Exposure to cigarette smoke in vitro has also been shown to increase the oxidative metabolism of alveolar macrophages (Hoidal et al. 1981). Subpopulations of higher-density alveolar macrophages, which are more common in the lungs of smokers, may be responsible for the increased production of $O_2\bullet^-$ that occurs in the macrophages of smokers (Schaberg et al. 1995).

Lung epithelial cells are another source of ROS. Type II alveolar epithelial cells have been shown to release both H_2O_2 and $O_2\bullet^-$ in quantities similar to the amounts released by alveolar macrophages (Rochelle et al. 1998). ROS released from type II cells are able, in the presence of MPO, to inactivate AAT in vitro (Wallaert et al. 1993).

ROS can also be generated intracellularly from several sources, such as mitochondrial respiration, which is the largest source of free radicals. In the mitochondria, electrons leak from the electron-transport chain onto oxygen to form $O_2\bullet^-$ (Halliwell and Gutteridge 1990). A further significant cytosolic source of superoxide is the enzyme xanthine dehydrogenase, which has been shown to be present at higher levels in cell-free BAL fluid in patients with COPD than in that of healthy persons, in association with increased production of superoxide and uric acid (Pinamonti et al. 1996). A substantial amount of superoxide is also produced by membrane oxidases, such as cytochrome P-450 and the NADPH oxidase system. In addition, NO is generated from arginine by the action of NOS. Depending on the relative amounts of ROS and RNS, particularly superoxide and NO, which are almost always produced simultaneously at sites of inflammation, these species can react together to produce the powerful oxidant $ONOO^-$ (Beckman and Koppenol 1996). The generation of $ONOO^-$ is thought to prolong the action of NO and to be responsible for most of the adverse effects of excess generation of NO.

Assessment of Oxidative Stress

Oxidative stress can be measured by direct measurements of the oxidative burden, indirectly as the responses to oxidative stress, and by examining the effects of oxidative stress on target molecules (Table 7.4). Assessments of the oxidative burden in the air spaces can be derived by measuring H_2O_2 in BAL fluid or in exhaled breath condensate (Dekhuijzen et al. 1996; Nowak et al. 1998). Air space leukocytes obtained by BAL can be assessed ex vivo for the ability to produce ROS. Spin trapping, a technique in which a radical reacts with a more stable molecule, can be used to measure oxidants in biologic systems; spin trapping has shown increased ROS in the BAL fluid from patients with COPD (Pinamonti et al. 1998). NO is produced in the lungs by the catalytic activity of NOS as a marker of inflammation and indirectly as a marker of oxidative stress, and it can be measured in exhaled breath. Among the indirect measures for assessing oxidative stress is an examination of the increased activity of the hemoxygenase system, which is reflected in the carbon monoxide levels in exhaled breath. Assessment of the effects of oxidative stress on target molecules may include measuring the reaction of ROS with lipids, proteins, or nucleic acids to form markers of oxidative stress. For example, ROS attack proteins to form protein carbonyls, $ONOO^-$ reacts with tyrosine to form nitrotyrosine, and ROS react with lipids to liberate ethane and isoprostane and with DNA to form base-paired adducts (e.g., 7-hydroxy-8-oxo-2'-deoxyguanosine) or with GSH to produce oxidized GSH. These markers can be measured in blood, breath condensate, BAL fluid, and lung tissue as an indicator of the effects of free radicals on target molecules.

Evidence of Smoking-Induced Oxidative Stress

In Vitro Studies

Studies have examined the consequences of acute (short-term) exposure to cigarette smoke for a wide range of cells (Table 7.5). Many studies have focused on oxidative stress and have shown an increase in markers of such stress after exposure to whole cigarette smoke or condensate of cigarette smoke. The cell types studied have included alveolar macrophages, type II alveolar epithelial cell lines consisting largely of A549 cells, and neutrophils. For exposure to cigarette smoke, most of the studies have used cigarette smoke extract (CSE) as the exposure agent; a smaller number have used cigarette smoke. The concentrations of CSE and the duration of exposure have differed among studies, and concentrations of CSE from that produced by one cigarette per milliliter to that produced by four cigarettes per milliliter. The exposure times have varied between 1 second and 24 hours. All of the studies have shown that acute exposure to cigarette smoke causes increased oxidative stress.

Exposure of plasma to cigarette smoke in vitro depletes antioxidants, including vitamin C, ubiniquol-10, α-tocopherol, cryptoxanthin, retinol, and beta-carotene and leads to lipid peroxidation (Eiserich et al. 1995; Handelman et al. 1996; Scott et al. 2005). In vivo, smokers are well documented to have lower serum levels of vitamin C and beta-carotene and perhaps α-tocopherol than do nonsmokers (Tribble et al. 1993; Faruque et al. 1995; Adams et al. 1997; Lykkesfeldt et al. 1997; Motoyama et al. 1997; Munro et al. 1997; Alberg 2002; Northrop-Clewes and Thurnham 2007). This relationship between smoking status and reduced vitamin C levels may be dose related (Tribble et al. 1993; Faruque et al. 1995; Marangon et al. 1998). The hypothesis was that reduced levels of vitamin C in smokers are due to the activation of leukocytes and subsequent generation of ROS (Winklhofer-Roob et al. 1997).

Table 7.4   Measurements of oxidative stress

Direct measurements of oxidative burden
Hydrogen peroxide in breath condensate or BAL fluid
Reactive oxygen species in BAL fluid and peripheral blood leukocytes
Nitric oxide in exhaled breath
Responses to oxidative stress
Carbon monoxide in breath, reflecting hemoxygenase activity
Antioxidants, antioxidant enzymes in blood, sputum, BAL fluid, and lung tissue
Effects of oxidative stress on target molecules
Oxidized proteins (e.g., carbonyl residues and oxidized and nitrated proteins)
Lipid peroxidation products (e.g., F_2-isoprostanes and 4-hydroxy-2-nonenal)
DNA oxidation products (e.g., 8-hydroxy-2'-deoxyguanosine)
Hydrocarbons in breath condensate, sputum, BAL fluid, blood, urine, and lung tissue

Note: **BAL** = bronchoalveolar lavage.

Table 7.5   Studies of oxidative stress in smokers

Study	Number of participants by smoking status	Abstinence time	Cigarettes smoked	Time between inhalation and measurement	Effect of smoking
Kharitonov et al. 1995	17 smokers	8 hours	1	5 and 15 minutes	Exhaled air: ENO decreased after 5 minutes (65 ± 6.3 to 44 ± 6.4 ppb); returned to control values within 15 minutes (53 ± 6.3 ppb)
Morrow et al. 1995	10 smokers 10 nonsmokers	10 hours	3	30 minutes	Blood: F_2-isoprostane showed no significant change
Rahman et al. 1996a	12 smokers 14 nonsmokers	Unknown	1	60 minutes	Blood: TEAC decreased; TBARS increased
Chambers et al. 1998	24 smokers	1 hour	1	1 and 10 minutes	Exhaled air: ENO increased
Morrison et al. 1999	14 smokers 7 nonsmokers	12 hours	2	60 minutes	BAL fluid: leukocyte superoxide anions increased; TBARS showed no significant change; TEAC increased; glutathione showed no significant change; oxidized glutathione showed no significant change; neutrophils increased Blood: TEAC decreased; TBARS increased Epithelial permeability increased
Guatura et al. 2000	12 smokers 10 nonsmokers	10 hours	1	30 minutes	Breath condensate: hydrogen peroxide increased
Montuschi et al. 2000	12 smokers	12 hours	2	15 hours	Breath condensate: 8-isoprostane increased after 15 minutes; no significant change after 5 hours
Balint et al. 2001	15 smokers 15 nonsmokers	4 hours	2	30 and 90 minutes	Breath condensate: nitrate + nitrite increased after 30 minutes; no significant change after 90 minutes; nitrite, peroxynitrite, and ENO showed no significant change
Tsuchiya et al. 2002	20 smokers	6 hours	1	5 and 60 minutes	Blood: nitrate, nitrite, ascorbic acid, cysteine, methionine, and uric acid decreased after 5 minutes; no significant change after 30 minutes

Source: Adapted from van der Vaart et al. 2004 with permission from BMJ Publishing Group Ltd., © 2004.
Note: **BAL** = bronchoalveolar lavage; **ENO** = exhaled nitric oxide; **ppb** = parts per billion; **TBARS** = thiobarbituric acid reactive substances; **TEAC** = trolox equivalent antioxidant capacity.

GSSG, the oxidized form of GSH, is released from endothelial cells after 30 minutes of exposure to cigarette smoke (Noronha-Dutra et al. 1993). Although intracellular GSH decreased within 3 hours of exposure to cigarette smoke (Bridgeman et al. 1991; Li et al. 1994; Carnevali et al. 2003), GSH and GCL increased 24 hours after exposure. This finding suggests a protective cellular mechanism against the oxidative stress induced by cigarette smoke (Rahman et al. 1996b). Immediately after

exposure to six puffs of cigarette smoke, H_2O_2 and superoxide molecules were detected in the membranes of epithelial cells in the tracheal explant model (Hobson et al. 1991), but this consequence of exposure was prevented by antioxidants. Twenty-four hours after exposure to CSE, NO was released from endothelial cells (Tuder et al. 2000). In contrast, inducible NOS (INOS) expression and release of nitrate from epithelial cells exposed to CSE were decreased (Hoyt et al. 2003). Exposure to cigarette smoke was also shown to activate the pentose phosphate pathway, which is a source of NADPH for the enzyme GRX in endothelial cells (Noronha-Dutra et al. 1993). The activities of the main enzymes in the GSH redox cycle have been shown to be decreased by the acute exposure of alveolar epithelial cells to cigarette smoke (Rahman et al. 1996a). Cigarette smoke causes depletion of intracellular GSH in cultured airway epithelial cells and transient decreases in GPX and glucose-6-phosphate activities (Rahman et al. 1998). Exposure to cigarette smoke also causes an increase in the expression of GPX (Rahman and MacNee 1999). In vitro studies also suggest that after initial GSH depletion, GSH levels increased, apparently due to GCL induction (Rahman et al. 1996a). Exposure of neutrophils and alveolar macrophages to cigarette smoke produces morphologic changes in the cells that result in cell blebbing, which indicates oxidant-induced damage (Lannan et al. 1994).

Animal Studies

Several studies have assessed the short-term effects of the inhalation of cigarette smoke on markers of oxidative stress in lung tissue, BAL fluid, and blood in animals (Table 7.6). These studies have found increased levels of oxidative stress after such exposure.

GSH, the major thiol antioxidant in the lungs, rapidly and immediately decreases in the lung tissue of rats and other laboratory animals after exposure to cigarette smoke (Cotgreave et al. 1987; Bilimoria and Ecobichon 1992; Ishizaki et al. 1996; Li et al. 1996). GSH levels may return to normal by two to six hours after exposure to smoke (Cotgreave et al. 1987; Bilimoria and Ecobichon 1992) or may remain at levels higher than baseline (Ishizaki et al. 1996). GSSG levels increased 1 hour after exposure to smoke in animal models and decreased at 6 hours after acute exposure, returning to normal levels after 24 hours (Li et al. 1996). Acute exposure to cigarette smoke in rats did not produce any change in the amount of cysteine in the lungs; cysteine is an essential amino acid for the synthesis of GSH (Cotgreave et al. 1987). Other markers of oxidative stress, including 4-hydroxy-2-nonenal (4-HNE) and 8-hydroxy-2'-deoxyguanosine (8-OH-dG), were elevated in lung tissue after acute exposure to cigarette smoke (Ishizaki et al. 1996; Aoshiba et al. 2003a). Furthermore, INOS messenger RNA (mRNA) and endothelial NOS are increased after acute exposure to cigarette smoke (Wright et al. 1999).

ELF is the initial target for oxidative stress, and extracellular GSH levels obtained by BAL in rats were reduced immediately (Cotgreave et al. 1987) and remained at reduced levels six hours after smoke inhalation (Li et al. 1996). Twenty-four hours after acute exposure to cigarette smoke, GSH concentrations return to baseline values (Li

et al. 1996). Evidence indicates that short-term cigarette smoking depletes intracellular GSH concentrations (Cotgreave et al. 1987) and increases levels of GSSG (Cavarra et al. 2001b) and 8-OH-dG (Aoshiba et al. 2003a) that are associated with decreased antioxidant capacity in BAL fluid (Cavarra et al. 2001b). Evidence of systemic oxidative stress has been shown in animal models after acute exposure to cigarette smoke, as shown by a decrease in antioxidants (Uotila 1982; Ishizaki et al. 1996). This finding is associated with an increase in products of lipid peroxidation such as 8-epi-prostaglandin$_{2\alpha}$ in blood (Cavarra et al. 2001b).

Consequences of Smoke-Induced Oxidative Stress

Epithelial Injury

Among the first injurious effects of cigarette smoke on the lungs is an increase in epithelial permeability, which has been demonstrated in animal models (Li et al. 1994). In the lung tissue of rats, increased epithelial permeability is associated with a decrease in GSH levels and an increase in GSSG levels. Depletion of GSH in the lungs increased epithelial permeability both in vivo and in vitro with use of cultured epithelial monolayers (Li et al. 1994).

Inflammatory Responses

Oxidative stress has been shown to enhance gene expression of proinflammatory mediators through the redox-sensitive transcription factors nuclear factor-kappa B (NF-κB) and activator protein-1 (AP-1). Animal studies have shown enhanced NF-κB nuclear binding after exposure to cigarette smoke, which was associated with increased gene expression and protein release of proinflammatory cytokines (Nishikawa et al. 1999). Furthermore, the molecular mechanisms associated with enhanced inflammatory responses after exposure to cigarette smoke are thought to involve an increase in histone acetylation and decreased histone deacetylase (HDAC) activity, resulting in enhanced histone acetylation, unwinding of chromatin, and hence, enhanced gene expression (Marwick et al. 2004). These effects have been demonstrated in animal models of exposure to cigarette smoke.

Susceptible Animal Models

The role of oxidative stress in the development of lung disease induced by cigarette smoke has been demonstrated in animal models: increasing oxidative stress has led to higher frequency of emphysema induced by cigarette smoke. NRF-2 is a controlling transcription factor

Table 7.6   Studies of oxidative stress in animals exposed to smoke

Study	Animals (number)	Smoke exposure			Route of administration	Effect
		Number of cigarettes	Exposure time	Time between exposure and measurement		
Uotila 1982	Syrian hamsters (NR)	5 12	1 hours 2 hours	20 hours Measurement during exposure	Smoking chamber	Experiment 1[a]—Blood: MUG increased after 20 hours Experiment 2[b]—Blood: MUG increased during smoking
Cotgreave et al. 1987	Sprague-Dawley rats (NR)	8	1 hour	0 hours	Nose only	BAL fluid: intracellular GSH decreased; free GSH decreased; extracellular GSH decreased Blood: GSH showed no significant change; cysteine increased Lung tissue: cysteine showed no significant change
Bilimoria and Ecobichon 1992	Sprague-Dawley rats (8) Hartley guinea pigs (NR)	40, 120, and 240 puffs	NR	0, 3, and 6 hours	Nose only	Lung homogenate: GSH decreased at 0 hours in rats but only at high exposures in guinea pigs; levels returned to preexposure within 3 hours Ascorbic acid: no reduction in either species
Wright et al. 1999	Rats (NR)	7	2 hours	24 hours	Nose only	Lung homogenate CNOS mRNA and protein showed no significant change; INOS mRNA increased, protein showed no significant change; ENOS mRNA increased, protein showed no significant change
Cavarra et al. 2001b	C57BL/6J mice with smoke exposure (35), controls (70)	5	20 minutes	0, 20, and 60 minutes	Smoking chamber	BAL fluid at 0 hours: trolox equivalent antioxidant capacity decreased, levels returned to preexposure within 20 minutes; glutathione disulfide increased; ascorbic acid decreased; protein thiols decreased; neither total glutathione nor vitamin E showed any significant change; 8-epi-PGF$_{2\alpha}$ increased; prevented in a subgroup of case/controls by pretreatment with N-acetylcysteine Plasma: 8-epi-PGF$_{2\alpha}$ increased at 0, 20, and 60 minutes; total cell count, alveolar macrophages, polymorphonuclear neutrophils, and lymphocytes showed no significant change; human secretory leukoprotease inhibitor inactivated

Table 7.6   Continued

		Smoke exposure				
Study	Animals (number)	Number of cigarettes	Exposure time	Time between exposure and measurement	Route of administration	Effect
Aoshiba et al. 2003a	C57BL/6 mice (6)	10	1 hour	1, 3, 16, and 24 hours	Smoking chamber	Lung tissue: 8-oxo-dG and 4-HNE increased after 1 hour in bronchial epithelial cells and type II alveolar cells; cellularity increased after 1–16 hours BAL fluid: 8-oxo-dG levels increased after 1 hour; no significant change after 24 hours

Source: Adapted from van der Vaart et al. 2004 with permission from BMJ Publishing Group Ltd., © 2004.

Note: **4-HNE** = 4-hydroxy-2-nonenal; **8-epi-PGF$_{2\alpha}$** = 8-epi-prostaglandin F$_{2\alpha}$; **8-oxo-dG** = 7-hydroxy-8-hydroxy-2'-deoxyguanosine; **BAL** = bronchoalveolar lavage; **CNOS** = constitutive nitric oxide synthase; **ENOS** = endothelial nitric oxide synthese; **GSH** = reduced glutathione; **INOS** = inducible nitric oxide synthase; **mRNA** = messenger RNA; **MUG** = methylumbelliferyl glucuronide; **NR** = data not reported.

[a]Lungs were isolated, ventilated with cigarette smoke, and perfused with 4-MUG.

[b]Isolated lungs were simultaneously ventilated with cigarette smoke and perfused with MUG.

for the expression of antioxidant genes. In NRF-2 knock-out mice, exposure to smoke produced more evidence of oxidative stress in the lungs, which was associated with an increased inflammatory response and enhanced development of emphysema compared with those in wild-type mice (Foronjy et al. 2006). Furthermore, a transgenic animal that overexpressed SOD showed diminished smoke-induced emphysema. These findings suggest a role for oxidative stress in the development of emphysema (Rangasamy et al. 2004).

Antioxidants have been shown to reduce the effects of oxidative stress after exposure to cigarette smoke. The thiol antioxidants nacystelyn and *N*-acetylcysteine have each been used to reduce the inflammatory responses after exposure to cigarette smoke and also the injurious effects, principally emphysema (Antonicelli et al. 2004; Rubio et al. 2004). After exposure to cigarette smoke, recombinant SOD has been shown to reduce the inflammatory response in several ways: by decreasing the inflammatory response in the lungs, reducing the influx of neutrophils, decreasing IL-8 gene expression and release, and decreasing NF-κB activation (Nishikawa et al. 1999).

Human Studies

Several studies have shown evidence of both local and systemic oxidative stress in humans after acute exposure to cigarette smoke (Table 7.7). Some studies were undertaken in long-term smokers with normal lung function, and some have been performed in smokers who were instructed to refrain from smoking before the acute exposure at intervals between 7 and 24 hours. Reports of other studies have not provided information on abstention, and in some studies, the participants were not instructed to refrain from smoking.

Local Oxidative Stress in Lungs

The acute effects of cigarette smoking on oxidative stress have been assessed with markers in exhaled air, BAL fluid, and blood. Most of these studies have shown an immediate increase in oxidative stress after acute exposure, but some have shown no effect (Table 7.7). Five studies have described the effects of acute exposure to cigarette smoke on markers of oxidative stress in breath condensate or exhaled air. In breath condensate, the lipid peroxidation product 8-isoprostane increased 15 minutes after acute exposure (Montuschi et al. 2000). In addition, lipid peroxides have been shown to increase in exhaled breath 30 minutes after exposure to smoke (Guatura et al. 2000). Furthermore, exhaled NO has been shown to increase 1 and 10 minutes after acute exposure to smoke (Chambers et al. 1998), but in another study it decreased 5 minutes after exposure (Kharitonov et al. 1995). The inconsistency between these studies probably relates to differences in the measurements of exhaled NO and among the groups studied. High levels of exhaled NO have not been observed at time points after exposure (15, 30, and 90 minutes) (Kharitonov et al. 1995; Balint et al. 2001). Nitrate, an end product of NO, increased 30 minutes after acute exposure,

Table 7.7   In vitro studies of oxidative stress

Study	Cell types	Source	Dose (cigarettes/ mL)	Exposure time	Time between exposure and measurement	Effect of smoke exposure
Powell and Green 1971	Rabbit AMs	CSE	NR	NR	NR	G3PD activity in AMs decreased, effect prevented by cysteine; G6PD and LDH activities not significantly different from controls
Bridgeman et al. 1991	Erythrocytes Neutrophils A549 cell line	CS	1, 3, and 5 puffs	NR	NR	Intracellular GSH decreased, not prevented by reducing agents
Hobson et al. 1991	Rat tracheal explants	CS	1, 3, and 6 puffs	10 minutes	40 minutes	Hydrogen peroxide and $O_2{}^{\bullet-}$ increased along epithelial cell membranes, prevented by SOD 3 and 6 puffs: cell separation, focal membrane blebbing, and loss of cilia, cell disintegration
Tsuchiya et al. 1992	Rat PMNs	CSE	1	20 minutes	20 minutes	Radical oxidant scavenger production from PMNs decreased, prevented by SOD; oxygen consumption from PMNs increased
Noronha-Dutra et al. 1993	HUVEC	CSE	0.5	30 minutes	30 minutes	Pentose phosphate pathway activated; GSSG release increased
Li et al. 1994	A549 cell line	CSE	1	1–6 hours	1, 4, 6, and 24 hours	Epithelial permeability increased at 1 hour, prevented by GSH, no significant change 24 hours after wash; intracellular GSH decreased, no significant change 24 hours after wash
Rahman et al. 1996b	A549 cell line	CSE	1 puff/3 mL	4, 16, or 28 hours	0 hours	Intracellular CSE GSH increased after 24 hours; GSSG no significant change; γGCS activity increased; γGCS-HS mRNA increased
Pinot et al. 1999	Human peripheral blood monocytes	CSE	0, 0.006, 0.024	Overnight	Directly after	$O_2{}^{\bullet-}$ production showed no significant change; HSP 70 increased; membrane pseudopodes decreased; submembrane vacuoles increased; surfactant prevented CSE effects
Tuder et al. 2000	Bovine artery endothelial cells Monocytic U937 Hep G2 A549 cell line	CSE	0.1	24 hours	24 hours	VEGF decreased protein and mRNA in all cells except A549 cell line; apoptosis increased bovine artery endothelial cells

Table 7.7   Continued

Study	Cell types	Source	Dose (cigarettes/mL)	Exposure time	Time between exposure and measurement	Effect of smoke exposure
			Smoke exposure			
Hoyt et al. 2003	LA-4 A549 cell line HBEC	CSE	0.0004–0.00008	4 and 24 hours	24 hours	Nitrate decreased at 4 and 24 hours in all cell types; INOS-positive LA-4 cells decreased at 24 hours; INOS mRNA decreased; ENOS and NNOS mRNA showed no change in LA-4 cells; ENOS in A549 cells showed no significant change
Kayyali et al. 2003	RPMEC	CSE	20 µg/mL	4 and 24 hours	4 and 24 hours	XO activity increased at 4 and 24 hours; mRNA XO increased at 6 hours
Wickenden et al. 2003	A549 cell line HUVEC Jurkat cells	CSE	0.05–0.1	24 hours	24 hours	Necrosis increased, no apoptosis;[a] GSH inhibits necrosis and apoptosis (Jurkat cells); GSH/GSSG decreased intracellularly; inhibition CASPASE-3 activation (Jurkat cells)

Source: Adapted from van der Vaart et al. 2004 with permission from BMJ Publishing Group Ltd., © 2004.

Note: **A549** = human lung adenocarcinoma epithelial cell line; **AMs** = alveolar macrophages; **CS** = cigarette smokers; **CSE** = cigarette smoke extract; **G3PD** = glyceraldehyde 3-phosphate dehydrogenase; **G6PD** = glucose 6-phosphate dehydrogenase; **γGCS** = gamma-glutamylcysteine synthetase; **γGCS-HS** = gamma-glutamylcysteine synthetase heavy subunit; **GSH** = reduced glutathione; **GSSG** = oxidized glutathione; **HBEC** = human bronchial epithelial cells; **Hep G2** = human hepatocellular carcinoma cell line; **HSP 70** = heat shock protein 70; **HUVEC** = human umbilical vein endothelial cells; **INOS** = inducible nitric oxide synthase; **LA-4** = mouse lung epithelial cell line; **LDH** = lactate dehydrogenase; **mL** = milliliter; **µg** = microgram; **mRNA** = messenger RNA; **NNOS** = neuronal nitric oxide synthase; **NR** = data not reported; $O_2 \bullet^-$ = superoxide anion; **PMN** = polymorphonuclear neutrophil; **RPMEC** = rat pulmonary microvascular endothelial cells; **SOD** = superoxide dismutase; **U937** = human leukemic monocyte lymphoma cell line; **VEGF** = vascular endothelial growth factor; **XO** = xanthine oxidase.

[a]Light microscopy, TUNEL (terminal dUTP nick-end labeling) assay, electron microscopy.

but nitrite and nitrotyrosine, which are also products of NO metabolism, did not increase (Balint et al. 2001). In humans, all the oxidative markers of oxidative stress increase within the first hour after acute exposure, and most markers return to normal within 90 minutes (van der Vaart et al. 2004).

Only one study has investigated the effects of smoking on markers of oxidative stress in ELF or BAL fluid. In this study, release of $O_2 \bullet^-$ by air space leukocytes increased after exposure to smoke (Morrison et al. 1999). In addition, systemic antioxidant capacity decreased, as measured by the Trolox Equivalent Antioxidant Capacity (Rahman et al. 1996a; Morrison et al. 1999). Surprisingly, however, the antioxidant capacity in BAL fluid increased after exposure to smoke, possibly because all of the participants were long-term smokers and already had a high antioxidant capacity in BAL fluid. After smoking, no differences were observed in levels of reduced or oxidized GSH in leukocytes or in thiobarbituric acid reactive substances

(TBARS), as evidenced by measuring lipid peroxidation in BAL fluid or in ELF.

Systemic Oxidative Stress

After just one cigarette has been smoked, nitrite, nitrate, and cysteine decrease in peripheral blood (Tsuchiya et al. 2002). In a study by Hockertz and colleagues (1994), no differences were observed in the production of reactive oxygen intermediates from circulating neutrophils after exposure to smoke, but an earlier study gave conflicting findings (Drost et al. 1992). In contrast to levels in BAL fluid, TBARS in plasma increased after exposure to smoke and antioxidant capacity was decreased when measured within one hour after smoking (Rahman et al. 1996a; Tsuchiya et al. 2002). However, in smokers, levels of the lipid peroxidation product F_2-isoprostane did not change in plasma after exposure to smoke (Morrow et al. 1995), possibly because all participants were long-term smokers who had already developed high F_2-isoprostane levels.

Epithelial Injury

Increased epithelial permeability, which can be measured by ^{99m}Tc-DTPA lung clearance (Morrison et al. 1998a), has been shown to increase in cigarette smokers one hour after exposure to smoke (Morrison et al. 1999). Another study (Gil et al. 1995), however, showed no difference in epithelial permeability 15 minutes after exposure to cigarette smoke in long-term smokers. Epithelial permeability, measured by radiolabeled urea, decreased after acute exposure to cigarette smoke (Ward et al. 2000), but no differences could be detected when measurements were made by positron emission tomography scanning with use of radiolabeled transferrin (Kaplan et al.1992).

Inflammatory Responses

The numbers of neutrophils in the blood and BAL fluid from long-term smokers are higher than in those from nonsmokers (Hunninghake and Crystal 1983; Kuschner et al. 1996; van Eeden and Hogg 2000). Findings on the effect of short-term cigarette smoking on the number of neutrophils in BAL fluid have been inconsistent. Some studies reported an increase (Morrison et al. 1999), and others reported no change (Janoff et al. 1983b). Exposure to smoke has not been shown to change the number of monocytes or the total number of leukocytes in BAL fluid (Janoff et al. 1983b). However, counts of peripheral blood granulocytes increase after acute exposure to cigarette smoke (Winkel and Statland 1981; Abboud et al. 1986; Hockertz et al. 1994), and counts of peripheral blood eosinophils decrease after such exposure (Winkel and Statland 1981). Acute exposure to cigarette smoke has also been shown to reduce the number of B cells (Hockertz et al. 1994) and the total number of lymphocytes in peripheral blood (Winkel and Statland 1981). In contrast, the number of CDB-positive cells and the ratio of CD4+ to CD8+ cells are not affected by acute exposure to cigarette smoke (Hockertz et al. 1994). In capillary blood, the total number of basophils decreased 10 minutes after the smoking of two cigarettes (Walter and Nancy 1980), and the number of degranulated basophils increased (Walter and Walter 1982).

Neutrophil kinetics in the lungs have been examined after exposure to cigarette smoke by using an assessment of the first pass of radiolabeled neutrophils through the pulmonary circulation. Retention of neutrophils in the lungs increased after acute exposure to cigarette smoke (MacNee et al. 1989). This increased retention was not due to an alteration of pulmonary hemodynamics (Skwarski et al. 1993) but resulted from decreased deformability of leukocytes (Drost et al. 1993) and/or the increased expression of the adhesion molecule L-selectin in blood neutrophils after acute exposure to cigarette smoke (Patiar et al. 2002).

After acute exposure to cigarette smoke, changes in GSH have been studied in human, animal, and in vitro models. The ratio of GSH to GSSG, which reflects oxidative stress, has been shown to decrease after acute exposure in both animal and in vitro studies but not in a single human study (Morrison et al. 1999). This discrepancy may be explained by differences in species and dose of smoke and differences between human BAL fluid and animal lung homogenate.

Exposure to cigarette smoke has been shown to damage fatty acids in cell membranes and thereby result in increased products of lipid peroxidation both in humans, as seen in exhaled air and plasma (Rahman et al. 1996a; Montuschi et al. 2000), and in animals, as seen in BAL fluid and lung tissue (Ishizaki et al. 1996; Aoshiba et al. 2003a).

Summary

The time courses of the changes in markers of oxidative stress after exposure to smoke have been studied in humans and in animal models. In humans, all the oxidative markers of oxidative stress increase within the first hour after acute exposure, and most markers return to normal quickly. In animal models, markers of oxidative stress generally increase during the first 6 hours after exposure to cigarette smoke and return to normal by 24 hours. These findings have been demonstrated in lung tissue, BAL fluid, and blood. In studies with in vitro models, only a few time points have been examined. Initial depletion of GSH after acute exposure to cigarette smoke is followed in most cases by an increase in GSH 24 hours later. This finding suggests a protective mechanism against oxidative stress from smoke that may reflect the increase in GSH seen in long-term cigarette smokers.

Oxidative Stress in Chronic Obstructive Pulmonary Disease

There is considerable evidence, largely indirect, for increased oxidative stress in the lungs of COPD patients. As explained previously, oxidative stress can be measured in several ways, including direct measurements of oxidant burden, indirect measures using response to oxidative stress, and measurements of the effects of oxidative stress on target molecules (see "Assessment of Oxidative Stress" earlier in this chapter). Spin trapping, a technique by which a radical reacts with a more stable molecule, can be used to measure oxidants in biologic systems. The technique of spin trapping has been applied to measure BAL fluid in patients with COPD and has shown increased ROS (Pinamonti et al. 1998).

Numerous studies have shown that markers of oxidative stress are increased in the lungs of COPD patients compared not only with those in healthy persons but also with those in smokers having a similar smoking history who have not developed COPD (MacNee 2000). Patients with COPD have higher levels of H_2O_2 in exhaled breath condensate, a direct measurement of air space oxidative burden, than do former smokers with COPD or nonsmokers (Dekhuijzen et al. 1996; Nowak et al. 1998). Elevated levels of H_2O_2 in the exhaled breath of smokers are thought to derive partly from increased release of $O_2 \bullet^-$ by alveolar macrophages (Hoidal et al. 1981).

NO has been used as a marker of airway inflammation and indirectly as a measure of oxidative stress. Increased NO in exhaled breath has been seen in some studies of patients with COPD, but the levels are not as high as those reported in asthma (Maziak et al. 1998; Delen et al. 2000). Other studies have found either normal or even lower-than-normal levels of exhaled NO in patients with stable COPD compared with those in healthy persons (Clini et al. 1998; Rutgers et al. 1999). Smoking directly increases exhaled NO levels, however, thereby limiting the usefulness of this marker in COPD. The rapid reaction of NO with $O_2 \bullet^-$, described previously, or with thiols may alter NO levels in breath (see "Generation of Reactive Oxygen Species" earlier in this chapter). Nitrosothiol levels have been shown to be higher in breath condensate in smokers and in COPD patients than those in nonsmokers (Corradi et al. 2001). $ONOO^-$, formed by the reaction of NO with $O_2 \bullet^-$, can cause nitration of tyrosine to produce nitrotyrosine (Petruzzelli et al. 1997). Nitrotyrosine levels are elevated in sputum leukocytes of patients with COPD, and they are correlated negatively with FEV_1 (Ichinose et al. 2000).

Exhaled carbon monoxide, as a measure of the response of heme oxygenase to oxidative stress, has been shown to be elevated in exhaled breath in persons with COPD compared with that in persons without COPD (Montuschi et al. 2001). Carbon monoxide is also present in cigarette smoke, however, which limits its usefulness as a marker of oxidative stress in persons who smoke.

Lipid peroxidation products such as TBARS or malondialdehyde are elevated in sputum from COPD patients, and the levels correlate negatively with FEV_1 (Nowak et al. 1999; Tsukagoshi et al. 2000; Corradi et al. 2003). Urinary levels of 8-isoprostane, another lipid peroxidation product, are also higher in persons with COPD (Praticò et al. 1998). Levels of 8-isoprostane in breath condensate are also higher in persons with COPD than in healthy persons and smokers who have not developed the disease, and they correlate with the degree of airway obstruction (Paredi et al. 2000a). Isoprostanes may also reflect systemic effects caused by ROS (Morrow et al. 1995). Plasma levels of free F_2-isoprostanes are higher in smokers than in nonsmokers and are decreased after cessation of smoking.

Lipid peroxides can interact with enzymatic or nonenzymatic antioxidants and can decompose by reacting with metal ions or iron-containing proteins, thereby forming hydrocarbon gases and unsaturated aldehydes. Hydrocarbons are thus by-products of fatty acid peroxidation (Paredi et al. 2000b). COPD patients have higher levels of exhaled ethane in breath than do persons in the control group, and these levels correlate negatively with lung function (Habib et al. 1995; Paredi et al. 2000b).

There is evidence that concentrations of these markers of oxidative stress are also increased in the lung tissue of COPD patients. The lipid peroxidation product 4-HNE reacts quickly with extracellular proteins to form adducts, which have been shown to be present at higher concentrations in airway epithelial and endothelial cells in the lungs of COPD patients than in those of smokers with a similar smoking history who have not developed the disease (Rahman et al. 2002). Other markers of oxidative stress, such as 8-OH-dG and 4-HNE, have been shown to have increased expression associated with emphysematous lesions in the lungs (Tuder et al. 2003c).

Pathogenesis of Chronic Obstructive Pulmonary Disease

Many studies have shown higher levels of biomarkers of oxidative stress in COPD patients than in healthy smokers. Furthermore, several studies show relationships between markers of oxidative stress and the degree of airflow limitation in COPD (Repine et al. 1997; MacNee 2000). However, the presence of oxidative stress and its relationship to airflow limitation may be an epiphenomenon because oxidative stress occurs in any inflammatory response. Cohort studies have not shown that the presence of enhanced oxidative stress relates to the decline in FEV_1 or to the progression of COPD.

Protease-Antiprotease Imbalance

In COPD, the protease burden in the lungs is increased because of the influx and activation of inflammatory leukocytes that release proteases. It has been proposed that a relative "deficiency" of antiproteases such as AAT, because of their inactivation by oxidants, creates a protease-antiprotease imbalance in the lungs. This hypothesis forms the basis of the protease-antiprotease theory of the pathogenesis of emphysema (Janoff et al. 1983a; Stockley 2001). Inactivation of AAT by oxidants occurs at a critical methionine residue in its active site and can be produced by oxidants from cigarette smoke or oxidants released from inflammatory leukocytes, resulting in a marked reduction in the inhibitory capacity of AAT in vitro (Bieth 1985; Evans and Pryor 1992). In vivo study of the acute effects of cigarette smoke on the functional activity of AAT show a transient but nonsignificant fall in the antiprotease activity of BAL fluid one hour after cigarette smoking (Abboud et al. 1985). In addition, in vitro exposure of lung epithelial cells to proteases leads to increased release of ROS, suggesting that proteases increase oxidative stress (Aoshiba et al. 2001b).

Hypersecretion of Mucus

Oxidant-generating systems such as xanthine and xanthine oxidase have been shown to cause the secretion of mucus from airway epithelial cells (Adler et al. 1990; Wright et al. 1996). Oxidants are also involved in the signaling pathways for EGF, which has an important role in the production of mucus (Nadel 2001). In addition, H_2O_2 and superoxide have been shown to cause a significant impairment of ciliary function after short-term exposure at low concentrations (Feldman et al. 1994). These effects may have important implications in the pathogenesis of COPD.

Lung Inflammation

Oxidative stress is present wherever inflammation exists. It may also be a mechanism for enhancing the air space inflammation that is characteristic of COPD (Pauwels et al. 2001). Oxidative stress can result in the release of chemotactic factors, such as IL-8, from airway epithelial cells (Gilmour et al. 2003), and epithelial cells from COPD patients have been shown to release more IL-8 than those of smokers or healthy persons (Profita et al. 2003). Lipid peroxidation products such as 8-isoprostane can also act as signaling molecules and cause the release of inflammatory mediators such as IL-8 from lung cells (Scholz et al. 2003). The lipid peroxidation product 4-HNE can cause increased production of TGFβ (Leonarduzzi et al. 1997) and increased expression of the gene encoding for the antioxidant enzyme γ-glutamylcysteine synthetase (Arsalane et al. 1997).

An enhanced inflammatory response in the lungs is characteristic of COPD (Di Stefano et al. 2004; Hogg 2004). Oxidative stress may have a fundamental role in enhancing inflammation through the increased production of redox-sensitive transcription factors, such as NF-κB and AP-1, and also by activation of the extracellular signal-regulated kinase, C-JUN *N*-terminal kinase, and p38 mitogen-activated protein kinase pathways (Rahman and MacNee 1998; MacNee and Rahman 2001). Cigarette smoke has been shown to activate all of these signaling mechanisms.

Genes for many inflammatory mediators are regulated by NF-κB, which is present in the cytosol in an inactive form linked to its inhibitory protein IκB. Many stimuli, including oxidants, result in activation of IκB kinase, producing phosphorylation and cleaving of IκB from NF-κB. The release of NF-κB is a critical event in the inflammatory response and is redox sensitive (Janssen-Heininger et al. 1999; MacNee 2000). Studies both in macrophage cell lines and in alveolar and bronchial epithelial cells show that oxidants cause the release of inflammatory mediators (e.g., IL-8, IL-1, and NO) and that these events are associated with increased expression of the genes for these inflammatory mediators and with increased nuclear binding and activation of NF-κB (Jiménez et al. 2000; Parmentier et al. 2000). The linking of NF-κB to its consensus site in the nucleus leads to enhanced transcription of proinflammatory genes and hence inflammation, which induces more oxidative stress, creating a vicious circle as enhanced inflammation and increased oxidative stress perpetuate each other.

Nuclear binding of NF-κB is increased in the airway macrophages and airway epithelial cells of COPD patients (Di Stefano et al. 2002). In a guinea pig model, exposure to cigarette smoke led to influx of neutrophils into the lungs and increased IL-8 gene expression, protein release, and NF-κB activation (Nishikawa et al. 1999). These increases and the neutrophil influx were reduced by pretreatment with superoxide dismutase, suggesting a role for oxidant stress. NF-κB is activated and translocated to the nucleus to a greater extent in lung tissue in smokers and in patients with COPD than in healthy persons (Szulakowski et al. 2006), and NF-κB activation in lung tissue has been shown to correlate with FEV_1 (Crowther et al. 1999).

A study of gene expression in rat epithelium after exposure to cigarette smoke showed that smoke causes rapid induction of antioxidant stress-response genes and drug-metabolizing enzymes, such as heme oxygenase and quinone oxidoreductase, all of which had decreased expression after long-term exposure to cigarettes (Gebel et al. 2004). The protein kinase C signaling pathway is also sensitive to tobacco smoke and increases its activity by twofold to threefold when stimulated by 5-percent CSE (Wyatt et al. 1999).

A further event controlling gene transcription that may be affected by oxidative stress and may enhance lung inflammation is chromatin remodeling. Under normal circumstances, DNA is wound tightly around a core of histone residues. This configuration prevents access for transcription factors to the transcriptional machinery and also reduces access of RNA polymerase to DNA, thereby resulting in transcriptional repression and gene silencing (Rahman and MacNee 1998; MacNee 2001). Histone acetyltransferases (HATs) cause the acetylation of histone residues, resulting in a change in their charge and unwinding of DNA and allowing access for transcription factors such as NF-κB and RNA polymerase to the transcriptional machinery, thereby enhancing gene expression. This process is reversed by HDACs, enzymes that deacetylate histone residues, resulting in the rewinding of DNA and gene silencing. The exact role of oxidative stress in modifying HAT and HDAC activity is unknown, but it appears that oxidative stress can result in increased HAT activity and decreased HDAC activity (Gilmour et al. 2003), which would enhance gene transcription.

Oxidative stress results in HAT activity in epithelial cells (Tomita et al. 2003). Histone acetylation can be shown to occur after the exposure of epithelial cells to cigarette smoke and is prevented by the antioxidant therapy *N*-acetylcysteine, indicating that the process is redox sensitive (Anderson et al. 2004). Furthermore, in animal models, exposure to cigarette smoke results in increased acetylated histone in the lung and decreased HDAC activity,

and both of these events would enhance gene expression (Marwick et al. 2002). In addition, HDAC activity in alveolar macrophages obtained from cigarette smokers has been shown to be decreased, which would also enhance gene expression (Ito et al. 2001). This event may be due to nitration of HDAC2 by $ONOO^-$ (Ito et al. 2001, 2004a). More recent studies have suggested that acetylate histone residues, such as H4, are present to a greater extent in lung tissue in smokers and in COPD patients who smoke. These increases in H4 are associated with a decrease in HDAC2 in COPD patients who smoke and in patients with severe COPD (Ito et al. 2005; Szulakowski et al. 2006). A correlation has also been shown between decreased HDAC activity in lung tissue and FEV_1 in patients with COPD.

Apoptosis

There are two types of cell death: apoptosis, which is organized and noninflammatory, and necrosis, which is unorganized, destructive, and proinflammatory. One hypothesis is that loss of alveolar endothelial cells by apoptosis may be an initial event in the development of emphysema (Tuder et al. 2003b). Apoptosis has been shown to occur to a greater extent in endothelial cells in emphysematous lungs than in lungs of nonsmokers (Kasahara et al. 2001).

Airway lymphocytes (Majo et al. 2001) and stimulated peripheral blood leukocytes (Hodge et al. 2003) from patients with COPD also show increased apoptosis. The process of endothelial apoptosis is thought to be under the influence of VEGFR-2 receptors. Decrease of VEGFR-2 has been shown to produce emphysema in animals, and reduced expression of VEGFR-2 is evident in emphysematous human lungs (Kasahara et al. 2001). Studies have also shown that the apoptosis and emphysema induced by VEGF inhibition in animal models is associated with increased markers of oxidative stress and is prevented by antioxidants, suggesting that oxidative stress is involved in this process (Tuder et al. 2003c).

Systemic Involvement

Although COPD predominantly affects the lungs, it has important systemic consequences, including cachexia and skeletal muscle function (Wouters et al. 2002; Langen et al. 2003). Increasing evidence suggests that similar mechanisms involving oxidative stress and inflammation in the lungs may also be responsible for many of the systemic effects of COPD (Langen et al. 2003).

Peripheral blood neutrophils from COPD patients have been shown to release more ROS than such neutrophils from unaffected persons (Rahman et al. 1996a). Products of lipid peroxidation are also increased in plasma in smokers and patients with COPD (Rahman et al. 1996a). In addition, increased levels of nitrotyrosine have been shown to occur in the plasma of COPD patients (Ichinose et al. 2000).

Patients with COPD often display weight loss, which correlates inversely with the occurrence of exacerbations and is seen as an independent indicator of outcome (Gray-Donald et al. 1996; Landbo et al. 1999). In addition, loss of fat-free mass results in peripheral muscle dysfunction, decreased exercise capacity, and reduced health status (Palange et al. 1995; Baarends et al. 1997; Engelen et al. 2000b). Several factors influence the loss of weight and fat-free mass in COPD patients, including malnutrition, imbalance in overall protein turnover and the hormones involved in this process, tissue hypoxia, and pulmonary inflammation (Jenkins and Ross 1996; Engelen et al. 2000b; Eid et al. 2001; Wouters et al. 2002).

Oxidative stress may also have a role in the cachexia and loss of fat-free mass that occurs in COPD. Skeletal muscle is exposed continuously to changes in the redox environment that occur during exercise. Several studies have shown evidence of increased oxidative stress in patients with COPD both locally and systemically, particularly during exercise (Couillard et al. 2002, 2003; Langen et al. 2003). Presence of lipid peroxidation products in the serum, accompanied by an increase in the ratio of oxidized to reduced GSH, occur during exercise in COPD patients to a greater extent than in healthy persons (Sastre et al. 1992; Viña et al. 1996; Heunks and Dekhuijzen 2000). Skeletal muscle cells adapt to oxidative stress by increasing production of antioxidant enzymes such as SOD, catalase, and GPX (Franco et al. 1999). Study findings also showed evidence of disturbed redox homeostasis in COPD associated with emphysema. GSH levels in skeletal muscle were lower in COPD patients with emphysema than in those who did not have emphysema and were associated with reduced concentrations of glutamate, an important substrate in the synthesis of glutamine and GSH (Engelen et al. 2000a). Other studies demonstrate a decrease in GPX activity, elevated GRX activity, and increased lipid peroxidation, which indicate oxidative damage in the skeletal muscle of experimental hamsters with emphysema (Mattson et al. 2002). These results suggest that GSH metabolism is impaired in COPD.

Increased ROS production in skeletal muscle during exercise may result from stimulation of the mitochondrial electron-transport chain by TNFα (Li et al. 1999), which is known to be elevated in the circulation of patients with COPD who lose weight (Di Francia et al. 1994). Leukocytes infiltrating skeletal muscles in COPD patients may be another source of ROS (Adams et al. 2002). In addition, exercise increases the activity of xanthine and xanthine oxidase, a further source of ROS (Andrade et al. 1998). ROS also contribute to oxidative stress in muscles, and inducible NO expression has been shown to increase in skeletal muscle in response to inflammatory cytokines and activation of NF-κB (Adams et al. 2002). Oxidative stress may directly compromise muscle function by decreasing contractility and by increasing the susceptibility of muscle to oxidants (Barclay and Hansel 1991; Andrade et al. 1998). ROS may also oxidize proteins in the contractile apparatus, such as sulfhydryl residues in the contractile proteins, which may impair muscle function (MacFarlane and Miller 1992). In addition to impairing muscle function, resulting in muscle fatigue, oxidative stress may induce muscle atrophy. Atrophy is the result of an imbalance in muscle protein metabolism, which has been described in studies showing that oxidative stress induced inhibition of muscle-specific protein expression (Buck and Chojkier 1996; Langen et al. 2004). Furthermore, oxidative stress may result in apoptosis of muscle cells, which has been described in skeletal muscle cells, and may contribute to muscle atrophy (Stangel et al. 1996).

Summary

Considerable evidence now exists for both local and systemic oxidative stress in COPD patients. Increasing evidence suggests that oxidative stress is involved in many of the pathogenic processes involved in COPD, as well as in systemic phenomena such as skeletal muscle dysfunction. Cigarette smoke provides an extraordinarily strong dose of free radicals to the lung, initiating processes of oxidative injury that involve multiple cell types and the entire lung. Local inflammation results and markers of inflammation are higher, both in smokers and in persons with COPD, than are those in nonsmokers. Oxidative stress unfavorably tips the protease-antiprotease balance toward protease, leading to tissue damage and COPD.

Genetics of Pulmonary Disease and Susceptibility to Tobacco Smoke

α1-Antitrypsin Deficiency

Genetic Etiology

AAT deficiency is a long-established genetic risk factor for COPD and a model for the determination of susceptibility to cigarette smoking by causing COPD through a genetic mutation. However, only a minority of patients with COPD (1 to 2 percent) inherit the severe AAT deficiency that places them at highly increased risk of COPD (Lieberman et al. 1986). Consequently, only a small proportion of COPD cases are thought to be attributable to this gene-environment interaction (Lieberman et al. 1986).

The AAT protein is encoded by the *SERPINA1* gene on chromosome 14q32.1. Approximately 100 protease inhibitor (PI) alleles have been identified, some resulting in decreased serum levels of AAT (*American Journal of Respiratory and Critical Care Medicine* 2003). The **M* allele accounts for more than 95 percent of the PI alleles in U.S. populations and is associated with normal serum levels of AAT (Brantly et al. 1988). The **S* allele, which leads to mildly reduced AAT levels, and the **Z* allele, which leads to severely reduced AAT levels, occur at frequencies above 1 percent in U.S. populations. A smaller percentage of people inherit **NULL* alleles, which lead to the absence of any AAT production through a heterogeneous set of mutational mechanisms. Persons with two **Z* alleles or one **Z* and one **NULL* allele are commonly referred to as having the *PI *Z* phenotype, because their serum samples cannot be distinguished by the isoelectric focusing technique commonly used to assess PI type (Ogushi et al. 1987). Persons with *PI *Z* alleles have approximately 15 percent of normal serum AAT levels, and this quantitative reduction in circulating AAT is the primary determinant of increased risk for emphysema. In addition, molecule by molecule, the Z protein is a slightly less effective serine PI than is the M protein.

Immunologic assay of the AAT level in serum is a common test for AAT deficiency, but confirmation of the diagnosis of AAT deficiency requires determination of PI type, which is typically performed by isoelectric focusing of serum in specialized laboratories. Molecular genotyping by polymerase chain reaction can distinguish the common PI alleles (**M*, **S*, and **Z*) with use of DNA from a variety of cellular sources (von Ahsen et al. 2000; Stockley and Campbell 2001). However, high-throughput complete sequencing tests for rare PI alleles are not yet widely available, so rare alleles that produce severe AAT deficiency (e.g., **NULL* alleles) can be misclassified as normal if comprehensive molecular tests are not used.

AAT is one of the serpin protease inhibitors (serpins), an important family of PIs. The association between inherited AAT deficiency and pulmonary emphysema was critical for the development of the protease-antiprotease hypothesis on the pathogenesis of emphysema (Janoff 1985; Niewoehner 1988; Churg and Wright 2005). AAT is the major serum PI of neutrophil elastase, which is encoded by the *ELA2* gene. Neutrophil elastase is a potent elastase considered to be involved in the elastin degradation that leads to emphysema (Travis and Salvesen 1983). Although AAT demonstrates some inhibitory activity against a range of proteases, it is an extremely effective inhibitor of neutrophil elastase (Beatty et al. 1980). The functional specificity of AAT is determined by a methionine at amino acid position 358 of the AAT protein, which is the PI residue at the active inhibitory site (Mahadeva and Lomas 1998). The **Z* allele encodes a single base substitution that replaces glutamic acid at amino acid position 342 in the M protein with lysine, thus eliminating a critical salt bridge in the AAT protein. The low serum AAT levels in *PI *Z* alleles occur because the Z protein polymerizes within the endoplasmic reticulum of hepatocytes, the primary site of AAT synthesis, preventing release of the protein.

The prevalence of AAT deficiency is particularly high in populations of Northern European descent. Molecular haplotype analysis of polymorphic loci adjacent to the *AAT *Z* allele suggests a single mutational origin for the majority of **Z* alleles in modern populations, an ancestral mutation that likely occurred in Northern Europe (Byth et al. 1994). Hutchison (1998), who reviewed the European screening studies for AAT deficiency, found that the highest frequencies of the **Z* allele were in northwestern Europe. Although screening studies have typically found low frequencies of the **Z* allele in populations of African and Asian descent (Kellermann and Walter 1970), the review of the worldwide screening literature in control cohorts, prepared by de Serres (2002), suggested that there could be significant numbers of *PI *Z* carriers in almost every region of the world. These estimates were based on calculations assuming Hardy-Weinberg equilibrium and accurate AAT typing in these control populations, but it remains to be determined how significantly these estimates were affected by PI typing errors, new mutations, or migration from populations in Northern Europe.

Natural History

Although increased risk for the development of COPD among persons with the *PI *Z* allele has been well established, the magnitude of this risk and the natural history of the entire population with the *PI *Z* allele remain unclear. This population in the United States is estimated at 80,000 to 100,000. Among persons known to have the *PI *Z* allele, early-onset COPD is often observed clinically. Classic emphysema with the greatest severity in the lower lobes has been described among adults with the *PI *Z* allele and COPD, but diffuse or upper lobe emphysema can also be observed in this population (Parr et al. 2004).

Several early studies of large numbers of persons with the *PI *Z* allele demonstrated that *PI *Z*-type persons who smoked cigarettes tended to develop more severe COPD at an earlier age than did *PI *Z*-type persons who were nonsmokers (Larsson 1978; Tobin et al. 1983; Janus et al. 1985). More recently, Seersholm and colleagues (1994) demonstrated significantly higher mortality rates in smokers with *PI *Z* than in nonsmokers with *PI *Z*. Silverman and colleagues (1992) demonstrated an interaction between PI type and cigarette smoking, by comparing the patterns of phenotypic expression in smokers by the percentage with specific predicted FEV_1 values and the patterns in participants with the *PI *M*, *PI *M/*Z*, or *PI *Z* allele, in the St. Louis Alpha-1-Antitrypsin Study.

The St. Louis Alpha-1-Antitrypsin Study also demonstrated the importance of ascertainment bias in limiting insight into the natural history of AAT deficiency. If most persons with the *PI *Z* allele are identified because they already have COPD, it would appear that most persons with this genotype will develop COPD. Among 52 persons with this allele, Silverman and colleagues (1989) confirmed the expected result that persons with the *PI *Z* allele who were tested for AAT deficiency because they already had COPD (index persons) all had significantly reduced FEV_1 values. However, marked variability in development of airflow obstruction was demonstrated in nonindex persons with the *PI *Z* allele whose genotype was ascertained, not because of existing COPD, but by genotyping in family studies or because they had liver disease. In Denmark, Seersholm and colleagues (1995) confirmed differences between lung function in index and nonindex persons with the *PI *Z* allele that were independent of age and smoking history.

The *PI *Z* type is a major risk factor for COPD, and cigarette smoking increases the risk for COPD in persons with the *PI *Z* allele (Silverman et al. 1989). Even so, some smokers with *PI *Z* maintain normal pulmonary function into older ages, whereas some nonsmokers with *PI *Z* develop COPD at an early age (Black and Kueppers 1978). For example, among 18 lifetime nonsmokers with the *PI *Z* allele, the investigators found significant variability in lung function and respiratory symptoms, despite the absence of a history of smoking or other significant environmental exposures.

In a study of 205 nonsmokers with the *PI *Z* allele in Sweden, Piitulainen and colleagues (1998) observed that using a kerosene heater and working in agriculture were associated with lower lung function. Among 128 persons with *PI *Z*, Mayer and associates (2000) found that high exposure to mineral dust was associated with increased cough symptoms and reduced FEV_1.

Because less than 10 percent of the estimated total of persons with the *PI *Z* genotype in the United States have been identified (*American Journal of Respiratory and Critical Care Medicine* 2003), the natural history of COPD in persons with the *PI *Z* allele remains uncertain. In addition to cigarette smoking, other environmental factors and genetic modifiers likely influence the development of COPD among persons with *PI *Z*. Largely in response to the underdiagnosis of persons with *PI *Z*, the American Thoracic Society and European Respiratory Society Task Force (*American Journal of Respiratory and Critical Care Medicine* 2003) recommended testing for AAT deficiency in all adults with COPD, emphysema, or asthma with chronic airflow obstruction.

Familial Aggregation of Phenotypes Related to Chronic Obstructive Pulmonary Disease

Pulmonary Function in the General Population

Several types of studies have suggested that genetic factors influence variation in spirometric measurements in the general population. Studies of twins who were not selected for lung disease have found greater correlations in the measure of lung function between monozygotic twins, who share all of their genetic variation, than between dizygotic twins, who share approximately one-half of their genetic variation. Comparison of correlations between monozygotic and dizygotic twins allows for estimating the heritability of lung function, the percentage of total phenotypic variation in lung function that is related to genetic factors. For example, in a study of 127 monozygotic and 141 dizygotic twin pairs by the National Heart, Lung, and Blood Institute (NHLBI), the estimated heritability for FEV_1 values, after adjustment for age, height, weight, and smoking was 74 percent (Hubert et al. 1982). Redline and colleagues (1987) also observed significantly higher correlations for FEV_1 between monozygotic twins than between dizygotic twins. Tishler and associates

(2002) studied 352 adult twin pairs and found evidence suggesting a relationship between history of cigarette smoking and unidentified potential susceptibility genes.

Studies in nuclear families have also supported a role for genetic determinants of pulmonary function in the general population; both path analysis and variance component analysis have been used. Lewitter and colleagues (1984), who used path analysis in a study of 404 nuclear families, estimated that 41 to 47 percent of variation in FEV$_1$ values was related to genetic factors. Using variance component analysis in a study of 439 persons from 108 families, Astemborski and associates (1985) estimated that after adjustment for age, gender, race, and smoking history, 28 percent of the variation in FEV$_1$ and 24 percent of the variation in FEV$_1$/FVC were related to genetic determinants. More recently, Palmer and colleagues (2001) performed variance component modeling of spirometric phenotypes in the Busselton Health Study and estimated the heritability of FEV$_1$ as 39 percent. Although these studies in the general population provide compelling evidence that genetic factors influence variation in level of pulmonary function, they do not necessarily provide insight into the role of genetic factors in the development of COPD.

Airflow Obstruction

Studies assessing the role of familial aggregation of phenotypes in the occurrence of airflow obstruction in relatives of patients with COPD have supported a role for genetic factors in the development of COPD. In an early study, Larson and colleagues (1970) reported higher rates of airflow obstruction in first-degree relatives of COPD patients than in the control group. Later, Kueppers and associates (1977), who studied 114 persons with COPD, compared the spirometric values in siblings with those in a matched control group and found that the siblings had significantly lower FEV$_1$ values after adjustment for smoking history.

In the Boston Early-Onset COPD Study, Silverman and colleagues (1998) focused on persons with severe, early-onset COPD without AAT deficiency. Among nonsmokers who were first-degree relatives of these probands with early-onset COPD, FEV$_1$ and FEV$_1$/FVC values were similar to those in nonsmokers in the control group. Using generalized estimating equations to adjust for age and pack-years of smoking, the investigators found, however, that current or former smokers among first-degree relatives of the probands with early-onset COPD had significantly higher risk for reduced FEV$_1$ values than did smokers in the control group. In Great Britain, McCloskey and associates (2001) compared the rates of airflow obstruction in 173 siblings of probands who had severe

COPD with those for a population-based control cohort. As was found in the Boston Early-Onset COPD Study, nonsmokers who were siblings of COPD patients had risk of airflow obstruction similar to that for nonsmokers in the control group. In contrast, current or former smokers who were siblings of probands with COPD had a significantly higher risk of airflow obstruction than did smokers from the general population. The significant familial aggregation of phenotypes for airflow obstruction in COPD families, which persists after adjustment for intensity of cigarette smoking, strongly suggests genetic influences on susceptibility to developing chronic airflow obstruction.

Chronic Bronchitis

Familial aggregation of chronic cough and production of phlegm (chronic bronchitis) has also been demonstrated. In a sample of 9,226 persons from the general population, Higgins and Keller (1975) found significantly higher rates of chronic bronchitis in offspring when at least one parent had chronic bronchitis than if neither parent had the disorder, but there was no adjustment for cigarette smoking. Speizer and colleagues (1976), using National Health Interview Survey data and adjusting for cigarette smoking, demonstrated significantly higher rates of bronchitis or emphysema among offspring when at least one parent had bronchitis or emphysema. Tager and associates (1978) also adjusted for history of cigarette smoking in their analysis and found that rates of chronic bronchitis or airflow obstruction in first-degree relatives of probands with chronic bronchitis or airflow obstruction were significantly higher than those in first-degree relatives of the control group. Finally, in the Boston Early-Onset COPD Study, Silverman and colleagues (1998) found significantly higher risk of chronic bronchitis among smokers who were first-degree relatives of probands with early-onset COPD than among control smokers. This analysis was adjusted for the intensity of cigarette smoking.

Linkage Analysis of Phenotypes Related to Chronic Obstructive Pulmonary Disease

Several studies of genetic linkage across the human genome were performed in families from the general population who were not selected because of the presence of particular respiratory disease (Table 7.8). The purpose was to examine the relationship between spirometric values and genetic determinants of pulmonary

Table 7.8   Genomewide linkage analysis studies in general-population samples and in families with chronic obstructive pulmonary disease (COPD)

Study	Study design	Sample size	Phenotype	Chromosomal region/ maximum limit of detection score[a]	Comments
General Population					
Joost et al. 2002	Framingham Heart Study pedigrees	1,578 persons 330 pedigrees	FEV_1	• 4p: 1.6 • 6q: 2.4	
Malhotra et al. 2003	Extended Utah Centre d'Etude du Polymorphisme Humain pedigrees	264 persons 26 pedigrees	FEV_1/FVC	• 2q: 2.0	Parametric limit of detection score without heterogeneity showed most significant linkage evidence on 2q
Wilk et al. 2003a	Family Heart Study pedigrees	2,178 persons 391 pedigrees	FEV_1 FEV_1/FVC	• 3q: 2.0 • 1p: 1.7 • 4p: 3.5 • 9p: 2.0 • 17p: 2.3	Untransformed values were reported; normalized values were also analyzed
Boston Early-Onset COPD Study					
Silverman et al. 2002a	Extended pedigrees ascertained in proband with early-onset COPD	585 persons 72 pedigrees	Moderate airflow obstruction	• 12p: 1.7 • 19q: 1.5	Some regions demonstrated increased limit of detection scores for smokers only
Palmer et al. 2003	Extended pedigrees ascertained in proband with early-onset COPD	Same population 560 persons with spirometry	FEV_1 (postbronchodilation) FEV_1/FVC (postbronchodilation)	• 1p: 2.2 • 8p: 3.3 • 8q: 2.0 • 19q: 1.9 • 1p: 2.5 • 2q: 4.4 • 17q: 2.4	
DeMeo et al. 2004	Extended pedigrees ascertained in proband with early-onset COPD	Same population	FEF25–75 (postbronchodilation) FEF25–75/FVC (postbronchodilation)	• 8p: 1.8 • 12p: 1.7 • 2q: 2.6	

Note: **FEF25–75** = forced expiratory flow between 25 and 75 percent of FVC; **FEV_1** = forced expiratory volume in 1 second; **FVC** = forced vital capacity.
[a]Limit of detection scores >1.5 are presented.

function. These genetic determinants may predispose family members to COPD, or they may only contribute to variation in pulmonary function within the normal range. Joost and colleagues (2002) analyzed linkage to quantitative spirometric measurements made before use of a bronchodilator in 1,578 persons from 330 pedigrees in the Framingham Heart Study. The largest linkage signal, which did not reach the criteria for genomewide significance, was on chromosome 6q for prebronchodilator FEV_1. The score of the logarithm of the odds (LOD) ratio, or likelihood ratio, was 2.4. In a subset of this study population, flanking short tandem repeat (STR) markers were genotyped to increase the information available for linkage analysis, and significant linkage of FEV_1 to chromosome 6q was identified with a maximum LOD score of 5.0 (Wilk et al. 2003b).

Wilk and colleagues (2003a) performed genomewide linkage analysis with prebronchodilator spirometric phenotypes in 2,178 participants in the NHLBI Family Heart Study, a population that partially overlapped that with the pedigrees from the Framingham Heart Study used by Joost and colleagues (2002). Even so, the linkage results differed substantially from those in the Framingham Heart Study. The most impressive signals suggested linkage of FEV_1 to chromosome 3q and FEV_1/FVC to chromosome 4p.

Finally, Malhotra and associates (2003) performed genomewide linkage analysis of quantitative prebronchodilator spirometric measurements in extended pedigrees. The findings suggested linkage of FEV_1/FVC values to chromosome 2q and to chromosome 5q but no linkage for either FEV_1 or FVC.

Chronic Obstructive Pulmonary Disease in Families

The Boston Early-Onset COPD Study includes extended pedigrees obtained through persons with severe early-onset COPD but without AAT deficiency. Genomewide linkage analysis has been performed with 585 members of 72 pedigrees involving early-onset COPD (Table 7.8). Initially, qualitative phenotypes of airflow obstruction and chronic bronchitis were analyzed, and no statistically significant or even suggestive regions of linkage were identified (Silverman et al. 2002a). Although limiting the sample to smokers only and genotyping of flanking STR markers identified several linkage regions of potential interest, linkage analysis of quantitative spirometric phenotypes provided more compelling evidence for linkage, especially with use of postbronchodilator spirometric values (Silverman et al. 2002b; Palmer et al. 2003). Findings suggested linkage of the postbronchodilator values of FEV_1 to chromosomes 8p (LOD = 3.30) and 1p (LOD = 2.24). Postbronchodilator FEV_1/FVC was also linked to multiple regions, most significantly to markers on chromosomes 2q (LOD = 4.42) and 1p (LOD = 2.52).

Genotyping additional STR markers and repeating linkage analysis of quantitative spirometric phenotypes provided stable-to-increased evidence for linkage on chromosomes 2q, 12p, and 19q (Celedón et al. 2004; DeMeo et al. 2004). Stratified linkage analysis of samples only from smokers also provided stable-to-increased evidence for linkage to these genomic regions. Findings suggested that genetic determinants in those regions confer increased risk for COPD because of a relationship between history of cigarette smoking and unidentified potential susceptibility genes.

Overall, the linkage results of quantitative spirometric measurements in the persons with pedigrees from the Boston Early-Onset COPD Study (Hersh et al. 2005) and samples from the general population have demonstrated only modest concordance. The most impressive linkage signals in the study have been obtained with postbronchodilator spirometric measures, which have not been used in the linkage studies of the general population. The Boston Early-Onset COPD Study demonstrated linkage of FEV_1/FVC to chromosome 2q. The suggestive linkages of FEV_1/FVC to chromosome 1p in the NHLBI Family Heart Study and the Boston Early-Onset COPD Study indicate a region that may influence spirometric measurements in both the general population and persons with COPD. One explanation for inconsistent linkage results in studies of COPD families and studies of pedigrees in the general population is that different genetic determinants could influence normal variation in spirometry and COPD. In addition, the lack of concordance among results from linkage studies in the general population could relate to genetic heterogeneity among study populations, false-positive evidence for linkage in some regions, or inadequate power of the study to replicate linkage signals.

Genetic Association with Chronic Obstructive Pulmonary Disease

A large number of studies to determine associations have assessed genetic variants in candidate genes hypothesized to be involved in the development of COPD. These were primarily case-control studies of patients with COPD and control groups. Candidate gene loci significantly associated with COPD in at least two studies are listed in Table 7.9. In addition to the *PI *M/*Z* genotype of AAT, which has been variably associated with COPD (Hersh et al. 2004), replicated associations have been demonstrated for genes of α1-antichymotrypsin (*SERPINA3*) (Poller et al. 1993; Sandford et al. 1998; Benetazzo et al. 1999; Ishii et al. 2000a), GSTM1 (*GSTM1*) (Baranova et al. 1997; Harrison et al. 1997; Yim et al. 2000; He et al. 2004), GSTP1 (*GSTP1*) (Ishii et al. 1999; Yim et al. 2002; He et al. 2004), vitamin D binding protein (*GC*) (Kauffmann et al. 1983; Horne et al. 1990; Schellenberg et al. 1998; Ishii et al. 2001; Sandford et al. 2001; Kasuga et al. 2003; Ito et al. 2004b), TGFβ1 (*TGFβ1*) (Celedón et al. 2004; Wu et al. 2004), TNF (*TNF*) (Huang et al. 1997; Higham et al. 2000; Ishii et al. 2000b; Patuzzo et al. 2000; Sakao et al. 2001;

Table 7.9   Replicated candidate gene associations in chronic obstructive pulmonary disease (COPD)

Study	Sample size	Genetic variants studied
α1-antitrypsin *PI *M/*Z* heterozygotes		
Hersh et al. 2004	>100 studies Meta-analysis	*PI *M/*Z* heterozygotes
TGF*β1*		
Celedon et al. 2004	585 persons in 72 pedigrees 304 cases vs. 441 controls	5 SNPs (including same exonic SNP)
Wu et al. 2004	165 cases vs. 146 blood donor controls 76 healthy smokers	1 exonic SNP
EPHX1		
Smith and Harrison 1997	68 COPD cases 94 emphysema cases vs. 203 blood donor controls	Exon 3 nonsynonymous SNP (slow) and Exon 4 nonsynonymous SNP (fast)
Takeyabu et al. 2000	79 emphysema cases vs. 58 smoking controls and 114 healthy controls	Exon 3 and 4 SNPs
Yim et al. 2000	83 cases vs. 76 smoking controls	Exon 3 and 4 SNPs
Yoshikawa et al. 2000	40 COPD cases and 140 controls among poison-gas workers	Exon 3 and 4 SNPs
Sandford et al. 2001	283 COPD persons with rapid FEV_1 decline vs. 308 COPD persons with slow FEV_1 decline in the U.S. Lung Health Study	Exon 3 and 4 SNPs
Hersh et al. 2005	949 persons in 127 pedigrees with early-onset COPD 304 cases vs. 441 smoking controls	8 SNPs including Exon 3 and 4 SNPs
TNFα		
Huang et al. 1997	42 cases vs. 42 smoking controls and 99 blood donor controls	1 promoter SNP at -308
Higham et al. 2000	86 cases vs. 63 smoking controls and 199 blood donor controls	-308 SNP
Ishii et al. 2000b	53 cases vs. 65 smoking controls	-308 SNP
Patuzzo et al. 2000	66 cases vs. 98 healthy controls and 45 cases of nonobstructive pulmonary disease	-308 SNP
Sakao et al. 2001	106 cases vs. 110 smoking controls and 129 blood donor controls	-308 SNP

Phenotype	Results/p value for association	Comments
α1-antitrypsin *PI *M/*Z* heterozygotes		
Presence or absence of COPD FEV$_1$ in persons with *PI *M/*Z* vs. *PI *M/*M* alleles	Typically positive Typically negative	No overall consensus on risk for lung disease in persons with *PI *M/*Z* alleles
TGFß1		
Families with early-onset COPD: qualitative and quantitative airflow obstruction phenotypes[a] Case/control: presence/absence of COPD	3 significant SNPs at p <0.05 (1 promoter and 2 in the 3′ genomic region) 3 significant SNPs at p <0.05 (2 promoter SNPs and 1 exonic SNP)	1 promoter SNP replicated in both study populations
Presence/absence of COPD	p ≤0.01 vs. both control groups	Exonic SNP replicated in both case-control studies but not in family-based study
EPHX1		
Presence/absence of COPD or emphysema	Significant associations of exon 3 SNP with emphysema group and of exon 4 SNP with COPD group	Several negative studies had small samples
Presence/absence of emphysema	No significant association	
Presence/absence of COPD	No significant association	
Presence/absence of COPD	No significant association	
Rapid vs. slow FEV$_1$ decline in persons with COPD	Significant association of exons 3 and 4 SNP haplotypes with rapid FEV$_1$ decline	
Families with early-onset COPD: quantitative and qualitative airflow obstruction phenotypes[a] Case/control: presence/absence of COPD	Significant association of exon 4 SNP only in case-control sample	
TNFα		
Presence/absence of COPD with chronic bronchitis	Significant association vs. both control groups (p <0.001)	Several studies with significant associations, but many negative studies; many studies had small sample sizes
Presence/absence of COPD	No significant association	
Presence/absence of COPD	No significant association	
Presence/absence of COPD	No significant association	
Presence/absence of COPD	Significant differences in allele frequencies in COPD cases vs. both control groups (p <0.01)	

Table 7.9   Continued

Study	Sample size	Genetic variants studied
Sandford et al. 2001	283 cases with rapid vs. 304 cases with slow FEV_1 decline U.S. Lung Health Study	-308 SNP
Kucukaycan et al. 2002	169 cases vs. 358 blood donor controls	4 SNPs including -308 and +489
Ferrarotti et al. 2003	63 cases vs. 86 smoking controls	-308 SNP
Hersh et al. 2005	949 members of 127 pedigrees with early-onset COPD and 304 cases vs. 441 smoking controls	5 SNPs including -308 and +489
	GSTM1	
Baranova et al. 1997	87 cases of severe chronic bronchitis vs. 102 cases of moderate chronic bronchitis vs. 172 smoking controls	Null variant
Harrison et al. 1997	111 lung cancer patients with emphysema vs. 57 without emphysema	Null variant (homozygous null vs. all others)
Yim et al. 2000	83 cases vs. 76 smoking controls	Null variant
He et al. 2004	544 persons with COPD and low FEV_1 vs. 554 with high FEV_1 U.S. Lung Health Study	Null variant
Hersh et al. 2005	Families with early-onset COPD: 949 persons in 127 pedigrees Case/control: 304 cases vs. 441 smoking controls	Null variant
	GSTP1	
Ishii et al. 1999	53 cases vs. 50 healthy controls	1 nonsynonymous SNP (*ILE105VAL*)
Yim et al. 2002	89 cases vs. 94 smoking controls	1 nonsynonymous SNP (*ILE105VAL*)
He et al. 2004	544 persons with COPD and low FEV_1 vs. 554 with high FEV_1 U.S. Lung Health Study	1 nonsynonymous SNP (*ILE105VAL*)
Hersh et al. 2005	949 members of 127 pedigrees with early-onset COPD and 304 cases vs. 441 smoking controls	2 nonsynonymous SNPs (*ILE105VAL* and *ALA114VAL*)

Phenotype	Results/p value for association	Comments
Rapid vs. slow FEV_1 decline in persons with COPD	No significant association	
Presence/absence of COPD	Significant association with +489 variant only	
Presence/absence of COPD with reduced $D_{L,CO}$	No significant association	
Families with early-onset COPD: quantitative and qualitative airflow obstruction phenotypes[a] Case/control: presence/absence of COPD	Significant associations with qualitative and quantitative airflow obstruction phenotypes with SNP -308 in COPD pedigrees only	
GSTM1		
Presence/absence of COPD	Higher null/null frequency in both cases of moderate and severe chronic bronchitis and severe chronic bronchitis vs. controls ($p < 0.001$)	
Presence/absence of emphysema in resected lung tissue	Significantly increased frequency of homozygosity for null variant in persons with emphysema ($p < 0.05$)	Only homozygosity for null variant was typically assessed
Presence/absence of COPD	No significant association	
High vs. low FEV_1 in persons with COPD	No significant association	
Families with early-onset COPD: qualitative and quantitative airflow obstruction phenotypes[a] Case/control: presence/absence of COPD	No significant association	
GSTP1		
Presence/absence of COPD	Homozygous *105ILE* more common in COPD cases	Several studies with significant associations, but different alleles, are associated at amino acid 105 SNP in different studies
Presence/absence of COPD	No significant association	
High vs. low FEV_1 in persons with COPD	Homozygous *105VAL* gene more common in low FEV_1 group	
Families with early-onset COPD: qualitative and quantitative airflow obstruction phenotypes[a] Case/control: presence/absence of COPD	Borderline higher frequency of *105VAL* allele in case-control analysis only	

Table 7.9   Continued

Study	Sample size	Genetic variants studied
	SFTPB	
Guo et al. 2001	97 cases vs. 82 smoking controls	4 SNPs, 1 promoter, and 3 intragenic indels
Seifart et al. 2002	118 cases vs. 118 matched controls and 110 population-based controls	SP-B *INTRON 4* indels
Hersh et al. 2005	949 members of 127 pedigrees with early-onset COPD and 304 cases vs. 441 smoking controls	1 nonsynonymous SNP (*THR131IL3*) and 1 short tandem repeat
	α1-antichymotrypsin	
Poller et al. 1993	100 COPD cases vs. 100 controls	2 nonsynonymous SNPs: *PRO229ALA* and *LEU55PRO*
Sandford et al. 1998	168 COPD cases vs. 61 controls	*PRO229ALA* and *LEU55PRO*
Benetazzo et al. 1999	66 COPD cases vs. 45 controls with nonobstructive pulmonary disease and 98 healthy volunteers	4 coding SNPs (*THR15ALA*, *LEU55PRO*, *PRO229ALA*, and *MET389VAL*) and 1 indel (*1258DELAA*)
Ishii et al. 2000a	53 COPD cases vs. 65 controls	2 coding SNPs in protein (*PRO229ALA* and *LEU55PRO*) and 1 coding SNP in signal peptide (*ALA15THR*)
Hersh et al. 2005	949 members of 127 pedigrees with early-onset COPD and 304 cases vs. 441 smoking controls	*ALA15THR*, *LEU55PRO*, and *PRO229ALA* polymorphisms
	Vitamin D binding protein (group-specific component [*GC*])	
Kauffmann et al. 1983	43 lifetime nonsmokers with low FEV_1 vs. 45 heavy smokers with high FEV_1	*GC*1S/F* and *GC*2* alleles
Horne et al. 1990	104 COPD cases vs. 413 controls	GC phenotype by isoelectric focusing
Schellenberg et al. 1998	75 COPD cases vs. 64 smoking controls	SNPs *THR420LYS* (*GC*2*) and *ASP416GLU* (*GC*1S*)
Ishii et al. 2001	63 COPD cases vs. 82 controls	*GC*1F/*1S* and *GC*2* alleles
Sandford et al. 2001	283 persons with COPD with rapid FEV_1 decline vs. 308 persons with COPD with slow FEV_1 decline	*THR420LYS* and *ASP416GLU* polymorphisms
Kasuga et al. 2003	537 persons with COPD with high FEV_1 vs. 533 with low FEV_1 U.S. Lung Health Study	*GC** haplotypes
Ito et al. 2004b	103 COPD cases vs. 88 smoking controls	*GC*1S/*1F* and *GC*2*

Phenotype	Results/p value for association	Comments
	SFTPB	
Presence/absence of COPD	Significant association with SNP at +1580 (p <0.05)	
Presence/absence of COPD and COPD severity	*INTRON 4* variants significantly associated (p <0.05) with respiratory failure subgroup	
Families with early-onset COPD: quantitative and qualitative airflow obstruction phenotypes[a] Case/control: presence/absence of COPD	Significant SNP association with moderate-to-severe airflow obstruction (p <0.05) Significant SNP association only with gene-x-smoking interaction term (p <0.01)	
	α1-antichymotrypsin	
Presence/absence of COPD	Significant SNP association (p <0.05) with *PRO229ALA*	No studies replicated associations of the same genetic variants
Presence/absence of COPD	No significant association	
Presence/absence of COPD	No significant association	
Presence/absence of COPD	Significant SNP association with *ALA15THR* only	
Families with early-onset COPD: quantitative and qualitative airflow obstruction phenotypes[a] Case/control: presence/absence of COPD	No significant association	
	Vitamin D binding protein (group-specific component [GC])	
Presence/absence of COPD	No significant association	
Presence/absence of COPD	Significant association with inferred *GC** allele (p <0.01)	
Presence/absence of COPD	Significant protection against COPD with *GC*2/GC*2* genotype	
Presence/absence of COPD	Significantly increased frequency of *GC*1F* allele in COPD cases	
Rapid vs. slow FEV_1 decline in COPD cases	No significant association	
High vs. low FEV_1 among COPD cases	No significant association	
Presence/absence of COPD	Significantly increased frequency of *GC*1F* allele in COPD cases	

Table 7.9   Continued

Study	Sample size	Genetic variants studied
Hersh et al. 2005	949 members of 127 pedigrees with early-onset COPD and 304 cases vs. 441 smoking controls	*THR420LYS* and *ASP416GLU*

Note: $D_{L,CO}$ = diffusing capacity of the lung for carbon monoxide; **FEV$_1$** = forced expiratory volume in 1 second; **FVC** = forced vital capacity; **indel** = DNA mutation; **PI** = protease inhibitor; **SNP** = single nucleotide polymorphism; **SP-B** = surfactant protein B.
[a]In families with early-onset COPD, quantitative spirometric phenotypes included FEV$_1$/FVC before and after use of a bronchodilator; qualitative phenotypes included mild-to-severe airflow obstruction (FEV$_1$ <80% predicted with FEV$_1$/FVC <90% predicted) and moderate-to-severe airflow obstruction (FEV$_1$ <60% predicted with FEV$_1$/FVC <90% predicted).

Sandford et al. 2001; Küçükaycan et al. 2002; Ferrarotti et al. 2003), surfactant protein B (*SFTPB*) (Guo et al. 2001; Seifart et al. 2002; Hersh et al. 2005), and microsomal epoxide hydrolase (*EPHX1*) (Smith and Harrison 1997; Takeyabu et al. 2000; Yim et al. 2000; Yoshikawa et al. 2000; Sandford et al. 2001). Although at least two studies support an association of a genetic variant with COPD in these candidate genes, every case also has at least one negative study.

Several factors could contribute to the inconsistent results from case-control studies of genetic association with COPD. Genetic heterogeneity in different populations could contribute to difficulty in replicating associations between studies, and false-positive or false-negative results could contribute to inconsistent replication. A potentially important factor is that case-control studies of association are susceptible to supporting associations based only on population stratification; that is, they reflect differences between populations rather than true associations (Freedman et al. 2004). Population stratification can result from incomplete matching between cases and controls, which might include failure to account for differences in ethnicity and geographic origin that may affect the results. In addition, most published studies on genetic associations of COPD have not focused on genomic regions linked to COPD-related phenotypes, regions in which association studies may be more fruitful.

As of 2008, only one study, a linkage analysis of family-based genetic association for COPD, has been reported (Celedón et al. 2004). The design of the study is typically not vulnerable to effects of population stratification. The study focused on genetic variants in *TGFβ1*, a gene that is located within the region of linkage to FEV$_1$ on chromosome 19q in the Boston Early-Onset COPD Study and that was associated with COPD in another case-control study of genetic association (Wu et al. 2004). Five *TGFβ1* single nucleotide polymorphisms (SNPs) were genotyped in families in the Boston Early-Onset COPD Study. Family-based

association analysis showed that one SNP in the promoter region of *TGFβ1* (*RS2241712*) and two SNPs in the 3′ untranslated region of *TGFβ1* (*RS2241718* and *RS6957*) were significantly associated with FEV$_1$ (p <0.05). Among 304 case patients with severe COPD from the National Emphysema Treatment Trial and 441 smokers in the control group from the Normative Aging Study, two SNPs in the promoter region of *TGFβ1* (*RS2241712* and *RS1800469*) and one SNP in exon 1 of *TGFβ1* (*RS1982073*) were significantly associated with COPD (p ≤0.02) (Celedón et al. 2004). Additional research to replicate the genetic associations in *TGFβ1* and identify the functional variants in or near *TGFβ1* is required.

A variety of candidate genes have been examined in genetic association studies focused on COPD, but no genetic loci other than the *SERPINA1* gene for severe AAT deficiency proved to be significant risk factors for COPD.

Mouse Models of Genetics for Chronic Obstructive Pulmonary Disease

Although rodent models have provided important insights into the potential biochemical mechanisms of COPD, there has been no publication of research using quantitive trait locus mapping to identify susceptibility loci through experimental crosses of relatively susceptible and relatively nonsusceptible strains. Significant differences between murine strains in susceptibility to the development of smoking-induced COPD have been demonstrated (Guerassimov et al. 2004), and use of these strain-specific differences to perform quantitative trait locus mapping may provide unique opportunities to uncover genetic determinants of COPD (Shapiro et al. 2004).

Phenotype	Results/p value for association	Comments
Families with early-onset COPD: quantitative and qualitative airflow obstruction phenotypes[a] Case/control: presence/absence of COPD	No significant association	

Summary

Severe AAT deficiency is a proven genetic risk factor for COPD. Although considerable insight into the pathogenesis of COPD has been provided by studies of AAT deficiency, fundamental questions about the natural history of this deficiency remain unanswered.

Only a small percentage of patients with COPD inherit severe AAT deficiency, and additional genetic factors likely influence the development of the disorder. Further efforts in linkage analysis, association studies, and research on animal models may lead to identification of such factors. To achieve a complete understanding of COPD pathophysiology, characterization of the interactions among genetic determinants, cigarette smoking, and possibly other environmental factors is required. Identification of genetic factors influencing the development of COPD unrelated to AAT deficiency could elucidate the biochemical mechanisms causing COPD, allow identification of more susceptible persons, and lead to new therapeutic interventions as pathways of injury are better characterized.

Pathogenesis of Emphysema

Sources of Information

The information on pathogenesis of emphysema discussed here was obtained from original research articles, most published since the early 1990s. These articles were found by consulting reviews of the literature (Pardo and Selman 1999; Mahadeva and Shapiro 2002; Barnes et al. 2003; Tuder et al. 2003a; Barnes 2004b; MacNee 2005b) and by searching the Internet with use of a variety of terms relevant to the pathogenesis of emphysema. The review includes citations through June 2005.

In reviewing the literature, special attention was paid to reports that distinguished between "emphysema" and the all-encompassing term "chronic obstructive pulmonary disease." In recent years this distinction has been made by using chest CT and microscopy of lung tissue.

Introduction

One long-accepted definition of emphysema is "a condition of the lung characterized by abnormal, permanent enlargement of air spaces distal to the terminal bronchiole, accompanied by destruction of their walls, and without obvious fibrosis" (Snider et al. 1985, p. 183). This definition emphasizes the loss of alveolar tissue. However, in emphysema induced by tobacco smoke, the lung tissue exhibits active synthesis of extracellular matrix (Lang et al. 1994; Wright and Churg 1995; Vlahovic et al. 1999), apoptosis, and proliferation of alveolar cells (Calabrese et al. 2005). Accordingly, emphysematous lung tissue should be viewed as undergoing remodeling rather than simply resulting from a destructive process.

The current model of the pathogenesis of emphysema, which involves diverse processes of varying importance, is summarized in Figure 7.18. In this pathogenetic

Figure 7.18   Pathogenesis of smoking-induced pulmonary emphysema

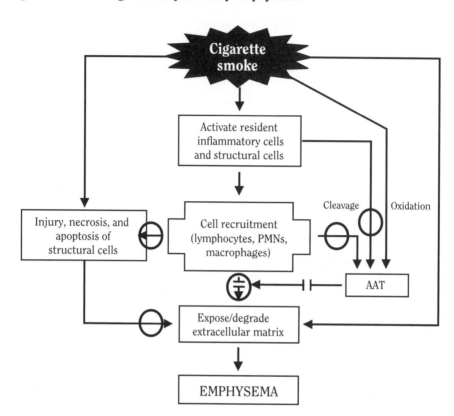

Note: Three pathways for pathogenesis are shown. The circles indicate steps in which proteases are or may be involved. (1) Smoke components recruit inflammatory cells to the lower respiratory system via factors released from alveolar macrophages and structural cells of the lungs. Recruited cells, macrophages, and structural cells release proteases and reactive oxygen species that degrade the extracellular matrix of the respiratory tissues. (2) Smoke components directly affect viability of lung cells, leading to liberation of proteases that can degrade lung matrix. (3) Smoke components may disrupt the function of protease inhibitors such as α1-antitrypsin, facilitating the activity of proteases. **AAT** = α1-antitrypsin; **PMNs** = polymorphonuclear neutrophils.

scheme, accumulation of inflammatory cells in the peripheral tissues of smokers' lungs appears to be pivotal (Finkelstein et al. 1995; Abboud et al. 1998), and proteases from inflammatory cells have multiple potential roles in causing injury.

Inflammatory cells linked to the development of emphysema include neutrophils, macrophages, and lymphocytes. How inflammatory cells are first recruited and activated in response to smoking remains incompletely understood, but the inflammatory process, once initiated, can persist for years after smoking has stopped. Thus, emphysematous tissues from transplant surgery and surgery to reduce lung volume show large numbers of inflammatory cells, even among persons who stopped smoking long before the surgery (Retamales et al. 2001; Shapiro 2001). In addition, some evidence from serial chest CT examinations indicates that emphysema also progresses

after the cessation of smoking (Soejima et al. 2000). Products of neutrophils and macrophages can degrade extracellular matrix, inactivate PIs, and convert proenzymes to their active matrix-degrading form.

The role of lymphocytes in emphysema has been a topic of research over the past decade (Finkelstein et al. 1995; Cosio et al. 2002; Boschetto et al. 2003), and findings indicate that T-cell factors can induce macrophages to express proteases (Grumelli et al. 2004). ROS, both in cigarette smoke and released by inflammatory cells or epithelial cells, impinge on protease-antiprotease balance in the lungs in multiple ways, including inactivation of AAT, increased expression of chemokines such as IL-8, activation of MMPs, and induction of the transcription of NF-κB, leading to increased expression of MMPs (MacNee 2005b).

Three discoveries in the 1960s linked elastases to emphysema: (1) association between early-age onset of emphysema and deficiency of AAT (Eriksson 1965); (2) production of emphysema in experimental animals by putting elastolytic proteases, such as papain, directly into the lung (Gross et al. 1965); and (3) demonstration that neutrophils contain and release a potent elastolytic enzyme (Janoff and Scherer 1968). Together, these discoveries led to formulation of the "elastase-antielastase" hypothesis for the pathogenesis of emphysema. This hypothesis posits development of emphysema in response to unchecked intrapulmonary activity of neutrophil elastase due to an excess of inflammatory cells, a deficiency of intrapulmonary elastase inhibition, or a combination of increased elastolytic burden and decreased elastase inhibitory capacity. This hypothesis remains tenable, but it does not incorporate more recent data indicating that

(1) MMPs, including collagenases from inflammatory cells and lung structural cells (Table 7.10) (Foronjy and D'Armiento 2001), are associated with emphysema and (2) the destruction of alveolar walls in emphysema may begin with death of alveolar cells rather than with degradation of the alveolar extracellular matrix (Kasahara et al. 2001; Aoshiba et al. 2003b; Tuder et al. 2003b).

Proteases

Data from Human Studies

Several types of data link proteases to the causation of emphysema in humans: (1) assays of proteolytic

Table 7.10   Matrix metalloproteinases in emphysema

Study	Emphysema detection	Test samples	Observations	Comments
Finlay et al. 1997a	Computed tomography	AM mRNA and culture media	• Increased collagenase 1 (MMP-1) • Increased gelatinase B (MMP-9)	No increase in expression of macrophage elastase (MMP-12)
Finlay et al. 1997b	Computed tomography	BAL fluid	• Increased collagenase activity • Increased gelatinase B (MMP-9)	MMPs probably neutrophil derived
Ohnishi et al. 1998	Histology	Lung tissue from LVRS	• Increased MT-MMP-1 (MMP-14) • Increased gelatinase A (MMP-2)	No increase in expression of macrophage elastase (MMP-12)
Betsuyaku et al. 1999	Computed tomography	BAL fluid and AM culture media	• Increased collagenase 2 (MMP-8) • Increased gelatinase B (MMP-9)	MMPs in BAL fluid from inflammatory cells; no increase in gelatinase B (MMP-9) in AM culture media in emphysema
Segura-Valdez et al. 2000	Histology	Lung tissue from autopsy and LVRS; BAL fluid	• Increased collagenases 1, 2, 3 (MMP-1, -8, -13) • Increased gelatinases A, B (MMP-2, -9)	MMPs expressed by both inflammatory cells and structural cells of lung
Imai et al. 2001	Histology	Lung tissue from lung transplantation and LVRS	• Increased collagenase 1 (MMP-1)	Collagenase expressed by type II cells; no increase in expression of macrophage elastase (MMP-12)
Minematsu et al. 2001	Computed tomography	Cellular DNA	• Increased gelatinase B (MMP-9) polymorphism in smokers with emphysema	Polymorphism also associated with increased incidence of coronary atherosclerosis

Source: Adapted from Hogg and Senior 2002 with permission from BMJ Publishing Group Ltd., © 2002.
Note: **AM** = alveolar macrophage; **BAL** = bronchoalveolar lavage; **LVRS** = lung volume reduction surgery; **MMP** = matrix metalloproteinase; **mRNA** = messenger RNA; **MT** = membrane type.

activity and protease content in BAL fluid; (2) measurements of protease proteins, proteolytic activities, and protease mRNAs associated with alveolar macrophages from emphysematous lung; (3) immunostains of proteases in emphysematous tissue; and (4) determinations of protease mRNAs in lung tissue. The association between AAT deficiency and emphysema is perhaps the strongest evidence (*American Journal of Respiratory and Critical Care Medicine* 2003).

Bronchoalveolar Lavage

The BAL technique samples cells and mediators from the lower respiratory tract, but in COPD the volumes of lavage recovered are often low (Linden et al. 1993; Soler et al. 1999), and the presence of emphysema adversely influences the recovery of BAL fluid (Löfdahl et al. 2005). In one study of patients with COPD who were scored for emphysema by chest CT, patients with high scores had recoveries of fluid less than one-half the volume for those with low scores.

Numerous studies have examined proteases in BAL fluid. In studies with evaluation for emphysema, it appears that protease levels were higher in some persons with emphysema than they were in control groups (Muley et al. 1994; Yoshioka et al. 1995; Betsuyaku et al. 1995, 1996, 1999, 2002, 2003; Finlay et al. 1997a,b; Abboud et al. 1998; Takeyabu et al. 1998). The proteases included elastase, both free and in complex with AAT; MMP-1, -8, -9, -12, and -14; and cysteine proteases. However, interpretation of these data is limited by three considerations: (1) although emphysema is documented by CT, quantification of the emphysema is not reported in most studies; (2) studies do not always explicitly state whether persons with emphysema are current smokers; and (3) some control groups included nonsmokers and smokers. Regardless of these problems, the presence of emphysema is associated with no more than modest, approximately twofold, increases in proteases.

Numerous factors are known to regulate MMPs, a class of proteases increasingly implicated in emphysema, but few studies have assessed the expression of MMP regulatory factors in the context of emphysema. In one study, levels of the extracellular MMP inducer, basigin, a transmembrane protein that stimulates production of several MMPs, were much higher in BAL fluid from current and former smokers than from those who never smoked (Betsuyaku et al. 2003). Among smokers, however, levels did not differ for persons with or without emphysema.

Alveolar Macrophages

Alveolar macrophages appear to have a central role in orchestrating inflammation in COPD through production of cytokines, chemokines, and ROS, in addition to being a source of proteases and PIs (Barnes 2004a; Shapiro 2005). However, few studies have focused on macrophages from lungs with documented emphysema (Muley et al. 1994; Betsuyaku et al. 1995; Finlay et al. 1997b), and in these studies the measurements have been from macrophages that have been in culture, making the relevance of the findings to the in vivo state unclear. Despite these caveats, studies of emphysema suggest an increase in alveolar macrophage mRNA for MMP-1 (collagenase 1) and MMP-9 (gelatinase B) (Finlay et al. 1997a; Betsuyaku et al. 1999). Regardless of the presence of emphysema, however, alveolar macrophages from smokers express more MMP-9, an elastolytic protease, than do those from nonsmokers (Russell et al. 2002a). MMPs appear to account for most of the elastolytic activity released from alveolar macrophages of persons with COPD (Russell et al. 2002b). MMP-12, a protease strongly implicated in smoke-induced emphysema in mice (Hautamaki et al. 1997), was more recently found to be increased in macrophages of persons with COPD (Molet et al. 2005). The role of current smoking is not clear in this observation, however, and diagnosis of emphysema was not documented in the study.

Promising techniques are becoming available for analysis of the products of alveolar macrophages in association with smoking, COPD, and emphysema (Koike et al. 2002; Wu et al. 2005). Considering that most of the macrophages within the lungs are associated with tissue, analysis of alveolar macrophages harvested by BAL may not represent all the phenotypes of macrophages in the lung. Laser-capture microdissection of pulmonary macrophages from histological lung sections is a method for procuring macrophages within the tissue, as well as in alveolar spaces (Fuke et al. 2004), and future use of this approach is expected to provide much more data on macrophage proteases in the context of emphysema.

Studies of Lung Tissue

Immunohistochemistry. Studies of emphysematous lung tissue support the hypothesis that proteases are involved in the pathogenic process. With use of antibody to human elastin, several types of abnormalities of elastic fiber were found in the lungs of persons with emphysema, including fragmented elastic fibers in AAT deficiency and poorly formed elastic fibers and clumps of elastin in smokers with centriacinar emphysema (Fukuda et al. 1989). The clumps appear to be from synthesis of new aberrant elastin, resembling changes observed in experimental elastase-induced emphysema (Kuhn et al. 1976). In lungs confirmed to have emphysema, alveolar macrophages, interstitial cells, and epithelial cells express immunore-active MMP-1 and MMP-2 (gelatinase A) (Segura-Valdez et al. 2000). Structural cells in emphysematous lungs express MMP-1 (Imai et al. 2001) and MMP-14 (membrane-type 1 MMP [MT1-MMP]) (Ohnishi et al. 1998).

Gene profiling. Gene profiling of emphysematous lung tissue has found only limited changes in proteases and PIs in comparisons with control lung tissue (Golpon et al. 2004; Ning et al. 2004; Spira et al. 2004). However, these data represent small numbers of lungs, and estimates of emphysema by chest CT or morphometry of fixed lung have not been uniformly provided. Also, the tissue analyzed has not always been limited to alveolar parenchyma. Gene profiling does not quantify neutrophil proteases and circulating PIs produced at sites other than the lungs.

Direct effects of cigarette smoke. Cigarette smoke has long been thought to induce protease expression in the lungs indirectly through cytokines (Churg et al. 2002, 2004), but smoke may act directly on structural cells of the lungs to induce protease expression. In response to exposure to smoke, human small airway epithelial cells (Mercer et al. 2004) and human lung fibroblasts (Kim et al. 2004) in culture increased expression of MMP-1 without a concomitant increase in the expression of tissue inhibitor of metalloproteinase (TIMP)-1. In some studies, cytokines enhanced the direct effects of smoke (Mercer et al. 2004).

Biomarkers of Protease Involvement in Emphysema

As noted previously, elastic fibers in emphysematous lung tissue show disruptions and fenestrations of the elastin (Fukuda et al. 1989; Finlay et al. 1996) that suggest degradative events (see "Studies of Lung Tissue" earlier in this chapter). Elastin-derived peptides (desmosines) in plasma, serum, and BAL fluid are markers of elastin breakdown. A number of desmosine assays have been devised, and a highly sensitive, precise assay method (Ma et al. 2003) has been applied in studies of AAT supplementation therapy (Stolk et al. 2005). Increased urinary desmosines have been reported in smokers (Stone et al. 1995) and in persons who had rapid declines in FEV_1 (Gottlieb et al. 1996), but the presence of emphysema was not determined. Similarly, levels of elastin-derived peptides found in BAL fluid from current smokers were higher than those from former smokers and lifetime nonsmokers, regardless of associated mild COPD or emphysema (Betsuyaku et al. 1996).

Therapy to Control Proteases

The most direct antiprotease therapy for control of emphysema is supplementation with AAT for patients with severe AAT deficiency (*American Journal of Respiratory and Critical Care Medicine* 2003). Usually given intravenously once a week, this therapy appears to slow the rate of decline in FEV_1, reduce the number of lung infections, enhance survival, and reduce lung inflammation as measured by sputum markers, although the optimal dose is still under study (Stoller and Aboussouan 2004; Stolk et al. 2005). In patients with moderate-to-advanced emphysema who are not AAT deficient, oral all-*trans* retinoic acid lowered plasma levels of MMP-9 and release of MMP-9 from alveolar macrophages without affecting levels of TIMP-1, so the balance of protease activity appeared to shift toward protease inhibition (Mao et al. 2003). Whether these effects translate into a therapeutic benefit for emphysema is uncertain.

Data from Animal Models

By incorporating measurements and experimental designs that are not possible in human studies, animal models have improved understanding of the role of proteases in emphysema and are useful in evaluating agents for antiprotease therapy in patients with emphysema (Hele 2002; Voelkel 2004).

Most recent models of emphysema have used mice. These animals provide the convenience of genetic manipulation, and findings indicate that humans and mice may have shared susceptibility factors for exposure to smoke (Shapiro et al. 2004). Emphysema can be induced in normal mice with cigarette smoke (Hautamaki et al. 1997) but significant differences in susceptibility exist among strains (Cavarra et al. 2001a; Guerassimov et al. 2004). By genetic manipulation, emphysema can be induced in resistant strains. For example, mice deficient in Nrf2, a transcription factor for antioxidant and detoxifying genes, develop emphysema in response to smoke, even though their ICR strain is normally resistant to the effect of smoke (Rangasamy et al. 2004). Overexpression of certain proteins in the lung (e.g., IL-13) can lead to emphysema without exposure to an exogenous factor (Table 7.11) (Zheng et al. 2000). However, deleting the expression of certain proteins, such as surfactant protein D (Wert et al. 2000) and TIMP-3 (Leco et al. 2001), in the lungs can also lead to the development of emphysema. Inflammation is a common feature of these and other models, but inflammation does not appear to be required in all models. Emphysema induced by an *MMP-1* transgene (D'Armiento et al. 1992) or by severe caloric restriction (Massaro and Massaro 2004) occurs without overt inflammation.

Although enlarged terminal air spaces are the hallmark of emphysema, it is important to distinguish between enlargement attributable to faulty alveolar formation during development and that occurring after normal

Table 7.11   Mouse models of overexpression of a protein leading to emphysema

Study	Mediator	Promoter	Lung pathology	Mechanism
D'Armiento et al. 1992	Human interstitial collagenase (MMP-1)	Haptoglobulin	Disruption of alveolar walls and coalescence of alveolar spaces	Degradation of collagen by collagenase
Wang et al. 2000	Interferon-gamma	CC10-rtTA	Emphysema with alveolar enlargement, enhanced lung volumes, and enhanced pulmonary compliance	Increased macrophages and neutrophils in BAL fluid; decreased secretory leukocyte proteinase inhibitor; increased MMP-9 and -12 and cathepsins B, D, H, L, and S
Zheng et al. 2000	Interleukin-13	CC10-rtTA	Emphysema with enhanced lung volumes and compliance, mucus metaplasia, and inflammation	Increased MMP-2, -9, -12, -13, and -14 and cathepsins B, H, K, L, and S; treatment with MMP or cysteine proteinase antagonists significantly decreased emphysema and inflammation but not mucus

Source: Adapted from Mahadeva and Shapiro 2002 with permission from BMJ Publishing Group Ltd., © 2002.
Note: **BAL** = bronchoalveolar lavage; **CC10-rtTA** = clara cell 10-kDa protein promoter-reversible tetracycline transactivator; **MMP** = matrix metalloproteinase.

lung development. Thus, models of enlargement in which alveolar development is abnormal, such as in MT1-MMP deficiency (Atkinson et al. 2005), may not be relevant to human emphysema associated with smoking, in which the presumption is that the lung was previously normal.

Despite strong evidence implicating elastases in the pathogenesis of emphysema, research findings beginning in 1992 (D'Armiento et al. 1992) indicate that collagenolytic enzymes that do not degrade elastin may also be involved in the pathogenesis of emphysema. The key discovery was the finding of emphysema in mice engineered to harbor a transgene consisting of a haptoglobin promoter linked to the human *MMP-1* (interstitial collagenase) gene. These mice show expression of the *Mmp-1* gene in lung tissue, enlarged air spaces, bullous lesions, and reduced collagen fibers in alveolar walls and pleura. Depending on the level of transgene expression, the lung lesions can start either soon after birth or later, indicating that the emphysema is clearly postdevelopmental (Foronjy et al. 2003). Apart from demonstrating that collagenase activity could lead to emphysema, results with these mice also suggest two conclusions: (1) lung inflammation was minimal, indicating that proteases causing emphysema could come from structural cells of the lungs; and (2) the elastic fibers in the lung showed minimal inflammation, indicating that emphysema can occur without obvious disruption and resynthesis of elastic fibers.

Models of Emphysema Involving Cigarette Smoke

Model systems for exposing mice to cigarette smoke to produce emphysema vary in the cigarettes used, the manner in which cigarette smoke is delivered, and assessment of the dose of smoke actually reaching the animals. Standard research cigarettes are commonly used, and the exposure is produced by directing smoke from a single cigarette to the nose of a mouse restrained in a single-body compartment or by exposing groups of mice that are free to move in a chamber in which cigarette smoke is put into the atmosphere. The intensity of exposure to smoke, if monitored, is typically indexed by the level of carboxyhemoglobin in the blood (Wright and Churg 1995). The smoking regimens usually require nearly daily exposures for months to achieve emphysema.

As noted previously, strains of mice can exhibit extremely different susceptibility to the development of emphysema from smoke inhalation (see "Susceptible Animal Models" earlier in this chapter). These differences in susceptibility are matched by differences in the accumulation of lymphocytes and neutrophils in the lung tissue. Higher numbers of these cell types in the tissue is associated with emphysema.

For four decades, elastases have been foremost in pathogenetic schemes linking proteases to the pathogenesis of emphysema, and in recent years, the importance of elastases has been supported in studies involving mice with deficiencies of macrophage elastase (Hautamaki et al. 1997) or neutrophil elastase (Shapiro et al. 2003). Mice with no macrophage elastase have virtually complete protection from smoke-induced emphysema; mice without neutrophil elastase have approximately 70 percent protection. The finding that a "knockout" of either of these elastolytic enzymes is protective indicates interplay between these enzymes in the pathogenesis of emphysema. The evidence suggests that neutrophil elastase is the principal culprit in matrix degradation and that macrophage elastase acts, at least partly, as a proinflammatory agent by facilitating release of TNFα (Churg et al. 2004) and as a shield for neutrophil elastase by the capacity to cleave AAT.

Although overexpression of collagenase, as described above, has been associated with emphysema, studies have performed only limited assessment of collagenase expression in response to smoke. In guinea pigs exposed to smoke, collagenase mRNA and protein were found in alveolar macrophages and structural cells of the lungs coincident with decreased lung collagen and enlarged air spaces (Selman et al. 1996).

Antiprotease Therapy for Experimental Smoke-Induced Emphysema

As noted previously, studies of gene disruption have shown that inactivating the genes for MMP-12 (Hautamaki et al. 1997) or neutrophil elastase (Shapiro et al. 2003) provides major protection against the development of emphysema from cigarette smoke (see "Alveolar Macrophages" earlier in this chapter). Similarly, PIs against

MMPs or neutrophil elastase have proved effective in mice, in limiting the enlargement of air spaces associated with exposure to cigarette smoke (Table 7.12). Various routes of administration have been tried; ilomastat, a broad-spectrum MMP inhibitor, produced highly significant protection when inhaled (Pemberton et al. 2005). These studies consistently show that compounds protecting against emphysema also produce a concurrent reduction of the typical inflammatory response to exposure to smoke. Accordingly, PIs should be regarded as anti-inflammatory agents, as well as antiproteases.

Apoptosis

In contrast to findings in the lungs of nonsmokers, apoptotic epithelial cells are identifiable in the lungs of smokers (Segura-Valdez et al. 2000; Kasahara et al. 2001; Calabrese et al. 2005), and they are found in isolated alveolar macrophages subjected to cigarette smoke in vitro (Aoshiba et al. 2001a). The apoptotic cell types include alveolar macrophages and lung structural cells. Apoptosis, proteases, and emphysema were linked when emphysema developed within six hours after the protease CASPASE-3 was instilled into the lungs of mice (Aoshiba et al. 2003b). Apoptosis and emphysema have also been produced by intrapulmonary instillation of VEGF receptor blockers (Kasahara et al. 2000) and by producing a temporary reduction in lung VEGF by intratracheal administration of an adeno-associated CRE recombinase virus to mice that have a floxed VEGF (Tang et al. 2004). The mechanisms by which apoptosis leads to emphysema are still not well

Table 7.12   Effects of protease inhibitors in experimental smoke-induced emphysema

Study	Animal	Drug/route/frequency	Smoking protocol	Protection against emphysema[a]
Wright et al. 2002	Guinea pig	ZD0892 Oral Twice a day	5 cigarettes/day 5 days/week	45% (6 months)
Churg et al. 2003	Mouse	AAT Intraparenteral 48-hour intervals	2 cigarettes/day 5 days/week	63% (6 months)
Selman et al. 2003	Guinea pig	CP-471,474 Subcutaneous Once a day	Group smoke chamber 5 days/week	30% (4 months)
Pemberton et al. 2005	Mouse	Ilomastat Aerosol Daily	2 cigarettes/day 6 days/week	96% (6 months)

Note: **AAT** = α1-antitrypsin.
[a]Graded by air space enlargement in comparison of animals exposed to tobacco smoke with unexposed animals.

understood. In the CASPASE-3 study (Aoshiba et al. 2003b), elastase activity was found in BAL fluid, and induction of apoptosis of alveolar type II cells in culture resulted in liberation of elastin peptides from an elastin substrate culture medium. Accordingly, in this model, apoptosis appears to induce emphysema by causing proteolytic degradation of extracellular matrix.

Summary

Since its inception about 40 years ago, the protease-antiprotease hypothesis of emphysema pathogenesis has gained increasing support from studies in persons with emphysema and from those using animal models of emphysema. The high risk of emphysema among persons with AAT deficiency, particularly current smokers, continues to be compelling evidence for the linking of smoking and neutrophil elastase to emphysema. However, other proteases, particularly certain MMPs, appear to be involved in emphysema. Success in protecting mice from smoke-induced emphysema through genetic manipulations of proteases or by treatment with PIs has reinforced the protease-antiprotease hypothesis. For many years, the hypothesis specifically focused on elastase-antielastase imbalance and inflammatory cells infiltrating the lung as the source of proteases. These ideas have been modified in recent years to encompass discoveries that collagenolytic activity may produce emphysema and that structural cells of the lungs may contribute to the protease burden of the lung. Despite great progress, much more needs to be known about the proteolytic mechanisms involved in the pathogenesis of emphysema, such as the role of immune cells in protease regulation in emphysema and the effects of proteases on structural cells of the lungs. New techniques for analyzing biologic materials, combined with the capacity to document and quantify emphysema noninvasively, offer promise for better understanding of the role of proteases in emphysema in the years ahead.

Summary

COPD is a rising cause of morbidity and mortality in the United States and elsewhere. Smoking has long been causally linked to COPD, and decades of clinical and experimental research have provided insights into the mechanisms underlying this causal linkage. The extensive evidence reviewed in this chapter highlights the critical role of oxidative injury, driven by the high level of ROS in cigarette smoke. COPD is the only disease caused by cigarette smoking that is associated with genetic mutations leading to AAT deficiency. This genetic association led to the protease-antiprotease hypothesis on the pathogenesis of emphysema that is now well supported by work in animal models. The ROS in cigarette smoke and secondarily released by epithelial and inflammatory cells can unfavorably tip the protease-antiprotease scale in multiple ways. Although these mechanisms are now well characterized, the factors leading to COPD in the minority of affected smokers are not completely understood.

Evidence Summary

This chapter addresses mechanisms of lung injury by tobacco smoke that lead to development of COPD and considers the role of genetic factors, including specific genes, in increasing risk for COPD. The chapter acknowledges that COPD is a broad phenotypic designation with underlying damage and structural changes in the lung's airways and alveoli. This section systematically evaluates the evidence related to genetic susceptibility and to the two major mechanisms of injury considered: oxidative stress and protease-antiprotease imbalance.

Oxidative Stress

Cigarette smoke contains massive quantities of free radicals in its gas and tar phases; concentrations of free radicals are 10^{15} per puff and 10^{17} per gram, respectively. The approximately 200 or more puffs inhaled daily by a typical smoker of one pack per day would lead to a sustained high-level daily dose of free radicals. The chemical pathways by which these free radicals produce damaging ROS have been well characterized, as have the chemical reactions by which ROS damage target molecules, including lipids, proteins, and DNA. The plausibility of oxidative stress as a mechanism of disease production is well documented and further affirmed through biomarker studies.

In various experimental systems, oxidative stress from exposure to cigarette smoke causes damage to components of the lung: the epithelium, the airways, and the alveoli. In humans, smoking is followed by a rise in markers of systemic oxidative stress and of oxidative stress affecting the lungs more specifically. The time course of the response to oxidative stress from smoking has also been characterized, showing a rise in markers after exposure to tobacco smoke. There is also substantial evidence for increased levels of oxidative stress markers in the lungs of persons with COPD. This large body of experimental and observational evidence is consistent in demonstrating that ROS can damage the lung and that evidence of oxidative stress is strongly linked with COPD. Oxidative stress is one of several mechanisms contributing to the development of COPD. However, the available evidence has not addressed whether oxidative stress is a necessary mechanism or sufficient by itself to cause COPD.

Genetic Susceptibility to Cigarette Smoke

All smokers do not develop COPD, indicating that smoking alone is not sufficient to cause COPD. A variety of lines of evidence support a role for genetic factors in determining susceptibility to cigarette smoke. Familial aggregation of phenotypes for lung function and for COPD has been repeatedly demonstrated. In addition, there is strong clinical and epidemiologic evidence on genetically inherited AAT deficiency and risk for emphysema. This chapter offers the conclusion that protease-antiprotease imbalance is involved in the development of emphysema and sufficient by itself to produce it.

The general observation that smoking alone does not lead universally to COPD, and the specific observation that genotypes associated with severe AAT deficiency lead to emphysema, imply a role for genetic factors in the pathogenesis of emphysema. To date, however, genetic

loci other than *SERPINA1* have not been linked to risk for COPD.

Protease-Antiprotease Imbalance

Emphysema is a prominent and highly prevalent component of the COPD phenotype. The potential role of a protease-antiprotease balance shifted toward unchecked proteolytic activity was first identified with the finding of enhanced risk for emphysema in persons with AAT and the supporting experimental demonstration that emphysema could be produced experimentally by proteolytic enzymes. These enzymes damage the elastin in the lung, which is essential to maintaining the lung's elasticity and ventilatory function. Thus, it is directly plausible that this mechanism has a role in producing emphysema.

Three lines of evidence support a role for protease-antiprotease imbalance in causing emphysema. First, in experimental models and in smokers, a shift of protease-antiprotease balance in a destructive direction has been repeatedly demonstrated, as has corresponding injury to elastin fibers. Second, in animal models, instillation of proteolytic enzymes can produce emphysema, as does exposure to cigarette smoke. Genetically engineered mice with deficient macrophage or neutrophil elastase are protected from smoke-induced emphysema. Third, persons with homozygous AAT deficiency who smoke develop emphysema at a young age.

This substantial consistent and complementary evidence supports a causal role for protease-antiprotease imbalance in the pathogenesis of emphysema, a critical element of the COPD phenotype. This mechanism is also substantially plausible because of the importance of elastin in determining ventilator function. The evidence further indicates that protease-antiprotease imbalance is sufficient to produce emphysema in smokers. Human evidence comes from the long-described and well-documented occurrence of early-onset emphysema in smokers with low levels of AAT consequent to mutations of *SERPINA1*. Findings in animal models confirm the sufficiency of this mechanism.

Conclusions

1. Oxidative stress from exposure to tobacco smoke has a role in the pathogenetic process leading to chronic obstructive pulmonary disease.

2. Protease-antiprotease imbalance has a role in the pathogenesis of emphysema.

3. Inherited genetic variation in genes such as *SERPINA3* is involved in the pathogenesis of tobacco-caused chronic obstructive pulmonary disease.

4. Smoking cessation remains the only proven strategy for reducing the pathogenetic processes leading to chronic obstructive pulmonary disease.

Implications

Two major mechanisms underlying the causation of COPD by cigarette smoking have been identified: oxidative stress (injury) and protease-antiprotease imbalance. These mechanisms are triggered by the inhalation of combustion products directly into the lungs of smokers. Although the lung has defense mechanisms that function to check injury by inhaled agents, these defenses are overwhelmed by the sustained inhalation of cigarette smoke. Doses of inhaled smoke that could be tolerated without resulting in oxidative injury and protease-antiprotease imbalance have not been identified. Smoking cessation remains the only way to check and halt these processes.

COPD is the only disease caused by smoking that is strongly associated with a specific genetic disorder, namely, AAT deficiency. The occurrence of COPD in young smokers should trigger testing for AAT deficiency, but such screening is not recommended for the general population. Studies in progress are expected to extend understanding of the genetic basis of COPD.

References

Abbas AK, Lichtman AH, Pober JS. Activation of T lymphocytes. In: *Cellular and Molecular Immunology*. 4th ed. Philadelphia: W.B. Saunders, 2000a:161–81.

Abbas AK, Lichtman AH, Pober JS. B cell activation and antibody production. In: *Cellular and Molecular Immunology*. 4th ed. Philadelphia: W.B. Saunders, 2000b:182–207.

Abbas AK, Lichtman AH, Pober JS. Innate immunity. In: *Cellular and Molecular Immunology*. 4th ed. Philadelphia: W.B. Saunders, 2000c:270–90.

Abboud RT, Fera T, Johal S, Richter A, Gibson N. Effect of smoking on plasma neutrophil elastase levels. *Journal of Laboratory and Clinical Medicine* 1986;108(4):294–300.

Abboud RT, Fera T, Richter A, Tabona MZ, Johal S. Acute effect of smoking on the functional activity of alpha1-protease inhibitor in bronchoalveolar lavage fluid. *American Review of Respiratory Disease* 1985;131(1):79–85.

Abboud RT, Ofulue AF, Sansores RH, Muller NL. Relationship of alveolar macrophage plasminogen activator and elastase activities to lung function and CT evidence of emphysema. *Chest* 1998;113(5):1257–63.

Adams MR, Jessup W, Celermajer DS. Cigarette smoking is associated with increased human monocyte adhesion to endothelial cells: reversibility with oral L-arginine but not vitamin C. *Journal of the American College of Cardiology* 1997;29(3):491–7.

Adams V, Nehrhoff B, Späte U, Linke A, Schulze PC, Baur A, Gielen S, Hambrecht R, Schuler G. Induction of iNOS expression in skeletal muscle by IL-1β and NFκB activation: an in vitro and in vivo study. *Cardiovascular Research* 2002;54(1):95–104.

Adler KB, Holden-Stauffer WJ, Repine JE. Oxygen metabolites stimulate release of high-molecular-weight glycoconjugates by cell and organ cultures of rodent respiratory epithelium via an arachidonic acid-dependent mechanism. *Journal of Clinical Investigation* 1990;85(1):75–85.

Agustí A, MacNee W, Donaldson K, Cosio M. Hypothesis: does COPD have an autoimmune component? *Thorax* 2003;58(10):832–4.

Alberg AJ. The influence of cigarette smoking on circulating concentrations of antioxidant micronutrients. *Toxicology* 2002;180(2):121–37.

American Journal of Respiratory and Critical Care Medicine. American Thoracic Society/European Respiratory Society statement: standards for the diagnosis and management of individuals with alpha-1 antitrypsin deficiency. *American Journal of Respiratory and Critical Care Medicine* 2003;168(7):818–900.

American Thoracic Society. ATS publishes asthma state-of-the-art report [press release]. New York: American Thoracic Society, May 2000; <http://www.thoracic.org/sections/publications/press-releases/journal/articles/may-2000.html>; accessed: April 13, 2007.

American Thoracic Society/European Respiratory Society Task Force. Standards for the diagnosis and management of patients with COPD [Internet]. Version 1.2. New York: American Thoracic Society, 2004 [updated September 8, 2005]; <http://www.thoracic.org/go/copd>; accessed: April 13, 2007.

Anderson C, Kilty I, Marwick JA, MacNee W, Rahman I. Cigarette smoke and H_2O_2-mediated decrease in histone deacetylase activity is attenuated by *N*-acetyl-L-cysteine but not by I-κB kinase inhibition in A549 cells [abstract]. *American Journal of Respiratory and Critical Care Medicine* 2004;169:A424.

Andrade FH, Reid MB, Allen DG, Westerblad H. Effect of hydrogen peroxide and dithiothreitol on contractile function of single skeletal muscle fibres from the mouse. *Journal of Physiology* 1998;509(Pt 2):565–75.

Anthonisen NR, Skeans MA, Wise RA, Manfreda J, Kanner RE, Connett JE, Lung Health Study Research Group. The effects of a smoking cessation intervention on 14.5-year mortality: a randomized clinical trial. *Annals of Internal Medicine* 2005;142(4):233–9.

Antonicelli F, Brown D, Parmentier M, Drost EM, Hirani N, Rahman I, Donaldson K, MacNee W. Regulation of LPS-mediated inflammation in vivo and in vitro by the thiol antioxidant Nacystelyn. *American Journal of Physiology – Lung Cellular and Molecular Physiology* 2004;286(6):L1319–L1327.

Anttila S, Hirvonen A, Vainio H, Husgafvel-Pursiainen K, Hayes JD, Ketterer B. Immunohistochemical localization of glutathione *S*-transferases in human lung. *Cancer Research* 1993;53(23):5643–8.

Aoshiba K, Koinuma M, Yokohori N, Nagai A. Immunohistochemical evaluation of oxidative stress in murine lungs after cigarette smoke exposure. *Inhalation Toxicology* 2003a;15(10):1029–38.

Aoshiba K, Koinuma M, Yokohori N, Nagai A, Respiratory Failure Research Group in Japan. Differences in the distribution of CD4+ and CD8+ T cells in emphysematous lungs. *Respiration* 2004;71(2):184–90.

Aoshiba K, Tamaoki J, Nagai A. Acute cigarette smoke exposure induces apoptosis of alveolar macrophages. *American Journal of Physiology – Lung Cellular and Molecular Physiology* 2001a;281(6):L1392–L1401.

Aoshiba K, Yasuda K, Yasui S, Tamaoki J, Nagai A. Serine proteases increase oxidative stress in lung cells. *American Journal of Physiology – Lung Cellular and Molecular Physiology* 2001b;281(3):L556–L564.

Aoshiba K, Yokohori N, Nagai A. Alveolar wall apoptosis causes lung destruction and emphysematous changes. *American Journal of Respiratory Cell and Molecular Biology* 2003b;28(5):555–62.

Arnér ESJ, Holmgren A. Physiological functions of thioredoxin and thioredoxin reductase. *European Journal of Biochemistry* 2000;267(20):6102–9.

Arsalane K, Dubois CM, Muanza T, Bégin R, Boudreau F, Asselin C, Cantin AM. Transforming growth factor-β1 is a potent inhibitor of glutathione synthesis in the lung epithelial cell line A549: transcriptional effect on the GSH rate-limiting enzyme γ-glutamylcysteine synthetase. *American Journal of Respiratory Cell and Molecular Biology* 1997;17(5):599–607.

Astemborski JA, Beaty TH, Cohen BH. Variance components analysis of forced expiration in families. *American Journal of Medical Genetics* 1985;21(4):741–53.

Atkinson JJ, Holmbeck K, Yamada S, Birkedal-Hansen H, Parks WC, Senior RM. Membrane-type 1 matrix metalloproteinase is required for normal alveolar development. *Developmental Dynamics* 2005;232(4):1079–90.

Baarends EM, Schols AM, Mostert R, Wouters EF. Peak exercise response in relation to tissue depletion in patients with chronic obstructive pulmonary disease. *European Respiratory Journal* 1997;10(12):2807–13.

Balint B, Donnelly LE, Hanazawa T, Kharitonov SA, Barnes PJ. Increased nitric oxide metabolites in exhaled breath condensate after exposure to tobacco smoke. *Thorax* 2001;56(6):456–61.

Baranova H, Perriot J, Albuisson E, Ivaschenko T, Baranova VS, Hemery B, Mouraire P, Riol N, Malet P. Peculiarities of the GSTM1 0/0 genotype in French heavy smokers with various types of chronic bronchitis. *Human Genetics* 1997;99(6):822–6.

Barberà JA, Peinado VI, Santos S. Pulmonary hypertension in chronic obstructive pulmonary disease. *European Respiratory Journal* 2003;21(5):892–905.

Barclay JK, Hansel M. Free radicals may contribute to oxidative skeletal muscle fatigue. *Canadian Journal of Physiology and Pharmacology* 1991;69(2):279–84.

Barnes PJ. Alveolar macrophages as orchestrators of COPD. *COPD* 2004a;1(1):59–70.

Barnes PJ. Mediators of chronic obstructive pulmonary disease. *Pharmacological Reviews* 2004b;56(4):515–48.

Barnes PJ, Shapiro SD, Pauwels RA. Chronic obstructive pulmonary disease: molecular and cellular mechanisms. *European Respiratory Journal* 2003;22(4):672–88.

Bast A, Haenen GR, Doelman CJ. Oxidants and antioxidants: state of the art. *American Journal of Medicine* 1991;91(3C):2S–13S.

Beatty K, Bieth J, Travis J. Kinetics of association of serine proteinases with native and oxidized α-1-proteinase inhibitor and α-1-antichymotrypsin. *Journal of Biological Chemistry* 1980;255(9):3931–4.

Becker K, Gui M, Schirmer RH. Inhibition of human glutathione reductase by *S*-nitrosoglutathione. *European Journal of Biochemistry* 1995;234(2):472–8.

Becker S, Soukup JM, Gilmour MI, Devlin RB. Stimulation of human and rat alveolar macrophages by urban air particulates: effects on oxidant radical generation and cytokine production. *Toxicology and Applied Pharmacology* 1996;141(2):637–48.

Beckman JS, Koppenol WH. Nitric oxide, superoxide, and peroxynitrite: the good, the bad, and ugly. *American Journal of Physiology – Cell Physiology* 1996;271(5 Pt 1):C1424–C1437.

Behzad AR, Chu F, Walker DC. Fibroblasts are in a position to provide directional information to migrating neutrophils during pneumonia in rabbit lungs. *Microvascular Research* 1996;51(3):303–16.

Benetazzo MG, Gilè LS, Bombieri C, Malerba G, Massobrio M, Pignatti PF, Luisetti M. α₁-Antitrypsin TAQ I polymorphism and α₁-antichymotrypsin mutations in patients with obstructive pulmonary disease. *Respiratory Medicine* 1999;93(9):648–54.

Bernstein D. A review of the influence of particle size, puff volume, and inhalation pattern on the deposition of cigarette smoke particles in the respiratory tract. *Inhalation Toxicology* 2004;16(10):675–89.

Betsuyaku T, Nishimura M, Takeyabu K, Tanino M, Venge P, Xu S, Kawakami Y. Neutrophil granule proteins in bronchoalveolar lavage fluid from subjects with subclinical emphysema. *American Journal of Respiratory and Critical Care Medicine* 1999;159(6):1985–91.

Betsuyaku T, Nishimura M, Yoshioka A, Takeyabu K, Miyamoto K, Kawakami Y. Elastin-derived peptides and neutrophil elastase in bronchoalveolar lavage fluid. *American Journal of Respiratory and Critical Care Medicine* 1996;154(3 Pt 1):720–4.

Betsuyaku T, Takeyabu K, Tanino M, Nishimura M. Role of secretory leukocyte protease inhibitor in the development of subclinical emphysema. *European Respiratory Journal* 2002;19(6):1051–7.

Betsuyaku T, Tanino M, Nagai K, Nasuhara Y, Nishimura M, Senior RM. Extracellular matrix metalloproteinase inducer is increased in smokers' bronchoalveolar lavage fluid. *American Journal of Respiratory and Critical Care Medicine* 2003;168(2):222–7.

Betsuyaku T, Yoshioka A, Nishimura M, Miyamoto K, Kondo T, Kawakami Y. Neutrophil elastase associated with alveolar macrophages from older volunteers. *American Journal of Respiratory and Critical Care Medicine* 1995;151(2 Pt 1):436–42.

Bieth JG. The antielastase screen of the lower respiratory tract. *European Journal of Respiratory Disease Supplement* 1985;139:57–61.

Bilimoria MH, Ecobichon DJ. Protective antioxidant mechanisms in rat and guinea pig tissues challenged by acute exposure to cigarette smoke. *Toxicology* 1992;72(2):131–44.

Black LF, Kueppers F. α1-Antitrypsin deficiency in nonsmokers. *American Review of Respiratory Disease* 1978;117(3):421–8.

Boschetto P, Miniati M, Miotto D, Braccioni F, De Rosa E, Bononi I, Papi A, Saetta M, Fabbri LM, Mapp CE. Predominant emphysema phenotype in chronic obstructive pulmonary disease patients. *European Respiratory Journal* 2003;21(3):450–4.

Bosken CH, Hards J, Gatter K, Hogg JC. Characterization of the inflammatory reaction in the peripheral airways of cigarette smokers using immunocytochemistry. *American Review of Respiratory Disease* 1992;145 (4 Pt 1):911–7.

Bowler RP, Barnes PJ, Crapo JD. The role of oxidative stress in chronic obstructive pulmonary disease. *COPD* 2004;1(2):255–77.

Brantly M, Nukiwa, T, Crystal RG. Molecular basis of alpha-1-antitrypsin deficiency. *American Journal of Medicine* 1988;84(Suppl 6A):13–31.

Breuer R, Christensen TG, Lucey EC, Bolbochan G, Stone PJ, Snider GL. Elastase causes secretory discharge in bronchi of hamsters with elastase-induced secretory cell metaplasia. *Experimental Lung Research* 1993;19(2):273–82.

Bridgeman MME, Marsden M, Drost E, Selby C, Ryle AP, Donaldson K, MacNee W. The effect of cigarette smoke on lung cells [abstract]. *American Review of Respiratory Disease* 1991;143:A737.

BMJ. Standardized questionaries [sic] on respiratory symptoms. *BMJ (British Medical Journal)* 1965;2(5213):1665.

Buck M, Chojkier M. Muscle wasting and dedifferentiation induced by oxidative stress in a murine model of cachexia is prevented by inhibitors of nitric oxide synthesis and antioxidants. *EMBO Journal* 1996;15(8):1753–65.

Burgel PR, Escudier E, Coste A, Dao-Pick T, Ueki IF, Takeyama K, Shim JJ, Murr AH, Nadel JA. Relation of epidermal growth factor receptor expression to goblet cell hyperplasia in nasal polyps. *Journal of Allergy and Clinical Immunology* 2000;106(4):705–12.

Burns AR, Smith CW, Walker DC. Unique structural features that influence neutrophil emigration into the lung. *Physiological Reviews* 2003;83(2):309–36.

Buzatu L, Chu F, Javadifard A, Elliot WM, Lee W, Cherniack RM, Rogers RM, Sciurba FC, Coxson HO, Pare PD, Hogg JC. The accumulation of dendritic and natural killer cells in the small airways at different levels of COPD severity. *Proceedings of the American Thoracic Society* 2005;2:A135.

Byth BC, Billingsley GD, Cox DW. Physical and genetic mapping of the serpin gene cluster at 14q32.1: allelic association and a unique haplotype associated with alpha 1-antitrypsin deficiency. *American Journal of Human Genetics* 1994;55(1):126–33.

Calabrese F, Giacometti C, Beghe B, Rea F, Loy M, Zuin R, Marulli G, Baraldo S, Saetta M, Valente M. Marked alveolar apoptosis/proliferation imbalance in end-stage emphysema. *Respiratory Research* 2005;6(1):14.

Cantin A, Crystal RG. Oxidants, antioxidants and the pathogenesis of emphysema. *European Journal of Respiratory Disease Supplement* 1985;139:7–17.

Cantin AM, North SL, Hubbard RC, Crystal RG. Normal alveolar epithelial lining fluid contains high levels of glutathione. *Journal of Applied Physiology* 1987;63(1):152–7.

Cantrell ET, Warr GA, Busbee DL, Martin RR. Induction of aryl hydrocarbon hydroxylase in human pulmonary alveolar macrophages by cigarette smoking. *Journal of Clinical Investigation* 1973;52(8):1881–4.

Carnevali S, Petruzzelli S, Longoni B, Vanacore R, Barale R, Cipollini M, Scatena F, Paggiaro P, Celi A, Giuntini C. Cigarette smoke extract induces oxidative stress and apoptosis in human lung fibroblasts. *American Journal of Physiology – Lung Cellular and Molecular Physiology* 2003;284(6):L955–L963.

Carter AB, Tephly LA, Venkataraman S, Oberley LW, Zhang Y, Buettner GR, Spitz DR, Hunninghake GW. High levels of catalase and glutathione peroxidase activity dampen H_2O_2 signaling in human alveolar macrophages. *American Journal of Respiratory Cell and Molecular Biology* 2004;31(1):43–53.

Cavarra E, Bartalesi B, Lucattelli M, Fineschi S, Lunghi B, Gambelli F, Ortiz LA, Martorana PA, Lungarella G. Effects of cigarette smoke in mice with different levels of α_1-proteinase inhibitor and sensitivity to oxidants. *American Journal of Respiratory and Critical Care Medicine* 2001a;164(5):886–90.

Cavarra E, Lucattelli M, Gambelli F, Bartalesi B, Fineschi S, Szarka A, Giannerini F, Martorana PA, Lungarella G. Human SLPI inactivation after cigarette smoke exposure in a new in vivo model of pulmonary oxidative stress. *American Journal of Physiology – Lung Cellular and Molecular Physiology* 2001b;281(2):L412–L417.

Celedón JC, Lange C, Raby BA, Litonjua AA, Palmer LJ, DeMeo DL, Reilly JJ, Kwiatkowski DJ, Chapman HA, Laird N, et al. The transforming growth factor-β1 (TGFB1) gene is associated with chronic obstructive pulmonary disease (COPD). *Human Molecular Genetics* 2004;13(15):1649–56.

Centers for Disease Control and Prevention. Annual smoking-attributable mortality, years of potential life lost, and productivity losses—United States, 1997–2001. *Morbidity and Mortality Weekly Report* 2005;54(25):625–8.

Chambers DC, Tunnicliffe WS, Ayres JG. Acute inhalation of cigarette smoke increases lower respiratory tract nitric oxide concentrations. *Thorax* 1998;53(8):677–9.

Chance B, Sies H, Boveris A. Hydroperoxide metabolism in mammalian organs. *Physiological Reviews* 1979;59(3):527–605.

Chan-Yeung M, Abboud R, Buncio AD, Vedal S. Peripheral leukocyte count and longitudinal decline in lung function. *Thorax* 1988;43(6):462–6.

Choi AM, Alam J. Heme oxygenase-1: function, regulation, and implication of a novel stress-inducible protein in oxidant-induced lung injury. *American Journal of Respiratory Cell and Molecular Biology* 1996;15(1):9–19.

Church DF, Pryor WA. Free-radical chemistry of cigarette smoke and its toxicological implications. *Environmental Health Perspectives* 1985;64:111–26.

Churg A, Dai J, Tai H, Xie C, Wright JL. Tumor necrosis factor-α is central to acute cigarette smoke–induced inflammation and connective tissue breakdown. *American Journal of Respiratory and Critical Care Medicine* 2002;166(6):849–54.

Churg A, Wang RD, Tai H, Wang X, Xie C, Wright JL. Tumor necrosis factor-α drives 70% of cigarette smoke–induced emphysema in the mouse. *American Journal of Respiratory and Critical Care Medicine* 2004;170(5):492–8.

Churg A, Wang RD, Xie C, Wright JL. α1-Antitrypsin ameliorates cigarette smoke–induced emphysema in the mouse. *American Journal of Respiratory and Critical Care Medicine* 2003;168(2):199–207.

Churg A, Wright JL. Proteases and emphysema. *Current Opinion in Pulmonary Medicine* 2005;11(2):153–9.

Clark RAF. Wound repair. In: Clark RAF, editor. *The Molecular and Cellular Biology of Wound Repair*. 2nd ed. New York: Plenum Press, 1996:3–50.

Clark AG, Debnam P. Inhibition of glutathione S-transferases from rat liver by S-nitroso-L-glutathione. *Biochemical Pharmacology* 1988;37(16):3199–201.

Clark-Lewis I, Mattioli I, Gong J-H, Loetscher P. Structure-function relationship between the human chemokine receptor CXCR3 and its ligands. *Journal of Biological Chemistry* 2003;278(1):289–95.

Clini E, Bianchi L, Pagani M, Ambrosino N. Endogenous nitric oxide in patients with stable COPD: correlates with severity of disease. *Thorax* 1998;53(10):881–3.

Cohen D, Arai SF, Brain JD. Smoking impairs long-term dust clearance from the lung. *Science* 1979;204(4392):514–7.

Comhair SAA, Bhathena PR, Farver C, Thunnissen FBJM, Erzurum SC. Extracellular glutathione peroxidase induction in asthmatic lungs: evidence for redox regulation of expression in human airway epithelial cells. *FASEB Journal* 2001;15(1):70–8.

Conner EM, Grisham MB. Inflammation, free radicals, and antioxidants. *Nutrition* 1996;12(4):274–7.

Conway EM, Collen D, Carmeliet P. Molecular mechanisms of blood vessel growth. *Cardiovascular Research* 2001;49(3):507–21.

Cook CL. Upper and lower respiratory tract infections. In: Mahon CR, Manuselis G, editors. *Textbook of Diagnostic Microbiology*. 2nd ed. Philadelphia: W.B. Saunders, 2000:878–917.

Corradi M, Montuschi P, Donnelly LE, Pesci A, Kharitonov SA, Barnes PJ. Increased nitrosothiols in exhaled breath condensate in inflammatory airway diseases. *American Journal of Respiratory and Critical Care Medicine* 2001;163(4):854–8.

Corradi M, Rubinstein I, Andreoli R, Manini P, Caglieri A, Poli D, Alinovi R, Mutti A. Aldehydes in exhaled breath condensate of patients with chronic obstructive pulmonary disease. *American Journal of Respiratory and Critical Care Medicine* 2003;167(10):1380–6.

Cosio MG, Majo J, Cosio MG. Inflammation of the airways and lung parenchyma in COPD: role of T cells. *Chest* 2002;121(5 Suppl):160S–165S.

Cotgreave IA, Johansson U, Moldeus P, Brattsand R. The effect of acute cigarette smoke inhalation on pulmonary and systemic cysteine and glutathione redox states in the rat. *Toxicology* 1987;45(2):203–12.

Couillard A, Koechlin C, Cristol JP, Varray A, Prefaut C. Evidence of local exercise-induced systemic oxidative stress in chronic obstructive pulmonary disease patients. *European Respiratory Journal* 2002;20(5):1123–9.

Couillard A, Maltais F, Saey D, Debigare R, Michaud A, Koechlin C, LeBlanc P, Prefant C. Exercise-induced quadriceps oxidative stress and peripheral muscle dysfunction in patients with chronic obstructive pulmonary disease. *American Journal of Respiratory and Critical Care Medicine* 2003;167(12):1664–9.

Cross CE, Halliwell B, Allen A. Antioxidant protection: a function of tracheobronchial and gastrointestinal mucus. *Lancet* 1984;323(8390):1328–30.

Cross CE, van der Vliet A, Eiserich JP, Wong J, Halliwell B. Oxidative stress and antioxidants in respiratory tract lining fluids. In: Clerch LB, Massaro DJ, editors. *Oxygen, Gene Expression, and Cellular Function.* New York: Marcel Dekker, 1997:367–98.

Cross KJ, Mustoe TA. Growth factors in wound healing. *Surgical Clinics of North America* 2003;83(3):531–45.

Crowther AJ, Rahman I, Antonicelli F, Jimenez LA, Salter D, MacNee W. Oxidative stress and transcription factors AP-1 and NF-κB in human lung tissue [abstract]. *American Journal of Respiratory and Critical Care Medicine* 1999;159:A816.

Curtis JL, Freeman CM, Hogg JC. The immunopathogenesis of chronic obstructive pulmonary disease: insights from recent research. *Proceedings of the American Thoracic Society* 2007;4(7):512–21.

D'Armiento J, Dalal SS, Okada Y, Berg RA, Chada K. Collagenase expression in the lungs of transgenic mice causes pulmonary emphysema. *Cell* 1992;71(6):955–61.

Davies KJ. Oxidative stress: the paradox of aerobic life. *Biochemical Society Symposium* 1995;61:1–31.

de Serres FJ. Worldwide racial and ethnic distribution of α_1-antitrypsin deficiency: summary of an analysis of published genetic epidemiologic surveys. *Chest* 2002;122(5):1818–29.

Dekhuijzen PN, Aben KK, Dekker I, Aarts LP, Wielders PL, van Herwaarden CL, Bast A. Increased exhalation of hydrogen peroxide in patients with stable and unstable chronic obstructive pulmonary disease. *American Journal of Respiratory and Critical Care Medicine* 1996;154(3 Pt 1):813–6.

Delen FM, Sippel JM, Osborne ML, Law S, Thukkani N, Holden WE. Increased exhaled nitric oxide in chronic bronchitis: comparison with asthma and COPD. *Chest* 2000;117(3):695–701.

DeMeo DL, Celedon JC, Lange C, Reilly JJ, Chapman MA, Sylvia JS, Speizer FE, Weiss ST, Silverman EK. Genome-wide linkage of forced mid-expiratory flow in chronic obstructive pulmonary disease. *American Journal of Respiratory and Critical Care Medicine* 2004;170(12):1294–301.

Deneke SM, Fanburg BL. Regulation of cellular glutathione. *American Journal of Physiology* 1989;257(4 Pt 1):L163–L173.

Di Francia M, Barbier D, Mege JL, Orehek J. Tumor necrosis factor-alpha levels and weight loss in chronic obstructive pulmonary disease. *American Journal of Respiratory and Critical Care Medicine* 1994;150 (5 Pt 1):1453–5.

Di Stefano A, Caramori G, Oates T, Capelli A, Lusuardi M, Gnemmi I, Ioli F, Chung KF, Donner CF, Barnes PJ, et al. Increased expression of nuclear factor-κB in bronchial biopsies from smokers and patients with COPD. *European Respiratory Journal* 2002;20(3):556–63.

Di Stefano A, Caramori G, Ricciardolo FL, Capelli A, Adcock IM, Donner CF. Cellular and molecular mechanisms in chronic obstructive pulmonary disease: an overview. *Clinical and Experimental Allergy* 2004;34(8):1156–67.

Di Stefano A, Turato G, Maestrelli P, Mapp CE, Ruggieri MP, Roggeri A, Boschetto P, Fabbri LM, Saetta M. Airflow limitation in chronic bronchitis is associated with T-lymphocyte and macrophage infiltration in the bronchial mucosa. *American Journal of Respiratory and Critical Care Medicine* 1996;153(2):629–32.

Doelman CJ, Bast A. Oxygen radicals in lung pathology. *Free Radical Biology & Medicine* 1990;9(5):381–400.

Donaldson GC, Seemungal TA, Bhowmik A, Wedzicha JA. Relationship between exacerbation frequency and lung function decline in chronic obstructive pulmonary disease. *Thorax* 2002;57(10):847–52.

Drannik AG, Pouladi MA, Robbins CS, Goncharova SI, Kianpour S, Stampfli MR. Impact of cigarette smoke on clearance and inflammation after *Pseudomonas aeruginosa* infection. *American Journal of Respiratory and Critical Care Medicine* 2004;170(11):1164–71.

Drost EM, Selby C, Bridgeman MM, MacNee W. Decreased leukocyte deformability after acute cigarette smoking in humans. *American Review of Respiratory Disease* 1993;148(5):1277–83.

Drost EM, Selby C, Lannan S, Lowe GD, MacNee W. Changes in neutrophil deformability following in vitro smoke exposure: mechanism and protection. *American Journal of Respiratory Cell and Molecular Biology* 1992;6(3):287–95.

Dunnill MS. Emphysema. In: Dunnill MS, editor. *Pulmonary Pathology.* New York: Churchill Livingston, 1982:81–112.

Eid AA, Ionescu AA, Nixon LS, Lewis-Jenkins V, Matthews SB, Griffiths TL, Shale DJ. Inflammatory response and body composition in chronic obstructive pulmonary disease. *American Journal of Respiratory and Critical Care Medicine* 2001;164(8 Pt 1):1414–8.

Eiserich JP, van der Vliet A, Handelman GJ, Halliwell B, Cross CE. Dietary antioxidants and cigarette smoke-induced biomolecular damage: a complex interaction. *American Journal of Clinical Nutrition* 1995;62 (6 Suppl):1490S–1500S

Ekberg-Jansson A, Bake B, Andersson B, Skoogh BE, Lofdahl CG. Respiratory symptoms relate to physiological changes and inflammatory markers reflecting central but not peripheral airways: a study in 60-year-old 'healthy' smokers and never-smokers. *Respiratory Medicine* 2001;95(1):40–7.

Engelen MP, Schols AM, Does JD, Deutz NE, Wouters EF. Altered glutamate metabolism is associated with reduced muscle glutathione levels in patients with emphysema. *American Journal of Respiratory and Critical Care Medicine* 2000a;161(1):98–103.

Engelen MP, Schols AM, Does JD, Wouters EF. Skeletal muscle weakness is associated with wasting of extremity fat-free mass but not with airflow obstruction in patients with chronic obstructive pulmonary disease. *American Journal of Clinical Nutrition* 2000b;71(3):733–8.

Eriksson S. Studies in α_1-antitrypsin deficiency. *Acta Medica Scandinavica Supplementum* 1965;432:1–85.

Evans MD, Pryor WA. Damage to human α-1-proteinase inhibitor by aqueous cigarette tar extracts and the formation of methionine sulfoxide. *Chemical Research in Toxicology* 1992;5(5):654–60.

Faruque MO, Khan MR, Rahman MM, Ahmed F. Relationship between smoking and antioxidant nutrition status. *British Journal of Nutrition* 1995;73(4):625–32.

Feldman C, Anderson R, Kanthakumar K, Vargas A, Cole PJ, Wilson R. Oxidant-mediated ciliary dysfunction in human respiratory epithelium. *Free Radical Biology & Medicine* 1994;17(1):1–10.

Ferrarotti I, Zorzetto M, Beccaria M, Gile LS, Porta R, Ambrosino N, Pignatti PF, Cerveri I, Pozzi E, Luisetti M. Tumour necrosis factor family genes in a phenotype of COPD associated with emphysema. *European Respiratory Journal* 2003;21(3):444–9.

Finkelstein R, Fraser RS, Ghezzo H, Cosio MG. Alveolar inflammation and its relation to emphysema in smokers. *American Journal of Respiratory and Critical Care Medicine* 1995;152(5 Pt 1):1666–72.

Finlay GA, O'Donnell MD, O'Connor CM, Hayes JP, FitzGerald MX. Elastin and collagen remodeling in emphysema: a scanning electron microscopy study. *American Journal of Pathology* 1996;149(4):1405–15.

Finlay GA, O'Driscoll LR, Russell KJ, D'Arcy EM, Masterson JB, FitzGerald MX, O'Connor CM. Matrix metalloproteinase expression and production by alveolar macrophages in emphysema. *American Journal of Respiratory and Critical Care Medicine* 1997a;156(1):240–7.

Finlay GA, Russell KJ, McMahon KJ, D'Arcy EM, Masterson JB, FitzGerald MX, O'Connor CM. Elevated levels of matrix metalloproteinases in bronchoalveolar lavage fluid of emphysematous patients. *Thorax* 1997b;52(6):502–6.

Fletcher CM, Peto R, Tinker C, Speizer FE. *The Natural History of Chronic Bronchitis and Emphysema: An Eight-Year Study of Early Chronic Obstructive Lung Disease in Working Men in London*. New York: Oxford University Press, 1976.

Foronjy R, D'Armiento J. The role of collagenase in emphysema. *Respiratory Research* 2001;2(6):348–52.

Foronjy RF, Mirochnitchenko O, Propokenko O, Lemaitre V, Jia Y, Inouye M, Okada Y, D'Armiento JM. Superoxide dismutase expression attenuates cigarette smoke- or elastase-generated emphysema in mice. *American Journal of Respiratory and Critical Care Medicine* 2006;173(6):623–31.

Foronjy RF, Okada Y, Cole R, D'Armiento J. Progressive adult-onset emphysema in transgenic mice expressing human MMP-1 in the lung. *American Journal of Physiology – Lung Cellular and Molecular Physiology* 2003;284(5):L727–L737.

Franco AA, Odom RS, Rando TA. Regulation of antioxidant enzyme gene expression in response to oxidative stress and during differentiation of mouse skeletal muscle. *Free Radical Biology & Medicine* 1999;27(9–10): 1122–32.

Freedman ML, Reich D, Penney KL, McDonald GJ, Mignault AA, Patterson N, Gabriel SB, Topol EJ, Smoller JW, Pato CN, et al. Assessing the impact of population stratification on genetic association studies. *Nature Genetics* 2004;36(4):388–93.

Friedlander AL, Lynch D, Dyar LA, Bowler RP. Phenotypes of chronic obstructive pulmonary disease. *COPD* 2007;4(4):301–2.

Fujii T, Hayashi S, Hogg JC, Mukae H, Suwa T, Goto Y, Vincent R, van Eeden SF. Interaction of alveolar macrophages and airway epithelial cells following exposure to particulate matter produces mediators that stimulate the bone marrow. *American Journal of Respiratory Cell and Molecular Biology* 2002;27(1):34–41.

Fujii T, Hayashi S, Hogg JC, Vincent R, van Eeden SF. Particulate matter induces cytokine expression in human bronchial epithelial cells. *American Journal of Respiratory Cell and Molecular Biology* 2001;25(3):265–71.

Fuke S, Betsuyaku T, Nasuhara Y, Morikawa T, Katoh H, Nishimura M. Chemokines in bronchiolar epithelium in the development of chronic obstructive pulmonary disease. *American Journal of Respiratory Cell and Molecular Biology* 2004;31(4):405–12.

Fukuda Y, Masuda Y, Ishizaki M, Masugi Y, Ferrans VJ. Morphogenesis of abnormal elastic fibers in lungs of patients with panacinar and centriacinar emphysema. *Human Pathology* 1989;20(7):652–9.

Gadek JE, Fells JA, Crystal RG. Cigarette smoking induces functional antiprotease deficiency in the lower respiratory tract of humans. *Science* 1979;206(4424):1315–6.

Gardner DE, Crapo JD, McClellan RO. *Toxicology of the Lung*. 3rd ed. Philadelphia: Taylor & Francis, 2000.

Gebel S, Gerstmayer B, Bosio A, Haussmann HJ, Van Miert E, Muller T. Gene expression profiling in respiratory tissues from rats exposed to mainstream cigarette smoke. *Carcinogenesis* 2004;25(2):169–78.

Gil E, Chen B, Kleerup E, Webber M, Tashkin DP. Acute and chronic effects of marijuana smoking on pulmonary alveolar permeability. *Life Sciences* 1995;56 (23–24):2193–9.

Gilmour PS, Rahman I, Donaldson K, MacNee W. Histone acetylation regulates epithelial IL-8 release mediated by oxidative stress from environmental particles. *American Journal of Physiology – Lung Cellular and Molecular Physiology* 2003;284(3):L533–L540.

Global Initiative for Chronic Obstructive Lung Disease. Guidelines: Global Strategy for Diagnosis, Management, and Prevention of COPD, November 2006; <http://www.goldcopd.org>; accessed: April 9, 2007.

Golpon HA, Coldren CD, Zamora MR, Cosgrove GP, Moore MD, Tuder RM, Geraci MW, Voelkel NF. Emphysema lung tissue gene expression profiling. *American Journal of Respiratory Cell and Molecular Biology* 2004;31(6):595–600.

Gonzáles S, Hards J, van Eeden S, Hogg JC. The expression of adhesion molecules in cigarette smoke-induced airways obstruction. *European Respiratory Journal* 1996;9(10):1995–2001.

Goto Y, Hogg JC, Shih CH, Ishii H, Vincent R, van Eeden SF. Exposure to ambient particles accelerates monocyte release from the bone marrow in atherosclerotic rabbits. *American Journal of Physiology – Lung Cellular and Molecular Physiology* 2004;287(1):L79–L85.

Gottlieb DJ, Stone PJ, Sparrow D, Gale ME, Weiss ST, Snider GL, O'Connor GT. Urinary desmosine excretion in smokers with and without rapid decline of lung function: the Normative Aging Study. *American Journal of Respiratory and Critical Care Medicine* 1996;154(5):1290–5.

Gray-Donald K, Gibbons L, Shapiro SH, Macklem PT, Martin JG. Nutritional status and mortality in chronic obstructive pulmonary disease. *American Journal of Respiratory and Critical Care Medicine* 1996; 153(3):961–6.

Greene CM, McElvaney NG. Toll-like receptor expression and function in airway epithelial cells. *Archives of Immunology and Experimental Therapy* 2005;53(5): 418–27.

Gromer S, Urig S, Becker K. The thioredoxin system—from science to clinic. *Medicinal Research Reviews* 2004;24(1):40–89.

Gross P, Babyak MA, Tolker E, Kaschak M. Enzymatically produced pulmonary emphysema: a preliminary report. *Journal of Occupational Medicine* 1964;6: 481–4.

Gross P, Pfitzer EA, Tolker E, Babyak MA, Kaschak M. Experimental emphysema: its production with papain in normal and silicotic rats. *Archives of Environmental Health* 1965;11:50–8.

Grumelli S, Corry DB, Song L-Z, Song L, Green L, Huh J, Hacken J, Espada R, Bag R, Lewis DE, et al. An immune basis for lung parenchymal destruction in chronic obstructive pulmonary disease and emphysema. *PLoS Medicine* 2004;1(1):e8. doi:10.1371/journal.pmed.0010008.

Guatura SB, Martinez JA, Santos Bueno PC, Santos ML. Increased exhalation of hydrogen peroxide in healthy subjects following cigarette consumption. *Sao Paulo Medical Journal* 2000;118(4):93–8.

Guerassimov A, Hoshino Y, Takubo Y, Turcotte A, Yamamoto M, Ghezzo H, Triantafillopoulos A, Whittaker K, Hoidal JR, Cosio MG. The development of emphysema in cigarette smoke-exposed mice is strain dependent. *American Journal of Respiratory and Critical Care Medicine* 2004;170(9):974–80.

Gum JR Jr. Mucin genes and the proteins they encode: structure, diversity, and regulation. *American Journal of Respiratory Cell and Molecular Biology* 1992; 7(6):557–64.

Guo X, Lin H-M, Lin Z, Montaño M, Sansores R, Wang G, DiAngelo S, Pardo A, Selman M, Floros J. Surfactant protein gene A, B, and D marker alleles in chronic obstructive pulmonary disease of a Mexican population. *European Respiratory Journal* 2001;18(3):482–90.

Gutteridge JM. Biological origin of free radicals, and mechanisms of antioxidant protection. *Chemico-Biological Interactions* 1994;91(2–3):133–40.

Habib MP, Clements NC, Garewal HS. Cigarette smoking and ethane exhalation in humans. *American Journal of Respiratory and Critical Care Medicine* 1995; 151(5):1368–72.

Hale KA, Ewing SL, Goxnell BA, Niewoehner DE. Lung disease in long-term cigarette smokers with and without chronic air-flow obstruction. *American Review of Respiratory Disease* 1984;130(5):716–21.

Halliwell B, Gutteridge JM. Role of free radicals and catalytic metal ions in human disease: an overview. *Methods in Enzymology* 1990;186:1–85.

Halliwell B, Gutteridge JMC. The definition and measurement of antioxidants in biological systems [letter]. *Free Radical Biology & Medicine* 1995;18(1):125–6.

Han J, Stamler JS, Li H, Griffith OW. Inhibition of γ-glutamylcysteine synthetase by S-nitrosylation. In: Moncada S, Stamler J, Gross S, Higgs EA, editors. *The Biology of Nitric Oxide Part 5: Proceedings of the 4th International Meeting on the Biology of Nitric Oxide*. London: Portland Press, 1996:114.

Handelman GJ, Packer L, Cross CE. Destruction of tocopherols, carotenoids, and retinol in human plasma by cigarette smoke. *American Journal of Clinical Nutrition* 1996;63(4):559–65.

Haniuda M, Kubo K, Fujimoto K, Honda T, Yamaguchi S, Yoshida K, Amano J. Effects of pulmonary artery remodeling on the pulmonary circulation after lung volume reduction surgery. *Thoracic and Cardiovascular Surgeon* 2003;51(3):154–8.

Harrison DJ, Cantlay AM, Rae F, Lamb D, Smith CA. Frequency of glutathione S-transferase M1 deletion in smokers with emphysema and lung cancer. *Human & Experimental Toxicology* 1997;16(7):356–60.

Hautamaki RD, Kobayashi DK, Senior RM, Shapiro SD. Requirement for macrophage elastase for cigarette smoke-induced emphysema in mice. *Science* 1997;277(5334):2002–4.

Hayes JD, Flanagan JU, Jowsey IR. Glutathione transferases. *Annual Review of Pharmacology and Toxicology* 2005;45:51–88.

He J-Q, Connett JE, Anthonisen NR, Paré PD, Sandford AJ. Glutathione S-transferase variants and their interaction with smoking on lung function. *American Journal of Respiratory and Critical Care Medicine* 2004;170(4):388–94.

Heffner JE, Repine JE. Pulmonary strategies of antioxidant defense. *American Review of Respiratory Disease* 1989;140(2):531–54.

Hele D. First Siena International Conference on Animal Models of Chronic Obstructive Pulmonary Disease, Certosa di Pontignano, University of Siena, Italy, September 30–October 2, 2001. *Respiratory Research* 2002;3(1):12.

Heppleston AG, Leopold JG. Chronic pulmonary emphysema: anatomy and pathogenesis. *American Journal of Medicine* 1961;31:279–91.

Hersh CP, Dahl M, Ly NP, Berkey CS, Nordestgaard BG, Silverman EK. Chronic obstructive pulmonary disease in α_1-antitrypsin PI MZ heterozygotes: a meta-analysis. *Thorax* 2004;59(10):843–9.

Hersh CP, DeMeo DL, Lange C, Litonjua AA, Reilly JJ, Kwiatkowski D, Laird N, Sylvia JS, Sparrow D, Speizer FE, et al. Attempted replication of reported chronic obstructive pulmonary disease candidate gene associations. *American Journal of Respiratory Cell and Molecular Biology* 2005;33(1):71–8.

Heunks LM, Dekhuijzen PN. Respiratory muscle function and free radicals: from cell to COPD. *Thorax* 2000;55(8):704–16.

Higgins M, Keller J. Familial occurrence of chronic respiratory disease and familial resemblance in ventilatory capacity. *Journal of Chronic Disease* 1975;28(4):239–51.

Higham MA, Pride NB, Alikhan A, Morrell NW. Tumour necrosis factor-α gene promoter polymorphism in chronic obstructive pulmonary disease. *European Respiratory Journal* 2000;15(2):281–4.

Hill JM, Zalos G, Halcox JP, Schenke WH, Waclawiw MA, Quyyumi AA, Finkel T. Circulating endothelial progenitor cells, vascular function, and cardiovascular risk. *New England Journal of Medicine* 2003;348(7):593–600.

Hobson J, Wright J, Churg A. Histochemical evidence for generation of active oxygen species on the apical surface of cigarette-smoke-exposed tracheal explants. *American Journal of Pathology* 1991;139(3):573–80.

Hockertz S, Emmendorffer A, Scherer G, Ruppert T, Daube H, Tricker AR, Adlkofer F. Acute effects of smoking and high experimental exposure to environmental tobacco smoke (ETS) on the immune system. *Cell Biology and Toxicology* 1994;10(3):177–90.

Hodge SJ, Hodge GL, Reynolds PN, Scicchitano R, Holmes M. Increased production of TGF-β and apoptosis of T lymphocytes isolated from peripheral blood in COPD. *American Journal of Physiology – Lung Cellular and Molecular Physiology* 2003;285(2):L492–L499.

Hogg JC. Pathophysiology of airflow limitation in chronic obstructive pulmonary disease. *Lancet* 2004;364(9435):709–21.

Hogg JC. The relationship of tobacco smoking to COPD: histopathogenesis. In: Rennard SI, Rodríguez-Roisin, Huchon G, Roche N, editors. *Clinical Management of Chronic Obstructive Pulmonary Disease*. Lung Biology in Health and Disease, 2nd ed., vol. 222. New York: Informa Healthcare, 2007:43–66.

Hogg JC. Lung structure and function in COPD. *International Journal of Tuberculosis and Lung Disease* 2008;12(5):467–79.

Hogg JC, Chu F, Utokaparch S, Woods R, Elliott WM, Buzatu L, Cherniack RM, Rogers RM, Sciurba FC, Coxson HO, et al. The nature of small-airway obstruction in chronic obstructive pulmonary disease. *New England Journal of Medicine* 2004;350(26):2645–53.

Hogg JC, Macklem PT, Thurlbeck WM. Site and nature of airways obstruction in chronic obstructive lung disease. *New England Journal of Medicine* 1968;278(25):1355–6.

Hogg JC, Senior RM. Chronic obstructive pulmonary disease c2: pathology and biochemistry of emphysema. *Thorax* 2002;57(9):830–4.

Hoidal JR, Fox RB, LeMarbe PA, Perri R, Repine JE. Altered oxidative metabolic responses in vitro of alveolar macrophages from asymptomatic cigarette smokers. *American Review of Respiratory Disease* 1981;123(1):85–9.

Holmgren A. Antioxidant function of thioredoxin and glutaredoxin systems. *Antioxidants & Redox Signaling* 2000;2(4):811–20.

Horne SL, Cockcroft DW, Dosman JA. Possible protective effect against chronic obstructive airways disease by the GC2 allele. *Human Heredity* 1990;40(3):173–6.

Horsfield K, Segel N, Bishop JM. Pulmonary circulation in chronic bronchitis at rest and during exercise breathing air and 80 percent oxygen. *Clinical Science* 1968;34(3):473–83.

Hoyt JC, Robbins RA, Habib M, Springall DR, Buttery LD, Polak JM, Barnes PJ. Cigarette smoke decreases inducible nitric oxide synthase in lung epithelial cells. *Experimental Lung Research* 2003;29(1):17–28.

Huang S-L, Su C-H, Chang S-C. Tumor necrosis factor-α gene polymorphism in chronic bronchitis. *American Journal of Respiratory and Critical Care Medicine* 1997; 156(5):1436–9.

Hubert HB, Fabsitz RR, Feinleib M, Gwinn C. Genetic and environmental influences on pulmonary function in adult twins. *American Review of Respiratory Disease* 1982;125(4):409–15.

Hulbert WC, Walker DC, Jackson A, Hogg JC. Airway permeability to horseradish peroxidase in guinea pigs: the repair phase after injury by cigarette smoke. *American Review of Respiratory Disease* 1981;123(3):320–6.

Hunninghake GW, Crystal RG. Cigarette smoking and lung destruction: accumulation of neutrophils in the lungs of cigarette smokers. *American Review of Respiratory Disease* 1983;128(5):833–8.

Hunninghake GW, Gadek JE, Kawanami O, Ferrans VJ, Crystal RG. Inflammatory and immune processes in the human lung in health and disease: evaluation by bronchoalveolar lavage. *American Journal of Pathology* 1979;97(1):149–206.

Hutchison DCS. α_1-Antitrypsin deficiency in Europe: geographical distribution of Pi types S and Z. *Respiratory Medicine* 1998;92(3):367–77.

Ichinose M, Sugiura H, Yamagata S, Koarai A, Shirato K. Increase in reactive nitrogen species production in chronic obstructive pulmonary disease airways. *American Journal of Respiratory and Critical Care Medicine* 2000;162(2 Pt 1):701–6.

Imai K, Dalal SS, Chen ES, Downey R, Schulman LL, Ginsburg M, D'Armiento J. Human collagenase (matrix metalloproteinase-1) expression in the lungs of patients with emphysema. *American Journal of Respiratory and Critical Care Medicine* 2001;163(3 Pt 1):786–91.

International Agency for Research on Cancer. *IARC Monographs on the Evaluation of Carcinogenic Risks to Humans: Tobacco Smoke and Involuntary Smoking*. Vol. 83. Lyon (France): International Agency for Research on Cancer, 2004.

International Commission on Radiological Protection. *Human Respiratory Tract Model for Radiological Protection*. Report of the Task Group of the International Commission on Radiological Protection. Tarrytown (NY): Elsevier Science, 1994. ICRP Publication 66.

Ishii T, Keicho N, Teramoto S, Azuma A, Kudoh S, Fukuchi Y, Ouchi Y, Matsuse T. Association of Gc-globulin variation with susceptibility to COPD and diffuse panbronchiolitis. *European Respiratory Journal* 2001;18(5):753–7.

Ishii T, Matsuse T, Teramoto S, Matsui H, Hosoi T, Fukuchi Y, Ouchi Y. Association between alpha-1-antichymotrypsin polymorphism and susceptibility to chronic obstructive pulmonary disease. *European Journal of Clinical Investigation* 2000a;30(6):543–8.

Ishii T, Matsuse T, Teramoto S, Matsui H, Miyao M, Hosoi T, Takahashi H, Fukuchi Y, Ouchi Y. Glutathione *S*-transferase P1 (GSTP1) polymorphism in patients with chronic obstructive pulmonary disease. *Thorax* 1999;54(8):693–6.

Ishii T, Matsuse T, Teramoto S, Matsui H, Miyao M, Hosoi T, Takahashi H, Fukuchi Y, Ouchi Y. Neither IL-1 β, IL-1 receptor antagonist, nor TNF-α polymorphisms are associated with susceptibility to COPD. *Respiratory Medicine* 2000b;94(9):847–51.

Ishizaki T, Kishi Y, Sasaki F, Ameshima S, Nakai T, Miyabo S. Effect of probucol, an oral hypocholesterolaemic agent, on acute tobacco smoke inhalation in rats. *Clinical Science (London)* 1996;90(6):517–23.

Ito K, Hanazawa T, Tomita K, Barnes PJ, Adcock IM. Oxidative stress reduces histone deacetylase 2 activity and enhances IL-8 gene expression: role of tyrosine nitration. *Biochemical and Biophysical Research Communications* 2004a;315(1):240–5.

Ito K, Ito M, Elliott WM, Cosio B, Caramori G, Kon OM, Barczyk A, Hayashi S, Adcock IM, Hogg JC, et al. Decreased histone deacetylase activity in chronic obstructive pulmonary disease. *New England Journal of Medicine* 2005;352(19):1967–76.

Ito K, Lim S, Caramori G, Chung KF, Barnes PJ, Adcock IM. Cigarette smoking reduces histone deacetylase 2 expression, enhances cytokine expression, and inhibits glucocorticoid actions in alveolar macrophages. *FASEB Journal* 2001;15(6):1110–2.

Ito I, Nagai S, Hoshino Y, Muro S, Hirai T, Tsukino M, Mishima M. Risk and severity of COPD is associated with the group-specific component of serum globulin 1F allele. *Chest* 2004b;125(1):63–70.

Janoff A. Elastases and emphysema: current assessment of the protease-antiprotease hypothesis. *American Review of Respiratory Disease* 1985;132(2):417–33.

Janoff A, Carp H, Laurent P, Raju L. The role of oxidative processes in emphysema. *American Review of Respiratory Disease* 1983a;127(2):S31–S38.

Janoff A, Raju L, Dearing R. Levels of elastase activity in bronchoalveolar lavage fluids of healthy smokers and nonsmokers. *American Review of Respiratory Disease* 1983b;127(5):540–4.

Janoff A, Scherer J. Mediators of inflammation in leukocyte lysosomes. IX: elastinolytic activity in granules of human polymorphonuclear leukocytes. *Journal of Experimental Medicine* 1968;128(5):1137–55.

Janssen-Heininger YMW, Macara I, Mossman BT. Cooperativity between oxidants and tumor necrosis factor in the activation of nuclear factor (NF)-κB: requirement of Ras/mitogen-activated protein kinases in the activation of NF-κB by oxidants. *American Journal of Respiratory Cell and Molecular Biology* 1999;20(5):942–52.

Janus ED, Phillips NT, Carrell RW. Smoking, lung function, and alpha 1-antitrypsin deficiency. *Lancet* 1985; 325(8421):152–4.

Jenkins RC, Ross RJ. Growth hormone therapy for protein catabolism. *Quarterly Journal of Medicine* 1996; 89(11):813–9.

Jezek V, Schrijen F, Sadoul P. Right ventricular function and pulmonary hemodynamics during exercise in patients with chronic obstructive bronchopulmonary disease. *Cardiology* 1973;58(1):20–31.

Jiménez LA, Thompson J, Brown DA, Rahman I, Antonicelli F, Duffin R, Drost EM, Hay RT, Donaldson K, MacNee W. Activation of NF-κB by PM$_{10}$ occurs via an iron-mediated mechanism in the absence of IκB degradation. *Toxicology and Applied Pharmacology* 2000;166(2):101–10.

Jones JG, Minty BD, Lawler P, Hulands G, Crawley JCW, Veall N. Increased alveolar epithelial permeability in cigarette smokers. *Lancet* 1980;315(8159):66–8.

Joost O, Wilk, JB, Cupples LA, Harmon M, Shearman AM, Baldwin CT, O'Connor GT, Myers RH, Gottlieb DJ. Genetic loci influencing lung function: a genome-wide scan in the Framingham Study. *American Journal of Respiratory and Critical Care Medicine* 2002;165(6):795–9.

Kanner RE, Anthonisen NR, Connett JE, Lung Health Study Research Group. Lower respiratory illnesses promote FEV$_1$ decline in current smokers but not ex-smokers with mild chronic obstructive pulmonary disease. *American Journal of Respiratory and Critical Care Medicine* 2001;164(3):358–64.

Kaplan JD, Calandrino FS, Schuster DP. Effect of smoking on pulmonary vascular permeability: a positron emission tomography study. *American Review of Respiratory Disease* 1992;145(3):712–5.

Kasahara Y, Tuder RM, Cool CD, Lynch DA, Flores SC, Voelkel NF. Endothelial cell death and decreased expression of vascular endothelial growth factor and vascular endothelial growth factor receptor 2 in emphysema. *American Journal of Respiratory and Critical Care Medicine* 2001;163(3 Pt 1):737–44.

Kasahara Y, Tuder RM, Taraseviciene-Stewart L, Le Cras TD, Abman S, Hirth PK, Waltenberger J, Voelkel NF. Inhibition of VEGF receptors causes lung cell apoptosis and emphysema. *Journal of Clinical Investigation* 2000;106(11):1311–9.

Kasuga I, Paré PD, Ruan J, Connett JE, Anthonisen NR, Sandford AJ. Lack of association of group specific component haplotypes with lung function in smokers. *Thorax* 2003;58(9):790–3.

Kauffmann F, Kleisbauer JP, Cambon-DeMouzon A, Mercier P, Constans J, Blanc M, Rouch Y, Feingold N. Genetic markers in chronic air-flow limitation: a genetic epidemiologic study. *American Review of Respiratory Disease* 1983;127(3):263–9.

Kayyali US, Budhiraja R, Pennella CM, Cooray S, Lanzillo JJ, Chalkley R, Hassoun PM. Upregulation of xanthine oxidase by tobacco smoke condensate in pulmonary endothelial cells. *Toxicology and Applied Pharmacology* 2003;188(1):59–68.

Keatings VM, Collins PD, Scott DM, Barnes PJ. Differences in interleukin-8 and tumor necrosis factor-alpha in induced sputum from patients with chronic obstructive pulmonary disease or asthma. *American Journal of Respiratory and Critical Care Medicine* 1996;153(2): 530–4.

Keicho N, Elliott WM, Hogg JC, Hayashi S. Adenovirus E1A gene dysregulates ICAM-1 expression in transformed pulmonary epithelial cells. *American Journal of Respiratory Cell and Molecular Biology* 1997;16(1):23–30.

Kellermann G, Walter H. Investigations on the population genetics of the alpha-1-antitrypsin polymorphism. *Humangenetik* 1970;10(2):145–50.

Kessler R, Faller M, Weitzenblum E, Chaouat A, Aykut A, Ducolone A, Ehrhart M, Oswald-Mammomosser M. "Natural history" of pulmonary hypertension in a series of 131 patients with chronic obstructive lung disease. *American Journal of Respiratory and Critical Care Medicine* 2001;164(2):219–24.

Kharitonov SA, Robbins RA, Yates D, Keatings V, Barnes PJ. Acute and chronic effects of cigarette smoking on exhaled nitric oxide. *American Journal of Respiratory and Critical Care Medicine* 1995;152(2):609–12.

Kim H, Liu X, Kohyama T, Kobayashi T, Conner H, Abe S, Fang Q, Wen F-Q, Rennard SI. Cigarette smoke stimulates MMP-1 production by human lung fibroblasts through the ERK1/2 pathway. *Chronic Obstructive Pulmonary Disease* 2004;1(1):13–23.

Kim V, Rogers TJ, Criner GJ. New concepts in the pathobiology of chronic obstructive pulmonary disease. *Proceedings of the American Thoracic Society* 2008; 5(4):478–85.

Kinnula VL, Crapo JD. Superoxide dismutases in the lung and human lung diseases. *American Journal of Respiratory and Critical Care Medicine* 2003;167(12): 1600–19.

Kinnula VL, Lehtonen S, Kaarteenaho-Wiik R, Lakari E, Paakko P, Kang SW, Rhee SG, Soini Y. Cell specific expression of peroxiredoxins in human lung and pulmonary sarcoidosis. *Thorax* 2002;57(2):157–64.

Klaassen CD, editor. *Casarett and Doull's Toxicology: The Basic Science of Poisons*. 6th ed. New York: McGraw-Hill, 2001.

Knowles MR, Boucher RC. Mucus clearance as a primary innate defense mechanism for mammalian airways. *Journal of Clinical Investigation* 2002;109(5):571–7.

Kohri K, Ueki IF, Nadel JA. Neutrophil elastase induces mucin production by ligand-dependent epidermal growth factor receptor activation. *American Journal of Physiology – Lung Cellular and Molecular Physiology* 2002;283(3):L531–L540.

Koike E, Hirano S, Shimojo N, Kobayashi T. cDNA microarray analysis of gene expression in rat alveolar macrophages in response to organic extract of diesel exhaust particles. *Toxicological Sciences* 2002;67(2):241–6.

Kreyling WG, Scheuch G. Clearance of particles deposited in the lungs. In: Gehr P, Heyder J, editors. *Particle–Lung Interactions*. Lung Biology in Health and Disease. Vol. 1143. New York: Marcel Dekker, 2000:323–76.

Kruh GD, Belinsky MG. The MRP family of drug efflux pumps. *Oncogene* 2003;22(47):7537–52.

Kubo H, Alitalo K. The bloody fate of endothelial stem cells. *Genes & Development* 2003;17(3):322–9.

Kubo K, Ge R-L, Koizumi T, Fujimoto K, Yamanda T, Haniuda M, Honda T. Pulmonary artery remodelling modifies pulmonary hypertension during exercise in severe emphysema. *Respiration Physiology* 2000;120(1):71–9.

Küçükaycan M, Van Krugten M, Pennings H-J, Huizinga TWJ, Buurman WA, Dentener MA, Wouters EFM. Tumor necrosis factor-α +489G/A gene polymorphism is associated with chronic obstructive pulmonary disease. *Respiratory Research* 2002;3(1):29.

Kueppers F, Miller RD, Gordon H, Hepper NG, Offord K. Familial prevalence of chronic obstructive pulmonary disease in a matched pair study. *American Journal of Medicine* 1977;63(3):336–42.

Kugelman A, Choy HA, Liu R, Shi MM, Gozal E, Forman HJ. gamma-Glutamyl transpeptidase is increased by oxidative stress in rat alveolar L2 epithelial cells. *American Journal of Respiratory Cell and Molecular Biology* 1994;11(5):586–92.

Kuhn C, Yu SY, Chraplyvy M, Linder HE, Senior RM. The induction of emphysema with elastase. II: changes in connective tissue. *Laboratory Investigation* 1976;34(4):372–80.

Kumar V, Abbas AK, Fausto N. Tissue renewal and repair: regeneration, healing, and fibrosis. In: *Robbins and Cotran Pathologic Basis of Disease*. 7th ed. Philadelphia: Elsevier, 2005:87–118.

Kuschner WG, D'Alessandro A, Wong H, Blanc PD. Dose-dependent cigarette smoking-related inflammatory responses in healthy adults. *European Respiratory Journal* 1996;9(10):1989–94.

Laënnec RTH. *A Treatise on the Diseases of the Chest and on Mediate Auscultation*. 4th ed. Translated by Forbes J. London: Longmans, 1834.

Lakari E, Paakko P, Kinnula VL. Manganese superoxide dismutase, but not CuZn superoxide dismutase, is highly expressed in the granulomas of pulmonary sarcoidosis and extrinsic allergic alveolitis. *American Journal of Respiratory and Critical Care Medicine* 1998;158(2):589–96.

Lakari E, Paakko P, Pietarinen-Runtti P, Kinnula VL. Manganese superoxide dismutase and catalase are coordinately expressed in the alveolar region in chronic interstitial pneumonias and granulomatous diseases of the lung. *American Journal of Respiratory and Critical Care Medicine* 2000;161(2 Pt 1):615–21.

Lancet. Definition and classification of chronic bronchitis for clinical and epidemiological purposes. *Lancet* 1965;285(7389):775–9.

Landbo C, Prescott E, Lange P, Vestbo J, Almdal TP. Prognostic value of nutritional status in chronic obstructive pulmonary disease. *American Journal of Respiratory and Critical Care Medicine* 1999;160(6):1856–61.

Lang MR, Fiaux GW, Gillooly M, Stewart JA, Hulmes DJ, Lamb D. Collagen content of alveolar wall tissue in emphysematous and non-emphysematous lungs. *Thorax* 1994;49(4):319–26.

Langen RC, Korn SH, Wouters EF. ROS in the local and systemic pathogenesis of COPD. *Free Radical Biology & Medicine* 2003;35(3):226–35.

Langen RCJ, Van Der Velden JLJ, Schols AMWJ, Kelders MCJM, Wouters EFM, Janssen-Heininger YMW. Tumor necrosis factor-alpha inhibits myogenic differentiation through MyoD protein destabilization. *FASEB Journal* 2004;18(2):227–37.

Lannan S, Donaldson K, Brown D, MacNee W. Effect of cigarette smoke and its condensates on alveolar epithelial cell injury in vitro. *American Journal of Physiology* 1994;266(1 Pt 1):L92–L100.

Larson RK, Barman ML, Kueppers F, Fudenberg HH. Genetic and environmental determinants of chronic obstructive pulmonary disease. *Annals of Internal Medicine* 1970;72(5):627–32.

Larsson C. Natural history and life expectancy in severe alpha1-antitrypsin deficiency, Pi Z. *Acta Medica Scandinavica* 1978;204(5):345–51.

Laurell CB, Eriksson S. The electrophoretic α_1-globulin pattern of serum in α_1-antitrypsin deficiency. *Scandinavian Journal of Clinical and Laboratory Investigation* 1963;15(2):132–40.

Leco KJ, Waterhouse P, Sanchez OH, Gowing KLM, Poole AR, Wakeham A, Mak TW, Khokha R. Spontaneous air space enlargement in the lungs of mice lacking tissue inhibitor of metalloproteinases-3 (TIMP-3). *Journal of Clinical Investigation* 2001;108(6):817–29.

Lee HM, Takeyama K, Dabbagh K, Lausier JA, Ueki IF, Nadel JA. Agarose plug instillation causes goblet cell metaplasia by activating EGF receptors in rat airways. *American Journal of Physiology – Lung Cellular and Molecular Physiology* 2000;278(1):L185–L192.

Leonarduzzi G, Scavazza A, Biasi F, Chiarpotto E, Camandola S, Vogel S, Dargel R, Poli G. The lipid peroxidation end product 4-hydroxy-2,3-nonenal up-regulates transforming growth factor β1 expression in the macrophage lineage: a link between oxidative injury and fibrosclerosis. *FASEB Journal* 1997;11(11):851–7.

Leopold JG, Gough J. The centrilobular form of hypertrophic emphysema and its relation to chronic bronchitis. *Thorax* 1957;12(3):219–35.

Lewitter FI, Tager IB, McGue M, Tishler PV, Speizer FE. Genetic and environmental determinants of level of pulmonary function. *American Journal of Epidemiology* 1984;120(4):518–30.

Li XY, Donaldson K, Rahman I, MacNee W. An investigation of the role of glutathione in increased epithelial permeability induced by cigarette smoke in vivo and in vitro. *American Journal of Respiratory and Critical Care Medicine* 1994;149(6):1518–25.

Li XY, Rahman I, Donaldson K, MacNee W. Mechanisms of cigarette smoke induced increased airspace permeability. *Thorax* 1996;51(5):465–71.

Li YP, Atkins CM, Sweatt JD, Reid MB. Mitochondria mediate tumor necrosis factor-α/NF-κB signaling in skeletal muscle myotubes. *Antioxidants & Redox Signaling* 1999;1(1):97–104.

Lieberman J, Winter B, Sastre A. Alpha$_1$-antitrypsin Pi-types in 965 COPD patients. *Chest* 1986;89(3):370–3.

Linden M, Rasmussen JB, Piitulainen E, Tunek A, Larson M, Tegner H, Venge P, Laitinen LA, Brattsand R. Airway inflammation in smokers with nonobstructive and obstructive chronic bronchitis. *American Review of Respiratory Disease* 1993;148(5):1226–32.

Löfdahl JM, Cederlund K, Nathell L, Eklund A, Sköld CM. Bronchoalveolar lavage in COPD: fluid recovery correlates with the degree of emphysema. *European Respiratory Journal* 2005;25(2):275–81.

Lowenstein CJ, Snyder SH. Nitric oxide, a novel biologic messenger. *Cell* 1992;70(5):705–7.

Lukacs NW, Hogaboam CM, Kunkel SL. Chemokines and their receptors in chronic pulmonary disease. *Current Drug Targets: Inflammation and Allergy* 2005; 4(3):313–7.

Lykkesfeldt J, Loft S, Nielsen JB, Poulsen HE. Ascorbic acid and dehydroascorbic acid as biomarkers of oxidative stress caused by smoking. *American Journal of Clinical Nutrition* 1997;65(4):959–63.

Ma S, Lieberman S, Turino GM, Lin YY. The detection and quantitation of free desmosine and isodesmosine in human urine and their peptide-bound forms in sputum. *Proceedings of the National Academy of Sciences of the United States of America* 2003;100(22):12941–3.

MacFarlane NG, Miller DJ. Depression of peak force without altering calcium sensitivity by the superoxide anion in chemically skinned cardiac muscle of rat. *Circulation Research* 1992;70(6):1217–24.

MacNee W. Oxidants/antioxidants and COPD. *Chest* 2000;117(5 Suppl 1):303S–317S.

MacNee W. Oxidative stress and lung inflammation in airways disease. *European Journal of Pharmacology* 2001;429(1–3):195–207.

MacNee W. Oxidants and COPD. *Current Drug Targets: Inflammation and Allergy* 2005a;4(6):627–41.

MacNee W. Pulmonary and systemic oxidant/antioxidant imbalance in chronic obstructive pulmonary disease. *Proceedings of the American Thoracic Society* 2005b; 2(1):50–60.

MacNee W, Rahman I. Is oxidative stress central to the pathogenesis of chronic obstructive pulmonary disease? *Trends in Molecular Medicine* 2001;7(2):55–62.

MacNee W, Wiggs B, Belzberg AS, Hogg JC. The effect of cigarette smoking on neutrophil kinetics in human lungs. *New England Journal of Medicine* 1989;321(14):924–8.

Mahadeva R. Lomas DA. Genetics and respiratory disease. 2: alpha$_1$-antitrypsin deficiency, cirrhosis and emphysema. *Thorax* 1998;53(6):501–5.

Mahadeva R, Shapiro SD. Chronic obstructive pulmonary disease. 3: experimental animal models of pulmonary emphysema. *Thorax* 2002;57(10):908–14.

Majo J, Ghezzo H, Cosio MG. Lymphocyte population and apoptosis in the lungs of smokers and their relation to emphysema. *European Respiratory Journal* 2001;17(5):946–53.

Malhotra A, Peiffer AP, Ryujin DT, Elsner T, Kanner RE, Leppert MF, Hasstedt SJ. Further evidence for the role of genes on chromosome 2 and chromosome 5 in the inheritance of pulmonary function. *American Journal of Respiratory and Critical Care Medicine* 2003;168(5):556–61.

Mall M, Grubb BR, Harkema JR, O'Neal WK, Boucher RC. Increased airway epithelial NA+ absorption produces cystic fibrosis-like lung disease in mice. *Nature Medicine* 2004;10(5):487–93.

Mao JT, Tashkin DP, Belloni PN, Baileyhealy I, Baratelli F, Roth MD. All-*trans* retinoic acid modulates the balance of matrix metalloproteinase-9 and tissue inhibitor of metalloproteinase-1 in patients with emphysema. *Chest* 2003;124(5):1724–32.

Marangon K, Herbeth B, Lecomte E, Paul-Dauphin A, Grolier P, Chancerelle Y, Artur Y, Siest G. Diet, antioxidant status, and smoking habits in French men. *American Journal of Clinical Nutrition* 1998;67(2):231–9.

Marklund SL. Extracellular superoxide dismutase in human tissues and human cell lines. *Journal of Clinical Investigation* 1984;74(4):1398–403.

Martin TR, Frevert CW. Innate immunity in the lungs. *Proceedings of the American Thoracic Society* 2005; 2(5):403–11.

Martonen TB. Deposition patterns of cigarette smoke in human airways. *American Industrial Hygiene Association Journal* 1992;53(1):6–18.

Marwick JA, Kirkham P, Gilmour PS, Donaldson K, MacNee W, Rahman I. Cigarette smoke-induced oxidative stress and TGF-β1 increase p21$^{waf1/cip1}$ expression in alveolar epithelial cells. *Annals of the New York Academy of Sciences* 2002;973:278–83.

Marwick JA, Kirkham PA, Stevenson CS, Danahay H, Giddings J, Butler K, Donaldson K, MacNee W, Rahman I. Cigarette smoke alters chromatin remodeling and induces proinflammatory genes in rat lungs. *American Journal of Respiratory Cell and Molecular Biology* 2004;31(6):633–42.

Mason RJ, Broaddus VC, Murray JF, Nadel JA. *Murray and Nadel's Textbook of Respiratory Medicine.* 4th ed. St. Louis: Elsevier, 2005.

Massaro D, Massaro GD. Hunger disease and pulmonary alveoli. *American Journal of Respiratory and Critical Care Medicine* 2004;170(7):723–4.

Matsuba K, Thurlbeck WM. The number and dimensions of small airways in emphysematous lungs. *American Journal of Pathology* 1972;67(2):265–75.

Mattson JP, Sun J, Murray DM, Poole DC. Lipid peroxidation in the skeletal muscle of hamsters with emphysema. *Pathophysiology* 2002;8(3):215–21.

Mayer AK, Dalpke AH. Regulation of local immunity by airway epithelial cells. *Archives of Immunology and Experimental Therapy* 2007;55(6):353–62.

Mayer AS, Stoller JK, Bartelson BB, Ruttenber AJ, Sandhaus RA, Newman LS. Occupational exposure risks in individuals with PI*Z α_1-antitrypsin deficiency. *American Journal of Respiratory and Critical Care Medicine* 2000;162(2 Pt 1):553–8.

Maziak W, Loukides S, Culpitt S, Sullivan P, Kharitonov SA, Barnes PJ. Exhaled nitric oxide in chronic obstructive pulmonary disease. *American Journal of Respiratory and Critical Care Medicine* 1998;157(3 Pt 1): 998–1002.

McCallum WG. Types of injury—obstruction of respiratory tract. In: MacCallum WG, editor. *A Textbook of Pathology.* 7th ed. Philadelphia: WB Saunders, 1940:419–28.

McCay PB. Vitamin E: interactions with free radicals and ascorbate. *Annual Review of Nutrition* 1985;5:323–40.

McCloskey SC, Patel BD, Hinchliffe SJ, Reid ED, Wareham NJ, Lomas DA. Siblings of patients with severe chronic obstructive pulmonary disease have a significant risk of airflow obstruction. *American Journal of Respiratory and Critical Care Medicine* 2001;164(8 Pt 1):1419–24.

McCord JM, Fridovich I. The utility of superoxide dismutase in studying free radical reactions. II: the mechanism of the mediation of cytochrome c reduction by a variety of electron carriers. *Journal of Biological Chemistry* 1970;245(6):1374–7.

McLean KH. The macroscopic anatomy of pulmonary emphysema. *Australian Annals of Medicine* 1956;5(2): 73–88.

Mead J, Turner JM, Macklem PT, Little JB. Significance of the relationship between lung recoil and maximum expiratory flow. *Journal of Applied Physiology* 1967;22(1):95–108.

Meister A, Anderson ME. Glutathione. *Annual Review of Biochemistry* 1983;52:711–60.

Mercer BA, Kolesnikova N, Sonett J, D'Armiento J. Extracellular regulated kinase/mitogen activated protein kinase is up-regulated in pulmonary emphysema and mediates matrix metalloproteinase-1 induction by cigarette smoke. *Journal of Biological Chemistry* 2004;279(17):17690–6.

Minematsu N, Nakamura H, Tateno H, Nakajima T, Yamaguchi K. Genetic polymorphism in matrix metalloproteinase-9 and pulmonary emphysema. *Biochemical and Biophysical Research Communications* 2001;289(1):116–9.

Molet S, Belleguic C, Lena H, Germain N, Bertrand CP, Shapiro SD, Planquois J-M, Delaval P, Lagente V. Increase in macrophage elastase (MMP-12) in lungs from patients with chronic obstructive pulmonary disease. *Inflammation Research* 2005;54(1):31–6.

Monto AS, Higgins MW, Ross HW. The Tecumseh Study of Respiratory Illness. VIII: acute infection in chronic respiratory disease and comparison groups. *American Review of Respiratory Disease* 1975;111(1):27–36.

Montuschi P, Collins JV, Ciabattoni G, Lazzeri N, Corradi M, Kharitonov SA, Barnes PJ. Exhaled 8-isoprostane as an in vivo biomarker of lung oxidative stress in patients with COPD and healthy smokers. *American Journal of Respiratory and Critical Care Medicine* 2000;162 (3 Pt 1):1175–7.

Montuschi P, Kharitonov SA, Barnes PJ. Exhaled carbon monoxide and nitric oxide in COPD. *Chest* 2001; 120(2):496–501.

Morgan MDL. Bullous lung disease. In: Calverley PMA, Pride NB, editors. *Chronic Obstructive Pulmonary Disease*. London: Chapman and Hall, 1995:547–60.

Morrison D, Rahman I, Lannan S, MacNee W. Epithelial permeability, inflammation, and oxidant stress in the air spaces of smokers. *American Journal of Respiratory and Critical Care Medicine* 1999;159(2):473–9.

Morrison D, Skwarski K, Millar AM, Adams W, MacNee W. A comparison of three methods of measuring ^{99m}Tc-DTPA lung clearance and their repeatability. *European Respiratory Journal* 1998a;11(5):1141–6.

Morrison D, Strieter RM, Donnelly SC, Burdick MD, Kunkel SL, MacNee W. Neutrophil chemokines in bronchoalveolar lavage fluid and leukocyte-conditioned medium from nonsmokers and smokers. *European Respiratory Journal* 1998b;12(5):1067–72.

Morrow JD, Frei B, Longmire AW, Gaziano JM, Lynch SM, Shyr Y, Strauss WE, Oates JA, Roberts LJ II. Increase in circulating products of lipid peroxidation (F_2-isoprostanes) in smokers: smoking as a cause of oxidative damage. *New England Journal of Medicine* 1995;332(18):1198–203.

Motoyama T, Kawano H, Kugiyama K, Hirashima O, Ohgushi M, Yoshimura M, Ogawa H, Yasue H. Endothelium-dependent vasodilation in the brachial artery is impaired in smokers: effect of vitamin C. *American Journal of Physiology* 1997;273(4 Pt 2):H1644–H1650.

Mukae H, Hogg JC, English D, Vincent R, van Eeden SF. Phagocytosis of particulate air pollutants by human alveolar macrophages stimulates the bone marrow. *American Journal of Physiology – Lung Cellular and Molecular Biology* 2000;279(5):L924–L931.

Mukae H, Vincent R, Quinlan K, English D, Hards J, Hogg JC, van Eeden SF. The effect of repeated exposure to particulate air pollution (PM_{10}) on the bone marrow. *American Journal of Respiratory and Critical Care Medicine* 2001;163(1):201–9.

Muley T, Wiebel M, Schulz V, Ebert W. Elastinolytic activity of alveolar macrophages in smoking-associated pulmonary emphysema. *Clinical Investigator* 1994; 72(4):269–76.

Mullen JB, Wright JL, Wiggs BR, Paré PD, Hogg JC. Reassessment of inflammation of airways in chronic bronchitis. *BMJ (British Medical Journal)* 1985; 291(6504):1235–9.

Munro LH, Burton G, Kelly FJ. Plasma RRR-alpha-tocopherol concentrations are lower in smokers than in non-smokers after ingestion of a similar oral load of this antioxidant vitamin. *Clinical Science (London)* 1997;92(1):87–93.

Murphy TF, Brauer AL, Grant BJ, Sethi S. *Moraxella catarrhalis* in chronic obstructive pulmonary disease: burden of disease and immune response. *American Journal of Respiratory and Critical Care Medicine* 2005; 172(2):195–9.

Nadel JA. Role of epidermal growth factor receptor activation in regulating mucin synthesis. *Respiratory Research* 2001;2(2):85–9.

Nagaishi C. Lymphatic system. In: Nagaishi, C, editor. *Functional Anatomy and Histology of the Lung*. Baltimore: University Park Press, 1972:102–79.

Nakayama T, Church DF, Pryor WA. Quantitative analysis of the hydrogen peroxide formed in aqueous cigarette tar extracts. *Free Radical Biology & Medicine* 1989; 7(1):9–15.

Nathan C, Xie Q-W. Regulation of biosynthesis of nitric oxide. *Journal of Biological Chemistry* 1994; 269(19):13725–8.

Niewoehner DE. Cigarette smoking, lung inflammation, and the development of emphysema. *Journal of Laboratory and Clinical Medicine* 1988;111(1):15–27.

Niewoehner DE, Kleinerman J, Rice DB. Pathologic changes in the peripheral airways of young cigarette smokers. *New England Journal of Medicine* 1974;291(15):755–8.

Ning W, Li C-J, Kaminski N, Feghali-Bostwick CA, Alber SM, Di YP, Otterbein SL, Song R, Hayashi S, Zhou Z, et al. Comprehensive gene expression profiles reveal pathways related to the pathogenesis of chronic obstructive pulmonary disease. *Proceedings of the National Academy of Sciences of the United States of America* 2004;101(41):14895–900.

Nishikawa M, Kakemizu N, Ito T, Kudo M, Kaneko T, Suzuki M, Udaua N, Ikeda H, Okubo T. Superoxide mediates cigarette smoke-induced infiltration of neutrophils into the airways through nuclear factor-κB activation and IL-8 mRNA expression in guinea pigs in vivo. *American Journal of Respiratory Cell and Molecular Biology* 1999;20(2):189–98.

Noronha-Dutra AA, Epperlein MM, Woolf N. Effect of cigarette smoking on cultured human endothelial cells. *Cardiovascular Research* 1993;27(5):774–8.

Northrop-Clewes CA, Thurnham DI. Monitoring micronutrients in cigarette smokers. *Clinica Chimica Acta* 2007;377(1–2):14–38.

Nowak D, Kasielski M, Antczak A, Pietras T, Bialasiewicz P. Increased content of thiobarbituric acid-reactive substances and hydrogen peroxide in the expired breath condensate of patients with stable chronic obstructive pulmonary disease: no significant effect of cigarette smoking. *Respiratory Medicine* 1999;93(6):389–96.

Nowak D, Kasielski M, Pietras T, Bialasiewicz P, Antczak A. Cigarette smoking does not increase hydrogen peroxide levels in expired breath condensate of patients with stable COPD. *Monaldi Archives for Chest Disease* 1998;53(3):268–73.

Oberdörster G, Oberdörster E, Oberdörster J. Nanotoxicology: an emerging discipline evolving from studies of ultrafine particles. *Environmental Health Perspectives* 2005;113(7):823–39.

Ogushi F, Fells GA, Hubbard RC, Straus SD, Crystal RG. Z-type α1-antitrypsin is less competent than M1-type α1-antitrypsin as an inhibitor of neutrophil elastase. *Journal of Clinical Investigation* 1987;80(5):1366–74.

Ohata M, Suzuki H. Pathogenesis of spontaneous pneumothorax with special reference to the ultrastructure of emphysematous bullae. *Chest* 1980;77(6):771–6.

Ohnishi K, Takagi M, Kurokawa Y, Satomi S, Konttinen YT. Matrix metalloproteinase-mediated extracellular matrix protein degradation in human pulmonary emphysema. *Laboratory Investigation* 1998;78(9):1077–87.

O'Shaughnessy TC, Ansari TW, Barnes NC, Jeffery PK. Inflammation in bronchial biopsies of subjects with chronic bronchitis: inverse relationship of CD8+ T lymphocytes with FEV_1. *American Journal of Respiratory and Critical Care Medicine* 1997;155(3):852–7.

Otis AB, McKerrow CB, Bartlett RA, Mead J, McIlroy MB, Selverstone NJ, Radford EP. Mechanical factors in distribution of pulmonary ventilation. *Journal of Applied Physiology* 1956;8(4):427–443.

Oury TD, Day BJ, Crapo JD. Extracellular superoxide dismutase: a regulator of nitric oxide bioavailability. *Laboratory Investigation* 1996;75(5):617–36.

Pabst R, Gehrke I. Is the bronchus-associated lymphoid tissue (BALT) an integral structure in the lung of normal mammals, including humans? *American Journal of Respiratory Cell and Molecular Biology* 1990;3(2):131–5.

Palange P, Forte S, Felli A, Galassetti P, Serra P, Carlone S. Nutritional state and exercise tolerance in patients with COPD. *Chest* 1995;107(5):1206–12.

Palmer LJ, Celedon JC, Chapman HA, Speizer FE, Weiss ST, Silverman EK. Genome-wide linkage analysis of bronchodilator responsiveness and post-bronchodilator spirometric phenotypes in chronic obstructive pulmonary disease. *Human Molecular Genetics* 2003;12(10):1199–210.

Palmer LJ, Knuiman MW, Divitini ML, Burton PR, James AL, Bartholomew HC, Ryan G, Musk AW. Familial aggregation and heritability of adult lung function: results from the Busselton Health Study. *European Respiratory Journal* 2001;17(4):696–702.

Pardo A, Selman M. Proteinase-antiproteinase imbalance in the pathogenesis of emphysema: the role of metalloproteinases in lung damage. *Histology and Histopathology* 1999;14(1):227–33.

Paredi P, Kharitonov S, Barnes PJ. Analysis of expired air for oxidation products. *American Journal of Respiratory and Critical Care Medicine* 2002;166(12 Pt 2):S31–S37.

Paredi P, Kharitonov SA, Barnes PJ. Elevation of exhaled ethane concentration in asthma. *American Journal of Respiratory and Critical Care Medicine* 2000a;162(4 Pt 1):1450–4.

Paredi P, Kharitonov SA, Leak D, Ward S, Cramer D, Barnes PJ. Exhaled ethane, a marker of lipid peroxidation, is elevated in chronic obstructive pulmonary disease. *American Journal of Respiratory and Critical Care Medicine* 2000b;162(2 Pt 1):369–73.

Parks NJ, Krohn KJ, Mathis CA, Chasko JH, Geiger KR, Gregor ME, Peek NF. Nitrogen-13-labeled nitrite and nitrate: distribution and metabolism after intratracheal administration. *Science* 1981;212(4490):58–60.

Parmentier M, Hirani N, Rahman I, Donaldson K, MacNee W, Antonicelli F. Regulation of lipopolysaccharide-mediated interleukin-1β release by *N*-acetyl-cysteine in THP-1 cells. *European Respiratory Journal* 2000;16(5):933–9.

Parr DG, Stoel BC, Stolk J, Stockley RA. Pattern of emphysema distribution in α1-antitrypsin deficiency influences lung function impairment. *American Journal of Respiratory and Critical Care Medicine* 2004;170(11):1172–8.

Patel RP, McAndrew J, Sellak H, White CR, Jo H, Freeman BA, Darley-Usmar VM. Biological aspects of reactive nitrogen species. *Biochimica et Biophysica Acta* 1999;1411(2–3):385–400.

Patiar S, Slade D, Kirkpatrick U, McCollum CN. Smoking causes a dose-dependent increase in granulocyte-bound L-selectin. *Thrombosis Research* 2002;106(1):1–6.

Patuzzo C, Gilè LS, Zorzetto M, Trabetti E, Malerba G, Pignatti PF, Luisetti M. Tumor necrosis factor gene complex in COPD and disseminated bronchiectasis. *Chest* 2000;117(5):1353–8.

Pauwels RA, Buist AS, Calverley PM, Jenkins CR, Hurd SS, GOLD Scientific Committee. Global strategy for the diagnosis, management, and prevention of chronic obstructive pulmonary disease: NHLBI/WHO Global Initiative for Chronic Obstructive Lung Disease (GOLD)

Workshop summary. *American Journal of Respiratory and Critical Care Medicine* 2001;163(5):1256–76.

Pemberton PA, Cantwell JS, Kim KM, Sundin DJ, Kobayashi D, Fink JB, Shapiro SD, Barr PJ. An inhaled matrix metalloproteinase inhibitor prevents cigarette smoke-induced emphysema in the mouse. *Chronic Obstructive Pulmonary Disease* 2005;2(3):303–10.

Petruzzelli S, Puntoni R, Mimotti P, Pulera N, Baliva F, Fornai E, Giuntini C. Plasma 3-nitrotyrosine in cigarette smokers. *American Journal of Respiratory and Critical Care Medicine* 1997;156(6):1902–7.

Pietarinen P, Raivio K, Devlin RB, Crapo JD, Chang LY, Kinnula VL. Catalase and glutathione reductase protection of human alveolar macrophages during oxidant exposure in vitro. *American Journal of Respiratory Cell and Molecular Biology* 1995;13(4):434–41.

Piitulainen E, Tornling G, Eriksson S. Environmental correlates of impaired lung function in non-smokers with severe α_1-antitrypsin deficiency (PiZZ). *Thorax* 1998;53(11):939–43.

Pinamonti S, Leis M, Barbieri A, Leoni D, Muzzoli M, Sostero S, Chicca MC, Carrieri A, Ravenna F, Fabbri LM, et al. Detection of xanthine oxidase activity products by EPR and HPLC in bronchoalveolar lavage fluid from patients with chronic obstructive pulmonary disease. *Free Radical Biology & Medicine* 1998;25(7):771–9.

Pinamonti S, Muzzoli M, Chicca MC, Papi A, Ravenna F, Fabbri LM, Ciaccia A. Xanthine oxidase activity in bronchoalveolar lavage fluid from patients with chronic obstructive pulmonary disease. *Free Radical Biology & Medicine* 1996;21(2):147–55.

Pinot F, Bachelet M, François D, Polla BS, Walti H. Modified natural porcine surfactant modulates tobacco smoke-induced stress response in human monocytes. *Life Sciences* 1999;64(2):125–34.

Poller W, Faber J-P, Weidinger S, Tief K, Scholz S, Fischer M, Olek K, Kirchgesser M, Heidtmann H-H. A leucine-to-proline substitution causes a defective α^1-antichymotrypsin allele associated with familial obstructive lung disease. *Genomics* 1993;17(3):740–3.

Postma DS, Timens W. Remodeling in asthma and chronic obstructive pulmonary disease. *Proceedings of the American Thoracic Society* 2006;3(5):434–9.

Powell GM, Green GM. Investigation on the effects of cigarette smoke on rabbit alveolar macrophages. *Biochemical Journal* 1971;124(2):26P–27P.

Powis G, Mustacich D, Coon A. The role of the redox protein thioredoxin in cell growth and cancer. *Free Radical Biology & Medicine* 2000;29(3–4):312–22.

Praticò D, Basili S, Vieri M, Cordova C, Violi F, FitzGerald GA. Chronic obstructive pulmonary disease is associated with an increase in urinary levels of isoprostane $F_{2\alpha}$-III, an index of oxidant stress. *American Journal of Respiratory and Critical Care Medicine* 1998;158(6):1709–14.

Profita M, Chiappara G, Mirabella F, Di Giorgi R, Chimenti L, Costanzo G, Riccobono L, Bellia V, Bousquet J, Vignola AM. Effect of cilomilast (Ariflo) on TNF-α, IL-8, and GM-CSF release by airway cells of patients with COPD. *Thorax* 2003;58(7):573–9.

Proudfoot AE. Chemokine receptors: multifaceted therapeutic targets. *Nature Reviews Immunology* 2002; 2(2):106–15.

Pryor WA, Stone K. Oxidants in cigarette smoke: radicals, hydrogen peroxide, peroxynitrate, and peroxynitrite. *Annals of the New York Academy of Sciences* 1993;686:12–27.

Quay JL, Reed W, Samet J, Devlin RB. Air pollution particles induce IL-6 gene expression in human airway epithelial cells via NF-κB activation. *American Journal of Respiratory Cell and Molecular Biology* 1998;19(1): 98–106.

Rabe KF, Hurd S, Anzueto A, Barnes PJ, Buist SA, Calverley P, Fukuchi Y, Jenkins C, Rodriquez-Roisin R, van Weel C, et al. Global strategy for the diagnosis, management, and preventing of chronic obstructive pulmonary disease: GOLD executive summary. *American Journal of Respiratory and Critical Care Medicine* 2007;176(6):532–55.

Rafii S, Meeus S, Dias S, Hattori K, Heissig B, Shmelkov S, Rafii D, Lyden D. Contribution of marrow-derived progenitors to vascular and cardiac regeneration. *Seminars in Cell & Developmental Biology* 2002;13(1):61–7.

Rahman I, Bel A, Mulier B, Donaldson K, MacNee W. Differential regulation of glutathione by oxidants and dexamethasone in alveolar epithelial cells. *American Journal of Physiology* 1998;275(1 Pt 1):L80–L86.

Rahman I, MacNee W. Role of transcription factors in inflammatory lung diseases. *Thorax* 1998;53(7): 601–12.

Rahman I, MacNee W. Lung glutathione and oxidative stress: implications in cigarette smoke-induced airway disease. *American Journal of Physiology* 1999;277 (6 Pt 1):L1067–L1088.

Rahman I, MacNee W. Regulation of redox glutathione levels and gene transcription in lung inflammation: therapeutic approaches. *Free Radical Biology & Medicine* 2000;28(9):1405–20.

Rahman I, Morrison D, Donaldson K, MacNee W. Systemic oxidative stress in asthma, COPD, and smokers. *American Journal of Respiratory and Critical Care Medicine* 1996a;154(4 Pt 1):1055–60.

Rahman I, Smith CAD, Lawson MF, Harrison DJ, MacNee W. Induction of γ-glutamylcysteine synthetase by cigarette smoke is associated with AP-1 in human alveolar epithelial cells. *FEBS Letters* 1996b;396(1):21–5.

Rahman I, van Schadewijk AA, Crowther AJ, Hiemstra PS, Stolk J, MacNee W, DeBoek WI. 4-Hydroxy-2-nonenal, a specific lipid peroxidation product, is elevated in lungs of patients with chronic obstructive pulmonary disease. *American Journal of Respiratory and Critical Care Medicine* 2002;166(4):490–5.

Ramezanian MS, Padmaja S, Koppenol WH. Nitration and hydroxylation of phenolic compounds by peroxynitrite. *Chemical Research in Toxicology* 1996;9(1):232–40.

Rangasamy T, Cho CY, Thimmulappa RK, Zhen L, Srisuma SS, Kensler TW, Yamamoto M, Petrache I, Tuder RM, Biswal S. Genetic ablation of Nrf2 enhances susceptibility to cigarette smoke–induced emphysema in mice. *Journal of Clinical Investigation* 2004;114(9):1248–59.

Redline S, Tishler PV, Lewitter FI, Tager IB, Munoz A, Speizer FE. Assessment of genetic and nongenetic influences on pulmonary function: a twin study. *American Review of Respiratory Disease* 1987;135(1):217–22.

Reid L. Measurement of the bronchial mucous gland layer: a diagnostic yardstick in chronic bronchitis. *Thorax* 1960;15:132–41.

Repine JE, Bast A, Lankhorst I. Oxidative stress in chronic obstructive pulmonary disease. Oxidative Stress Study Group. *American Journal of Respiratory and Critical Care Medicine* 1997;156(2 Pt 1):341–57.

Retamales I, Elliott WM, Meshi B, Coxson HO, Paré PD, Sciurba FC, Rogers RM, Hayashi S, Hogg JC. Amplification of inflammation in emphysema and its association with latent adenoviral infection. *American Journal of Respiratory and Critical Care Medicine* 2001;164(3):469–73.

Reyes M, Dudek A, Jahagirdar B, Koodie L, Marker PH, Verfaillie CM. Origin of endothelial progenitors in human postnatal bone marrow. *Journal of Clinical Investigation* 2002;109(3):337–46.

Reynolds HY. Bronchoalveolar lavage. *American Review of Respiratory Disease* 1987;135(1):250–63.

Rhee SG, Kang SW, Netto LE, Seo MS, Stadtman ER. A family of novel peroxidases, peroxiredoxins. *Biofactors* 1999;10(2–3):207–9.

Richmond I, Pritchard GE, Ashcroft T, Avery A, Corris PA, Walters EH. Bronchus associated lymphoid tissue (BALT) in human lung: its distribution in smokers and non-smokers. *Thorax* 1993;48(11):1130–4.

Rochelle LG, Fischer BM, Adler KB. Concurrent production of reactive oxygen and nitrogen species by airway epithelial cells in vitro. *Free Radical Biology & Medicine* 1998;24(5):863–8.

Rowley DA, Halliwell B. Formation of hydroxyl radicals from hydrogen peroxide and iron salts by superoxide- and ascorbate-dependent mechanisms: relevance to the pathology of rheumatoid disease. *Clinical Science (London)* 1983;64(6):649–53.

Rubio ML, Martin-Mosquero MC, Ortega M, Peces-Barba G, González-Mangado N. Oral N-acetylcysteine attenuates elastase-induced pulmonary emphysema in rats. *Chest* 2004;125(4):1500–6.

Russell REK, Culpitt SV, DeMatos C, Donnelly L, Smith M, Wiggins J, Barnes PJ. Release and activity of matrix metalloproteinase-9 and tissue inhibitor of metalloproteinase-1 by alveolar macrophages from patients with chronic obstructive pulmonary disease. *American Journal of Respiratory Cell and Molecular Biology* 2002a;26(5):602–9.

Russell REK, Thorley A, Culpitt SV, Dodd S, Donnelly LE, Demattos C, Fitzgerald M, Barnes PJ. Alveolar macrophage-mediated elastolysis: roles of matrix metalloproteinases, cysteine, and serine proteases. *American Journal of Physiology – Lung Cellular and Molecular Physiology* 2002b;283(4):L867–L873.

Rutgers SR, Postma DS, ten Hacken NH, Kauffman HF, van der Mark TW, Koëter GH, Timens W. Ongoing airway inflammation in patients with COPD who do not currently smoke. *Chest* 2000;117(5 Suppl 1):262S.

Rutgers SR, van der Mark TW, Coers W, Moshage H, Timens W, Kauffman HF, Koëter GH, Postma DS. Markers of nitric oxide metabolism in sputum and exhaled air are not increased in chronic obstructive pulmonary disease. *Thorax* 1999;54(7):576–80.

Ryder RC, Dunnill MS, Anderson JA. A quantitative study of bronchial mucus gland volume, emphysema and smoking in a necropsy population. *Journal of Pathology* 1971;104(1):59–71.

Sabatini F, Petecchia L, Tavian M, Jodon de Villeroche V, Rossi GA, Brouty-Boye D. Human bronchial fibroblasts exhibit a mesenchymal stem cell phenotype and multilineage differentiating potentialities. *Laboratory Investigation* 2005;85(8):962–71.

Sabroe I, Parker LC, Dockrell DH, Davies DE, Dower SK, Whyte MKB. Targeting the networks that underpin contiguous immunity in asthma and chronic obstructive pulmonary disease. *American Journal of Respiratory and Critical Care Medicine* 2007;175(4):306–11.

Saetta M, Mariani M, Panina-Bordignon P, Turato G, Buonsanti C, Baraldo S, Bellettato CM, Papi A, Corbetta L, Zuin R, et al. Increased expression of the chemokine receptor CXCR3 and its ligand CXCL10 in peripheral airways of smokers with chronic obstructive pulmonary disease. *American Journal of Respiratory and Critical Care Medicine* 2002;165(10):1404–9.

Saetta M, Turato G, Facchini FM, Corbino L, Lucchini RE, Casoni G, Maestrelli P, Mapp CE, Ciaccia A, Fabbri LM. Inflammatory cells in the bronchial glands of smokers with chronic bronchitis. *American Journal of Respiratory and Critical Care Medicine* 1997;156(5):1633–9.

Sakao S, Tatsumi K, Igara H, Shino Y, Shirasawa H, Kuriyama T. Association of tumor necrosis factor α gene promoter polymorphism with the presence of chronic obstructive pulmonary disease. *American Journal of Respiratory and Critical Care Medicine* 2001; 163(2):420–2.

Sandford AJ, Chagani T, Weir TD, Connett JE, Anthonisen NR, Paré PD. Susceptibility genes for rapid decline of lung function in the Lung Health Study. *American Journal of Respiratory and Critical Care Medicine* 2001;163(2):469–73.

Sandford AJ, Chagani T, Weir TD, Paré PD. α_1-Antichymotrypsin mutations in patients with chronic obstructive pulmonary disease. *Disease Markers* 1998; 13(4):257–60.

Sastre J, Asensi M, Gasco E, Pallardo FV, Ferrero JA, Furukawa T, Vina J. Exhaustive physical exercise causes oxidation of glutathione status in blood: prevention by antioxidant administration. *American Journal of Physiology* 1992;263(5 Pt 2):R992–R995.

Schaberg T, Haller H, Rau M, Kaiser D, Fassbender M, Lode H. Superoxide anion release induced by platelet-activating factor is increased in human alveolar macrophages from smokers. *European Respiratory Journal* 1992;5(4):387–93.

Schaberg T, Klein U, Rau M, Eller J, Lode H. Subpopulations of alveolar macrophages in smokers and non-smokers: relation to the expression of CD11/CD18 molecules and superoxide anion production. *American Journal of Respiratory and Critical Care Medicine* 1995;151(5):1551–8.

Schellenberg D, Paré PD, Weir TD, Spinelli JJ, Walker BA, Sandford AJ. Vitamin D binding protein variants and the risk of COPD. *American Journal of Respiratory and Critical Care Medicine* 1998;157(3 Pt 1):957–61.

Scholz H, Yndestad A, Damås JK, Wæhre T, Tonstad S, Aukrust P, Halvorsen B. 8-Isoprostane increases expression of interleukin-8 in human macrophages through activation of mitogen-activated protein kinases. *Cardiovascular Research* 2003;59(4):945–54.

Schulz H, Brand P, Heyder J. Particle deposition in the respiratory tract. In: Gehr P, Heyder J, editors. *Particle-Lung Interactions*. Lung Biology in Health and Disease. Vol. 143. New York: Marcel Dekker, 2000:229–90.

Scott DA, Poston RN, Wilson RF, Coward PY, Palmer RM. The influence of vitamin C on systemic markers of endothelial and inflammatory cell activation in smokers and non-smokers. *Inflammation Research* 2005;54(3):138–44.

Seemungal T, Harper-Owen R, Bhowmik A, Moric I, Sanderson G, Message S, Maccallum P, Meade TW, Jeffries DJ, Johnston SL, et al. Respiratory viruses, symptoms, and inflammatory markers in acute exacerbations and stable chronic obstructive pulmonary disease. *American Journal of Respiratory and Critical Care Medicine* 2001;164(9):1618–23.

Seersholm N, Kok-Jensen A, Dirksen A. Survival of patients with severe alpha 1-antitrypsin deficiency with special reference to non-index cases. *Thorax* 1994;49(7): 695–8.

Seersholm N, Kok-Jensen A, Dirksen A. Decline in FEV1 among patients with severe hereditary alpha 1-antitrypsin deficiency type PiZ. *American Journal of Respiratory and Critical Care Medicine* 1995;152 (6 Pt 1):1922–5.

Segura-Valdez L, Pardo A, Gaxiola M, Uhal BD, Becerril C, Selman M. Upregulation of gelatinases A and B, collagenases 1 and 2, and increased parenchymal cell death in COPD. *Chest* 2000;117(3):684–94.

Seifart C, Plagens A, Brodje D, Muller B, von Wichert P, Floros J. Surfactant protein B intron 4 variation in German patients with COPD and acute respiratory failure. *Disease Markers* 2002;18(3):129–36.

Selman M, Cisneros-Lira J, Gaxiola M, Ramirez R, Kudlacz EM, Mitchell PG, Pardo A. Matrix metalloproteinases inhibition attenuates tobacco smoke-induced emphysema in guinea pigs. *Chest* 2003;123(5):1633–41.

Selman M, Montaño M, Ramos C, Vanda B, Becerril C, Delgado J, Sansores R, Barrios R, Pardo A. Tobacco smoke-induced lung emphysema in guinea pigs is associated with increased interstitial collagenase. *American Journal of Physiology – Lung Cellular and Molecular Physiology* 1996 Nov;271(5 Pt 1):L734–L743.

Sethi S, Evans N, Grant BJB, Murphy TF. New strains of bacteria and exacerbations of chronic obstructive pulmonary disease. *New England Journal of Medicine* 2002;347(7):465–71.

Shapiro SD. End-stage chronic obstructive pulmonary disease: the cigarette is burned out but inflammation rages on [editorial]. *American Journal of Respiratory and Critical Care Medicine* 2001;164(3):339–40.

Shapiro SD. COPD unwound. *New England Journal of Medicine* 2005;352(19):2016–9.

Shapiro SD, DeMeo DL, Silverman EK. Smoke and mirrors: mouse models as a reflection of human chronic obstructive pulmonary disease. *American Journal of Respiratory and Critical Care Medicine* 2004;170(9): 929–31.

Shapiro SD, Goldstein NM, Houghton AM, Kobayashi DK, Kelley D, Belaaouaj A. Neutrophil elastase contributes to cigarette smoke-induced emphysema in mice. *American Journal of Pathology* 2003;163(6):2329–35.

Silverman EK, Chapman HA, Drazen JM, Weiss ST, Rosner B, Campbell EJ, O'Donnell WJ, Reilly JJ, Ginns L, Mentzer S, et al. Genetic epidemiology of severe, early-onset chronic obstructive pulmonary disease: risk to relatives for airflow obstruction and chronic bronchitis. *American Journal of Respiratory and Critical Care Medicine* 1998;157(6 Pt 1):1770–8.

Silverman EK, Mosley JD, Palmer LJ, Barth M, Senter JM, Brown A, Drazen JM, Kwiatkowski DJ, Chapman HA, Campbell EJ, et al. Genome-wide linkage analysis of severe, early-onset chronic obstructive pulmonary disease: airflow obstruction and chronic bronchitis phenotypes. *Human Molecular Genetics* 2002a;11(6):623–32.

Silverman EK, Palmer LJ, Mosley JD, Barth M, Senter JM, Brown A, Drazen JM, Kwiatkowski DJ, Chapman HA, Campbell EJ, et al. Genomewide linkage analysis of quantitative spirometric phenotypes in severe early-onset chronic obstructive pulmonary disease. *American Journal of Human Genetics* 2002b;70(5):1229–39.

Silverman EK, Pierce JA, Province MA, Rao DC, Campbell EJ. Variability of pulmonary function in alpha-1-antitrypsin deficiency: clinical correlates. *Annals of Internal Medicine* 1989;111(12):982–91.

Silverman EK, Province MA, Campbell EJ, Pierce JA, Rao DC, Boerwinkle E. Family study of α1-antitrypsin deficiency: effects of cigarette smoking, measured genotype, and their interaction on pulmonary function and biochemical traits. *Genetic Epidemiology* 1992; 9(5):317–31.

Singh S, Evans TW. Nitric oxide, the biological mediator of the decade: fact or fiction? *European Respiratory Journal* 1997;10(3):699–707.

Skwarski KM, Gorecka D, Sliwinski P, Hogg JC, MacNee W. The effects of cigarette smoking on pulmonary hemodynamics. *Chest* 1993;103(4):1166–72.

Slot JW, Geuze HJ, Freeman BA, Crapo JD. Intracellular localization of the copper-zinc and manganese superoxide dismutases in rat liver parenchymal cells. *Laboratory Investigation* 1986;55(3):363–71.

Smith CA, Harrison DJ. Association between polymorphism in gene for microsomal epoxide hydrolase and susceptibility to emphysema. *Lancet* 1997;350(9078):630–3.

Smith CB, Golden CA, Kanner RE, Renzetti AD Jr. Association of viral and Mycoplasma pneumoniae infections with acute respiratory illness in patients with chronic obstructive pulmonary diseases. *American Review of Respiratory Disease* 1980;121(2):225–32.

Snider GL, Kleinerman J, Thurlbeck WM, Bengali ZH. The definition of emphysema: report of a National Heart, Lung, and Blood Institute, Division of Lung Diseases Workshop. *American Review of Respiratory Disease* 1985;132(1):182–5.

Soejima K, Yamaguchi K, Kohda E, Takeshita K, Ito Y, Mastubara H, Oguma T, Inoue T, Okubo Y, Amakawa K, et al. Longitudinal follow-up study of smoking-induced lung density changes by high-resolution computed tomography. *American Journal of Respiratory and Critical Care Medicine* 2000;161(4 Pt 1):1264–73.

Soini Y, Näpänkangas U, Jarvinen K, Kaarteenaho-Wiik R, Pääkkö P, Kinnula VL. Expression of γ-glutamyl cysteine synthetase in nonsmall cell lung carcinoma. *Cancer* 2001;92(11):2911–9.

Soler N, Ewig S, Torres A, Filella X, Gonzalez J, Zaubet A. Airway inflammation and bronchial microbial patterns in patients with stable chronic obstructive pulmonary disease. *European Respiratory Journal* 1999; 14(5):1015–22.

Speizer FE, Rosner B, Tager I. Familial aggregation of chronic respiratory disease: use of National Health Interview Survey data for specific hypothesis testing. *International Journal of Epidemiology* 1976;5(2): 167–72.

Spira A, Beane J, Pinto-Plata V, Kadar A, Liu G, Shah V, Celli B, Brody JS. Gene expression profiling of human lung tissue from smokers with severe emphysema. *American Journal of Respiratory Cell and Molecular Biology* 2004;31(6):601–10.

Stangel M, Zettl UK, Mix E, Zielasek J, Toyka KV, Hartung HP, Gold R. H2O2 and nitric oxide-mediated oxidative stress induce apoptosis in rat skeletal muscle myoblasts. *Journal of Neuropathology and Experimental Neurology* 1996;55(1):36–43.

Stockley RA. Proteases and antiproteases. *Novartis Foundation Symposium* 2001;234:189–99.

Stockley RA, Campbell EJ. Alpha-1-antitrypsin genotyping with mouthwash specimens. *European Respiratory Journal* 2001;17(3):356–9.

Stolk J, Nieuwenhuizen W, Stoller JK, Aboussouan L. High dose intravenous AAT and plasma neutrophil derived fibrinogen fragments. *Thorax* 2005;60(1):84.

Stoller JK, Aboussouan LS. α_1-Antitrypsin deficiency. 5: intravenous augmentation therapy: current understanding. *Thorax* 2004;59(8):708–12.

Stone PJ, Gottlieb DJ, O'Connor GT, Ciccolella DE, Breuer R, Bryan-Rhadfi J, Shaw HA, Franzblau C, Snider GL. Elastin and collagen degradation products in urine of smokers with and without chronic obstructive pulmonary disease. *American Journal of Respiratory and Critical Care Medicine* 1995;151(4):952–9.

Szulakowski P, Crowther AJL, Jiménez LA, Donaldson K, Mayer R, Leonard TB, MacNee W, Drost E. The effect of smoking on the transcriptional regulation of lung inflammation in patients with chronic obstructive pulmonary disease. *American Journal of Respiratory and Critical Care Medicine* 2006;174(1):41–50.

Tager I, Tishler PV, Rosner B, Speizer FE, Litt M. Studies of the familial aggregation of chronic bronchitis and obstructive airways disease. *International Journal of Epidemiology* 1978;7(1):55–62.

Takeyabu K, Betsuyaku T, Nishimura M, Yoshioka A, Tanino M, Miyamoto K, Kawakami Y. Cysteine proteinases and cystatin C in bronchoalveolar lavage fluid from subjects with subclinical emphysema. *European Respiratory Journal* 1998;12(5):1033–9.

Takeyabu K, Yamaguchi E, Suzuki I, Nishimura M, Hizawa N, Kamakami Y. Gene polymorphism for microsomal epoxide hydrolase and susceptibility to emphysema in a Japanese population. *European Respiratory Journal* 2000;15(5):891–4.

Takeyama K, Dabbagh K, Jeong Shim J, Dao-Pick T, Ueki IF, Nadel JA. Oxidative stress causes mucin synthesis via transactivation of epidermal growth factor receptor: role of neutrophils. *Journal of Immunology* 2000;164(3):1546–52.

Takeyama K, Dabbagh K, Lee HM, Agustí C, Lausier JA, Ueki IF, Grattan KM, Nadel JA. Epidermal growth factor system regulates mucin production in airways. *Proceedings of the National Academy of Sciences of the United States of America* 1999;96(6):3081–6.

Takeyama K, Fahy JV, Nadel JA. Relationship of epidermal growth factor receptors to goblet cell production in human bronchi. *American Journal of Respiratory and Critical Care Medicine* 2001a;163(2):511–6.

Takeyama K, Jung B, Shim JJ, Burgel P-R, Dao-Pick T, Ueki IF, Protin U, Kroschel P, Nadel JA. Activation of epidermal growth factor receptors is responsible for mucin synthesis induced by cigarette smoke. *American Journal of Physiology – Lung Cellular and Molecular Physiology* 2001b;280(1):L165–L172.

Tan WC, Qui D, Liam BL, Ng TP, Lee SH, Van Eeden SF, D'Yachkova Y, Hogg JC. The human bone marrow response to acute air pollution caused by forest fires. *American Journal of Respiratory and Critical Care Medicine* 2000;161(4):1213–7.

Tang K, Rossiter HB, Wagner PD, Breen EC. Lung-targeted VEGF inactivation leads to an emphysema phenotype in mice. *Journal of Applied Physiology* 2004; 97(4):1559–66.

Thurlbeck WM The incidence of pulmonary emphysema, with observations on the relative incidence and spatial distribution of various types of emphysema. *American Review of Respiratory Disease* 1963;87:207–15.

Tiitto L, Kaarteenaho-Wiik R, Sormunen R, Holmgren A, Pääkkö P, Soini Y, Kinnula VL. Expression of the thioredoxin system in interstitial lung disease. *Journal of Pathology* 2003;201(3):363–70.

Tishler PV, Carey VJ, Reed T, Fabsitz RR. The role of genotype in determining the effects of cigarette smoking on pulmonary function. *Genetic Epidemiology* 2002;22(3):272–82.

Tobin MJ, Cook PJL, Hutchison DCS. Alpha$_1$ antitrypsin deficiency: the clinical and physiological features of pulmonary emphysema in subjects homozygous for Pi type Z: a survey by the British Thoracic Association. *British Journal of Diseases of the Chest* 1983;77(1): 14–27.

Tomasek JJ, Gabbiani G, Hinz B, Chaponnier C, Brown RA. Myofibroblasts and mechano-regulation of connective tissue remodeling. *Nature Reviews Molecular Cell Biology* 2002;3(5):349–63.

Tomita K, Barnes PJ, Adcock IM. The effect of oxidative stress on histone acetylation and IL-8 release. *Biochemical and Biophysical Research Communications* 2003;301(2):572–7.

Torrelles JB, Azad AK, Henning LN, Carlson TK, Schlesinger LS. Role of C-type lectins in mycobacterial infections. *Current Drug Targets* 2008;9(2):102–12.

Traves SL, Culpitt SV, Russell REK, Barnes PJ, Donnelly LE. Increased levels of the chemokines GRO-alpha and MCP-1 in sputum samples from patients with COPD. *Thorax* 2002;57(7):590–5.

Travis J, Salvesen GS. Human plasma proteinase inhibitors. *Annual Review of Biochemistry* 1983;52:655–709.

Tribble DL, Giuliano LJ, Fortmann SP. Reduced plasma ascorbic acid concentrations in non-smokers regularly exposed to environmental tobacco smoke. *American Journal of Clinical Nutrition* 1993;58(6):886–90.

Tsuchiya M, Asada A, Kasahara E, Sato EF, Shindo M, Inoue M. Smoking a single cigarette rapidly reduces combined concentrations of nitrate and nitrite and concentrations of antioxidants in plasma. *Circulation* 2002;105(10):1155–7.

Tsuchiya M, Thompson DF, Suzuki YJ, Cross CE, Packer L. Superoxide formed from cigarette smoke impairs polymorphonuclear leukocyte active oxygen generation activity. *Archives of Biochemistry and Biophysics* 1992;299(1):30–7.

Tsukagoshi H, Shimizu Y, Iwamae S, Hisada T, Ishizuka T, Iizuka K, Dobashi K, Mori M. Evidence of oxidative stress in asthma and COPD: potential inhibitory effect of theophylline. *Respiratory Medicine* 2000;94(6): 584–8.

Tuder RM, McGrath S, Neptune E. The pathobiological mechanisms of emphysema models: what do they have in common? *Pulmonary Pharmacology & Therapeutics* 2003a;16(2):67–78.

Tuder RM, Petrache I, Elias JA, Voelkel NF, Henson PM. Apoptosis and emphysema: the missing link. *American Journal of Respiratory Cell and Molecular Biology* 2003b;28(5):551–4.

Tuder RM, Wood K, Taraseviciene L, Flores SC, Voelkel NF. Cigarette smoke extract decreases the expression of vascular endothelial growth factor by cultured cells and triggers apoptosis of pulmonary endothelial cells. *Chest* 2000;117(5 Suppl 1):241S–242S.

Tuder RM, Zhen L, Cho CY, Taraseviciene-Stewart L, Kasahara Y, Salvemini D, Voelkel NF, Flores SC. Oxidative stress and apoptosis interact and cause emphysema due to vascular endothelial growth factor receptor blockade. *American Journal of Respiratory Cell and Molecular Biology* 2003c;29(1):88–97.

Uotila P. Effect of cigarette smoke on glucuronide conjugation in hamster isolated lungs. *Research Communications in Chemical Pathology and Pharmacology* 1982;38(1):173–6.

U.S. Department of Health and Human Services. *The Health Consequences of Smoking: Chronic Obstructive Lung Disease. A Report of the Surgeon General*. Rockville (MD): U.S. Department of Health and Human Services, Public Health Service, Office on Smoking and Health, 1984. DHHS Publication No. (PHS) 84-50205.

U.S. Department of Health and Human Services. *The Health Benefits of Smoking Cessation. A Report of the Surgeon General*. Atlanta: U.S. Department of Health and Human Services, Public Health Service, Centers for Disease Control, National Center for Chronic Disease Prevention and Health Promotion, Office on Smoking and Health, 1990. DHHS Publication No. (CDC) 90-8416.

U.S. Department of Health and Human Services. *9th Report on Carcinogens*. Research Triangle Park (NC): U.S. Department of Health and Human Services, Public Health Service, National Toxicology Program, 2000.

U.S. Department of Health and Human Services. *The Health Consequences of Smoking: A Report of the Surgeon General*. Atlanta: U.S. Department of Health and Human Services, Centers for Disease Control and Prevention, National Center for Chronic Disease Prevention and Health Promotion, Office on Smoking and Health, 2004.

U.S. Department of Health and Human Services. *The Health Consequences of Involuntary Exposure to Tobacco Smoke: A Report of the Surgeon General*. Atlanta: U.S. Department of Health and Human Services, Centers for Disease Control and Prevention, Coordinating Center for Health Promotion, National Center for Chronic Disease Prevention and Health Promotion, Office on Smoking and Health, 2006.

U.S. Department of Health, Education, and Welfare. *Smoking and Health: Report of the Advisory Committee to the Surgeon General of the Public Health Service*. Washington: U.S. Department of Health, Education, and Welfare, Public Health Service, Center for Disease Control, 1964. PHS Publication No. 1103.

U.S. Environmental Protection Agency. *Air Quality Criteria for Oxides of Nitrogen*. Washington: U.S. Environmental Protection Agency, 1993. Publication No. EPA/600/8-91/049AF.

U.S. Environmental Protection Agency. *Air Quality Criteria for Carbon Monoxide*. Washington: U.S. Environmental Protection Agency, Office of Research and Development, 2000. Publication No. EPA 600/P-99/001F.

van Acker SA, Koymans LM, Bast A. Molecular pharmacology of vitamin E: structural aspects of antioxidant activity. *Free Radical Biology & Medicine* 1993;15(3):311–28.

van Brabandt H, Cauberghs M, Verbeken E, Moerman P, Lauweryns JM, Van de Woestijne KP. Partitioning of pulmonary impedance in excised human and canine lungs. *Journal of Applied Physiology* 1983;55(6):1733–42.

van der Vaart H, Postma DS, Timens W, Ten Hacken NHT. Acute effects of cigarette smoke on inflammation and oxidative stress: a review. *Thorax* 2004;59(8):713–21.

van der Vliet A, Eiserich JP, Shigenaga MK, Cross CE. Reactive nitrogen species and tyrosine nitration in the respiratory tract: epiphenomena or a pathobiologic mechanism of disease? *American Journal of Respiratory and Critical Care Medicine* 1999;160(1):1–9.

van Eeden SF, Hogg JC. The response of human bone marrow to chronic cigarette smoking. *European Respiratory Journal* 2000;15(5):915–21.

van Eeden SF, Tan WC, Suwa T, Mukae H, Terashima T, Fujii T, Qui D, Vincent R, Hogg JC. Cytokines involved in the systemic inflammatory response induced by exposure to particulate matter air pollutants (PM_{10}). *American Journal of Respiratory and Critical Care Medicine* 2001;164(5):826–30.

Vestbo J, Lange P. Can GOLD Stage 0 provide information of prognostic value in chronic obstructive pulmonary disease? *American Journal of Respiratory and Critical Care Medicine* 2002;166(3):329–32.

Vestbo J, Prescott E, Lange P. Association of chronic mucus hypersecretion with FEV_1 decline and chronic obstructive pulmonary disease morbidity. The Copenhagen City Heart Study Group. *American Journal of Respiratory and Critical Care Medicine* 1996;153(5):1530–5.

Viña J, Servera E, Asensi M, Sastre J, Pallardó FV, Ferrero JA, García-De-La-Asunción J, Antón V, Marín J. Exercise causes blood glutathione oxidation in chronic obstructive pulmonary disease: prevention by O_2 therapy. *Journal of Applied Physiology* 1996;81(5):2199–202.

Vlahovic G, Russell ML, Mercer RR, Crapo JD. Cellular and connective tissue changes in alveolar septal walls in emphysema. *American Journal of Respiratory and Critical Care Medicine* 1999;160(6):2086–92.

Voelkel NF. A conference report: the second Siena International Conference on animal models of chronic obstructive pulmonary disease. *Pulmonary Pharmacology & Therapeutics* 2004;17(2):61–3.

Voelkel N, Taraseviciene-Stewart L. Emphysema: an autoimmune vascular disease? *Proceedings of the American Thoracic Society* 2005;2(1):23–5.

von Ahsen N, Oellerich M, Schütz E. Use of two reporter dyes without interference in a single-tube rapid-cycle PCR: α_1-antitrypsin genotyping by multiplex real-time fluorescence PCR with the LightCycler. *Clinical Chemistry* 2000;46(2):156–61.

Walker DC, Behzad A, Chu F. Neutrophil migration through preexisting holes in the basal laminae of alveolar capillaries and epithelium during streptococcal pneumonia. *Microvascular Research* 1995;50(3): 397–416.

Wallaert B, Gressier B, Marquette CH, Gosset P, Remy-Jardin M, Mizon J, Tonnel AB. Inactivation of alpha 1-proteinase inhibitor by alveolar inflammatory cells from smoking patients with or without emphysema. *American Review of Respiratory Disease* 1993;147 (6 Pt 1):1537–43.

Walter S, Nancy NR. Basopenia following cigarette smoking. *Indian Journal of Medical Research* 1980;72: 422–5.

Walter S, Walter A. Basophil degranulation induced by cigarette smoking in man. *Thorax* 1982;37(10):756–9.

Wang Z, Zheng T, Zhu Z, Homer RJ, Riese RJ, Chapman HA Jr, Shapiro SD, Elias JA. Interferon γ induction of pulmonary emphysema in the adult murine lung. *Journal of Experimental Medicine* 2000;192(11):1587–99.

Ward C, Thien F, Secombe J, Gollant S, Walters EH. Bronchoalveolar lavage fluid urea as a measure of pulmonary permeability in healthy smokers. *European Respiratory Journal* 2000;15(2):285–90.

Weiss SJ, Test ST, Eckmann CM, Roos D, Regiani S. Brominating oxidants generated by human eosinophils. *Science* 1986;234(4773):200–3.

Weiss ST, Segal MR, Sparrow D, Wager C. Relation of FEV_1 and peripheral blood leukocyte count to total mortality: the normative aging study. *American Journal of Epidemiology* 1995;142(5):493–8.

Weitzenblum E, Hirth C, Ducolone A, Mirhom R, Rasaholinjanahary J, Ehrhart M. Prognostic value of pulmonary artery pressure in chronic obstructive pulmonary disease. *Thorax* 1981;36(10):752–8.

Werner S, Grose R. Regulation of wound healing by growth factors and cytokines. *Physiological Reviews* 2003;83(3):835–70.

Wert SE, Yoshida M, LeVine AM, Ikegami M, Jones T, Ross GF, Fisher JH, Korfhagen TR, Whitsett JA. Increased metalloproteinase activity, oxidant production, and emphysema in surfactant protein D gene-inactivated mice. *Proceedings of the National Academy of Sciences of the United States of America* 2000;97(11):5972–7.

Wickenden JA, Clarke MC, Rossi AG, Rahman I, Faux SP, Donaldson K, MacNee W. Cigarette smoke prevents apoptosis through inhibition of caspase activation and induces necrosis. *American Journal of Respiratory Cell and Molecular Biology* 2003;29(5):562–70.

Wilk JB, DeStefano AL, Arnett DK, Rich SS, Djousse L, Crapo RO, Leppert MF, Province MA, Cupples LA, Gottlieb DJ, et al. A genome-wide scan of pulmonary function measures in the National Heart, Lung, and Blood Institute Family Heart Study. *American Journal of Respiratory and Critical Care Medicine* 2003a;167(11): 1528–33.

Wilk JB, DeStefano AL, Joost O, Myers RH, Cupples LA, Slater K, Atwood LD, Heard-Costa NL, Herbert A, O'Connor GT, et al. Linkage and association with pulmonary function measures on chromosome 6q27 in the Framingham Heart Study. *Human Molecular Genetics* 2003b;12(21):2745–51.

Wilkinson TMA, Patel IS, Wilks M, Donaldson GC, Wedzicha JA. Airway bacterial load and FEV_1 decline in patients with chronic obstructive pulmonary disease. *American Journal of Respiratory and Critical Care Medicine* 2003;167(8):1090–5.

Wink DA, Hanbauer I, Grisham MB, Laval F, Nims RW, Laval J, Cook J, Pacelli R, Liebmann J, Krishna M, et al. Chemical biology of nitric oxide: regulation and protective and toxic mechanisms. *Current Topics in Cellular Regulation* 1996;34:159–87.

Winkel P, Statland BE. The acute effect of cigarette smoking on the concentrations of blood leukocyte types in healthy young women. *American Journal of Clinical Pathology* 1981;75(6):781–5.

Winklhofer-Roob BM, Ellmunter H, Frühwirth M, Schlegel-Haueter SE, Khoschsorur G, van't Hof MA, Shmerling DH. Plasma vitamin C concentrations in patients with cystic fibrosis: evidence of associations with lung inflammation. *American Journal of Nutrition* 1997;65(6):1858–66.

Wouters EF, Creutzberg EC, Schols AM. Systemic effects in COPD. *Chest* 2002;121(5 Suppl):127S–130S.

Wright DT, Fischer BM, Li C, Rochelle LG, Akley NJ, Adler KB. Oxidant stress stimulates mucin secretion and PLC in airway epithelium via a nitric oxide-dependent mechanism. *American Journal of Physiology* 1996;271 (5 Pt 1):L854–L861.

Wright JL, Churg A. Smoke-induced emphysema in guinea pigs is associated with morphometric evidence of collagen breakdown and repair. *American Journal of Physiology* 1995;268(1 Pt 1):L17–L20.

Wright JL, Dai J, Zay K, Price K, Gilks CB, Churg A. Effects of cigarette smoke on nitric oxide synthase expression in the rat lung. *Laboratory Investigation* 1999; 79(8):975–83.

Wright JL, Farmer SG, Churg A. Synthetic serine elastase inhibitor reduces cigarette smoke–induced emphysema in guinea pigs. *American Journal of Respiratory and Critical Care Medicine* 2002;166(7):954–60.

Wright JL, Lawson L, Paré PD, Hooper RO, Peretz DI, Nelems JM, Schulzer M, Hogg JC. The structure and function of the pulmonary vasculature in mild chronic obstructive pulmonary disease: the effect of oxygen and exercise. *American Review of Respiratory Disease* 1983a;128(4):702–7.

Wright JL, Lawson LM, Paré PD, Wiggs BJ, Kennedy S, Hogg JC. Morphology of peripheral airways in current smokers and ex-smokers. *American Review of Respiratory Disease* 1983b;127(4):474–7.

Wright JL, Petty T, Thurlbeck WM. Analysis of the structure of the muscular pulmonary arteries in patients with pulmonary hypertension and COPD: National Institutes of Health Nocturnal Oxygen Therapy Trial. *Lung* 1992;170(2):109–24.

Wu HM, Jin M, Marsh CB. Toward functional proteomics of alveolar macrophages. *American Journal of Physiology – Lung Cellular and Molecular Physiology* 2005; 288(4):L585–L595.

Wu L, Chau J, Young RP, Pokorny V, Mills GD, Hopkins R, McLean L, Black PN. Transforming growth factor-β_1 genotype and susceptibility to chronic obstructive pulmonary disease. *Thorax* 2004;59(2):126–9.

Wyatt JP, Fischer VW, Sweet HC. Panlobular emphysema: anatomy and pathodynamics. *Diseases of the Chest* 1962;41(3):239–59.

Wyatt TA, Heires AJ, Sanderson SD, Floreani AA. Protein kinase C activation is required for cigarette smoke-enhanced C5a-mediated release of interleukin-8 in human bronchial epithelial cells. *American Journal of Respiratory Cell and Molecular Biology* 1999; 21(2):283–8.

Yamamoto C, Yoneda T, Yoshikawa M, Fu A, Tokuyama T, Tsukaguchi K, Narita N. Airway inflammation in COPD assessed by sputum levels of interleukin-8. *Chest* 1997;112(2):505–10.

Yanai M, Sekizawa K, Ohrui T, Sasaki H, Takishima T. Site of airway obstruction in pulmonary disease: direct measurement of intrabronchial pressure. *Journal of Applied Physiology* 1992;72(3):1016–23.

Yim J-J, Park GY, Lee C-T, Kim YW, Han SK, Shim Y-S, Yoo C-G. Genetic susceptibility to chronic obstructive pulmonary disease in Koreans: combined analysis of polymorphic genotypes for microsomal epoxide hydrolase and glutathione *S*-transferase M1 and T1. *Thorax* 2000;55(2):121–5.

Yim J-J, Yoo CG, Lee C-T, Kim YW, Han SK, Shim Y-S. Lack of association between glutathione *S*-transferase P1 polymorphism and COPD in Koreans. *Lung* 2002;180(2):119–25.

Yoshikawa M, Hiyama K, Ishioka S, Maeda H, Maeda A, Yamakido M. Microsomal epoxide hydrolase genotypes and chronic obstructive pulmonary disease in Japanese. *International Journal of Molecular Medicine* 2000;5(1):49–53.

Yoshioka A, Betsuyaku T, Nishimura M, Miyamoto K, Kondo T, Kawakami Y. Excessive neutrophil elastase in bronchoalveolar lavage fluid in subclinical emphysema. *American Journal of Respiratory and Critical Care Medicine* 1995;152(6 Pt 1):2127–32.

Zang LY, Stone K, Pryor WA. Detection of free radicals in aqueous extracts of cigarette tar by electron spin resonance. *Free Radical Biology & Medicine* 1995; 19(2):161–7.

Zheng T, Zhu Z, Wang Z, Homer RJ, Ma B, Riese RJ Jr, Chapman HA Jr, Shapiro SD, Elias JA. Inducible targeting of IL-13 to the adult lung causes matrix metalloproteinase– and cathepsin-dependent emphysema. *Journal of Clinical Investigation* 2000;106(9):1081–93.

Chapter 8
Reproductive and Developmental Effects

Introduction

Health professionals have long considered exposure to tobacco smoke harmful to reproduction, affecting aspects from fertility and pregnancy outcome to fetal and child development. Tobacco smoke contains thousands of compounds, some of which are known to have toxic effects on reproductive health, such as carbon monoxide (CO), nicotine, and metals. Along with more than four million births in the United States annually, 10 to 20 percent of pregnancies end in miscarriage or stillbirth before delivery, and another 10 percent of couples who want to conceive a child experience infertility or reduced fertility. In 2007, 17.4 percent of all women and approximately 19 percent of women of reproductive age (18 through 44 years) smoked cigarettes (Centers for Disease Control and Prevention [CDC] 2008). Smoking rates among women of reproductive age vary by other factors such as education, race, and geographic area, ranging from about 10 percent in Utah to nearly 30 percent in Kentucky and West Virginia (CDC 2005). From 2002 to 2005, 17.3 percent of pregnant women reported smoking cigarettes in the past month (*NSDUH Report* 2007). CDC's Pregnancy Risk Assessment Monitoring System is an ongoing, population-based surveillance system designed to identify and monitor selected self-reported maternal behaviors and experiences that occur before, during, and after pregnancy among women who deliver a live infant. In 2002, the prevalence of smoking in the three months before pregnancy ranged from 13.6 percent (Utah) to 37.0 percent (West Virginia); in the last three months of pregnancy, from 6.8 percent (Utah) to 25.3 percent (West Virginia); and after pregnancy, from 9.0 percent (Utah) to 33.7 percent (West Virginia) (Williams et al. 2006). Prevalence of smoking is generally higher among men. In 2003, 24.1 percent reported smoking and prevalence was higher among younger men than among older men. This chapter examines reproductive and developmental outcomes, although the term "reproductive" may be used generally to describe both, in relation to smoking.

The reproductive endpoints include aspects affecting a person's ability to conceive a child, such as menstrual cycle function, semen quality, fertility, and menopause, in addition to complications of pregnancy, such as miscarriage, ectopic pregnancy, and preterm delivery. Developmental endpoints that affect child health status include birth weight, congenital anomalies, and perinatal and infant deaths—especially sudden infant deaths and sudden unexplained infant deaths which have been associated with exposure to secondhand smoke—and they extend into childhood with neurobehavioral endpoints and puberty. Previous Surgeon General's reports have examined epidemiologic data for most of these endpoints. This chapter cites conclusions from those earlier reports, examines in more detail endpoints for which the evidence was not sufficient to establish causality, and provides an updated review of the epidemiologic literature for these endpoints. Other sections explore the possible biologic basis for an effect of smoking on reproduction and development from the pathophysiological levels to the cellular and genetic levels.

When studying the reproductive effects of smoking in humans, there are several exposure issues to bear in mind. Most studies have examined the effects of active smoking on fertility or pregnancy. For the past decade, interest has also increased in the effects of secondhand exposure to tobacco smoke, so these studies are mentioned when available (U.S. Department of Health and Human Services [USDHHS] 2006). Because smoking rates have declined, persons who are involuntarily exposed to tobacco smoke probably now outnumber active smokers. Thus, many nonsmokers are exposed to some of the same toxins to which smokers are exposed. The problem of involuntary exposure may be particularly pervasive for women who stop smoking during pregnancy. They may live with partners or family members who continue to smoke, so the potential still exists for exposure to tobacco smoke in the household. Such an exposure may also occur in the workplace. However, local, state, and federal laws against smoking in the workplace have led to a decline in this type of exposure. The critical exposure periods may be very specific for certain pregnancy outcomes or congenital anomalies, but most epidemiologic studies do not seek such detailed information about exposure to tobacco smoke. For endpoints of child development, postnatal exposure to tobacco smoke may also be important but difficult to separate from prenatal exposure, because the two are correlated.

Current smoking may be assessed for reproductive endpoints such as fertility, but this timing may not reflect exposure during the critical period when fertility began if the woman has stopped smoking as a result of ongoing fertility problems. Fertility may also be affected by her partner's smoking, either directly or indirectly as exposure to secondhand smoke. Research shows the long-lasting effects of prenatal exposures on later health, even in adulthood. Thus, age at puberty, fertility, or even maintenance of a pregnancy may be affected by in utero exposure to tobacco smoke, but this relationship is rarely studied. For age at menopause, patterns of exposure to tobacco smoke over a lifetime may be important.

Review of Epidemiologic Literature on Smoking

Reproductive Endpoints

Menstrual Function, Menarche, and Menopause

Menstrual Cycling

The effects of exogenous exposures on menstrual function have become the focus of much research. Studies of these effects are hindered because cyclic patterns of menstruation vary and do not have one well-defined health endpoint. For example, some menstrual disturbances such as irregularity do not have standard definitions, and others, such as dysmenorrhea (painful menstruation), may be subjective. However, menstrual morbidity has a significant impact on women's health and economics (e.g., physician visits and time lost from work) (Harlow and Ephross 1995). Furthermore, menstrual cycle patterns are a useful marker of ovarian function and reproductive health and may affect risks of chronic disease. The 2004 Surgeon General's report on the health consequences of smoking did not examine menstrual function or menopause, but the 2001 report on women and smoking reached suggestive conclusions that are expanded upon here (USDHHS 2001, 2004).

Beginning in the 1960s, numerous studies have examined menstrual function in relation to smoking, but most were focused on dysmenorrhea or other self-reported symptoms. As summarized in the 2001 Surgeon General's report on women and smoking (USDHHS 2001), the prevalence of dysmenorrhea was increased with current smoking, with intermediate effects among former smokers (Brown et al. 1988; Parazzini et al. 1994; Harlow and Park 1996; Mishra et al. 2000), but not in all studies (Andersch and Milsom 1982). A Chinese study of exposure to secondhand smoke in nonsmoking women reported an adjusted risk for dysmenorrhea that increased with higher exposure levels (Chen et al. 2000). In examining multiple endpoints or symptoms, a community survey in Los Angeles, California, revealed that the prevalence of physician-attended menstrual disorders (e.g., dysmenorrhea and oligomenorrhea) was higher among heavy smokers (≥15 cigarettes per day) than among nonsmokers (Sloss and Frerichs 1983). A postal survey in England found that compared with nonsmokers, smokers more frequently reported six of seven aspects of "abnormal" menstruation, including frequent, short, or irregular periods and prolonged and heavy bleeding (Brown et al. 1988).

Similarly, other worldwide studies have reported higher risks of multiple symptoms, including premenstrual tension, heavy periods, severe pain, and frequent and irregular periods among smokers, especially heavy smokers (Kritz-Silverstein et al. 1999; Mishra et al. 2000). Additional studies reported increased risks of short and/or irregular cycles among smokers, with some dose-response relationships observed (Kato et al. 1999; Rowland et al. 2002). Using prospective menstrual diaries to improve ascertainment, Hornsby and colleagues (1998) found more reporting of dysmenorrhea, an increased daily amount of bleeding, and a shorter duration of bleeding among smokers. The findings suggested that heavy smokers (>10 cigarettes per day) had irregularity or greater variability in cycle length than did nonsmokers. However, the study had limited power to examine higher smoking levels, and the study sample was selective in that the participants' mothers had participated in a clinical trial of diethylstilbestrol while pregnant with them.

Other studies have assessed menstrual cycle parameters by measuring hormone levels to define lengths of phases in the cycle. A small study noted cycles of heavy smokers that were, on average, 1.6 days shorter than cycles of nonsmokers, and the mean follicular phase was shorter by 1.4 days (Zumoff et al. 1990). A study based on diaries and daily measurement of urinary levels of hormone metabolites reported that heavy smoking (≥20 cigarettes per day) was also associated with menstrual cycle lengths that were shorter by 2.6 days and more variable than those of nonsmokers (Windham et al. 1999b). The shortening of the cycle occurred primarily during the follicular phase. The findings also suggested an increased risk of a short luteal phase (<11 days) and anovulation, but the confidence intervals (CIs) for these endpoints were wide and not significant. The mean duration of bleeding in smokers was not different. Another study, based on diaries of workers in the semiconductor industry, as well as levels of hormone metabolites, found little difference in cycle length among smokers compared with nonsmokers (Liu et al. 2004a). However, this finding was modified by age: shorter follicular phases were associated with smoking only among women older than 35 years of age. The data also revealed a nonsignificant increase in risk of anovulation among smokers. Dose-response relationships were not examined (Liu et al. 2004b).

Alterations in menstrual cycle function may have several ramifications, including a burden on the health care system. Dysmenorrhea may lead to a loss of work productivity. Women with variable cycle lengths may have difficulty trying to conceive, because the timing of ovulation is less predictable. Anovulation has an obvious relevance for time to conception or fertility. Cycles that are shortened during the follicular phase might indicate abnormal folliculogenesis and ovum maturation. A short luteal phase may indicate a progesterone response that is inadequate for implantation and maintenance of the trophoblast. Studies have implicated a luteal phase defect as a cause of infertility as well as a cause of recurrent spontaneous abortion (SAB) (Regan et al. 1990; Tulppala et al. 1991). These effects are consistent with evidence for association of smoking with decreased fertility (see "Fertility" later in this chapter). Women with short menstrual cycles may also be at a higher risk of breast cancer (Kelsey et al. 1993).

Reproductive Life Span—Menarche to Menopause

Smoking may also affect the duration of menstrual cycling (reproductive life span). The 2001 Surgeon General's report on women and smoking summarized numerous studies that consistently found a younger age at natural menopause among women who smoked than that for nonsmokers (USDHHS 2001). The studies also concluded that smokers may have more menopausal symptoms. In an earlier meta-analysis, the difference in the mean age at natural menopause ranged from 0.8 to 1.7 years (Midgette and Baron 1990). This same meta-analysis showed a prevalence ratio for being postmenopausal that was nearly doubled among current smokers versus lifetime nonsmokers, with dose-response trends by the number of cigarettes smoked. Later studies confirmed these findings (Cooper et al. 1999; Harlow and Signorello 2000; Meschia et al. 2000; Brett and Cooper 2003). One study reported a decrease in mean age at natural menopause with current active smoking but did not find an association among former smokers or with exposure to secondhand smoke (Cooper et al. 1999). However, two studies that were more briefly described found an earlier age at menopause with exposure to secondhand tobacco smoke (Everson et al. 1986; Tajtakova et al. 1990). In a population-based study in the United States, smoking was weakly associated with transition to menopausal status and strongly associated with postmenopausal status (Brett and Cooper 2003). This finding led the authors to suggest that the menopausal transition period may be shortened in smokers.

On the other end of the spectrum, some studies have examined age at menarche (start of menstrual periods) in relation to parental smoking. On the basis of data from a longitudinal birth cohort study, daughters whose mothers had smoked heavily during pregnancy had an earlier mean age at menarche by several months (Windham et al. 2004). This effect was greater among non-Whites than among Whites. Two studies from Poland reported a younger age at menarche for daughters of smoking mothers than

that for daughters of nonsmoking mothers (Kolasa 1997; Kolasa et al. 1998). A retrospective study of teachers found a slightly higher risk of early menarche among women who reported that during their childhoods, their parents had smoked at home (Reynolds et al. 2004). These later studies primarily examined exposure to secondhand smoke, and the timing with respect to puberty was not established. However, mothers who smoked postnatally, especially before smoking was socially prohibited, may have smoked during pregnancy as well. Windham and colleagues (2004) showed that girls with high prenatal and childhood exposure to secondhand smoke had the earliest mean age at menarche. One study examined the effects of parental smoking on puberty in both boys and girls and reported earlier pubertal milestones in boys whose mothers had smoked during pregnancy, but not in girls. However, the study had such small numbers that the power to examine age at menarche was insufficient (Fried et al. 2001).

Changes that affect the reproductive life span can have an impact on other aspects of a woman's health. Shorter cycles may lead to a more rapid depletion of oocytes, shortening the reproductive life span and leading to earlier menopause (Whelan et al. 1990; Bromberger et al. 1997). Early menopause is associated with other hormone-related health problems such as osteoporosis and cardiovascular disease (Harlow and Ephross 1995; Sowers and La Pietra 1995; Cooper and Sandler 1998). Early menarche or puberty may lead to psychosocial problems, adolescent pregnancy and attendant risks, other adverse reproductive outcomes, and breast cancer (Hardy et al. 1978; Liestol 1980; MacMahon et al. 1982a; Martin et al. 1983; Sandler et al. 1984; Wilson et al. 1994; Ge et al. 1996; He and Karlberg 2001).

Fertility

Fertility is an endpoint that is difficult to compare across studies, because no standard definition exists. Fecundity refers to the biologic ability to conceive, given unprotected intercourse, and depends on the reproductive capacity of both sexual partners. The clinical definition of infertility in the United States usually connotes lack of conception after one year of unprotected intercourse during the fertile phase. However, couples who delay childbearing may seek treatment before one year, which further complicates studies. Subfertility refers to any form of reduced fertility in couples trying to conceive, and one way to study it is by measuring time to conception or pregnancy. One commentary indicated that about 20 percent of couples experience subfertility, defined as the inability to conceive within six months (Gnoth et al. 2005). About 50 percent of these couples conceive in the next six months, leaving

10 percent of couples that match the clinical definition of infertility. Another 50 percent will likely conceive spontaneously in the next three years, leaving 5 percent infertile. Smoking affects fertility in men and women, as well as the success of in vitro fertilization (IVF).

Fertility in Females

Numerous studies have found associations of smoking with reduced fertility. The 2001 Surgeon General's report concluded that "women who smoke have increased risks for conception delay and for both primary and secondary infertility" (USDHHS 2001, p. 14). The 2004 Surgeon General's report also reviewed the literature and concluded that "the evidence is sufficient to infer a causal relationship between smoking and reduced fertility in women" (USDHHS 2004, p. 7). Other reviews have found consistent decrements in fertility associated with smoking, as well as evidence for dose-response trends. In a meta-analysis of data from 12 studies, the odds ratio (OR) was 1.6 (95 percent CI, 1.3–1.9) for infertility among smokers (Augood et al. 1998). Furthermore, meta-analyses of data on IVF treatment indicated a reduction in fecundity (conception rate per cycle) among women smokers ranging from 0.57 (95 percent CI, 0.42–0.78) to 0.66 (95 percent CI, 0.49–0.88) (Hughes and Brennan 1996; Augood et al. 1998). In a later qualitative review of 22 studies, all but 3 of the studies indicated a detrimental effect of smoking on female fecundity (Wilks and Hay 2004). The Practice Committee of the American Society for Reproductive Medicine (PCASRM) also issued a statement strongly supporting evidence for an association between smoking and infertility, estimating that 13 percent of infertility may be attributable to smoking (PCASRM 2004).

Several studies also examined the effects of exposure to secondhand tobacco smoke on fertility, but these effects may be difficult to separate from the direct effects of smoking on the partner's fecundity. Researchers have reviewed these studies and found suggestive but inconsistent results (National Cancer Institute [NCI] 1999; USDHHS 2001, 2006), so there are insufficient data to reach conclusions. A study published since two of those reviews examined the effects of exposure to mainstream and sidestream smoke on IVF outcomes. The researchers found that implantation and pregnancy rates were reduced by about one-half from both types of exposure to tobacco smoke among smokers compared with nonsmokers (Neal et al. 2005). The investigators noted that the association of exposure to sidestream smoke may reflect some direct effect of smoking on the male partners. However, they claimed that this could not explain the entire effect in that they observed no difference in implantation and pregnancy rates by the partner's smoking level.

Intriguingly, some studies have also examined the effects of in utero exposure to maternal smoking on later fertility or fecundability. One study found a significantly reduced likelihood of conception in smokers versus nonsmokers (fecundability ratio [FR]) of 0.5 (Weinberg et al. 1989); another study found a slightly reduced FR of 0.9 (Wilcox et al. 1989); and a third study found a slightly increased FR of 1.1 but also observed no effect of active smoking among the women (Schwingl 1992). In the range of these studies, a Danish study reported FRs for in utero exposure to cigarette smoking of 0.70 among adult nonsmokers and 0.53 among smokers, as well as 0.67 for female smokers with no in utero exposure, all compared with that for nonsmokers who had no in utero exposure (Jensen et al. 1998b). This study also found a similarly decreased fecundability in males exposed to smoking in utero.

Effects on Semen Quality and Male Fertility

For decades, epidemiologic studies have investigated the effects of cigarette smoking on semen quality, because of its relationship to male fertility (Campana et al. 1996; Eggert-Kruse et al. 1996; Bonde et al. 1998; Chia et al. 2000), although this relationship is not always predictive (Polansky and Lamb 1988; Guzick et al. 2001). Semen quality is measured by seminal plasma constituents and sperm cell characteristics such as ejaculate volume, sperm count, sperm motility, and sperm morphology. The *World Health Organization (WHO) Laboratory Manual for the Examination of Human Semen and Sperm-Cervical Mucus Interaction* (WHO 1980, 1987, 1992, 1999b) provides reference values for many semen parameters associated with fertility. A number of epidemiologic studies of smoking effects have used WHO reference values to categorize participants by their fertility status. Reproductive hormones are important determinants of normal sperm production and male sexual function and have thus also been studied in relation to exposure to cigarette smoking (see "Endocrine System" later in this chapter).

The 2004 Surgeon General's report reviewed the published epidemiologic literature evaluating semen quality and fertility and concluded that "the evidence is inadequate to infer the presence or absence of a causal relationship between active smoking and sperm quality" (USDHHS 2004, p. 28). However, "the evidence suggests that smokers may have decreased semen volume and sperm number and increased abnormal [morphologic] forms, although any clinical relevance of these findings is not clear" (USDHHS 2004, p. 534). A stronger causal statement could not be made at that time because of variability in published findings across studies. Reviews on this topic (Mattison 1982; Stillman et al. 1986; Little and

Vainio 1994; Vine 1996; Marinelli et al. 2004; PCASRM 2004) and one meta-analysis of data from 20 studies covering 1966–1992 (Vine et al. 1994) attribute this variation in the findings across studies to weaknesses in study designs. These weaknesses include a failure to adjust for potential confounders, small sample sizes, inadequate exposure assessments, and the use of fertility clinic populations.

Subsequent to the 2004 Surgeon General's report (USDHHS 2004), the PCASRM review (2004), and the review by Marinelli and colleagues (2004), some publications have strengthened the evidence for decrements in adult semen quality and fertility associated with exposure to tobacco smoke either prenatally or in adulthood (Table 8.1). Both studies in Table 8.1 that evaluated adult semen quality after in utero exposure found decrements in sperm concentration (Storgaard et al. 2003; Jensen et al. 2004). Studies conducted in clinical settings using assisted reproductive technology with extremely sensitive measures of fertilization and very early pregnancy loss also reported adverse effects from paternal smoking. Some studies had low power for detecting effects, but one of the largest studies, which was based on a retrospective review of records, did not find independent effects of cigarette smoking. However, the researchers reported a reduction in seminal volume, sperm concentration, and the percentage of motile sperm in men who smoked and consumed alcohol, behaviors that tend to be correlated (Martini et al. 2004). Another study based on a retrospective review of medical records for exposure assessments could not include more than 46 percent of the medical records initially reviewed, because of insufficient data, particularly data related to smoking (Ozgur et al. 2005). Although the study found no significant differences in sperm density, normal sperm tail morphology decreased or abnormal forms increased.

Spermatogenesis in the adult testes depends on a hormonal milieu that is temporally and compartmentally specific (e.g., seminiferous tubule, interstitial space, and epididymis). Thus, factors likely to be responsible for the decrements seen in semen quality and male fertility are constituents of cigarette smoke that influence the normal development and adult function of the hypothalamus and pituitary gland or that influence the differentiation, development, and adult function of Leydig and/or Sertoli cells that secrete hormones (see "Endocrine System" later in this chapter). Support for the contribution of smoking effects on hormonal factors to male fertility is still evolving (Meikle et al. 1989; Michnovicz et al. 1989; Sofikitis et al. 1995; Chapin et al. 2004). Other potential mechanisms of smoking for male infertility include effects on the sperm plasma membrane (Belcheva et al. 2004) and tobacco-related damage to DNA and/or chromosomes in

gametes (PCASRM 2004) (see "Genetic Damage to Sperm" later in this chapter). Studies have associated in utero exposure to polycyclic aromatic hydrocarbons (PAHs) in tobacco smoke with adverse effects on male fertility and on testes (see "Polycyclic Aromatic Hydrocarbons" later in this chapter). Additional targeted research in human populations with use of molecular laboratory tools will help to elucidate the mechanisms underlying these observations.

Study designs have not addressed the timing of exposures in relation to sperm cell maturation in the testes, the formation and secretion of fluids contributed by accessory organs outside the testes, and events during fertilization. This information is critical to unraveling mechanisms of the toxic effects of tobacco smoke, determining whether these exposures result in long-term risks to male reproductive health, and documenting the benefits of smoking cessation. For example, if spermatogonial stem cells prove to be the cells most sensitive to exposure to tobacco smoke, then long-term consequences might be observed even after smoking cessation. However, if mechanisms of toxic effects relate primarily to effects on epididymal sperm or to direct effects on mature sperm in the ejaculate from seminal plasma constituents, then smoking cessation could result in immediate benefits.

Pregnancy Complications

This section addresses a variety of complications that may occur during pregnancy. These complications primarily represent difficulties the pregnant mother may experience trying to maintain a healthy pregnancy, but there also may be wide-ranging effects on the health of the fetus or the offspring. In general, these conditions may be influenced by maternal age, reproductive history, and medical history or conditions affecting the maternal endocrine or immune systems, uterine structure, and cardiovascular system, among others. Exogenous exposures may also play a role in causing or exacerbating these conditions. This section briefly presents the etiology of these complications and puts potential smoking-induced mechanisms into context. (For details on the mechanisms of these complications, see "Pathophysiological and Cellular and Molecular Mechanisms of Smoking" later in this chapter.)

Spontaneous Abortion

SAB is typically defined as the involuntary termination of an intrauterine pregnancy before 20 weeks of gestation. Studies have reported recognized SABs in approximately 12 percent of pregnancies, and most occur

Table 8.1 **Association of adult cigarette smoking and in utero exposure to cigarette smoke with semen parameters and fertility in adults**[a]

Study	Population	Study period	Definition of smoking
	Effects from adult smoking		
Chia et al. 2000	240 fertile and 218 infertile men from obstetric and andrology clinic populations	NR	Self-reported number of cigarettes/day and smoking history
Trummer et al. 2002	260 smokers, 70 former smokers, and 258 nonsmokers from infertility clinic population	1993–2000	Self-reported number of cigarettes/day
Gaspari et al. 2003	69 current smokers, 22 former smokers, and 88 lifetime nonsmokers from infertility clinic population, 75 with 1-year follow-up for fertility	2001	Self-reported number of cigarettes/day and smoking history
Künzle et al. 2003	655 smokers and 1,131 nonsmokers from infertility clinic population	1991–1997	Self-reported >1 cigarette/day
Loft et al. 2003	225 women with first pregnancy, 74 male smokers, and 151 male nonsmokers	1992–1994	Self-reported number of cigarettes/day
Zitzmann et al. 2003	48 IVF couples and 153 ICSI couples	1999–2001	Self-reported lifetime nonsmoker or smoker (≥5 cigarettes/day for 2 years)
Chen et al. 2004	22 smokers, 57 former smokers, and 227 nonsmokers from infertility clinic population in study of seasonal effects and environmental exposures	2000–2002	Self-reported current smoker, former smoker, or lifetime nonsmoker
Jurasović et al. 2004	61 smokers and 62 nonsmokers from infertility clinic population	NR	Self-reported number of cigarettes/day
Martini et al. 2004	3,430 nonsmokers, 422 light smokers, and 124 heavy smokers from infertility clinic population	1990–1999	Retrospective review of records for cigarettes/day: 0, 1–20, >20

Findings	OR, RR, or % (95% CI or p value)	Comments
	Effects from adult smoking	
• Smoking predictive of risk of infertility	Infertility in smokers compared with nonsmokers = 2.96 (1.98–4.42)	None
• NS difference in density, motility, and morphology	NR	None
• PAH-DNA adducts in sperm associated with infertility but not cigarette smoking • PAH-DNA adducts associated directly with abnormal forms of sperm and inversely with asthenospermia	Smokers = 1.58 Nonsmokers = 1.62 in relative staining intensity (NS) PAH-DNA adducts associated with abnormal head (r = 0.3), abnormal neck (r = -0.2), and abnormal physiological forms (r = -0.2)	None
• Lower sperm density, total motile cells, and citrate concentration • Fewer morphologically normal cells • Higher pH • No significant difference in volume, vitality, and fructose concentration	Decreased density by 15.3%, p = 0.0001 Decreased total motile cells by 16.6%, p = 0.002 Decreased normal forms by 10.6%, p = 0.0007 Decreased citrate concentration by 22.4%, p = 0.007	Correlation of alcohol intake and smoking (p = 0.002) after removing heavy drinkers because moderate alcohol intake has not been associated with infertility; no adjustment
• Likelihood of pregnancy in a menstrual cycle inversely associated with 8-oxo-dG concentrations, but levels not associated with smoking status	Correlation of smoking and 8-oxo-dG concentrations Spearman correlation 0.02 (NS)	Adequate semen count required to extract enough DNA for bioassay because variance by smoking may bias findings

• Paternal smoking predictive of fertilization in IVF but not in ICSI
• Paternal smoking predictive of clinical pregnancy in ICSI and IVF
• Increased progressive motility and decreased normal forms of sperm among smokers
	ICSI pregnancy failures in partners of male smokers compared with partners of nonsmokers
	  2.95 (1.32–6.59)
	IVF pregnancy failures in partners of male smokers compared with partners of nonsmokers
	  2.65 (1.33–5.30)
		None

• NS differences in concentration, motility, and morphology of sperm	NS 20% decrease in sperm density in current smokers compared with lifetime nonsmokers	Small number of smokers

• Decreased blood prolactin
• Positive correlation with blood cadmium
• NS differences in concentration, motility, and morphology of sperm
	Decreased blood prolactin (p = 0.02)
	Correlations with blood:
	  Cadmium, +0.80 (p <0.001)
	  Selenium, -0.26 (p <0.01)
	  Selenium-glutathione peroxidase, -0.30 (p <0.001)
		None

• NS differences in concentration, motility, and morphology of sperm across categories of smoking independent of alcohol intake	Significantly decreased density by 11%, decreased total motile sperm 10%, decreased rapid sperm by 14% for men who smoked >1 cigarette and drank ≤52 grams of ethanol/day compared with no smoking or drinking	Retrospective review of record with no exposure validation measures

Table 8.1   Continued

Study	Population	Study period	Definition of smoking
Ozgur et al. 2005	116 heavy smokers, 82 light smokers, and 98 nonsmokers from infertility clinic patients	2000–2002	Retrospective review of records for cigarettes/day: 0, 1–19, ≥20

Effects during adulthood of in utero exposure to cigarette smoke			
Storgaard et al. 2003	265 Danish men identified from population-based birth registries	1999–2000	Maternal recall of smoking during pregnancy: 0, 1–10, 11–20, >20 cigarettes/day
Jensen et al. 2004	1,770 military inductees from Denmark, Estonia, Finland, Lithuania, and Norway	1996–1999	Maternal recall of maternal and paternal smoking during pregnancy: yes, no

Note: **8-oxo-dG** = 7-hydroxy-8-oxo-2′-deoxyguanosine; **CI** = confidence interval; **ICSI** = intracytoplasmic sperm injection; **IVF** = in vitro fertilization; **NR** = not reported; **NS** = not statistically significant; **OR** = odds ratio; **PAH** = polycyclic aromatic hydrocarbon; **RR** = rate ratio.
[a]Not included in the 2004 Surgeon General's report on the health consequences of smoking.

before 12 weeks of gestation (Regan et al. 1989). However, very early pregnancy loss may go unrecognized and/or unreported. An estimated 30 to 45 percent of conceptions actually end in pregnancy loss (Wilcox et al. 1988; Eskenazi et al. 1995). Studies of tissue from SABs suggest that 50 to 80 percent of losses have an abnormal karyotype, depending on the mother's age and the gestational age at the time of the loss; a higher proportion of abnormalities is found in losses at earlier gestational ages (Kajii et al. 1980; Hogge et al. 2003; Philipp et al. 2003). In addition to fetal abnormalities, other factors that likely contribute to SAB include maternal anatomical abnormalities of the uterus, immunologic disturbances, thrombotic disorders, and endocrine abnormalities (Christianson 1979; Cramer and Wise 2000; Regan and Rai 2000). Infections may also play a role, but data are limited and inconsistent (Cramer and Wise 2000; McDonald and Chambers 2000; Matovina et al. 2004).

Several studies have demonstrated a moderate association between smoking and SAB (DiFranza and Lew 1995). The 2004 Surgeon General's report on the health consequences of smoking found the evidence suggestive but not sufficient to infer a causal relationship between smoking and SAB (USDHHS 2004). However, numerous studies are available since the handful reviewed at that time (Table 8.2), and most show positive associations. These results represent both retrospective and prospective study designs from a number of different countries, with adjustment for various confounders. One study found an association with amount smoked before pregnancy (Nielsen et al. 2006), and another reported an association among former smokers (Mishra et al. 2000), but others did not observe these associations (Chatenoud et al. 1998; Wisborg et al. 2003). The later study had a very low SAB rate of approximately 1 percent, so many SABs were likely missed, particularly early in pregnancy. Two studies used a measurement of cotinine to verify exposure to tobacco smoke and found relatively high risks of SAB (Ness et al. 1999; George et al. 2006). Estimates of the increase in risk of SAB from smoking are 30 to 100 percent, some in a dose-response pattern (Kline et al. 1977; Chatenoud et al. 1998; USDHHS 2004; George et al. 2006; Nielsen et al. 2006). In a meta-analysis of data from 13 studies, the pooled ORs for SAB in smokers were 1.24 (95 percent CI, 1.19–1.30) for cohort studies and 1.32 (95 percent CI, 1.18–1.48) for case-control studies (DiFranza and Lew 1995). In one study, the association with smoking appeared stronger in chromosomally normal SABs (Kline

Findings	OR, RR, or % (95% CI or p value)	Comments
• Increased rapidly motile cells among smokers of ≥20 compared with 1–19 cigarettes/day • Increased coiled-tail defects among smokers • NS difference in density and total motile cells in nonsmokers compared with heavy smokers	Decreased rapidly motile cells by 30% at ≥20 compared with 1–19 cigarettes/day (p <0.05) Decreased normal tail morphology by 18% for smokers of ≥20 cigarettes/day compared with nonsmokers (p <0.05)	Retrospective review of records with no exposure validation measures; missing data on more than 46% of records
Effects during adulthood of in utero exposure to cigarette smoke		
• In utero exposure to >10 cigarettes/day associated with lower sperm density (48%), lower inhibin B, and higher follicle-stimulating hormone • No dose-response relationship or significant change in other semen parameters or hormones	Decreased sperm concentration by 48% (-69 to -11%) at exposure of >10 cigarettes/day	None
• Lower sperm concentration and total sperm count among those exposed to smoking • NS difference in sperm motility, morphology, or testis size	Decreased sperm concentration by 20.1% (6.8–33.5%) Decreased total sperm count by 24.5% (9.5–39.5%)	None

et al. 1995), but another study did not find a differential effect by chromosomal abnormality (George et al. 2006).

In examining exposure to secondhand smoke, the 2006 Surgeon General's report on the health consequences of involuntary exposure to tobacco smoke concluded that the evidence was "inadequate to infer the presence or absence of a causal relationship" with SAB, on the basis of a few studies with inconsistent results (USDHHS 2006, p. 13). Since then, two studies have found an association with secondhand smoke on the order of 60 to 80 percent, one with a biomarker of cotinine (George et al. 2006) and one that examined very early fetal loss (Venners et al. 2004). Another study did not find an association in examining only paternal smoking (Chatenoud et al. 1998), and one found an effect of exposure to secondhand smoke at either home or work only among women who also consumed alcohol or high amounts of caffeine (Windham et al. 1999c).

Proposed mechanisms for an effect from tobacco smoke include fetal hypoxia from exposure to CO, vasoconstrictive and antimetabolic effects resulting in placental insufficiency and the subsequent death of the embryo or fetus (PCASRM 2004), and direct toxic effects of constituents of cigarette smoke.

Ectopic Pregnancy

Ectopic pregnancy occurs when a fertilized egg is implanted outside the uterus, usually within the fallopian tube. It is estimated to occur in 1 to 2 percent of pregnancies (Chow et al. 1987; Goldner et al. 1993; Van Den Eeden et al. 2005) and accounts for approximately 6 percent of pregnancy-related deaths in the United States (Berg et al. 2003; Chang et al. 2003). Factors associated with ectopic pregnancy include a history of sexually transmitted diseases and pelvic inflammatory disease, increased number of sexual partners, maternal age, history of SAB, history of surgical procedures affecting the fallopian tubes, previous use of an intrauterine device, and vaginal douching (Kendrick et al. 1997; Pisarska et al. 1998; Bouyer et al. 2003). Affected women are at increased risk of infertility and recurrent ectopic pregnancy in subsequent pregnancies (Chow et al. 1987; Coste et al. 1991; Washington and Katz 1993; Skjeldestad et al. 1998), as would be expected among women with tubal damage.

The 2004 Surgeon General's report found the evidence suggestive but not sufficient to infer a causal relationship between smoking and ectopic pregnancy (USDHHS 2004). A number of studies have associated

Table 8.2   Association between maternal smoking and spontaneous abortion (SAB), 1998–2006

Study	Design/population	Definition of smoking	OR (95% CI)	Comments
Chatenoud et al. 1998	Case-control study 782 cases of SAB by 12 weeks' gestation, confirmed pathologic examination 1,543 women who delivered term healthy infants in same hospitals as cases Italy	Lifetime nonsmokers vs. women who smoked during pregnancy None, 1–4, 5–9, ≥10 cigarettes/day Any smoking ≥10 cigarettes/day	 1.3 (1.0–1.6) 1.4 (1.0–2.1)	No association with smoking before pregnancy or with paternal smoking; adjustment for center, age, marital status, history of SAB, nausea, and use of alcohol and coffee
Ness et al. 1999	Case-control study 400 adolescents or women with SAB <22 weeks' gestation at initial visit or during follow-up 570 adolescents or women with pregnancies beyond 22 weeks' gestation seeking care at inner-city emergency room Low SES population Pennsylvania	Urinary cotinine >500 ng/mL used to identify heavy smokers Self-reported smoking during pregnancy	 1.8 (1.3–2.6) 1.4 (1.0–1.9) Crude data	Adjustment for use of cocaine, marijuana, and alcohol, and living with partner, weeks of gestation at interview, and prenatal care; stronger among SABs during follow-up (OR 2.4)
Windham et al. 1999c	Prospective study of women seeking prenatal care at large health maintenance organization (Kaiser) by 12 weeks' gestation 499 SABs by 20 weeks' gestation, from medical records 5,144 pregnancies after excluding therapeutic abortions California	Smoking at 8 weeks of gestation and amount vs. nonsmoking ≥5 cigarettes/day Spouse smoking status Hours of exposure to SHS at home and work for nonsmokers	 1.3 (0.9–1.9) No association No association, unless consumption of caffeine or alcohol OR ~3 for any exposure to SHS	Adjustment for age, previous fetal loss, gestational age at interview, use of alcohol and caffeine; effect modification with high use of caffeine or alcohol (>3 drinks/week)

Mishra et al. 2000	Prospective study
	
	14,779 women (aged 18–23 years), from baseline survey
	
	Self-reported SABs (≥1)
	
	Australia
		Lifetime nonsmokers vs. current and former smokers
		
		Amount (cigarettes/day)
		  Former smokers
		  Current smokers
		    1–9
		    10–19
		    ≥20
			
			1.6 (1.3–2.2)
			
			1.7 (1.1–2.5)
			1.6 (1.6–2.3)
			2.0 (1.5–2.8)
				Adjustment for parity, therapeutic abortion, age, education, marital status, and area of residence; higher risk for smoking initiation at younger age

Table 8.2   Continued

Study	Design/population	Definition of smoking	OR (95% CI)	Comments
Rasch 2003	Case-control study 330 women with SAB ascertained by evacuation procedure at hospital, 6–16 weeks' gestation 1,168 pregnant women receiving prenatal care in weeks 6–16 Denmark	Smoking during pregnancy and amount vs. none ≥20 cigarettes/day vs. none	0.95 (0.4–2.2) Adjusted data 2.2 (1.1–4.8) Crude data	Large effect of adjustment for age, parity, occupation, and use of alcohol and caffeine; dose-response relationship before adjustment; 40% of original eligible subjects not included in study
Wisborg et al. 2003	Prospective study among women seeking prenatal care 24,608 pregnant women who completed questionnaire by 28 weeks' gestation 321 SABs by 28 weeks (104 first trimester, 217 second trimester) from Danish patient registry Denmark	Smoking before or during pregnancy (and amount) vs. nonsmokers ≥10 cigarettes/day during pregnancy for second trimester SABs First trimester	0.88 (0.59–1.31) 0.92 (0.55–1.54)	Crude estimates; adjustment made no difference; very low SAB rate (~1%), especially with extended definition (28 weeks); median entry time was second trimester, so most earlier SABs were missed
George et al. 2006	Case-control population-based study 463 women with SAB at 6–12 weeks' gestation, interviewed after SAB (most within 2 weeks) 864 pregnant women with viable pregnancy, matched to cases by gestational week Sweden	Plasma cotinine >15.0 ng/mL = active smoking 0.1–15.0 ng/mL for exposure to SHS vs. <0.1 ng/mL No exposure to cigarette smoke	2.1 (1.4–3.3) 1.7 (1.2–2.4)	Adjustment for age, country of birth, education, marital status, shift work, parity, previous SAB, caffeine intake, folate level, change of eating habits, pregnancy symptoms; SHS exposed may include light smokers
Nielsen et al. 2006	Nested case-control study from population-based cohort of 11,088 women with baseline survey and 2-year follow-up 343 SAB or fetal loss by 28 weeks' gestation, self-reported or in Danish registry 1,578 women with pregnancy of >28 weeks during follow-up period Denmark	Smoking at baseline, before pregnancy, by amount and number of years of smoking Amount (cigarettes/day) 1–14 15–19 ≥20 Each additional 5	1.0 (current smokers vs. never smoked) Reference group 1.4 (0.9–2.1) 1.6 (1.1–2.5) 1.2 (1.0–1.4)	Adjustment for age, marital status, previous SAB, oral contraceptive use, IUD use, and smoking status and duration of smoking—but did not affect ORs; no association for former smokers or by duration of smoking; odd reference group

Note: **CI** = confidence interval; **IUD** = intrauterine device; **ng/mL** = nanograms per milliliter; **OR** = odds ratio; **SES** = socioeconomic status; **SHS** = secondhand smoke.

smoking with ectopic pregnancy, and in a meta-analysis of data from nine studies, the OR from pooled data on ectopic pregnancy from smoking was 1.77 (95 percent CI, 1.31–2.22) (Castles et al. 1999). In addition, two other studies also reported significant associations between smoking and ectopic pregnancy (Bouyer et al. 2003; Karaer et al. 2006). Both found evidence of a dose-response relationship, even after adjustment for important potential confounders, such as a history of sexually transmitted diseases and infertility. In one study, the magnitude of the association of ectopic pregnancy and smoking was similar to that seen with infectious causes (Bouyer et al. 2003). In addition, plausible mechanisms for a relationship between smoking and ectopic pregnancy exist. The oviduct plays a critical role in the pickup and transport of the oocyte, and failure of this function can result in ectopic pregnancy. Both in vivo and in vitro studies showed that smoking impairs mammalian oviduct function (Talbot and Riveles 2005).

Preeclampsia

Preeclampsia is a syndrome of reduced organ perfusion attributable to vasospasm and endothelial activation with an onset after 20 weeks of gestation that is marked by proteinuria, hypertension, and dysfunction of the endothelial cells lining the uterus (National High Blood Pressure Education Program 2000; Sibai et al. 2005). The disease can be mild or severe. When accompanied by seizures that cannot be attributed to other causes, the diagnosis is established as eclampsia by exclusion. Preeclampsia affects approximately 2 to 8 percent of pregnancies (*American Journal of Obstetrics and Gynecology* 1988; Duley 2003; Zhang et al. 2003; Villar et al. 2004), and the incidence is highest in nulliparous women. The reported incidence varies widely, likely because of variation in population characteristics such as parity, race and/or ethnicity, and environmental factors (Zhang et al. 1997), as well as heterogeneity in classification systems (*American Journal of Obstetrics and Gynecology* 1988; Villar et al. 2004). Preeclampsia is a leading cause of pregnancy-related mortality in the United States (Berg et al. 2003). Morbidity and mortality are particularly high with early-onset disease (<33 weeks of gestation) (Sibai 2003; von Dadelszen et al. 2003). Preeclampsia is also associated with fetal growth restriction, placental abruption, and perinatal death (Sibai et al. 2005).

Risk factors for preeclampsia include preexisting medical conditions, multifetal gestation, an elevated body mass index (BMI), and older maternal age (Sibai et al. 2005). Immunologic factors have also been implicated (Zhang et al. 1997; Dekker and Robillard 2003; Einarsson et al. 2003), as have infectious and/or inflammatory

conditions (Sibai et al. 2005). Evidence from epidemiologic and physiological studies has led to several hypotheses on the cause of preeclampsia. First, preeclampsia seems to be characterized by poor formation of the placenta (placentation) with a shallow invasion of the decidua and myometrium by trophoblast cells, resulting in an incomplete transformation of maternal spiral arteries that then retain their muscular characteristics (Brosens et al. 1972; Naicker et al. 2003). This process leads to placental ischemia and reperfusion and results in increased oxidative stress and vascular disease. Poor placentation in preeclamptic pregnancies could be the result of maternal-fetal immune maladaptation (Sibai et al. 2005). Researchers think that the clinical manifestations of preeclampsia result from the release of placental factors in response to ischemic conditions, resulting in the endothelial dysfunction of maternal circulation (Roberts and Redman 1993). Endothelial dysfunction is characterized by a disruption in regulatory functions of vasomotor tone through coagulation, by platelet activity, and by fibrinolysis in the vascular endothelium (Roberts et al. 1989, 1991). It is unclear which placental factors may be involved, but one hypothesis is that an imbalance between proangiogenic and antiangiogenic factors may contribute. Animal and human studies support the hypothesis that angiogenic proteins may play a role in the etiology of preeclampsia (Maynard et al. 2003; Levine et al. 2004).

Smoking is inversely associated with preeclampsia; the pooled risk reduction is 32 percent (Conde-Agudelo et al. 1999). The 2004 Surgeon General's report found the evidence sufficient to infer a causal relationship between smoking and a reduced risk of preeclampsia (USDHHS 2004). Whether a dose-response relationship exists is unclear because study results are conflicting (Marcoux et al. 1989; Klonoff-Cohen et al. 1993; Zhang et al. 1999). Investigators have proposed three mechanisms through which smoking could reduce the risk of preeclampsia (Maynard et al. 2003; Fisher 2004):

1. exposure to thiocyanate, which has a hypotensive effect (Andrews 1973);

2. inhibition of thromboxane A_2 production, a potent vasoconstrictor and platelet aggregation stimulator, or increase in levels of prostacyclin, a vasodilator and platelet aggregation inhibitor (Ylikorkala et al. 1985; Davis et al. 1987; Marcoux et al. 1989), both of which would improve the ratio of thromboxane A_2 to prostacyclin (Lindqvist and Maršál 1999); and

3. stimulation of proangiogenic factors, such as vascular endothelial growth factor (VEGF), and/or

reduction in antiangiogenic factors, such as soluble VEGF receptor Flt-1 (sFlt-1) (Maynard et al. 2003; Fisher 2004; Jeyabalan et al. 2008).

Placenta Previa

Placenta previa is the complete or partial obstruction of the cervical os by the placenta that affects approximately 0.4 percent of all births (Comeau et al. 1983; Iyasu et al. 1993; Faiz and Ananth 2003). Placenta previa has been associated with maternal and infant complications, such as preterm delivery, a hemorrhage that requires a blood transfusion, maternal death, and fetal or neonatal death (Salihu et al. 2003; Creasy et al. 2004). Neonatal mortality in pregnancies complicated by placenta previa may be up to three times higher than that in the general obstetric population (Salihu et al. 2003). The cause of placenta previa is unknown. However, risk factors with plausible etiologic mechanisms include advanced maternal age, multiparity, multifetal gestation, and a history of a cesarean section or a previous abortion (Ananth et al. 2003; Faiz and Ananth 2003; Creasy et al. 2004).

Epidemiologic studies have consistently reported an increased risk of placenta previa among smokers, and many studies show a dose-response relationship (Meyer et al. 1976; Zhang and Fried 1992; Monica and Lilja 1995). The estimated relative risks (RRs) from smoking are 1.3 to 3.0 (Castles et al. 1999; Andres and Day 2000; Cnattingius 2004). The 2004 Surgeon General's report found the evidence sufficient to infer a causal relationship between smoking and placenta previa (USDHHS 2004). A mechanism commonly proposed to explain this association is the chronic hypoxemia and ischemia that result from smoking, with compensatory placental enlargement. However, not all studies have shown a clinically significant increase in placental size in smokers (Zhang et al. 1999; Larsen et al. 2002).

Placental Abruption

Placental abruption, the premature separation of the placenta from the uterine wall, affects 0.5 to 2 percent of pregnancies (Rasmussen et al. 1996a; Ananth et al. 2001, 2005; Kyrklund-Blomberg et al. 2001). However, reported perinatal mortality in affected women is 8 to 12 percent (Raymond and Mills 1993; Ananth and Wilcox 2001; Kyrklund-Blomberg et al. 2001). Abruption may account for up to 14 percent of perinatal deaths (Rasmussen et al. 1996b; Ananth and Wilcox 2001). Ananth and Wilcox (2001) estimated that the perinatal mortality rate associated with abruption was 119 per 1,000 births compared with 8.2 per 1,000 among all births. Abruption can also result in neonatal asphyxia (Heinonen and Saarikoski

2001), preterm delivery, and maternal disseminated intravascular coagulation if thromboplastic material is released into the mother's circulatory system (Hladky et al. 2002).

It is likely that the etiology of placental abruption is multifactorial (Misra and Ananth 1999). Potential risk factors include advanced maternal age (35 years or older), high parity, previous abruption, a history of infertility, preterm premature rupture of membranes (PPROM), small for gestational age (SGA), infant congenital malformations, multifetal pregnancy, hypertensive disorders, polyhydramnios, thrombophilia, diabetes, trauma, sudden uterine decompression, previous cesarean section, and uterine infections (Abdella et al. 1984; Williams et al. 1991; Raymond and Mills 1993; Ananth et al. 1996a,b; Kramer et al. 1997; Rasmussen et al. 1999; Cunningham et al. 2001; Kyrklund-Blomberg et al. 2001). Underlying causes of abruption could include vessel fragility, vascular malformations, uterine scarring from previous cesarean section, and placentation abnormalities (Dommisse and Tiltman 1992; Rasmussen et al. 1999; Hladky et al. 2002). In addition, failure of the maternal spiral arteries to transform into low-resistance dilated vessels could predispose the mother to ischemia and vessel rupture (Eskes 1997). In one study, a high percentage of placentas from women with severe abruption showed an absence of trophoblastic transformation, and not all cases were attributable to preeclampsia (Dommisse and Tiltman 1992).

Studies have consistently associated smoking with an increased risk of placental abruption. Relative risks range from 1.4 to 1.9 (Raymond and Mills 1993; Ananth et al. 1999; Castles et al. 1999; Andres and Day 2000). The 2004 Surgeon General's report found the evidence sufficient to infer a causal relationship (USDHHS 2004). In addition, study findings support a dose-response relationship (Ananth et al. 1999). Raymond and Mills (1993) found a 20-percent increase in the risk of abruption for every 10 cigarettes the mother smoked per day. Etiologic mechanisms proposed by researchers to explain this relationship include smoking-related degenerative and/or inflammatory changes in the placenta (Cnattingius 2004); decreased vitamin C (ascorbic acid) levels in smokers (Faruque et al. 1995), leading to impaired collagen synthesis (Cnattingius 2004); microinfarcts; and atheromatous changes in placental vessels (Naeye 1979; Andres and Day 2000) (see "Placenta" and "Maternal and Fetal Cardiovascular System" later in this chapter). Analyses of consecutive pregnancies indicate that abruption risk is decreased when women stop smoking between pregnancies, suggesting that effects of smoking are transient and not cumulative across pregnancies (Ananth and Cnattingius 2007).

Preterm Delivery

Delivery at less than 37 completed weeks of gestation (preterm delivery) is a leading cause of neonatal mortality and morbidity in developed countries and is often divided into categories of moderate preterm (32 to 36 weeks) and very preterm (<32 weeks) delivery. Preterm delivery complicated 12.3 percent of pregnancies in the United States in 2003 (Hamilton et al. 2004). Rates of preterm delivery in the United States and other industrialized countries have been increasing in the past decade and are partially attributable to an increase in the frequency of multiple births (Hamilton et al. 2004).

The underlying causes of preterm delivery are complex and multifactorial. Contributing factors include multigestational pregnancy, preeclampsia, placental abruption, placenta previa, intrauterine infections, uterine overdistension, and abnormal uterine anatomy, in addition to disorders of the cervix, endocrine system, and placenta. Other risk factors include race (e.g., African Americans have higher risk), low socioeconomic status (SES), underlying maternal medical conditions, genitourinary infections, poor maternal weight gain or nutrition, young or advanced maternal age, short maternal stature, and fetal abnormalities (Haram et al. 2003; Iams 2003). Approximately 25 percent of preterm deliveries are medically indicated and are attributable to conditions affecting the mother and/or the fetus, and the remaining 75 percent are spontaneous (Meis et al. 1995; Iams 2003). A substantial body of evidence indicates that intrauterine bacterial infections are associated with preterm labor and delivery, especially at earlier gestational ages (Cassell et al. 1993; Kimberlin and Andrews 1998; Andrews et al. 2000; Goldenberg and Culhane 2003). Most intrauterine infections are believed to result from ascending infection, resulting from changes in vaginal/cervical flora, including bacterial vaginosis, or from the introduction of pathologic organisms. If these organisms ascend to the intrauterine cavity, they can cause an inflammatory reaction. The infection may progress to involve the chorion and/or amnion, fetal vessels, or the amniotic cavity, and even the fetus (review by Gonçalves et al. 2002; Romero et al. 2002). Systemic maternal infection or maternal infections remote from the genitourinary tract have also been associated with preterm labor and delivery, but the risk of preterm labor and delivery attributable to these conditions is thought to be low (Romero et al. 2002). One mechanism proposed to explain the onset of preterm labor attributable to intrauterine infection is that bacterial invasion of the choriodecidual space results in the release of endotoxins and exotoxins, which, in turn, stimulate the production of cytokines such as TNFα, interleukin-6 (IL-6), IL-8, IL-1α, IL-1β, and granulocyte colony-stimulating factor.

One hypothesis is that cytokines, endoxins, and exotoxins stimulate the release of prostaglandins and initiate neutrophil activation, which results in the release of metalloproteases. This process results in stimulation of uterine contractions by prostaglandins, rupture of chorioamniotic membranes, and softening of the cervix by metalloproteinases (review by Goldenberg et al. 2000).

Researchers have consistently associated smoking with preterm delivery, and smoking likely increases the risk of both very preterm and moderate preterm births (Kyrklund-Blomberg and Cnattingius 1998; Ancel et al. 1999; Cnattingius et al. 1999; Gardosi and Francis 2000). The 2004 Surgeon General's report found that the evidence was sufficient to infer a causal relationship between smoking and preterm delivery (USDHHS 2004). Smoking appears to increase the risk of both medically indicated and spontaneous preterm delivery (Kyrklund-Blomberg and Cnattingius 1998). However, estimates of the magnitude of the association vary among studies. In a meta-analysis of pooled data from 20 prospective studies, the estimate for any maternal smoking versus none was 1.27 (95 percent CI, 1.21–1.33), and the ORs were 1.25, 1.38, and 1.31 for light, moderate, and heavy maternal smoking, respectively (Shah and Bracken 2000), suggesting a truncated dose-response relationship.

Exposure to secondhand smoke is also associated with preterm delivery in several studies. The 2006 Surgeon General's report concluded that the evidence was suggestive but not sufficient to infer a causal relationship (USDHHS 2006). A study by Kharrazi and colleagues (2004) included measurement of cotinine and found that nonsmokers with higher levels had earlier delivery than did those with no measurable exposure to secondhand smoke. The risk increased about 30 percent with each log increase in cotinine (adjusted OR [AOR] = 1.29 [95 percent CI, 0.97–1.72]).

Parity may modify the association between preterm delivery and smoking. As previously stated, the incidence of preeclampsia is highest among nulliparous women (see "Preeclampsia" earlier in this chapter). Because smoking protects against preeclampsia and preeclampsia can result in preterm delivery, the adverse effects of smoking on risk of preterm delivery may be masked in nulliparous women (Burguet et al. 2004).

Mechanisms through which smoking may contribute to preterm delivery are unknown. Researchers have proposed that smoking could increase risk of intrauterine infections (review by Cnattingius 2004). Smokers have a twofold-to-threefold increase in risk for bacterial vaginosis, which is a risk factor for preterm delivery (Morris et al. 2001). Researchers have hypothesized that smoking increases this risk through its effects on vaginal flora or through depletion of Langerhans cells, resulting in local immunosuppression (Smart et al. 2004). Alterations in the cervical cytokine profile have been associated with increased risk of preterm delivery; women with a high anti-inflammatory and low proinflammatory profile are at highest risk (Simhan and Krohn 2009). Cigarette smoking has been associated with increased cervical anti-inflammatory cytokines in early pregnancy, which could make women who smoke more vulnerable to reproductive tract infections and subsequent preterm delivery (Simhan et al. 2005). Smoking can also reduce zinc levels, which could increase susceptibility to vaginal infections (Edman et al. 1986; Sikorski et al. 1990; Shubert et al. 1992). Immunosuppressive effects of smoking could also increase the risk of upper genital infections, known to be associated with preterm labor and PPROM. Neonates born to smokers have been noted to have a decrease in all leukocytes, indicating possible fetal immune dysregulation (Pachlopnik Schmid et al. 2007). Pathways other than those involving infections have also been proposed. For example, investigators have suggested that smoking during pregnancy increases contractile sensitivity and activity of the myometrium, with exposure to oxytocin by upregulating expression of messenger RNA (mRNA) for oxytocin receptor (Egawa et al. 2003). Compared with unexposed pregnant rats, those with exposure to cigarette smoke were found to have higher contractile sensitivity and activity in response to oxytocin (Egawa et al. 2003).

Finally, findings have also suggested that smoking may disrupt the integrity of type III collagen, leading to weakening and rupture of the membranes and an increased risk of medical indications for preterm delivery, such as placental abruption and intrauterine growth restriction (IUGR) (Cnattingius 2004).

Preterm Premature Rupture of Membranes

PPROM is defined as the rupture of amniotic membranes before the onset of labor and before 37 completed weeks of gestation. PPROM occurs in up to 4.5 percent of deliveries and in approximately 40 percent of preterm births (Mercer et al. 2000). Pregnancies complicated by PPROM have higher rates of neonatal morbidity than do pregnancies complicated by idiopathic preterm labor (Arias and Tomich 1982).

Factors that researchers have associated with PPROM include (1) nutritional deficiencies in vitamin C (Hadley et al. 1990; Casanueva et al. 1993), copper (Artal et al. 1979; Kiilholma et al. 1984), and zinc (Sikorski et al. 1990; Scholl et al. 1993); (2) vaginal bleeding (Harger et al. 1990; Ekwo et al. 1992); (3) multifetal pregnancies (Mercer et al. 1993); (4) a history of preterm delivery or PPROM in a previous pregnancy (Naeye 1982; Harger et al.

1990; Ekwo et al. 1992; Mercer et al. 2000); (5) obstetric complications involving uterine overdistension (French and McGregor 1996); and (6) bacterial vaginosis (Kurki et al. 1992; Mercer et al. 2000) and intra-amniotic infections (Naeye and Peters 1980; Ekwo et al. 1993; Heffner et al. 1993). However, it can be difficult to determine whether an intra-amniotic infection precedes or follows the rupture of membranes. A review by Lee and Silver (2001) discusses in detail the risk factors for PPROM.

Researchers suggest that structural deficiencies in the architecture of the amniotic membrane could increase the risk of PPROM (Shubert et al. 1992; Lee and Silver 2001). Studies of spontaneously ruptured membranes demonstrate that membranes are thinner and collagen content is lower near the site of rupture. Moreover, these alterations appear to be focal rather than generalized (Skinner et al. 1981; Kanayama et al. 1985; French and McGregor 1996). The tensile strength of tissue depends on the collagens, especially types I and III. The amniotic membranes of women with PPROM have decreased amounts of type III, type V, and total collagen (Skinner et al. 1981; Kanayama et al. 1985; al-Zaid et al. 1988). In addition, Athayde and colleagues (1998) found that women with PPROM had higher amniotic fluid levels of metalloproteinases that degrade collagen types IV and V than did women with term labor. These researchers also suggested that infection could be an additional trigger if the host responds to an infection by activating matrix-degrading enzymes (Athayde et al. 1998).

Many studies have associated smoking with an increased risk of PPROM (Lee and Silver 2001). The 2004 Surgeon General's report found sufficient evidence to infer a causal relationship between smoking and PPROM (USDHHS 2004). Researchers have hypothesized that smoking increases the risk of PPROM through several pathways. The effects of smoking on the immune system could increase the risk of genital tract infection or disrupt the cytokine system (French and McGregor 1996). Smoking could increase the inflammatory response and reduce the availability of nutrients such as vitamin C or decrease the uptake of nutrients by the placenta (French and McGregor 1996; Lykkesfeldt et al. 1996, 2000) (see "Other Molecular Mechanisms" later in this chapter).

Developmental Endpoints

This section on developmental effects summarizes the epidemiologic evidence for prenatal effects of maternal smoking on the infant and child, including endpoints such as birth weight, perinatal or infant mortality, birth defects, and neurobehavioral. The discussion also briefly notes the evidence for effects from exposure to second-hand smoke on these outcomes. Studies have examined the effects of smoking on child growth, but this topic is not addressed in this report. Studying childhood health in relation to prenatal smoking is complicated by the possibility of exposure to secondhand smoke subsequent to birth, as well as other intervening factors between birth and some later outcomes that are difficult to assess.

Fetal Size and Growth

The first and the most widely studied effect of maternal smoking is the influence on fetal growth. Fetal growth cannot be directly assessed, so birth weight is used as a surrogate. However, birth weight reflects not only growth but also gestational age, as well as genetic potential, which is not commonly assessed. To account for gestational age, studies may examine IUGR, which is usually assessed from the distribution of birth weight by gestational week, in a standard population. The common definition of SGA is less than the 10th percentile of weight for the age. Another parameter that is examined includes low birth weight (LBW) (<2,500 grams [g]), sometimes among term births only (≥37 weeks).

The first Surgeon General's report on smoking and health in 1964 noted an association of maternal smoking with LBW (U.S. Department of Health, Education, and Welfare 1964). The 2001 Surgeon General's report on women and smoking concluded that "infants born to women who smoke during pregnancy have a lower average birth weight and are more likely to be SGA than are infants born to women who do not smoke" (USDHHS 2004, p. 15). Furthermore, the 2004 Surgeon General's report concluded that "the evidence is sufficient to infer a causal relationship between maternal active smoking and fetal growth restriction and low birth weight" (USDHHS 2004, p. 28). These conclusions are based on a multitude of studies with consistent evidence of a dose-response relationship, confirmed by more recent studies using a biomarker of exposure to tobacco smoke.

Infants of smokers typically weigh 150 to 200 g less than infants of nonsmokers and are twice as likely (ORs = 1.5 to 2.5) to be LBW or SGA. Maternal smoking appears to have the strongest effect on birth weight through growth retardation and, to a lesser extent, through a shortened gestation (Ananth and Platt 2004; USDHHS 2004). On the basis of a maternal smoking rate of about 12 percent during pregnancy, the etiologic fraction (EF) for LBW from smoking was calculated as 6.4 percent for all births and 10.9 percent for single births (Magee et al. 2004). The EF for LBW from smoking among births at full term was slightly higher at 13.4 percent or 16.7 percent for single births, which comprise most births. The authors also

reported that 60 percent of the effect of smoking on LBW in the overall population was among light smokers.

Because of the established effects of maternal active smoking, many studies have also examined fetal growth in relation to exposure of the mother to secondhand smoke. Several reviews concluded that exposure to secondhand smoke is associated with adverse effects on infant growth or an increased risk of LBW and SGA (NCI 1999; WHO 1999a; USDHHS 2001; British Medical Association 2004). Moreover, the 2006 Surgeon General's report concludes that "the evidence is sufficient to infer a causal relationship between exposure to secondhand smoke and a small reduction in birth weight" (USDHHS 2006, p. 13). The highest quality studies indicate birth weight decrements of 15 to 100 g and an OR for LBW or SGA of 1.1 to 1.7 from exposure to secondhand smoke (NCI 1999). A meta-analysis of pooled data conducted through 1995 calculated a mean weight decrement of 28 g (95 percent CI, 16–40) among infants of mothers who did not smoke but were exposed to secondhand smoke and ORs of 1.2 for IUGR and 1.4 for LBW (Windham et al. 1999a). One study based on a sensitive assay for cotinine showed a birth weight decrement of 27.2 g (95 percent CI, 0.6–53.7) per unit change in log cotinine, which represented a decrement of about 100 g between the highest and lowest cotinine quintiles (Kharrazi et al. 2004).

Several studies have shown that the effects of exposure to tobacco smoke, primarily active but also involuntary exposure, appear to be stronger among older mothers (Wen et al. 1990; Wisborg et al. 1996; Haug et al. 2000; Windham et al. 2000; Salihu et al. 2005). Risk may also vary by racial and ethnic groups, and some studies (Mainous and Hueston 1994; USDHHS 1998; Windham et al. 2000) noted stronger effects among non-Whites or Blacks. Some of these variations may be a result of differences in nicotine metabolism among racial groups or differences in smoking and exposure patterns. Smoking may cause reduced birth weight or fetal growth due to fetal hypoxia resulting from exposure to CO, other effects on fetal nutrition, or the action of PAHs (see "Tobacco Smoke Toxicants and the Reproductive System" and "Other Molecular Mechanisms" later in this chapter).

Perinatal and Infant Mortality

The definition of perinatal mortality may vary slightly across studies, but it commonly includes stillbirth at more than 28 weeks of gestation and early neonatal deaths (first 7 days of life). Infant mortality includes death of a live-born child in the first year of life and can be divided into the neonatal (first month) and postneonatal (1 month to 1 year) periods. Neonatal mortality is more related to prenatal conditions. Previous reports of the Surgeon General have reviewed the data for an effect of smoking on mortality. The 2001 report concluded, "the risk for perinatal mortality—both stillbirth and neonatal deaths—and the risk for sudden infant death syndrome (SIDS) are increased among the offspring of women who smoke during pregnancy" (USDHHS 2001, p. 15). The 2004 Surgeon General's report also concluded, "the evidence is sufficient to infer a causal relationship between sudden infant death syndrome and maternal smoking during and after pregnancy" (USDHHS 2004, p. 7). However, the report noted the difficulty of separating prenatal from postnatal effects of maternal smoking.

Many studies have found a slightly increased risk of approximately 20 to 30 percent for stillbirth or neonatal mortality associated with smoking (USDHHS 2004). A meta-analysis of pooled data from 23 cohort studies of perinatal mortality calculated a RR of 1.26 (95 percent CI, 1.19–1.34) (DiFranza and Lew 1995). In one study, the risk was higher for postneonatal death (AOR = 1.6; 95 percent CI, 1.41–1.85) than for neonatal death (AOR = 1.2; 95 percent CI, 1.05–1.30), which was primarily attributable to two causes: respiratory disease and SIDS (Malloy et al. 1988). A study in India (Gupta and Subramoney 2006) reports an adjusted risk for stillbirth three times higher for mothers who use smokeless tobacco than for those who do not use smokeless tobacco. Some evidence for a dose-response relationship was shown for frequency of use. Two previous studies from India had also reported an increased risk of stillbirth or perinatal death with use of smokeless tobacco (primarily chewing tobacco) (Krishna 1978; Shah et al. 2000). These investigations lend further support to the literature on the adverse effects of tobacco use, which may be related to heavy metals or nicotine, because CO from tobacco smoke would not be present (see "Tobacco Smoke Toxicants and the Reproductive System" later in this chapter).

Studies of SIDS and maternal smoking that controlled for other factors showed ORs of 1.8 to 3.1. Several of those studies also report a dose-response relationship (NCI 1999; USDHHS 2004). A meta-analysis comparing women who did or did not smoke during pregnancy, regardless of smoking status after delivery, calculated a pooled OR of 2.98 (95 percent CI, 2.51–3.54) (DiFranza and Lew 1995). Some studies have attempted to separate the effects of prenatal exposure from those of postnatal exposure. In one study, the risk of SIDS was increased in infants with only postpartum exposure to tobacco smoke but was even greater with both prenatal and postnatal exposures (Schoendorf and Kiely 1992). A large study in which participants were asked detailed questions on exposure to tobacco smoke found similar risks for maternal or paternal smoking, but the risks increased with more smokers in the household (Klonoff-Cohen et al. 1995).

In addition, some studies that attempted to examine the independent effects of paternal smoking observed elevated risks of SIDS (Mitchell et al. 1993; Blair et al. 1996). Rates of SIDS have decreased over time with strong public education campaigns to place infants in the supine position while they sleep. Subsequent studies found that the risk attributable to maternal smoking has concomitantly increased and smoking may now be the greatest preventable cause of SIDS (Chong et al. 2004; Anderson et al. 2005).

Birth weight is one of the strongest predictors of infant survival. However, the effects of reduced growth versus shortened gestation are important to consider in determining etiology. Both reduced growth and shortened gestation appear to be related to infant mortality and SIDS (McCormick 1985; Oyen et al. 1995; Paneth 1995; Ananth and Platt 2004). The longer the gestation for a given birth weight, the lower is the mortality (McCormick 1985; Wilcox and Skjærven 1992). The increased risk of mortality associated with LBW appears to continue beyond infancy into childhood (Samuelson et al. 1998; Xu et al. 1998). Furthermore, studies suggest an association of maternal smoking with a higher mortality rate that continues beyond infancy. This effect was greater after adjustment for birth weight (Hofvendahl 1995). Infants who experience symmetrical growth retardation (in weight, length, and head circumference) associated with maternal smoking may be less likely to exhibit later "catch-up" growth and appear to be more likely to have cognitive deficits and difficulties in school (McCormick 1985). Thus, other effects associated with maternal smoking, such as perinatal mortality, may be mediated through reduced fetal growth and, to some extent, through a shortened gestation period (Ananth and Platt 2004). Some studies have found higher risks of infant mortality associated with smoking among mothers who are 35 years of age or older or of certain racial groups (Cnattingius et al. 1988; Li and Daling 1991). Studies have also found an increased risk of SIDS with placental abnormalities (Li and Wi 1999), thus suggesting another mechanism by which smoking may lead to SIDS.

Birth Defects

The 2004 Surgeon General's report summarized epidemiologic studies published between 1974 and 1998 on the relationship between maternal smoking during pregnancy and the risk for congenital malformations (USDHHS 2004). The report concluded that "the evidence is inadequate to infer the presence or absence of a causal relationship between maternal smoking and congenital malformations in general" (USDHHS 2004, p. 28). For oral clefts, however, several studies reported increased risks, and the evidence was considered to be suggestive, but not sufficient, to infer a causal relationship with smoking.

Since the 2004 Surgeon General's report, additional studies have examined possible associations of maternal smoking with major birth malformations. The evidence in support of an association between smoking and an increased risk for oral clefts has become stronger (Table 8.3). A meta-analysis of data from studies published between 1974 and 2001 focused on 9 studies that examined total orofacial clefts and 15 that examined cleft lip with or without cleft palate and cleft palate alone. The study found an association between maternal smoking and a 34-percent increase in the risk of cleft lip with or without cleft palate and a 22-percent increase in the risk of cleft palate alone (Little et al. 2004a). More recently, similar findings were also observed by Honein and colleagues (2007). Other studies provide evidence of a dose-response relationship for maternal smoking and the risk for cleft lip with or without cleft palate (Wyszynski and Wu 2002; Little et al. 2004b; Honein et al. 2007) and for cleft palate alone (Little et al. 2004b). A recent study assessing maternal tobacco exposure by cotinine levels in mid-pregnancy serum samples found an OR of 2 for cleft lip with or without cleft palate (Shaw et al. 2009).

Studies on interactions between genes and smoking and between vitamin use and smoking contribute to an understanding of the etiology of oral clefts (van Rooij et al. 2002; Jugessur et al. 2003; Shi et al. 2007) (see "Fetal Tissue and Organogenesis" and "Smoking and Maternal and Neonatal Genetic Polymorphisms" later in this chapter). One study reported an increase in the risk for cleft lip with or without cleft palate that was strongest among offspring whose mothers had smoked but had not consumed multivitamins during the periconceptive period (Shaw et al. 2002). Results did not suggest an interaction for isolated cleft palate. Study findings also supported an increased risk of clefting with paternal smoking or involuntary exposure to tobacco smoke (Savitz et al. 1991; Zhang et al. 1992; Shaw et al. 1996). Whether paternal smoking acts through exposure of the mother to secondhand smoke or directly on male gametes is not clear.

A number of studies have also investigated maternal smoking in relation to cardiovascular malformations. A review of data from 13 studies published between 1971 and 1999 found mixed results. Twelve of the studies provided results for cardiovascular malformations combined and seven studies for specific subgroups of cardiovascular defects examined separately (Källén 2002a). Combining all cardiovascular malformations represents a heterogeneous group but examining subgroups resulted in low power for several studies. The conflicting results probably reflect differences in research methods, including case ascertainment, classification, control of confounding, and

sample size of the case group. Other studies have reported associations of maternal smoking with cardiovascular malformations (Table 8.4), including conotruncal defects, atrial septal defects, and atrioventricular septal defects (Torfs and Christianson 1999); L-transposition of the great arteries (Steinberger et al. 2002; Kuehl and Loffredo 2003); and conotruncal defects among offspring whose mothers did not use vitamins (Shaw et al. 2002). Steinberger and colleagues (2002) found an association between paternal smoking and single-ventricle defects. These more recent exploratory studies present methodologic issues similar to those noted in the meta-analysis by Källén (2002a). In addition, Malik and colleagues (2008) found an association between periconceptual smoking and septal heart defects. There is a need for further research with large, population-based studies that incorporate standardized methods for case ascertainment and classification to determine whether a relationship exists between maternal smoking and the risk of cardiovascular malformations.

Studies of other birth defects have found an association between maternal smoking and an increased risk for clubfoot (Honein et al. 2000; Skelly et al. 2002), craniosynostosis (Källén 1999; Carmichael et al. 2008), and gastroschisis (Werler et al. 2003), but not for spina bifida (Table 8.5) (Shaw et al. 2002; van Rooij et al. 2002). Studies report mixed results for maternal smoking and limb deficiency defects (Hwang et al. 1998; Shaw et al. 2002; Carmichael et al. 2004), Down syndrome (Chen et al. 1999; Yang et al. 1999), and for cryptorchidism and hypospadias (Akre et al. 1999; Källén 2002b; Pierik et al. 2004).

Maternal smoking may interfere with normal organ development in offspring in several ways, including through fetal hypoxia, alterations in essential nutrients, teratogenic effects, and DNA damage. Those effects may be related to exposure to tobacco smoke components such as CO, nicotine, cadmium, and PAHs (Chernoff 1973; Mochizuki et al. 1984; Lammer et al. 2004; Munger et al. 2004; Ziaei et al. 2005). In addition, certain populations with genetic polymorphisms may be more susceptible to damage attributable to exposure to tobacco smoke because of alterations in metabolic pathways (see "Fetal Tissue and Organogenesis" and "Smoking and Maternal and Neonatal Genetic Polymorphisms" later in this chapter).

Neurodevelopment

Maternal smoking and exposure to secondhand tobacco smoke during pregnancy affect infant health status at birth as described earlier and are hypothesized to affect physical and mental development in infancy and early childhood as well. Studies have reported evidence of lower weights and shorter heights into the preschool period (Fox et al. 1990), in addition to correlations of maternal smoking with microcephaly and hydrocephaly, particularly among female infants (Honein et al. 2001). Reviews have also examined the links between maternal smoking and mental development in offspring (Hardy and Mellits 1972; Lassen and Oei 1998). Earlier Surgeon General's reports examined this topic and reported possible effects. However, at the time of the 2004 Surgeon General's report, the evidence was considered "inadequate to infer the presence or absence of a causal relationship between maternal smoking and physical growth and neurocognitive development of children" (USDHHS 2004, p. 601), and this conclusion was echoed in the examination of secondhand smoke (USDHHS 2006). Some key studies, as well as others published since those included in the prior reports of the Surgeon General (e.g., 2004 and later), are summarized below.

Researchers have suggested that prenatal exposure to smoking poses a unique risk for neurologic development and intellectual abilities attributable to impairments of the central nervous system (Olds et al. 1994). Drews and colleagues (1996) studied a sample of 221 children aged 10 years and reported that those with mental retardation were more likely than control participants with no mental retardation to have mothers who had smoked during pregnancy. Moreover, the rates of retardation increased with the number of cigarettes mothers smoked. McCartney and colleagues (1994) speculated that intrauterine exposure to nicotine specifically affects the physiology of outer hair cells in the ear that underlies language ability and leads to poorer performance scores among offspring on assessments that rely heavily on verbal abilities.

Investigators have found it difficult to document a consistent impact of maternal smoking on cognitive development in infants and young children, because many factors affect cognitive development. For example, in a study of two- and four-year-old children of mothers who smoked compared with children in the same age groups whose mothers did not smoke, Baghurst and colleagues (1992) reported small but significant group differences on the Bayley Scales of Infant Development (BSID) and the McCarthy Scales of Children's Abilities (MSCA). However, group differences were not significant after controlling for SES, maternal intelligence quotient, and quality of the home learning environment. Sexton and colleagues (1990) also reported better scores among three-year-olds whose mothers had stopped smoking during pregnancy compared with children whose mothers had smoked more than 10 cigarettes a day during pregnancy. Group differences in performance on the Minnesota Child Development Inventory and the MSCA were small, but differences remained significant after adjustment for birth weight, SES, and certain maternal and child characteristics. Trasti and colleagues (1999) reported lower scores

on the Wechsler Preschool and Primary Scale of Intelligence-Revised for a sample of 369 children aged five years whose mothers had smoked during pregnancy compared with children of mothers who did not smoke. However, significant group differences were not found after adjustment for maternal education level. These researchers also reported no differences on the BSID in a sample of 376 children from the same population at 13 months of age by mothers' smoking status.

Batstra and colleagues (2003) reported poorer performance on mathematics and spelling achievement tests among a group of 1,186 children aged 5 through 11 years whose mothers smoked, and differences remained after adjustment for SES and for prenatal and perinatal complications. A Danish study found effects of prenatal smoking during the third trimester on adult intelligence even after adjustment for sociodemographic variables (Mortensen et al. 2005). In contrast to other studies, Eskenazi and Trupin (1995) reported slightly higher but nonsignificant scores on the Peabody Picture Vocabulary Test and the Raven Progressive Matrices Test for five-year-old children whose mothers had smoked during pregnancy compared with those for children of mothers who had not smoked, even after adjustment for parental education, SES, age, race, and preschool attendance. Some significant decrements in performance on these same measures and significant differences in the maternal-rated activity levels were attributable to exposure to secondhand tobacco smoke during childhood. Other studies show cognitive deficits with prenatal exposure to secondhand smoke that are exacerbated by conditions of material hardship (Rauh et al. 2004). After adjustment, decrements in cognitive and academic abilities were reported with increasing cotinine levels within the range indicating exposure to secondhand smoke during childhood (Yolton et al. 2005).

Despite these inconsistent findings on general assessments of children's cognition and intelligence, findings more consistently show an association between maternal smoking and children's lower performance on assessments of verbal skills in general, as well as on specific language and auditory tests. For example, a sample of 110 children aged 6 to 11 years whose mothers had smoked during pregnancy performed more poorly on tasks tapping phonologic processing skills that are known to be related to both language and reading abilities (McCartney et al. 1994). Follow-up studies of the same cohort reported that maternal smoking and maternal involuntary exposure to tobacco smoke negatively affected the performance of children aged 9 and 12 years on standardized assessments of language and reading, as well as on assessments of general intelligence skills (Fried et al. 1997). Butler and Goldstein (1973) studied a sample of more than 9,000 children aged 7 and 11 years whose

Table 8.3   Association between maternal smoking and orofacial clefts (OFCs), 1999–2009[a]

Study	Design/population	Definition of smoking (smoking rate in controls)
van Rooij et al. 2001	Case-control study 113 infants with nonsyndromic OFCs 104 infants with no defects White, aged 9 months–3 years The Netherlands Study period not specified	Smokers (20.2%) vs. nonsmokers
Shaw et al. 2002	Case-control study 489 infants and fetal deaths with OFCs 734 control infants with no malformation California Birth Defects Monitoring Program 1987–1989	Smoking in periconceptional period—1 month before to 3 months after conception—(24%) vs. none
van Rooij et al. 2002	Case-control study 45 mothers of children with OFCs 39 mothers of children with spina bifida 75 control mothers DNA for possible effect modification The Netherlands 1997–1999	Smokers (18.1%) vs. nonsmokers Smoking in periconceptional period Number of cigarettes/day

Wyszynski and Wu 2002	Case-control study
	2,029 births with nonsyndromic oral clefts
	4,050 control infants with no malformation, matched on maternal and paternal race and child's gender, county of birth, and month of birth
	United States Natality database
	1997
		Smoking
		  Any (16.9%) vs. none
		Number of cigarettes/day
		  1–10 (10.8%)
		  11–20 (4.9%)
		  >20 (1.1%)

Jugessur et al. 2003	Case-parent triad study
	261 case-parent triads (88 CPO and 173 CL/P)
	Norway
	1996–1998
		Smoking in last year or during first trimester
		  Before pregnancy (31%)
		  First trimester (27%)

Little et al. 2004a	Meta-analysis of data from 24 case-control and cohort studies 9 studies addressed only OFCs 15 studies assessed CL/P and CP separately Studies published between 1974 and 2001	Smokers vs. nonsmokers varied by study

Findings	OR (95% CI)	Comments
• Maternal smoking not associated with oral clefting	1.1 (0.6–2.2)	See Table 8.13 for polymorphism results
• Association of maternal smoking with isolated CL/P among women not using vitamins Vitamins/Smoking		Adjustment for maternal body mass index, education, race, and ethnicity
Yes/No	1.0	
No/Yes	2.8 (1.8–4.3)	
No/No	1.9 (1.3–2.7)	
Yes/Yes	1.5 (1.0–2.2)	
• Relationship marginally significant for isolated CP Vitamins/Smoking		
Yes/No	1.0	
No/Yes	2.0 (1.0–3.9)	
No/No	1.6 (1.0–2.6)	
Yes/Yes	1.7 (1.0–2.9)	
• Association with OFCs	2.0 (0.8–5.0)	Adjustment for maternal education
• No association between maternal NAT2 acetylator status and OFCs		
• No interaction between NAT2 acetylator status and maternal smoking		
• Maternal smoking associated with CL/P in infants Any vs. none	1.16 (1.01–1.33)	Did not distinguish cases with isolated CP; adjusted for maternal education, age, race, diabetes mellitus, and pregnancy-associated hypertension
• Number of cigarettes/day vs. none		
1–10	1.10 (0.93–1.30)	
11–20	1.11 (0.87–1.41)	
>20	1.55 (0.88–2.70)	
	Trend test, $p = 0.072$	
• Risk for smoking alone not stated		None
• No interaction between maternal smoking and *TGFα* gene *TAQ1 *A2/*A2* genotype in infant		
• Consistent, moderate, and statistically significant associations between maternal smoking and CL/P	1.34 (1.25–1.44)	None
• Evidence of a dose-response relationship between maternal smoking and CP	1.22 (1.10–1.35)	

Table 8.3   Continued

Study	Design/population	Definition of smoking (smoking rate in controls)

Little et al. 2004b	Case-control study
	190 children with OFCs
	248 children with no malformation
	Scotland and Manchester and Merseyside regions of England
	1997–2000
		Number of cigarettes/day
		Active smoking and involuntary exposure to cigarette smoke
		Maternal smoking
		    Ever (37.5%)
		    During pregnancy (24.2%)
		    First trimester (23.8%)
		Exposure to cigarette smoke among mothers who did not smoke (28.2%)
		Exposure to cigarette smoke among mothers who smoked (31.0%)

Honein et al. 2007	Case-control study 933 CL/P 528 CPO 3,390 controls with no defects 8 sites in the United States Oct 1997–Dec 2001 births	Periconceptual smoking (1 month before to 3 months after conception) 20% controls exposed
Shi et al. 2007	Case-control study DNA samples from 1,244 children with CL/P, CPO 4,183 parents, siblings, and unrelated population controls Danish samples from two independent case-control studies (Dec 1991–Aug 1994; born between 1981–1990) Iowa samples from cases in Iowa Registry for Congenital and Inherited Disorders Control children born without major anomalies were matched by birth month, year, and gender	Number of cigarettes/day 0 1–9 10–19 ≥20
Shaw et al. 2009	Case-control study nested within a cohort of pregnancies with mid-pregnancy serum specimens 89 pregnancies with CL/P 409 pregnancies without malformations	Mid-pregnancy serum cotinine levels No smoke exposure: cotinine value <2 µg/mL Any exposure: cotinine value ≥2 µg/mL

Note: **CI** = confidence interval; **CL/P** = cleft lip with or without cleft palate; **CP** = cleft palate; **CPO** = cleft palate only; **mL** = milliliter; **OR** = odds ratio; **µg** = micrograms.
[a]Not included in 2004 Surgeon General's report on the health consequences of smoking.

Findings	OR (95% CI)	Comments
• First trimester smoking associated with CL/P		Adjustment for gender, season of
Any vs. none	1.9 (1.1–3.1)	birth, maternal education, and
≤10 cigarettes/day	1.7 (0.9–3.0)	infant's ethnic group
>10 cigarettes/day	2.5 (1.1–5.6)	
• First trimester smoking associated with CP		
Any vs. none	2.5 (1.3–4.1)	
≤10 cigarettes/day	2.1 (1.1–3.9)	
>10 cigarettes/day	3.1 (1.2–7.8)	
• An effect of involuntary smoking could not be excluded in mothers who did not smoke		
• CL/P	1.3 (1.0–1.6)	Strong effects for bilateral CL/P and
• CPO	1.2 (0.9–1.5)	heavy smoking
• Maternal smoking was associated with OFC in both Danish and Iowa data		Suggestive effects of variants in the *NAT2* and *CYP1A1* genes were
CL/P		observed in both the Iowan and
Danish		Danish participants
10–19	1.71 (1.14–2.56)	
≥20	1.16 (0.51–2.64)	
Iowa		
1–4	0.93 (0.42–2.57)	
5–14	2.24 (1.11–4.50)	
≥15	2.78 (1.42–5.44)	
CPO		
Danish		
10–19	1.17 (0.61–2.23)	
≥20	0.35 (0.05–2.67)	
Iowa		
1–4	0.91 (0.30–2.75)	
5–14	2.52 (1.09–5.81)	
≥15	1.58 (0.59–4.21)	
• There was an interaction between maternal smoking and fetal inheritance of a *GSTT1 null* deletion (Fisher combined p value <0.001)		
• Association of maternal serum mid-pregnancy cotinine levels with CL/P	2.1 (1.0–4.4)	Exposure assessment based on biomarker

Table 8.4   Association between maternal smoking and cardiovascular malformations, by phenotype, 1999–2008

Study	Design/population	Definition of smoking (prevalence of smoking)

Torfs and Christiansen 1999	Case-control study
	687 infants with Down syndrome
	385 case infants with cardiac defects also
	302 control infants with no heart defects and no other specific defect
	California Birth Defects Monitoring Program
	1991 and 1993
		First trimester participants
		  Yes vs. no
		Smoking during pregnancy
		  12% of all participants
		  8% of controls for cardiac defects

Woods and Raju 2001	Retrospective cohort study of 18,016 live births in TriHealth Hospital System (Cincinnati, Ohio) Congenital defects grouped in 22 categories, including oral clefts 1987–1999	Smokers vs. nonsmokers Cohort included 1,943 mothers who were smokers

Källén 2002a	Meta-analysis of 13 case-control studies published in 1971–1999	Smokers vs. nonsmokers
		  None, 1–20 cigarettes/day, and
		  >20 cigarettes/day
		Prevalence varied by study

Shaw et al. 2002	Case-control study 207 infants and fetal deaths with conotruncal defects 489 infants and fetal deaths with orofacial clefts 265 infants and fetal deaths with neural tube defects 734 control infants with no malformation California Birth Defects Monitoring Program 1987–1989	Maternal smoking during periconceptional period (1 month before to 3 months after conception) Smoking among case mothers Smoking among controls
Steinberger et al. 2002	Case-control study 48 infants with single ventricle and abnormal situs 3,572 infants without cardiac defects Baltimore-Washington Infant Study (Maryland; northern Virginia; and Washington, DC) 1981–1989	Parental smoking of >1 pack/day (maternal 4.9%, paternal 9%) vs. no smoking Exposure period during gestation not stated
Kuehl and Loffredo 2003	Case-control study 36 infants with single L-transposition of great arteries 3,495 infants without cardiac defects Baltimore-Washington Infant Study Maryland; northern Virginia; and Washington, DC) 1981–1989	Not stated Prevalence of maternal smoking for control infants not mentioned
Malik et al. 2008	Case-control study 3,067 infants with congenital heart defects 3,947 controls without defects	Those who reported smoking any time from 1 month before conception and through each month of pregnancy <1 cigarette/day to >2 packs/day

Findings by type of cardiovascular defect	Odds ratio (95% confidence interval)	Comments

• Maternal smoking associated with grouped cardiac defects
• Maternal smoking associated with
  Atrioventricular septal defects
  Tetralogy of Fallot
  Atrial septal defects
	2.1 (1.2–3.5)
	
	2.3 (1.2–4.5)
	4.6 (1.2–17.0)
	2.2 (1.1–4.3)
		Adjustment for maternal race; all infants had Down syndrome

• Smoking associated with increased risk of cardiovascular system abnormalities • Patent ductus arteriosus (n = 153) and ventricular septal defect (n = 48) most common abnormalities • Maternal smoking not associated with 21 other defects	1.56 (1.12–1.82)	Adjustment for maternal age, race, and diabetes mellitus but not for gestational age
• Mixed results for cardiovascular defects overall • Mixed results for specific cardiovascular defects	Data not reported	Different methods of case ascertainment, classification, control of confounding, and small case groups

• Smoking associated with conotruncal defects among infants of women who did not use vitamins
  Vitamins/Smoking
    Yes/No
    No/Yes
    No/No
    Yes/Yes
	
	1.0
	2.2 (1.3–4.0)
	1.4 (0.9–2.2)
	1.0 (0.6–1.7)
		Adjustment for maternal body mass index, education, race, and ethnicity

• No association with maternal smoking
• Increased risk with paternal smoking of >1 pack/day
• Increased risk with paternal smoking of increasing number of cigarettes/day
  1–19
  20–39
  ≥40
	1.9 (0.6–6.3)
	2.2 (1.1–5.1)
	
	1.0
	1.9
	3.7
	trend test, p = 0.02
		Source of information on paternal smoking not specified; small case sample size; estimates based on exact methods but not adjusted for potential confounders

• Maternal cigarette smoking associated with increased risk of L-transposition of great arteries	1.6 (1.1–2.4)	Maternal smoking highly correlated with use of hair dyes; adjustment for maternal use of hair dyes, paternal exposure to laboratory chemicals, and residence in spatial cluster

• Septal heart defects
  Light smoking
  Medium smoking
  Heavy smoking
	
	1.44 (1.18–1.76)
	1.50 (1.11–2.03)
	2.06 (1.20–3.54)
		None

Table 8.5   Association between maternal smoking and noncardiovascular congenital malformations, by type of malformation, 1998–2008

Study	Design/population	Analysis and definition of smoking (smoking rate in controls)
Hwang et al. 1998	Case-control study 34 infants with isolated LDD 482 control infants with other isolated defects Maryland Birth Defects Reporting and Information System 1984–1992	Maternal smoking during pregnancy (27.5% among all participants) Any vs. none Effect modification by *MSX1* gene
Reefhuis et al. 1998	Case-control study 3,662 children with foot deformities 7,829 control children with chromosomal or monogenic disorder 26 European Surveillance of Congenital Anomalies registries 1980–1994	During pregnancy Any (18.1%) vs. none
Akre et al. 1999	2 population-based case-control studies 2,782 boys operated on for cryptorchidism 1,220 boys operated on for hypospadias (5 matched controls per case) Linkage of Inpatient and Birth Registries Sweden birth cohort 1983–1993	Prenatal clinic record on maternal smoking Yes (38.1%) vs. no
Chen et al. 1999	Case-control study 775 children with Down syndrome 7,750 control children with no malformation, matched by birth year Washington State Birth Events Records Database 1984–1994	Any maternal smoking during pregnancy vs. none (age) <35 years (20.2%) ≥35 years (14.2%)
Källén 1999	Case-control studies 304 infants with craniosynostosis, no information available on type or number of controls Linkages of Swedish Registry of Congenital Malformations and National Board of Health Medical Birth Registry Sweden 1983–1996	Smoking at first prenatal visit Any (% not stated) vs. none Categories None <10 cigarettes/day ≥10 cigarettes/day

Findings by type of defect	Odds ratio (95% confidence interval)	Comments
• Interaction with *MSX1* *rare* alleles and risk of isolated limb deficiency		Passive surveillance system, so incomplete case ascertainment; small sample; unadjusted
Smoking only	0.7 (0.03–6.72)	
1 or 2 alleles only	2.4 (0.73–8.71)	
Smoking and 1 or 2 alleles	4.8 (1.37–18.4)	
• Maternal smoking during pregnancy associated with increased risk of foot deformities	1.2 (1.1–1.3)	Adjustment for maternal age, registry, parity, and year of birth; control infants with malformation
• Maternal smoking associated with increased risk of cryptorchidism	1.19 (1.06–1.33)	Adjustment for maternal age, parity, height, history of subfertility, preeclampsia, twinning, Apgar score, other malformations, gestation, and birth weight
• Maternal smoking not associated with increased risk of hypospadias	0.85 (0.71–1.02)	
• Maternal smoking during pregnancy not associated with Down syndrome	1.00 (0.82–1.24)	Adjustment for exact year of maternal age, race, and parity
• Associated with craniosynostosis	1.45 (1.13–1.87)	Adjustment for year of birth, maternal age, parity, and educational level; no information on smoking prevalence
• Associated with isolated craniosynostosis	1.67 (1.27–2.19)	
• Not associated with syndromes	0.61 (0.29–1.30)	
• Dose-response effect for isolated craniosynostosis		
<10 cigarettes/day	1.48 (1.04–2.02)	
≥10 cigarettes/day	2.12 (1.50–2.99)	
• Associated with sagittal but not other suture synostosis	1.48 (1.02–2.14)	

Table 8.5   Continued

Study	Design/population	Analysis and definition of smoking (smoking rate in controls)
Yang et al. 1999	Population-based case-control study 285 children with Down syndrome 329 control children with no defects Cases ascertained from Metropolitan Atlanta Congenital Defects Program 5 counties in Georgia 1989–1996	Lifetime nonsmokers (71.0%) Ever smoked (28.9%) Current smoker (15.8%) Total pack-years[a] <5 (16.4%) ≥5 (12.2%) Effect modification by timing and origin of meiotic error and OC use
Honein et al. 2000	Population-based case-control study 346 infants with isolated clubfoot 3,029 infants with no defects Frequency matched to cases by year and hospital of birth Atlanta Birth Defects Case-Control Study 1968–1980	First trimester Any (28.6%) vs. none
Källén 2002b	Case-control study 3,262 infants with hypospadias 1,413,811 infants with no malformation Linkages of Swedish Registry of Congenital Malformations, National Board of Health Medical Birth Registry, and Hospital Discharge Registry Sweden 1983–1996	Smokers (24.6%) vs. nonsmokers Cigarettes/day <10 (15.2%) ≥10 (9.3%)
Shaw et al. 2002	Case-control study 265 infants and fetal deaths with neural tube defects 165 infants with LDD 734 control infants with no malformation California Birth Defects Monitoring Program 1987–1989	During the periconceptional period (1 month before to 3 months after conception) (24%) vs. none

Findings by type of defect	Odds ratio (95% confidence interval)	Comments
• No association in presence of maternal meiosis I nondisjunction error Current smoker (age)		60–63% participation rates; interaction of smoking with type of nondisjunction error and OC use
<35 years	0.69 (0.35–1.37)	
≥35 years	0.81 (0.20–3.29)	
• Associated with Down syndrome in young mothers with meiosis II nondisjunction error Ever smoked (age)		
<35 years	2.43 (0.89–6.63)	
≥35 years	0.37 (0.07–1.87)	
Current smoker (age)		
<35 years	2.98 (1.01–8.87)	
≥35 years	0.65 (0.06–7.48)	
• Associated with Down syndrome in young mothers with OC use and maternal meiosis II nondisjunction error		
OC use alone	0.38 (0.05–3.01)	
Smoking without OC use	1.54 (0.45–5.27)	
Smoking with OC use	7.92 (1.63–35.6)	
• Interaction between maternal smoking and family history of clubfoot		Adjustment for gravidity and gender
Smoking only	1.32 (1.04–1.72)	
Family history only	6.52 (2.95–14.41)	
Both	20.30 (7.90–52.17)	
• Maternal smoking negatively associated with hypospadias Smokers vs. nonsmokers	0.83 (0.76–0.90)	Stratification by maternal age, parity, educational level, and year of birth
<10 cigarettes/day	0.84 (0.76–0.93)	
≥10 cigarettes/day	0.81 (0.71–0.92)	
• Little association with LDD Vitamins/Smoking		Adjustment for maternal BMI, education, race, and ethnicity
Yes/No	1.0	
No/Yes	1.5 (0.8–2.8)	
No/No	1.1 (0.7–1.8)	
Yes/Yes	0.8 (0.5–1.4)	

Table 8.5   Continued

Study	Design/population	Analysis and definition of smoking (smoking rate in controls)
Skelly et al. 2002	Case-control study 239 children with clubfoot 365 control children with no malformation Western Washington State 1986–1994	Average number of cigarettes/day during pregnancy None (81.7%) 0.01–9.9 (11.2%) 10–19.9 (4.8%) ≥20 (2.3%)
van Rooij et al 2002	Case-control study 45 case mothers of children with orofacial clefts 39 case mothers of children with spina bifida 75 control mothers The Netherlands 1997–1999	Smokers (18.1%) vs. nonsmokers Cigarettes/day Effect modification by NAT2 acetylator status
Werler et al. 2003	Population-based case-control study Mothers of 205 case children with gastroschisis 127 case children with small intestinal atresia 381 malformed control children 416 control children with no malformation 15 cities across the United States and Canada 1995–1999	Maternal smoking during first trimester Cigarettes/day Control children with malformation Any (34%) 1–9 (10%) 10–19 (11%) >19 (13%) Control children with no malformation Any (34%) 1–9 (9%) 10–19 (9%) >19 (16%)
Carmichael et al. 2004	Population-based case-control study 92 infants with LDD 180 control infants with no malformation California Birth Defects Monitoring Program 1987–1988	Maternal and paternal smoking and infant *MSX1* genotype Neither (50.0%) Mother only (11.7%) Father only (20.6%) Both (14.4%)
Pierik et al. 2004	Population-based nested case-control study 78 case children with cryptorchidism 56 case newborns with hypospadias 313 control newborns with no defects in a cohort of 8,698 male newborns Rotterdam, The Netherlands 1999–2001	Current smoking (maternal 22.7%, paternal 41.5%) vs. no current smoking

Findings by type of defect	Odds ratio (95% confidence interval)	Comments
• Associated with idiopathic clubfoot		No confounders noted or adjusted for; no information collected on vitamin supplement intake
Smoking vs. none (cigarettes/day)	2.1 (1.5–3.3)	
0.01–9.9	1.5 (0.9–2.5)	
10–19.9	3.1 (1.7–5.8)	
≥20	3.9 (1.6–9.2)	
Risk (any vs. none) varied by infant gender		
Boys	1.8 (1.2–3.0)	
Girls	2.8 (1.4–5.4)	
• Associated with isolated idiopathic clubfoot		
Any vs. none (cigarettes/day)	2.4 (1.7–3.6)	
0.01–9.9	1.4 (0.9–2.5)	
10–19.9	3.5 (1.8–6.7)	
≥20	4.6 (1.9–11.0)	
• Maternal smoking not associated with spina bifida	Data not reported	Adjustment for maternal education
• No association between maternal NAT2 acetylator status and spina bifida		
• No interaction		
• Associated with gastroschisis		Adjustment for vasoconstrictive drug use and maternal age
Any vs. none (cigarettes/day)	1.5 (1.1–2.2)	
1–9	1.3 (0.7–2.2)	
10–19	1.4 (0.9–2.4)	
>19	1.8 (1.1–2.8)	
• Not associated with small intestinal atresia		Adjustment for age, education, family income, and use of vasoconstrictive drugs, other medications, alcohol, and marijuana
Any vs. none (cigarettes/day)	1.0 (1.6–1.7)	
1–9	1.4 (0.6–1.7)	
10–19	0.8 (0.3–2.0)	
>19	1.2 (0.6–2.4)	
• No association of maternal smoking and LDD risk	1.0 (0.4–2.3)	None
• No association of paternal smoking and LDD risk	1.1 (0.6–2.2)	
• No association between *MSX1* genotype and LDD		
• No interaction between parental smoking, infant's *MSX1* genotype, and LDD risk		
• Maternal smoking not associated with cryptorchidism	1.3 (0.8–2.3)	Adjustment for small-for-gestational-age status, self-reported exposure to solvents, and time to pregnancy
• Maternal smoking not associated with hypospadias	1.6 (0.8–2.3)	
• Paternal smoking not associated with cryptorchidism	1.2 (0.6–2.1)	
• Paternal smoking associated with hypospadias	3.8 (1.8–8.2)	

Table 8.5   Continued

Study	Design/population	Analysis and definition of smoking (smoking rate in controls)

Carmichael et al. 2008	Case-control study
	531 cases of craniosynostosis
	5,008 control children without malformation matched by birth cohort
	National Birth Defects Prevention Study
	10 states
	1997–2003
		Smoking before pregnancy, 1st, 2nd, and 3rd month of pregnancy
		2nd and 3rd trimesters
		Categories
		    None
		    Smoked <5 cigarettes/day
		    Smoked 5–14 cigarettes/day
		    Smoked ≥15 cigarettes/day

Note: **Apgar** = appearance, pulse, grimace, activity, respiration; **BMI** = body mass index; **LDD** = limb deficiency defects; **OC** = oral contraceptive.
[a]Pack-years = the number of years of smoking multiplied by the number of packs of cigarettes smoked per day.

mothers had smoked during pregnancy. These children were three to five months behind children of nonsmoking mothers in reading, mathematics, and general cognitive abilities. In more than 5,000 youth aged 6 through 16 years from the Third National Health and Nutrition Examination Survey, deficits in reading and mathematics scores were associated with higher current exposure to secondhand smoke (Yolton et al. 2005).

Researchers have used various types of tests that measure both cognitive and behavioral aspects of development to study the relationship between possible language impairments and maternal smoking. Data from studies using evoked brain responses indicate that infants born to mothers who smoked approximately one pack of cigarettes per day showed atypical patterns of brain organization, which reflected poorer speech discrimination than that of infants born to mothers who did not smoke. Compared with infants of smokers, the unexposed infants exhibited more common forms of brain lateralization for speech

and showed evidence of better discrimination of consonant and vowel syllables (Molfese et al. 2004). This finding parallels findings in studies that reported long-term impacts on language and cognitive domains in children whose mothers smoked (Makin et al. 1991; McCartney et al. 1994). These results indicate that prenatal exposure to smoking in otherwise healthy infants can be linked to significant changes in brain physiology associated with basic perceptual skills. These effects may be long term, with impacts noted in later school performance. A study of gravid mice exposed to tobacco smoke supports these findings. The study revealed that the offspring had a developmental delay in neonatal reflexes and notable behavioral deficits in adulthood, including impaired learning and memory abilities (Li and Wang 2004). CO in tobacco smoke induces fetal hypoxia and may contribute to these effects (see "Carbon Monoxide" later in this chapter).

Findings by type of defect	Odds ratio (95% confidence interval)	Comments
• Smoking during first month of pregnancy was not associated with craniosynostosis		Adjustment for maternal age, education, race/ethnicity, subfertility, parity, folic acid supplement intake, BMI, and study center
• Smoking later in pregnancy (2nd or 3rd trimester) was associated with increased risk but only among mothers who smoked at least 1 pack per day		
• Smoked ≥15 cigarettes/day		
2nd trimester	1.6 (0.9–2.8)	
3rd trimester	1.4 (0.7–2.5)	
• Most confidence intervals include 1.0		

Pathophysiological and Cellular and Molecular Mechanisms of Smoking

This section explores various mechanisms by which smoking may affect reproductive and developmental outcomes at the pathophysiological and cellular levels.

Endocrine System

One mechanism by which smoking may contribute to various reproductive outcomes is alterations in hormone function. Researchers have suggested that smoking has antiestrogenic effects (Baron et al. 1990). However, there is also evidence of effects on hormones other than estrogen, which may vary by gender and the stage of life.

Premenopausal Women

Hormone function has been difficult to study in non-clinic-based populations, because of the cyclic nature of hormone excretion and day-to-day variations in premenopausal women. During regular menstrual cycles, the hormone dynamics are predictable in a pattern that reflects the integrity of the hypothalamic-pituitary-gonadal (HPG) axis. Excretion of the follicle-stimulating hormone (FSH) from the pituitary gland is critical for ovarian follicle recruitment, development, and maturation (van Santbrink et al. 1995). The synthesis and excretion of estrogen by the follicles reflect ovarian activity that then modulates the release of gonadotropins from the pituitary through a negative-feedback loop. After ovulation has occurred, the follicle undergoes luteinization, and the corpus luteum excretes progesterone and some estrogen to prepare the uterine lining for implantation. In the absence of conception, estrogen and progesterone levels decline, followed by menstruation. Should fertilization occur, the steroid levels continue to rise along with levels of other hormones, such as human chorionic gonadotropin (hCG), to maintain the pregnancy. The placenta takes over hormone production during pregnancy.

Smoking has been considered potentially antiestrogenic (Baron et al. 1990), primarily because of the nature of its association with hormonally related diseases such as reproductive cancers. However, the 2001 Surgeon General's report on women and smoking concluded that circulating levels of the major endogenous estrogens are not altered among smokers (USDHHS 2001). Some studies were hampered by a lack of biosampling points, small numbers of participants, or the inclusion of postmenopausal or potentially perimenopausal women. Details on 15 studies of premenopausal women are provided in Table 8.6. Most of these studies excluded women who were taking hormones or who were known to have menstrual problems. Nevertheless, the studies represent a variety of ages and did not always adjust for factors such as age and obesity. Two studies (MacMahon et al. 1982b; Westhoff et al. 1996) reported levels of urinary excretion of estrone, estradiol, and/or estriol in the luteal phase among smokers that were lower than those among nonsmokers, suggesting reduced estrogen production. However, several other studies did not observe significant differences in serum levels of estradiol by smoking status among premenopausal women (Longcope and Johnston 1988; Key et al. 1991; Berta et al. 1992). The study by Michnovicz and colleagues (1986) is often cited for the discovery that smoking induced the 2-hydroxylation of estrone to relatively inactive metabolites and decreased estriol excretion. A later, much larger study, however, did not find differences in the circulating levels of the 2α- or 16α-hydroxy metabolites in nulliparous smokers versus nonsmokers after adjustment for age, ethnicity, and length of menstrual cycle (Jernström et al. 2003). Zumoff and colleagues (1990) measured serum at multiple points during the cycle and found that estradiol was actually increased among heavy smokers in the follicular phase, particularly early, at baseline. A study with only a single serum sample obtained in the early follicular phase (Lucero et al. 2001) found that current smokers had higher baseline estradiol levels than did former olifetime nonsmokers, but this finding was not significant after adjustment. Examination of dose by pack-years[1] did not indicate a dose-response pattern, but this analysis may have been diluted by including former smokers with smokers if the effects do not persist after smoking cessation.

Among women who had IVF, smokers had higher baseline levels of 17-β-estradiol than did nonsmokers (Weigert et al. 1999). A later study examined hormonal dynamics by daily measurement of urinary levels of estrone and progesterone metabolites throughout the cycle, in relation to smoking level that was verified by cotinine bioassay (Windham et al. 2005). This analysis showed that heavy smokers had elevated baseline (e.g., early follicular phase) levels of the steroid metabolites, a finding consistent with results in other studies (Longcope and Johnston 1988; Zumoff et al. 1990; Key et al. 1996; Lucero et al. 2001). A study of Chinese nonsmokers examined the effects of secondhand smoke on urinary levels of hormone metabolites and found an association with lower mean levels of estrone conjugates only for nonconceptive cycles (Chen et al. 2005).

Some of the disease patterns observed with smoking may reflect changes in androgen or progesterone levels, rather than estrogen levels, or changes in the ratio of androgens to estrogens. Some studies have reported that smoking increases adrenal activity and have found elevations in adrenal androgens among postmenopausal smokers (Friedman et al. 1987; Khaw et al. 1988; Longcope and Johnston 1988; Key et al. 1991). Researchers have found elevated serum testosterone levels in female smokers that were positively correlated with estradiol levels in menstrual cycling women who had IVF (pre-hCG treatment) (Barbieri et al. 2005). Elevated testosterone levels in female smokers were also positively correlated with obesity (Longcope and Johnston 1988; Sowers et al. 2001). Zumoff and colleagues (1990) reported elevated serum levels of progesterone among heavy smokers during the early follicular phase, a time when most progesterone is from the adrenal cortex. This finding is again consistent with the urine metabolite results reported by Windham and colleagues (2005) (Table 8.6). However, Zumoff and colleagues (1990) observed little difference in progesterone levels in the luteal phase. Windham and colleagues (2005) observed dampened progesterone metabolites in the luteal phase with heavy smoking. Berta and colleagues (1992) found that regular smokers had lower plasma levels of progesterone in a single sample per day during the mid-luteal phase. However, the small study by Westhoff and colleagues (1996) did not find these differences in examining data on all smokers without considering the amount smoked. In addition, the study on exposure to secondhand smoke did not report reductions in progesterone metabolite levels with exposure (Chen et al. 2005).

In vitro experiments support the effects on progesterone by showing that granulosa and tumor cells treated with alkaloids found in cigarette smoke or with an aqueous extract of cigarette smoke showed a dose-dependent inhibition of progesterone production (Bódis et al. 1997; Gocze et al. 1999; Gocze and Freeman 2000; Miceli et al. 2005). In contrast, estradiol production was little affected or was slightly stimulated. Cell growth and DNA content

---

[1]Pack-years = the number of years of smoking multiplied by the number of packs of cigarettes smoked per day.

also decreased with treatment, leading the authors to suggest that smoking directly inhibits cellular progesterone synthesis through less specific cytotoxic effects on progesterone-producing cells (Gocze and Freeman 2000). Other proposed mechanisms include modulations in the prostaglandin system (Miceli et al. 2005) or inhibition of aromatase enzymes.

Some studies examined gonadotropin FSH levels by smoking status (Table 8.6). Three studies that measured a single serum FSH level in the first few days of the cycle found higher levels associated with smoking (Cramer et al. 1994; Cooper et al. 1995; Lucero et al. 2001). Another study with a similar finding of higher FSH in smokers did not include the time during the menstrual cycle when the single serum sample was obtained (Backer et al. 1999). In addition to the limitation of single serum samples, these studies tended to include some perimenopausal or postmenopausal older women even though FSH levels naturally rise during and after menopause. Another study measured daily urinary levels of FSH metabolites in women of reproductive age. These findings also showed mean FSH levels among moderate-to-heavy smokers (≥10 cigarettes per day) that were higher than those among nonsmokers during the luteal-follicular phase transition between cycles (Windham et al. 2005).

Serum levels of FSH increase with age, and researchers think this increase reflects the diminishing supply of oocyte- and gonadotropin-responsive follicles that leads to the release of the HPG axis from ovarian control (Marcus et al. 1993; Cramer et al. 1994; Westhoff et al. 1996). The FSH level is thus considered a marker of ovarian reserve or competence, and as such, it may also be useful for identifying agents with toxic effects on the ovaries (Scott et al. 1989; Scott and Hofmann 1995). As progesterone modulates FSH in the endocrine feedback loop, the lower levels of luteal phase progesterone metabolites observed in some studies are consistent with the decreased entrainment of FSH, which would lead to the observed elevations. The increase in FSH may accelerate the recruitment and development of follicles, moving ovulation earlier, and perhaps leading to inadequate follicle development followed by inadequate function of the corpus luteum. Progesterone controls the endometrial response and is critical for early maintenance of pregnancy. Studies have implicated a luteal phase deficiency as a cause of infertility and fetal loss (Pittaway et al. 1983; Tulppala et al. 1991). Earlier ovulation would also be consistent with the shortening of the menstrual cycle or of the follicular phase observed in smokers (see "Menstrual Function, Menopause, and Menarche" earlier in this chapter). The pattern of higher FSH levels, shorter cycles, and thus more frequent ovulation in smokers is also consistent with the observation that smokers tend to experience earlier menopause (see

"Menstrual Function, Menopause, and Menarche" earlier in this chapter).

Pregnant Women

The 2001 Surgeon General's report noted that smoking more clearly affects estrogen levels during pregnancy than when a woman is not pregnant (USDHHS 2001). Several studies show that smokers have lower circulating levels of estriol and estradiol than do nonsmokers (USDHHS 2001), confirmed for estriol measured multiple times throughout pregnancy (Kaijser et al. 2000). Furthermore, the study found a positive correlation of estriol and birth weight. This study's results support the hypothesis of Michnovicz and colleagues (1986) that smokers and nonsmokers may metabolize estrogens differently, with acceleration of the 2-hydroxylation versus the 16α-hydroxylation pathway in smokers. In addition, some studies show an increase in 2-hydroxylation and 4-hydroxylation activity in placental tissues of smokers (Chao et al. 1981; Juchau et al. 1982). In a later study using placental microsomes, smokers had increased placental formation of 4-hydroxyestradiol, 7α-hydroxyestradiol, and most markedly, 15α-hydroxyestradiol, but little or no difference in the overall rate of placental estradiol metabolism or in the formation of the estrone, 2α-hydroxyestradiol, and other metabolites (Zhu et al. 2002). A study of progesterone in placental tissue samples revealed that levels among smokers were lower than those among nonsmokers (Piasek et al. 2001), a finding consistent with the data for nonpregnant women.

Using stored serum samples, Kandel and Udry (1999) found that the cotinine levels were positively correlated with the testosterone levels, especially in samples obtained during the second trimester of pregnancy. In turn, maternal testosterone levels were correlated with those in adult daughters. An animal study also showed that nicotine infusion resulted in increased plasma testosterone in ovine fetuses. This study also associated maternal exposure to nicotine with increased testosterone levels in 30-day-old (adolescent) female offspring of rats but not in male offspring (Smith et al. 2003). Changes in hormone patterns during pregnancy may therefore affect both pregnancy outcome and the endocrine profile of the offspring, thus relating to possible effects on neurobehavioral endpoints, puberty, or later reproductive status, including semen quality.

Men

Numerous studies have also examined hormone levels in men in relation to smoking (Table 8.7). Some studies examined the acute effects of smoking cigarettes in a standardized protocol, and others studied baseline

Table 8.6   Association between smoking and reproductive hormones in women

Study	Population	Sample/period	Definition of smoking (number of smokers)
MacMahon et al. 1982b	106 White women Aged 25–49 years	Overnight urine sample FP (days 10–11) LP (days 21–22)	Nonsmokers: ≤100 cigarettes in lifetime Former smokers (n = 23) Current smokers (n = 39)
Michnovicz et al. 1986	27 nonobese women with normal cycle length Mean age ~30 years	Blood and urine samples over 48 hours after administration of radiolabeled estradiol FP (days 1–10) in morning 5 samples in LP (days 19–25)	Smokers (14) ≥15 cigarettes/day
Longcope and Johnston 1988	88 women (47 premenopausal) Mean age 50 years	Radiolabeled steroid infusion Blood and urine samples at baseline	Smokers (23) 10 cigarettes/day for ≥10 years
Zumoff et al. 1990	16 volunteers with normal ovulatory and luteal function Aged 25–35 years	Blood samples on 17 days over cycle, more frequently around mid-cycle (ovulation)	Smokers (8) ≥20 cigarettes/day for ≥3 years
Key et al. 1991	147 women with cycle lengths of 21–35 days tested for estradiol and progesterone Aged ≥35 years Guernsey Breast Cancer Study 105 women tested for urinary steroids	24-hour urine and 1 blood sample	Current smokers (1–10, 11–20, ≥21 cigarettes/day) 69 smokers tested for estradiol and progesterone 20 smokers tested for urinary steroids
Berta et al. 1992	684 nonobese fertile women Aged 25–52 years	24-hour urine sample and 3 blood samples on days 21–24 of LP	Smokers (237) >10 cigarettes/day for ≥5 years
Cramer et al. 1994	224 women Aged 26–50 years Some with family history of ovarian cancer	1 blood sample in early FP (days 1–3)	Not defined, except "current, past, none" Current smokers (42)
Cooper et al. 1995	290 women Aged 38–49 years	1 blood sample in early FP (days 2–4)	Self-reports on current smoking (31), former smoking, and involuntary and prenatal exposure

Findings in smokers	Estimate of effect (95% CI or p value)	Comments
• Estrone, estradiol, and estriol levels in FP similar to those in nonsmokers • All 3 decreased in LP • Little difference from levels in former smokers	LP decreased 29% (10–43%)	Stronger effects in ovulatory cycles; adjustment for age; data on progesterone not presented
• 2-hydroxylation increased • Urine estriol and estriol/estrone decreased	Increased 50%, p <0.001 Decreased 40%, p <0.01	No difference in FP vs. LP; age and BMI similar in nonsmokers and smokers, so no adjustments made
• Metabolic clearance rates for testosterone, androstenedione, and estrone decreased • Plasma testosterone, androstenedione increased • No difference in estrone and estradiol or conversion from androgens	p <0.05 for metabolic clearance rates NS in only premenopausal women	No difference with adjustment for weight
• Progesterone increased in FP, not LP • Estradiol increased in early FP, slightly through FP • Mean LH slightly decreased	Increased 37% (p <0.0001) Increased 23% (p <0.001) in early FP Increased 12.5% (p ~0.05) through FP NS	Suggests that smoking stimulates adrenocorticol hormone secretion
• No difference in serum estradiol or progesterone • No difference in 6 urinary steroids (primarily androgens)	NS	Adjustment of serum values for cycle day, age, and BMI; adjustment of urine values for age, BMI, and parity
• Plasma progesterone decreased • Plasma prolactin decreased • No difference in estrone, estradiol, FSH, and LH	Decreased 15% (p <0.05) Decreased 20% (p <0.002)	Results not affected by age
• Mean FSH increased in current and former smokers (≥10 pack-years)[a]	Increased 14–21% (p = 0.03)	Effect of smoking still significant after adjustment for age
• Mean FSH increased in current smokers and those exposed to SHS • No difference in FSH in former smokers or prenatal exposure	Increased 66% (28–116%) Increased 57% at <10 cigarettes/day Increased 76% at 10–20 cigarettes/day Increased 39% (4–86%) with involuntary exposure	None of factors examined were confounders; significant interaction with age

Table 8.6   Continued

Study	Population	Sample/period	Definition of smoking (number of smokers)
Key et al. 1996	167 women Aged ≥34 years Guernsey Breast Cancer Study	24-hour urine sample with timing known and periovulatory period excluded	Self-reports, not defined (53)
Westhoff et al. 1996	175 parous women with normal cycles Aged 21–36 years	Urine sample on day 10 to menses Blood sample 3 times in LP	Self-reports, not defined (48)
Backer et al. 1999	3,114 women Aged 35–60 years National Health and Nutrition Examination Survey (U.S. national sample)	1 convenient blood sample	Smoking during 5 days before examination
Lucero et al. 2001	498 women not in depressive state Aged 36–44 years Harvard Study of Moods and Cycles	1 blood sample in early FP (days 1–5)	Smoking not defined; current smokers (52); former smokers (172)
Sowers et al. 2001	511 White women Aged 24–45 years	1 blood sample in FP (days 3–7) annually for 3 years	Lifetime nonsmokers, former smokers, current smokers (~20%)
Jernström et al. 2003	513 nulliparous women Aged 17–35 years	Morning blood sample on random day (timing calculated)	Current smoker (yes/no)
Windham et al. 2005	403 women in reproductive years Aged 18–39 years Members of Kaiser Permanente health maintenance organization	Daily urine collection through 2–7 cycles Adjustment of hormone values for creatinine	Cigarettes/day from daily diary, averaged over cycle Validated by cotinine 100–150 cycles of smokers

Note: **BMI** = body mass index; **CI** = confidence interval; **FP** = follicular phase; **FSH** = follicle-stimulating hormone; **LH** = luteinizing hormone; **LP** = luteal phase; **NS** = not statistically significant; **SHS** = secondhand smoke.

[a]Pack-years = the number of years of smoking multiplied by the number of packs of cigarettes smoked per day.

hormone levels in smokers compared with those in non-smokers. The results from studies spanning many years are inconsistent. These studies also vary in considering obesity, which may be important because increased weight is associated with the peripheral conversion of androgens to estrogens. Also, studies generally report total circulating levels of hormones but vary in reports of free or bioavailable levels.

The most consistent finding is an increase of androstenedione in smokers in three studies (Barrett-Connor and Khaw 1987; Dai et al. 1988; Field et al. 1994). Testosterone levels also increased with smoking in many studies, but some studies found decreases or no differences (Table 8.7). The study by Sofikitis and colleagues (1995) is noteworthy for demonstrating differences between apparent endocrine versus paracrine levels of testosterone related to effects from smoking. Animal studies show that prenatal exposure to nicotine is related to decreased testosterone levels in adult male rats (Segarra and Strand 1989)

Findings in smokers	Estimate of effect (95% CI or p value)	Comments
• Estrone and estradiol slightly decreased • Estriol decreased in early FP, but less so later	0–16% for estrone 4–15% for estradiol 30% for estriol in early FP 5–22% for estriol later in cycle	NS after adjustment for time of cycle, age, and BMI
• No difference in mean LP progesterone in blood or urine • Urine estradiol decreased in LP	21% decreased, p = 0.04	4 anovulatory women excluded; adjustment for creatinine (decreased differences in estradiol); some dose-response effects
• FSH increased	p <0.001	Cycle timing unknown, but tried to exclude samples obtained close to time of ovulation on basis of LH to FSH ratio
• FSH increased • Estradiol increased • LH increased • No difference in sex hormone binding globulin	12% increased, p <0.05 8% increased, p <0.05 42% increased, NS	No difference with former smoking; estradiol NS in adjusted model, but FSH values not adjusted; adjustment for age, BMI, calories, use of alcohol and caffeine, cholesterol, and cycle day
• Increased serum testosterone • Intermediate effect among former smokers	30–40% increased (by year), p <0.01	Significant after adjustment for BMI, year, and reproductive status
• 2α- and 16α-hydroxyestrone slightly increased before adjustment, but not after adjustment • No effect on either metabolite alone	19% increased, p = 0.06 unadjusted, p = 0.76 adjusted	Adjustment for age, race, and cycle day
• Mean FSH increased in smokers ≥10 cigarettes/day • Estrone and progesterone metabolites increased in early FP in smokers of ≥10 cigarettes/day • Progesterone decreased in LP in smokers of ≥20 cigarettes/day	20–35% increased, significant on some days 25% and 35% increased, p <0.05 25% decreased, p = 0.06	Adjustment for age, race, pregnancy history, BMI, and use of alcohol and caffeine; some dose-response effects

and that cotinine, but not nicotine, inhibits testosterone synthesis in testes of neonatal rats (Sarasin et al. 2003).

Four studies that measured estradiol or estrone had inconsistent results. However, results from one of the studies showing an association with smoking were not adjusted for BMI or weight, although adjustment was made for age. The findings for the gonadotropins, FSH and luteinizing hormone (LH), tend to show no effect of smoking.

In 1990, one study (Barrett-Connor 1990) suggested that the ratio of androgen to estrogen is critical in determining the gender-specific risk of some hormone-related diseases and that smoking may alter this ratio. Nicotine or its metabolites may influence endocrine profiles directly and indirectly. PAHs also act on the cytochrome P-450 systems involved in the metabolism of endogenous hormones and of xenobiotics such as those found in tobacco smoke.

Table 8.7   Association between smoking and reproductive hormones in healthy men

Study	Population	Study period	Definition of smoking
Briggs 1973	6 healthy smokers 6 healthy nonsmokers	7 days	>30 cigarettes/day
Dotson et al. 1975	91 university students attending simulated party	4 hours	Number of cigarettes smoked
Winternitz and Quillen 1977	17 long-term male smokers	2 days smoking followed by day not smoking	8 cigarettes 2.8 mg of nicotine within 2 hours vs. baseline on day of abstinence
Shaarawy and Mahmoud 1982	25 healthy smokers 20 healthy nonsmokers All fathers of ≥2 children	3 consecutive days	>20 cigarettes/day
Wilkins et al. 1982	10 long-term male smokers (≥1 pack/day of cigarettes with 1.0 mg of nicotine)	2 days	2 cigarettes 2.0 mg vs. 0.2 mg of nicotine in 10 minutes
Deslypere and Vermeulen 1984	75 healthy smokers 73 healthy nonsmokers 33 former smokers	Single blood sample	>5 cigarettes/day for >2 years

Klaiber et al. 1984	Group I
	    23 healthy smokers
	    18 healthy nonsmokers
	
	Group II
	    18 smokers
	    17 nonsmokers
	    Attending infertility clinic
		Single fasting blood sample for estradiol	Not defined

Gossain et al. 1986	6 healthy smokers 6 healthy nonsmokers	Experimental session with blood sample obtained 120 minutes after smoking first cigarette	2 unfiltered cigarettes smoked in 10 minutes
Seyler et al. 1986	4 healthy smokers Average 22.5 cigarettes/day	2 experimental sessions	15 hours with no smoking followed by 2 low-dose (0.48 mg) cigarettes smoked 5 minutes apart or 2 high-dose (2.87 mg) nicotine cigarettes smoked in rapid succession

Findings	Odds ratio/response rate and 95% CI or p value	Comments
• Serum testosterone lower in smokers (5.15 ± 0.7 ng/mL) than in nonsmokers (7.47 ± 0.53 ng/mL)	NR	No men obese
• Mean increase in testosterone after 7 days abstinence for smokers (1.65 + 0.5 ng/mL) but no change for nonsmokers	p <0.005	
• Testosterone positively correlated with number of cigarettes smoked, r = 0.24	p <0.05	Study designed to look at testosterone levels, aggressive behavior, alcohol use, and smoking
• LH, FSH, testosterone, and thyroid-stimulating hormone showed no significant change during 4-hour study	NS	None
• Smokers had higher serum FSH (18.3 vs. 12.2 milli-international units per milliliter)	p <0.0025	None
• Serum testosterone was lower in smokers than in non-smokers (3.6 vs. 6.2 ng/mL)	p <0.0005	
• LH not different between groups		
• Prolactin concentrations were significantly higher with high- vs. low-nicotine cigarettes	p <0.0001	None
• 150% increase in prolactin concentrations 30 minutes after smoking cigarette with 2 mg of nicotine and remained above baseline at 60 minutes		
• Plasma testosterone and free testosterone levels were higher in smokers than in nonsmokers for three age groups	Aged 20–39 years, p <0.001 Aged 40–59 years, p <0.01 Aged 60–80 years, p <0.05	Decrease in difference in plasma levels of testosterone and free testosterone in smokers vs. nonsmokers with increasing age
• LH did not differ between smokers and nonsmokers		
• Higher mean serum estradiol levels in both groups of smokers	Group I: p <0.03 Group II: p <0.001	Adjustment for age and alcohol intake
• Number of cigarettes smoked/day not associated with estradiol concentrations in smokers		
• Positive correlation with number of cigarettes smoked/day in analysis of pooled data from smokers and nonsmokers	Group I: r = 0.35, p <0.03 Group II: r = 0.73, p <0.001	
• Mean prolactin concentrations of 8.3 ng/mL for smokers and 15.4 ng/mL for nonsmokers	Integrated curves for 2 groups differed at p <0.001	None
• No differences in FSH, LH, prolactin, or thyroid-stimulating hormone concentrations between baseline and either high-dose or low-dose exposures	NS	None

Table 8.7   Continued

Study	Population	Study period	Definition of smoking
Barrett-Connor and Khaw 1987	590 men No history of heart disease or stroke Rancho Bernardo, California	Enrollment 1972–1974	Lifetime nonsmokers, former smokers, or current smokers (number of cigarettes/day)
Dai et al. 1988	121 men Pittsburgh Multiple Risk Factor Intervention Trial	Baseline and 4 years later	Cigarettes/day None 1–30 31–70
Meikle et al. 1989	75 healthy monozygotic twins 85 healthy dizygotic twins 1 set of healthy triplets		Nonsmokers, former smokers, current smokers Packs/day for current smokers
Michnovicz et al. 1989	20 healthy smokers 16 healthy nonsmokers	48 hours	Lifetime nonsmokers vs. ≥15 cigarettes/day
Field et al. 1994	1,241 healthy men Boston area 341 male smokers	Enrollment 1987–1989	Cigarettes smoked/day
Sofikitis et al. 1995	Healthy men presenting for hernia repair 49 smokers 18 lifetime nonsmokers 9 former smokers	19 months Presurgery and postsurgery sampling and postcessation sampling	≥20 cigarettes/day for >3 years
English et al. 2001	25 smokers 25 lifetime nonsmokers	NR	Self-reported ≥10 cigarettes/day
Trummer et al. 2002	260 smokers 70 former smokers 258 lifetime nonsmokers Infertility clinic population	1993–2000	Self-reported number of cigarettes/day

Note: **BMI** = body mass index; **CI** = confidence interval; **DHT** = dihydrotestosterone; **FSH** = follicle-stimulating hormone; **LH** = luteinizing hormone; **mg** = milligrams; **ng/mL** = nanograms per milliliter; **NR** = not reported; **NS** = no significant difference; **SHBG** = sex hormone binding globulin.

Findings	Odds ratio/response rate and 95% CI or p value	Comments
• No significant differences between groups in concentrations of testosterone or SHBG • Androstenedione was higher in smokers • Estrone was higher in smokers • Estradiol was higher in smokers • Dose-response effect for number of cigarettes/day for androstenedione, estrone, and estradiol, but not for testosterone and SHBG	p <0.001 p <0.001 p <0.02 p <0.001	Adjustment for age, BMI, alcohol and caffeine intake, and exercise
• Testosterone positively associated with number of cigarettes/day • Androstenedione positively associated with number of cigarettes/day	p <0.05 p <0.05	Adjustment for age, alcohol use, high-density lipoprotein cholesterol, blood pressure, and relative weight
• Higher DHT concentrations for current smokers than for nonsmokers • No adjusted, independent effect of smoking for estrone, estradiol, testosterone, SHBG, LH, and FSH	p = 0.03	Study of effects of smoking on concentrations of sex steroid hormone through BMI
• Estradiol 2-hydroxylation increased ~70% in smokers • Urinary catechol estrogen index significantly higher for smokers	p <0.001 p = 0.006	None
• Higher androstenedione, testosterone, DHT, and SHBG for smokers	Androstenedione p = 0.0001 Testosterone p = 0.009 DHT p = 0.004 SHBG p = 0.0004	Adjustment for age and BMI
• Testicular androgen-binding protein lower in smokers • Testicular venous testosterone lower in smokers • Circulating serum FSH, LH, and testosterone concentrations not statistically different between smokers and nonsmokers	p <0.05 p <0.05	Included examination of testicular biopsy specimens
• Cotinine correlated with SHBG (r = 0.49) • Free testosterone and total testosterone higher in smokers • Bioavailable testosterone did not differ between groups • 17-β estradiol did not differ between groups	p <0.05 p = 0.03 p = 0.01	Matched on age and BMI
• Increased LH and testosterone and decreased prolactin in smokers compared with those for nonsmokers	Increased total and free testosterone, p <0.001 Increased LH, p = 0.035 Decreased prolactin, p <0.001	Testosterone lower in men who were able to stop smoking

Tubal Function

The mammalian oviduct transports gametes to the fertilization site and provides a suitable environment for fertilization and development before implantation. Factors that impair oviductal physiology can lead to reproductive problems, such as fertilization failure, ectopic pregnancy, and failure of implantation. Numerous epidemiologic studies have correlated maternal smoking with reproductive problems that can originate in the oviduct, including increased infertility and ectopic pregnancy (Stillman et al. 1986; Buck et al. 1997) (see "Review of Epidemiologic Literature on Smoking" earlier in this chapter).

The mammalian oviduct has three anatomic regions: (1) the infundibulum, which picks up the oocyte cumulus complex after it is ovulated from the ovary; (2) the ampulla, where fertilization occurs; and (3) the isthmus, which conducts sperm to the ampulla and provides a site for preimplantation development. Proper functioning of each region is necessary for normal reproduction.

The oviduct is an in vivo target of cigarette smoke and its components. Contraction of both the human oviduct (Neri and Eckerling 1969) and the rabbit oviduct (Ruckebusch 1975) is altered by exposure to tobacco smoke. Inhalation of mainstream or sidestream smoke at doses that produce serum cotinine levels within the range of those found in active smokers and persons involuntarily exposed to tobacco smoke caused blebbing of the oviductal epithelium and decreased the ratio of ciliated to secretory cells in hamsters (Magers et al. 1995). In another study of hamsters, in which the oviduct was directly observed before, during, and after inhalation of tobacco smoke at doses equivalent to those received by humans, both mainstream and sidestream smoke decreased ampullary smooth muscle contractions and slowed embryo transport through the oviduct (DiCarlantonio and Talbot 1999). Nicotine altered the motility of oviducts of rhesus monkeys (Neri and Marcus 1972), decreased oviductal blood flow (Mitchell and Hammer 1985), decreased sodium and potassium levels in oviductal epithelial cells of mice (Jin et al. 1998), and increased lactate dehydrogenase levels in oviductal epithelium of rats (Rice and Yoshinaga 1980).

In vitro studies using oviductal explants have been valuable in characterizing the effects of cigarette smoke on various biologic processes, including ciliary beat frequency, oocyte pickup rate, and smooth muscle contraction (Huang et al. 1997; Riveles et al. 2003). Solutions of particulate matter, whole mainstream smoke, and mainstream and sidestream smoke in the gas phase inhibited ciliary beat frequency, oocyte pickup rate, and smooth muscle contraction in a dose-dependent manner in hamsters (Knoll and Talbot 1998). Although this inhibition was originally reported for unfiltered (2R1) research cigarettes, a similar inhibition was subsequently shown for filter-tipped (1R4F) research cigarettes, unfiltered and filter-tipped commercial cigarettes, and "harm-reduction" cigarettes that are lower in carcinogens than are traditional brands (Riveles 2004). The data on harm-reduction cigarettes are important in demonstrating that these cigarettes still contain toxicants that can adversely affect diverse biologic processes. Exposure to sidestream whole smoke, in contrast to mainstream smoke, stimulated ciliary beat frequency (Knoll and Talbot 1998). The oocyte pickup rate was inhibited even in samples in which beat frequency was stimulated, which shows that pickup depends on factors other than ciliary beating. Adhesion between the extracellular matrix of the oocyte cumulus complex and the tips of the cilia is an additional factor essential for pickup (Talbot et al. 1999; Lam et al. 2000). If adhesion is too strong or too weak, oocyte pickup can fail (Lam et al. 2000). Exposure to both mainstream and sidestream smoke increases adhesion (Gieseke and Talbot 2003), which could account for decreased pickup rates even when cilia beat at normal or accelerated rates. Exposure to tobacco smoke adversely affects other adhesive processes involving cells, asbestos, and bacteria (Cantral et al. 1995; Churg et al. 1998; El Ahmer et al. 1999).

Therefore, in vitro studies demonstrate that exposure to tobacco smoke adversely affects oviductal structure and functioning and that nicotine can impair oviductal physiology. Together with in vitro data, in vivo studies demonstrate that maternal smoking adversely affects the oviduct in ways that could impair fertility and complicate pregnancy.

Placenta

Normal Development

Formation of the placenta in the uterus (placentation) is a complex process that is not fully understood. Fetal stem cells (cytotrophoblasts) form a polarized epithelium attached to a basement membrane that surrounds a stromal core containing the placental vasculature and forming chorionic villi. These villi are surrounded by a multinucleate syncytial covering. Floating villi are attached only to the fetal side of the placenta. In contrast, anchoring villi are formed when cytotrophoblastic cells detach from the basement membrane, penetrate the uterine wall, and invade maternal arteries and veins. Cytotrophoblasts travel deeply into uterine arterioles, replace the maternal endothelial lining, and disrupt the smooth muscle wall. This physiological transformation converts the maternal vasculature from a high-resistance, low-capacitance system to a low-resistance, high-capacitance system that allows for increased blood flow to the fetus. Blood from the spiral arteries then enters the intervillous space where an exchange of substances between the mother and the fetus occurs (Khong 2004). As the placenta develops, the villous system also undergoes remodeling. The terminal villi elongate, and there is a large increase in the peripheral villi capillary volume (Mayhew 2002; Torry et al. 2004). In addition, the thickness of the collective layers of the villi that separate maternal and fetal circulatory systems (villous membrane) decreases, enhancing the exchange of nutrients and metabolic products between the mother and fetus (Mayhew 1998). Interference with the development and remodeling of the placental vasculature likely contributes to adverse pregnancy outcomes.

Effects of Smoking

Studies have examined the effects of maternal smoking on the placenta, but the results are often conflicting. Real or apparent inconsistencies among studies may reflect differences in laboratory techniques and terminology. However, many studies appear to fall into one of three general areas of research: (1) cytotrophoblastic invasion of the uterus and subsequent transformation of uterine blood vessels; (2) development of the fetal capillary and villous system, particularly with respect to whether the placenta can compensate for maternal hypoxia by increasing the supply of oxygen (O_2) and nutrients to the fetus; and (3) transportation of nutrients across the placenta (see "Amino Acids" later in this chapter).

As previously stated, cytotrophoblastic cells in normal pregnancy invade the uterine arterioles and transform them into a high-capacitance system that allows for an increase in blood flow to the fetus. Incomplete transformation of the spiral arteries results in a high vascular resistance in the placenta and a decrease in blood flow to the intervillous space. Studies have described a diminished physiological transformation in placentas from women with preeclampsia (Brosens et al. 1972; Naicker et al. 2003), SAB (Khong et al. 1987), IUGR (Khong et al. 1986), PPROM (Kim et al. 2002), preterm labor (Kim et al. 2003), preterm birth (Kim et al. 2003), or placental abruption (Dommisse and Tiltman 1992).

Physiological transformation appears to be disturbed in women who smoke cigarettes during pregnancy. In vitro studies have shown that formation of cytotrophoblastic cell columns, which is necessary for the invasion of the uterine wall, is disrupted, perhaps from the effects of exposure to nicotine (Genbacev et al. 1995). Among women who smoke, there also appears to be a reduction in the number of cytotrophoblastic stem cells in the floating villi and a reduction in the number of anchoring villi that successfully invade the uterine wall, which may reflect a premature depletion of cytotrophoblastic stem cells (Genbacev et al. 1995). The interference by smoking in cytotrophoblastic invasion of the uterine wall could lead to increased risk of adverse pregnancy outcomes.

Paradoxically, maternal smoking is protective against preeclampsia, which is also characterized by an incomplete transformation of the spiral arteries. As previously noted, an imbalance between proangiogenic and antiangiogenic placental factors may contribute to manifestations of preeclampsia, and smoking may exert its protective effects by affecting this imbalance (Genbacev et al. 2003; Maynard et al. 2003) (see "Pregnancy Complications" earlier in this chapter). In a normal pregnancy, the placenta releases proangiogenic factors, VEGF, and the placental growth factor (PlGF). Placental soluble FMS-like sFlt-1, which is elevated in preeclampsia, is an antagonist of both VEGF and PlGF. An elevated sFlt-1 level is associated with lower levels of VEGF and PlGF and leads to endothelial dysfunction. Maternal smoking appears to increase the placental expression of VEGF-A (Zhou et al. 2002), a major regulator of cytotrophoblastic differentiation along the invasive pathway that is decreased in the preeclamptic placenta. In contrast, studies have found decreased levels of sFlt-1 in the plasma of smokers (Belgore et al. 2000), but not in pregnant smokers (Kämäräinen et al. 2009). The 2004 Surgeon General's report on the health consequences of smoking noted that "the decreased risk of preeclampsia among smokers compared with nonsmokers does not outweigh the adverse outcomes that can result from prenatal smoking" (USDHHS 2004, p. 576). Additional research is needed to confirm or refute the notion that the effects on VEGF-A and/or sFlt-1 explain the reduced risk of preeclampsia in smokers.

Findings on the effects of maternal smoking on the development of the villous capillary system are inconsistent. The fetus of a smoker develops under conditions of reduced partial pressure of O_2, because hemoglobin has an affinity for CO from cigarette smoke that greatly exceeds its affinity for O_2. Thus, the expectation is to see compensatory responses in the placenta similar to those observed with other hypoxic conditions. Such compensatory responses to hypoxia could include increased volume density, branching, and dilation of the fetal capillary system; increased density and proliferation of the cytotrophoblasts; thinning of the villous membrane (Kingdom and Kaufmann 1997; Mayhew 1998; Bush et al. 2000); and increased maternal and fetal hematocrits. Studies have documented increases in both the maternal and fetal hematocrits among smokers (Bodnar et al. 2004), which should lead to increased delivery of O_2 to the fetus.

In addition, several studies have found that the placentas of smokers are heavier or larger than those in nonsmokers (Naeye 1978; van der Veen and Fox 1982; Howe et al. 1995; Williams et al. 1997), which suggests an expansion of the peripheral villous tree. However, other researchers have found no increase or only a small increase in placental size and/or weight in smokers (Spira et al. 1975; Picone et al. 1982; Demir et al. 1994; Sanyal et al. 1994; Williams et al. 1997; Zhang et al. 1999; Larsen et al. 2002). In many of these studies, the ratio of placental to fetal weight was higher in smokers than in nonsmokers even when the placental weight did not increase. This increase in the ratio of placental to fetal weight could result from a compensatory response to hypoxia, but this explanation has not been established. Studies of morphology have described increase (Pfarrer et al. 1999), decrease (Asmussen 1980; Burton et al. 1989; Teasdale and Ghislaine 1989; Bush et al. 2000; Larsen et al. 2002), and no appreciable difference (van der Velde et al. 1983; Mayhew 1996) in dimensions of the villous capillary system of smokers.

In contrast, studies have consistently shown that maternal smoking is associated with a thickening of the villous membrane, which would decrease the ability of nutrients to diffuse through the placenta (Burton et al. 1989; Jauniaux and Burton 1992; Demir et al. 1994; Bush et al. 2000; Larsen et al. 2002). This increased thickness was attributed to the increased thickness of the trophoblastic component (Jauniaux and Burton 1992; Bush et al. 2000) and to a thickening of the basement membrane (Asmussen 1980; Demir et al. 1994). The thickening of the villous membrane is opposite from an expected compensatory thinning in response to a hypoxic environment and could contribute to fetal growth restriction. Researchers have hypothesized that direct toxic effects of maternal smoking on the placenta are responsible for the thickening of the villous membrane, perhaps due to the accumulation of cadmium that is associated with a reduction in fetal capillary volume (Burton et al. 1989; Bush et al. 2000).

Studies have also explored other effects of maternal smoking on the cellular and noncellular composition of the villous system. Researchers have described changes in placental morphology of smokers, including cytotrophoblastic hyperplasia, focal syncytial necrosis, the loss or distortion of syncytial microvilli, decreased vasculosyncytial membranes, decreased syncytial pinocytotic vesicles, the degeneration of cytoplasmic organelles, increased syncytial knots and decreased syncytial buds, and increased collagen levels in the villous stroma (van der Veen and Fox 1982; van der Velde et al. 1983, 1985; Demir et al. 1994). Evidence of increases in syncytial knots and necrotic areas suggests an increase in syncytial damage among smokers (Demir et al. 1994). However, these effects are not consistent in all studies (Teasdale and

Ghislaine 1989; Ashfaq et al. 2003). Researchers have found it difficult to clearly connect these findings with adverse pregnancy outcomes, because the observed changes are not pathognomonic for any particular disorder. However, these cellular and molecular abnormalities of the villous system could lead to an impaired exchange of metabolic products, O_2, and nutrients between the mother and fetus.

Maternal and Fetal Cardiovascular Systems

Smoking acutely increases the heart rate and blood pressure of smokers, particularly after a period of abstinence from smoking (e.g., first cigarette of the day). This finding has led to the suggestion that changes in blood flow may be a mechanism for the lower birth weight observed in infants of smokers. Numerous studies have investigated the effect of cigarette smoke on the cardiovascular system of pregnant women or their fetuses. The studies can be broadly divided into those that examined differences in basal cardiovascular parameters between nonsmokers and smokers after an interval of abstinence and those that examined the acute cardiovascular effects immediately after the pregnant women had each smoked one or two cigarettes. A body of work investigating the relationships of smoking with maternal blood pressure and preeclampsia is not presented here, as preeclampsia is described above.

Seven studies investigated the basal cardiovascular state of mothers who smoked and their fetuses compared with those in a control group of mothers who did not smoke and their fetuses (Table 8.8). Four studies used a radioisotope to study blood flow through the placenta (Table 8.9). In 28 studies, the acute maternal and fetal cardiovascular effects of maternal smoking were examined, and some of these studies also reported baseline differences (Table 8.10). The participants in these 39 studies had healthy singleton pregnancies unless otherwise noted. Most of the percentage differences in the parameters were calculated for this Surgeon General's report from data and graphs in the original articles, but the statistically significant data are those of the original investigators.

Basal Function

Maternal Heart Rate and Blood Pressure During Smoking Abstinence

One prospective study of 203 smokers and 292 nonsmokers at 18, 24, 28, and 34 weeks of gestation found no differences in maternal heart rate during abstinence from smoking (Table 8.8) (Newnham et al. 1990). Two smaller

Table 8.8   Basal maternal and fetal cardiovascular effects of smoking

Study	Design/population	Outcome and comments
MacGillivray et al. 1969	226 women 144 nonsmokers, 82 smokers Gestational age ≥20 weeks Healthy and high-risk pregnancies Lifetime nonsmokers vs. smokers Unadjusted data	**Maternal heart rate:** no data collected; **Maternal blood pressure:** diastolic blood pressure at first prenatal clinic visit during abstinence 9% lower (p <0.05) in smokers than in nonsmokers; systolic blood pressure higher in smokers than in nonsmokers but no significant data or actual numbers given
Phelan 1980	478 women 350 nonsmokers, 128 smokers Gestational age 32–40 weeks All high-risk pregnancies Repeated NST between 32 and 40 weeks' gestation	**NST:** smokers had higher rate of nonreactive NST (21% vs. 13%, p <0.005), but nonreactive NST in nonsmokers stayed nonreactive on subsequent NST; usually, nonreactive NST in a smoker may or may not be nonreactive on subsequent NST
Eldridge et al. 1986	24 women 19 nonsmokers, 5 smokers Gestational age 20–38 weeks	**Fetal heart rate:** no difference in second or early third trimester; heart rate 9% higher in smokers than in nonsmokers (p <0.01) in late pregnancy; **Fetal blood flow: aorta**—significant increase in blood flow (30–50% depending on gestational age) in smokers vs. nonsmokers (no p value given)
Newnham et al. 1990	495 women 292 nonsmokers, 203 smokers Gestational age 18–34 weeks Study conducted at 18, 24, 28, and 34 weeks' gestation	**Maternal heart rate:** no difference between smokers and nonsmokers during abstinence; **Maternal blood pressure:** no difference between smokers and nonsmokers; **Fetal heart rate:** no difference between smokers and nonsmokers; **Blood flow:** no difference in umbilical artery or uteroplacental S/D ratio between smokers and nonsmokers
Matkin et al. 1999	5,369 women 2,478 smokers, 2,891 nonsmokers Gestational age 20–40 weeks	**Maternal blood pressure:** in general, lower mean diastolic blood pressure and higher mean systolic blood pressure in smokers; no significant differences between nonsmokers and any of smokers' groups (p >0.05); no dose-response relationship demonstrable between smoking levels and blood pressure
Lees et al. 2001	5,121 women 4,821 nonsmokers, 800 smokers Gestational age 23 weeks	**Uterine artery:** at pulsatile index of ≥1.45 (≥95% for cohort), likelihood ratio for severe adverse outcome was 5 for nonsmokers and 10 for smokers; odds ratio for severe adverse outcome for smokers, after adjustment for pulsatile index, was 2.18 (95% confidence interval, 1.27–3.74; p <0.005)
Albuquerque et al. 2004	143 women 69 nonsmokers, 74 smokers 28 smokers ≤10 cigarettes/day 45 smokers >10 cigarettes/day Median gestational age 34–35 weeks Abstinence 20 minutes–4 hours before study	**Blood flow: uterine arteries**—no difference in S/D ratio or RI values in smokers vs. nonsmokers; **umbilical arteries**—median S/D ratio 13% greater and median RI value 5% greater in smokers than in nonsmokers (p <0.05); **Fetal middle cerebral artery:** no difference in S/D ratio or RI values between smokers and nonsmokers

Note: Sonographic technology (ultrasound/Doppler) was used to determine maternal heart rate and blood pressure and for fetal monitoring. Prospective studies were conducted during variable periods of abstinence (no smoking before or during protocol). Most percentages were calculated for this Surgeon General's report from data in the study articles or estimated from graphs in the articles. **NST** = nonstress test; **RI** = resistance index; **S/D** = systolic/diastolic.

Table 8.9   Maternal and fetal cardiovascular effects: radioisotope studies of placental intervillous blood flow (IBF) conducted before and after smoking

Study	Design/population	Outcome and comments
Lehtovirta and Forss 1978[a]	12 nonsmokers Gestational age 35–40 weeks	**Xenon[133] IBF:** overall mean decrease in IBF of 21% (p <0.05) resolved within 15 minutes, but 7 with decreased IBF and 5 with increased IBF
Lehtovirta and Forss 1980[a]	12 healthy women Unknown smoking status 11 women with hypertension (9 nonsmokers, 2 smokers) Gestational age 34–40 weeks	**Maternal heart rate:** mean increase of 15% in both groups (p >0.001); **Maternal blood pressure:** increase of 6% (p <0.001) in healthy women and 2.5% (p <0.05) in women with hypertension; **Xenon[133] IBF:** baseline IBF 19% lower in women with hypertension; smoking resulted in mean 21% (p <0.05) decrease in IBF in healthy women, and a 28% (p <0.05) increase in IBF in women with hypertension; no change in myometrial blood flow in either group
Rauramo et al. 1983[a]	7 women 1 smoker, 6 nonsmokers Gestational age 37–38 weeks	**Xenon[133] IBF:** decrease in mean IBF of 20% in 7 measurements (p <0.001), with a concomitant 54% fall in mean differential indices and 45% fall in interval indices; in 5 measurements, an increase in mean IBF, differential indices, and interval indices (24%, p not significant; 37%, p <0.001; and 45%, p <0.01, respectively); relationship between change in IBF and smoking was not clearly stated, but it appears that rise in IBF occurred after fall in IBF; IBF returned to baseline within 20 minutes
Philipp et al. 1984	40 women 20 smokers, 20 nonsmokers Gestational age 32–38 weeks Smokers studied after smoking 2 cigarettes and compared with nonsmokers	**Uteroplacental blood flow measured by indium[113] labeled transferrin:** significant difference in distribution of scan types (p <0.005); normal flow in 15% of smokers vs. 55% of nonsmokers; intermediate flow in 65% of smokers vs. 30% of nonsmokers; and abnormal flow in 20% of smokers vs. 15% of nonsmokers

[a]Same group of investigators.

studies also found no differences in the maternal heart rate in smokers and nonsmokers at baseline (Table 8.10) (Bruner and Forouzan 1991; Kimya et al. 1998). Many other studies that investigated maternal blood pressure or fetal heart rate did not report data on maternal heart rate, possibly indicating that they did not find a difference between smokers and nonsmokers.

The first study that prospectively evaluated maternal blood pressure during abstinence from smoking found a significantly lower diastolic blood pressure among smokers than among nonsmokers (MacGillivray et al. 1969). Three later studies have not replicated these results (Newnham et al. 1990; Kimya et al. 1998; Matkin et al. 1999). The largest study, of more than 5,000 participants, also found that smokers tended to have a lower mean diastolic blood pressure of 1 to 3 millimeters of mercury, but this difference was not statistically significant and is unlikely to be clinically significant (Table 8.8) (Matkin et al. 1999). The study by Newnham and colleagues (1990) was larger than that by MacGillivray and colleagues (1969) and of a similar design, but no significant differences in maternal diastolic or systolic blood pressure were

observed. Two investigations found that the systolic blood pressure of smokers was higher than that of nonsmokers (MacGillivray et al. 1969; Matkin et al. 1999). However, MacGillivray and colleagues (1969) did not report significance data, and Matkin and colleagues (1999) found the difference to be nonsignificant.

Sufficient clinical data indicate that there is no clinically significant difference in the mean maternal heart rate or blood pressure in healthy pregnant nonsmokers and smokers during abstinence from smoking. Further study of the blood pressure distribution, especially in the tails of the statistical distribution, may be warranted, because the percentage of women with blood pressure at or near the hypertensive range is most important clinically, and this group is at a higher risk of adverse pregnancy outcomes (Lees et al. 2001).

Fetal Heart Rate

Four studies provide data on fetal heart rate collected from smokers during periods of abstinence and compared with data from nonsmokers (Eldridge et al. 1986;

Table 8.10   Acute maternal and fetal cardiovascular effects of smoking

Study	Design/population	Outcome and comments
Gennser et al. 1975[a]	12 smokers Gestational age 33–39 weeks	**Maternal heart rate:** median increase of 29% (p <0.01) and correlated with nicotine plasma level; **Fetal heart rate:** no consistent change
Nylund et al. 1979	12 smokers Gestational age 39–45 weeks Hospitalization, high-risk pregnancies Data graphically displayed	**Maternal heart rate:** mean increase of 27% (p <0.001); **Maternal blood pressure:** mean increase in systolic blood pressure of 12% (p <0.05) and in diastolic blood pressure of 14% (p <0.05); **Fetal heart rate:** mean increase of 15% (p <0.001)
Quigley et al. 1979	8 smokers 20–40 cigarettes/day Gestational age 34 weeks	**Maternal heart rate:** mean increase of 35% during smoking and 25% after smoking (p <0.01); **Maternal blood pressure:** mean increase in systolic blood pressure and diastolic blood pressure of 7% and 13%, respectively, during smoking (p <0.01); return to baseline by 20 minutes after smoking; **Fetal heart rate:** mean increase of 17% (p <0.01); return to baseline by 30 minutes after smoking
Barrett et al. 1981	26 smokers Gestational age 31–44 weeks All high-risk pregnancies 1 hour abstinence before testing	**NST:** none developed a nonreactive NST after smoking; **Fetal heart rate:** slight transient increase in 7 smokers, no change in 18 smokers, and decrease in 1 smoker
Kariniemi et al. 1982[a]	N = 8: 1 smoker, 7 nonsmokers Gestational age 37–41 weeks	**Maternal heart rate:** mean increase of 17% (p <0.001); **Maternal blood pressure:** mean systolic blood pressure increase of 11% (p <0.001) and mean diastolic blood pressure increase of 20% (p <0.001); fetal heart rate and variability data not given in relationship to smoking
Forss et al. 1983[a]	8 women 3 smokers, 5 nonsmokers Gestational age 22–26 weeks Data provided only graphically	**Maternal heart rate:** increased (p <0.001); **Maternal blood pressure:** increased (p <0.01); **Fetal heart rate and variability:** heart rate increased (p <0.01); no change in short-term variability, decreased long-term variability
Jouppila et al. 1983	19 smokers Gestational age 29–39 weeks	**Maternal heart rate:** 13% increase (p >0.05); **Fetal heart rate:** 4% increase (p >0.05); **Fetal blood flow: aorta**—no change in diameter, 1% decrease in blood flow (p not significant); **umbilical vein**—no change in diameter, 10% increase in blood flow (p not significant)
Lehtovirta et al. 1983[a]	8 women 1 smoker, 7 nonsmokers Gestational age 37–40 weeks Data provided only graphically	**Maternal heart rate:** increased (p <0.001); **Maternal blood pressure:** increased (p <0.001); **Fetal heart rate and variability:** no significant increase in heart rate but significant decreases in short- and long-term variability
Goodman et al. 1984	10 smokers 10–20 cigarettes/day Gestational age 37–40 weeks Studied on 2 days, smoking on 1 day and no smoking on 1 day Order of smoking randomized	**Fetal heart rate:** increase of 2% with smoking (p not significant); **Fetal heart rate variability:** decrease of 63% in number of accelerations lasting ≥40 minutes (p <0.01)
Kariniemi et al. 1984[a]	8 women Smoking status not given Gestational age 27–32 weeks	**Maternal heart rate:** 24% increase (p <0.001); **Maternal blood pressure:** 9% increase in systolic blood pressure (p <0.01), 15% increase in diastolic blood pressure (p <0.001); **Fetal heart rate and variability:** 11% increase in heart rate (p <0.001), decrease in both DI and II of 24% (p <0.001)

Table 8.10   Continued

Study	Design/population	Outcome and comments
Pijpers et al. 1984	14 smokers Gestational age 34–38 weeks All abstained for 24 hours 7 smoked cigarette and were studied before, during, and after smoking, and 7 abstained Both studied at similar time points	**Maternal heart rate:** 11% increase for smokers (p <0.05) compared with women who abstained; **Maternal blood pressure:** 5% and 10% increase in systolic and diastolic blood pressure, respectively (p <0.05), with no change in women who abstained; **Fetal heart rate:** 4.5% increase (p <0.05) compared with women who abstained; **Fetal blood flow: aorta**—no significant change in velocity or in systolic or diastolic diameters
Sindberg Eriksen et al. 1984	10 smokers Gestational age 34–40 weeks	**Fetal heart rate:** 14% increase (p <0.01), returned to baseline by 20 minutes after smoking; **Fetal heart rate variability:** significant decrease in short-term variability of fetal heart rate but no significant change in long-term variability
Sindberg Eriksen and Gennser 1984	17 smokers Gestational age 33–37 weeks	**Maternal heart rate:** median increase of 42% (p <0.01); **Fetal heart rate:** median increase of 14% (p <0.01); **Fetal blood flow: aorta**—11.6% increase in median diastolic diameter (p <0.01); 13.8% increase in median pulsatile index (p <0.01); significant changes in aorta waveform with smoking; no signs of fetal hypoxia
Sindberg Eriksen and Marsál 1984	30 smokers Gestational age 31–40 weeks	**Maternal heart rate:** median increase of 29% (p <0.01); **Maternal blood pressure:** median increase in systolic and diastolic blood pressure of 14% and 12.5%, respectively (p <0.01); **Fetal heart rate:** median increase of 13% (p <0.01); **Fetal blood flow: aorta**—5% increase in median diameter, 15% increased peak, 20% increased mean blood velocity, and 30% increased flow (p <0.01); **umbilical vein**—9% increase in median diameter, 38.5% increase in flow (both p <0.05), and no change in velocity
Sindberg Eriksen and Marsál 1987[a]	10 smokers Gestational age 33–40 weeks	**Fetal heart rate:** 15% increase (p <0.05), return to baseline by 30 minutes after smoking; **Fetal blood flow: aorta**—5 minutes after smoking, pulsatile index decreased by 9%, and least diastolic blood velocity increased by 22% (p <0.05 for both), but mean peak velocity was unchanged
Sorensen and Borlum 1987	21 smokers 6–20 cigarettes/day Gestational age 24–39 weeks Abstinence 2–12 hours	**Maternal heart rate:** 15% median increase (p <0.05); **Maternal blood pressure:** 8.7% median increase in systolic blood pressure (p <0.05), and no increase in diastolic blood pressure; **Fetal heart rate:** 4.3% median increase (p <0.05); **Blood flow:** no change in fetal cardiac output
Lindblad et al. 1988[a]	24 smokers Gestational age 33–36 weeks	**Maternal heart rate:** 16% increase (p <0.01); **Maternal blood pressure:** no significant increase in systolic blood pressure; 11% increase in diastolic blood pressure (p <0.01); **Fetal heart rate:** 14% increase (p <0.001); **Fetal blood flow: aorta**—11% increase in flow (p <0.01); **umbilical vein**—20% increase in flow (p <0.01)
Morrow et al. 1988	15 smokers Gestational age 36–41 weeks	**Maternal heart rate:** 30% increase (p <0.0001); **Maternal blood pressure:** slight increase in systolic blood pressure (p not significant), and 14% increase in diastolic blood pressure (p = 0.0002); **Fetal heart rate:** 7% increase (p = 0.001); **Blood flow: uterine artery**—increase in S/D ratio (p = 0.08, powered [80%] to detect 17% change in S/D ratio); **umbilical artery**—26% increase in S/D ratio (p = 0.0001)

Table 8.10   Continued

Study	Design/population	Outcome and comments
Bruner and Forouzan 1991	47 women 24 nonsmokers, 23 smokers Gestational age 26–34.5 weeks Smokers studied before and after smoking and compared with control nonsmokers	**Maternal heart rate and fetal heart rate:** no significant difference at baseline between nonsmokers and smokers; no significant change after smoking; **Uterine artery and umbilical artery blood flow:** no significant difference at baseline between nonsmokers and smokers; no difference after smoking in flow velocity waveform or S/D ratio
Graca et al. 1991	51 women Gestational age 34–38 weeks	**Fetal heart rate:** increase of >10 beats per minute in most fetuses after maternal smoking (estimated to be increase of approximately 6–8%) and decreased short-term variability
Castro et al. 1993	19 smokers Mean gestational age 28 weeks ±1 week	**Maternal heart rate:** 27% increase (p < 0.001); **Maternal blood pressure:** 8% increase in systolic and 19% increase in diastolic blood pressure (p <0.001); **Uterine artery blood flow:** baseline S/D ratio >90% in 13 subjects; significant decrease in S/D ratio (15%) and resistance index (12%)
Oncken et al. 1996	9 smokers Gestational age 24–36 weeks Percentages estimated from graphs No p value or statement of significance given	**Maternal heart rate:** 17% increase; **Maternal blood pressure:** 4% increase in mean arterial pressure; **Fetal heart rate:** 2% increase; **Blood flow:** umbilical artery—8% decrease in resistance index; uterine artery—1% decrease in resistance index
Huisman et al. 1997	5 smokers Gestational age 8–16 weeks (studied weekly) All twin pregnancies	**Maternal heart rate:** 12% increase (p <0.005); **Maternal blood pressure:** no significant change; **Fetal heart rate:** no significant change; **Umbilical artery blood flow:** 13% increase in pulsatile index (p <0.01)
Oncken et al. 1997	15 smokers Gestational age 24–34 weeks Overnight abstinence, then studied every 2 hours during 8 hours of ad lib smoking	**Maternal heart rate:** significant increase 2 hours after baseline (p <0.001); **Maternal blood pressure:** approximately 6% mean increase in systolic blood pressure at 2 hours after baseline (p <0.001); **Fetal heart rate:** 0.7% increase (p not significant); **Fetal heart rate reactivity:** nonsignificant change: 1 loss of reactivity at 4 hours, 2 gained reactivity, and 12 had no change in reactivity; **Blood flow:** fetal MCA—2.4% decrease in resistance index at 4 hours (p = 0.02); umbilical artery—3% increase in resistance index at 2 hours (significance not stated); uterine artery—nonsignificant fluctuation (decrease and increase) in mean resistance index over 8 hours
Kimya et al. 1998	43 women 22 smokers, 21 nonsmokers Gestational age 20–40 weeks Smokers studied before and after smoking and compared with control nonsmokers	**Maternal heart rate:** no difference at baseline between smokers and nonsmokers, 23% increase (p <0.01) after smoking; **Maternal blood pressure:** no difference at baseline, systolic and diastolic blood pressure increased by 11% and 23%, respectively, after smoking (p <0.05); **Blood flow:** uterine artery—at baseline, smokers had 12% lower S/D ratio, 19% lower pulsatile index, and 19% lower resistance index compared with those of smokers (p <0.001); after smoking—no significant change in S/D ratio, pulsatile index, or resistance index; **umbilical artery**—no difference in pulsatile index or resistance index for nonsmokers vs. smokers at baseline and after smoking; S/D ratio was 13% lower in nonsmokers, with no change in S/D ratio after smoking

Table 8.10   Continued

Study	Design/population	Outcome and comments
Coppens et al. 2001	26 women 13 smokers, 13 nonsmokers >10 cigarettes/day Mean gestational age 37–38 weeks Smokers studied before and after smoking and compared with control nonsmokers	**Fetal heart rate:** no difference between smokers and nonsmokers at baseline or after smoking; **Fetal heart rate variability:** at baseline, percentage of time in high variability was 31% lower in smokers than in nonsmokers (p <0.05); similar differences remained after smoking; **Blood flow: umbilical artery**—at baseline, no difference in pulsatile index between nonsmokers and smokers; pulsatile index increased by 76% after smoking (p <0.05)
Oncken et al. 2002	15 smokers Gestational age 29–36 weeks Smoked 1 cigarette/hour for 8 hours Studied at baseline and at 4 hours, just before 4th cigarette	**Fetal heart rate:** baseline vs. 4 hours—no change (p = 0.17); **Fetal heart rate variability: nonstress test**—20% were nonreactive at baseline, and 73% were nonreactive at 4 hours (p = 0.013); nonreactive tests at baseline were also nonreactive at 4 hours; all fetuses demonstrated fetal breathing movements indicating fetal well-being
Ates et al. 2004	67 smokers Gestational age 32–40 weeks	**Maternal heart rate:** 6% increase (p <0.001); **Maternal blood pressure:** no significant increase (p = 0.2); **Fetal heart rate:** no significant increase; **Fetal heart rate variability:** 7% decrease in variability (p = 0.08) and 19% decrease in number of accelerations (p = 0.035); **Blood flow: umbilical artery and fetal MCA**—no significant change in resistance index, pulsatile index, S/D ratio, or maximum and minimum velocity

Note: Maternal heart rate and blood pressure measurements and fetal monitoring used sonographic technology (ultrasound/ Doppler). Prospective studies were conducted before and after smoking. Unless noted otherwise in description of study design, the following applies to all studies: overnight (>8 hours) smoking abstinence before smoking study cigarette. All were healthy singleton pregnancies, and percentage changes are for means. Most percentages were calculated for this Surgeon General's report from numeric data in article or estimated from graphs. **DI** = differential index or indices; **II** = interval index or indices; **MCA** = middle cerebral artery; **S/D** = systolic/diastolic.
[a]Same group of investigators.

Newnham et al. 1990; Bruner and Forouzan 1991; Coppens et al. 2001). These studies found no differences except for the small study by Eldridge and colleagues (1986). This study compared 19 nonsmokers with 5 smokers and found no difference in fetal heart rate during the second or early third trimester, but it did find a significant 9-percent elevation among smokers late in the pregnancy.

Acute Effects of Smoking

Maternal Heart Rate

Twenty-one studies provide data on the immediate effect of smoking one or two cigarettes on maternal heart rate (Table 8.10). The general design of these studies is similar. Healthy active smokers with singleton births in the latter half of pregnancy abstained from smoking overnight and were then studied before and after smoking one or two cigarettes. The different designs of the studies are noted in Table 8.10. All but two of the studies (Jouppila et

al. 1983; Bruner and Forouzan 1991) found a statistically significant transient increase in maternal heart rate immediately after smoking. The largest study, with 67 pregnant smokers, found a significant increase of 6 percent in maternal heart rate (Ates et al. 2004), and one smaller study, with 17 pregnant smokers, found a significant 42-percent increase in maternal heart rate immediately after smoking (Sindberg Eriksen and Gennser 1984). Other increases in maternal heart rate ranged from 10 to 30 percent, which were similar to the nonsignificant effect in the study conducted by Jouppila and colleagues (1983).

Sufficient clinical data establish that smoking a cigarette after a period of abstinence transiently elevates maternal heart rate, although the magnitude of the increase varies. This finding holds true even when studies involving nonsmokers are excluded. Only one study (Oncken et al. 1997), however, addressed the effect of ad lib smoking throughout the day on maternal heart rate. Oncken and colleagues (1997) found a maximal increase of 11 beats per minute in maternal heart rate two hours after baseline—an increase of approximately 13 percent—with ad lib smoking. The clinical significance of a transiently elevated maternal heart rate during pregnancy is unknown.

Maternal Blood Pressure

Of the 16 studies that examined the acute effects of smoking on maternal blood pressure (Table 8.10), all but 2 (Huisman et al. 1997; Ates et al. 2004) reported a transient but significant elevation in the mean or median diastolic or systolic blood pressure or in the mean arterial pressure. The largest increases, ranging from 10 to 23 percent, were observed for diastolic blood pressure, but most studies found an increase of less than 15 percent. The largest study, with 67 participants, found a small but nonsignificant increase in diastolic blood pressure after smoking (Ates et al. 2004). In general, the acute effect of smoking on maternal systolic blood pressure was less than the effect on diastolic blood pressure. Three studies reported no significant increase in systolic blood pressure, and the largest study found a small but nonsignificant (p = 0.2) increase (Table 8.10) (Ates et al. 2004). In the remaining 10 studies, transient increases ranged from 5 to 14 percent. These data indicate that smoking after abstinence transiently increases diastolic blood pressure and, to a lesser extent, systolic blood pressure. Because one large study (Ates et al. 2004) found a nonsignificant effect of smoking on maternal blood pressure, additional large studies may be needed.

The release of catecholamine may mediate the elevations in maternal heart rate and blood pressure reported in these studies. In a study of pregnant women, smoking was associated with an acute rise in plasma levels of norepinephrine, epinephrine, and dopamine and an associated acute rise in maternal heart rate and blood pressure (Quigley et al. 1979).

Fetal Heart Rate

Twenty-five studies (Table 8.10) collected data on fetal heart rate before and after mothers smoked one or two cigarettes. Ten studies, including the largest study (Ates et al. 2004) and two studies with a control group of nonsmokers (Bruner and Forouzan 1991; Coppens et al. 2001), found no effect of smoking on fetal heart rate. Five studies reported that smoking after abstinence was associated with a 2- to 8-percent transient increase in fetal heart rate, and eight studies reported an increase of 11 to 17 percent in fetal heart rate. The studies that found mean elevations in the fetal heart rate above 10 percent were conducted between 1979 and 1988. The five studies published after 1996 reported no statistically significant difference.

Variability in Fetal Heart Rate

Healthy fetal heart rate is variable, and there are short- and long-term patterns to this variability. The "differential index" is an alternative term for short-term variability, and the "interval index" is an alternative term for long-term variability. Healthy fetal heart rate also has episodes of accelerations. Researchers use the variability in fetal heart rate and the presence of episodes of accelerations to measure fetal well-being. This variability and acceleration are measured in the noninvasive nonstress test (NST). A reactive NST is a sign of fetal well-being, and a nonreactive NST is a sign of fetal distress. The NST is routinely used in the third trimester of pregnancy and during labor to monitor high-risk pregnancies and to assess low-risk pregnancies if concerns develop. Healthy fetuses have transient periods of decreased variability and accelerations, which would appear as a transiently nonreactive NST.

Data on fetal heart rate reactivity and accelerations and the NST are presented in Tables 8.8 and 8.10. A large cohort of mothers with high-risk pregnancies among smokers and nonsmokers was studied repeatedly over the course of the pregnancies (Table 8.8) (Phelan 1980). Although smokers had a high rate of nonreactive NSTs, many were reactive at a subsequent visit. A nonreactive NST in a pregnant smoker should generally be repeated to rule out a false nonreactive result. There are no reports on the prevalence of nontransient, abnormal NSTs among healthy smokers versus healthy nonsmokers.

Nine studies investigated variability in fetal heart rate before and after maternal smoking (Table 8.10). All but two studies (Oncken et al. 1997; Coppens et al. 2001) found that either maternal smoking transiently decreased short- and long-term variability or the NST became nonreactive. Three of the studies with positive findings were conducted with a control group of nonsmokers by the same team of investigators (Forss et al. 1983; Lehtovirta et al. 1983; Kariniemi et al. 1984). One investigator did not find a loss of reactivity from smoking one cigarette but did find a large increase in nonreactive NSTs with additional smoking (Oncken et al. 2002). The two largest studies (Graca et al. 1991; Ates et al. 2004) found a significant decrease in variability of fetal heart rate and an accelerated increase after smoking.

These data indicate that maternal smoking transiently decreases variability of fetal heart rate. However, the clinical significance of these transient decreases in the heart rate of fetuses of smokers is not clear. Generally, the nontransient changes in these parameters are the clinically important changes.

Blood Flow in Uterus, Placenta, and Fetus

Table 8.9 presents data on blood flow in the uterus and placenta from studies that used a radioisotope, which is considered the "gold standard" because it directly measures flow. The development of fetal sonographic technology has replaced radioisotope studies, because radioisotopes measure only maternal blood flow and expose the mother and fetus to radiation. Sonography is noninvasive and can be used to assess blood flow in both the fetus and the mother. Table 8.10 presents data from ultrasound and Doppler sonography on vessel diameter and blood velocity. These data are then used to calculate blood flow, which is difficult to measure, because the sonographer must visually mark the diameter of a vessel. Flow is proportional to the fourth power of the vessel radius, so even very small changes in the measurement of the diameter have a large effect on the calculation. Furthermore, all of the studies are unblinded. Sonographic technology advanced greatly between 1978 and 2004, which may partly explain the variations in the results from more than 25 years of publications, as is discussed here.

The most commonly used surrogate measures of blood flow are the ratio of systolic to diastolic blood flow velocity (S/D ratio), pulsatile index, and resistance index (RI). The S/D ratio is defined as the ratio of the time-averaged maximal systolic and diastolic blood flow velocities. The pulsatile index is defined as the difference between peak velocity and the lowest diastolic velocity, divided by the mean velocity during the heart cycle. The RI is defined as the difference between the maximal systolic and diastolic flow velocities, divided by the systolic flow velocity.

Independent of studies of smoking, researchers have used the S/D ratio, pulsatile index, and RI measures to monitor high-risk pregnancies and to predict outcomes (Maulik et al. 1990; Alatas et al. 1996; Fong et al. 1999; Özeren et al. 1999; Coleman et al. 2000; Gudmundsson et al. 2003; Axt-Fliedner et al. 2005; Li et al. 2005). In low-risk pregnancies, these measures of blood flow are not sensitive to or specific predictors of adverse outcomes such as preeclampsia or IUGR (Kurmanavichius et al. 1990; Irion et al. 1998; Albaiges et al. 2000; Harrington et al. 2004; Schwarze et al. 2005), except when the measures are markedly abnormal (Becker et al. 2002; Papageorghiou et al. 2005).

Four radioisotope studies of placental intervillous blood flow (IBF) have been performed (Table 8.9). Historically, these four studies have provided the initial data for the hypothesis that decreased maternal blood flow through the placenta caused fetal growth retardation. Three studies by the same group of investigators used xenon[133] to determine the acute effect of smoking on IBF among nonsmokers (Lehtovirta and Forss 1978, 1980; Rauramo et al. 1983). The results of the three studies are contradictory. Smoking resulted in either an acute increase or a decrease in IBF, depending on the patient and the study. The fourth radioisotope study used indium[113]-labeled transferrin to compare smokers immediately after smoking with nonsmokers (Philipp et al. 1984). This study found a significant difference in the distribution of normal and abnormal blood flow between the two groups, and a smaller proportion of scans were normal among the smokers.

Of four studies conducted during abstinence from smoking, two found no difference in blood flow parameters of uterine arteries between nonsmokers and smokers (Table 8.8) (Newnham et al. 1990; Albuquerque et al. 2004); the latter did find a difference in blood flow in umbilical arteries, but the larger Newnham study did not. The very small study by Eldridge and colleagues (1986) found an increase in aortic blood flow. The most important study found an association between the risk of a severe adverse pregnancy outcome and a pulsatile index for the uterine artery that doubled among smokers (Lees et al. 2001).

Sixteen studies used Doppler sonography to examine blood flow parameters in maternal smokers and their fetuses before and after smoking or in smokers after smoking compared with nonsmokers and their fetuses (Table 8.10). Four studies by the same group of investigators found that smoking dramatically increased four parameters (blood flow, velocity, diameter, and pulsatile index) (Sindberg Eriksen et al. 1984; Sindberg Eriksen and Marsal 1984, 1987; Lindblad et al. 1988). One study found an acute 76-percent increase in the pulsatile index of the umbilical artery after maternal smoking (Coppens et al. 2001). Six studies found no effect on blood flow, velocity, diameter, S/D ratio, pulsatile index, and RI in the uteroplacental or fetal blood vessels (Jouppila et al. 1983; Pijpers et al. 1984; Sorensen and Borlum 1987; Bruner and Forouzan 1991; Kimya et al. 1998; Ates et al. 2004). However, Oncken and colleagues (1997) found a negligible change, and four studies found either increases or decreases in the S/D ratio and the pulsatile index (Table 8.10) (Morrow et al. 1988; Castro et al. 1993; Oncken et al. 1996; Huisman et al. 1997).

In summary, differences between blood flow in smokers during abstinence and that in nonsmokers do not appear to be significant. However, the study by Lees and colleagues (2001) raises concerns because it indicates that with an elevated pulsatile index in the uterine artery, maternal cigarette smoking doubles the risk of a severe, adverse pregnancy outcome. The data on the acute effects of smoking on maternal and fetal blood flow are more contradictory, and no generalizations can be made at this time.

Fetal Tissue and Organogenesis

Timing and Critical Periods

The embryonic period includes the first eight weeks after fertilization and constitutes a significant period in human development. During this time, all major internal and external structures start to develop, involving many complex interactions that must occur in an orderly sequence. The embryonic period is a time of rapid differentiation, and the developing organs are particularly susceptible to the effects of exogenous agents. The stage of embryonic development determines the embryo's susceptibility to unfavorable environmental factors. The embryo is most easily disturbed during the organogenesis period, from day 15 to day 60 after conception. In addition, each system or organ of an embryo has a critical period when its development may be altered. The effects of some environmental toxins on the developing embryo and fetus can be direct and lethal or subtle with delayed but serious consequences. Thus, multiple factors are involved in identifying and evaluating the effects of exposure to tobacco smoke on the developing baby.

Evidence on Effects of Smoking

Some epidemiologic studies report an association between maternal smoking and various congenital malformations. In this area of research, the associations with smoking most frequently examined and published relate to nonsyndromic orofacial clefting, congenital heart disease, malformations of the lower extremities such as clubfoot or limb deficiency defects, hypospadias, gastroschisis, and craniosynostosis (see "Birth Defects" earlier in this chapter). Data supporting a causal association between nonsyndromic orofacial clefting and maternal smoking have strengthened, but few studies have addressed possible pathogenetic mechanisms.

Traditionally, investigators have used animal models and postmortem tissues to detect the effects on organogenesis of exposure to tobacco smoke by conducting gross morphologic, soft tissue, and skeletal examinations. Early studies of this type involving exposure to mainstream cigarette smoke provide little data supporting an effect on organogenesis. Of seven studies, four did not find any effects (Wagner et al. 1972; Reznik and Marquard 1980; Peterson et al. 1981; Bassi et al. 1984), and three mentioned limited findings but lacked sufficient details for a full evaluation (Schoeneck 1941; Tachi and Aoyama 1983; Amankwah et al. 1985).

A subsequent set of experiments exposed pregnant Wistar rats to sidestream cigarette smoke, and the pups were then examined for gross morphologic changes (Table 8.11). Researchers observed a dose-dependent reduction in birth weight (p <0.001) but no increase in macroscopically visible gross anomalies (Nelson et al. 1999a). Ossification was delayed throughout the skeleton in all exposed groups regardless of the dose. The second part of the experiment studied the histopathologic changes in tissues such as the lung, liver, stomach, kidney, and intestines (Nelson et al. 1999b). The lung tissues of pups of dams exposed to smoke showed increased apoptosis, mesenchymal changes, and hyperplasia of bronchial muscles. Researchers found abnormal hematopoiesis, proliferation of bile ducts in the liver, and delayed maturation of the glomeruli, gastric epithelia, and intestinal villi. Another study exposed Sprague-Dawley rats to mainstream tobacco smoke by nose-only inhalation (Carmines et al. 2003). Males were exposed four weeks before and during mating, and females were exposed two weeks before and during mating and through gestational day 20. Exposure to tobacco smoke was confirmed by biomarker evaluation. Researchers evaluated external and internal abnormal macroscopic findings, histopathology of the placenta and fetal tissue, and skeletal radiograms. They concluded that exposure to tobacco smoke was not associated with any congenital malformations in the offspring. However, numerous abnormalities were described, including hypoplasia of the internal genital structures in the exposed adult male rats and decreased ossification in the fetuses of the exposed dams.

Epidemiologic studies show that offspring of maternal smokers have abnormal lung function and associated higher incidences of lower respiratory disorders. The identification of nicotinic acetylcholine receptors in fetal lung suggests a mechanism that may underlie the observed postnatal pulmonary abnormalities. This hypothesis was tested in monkeys to determine whether maternal exposure to nicotine would produce changes in lung function or morphology in newborn monkeys similar to the changes observed in human infants (Sekhon et al. 2001). Pregnant rhesus monkeys were infused with either nicotine comparable to heavy smoking in humans (1.5 milligrams per kilogram per day [mg/kg/day], $n = 7$) or saline ($n = 7$) timed to days 26 through 160 of gestation. The fetuses were delivered by cesarean section and on the next day had pulmonary function testing. They were then sacrificed, and their lungs were weighed and fixed. There was a significant decrease in fetal lung weight (16 percent) and fixed lung volume (14 percent) after in utero exposure to nicotine. All lung function tests (e.g., peak tidal expiratory volume, mean mid-expiratory volume, and forced expiratory volume at peak expiratory flows) were also

Table 8.11 **Animal and in vitro studies on association between maternal smoking and congenital abnormalities with relevant genetic and/or molecular hypotheses**

Study	Design	Developmental defect studied	Proposed mechanism or hypothesis	Findings
Nelson et al. 1999a	Pregnant Wistar rats were exposed to sidestream cigarette smoke (13 mg of tar, 0.9 mg of nicotine) Pups examined	Histopathologic changes in tissues such as lung, liver, stomach, kidney, and intestines	Define microscopic morphology after exposure to cigarette smoke	• Lung tissues showed increased apoptosis, mesenchymal changes, and hyperplasia of bronchial muscles • Abnormal hematopoiesis and proliferation of bile ducts in liver • Delayed maturation of glomeruli, gastric epithelia, and intestinal villi
Nelson et al. 1999b	Pregnant Wistar rats were exposed to sidestream cigarette smoke (13 mg of tar, 0.9 mg of nicotine) Pups examined	Gross morphologic changes in tissues	Define macroscopic morphology after exposure to cigarette smoke	• Dose-dependent reduction of birth weight was observed (p <0.001) • No macroscopically visible gross anomaly was observed • Delay in ossification in entire skeleton was observed in all exposed, regardless of dose
Subrama-niam et al. 1999	12-week-old female Sprague-Dawley rats exposed to sidestream cigarette smoke and unexposed control group 2 weeks after exposure, females inseminated by unexposed males Exposure continued during mating and pregnancy Pups from the exposed group continued to be exposed to cigarette smoke until examination	Lung surfactant proteins SP-A and SP-B in bronchoalveolar lavage fluids, preparations from postnatal days 1, 3, 7, 14, 21, and 35 from sham- and smoke-exposed pups	Determine whether perinatal exposure to sidestream cigarette smoke decreases amount of surfactant in developing rat pups	• Smoke-exposed pups showed reduced level of SP-A on day 1 and a higher level of SP-A and phospholipids on day 21 • Perinatal exposure to sidestream smoke can have deleterious effects on the developing lung

Table 8.11   Continued

Study	Design	Developmental defect studied	Proposed mechanism or hypothesis	Findings
Panter et al. 2000	27 Spanish-type female goats and 28 Western ewes were given *Nicotiana glauca* during pregnancy Concentration of anabasine in the dried plants was 0.175–0.23% vs. 2.4% in extracts Treatment groups divided into 6 subgroups and fed dried plant by gavage or anabasine-rich extract by capsule on days 32 and 41 of gestation Low initial dose (5–8 mg/kg) titrated until clinical signs of toxicity (maximum 18 mg/kg)	Intrauterine growth, presence or absence of CP, facial asymmetry, and skeletal contractures in newborn goats and sheep	Compare incidence of plant-induced CP formation between sheep and goat treatment groups Determine differences in sensitivity of study animals exposed to same toxicants in similar doses and manner Determine other variables that might explain cause of CP formation	• Fetuses from both study groups showed decreased fetal movement, as determined by ultrasound • 21 of 45 (47%) newborn goats exposed during the early part of pregnancy (32–41 gestational days) had CP; only 1 of 45 (2.2%) had skeletal contractures • 1 of 35 (2.9%) lambs had CP, and 6 of 35 (17%) had contractures • Goat model is more efficient and reliable for studying CP deformities • Tobacco plant and its extract is a well-established cause of congenital cleft formation • Exact mechanism is undetermined, but neuromuscular blockade may play a role
Sekhon et al. 2001	Pregnant rhesus monkeys received subcutaneous infusion of nicotine (1.5 mg/kg per day (n = 7) or saline (n = 7) on gestational days 26–160 After delivery by cesarean section, fetuses had pulmonary function testing on next day	Pulmonary function before and after exposure to nicotine Lung weight and morphology	Interaction of nicotine with nicotinic acetylcholine receptor in developing lung responsible for altered pulmonary morphogenesis and mechanics observed in human infants whose mothers smoked during pregnancy	• Lung weight and fixed lung volume were significantly decreased in exposed monkeys (16% and 14%, respectively) • Fixed lung volume and lung volume normalized to body weight decreased (14%, p = 0.001; 11%, p = 0.006, respectively) • All lung function test results were significantly lower in newborns exposed to nicotine during gestation

Table 8.11   Continued

Study	Design	Developmental defect studied	Proposed mechanism or hypothesis	Findings
Carmines et al. 2003	Potential developmental effects of smoke from 1R4F reference cigarette examined Sprague-Dawley rats exposed for 2 hours/day, 7 days/week, by nose-only inhalation at target mainstream smoke levels of 150, 300, and 600 mg/m^3 of total particulate matter Males exposed 4 weeks before and during mating and females for 2 weeks before and during mating and through gestational day 20 Sham controls: filtered air to simulate nose-only exposure, and cage controls maintained untreated Smoke exposure confirmed through biomarker evaluation	Histopathologic evaluation of placenta and fetal tissue External and internal malformations Macroscopic and microscopic findings and changes determined by skeletal radiograms	Parental exposure to tobacco smoke may cause congenital malformations	• Exposure duration was limited • Number of study and control subjects was inadequate • Morphologic and dysmorphic evaluations were not thorough • Adult male rats showed hypoplasia of the internal male genital structures • Fetuses from dams exposed to tobacco smoke showed decreased ossification • Possibility of an association
Lavezzi et al. 2004	54 sudden and unexplained fetal and infant deaths (13 stillbirths, 7 neonatal deaths, and 34 from sudden infant death syndrome) Postmortem examination 33 (61%) nonsmokers 21 (39%) smokers Sections of brainstem and medulla oblongata examined with morphometric methods	Brainstem histopathology and morphometric analysis of arcuate nucleus	Decrease in size of the arcuate nucleus of brainstem was expected in group exposed to smoke	• Mothers of 18 of 34 infants with hypoplasia in >20% of arcuate nucleus were smokers (p <0.05) • Homeobox-containing gene • *EN2* is a candidate gene thought to regulate development of arcuate nucleus • Cigarette smoke may directly affect this gene, resulting in brainstem abnormalities

Table 8.11   Continued

Study	Design	Developmental defect studied	Proposed mechanism or hypothesis	Findings
de la Chica et al. 2005	Prospective study 25 control mothers and 25 mothers who smoked (≥10 cigarettes/day for ≥10 years) Amniocytes obtained by routine amniocentesis for prenatal diagnosis Questionnaire about smoking patterns used	Chromosomal instability in routine chromosome spreads Breakpoints implicated in chromosomal abnormalities identified by G-banding	Determine whether maternal smoking has a genotoxic effect on amniotic cells, expressed as increased chromosomal instability Analyze whether any chromosomal regions are especially affected by tobacco	• Smoking as defined and during pregnancy is associated with increased chromosomal instability in amniocytes • Band 11q23, known to be involved in leukemogenesis, seems especially sensitive to genotoxic compounds contained in tobacco
Ejaz et al. 2005	Chicken embryo model In vivo examination of neonatal development Effects examined of different preparations of nicotine and solutions of whole mainstream smoke on embryonic movements during neonatal development Activity level before and after exposure to nicotine was measured	Kinematic analysis	Evaluate effects of nicotine and solutions of whole mainstream smoke on embryonic movements	• Low doses of nicotine induced hyperactivity, and higher doses induced hypoactivity • Significant (p <0.01) decrease in movements with application of 10 mg of nicotine and different preparations of solution of whole mainstream smoke

Table 8.11   Continued

Study	Design	Developmental defect studied	Proposed mechanism or hypothesis	Findings
Lavezzi et al. 2005	Postmortem examination of 42 stillborn babies In 30 of 42, no cause of death was identified (sudden intrauterine unexplained death) In 12 of 42, causes of death were known (intrauterine explained death) 15 sudden intrauterine unexplained deaths and 1 intrauterine explained death of infants born to maternal smokers 16 maternal smokers 25 nonsmokers Brainstems studied by immunohistochemistry to assay expression of *EN2* gene, somatostatin, and tyrosine hydroxylase enzyme	Brainstem histopathology/ morphology	Morphologic changes of brainstem expected in the smoke-exposed group	• Brainstem sections from 13 stillbirths with no definite cause of death but with known exposure to tobacco smoke showed varying degrees of hypoplasia of arcuate nucleus and abnormal staining pattern with antibodies applied • Exposure in utero to maternal smoking may strongly interfere with brain biologic parameters, including decrease in noradrenergic activity in brainstem

Note: **CP** = cleft palate; **mg** = milligrams; **mg/kg** = milligrams per kilogram; **mg/m^3** = milligrams per cubic meter.

significantly lower in the newborns exposed to nicotine, demonstrating that prenatal exposure to nicotine compromises lung growth and pulmonary function. Although there was no histopathologic description of the examined lungs, researchers have described changes in lung morphology in humans (DiFranza et al. 2004), as well as in rats (Nelson et al. 1999b). Another experiment exposed female Sprague-Dawley rats aged 12 weeks to tobacco smoke and then mated them to unexposed males. Postnatal measurements of the pups' lung surfactant levels of protein (SP-A and SP-B) in bronchoalveolar lavage fluids showed a reduced level of SP-A on day 1 and a higher level of SP-A and phospholipid on day 21 among pups exposed to smoke (Subramaniam et al. 1999).

One study examined the induction of cleft palate by *Nicotiana glauca* (wild-tree tobacco) or anabasine-rich extracts during the first trimester of pregnancy and compared Spanish-type goats with crossbred Western-type sheep (Panter et al. 2000). Bilateral cleft palate was induced in 100 percent of the embryonic and fetal goats by gavage of the pregnant mothers with anabasine-rich extracts. Eleven percent of the newborn goats showed extracranial abnormalities, mainly contractures of the metacarpal joints, in addition to bilateral cleft palate. Most of these contractures resolved spontaneously within four to six weeks after delivery. In contrast, only two lambs from ewes exposed to both substances had cleft palate. However, all lambs exposed to both substances had contractures, which indicated differential susceptibility of the species. The researchers postulated that an alkaloid-induced reduction in fetal movement during the period of normal palate closure caused the cleft palate and the multiple flexion contractures. This postulation is supported by a later study that used the chick embryo model to conduct an in vivo examination of the effects of different preparations of solutions of nicotine and of mainstream whole smoke on embryonic movements during neonatal development (Ejaz et al. 2005). In this experiment, low doses of nicotine induced hyperactivity and high doses induced hypoactivity. Accordingly, there was a significant (p <0.01) decrease in movements after applying 10 mg of nicotine and different preparations of whole mainstream smoke solutions. The decrease in embryonic movements was dose dependent and did not resolve by the end of the experiment. The researchers concluded that nicotine could alter embryonic movements that are important during embryogenesis for the differentiation and maturation of the body systems.

In a clinical study, researchers collected amniocytes from routine amniocenteses of 25 control women and 25 women who smoked (≥10 cigarettes per day for ≥10 years). Amniocytes of the smokers showed increased chromosomal instability; breakpoints involving band 11q23, which is commonly implicated in hematopoietic malignancies, was the chromosomal region most affected (de la Chica et al. 2005). Another study examined autopsy specimens from 42 stillborn infants (Lavezzi et al. 2005). Researchers studied the brainstem tissue by immunohistochemistry to evaluate the expression of the *EN2* gene, somatostatin, and the tyrosine hydroxylase enzyme. Brainstem sections from stillborn infants whose mothers had smoked during pregnancy showed hypoplasia of the arcuate nucleus and an abnormal staining pattern with the antibodies applied. Thus, in utero exposure to maternal smoking may strongly interfere with brain biologic parameters of brain development, including a decrease in the noradrenergic activity in the brainstem, resulting in pulmonary hypodevelopment and even an apparently unexplained sudden death of the fetus (Lavezzi et al. 2005).

Researchers have identified an increasing number of polymorphisms of genes encoding drug- and/or toxin-metabolizing enzymes, transporters, and receptors. Some of these genetic factors have a major impact on drug sensitivity, adverse reactions, or variations of responses to environmental toxins. As a result, many investigators have studied polymorphisms of certain candidate genes to elucidate the pathogenesis of the effects of maternal smoking on the developing embryo and fetus (see "Smoking and Maternal and Neonatal Genetic Polymorphisms" later in this chapter).

Investigators have proposed other mechanisms for the adverse effects of smoking on organogenesis, particularly orofacial clefting. CO contributes to fetal hypoxia, which investigators have associated with an increased risk for cleft lip and cleft palate in susceptible strains of mice (Millicovsky and Johnston 1981; Bronsky et al. 1986; Bailey et al. 1995). Impaired uteroplacental circulation may result in a reduced supply of essential nutrients for embryonic tissues (van Rooij et al. 2001). Studies have associated poor intake of vitamin B_6 and multivitamins with a risk of oral clefts (Botto et al. 2004; Munger et al. 2004). Other possible mechanisms include (1) reductions in serum folate levels mediated by maternal smoking (McDonald et al. 2002; Mannino et al. 2003; Ortega et al. 2004), (2) exposure to cadmium that is present in increased amounts in the placentas of smokers (Ronco et al. 2005) and is associated with teratogenic effects in certain rats (Ferm 1971; Chernoff 1973), and (3) DNA damage by PAHs (Lammer et al. 2004; Perera et al. 2004). Further work is needed to elucidate the extent to which these or other mechanisms involving the complex mixture of chemicals in cigarette smoke account for the increased risk of oral clefts.

Immune System

Cigarette smoking is associated with an increased risk for many types of infectious diseases including pneumococcal pneumonia, Legionnaires' disease, meningococcal disease, influenza, the common cold, and infection with *Helicobacter pylori* (Arcavi and Benowitz 2004). In addition, studies have associated smoking with seropositivity for human immunodeficiency virus (HIV) and an increase in the transmission of HIV from infected mothers to their offspring (Boulos et al. 1990; Royce and Winkelstein 1990; Burns et al. 1991, 1994).

The mechanisms through which smoking increases the risk of infection are not well defined and are likely complex, involving both innate and adaptive immune responses. Compared with nonsmokers, smokers appear to have a leukocytosis (Corre et al. 1971; Friedman et al. 1973; Yeung and Buncio 1984; Hughes et al. 1985; Calori et al. 1996; Jensen et al. 1998a) and elevations in levels of all major blood cell types (Corre et al. 1971). This leukocytosis could be a result of nicotine-induced increases in the release of catecholamine (Friedman et al. 1973). However, the consequences of an increased white blood cell count are unclear. It appears that there are increases in both CD4+ (an HIV-helper white blood cell) and CD8+ (an HIV-suppressor white blood cell) T-cell populations in smokers, although heavy smokers may have reduced CD4+ cell counts, and effects may vary by race (Sopori 2002; Arcavi and Benowitz 2004). A decline in CD4+ cell counts could contribute to a decrease in B-cell proliferation and immunoglobulin (Ig) synthesis, which would increase the risk of infection (Arcavi and Benowitz 2004). However, in a study of pregnant smokers compared with pregnant nonsmokers, a decline in CD4+ count was not described (Luppi et al. 2007).

In general, smoking appears to have immunosuppressive effects. For example, lymphocytes in smokers appear to have a decreased response to T-cell mitogens (Sopori 2002), and polymorphonuclear leukocytes show decreases in chemotaxis and migration (Noble and Penny

1975; Corberand et al. 1979), which do not appear to be attributable to exposure to nicotine (Sasagawa et al. 1985). Study findings suggest that smokers have reduced titers of antibodies to the influenza virus and low serum levels of all Ig classes except IgE (Gerrard et al. 1980; Sopori 2002). In addition, smoking may increase levels of autoantibodies, perhaps contributing to some autoimmune disorders (Mathews et al. 1973; Másdóttir et al. 2000; Sopori 2002). Smoking may also affect the balance of function between helper T-cell subsets 1 and 2 (Th1 and Th2), because researchers have observed increases in Th2- and/or Th1-related cytokines in smokers (Tsunoda et al. 2003; Cozen et al. 2004). In vitro experiments suggest that nicotine impairs the immunostimulatory activity of dendritic cells (antigen-presenting cells) and adversely affects the differentiation of monocytes into dendritic cells (Nouri-Shirazi and Guinet 2003; Guinet et al. 2004). Finally, studies have also associated smoking with low counts and reduced cytotoxic activity of natural killer cells, which are important components of innate immunity (Tollerud et al. 1989; Zeidel et al. 2002). Potential mechanisms through which exposure to tobacco or nicotine might result in an altered immune function include the induction of glucocorticoid hypersecretion and the increased release of catecholamines, which both inhibit the immune response or the activation of the autonomic nervous system (Sopori and Kozak 1998; Borovikova et al. 2000; Sopori 2002). Activation of the parasympathetic arm of the autonomic nervous system attenuates the systemic inflammatory response.

Studies suggest that smoking also induces systemic chronic inflammatory effects, which is possibly a consequence of increased oxidative stress (Cross et al. 1999; Hecht 1999; van der Vaart et al. 2005). As described earlier in this section, smokers have a leukocytosis compared with white blood cell counts in nonsmokers, and studies have associated smoking with elevated levels of C-reactive protein (Tracy et al. 1997; Wong et al. 2001; Bermudez et al. 2002). However, findings in studies of cytokine profiles in blood are not consistent (van der Vaart et al. 2005). Some studies suggest that smoking suppresses the production of proinflammatory cytokines such as IL-1, IL-6, and TNFα, which are important components of the immune response to intracellular pathogens such as viruses and fungi (Sopori and Kozak 1998; Ouyang et al. 2000). However, other studies have shown an enhanced production of IL-6 and TNFα, as well as other cytokines including IL-1β (Zeidel et al. 2002; van der Vaart et al. 2005).

Smoking could contribute to an increased risk of adverse pregnancy outcomes by its effects on the immune system through an increased risk of maternal infection, an alteration of the inflammatory response, or both. For example, studies have consistently associated smoking with a twofold-to-threefold increase in risk for bacterial vaginosis (Morris et al. 2001), which is a risk factor for preterm delivery. Researchers have hypothesized that smoking increases this risk through its effects on vaginal flora or through the depletion of Langerhans cells, resulting in local immunosuppression (Smart et al. 2004). Smoking can also reduce zinc levels, which could increase susceptibility to vaginal infections (Edman et al. 1986; Sikorski et al. 1990; Shubert et al. 1992). Cigarette smoking has been associated with increased cervical anti-inflammatory cytokines in early pregnancy, which could make women who smoke more vulnerable to reproductive tract infections and subsequent preterm delivery (Simhan et al. 2005, 2009). Finally, the immunosuppressive effects of smoking could contribute to protective effects against preeclampsia, because preeclampsia appears to involve an exaggerated or inappropriate immune response. More research is needed to fully define these potential relationships and pathways.

Tobacco Smoke Toxicants and the Reproductive System

Carbon Monoxide

Toxicity

CO is formed as a by-product of combustion and is thus present in tobacco smoke. It is a potent and even lethal toxin whose primary target organ is the brain. The fetus is more susceptible to the toxic effects of CO than is the mother. Symptomatic exposures to CO that the mother will fully recover from may end in permanent neurologic damage to the fetus or even fetal death (e.g., stillbirth) (Norman and Halton 1990; Koren et al. 1991). The fetal effects of CO are well studied (Koren et al. 1991; Penney 1996).

CO is the toxin found in the highest concentration in cigarette smoke. The dose per cigarette is 10 to 20 times the dose of nicotine (Hoffman et al. 1997). Furthermore, CO is not found in unsmoked tobacco products. The toxic effects of CO result predominantly from its binding to hemoglobin (Longo 1976, 1977). Each molecule of hemoglobin can carry four molecules of O_2 (Hsia 1998). The binding and unbinding of O_2 to hemoglobin depends on the local level of O_2. High levels of O_2 facilitate binding to hemoglobin, and low levels (hypoxia) facilitate the release of O_2 from hemoglobin. The O_2 binds to hemoglobin as blood passes through the O_2-rich lungs and is delivered to tissues as blood traverses the capillary beds. When one molecule of O_2 is released from hemoglobin, a conformational change in hemoglobin facilitates the release of further O_2 molecules.

Hypoxia, Fetal Growth, and Other Abnormalities

CO binds to hemoglobin with an affinity more than 200 times that of O_2 (Sauter 1994). Once CO binds to one of the four binding sites of hemoglobin, the hemoglobin is altered so greater tissue hypoxia is required before O_2 will be released from the other binding sites (Hsia 1998). In addition, CO prevents the conformational change in hemoglobin that occurs with O_2 unbinding. The release of one O_2 molecule does not facilitate the release of subsequent O_2 molecules when hemoglobin also binds CO.

The binding of CO to hemoglobin is tenacious, with a half-life of five to six hours. Fetal hemoglobin binds CO more tightly than does adult hemoglobin, and the fetus has higher levels of carboxyhemoglobin than those of the mother; the average ratio of fetal to maternal carboxyhemoglobin is 1.8 (Cole et al. 1972; Longo 1977; Bureau et al. 1982). It takes approximately seven hours for CO to equilibrate between the mother and the fetus (Bureau et al. 1982). The net effect of the CO and hemoglobin interaction is chronic hypoxia in fetal tissue (Longo 1977) or, more accurately, chronic cellular hypoxia that persists during periods of maternal abstinence from smoking, such as during sleep. Simply put, CO from cigarette smoke deprives the fetus of O_2, which is essential for the aerobic metabolism that produces adenosine triphosphate (ATP). ATP stores chemical energy that is ubiquitously used to drive all manner of chemical reactions in the body. This chronic yet mild O_2 deprivation in the fetus is likely a major underlying mechanism of smoking-associated fetal growth retardation (Longo 1976, 1977).

Data from both clinical and animal studies indicate that CO is probably the foremost toxin responsible for the LBW associated with maternal smoking (Garvey and Longo 1978; Lynch and Bruce 1989; Penney 1996; England et al. 2003). A well-designed study found a decrease in birth weight that was almost five times greater for infants of smokers than for infants of snuff users, even after adjustment for variables (England et al. 2003). The mean adjusted decrease in birth weight was 39 g for infants of snuff users and 190 g for infants of smokers compared with infants of nonsmokers. Because CO is the main toxin in cigarette smoke but not in snuff, this difference in birth weight implicates CO as the likely hazard. Even mild, long-term exposure to CO in animals resulted in fetal growth retardation; maternal carboxyhemoglobin levels were 4 to 9 percent (Garvey and Longo 1978; Penney 1996). The carboxyhemoglobin levels associated with smoking are 5 to 10 percent.

Studies have found central nervous system abnormalities in fetuses and pups of pregnant rats with long-term exposure to CO (Storm and Fechter 1985a,b; Storm et al. 1986; Fechter 1987; Carratù et al. 1993a,b; Packianathan et al. 1993). Behavioral studies of prenatally exposed animals have revealed persistent postnatal effects associated with CO exposure that produced maternal carboxyhemoglobin levels of 6 to 16 percent. These levels were not associated with small litter size or altered duration of gestation but with LBW (Fechter and Annau 1976, 1980, 1997; Abbatiello and Mohrmann 1979; Mactutus and Fechter 1984, 1985; Singh 1986; Fechter 1987). CO-induced hypoxia appears related to other congenital anomalies including cleft lip and cleft palate in susceptible strains of mice (Millicovsky and Johnston 1981; Bronsky et al. 1986; Bailey et al. 1995). Subsequent epidemiologic studies of birth defects in relation to CO levels from air pollution early in gestation found associations between higher CO levels and various cardiac defects, but the findings were not consistent (Ritz et al. 2002; Gilboa et al. 2005).

Blood Hyperviscosity

Carboxyhemoglobin results in functional anemia in both the mother and fetus that stimulates production of red blood cells and elevates maternal and fetal hematocrits (Meberg et al. 1979; Bureau et al. 1983; Bili et al. 1996). As the hematocrit increases, the viscosity of the blood increases. At birth, the healthy newborn hematocrit is normally 44 to 64 percent, which is well above adult values. Because of the increased viscosity, healthy newborns are at risk for stroke if the hematocrit is above 65 percent. The hematocrit can be lowered with partial-exchange transfusions. Compared with newborns of nonsmokers, newborns of smokers have higher hematocrits that therefore increase the risk of stroke and a need for exchange transfusion (D'Souza et al. 1978; Buchan 1983). Elevated maternal hematocrits and a consequently higher blood viscosity in the mother may also be risk factors for suboptimal placental perfusion (Bureau et al. 1983; Knottnerus et al 1990).

Preeclampsia

Data indicate that CO functions as a gaseous localized messenger (Ryter et al. 2004). CO appears to activate guanylate cyclase and modulate the mitogen-activated protein kinase signaling pathway (Ryter et al. 2004). Heme oxygenases (HO-1, HO-2, and HO-3) degrade heme into ferrous ion, CO, and biliverdin, which all have important physiological functions at low concentrations but are toxic in high concentrations (Ryter et al. 2004). CO appears to have localized functions similar to those of nitric oxide (NO), a gas that affects vascular tone and platelet aggregation (Ryter et al. 2004). CO also appears to have cytoprotective effects against oxidative stress by reducing inflammation and suppressing apoptosis (Ryter et al. 2004; Tsuchihashi et al. 2004).

Researchers think it is likely that the CO from cigarette smoke is responsible for the reduced risk of preeclampsia associated with smoking. The basis for this rationale is that users of snuff, which does not contain CO, have an increased risk of preeclampsia (England et al. 2003). The pathophysiology of preeclampsia remains to be elucidated, but the transformation of the spiral arterioles, which supply blood to the placenta, into low-resistance high-flow vessels appears to be incomplete (see "Preeclampsia" and "Placenta" earlier in this chapter). Spiral arteries may still be responsive to vasoconstrictive stimuli. Episodic constriction resulting in reduced blood flow to the placenta can cause hypoxia-reperfusion injury, which elicits endothelial damage and an inflammatory response. A hypoxic uterine environment appears to be a normal stimulus for the transformation of spiral arterioles during pregnancy (Lyall 2003). CO via carboxyhemoglobin can augment this tissue hypoxia and may stimulate the normal transformation of spiral arterioles. Additionally, CO functions similarly to NO as a vasorelaxant and may counteract the effects of circulating vasoconstrictive agents on preeclamptic spiral arterioles. Both hypoxic environment and vasorelaxation may help to prevent hypoxia-reperfusion injury and the consequential inflammation and endothelial damage, thereby reducing the risk of preeclampsia (Bainbridge et al. 2005).

Independent of preventing hypoxia-reperfusion injury, CO may function similarly to NO in maintaining normal endothelial function and preventing platelet aggregation. Also, research in the area of tissue transplantation has found that exogenous CO significantly reduces the inflammatory environment in allograft rejections (Tsuchihashi et al. 2004). Researchers postulate that CO may have a similar role in the heightened inflammatory environment of the preeclamptic placenta. Although some evidence supports this model of CO and preeclampsia, the data are not extensive (Barber et al. 2001; McLaughlin et al. 2001). Investigators do not know how important CO is as a local messenger during pregnancy or how exogenous CO supplements endogenous CO.

Summary

CO is the toxin in cigarette smoke that is found in the highest concentrations. The major effect of CO is to deprive the fetus of O_2 by binding to hemoglobin. The binding of CO to hemoglobin also results in functional anemia that eventually produces a rise in the hematocrit. Elevated hematocrit in the mother may adversely affect blood flow in the placenta, leading to placental problems and potentially to fetal growth retardation. CO appears

to prevent preeclampsia by augmenting uterine hypoxia and, thus, development of arterioles or other local effects similar to those of NO. However, this possibly beneficial role for CO is far outweighed by its hypoxic effects involving hemoglobin.

Nicotine

Nicotine, the principal alkaloid in tobacco, is a major contributor to the addictive properties of smoking. The diverse pharmacologic and toxicologic properties of nicotine are discussed in Chapter 4, "Nicotine Addiction: Past and Present," and are only briefly touched on here. Nicotine has both short- and long-term effects and is likely causally related to several of the endpoints discussed in this chapter. The Office of Environmental Health Hazard Assessment of the California Environmental Protection Agency (Cal/EPA) lists nicotine as a developmental toxicant. Nicotine is known to cross the placenta and concentrate in the fetus at levels slightly higher than those in the mother. Nicotine may decrease placental perfusion, leading to hypoxia of the fetus and acidosis.

As noted earlier in this chapter, nicotine may be involved in the development of various congenital anomalies or neurobehavioral problems. Experimental studies of rhesus monkeys exposed to nicotine in utero showed decreases in fetal lung weight, volume, and function (Sekhon et al. 2001) similar to those observed in offspring of maternal smokers (see "Fetal Tissue and Organogenesis" earlier in this chapter). Thus, nicotine may be the key constituent of tobacco smoke to impair fetal lung development and lead to altered lung function and perhaps increased respiratory illness. In an experiment with chick embryos, low doses of nicotine induced hyperactivity and higher doses induced hypoactivity (Ejaz et al. 2005). The researchers concluded that nicotine could alter embryonic movements that are important during embryogenesis for the differentiation and maturation of the embryo's organ systems. McCartney and colleagues (1994) speculated that intrauterine exposure to nicotine specifically affects the outer hair cells in the ear, which influence language ability, leading to poorer performance scores on assessments that rely heavily on verbal abilities.

Nicotine may also interfere with pregnancy by affecting oviduct function, which may lead to ectopic pregnancy or problems with fertilization and implantation, or by affecting transport of essential nutrients, which could affect fetal growth (see earlier sections). For example, nicotine altered oviduct motility in rhesus monkeys (Neri and Marcus 1972), decreased oviductal blood flow in rats (Mitchell and Hammer 1985), and decreased sodium and potassium concentrations in oviductal epithelial cells of mice (Jin et al. 1998). In vitro studies report that nicotine, CO, and cyanide impair amino acid uptake in placental microvilli (Rowell and Sastry 1978; Horst and Sastry 1988; Sastry 1991). In addition, nicotine may impair amino acid transport (Fisher et al. 1984). Studies show reduced levels of several amino acids in fetal plasma, umbilical plasma, and placental villi in maternal smokers compared with those in nonsmokers (Jauniaux et al. 1999, 2001), and nicotine inhibits in vitro transport of arginine in human placentas (Pastrakuljic et al. 2000) (see "Amino Acids" later in this chapter). The reports of associations of smokeless tobacco use with several adverse pregnancy outcomes, such as LBW, preterm delivery, stillbirth, and placental morphologic changes (Agrawal et al. 1983; Gupta and Sreevidya 2004; Gupta and Subramoney 2006), suggest that a component of tobacco smoke in addition to CO, perhaps nicotine, contributes to these toxic effects.

Nicotine appears to be one of the components of tobacco smoke that has endocrine-disrupting effects, which, in turn, may affect several other reproductive and developmental endpoints. In vitro experiments show that treatment of cells with alkaloids found in tobacco smoke (namely, nicotine, cotinine, anabasine, or a combination of these substances) or with an aqueous extract of cigarette smoke resulted in a dose-dependent inhibition of progesterone production (Bódis et al. 1997; Gocze et al. 1999; Gocze and Freeman 2000; Miceli et al. 2005), whereas estradiol production showed little effect or was slightly stimulated. These findings support the effects of smoking on progesterone observed in epidemiologic studies. Cell growth and DNA content also decreased with treatment, leading the authors to suggest that smoking directly inhibits cellular progesterone synthesis through less specific cytotoxic effects on progesterone-producing cells (Gocze and Freeman 2000). Other scientists concluded that nicotine and M-nicotine, the methylated metabolite, can induce a type of luteal insufficiency by inhibiting progesterone release, probably through modulations in the prostaglandin system (Miceli et al. 2005) or inhibition of aromatase enzymes.

In animal models, nicotine acts on the HPG axis to increase secretion of adrenocorticotropic hormone from the pituitary gland, which then stimulates production of adrenocortical hormone (Matta et al. 1998). This finding is consistent with hormone profiles observed in clinical studies (see "Endocrine System" earlier in this chapter). Studies have also reported that nicotine acts directly on steroidogenesis by inhibiting various hydroxylases involved in their metabolism and on aromatases involved in converting androgens to estrogens (Barbieri et al. 1986a,b, 1987). Animal studies show that prenatal exposure to nicotine is related to decreased testosterone levels in adult male rats (Segarra and Strand 1989). They also report that cotinine, but not nicotine, inhibits testosterone synthesis in testes of neonatal rats (Sarasin et al. 2003). A small study of administration of nicotine to men and women by a transdermal patch found that the patch significantly lengthened the interpulse interval of pulsatile LH secretion in male nonsmokers but not in female nonsmokers or in smokers (Funabashi et al. 2005).

Metals

Presence in Tobacco Smoke

The particulate component of tobacco smoke contains metals. Their presence depends on the origin of the tobacco, the formulation of the cigarette product, and the method of smoking; detection depends on the method and sensitivity of the analysis. Analyses have quantified cadmium (<1.2 to 90.3 nanograms [ng] per cigarette), lead (0 to 41.4 ng/microgram [µg]), and mercury (<0.25 to 4.3 ng/µg) in mainstream smoke (Houlgate 2003). Nickel and chromium were not detectable (limit of detection = 1.8 and 1.7 ng per cigarette, respectively), although other studies have identified these metals in tobacco smoke (Smith et al. 1997; Torjussen et al. 2003). Arsenic was detectable but not quantifiable (limit of quantitation = 2.7 ng per cigarette). Studies have also detected additional metals such as zinc (U.S. Environmental Protection Agency [USEPA] 1992) and beryllium (Smith et al. 1997) in cigarette smoke. In sidestream smoke, there are estimated amounts only for cadmium, nickel, and zinc (National Research Council 1986). Very few animal toxicology studies of metals, which are reviewed here, used inhalation exposure. Clinical data are available on the bioavailability of cadmium and nickel from cigarette smoke, but researchers have studied only cadmium in connection with smoking-induced toxic effects on reproduction and development.

Exposure of reproductive organs to metals from cigarette smoke depends on (1) the uptake from the lung to the circulation, (2) the presence of transporters at blood-tissue barriers, and (3) the regulation of uptake and egress at the cellular level. In the fetus and the testes, there are physical barriers to blood flow (the placenta and the blood-testes barrier) and highly selective metal transport mechanisms (Hidiroglou and Knipfel 1984; Sylvester and Griswold 1994; Ballatori 2002; Asano et al. 2004; Gruper et al. 2005).

General Mechanisms

Metals reaching the cells and reproductive organs of the fetus can act through several common mechanisms. Transition metals, which can assume more than one valence state, can influence electron-exchange reactions and oxidative stress within cells. Metals can also substitute for the appropriate trace element at sites where nutritionally essential trace elements are important, such as active sites of enzymes, sites for regulatory elements of transcription factors, and metal-binding sites in receptor complexes or ion channels. Metals can also displace essential trace elements at storage sites, such as the bone matrix or heme molecules. Most mechanisms are posited for metals in the ionic form. Various compounds that incorporate metals may take metals from cigarette smoke before reaching the circulatory system and reproductive organs. However, the relevance of the various biologic actions of metals in smoking-related reproductive disease awaits further research. Current assessments must rely on parallels between smoking-related and metal-induced adverse reproductive effects.

Reproductive Effects of Specific Metals

The toxic effects of the heavy metals lead, mercury, and cadmium on reproduction and development are well known and widely reviewed in both clinical and animal studies (Clarkson et al. 1985; Andrews et al. 1994; Goyer and Clarkson 2001). The toxicity of mercury and lead is highly dependent on whether the metal is organic or inorganic. The most sensitive endpoint for lead and methyl mercury is the neurobehavior of children (Mendola et al. 2002). In addition, male and female reproductive effects from metal toxicity are well documented, including effects on fertility, menstrual cycle function, and adverse pregnancy outcomes (Ward et al. 1987; Golub 2005b; Hoyer 2005; Sokol 2005). At low levels of exposure that are potentially relevant to cigarette smoke, studies have not demonstrated effects on fertility in women but have associated infertility with paternal occupational exposure to lead (Sallmén et al. 2000). Literature reviews have indicated associations between prenatal exposure to lead and SAB, preterm delivery, and reduced birth weight (Andrews et al. 1994; Antilla and Sallmén 1995; Borja-Aburto et al. 1999). One study associated exposure to lead with delayed puberty (Selevan et al. 2003), but exposure to mercury had little effect on the timing of puberty (Denham et al. 2005).

An extensive number of studies on exposure to lead in male animals all report abnormalities in spermatogenesis and production of reproductive hormones. Studies of men report an inverse relationship between levels of lead in blood and levels in sperm, in addition to adverse pregnancy outcomes in their partners (Anttila and Sallmén 1995; Lin et al. 1998; Sokol 2005). The use of mercury in dental amalgams has led to studies of dentists and dental assistants, but evidence for reproductive effects in either

males or females is limited. One study found decreased fertility in female dental assistants with greater exposure to lead (Rowland et al. 1994). Sperm production is affected in animal models with exposure to some mercury doses. Finally, experimental studies of exposure to mercury in birds and fish demonstrate hormonal effects relevant to endocrine disruption (Golub 2005b).

Researchers have investigated cadmium as the agent in cigarette smoke responsible for LBW in newborns of smokers. Studies document that cadmium accumulation in the blood and placentas of pregnant smokers correlated with LBW (Kuhnert et al. 1982, 1987a). Other studies associated placental cadmium, but not blood cadmium, with LBW of newborns of smokers (Ward et al. 1987; Sikorski et al. 1988). Studies have reported inconsistent associations between exposure to cadmium and birth weight in newborns of women exposed to cigarette smoke in the workplace or by environmental contamination (Huel et al. 1981, 1984; Bonithon-Kopp et al. 1986; Berlin et al. 1992; Loiacono et al. 1992; Fréry et al. 1993; Nishijo et al. 2002). LBW was a significant finding in some studies that administered cadmium, usually as cadmium chloride, to rats and mice by injection, inhalation, or orally in food and drinking water (Cal/EPA 1996). Many of these studies found delayed ossification, another indicator of developmental delay. At higher doses, fetal viability was affected.

One proposed mechanism of the effect of cadmium on birth weight is interference with the placental transfer of the essential trace elements zinc and copper (Sowa et al. 1982; Steibert et al. 1984; Sasser et al. 1985; Sowa and Steibert 1985; Kuhnert et al. 1987a; Chmielnicka and Sowa 1996). Researchers hypothesize that cadmium also interferes with progesterone production in the placenta (Jolibois et al. 1999a,b; Piasek et al. 2001; Kawai et al. 2002; Henson and Chedrese 2004). Studies have found that cadmium acts as an estrogenic agent. Initially, in vitro studies demonstrated that cadmium binds to a specific site on the estrogen receptor and mimics estradiol-induced gene transcription (Garcia-Morales et al. 1994; Choe et al. 2003; Johnson et al. 2003b). Other studies found that the effects of in vivo administration of cadmium on the uterus and mammary glands could be blocked by antiestrogenic agents (Johnson et al. 2003b). Animal studies show that cadmium accumulates in ovaries, that there is a loss of ovarian follicles, and that steroid production declines (Hoyer 2005). Elevated levels of cadmium in the follicular fluid of smokers (Zenzes et al. 1995) were not associated with impaired fertility (Drbohlav et al. 1998; Younglai et al. 2002). Studies have also associated smoking with elevated cadmium levels in seminal fluid. At least one study noted a negative correlation with cadmium levels and semen quality, but another found no correlation (Saaranen et al. 1989; Chia et al. 1994). Animal studies have shown some negative effects on spermatogenesis.

Chromium, nickel, and zinc are essential human dietary nutrients (Institute of Medicine 2000). They are present in tobacco and have been studied for their toxic effects on reproduction and development (Keen 1996; Golub 2005a). Almost all information on toxicity comes from laboratory animal studies, and very little is known about exposure through inhalation. Exposure to chromium (as Cr^{+6}) produced embryo and fetal loss, growth restrictions, and malformations when administered in drinking water to mice at a minimum dose of 60 mg/kg per day (Trivedi et al. 1989; Junaid et al. 1995, 1996). Studies show that chromium is a testicular and ovarian toxicant that also affects fertility when administered in drinking water to rodents (Saxena et al. 1990; Zahid et al. 1990; Murthy et al. 1991, 1996; Bataineh et al. 1997). Nickel is teratogenic in mice and rats when it is injected (Lu et al. 1979; Mas et al. 1985). When nickel was administered over a long period in drinking water, perinatal mortality was a common finding (Smith et al. 1993). Studies have also demonstrated the testicular toxicity of nickel that was injected intraperitoneally or administered orally to rodents, but ovarian toxicity and male fertility were not studied (Kakela et al. 1999; Doreswamy et al. 2004). Long-term studies that administered zinc to male and female rodents found no effects on fertility (Ogden et al. 2002; Johnson et al. 2003a).

Growing evidence suggests adverse effects on human pregnancy outcomes (e.g., stillbirth, SAB, and LBW) from exposure to arsenic in drinking water (Hopenhayn-Rich et al. 2000; Ahmad et al. 2001; Hopenhayn et al. 2003; Yang et al. 2003). Animal studies demonstrate toxic effects on ovaries and testicles from arsenic in drinking water (Chattopadhyay et al. 1999, 2001; Pant et al. 2001), and earlier literature discusses arsenic teratogenesis (Golub et al. 1998). These studies support further efforts to assess the bioavailability of arsenic from cigarette smoke.

Most of these metals, such as lead, cadmium, mercury and mercury compounds, nickel carbonyl, and inorganic oxides of arsenic, are listed as "known by the state to cause reproductive toxicity" under California's Proposition 65 program, affecting a variety of endpoints. (Information supporting the listings can be found at the agency's web site [http://www.oehha.ca.gov].) Thus, some or all of these compounds may contribute to the adverse effects of smoking on reproduction, but direct links in smokers have not been established.

Polycyclic Aromatic Hydrocarbons

Formation and Toxicity

PAHs are ubiquitous products of the partial combustion of carbon-containing materials, and they appear as important components of environmental pollution. Although some sources are natural, the predominant sources of PAHs found in the air are usually anthropogenic. Examples include vehicle exhausts, products from industrial processes, and emissions from fossil fuel power plants (International Agency for Research on Cancer [IARC] 1983), as well as tobacco smoke (IARC 1986, 2004; USEPA 1992). The usual definition of a PAH specifies hydrocarbons with no heteroatom substitutents or ring members that include at least two or, according to some authors, three concatenated aromatic (usually benzene-like) rings. The two-ring members of the class, primarily naphthalenes, are included within the definition used in EPA's identification of "polycyclic organic material" as a hazardous air pollutant. These two-ring members are abundant in tobacco smoke and show some chemical and toxicologic differences from other PAHs. This discussion primarily addresses the effects of PAHs with three or more rings, while also noting some specific effects of naphthalenes. The five-ring compound benzo[a]pyrene (B[a]P) is one of the most extensively studied PAHs. In addition to carcinogenesis, studies have reported direct fetotoxic and teratogenic effects associated with PAHs, as well as adverse effects on reproduction. Other notable effects include immunotoxicity, endocrine effects, and toxic effects on the lungs. Key studies are summarized in Table 8.12, and the results are discussed in detail here.

The toxic effects and dose-response relationships described for specific PAHs are primarily based on experiments on toxic effects in animals, which are the focus of this summary. Several corresponding effects in humans result from exposure to pollutant mixtures containing PAHs, such as diesel exhaust. Human exposure to PAHs generally involves mixtures that are ill defined and poorly quantified, so it is difficult to separate the effects of PAHs from those of other components of the mixtures.

Most of the toxic endpoints described for PAHs appear to result from the generation of reactive intermediate agents by metabolism, followed by reactions of these intermediates (e.g., as B[a]P 7,8,9,10-dihydrodiol) with the cellular components, particularly DNA, in both adult and fetal tissues (Kleihues et al. 1980; Bolognesi et al. 1985; Shugart and Matsunami 1985). Unless repaired, the adducts that are produced give rise to mutations that

Table 8.12   Reproductive and developmental effects of polycyclic aromatic hydrocarbons (PAHs), by endpoint

Study	Design: animal model or population	Endpoint
Krarup 1969	Direct application of 9:0-dimethyl-1:2-benzanthrene to mouse ovary	Toxic effects to reproductive system in adults
Mattison and Thorgeirsson 1979	PAH treatment (80 mg/kg) of juvenile mice (4–6 weeks old): C57BL/6N (AHH inducible) and DBA/2N (AHH noninducible)	Toxic effects to reproductive system in adults
Shum et al. 1979	C57BL/6 (AHH responsive) or AKR (nonresponsive) mice exposed to B[a]P (50–300 mg/kg intraperitoneally) at day 7, 10, or 12 of gestation	Teratogenicity

Mackenzie and Angevine 1981	Mice exposed prenatally to B[a]P (10, 40, or 160 mg/kg per day) on days 7–16 of gestation
	Fertility study
	  Beginning at 7 weeks of age, each F_1 male was placed with 10 untreated females for 25 days
	  Beginning at 6 weeks of age, each F_1 female was cohabitated continuously with an untreated male for 6 months
	Fertility index = females pregnant/females exposed to males × 100
		Birth weight
		
		Adult reproductive function after prenatal exposure

Mattison and Nightingale 1982	Mice (AHH responsive or nonresponsive) exposed to B[a]P (100 mg/kg intraperitoneally)	Toxic effects to reproductive system in adults
Urso and Gengozian 1982; Urso and Johnson 1988; Urso et al. 1992	Series of experiments in mice: single exposure to B[a]P during pregnancy (150 mg/kg intraperitoneally)	Developmental immunotoxicity Immune response measure: degree of anti–sheep erythrocyte plaque-forming response, mixed lymphocyte response of cultured lymphocytes, measures of T-cell function

Findings	Comments
• Oocyte destruction and ovarian tumorigenesis	A typical effect reported early, although the route of application is artificial
• Number of primordial oocytes severely depleted in ovaries of mice exposed to carcinogenic PAHs (B[a]P, 3-methylcholanthrene, 7,12-dimethylbenz[a]anthracene, but not by a noncarcinogenic PAH or an AHH inducer (pyrene, β-naphthoflavone) • PAHs eventually resulted in complete destruction of oocytes in both strains, but effect is faster in AHH inducible strain	Destruction of oocytes is related to inducibility of AHH; researchers assumed in this case that activation of the enzyme led to generation of more reactive metabolites, which caused greater oocyte destruction: this is supported by the inactivity of β-naphthoflavone, an AHH inducer not metabolized to reactive intermediates; however, other AH receptor actions may also be involved
• In utero toxicity and teratogenicity: stillbirths, resorptions, malformations increased in exposed mice • Effects approximately 2–3 times as severe in C57BL/6 mice, which are responsive to AHH induction at all exposure times • B[a]P (200 mg/kg intraperitoneally)	
• Pup weights significantly reduced compared with those for controls at all doses (p <0.01) at 20 and 42 days; decreasing trend in pup weight with dose at day 4 • Exposed mice of both sexes as adults showed loss of fertility in controlled breeding studies with untreated partners • Mice given B[a]P at 40 or 160 mg/kg per day essentially infertile (p <0.01) with histologic abnormalities of gonads • Testes of males exposed to B[a]P at 40 mg/kg showed severe atrophy and aspermic seminiferous tubules • Ovaries of exposed females hypoplastic or atrophied with few follicles or corpora lutea • Mean litter size reduced (p <0.01) with treatment of females but not with treatment of males	
• 30% oocyte destruction of primordial oocytes	Effect was not linked to AHH induction in this experiment
• Increases in Lyt2 cells in fetal liver • Often profound immunosuppression in neonatal offspring and later in life; postnatal thymic and splenic suppression • Approximately 50% reduction in plaque-forming cells in sheep erythrocyte assay in 1-week-old offspring after mid- or late-gestational treatment with 150 μg of B[a]P • Changes in maternal immune system, which may affect maintenance of pregnancy: thymic suppression, including reduction in several classes of T lymphocytes and inhibition of mixed lymphocyte response	

Table 8.12   Continued

Study	Design: animal model or population	Endpoint
Holladay and Smith 1994	B6C3F$_1$ mice exposed to B[a]P (maternal dose of 50, 100, or 150 mg/kg/day) on days 13–17 of gestation	Developmental immunotoxicity
		Offspring examined for T-cell and fetal liver cell markers on gestational day 18
Lummus and Henningsen 1995	BALB/c mice exposed to B[a]P in utero: single dose of 150 mg/kg of B[a]P on days 11–13 of gestation	Developmental immunotoxicity
Nicol et al. 1995	Exposure to B[a]P in utero Normal mice and mice deficient in the *P53* tumor suppressor gene	Teratogenicity
Perera et al. 1998	Epidemiologic exposure to PAHs by ambient air pollution in Poland 70 newborns from Krakow (industrialized) and 90 from Limanowa (rural but coal used for home heating) PAH-DNA adducts in leukocytes and plasma cotinine measured in umbilical cord blood	Birth weight and developmental delay

Findings	Comments
• Severe depletion of T cells in both thymus and liver • Changes in proportions of surface antigens (CD4, CD8, and heat stable) in isolated thymocytes • Reduction in total cellularity of thymus and liver	Researchers suggested that these changes indicated impaired maturation in surviving thymocytes consistent with long-term immunosuppression seen in mice exposed to B[*a*]P in utero
• Numbers of T cells in fetal liver severely reduced compared with those for untreated controls; severe atrophy of fetal thymus • Neonates showed decreased overall thymic cells and increases in some splenic cells • 6-week-old juvenile mice showed recovery of total T cells to control levels in spleen and thymus but depletion of thymic cells bearing fetal liver T-cell antigen	Changes in relative proportions of different types of T cells, distinguished by various surface antigens, result in disturbance of immune system development; some apparently B[*a*]P-resistant cell types repopulate depleted lymphoid organs, but overall function of the immune system is changed and remains depressed
• Malformations and increased rate of fetal death • Embryotoxicity and teratogenicity 2- to 4-fold higher in *P53*-deficient mice than in controls	The *P53* gene, which is important in regulation of DNA repair and apoptosis, has a significant embryo-protective effect in the B[*a*]P-exposed fetus

• In newborns with high (>median) versus low (≤median) levels of PAH-DNA adducts:
  – Mean birth weight reduced by 147 g (p <0.05)
  – Birth length reduced by 1.1 cm (p <0.02)
  – Head circumference reduced by 0.9 cm (p <0.001)
• Cotinine also significantly and inversely associated with low birth weight and reduced length	

Table 8.12   Continued

Study	Design: animal model or population	Endpoint
Dejmek et al. 2000	Epidemiologic exposure to PAHs and PM by ambient pollution in Czech Republic 3,349 births in Teplice and 1,505 in Prachatice between April 1994 and March 1998 Continuous measurement of PAH, PM_{10}, and $PM_{2.5}$ AOR for IUGR correlated monthly with PAH and PM pollution levels	Birth weight and developmental delay
Matikainen et al. 2001	Young mice, oocytes, and human ovarian tissue explants exposed to 7,12-dimethylbenz[*a*]anthracene	Toxic effects to reproductive system in adults

Note: **AH** = aryl hydrocarbon; **AHH** = aryl hydrocarbon hydroxylase; **AOR** = adjusted odds ratio; **B[*a*]P** = benzo[*a*]pyrene; **CI** = confidence interval; **cm** = centimeters; **g** = grams; **IUGR** = intrauterine growth retardation, where birth weight is <10th percentile by gender and gestational week; **mg/kg** = milligrams per kilogram; **ng** = nanograms; **ORs** = odds ratios; **PM** = particulate material; **PM_{10}** = particulate matter in which particles are ≤10 micrometers; **$PM_{2.5}$** = particulate matter in which particles are ≤2.5 micrometers; **µg** = micrograms.

Findings	Comments
• AORs for IUGR show significant increases with levels of PAH at both locations early in pregnancy during first month of gestation; AOR for medium exposure = 1.63 (95% CI = 0.87–3.06) and for high exposure, 2.39) (95% CI = 1.01–5.65) • In Prachatice, relationship was more noticeable (AOR 2.44 [95% CI, 0.6–9.83]) in subset closer to pollutant source • Pollution in Teplice high in both PM and PAH, but in Prachatice, high in PAH and generally lower in PM • IUGR was observed in 9.6% of pregnancies in Teplice and 8.2% in Prachatice	Because the ratio of PM and PAH varied between locations and with time, the continuous model was able to show that the risk of IUGR increased with level of PAH exposure, rather than with PM, and resulted from an early developmental defect

Risk of IUGR with level of exposure to pollutant in first month

Pollutant/ location	Comparison by exposure	AOR	95% CI
PM_{10}			
Teplice	Medium : low	1.44	1.03–2.02
	High : low	2.14	1.42–3.23
Prachatice	Medium : low	2.11	1.03–4.33
	High : low	1.09	0.49–2.46
PAH			
Teplice	Medium : low	1.59	1.06–2.39
	High : low	2.15	1.27–3.63
Prachatice	Medium : low	1.49	0.81–2.73
	High : low	1.26	0.60–2.63

Increase in AOR for IUGR for each 10 µg of PM_{10} or 10 ng of PAH during first month*

Pollutant/ location	AOR	95% CI
PM_{10}		
Teplice	1.19	1.06–1.33
Prachatice	1.04	0.86–1.27
PAH		
Teplice	1.22	1.07–1.39
Prachatice	1.17	0.92–1.89

*ORs adjusted for parity, maternal age and height, prepregnancy weight, education, marital status, season, year of study, and maternal smoking per month

• Oocyte destruction and ovarian failure; mechanism involves enhancement of apoptosis	Effect is dependent on the *BAX* promoter gene and the AH receptor

are then followed by cytotoxicity and/or cancer and possibly teratogenicity (Wells and Winn 1996). Both phase I (activation) enzymes and phase II (detoxification and conjugation) enzymes are important in the metabolism and toxicity of PAHs, and both are inducible by PAHs. The structural genes determining the stability and activity of the enzymes and the regulatory genes controlling the expression of the enzymes, show polymorphisms in both humans and animals. One of these enzymes is aryl hydrocarbon hydroxylase (AHH), which is influenced by induction of cytochrome P-450 activity. Animals are described as genetically "responsive" when AHH activity is induced by exposure to PAHs and to other activators of the AH receptor. There are also important changes in the levels and types of enzymes expressed at different developmental stages, particularly during the latter part of fetal development and the immediate postnatal period (Cresteil et al. 1986). Researchers have used the resulting variations in metabolic capabilities of the fetus and young animal to investigate the mechanisms of and differential susceptibility to PAH toxicity.

Toxic Effects on Reproduction

Investigators have known for some time that exposure of the adult female rodent to PAHs damages the resting ovarian follicle complexes, leading to oocyte destruction (Krarup 1969; Mattison and Thorgeirsson 1979; Mattison and Nightingale 1982) (Table 8.12). Studies have revealed similar effects in women, primarily as premature reproductive senescence (menopause), after exposure to mixed pollutants. As noted previously, premature senescence is associated with smoking (Jick et al. 1977; USDHHS 1980) (see "Menstrual Function, Menarche, and Menopause" earlier in this chapter).

Mattison and Nightingale (1982) reported a 30-percent destruction of primordial oocytes in adult mice exposed to a single dose of B[a]P. After comparing susceptibility to this effect in different strains of mice that were responsive or unresponsive to inducers of cytochrome P-450 enzymes, these researchers suggested that the determining factor for oocyte destruction involves the ratio of phase II (detoxifying) to phase I (activating) enzyme activities. Later investigations have shown the involvement of mechanisms that control apoptosis in oocyte destruction (e.g., Matikainen et al. 2001). The researchers described three sets of studies using treatment with 7,12-dimethylbenz[a]anthracene in young mice, isolated oocytes, or xenografts of human ovary tissue. They found that both a functional AH receptor and a functional *BAX* promoter gene were necessary for oocyte destruction in mice. Moreover, this apoptosis control system was induced in oocytes by the activation of

the aryl-hydrocarbon-responsive AH receptor. This finding provides an alternative direct route for triggering the cytotoxic response to PAHs, which is in contrast to the earlier proposal involving reactive PAH metabolites.

Toxic Effects on Development

Teratogenicity. Many fetotoxins, including PAHs, produce a spectrum of effects: anatomic and functional teratogenesis; prenatal, perinatal, and postnatal mortality; growth retardation; and developmental delay. To observe the combination of these outcomes in a particular experiment may depend on dose level and timing, the test species used, and other experimental conditions. The most commonly observed effects of PAHs in animal studies are growth retardation and fetal mortality, but a few experiments have demonstrated anatomic teratogenic effects. The number of surviving offspring is reduced in these experiments, so it appears that the dose range over which surviving, but malformed, offspring are produced is narrow.

Intraperitoneal B[a]P given to mice at day 7 or 10 of gestation causes toxic effects in utero (e.g., a reduction in the number of surviving offspring) and teratogenicity (Table 8.12) (Shum et al. 1979). The severity of the effect was correlated with the ability of the fetus and the maternal systems to metabolize B[a]P. A greater impact on prenatal and postnatal mortality was noted in C57BL/6 mice, which are responsive to induction of AHH, than in unresponsive AKR inbred mice. This finding suggests a role for reactive intermediate agents of PAHs. Malformations observed only in the responsive mice included clubfoot, hemangioendothelioma, cleft palate, and other anomalies of the skeleton and soft tissues.

Nicol and colleagues (1995) also observed malformations and an increased rate of fetal death after in utero exposure to B[a]P. The embryotoxicity and teratogenicity were twofold-to-fourfold higher in mice deficient in the *P53* tumor-suppressor gene than in the controls with the normal *P53* gene. The *P53* gene, which is important in the regulation of DNA repair and apoptosis, thus has a significant embryoprotective effect in the fetus exposed to B[a]P, which is also characteristic in relation to other DNA-damaging teratogens such as phenytoin (Nicol et al. 1995; Wells and Winn 1996).

Prenatal impacts on adult reproductive function. Animal studies have demonstrated similar but more drastic reproductive effects in both males and females exposed to PAHs in utero rather than as adults. As adults, offspring exposed to B[a]P in utero showed a loss of fertility in controlled breeding studies with untreated partners (Table 8.12). High doses of B[a]P resulted in complete infertility and histologic abnormalities of the gonads

(Mackenzie and Angevine 1981). Although most observations of reduced fertility in adults focused on females, this experiment also showed a clear reduction in fertility among the treated F_1 males. Examination of the testes showed severely atrophied and essentially aspermic seminiferous tubules. The ovaries of females were hypoplastic and had very few follicles or corpora lutea. Most of the animals exposed to the high doses had no identifiable ovaries or only remnants of ovarian tissue.

Kristensen and colleagues (1995) also reported reductions in fertility among female NMRI mice after exposure in utero to 10 mg of B[*a*]P/kg per day given orally. Watanabe (2005) reported decreases in the number of spermatozoa and Sertoli cells in the testes of adult rats exposed in utero to diesel exhaust.

Investigations of the mechanism of oocyte depletion have emphasized the importance of the AH receptor and *BAX* activation in the induction of apoptotic destruction of oocytes and in the natural process that reduces the initial fetal complement of primordial oocytes early in their development to the lower levels that characterize the adult female. These findings do not necessarily exclude a separate role for cytotoxic effects from DNA damage by reactive PAH metabolites in the destruction of germ cells. The mechanisms involved in the induction of impaired sperm quality and male infertility after adult or fetal exposure to PAHs are less extensively studied. Therefore, it is unclear whether other factors and/or mechanisms apply.

Effects on birth weight and developmental delay. Clinical studies of exposure to PAH-containing mixtures of pollutants in utero have reported reductions in birth weight, apparently attributable to both premature birth and IUGR, as well as variations in other size measures, such as length and head circumference at birth. More recent studies have used correlations with PAH-derived DNA adducts and the differential impact of pollution sources with high versus low PAH levels to more clearly establish the role of PAHs on LBW.

Perera and colleagues (1998) studied developmental effects of fetal exposure to PAHs through ambient pollution from burning coal in Poland (Table 8.12). Plasma cotinine and PAH-DNA adducts in leukocytes were measured in umbilical cord blood as dosimeters of cigarette smoke and transplacental PAH, respectively. Newborns whose levels of PAH-DNA adducts were above the median (3.85 per 10^8 nucleotides) had a significantly decreased birth weight, length, and head circumference. Cotinine was also significantly and inversely associated with birth weight and length. Similarly, Dejmek and colleagues (2000) studied birth outcomes in relation to air pollution in two towns in the Czech Republic, one industrialized (Teplice) and one rural (Prachatice) (Table 8.12). The

authors defined IUGR as a birth weight below the 10th percentile by gender and gestational week. In Teplice, IUGR was observed in 9.6 percent of pregnancies, while at Prachatice, 8.2 percent were affected. There was a significant association of IUGR with exposure to air pollution, particularly to PAHs rather than to particulate matter (Table 8.12). The association between PAH exposure and IUGR was only significant during the first month of gestation. The AOR was 1.63 (95 percent CI, 0.87–3.06) for a medium exposure and 2.39 (95 percent CI, 1.01–5.65) for a high exposure. Researchers interpreted these findings as indications that the induction of IUGR by a PAH exposure resulted from an early developmental effect.

Despite the exposures to mixed pollutants, these studies provide specific correlations of impacts on birth weight and development with PAH exposure either through a determination of specific DNA adducts or on the basis of differential exposures to PAHs and other pollutants. Extensive evidence from other studies shows an impact of air pollution on birth weight and other pregnancy outcomes (Šrám et al. 2005), supporting the plausibility of a causal relationship between LBW and exposure to PAHs, in spite of the difficulties in assigning causality to specific compounds within mixtures.

Animal studies also show developmental delay and LBW after in utero exposure to pure PAHs, thus strengthening the epidemiologic data. MacKenzie and Angevine (1981) reported statistically significant reductions in weights of exposed pups compared with those of controls for all in utero doses of B[*a*]P, as well as evidence of a progressive dose response. Similarly, Bui and colleagues (1986) observed reductions in fetal weight in a mechanistic study that compared the effects of B[*a*]P with those of methadone, another known fetotoxicant. These authors also observed reductions in uterine weight among the pregnant dams, which suggest that B[*a*]P treatment affects both the fetus and the maternal system.

Developmental Immunotoxicity

PAH exposures have a variety of effects on the immune system. Extensive literature describes the effects of exposure to pollutant mixtures containing PAHs in adult humans. Researchers have demonstrated interest in performing studies on the initiation and exacerbation of asthma and other allergic respiratory conditions from exposure to diesel exhaust, often in combination with other allergens (Riedl and Diaz-Sanchez 2005). Findings suggest that these exposures can potentiate allergic reactions to antigens such as pollen. Exposure early in life may result in a shift in T-cell activity patterns toward a more atopic profile. Studies have also linked these effects to exposures to other pollutant mixtures that contain PAHs, including tobacco smoke (NCI 1999). Literature reviews also describe mechanistic studies of similar processes in animals. As noted earlier, the presence of PAHs in these pollutant mixtures raises the likelihood that these substances are among the causative agents. However, it is not generally possible to separate the PAH effects from those of other components in the mixture. Synergistic interactions among these components may also be a significant factor.

In contrast to the stimulatory or adjuvant effects at comparatively low exposure levels, higher doses of PAHs in humans have immunosuppressive effects (Karakaya et al. 2004). Similar findings and investigations of the mechanisms involved have been extensively described in adult animals (Table 8.12). The primary effects noted after fetal and neonatal exposures involved immunosuppression, which is often profound and persistent (Urso and Gengozian 1982; Urso and Johnson 1988; Urso et al. 1992), and includes both selective and overall reductions in various cellular components of the immune system, particularly T cells (Holladay and Smith 1994; Lummus and Henningsen 1995). Holladay and Luster (1996) have reviewed the effects of B[a]P on T-cell development and the long-term consequences on the development of the immune system. Although development of the immune system begins in utero, important structural and functional changes occur after birth. In view of this continuing development, enhanced sensitivity to exposures to immunotoxicants both during gestation and infancy is to be expected.

Toxic Effects of Naphthalene

Studies have not widely reported or characterized naphthalene as a cause of toxic effects on reproduction and fetotoxic or teratogenic effects. However, Plasterer and colleagues (1985) did report a slight reduction in the number of pups per litter, as well as toxic effects in the mother after high oral doses of naphthalene, that is, the lethal dose for 50 percent of the population (LD_{50}). However, the reports of preferential toxic effects in the neonate or infant described here are examples of toxic effects on postnatal development.

Researchers have reported hemolysis in infants exposed to very high doses of naphthalene (Siegel and Wason 1986). This effect appears to be caused by the metabolites (1- and 2-naphthol and 1- and 2-naphthoquinones) that produce methemoglobinemia. Also, naphthalene damaged both ciliated and Clara cells of the bronchiolar epithelium in mice (Plopper 1992a,b; Van Winkle et al. 1995). Neonatal mice were more sensitive to this damage than were adult mice (Fanucchi et al. 1997). Although the

experiment involved intraperitoneal dosing, the effects appear to depend on the metabolism of naphthalene in the target tissues and are therefore probably independent of the route of administration.

Endocrine Disruption

Many investigators have reported that PAHs disrupt reproductive and developmental events and other physiological processes under endocrine control. Some of these effects appear to reflect direct action on hormones and their receptors as opposed to the cytotoxic action of reactive metabolites noted earlier. The nuclear AH receptor is responsible for regulating several cytochrome P-450 isoenzymes and triggering their induction in the presence of various xenobiotics, including PAHs, chlorinated dioxins, and coplanar polychlorinated biphenyls. This receptor also appears to have a range of other functions, including the modulation and proliferation of cell growth. The role of this receptor in the regulation of apoptosis, which includes the *BAX* gene product, has already been noted in the context of oocyte loss and may be involved in other processes in which apoptosis occurs.

The AH receptor also appears to interact with and in some cases control the expression of other nuclear receptors. B[a]P reduces the expression of receptors for the epidermal growth factor and the in vitro secretion of chorionic gonadotropin by human placental cells (Zhang et al. 1995). PAHs reportedly have antiestrogenic effects. Chaloupka and colleagues (1992) used MCF-7 human breast cancer cells to investigate in vitro the inhibition by 3-methylcholanthrene (a synthetic PAH) of estradiol-stimulated cell growth. Subsequently, Navas and Segner (2000) described antiestrogenic effects of various PAHs on synthesis of vitellogenin in cultured hepatocytes of rainbow trout by 17-β-estradiol. In both systems, the binding of the PAH to the AH receptor appears to be the event that triggers a range of cellular responses, including a reduced expression of the estrogen receptor.

Other Compounds

Tobacco smoke contains thousands of compounds, some of which have also been identified as known or suspected reproductive toxicants, in addition to the compounds already described here in detail. Examples include toluene, carbon disulfide, dichlorodiphenyltrichloroethane, styrene, benzene, and vinyl chloride.

Other compounds that are less well studied may also influence reproductive outcomes. As noted earlier in this chapter (see "Tubal Function"), cigarette smoke impairs oviductal functioning (Knoll and Talbot 1998) and inhibits the growth of the chick chorioallantoic membrane (CAM)

(Melkonian et al. 2000, 2002). To identify which chemicals in tobacco smoke are responsible for these toxic effects, solutions of mainstream smoke were fractionated and the eluates were screened for inhibitory activity in the CAM and oviductal assays. The CAM assay measures CAM and embryonic growth, and the oviductal assays measure ciliary beat frequency, oocyte pickup rate, and rate of smooth muscle contraction. The chemicals in each eluate that retained 80 percent or more of the inhibitory activity were identified by gas chromatography and mass spectrometry. This approach identified pyridine, pyrazine, phenol, indole, and quinoline derivatives as the major groups of inhibitory compounds (Ji et al. 2002; Melkonian et al. 2003; Riveles et al. 2003, 2004, 2005). Members of each group were highly effective in both the CAM and oviductal assays that measure diverse biologic processes. In every group, some chemicals were inhibitory at nanodoses and picomolar doses, and indole was inhibitory in the oviductal assays at femtomolar doses. In general, methyl and ethyl substitutions increased the toxicity of these compounds. Some of the inhibitory chemicals (e.g., 3-ethylpyridine and pyrazine) are on the Flavor and Extract Manufacturer's Association's Generally Recognized as Safe list and the "Everything" Added to Food in the United States list from the U.S. Food and Drug Administration (FDA); some are added to cigarettes to enhance flavor.

Other Molecular Mechanisms

In addition to the molecular mechanisms of specific toxins outlined here, researchers have conducted general investigations of smoking in relation to pathways for molecular mechanisms.

Genetic Damage to Sperm

Concern exists that exposures to toxins such as those in cigarette smoke may cause damage to sperm DNA that could be transmitted to offspring (Chapin et al. 2004). This important question of male-mediated toxic effects on development can now be addressed directly through use of tools of molecular genetics that detect and measure chromosomal changes and DNA damage in ejaculated sperm cells (Perreault et al. 2003). Studies have reported significant increases in sperm DNA and chromatin damage, including oxidative DNA damage, in smokers compared with nonsmokers from both infertility clinic and nonclinic populations (Fraga et al. 1996; Shen et al. 1997); strand breaks (Sun et al. 1997; Potts et al. 1999); native DNA stainability (Sofikitis et al. 1995; Spanò et al. 1998); denaturation of labile sites (Potts et al. 1999); DNA adducts (Zenzes et al. 1999a,b; Horak et al. 2003);

and apoptosis (Belcheva et al. 2004). Only a few studies did not find statistically significant differences related to exposure to cigarette smoke. One of these studies focused on DNA strand breaks (Sergerie et al. 2000) and another on oxidative DNA damage (Loft et al. 2003). Both studies were conducted in nonclinical populations.

Researchers have determined a statistically significant trend across published studies (p <0.001) for sperm aneuploidy associated with smoking (Robbins et al. 2005). Sperm carrying aberrant chromosomes are capable of fertilizing eggs that result in aneuploid offspring. For example, the father contributes the extra Y chromosome in 100 percent of XYY offspring, the extra chromosome in approximately 30 to 50 percent of XXY offspring with Klinefelter syndrome, and in up to an estimated 80 percent of the offspring with missing X in Turner's syndrome (Hassold 1998; Martínez-Pasarell et al. 1999). In addition to congenital anomalies, damage to genetic material could affect sperm quality and could be manifested as infertility or very early pregnancy loss if the damage is incompatible with survival.

Nutrient Deficiencies

Micronutrients

Deficiencies of micronutrients may contribute to adverse pregnancy outcomes, and smoking could act through this relationship. As previously mentioned, a decrease in the amount of collagen III likely leads to a weakening of the tensile strength of amniotic membranes, which could increase the risk of PPROM. Vitamin C is required for collagen formation in amnion epithelial cells, and studies have noted reduced vitamin C in women with PPROM (Wideman et al. 1964; Casanueva et al. 1993). Studies consistently show that plasma vitamin C levels are lower in smokers than in nonsmokers, a finding that appears to be attributable to a lower intake as well as increased utilization in the body (Preston 1991; Lykkesfeldt et al. 2000; Cogswell et al. 2003). Vitamin C levels in the amniotic fluid of smokers are also lower than those in nonsmokers (Barrett et al. 1991). Vitamin C is important for normal immune functioning. Deficiencies of vitamin C are associated with impaired immunocompetence, reduced counts of polymorphonuclear leukocytes, phagocytosis, and depressed cell-mediated immunity (Long and Santos 1999). A vitamin C deficiency in smokers could contribute to adverse pregnancy outcomes by impairing maternal immune responses to genital tract infections. Data on other antioxidant levels in smokers are conflicting (Cogswell et al. 2003).

Zinc deficiency may also play a causal role in PPROM and other adverse outcomes. Zinc is necessary for DNA synthesis, transcription, and translation, as well as cell division and cell growth (Fisher 1975; Vallee and Falchuk 1993; Prasad 1996). Low zinc levels result in impaired immune function (Fraker and King 2004), increased susceptibility to infectious diseases (Fischer Walker and Black 2004), and cell death (Fraker 2005). Researchers have found reduced serum and amniotic fluid levels of zinc in pregnant women with PPROM (Anderson 1979; Kiilholma et al. 1984). A prospective study of pregnant women associated a low zinc intake with a threefold increase in PPROM (Scholl et al. 1993). Some data suggest that smokers are more likely to experience a zinc deficiency than are nonsmokers (Cogswell et al. 2003). Levels of maternal dietary zinc, plasma zinc, and zinc in red blood cells are similar in smokers and nonsmokers close to the time of delivery. However, shortly after delivery, zinc levels in cord blood and polymorphonuclear cells, which may be a more sensitive indicator of zinc depletion, were lower in smokers than in nonsmokers (Simmer and Thompson 1985; Kuhnert et al. 1987b). Cadmium, which accumulates in the placenta and binds to zinc, may contribute to a local zinc deficiency in smokers (Kuhnert et al. 1987a,b, 1988a,b; Preston 1991).

Amino Acids

In addition to a supply of nutrients delivered to the fetus through the uteroplacental circulation, fetal growth depends on nutrient transport across the syncytiotrophoblast. Because the placenta is impermeable to most proteins, almost all of the fetal proteins are synthesized by the fetus from amino acids supplied by the mother. Amino acids from the mother's blood are taken up by the active transport of placental trophoblasts and then diffused into the umbilical venous blood. There is accumulating evidence that abnormalities in amino acid transport across the placenta can contribute to impaired fetal growth (Pastrakuljic et al. 1999). In addition, many studies suggest that maternal smoking adversely affects this transport, and this effect may be one mechanism by which smoking restricts fetal growth. Levels of several amino acids in fetal plasma, umbilical plasma, and placental villi are lower in smokers than in nonsmokers (Jauniaux et al. 1999, 2001) (see "Carbon Monoxide" and "Nicotine" earlier in this chapter). Additional research is needed to determine more precisely how the results of the in vivo and in vitro studies may be related to adverse pregnancy outcomes among maternal smokers.

Nitric Oxide Activity

Researchers have also studied the effects of smoking on NO activity. Endothelial NO is a potent vasodilator synthesized by NO synthase in vascular endothelial cells (ENOS) (Moncada and Higgs 1993). NO regulates blood pressure by its effects on vascular resistance. Evidence suggests that a decrease in the release of basal NO may predispose a person to hypertension, vasospasm, and thrombosis, whereas elevated levels may be associated with shock (Moncada and Higgs 1993; Änggård 1994; Cooke and Dzau 1997; Oemar et al. 1998). In pregnancy, NO is also present in placental villi and is believed to play an important role in the vasodilatory response of the maternal, uteroplacental, and fetoplacental circulatory systems (Myatt et al. 1991, 1992; Poston et al. 1995). Reductions of NO activity in placental villi from pregnancies with preeclampsia and IUGR suggest a role for NO in pregnancy complications (Sooranna et al. 1995). In vitro research indicates that the mRNA and the protein expression of ENOS are decreased in endothelial cells from preeclamptic pregnancies (Wang et al. 2004).

Studies have associated maternal smoking with a dose-dependent decrease in endothelial-dependent vessel dilation (Lekakis et al. 1998; Poredoš et al. 1999) and with an inhibition of ENOS activity, depending on the *ENOS* genotype (Wang et al. 2000b). Researchers have reported that endothelial cells from the umbilical cords of infants born to smokers had a 40-percent reduction in ENOS activity and a 32-percent reduction in ENOS levels compared with those in cells from infants born to nonsmokers. Furthermore, the ENOS activity level was associated with the number of cigarettes smoked per day (Andersen et al. 2004). The effects of maternal smoking on ENOS activity could lead to lower NO levels, resulting in a loss of dilatory capacity and contributing to IUGR.

Smoking and Maternal and Neonatal Genetic Polymorphisms

Investigators have reported differences in the human metabolism of toxic constituents in tobacco smoke (Benowitz et al. 1999; Lee et al. 2000; Yang et al. 2001). These metabolic differences may reflect a differential induction of toxins and drug-metabolizing enzymes, such as phase I cytochrome P-450; phase II glutathione-*S*-transferase (GST); NAT1 and 2; placental alkaline phospholipase; lysyl oxidase; the platelet-activating factor acetylhydrolase; TGFα; TGFβ3; and microsomal epoxide hydrolase. Genetic polymorphisms that alter the expression of these enzymes are in the pathway of development of disease such as lung cancer. These polymorphisms also appear to modify the relationship between prenatal exposure to tobacco smoke and birth outcomes. Studies of prenatal exposure to fetotoxins present in tobacco smoke (e.g., PAHs, AH, and benzene) have linked these toxins to adverse pregnancy outcomes through the inducibility of phase I enzymes such as CYP1A1 (Huel et al. 1993; Lagueux et al. 1999; Dejmek et al. 2000; Wang et al. 2000a), which can vary by host genotype.

Birth Defects

Initial investigations of the mechanisms of maternal or neonatal metabolism of tobacco smoke toxins and adverse birth outcomes were conducted in studies of birth defects. Several studies examined the potential interaction of maternal exposure to tobacco smoke and maternal and/or neonatal genotypes in association with orofacial cleft in newborns (Table 8.13). The genetic polymorphisms that code for the expression of tissue damage, inflammatory response, and immune mediator enzymes and that were examined in those studies include *TGFα* and *TGFß3*, *MSX1*, and *EPHX1*, as well as gene variants of both phase I activation and phase II detoxification enzymes *CYP1A1, GSTM1, GSTT1, NAT1,* and *NAT2*. Prenatal exposure to tobacco smoke was measured by self-reports of maternal active smoking, maternal exposure to secondhand smoke, and paternal active smoking. Most of these studies examined the *TGFα* genotype in neonates. In one study, genotyping was performed in both neonates and parents.

A case-control study of infants with a *TGFα *TAQ1* genotype that contained a rare allele and whose mothers had smoked during pregnancy found a significantly elevated risk for cleft palate in offspring (Table 8.13) (Hwang et al. 1995). In a large, population-based, case-control study conducted by the California Birth Defects Monitoring Program registry, the risks of cleft palate and cleft lip with or without cleft palate were significantly elevated among White infants with *TGFα *rare* genotypes (*A2*) whose mothers were heavy smokers (Shaw et al. 1996). However, three subsequent case-control studies (Christensen et al. 1999; Romitti et al. 1999; Beaty et al. 2001) that failed to replicate these findings had fewer cases and one study had used a lower cutpoint for smoking than that used by Shaw and colleagues (1996). None of the five studies cited above presented regression models with terms for estimating maternal smoking levels and the *TGFα* genotype interactions. Zeiger and colleagues (2005) conducted a meta-analysis of data from these five studies and found a marginally significant interaction between maternal smoking and infant *TGFα *allele* genotypes (*A2*) in relation to cleft palate (OR = 1.95 [95 percent CI, 1.22–3.10]). There was no evidence of an interaction in relation to cleft lip and cleft palate (OR = 0.86 [95 percent CI, 0.53–1.40]).

Romitti and colleagues (1999) also examined the *TGFß3* genotype and maternal smoking in relation to the risk of cleft palate or cleft lip and cleft palate (Table 8.13). These researchers found a significantly elevated risk for the conditions among infants who were homozygous for the common *1* allele at the X5.1 or 5'UTR.1 site and whose mothers had smoked 10 or more cigarettes per day. There was no evidence of an interaction for infant genotypes that included the rare *2* allele.

Hartsfield and colleagues (2001) did not observe any significant interaction between maternal smoking and *EPHX1* (codon 113) or *null GSTM1* genotypes in a case-control study of isolated cleft lip and cleft palate (Table 8.13). van Rooij and colleagues (2001) examined the association of maternal prenatal smoking and the maternal *GSTT1* genotype. The researchers found that mothers who smoked and carried the *GSTT1 null* genotype had a marginally higher risk for delivering an infant with oral clefting than that of nonsmokers who carried the wild-type genotype. Although the RR was not statistically significant, it was almost five times greater when both mothers and their infants carried the *GSTT1 null* genotype. There was no evidence of an interaction between maternal smoking and the *CYP1A1* genotype with a recessive allele in relation to oral clefting. In a case-control study, the *CYP1A1, GSTT1,* and *GSTM1* polymorphisms were also examined as risk factors for hypospadias, a congenital anomaly of the male reproductive organs (Kurahashi et al. 2005). The study did not observe any increased risk of hypospadias among children born to mothers who smoked and had various genotypes, including *CYP1A1 *MSPI* variant allele genotype or the *GSTT1 null* genotype or *GSTM1 null* genotype. In a case-only, haplotypic analysis of an intronic CA repeat of the *MSX1* gene in 206 infants with oral clefting, there was evidence for an interaction with maternal prenatal smoking (Fallin et al. 2003). In the Iowa study (Romitti et al. 1999), infants whose *MSX1 X1.3* or *MSX1 X2.4* genotype contained the *2* allele and whose mothers smoked 10 or more cigarettes per day also had a significantly elevated risk of cleft palate (Table 8.13). In a study of limb deficiency defects, Carmichael and colleagues (2004) did not observe any significantly elevated risk for infants with *MSX1* intronic CA repeat genotype whose mothers smoked during pregnancy. In another case-control study from the California Birth Defects Monitoring Program, the *NAT1 1088* genotype *A/*A and the *NAT1 1095* genotype *A/*A, but not *NAT2* polymorphisms, were strongly associated with isolated oral clefting in infants whose mothers had smoked during pregnancy (Table 8.13) (Lammer et al. 2004).

Other Reproductive Endpoints

Several studies have also examined the potential interaction among phase I and II toxins, genes for drug metabolism, and prenatal exposure to tobacco smoke in

Table 8.13   Studies of interactions between genotype and exposure to tobacco related to oral clefting

Study	Study period	Population	Definition of smoking	Key results
Hwang et al. 1995	1984–1992	69 case infants with CP 114 case infants with CL/P 284 control infants with no cleft defects	Pregnant smokers Pregnant nonsmokers Light smokers: ≤10 cigarettes/day Heavy smokers: >10 cigarettes/day	• Among White infants with *TGFα* genotype containing the *A2 (rare)* allele at the *TAQ1* site whose mothers were heavy smokers, risks of CP and CL/P were significantly elevated (OR = 5.60 [95% CI, 1.36–22.9]) in infants with no family history of birth defects • By amount smoked, risk for CP was elevated among infants with *A2 allele born to light smokers (OR = 6.16 [95% CI, 1.09–34.7]) as well as infants whose mothers were heavy smokers (OR = 8.69 [95% CI, 1.57-47.7])
Shaw et al. 1996	1987–1989	731 case infants with orofacial clefting 348 with isolated CL/P 141 with isolated CP 99 with multiple CL/P 74 with multiple CP 69 with known cause 939 control infants California Birth Defects Monitoring Program	Smokers: 1–19 cigarettes/day, ≥20 cigarettes/day Nonsmokers exposed to secondhand smoke from anyone inside mother's home who smoked daily during 4 months after conception or from regularly frequented places where others smoked	• White infants whose *TGFα* genotype contained the *A2 allele born to maternal heavy smokers had increased risk of isolated CL/P (OR = 6.1 [95% CI, 1.1–36.6]) • Risks were also elevated in the same group for isolated CP (OR = 9.0 [95% CI, 1.4–61.9]) and for "known etiology clefts" (OR = 10.8 [95% CI, 1.2–111.7]) • Sample size in non-White racial groups was too small to permit reliable estimates of effect
Christensen et al. 1999	1991–1994	316 case infants 233 with CL/P 83 with CP 604 control infants	Smokers (before conception and/or during pregnancy): mean cigarettes/day Nonsmokers	• No evidence was found for increased risk of CP or CL/P among infants with the *rare allele for *TGFα* whose mothers had smoked while pregnant
Romitti et al. 1999	1987–1994	225 case infants 161 with CL/P 64 with CP 393 control infants	Smokers (before conception and/or during pregnancy): 1–9 cigarettes/day, ≥10 cigarettes/day Nonsmokers	• For infants whose genotype contained the *rare allele for *TGFα* or *TGFß3*, maternal smoking did not increase risk of having CP or CL/P • Infants whose genotype contained common *1 allele for *TGFß3* (*X5.1* or *5'UTR.1* sites) were at increased risk of having CP or CL/P • With maternal smoking of ≥10 cigarettes/day, infants whose *MSX1 X1.3* genotype contained *A2 allele had elevated risk of CP (OR = 2.7 [95% CI, 1.1–6.3]) • Similar results were found among infants whose *MSX1 X2.4* genotype contained *A2 allele (OR = 2.8 [95% CI, 1.1–6.9])

Table 8.13   Continued

Study	Study period	Population	Definition of smoking	Key results
Beaty et al. 2001	1992–1998	175 infants 111 with CL/P 64 with CP 182 control infants	Smokers (before conception and/or during pregnancy) Nonsmokers (survey of passive exposure to cigarette smoke)	• No evidence was found for increased risk of isolated CL, CP, or CL/P among infants with *rare allele for *TGFα* whose mothers had smoked while pregnant
Hartsfield et al. 2001	1987–1989	85 case infants with CL/P 110 control infants	Pregnant smokers	• With maternal smoking, infants whose genotype was homozygous for *EPHX1* codon 113 *H allele were not at higher risk of CL/P than were infants with *EPHX1* codon 113 wild-type allele (OR = 0.4 [95% CI, 0.1–1.3])
van Rooij et al. 2001	Not reported	113 infants with nonsyndromic oral clefts 104 control infants	Smokers (before conception and/or during pregnancy and/or postpartum) Nonsmokers	• Attributable fraction for oral clefting in maternal smokers with *GSTT1 null* genotype was 7.3%, increased to 7.7% when both mother and infant had *GSTT1 null* genotype • No interaction was observed with maternal smoking and *CYP1A1* polymorphism (maternal or infant) associated with risk of oral clefting
Fallin et al. 2003	1992–1998	206 case infants with oral clefting No controls	Smokers (before conception and/or during pregnancy) Nonsmokers (survey of passive exposure to secondhand smoke)	• Case-only (combined CP and CL/P) tests of association between *MSX1* haplotypes and maternal smoking during first trimester showed excess cases of haplotype containing intronic CA repeat marker among infants of mothers who smoked
Lammer et al. 2004	1987–1989	437 case infants 309 with isolated CL/P 128 with CP California Birth Defects Monitoring Program	Smokers: 1–19 cigarettes/day or ≥20 cigarettes/day Nonsmokers exposed to secondhand smoke from anyone inside mother's home who smoked daily during 4 months after conception or from regularly frequented places where others smoked	• *NAT1 1088* homozygous *A/*A genotype among infants whose mothers smoked was strongly associated with CL/P (OR = 3.9 [95% CI, 1.1–17.2]) • *NAT1 1095* homozygous *A/*A genotype was also strongly associated with CL/P (OR = 4.2 [95% CI, 1.2–18.0]) • No significant interaction was observed for *NAT2* polymorphisms and maternal smoking in relation to CL/P or CP
Zeiger et al. 2005	1984–1998 Meta-analysis of data from 5 studies	726 case infants with CL/P 335 with CP 1,565 control infants (meta-analysis)	Smokers (before conception and/or during pregnancy and/or postpartum) Nonsmokers	• Meta-analysis results indicated that with maternal smoking at any level during pregnancy, risk of CP increased for infants whose *TGFα* genotype contained *A2 allele (OR = 1.95 [95% CI, 1.22–3.10]) • No significant interaction for maternal smoking and infant carrying *TGFα* *A2 allele was associated with CL/P

Note: **CI** = confidence interval; **CL/P** = cleft lip with or without cleft palate; **CP** = cleft palate; **OR** = odds ratio.

Table 8.14 **Decreased birth weight, preterm delivery, intrauterine growth retardation, and neonatal oxidative damage: interactions between host genotype and exposure to tobacco smoke**

Study	Study period	Population	Definition of smoking	Key results
Hong et al. 2001	1999	81 maternal and infant pairs measured for neonatal oxidative damage	Nonsmokers exposed and unexposed to secondhand smoke during pregnancy, determined by measuring cotinine levels	• Urinary concentrations of neonatal oxidative damage from 8-OH-dG were correlated with maternal exposure to secondhand smoke • Infants of mothers with *GSTM1 null* genotype and exposure to secondhand smoke had significantly higher concentrations of 8-OH-dG than did infants of mothers with *GSTM1 present* genotype and no exposure to secondhand smoke
Wang et al. 2002	1998–2000	207 mothers of preterm and/or LBW infants 534 control infants	Smokers (continuously or with cessation during pregnancy) Self-reported lifetime nonsmokers	• Mothers with *CYP1A1 MSPI* genotype containing the **a* allele who smoked throughout pregnancy had infants with mean birth weight decrements of -520 g compared with mothers with *CYP1A1 MSPI *A/*A* genotype who never smoked (from stratified models: LBW OR = 3.2 [95% CI, 1.6–6.4]; from interaction term model: LBW OR = 3.1 [95% CI, 1.2–7.8]) • Infants of mothers with *GSTT1 null* genotype who smoked throughout pregnancy had mean birth weight decrements of -642 g compared with mothers with the *GSTT1 present* genotype who never smoked (from stratified models: LBW OR = 3.5 [95% CI, 1.5–8.3]; from interaction term model: LBW OR = 2.4 [95% CI, 0.9–6.6]) • Among mothers with *CYP1A1 MSPI *Aa/*aa* and *GSTT1 null* genotypes, infants of mothers who smoked throughout pregnancy had mean birth weight decrements of -1,285 g (test of interaction: -1086 g, p <0.001) • Interaction between maternal *GSTT1* genotype and maternal smoking in relation to preterm birth was significant (OR = 2.9 [95% CI, 1.0–8.2]) • Interaction between maternal *CYP1A1 MSPI* genotype and maternal smoking in relation to intrauterine growth retardation was significant (OR = 3.0 [95% CI, 1.2–7.8])
Hong et al. 2003	1999	266 maternal and infant pairs measured for birth weight	Nonsmokers exposed or unexposed to secondhand smoke during pregnancy, determined by measuring cotinine levels	• Mothers exposed to secondhand smoke during pregnancy and having *GSTM1 null* genotype delivered infants with mean birth weight decrements of -158 g compared with unexposed women with *GSTM1 present* genotype, after adjustment for gestational age • Similarly, women exposed to tobacco as secondhand smoke and having *GSTT1 null* genotype delivered infants with mean birth weight decrements of -203 g compared with unexposed women with *GSTT1 present* genotype, after adjustment for gestational age

Table 8.14   Continued

Study	Study period	Population	Definition of smoking	Key results
Magrini et al. 2003	NR	214 maternal and infant pairs measured for birth weight	Smokers Nonsmokers	• Placental specimens from maternal smokers who did not have *PLAP *1/*1* genotype were associated with elevated risk of LBW infants (OR = 6.02 [95% CI, 1.65–23.02]) • This effect was more marked in mothers aged >28 years
Nukui et al. 2004	NR	955 mother and infant pairs assessed for preterm birth and LBW	Smokers (cigarettes/day for first and third trimesters) Nonsmokers (hours of exposure to secondhand smoke)	• Maternal smokers during third trimester and their infants, both with *GSTT1 null* genotype, had higher risk of premature birth than did mothers and infants with *GSTT1 present* genotype among nonsmokers in third trimester (OR = 4.0 [95% CI, 1.7–9.5]) • When both mother and infant had *GSTT1 null* genotype, the risk of premature birth was elevated for smokers and nonsmokers and their infants

Note: **8-OH-dG** = 8-hydroxy-2'-deoxyguanosine; **CI** = confidence interval; **g** = grams; **LBW** = low birth weight; **NR** = data not reported; **OR** = odds ratio.

relation to other outcomes, such as LBW, preterm birth, IUGR, and neonatal oxidative damage (Table 8.14).

A large case-control study described an interaction between self-reported smoking during pregnancy and maternal genetic polymorphisms for *CYP1A1 MSPI* and *GSTT1*, which were associated with reduced birth weight, preterm delivery, reduced gestation, and IUGR (Table 8.14) (Wang et al. 2002). Mothers who had smoked continuously during pregnancy and who were heterozygous variant type (**A/*a*) or homozygous variant type (**a/*a*) for *CYP1A1 MSPI*, were at a threefold higher risk of having a LBW (<2,500 g) infant compared with lifetime nonsmokers who were homozygous wild type (**A/*A*). In these genotype-exposure groups, gestation was reduced on average by 1.5 weeks among smokers who were *CYP1A1 MSPI *A/*a* or **a/*a*. Smokers with the *GSTT1 null* genotype gave birth to infants with significant decrements in birth weight compared with birth weight of infants of nonsmokers who carried at least one *GSTT1* allele. The risk of growth retardation, defined as less than 85 percent of the ratio of observed birth weight to mean birth weight for gestational age, was associated with smoking in mothers who carried the *CYP1A1 MSPI *A/*a* or **a/*a*. This study was unique because it presented regression models that evaluated interaction terms along with analyses stratified by gene variant and smoking status, but it lacked an objective measure of smoking.

In a study conducted in Korea, Hong and colleagues (2003) examined the potential interaction of the *GST* family gene variants and exposure to secondhand smoke in

association with mean birth weight (Table 8.14). Women classified as exposed to secondhand smoke, as determined by assays of urinary levels of cotinine, who carried the *GSTM1 null* genotype delivered infants with a mean birth weight decrement of -158 g, after adjustment for gestational age. A similar pattern was observed among mothers with the *GSTT1 null* genotype (decrement of -203 g). In a subsample of 81 women in the same study population, Hong and colleagues (2001) examined the effect of exposure to secondhand smoke and maternal *GST* family genotypes in relation to measurements of neonatal oxidative damage as urinary levels of 8-hydroxy-2'-deoxyguanosine (8-OH-dG). Infants born to women classified as exposed to secondhand smoke who carried the *GSTM1 null* genotype had significantly higher levels of log urinary 8-OH-dG (geometric mean level = 4.03 [95 percent CI, 2.13–7.61]) than did women classified as unexposed who carried the *GSTM1* wild type. Significant differences in 8-OH-dG remained after adjusting for confounders.

One study evaluated phase I and II metabolic enzyme gene variants (Table 8.14) (Nukui et al. 2004). The authors reported that the most significantly elevated risk of premature birth occurred when both mother and infant carried the *GSTT1 null* genotype. The results were the same for smokers and nonsmokers, so no interaction was observed. Phase I genetic polymorphisms (e.g., *CYP1A1*) were not associated with an elevated risk of a premature birth. A study that examined *PLAP* polymorphisms found an elevated risk of LBW when the *PLAP *1/*1* genotype was absent in mothers who smoked (Magrini et al. 2003).

Implications

The evidence of a causal relationship between smoking during pregnancy and increased risk for adverse pregnancy outcomes is sufficient to warrant promoting smoking cessation among women early in pregnancy or before they become pregnant, because the critical period may be quite early. For example, the impact of smoking on oral clefts could be lessened by 5 to 22 percent if women stopped smoking before pregnancy. Thus, there is a need for widespread implementation of interventions for effective smoking cessation that target all women of childbearing age.

Smoking may have several ramifications of alterations in fertility, menstrual cycle function, or sperm quality, including a burden on the health care system and loss of work productivity. These changes may affect a woman's ability to conceive and maintain a pregnancy at a desired time in a couple's life. The reproductive life span may be shortened, and early menopause is associated with other hormone-related health problems such as osteoporosis and cardiovascular disease (Harlow and Ephross 1995; Sowers and La Pietra 1995; Cooper and Sandler 1998). Women with short menstrual cycles may also be at a higher risk of breast cancer (Kelsey et al. 1993). Such effects warrant smoking cessation early in the reproductive age span, or ideally, prevention of smoking initiation among youth.

Smoking Prevention and Cessation

Smoking cessation is one of the most important actions a woman can take to improve the outcome of her pregnancy, and most women who stop smoking during pregnancy do so on their own. Because women know about the adverse effects of smoking on their health and that of a fetus, pregnancy may be a time when smoking cessation efforts and interventions are potentially more effective (Mullen 1999; Fiore et al. 1996, 2008). Nevertheless, most smokers do not stop smoking during pregnancy. Tobacco addiction is progressive and chronic and, in consequence, smoking cessation interventions focusing on the prenatal period have failed to achieve long-term abstinence among most pregnant smokers. Two-thirds of women who smoke during the first pregnancy also smoke during the second, exposing the first infant to tobacco smoke both in utero and postnatally (Dietz et al. 1997).

Population-based, cross-sectional surveys have been widely used to monitor prenatal smoking rates (Connor and McIntyre 1999; Owen and Penn 1999; Ebrahim et al. 2000). However, such data do not provide information on changes in smoking behaviors during pregnancy, in contrast to data collected during prenatal care, in which smoking behaviors are recorded on more than one occasion, as described by Kirkland and colleagues (2000). Such longitudinal data can usefully supplement survey data to monitor progress in control of prenatal exposure to tobacco smoke. Because of the social desirability of nonsmoking status, which is greater during pregnancy, the actual prevalence of smoking may be even higher than is self-reported. In the United Kingdom, 16 percent of respondents to a survey reported that they did not admit to their physicians that they smoked (*Bulletin of the World Health Organization* 1999). A study in the United States found nondisclosure rates of 28 percent at enrollment into prenatal care and 35 percent at follow-up (Kendrick et al. 1995). Therefore, biochemical verification of smoking status of each woman during each contact with a clinician is needed to evaluate cessation interventions.

Clinicians who provide health care to women have an important role in reducing the burden of smoking among women. Clinically proven programs for smoking cessation that can be delivered in primary care settings are now available. However, there is a dearth of information specifically addressing the most effective smoking prevention and cessation interventions for women of childbearing age, especially those of low socioeconomic status. For this reason NC1 has implemented the TReND: Low SES Women and Girls Project. This project was created to strategically address and examine the effects of multiple tobacco control policies on diverse populations of low SES women and girls. In addition, the USDHHS Office of Women's Health has developed an interagency work group to address this issue. The FDA Office of Women's Health has also developed a guide for providers to educate women about medications available to assist them if they are ready to quit smoking.

Experts attending the 1998 Consensus Workshop on Smoking Cessation During Pregnancy reviewed the evidence related to counseling on smoking cessation during pregnancy, including the U.S. Public Health Service Clinical Practice Guideline, *Treating Tobacco Use and Dependence* (Fiore et al. 1996; Mullen 1999). This group concluded that brief cessation counseling (5 to 15 minutes), delivered by a trained provider with pregnancy-specific self-help materials, significantly increases rates of cessation among pregnant smokers. The 5A strategy of smoking intervention—Ask, Advise, Assess, Assist, and Arrange—and recommended procedures are outlined in the one-page form, *Brief Smoking Cessation Counseling for Pregnant Patients*. More intense efforts may be needed for groups of women who are less likely to stop smoking and more likely to relapse (Connor and McIntyre 1999). Smoking cessation interventions should be continued after delivery to prevent relapse, and partners who smoke should be included in such interventions. More than 50 percent of women do not recognize that they are pregnant until after the fourth week of gestation. Therefore, efforts to prevent exposure to tobacco smoke should begin before conception to avoid pregnancy complications or to avoid exposing the fetus to tobacco smoke. Furthermore, to prevent subfertility, cessation efforts should begin even earlier in the reproductive period.

Despite evidence that provider-administered cessation counseling significantly increases rates of cessation among pregnant smokers, evidence suggests that such interventions may do little to decrease overall prenatal smoking prevalence. It has been estimated that universal implementation of a provider-administered psychosocial cessation intervention on a national level would result in only a modest decline (0.8 percentage points) in the overall prevalence of smoking among pregnant women (Kim et al. 2009). Larger reductions in prenatal smoking prevalence will likely require implementation of comprehensive tobacco control policies that effectively decrease smoking prevalence among women of reproductive age.

Unfortunately, pregnant women who smoke most heavily do not appear to respond to the type of behavioral intervention indicated here. The U.S. Public Health Service has suggested, as have others, the need to explore the use of pharmacologic approaches to achieve cessation in women who are unable to stop smoking (Fiore et al. 1996, 2000, 2008). These approaches include nicotine replacement therapy (e.g., gum, patch, inhaler, or spray); nonnicotine products, such as varenicline and bupropion hydrochloride; and second-line pharmacotherapies, such as clonidine and nortriptyline. However, the efficacy and safety of these approaches during pregnancy are not well documented. Pharmacologic interventions should be considered on an individual basis as an adjunct to behavioral interventions. These interventions should be considered for pregnant women only if the increased likelihood of smoking cessation outweighs the harmful effects on the fetus of nicotine replacement therapy and possible continued smoking.

To minimize the effects of smoking among all women and to foster effective perinatal tobacco control, focus and efforts should expand beyond prenatal care to include both the whole family and the entire reproductive life span of women. The complexities associated with smoking cessation among established smokers are underscored by reports of persistent high smoking rates among pregnant women in Canada, the United Kingdom, and the United States (Connor and McIntyre 1999; Owen and Penn 1999; Ebrahim et al. 2000). Long-term reduction in tobacco exposure during pregnancy can be achieved only by encouraging adolescent girls and young women not to start smoking.

Regulation and Policy

Ranking of infant mortality rates in established market economies placed the United States twenty-eighth in 2005 compared with twelfth in 1960. Rates of smoking remain high among women in three categories related to pregnancy—pregnant, planning a pregnancy, and at risk of pregnancy. Substantial efforts would be needed to reduce known risks to pregnancy and infant health, to reverse the stagnant trends in infant mortality rates in the near future. Because only about 20 percent of women successfully control tobacco dependence during pregnancy, smoking cessation is recommended before pregnancy (U.S. Preventive Services Task Force [USPSTF] 2003). National recommendations to support preconception care as an opportunity to reduce maternal risks during pregnancy have been introduced (USPSTF 2003). Therefore, high rates of smoking in the preconception period, almost the same as that among all women of childbearing age, pose both a challenge and an opportunity to the implementation of the preconception care initiative. After childbirth, smoking does not usually decline below the level achieved during pregnancy (USPSTF 2003). Therefore, further challenges to preventing smoking-related harm to infant health include continued postnatal exposure to secondhand tobacco smoke from maternal smoking.

Intervention tools to aid smoking cessation among pregnant women are now available. One report estimated that the costs of implementing such interventions range from $24 to $34 per pregnant smoker counseled (Ayadi et al. 2006). Potential neonatal cost savings that could be accrued for women who stop smoking during pregnancy were estimated at $881 per maternal smoker (Ayadi et al. 2006). A woman's contact with the health care system during and after pregnancy provides enough opportunities to engage women for smoking cessation and provide follow-up and support services to prevent relapse during the interconception period. Furthermore, women of childbearing age in the United States have on average 6.4 health care visits per year (Adams and Marano 1995), and such opportunities can be used to improve access to the 5A strategy of smoking intervention.

Smoking behaviors of partners of women who smoke are important considerations for achieving cessation and prevention of relapse. Extension of services or facilitation of use of services by the partners would be needed to maintain the benefit from smoking cessation services provided to the women. Because men have fewer contacts with the health care system than do women (Everett et al. 2005), smoking cessation efforts among women provide an opportunity for access to health care for their male partners also for cessation efforts.

Efforts to reduce smoking in the United States have shifted from a primary focus on smoking cessation for individuals to more population-based interventions that emphasize prevention of smoking initiation, reduction of exposure to secondhand tobacco smoke, and policy changes in health care systems to promote cessation. Parallel to these efforts, concerted efforts are needed to reduce the disparity in smoking rates among socially disadvantaged women and White women; targeted efforts aimed at women in the preconception period and those at risk for pregnancy; and efforts to promote smoking cessation among women who are pregnant. One report indicated that bundling of services to address common preventable risks, such as tobacco and alcohol use and risks for sexually transmitted diseases, through a preconceptional approach, would benefit about one-half of all women of childbearing age in the United States (CDC 2006). Tobacco use in women coexists with other risk behaviors or morbidities, including mental health disorders and substance use. Some factors, such as illicit drug use or alcohol use, may synergistically elevate the risk from other factors such as tobacco use or acquisition of sexually transmitted infections, requiring intervention approaches through case management that address more than one risk factor. Use of tobacco and alcohol are comorbidities that can benefit from many efforts to provide several interventions to a woman simultaneously. Such case-management approaches may help to increase adherence to treatment and reduce relapse to smoking after delivery.

Earlier data have indicated that the observed declines during the past four decades in the United States in smoking rates among pregnant women reflect declines that occurred in general among women and were not specific to pregnancy. Therefore, efforts to close the gaps in the diffusion of smoking cessation intervention to individual smokers are still needed and should be a priority. However, large reductions in smoking rates among pregnant women over time are more likely to come from efforts to reduce smoking initiation by young women.

Evidence Summary

Health professionals have long considered exposure to tobacco smoke harmful to reproduction, affecting aspects from fertility to fetal and child development and pregnancy outcome. Tobacco smoke contains thousands of compounds, some of which are known toxicants to reproductive health, such as CO, nicotine, and metals. About 10 percent of couples who want to conceive a child experience infertility or reduced fertility, approximately 10 to 20 percent of women who do conceive have miscarriage or stillbirth before delivery, and others have pregnancy complications and adverse outcomes that affect infant health and survival (CDC 2005).

In 2007, 17.4 percent of women and approximately 19 percent of women of reproductive age (18 through 44 years) smoked cigarettes (CDC 2008). From 2002 to 2005, 17.3 percent of pregnant women reported smoking cigarettes in the past month (*NSDUH Report* 2007). Because smoking rates have declined, persons involuntarily exposed to tobacco smoke probably now outnumber active smokers and they are exposed to some of the same toxins to which smokers are exposed.

Previous Surgeon General's reports and subsequent studies have found that smoking is related to several reproductive health endpoints. The 2001 report on women and smoking and the 2004 report on the health consequences of smoking noted a causal link between smoking and reduced fertility in women. Smoking may contribute to reduced fertility and other related reproductive endpoints, including earlier menopause or altered menstrual cycle parameters, through similar mechanisms such as by producing alterations in hormone function. Study findings suggest effects of smoking on estrogen and other hormones, which may vary by gender and the stage of life. Researchers have suggested that smoking has antiestrogenic effects, but more recent data are less consistent, at least for nonpregnant, premenopausal women. Studies implicate smoking and its effects on other hormones, such as progesterone, gonadotropins (FSH), and androgens (including in men). In animal studies, cells treated with alkaloids found in tobacco smoke, including nicotine, showed a dose-dependent inhibition of progesterone production, whereas estradiol production showed little effect or was slightly stimulated (Bódis et al. 1997; Gocze et al. 1999; Gocze and Freeman 2000; Miceli et al. 2005). Other scientists concluded that nicotine affects the menstrual cycle by inhibiting progesterone release just after ovulation. In animal models, nicotine acts on the HPG axis, which is involved in normal sexual development and control of reproductive function (Matta et al. 1998). Studies show that prenatal exposure to nicotine is related to decreased testosterone levels in adult male rats and that cotinine, but not nicotine, inhibits testosterone synthesis in testes of neonatal rats (Sarasin et al. 2003).

Spermatogenesis is also affected by the hormonal milieu. Recent studies have provided more evidence that tobacco smoke exposure is associated with reduced sperm quality, which, in turn, may be a mechanism leading to reduced fertility in couples. Smoking-associated DNA damage in sperm could also be related to birth defects in offspring or producing nonviable gametes, resulting in apparent infertility or early fetal loss.

Many epidemiologic studies have related maternal smoking to reproductive problems that can originate in the oviduct (e.g., fallopian tube) (Stillman et al. 1986; Buck et al. 1997), including infertility and ectopic pregnancy. Studies have shown that exposure to tobacco smoke diminishes oviductal functioning. Exposure to cigarette smoke and its components has been shown to alter contraction in human and rabbit oviducts (Neri and Eckerling 1969; Ruckebusch 1975) and to form blebs on the oviductal epithelium in hamsters (Magers et al. 1995). In other studies of hamster oviducts, effects included decreased smooth muscle contractions and changed the ratio of ciliated to secretory cells, both of which would affect transit time of the egg through the oviduct (Huang et al. 1997; Knoll and Talbot 1998; DiCarlantonio and Talbot 1999; Riveles et al. 2003). Adhesion between the extracellular matrix of the oocyte cumulus complex and the tips of the cilia is essential for pickup of the oocyte and transport through the oviduct (Talbot et al. 1999; Lam et al. 2000). Exposure to both mainstream and sidestream smoke increases adhesion, which could account for decreased pickup rates even when cilia beat at normal or accelerated rates.

Ectopic pregnancy occurs when a fertilized egg is implanted outside the uterus, usually in the fallopian tube; it is estimated to occur in 1 to 2 percent of pregnancies. This condition accounts for approximately 6 percent of pregnancy-related deaths in the United States (Chow et al. 1987; Goldner et al. 1993; Berg et al. 2003; Chang et al. 2003; Van Den Eeden et al. 2005). Affected women are at increased risk of subsequent infertility and recurrent ectopic pregnancy, as would be expected among women with tubal damage (Chow et al. 1987; Coste et al. 1991; Washington and Katz 1993; Skjeldestad et al. 1998). The 2004 Surgeon General's report found the evidence suggestive but not sufficient to infer a causal relationship between smoking and ectopic pregnancy (USDHHS 2004) on the basis of a number of studies with significant associations between smoking and increased risk of ectopic pregnancy, yielding a pooled OR of 1.8 or an 80-percent increase with smoking (Castles et al. 1999). Two subsequent methodologically strong studies also indicate an increased risk with dose-response effects, further strengthening the evidence.

Studies have found evidence of a dose-response relationship even after adjustment for important potential confounders such as a history of sexually transmitted diseases and infertility (Bouyer et al. 2003; Karaer et al. 2006). In addition, plausible mechanisms for a relationship between smoking and ectopic pregnancy exist. As noted, the oviduct plays a critical role in the pickup and transport of the oocyte, and failure of this function can result in ectopic pregnancy (Talbot and Riveles 2005).

Spontaneous abortion, the involuntary termination of an intrauterine pregnancy before 20 weeks of gestation, has been reported in approximately 12 percent of recognized pregnancies; the majority occur before 12 weeks of gestation. Including very early pregnancy loss that may be unreported suggests an estimated 30 to 45 percent of conceptions actually end in pregnancy loss, some before implantation (Wilcox et al. 1988; Eskenazi et al. 1995). In addition to fetal abnormalities, other factors that likely contribute to SAB include maternal anatomic abnormalities of the uterus, immunologic disturbances, thrombotic disorders, and endocrine abnormalities (Christianson 1979; Cramer and Wise 2000; Regan and Rai 2000), some of which are affected by tobacco smoke. The 2004 Surgeon General's report (USDHHS 2004) found the evidence suggestive but not sufficient to infer a causal relationship between tobacco and SAB. Additional studies have shown positive associations, including two with measurement of cotinine (Ness et al. 1999; George et al. 2006) and two showing associations with secondhand smoke (Venners et al. 2004; George et al. 2006). Proposed mechanisms for an effect from tobacco smoke include vasoconstrictive and antimetabolic effects resulting in placental insufficiency and the subsequent demise of the embryo or fetus, fetal hypoxia from CO exposure, and direct toxic effects of cigarette smoke constituents.

Preeclampsia, marked by proteinuria, hypertension, and dysfunction of the cells lining the uterus, is a leading cause of pregnancy-related mortality in the United States (Berg et al. 2003). The 2004 Surgeon General's report found the evidence sufficient to infer a causal relationship between smoking and a reduced risk of preeclampsia (USDHHS 2004). Smoking has been proposed to reduce the risk of preeclampsia by effects of exposure to thiocyanate, which has a hypotensive effect (Andrews 1973), by changing the thromboxane A_2 to prostacyclin ratio, which would alter the way blood vessels constrict and dilate (Ylikorkala et al. 1985; Davis et al. 1987; Marcoux et al. 1989; Lindqvist and Maršál 1999), or by stimulating the growth of new blood vessels in the placenta (Maynard et al. 2003; Fisher 2004; Jeyabalan et al. 2008).

Numerous studies have demonstrated the immediate effect of smoking one or two cigarettes on maternal heart rate and blood pressure (Lindblad et al. 1988; Morrow et al. 1988; Castro et al. 1993; Kimya et al. 1998; Ates et al. 2004). The clinical significance of a transiently elevated maternal heart rate on pregnancy is unknown. Studies that examined the acute effects of smoking after abstinence reported a transient increase in diastolic blood pressure and, to a lesser extent, systolic blood pressure. The release of catecholamine may trigger the elevations in maternal heart rate and blood pressure reported in these studies. However, smoking was also associated with an acute rise in plasma levels of norepinephrine, epinephrine, and dopamine, which could mediate the rise in maternal heart rate and blood pressure (Quigley et al. 1979). The literature indicates a transient increase in fetal heart rate with acute maternal smoking that was not statistically significant, although fetal heart rate variability, used to assess fetal well-being, was significantly transiently decreased (Graca et al. 1991; Ates et al. 2004). The clinical significance of these transient changes is not known. Studies on uterine and placental blood flow did not indicate basal differences between smokers and non-smokers and results were inconsistent with respect to acute changes from smoking, so this mechanism is not supported as a possible cause of the well-documented fetal growth retardation among smokers.

Maintenance of pregnancy and fetal growth and development are dependent on normal formation of the placenta for exchange of nutrients and metabolic products between the mother and fetus. Studies have consistently shown that maternal smoking is associated with a thickening of the villous membrane of the placenta, which would decrease the ability of nutrients to pass through the placenta by diffusion (Burton et al. 1989; Jauniaux and Burton 1992; Demir et al. 1994; Bush et al. 2000; Larsen et al. 2002). The thickening of the villous membrane could contribute to fetal growth restriction. Researchers have hypothesized that toxic effects of maternal smoking on the placenta are responsible for the thickening of the villous membrane, perhaps caused by the accumulation of cadmium that is associated with a reduction in fetal capillary volume (Burton et al. 1989; Bush et al. 2000). Smoking appears to interfere with transformation of uterine spiral arteries, which is critical for the formation of the high-capacitance system that allows increased blood flow from the mother to the fetus. Such interference could lead to increased risk of adverse pregnancy outcomes such as miscarriage.

Epidemiologic studies have consistently found an increased risk of partial obstruction of the cervix by the placenta (placenta previa) among maternal smokers, which may lead to preterm delivery or maternal or fetal or neonatal death (Meyer et al. 1976; Zhang and Fried 1992; Monica and Lilja 1995). One mechanism commonly proposed to explain this association is the lower blood levels of O_2 and reduced blood flow that result from smoking, with compensatory placental enlargement.

Premature separation of the placenta from the uterus (placental abruption) increases the risk of perinatal mortality, and although several factors are involved (Misra and Ananth 1999), studies have consistently associated smoking with an increased risk (Raymond and Mills 1993; Ananth et al. 1999; Castles et al. 1999; Andres and Day 2000). The 2004 Surgeon General's report found the evidence sufficient to infer a causal relationship (USDHHS 2004), and researchers have observed a dose-response relationship (Raymond and Mills 1993; Ananth et al. 1999). One researcher has hypothesized that smoking-related degenerative and/or inflammatory changes in the placenta are factors related to abruption (Cnattingius 2004). Other hypotheses include low levels of vitamin C in maternal smokers (Faruque et al. 1995), leading to impaired collagen synthesis (Cnattingius 2004), microinfarcts, and accumulation of fatty deposits in placental vessels (Naeye 1979; Andres and Day 2000).

The 2004 Surgeon General's report found that the evidence was sufficient to infer a causal relationship between smoking and preterm delivery, a leading cause of neonatal morbidity and mortality in developed countries (USDHHS 2004). Smoking appears to increase the risk of both medically indicated and spontaneous preterm delivery (Kyrklund-Blomberg and Cnattingius 1998). Mechanisms through which smoking may contribute to preterm delivery include placental abruption or effects on the integrity of collagen, leading to a weakening and rupture of the membranes and increased risk of infections.

The same Surgeon General's report found sufficient evidence to infer a causal relationship between smoking and preterm premature rupture of membranes (PPROM) (USDHHS 2004). Researchers have hypothesized that smoking increases the risk of PPROM through several pathways. The effects of smoking on the immune system could increase the risk of genital tract infection or disrupt the cytokine system (French and McGregor 1996). Smoking could also increase the inflammatory response and reduce the availability of nutrients such as vitamin C or decrease the uptake of nutrients by the placenta (French and McGregor 1996; Lykkesfeldt et al. 1996, 2000), which would affect collagen content and membrane structure.

Maternal smoking has also been investigated for an association with birth defects, and although the 2004 Surgeon General's report (USDHHS 2004) found inadequate evidence for birth defects in general, maternal smoking was considered suggestive for oral clefts. Evidence accumulated since the studies in that report is even stronger in supporting an association with smoking and cleft lip and/or palate (Little et al. 2004a), with some dose-response effects noted (Little et al. 2004b). Animal studies support these findings with evidence that nicotine can alter embryonic movements that are important during embryogenesis for the differentiation and maturation of organ systems, including palate closure (Panter et al. 2000; Ejaz et al. 2005). Other possible mechanisms include smoking-induced reductions in supply of essential nutrients for embryonic tissues, such as multivitamins and folate, fetal hypoxia from CO, or DNA damage from PAHs.

Deficiencies of micronutrients may contribute to adverse pregnancy outcomes, and smoking may contribute to this relationship. Vitamin C is required for collagen formation in amnion epithelial cells, and studies have noted reduced vitamin C levels in women with PPROM (Wideman et al. 1964; Casanueva et al. 1993). A decrease in the amount of collagen III likely leads to a weakening of the tensile strength of amniotic membranes, which could increase the risk of PPROM. Studies consistently show that smokers consume less and metabolize more vitamin C than do nonsmokers and thus have lower levels of vitamin C in plasma (Preston 1991; Lykkesfeldt et al. 2000; Cogswell et al. 2003) and in amniotic fluid (Barrett et al. 1991). Vitamin C is important for normal immune functioning, and a vitamin C deficiency in maternal smokers could contribute to adverse pregnancy outcomes by impairing maternal immune responses to genital tract infections. Because the placenta is impermeable to most proteins, proteins are usually synthesized by the fetus from amino acids supplied by the mother. Abnormalities in amino acid transport across the placenta can contribute to impaired fetal growth. Compared with nonsmokers, smokers have reduced levels of several amino acids in fetal plasma, umbilical plasma, and placental villi (Jauniaux et al. 1999, 2001).

CO forms as a by-product of combustion and is the toxin found in the highest concentration in cigarette smoke—10 to 20 times the dose of nicotine (Hoffman et al. 1997). The toxic effects of CO result predominantly from its binding to hemoglobin (Longo 1976, 1977), which is more than 200 times that of O_2 to hemoglobin (Hsia 1998). Fetal hemoglobin binds CO more tightly than

does adult hemoglobin, so the fetus of a smoking mother has much higher levels of carboxyhemoglobin than those of the mother. The fetus experiences chronic hypoxia of fetal tissue, which persists for five or six hours of maternal smoking abstinence, such as during sleeping (Cole et al. 1972; Longo 1977; Bureau et al. 1982). CO from cigarette smoke deprives the fetus of O_2, which is essential for the aerobic metabolism that produces ATP, a coenzyme that stores the energy to fuel cellular activity throughout the body. Chronic mild O_2 deprivation in the fetus is likely a major underlying mechanism of smoking-associated fetal growth retardation, one of the most consistent and earliest identified adverse effects in infants of maternal smokers (Longo 1976, 1977; USDHHS 1980, 2004). Furthermore, infants of maternal smokers showed a decrease in birth weight nearly five times lower than that in infants of snuff users, even after adjustment for variables, implicating CO as the likely hazard (Longo 1976, 1977; England et al. 2003). Reduced fetal growth is associated with adverse effects on other endpoints, including perinatal mortality, birth defects, and neurodevelopment, which may also be directly affected by CO exposure.

Other components of tobacco smoke, including nicotine (see Chapter 3, "Chemistry and Toxicology of Cigarette Smoke and Biomarkers of Exposure and Harm"); heavy metals such as cadmium, lead, and mercury; and PAHs have been found to be causally associated with several adverse reproductive outcomes described here. Furthermore, levels of these components are found to be higher in smokers than in nonsmokers. It is more difficult to determine whether the levels generated from tobacco smoke are sufficient to cause these outcomes, but the evidence is suggestive for several of the components. The metabolism of these toxic constituents likely varies by genetic polymorphisms that reflect differential induction of drug- or toxin-metabolizing enzymes, such as cytochrome P-450s and GSTs, which, in turn, may modify the relationship between maternal smoking and birth outcomes, such as LBW or congenital anomalies. Genetic polymorphisms coding for the expression of tissue damage, inflammatory response, and immune mediator enzymes have been examined for interaction with maternal smoking in several studies of oral facial clefts, with *TGFα* and *TGFβ3* alleles most often implicated.

Conclusions

1. There is consistent evidence that links smoking in men to chromosome changes or DNA damage in sperm (germ cells), affecting male fertility, pregnancy viability, and anomalies in offspring.

2. There is consistent evidence for association of periconceptional smoking to cleft lip with or without cleft palate.

3. There is consistent evidence that increases in follicle-stimulating hormone levels and decreases in estrogen and progesterone are associated with cigarette smoking in women, at least in part due to effects of nicotine on the endocrine system.

4. There is consistent evidence that maternal smoking leads to transient increases in maternal heart rate and blood pressure (primarily diastolic), probably mediated by the release of norepinephrine and epinephrine into the circulatory system.

5. There is consistent evidence that links maternal smoking to interference in the physiological transformation of spiral arteries and thickening of the villous membrane in forming the placenta; placental problems could lead to fetal loss, preterm delivery, or low birth weight.

6. There is consistent evidence of the presence of histopathologic changes in the fetus from maternal smoking, particularly in the lung and brain.

7. There is consistent evidence that suggests smoking leads to immunosuppressive effects, including dysregulation of the inflammatory response, that may lead to miscarriage and preterm delivery.

8. There is consistent evidence that suggests a role for polycyclic aromatic hydrocarbons from tobacco smoke in the adverse effects of maternal smoking on a variety of reproductive and developmental endpoints.

9. There is consistent evidence that tobacco smoke exposure leads to diminished oviductal functioning, which could impair fertilization.

10. There is consistent evidence that links prenatal smoke exposure and genetic variations in metabolizing enzymes such as GSTT1 with increased risk of adverse pregnancy outcomes such as lowered birth weight and reduced gestation.

11. There is consistent evidence that genetic polymorphisms, such as variants in transforming growth factor-alpha, modify the risks of oral clefting in offspring related to maternal smoking.

12. There is consistent evidence that carbon monoxide leads to birth weight deficits and may play a role in neurologic deficits (cognitive and neurobehavioral endpoints) in the offspring of smokers.

References

Abbatiello ER, Mohrmann K. Effects on the offspring of chronic low exposure carbon monoxide during mice pregnancy. *Clinical Toxicology* 1979;14(4):401–6.

Abdella TN, Sibai BM, Hays JM Jr, Anderson GD. Relationship of hypertensive disease to abruptio placentae. *Obstetrics and Gynecology* 1984;63(3):365–70.

Adams PF, Marano MA. Current estimates from the National Health Interview Survey, 1994. *Vital Health Statistics* 1995;10(193 Pt 1):1–260.

Agrawal P, Chansoriya M, Kaul KK. Effect of tobacco chewing by mothers on placental morphology. *Indian Pediatrics* 1983;20(8):561–5.

Ahmad SA, Sayed MHSU, Barua S, Khan MH, Faruquee MH, Jalil A, Hadi SA, Talukder HK. Arsenic in drinking water and pregnancy outcomes. *Environmental Health Perspectives* 2001;109(6):629–31.

Akre O, Lipworth L, Cnattingius S, Sparen P, Ekbom A. Risk factor patterns for cryptorchidism and hypospadias. *Epidemiology* 1999;10(4):364–9.

Alatas C, Aksoy E, Akarsu C, Yakin K, Bahceci M. Prediction of perinatal outcome by middle cerebral artery Doppler velocimetry. *Archives of Gynecology and Obstetrics* 1996;258(3):141–6.

Albaiges G, Missfelder-Lobos H, Lees C, Parra M, Nicolaides KH. One-stage screening for pregnancy complications by color Doppler assessment of the uterine arteries at 23 weeks' gestation. *Obstetrics and Gynecology* 2000;96(4):559–64.

Albuquerque CA, Smith KR, Johnson C, Chao R, Harding R. Influence of maternal tobacco smoking during pregnancy on uterine, umbilical and fetal cerebral artery blood flows. *Early Human Development* 2004; 80(1):31–42.

al-Zaid NS, Gumaa KA, Bou-Resli MN, Ibrahim MEA. Premature rupture of fetal membranes changes in collagen type. *Acta Obstetricia et Gynecologica Scandinavica* 1988;67(4):291–5.

Amankwah KS, Kaufmann RC, Weberg AD. Ultrastructural changes in neonatal sciatic nerve tissue: effects of passive maternal smoking. *Gynecologic and Obstetric Investigation* 1985;20(4):186–93.

American Journal of Obstetrics and Gynecology. Geographic variation in the incidence of hypertension in pregnancy. *American Journal of Obstetrics and Gynecology* 1988;158(1):80–3.

Ananth CV, Cnattingius S. Influence of maternal smoking on placental abruption in successive pregnancies: a population-based prospective cohort study in Sweden. *American Journal of Epidemiology* 2007;166(3): 289–95.

Ananth CV, Demissie K, Smulian JC, Vintzileos AM. Placenta previa in singleton and twin births in the United States, 1989 through 1998: a comparison of risk factor profiles and associated conditions. *American Journal of Obstetrics and Gynecology* 2003;188(1):275–81.

Ananth CV, Oyelese Y, Yeo L, Pradhan A, Vintzileos AM. Placental abruption in the United States, 1979 through 2001: temporal trends and potential determinants. *American Journal of Obstetrics and Gynecology* 2005; 192(1):191–8.

Ananth CV, Platt RW. Reexamining the effects of gestational age, fetal growth, and maternal smoking on neonatal mortality. *BMC Pregnancy and Childbirth* 2004; 4(1):22.

Ananth CV, Savitz DA, Williams MA. Placental abruption and its association with hypertension and prolonged rupture of membranes: a methodologic review and meta-analysis. *Obstetrics and Gynecology* 1996a; 88(2):309–18.

Ananth CV, Smulian JC, Demissie K, Vintzileos AM, Knuppel RA. Placental abruption among singleton and twin births in the United States: risk factor profiles. *American Journal of Epidemiology* 2001;153(8):771–8.

Ananth CV, Smulian JC, Vintzileos AM. Incidence of placental abruption in relation to cigarette smoking and hypertensive disorders during pregnancy: a meta-analysis of observational studies. *Obstetrics and Gynecology* 1999;93(4):622–8.

Ananth CV, Wilcox AJ. Placental abruption and perinatal mortality in the United States. *American Journal of Epidemiology* 2001;153(4):332–7.

Ananth CV, Wilcox AJ, Savitz DA, Bowes WA Jr, Luther ER. Effect of maternal age and parity on the risk of uteroplacental bleeding disorders in pregnancy. *Obstetrics and Gynecology* 1996b;88(4 Pt 1):511–6.

Ancel P-Y, Saurel-Cubizolles M-J, Di Renzo GC, Papiernik E, Bréart G. Very and moderate preterm births: are the risk factors different? *British Journal of Obstetrics and Gynaecology* 1999;106(11):1162–70.

Andersch B, Milsom I. An epidemiologic study of young women with dysmenorrhea. *American Journal of Obstetrics and Gynecology* 1982;144(6):655–60.

Andersen MR, Walker LR, Stender S. Reduced endothelial nitric oxide synthase activity and concentration in fetal umbilical veins from maternal cigarette smokers. *American Journal of Obstetrics and Gynecology* 2004;191(1):346–51.

Anderson R. Effects of ascorbate on leucocytes. Part II: effects of ascorbic acid and calcium and sodium ascorbate on neutrophil phagocytosis and post-phagocytic metabolic activity. *South African Medical Journal* 1979; 56(10):401–4.

Anderson ME, Johnson DC, Batal HA. Sudden infant death syndrome and prenatal maternal smoking: rising attributed risk in the *Back to Sleep* era. *BMC Medicine* 2005;3(1):4.

Andres RL, Day M-C. Perinatal complications associated with maternal tobacco use. *Seminars in Neonatology* 2000;5(3):231–41.

Andrews J. Thiocyanate and smoking in pregnancy. *Journal of Obstetrics and Gynaecology of the British Commonwealth* 1973;80(9):810–4.

Andrews KW, Savitz DA, Hertz-Picciotto I. Prenatal lead exposure in relation to gestational age and birth weight: a review of epidemiologic studies. *American Journal of Industrial Medicine* 1994;26(1):13–32.

Andrews WW, Hauth JC, Goldenberg RL. Infection and preterm birth. *American Journal of Perinatology* 2000; 17(7):357–65.

Änggård E. Nitric oxide: mediator, murderer, and medicine. *Lancet* 1994;343(8907):1199–206.

Anttila A, Sallmén M. Effects of parental occupational exposure to lead and other metals on spontaneous abortion. *Journal of Occupational and Environmental Medicine* 1995;37(8):915–21.

Arcavi L, Benowitz NL. Cigarette smoking and infection. *Archives of Internal Medicine* 2004;164(20):2206–16.

Arias F, Tomich P. Etiology and outcome of low birth weight and preterm infants. *Obstetrics and Gynecology* 1982;60(3):277–81.

Artal R, Burgeson R, Fernandez FJ, Hobel CJ. Fetal and maternal copper levels in patients at term with and without premature rupture of membranes. *Obstetrics and Gynecology* 1979;53(5):608–10.

Asano N, Kondoh M, Ebihara C, Fujii M, Nakanishi T, Soares MJ, Nakashima E, Tanaka K, Sato M, Watanabe Y. Expression profiles of zinc transporters in rodent placental models. *Toxicology Letters* 2004;154(1–2): 45–53.

Ashfaq M, Janjua MZ, Nawaz M. Effects of maternal smoking on placental morphology. *Journal of Ayub Medical College, Abbottabad* 2003;15(3):12–5.

Asmussen I. Ultrastructure of the villi and fetal capillaries in placentas from smoking and nonsmoking mothers. *British Journal of Obstetrics and Gynaecology* 1980; 87(3):239–45.

Ates U, Ata B, Armagan F, Has R, Sidal B. Acute effects of maternal smoking on fetal hemodynamics. *International Journal of Gynaecology and Obstetrics* 2004; 87(1):14–8.

Athayde N, Edwin SS, Romero R, Gomez R, Maymon E, Pacora P, Menon R. A role for matrix metalloproteinase-9 in spontaneous rupture of the fetal membranes. *American Journal of Obstetrics and Gynecology* 1998; 179(5):1248–53.

Augood C, Duckitt K, Templeton AA. Smoking and female infertility: a systematic review and meta-analysis. *Human Reproduction* 1998;13(6):1532–9.

Axt-Fliedner R, Schwarze A, Nelles I, Altgassen C, Friedrich M, Schmidt W, Diedrich K. The value of uterine artery Doppler ultrasound in the prediction of severe complications in a risk population. *Archives of Gynecology and Obstetrics* 2005;271(1):53–8.

Ayadi MF, Adams EK, Melvin CL, Rivera CC, Gaffney CA, Pike J, Rabius V, Ferguson JN. Costs of a smoking cessation counseling intervention for pregnant women: comparison of three settings. *Public Health Reports* 2006;121(2):120–6.

Backer LC, Rubin CS, Marcus M, Kieszak SM, Schober SE. Serum follicle-stimulating hormone and luteinizing hormone levels in women aged 35–60 in the U.S. population: The Third National Health and Nutrition Examination Survey (NHANES III, 1988–1994). *Menopause* 1999;6(1):29–35.

Baghurst PA, Tong SL, Woodward A, McMichael AJ. Effects of maternal smoking upon neuropsychological development in early childhood: importance of taking account of social and environmental factors. *Paediatric and Perinatal Epidemiology* 1992;6(4):403–15.

Bailey LJ, Johnston MC, Billet J. Effects of carbon monoxide and hypoxia on cleft lip in A/J mice. *Cleft Palate-Craniofacial Journal* 1995;32(1):14–9.

Bainbridge SA, Sidle EH, Smith GN. Direct placental effects of cigarette smoke protect women from preeclampsia: the specific roles of carbon monoxide and antioxidant systems in the placenta. *Medical Hypotheses* 2005;64(1):17–27.

Ballatori N. Transport of toxic metals by molecular mimicry. *Environmental Health Perspectives* 2002; 110(Suppl 5):689–94.

Barber A, Robson SC, Myatt L, Bulmer JN, Lyall F. Heme oxygenase expression in human placenta and placental bed: reduced expression of placenta endothelial HO-2 in preeclampsia and fetal growth restriction. *FASEB Journal* 2001;15(7):1158–68.

Barbieri RL, Gochberg J, Ryan KJ. Nicotine, cotinine, and anabasine inhibit aromatase in human trophoblast in vitro. *Journal of Clinical Investigation* 1986a; 77(6):1727–33.

Barbieri RL, McShane PM, Ryan KJ. Constituents of cigarette smoke inhibit human granulosa cell aromatase. *Fertility and Sterility* 1986b;46(2):232–6.

Barbieri RL, Sluss PM, Powers RD, McShane PM, Bitonis A, Ginsburg E, Cramer DC. Association of body mass index, age, and cigarette smoking with serum testosterone levels in cycling women undergoing in vitro fertilization. *Fertility and Sterility* 2005;83(2):302–8.

Barbieri RL, York CM, Cherry ML, Ryan KJ. The effects of nicotine, cotinine and anabasine on rat adrenal 11 beta-hydroxylase and 21-hydroxylase. *Journal of Steroid Biochemistry* 1987;28(1):25–8.

Baron JA, La Vecchia C, Levi F. The antiestrogenic effect of cigarette smoking in women. *American Journal of Obstetrics and Gynecology* 1990;162(2):502–14.

Barrett B, Gunter E, Jenkins J, Wang M. Ascorbic acid concentration in amniotic fluid in late pregnancy. *Biology of the Neonate* 1991;60(5):333–5.

Barrett JM, Vanhooydonk JE, Boehm FH. Acute effect of cigarette smoking on the fetal heart nonstress test. *Obstetrics and Gynecology* 1981;57(4):422–5.

Barrett-Connor E. Smoking and endogenous sex hormones in men and women. In: Wald N, Baron JA, editors. *Smoking and Hormone-Related Disorders*. New York: Oxford University Press, 1990:183–96.

Barrett-Connor E, Khaw K-T. Cigarette smoking and increased endogenous estrogen levels in men. *American Journal of Epidemiology* 1987;126(2):187–92.

Bassi JA, Rosso P, Moessinger AC, Blanc WA, James LS. Fetal growth retardation due to maternal tobacco smoke exposure in the rat. *Pediatric Research* 1984;18(2):127–30.

Bataineh H, al-Hamood MH, Elbetieha A, Bani Hani I. Effect of long-term ingestion of chromium compounds on aggression, sex behavior and fertility in adult male rat. *Drug and Chemical Toxicology* 1997;20(3):133–49.

Batstra L, Hadders-Algra M, Neeleman J. Effect of antenatal exposure to maternal smoking on behavioural problems and academic achievement in childhood: prospective evidence from a Dutch birth cohort. *Early Human Development* 2003;75(1–2):21–33.

Beaty TH, Wang H, Hetmanski JB, Fan YT, Zeiger JS, Liang KY, Chiu YF, Vanderkolk CA, Seifert KC, Wulfsberg EA, et al. A case-control study of nonsyndromic oral clefts in Maryland. *Annals of Epidemiology* 2001;11(6):434–42.

Becker R, Vonk R, Vollert W, Entezami M. Doppler sonography of uterine arteries at 20–23 weeks: risk assessment of adverse pregnancy outcome by quantification of impedance and notch. *Journal of Perinatal Medicine* 2002;30(5):388–94.

Belcheva A, Ivanova-Kicheva M, Tzvetkova P, Marinov M. Effects of cigarette smoking on sperm plasma membrane integrity and DNA fragmentation. *International Journal of Andrology* 2004;27(5):296–300.

Belgore FM, Lip GYH, Blann AD. Vascular endothelial growth factor and its receptor, Flt-1, in smokers and non-smokers. *British Journal of Biomedical Science* 2000;57(3):207–13.

Benowitz NL, Perez-Stable EJ, Fong I, Modin G, Herrera B, Jacob P III. Ethnic differences in *N*-glucuronidation of nicotine and cotinine. *Journal of Pharmacology and Experimental Therapeutics* 1999;291(3):1196–203.

Berg CJ, Chang J, Callaghan WM, Whitehead SJ. Pregnancy-related mortality in the United States, 1991–1997. *Obstetrics and Gynecology* 2003;101(2):289–96.

Berlin M, Blanks R, Catton M, Kazantzis G, Mottet NK, Samiullah Y. Birth weight of children and cadmium accumulation in placentas of female nickel-cadmium (long-life) battery workers. *IARC Scientific Publications* 1992;(118):257–62.

Bermudez EA, Rifai N, Buring JE, Manson JE, Ridker PM. Relation between markers of systemic vascular inflammation and smoking in women. *American Journal of Cardiology* 2002;89(9):1117–9.

Berta L, Frairia R, Fortunati N, Fazzari A, Gaidano G. Smoking effects on the hormonal balance of fertile women. *Hormone Research* 1992;37(1–2):45–8.

Bili H, Mamopoulos M, Tsantali C, Tzevelekis P, Malaka K, Mantalenakis S, Farmakides G. Elevated umbilical erythropoietin levels during labor in newborns of smoking mothers. *American Journal of Perinatology* 1996;13(2):85–7.

Blair PS, Fleming PJ, Bensley D, Smith I, Bacon C, Taylor E, Berry J, Golding J, Tripp J. Smoking and the sudden infant death syndrome: results from 1993–5 case-control study for confidential inquiry into stillbirths and deaths in infancy. *BMJ (British Medical Journal)* 1996;313(7051):195–8.

Bódis J, Hanf V, Török A, Tinneberg HR, Borsay P, Szabó I. Influence of nicotine on progesterone and estradiol production of cultured human granulose cells. *Early Pregnancy* 1997;3(1):34–7.

Bodnar LM, Siega-Riz AM, Arab L, Chantala K, McDonald T. Predictors of pregnancy and postpartum haemoglobin concentrations in low-income women. *Public Health Nutrition* 2004;7(6):701–11.

Bolognesi C, Rossi L, Barbieri O, Santi L. Benzo[*a*]pyrene-induced DNA damage in mouse fetal tissues. *Carcinogenesis* 1985;6(8):1091–5.

Bonde JPE, Ernst E, Jensen RK, Hjollund NHI, Kolstad H, Henriksen TB, Scheike T, Giwercman A, Olsen J, Skakkebaek NE. Relation between semen quality and fertility: a population-based study of 430 first-pregnancy planners. *Lancet* 1998;352(9135):1172–7.

Bonithon-Kopp C, Huel G, Grasmick C, Sarmini H, Moreau T. Effects of pregnancy on the inter-individual variations in blood levels of lead, cadmium and mercury. *Biological Research in Pregnancy and Perinatology* 1986;7(1):37–42.

Borja-Aburto VH, Hertz-Picciotto I, Rojas Lopez M, Farias P, Rios C, Blanco J. Blood lead levels measured prospectively and risk of spontaneous abortion. *American Journal of Epidemiology* 1999;150(6):590–7.

Borovikova LV, Ivanova S, Zhang M, Yang H, Botchkina GI, Watkins LR, Wang H, Abumrad N, Eaton JW, Tracey KJ. Vagus nerve stimulation attenuates the systemic inflammatory response to endotoxin. *Nature* 2000; 405(6785):458–62.

Botto LD, Olney RS, Erickson JD. Vitamin supplements and the risk for congenital anomalies other than neural tube defects. *American Journal of Medical Genetics Part C, Seminars in Medical Genetics* 2004;125C(1):12–21.

Boulos R, Halsey NA, Holt E, Ruff A, Brutus J-R, Quinn TC, Adrien M, Boulos C. HIV-1 in Haitian women 1982–1988. The Cite Coleil/JHU AIDS Project Team. *Journal of Acquired Immune Deficiency Syndromes* 1990;3(7):721–8.

Bouyer J, Coste J, Shojaei T, Pouly J-L, Fernandez H, Gerbaud L, Job-Spira N. Risk factors for ectopic pregnancy: a comprehensive analysis based on a large case-control, population-based study in France. *American Journal of Epidemiology* 2003;157(3):185–94.

Brett KM, Cooper GS. Associations with menopause and menopausal transition in a nationally representative US sample. *Maturitas* 2003;45(2):89–97.

Briggs MH. Cigarette smoking and infertility in men [letter]. *Medical Journal of Australia* 1973;1(12):616–7.

British Medical Association. *Smoking and Reproductive Life: The Impact of Smoking on Sexual, Reproductive and Child Health*. London: British Medical Association, Board of Science and Education and Tobacco Control Resource Centre, 2004; <http://www.bma.org.uk>; accessed: February 2, 2006.

Bromberger JT, Matthews KA, Kuller LH, Wing RR, Meilahn EN, Plantinga P. Prospective study of the determinants of age at menopause. *American Journal of Epidemiology* 1997;145(2):124–33.

Bronsky PT, Johnston MC, Sulik KK. Morphogenesis of hypoxia-induced cleft lip in CL/Fr mice. *Journal of Craniofacial Genetics and Developmental Biology Supplement* 1986;2:113–28.

Brosens IA, Robertson WB, Dixon HG. The role of the spiral arteries in the pathogenesis of preeclampsia. *Obstetrics and Gynecology Annual* 1972;1:177–91.

Brown S, Vessey M, Stratton I. The influence of method of contraception and cigarette smoking on menstrual patterns. *British Journal of Obstetrics and Gynaecology* 1988;95(9):905–10.

Bruner JP, Forouzan I. Smoking and buccally administered nicotine: acute effect on uterine and umbilical artery Doppler flow velocity waveforms. *Journal of Reproductive Medicine* 1991;36(6):435–40.

Buchan PC. Cigarette smoking in pregnancy and fetal hyperviscosity. *BMJ (British Medical Journal)* 1983;286(6374):1315.

Buck GM, Sever LE, Batt RE, Mendola P. Life-style factors and female infertility. *Epidemiology* 1997;8(4):435–41.

Bui QQ, Tran MB, West WL. A comparative study of the reproductive effects of methadone and benzo[a]pyrene in the pregnant and pseudopregnant rat. *Toxicology* 1986;42(2–3):195–204.

Bulletin of the World Health Organization. Antismoking campaigns fail in industrialized countries. *Bulletin of the World Health Organization* 1999;77(5):449.

Bureau MA, Monette J, Shapcott D, Pare C, Mathieu JL, Lippe J, Blovin D, Berthiaume Y, Begin R. Carboxyhemoglobin concentration in fetal cord blood and in blood of mothers who smoked during labor. *Pediatrics* 1982;69(3):371–3.

Bureau MA, Shapcott D, Berthiaume Y, Monette J, Blouin D, Blanchard P, Begin R. Maternal cigarette smoking and fetal oxygen transport: a study of P50, 2,3-diphosphoglycerate, total hemoglobin, hematocrit, and type F hemoglobin in fetal blood. *Pediatrics* 1983;72(1):22–6.

Burguet A, Kaminski M, Abraham-Lerat L, Schaal J-P, Cambonie G, Fresson J, Grandjean H, Truffert P, Marpeau L, Voyer M, et al. The complex relationship between smoking in pregnancy and very preterm delivery: results of the Epipage study. *BJOG* 2004; 111(3):258–65.

Burns DN, Kramer A, Yellin F, Fuchs D, Wachter H, DiGioia RA, Sanchez WC, Grossman RJ, Gordin FM, Biggar RJ, et al. Cigarette smoking: a modifier of human immunodeficiency virus type 1 infection? *Journal of Acquired Immune Deficiency Syndromes* 1991;4(1):76–83.

Burns DN, Landesman S, Muenz LR, Nugent RP, Goedert JJ, Minkoff H, Walsh JH, Mendez H, Rubinstein A, Willoughby A. Cigarette smoking, premature rupture of membranes, and vertical transmission of HIV-1 among women with low CD4+ levels. *Journal of Acquired Immune Deficiency Syndromes* 1994;7(7):718–26.

Burton GJ, Palmer ME, Dalton KJ. Morphometric differences between the placental vasculature of nonsmokers, smokers and ex-smokers. *British Journal of Obstetrics and Gynaecology* 1989;96(8):907–15.

Bush PG, Mayhew TM, Abramovich DR, Aggett PJ, Burke MD, Page KR. A quantitative study on the effects of maternal smoking on placental morphology and cadmium concentration. *Placenta* 2000;21(2–3):247–56.

Butler NR, Goldstein H. Smoking in pregnancy and subsequent child development. *BMJ (British Medical Journal)* 1973;4(5892):537–75.

California Environmental Protection Agency. *Evidence on Developmental and Reproductive Toxicity of Cadmium*. Sacramento (CA): California Environmental Protection Agency, Office of Environmental Health Hazard Assessment, Reproductive and Cancer Hazard Assessment Section, 1996.

Calori G, D'Angelo A, Della Valle P, Ruotolo G, Ferini-Strambi L, Giusti C, Errera A, Gallus G. The effect of cigarette-smoking on cardiovascular risk factors: a study of monozygotic twins discordant for smoking. *Thrombosis and Haemostasis* 1996;75(1):14–8.

Campana A, Sakkas D, Stalberg A, Bianchi PG, Comte I, Pache T, Walker D. Intrauterine insemination: evaluation of the results according to the woman's age, sperm quality, total sperm count per insemination and life table analysis. *Human Reproduction* 1996;11(4):732–6.

Cantral DE, Sisson JH, Veys T, Rennard SI, Spurzem JR. Effects of cigarette smoke extract on bovine bronchial epithelial cell attachment and migration. *American Journal of Physiology* 1995;268(5 Pt 1):L723–L728.

Carmichael SL, Ma C, Rasmussen SA, Honein MA, Lammer EJ, Shaw GM, National Birth Defects Prevention Study: craniosynostosis and maternal smoking. *Birth Defects Research Part A, Clinical and Molecular Teratology* 2008;82(2):78–85.

Carmichael SL, Shaw GM, Yang W, Lammer EJ, Zhu H, Finnell RH. Limb deficiency defects, *MSX1*, and exposure to tobacco smoke. *American Journal of Medical Genetics Part A* 2004;125A(3):285–9.

Carmines EL, Gaworski CL, Faqi AS, Rajendran N. *In utero* exposure to 1R4F reference cigarette smoke: evaluation of developmental toxicity. *Toxicological Sciences* 2003;75(1):134–47.

Carratù MR, Cagiano R, De Salvia MA, Cuomo V. Wallerian degeneration in rat sciatic nerve: comparative evaluation between prenatal and postnatal exposure to carbon monoxide [abstract]. *Society for Neuroscience Abstracts* 1993a;19(Part 1):834.

Carratù MR, Renna G, Giustino A, De Salvia MA, Cuomo V. Changes in peripheral nervous system activity produced in rats by prenatal exposure to carbon monoxide. *Archives of Toxicology* 1993b;67(5):297–301.

Casanueva E, Polo E, Tejero E, Meza C. Premature rupture of amniotic membranes as functional assessment of vitamin C status during pregnancy. *Annals of the New York Academy of Sciences* 1993;678:369–70.

Cassell G, Hauth J, Andrews W, Cutter G, Goldenberg R. Chorioamnion colonization: correlation with gestational age in women following spontaneous versus indicated delivery [abstract]. *American Journal of Obstetrics and Gynecology* 1993;168:425.

Castles A, Adams EK, Melvin CL, Kelsch C, Boulton ML. Effects of smoking during pregnancy: five meta-analyses. *American Journal of Preventive Medicine* 1999;16(3):208–15.

Castro LC, Allen R, Ogunyemi D, Roll K, Platt LD. Cigarette smoking during pregnancy: acute effects on uterine flow velocity waveforms. *Obstetrics and Gynecology* 1993;81(4):551–5.

Centers for Disease Control and Prevention. Smoking during pregnancy—United States, 1990–2002. *Morbidity and Mortality Weekly Report* 2004;53(39):911–5.

Centers for Disease Control and Prevention. Cigarette smoking among adults—United States, 2003. *Morbidity and Mortality Weekly Report* 2005;54(20):509–13.

Centers for Disease Control and Prevention. Recommendations to improve preconception health and health care—United States: a report of the CDC/ATSDR Preconception Care Work Group and the Select Panel on Preconception Care. *Morbidity and Mortality Weekly Report* 2006;55(RR-6):1–23.

Centers for Disease Control and Prevention. Cigarette smoking among adults—United States, 2007. *Morbidity and Mortality Weekly Report* 2008;57(45):1221–6.

Chaloupka K, Krishnan V, Safe S. Polynuclear aromatic hydrocarbon carcinogens as antiestrogens in MCF-7 human breast cancer cells: role of the Ah receptor. *Carcinogenesis* 1992;13(12):2233–9.

Chang J, Elam-Evans LD, Berg CJ, Herndon J, Flowers L, Seed KA, Syverson CJ. Pregnancy-related mortality surveillance—United States, 1991–1999. *Morbidity and Mortality Weekly Report* 2003;52(SS-2):1–8.

Chao ST, Omiecinski CJ, Namkung MJ, Nelson SD, Dvorchik BH, Juchau MR. Catechol estrogen formation in placental and fetal tissues of humans, macaques, rats and rabbits. *Developmental Pharmacology and Therapeutics* 1981;2(1):1–16.

Chapin RE, Robbins WA, Schieve LA, Sweeney AM, Tabacova SA, Tomashek KM. Off to a good start: the influence of pre- and periconceptional exposures, parental fertility, and nutrition on children's health. *Environmental Health Perspectives* 2004;112(1):69–78.

Chatenoud L, Parazzini F, di Cintio E, Zanconato G, Benzi G, Bortolus R, La Vecchia C. Paternal and maternal smoking habits before conception and during the first trimester: relation to spontaneous abortion. *Annals of Epidemiology* 1998;8(8):520–6.

Chattopadhyay S, Ghosh S, Chaki S, Debnath J, Ghosh D. Effect of sodium arsenite on plasma levels of gonadotrophins and ovarian steroidogenesis in mature albino rats: duration-dependent response. *Journal of Toxicological Sciences* 1999;24(5):425–31.

Chattopadhyay S, Ghosh S, Debnath J, Ghosh D. Protection of sodium arsenite-induced ovarian toxicity by coadministration of L-ascorbate (vitamin C) in mature wistar strain rat. *Archives of Environmental Contamination and Toxicology* 2001;41(1):83–9.

Chen C, Cho SI, Damokosh AI, Chen D, Li G, Wang X, Xu X. Prospective study of exposure to environmental tobacco smoke and dysmenorrhea. *Environmental Health Perspectives* 2000;108(11):1019–22.

Chen C, Wang X, Wang L, Yang F, Tang G, Xing H, Ryan L, Lasley B, Overstreet JW, Stanford JB, et al. Effect of environmental tobacco smoke on levels of urinary hormone markers. *Environmental Health Perspectives* 2005;113(4);412–7.

Chen CL, Gilbert TJ, Daling JR. Maternal smoking and Down syndrome: the confounding effect of maternal age. *American Journal of Epidemiology* 1999;149(5):442–6.

Chen Z, Godfrey-Bailey L, Schiff I, Hauser R. Impact of seasonal variation, age and smoking status on human semen parameters: the Massachusetts General Hospital experience. *Journal of Experimental and Clinical Assisted Reproduction* 2004;1(1):2.

Chernoff N. Teratogenic effects of cadmium in rats. *Teratology* 1973;8(1):29–32.

Chia S-E, Lim S-TA, Tay S-K, Lim S-T. Factors associated with male infertility: a case-control study of 218 infertile and 240 fertile men. *BJOG* 2000;107(1):55–61.

Chia S-E, Xu B, Ong CN, Tsakok FMH, Lee ST. Effect of cadmium and cigarette smoking on human semen quality. *International Journal of Fertility and Menopausal Studies* 1994;39(5):292–8.

Chmielnicka J, Sowa B. Cadmium interaction with essential metals (Zn, Cu, Fe), metabolism metallothionein, and ceruloplasmin in pregnant rats and fetuses. *Ecotoxicology and Environmental Safety* 1996;35(3):277–81.

Choe S-Y, Kim S-J, Kim H-G, Lee JH, Choi Y, Lee H, Kim Y. Evaluation of estrogenicity of major heavy metals. *Science of the Total Environment* 2003;312(1–3):15–21.

Chong DS, Yip PS, Karlberg J. Maternal smoking: an increasing unique risk factor for sudden infant death syndrome in Sweden. *Acta Paediatrica* 2004;93(4):471–8.

Chow W-H, Daling JR, Cates W Jr, Greenberg RS. Epidemiology of ectopic pregnancy. *Epidemiologic Reviews* 1987;9:70–94.

Christensen K, Olsen J, Norgaard-Pedersen B, Basso O, Stovring H, Milhollin-Johnson L, Murray JC. Oral clefts, transforming growth factor alpha gene variants, and maternal smoking: a population-based case-control study in Denmark, 1991–1994. *American Journal of Epidemiology* 1999;149(3):248–55.

Christianson RE. Gross differences observed in the placentas of smokers and nonsmokers. *American Journal of Epidemiology* 1979;110(2):178–87.

Churg A, Sun J-P, Zay K. Cigarette smoke increases amosite asbestos fiber binding to the surface of tracheal epithelial cells. *American Journal of Physiology* 1998;275(3):L502–L508.

Clarkson TW, Nordberg GF, Sager PR. Reproductive and developmental toxicity of metals. *Scandinavian Journal of Work, Environment & Health* 1985;11(3 Spec No):145–54.

Cnattingius S. The epidemiology of smoking during pregnancy: smoking prevalence, maternal characteristics, and pregnancy outcomes. *Nicotine & Tobacco Research* 2004;6(Suppl 2):S125–S140.

Cnattingius S, Granath F, Petersson G, Harlow BL. The influence of gestational age and smoking habits on the risk of subsequent preterm deliveries. *New England Journal of Medicine* 1999;341(13):943–8.

Cnattingius V, Haglund B, Meirik O. Cigarette smoking as risk factor for late fetal and early neonatal death. *BMJ (British Medical Journal)* 1988;297(6643):258–61.

Cogswell ME, Weisberg P, Spong C. Cigarette smoking, alcohol use and adverse pregnancy outcomes: implications for micronutrient supplementation. *Journal of Nutrition* 2003;133(5 Suppl 2):1722S–1731S.

Cole PV, Hawkins LH, Roberts D. Smoking during pregnancy and its effects on the fetus. *Journal of Obstetrics and Gynaecology of the British Commonwealth* 1972;79(9):782–7.

Coleman MAG, McCowan LME, North RA. Mid-trimester uterine artery Doppler screening as a predictor of adverse pregnancy outcome in high-risk women. *Ultrasound in Obstetrics & Gynecology* 2000;15(1):7–12.

Comeau J, Shaw L, Marcell CC, Lavery JP. Early placenta previa and delivery outcome. *Obstetrics and Gynecology* 1983;61(5):577–80.

Conde-Agudelo A, Althabe F, Belizán JM, Kafury-Goeta AC. Cigarette smoking during pregnancy and risk of preeclampsia: a systematic review. *American Journal of Obstetrics and Gynecology* 1999;181(4):1026–35.

Connor SK, McIntyre L. The sociodemographic predictors of smoking cessation among pregnant women in Canada. *Canadian Journal of Public Health* 1999;90(5):352–5.

Cooke JP, Dzau VJ. Nitric oxide synthase: role in the genesis of vascular disease. *Annual Review of Medicine* 1997;48:489–509.

Cooper GS, Baird DD, Hulka BS, Weinberg CR, Savitz DA, Hughes CL Jr. Follicle-stimulating hormone concentrations in relation to active and passive smoking. *Obstetrics and Gynecology* 1995;85(3):407–11.

Cooper GS, Sandler DP. Age at natural menopause and mortality. *Annals of Epidemiology* 1998;8(4):229–35.

Cooper GS, Sandler DP, Bohlig M. Active and passive smoking and the occurrence of natural menopause. *Epidemiology* 1999;10(6):771–3.

Coppens M, Vindla S, James DK, Sahota DS. Computerized analysis of acute and chronic changes in fetal heart rate variation and fetal activity in association with maternal smoking. *American Journal of Obstetrics and Gynecology* 2001;185(2):421–6.

Corberand J, Nguyen F, Do AH, Dutau G, Laharrague P, Fontanilles AM, Gleizes B. Effect of tobacco smoking on the functions of polymorphonuclear leukocytes. *Infection and Immunity* 1979;23(3):577–81.

Corre F, Lellouch J, Schwartz D. Smoking and leucocyte-counts: results of an epidemiological survey. *Lancet* 1971;2(7725):632–4.

Coste J, Job-Spira N, Fernandez H, Papiernik E, Spira A. Risk factors for ectopic pregnancy: a case-control study in France, with special focus on infectious factors. *American Journal of Epidemiology* 1991;133(9): 839–49.

Cozen W, Diaz-Sanchez D, Gauderman WJ, Zadnick J, Cockburn MG, Gill PS, Masood R, Hamilton AS, Jyrala M, Mack TM. Th1 and Th2 cytokines and IgE levels in identical twins with varying levels of cigarette consumption. *Journal of Clinical Immunology* 2004; 24(6):617–22.

Cramer DW, Barbieri RL, Xu H, Reichardt JKV. Determinants of basal follicle-stimulating hormone levels in premenopausal women. *Journal of Clinical Endocrinology and Metabolism* 1994;79(4):1105–9.

Cramer DW, Wise LA. The epidemiology of recurrent pregnancy loss. *Seminars in Reproductive Medicine* 2000; 18(4):331–9.

Creasy RK, Resnik R, Iams JD, editors. Placenta previa and abruptio placentae. In: *Maternal-Fetal Medicine*. 5th ed. Philadelphia: W.B. Saunders Company, 2004:709.

Cresteil T, Beaune P, Celier C, Leroux JP, Guengerich FP. Cytochrome P-450 isoenzyme content and monooxygenase activities in rat liver: effect of ontogenesis and pretreatment by phenobarbital and 3-methylcholanthrene. *Journal of Pharmacology and Experimental Therapeutics* 1986;236(1):269–76.

Cross CE, Traber M, Eiserich J, van der Vliet A. Micronutrient antioxidants and smoking. *British Medical Bulletin* 1999;55(3):691–704.

Cunningham FG, Gant NF, Leveno KJ, Gilstrap LC III, Hauth JC, Wenstrom KD, editors. Abortion. In: *Williams Obstetrics*. 21st ed. New York: McGraw-Hill, 2001:868.

Dai WS, Gutai JP, Kuller LH, Cauley JA. Cigarette smoking and serum sex hormones in men. *American Journal of Epidemiology* 1988;128(4):796–805.

Davis RB, Leuschen MP, Boyd D, Goodlin RC. Evaluation of platelet function in pregnancy: comparative studies in non-smokers and smokers. *Thrombosis Research* 1987;46(2):175–86.

de la Chica RA, Ribas I, Giraldo J, Egozcue J, Fuster C. Chromosomal instability in amniocytes from fetuses of mothers who smoke. *JAMA: the Journal of the American Medical Association* 2005;293(10):1212–22.

Dejmek J, Solanský I, Beneš I, Leníček J, Šrám RJ. The impact of polycyclic aromatic hydrocarbons and fine particles on pregnancy outcome. *Environmental Health Perspectives* 2000;108(12):1159–64.

Dekker G, Robillard P-Y. The birth interval hypothesis—does it really indicate the end of the primipaternity hypothesis. *Journal of Reproductive Immunology* 2003; 59(2):245–51.

Demir R, Demir AY, Yinanc M. Structural changes in placental barrier of smoking mother: a quantitative and ultrastructural study. *Pathology, Research and Practice* 1994;190(7):656–67.

Denham M, Schell LM, Deane G, Gallo MV, Ravenscroft J, DeCaprio AP, Akwesasne Task Force on the Environment. Relationship of lead, mercury, mirex, dichlorodiphenyldichloroethylene, hexachlorobenzene, and polychlorinated biphenyls to timing of menarche among Akwesasne Mohawk girls. *Pediatrics* 2005; 115(2):e127–e134.

Deslypere JP, Vermeulen A. Leydig cell function in normal men: effect of age, life-style, residence, diet, and activity. *Journal of Clinical Endocrinology and Metabolism* 1984;59(5):955–62.

DiCarlantonio G, Talbot P. Inhalation of mainstream and sidestream cigarette smoke retards embryo transport and slows muscle contraction in oviducts of hamsters (*Mesocricetus auratus*). *Biology of Reproduction* 1999; 61(3):651–6.

Dietz PM, Adams MM, Rochat RW, Mathis MP. Prenatal smoking in two consecutive pregnancies: Georgia, 1989–1992. *Maternal and Child Health Journal* 1997; 1(1):43–51.

DiFranza JR, Aligne CA, Weitzman M. Prenatal and postnatal environmental tobacco smoke exposure and children's health. *Pediatrics* 2004;113(4 Suppl):1007–15.

DiFranza JR, Lew RA. Effect of maternal cigarette smoking on pregnancy complications and sudden infant death syndrome. *Journal of Family Practice* 1995;40(4): 385–94.

Dommisse J, Tiltman AJ. Placental bed biopsies in placental abruption. *British Journal of Obstetrics and Gynaecology* 1992;99(8):651–4.

Doreswamy K, Shrilatha B, Rajeshkumar T, Muralidhara. Nickel-induced oxidative stress in testis of mice: evidence of DNA damage and genotoxic effects. *Journal of Andrology* 2004;25(6):996–1003.

Dotson LE, Robertson LS, Tuchfeld B. Plasma alcohol, smoking, hormone concentrations and self-reported aggression: a study in a social-drinking situation. *Journal of Studies on Alcohol* 1975;36(5):578–86.

Drbohlav P, Bencko V, Masata J, Bendl J, Rezacova J, Zouhar T, Cerny V, Halkova E. Detection of cadmium and zinc in the blood and follicular fluid in women in the IVF and ET program [Czech]. *Ceska Gynekologie* 1998;63(4):292–300.

Drews CD, Murphy CC, Yeargin-Allsopp M, Decoufle P. The relationship between idiopathic mental retardation and maternal smoking during pregnancy. *Pediatrics* 1996;97(4):547–53.

D'Souza SW, Black PM, Williams N, Jennison RF. Effect of smoking during pregnancy upon the haematological values of cord blood. *British Journal of Obstetrics and Gynaecology* 1978;85(7):495–9.

Duley L. Pre-eclampsia and hypertension. *Clinical Evidence* 2003;(9):1584–600.

Ebrahim SH, Floyd RL, Merritt RK II, Decoufle P, Holtzman D. Trends in pregnancy-related smoking rates in the United States, 1987–1996. *JAMA: the Journal of the American Medical Association* 2000;283(3):361–6.

Edman J, Sobel JD, Taylor ML. Zinc status in women with recurrent vulvovaginal candidiasis. *American Journal of Obstetrics and Gynecology* 1986;155(5):1082–5.

Egawa M, Yasuda K, Nakajima T, Okada H, Yoshimura T, Yuri T, Yasuhara M, Nakamoto T, Nagata F, Kanzaki H. Smoking enhances oxytocin-induced rhythmic myometrial contraction. *Biology of Reproduction* 2003; 68(6):2274–80.

Eggert-Kruse W, Schwarz H, Rohr G, Demirakca T, Tilgen W, Runnebaum B. Sperm morphology assessment using strict criteria and male fertility under in-vivo conditions of conception. *Human Reproduction* 1996;11(1):139–46.

Einarsson JI, Sangi-Haghpeykar H, Gardner MO. Sperm exposure and development of preeclampsia. *American Journal of Obstetrics and Gynecology* 2003; 188(5):1241–3.

Ejaz S, Seok KB, Woong LC. Toxicological effects of mainstream whole smoke solutions on embryonic movements of the developing embryo. *Drug and Chemical Toxicology* 2005;28(1):1–14.

Ekwo EE, Gosselink CA, Moawad A. Unfavorable outcome in penultimate pregnancy and premature rupture of membranes in successive pregnancy. *Obstetrics and Gynecology* 1992;80(2):166–72.

Ekwo EE, Gosselink CA, Woolson R, Moawad A. Risks for premature rupture of amniotic membranes. *International Journal of Epidemiology* 1993;22(3):495–503.

El Ahmer OR, Essery SD, Saadi AT, Raza MW, Ogilvie MM, Weir DM, Blackwell CC. The effect of cigarette smoke on adherence of respiratory pathogens to buccal epithelial cells. *FEMS Immunology and Medical Microbiology* 1999;23(1):27–36.

Eldridge MW, Berman W Jr, Greene ER. Chronic maternal cigarette smoking and fetal abdominal aortic blood flow in humans. *Journal of Ultrasound in Medicine* 1986;5(3):131–6.

England LJ, Levine RJ, Mills JL, Klebanoff MA, Yu KF, Cnattingius S. Adverse pregnancy outcomes in snuff users. *American Journal of Obstetrics and Gynecology* 2003;189(4):939–43.

English KM, Pugh PJ, Parry H, Scutt NE, Channer KS, Jones TH. Effect of cigarette smoking on levels of bioavailable testosterone in healthy men. *Clinical Science (London)* 2001;100(6):661–5.

Eskenazi B, Gold EB, Lasley BL, Samuels SJ, Hammond SK, Wight S, Rasnor MO, Hines CJ, Schenker MB. Prospective monitoring of early fetal loss and clinical spontaneous abortion among female semiconductor workers. *American Journal of Industrial Medicine* 1995;28(6):833–46.

Eskenazi B, Trupin L. Passive and active maternal smoking during pregnancy, as measured by serum cotinine, and postnatal exposure. II: effects on neurodevelopment at age 5 years. *American Journal of Epidemiology* 1995;142(9 Suppl):S19–S29.

Eskes TKAB. Abruptio placentae: a "classic" dedicated to Elizabeth Ramsey. *European Journal of Obstetrics, Gynecology, and Reproductive Biology* 1997;75(1): 63–70.

Everett KD, Gage J, Bullock L, Longo DR, Geden E, Madsen RW. A pilot study of smoking and associated behaviors of low-income expectant fathers. *Nicotine & Tobacco Research* 2005;7(2):269–76.

Everson RB, Sandler DP, Wilcox AJ, Schreinemachers D, Shore DL, Weinberg C. Effect of passive exposure to smoking on age at natural menopause. *BMJ (British Medical Journal)* 1986;293(6550):792.

Faiz AS, Ananth CV. Etiology and risk factors for placenta previa: an overview and meta-analysis of observational studies. *Journal of Maternal-Fetal & Neonatal Medicine* 2003;13(3):175–90.

Fallin MD, Hetmanski JB, Park J, Scott AF, Ingersoll R, Fuernkranz HA, McIntosh I, Beaty TH. Family-based analysis of MSX1 haplotypes for association with oral clefts. *Genetic Epidemiology* 2003;25(2):168–75.

Fanucchi MV, Buckpitt AR, Murphy ME, Plopper CG. Naphthalene cytotoxicity of differentiating Clara cells in neonatal mice. *Toxicology and Applied Pharmacology* 1997;144(1):96–104.

Faruque MO, Khan MR, Rahman M, Ahmed F. Relationship between smoking and antioxidant nutrient status. *British Journal of Nutrition* 1995;73(4):625–32.

Fechter LD. Neurotoxicity of prenatal carbon monoxide exposure. *Research Report (Health Effects Institute)* 1987;(12):3–22.

Fechter LD, Annau Z. Effects of prenatal carbon monoxide exposure on neonatal rats. In: Horvath M, editor. *Adverse Effects of Environmental Chemicals and Psychotropic Drugs*. Vol. 2. New York: Elsevier, 1976:219.

Fechter LD, Annau, Z. Prenatal carbon monoxide exposure alters behavioral development. *Neurobehavioral Toxicology* 1980;2(1):7–11.

Fechter LD, Annau, Z. Toxicity of mild prenatal carbon monoxide exposure. *Science* 1997;197(4304):680–2.

Ferm VH. Developmental malformations induced by cadmium: a study of timed injections during embryogenesis. *Biology of the Neonate* 1971;19(1):101–7.

Field AE, Colditz GA, Willett WC, Longcope C, McKinlay JB. The relation of smoking, age, relative weight, and dietary intake to serum adrenal steroids, sex hormones, and sex hormone-binding globulin in middle-aged men. *Journal of Clinical Endocrinology and Metabolism* 1994;79(5):1310–6.

Fiore MC, Bailey WC, Cohen SJ, Dorfman SF, Goldstein MG, Gritz ER, Heyman RB, Holbrook J, Jaén CR, Kottke TE, et al. *Smoking Cessation*. Clinical Practice Guideline No. 18. Rockville (MD): U.S. Department of Health and Human Services, Public Health Service, Agency for Health Care Policy and Research, 1996. AHCPR Publication No 96-0692.

Fiore MC, Bailey WC, Cohen SJ, Dorfman SF, Goldstein MG, Gritz ER, Heyman RB, Jaén CR, Kottke TE, Lando HA, et al. *Treating Tobacco Use and Dependence*. Clinical Practice Guideline. Rockville (MD): U.S. Department of Health and Human Services, Public Health Service, 2000.

Fiore MC, Jaén CR, Baker TB, Bailey WC, Benowitz NL, Curry SJ, Dorfma SF, Froelicher ES, Goldstein MG, Healton CG, et al. *Treating Tobacco Use and Dependence: 2008 Update*. Clinical Practice Guideline. Rockville (MD): U.S. Department of Health and Human Services, 2008.

Fischer Walker CF, Black RE. Zinc and the risk for infectious disease. *Annual Review of Nutrition* 2004;24:255–75.

Fisher GL. Function and homeostasis of copper and zinc in mammals. *Science of the Total Environment* 1975;4(4):373–412.

Fisher SJ. The placental problem: linking abnormal cytotrophoblast differentiation to the maternal symptoms of preeclampsia. *Reproductive Biology and Endocrinology* 2004;2:53.

Fisher SE, Atkinson M, Van Thiel DH. Selective fetal malnutrition: the effect of nicotine, ethanol, and acetaldehyde upon in vitro uptake of alpha-aminoisobutyric acid by human term placental villous slices. *Developmental Pharmacology and Therapeutics* 1984;7(4):229–38.

Fong KW, Ohlsson A, Hannah ME, Grisaru S, Kingdom J, Cohen H, Ryan M, Windrim R, Foster G, Amankwah K. Prediction of perinatal outcome in fetuses suspected to have intrauterine growth restriction: Doppler US study of fetal cerebral, renal, and umbilical arteries. *Radiology* 1999;213(3):681–9.

Forss M, Lehtovirta P, Rauramo I, Kariniemi V. Midtrimester fetal heart rate variability and maternal hemodynamics in association with smoking. *American Journal of Obstetrics and Gynecology* 1983;146(6):693–5.

Fox NL, Sexton M, Hebel JR. Prenatal exposure to tobacco. I: effects on physical growth at age three. *International Journal of Epidemiology* 1990;19(1):66–71.

Fraga CG, Motchnik PA, Wyrobek AJ, Rempel DM, Ames BN. Smoking and low antioxidant levels increase oxidative damage to sperm DNA. *Mutation Research* 1996;351(2):199–203.

Fraker PJ. Roles for cell death in zinc deficiency. *Journal of Nutrition* 2005;135(3):359–62.

Fraker PJ, King LE. Reprogramming of the immune system during zinc deficiency. *Annual Review of Nutrition* 2004;24:277–98.

French JI, McGregor JA. The pathobiology of premature rupture of membranes. *Seminars in Perinatology* 1996;20(5):344–68.

Fréry N, Nessmann C, Girard F, Lafond J, Moreau T, Blot P, Lellouch J, Huel G. Environmental exposure to cadmium and human birthweight. *Toxicology* 1993;79(2):109–18.

Fried PA, James DS, Watkinson B. Growth and pubertal milestones during adolescence in offspring prenatally exposed to cigarettes and marihuana. *Neurotoxicology and Teratology* 2001;23(5):431–6.

Fried PA, Watkinson B, Siegel LS. Reading and language in 9- to 12-year olds prenatally exposed to cigarettes and marijuana. *Neurotoxicology and Teratology* 1997;19(3):171–83.

Friedman AJ, Ravnikar VA, Barbieri RL. Serum steroid hormone profiles in postmenopausal smokers and nonsmokers. *Fertility and Sterility* 1987;47(3):398–401.

Friedman GD, Siegelaub AB, Seltzer CC, Feldman R, Collen MF. Smoking habits and the leukocyte count. *Archives of Environmental Health* 1973;26(3):137–43.

Funabashi T, Sano A, Mitsushima D, Kimura F. Nicotine inhibits pulsatile luteinizing hormone secretion in human males but not in human females, and tolerance to this nicotine effect is lost within one week of quitting smoking. *Journal of Clinical Endocrinology and Metabolism* 2005;90(7):3908–13.

Garcia-Morales P, Saceda M, Kenney N, Kim N, Salomon DS, Gottardis MM, Solomon HB, Sholler PF, Jordan VC, Martin MB. Effect of cadmium on estrogen receptor levels and estrogen-induced responses in human breast cancer cells. *Journal of Biological Chemistry* 1994;269(24):16896–901.

Gardosi J, Francis A. Early pregnancy predictors of preterm birth: the role of a prolonged menstruation–conception interval. *BJOG* 2000;107(2):228–37.

Garvey DJ, Longo LD. Chronic low level maternal carbon monoxide exposure and fetal growth and development. *Biology of Reproduction* 1978;19(1):8–14.

Gaspari L, Chang S-S, Santella RM, Garte S, Pedotti P, Taioli E. Polycyclic aromatic hydrocarbon-DNA adducts in human sperm as a marker of DNA damage and infertility. *Mutation Research* 2003;535(2):155–60.

Ge X, Conger RD, Elder GH Jr. Coming of age too early: pubertal influences on girls' vulnerability to psychological distress. *Child Development* 1996;67(6):3386–400.

Genbacev O, Bass KE, Joslin RJ, Fisher SJ. Maternal smoking inhibits early human cytotrophoblast differentiation. *Reproductive Toxicology* 1995;9(3):245–55.

Genbacev O, McMaster MT, Zdravkovic T, Fisher SJ. Disruption of oxygen-regulated responses underlies pathological changes in the placentas of women who smoke or who are passively exposed to smoke during pregnancy. *Reproductive Toxicology* 2003;17(5):509–18.

Gennser G, Marsal K, Brantmark B. Maternal smoking and fetal breathing movements. *American Journal of Obstetrics and Gynecology* 1975;123(8):861–7.

George L, Granath F, Johansson AL, Anneren G, Cnattingius S. Environmental tobacco smoke and risk of spontaneous abortion. *Epidemiology* 2006;17(5):500–5.

Gerrard JW, Heiner DC, Ko CG, Mink J, Meyers A, Dosman JA. Immunoglobulin levels in smokers and nonsmokers. *Annals of Allergy* 1980;44(5):261–2.

Gieseke C, Talbot P. Cigarette smoke affects hamster oocyte cumulus complex pickup rate, adhesion and ciliary beat frequency [abstract]. *Molecular Biology of the Cell* 2003;14(Suppl):388a–389a.

Gilboa SM, Mendola P, Olshan AF, Langlois PH, Savitz DA, Loomis D, Herring AH, Fixler DE. Relation between ambient air quality and selected birth defects, Seven County Study, Texas, 1997–2000. *American Journal of Epidemiology* 2005;162(3):238–52.

Gnoth C, Godehardt E, Frank-Herrmann P, Friol K, Tigges J, Freundl G. Definition and prevalence of subfertility and infertility. *Human Reproduction* 2005;20(5):1144–7.

Gocze PM, Freeman DA. Cytotoxic effects of cigarette smoke alkaloids inhibit the progesterone production and cell growth of cultured MA-10 Leydig tumor cells. *European Journal of Obstetrics, Gynecology, and Reproductive Biology* 2000;93(1):77–83.

Gocze PM, Szabo I, Freeman DA. Influence of nicotine, cotinine, anabasine and cigarette smoke extract on human granulosa cell progesterone and estradiol synthesis. *Gynecological Endocrinology* 1999;13(4):266–72.

Goldenberg RL, Culhane JF. Infection as a cause of preterm birth. *Clinics in Perinatology* 2003;30(4):677–700.

Goldenberg RL, Hauth JC, Andrews WW. Intrauterine infection and preterm delivery. *New England Journal of Medicine* 2000;342(20):1500–7.

Goldner TE, Lawson HW, Xia Z, Atrash HK. Surveillance for ectopic pregnancy—United States, 1970–1989. *Morbidity and Mortality Weekly Report* 1993;42(SS-6):73–85.

Golub MS. Intrauterine and reproductive toxicity of nutritionally essential metals. In: Golub MS, editor. *Metals, Fertility, and Reproductive Toxicity.* Boca Raton (FL): CRC Press, 2005a:93–115.

Golub MS. Reproductive toxicity of mercury, cadmium, and arsenic. In: Golub MS, editor. *Metals, Fertility, and Reproductive Toxicity.* Boca Raton (FL): CRC Press, 2005b:6–22.

Golub MS, Macintosh MS, Baumrind N. Developmental and reproductive toxicity of inorganic arsenic: animal studies and human concerns. *Journal of Toxicology and Environmental Health Part B, Critical Reviews* 1998;1(3):199–241.

Gonçalves L, Chaiworapongsa T, Romero R. Intrauterine infection and prematurity. *Mental Retardation and Developmental Disabilities Research Reviews* 2002;8(1):3–13.

Goodman JD, Visser FG, Dawes GS. Effects of maternal cigarette smoking on fetal trunk movements, fetal breathing movements and the fetal heart rate. *British Journal of Obstetrics and Gynaecology* 1984;91(7):657–61.

Gossain VV, Sherma NK, Srivastava L, Michelakis AM, Rovner DR. Hormonal effects of smoking—II: effects on plasma cortisol, growth hormone, and prolactin. *American Journal of the Medical Sciences* 1986;291(5):325–7.

Goyer RA, Clarkson TW. Toxic effects of metals. In: Klaassen CD, editor. *Casarett and Doull's Toxicology: The Basic Science of Poisons.* 6th ed. New York: McGraw-Hill, 2001:811–67.

Graca LM, Cardoso CG, Clode N, Calhaz-Jorge C. Acute effects of maternal cigarette smoking on fetal heart rate and fetal body movements felt by the mother. *Journal of Perinatal Medicine* 1991;19(5):385–90.

Gruper Y, Bar J, Bacharach E, Ehrlich R. Transferrin receptor co-localizes and interacts with the hemochromatosis factor (HFE) and the divalent metal transporter-1 (DMT1) in trophoblast cells. *Journal of Cellular Physiology* 2005;204(3):901–12.

Gudmundsson S, Korszun P, Olofsson P, Dubiel M. New score indicating placental vascular resistance. *Acta Obstetricia et Gynecologica Scandinavica* 2003; 82(9):807–12.

Guinet E, Yoshida K, Nouri-Shirazi M. Nicotinic environment affects the differentiation and functional maturation of monocytes derived dendritic cells (DCs). *Immunology Letters* 2004;95(1):45–55.

Gupta PC, Sreevidya S. Smokeless tobacco use, birth weight, and gestational age: population based, prospective cohort study of 1217 women in Mumbai, India. *BMJ (British Medical Journal)* 2004;328(7455):1538–42.

Gupta PC, Subramoney S. Smokeless tobacco use and risk of stillbirth: a cohort study in Mumbai, India. *Epidemiology* 2006;17(1):47–51.

Guzick DS, Overstreet JW, Factor-Litvak P, Brazil CK, Nakajima ST, Coutifaris C, Carson SA, Cisneros P, Steinkampf MP, Hill JA, et al. Sperm morphology, motility, and concentration in fertile and infertile men. *New England Journal of Medicine* 2001;345(19): 1388–93.

Hadley CB, Main DM, Gabbe SG. Risk factors for preterm premature rupture of the fetal membranes. *American Journal of Perinatology* 1990;7(4):374–9.

Hamilton BE, Martin JA, Sutton PD. Births: preliminary data for 2003. *National Vital Statistics Reports* 2004;53(9):1–17.

Haram K, Mortensen JHS, Wollen A-L. Preterm delivery: an overview. *Acta Obstetricia et Gynecologica Scandinavica* 2003;82(8):687–704.

Hardy BJ, Welcher DW, Stanley J, Dallas JR. Long-range outcome of adolescent pregnancy. *Clinical Obstetrics and Gynecology* 1978;21(4):1215–32.

Hardy JB, Mellits ED. Does maternal smoking during pregnancy have a long-term effect on the child? *Lancet* 1972; 2(7791):1332–6.

Harger JH, Hsing AW, Tuomala RE, Gibbs RS, Mead PB, Eschenbach DA, Knox GE, Polk BF. Risk factors for preterm premature rupture of fetal membranes: a multicenter case-control study. *American Journal of Obstetrics and Gynecology* 1990;163(1 Pt 1):130–7.

Harlow BL, Signorello LB. Factors associated with early menopause. *Maturitas* 2000;35(1):3–9.

Harlow SD, Ephross SA. Epidemiology of menstruation and its relevance to women's health. *Epidemiologic Reviews* 1995;17(2):265–86.

Harlow SD, Park M. A longitudinal study of risk factors for the occurrence, duration and severity of menstrual cramps in a cohort of college women. *British Journal of Obstetrics and Gynaecology* 1996;103(11):1134–42.

Harrington K, Fayyad A, Thakur V, Aquilina J. The value of uterine artery Doppler in the prediction of uteroplacental complications in multiparous women. *Ultrasound in Obstetrics & Gynecology* 2004;23(1):50–5.

Hartsfield JK Jr, Hickman TA, Everett ET, Shaw GM, Lammer EJ, Finnell RA. Analysis of the *EPHX1* 113 polymorphism and *GSTM1* homozygous null polymorphism and oral clefting associated with maternal smoking. *American Journal of Medical Genetics* 2001;102(1):21–4.

Hassold TJ. Nondisjunction in the human male. *Current Topics in Developmental Biology* 1998;37:383–406.

Haug K, Irgens LM, Skjaerven R, Markestad T, Baste V, Schreuder P. Maternal smoking and birthweight: effect modification of period, maternal age and paternal smoking. *Acta Obstetricia et Gynecologica Scandinavica* 2000;79(6):485–9.

He Q, Karlberg J. BMI in childhood and its association with height gain, timing of puberty, and final height. *Pediatric Research* 2001;49(2):244–51.

Hecht SS. Tobacco smoke carcinogens and lung cancer. *Journal of the National Cancer Institute* 1999; 91(14):1194–210.

Heffner LJ, Sherman CB, Speizer FE, Weiss ST. Clinical and environmental predictors of preterm labor. *Obstetrics and Gynecology* 1993;81(5 Pt 1):750–7.

Heinonen S, Saarikoski S. Reproductive risk factors of fetal asphyxia at delivery: a population based analysis. *Journal of Clinical Epidemiology* 2001;54(4):407–10.

Henson MC, Chedrese PJ. Endocrine disruption by cadmium, a common environmental toxicant with paradoxical effects on reproduction. *Experimental Biology and Medicine (Maywood, N.J.)* 2004;229(5):383–92.

Hidiroglou M, Knipfel JE. Zinc in mammalian sperm: a review. *Journal of Dairy Science* 1984;67(6):1147–56.

Hladky K, Yankowitz J, Hansen WF. Placental abruption. *Obstetrical & Gynecological Survey* 2002;57(5): 299–305.

Hoffmann D, Djordjevic MV, Hoffmann I. The changing cigarette. *Preventive Medicine* 1997;26(4):427–34.

Hofvendahl EA. Smoking in pregnancy as a risk factor for long-term mortality in the offspring. *Paediatric and Perinatal Epidemiology* 1995;9(4):381–90.

Hogge WA, Byrnes AL, Lanasa MC, Surti U. The clinical use of karyotyping spontaneous abortions. *American Journal of Obstetrics and Gynecology* 2003;189(2):397–402.

Holladay SD, Luster MI. Alterations in fetal thymic and liver hematopoietic cells as indicators of exposure to developmental immunotoxicants. *Environmental Health Perspectives* 1996;104(Suppl 4):809–13.

Holladay SD, Smith BJ. Fetal hematopoietic alterations after maternal exposure to benzo[*a*]pyrene: a cytometric evaluation. *Journal of Toxicology and Environmental Health* 1994;42(3):259–73.

Honein MA, Paulozzi LJ, Moore CA. Family history, maternal smoking, and clubfoot: an indication of a gene-environment interaction. *American Journal of Epidemiology* 2000;152(7):658–65.

Honein MA, Paulozzi LJ, Watkins ML. Maternal smoking and birth defects: validity of birth certificate data for effect estimation. *Public Health Reports* 2001; 116(4):327–35.

Honein MA, Rasmussen SA, Reefhuis J, Romitti PA, Lammer EJ, Sun L, Correa A. Maternal smoking and environmental tobacco smoke exposure and the risk of orofacial clefts. *Epidemiology* 2007;18(2):226–33.

Hong Y-C, Kim H, Im M-W, Lee K-H, Woo B-H, Christiani DC. Maternal genetic effects on neonatal susceptibility to oxidative damage from environmental tobacco smoke. *Journal of the National Cancer Institute* 2001; 93(8):645–7.

Hong Y-C, Lee K-H, Son B-K, Ha E-H, Moon H-S, Ha M. Effects of the GSTM1 and GSTT1 polymorphisms on the relationship between maternal exposure to environmental tobacco smoke and neonatal birth weight. *Journal of Occupational and Environmental Medicine* 2003;45(5):492–8.

Hopenhayn C, Ferreccio C, Browning SR, Huang B, Peralta C, Gibb H, Hertz-Picciotto I. Arsenic exposure from drinking water and birth weight. *Epidemiology* 2003; 14(5):593–602.

Hopenhayn-Rich C, Browning SR, Hertz-Picciotto I, Ferreccio C, Peralta C, Gibb H. Chronic arsenic exposure and risk of infant mortality in two areas of Chile. *Environmental Health Perspectives* 2000;108(7): 667–73.

Horak S, Polanska J, Widlak P. Bulky DNA adducts in human sperm: relationship with fertility, semen quality, smoking, and environmental factors. *Mutation Research* 2003;537(1):53–65.

Hornsby PP, Wilcox AJ, Weinberg CR. Cigarette smoking and disturbance of menstrual function. *Epidemiology* 1998;9(2):193–8.

Horst MA, Sastry BV. Maternal tobacco smoking and alterations in amino acid transport in human placenta: induction of transport systems. *Progress in Clinical and Biological Research* 1988;258:249–62.

Houlgate P. *UK Smoke Constituents Study. Part 11: Determination of Metals Yields in Cigarette Smoke by ICP-MS & CVAAS*. Kingston upon Thames (UK): Arista Laboratories Europe, 2003.

Howe DT, Wheeler T, Osmond C. The influence of maternal haemoglobin and ferritin on mid-pregnancy placental volume. *British Journal of Obstetrics and Gynaecology* 1995;102(3):213–9.

Hoyer PB. Impact of metals on ovarian function. In: Golub MJ, editor. *Metals, Fertility, and Reproductive Toxicity*. Boca Raton (FL): CRC Press, 2005:155–73.

Hsia CC. Respiratory function of hemoglobin. *New England Journal of Medicine* 1998;338(4):239–47.

Huang S, Driessen N, Knoll M, Talbot P. In vitro analysis of oocyte cumulus complex pickup rate in the hamster *Mesocricetus auratus*. *Molecular Reproduction and Development* 1997;47(3):312–22.

Huel G, Boudene C, Ibrahim MA. Cadmium and lead content of maternal and newborn hair: relationship to parity, birth weight, and hypertension. *Archives of Environmental Health* 1981;36(5):221–7.

Huel G, Everson RB, Menger I. Increased hair cadmium in newborns of women occupationally exposed to heavy metals. *Environmental Research* 1984;35(1):115–21.

Huel G, Godin J, Fréry N, Girard F, Moreau T, Nessman C, Blot P. Aryl hydrocarbon hydroxylase activity in human placenta and threatened preterm delivery. *Journal of Exposure Analysis and Environmental Epidemiology* 1993;3(Suppl 1):187–99.

Hughes DA, Haslam PL, Townsend PJ, Turner-Warwick M. Numerical and functional alterations in circulatory lymphocytes in cigarette smokers. *Clinical and Experimental Immunology* 1985;61(2):459–66.

Hughes EG, Brennan BG. Does cigarette smoking impair natural or assisted fecundity? *Fertility and Sterility* 1996;66(5):679–89.

Huisman M, Risseeuw B, van Eyck J, Arabin B. Nicotine and caffeine: influence on prenatal hemodynamics and behavior in early twin pregnancy. *Journal of Reproductive Medicine* 1997;42(11):731–4.

Hwang S-J, Beaty TH, McIntosh I, Hefferon T, Panny SR. Association between homeobox-containing gene *MSX1* and the occurrence of limb deficiency. *American Journal of Medical Genetics* 1998;75(4):419–23.

Hwang S-J, Beaty TH, Panny SR, Street NA, Joseph JM, Gordon S, McIntosh I, Francomano CA. Association study of transforming growth factor alpha (TGF α) *TaqI* polymorphism and oral clefts: indication of gene-environment interaction in a population-based sample of infants with birth defects. *American Journal of Epidemiology* 1995;141(7):629–36.

Iams JD. The epidemiology of preterm birth. *Clinical Perinatology* 2003;30(4):651–64.

Institute of Medicine. *Dietary Reference Intakes for Vitamin A, Vitamin K, Arsenic, Boron, Chromium, Copper, Iodine, Iron, Manganese, Molybdenum, Nickel, Silica, Vanadium, and Zinc*. Washington: National Academy Press, 2000.

International Agency for Research on Cancer. *IARC Monographs on the Evaluation of Carcinogenic Risks of Chemicals to Humans: Polynuclear Aromatic Compounds, Part 1: Chemical, Environmental and Experimental Data*. Vol. 32. Lyon (France): International Agency for Research on Cancer, 1983.

International Agency for Research on Cancer. *IARC Monographs on the Evaluation of Carcinogenic Risks to Humans: Tobacco Smoking*. Vol. 38. Lyon (France): International Agency for Research on Cancer, 1986.

International Agency for Research on Cancer. *IARC Monographs on the Evaluation of Carcinogenic Risks to Humans: Tobacco Smoke and Involuntary Smoking*. Vol. 83. Lyon (France): International Agency for Research on Cancer, 2004.

Irion O, Masse J, Forest JC, Moutquin JM. Prediction of preeclampsia, low birthweight for gestation and prematurity by uterine artery blood flow velocity waveforms analysis in low risk nulliparous women. *British Journal of Obstetrics and Gynaecology* 1998;105(4):422–9.

Iyasu S, Saftlas AK, Rowley DL, Koonin LM, Lawson HW, Atrash HK. The epidemiology of placenta previa in the United States, 1979 through 1987. *American Journal of Obstetrics and Gynecology* 1993;168(5):1424–9.

Jauniaux E, Biernaux V, Gerlo E, Gulbis B. Chronic maternal smoking and cord blood amino acid and enzyme levels at term. *Obstetrics and Gynecology* 2001;97(1):57–61.

Jauniaux E, Burton GJ. The effect of smoking in pregnancy on early placental morphology. *Obstetrics and Gynecology* 1992;79(5 Pt 1):645–8.

Jauniaux E, Gulbis B, Acharya G, Gerlo E. Fetal amino acid and enzyme levels with maternal smoking. *Obstetrics and Gynecology* 1999;93(5 Pt 1):680–3.

Jensen EJ, Pedersen B, Frederiksen R, Dahl R. Prospective study on the effect of smoking and nicotine substitution on leucocyte blood counts and relation between blood leucocytes and lung function. *Thorax* 1998a;53(9):784–9.

Jensen TK, Henriksen TB, Hjollund NHI, Scheike T, Kolstad H, Giwercman A, Ernst E, Bonde JP, Skakkebæk NE, Olsen J. Adult and prenatal exposures to tobacco smoke as risk indicators of fertility among 430 Danish couples. *American Journal of Epidemiology* 1998b;148(10):992–7.

Jensen TK, Jørgensen N, Punab M, Haugen TB, Suominen J, Zilaitiene B, Horte A, Andersen A-G, Carlsen E, Magnus Ø, et al. Association of in utero exposure to maternal smoking with reduced semen quality and testis size in adulthood: a cross-sectional study of 1,770 young men from the general population in five European countries. *American Journal of Epidemiology* 2004;159(1):49–58.

Jernström H, Klug TL, Sepkovic DW, Bradlow HL, Narod SA. Predictors of the plasma ratio of 2-hydroxyestrone to 16α-hydroxyestrone among pre-menopausal, nulliparous women from four ethnic groups. *Carcinogenesis* 2003;24(5):991–1005.

Jeyabalan A, Powers RW, Durica AR, Harger GF, Roberts JM, Ness RB. Cigarette smoke exposure and angiogenic factors in pregnancy and preeclampsia. *American Journal of Hypertension* 2008;21(8):943–7.

Ji L, Melkonian G, Riveles K, Talbot P. Identification of pyridine compounds in cigarette smoke solution that inhibit growth of the chick chorioallantoic membrane. *Toxicological Sciences* 2002;69(1):217–25.

Jick H, Porter J, Morrison AS. Relation between smoking and age of natural menopause: report from the Boston Collaborative Drug Surveillance Program, Boston University Medical Center. *Lancet* 1977;309(8026):1354–5.

Jin Z, Jin M, Nilsson BO, Roomans GM. Effects of nicotine administration on elemental concentrations in mouse granulosa cells, maturing oocytes and oviduct epithelium studied by X-ray microanalysis. *Journal of Submicroscopic Cytology and Pathology* 1998;30(4):517–20.

Johnson F, Ogden L, Graham T, Thomas T, Gilbreath E, Hammersley M, Wilson L, Knight Q, DeJan B. Developmental effects of zinc chloride in rats. *Toxicologist* 2003a;72(1 Suppl):75.

Johnson MD, Kenney N, Stoica A, Hilakivi-Clarke L, Singh B, Chepko G, Clarke R, Sholler PF, Lirio AA, Foss C, et al. Cadmium mimics the *in vivo* effects of estrogen in the uterus and mammary gland. *Nature Medicine* 2003b;9(8):1081–4.

Jolibois LS Jr, Burow ME, Swan KF, George WJ, Anderson MB, Henson MC. Effects of cadmium on cell viability, trophoblastic development, and expression of low density lipoprotein receptor transcripts in cultured human placental cells. *Reproductive Toxicology* 1999a;13(6):473–80.

Jolibois LS Jr, Shi W, George WJ, Henson MC, Anderson MB. Cadmium accumulation and effects on progesterone release by cultured human trophoblast cells. *Reproductive Toxicology* 1999b;13(3):215–21.

Jouppila P, Kirkinen P, Eik-Nes S. Acute effect of maternal smoking on the human fetal blood flow. *British Journal of Obstetrics and Gynaecology* 1983;90(1):7–10.

Juchau MR, Namkung J, Chao ST. Mono-oxygenase induction in the human placenta: interrelationships among position-specific hydroxylations of 17 beta-estradiol and benzo[*a*]pyrene. *Drug Metabolism and Disposition* 1982;10(3):220–4.

Jugessur A, Lie RT, Wilcox AJ, Murray JC, Taylor JA, Saugstad OD, Vindenes HA, Åbyholm FE. Cleft palate, transforming growth factor alpha gene variants, and maternal exposures: assessing gene-environment interactions in case-parent triads. *Genetic Epidemiology* 2003;25(4):367–74.

Junaid M, Murthy RC, Saxena DK. Chromium fetotoxicity in mice during late pregnancy. *Veterinary and Human Toxicology* 1995;37(4):320–3.

Junaid M, Murthy RC, Saxena DK. Embryotoxicity of orally administered chromium in mice: exposure during the period of organogenesis. *Toxicology Letters* 1996;84(3): 143–8.

Jurasović J, Cvitković P, Pizent A, Čolak B, Telišman S. Semen quality and reproductive endocrine function with regard to blood cadmium in Croatian male subjects. *Biometals* 2004;17(6):735–43.

Kaijser M, Granath F, Jacobsen G, Cnattingius S, Ekbom A. Maternal pregnancy estriol levels in relation to anamnestic and fetal anthropometric data. *Epidemiology* 2000;11(3):315–9.

Kajii T, Ferrier A, Niikawa N, Takahara H, Ohama K, Avirachan S. Anatomic and chromosomal anomalies in 639 spontaneous abortuses. *Human Genetics* 1980; 55(1):87–98.

Kakela R, Kakela A, Hyvarinen H. Effects of nickel chloride on reproduction of the rat and possible antagonistic role of selenium. *Comparative Biochemistry and Physiology Part C, Pharmacology, Toxicology & Endocrinology* 1999;123(1):27–37.

Källén K. Maternal smoking and craniosynostosis. *Teratology* 1999;60(3):146–50.

Källén K. Maternal smoking and congenital malformations. *Fetal and Maternal Medicine Review* 2002a; 13(1):63–86.

Källén K. Role of maternal smoking and maternal reproductive history in the etiology of hypospadias in the offspring. *Teratology* 2002b;66(4):185–91.

Kämäräinen M, Soini T, Wathén K-A, Leinonen E, Stenman U-H, Vuorela P. Smoking and sVEGFR-1: circulating maternal concentrations and placental expression. *Molecular and Cellular Endocrinology* 2009;299(2):261–5.

Kanayama N, Terao T, Kawashima Y, Horiuchi K, Fujimoto D. Collagen types in normal and prematurely ruptured amniotic membranes. *American Journal of Obstetrics and Gynecology* 1985;153(8):899–903.

Kandel DB, Udry JR. Prenatal effects of maternal smoking on daughters' smoking: nicotine or testosterone exposure? *American Journal of Public Health* 1999; 89(9):1377–83.

Karaer A, Avsar FA, Batioglu S. Risk factors for ectopic pregnancy: a case-control study. *Australian and New Zealand Journal of Obstetrics and Gynaecology* 2006;46(6):521–7.

Karakaya A, Ates I, Yucesoy B. Effects of occupational polycyclic aromatic hydrocarbon exposure on T-lymphocyte functions and natural killer cell activity in asphalt and coke oven workers. *Human & Experimental Toxicology* 2004;23(7):317–22.

Kariniemi V, Forss M, Lehtovirta P, Rauramo I. Significant correlation between maternal hemodynamics and fetal heart rate variability. *American Journal of Obstetrics and Gynecology* 1982;144(1):43–6.

Kariniemi V, Lehtovirta P, Rauramo I, Forss M. Effects of smoking on fetal heart rate variability during gestational weeks 27 to 32. *American Journal of Obstetrics and Gynecology* 1984;149(5):575–6.

Kato I, Toniolo P, Koenig KL, Shore RE, Zeleniuch-Jacquotte A, Akhmedkhanov A, Riboli E. Epidemiologic correlates with menstrual cycle length in middle aged women. *European Journal of Epidemiology* 1999; 15(9):809–14.

Kawai M, Swan KF, Green AE, Edwards DE, Anderson MB, Henson MC. Placental endocrine disruption induced by cadmium: effects on P450 cholesterol side-chain cleavage and 3β-hydroxysteroid dehydrogenase enzymes in cultured human trophoblasts. *Biology of Reproduction* 2002;67(1):178–83.

Keen CL. Teratogenic effects of essential trace metals: deficiencies and excesses. In: Chang LW, editor. *Toxicology of Metals*. Boca Raton (FL): CRC Press, 1996:977–1001.

Kelsey JL, Gammon MD, John EM. Reproductive factors and breast cancer. *Epidemiologic Reviews* 1993; 15(1):36–47.

Kendrick JS, Atrash HK, Strauss LT, Gargiullo OM, Ahn YW. Vaginal douching and the risk of ectopic pregnancy among black women. *American Journal of Obstetrics and Gynecology* 1997;176(5):991–7.

Kendrick JS, Zahniser SC, Miller N, Salas N, Stine J, Gargiullo PM, Floyd RL, Spierto FW, Sexton M, Merzger RW, et al. Integrating smoking cessation into routine public prenatal care: the Smoking Cessation in Pregnancy project. *American Journal of Public Health* 1995;85(2):217–22.

Key TJ, Pike MC, Baron JA, Moore JW, Wang DY, Thomas BS, Bulbrook RD. Cigarette smoking and steroid hormones in women. *Journal of Steroid Biochemistry and Molecular Biology* 1991;39(4A):529–34.

Key TJ, Pike MC, Brown JB, Hermon C, Allen DS, Wang DY. Cigarette smoking and urinary oestrogen excretion in premenopausal and post-menopausal women. *British Journal of Cancer* 1996;74(8):1313–6.

Kharrazi M, DeLorenze GN, Kaufman FL, Eskenazi B, Bernert JT Jr, Graham S, Pearl M, Pirkle J. Environmental tobacco smoke and pregnancy outcome. *Epidemiology* 2004;15(6):660–70.

Khaw KT, Tazuke S, Barrett-Connor E. Cigarette smoking and levels of adrenal androgens in postmenopausal women. *New England Journal of Medicine* 1988; 318(26):1705–9.

Khong TY. Placental vascular development and neonatal outcome. *Seminars in Neonatology* 2004;9(4):255–63.

Khong TY, De Wolf F, Robertson WB, Brosens I. Inadequate maternal vascular response to placentation in pregnancies complicated by pre-eclampsia and by small-for-gestational age infants. *British Journal of Obstetrics and Gynaecology* 1986;93(10):1049–59.

Khong TY, Liddell HS, Robertson WB. Defective haemochorial placentation as a cause of miscarriage: a preliminary study. *British Journal of Obstetrics and Gynaecology* 1987;94(7):649–55.

Kiilholma P, Grönroos M, Erkkola R, Pakarinen P, Näntö V. The role of calcium, copper, iron and zinc in preterm delivery and premature rupture of fetal membranes. *Gynecologic and Obstetric Investigation* 1984; 17(4):194–201.

Kim SY, England LJ, Kendrick JS, Dietz PM, Callaghan WM. The contribution of clinic-based interventions to reduce prenatal smoking prevalence among US women. *American Journal of Public Health* 2009;99(5):893–8.

Kim YM, Bujold E, Chaiworapongsa T, Gomez R, Yoon BH, Thaler HT, Rotmensch S, Romero R. Failure of physiologic transformation of the spiral arteries in patients with preterm labor and intact membranes. *American Journal of Obstetrics and Gynecology* 2003; 189(4):1063–9.

Kim YM, Chaiworapongsa T, Gomez R, Bujold E, Yoon BH, Rotmensch S, Thaler HT, Romero R. Failure of physiologic transformation of the spiral arteries in the placental bed in preterm premature rupture of membranes. *American Journal of Obstetrics and Gynecology* 2002;187(5):1137–42.

Kimberlin DF, Andrews WW. Bacterial vaginosis: association with adverse pregnancy outcome. *Seminars in Perinatology* 1998;22(4):242–50.

Kimya Y, Cengiz C, Ozan H, Kolsal N. Acute effects of maternal smoking on the uterine and umbilical artery blood velocity waveforms. *Journal of Maternal-Fetal Investigation* 1998;8(2):79–81.

Kingdom JC, Kaufmann P. Oxygen and placental villous development: origins of fetal hypoxia. *Placenta* 1997;18(8):613–21.

Kirkland SA, Dodds LA, Brosky G. The natural history of smoking during pregnancy among women in Nova Scotia. *Canadian Medical Association Journal* 2000;163(3):281–2.

Klaiber EL, Broverman DM, Dalen JE. Serum estradiol levels in male cigarette smokers. *American Journal of Medicine* 1984;77(5):858–62.

Kleihues P, Doerjer G, Ehret M, Guzman J. Reaction of benzo(a)pyrene and 7,12-dimethylbenz(a)anthracene with DNA of various rat tissues in vivo. *Archives of Toxicology Supplement* 1980;Suppl 3:237–46.

Kline J, Levin B, Kinney A, Stein Z, Susser M, Warburton D. Cigarette smoking and spontaneous abortion of known karyotype: precise data but uncertain inferences. *American Journal of Epidemiology* 1995;141(5):417–27.

Kline J, Stein ZA, Susser M, Warburton D. Smoking: a risk factor for spontaneous abortion. *New England Journal of Medicine* 1977;297(15):793–6.

Klonoff-Cohen H, Edelstein S, Savitz D. Cigarette smoking and preeclampsia. *Obstetrics and Gynecology* 1993; 81(4):541–4.

Klonoff-Cohen HS, Edelstein SL, Lefkowitz ES, Srinivasan IP, Kaegi D, Chang JC, Wiley KJ. The effect of passive smoking and tobacco exposure through breast milk on sudden infant death syndrome. *JAMA: the Journal of the American Medical Association* 1995;273(10):795–8.

Knoll M, Talbot P. Cigarette smoke inhibits oocyte cumulus complex pick-up by the oviduct in vitro independent of ciliary beat frequency. *Reproductive Toxicology* 1998;12(1):57–68.

Knottnerus JA, Delgado LR, Knipschild PG, Essed GG, Smits F. Haematologic parameters and pregnancy outcome: a prospective cohort study in the third trimester. *Journal of Clinical Epidemiology* 1990;43(5):461–6.

Kolasa E. Constitution corporelle et âge à la puberté chez les étudiantes polonaises dans les années 1974–1994 (Body composition and age among Polish students in years 1974–1994) [French]. *Anthropologie et Préhistoire* 1997;108:35–42.

Kolasa E, Hulanicka B, Waliszko A. Does exposure to cigarette smoke influence girls maturation [Polish]. *Przeglad Epidemiologiczny* 1998;52(3):339–50.

Koren G, Sharav T, Pastuszak A, Garrettson LK, Hill K, Samson I, Rorem M, King A, Dolgin JE. A multicenter, prospective study of fetal outcome following accidental carbon monoxide poisoning in pregnancy. *Reproductive Toxicology* 1991;5(5):397–403.

Kramer MS, Usher RH, Pollack R, Boyd M, Usher S. Etiologic determinants of abruptio placentae. *Obstetrics and Gynecology* 1997;89(2):221–6.

Krarup T. Oocyte destruction and ovarian tumorigenesis after direct application of a chemical carcinogen (9:10-dimethyl-1:2-benzanthrene) to the mouse ovary. *International Journal of Cancer* 1969;4(1):61–75.

Krishna K. Tobacco chewing in pregnancy. *British Journal of Obstetrics and Gynaecology* 1978;85(10):726–8.

Kristensen P, Eilertsen E, Einarsdóttir E, Haugen A, Skaug V, Øvrebø S. Fertility in mice after prenatal exposure to benzo[*a*]pyrene and inorganic lead. *Environmental Health Perspectives* 1995;103(6):588–90.

Kritz-Silverstein D, Wingard DL, Garland FC. The association of behavior and lifestyle factors with menstrual symptoms. *Journal of Women's Health & Gender-Based Medicine* 1999;8(9):1185–93.

Kuehl KS, Loffredo CA. Population-based study of l-transposition of the great arteries: possible associations with environmental factors. *Birth Defects Research Part A, Clinical and Molecular Teratology* 2003;67(3):162–7.

Kuhnert BR, Kuhnert PM, Debanne S, Williams TG. The relationship between cadmium, zinc, and birth weight in pregnant women who smoke. *American Journal of Obstetrics and Gynecology* 1987a;157(5):1247–51.

Kuhnert BR, Kuhnert PM, Lazebnik N, Erhard P. The effect of maternal smoking on the relationship between maternal and fetal zinc status and infant birth weight. *Journal of the American College of Nutrition* 1988a;7(4):309–16.

Kuhnert BR, Kuhnert PM, Zarlingo TJ. Associations between placental cadmium and zinc and age and parity in pregnant women who smoke. *Obstetrics and Gynecology* 1988b;71(1):67–70.

Kuhnert PM, Kuhnert BR, Bottoms SF, Erhard P. Cadmium levels in maternal blood, fetal cord blood, and placental tissues of pregnant women who smoke. *American Journal of Obstetrics and Gynecology* 1982;142(8):1021–5.

Kuhnert PM, Kuhnert BR, Erhard P, Brashear WT, Groh-Wargo SL, Webster S. The effect of smoking on placental and fetal zinc status. *American Journal of Obstetrics and Gynecology* 1987b;157(5):1241–6.

Künzle R, Mueller MD, Hänggi W, Birkhäuser MH, Drescher H, Bersinger NA. Semen quality of male smokers and nonsmokers in infertile couples. *Fertility and Sterility* 2003;79(2):287–91.

Kurahashi N, Sata F, Kasai S, Shibata T, Moriya K, Yamada H, Kakizaki H, Minakami H, Nonomura K, Kishi R. Maternal genetic polymorphisms in *CYP1A1*, *GSTM1* and *GSTT1* and the risk of hypospadias. *Molecular Human Reproduction* 2005;11(2):93–8.

Kurki T, Sivonen A, Renkonen O-V, Savia E, Ylikorkala O. Bacterial vaginosis in early pregnancy and pregnancy outcome. *Obstetrics and Gynecology* 1992;80(2):173–7.

Kurmanavichius J, Baumann H, Huch R, Huch A. Uteroplacental blood flow velocity waveforms as a predictor of adverse fetal outcome and pregnancy-induced hypertension. *Journal of Perinatal Medicine* 1990;18(4):255–60.

Kyrklund-Blomberg NB, Cnattingius S. Preterm birth and maternal smoking: risks related to gestational age and onset of delivery. *American Journal of Obstetrics and Gynecology* 1998;179(4):1051–5.

Kyrklund-Blomberg NB, Gennser G, Cnattingius S. Placental abruption and perinatal death. *Paediatric and Perinatal Epidemiology* 2001;15(3):290–7.

Lagueux J, Pereg D, Ayotte P, Dewailly E, Poirier GG. Cytochrome P450 *CYP1A1* enzyme activity and DNA adducts in placenta of women environmentally exposed to organochlorines. *Environmental Research* 1999;80(4):369–82.

Lam X, Gieseke C, Knoll M, Talbot P. Assay and importance of adhesive interaction between hamster (*Mesocricetus auratus*) oocyte-cumulus complexes and the oviductal epithelium. *Biology of Reproduction* 2000;62(3):579–88.

Lammer EJ, Shaw GM, Iovannisci DM, Van Waes J, Finnell RH. Maternal smoking and the risk of orofacial clefts: susceptibility with NAT1 and NAT2 polymorphisms. *Epidemiology* 2004;15(2):150–6.

Larsen LG, Clausen HV, Jønsson L. Stereologic examination of placentas from mothers who smoke during pregnancy. *American Journal of Obstetrics and Gynecology* 2002;186(3):531–7.

Lassen K, Oei TPS. Effects of maternal cigarette smoking during pregnancy on long-term physical and cognitive parameters of child development. *Addictive Behaviors* 1998;23(5):635–53.

Lavezzi AM, Ottaviani G, Matturri L. Adverse effects of prenatal tobacco smoke exposure on biological parameters of the developing brainstem. *Neurobiology of Disease* 2005;20(2):601–7.

Lavezzi AM, Ottaviani G, Mauri M, Matturri L. Hypoplasia of the arcuate nucleus and maternal smoking during pregnancy in sudden unexplained perinatal and infant death. *Neuropathology* 2004;24(4):284–9.

Lee CZ, Royce FH, Denison MS, Pinkerton KE. Effect of in utero and postnatal exposure to environmental tobacco smoke on the developmental expression of pulmonary cytochrome P450 monooxygenases. *Journal of Biochemical and Molecular Toxicology* 2000;14(3):121–30.

Lee T, Silver H. Etiology and epidemiology of preterm premature rupture of the membranes. *Clinics in Perinatology* 2001;28(4):721–34.

Lees C, Parra M, Missfelder-Lobos H, Morgans A, Fletcher O, Nicolaides KH. Individualized risk assessment for adverse pregnancy outcome by uterine artery Doppler at 23 weeks. *Obstetrics and Gynecology* 2001;98(3):369–73.

Lehtovirta P, Forss M. The acute effect of smoking on intervillous blood flow of the placenta. *British Journal of Obstetrics and Gynaecology* 1978;85(10):729–31.

Lehtovirta P, Forss M. The acute effect of smoking on uteroplacental blood flow in normotensive and hypertensive pregnancy. *International Journal of Gynaecology and Obstetrics* 1980;18(3):208–11.

Lehtovirta P, Forss M, Kariniemi V, Rauramo I. Acute effects of smoking on fetal heart-rate variability. *British Journal of Obstetrics and Gynaecology* 1983;90(1):3–6.

Lekakis J, Papamichael C, Vemmos C, Stamatelopoulos K, Voutsas A, Stamatelopoulos S. Effects of acute cigarette smoking on endothelium-dependent arterial dilatation in normal subjects. *American Journal of Cardiology* 1998;81(10):1225–8.

Levine RJ, Maynard SE, Qian C, Lim K-H, England LJ, Yu KF, Schisterman EF, Thadhani R, Sacks BP, Epstein FH, et al. Circulating angiogenic factors and the risk of preeclampsia. *New England Journal of Medicine* 2004;350(7):672–83.

Li DK, Daling JR. Maternal smoking, low birth weight, and ethnicity in relation to sudden infant death syndrome. *American Journal of Epidemiology* 1991;134(9):958–64.

Li DK, Wi S. Maternal placental abnormality and the risk of sudden infant death syndrome. *American Journal of Epidemiology* 1999;149(7):608–11.

Li H, Gudnason H, Olofsson P, Dubiel M, Gudmundsson S. Increased uterine artery vascular impedance is related to adverse outcome of pregnancy but is present in only one-third of late third-trimester pre-eclamptic women. *Ultrasound in Obstetrics & Gynecology* 2005;25(5):459–63.

Li Y, Wang H. In utero exposure to tobacco and alcohol modifies neurobehavioral development in mice offspring: considerations a role of oxidative stress. *Pharmacological Research* 2004;49(5):467–73.

Liestøl K. Menarcheal age and spontaneous abortion: a causal connection? *American Journal of Epidemiology* 1980;111(6):753–8.

Lin S, Hwang SA, Marshall EG, Marion D. Does paternal occupational lead exposure increase the risks of low birth weight or prematurity? *American Journal of Epidemiology* 1998;148(2):173–81.

Lindblad A, Maršál K, Andersson KE. Effect of nicotine on human fetal blood flow. *Obstetrics and Gynecology* 1988;72(3 Pt 1):371–82.

Lindqvist PG, Maršál K. Moderate smoking during pregnancy is associated with a reduced risk of preeclampsia. *Acta Obstetricia et Gynecologica Scandinavica* 1999; 78(8):693–7.

Little J, Cardy A, Munger RG. Tobacco smoking and oral clefts: a meta-analysis. *Bulletin of the World Health Organization* 2004a;82(3):213–8.

Little J, Vainio H. Mutagenic lifestyles: a review of evidence of associations between germ-cell mutations in humans and smoking, alcohol consumption and use of 'recreational' drugs. *Mutation Research* 1994;313 (2–3):131–51.

Little L, Cardy A, Arslan MT, Mossey PA. Smoking and orofacial clefts: a United Kingdom–based case-control study. *Cleft Palate-Craniofacial Journal* 2004b;41(4):381–6.

Liu Y, Gold EB, Lasley BL, Johnson WO. Factors affecting menstrual cycle characteristics. *American Journal of Epidemiology* 2004a;160(2):131–40.

Liu Y, Johnson WO, Gold EB, Lasley BL. Bayesian analysis of risk factors for anovulation. *Statistics in Medicine* 2004b;23(12):1901–19.

Loft S, Kold-Jensen T, Hjollund NH, Giwercman A, Gyllemborg J, Ernst E, Olsen J, Scheike T, Poulsen HE, Bonde JP. Oxidative DNA damage in human sperm influences time to pregnancy. *Human Reproduction* 2003;18(6):1265–72.

Loiacono NJ, Graziano JH, Kline JK, Popovac D, Ahmedi X, Gashi E, Mehmeti A, Rajovic B. Placental cadmium and birthweight in women living near a lead smelter. *Archives of Environmental Health* 1992;47(4):250–5.

Long KZ, Santos JI. Vitamins and the regulation of the immune response. *Pediatric Infectious Disease Journal* 1999;18(3):283–90.

Longcope C, Johnston CC Jr. Androgen and estrogen dynamics in pre- and postmenopausal women: a comparison between smokers and nonsmokers. *Journal of Clinical Endocrinology and Metabolism* 1988; 67(2):379–83.

Longo LD. Carbon monoxide: effects on oxygenation of the fetus in utero. *Science* 1976;194(4264):523–5.

Longo LD. The biological effects of carbon monoxide on the pregnant woman, fetus, and newborn infant. *American Journal of Obstetrics and Gynecology* 1977; 129(1):69–103.

Lu CC, Matsumoto N, Iijima S. Teratogenic effects of nickel chloride on embryonic mice and its transfer to embryonic mice. *Teratology* 1979;19(2):137–42.

Lucero J, Harlow BL, Barbieri RL, Sluss P, Cramer DW. Early follicular phase hormone levels in relation to patterns of alcohol, tobacco, and coffee use. *Fertility and Sterility* 2001;76(4):723–9.

Lummus ZL, Henningsen G. Modulation of T-cell ontogeny by transplacental benzo(a)pyrene. *International Journal of Immunopharmacology* 1995;17(4):339–50.

Luppi P, Lain KY, Jeyabalan A, DeLoia JA. The effects of cigarette smoking on circulating maternal leukocytes during pregnancy. *Clinical Immunology* 2007; 122(2):214–9.

Lyall F. Development of the utero-placental circulation: the role of carbon monoxide and nitric oxide in trophoblast invasion and spiral artery transformation. *Microscopy Research and Technique* 2003;60(4):402–11.

Lykkesfeldt J, Christen S, Wallock LM, Chang HH, Jacob RA, Ames BN. Ascorbate is depleted by smoking and repleted by moderate supplementation: a study in male smokers and nonsmokers with matched dietary antioxidant intakes. *American Journal of Clinical Nutrition* 2000;71(2):530–6.

Lykkesfeldt J, Prieme H, Loft S, Poulsen HE. Effect of smoking cessation on plasma ascorbic acid concentration. *BMJ (British Medical Journal)* 1996;313(7049):91.

Lynch AM, Bruce NW. Placental growth in rats exposed to carbon monoxide at selected stages of pregnancy. *Biology of the Neonate* 1989;56(3):151–7.

MacGillivray I, Rose GA, Rowe B. Blood pressure survey in pregnancy. *Clinical Science* 1969;37(2):395–407.

Mackenzie KM, Angevine DM. Infertility in mice exposed in utero to benzo(a)pyrene. *Biology of Reproduction* 1981;24(1):183–91.

MacMahon B, Trichopoulos D, Brown J, Andersen AP, Cole P, deWaard F, Kauraniemi T, Polychronopoulou A, Ravnihar B, Stormby N, et al. Age at menarche, urine estrogens and breast cancer risk. *International Journal of Cancer* 1982a;30(4):427–31.

MacMahon B, Trichopoulos D, Cole P, Brown J. Cigarette smoking and urinary estrogens. *New England Journal of Medicine* 1982b;307(17):1062–5.

Mactutus CF, Fechter LD. Prenatal exposure to carbon monoxide: learning and memory deficits. *Science* 1984;223(4634):409–11.

Mactutus CF, Fechter LD. Moderate prenatal carbon monoxide exposure produces persistent, and apparently permanent, memory deficits in rats. *Teratology* 1985; 31(1):1–12.

Magee BD, Hattis D, Kivel NM. Role of smoking in low birth weight. *Journal of Reproductive Medicine* 2004; 49(1):23–7.

Magers T, Talbot P, DiCarlantonio G, Knoll M, Demers D, Tsai I, Hoodbhoy T. Cigarette smoke inhalation affects the reproductive system of female hamsters. *Reproductive Toxicology* 1995;9(6):513–25.

Magrini A, Bottini N, Gloria-Bottini F, Stefanini L, Bergamaschi A, Cosmi E, Bottini E. Enzyme polymorphisms, smoking, and human reproduction: a study of human placental alkaline phosphatase. *American Journal of Human Biology* 2003;15(6):781–5.

Mainous AG 3rd, Hueston WJ. Passive smoke and low birth weight: evidence of a threshold effect. *Archives of Family Medicine* 1994;3(10):875–8.

Makin J, Fried PA, Watkinson B. A comparison of active and passive smoking during pregnancy: long-term effects. *Neurotoxicology and Teratology* 1991;13(1): 5–12.

Malik S, Cleves MA, Honein MA, Romitti PA, Botto LD, Yang S, Hobbs CA, National Birth Defects Prevention Study. Maternal smoking and congenital heart defects. *Pediatrics* 2008;121(4):e810–e816.

Malloy MH, Kleinman JC, Land GH, Schramm WF. The association of maternal smoking with age and cause of infant death. *American Journal of Epidemiology* 1988;128(1):46–55.

Mannino DM, Mulinare J, Ford ES, Schwartz J. Tobacco smoke exposure and decreased serum and red blood cell folate levels: data from the Third National Health and Nutrition Examination Survey. *Nicotine & Tobacco Research* 2003;5(3):357–62.

Marcoux S, Brisson J, Fabia J. The effect of cigarette smoking on the risk of preeclampsia and gestational hypertension. *American Journal of Epidemiology* 1989; 130(5):950–7.

Marcus M, Grunfeld L, Berkowitz G, Kaplan P, Godbold J. Urinary follicle-stimulating hormone as a biological marker of ovarian toxicity. *Fertility and Sterility* 1993;59(4):931–3.

Marinelli D, Gaspari L, Pedotti P, Taioli E. Mini-review of studies on the effect of smoking and drinking habits on semen parameters. *International Journal of Hygiene and Environmental Health* 2004;207(3):185–92.

Martin EJ, Brinton LA, Hoover R. Menarcheal age and miscarriage. *American Journal of Epidemiology* 1983; 117(5):634–6.

Martínez-Pasarell O, Nogués C, Bosch M, Egozcue J, Templado C. Analysis of sex chromosome aneuploidy in sperm from fathers of Turner syndrome patients. *Human Genetics* 1999;104(4):345–9.

Martini AC, Molina RI, Estofán D, Senestrari D, Fiol de Cuneo M, Ruiz RD. Effects of alcohol and cigarette consumption on human seminal quality. *Fertility and Sterility* 2004;82(2):374–7.

Mas A, Holt D, Webb M. The acute toxicity and teratogenicity of nickel in pregnant rats. *Toxicology* 1985; 35(1):47–57.

Másdóttir B, Jónsson T, Manfreosdóttir V, Víkingsson Á, Brekkan A, Valdimarsson H. Smoking, rheumatoid factor isotypes and severity of rheumatoid arthritis. *Rheumatology (Oxford)* 2000;39(11):1202–5.

Mathews JD, Whittingham S, Hooper BM, Mackay IR, Stenhouse NS. Association of autoantibodies with smoking, cardiovascular morbidity, and death in the Busselton population. *Lancet* 1973;2(7832):754–8.

Matikainen T, Perez GI, Jurisicova A, Pru JK, Schlezinger JJ, Ryu H-Y, Laine J, Sakai T, Korsmeyer SJ, Casper RF, et al. Aromatic hydrocarbon receptor-driven *Bax* gene expression is required for premature ovarian failure caused by biohazardous environmental chemicals. *Nature Genetics* 2001;28(4):355–60.

Matkin CC, Britton J, Samuels S, Eskenazi B. Smoking and blood pressure patterns in normotensive pregnant women. *Paediatric and Perinatal Epidemiology* 1999;13(1):22–34.

Matovina M, Husnjak K, Milutin N, Ciglar S, Grce M. Possible role of bacterial and viral infections in miscarriages. *Fertility and Sterility* 2004;81(3):662–9.

Matta SG, Fu Y, Valentine JD, Sharp BM. Response of the hypothalamo-pituitary-adrenal axis to nicotine. *Psychoneuroendocrinology* 1998;23(2):103–13.

Mattison DR. The effects of smoking on fertility from gametogenesis to implantation. *Environmental Research* 1982;28(2):410–33.

Mattison DR, Nightingale MS. Oocyte destruction by polycyclic aromatic hydrocarbons is not linked to the inducibility of ovarian aryl hydrocarbon (benzo(*a*) pyrene) hydroxylase activity in (DBA/2N × C57BL/6N) F_1 × DBA/2N backcross mice. *Pediatric Pharmacology* 1982;2(1):11–21.

Mattison DR, Thorgeirsson SS. Ovarian aryl hydrocarbon hydroxylase activity and primordial oocyte toxicity of polycyclic aromatic hydrocarbons in mice. *Cancer Research* 1979;39(9):3471–5.

Maulik D, Yarlagadda P, Youngblood JP, Ciston P. The diagnostic efficacy of the umbilical arterial systolic/diastolic ratio as a screening tool: a prospective blinded study. *American Journal of Obstetrics and Gynecology* 1990;162(6):1518–23.

Mayhew TM. Patterns of villous and intervillous space growth in human placentas from normal and abnormal pregnancies. *European Journal of Obstetrics, Gynecology, and Reproductive Biology* 1996;68(1–2):75–82.

Mayhew TM. Thinning of the intervascular tissue layers of the human placenta is an adaptive response to passive diffusion in vivo and may help to predict the origins of fetal hypoxia. *European Journal of Obstetrics, Gynecology, and Reproductive Biology* 1998;81(1): 101–9.

Mayhew TM. Fetoplacental angiogenesis during gestation is biphasic, longitudinal and occurs by proliferation and remodelling of vascular endothelial cells. *Placenta* 2002;23(10):742–50.

Maynard SE, Min J-Y, Merchan J, Lim K-H, Li J, Mondal S, Libermann TA, Morgan JP, Sellke FW, Stillman IE, et al. Excess placental soluble fms-like tyrosine kinase 1 (sFlt1) may contribute to endothelial dysfunction, hypertension, and proteinuria in preeclampsia. *Journal of Clinical Investigation* 2003;111(5):649–58.

McCartney JS, Fried PA, Watkinson B. Central auditory processing in school-age children prenatally exposed to cigarette smoke. *Neurotoxicology and Teratology* 1994; 16(3):269–76.

McCormick MC. The contribution of low birth weight to infant mortality and childhood morbidity. *New England Journal of Medicine* 1985;313(2):82–90.

McDonald HM, Chambers HM. Intrauterine infection and spontaneous midgestation abortion: is the spectrum of microorganisms similar to that in preterm labor? *Infectious Diseases in Obstetrics and Gynecology* 2000; 8(5–6):220–7.

McDonald SD, Perkins SL, Jodouin CA, Walker MC. Folate levels in pregnant women who smoke: an important gene/environment interaction. *American Journal of Obstetrics and Gynecology* 2002;187(3):620–5.

McLaughlin BE, Lash GE, Graham CH, Smith GN, Vreman HJ, Stevenson DK, Marks GS, Nakatsu K, Brien JF. Endogenous carbon monoxide formation by chorionic villi of term human placenta. *Placenta* 2001; 22(10):886–8.

Meberg A, Haga P, Sande H, Foss OP. Smoking during pregnancy—hematological observations in the newborn. *Acta Paediatrica Scandinavica* 1979;68(5):731–4.

Meikle AW, Bishop DT, Stringham JD, Ford MH, West DW. Relationship between body mass index, cigarette smoking, and plasma sex steroids in normal male twins. *Genetic Epidemiology* 1989;6(3):399–412.

Meis PJ, Michielutte R, Peters TJ, Wells HB, Sands RE, Coles EC, Johns KA. Factors associated with preterm birth in Cardiff, Wales. I: univariable and multivariable analysis. *American Journal of Obstetrics and Gynecology* 1995;173(2):590–6.

Melkonian G, Cheung L, Marr R, Tong C, Talbot O. Mainstream and sidestream cigarette smoke inhibit growth and angiogenesis in the day 5 chick chorioallantoic membrane. *Toxicological Sciences* 2002;68(1):237–48.

Melkonian G, Eckelhofer H, Wu M, Wang Y, Tong C, Riveles K, Talbot P. Growth and angiogenesis are inhibited *in vivo* in developing tissues by pyrazine and its derivatives. *Toxicological Sciences* 2003;75(2):393–401.

Melkonian G, Le C, Zheng W, Talbot P, Martins-Green M. Normal patterns of angiogenesis and extracellular matrix deposition in chick chorioallantoic membranes are disrupted by mainstream and sidestream cigarette smoke. *Toxicology and Applied Pharmacology* 2000; 163(1):26–37.

Mendola P, Selevan SG, Gutter S, Rice D. Environmental factors associated with a spectrum of neurodevelopmental deficits. *Mental Retardation and Developmental Disabilities Research Reviews* 2002;8(3):188–97.

Mercer BM, Crocker LG, Pierce WF, Sibai BM. Clinical characteristics and outcome of twin gestation complicated by preterm premature rupture of the membranes. *American Journal of Obstetrics and Gynecology* 1993; 168(5):1467–73.

Mercer BM, Goldenberg RL, Meis PJ, Moawad AH, Shellhaas C, Das A, Menard MK, Caritis SN, Thurnau GR, Dombrowski MP, et al. The Preterm Prediction Study: prediction of preterm premature rupture of membranes through clinical findings and ancillary testing. The National Institute of Child Health and Human Development Maternal-Fetal Medicine Units Network. *American Journal of Obstetrics and Gynecology* 2000; 183(3):738–45.

Meschia M, Pansini F, Modena AB, de Aloysio D, Gambacciani M, Parazzini F, Campagnoli C, Maiocchi G, Peruzzi E. Determinants of age at menopause in Italy: results from a large cross-sectional study. ICARUS Study Group, Italian Climacteric Research Study Group. *Maturitas* 2000;34(2):119–25.

Meyer MB, Jonas BS, Tonascia JA. Perinatal events associated with maternal smoking during pregnancy. *American Journal of Epidemiology* 1976;103(5):464–76.

Miceli F, Minici F, Tropea A, Catino S, Orlando M, Lamanna G, Sagnella F, Tiberi F, Bompiani A, Mancuso S, Lanzone A, Apa R. Effects of nicotine on human luteal cells in vitro: a possible role on reproductive outcome for smoking women. *Biology of Reproduction* 2005;72(3):628–32.

Michnovicz JJ, Hershcopf RJ, Haley NJ, Bradlow HL, Fishman J. Cigarette smoking alters hepatic estrogen metabolism in men: implications for atherosclerosis. *Metabolism* 1989;38(6):537–41.

Michnovicz JJ, Hershcopf RJ, Naganuma H, Bradlow HL, Fishman J. Increased 2-hydroxylation of estradiol as a possible mechanism for the anti-estrogenic effect of cigarette smoking. *New England Journal of Medicine* 1986;315(21):1305–9.

Midgette AS, Baron JA. Cigarette smoking and the risk of natural menopause. *Epidemiology* 1990;1(6):474–80.

Millicovsky G, Johnston MC. Maternal hyperoxia greatly reduces the incidence of phenytoin-induced cleft lip and palate in A/J mice. *Science* 1981;212(4495):671–2.

Mishra GD, Dobson AJ, Schofield MJ. Cigarette smoking, menstrual symptoms and miscarriage among young women. *Australian and New Zealand Journal of Public Health* 2000;24(4):413–20.

Misra DP, Ananth CV. Risk factor profiles of placental abruption in first and second pregnancies: heterogeneous etiologies. *Journal of Clinical Epidemiology* 1999; 52(5):453–61.

Mitchell EA, Ford RPK, Stewart AW, Taylor BJ, Becroft DMO, Thompson JMD, Scragg R, Hassall IB, Barry DMJ, Allen EM, et al. Smoking and the sudden infant death syndrome. *Pediatrics* 1993;91(5):893–6.

Mitchell JH, Hammer RE. Effects of nicotine on oviducal blood flow and embryo development in the rat. *Journal of Reproduction and Fertility* 1985;74(1):71–6.

Mochizuki M, Maruo T, Masuko K, Ohtsu T. Effects of smoking on fetoplacental-maternal system during pregnancy. *American Journal of Obstetrics and Gynecology* 1984;149(4):413–20.

Molfese DL, Molfese VJ, Ferguson M, Key APF, Straub S, Peach K, Pratt N. Birth defects and their association with tobacco smoke. Abstract presented at the International Society for the Prevention of Tobacco Induced Diseases Conference; Oct. 29–Nov. 1, 2004; Louisville (KY).

Moncada S, Higgs A. The L-arginine-nitric oxide pathway. *New England Journal of Medicine* 1993;329(27): 2002–12.

Monica G, Lilja C. Placenta previa, maternal smoking and recurrence risk. *Acta Obstetricia et Gynecologica Scandinavica* 1995;74(5):341–5.

Morris M, Nicoll A, Simms I, Wilson J, Catchpole M. Bacterial vaginosis: a public health review. *BJOG* 2001;108(5):439–50.

Morrow RJ, Ritchie JW, Bull SB. Maternal cigarette smoking: the effects on umbilical and uterine blood flow velocity. *American Journal of Obstetrics and Gynecology* 1988;159(5):1069–71.

Mortensen EL, Michaelsen KF, Sanders SA, Reinisch JM. A dose-response relationship between maternal smoking during late pregnancy and adult intelligence in male offspring. *Paediatric and Perinatal Epidemiology* 2005;19(1):4–11.

Mullen PD. Maternal smoking during pregnancy and evidence-based intervention to promote cessation. *Primary Care* 1999;26(3):577–89.

Munger RG, Sauberlich HE, Corcoran C, Nepomuceno B, Daack-Hirsch S, Solon FS. Maternal vitamin B-6 and folate status and risk of oral cleft birth defects in the Philippines. *Birth Defects Research Part A, Clinical and Molecular Teratology* 2004;70(7):464–71.

Murthy RC, Junaid M, Saxena DK. Ovarian dysfunction in mice following chromium (VI) exposure. *Toxicology Letters* 1996;89(2):147–54.

Murthy RC, Saxena DK, Gupta SK, Chandra SV. Ultrastructural observations in testicular tissue of chromium-treated rats. *Reproductive Toxicology* 1991;5(5):443–7.

Myatt L, Brewer A, Brockman DE. The action of nitric oxide in the perfused human fetal-placental circulation. *American Journal of Obstetrics and Gynecology* 1991;164(2):687–92.

Myatt L, Brewer AS, Langdon G, Brockman DE. Attenuation of the vasoconstrictor effects of thromboxane and endothelin by nitric oxide in the human fetal-placental circulation. *American Journal of Obstetrics and Gynecology* 1992;166(1 Pt 1):224–30.

Naeye RL. Effects of maternal cigarette smoking on the fetus and placenta. *British Journal of Obstetrics and Gynaecology* 1978;85(10):732–7.

Naeye RL. The duration of maternal cigarette smoking, fetal and placental disorders. *Early Human Development* 1979;3(3):229–37.

Naeye RL. Factors that predispose to premature rupture of the fetal membranes. *Obstetrics and Gynecology* 1982;60(1):93–8.

Naeye RL, Peters EC. Causes and consequences of premature rupture of fetal membranes. *Lancet* 1980;1(8161): 192–4.

Naicker T, Khedun SM, Moodley J, Pijnenborg R. Quantitative analysis of trophoblast invasion in preeclampsia. *Acta Obstetricia et Gynecologica Scandinavica* 2003;82(8):722–9.

National Cancer Institute. *Health Effects of Exposure to Environmental Tobacco Smoke: The Report of the California Environmental Protection Agency*. Smoking and Tobacco Control Monograph No. 10. Bethesda (MD): U.S. Department of Health and Human Services, Public Health Service, National Institutes of Health, National Cancer Institute, 1999. NIH Publication No. 99-4645.

National High Blood Pressure Education Program. Report of the National High Blood Pressure Education Program Working Group on High Blood Pressure in Pregnancy. *American Journal of Obstetrics and Gynecology* 2000;183(1):S1–S22.

National Research Council. *Environmental Tobacco Smoke: Measuring Exposures and Assessing Health Effects*. Washington: National Academy Press, 1986.

Navas JM, Segner H. Antiestrogenicity of β-naphthoflavone and PAHs in cultured rainbow trout hepatocytes: evidence for a role of the arylhydrocarbon receptor. *Aquatic Toxicology* 2000;51(1):79–92.

Neal MS, Hughes EG, Holloway AC, Foster WG. Sidestream smoking is equally as damaging as mainstream smoking on IVF outcomes. *Human Reproduction* 2005; 20(9):2531–5.

Nelson E, Goubet-Wiemers C, Guo Y, Jodscheit K. Maternal passive smoking during pregnancy and fetal developmental toxicity. Part 2: histological changes. *Human & Experimental Toxicology* 1999a;18(4): 257–64.

Nelson E, Jodscheit K, Guo Y. Maternal passive smoking during pregnancy and fetal developmental toxicity. Part 1: gross morphological effects. *Human & Experimental Toxicology* 1999b;18(4):252–6.

Neri A, Eckerling B. Influence of smoking and adrenaline (epinephrine) on the uterotubal insufflation test (Rubin test). *Fertility and Sterility* 1969;20(5):818–27.

Neri A, Marcus SL. Effect of nicotine on the motility of the oviducts in the rhesus monkey: a preliminary report. *Journal of Reproduction and Fertility* 1972;31(1):91–7.

Ness RB, Grisso JA, Hirschinger N, Markovic N, Shaw LM, Day NL, Kline J. Cocaine and tobacco use and the risk of spontaneous abortion. *New England Journal of Medicine* 1999;340(5):333–9.

Newnham JP, Patterson L, James I, Reid SE. Effects of maternal cigarette smoking on ultrasonic measurements of fetal growth and on Doppler flow velocity waveforms. *Early Human Development* 1990;24(1): 23–36.

Nicol CJ, Harrison ML, Laposa RR, Gimelshtein IL, Wells PG. A teratologic suppressor role for *p53* in benzo[*a*] pyrene-treated transgenic *p53*-deficient mice. *Nature Genetics* 1995;10(2):181–7. [See also erratum in *Nature Genetics* 1995;11(1):104.]

Nielsen A, Hannibal CG, Lindekilde BE, Tolstrup J, Frederiksen K, Munk C, Bergholt T, Buss L, Ottesen B, Gronback M, et al. Maternal smoking predicts the risk of spontaneous abortion. *Acta Obstetricia et Gynecologica Scandinavica* 2006;85(9):1057–65.

Nishijo M, Nakagawa H, Honda R, Tanebe K, Saito S, Teranishi H, Tawara K. Effects of maternal exposure to cadmium on pregnancy outcome and breast milk. *Occupational and Environmental Medicine* 2002;59(6):394–7.

Noble RC, Penny BB. Comparison of leukocyte count and function in smoking and nonsmoking young men. *Infection and Immunity* 1975;12(3):550–5.

Norman CA, Halton DM. Is carbon monoxide a workplace teratogen: a review and evaluation of the literature. *Annals of Occupational Hygiene* 1990;34(4):335–47.

Nouri-Shirazi M, Guinet E. Evidence for the immunosuppressive role of nicotine on human dendritic cell functions. *Immunology* 2003;109(3):365–73.

NSDUH Report. Cigarette use among pregnant women and recent mothers. *NSDUH Report* February 9, 2007.

Nukui T, Day RD, Sims CS, Ness RB, Romkes M. Maternal/newborn *GSTT1* null genotype contributes to risk of preterm, low birthweight infants. *Pharmacogenetics* 2004; 14(9):569–76.

Nylund L, Lunell NO, Persson B, Fredholm BB, Lagercrantz H. Acute metabolic and circulatory effects of cigarette smoking in late pregnancy. *Gynecologic and Obstetric Investigation* 1979;10(1):39–45.

Oemar BS, Tschudi MR, Godoy N, Brovkovich V, Malinski T, Lüscher TF. Reduced endothelial nitric oxide synthase expression and production in human atherosclerosis. *Circulation* 1998;97(25):2494–8.

Ogden L, Graham T, Mahboob M, Atkinson A, Hammersley M, Sarkar N. Effects of zinc chloride on reproductive parameters of cd-1 mice. *Toxicologist* 2002;66(1–S):33.

Olds DL, Henderson CR Jr, Tatelbaum R. Intellectual impairment in children of women who smoke cigarettes during pregnancy. *Pediatrics* 1994;93(2):221–7.

Oncken C, Kranzler H, O'Malley P, Gendreau P, Campbell WA. The effect of cigarette smoking on fetal heart rate characteristics. *Obstetrics and Gynecology* 2002; 99(5):751–5.

Oncken CA, Hardardottir H, Hatsukami DK, Lupo VR, Rodis JF, Smeltzer JS. Effects of transdermal nicotine or smoking on nicotine concentrations and maternal-fetal hemodynamics. *Obstetrics and Gynecology* 1997;90(4 Pt 1):569–74.

Oncken CA, Hatsukami DK, Lupo VR, Lando HA, Gibeau LM, Hansen RJ. Effects of short-term use of nicotine gum in pregnant smokers. *Clinical Pharmacology and Therapeutics* 1996;59(6):654–61.

Ortega RM, Requejo AM, López-Sobaler AM, Navia B, Mena MC, Basabe B, Andrés P. Smoking and passive smoking as conditioners of folate status in young women. *Journal of the American College of Nutrition* 2004;23(4):365–71.

Ouyang Y, Virasch N, Hao P, Aubrey MT, Mukerjee N, Bierer BE, Freed BM. Suppression of human IL-1β, IL-2, IFN-γ, and TNF-α production by cigarette smoke extracts. *Journal of Allergy and Clinical Immunology* 2000;106(2):280–7.

Owen L, Penn G. *Smoking in Pregnancy: A Survey of Knowledge, Attitudes and Behaviours, 1992–1999*. London: Health Education Authority, 1999.

Oyen N, Skjaerven R, Little RE, Wilcox AJ. Fetal growth retardation in sudden infant death syndrome (SIDS) babies and their siblings. *American Journal of Epidemiology* 1995;142(1):84–90.

Özeren M, Dinç H, Ekmen Ü, Senekayli C, Aydemir V. Umbilical and middle cerebral artery Doppler indices in patients with preeclampsia. *European Journal of Obstetrics, Gynecology, and Reproductive Biology* 1999; 82(1):11–6.

Ozgur K, Isikoglu M, Seleker M, Donmez L. Semen quality of smoking and non-smoking men in infertile couples in a Turkish population. *Archives of Gynecology and Obstetrics* 2005;271(2):109–12.

Pachlopnik Schmid JM, Kuehni CE, Strippoli MP, Roiha HL, Pavlovic R, Latzin P, Gallati S, Kraemer R, Dahinden C, Frey U, et al. Maternal tobacco smoking and decreased leukocytes, including dendritic cells, in neonates. *Pediatric Research* 2007;61(4):462–6.

Packianathan S, Cain CD, Stagg RB, Longo LD. Ornithine decarboxylase activity in fetal and newborn rat brain: responses to hypoxic and carbon monoxide hypoxia. *Brain Research Developmental Brain Research* 1993;76(1):131–40.

Paneth NS. The problem of low birth weight. *The Future of Children: Low Birth Weight* 1995;5(1):19–34; <http://www.futureofchildren.org>.

Pant N, Kumar R, Murthy RC, Srivastava SP. Male reproductive effect of arsenic in mice. *Biometals* 2001; 14(2):113–7.

Panter KE, Weinzweig J, Gardner DR, Stegelmeier BL, James LF. Comparison of cleft palate induction by *Nicotiana glauca* in goats and sheep. *Teratology* 2000; 61(3):203–10.

Papageorghiou AT, Yu CKH, Erasmus IE, Cuckle HS, Nicolaides KH. Assessment of risk for the development of pre-eclampsia by maternal characteristics and uterine artery Doppler. *BJOG* 2005;112(6):703–9.

Parazzini F, Tozzi L, Mezzopane R, Luchini L, Marchini M, Fedele L. Cigarette smoking, alcohol consumption and risk of primary dysmenorrhea. *Epidemiology* 1994;5(4):469–72.

Pastrakuljic A, Derewlany LO, Knie B, Koren G. The effects of cocaine and nicotine on amino acid transport across the human placental cotyledon perfused in vitro. *Journal of Pharmacology and Experimental Therapeutics* 2000;294(1):141–6.

Pastrakuljic A, Derewlany LO, Koren G. Maternal cocaine use and cigarette smoking in pregnancy in relation to amino acid transport and fetal growth. *Placenta* 1999;20(7):499–512.

Penney DG. Effects of carbon monoxide exposure on developing animals and humans. In: Penney DG, editor. *Carbon Monoxide*. Boca Raton (FL): CRC Press, 1996:109–44.

Perera FP, Tang D, Tu Y-H, Cruz LA, Borjas M, Bernert T, Whyatt RM. Biomarkers in maternal and newborn blood indicate heightened fetal susceptibility to procarcinogenic DNA damage. *Environmental Health Perspectives* 2004;112(10):1133–6.

Perera FP, Whyatt RM, Jedrychowski W, Rauh V, Manchester D, Santella RM, Ottman R. Recent developments in molecular epidemiology: a study of the effects of environmental polycyclic aromatic hydrocarbons on birth outcomes in Poland. *American Journal of Epidemiology* 1998;147(3):309–14.

Perreault SD, Aitken RJ, Baker HWG, Evenson DP, Huszar G, Irvine DS, Morris ID, Morris RA, Robbins WA, Sakkas D, et al. Integrating new tests of sperm genetic integrity into semen analysis: breakout group discussion. In: Robaire B, Hales BF, editors. *Advances in Male Mediated Developmental Toxicity*. Advances in Experimental Medicine and Biology. Vol. 518. New York: Kluwer Academic, 2003:253–68.

Peterson KL, Heninger RW, Seegmiller RE. Fetotoxicity following chronic prenatal treatment of mice with tobacco smoke and ethanol. *Bulletin of Environmental Contamination and Toxicology* 1981;26(6):813–9.

Pfarrer C, Macara L, Leiser R, Kingdom J. Adaptive angiogenesis in placentas of heavy smokers. *Lancet* 1999; 354(9175):303.

Phelan JP. Diminished fetal reactivity with smoking. *American Journal of Obstetrics and Gynecology* 1980; 136(2):230–3.

Philipp K, Pateisky N, Endler M. Effects of smoking on uteroplacental blood flow. *Gynecologic and Obstetric Investigation* 1984;17(4):179–82.

Philipp T, Philipp K, Reiner A, Beer F, Kalousek DK. Embryoscopic and cytogenetic analysis of 233 missed abortions: factors involved in the pathogenesis of developmental defects of early failed pregnancies. *Human Reproduction* 2003;18(8):1724–32.

Piasek M, Blanuša M, Kostial K, Laskey JW. Placental cadmium and progesterone concentrations in cigarette smokers. *Reproductive Toxicology* 2001;15(6):673–81.

Picone TA, Allen LH, Olsen PN, Ferris ME. Pregnancy outcome in North American women. II: effects of diet, cigarette smoking, stress, and weight gain on placentas, and on neonatal physical and behavioral characteristics. *American Journal of Clinical Nutrition* 1982; 36(6):1214–24.

Pierik FH, Burdorf A, Deddens JA, Juttmann RE, Weber RFA. Maternal and paternal risk factors for cryptorchidism and hypospadias: a case-control study in newborn boys. *Environmental Health Perspectives* 2004; 112(15):1570–6.

Pijpers L, Wladimiroff JW, McGhie JS, Bom N. Acute effect of maternal smoking on the maternal and fetal cardiovascular system. *Early Human Development* 1984; 10(1–2):95–105.

Pisarska MD, Carson SA, Buster JE. Ectopic pregnancy. *Lancet* 1998;351(9109):1115–20.

Pittaway DE, Maxson W, Daniell J, Herbert C, Wentz AC. Luteal phase defects in infertility patients with endometriosis. *Fertility and Sterility* 1983;39(5):712–3.

Plasterer MR, Bradshaw WS, Booth GM, Carter MW, Schuler RL, Hardin BD. Developmental toxicity of nine selected compounds following prenatal exposure in the mouse: naphthalene, *p*-nitrophenol, sodium selenite, dimethyl phthalate, ethylenethiourea, and four glycol ether derivatives. *Journal of Toxicology and Environmental Health* 1985;15(1):25–38.

Plopper CG, Macklin J, Nishio SJ, Hyde DM, Buckpitt AR. Relationship of cytochrome P-450 to Clara cell cytotoxicity. III: morphometric comparison of changes in the epithelial populations of terminal bronchioles and lobar bronchi in mice, hamsters, and rats after parenteral administration of naphthalene. *Laboratory Investigation* 1992a;67(5):553–65.

Plopper CG, Suverkropp C, Morin D, Nishio S, Buckpitt A. Relationship of cytochrome P-450 to Clara cell cytotoxicity. I: hisopathological comparison of the respiratory tract of mice, rats and hamsters after parenteral administration of naphthalene. *Journal of Pharmacology and Experimental Therapeutics* 1992b;261(1):353–63.

Polansky FF, Lamb EJ. Do the results of semen analysis predict future fertility: a survival analysis study. *Fertility and Sterility* 1988;49(6):1059–65.

Poredoš P, Orehek M, Tratnik E. Smoking is associated with dose-related increase of intima-media thickness and endothelial dysfunction. *Angiology* 1999;50(3):201–8.

Poston L, McCarthy AL, Ritter JM. Control of vascular resistance in the maternal and feto-placental arterial beds. *Pharmacology & Therapeutics* 1995;65(2): 215–39.

Potts RJ, Newbury CJ, Smith G, Notarianni LJ, Jefferies TM. Sperm chromatin damage associated with male smoking. *Mutation Research* 1999;423(1–2):103–11.

Practice Committee of the American Society for Reproductive Medicine. Smoking and infertility. *Fertility and Sterility* 2004;81(4):1181–6.

Prasad AS. Zinc deficiency in women, infants and children. *Journal of the American College of Nutrition* 1996;15(2):113–20.

Preston AM. Cigarette smoking-nutritional implications. *Progress in Food & Nutrition Science* 1991;15(4): 183–217.

Quigley ME, Sheehan KL, Wilkes MM, Yen SS. Effects of maternal smoking on circulating catecholamine levels and fetal heart rates. *American Journal of Obstetrics and Gynecology* 1979;133(6):685–90.

Rasch V. Cigarette, alcohol, and caffeine consumption: risk factors for spontaneous abortion. *Acta Obstetricia et Gynecologica Scandinavica* 2003;82(2):182–8.

Rasmussen S, Irgens LM, Bergsjø P, Dalaker K. Perinatal mortality and case fatality after placental abruption in Norway 1967–1991. *Acta Obstetricia et Gynecologica Scandinavica* 1996a;75(3):229–34.

Rasmussen S, Irgens LM, Bergsjø P, Dalaker K. The occurrence of placental abruption in Norway 1967–1991. *Acta Obstetricia et Gynecologica Scandinavica* 1996b; 75(3):222–8.

Rasmussen S, Irgens LM, Dalaker K. A history of placental dysfunction and risk of placental abruption. *Paediatric and Perinatal Epidemiology* 1999;13(1):9–21.

Rauh VA, Whyatt RM, Garfinkel R, Andrews H, Hoepner L, Reyes A, Diaz D, Camann D, Perera FP. Developmental effects of exposure to environmental tobacco smoke and material hardship among inner-city children. *Neurotoxicology and Teratology* 2004;26(3):373–85.

Rauramo I, Forss M, Kariniemi V, Lehtovirta P. Antepartum fetal heart rate variability and intervillous placental blood flow in association with smoking. *American Journal of Obstetrics and Gynecology* 1983;146(8):967–9.

Raymond EG, Mills JL. Placental abruption: maternal risk factors and associated fetal conditions. *Acta Obstetricia et Gynecologica Scandinavica* 1993;72(8):633–9.

Reefhuis J, de Walle HE, Cornel MC. Maternal smoking and deformities of the foot: results of the EUROCAT Study. European Registries of Congenital Anomalies. *American Journal of Public Health* 1998;88(10):1554–5.

Regan L, Braude PR, Trembath PL. Influence of past reproductive performance on risk of spontaneous abortion. *BMJ (British Medical Journal)* 1989;299(6698):541–5.

Regan L, Owen EJ, Jacobs HS. Hypersecretion of luteinising hormone, infertility, and miscarriage. *Lancet* 1990;336(8724):141–4.

Regan L, Rai R. Epidemiology and the medical causes of miscarriage. *Bailliere's Best Practice & Research Clinical Obstetrics & Gynaecology* 2000;14(5):839–54.

Reynolds P, Hurley SE, Hoggatt K, Anton-Culver H, Bernstein L, Deapen D, Peel D, Pinder R, Ross RK, West D, et al. Correlates of active and passive smoking in the California Teachers Study Cohort. *Journal of Women's Health* 2004;13(7):778–90.

Reznik G, Marquard G. Effect of cigarette smoke inhalation during pregnancy in Sprague-Dawley rats. *Journal of Environmental Pathology and Toxicology* 1980;4(5–6):141–52.

Rice C, Yoshinaga K. Effect of nicotine on oviducal lactate dehydrogenase during early pregnancy in the rat. *Biology of Reproduction* 1980;23(2):445–51.

Riedl M, Diaz-Sanchez D. Biology of diesel exhaust effects on respiratory function. *Journal of Allergy and Clinical Immunology* 2005;115(2):221–8.

Ritz B, Yu F, Fruin S, Chapa G, Shaw GM, Harris JA. Ambient air pollution and risk of birth defects in southern California. *American Journal of Epidemiology* 2002;155(1):17–25.

Riveles KA. Identification and quantification of toxicants in mainstream and sidestream smoke that affect hamster oviductal functioning [dissertation]. Riverside (CA): University of California, 2004.

Riveles K, Iv M, Arey J, Talbot P. Pyridines in cigarette smoke inhibit hamster oviductal functioning in picomolar doses. *Reproductive Toxicology* 2003;17(2):191–202.

Riveles K, Roza R, Arey J, Talbot P. Pyrazine derivatives in cigarette smoke inhibit hamster oviductal functioning. *Reproductive Biology and Endocrinology* 2004;2:23.

Riveles K, Roza R, Talbot P. Phenols, quinolines, indoles, benzene, and 2-cyclopenten-1-ones are oviductal toxicants in cigarette smoke. *Toxicological Sciences* 2005;86(1):141–51.

Robbins WA, Elashoff DA, Xun L, Jia J, Li N, Wu G, Wei F. Effect of lifestyle exposures on sperm aneuploidy. *Cytogenetic and Genome Research* 2005;111(3–4):371–7.

Roberts JM, Redman CWG. Pre-eclampsia: more than pregnancy-induced hypertension. *Lancet* 1993;341(8858):1447–51.

Roberts JM, Taylor RN, Goldfien A. Clinical and biochemical evidence of endothelial cell dysfunction in the pregnancy syndrome preeclampsia. *American Journal of Hypertension* 1991;4(8):700–8.

Roberts JM, Taylor RN, Musci TJ, Rodgers GM, Hubel CA, McLaughlin MK. Preeclampsia: an endothelial cell disorder. *American Journal of Obstetrics and Gynecology* 1989;161(5):1200–4.

Romero R, Espinoza J, Chaiworapongsa T, Kalache K. Infection and prematurity and the role of preventive strategies. *Seminars in Neonatology* 2002;7(4):259–74.

Romitti PA, Lidral AC, Munger RG, Daack-Hirsch S, Burns TL, Murray JC. Candidate genes for nonsyndromic cleft lip and palate and maternal cigarette smoking and alcohol consumption: evaluation of genotype-environment interactions from a population-based case-control study of orofacial clefts. *Teratology* 1999;59(1):39–50.

Ronco AM, Arguello G, Muñoz L, Gras N, Llanos M. Metals content in placentas from moderate cigarette consumers: correlation with newborn birth weight. *Biometals* 2005;18(3):233–41.

Rowell PP, Sastry BVR. The influence of cholinergic blockade on the uptake of α-aminoisobutyric acid by isolated human placental villi. *Toxicology and Applied Pharmacology* 1978;45(1):79–93.

Rowland AS, Baird DD, Long S, Wegienka G, Harlow SD, Alavanja M, Sandler DP. Influence of medical conditions and lifestyle factors on the menstrual cycle. *Epidemiology* 2002;13(6):668–74.

Rowland AS, Baird DD, Weinberg CR, Shore DL, Shy CM, Wilcox AJ. The effect of occupational exposure to mercury vapour on the fertility of female dental assistants. *Occupational and Environmental Medicine* 1994;51(1):28–34.

Royce RA, Winkelstein W Jr. HIV infection, cigarette smoking and CD4+ T-lymphocyte counts: preliminary results from the San Francisco Men's Health Study. *AIDS* 1990;4(4):327–33.

Ruckebusch Y. Relationship between the electrical activity of the oviduct and the uterus of the rabbit *in vivo*. *Journal of Reproduction and Fertility* 1975;45(1):73–82.

Ryter SW, Morse D, Choi AM. Carbon monoxide: to boldly go where NO has gone before. *Science's STKE* 2004(230):RE6.

Saaranen M, Kantola M, Saarikoski S, Vanha-Perttula T. Human seminal plasma cadmium: comparison with fertility and smoking habits. *Andrologia* 1989;21(2): 140–5.

Salihu HM, Li Q, Rouse DJ, Alexander GR. Placenta previa: neonatal death after live births in the United States. *American Journal of Obstetrics and Gynecology* 2003;188(5):1305–9.

Salihu HM, Shumpert MN, Aliyu MH, Kirby RS, Alexander GR. Smoking-associated fetal morbidity among older gravidas: a population study. *Acta Obstetricia et Gynecologica Scandinavica* 2005;84(4):329–34.

Sallmén M, Lindbohm ML, Nurminen M. Paternal exposure to lead and infertility. *Epidemiology* 2000;11(2):148–52.

Samuelson SO, Magnus P, Bakketeig LS. Birth weight and mortality in childhood in Norway. *American Journal of Epidemiology* 1998;148(10):983–91.

Sandler DP, Wilcox AJ, Horney LF. Age at menarche and subsequent reproductive events. *American Journal of Epidemiology* 1984;119(5):765–74.

Sanyal MK, Li Y-L, Belanger K. Metabolism of polynuclear aromatic hydrocarbon in human term placenta influenced by cigarette smoke exposure. *Reproductive Toxicology* 1994;8(5):411–8.

Sarasin A, Schlumpf M, Müller M, Fleischmann I, Lauber ME, Lichtensteiger W. Adrenal-mediated rather than direct effects of nicotine as a basis of altered sex steroid synthesis in fetal and neonatal rat. *Reproductive Toxicology* 2003;117(2):153–62.

Sasagawa S, Suzuki K, Sakatani T, Fujikura T. Effects of nicotine on the functions of human polymorphonuclear leukocytes in vitro. *Journal of Leukocyte Biology* 1985;37(5):493–502.

Sasser LB, Kelman BJ, Levin AA, Miller RK. The influence of maternal cadmium exposure or fetal cadmium injection on hepatic metallothionein concentrations in the fetal rat. *Toxicology and Applied Pharmacology* 1985;80(2):299–307.

Sastry BVR. Placental toxicology: tobacco smoke, abused drugs, multiple chemical interactions, and placental function. *Reproduction, Fertility, and Development* 1991;3(4):355–72.

Sauter D. Hematologic principles. In: Goldfrank LR, Weisman RS, Flomenbaum NE, Howland MA, Lewin NA, Hoffman RS, editors. *Goldfrank's Toxicologic Emergencies*. 5th ed. Norwalk (CT): Appleton & Lange, 1994:345–64.

Savitz DA, Schwingl PJ, Keels MA. Influence of paternal age, smoking, and alcohol consumption on congenital anomalies. *Teratology* 1991;44(4):429–40.

Saxena DK, Murthy RC, Lal B, Srivastava RS, Chandra SV. Effect of hexavalent chromium on testicular maturation in the rat. *Reproductive Toxicology* 1990;4(3):223–8.

Schoendorf KC, Kiely JL. Relationship of sudden infant death syndrome to maternal smoking during and after pregnancy. *Pediatrics* 1992;90(6):905–8.

Schoeneck JF. Cigarette smoking in pregnancy. *New York State Journal of Medicine* 1941;41:1945–48.

Scholl TO, Hediger ML, Schall JI, Fischer RL, Khoo C-S. Low zinc intake during pregnancy: its association with preterm and very preterm delivery. *American Journal of Epidemiology* 1993;137(10):1115–24.

Schwarze A, Nelles I, Krapp M, Friedrich M, Schmidt W, Diedrich K, Axt-Fliedner R. Doppler ultrasound of the uterine artery in the prediction of severe complications during low-risk pregnancies. *Archives of Gynecology and Obstetrics* 2005;271(1):46–52.

Schwingl PJ. Prenatal smoking exposure in relation to female adult fecundability [dissertation]. Ann Arbor (MI): United Microfilms International, 1992.

Scott RT Jr, Hofmann GE. Prognostic assessment of ovarian reserve. *Fertility and Sterility* 1995;63(1):1–11.

Scott RT, Toner JP, Muasher SJ, Oehninger S, Robinson S, Rosenwaks Z. Follicle-stimulating hormone levels on cycle day 3 are predictive of in vitro fertilization outcome. *Fertility and Sterility* 1989;51(4):651–4.

Segarra AC, Strand FL. Perinatal administration of nicotine alters subsequent sexual behavior and testosterone levels of male rats. *Brain Research* 1989;480(1–2): 151–9.

Sekhon HS, Keller JA, Benowitz NL, Spindel ER. Prenatal nicotine exposure alters pulmonary function in newborn rhesus monkeys. *American Journal of Respiratory and Critical Care Medicine* 2001;164(6):989–94.

Selevan SG, Rice DC, Hogan KA, Euling SY, Pfahles-Hutchens A, Bethel J. Blood lead concentration and delayed puberty in girls. *New England Journal of Medicine* 2003;348(16):1527–36.

Sergerie M, Ouhilal S, Bissonnette F, Brodeur J, Bleau G. Lack of association between smoking and DNA fragmentation in the spermatozoa of normal men. *Human Reproduction* 2000;15(6):1314–21.

Sexton M, Fox NL, Hebel JR. Prenatal exposure to tobacco. II: effects on cognitive functioning at age three. *International Journal of Epidemiology* 1990;19(1):72–7.

Seyler LE Jr, Pomerleau OF, Fertig JB, Hunt D, Parker K. Pituitary hormone response to cigarette smoking. *Pharmacology, Biochemistry, and Behavior* 1986; 24(1):159–62.

Shaarawy M, Mahmoud KZ. Endocrine profile and semen characteristics in male smokers. *Fertility and Sterility* 1982;38(2):255–7.

Shah D, Shroff S, Gania K. Factors affecting perinatal mortality in India (perinatal audit). *Prenatal and Neonatal Medicine* 2000;5(5):288–302.

Shah NR, Bracken MB. A systematic review and meta-analysis of prospective studies on the association between maternal cigarette smoking and preterm delivery. *American Journal of Obstetrics and Gynecology* 2000;182(2):465–72.

Shaw GM, Carmichael SL, Vollset SE, Yang W, Finnell RH, Blom H, Midttun Ø, Ueland PM. Mid-pregnancy cotinine and risks of orofacial clefts and neural tube defects. *Journal of Pediatrics* 2009;154(1):17–9.

Shaw GM, Nelson V, Carmichael SL, Lammer EJ, Finnell RH, Rosenquist TH. Maternal periconceptional vitamins: interactions with selected factors and congenital anomalies? *Epidemiology* 2002;13(6):625–30.

Shaw GM, Wasserman CR, Lammer EJ, O'Malley CD, Murray JC, Basart AM, Tolarova MM. Orofacial clefts, parental cigarette smoking, and transforming growth factor-alpha gene variants. *American Journal of Human Genetics* 1996;58(3):551–61.

Shen H-M, Chia S-E, Ni Z-Y, New A-L, Lee B-L, Ong C-N. Detection of oxidative DNA damage in human sperm and the association with cigarette smoking. *Reproductive Toxicology* 1997;11(5):675–80.

Shi M, Christensen K, Weinberg CR, Romitti P, Bathum L, Lozada A, Morris RW, Lovett M, Murray JC. Orafacial cleft risk is increased with maternal smoking and specific detoxification-gene variants. *American Journal of Human Genetics* 2007;80(1):76–90

Shubert PJ, Diss E, Iams JD. Etiology of preterm premature rupture of membranes. *Obstetrics and Gynecology Clinics of North America* 1992;19(2):251–63.

Shugart L, Matsunami R. Adduct formation in hemoglobin of the newborn mouse exposed in utero to benzo[*a*]pyrene. *Toxicology* 1985;37(3–4):241–5.

Shum S, Jensen NM, Nebert DW. The murine *Ah* locus: in utero toxicity and teratogenesis associated with genetic differences in benzo[*a*]pyrene metabolism. *Teratology* 1979;20(3):365–76.

Sibai BM. Diagnosis and management of gestational hypertension and preeclampsia. *Obstetrics and Gynecology* 2003;102(1):181–92.

Sibai B, Dekker G, Kupferminc M. Pre-eclampsia. *Lancet* 2005;365(9461):785–99.

Siegel E, Wason S. Mothball toxicity. *Pediatric Clinics of North America* 1986;33(2):369–74.

Sikorski R, Juszkiewicz T, Paszkowski T. Zinc status in women with premature rupture of membranes at term. *Obstetrics and Gynecology* 1990;76(4):675–7.

Sikorski R, Radomanski T, Paszkowski T, Skoda J. Smoking during pregnancy and the perinatal cadmium burden. *Journal of Perinatal Medicine* 1988;16(3):225–31.

Simhan HN, Caritis SN, Hillier SL, Krohn MA. Cervical anti-inflammatory cytokine concentrations among first-trimester pregnant smokers. *American Journal of Obstetrics and Gynecology* 2005;193(6):1999–2003.

Simhan HN, Krohn MA. First-trimester cervical inflammatory milieu and subsequent early preterm birth. *American Journal of Obstetrics and Gynecology* 2009; 200(4):377.e1–377.e4.

Simmer K, Thompson RPH. Maternal zinc and intrauterine growth retardation. *Clinical Science (London)* 1985;68(4):395–9.

Sindberg Eriksen P, Gennser G. Acute responses to maternal smoking of the pulsatile movements in fetal aorta. *Acta Obstetricia et Gynecologica Scandinavica* 1984; 63(7):647–54.

Sindberg Eriksen P, Gennser G, Lindvall R, Nilsson K. Acute effects of maternal smoking on fetal heart beat intervals. *Acta Obstetricia et Gynecologica Scandinavica* 1984;63(5):385–90.

Sindberg Eriksen P, Marsál K. Acute effects of maternal smoking on fetal blood flow. *Acta Obstetricia et Gynecologica Scandinavica* 1984;63(5):391–7.

Sindberg Eriksen P, Marsál K. Circulatory changes in the fetal aorta after maternal smoking. *British Journal of Obstetrics and Gynaecology* 1987;94(4):301–5.

Singh J. Early behavioral alterations in mice following prenatal carbon monoxide exposure. *Neurotoxicology* 1986;7(2):475–81.

Skelly AC, Holt VL, Mosca VS, Alderman BW. Talipes equinovarus and maternal smoking: a population-based case-control study in Washington state. *Teratology* 2002;66(2):91–100.

Skinner SJM, Campos GA, Liggins GC. Collagen content of human amniotic membranes: effect of gestation length and premature rupture. *Obstetrics and Gynecology* 1981;57(4):487–9.

Skjeldestad FE, Hadgu A, Eriksson N. Epidemiology of repeat ectopic pregnancy: a population-based prospective cohort study. *Obstetrics and Gynecology* 1998; 91(1):129–35.

Sloss EM, Frerichs RR. Smoking and menstrual disorders. *International Journal of Epidemiology* 1983;12(1): 107–9.

Smart S, Singal A, Mindel A. Social and sexual risk factors for bacterial vaginosis. *Sexually Transmitted Infections* 2004;80(1):58–62.

Smith CJ, Livingston SD, Doolittle DJ. An international literature survey of "IARC Group I carcinogens" reported in mainstream cigarette smoke. *Food and Chemical Toxicology* 1997;35(10–11):1107–30.

Smith LM, Cloak CC, Poland RE, Torday J, Ross MG. Prenatal nicotine increases testosterone levels in the fetus and female offspring. *Nicotine & Tobacco Research* 2003;5(3):369–74.

Smith MK, George EL, Stober JA, Feng HLA, Kimmel GL. Perinatal toxicity associated with nickel chloride exposure. *Environmental Research* 1993;61(2):200–11.

Sofikitis N, Miyagawa I, Dimitriadis D, Zavos P, Sikka S, Hellstrom W. Effects of smoking on testicular function, semen quality and sperm fertilizing capacity. *Journal of Urology* 1995;154(3):1030–4.

Sokol RZ. Lead exposure and its effects on the reproductive system. In: Golub MS, editor. *Metals, Fertility, and Reproductive Toxicity.* Boca Raton (FL): CRC Press, 2005:118–54

Sooranna SR, Morris NH, Steer PJ. Placental nitric oxide metabolism. *Reproduction, Fertility, and Development* 1995;7(6):1525–31.

Sopori M. Effects of cigarette smoke on the immune system. *Nature Reviews Immunology* 2002;2(5):372–7.

Sopori ML, Kozak W. Immunomodulatory effects of cigarette smoke. *Journal of Neuroimmunology* 1998;83 (1–2):148–56.

Sorensen KE, Borlum KG. Acute effects of maternal smoking on human fetal heart function. *Acta Obstetricia et Gynecologica Scandinavica* 1987;66(3):217–20.

Sowa B, Steibert E. Effect of oral cadmium administration to female rats during pregnancy on zinc, copper, and iron content in placenta, foetal liver, kidney, intestine, and brain. *Archives in Toxicology* 1985;56(4):256–62.

Sowa B, Steibert E, Gralewska K, Piekarski M. Effect of oral cadmium administration to female rats before and/ or during pregnancy on the metallothionein level in the fetal liver. *Toxicology Letters* 1982;11(3–4):233–6.

Sowers MF, Beebe JL, McConnell D, Randolph J, Jannausch M. Testosterone concentrations in women aged 25–50 years: associations with lifestyle, body composition, and ovarian status. *American Journal of Epidemiology* 2001;153(3):256–64.

Sowers MR, La Pietra MT. Menopause: its epidemiology and potential association with chronic diseases. *Epidemiologic Reviews* 1995;17(2):287–302.

Spanò M, Kolstad AH, Larsen SB, Cordelli E, Leter G, Giwercman A, Bonde JP, Asclepios. The applicability of the flow cytometric sperm chromatin structure assay in epidemiological studies. *Human Reproduction* 1998;13(9):2495–505.

Spira A, Spira N, Goujard J, Schwartz D. Smoking during pregnancy and placental weight: a multivariate analysis on 3759 cases. *Journal of Perinatal Medicine* 1975;3(4):237–41.

Šrám RJ, Binková B, Dejmek J, Bobak M. Ambient air pollution and pregnancy outcomes: a review of the literature. *Environmental Health Perspectives* 2005; 113(4):375–82.

Steibert E, Król B, Sowa B, Gralewska K, Kamiński M, Kamińska O, Kusz E. Cadmium-induced changes in the histoenzymatic activity in liver, kidney and duodenum of pregnant rats. *Toxicology Letters* 1984;20(2):127–32.

Steinberger EK, Ferencz C, Loffredo CA. Infants with single ventricle: a population-based epidemiological study. *Teratology* 2002;65(3):106–15.

Stillman RJ, Rosenberg MJ, Sachs BP. Smoking and reproduction. *Fertility and Sterility* 1986;46(4): 545–66.

Storgaard L, Bonde JP, Ernst E, Spanô M, Andersen CY, Frydenberg M, Olsen J. Does smoking during pregnancy affect sons' sperm counts? *Epidemiology* 2003; 14(3):278–86.

Storm JE, Fechter LD. Alteration in the postnatal ontogeny of cerebellar norepinephrine content following chronic prenatal carbon monoxide. *Journal of Neurochemistry* 1985a;45(3):965–9.

Storm JE, Fechter LD. Prenatal carbon monoxide exposure differentially affects postnatal weight and monoamine concentration of rat brain regions. *Toxicology and Applied Pharmacology* 1985b;81(1):139–46.

Storm JE, Valdes JJ, Fechter LD. Postnatal alterations in cerebellar GABA content, GABA uptake and morphology following exposure to carbon monoxide early in development. *Developmental Neuroscience* 1986; 8(4):251–61.

Subramaniam S, Srinivasan S, Bummer PM, Gairola CG. Perinatal sidestream cigarette smoke exposure and the developing pulmonary surfactant system in rats. *Human & Experimental Toxicology* 1999;18(4): 206–11.

Sun J-G, Jurisicova A, Casper RF. Detection of deoxyribonucleic acid fragmentation in human sperm: correlation with fertilization in vitro. *Biology of Reproduction* 1997;56(3):602–7.

Sylvester SR, Griswold MD. The testicular iron shuttle: a "nurse" function of the Sertoli cells. *Journal of Andrology* 1994;15(5):381–5.

Tachi N, Aoyama M. Effect of cigarette smoke and carbon monoxide inhalation by gravid rats on the conceptus weight. *Bulletin of Environmental Contamination and Toxicology* 1983;31(1):85–92.

Tajtakova M, Farkasova E, Klubertova M, Konradova I, Machovcakova L. [The effect of smoking on menopause] [Slovak]. *Vnitřní Lékařství* 1990;36(7):649–53.

Talbot P, Geiske C, Knoll M. Oocyte pickup by the mammalian oviduct. *Molecular Biology of the Cell* 1999; 10(1):5–8.

Talbot P, Riveles K. Smoking and reproduction: the oviduct as a target of cigarette smoke. *Reproductive Biology and Endocrinology* 2005;3:52.

Teasdale F, Ghislaine J-J. Morphological changes in the placentas of smoking mothers: a histomorphometric study. *Biology of the Neonate* 1989;55(4–5):251–9.

Tollerud DJ, Clark JW, Brown LM, Neuland CY, Mann DL, Pankiw-Trost LK, Blattner WA, Hoover RN. Association of cigarette smoking with decreased numbers of circulating natural killer cells. *American Review of Respiratory Disease* 1989;139(1):194–8.

Torfs CP, Christianson RE. Maternal risk factors and major associated defects in infants with Down syndrome. *Epidemiology* 1999;10(3):264–70.

Torjussen W, Zachariasen H, Andersen I. Cigarette smoking and nickel exposure. *Journal of Environmental Monitoring* 2003;5(2):198–201.

Torry DS, Hinrichs M, Torry RJ. Determinants of placental vascularity. *American Journal of Reproductive Immunology* 2004;51(4):257–68.

Tracy RP, Psaty BM, Macy E, Bovill EG, Cushman M, Cornell ES, Kuller LH. Lifetime smoking exposure affects the association of C-reactive protein with cardiovascular disease risk factors and subclinical disease in healthy elderly subjects. *Arteriosclerosis, Thrombosis, and Vascular Biology* 1997;17(10):2167–76.

Trasti N, Vik T, Jacobsen G, Bakketeig L. Smoking in pregnancy and children's mental and motor development at age 1 and 5 years. *Early Human Development* 1999;55(2):137–47.

Trivedi B, Saxena DK, Murthy RC, Chandra SV. Embryotoxicity and fetotoxicity of orally administered hexavalent chromium in mice. *Reproductive Toxicology* 1989; 3(4):275–8.

Trummer H, Habermann H, Haas J, Pummer K. The impact of cigarette smoking on human semen parameters and hormones. *Human Reproduction* 2002;17(6):1554–9.

Tsuchihashi S, Fondevila C, Kupiec-Weglinski JW. Heme oxygenase system in ischemia and reperfusion injury. *Annals of Transplantation* 2004;9(1):84–7.

Tsunoda M, Litonjua AA, Kuniak MP, Weiss ST, Satoh T, Guevarra L, Tollerud DJ. Serum cytokine levels, cigarette smoking and airway responsiveness among pregnant women. *International Archives of Allergy and Immunology* 2003;130(2):158–64.

Tulppala M, Bjorses UM, Stenman UH, Wahlstrom T, Ylikorkala O. Luteal phase defect in habitual abortion: progesterone in saliva. *Fertility and Sterility* 1991; 56(1):41–4.

U.S. Department of Health and Human Services. *The Health Consequences of Smoking for Women. A Report of the Surgeon General*. Washington: U.S. Department of Health and Human Services, Public Health Service, Office of the Assistant Secretary for Health, Office on Smoking and Health, 1980.

U.S. Department of Health and Human Services. *Tobacco Use Among U.S. Racial/Ethnic Minority Groups—African Americans, American Indians and Alaska Natives, Asian Americans and Pacific Islanders, and Hispanics. A Report of the Surgeon General*. Atlanta: U.S. Department of Health and Human Services, Public Health Service, Centers for Disease Control and Prevention, National Center for Chronic Disease Prevention and Health Promotion, Office on Smoking and Health, 1998.

U.S. Department of Health and Human Services. *Women and Smoking: A Report of the Surgeon General*. Rockville (MD): U.S. Department of Health and Human Services, Public Health Service, Office of the Surgeon General, 2001.

U.S. Department of Health and Human Services. *The Health Consequences of Smoking: A Report of the Surgeon General*. Atlanta: U.S. Department of Health and Human Services, Centers for Disease Control and Prevention, National Center for Chronic Disease Prevention and Health Promotion, Office on Smoking and Health, 2004.

U.S. Department of Health and Human Services. *The Health Consequences of Involuntary Exposure to Tobacco Smoke: A Report of the Surgeon General*. Atlanta: U.S. Department of Health and Human Services, Centers for Disease Control and Prevention, National Center for Chronic Disease Prevention and Health Promotion, Office on Smoking and Health, 2006.

U.S. Department of Health, Education, and Welfare. *Smoking and Health: Report of the Advisory Committee to the Surgeon General of the Public Health Service*. Washington: U.S. Department of Health, Education, and Welfare, Public Health Service, Center for Disease Control, 1964. PHS Publication No. 1103.

U.S. Environmental Protection Agency. *Respiratory Health Effects of Passive Smoking: Lung Cancer and Other Disorders*. Washington: U.S. Environmental Protection Agency, Office of Health and Environmental Assessment, Office of Research and Development, 1992. Publication No. EPA/600/6-90/006F.

U.S. Preventive Services Task Force. *Counseling to Prevent Tobacco Use and Tobacco-Caused Disease*. Rockville (MD): U.S. Department of Health and Human Services, Agency for Healthcare Research and Quality, U.S. Preventive Services Task Force, 2003. AHRQ Publication No. 04-0526. <http://www.ahrq.gov/clinic/3rduspstf/tobacccoun/tobcounrs.pdf>; accessed: January 7, 2008.

Urso P, Gengozian N. Alterations in the humoral immune response and tumor frequencies in mice exposed to benzo[a]pyrene and x-rays before or after birth. *Journal of Toxicology and Environmental Health* 1982;10(4–5): 817–35.

Urso P, Johnson RA. Quantitative and functional change in T cells of primiparous mice following injection of benzo(a)pyrene at the second trimester of pregnancy. *Immunopharmacology and Immunotoxicology* 1988; 10(2):195–217.

Urso P, Zhang W, Cobb JR. Immunological consequences from exposure to benzo(a)pyrene during pregnancy. *Scandinavian Journal of Immunology* 1992;Supplement 11:203–6.

Vallee BL, Falchuk KH. The biochemical basis of zinc physiology. *Physiological Reviews* 1993;73(1):79–118.

Van Den Eeden SK, Shan J, Bruce C, Glasser M. Ectopic pregnancy rate and treatment utilization in a large managed care organization. *Obstetrics and Gynecology* 2005;105(5 Part 1):1052–7.

van der Vaart H, Postma DS, Timens W, Hylkema MN, Willemse BWM, Boezen HM, Vonk JM, de Reus DM, Kauffman HF, Ten Hacken NHT. Acute effects of cigarette smoking on inflammation in healthy intermittent smokers. *Respiratory Research* 2005;6(1):22.

van der Veen F, Fox H. The effects of cigarette smoking on the human placenta: a light and electron microscopic study. *Placenta* 1982;3(3):243–56.

van der Velde WJ, Copius Peereboom-Stegeman JHJ, Treffers PE, James J. Structural changes in the placenta of smoking mothers: a quantitative study. *Placenta* 1983;4(3):231–40.

van der Velde WJ, Copius Peereboom-Stegeman JHJ, Treffers PE, James J. Basal lamina thickening in the placentae of smoking mothers. *Placenta* 1985;6(4):329–40.

van Rooij IALM, Groenen PMW, Van Drongelen M, Te Morsche RHM, Peters WHM, Steegers-Theunissen RPM. Orofacial clefts and spina bifida: *N*-acetyltransferase phenotype, maternal smoking, and medication use. *Teratology* 2002;66(5):260–6.

van Rooij IALM, Wegerif MJM, Roelofs HMJ, Peters WHM, Kuijpers-Jagtman A-M, Zielhuis GA, Merkus HMWM, Steegers-Theunissen RPM. Smoking, genetic polymorphisms in biotransformation enzymes, and nonsyndromic oral clefting: a gene-environment interaction. *Epidemiology* 2001;12(5):502–7.

Van Santbrink EJ, Hop WC, van Dessel TJ, de Jong FH, Fauser BC. Decremental follicle-stimulating hormone and dominant follicle development during the normal menstrual cycle. *Fertility and Sterility* 1995;64(1): 37–43.

Van Winkle LS, Buckpitt AR, Nishio SJ, Isaac JM, Plopper CG. Cellular response in naphthalene-induced Clara cell injury and bronchiolar epithelial repair in mice. *American Journal of Physiology* 1995;269(6 Pt 1):L800–L818.

Venners SA, Wang X, Chen C, Wang L, Chen D, Guang W, Huang A, Ryan L, O'Connor J, Lasley B, et al. Paternal smoking and pregnancy loss: a prospective study using a biomarker of pregnancy. *American Journal of Epidemiology* 2004;159(10):993–1001.

Villar J, Say L, Shennan A, Lindheimer M, Duley L, Conde-Agudelo A, Merialdi M. Methodological and technical issues related to the diagnosis, screening, prevention, and treatment of pre-eclampsia and eclampsia. *International Journal of Gynaecology and Obstetrics* 2004;85(Suppl 1):S28–S41.

Vine MF. Smoking and male reproduction: a review. *International Journal of Andrology* 1996;19(6):323–37.

Vine MF, Margolin BH, Morrison HI, Hulka BS. Cigarette smoking and sperm density: a meta-analysis. *Fertility and Sterility* 1994;61(1):35–43.

von Dadelszen P, Magee LA, Roberts JM. Subclassification of preeclampsia. *Hypertension in Pregnancy* 2003; 22(2):143–8.

Wagner B, Lazar P, Chouroulinkov I. The effects of cigarette smoke inhalation upon mice during pregnancy. *Revue Europeenne D'Etudes Cliniques et Biologiques* 1972;17(10):943–8.

Wang X, Chen D, Niu T, Wang Z, Wang L, Ryan L, Smith T, Christiani DC, Zuckerman B, Xu X. Genetic susceptibility to benzene and shortened gestation: evidence of gene-environment interaction. *American Journal of Epidemiology* 2000a;152(8):693–700.

Wang X, Zuckerman B, Pearson C, Kaufman G, Chen C, Wang G, Niu T, Wise PH, Bauchner H, Xu X. Maternal cigarette smoking; metabolic gene polymorphism, and infant birth weight. *JAMA: the Journal of the American Medical Association* 2002;287(2):195–202.

Wang XL, Sim AS, Wang MX, Murrell GAC, Trudinger B, Wang J. Genotype dependent and cigarette specific effects on endothelial nitric oxide synthase gene expression and enzyme activity. *FEBS Letters* 2000b; 471(1):45–50.

Wang Y, Gu Y, Zhang Y, Lewis DF. Evidence of endothelial dysfunction in preeclampsia: decreased endothelial nitric oxide synthase expression is associated with increased cell permeability in endothelial cells from preeclampsia. *American Journal of Obstetrics and Gynecology* 2004;190(3):817–24.

Ward NI, Watson R, Bryce-Smith C. Placental elemental levels in relation to fetal development for obstetrically 'normal' births: a study of 37 elements. Evidence for effects of cadmium, lead and zinc on fetal growth, and for smoking as a source of cadmium. *International Journal of Biosocial Research* 1987;9(1):63–81.

Washington AE, Katz P. Ectopic pregnancy in the United States: economic consequences and payment source trends. *Obstetrics and Gynecology* 1993;81(2):287–92.

Watanabe N. Decreased number of sperms and Sertoli cells in mature rats exposed to diesel exhaust as fetuses. *Toxicology Letters* 2005;155(1):51–8.

Weigert M, Hofstetter G, Kaipl D, Gottlich H, Krischker U, Bichler K, Poehl M, Feichtinger W. The effect of smoking on oocyte quality and hormonal parameters of patients undergoing in vitro fertilization-embryo transfer. *Journal of Assisted Reproduction and Genetics* 1999;16(6):287–93.

Weinberg CR, Wilcox AJ, Baird DD. Reduced fecundability in women with prenatal exposure to cigarette smoking. *American Journal of Epidemiology* 1989;129(5): 1072–8.

Wells PG, Winn LM. Biochemical toxicology of chemical teratogenesis. *Critical Reviews in Biochemistry and Molecular Biology* 1996;31(1):1–40.

Wen SW, Goldenberg RL, Cutter GR, Hoffman HJ, Cliver SP, Davis RO, DuBard MB. Smoking, maternal age, fetal growth, and gestational age at delivery. *American Journal of Obstetrics and Gynecology* 1990;162(1):53–8.

Werler MM, Sheehan JE, Mitchell A. Association of vasoconstrictive exposures with risks of gastroschisis and small intestinal atresia. *Epidemiology* 2003;14(3): 349–54.

Westhoff C, Gentile G, Lee J, Zacur H, Helbig D. Predictors of ovarian steroid secretion in reproductive-age women. *American Journal of Epidemiology* 1996;144(4):381–8.

Whelan EA, Sandler DP, McConnaughey DR, Weinberg CR. Menstrual and reproductive characteristics and age at natural menopause. *American Journal of Epidemiology* 1990;131(4):625–32.

Wideman GL, Baird GH, Bolding OT. Ascorbic acid deficiency and premature rupture of fetal membranes. *American Journal of Obstetrics and Gynecology* 1964; 88:592–5.

Wilcox AJ, Baird DD, Weinberg CR. Do women with childhood exposure to cigarette smoking have increased fecundability? *American Journal of Epidemiology* 1989; 129(5);1079–83.

Wilcox AJ, Skjaerven R. Birth weight and perinatal mortality: the effect of gestational age. *American Journal of Public Health* 1992;82(3):378–82.

Wilcox AJ, Weinberg CR, O'Connor JF, Baird DD, Schlatterer JP, Canfield RE, Armstrong EG, Nisula BC. Incidence of early loss of pregnancy. *New England Journal of Medicine* 1988;319(4):189–94.

Wilkins JN, Carlson HE, Van Vunakis H, Hill MA, Gritz E, Jarvik ME. Nicotine from cigarette smoking increases circulating levels of cortisol, growth hormone, and prolactin in male chronic smokers. *Psychopharmacology* 1982;78(4):305–8.

Wilks DJ, Hay AW. Smoking and female fecundity: the effect and importance of study design. *European Journal of Obstetrics, Gynecology, and Reproductive Biology* 2004;112(2):127–35.

Williams L, Morrow B, Shulman H, Stephens R, D'Angelo D, Fowler CI. *PRAMS 2002 Surveillance Report*. Atlanta: U.S. Department of Health and Human Services, Centers for Disease Control and Prevention, National Center for Chronic Disease Prevention and Health Promotion, Division of Reproductive Health, 2006.

Williams LA, Evans SF, Newnham JP. Prospective cohort study of factors influencing the relative weights of the placenta and the newborn infant. *BMJ (British Medical Journal)* 1997;314(7098):1864–8.

Williams MA, Lieberman E, Mittendorf R, Monson RR, Schoenbaum SC. Risk factors for abruptio placentae. *American Journal of Epidemiology* 1991;134(9): 965–72.

Wilson DM, Killen JD, Hayward C, Robinson TN, Hammer LD, Kraemer HC, Varady A, Taylor CB. Timing and rate of sexual maturation and the onset of cigarette and alcohol use among teenage girls. *Archives of Pediatric & Adolescent Medicine* 1994;148(8):789–95.

Windham GC, Bottomley C, Birner C, Fenster L. Age at menarche in relation to maternal use of tobacco, alcohol, coffee, and tea during pregnancy. *American Journal of Epidemiology* 2004;159(9);862–71.

Windham GC, Eaton A, Hopkins B. Evidence for an association between environmental tobacco smoke exposure and birthweight: a meta-analysis and new data. *Paediatric and Perinatal Epidemiology* 1999a;13(1):35–57.

Windham GC, Elkin EP, Swan SH, Waller KO, Fenster L. Cigarette smoking and effects on menstrual function. *Obstetrics and Gynecology* 1999b;93(1):59–65.

Windham GC, Hopkins B, Fenster L, Swan SH. Prenatal active or passive tobacco smoke exposure and the risk of preterm delivery or low birth weight. *Epidemiology* 2000;11(4):427–33.

Windham GC, Mitchell P, Anderson M, Lasley BL. Cigarette smoking and effects on hormone function in premenopausal women. *Environmental Health Perspectives* 2005;113(10):1285–90.

Windham GC, Von Behren J, Waller K, Fenster L. Exposure to environmental and mainstream tobacco smoke and risk of spontaneous abortion. *American Journal of Epidemiology* 1999c;149(3):243–7.

Winternitz WW, Quillen D. Acute hormonal response to cigarette smoking. *Journal of Clinical Pharmacology* 1977;17(7):389–97.

Wisborg K, Kesmodel U, Henriksen TB, Hedegaard M, Secher NJ. A prospective study of maternal smoking and spontaneous abortion. *Acta Obstetricia et Gynecologica Scandinavica* 2003;82(10):936–41.

Wisborg K, Henriksen TB, Hedegaard M, Secher NJ. Smoking during pregnancy and preterm birth. *British Journal of Obstetrics and Gynaecology* 1996;103(8):800–5.

Wong ND, Pio J, Valencia R, Thakal G. Distribution of C-reactive protein and its relation to risk factors and coronary heart disease risk estimation in the National Health and Nutrition Examination Survey (NHANES) III. *Preventive Cardiology* 2001;4(3):109–14.

Woods SE, Raju U. Maternal smoking and the risk of congenital birth defects: a cohort study. *Journal of the American Board of Family Medicine* 2001;14(5):330–4.

World Health Organization. *WHO Laboratory Manual for the Examination of Human Semen and Sperm-Cervical Mucus Interaction*. Singapore: Press Concern, 1980.

World Health Organization. *WHO Laboratory Manual for the Examination of Human Semen and Sperm-Cervical Mucus Interaction*. 2nd ed. Cambridge: Cambridge University Press, 1987.

World Health Organization. *WHO Laboratory Manual for the Examination of Human Semen and Sperm-Cervical Mucus Interaction*. 3rd ed. Cambridge: Cambridge University Press, 1992.

World Health Organization, International Consultation on Environmental Tobacco Smoke (ETS) and Child Health. Geneva: World Health Organization, Division of Communicable Diseases, Tobacco Free Initiative, 1999a. WHO/NCD/TF1//99.10.

World Health Organization. *WHO Laboratory Manual for the Examination of Human Semen and Sperm-Cervical Mucus Interaction*. 4th ed. Cambridge: Cambridge University Press, 1999b.

Wyszynski DF, Wu T. Use of U.S. birth certificate data to estimate the risk of maternal cigarette smoking for oral clefting. *Cleft Palate-Craniofacial Journal* 2002;39(2):188–92.

Xu B, Rantakallio P, Jarvelin MR. Mortality and hospitalizations of 24-year old members of the low-birthweight cohort in Northern Finland. *Epidemiology* 1998;9(6):662–5.

Yang C-Y, Chang C-C, Tsai S-S, Chuang H-Y, Ho C-K, Wu T-N. Arsenic in drinking water and adverse pregnancy outcome in an arseniasis-endemic area in northeastern Taiwan. *Environmental Research* 2003;91(1):29–34.

Yang M, Kunugita N, Kitagawa K, Kang S-H, Coles B, Kadlubar FF, Katoh T, Matsuno K, Kawamoto T. Individual differences in urinary cotinine levels in Japanese smokers: relation to genetic polymorphism of drug-metabolizing enzymes. *Cancer Epidemiology, Biomarkers & Prevention* 2001;10(6):589–93.

Yang Q, Sherman SL, Hassold TJ, Allran K, Taft L, Pettay D, Khoury MJ, Erickson JD, Freeman SB. Risk factors for trisomy 21: maternal cigarette smoking and oral contraceptive use in a population-based case-control study. *Genetics in Medicine* 1999;1(3):80–8.

Yeung MC, Buncio AD. Leukocyte count, smoking, and lung function. *American Journal of Medicine* 1984;76(1):31–7.

Ylikorkala O, Viinikka L, Lehtovirta P. Effect of nicotine on fetal prostacyclin and thromboxane in humans. *Obstetrics and Gynecology* 1985;66(1):102–5.

Yolton K, Dietrich K, Auinger P, Lanphear BP, Hornung R. Exposure to environmental tobacco smoke and cognitive abilities among U.S. children and adolescents. *Environmental Health Perspectives* 2005;113(1):98–103.

Younglai EV, Foster WG, Hughes EG, Trim K, Jarrell JF. Levels of environmental contaminants in human follicular fluid, serum, and seminal plasma of couples undergoing in vitro fertilization. *Archives of Environmental Contamination and Toxicology* 2002;43(1):121–6.

Zahid ZR, Al-Hakkak ZS, Kadhim AHH, Elias EA, Al-Jumaily IS. Comparative effects of trivalent and hexavalent chromium on spermatogenesis of the mouse. *Toxicology and Environmental Chemistry* 1990;25(2–3):131–6.

Zeidel A, Beilin B, Yardeni I, Mayburd E, Smirnov G, Bessler H. Immune response in asymptomatic smokers. *Acta Anaesthesiologica Scandinavica* 2002;46(8):959–64.

Zeiger JS, Beaty TH, Liang K-Y. Oral clefts, maternal smoking, and TGFA: a meta-analysis of gene-environment interaction. *Cleft Palate-Craniofacial Journal* 2005; 42(1):58–63.

Zenzes MT, Bielecki R, Reed TE. Detection of benzo(*a*) pyrene diol epoxide–DNA adducts in sperm of men exposed to cigarette smoke. *Fertility and Sterility* 1999a;72(2):330–5.

Zenzes MT, Krishnan S, Krishnan B, Zhang H, Casper RF. Cadmium accumulation in follicular fluid of women in in vitro fertilization-embryo transfer is higher in smokers. *Fertility and Sterility* 1995;64(3):599–603.

Zenzes MT, Puy LA, Bielecki R, Reed TE. Detection of benzo[a]pyrene diol epoxide-DNA adducts in embryos from smoking couples: evidence for transmission by spermatozoa. *Molecular Human Reproduction* 1999b; 5(2):125–31.

Zhang J, Fried DB. Relationship of maternal smoking during pregnancy to placenta previa. *American Journal of Preventive Medicine* 1992;8(5):278–82.

Zhang J, Klebanoff MA, Levine RJ, Puri M, Moyer P. The puzzling association between smoking and hypertension during pregnancy. *American Journal of Obstetrics and Gynecology* 1999;181(6):1407–13.

Zhang J, Meikle S, Trumble A. Severe maternal morbidity associated with hypertensive disorders in pregnancy in the United States. *Hypertension in Pregnancy* 2003;22(2):203–12.

Zhang J, Savitz DA, Schwingl PJ, Cai WW. A case-control study of paternal smoking and birth defects. *International Journal of Epidemiology* 1992; 21(2):273–8.

Zhang J, Zeisler J, Hatch MC, Berkowitz G. Epidemiology of pregnancy-induced hypertension. *Epidemiologic Reviews* 1997;19(2):218–32.

Zhang L, Connor EE, Chegini N, Shiverick KT. Modulation by benzo[a]pyrene of epidermal growth factor receptors, cell proliferation, and secretion of human chorionic gonadotropin in human placental cell lines. *Biochemical Pharmacology* 1995; 50(8):1171–80.

Zhou Y, McMaster M, Woo K, Janatpour M, Perry J, Karpanen T, Alitalo K, Damsky C, Fisher SJ. Vascular endothelial growth factor ligands and receptors that regulate human cytotrophoblast survival are dysregulated in severe preeclampsia and hemolysis, elevated liver enzymes, and low platelets syndrome. *American Journal of Pathology* 2002;160(4):1405–23.

Zhu BT, Cai MX, Spink DC, Hussain MM, Busch CM, Ranzini AC, Lai Y-L, Lambert GH, Thomas PE, Conney AH. Stimulatory effect of cigarette smoking on the 15 α-hydroxylation of estradiol by human term placenta. *Clinical Pharmacology and Therapeutics* 2002;71(5):311–24.

Ziaei S, Nouri K, Kazemnejad A. Effects of carbon monoxide air pollution in pregnancy on neonatal nucleated red blood cells. *Paediatric and Perinatal Epidemiology* 2005;19(1):27–30.

Zitzmann M, Rolf C, Nordhoff V, Schräder G, Rickert-Föhring M, Gassner P, Behre HM, Greb RR, Kiesel L, Nieschlag E. Male smokers have a decreased success rate for in vitro fertilization and intracytoplasmic sperm injection. *Fertility and Sterility* 2003;79 (Suppl 3):1550–4.

Zumoff B, Miller L, Levit CD, Miller EH, Heinz U, Kalin M, Denman H, Jandorek R, Rosenfeld RS. The effect of smoking on serum progesterone, estradiol, and luteinizing hormone levels over a menstrual cycle in normal women. *Steroids* 1990;55(11):507–11.

Chapter 9
A Vision for the Future

The Global Tobacco Epidemic

Tobacco use *remains* the leading preventable cause of premature death in the United States, and the World Health Organization (WHO) has called tobacco use "the single most preventable cause of death in the world today" (WHO 2008, p. 8). Predictions based on large population studies indicate that one-half of all long-term smokers, particularly those who began smoking in adolescence, will eventually die from their use of tobacco. Furthermore, one-half of the deaths caused by smoking will occur in middle age (35 through 69 years), resulting in the loss of 20 to 25 years of normal life expectancy (Peto et al. 1992, 2006; Doll et al. 1994). In the 45 years since the first U.S. Surgeon General's report on smoking and health was published in 1964 (U.S. Department of Health, Education, and Welfare [USDHEW] 1964), smoking has been the primary underlying cause of more than 12 million U.S. deaths. Each year since 2004, more than 430,000 additional smoking-attributable deaths have been added to the national total (U.S. Department of Health and Human Services [USDHHS] 2004; Bonnie et al. 2007; Centers for Disease Control and Prevention [CDC] 2008a). It has been estimated that worldwide, tobacco use caused 100 million deaths during the twentieth century, and that tobacco use may cause as many as 1 billion deaths in the twenty-first century, unless urgent and effective action is taken (WHO 2008).

Understanding the health consequences and diseases caused by tobacco use has provided the scientific foundation for public health actions aimed at tobacco use prevention, cessation, and protection from secondhand smoke exposure. Since the first Surgeon General's report, this series has considered research findings on mechanisms of disease production in assessing the biologic plausibility of associations observed in epidemiologic studies. The important contribution of evidence on biologic plausibility and coherence in evaluation of causality has been reviewed in recent reports (USDHHS 2004, 2006). For example, evidence regarding the biologic plausibility of the observed relationship between exposure to secondhand smoke and coronary heart disease (CHD) has been very important in the evaluation of causality (USDHHS 2001, 2006). In initial studies (e.g., Hirayama 1984; Garland et al. 1985), the estimated magnitude of the association between exposure to secondhand smoke and CHD seemed large compared with the association between active smoking and CHD. However, further findings on mechanisms linking tobacco smoke exposure to CHD risk—in particular, the impact of tobacco smoke exposure on platelet aggregation and acute endothelial dysfunction—provided plausible and quantitatively consistent mechanisms for the observed nonlinear relationship with exposure levels to tobacco smoke (Glantz and Parmley 1991, 1995; Law et al. 1997). More recently, the potential effect of active smoking and exposure to secondhand smoke on breast cancer risk is an area for which data on biologic plausibility and mechanisms are critically needed in the evaluation of potential causality (USDHHS 2006; International Agency for Research on Cancer [IARC] 2004; Miller et al. 2007; Phillips and Garte 2008).

Despite the wealth of scientific evidence on the adverse health effects of exposure to tobacco smoke, many gaps remain in our understanding of the molecular and cellular mechanisms of tobacco-induced diseases. It has been suggested that "given the obvious dangers of tobacco and the associated imperative to eliminate it, research undertaken purely to unravel mechanisms of tobacco-related cancer is difficult to justify" (Carlsten and Burke 2006, p. 2481). However, as discussed in Chapter 1, research to further understand the biologic mechanisms by which exposure to tobacco smoke causes disease has several important applications beyond assisting in the determination of causal relationships, including

- developing biomarkers of injury to identify smokers at early stages of disease development;

- providing a basis for preventive therapies that block or reverse the underlying process of injury;

- identifying the contribution of exposure to tobacco smoke to causation of diseases with multiple etiologic factors; and

- assessing tobacco products for their potential to cause injury through a particular mechanism.

Expanding our knowledge of several common molecular and cellular mechanisms underlying seemingly diverse smoking-induced diseases—such as dysregulation of inflammatory and immune processes (including oxidative stress, altered antibody production, endothelial cell dysfunction, suppression of T cells) and the dysregulation of inflammatory cells—could have important implications in the potential development of novel therapeutic targets for various environmentally induced diseases (Wang and Scott 2005). For example, with growing understanding of genetic and epigenetic mechanisms, opportunities are expanding to address the broader applications of disease mechanisms related to exposure to tobacco smoke (Esteller 2008; Herbst et al. 2008; Caporaso et al. 2009; Breton et al. 2009; National Cancer Institute [NCI] 2009). As noted in the 2007–2008 Annual Report of the President's Cancer Panel, "...even if all current smokers cease using tobacco today and no new smokers take up the habit, the latency of tobacco-caused cancer and other diseases dictates that cancer and other morbidity and mortality from tobacco will still be affecting our population for at least another two decades" (Reuben 2008, p. 57). A list of research priorities identified in this report is provided in Appendix 9.1.

A key feature of tobacco use is the development of nicotine addiction, which often leads to chronic, daily exposure to tobacco that typically persists for many years. As reviewed in Chapter 4 of this report, addiction, or more technically the diseases of dependence and withdrawal, make it essential to ensure that effective behavioral and pharmacological cessation treatments are widely available and accessible to diverse populations of smokers (Zaza et al. 2005; National Institutes of Health [NIH] State-of-the-Science Panel 2006). The various treatments for tobacco use have targeted different aspects of nicotine addiction, such as reinforcement, withdrawal, and cue-associated learning. Pharmacologic treatments have included nicotinic acetylcholine receptor ligands (nicotine replacement, and varenicline, a partial α4β2 agonist) or have involved alterations in signal transduction to stimulate the release of the same neurochemicals that are released by nicotine (e.g., bupropion and nortriptyline). Ideally, those who smoke would find it as easy to access cessation services as they do commercial tobacco products (Fiore et al. 2008).

Effective public health and clinical approaches to increase smoking cessation rates have been developed (USDHHS 2000; Zaza et al. 2005; Bonnie et al. 2007; Reuben 2007; Fiore et al. 2008). These public health strategies and the clinical treatments need to be more fully implemented.

Significant progress has been achieved in the United States during the last 50 years in reducing smoking initiation and increasing smoking cessation (Bonnie et al. 2007; Reuben 2007; Cokkinides et al. 2009). After 30 years of declining rates of smoking, particularly among men, the total U.S. cancer deaths began to decline in the late 1990s, driven largely by a reduction in male lung cancer deaths (Cokkinides et al. 2009). Moreover, the declines in lung cancer death rates among men and women in California declined more rapidly than in the rest of the country after the implementation of a comprehensive and sustained statewide tobacco control program (Barnoya and Glantz 2004; Jemal et al. 2008).

Today, an estimated one-half of all Americans who have ever smoked have quit (CDC 2008a, 2009a), and the benefits of cessation have been documented for smokers of all ages (USDHHS 1990; IARC 2007a). However, as a group, smokers who successfully quit early in life can avoid a large proportion of the excess mortality caused by smoking (USDHHS 1990; IARC 2007a). Data from the British Doctors' Study have been used to demonstrate the lifetime risks of smoking and the amount of that risk that can be avoided by sustained cessation at various ages (Doll et al. 2004). Figure 9.1 contrasts the cumulative survival curves for all-cause mortality of continuing smokers (blue lines), with never smokers (red lines), and with smokers who quit by various ages (e.g., effect from sustained quitting at ages 35, 40, 50, and 60 years). The survival curves demonstrate that even at older ages, a substantial and important fraction of the excess all-cause mortality due to smoking can be averted by sustained quitting. Nonetheless, smokers who quit after the age of 44 years continue to have excess risk for tobacco-related diseases.

As noted in Chapter 6, cigarette smoking is a major cause of cardiovascular disease (CVD) and has multiplicative interactions with the other major risk factors for CHD. Importantly, although there is a strong dose-response relationship between the number of cigarettes smoked per day and cardiovascular risk, the relationship is not linear, with those who smoke few cigarettes per day or who do not smoke every day remaining at significantly elevated risk for CVD. It has been estimated that one-fifth of U.S. smokers are intermittent or occasional smokers (CDC 2008a), and this pattern of use is more common among some racial and ethnic groups, including Blacks and Hispanics, and smokers living below the poverty level (Fagan and Rigotti 2009). This emphasizes the importance of increasing our understanding of the process of smoking and quitting and of providing appropriate cessation services to this group of smokers.

The time course of reduction of risk after quitting smoking varies substantially across disease outcomes, with the risk of CHD declining more rapidly than the risk of tobacco-related cancers, particularly among those with a longer duration of smoking before sustained quitting (USDHHS 1990; IARC 2007a). The continued excess risk of lung cancer among former smokers has focused attention on the need to better identify those at greatest risk and to develop effective methods of early detection (Black and Baron 2007; Dubey and Powell 2008; Field and Duffy 2008). More than one-half of all cases of lung cancer are diagnosed at an advanced stage, and the five-year survival rate for lung cancer remains at about 15 percent (Jemal et al. 2008). At present, the efficacy of screening for lung cancer with low-dose computed tomography or

Figure 9.1   Effects on survival of stopping smoking cigarettes at ages 25–34 years (effect from age 35), ages 35–44 years (effect from age 40), ages 45–54 years (effect from age 50), and ages 55–64 years (effect from age 60)

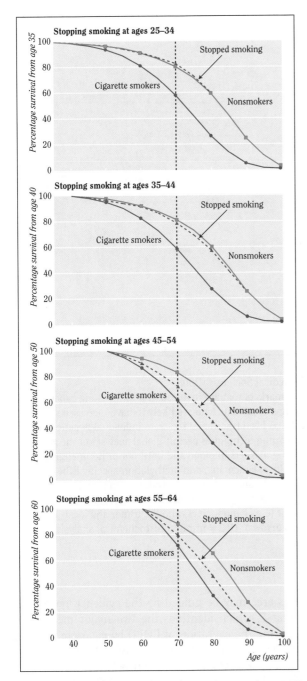

Source: Doll et al. 2004. Reprinted with permission from BMJ Publishing Group Ltd., © 2004.

other methodologies remains controversial (Black and Baron 2007). A better understanding of the molecular and cellular pathways involved in respiratory carcinogenesis could increase the feasibility of chemoprevention trials or of more cost-effective application of lung cancer screening (Alberg et al. 2005; Dubey and Powell 2008; Field 2008).

Recent advances in the understanding of the molecular origins of lung cancer have focused attention on the possibility that molecular profiling of genes and proteins could lead to the development of biomarkers for defining cancer risk, prognosis, and potentially improved treatment for some of the even more difficult to manage types of lung cancer (Herbst et al. 2008). The evidence reviewed in Chapter 5 on the major established pathways of cancer causation by cigarette smoking identifies important steps along these mechanistic pathways that could be used in potential biomarkers for defining cancer risk, prognosis, and potentially improved treatment. Figure 9.2 graphically presents how molecular profiling and assessments of genes and proteins could influence decisions regarding lung cancer treatment options for individual patients.

Chronic obstructive pulmonary disease (COPD) remains a leading cause of death in the United States, and in 2005, approximately 1 in 20 deaths in the United States had COPD as the underlying cause, with an estimated 75 percent of these COPD deaths attributable to smoking (CDC 2008b). While the U.S. trend in COPD deaths has remained fairly stable from 2000 to 2005 (CDC 2008b), the global burden of COPD is increasing (Mannino and Buist 2007; Barnes 2007). Importantly, the evidence indicates that in the United States, COPD could be almost completely prevented by the elimination of smoking (USDHHS 2004). Although the risks for COPD morbidity and mortality decline with smoking cessation, they may not return to the levels of nonsmokers (USDHHS 2004). The U.S. Lung Health Study documented the benefits of substantially reduced mortality among individuals with asymptomatic airway obstruction who quit smoking (Anthonisen et al. 2005). The U.S. Lung Health Study also documented the benefits of providing an intensive 10-week smoking cessation program to this at-risk population; nearly 22 percent of intervention participants succeeded in quitting smoking compared with only 5.4 percent of participants who received usual care (Anthonisen et al. 2005). These results emphasize that rates of smoking cessation among patients most at risk of COPD could be increased up to fourfold if current available smoking cessation treatment options were delivered more routinely.

Numerous studies have shown that COPD is associated with lung cancer risk; this association may be

Figure 9.2   Molecular-profiling approaches to the development of personalized therapy

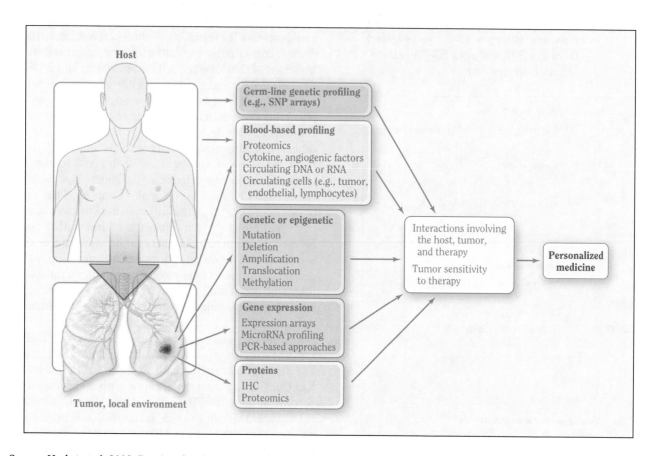

Source: Herbst et al. 2008. Reprinted with permission from Massachusetts Medical Society, © 2008.
Note: Host profiling involves innate characteristics of the cancer patient. All markers that are involved in profiling lung cancer can apply to the tumor or its local environment. Predictive markers identify groups of patients who are likely to have increased sensitivity or resistance to a given therapy, a critical step in personalizing treatment. It has been traditional to assess individual genetic or protein prognostic or predictive markers (e.g., HER2 for breast cancer), but emerging techniques permit global analyses of the genomic, gene-expression, epigenetic, and protein profiles of the host (innate), including markers in blood and in tumor or nonmalignant lung tissue. These methods include SNP arrays to assess genomic alterations, bisulfite sequencing, and methylation-specific PCR to assess epigenetic changes, microarrays for assessing gene expression or microRNA levels, and proteomic methods (such as mass spectroscopy, reverse-phase protein arrays, and multiplex beads) to assess intracellular signaling in tumor tissue and cytokines and angiogenic factors in blood. Blood-based profiling includes markers derived from the host (e.g., lymphocytes) and the tumor and local environment (e.g., circulating tumor cells and tumor-derived cytokines) (red arrows); **IHC** = immunohistochemical analysis; **PCR** = polymerase chain reaction; **SNP** = single nucleotide polymorphism.

attributed to shared exposure to cigarette smoke, to shared genetic susceptibility, and/or to facilitation of tumor initiation and promotion by inflammation (Dubey and Powell 2008). The growing global burden of COPD emphasizes the need for research to develop biomarkers of injury to identify smokers at early stages of disease development and to provide a basis for preventive therapies that block or reverse the underlying process of injury, particularly among former smokers. Research

in this area may be guided by the evidence reviewed in Chapter 7, which identifies the two major mechanisms underlying the causation of COPD by cigarette smoking, oxidative stress (injury) and protease-antiprotease imbalance, and the strong association between COPD occurrence and a specific genetic disorder: AAT deficiency.

As noted in Chapter 8, health professionals have long known that exposure to tobacco smoke during pregnancy poses serious risks to fetal development.

Despite this, approximately 19 percent of women of reproductive age smoke cigarettes, and based on birth certificate data, more than 1 in 10 (11.4 percent) women reported smoking during pregnancy (CDC 2004, 2008a). However, birth certificate data often underreport smoking during pregnancy. In survey data from 2002 to 2005, 17.3 percent of pregnant women reported smoking cigarettes in the month preceding the survey (*NSDUH Report* 2007). In addition, many pregnant women who do not smoke are exposed to secondhand smoke in workplaces, public places, and in their own homes. Recommendations have been made regarding the types of smoking cessation services that should be provided to all pregnant smokers (Fiore et al. 2008). Despite the documented costs of poor infant outcomes caused by smoking during pregnancy, and the higher prevalence of prenatal tobacco use found among lower income women, in 2006 only 27 states covered tobacco cessation counseling services for pregnant women in their Medicaid populations (CDC 2008e).

Reducing the Risks from Smoking

The benefits of quitting have been shown for smokers of all ages (USDHHS 1990, 2004; IARC 2007a). Smokers who quit completely and permanently early in life have a risk of premature death very similar to lifetime nonsmokers (Figure 9.1) (USDHHS 1990, 2004; IARC 2007a). However, for lung cancer, there is a persistent elevated risk in former smokers compared with lifetime nonsmokers of the same age even after a long abstinence (IARC 2007a). Evidence indicates that lung cancer risk increases far more strongly with each additional year of smoking than it increases for a higher average number of cigarettes smoked per day (Flanders et al. 2003; IARC 2007a). Although sustained smoking cessation at any age produces substantial reductions in risk, significant health benefits (other than for the fetus during pregnancy) from reducing the amount smoked or from short-term cessation have not been demonstrated (Benhamou et al. 1989; Godtfredsen et al. 2002; Anthonisen et al. 2005; Tverdal and Bjartveit 2006; IARC 2007a; Bjartveit and Tverdal 2009). The evidence presented in this report on the biologic mechanisms by which exposure to tobacco smoke causes cancers, cardiovascular and chronic obstructive pulmonary diseases, and reproductive and developmental effects document the importance of smokers quitting completely early in life and avoiding even occasional or infrequent smoking.

As reviewed in Chapter 2, in recent years a range of new products have been introduced and marketed to smokers as an alternative to conventional cigarettes, sometimes accompanied by messages, explicit or implied, that they offer reduced exposure to toxic substances or risk of disease. Evidence reviewed in this and previous reports indicates that five decades of evolving cigarette design have not reduced overall disease risk among smokers, and new designs can be used to undermine prevention and cessation efforts. It is now recognized that substantial risks may be associated with new tobacco products:

1. Smokers who might have otherwise stopped smoking may continue to smoke because of perceived reduction in risk with use of new products.

2. Former smokers may resume smoking because of perceived reduction in risk with use of new products.

3. Nonsmokers, particularly youth, may start to use new products because of their perceived safety.

The evidence reviewed in this report highlights many of the scientific challenges that will be faced in evaluating new cigarette products presented as alternatives to conventional cigarettes, because of the diversity of such products, the multitude of smoking-related diseases, the impact of these products on nonusers, and the dearth of empirical data on their effects. The Institute of Medicine (IOM) Committee to Assess the Science Base for Tobacco Harm Reduction (Stratton et al. 2001) and more recent reviews (Gray et al. 2005; Royal College of Physicians of London 2007; European Commission 2008) have discussed the potential role in tobacco control of a wider range of alternatives to the current cigarette. Several questions need to be carefully considered when proposing novel tobacco products as strategies to reducing smoking-attributable mortality: Do these products decrease individual risk? Do they increase initiation of tobacco use or promote relapse? Do they delay cessation? Do they lead to dual product use? How does their use compare to cessation? As discussed in Chapter 2, in the absence of a sound science base to support such alternative strategies, the primary public health approaches remain prevention and cessation of all forms of tobacco products.

Chapter 4 in this report documents the importance of nicotine as the drug causing the addiction that is the fundamental reason that individuals persist in using tobacco products. However, other constituents in tobacco and tobacco smoke may also be reinforcing or may facilitate the reinforcing effects of nicotine. The factors contributing to the high addiction potential of tobacco products are multiple and complex. Understanding these relationships is critical in developing better treatments for cessation and for determining appropriate strategies to reduce use of tobacco products (Benowitz and Henningfield 1994; Henningfield et al. 1998, 2004; Gray et al. 2005; Benowitz et al. 2006; Royal College of Physicians of London 2007; Benowitz 2008; Zeller et al. 2009).

The evidence on the CVD risks of low levels of tobacco smoke exposure in Chapter 6 of this report clearly demonstrate that the dose response for CVD is not linear, with risk rising rapidly at low doses and then plateauing at relatively low levels of exposure. The data on CVD also demonstrates the potential for dual tobacco product use resulting in a greater risk of disease than either product alone (Teo et al. 2006). Additional research to identify those toxicants in tobacco products that are most

responsible for acute cardiac risks is critically needed (Boffetta and Straif 2009).

As reviewed in this and prior reports, the risk of lung and other cancers, as well as COPD, increases dramatically with greater duration of smoking. In addition, dual use of cigarettes along with other tobacco products could not only result in delays in sustained smoking cessation but may also increase the risk of disease more than cigarette smoking alone. If the use of alternative tobacco products hinders tobacco prevention and cessation efforts and results in longer durations of smoking among some smokers, the population burden of tobacco-related morbidity and mortality would be higher than for an approach focused on helping these smokers quit completely. In addition, tobacco products used in places where smoking is not allowed may defeat public health efforts to reduce smoking rates. Thus, there are continuing concerns about the population health impact of tobacco product modification or alternatives to cigarettes (Stratton et al. 2001; European Commission 2008).

Ending the Tobacco Epidemic

Since the health risks of tobacco use were first identified, the public health response has focused on preventing initiation of tobacco use, encouraging cessation among existing users, and more recently, protecting nonsmokers from exposure to secondhand smoke. Although the primary focus of previous Surgeon General's reports has been a review of scientific evidence related to health effects of tobacco use, numerous reports have provided specific recommendations to reduce the use of tobacco and exposure to secondhand smoke (Lynch and Bonnie 1994; USDHHS 2000; Zaza et al. 2005; NIH State-of-the-Science Panel 2006; Bonnie et al. 2007; Reuben 2007; Fiore et al. 2008). Effective public health and clinical approaches to increase smoking cessation rates have been developed and need to be more fully implemented (USDHHS 2000; Zaza et al. 2005; Bonnie et al. 2007; Reuben 2007; Fiore et al. 2008).

The IOM report, *Ending the Tobacco Problem: A Blueprint for the Nation*, concluded that the ultimate goal is "to reduce smoking so substantially that it is no longer a significant public health problem" (Bonnie et al. 2007, p. 1). The report proposed a two-pronged strategy to accomplish this goal: first, to strengthen and fully implement traditional tobacco control measures known to be effective, and second, to change the regulatory

landscape to permit policy innovations such as strong federal regulation of tobacco products and their marketing and distribution (Bonnie et al. 2007). A complete list of the 42 recommendations made by the IOM report is provided in Appendix 9.2. In addition, the President's Cancer Panel has highlighted the critical importance of reducing tobacco use stating that "ridding the nation of tobacco is the single most important action needed to dramatically reduce cancer mortality and morbidity" (Reuben 2008, p. iii) and that "if the population ceased smoking, this single behavior change would be tantamount to a vaccine against one-third of cancer deaths" (Reuben 2007, p. vi).

In its 2006–2007 Annual Report, the President's Cancer Panel provided a detailed review of the status of tobacco control efforts in this country to address tobacco use prevention and treatment (Chapter 4) and environmental tobacco smoke exposure (Chapter 5). In this review, the President's Cancer Panel outlined the important roles in reducing tobacco-caused death and disease that could be undertaken by federal, state, and local governments; nongovernmental organizations and other partners; the educational system; employers, insurance, and the health care system; and individuals and families (Reuben 2007). Many of these actions are very consistent with the 42 recommendations made by IOM (Appendix

9.2) and emphasize the evidence-based methods identified by the 2006 NIH State-of-the-Science consensus conference (NIH State-of-the-Science Panel 2006). The 15 recommendations from the President's Cancer Panel are provided in Appendix 9.3.

Since the release of the recommendations from IOM (Bonnie et al. 2007) and the President's Cancer Panel review of the status of tobacco control in this country (Reuben 2007), additional actions have been taken at the federal, state, and local levels. Below is a summary of the status of tobacco control efforts in this country within the WHO MPOWER framework (WHO 2008):

- **Monitor** tobacco use and prevention policies.

- **Protect** people from tobacco smoke.

- **Offer** help to quit tobacco use.

- **Warn** about the dangers of tobacco use.

- **Enforce** comprehensive restrictions on tobacco advertising, promotion, and sponsorship.

- **Raise** taxes on tobacco.

MONITOR. The monitoring of the population pattern of tobacco use and the status of prevention and control policies and programs has been defined as essential in national efforts to counter the tobacco epidemic (WHO 2008; Giovino et al. 2009). Current efforts to monitor the tobacco use epidemic and identify additional steps to optimize measurement of tobacco use and factors influencing use in the United States have been reviewed (Cruz 2009; Delnevo and Bauer 2009; Farrelly 2009; Giovino et al. 2009; Stellman and Djordjevic 2009). These papers provide detailed analysis of national tobacco monitoring, research, and evaluation under the classic Agent, Host, Vector, and Environment framework. These reviews indicate that many of the most important basic elements of a national monitoring system are in place but that several key elements are needed to improve the system.

PROTECT. This report provides additional scientific evidence that there is no risk-free level of exposure to tobacco smoke. Although progress has been made to increase protection of nonsmokers in the United States from secondhand smoke exposure since the release of the 2006 Surgeon General's report on the health consequences of involuntary exposure to tobacco smoke (CDC 2008f), biomonitoring of exposure indicates that almost one-half of nonsmokers, and more than 60 percent of young children, continue to be exposed (CDC 2008c).

Wide geographic, occupational, and demographic disparities remain (CDC 2008c,f). It has been estimated that only about one in three residents of the United States live under state or local laws that make worksites, restaurants, and bars completely smoke-free (CDC 2008f).

OFFER. The U.S. Tobacco Use and Dependence Guideline Panel has identified the most effective interventions to assist tobacco users to successfully quit (Fiore et al. 2008). Moreover, a systematic review and analysis of recommended clinical preventive services has identified clinical smoking cessation services as one of the most successful and cost-effective recommendations (Maciosek et al. 2006). However, data indicate that less than 30 percent of smokers are offered assistance in quitting annually (Partnership for Prevention 2008). Both IOM and the President's Cancer Panel address this issue in their recommendations (Appendices 9.2 and 9.3).

WARN. WHO recommends that national efforts to warn about the dangers of tobacco should create high levels of awareness of the health risks of tobacco use across age groups, genders, and places of residence so all people understand that the result of tobacco use is often suffering, disfigurement, and early death (WHO 2008). The President's Cancer Panel noted that the warning labels on tobacco products in many other countries are larger and more graphic than those on U.S. cigarette packages (see figure 17, page 74, Reuben 2007). The *Federal Cigarette Labeling and Advertising Act of 1965* (the Cigarette Act) and the *Comprehensive Smokeless Tobacco Health Education Act of 1986* (the Smokeless Act), as amended by the *Family Smoking Prevention and Tobacco Control Act* (Tobacco Control Act) (2009), require new, stronger warning statements on cigarette and smokeless tobacco packages and advertising and require color graphics depicting the negative health consequences of smoking on cigarette packages and advertising. The Tobacco Control Act further amends the Cigarette Act and the Smokeless Act to give the U.S. Food and Drug Administration the authority to revise the warning label statements and the color graphics for both cigarettes and smokeless tobacco through rulemaking. In addition to potential changes in package warning labels, evidence supports the effectiveness of health communication and countermarketing strategies employing a wide range of efforts, including paid television, radio, billboard, print, and Web-based advertising at the national, state, and local levels; media advocacy through public relations efforts; and efforts to reduce or replace tobacco industry sponsorship and promotions (CDC 2007; NCI 2008). Recommendations 15 and 16 from IOM address the need for a national, youth-oriented, countermarketing campaign as well as increased mass media and other general and targeted public education programs to promote effective cessation programs and activities (Appendix 9.2) (Bonnie et al. 2007).

ENFORCE. Both the 2007 IOM and 2006–2007 President's Cancer Panel reports have identified the sophisticated strategies used by the tobacco industry to counter policies and programs to reduce tobacco consumption (Bonnie et al. 2007; Reuben 2007). Cigarettes remain one of the most heavily marketed products in the United States, with more than $250 billion (in 2006 dollars) expended between 1940 and 2005 on cigarette advertising and promotion (NCI 2008). The influence of these tobacco industry efforts in shaping tobacco-related knowledge, opinions, attitudes, and behavior was reviewed in detail, and it was concluded that the total weight of evidence demonstrated a causal relationship between tobacco advertising and promotion and increased tobacco use (NCI 2008). The Tobacco Control Act will enable new actions to be taken at the federal, state, and local levels to counteract the influence of tobacco advertising, promotions, and sponsorship.

RAISE. With the increase in the federal excise tax on cigarettes from $0.24 to $1.01 on April 1, 2009, the combined federal and average state cigarette excise tax increased to $2.21 per pack (CDC 2009b). Evidence-based reviews have concluded that increases in the price of cigarettes through excise taxes or other strategies are an effective policy intervention to prevent smoking initiation among adolescents and young adults, reduce cigarette consumption, and increase the number of smokers who quit (USDHHS 2000; Zaza et al. 2005; NIH State-of-the-Science 2006; Bonnie et al. 2007; CDC 2007; Reuben 2007). Additionally, the WHO MPOWER recommendations emphasize the importance of ensuring that the tax rates on tobacco products are adjusted periodically to keep pace with inflation and rise faster than consumer purchasing power. WHO also stresses that implementation of effective strategies to limit smuggling and the availability of untaxed tobacco products is essential to maximizing the effectiveness of higher taxes in reducing tobacco use (WHO 2008).

Concluding Remarks

In 1964, the Surgeon General's Advisory Committee concluded: "Cigarette smoking is a health hazard of sufficient importance in the United States to warrant appropriate remedial action" (USDHEW 1964, p. 33). Evidence-based recommendations have helped to define appropriate remedial actions, including those from the 2000 Surgeon General's report on reducing tobacco use (USDHHS 2000), NIH (NIH State-of-the-Science Panel 2006), the Task Force on Community Preventive Services (Zaza et al. 2005), IOM reports (Stratton et al. 2001; Bonnie et al. 2007), and President's Cancer Panel reports (Reuben 2007, 2008). The specific scientific conclusions from this report may provide further guidance for developing additional remedial actions.

Despite significant progress, tobacco use remains the single most preventable cause of death and disease in the United States. It is worth noting that lung cancer was once a very rare disease. *Primary Malignant Growths of the Lungs and Bronchi*, published in 1912, reviewed the worldwide scientific literature and was able to identify only 374 verified cases of lung cancer (Adler 1912; Spiro and Silvestri 2005). In stark contrast, lung cancer is today the nation's leading cause of cancer death among both men and women, killing an estimated 160,000 people in the United States, and an estimated 1.34 million people worldwide each year (Jemal et al. 2008; WHO 2008). An estimated 90 percent of U.S. lung cancer deaths in men and 80 percent of U.S. lung cancer deaths in women are caused by smoking and exposure to secondhand smoke (CDC 2009c). In addition, more than 100,000 deaths from pulmonary diseases and more than 140,000 deaths from heart disease and stroke in the United States are caused each year by active smoking and exposure to secondhand smoke (CDC 2008d).

Since the publication of the 1964 Surgeon General's report on smoking and health, this series of reports has provided an incontrovertible body of research evidence documenting the burden of sickness and death caused by tobacco use. Faced with these facts, it is appropriate to restate the challenge issued by a former Director-General of WHO, Dr. Gro Harlem Brundtland, at the start of the international negotiations that led to the landmark Framework Convention on Tobacco Control:

> If we do not act decisively today, a hundred years from now our grandchildren and their children will look back and seriously question how people claiming to be committed to public health and social justice allowed the tobacco epidemic to unfold unchecked (Brundtland 1999).

Appendix 9.1
Recommendations for Future Research

The evidence reviewed within this report identified important gaps in our scientific knowledge that merit greater attention in future research. Below is a listing of areas of research that can substantially contribute to a better understanding of how tobacco use causes disease.

Nicotine Addiction

With the emerging science base for understanding the physiological, behavioral, and cognitive bases for addiction and for identifying the genetics and other host factors that may moderate the effects of nicotine, new types of interventions are being developed that are expanding the treatment armamentarium, thus providing more effective interventions for those who continue to have difficulty in quitting smoking. For example, pharmacologic treatments are being marketed that target specific nicotinic receptors responsible for the reinforcing effects of nicotine, such as varenicline (Gonzales et al. 2006; Jorenby et al. 2006; Nides et al. 2006; Oncken et al. 2006). Nicotine immunotherapies (vaccines) under development also offer potential treatments for nicotine addiction. Nicotine immunotherapies stimulate the immune system to develop antibodies to nicotine that reduce the level and speed of nicotine entering the brain, potentially changing the pharmacokinetics of nicotine and thereby reducing the reinforcing effects of nicotine (Pentel 2004; Hatsukami et al. 2005). Another area of major development in the treatment of smokers, as with the treatment of other diseases, involves tailoring treatments to the phenotype and genotype of the individuals to select the most efficacious treatments (Lerman and Niaura 2002). All of these treatment developments have been aided by greatly expanded understanding of the mechanisms of dependence and withdrawal during the past two decades.

Valid indicators and biomarkers of addiction are needed to assess future "less addictive" or "less toxic" tobacco products and treatments and to provide a better understanding of the addictive process. Many subjective and behavioral measures and some cognitive measures have been developed and used to test addiction to tobacco. However, fundamental gaps in knowledge exist, and other areas need to be more vigorously pursued.

Biomarkers for Addiction Potential

Table 9.1 summarizes the methods used for animal and human testing to assess the addiction potential of a nicotine product. Most of these methods have been referred to in Chapter 4 of this report. Although there are many subjective and behavioral methods, researchers have devoted little attention to cognitive and neurophysiological measures of addiction through the use of functional magnetic resonance imaging or positron emission tomography. Using more precise tools to assess and better understand learning processes, decision making, and brain changes associated with addiction will lead to the development of measurements in these areas. The limitations and questions associated with the measures listed in Table 9.1 are similar to those concerning the diagnosis of tobacco addiction or, for that matter, biomarkers for disease in general. That is, other than relative terms (e.g., product A has a greater abuse potential than does product B) or the occurrence of addiction, the threshold or criterion that determines the extent of abuse potential is unknown.

Future Directions in Understanding Addiction

Several areas of research that can substantially contribute to a better understanding of nicotine addiction include—but are not limited to—the following:

- Improve understanding of the criteria for and measures of nicotine addiction or dependence and how they might differ across various populations, including youth and ethnic minorities.

- Adapt commonly used measures of assessing addiction to cigarettes to other tobacco products as demonstrated by preliminary efforts to develop and validate scales for smokeless tobacco dependence and, most recently, to waterpipe smoking.

- Develop a better understanding of the contribution of the design features of tobacco products and of constituents other than nicotine that play an important role in all aspects of nicotine addiction, including initiation, maintenance, withdrawal, and relapse.

Table 9.1   Behavioral indicators of addiction potential of a drug or addiction to a drug

Animal models

- Conditioned place preference
- Drug self-administration
- Drug discrimination
- Withdrawal
  - Somatic signs
  - Reward threshold

Human models

- Choice of drug compared with other reinforcers
- Breakpoint on a progressive ratio task relative to other reinforcers
- Level of nicotine or tobacco self-administration and pattern of self-administration
- Compensatory tobacco use behavior
- Time to use drug after a period of deprivation
- Withdrawal symptoms
  - Negative affect
  - Performance
  - Physiological (e.g., heart rate, weight)
  - Acoustic startle response
- Physiological reactivity toward smoking-related stimuli
- Cue-induced craving

Subjective measures of addiction potential

- Drug liking
- Drug effects (e.g., good effects, bad effects, strength of effects)
- Visual analog scale for drug effects (e.g., high, dizzy)
- Amount of monetary expenditure for a drug

Biochemical measures of addiction

- Cotinine/nicotine level

Cognitive indications of addiction

- Attentional bias toward smoking-related stimuli

Neurophysiological biomarkers of addiction potential or addiction

- Extent of brain activity in response to nicotine
- Extent of brain activity in response to cues

- Use current knowledge of the neurosystems associated with the reinforcement, withdrawal, and conditioning effects of nicotine addiction to develop a strategic road map for future discoveries in this area.

- Move toward a better understanding of the role and neurobiology of associative learning and cognitive processing in the development of and recovery from nicotine addiction.

- Foster an interdisciplinary effort to develop links among genotypes, endophenotypes, phenotypes, and the neurobiologic effects of nicotine.

- Explore the differences between adolescents and adults in their sensitivity to nicotine and to other factors associated with tobacco use, and find out which factors contribute to these differences (e.g., stage of neurodevelopment, sex hormones).

- Increase understanding of the relationship between comorbid disorders and nicotine addiction, including the common neural pathways and psychosocial vulnerabilities, and the mechanisms associated with an increased risk of nicotine addiction.

Cancer

Even though the evidence has long been sufficient to infer that both active and involuntary smoking cause at least 15 types of cancer, the long latency of tobacco-caused cancers emphasizes the need for further research on the mechanisms by which exposure to tobacco causes cancer. Several areas of research that can substantially contribute to a better understanding of these mechanisms include—but are not limited to—the following:

- Investigate genetic polymorphisms and phenotypic variations among smokers in critical aspects of the carcinogenic process that may lead to variations in susceptibility to the carcinogens in tobacco smoke. Examples include differences in carcinogen- and nicotine-metabolizing enzymes and their products, DNA repair genes, and cell cycle genes. This research could lead to the identification of individuals who are particularly susceptible to the effects of tobacco smoke and who could be targeted for preventive interventions.

- Develop a panel of quantitative biomarkers of carcinogens or their metabolites in blood or urine. Apply this panel of biomarkers to determine carcinogen dose in smokers and its relationship to cancer. Such a panel could be extremely useful in determining individual risk of tobacco-induced cancer and potentially useful for regulation.

- Develop quantitative reproducible and reliable methods for assessing levels of DNA adducts specific to all major carcinogens in tobacco smoke, and carry out biomarker studies to investigate the relationship between DNA adducts and cancer in smokers. This approach could potentially identify highly susceptible smokers and further define mechanisms of cancer induction in general, beyond the effects of tobacco products.

- Further study the role of nicotine, 4-(methylnitrosamino)-1-(3-pyridyl)-1-butanone, and other toxicants in tobacco smoke in the activation of nicotinic acetylcholine receptors in lung epithelial cells, as well as similar key intracellular proteins and related epigenetic events that can lead to tumor promotion, cocarcinogenesis, progression, and maintenance of cancer.

- Conduct additional studies of the potential mechanisms by which carcinogens in tobacco smoke affect breast tissue, and how various other effects from tobacco smoke exposure, including possible antiestrogenic effects, could modulate or reduce the carcinogenic effects of tobacco smoke exposure.

- Develop a predictive algorithm—including tobacco carcinogen and DNA biomarker data and related parameters such as polymorphisms in DNA repair genes—to identify those smokers most susceptible to cancer induction by cigarette smoke. This algorithm would be analogous to the Gail model for breast cancer susceptibility.

- Investigate the mechanisms by which alcohol consumption and asbestos exposure enhance the risk for tobacco-related cancers.

- Study the major pathway by which tobacco smoke induces cancer through DNA adduct formation by tobacco smoke carcinogens and other contributing factors such as tumor promotion, cocarcinogenesis, direct receptor binding effects of nicotine and tobacco-specific nitrosamines, and hypermethylation of tumor suppressor gene promoter regions that clearly contribute. Further research is necessary to elucidate the relevant mechanisms involved in these pathways.

Cardiovascular Diseases

Even though the evidence has long been sufficient to infer that both active and involuntary smoking cause coronary heart disease, the observed risks from exposure to toxicants in combustible and noncombustible tobacco products emphasize the need for further research on the mechanisms by which exposure to tobacco adversely affects the cardiovascular system. Several areas of research that can substantially contribute to a better understanding of these mechanisms include—but are not limited to—the following:

- Conduct further study of the role of oxidizing chemicals, nicotine, or other toxicants in tobacco smoke in the development of endothelial dysfunction.

- Promote additional study of the role of specific toxicants in tobacco smoke in the development of acute and chronic inflammatory reactions and the development of reliable biomarkers of these reactions predictive of acute cardiovascular events and atherosclerosis.

- Identify the toxicants in tobacco smoke most responsible for the nonlinear dose response between exposure dose to tobacco smoke (including second-hand smoke) and indicators of acute cardiovascular risk and related cardiovascular events.

- Identify the toxicants in tobacco smoke most responsible for platelet activation effects.

- Analyze the toxicants in various forms of smokeless tobacco products that could produce acute or chronic changes in mechanisms related to cardiovascular risk.

- Conduct further study of the differential effects of alveolar deposition of particulate constituents from tobacco smoke and other ambient air sources on biochemical and physiological acute and chronic reactions related to cardiovascular risk and related cardiovascular events.

- Further explore the role of nicotine and other toxicants in tobacco smoke in the development of insulin resistance.

Pulmonary Diseases

Chronic obstructive pulmonary disease (COPD) remains a major public health problem that is increasing, but evidence indicates that COPD could be almost completely prevented with the elimination of smoking (U.S. Department of Health and Human Services 2004). Although there are substantial and rapid benefits to lung function after smoking cessation, evidence indicates that morbidity related to COPD persists long after cessation of smoking (International Agency for Research on Cancer 2007a). Several areas of research that can substantially contribute to a better understanding of the mechanisms by which exposure to tobacco smoke increase the risk of COPD include—but are not limited to—the following:

- Promote further research in characterizing the genetic basis of susceptibility to tobacco smoke in the causation of COPD.

- Further explore the role of oxidative stress in the pathogenesis of COPD and the potential to modulate this mechanism of disease production.

- Investigate more deeply the role of protease-antiprotease imbalance in the pathogenesis of COPD and the potential to modulate this mechanism of disease production.

Reproductive and Developmental Effects

Epidemiologic Studies

Numerous adverse pregnancy outcomes or maternal complications have been causally associated with maternal smoking. Research to better define dose-response relationships, especially for preeclampsia, preterm delivery, and premature rupture of membranes, would be informative. This information could be used to establish more accurate estimates of individual risk and of population-attributable risk percentage. In general, research is needed to better define the effects of smoking cessation (before or during pregnancy) on risk of pregnancy complications or outcomes such as spontaneous abortion, placenta previa, placental abruption, preterm delivery, and premature rupture of membranes. This information could be used to help refine public health strategies for decreasing the contribution of maternal smoking to adverse pregnancy outcomes.

Smoking should continue to be examined in studies of birth defects, particularly in geographic areas in which smoking during pregnancy remains prevalent, as the evidence so far is suggestive, but not conclusive. These studies would be most beneficial if they also examine interactions with genetic polymorphisms (see below), requiring additional subjects and funding. Animal studies that better simulate smoke exposure would also be very useful in this regard.

Evidence is increasing that exposures during pregnancy may have long-lasting effects on offspring. Furthermore, developmental delays and disabilities are increasing in the population, so additional studies of smoking effects (in utero and postnatal exposure) on neurobehavioral endpoints, including cognition and behavior, are needed, perhaps as large cohort studies. In the context of some suggestive or early studies, it is important to pursue examination of in utero exposure to smoking and later reproductive effects in the offspring, including pubertal development, sperm quality, and female fertility. Studies of in utero exposure in offspring, either as children or adults, are difficult to carry out logistically because of long follow-up times or lack of retrospective data on parental tobacco use or secondhand smoke exposure during pregnancy if adults are studied. Such studies should also consider postnatal secondhand smoke exposure. Studies in adult offspring would need to be limited to nonsmokers, while considering secondhand smoke exposure in adults as well, requiring larger numbers of study subjects for stratification. In addition, numerous other factors may affect these endpoints after birth. Because of some of these methodological difficulties, further studies on mechanisms related to endocrine function would help support causal relationships (see below).

Research on humans would be improved with measurement of a biomarker of exposure, such as cotinine. Studies tend to show higher cotinine levels in young children exposed to secondhand smoke relative to older children and adults, so studying the pharmacokinetics of cotinine in the very young (birth to five years) would be of interest to determine whether this is attributable to slower metabolism of nicotine and cotinine or to greater exposure to secondhand smoke.

Pathophysiological and Cellular/Molecular Mechanisms

Effects on Organ Systems

1. Smoking has often been considered antiestrogenic, but studies measuring hormone levels in nonpregnant women or in men do not support this hypothesis. Therefore, studies of effects of smoking and secondhand smoke exposure on levels of other hormones in males and females would help elucidate the mechanism of effects of smoking on reproductive function and some pregnancy outcomes.

2. Research is needed to better understand mechanisms underlying causal relationships between maternal smoking and placental damage such as placenta previa, placental abruption, preeclampsia, preterm delivery, and premature rupture of membranes. Specifically needed are studies

   - to better characterize the effects of maternal smoking on physiological transformation and on the development of the villous capillary system of the placenta;

   - of the effects of maternal smoking on the balance between pro- and antiangiogenic factors; and

   - of the effects of maternal smoking on nutrient transport in uteroplacental circulation and the potential consequences for fetal growth and development.

3. The possible mechanisms of smoke exposure affecting organogenesis that may lead to birth defects require more research, particularly on the histopathologic changes in the brain and lung.

4. Research is needed to better define effects of active smoking on immunoregulation in general. In addition, research is needed to better understand the contribution of tobacco-related dysregulation of the immune response to adverse pregnancy outcomes, such as preterm delivery and preterm premature rupture of membranes, and to determine what mechanisms are involved, such as increased risk of infection of the upper genital tract or modification of the inflammatory response.

Molecular Mechanisms and Specific Toxicants

1. Cigarette smoke contains thousands of toxicants, but more data documenting exposure to toxicants in the fetus of maternal active and involuntary smokers are necessary to link effects of smoking to specific toxic mechanisms or models. Some of the primary toxicants of interest are heavy metals (e.g., lead, mercury, cadmium, arsenic), polycyclic aromatic hydrocarbons, solvents, and other less studied compounds such as pyrazines and phenols. Additional media could be used as substrate, including placenta, umbilical cord, amniotic fluid, urine excretion in the first days, and meconium for metals only (atomic absorption).

2. In addition, the bioavailability and bioaccumulation of these compounds (particularly metals) from inhalation of smoke in adults or children should be studied, including animal studies to interpret toxicologic data on these compounds.

3. Research is needed to establish whether deficiencies of micronutrients such as vitamin C and zinc contribute to adverse pregnancy outcomes and if mechanisms exist to compensate for the deficiencies, leading to better pregnancy outcomes.

4. Research on the effects of smoking and its components on DNA damage should be conducted.

5. Further studies that include information on genetic polymorphisms affecting drug- and carcinogen-metabolizing enzymes are critical to uncovering mechanisms of smoking effects in many areas, including birth defects, other adverse pregnancy outcomes, and developmental effects.

6. In addition, a potential genetic basis for the population of women who have difficulty quitting smoking during pregnancy, including polymorphisms for nicotine-metabolizing enzymes or for central nervous system receptors, should be investigated to develop new pharmacologic treatments.

Appendix 9.2
Ending the Tobacco Problem: A Blueprint for the Nation

Committee on Reducing Tobacco Use: Strategies, Barriers, and Consequences
Institute of Medicine, 2007
Richard J. Bonnie, Kathleen Stratton, and Robert B. Wallace, editors

Complete List of Recommendations

Strengthening Traditional Tobacco Control Measures

Recommendation 1: Each state should fund state tobacco control activities at the level recommended by the CDC [Centers for Disease Control and Prevention]. A reasonable target for each state is in the range of $15 to $20 per capita, depending on the state's population, demography, and prevalence of tobacco use. If it is constitutionally permissible, states should use a statutorily prescribed portion of their tobacco excise tax revenues to fund tobacco control programs.

Recommendation 2: States with excise tax rates below the level imposed by the top quintile of states should also substantially increase their own rates to reduce smuggling and tax evasion. State excise tax rates should be indexed to inflation.

Recommendation 3: The federal government should substantially raise federal tobacco excise taxes, currently set at 39 cents a pack. Federal excise tax rates should be indexed to inflation.

Recommendation 4: States and localities should enact complete bans on smoking in all nonresidential indoor locations, including workplaces, malls, restaurants, and bars. States should not preempt local governments from enacting bans more restrictive than the state ban.

Recommendation 5: All health care facilities, including nursing homes, psychiatric hospitals, and medical units in correctional facilities, should meet or exceed JCAHO [Joint Commission on the Accreditation of Healthcare Organizations] standards in banning smoking in all indoor areas.

Recommendation 6: The American Correctional Association should require through its accreditation standards that all correctional facilities (prisons, jails, and juvenile detention facilities) implement bans on indoor smoking.

Recommendation 7: States should enact legislation requiring leases for multiunit apartment buildings and condominium sales agreements to include the terms governing smoking in common areas and residential units. States and localities should also encourage the owners of multiunit apartment buildings and condominium developers to include nonsmoking clauses in these leases and sales agreements and to enforce them.

Recommendation 8: Colleges and universities should ban smoking in indoor locations, including dormitories, and should consider setting a smoke-free campus as a goal. Further, colleges and universities should ban the promotion of tobacco products on campus and at all campus-sponsored events. Such policies should be monitored and evaluated by oversight committees, such as those associated with the American College Health Association.

Recommendation 9: State health agencies, health care professionals, and other interested organizations should undertake strong efforts to encourage parents to make their homes and vehicles smoke free.

Recommendation 10: States should not preempt local governments from restricting smoking in outdoor public spaces, such as parks and beaches.

Recommendation 11: All states should license retail sales outlets that sell tobacco products. Licensees should be required to (1) verify the date of birth, by means of photographic identification, of any purchaser appearing to be 25 years of age or younger; (2) place cigarettes exclusively behind the counter and sell cigarettes only in a direct face-to-face exchange; and (3) ban the use of self-service displays and vending machines. Repeat violations of laws restricting youth access should be subject to license suspension or revocation. States should not preempt local governments from licensing retail outlets that sell tobacco products.

Recommendation 12: All states should ban the sale and shipment of tobacco products directly to consumers through mail order or the Internet or other electronic systems. Shipments of tobacco products should be permitted only to licensed wholesale or retail outlets.

Recommendation 13: School boards should require all middle schools and high schools to adopt evidence-based smoking prevention programs and implement them with fidelity. They should coordinate these in-school programs with public activities or mass media programming, or both. Such prevention programs should be conducted annually. State funding for these programs should be supplemented with funding from the U.S. Department of Education under the Safe and Drug-Free School Act or by an independent body administering funds collected from the tobacco industry through excise taxes, court orders, or litigation agreements.

Recommendation 14: All physicians, dentists, and other health care providers should screen and educate youth about tobacco use during their annual health care visits and any other visit in which a health screening occurs. Physicians should refer youth who smoke to counseling services or smoking cessation programs available in the community. Physicians should also urge parents to keep a smoke-free home and vehicles, to discuss tobacco use with their children, to convey that they expect their children to not use tobacco, and to monitor their children's tobacco use. Professional societies, including the American Medical Association, the American Nursing Association, the American Academy of Family Physicians, the American College of Physicians, and the American Academy of Pediatrics, should encourage physicians to adopt these practices.

Recommendation 15: A national, youth-oriented media campaign should be funded on an ongoing basis as a permanent component of the nation's strategy to reduce tobacco use. State and community tobacco control programs should supplement the national media campaign with coordinated youth prevention activities.

The campaign should be implemented by an established public health organization with funds provided by the federal government, public-private partnerships, or the tobacco industry (voluntarily or under litigation settlement agreements or court orders) for media development, testing, and purchases of advertising time and space.

Recommendation 16: State tobacco control agencies should work with health care partners to increase the demand for effective cessation programs and activities through mass media and other general and targeted public education programs.

Recommendation 17: Congress should ensure that stable funding is continuously provided to the national quitline network.

Recommendation 18: The Secretary of the U.S. Department of Health and Human Services [HHS], through the National Cancer Institute, the Centers for Disease Control and Prevention, and other relevant federal health agencies, should fund a program of developmental research and demonstration projects combining media techniques, other social marketing methods, and innovative approaches to disseminating smoking cessation technologies.

Recommendation 19: Public and private health care systems should organize and provide access to comprehensive smoking cessation programs by using a variety of successful cessation methods and a staged disease management model (i.e. stepped care), and should specify the successful delivery of these programs as one criterion for quality assurance within those systems.

Recommendation 20: All insurance, managed care, and employee benefit plans, including Medicaid and Medicare, should cover reimbursement for effective smoking cessation programs as a lifetime benefit.

Recommendation 21: While sustaining their own valuable tobacco control activities, state tobacco control programs, CDC, philanthropic foundations, and voluntary organizations should continue to support the efforts of community coalitions promoting, disseminating, and advocating for tobacco use prevention and cessation, smoke-free environments, and other policies and programs for reducing tobacco use.

Recommendation 22: Tobacco control programs should consider populations disproportionately affected by tobacco addiction and tobacco-related morbidity and mortality when designing and implementing prevention and treatment programs. Particular attention should be paid to ensuring that health communications and other materials are culturally-appropriate and that special outreach efforts target all high-risk populations. Standard prevention or treatment programs that are modified to reach high-risk populations should be evaluated for effectiveness.

Changing the Regulatory Landscape

Recommendation 23: Congress should repeal the existing statute preempting state tobacco regulation of advertising and promotion "based on smoking and health" and should enact a new provision that precludes all direct state regulation only in relation to tobacco product characteristics and packaging while allowing complementary state regulation in all other domains of tobacco regulation, including marketing and distribution. Under this approach, federal regulation sets a floor while allowing states to be more restrictive.

Recommendation 24: Congress should confer upon the FDA [U. S. Food and Drug Administration] broad regulatory authority over the manufacture, distribution, marketing, and use of tobacco products.

Recommendation 25: Congress should empower the FDA to regulate the design and characteristics of tobacco products to promote the public health. Specific authority should be conferred

- to require tobacco manufacturers to disclose to the agency all chemical compounds found in both product and the product's smoke, whether added or occurring naturally, by quantity; to disclose to the public the amount of nicotine in the product and the amount delivered to the consumer based on standards established by the agency; to disclose to the public research on their product, as well as behavioral aspects of its use; and to notify the agency whenever there is a change in a product;

- to prescribe cigarette testing methods, including how the cigarettes are tested and which smoke constituents must be measured;

- to promulgate tobacco product standards, including reduction of nicotine yields and reduction or elimination of other constituents, wherever such a standard is found to be appropriate for protection of the public health, taking into consideration the risks and benefits to the population as a whole, including users and non-users of tobacco products; and

- to develop specific standards for evaluating novel products that companies intend to promote as reduced-exposure or reduced-risk products, and to

regulate reduced-exposure and reduced-risk health claims, assuring that there is a scientific basis for claims that are permitted.

Recommendation 26: Congress should strengthen the federally mandated warning labels for tobacco products immediately and should delegate authority to the FDA to update and revise these warnings on a regular basis upon finding that doing so would promote greater public understanding of the risks of using tobacco products or reduce tobacco consumption. Congress should require or authorize the FDA to require rotating color graphic warnings covering 50 percent of the package equivalent to those required in Canada.

Recommendation 27: Congress should empower the FDA to require manufacturers to include in or on tobacco packages information about the health effects of tobacco use and about products that can be used to help people quit.

Recommendation 28: Congress should ban, or empower the FDA to ban, terms such as "mild," "lights," "ultralights," and other misleading terms mistakenly interpreted by consumers to imply reduced risk, as well as other techniques, such as color codes, that have the purpose or effect of conveying false or misleading impressions about the relative harmfulness of the product.

Recommendation 29: Whenever a court or administrative agency has found that a tobacco company has made false or misleading communications regarding the effects of tobacco products, or has engaged in conduct promoting tobacco use among youth or discouraging cessation by tobacco users of any age, the court or agency should consider using its remedial authority to require manufacturers to include corrective communications on or with the tobacco package as well as at the point of sale.

Recommendation 30: Congress and state legislatures should enact legislation regulating the retail point of sale of tobacco products for the purpose of discouraging consumption of these products and encouraging cessation. Specifically:

- All retail outlets choosing to carry tobacco products should be licensed and monitored. (See also youth access section in Chapter 5.)

- Commercial displays or other activity promoting tobacco use by or in retail outlets should be banned, although text-only informational displays (e.g., price or health-related product characteristics) may be permitted within prescribed regulatory constraints.

- Retail outlets choosing to carry tobacco products should be required to display and distribute prescribed warnings about the health consequences of tobacco use, information regarding products and services for cessation, and corrective messages designed to offset misstatements or implied claims regarding the health effects of tobacco use (e.g., that "light" cigarettes are less harmful than other cigarettes).

- Retail outlets choosing to carry tobacco products should be required to allocate a proportionate amount of space to cessation aids and nicotine replacement products and, after regulatory clearance by the FDA or a designated state agency, to "qualifying" exposure-reduction products. (The FDA or a suitable state health agency should promulgate a list of "qualifying" exposure-reducing products.)

Recommendation 31: Congress should explicitly and unmistakably include production, marketing, and distribution of tobacco products on Indian reservations by Indian tribes within the regulatory jurisdiction of FDA. Authority to investigate and enforce the Jenkins Act should be transferred to the Bureau of Alcohol, Tobacco, Firearms and Explosives. State restrictions on retail outlets should apply to all outlets on Indian reservations.

Recommendation 32: State governments should develop and, if feasible, implement and evaluate legal mechanisms for restructuring retail tobacco sales and restricting the number of tobacco outlets.

Recommendation 33: Congress should empower the FDA to restrict outlets in order to limit access and facilitate regulation of the retail environment, and thereby protect the public health.

Recommendation 34: If most states fail to increase tobacco control funding and reduce variations in tobacco excise tax rates as proposed in Recommendations 1 and 2, Congress should enact a National Tobacco Control Funding Plan raising funds through a per-pack remedial assessment on cigarettes sold in the United States. Part of the proceeds should be used to support national tobacco control programs and the remainder of the funds should be distributed to the states to subsidize state tobacco control programs according to a formula based on the level of state tobacco control expenditures and state tobacco excise rates. The plan should be designed to give states an incentive, not only to increase state spending on tobacco control, but also to raise cigarette taxes, especially in low-tax states. Congress should assure that any

federal coordination mechanism affecting the coverage and collection of state tobacco excise taxes applies to Indian tribes.

Recommendation 35: Congress and state legislatures should enact legislation limiting visually displayed tobacco advertising in all venues, including mass media and at the point-of-sale, to a text-only, black-and-white format.

Recommendation 36: Congress and state legislatures should prohibit tobacco companies from targeting youth under 18 for any purpose, including dissemination of messages about smoking (whether ostensibly to promote or discourage it) or to survey youth opinions, attitudes and behaviors of any kind. If a tobacco company wishes to support youth prevention programs, the company should contribute funds to an independent non-profit organization with expertise in the prevention field. The independent organization should have exclusive responsibility for designing, executing, and evaluating the program.

Recommendation 37: The Motion Picture Association of America (MPAA) should encourage and facilitate the showing of anti-smoking advertisements before any film in which smoking is depicted in more than an incidental manner. The film rating board of the MPAA should consider the use of tobacco in the movies as a factor in assigning mature film ratings (e.g., an R-rating indicating Restricted: no one under age 17 admitted without parent or guardian) to films that depict tobacco use.

Recommendation 38: Congress should appropriate the necessary funds to enable the U.S. Department of Health and Human Services to conduct a periodic review of a representative sample of movies, television programs, and videos that are offered at times or in venues in which there is likely to be a significant youth audience (e.g., 15 percent) in order to ascertain the nature and frequency of images portraying tobacco use. The results of these reviews should be reported to Congress and to the public.

Recommendation 39: State tobacco control agencies should conduct surveillance of tobacco sales and use and the effects of tobacco control interventions in order to assess local trends in usage patterns; identify special groups at high risk for tobacco use; determine compliance with state and local tobacco-related laws, policies, and ordinances; and evaluate overall programmatic success.

Recommendation 40: The Secretary of HHS, through FDA or other agencies, should establish a national comprehensive tobacco surveillance system to collect information on a broad range of elements needed to understand and track the population impact of all tobacco products and the effects of national interventions (such as attitudes, beliefs, product characteristics, product distribution and usage patterns, and marketing messages and exposures to them).

New Frontiers in Tobacco Control

Recommendation 41: Congress should direct the Centers for Disease Control and Prevention to undertake a major program of tobacco control policy analysis and development and should provide sufficient funding to support the program. This program should develop the next generation of macro-level simulation models to project the likely effects of various policy innovations, taking into account the possible initiatives and responses of the tobacco industry as well as the impacts of the innovations on consumers.

Recommendation 42: Upon being empowered to regulate tobacco products, the FDA should give priority to exploring the potential effectiveness of a long-term strategy for reducing the amount of nicotine in cigarettes and should commission the studies needed to assess the feasibility of implementing such an approach. If such a strategy appears to be feasible, the agency should develop a long-term plan for implementing the strategy as part of a comprehensive plan for reducing tobacco use.

Appendix 9.3
Promoting Healthy Lifestyles: Policy, Program, and Personal Recommendations for Reducing Cancer Risk

President's Cancer Panel
2006–2007 Annual Report

Recommendations Addressing Tobacco Use Prevention and Treatment; Environmental Tobacco Smoke Exposure

1. Ratify and fully implement the Framework Convention for Tobacco Control. Key provisions include: comprehensive bans on tobacco advertising, promotion, and sponsorship, larger and stronger warning labels on tobacco product packaging, provision of tobacco addiction treatment, disclosure of tobacco product ingredients, and public protection against environmental tobacco smoke exposure.

   • President
   • Congress

2. Authorize the Food and Drug Administration (FDA) to strictly regulate tobacco products and product marketing. FDA must receive sufficient funding and personnel to carry out this crucial role.

   • President
   • Congress

3. Increase the Federal excise tax on tobacco products.

   • Congress

4. Require all Federal facilities to be smoke-free.

   • Congress
   • Federal agencies

5. Reallocate existing National Cancer Institute, Centers for Disease Control and Prevention, and other Federal resources to better mirror the tobacco-related disease burden and capitalize on opportunities for progress.

- Congress
- Department of Health and Human Services (National Institutes of Health, Centers for Disease Control and Prevention, Health Resources and Services Administration, Substance Abuse and Mental Health Services Administration)
- Veterans Administration

6. Add the conduct of meaningful tobacco-related activities to the evaluation criteria for NCI-designated Cancer Centers.

- National Cancer Institute

7. Reduce the influence of the tobacco industry:
   - U.S. political parties and individual candidates should refuse campaign contributions from the tobacco industry or its subsidiaries.
   - Prohibit recipients of National Cancer Institute grants and contracts from accepting money from tobacco companies or their subsidiaries. Other Federal agencies should consider similar requirements.

- All U.S. political parties
- National Cancer Institute

8. Strengthen anti-tobacco efforts at the state and local levels:
   - Increase state commitment of Master Settlement Agreement funds and/or tobacco tax funds for tobacco control programs to at least the minimum level recommended by the Centers for Disease Control and Prevention for each state.
   - Pass smoke-free ordinances for all public and private workplaces and public spaces.
   - Encourage state governments to further increase tobacco excise taxes to discourage purchase of cigarettes and other tobacco products.
   - Require all public schools and universities to be 100 percent smoke-free.
   - Require state-funded programs (e.g., Medicaid, corrections, mental health) to offer smoking cessation services.
   - Ensure that all state cancer control plans include a tobacco control component.

- State and local governments

9. Develop and provide evidence-based multimedia curricula and educational materials in grades K-12 on the dangers of tobacco use and tobacco smoke exposure and the role of the tobacco industry in promoting tobacco use. Encourage colleges and universities to disseminate tested anti-tobacco messages for the 18 to 24 year-old age group through campus radio and television stations, Web sites, and print publications.

- Department of Health and Human Services (National Institutes of Health, Centers for Disease Control and Prevention, Food and Drug Administration)
- State and local boards of education
- Non-governmental organizations

10. Cease including images of smoking in movies, television, music videos, video games, and other visual media with child, adolescent, and young adult audiences.

- All visual media producers

11. Prohibit smoking in and around the workplace. Support worker efforts to quit smoking; provide incentives for cessation.

- Employers

12. Make coverage of tobacco use cessation services and medications a standard benefit in all comprehensive health benefit packages.

- Health insurance companies
- Centers for Medicare and Medicaid Services
- Veterans Administration
- Civilian Health and Medical Program of the Uniformed Services
- Indian Health Service

13. Incorporate smoking cessation services into the comprehensive care of cancer patients, survivors, and their family members.

- Cancer centers
- Academic and community hospitals and medical centers
- Private oncology offices/practices
- All publicly-funded clinics and health centers

14. Adopt the Agency for Healthcare Research and Quality *Guidelines for Clinicians Treating Tobacco Use and Dependence* as part of the standard of care for all health care providers.

- Primary and other health care providers

15. Quit smoking and use of any smokeless tobacco products. Prohibit smoking in the home and car. Protect children from exposure to smoking in movies and smoking role models. Patronize only smoke-free restaurants and other businesses.

- Individuals and families

References

Adler I. *Primary Malignant Growths of the Lungs and Bronchi: A Pathological and Clinical Study*. New York: Longmans, Green, and Company, 1912.

Alberg AJ, Brock MV, Samet JM. Epidemiology of lung cancer: looking to the future. *Journal of Clinical Oncology* 2005;23(14):3175–85.

Anthonisen NR, Skeans MA, Wise RA, Manfreda J, Kanner RE, Connett JE, Lung Health Study Research Group. The effects of a smoking cessation intervention on 14.5-year mortality: a randomized clinical trial. *Annals of Internal Medicine* 2005;142(4):233–9.

Barnes PJ. Chronic obstructive pulmonary disease: a growing but neglected global epidemic. *PLoS Medicine* 2007;4(5):e112.doi:10.1371/journal.pmed.0040112.

Barnoya J, Glantz S. Association of the California tobacco control program with declines in lung cancer incidence. *Cancer Causes and Control* 2004;15(7)689–95.

Benhamou E, Benhamou S, Auquier A, Flamant R. Changes in patterns of cigarette smoking and lung cancer risk: results of a case-control study. *British Journal of Cancer* 1989;60(4):601–4.

Benowitz NL. Clinical pharmacology of nicotine: implications for understanding, preventing, and treating tobacco addiction. *Clinical Pharmacology & Therapeutics* 2008;83(4):531–41.

Benowitz NL, Henningfield JE. Establishing a nicotine threshold for addiction: the implications for tobacco regulation. *New England Journal of Medicine* 1994;331(2):123–5.

Benowitz NL, Jacob P III, Herrera B. Nicotine intake and dose response when smoking reduced–nicotine content cigarettes. *Clinical Pharmacology & Therapeutics* 2006;80(6):703–14.

Bjartveit K, Tverdal A. Health consequences of sustained smoking cessation. *Tobacco Control* 2009;18(3):197–205.

Black WC, Baron JA. CT screening for lung cancer: spiraling into confusion? *JAMA: the Journal of the American Medical Association* 2007;297(9):995–7.

Boffetta P, Straif K. Use of smokeless tobacco and risk of myocardial infarction and stroke: systematic review with meta-analysis. BMJ (*British Medical Journal*) 2009;339:b3060. doi: 10.1136/bmj.b3060.

Bonnie RJ, Stratton K, Wallace RB, editors. *Ending the Tobacco Problem: A Blueprint for the Nation*. Washington: National Academies Press, 2007.

Breton CV, Byun H-M, Wenten M, Pan F, Yang A, Gilliland FD. Prenatal tobacco smoke exposure affects global and gene-specific DNA methylation. *American Journal of Respiratory and Critical Care Medicine* 2009;180(5):462–7.

Brundtland GH. Speech to the WHO International Conference on Tobacco and Health; November 15, 1999; Kobe, Japan. <http://www.who.int/director-general/speeches/1999/english/19991115_kobe.html>; accessed: March 25, 2009.

Caporaso N, Gu F, Chatterjee N, Sheng-Chih J, Yu K, Yeager M, Chen C, Jacobs K, Wheeler W, Landi MT, et al. Genome-wide and candidate gene association study of cigarette smoking behaviors. *PLoS ONE* 2009;4(2):e4653. doi:10.1371/journal.pone.0004653.

Carlsten C, Burke W. Potential for genetics to promote public health: genetics research on smoking suggests caution about expectations. *JAMA: the Journal of the American Medical Association* 2006;296(20):2480–2.

Centers for Disease Control and Prevention. Smoking during pregnancy—United States, 1990–2002. *Morbidity and Mortality Weekly Report* 2004;53(39):911–5.

Centers for Disease Control and Prevention. *Best Practices for Comprehensive Tobacco Control Programs—2007*. Atlanta: U.S. Department of Health and Human Services, Centers for Disease Control and Prevention, National Center for Chronic Disease Prevention and Health Promotion, Office on Smoking and Health, 2007.

Centers for Disease Control and Prevention. Cigarette smoking among adults—United States, 2007. *Morbidity and Mortality Weekly Report* 2008a;57(45):1221–6.

Centers for Disease Control and Prevention. Deaths from chronic obstructive lung disease—United States, 2000–2005. *Morbidity and Mortality Weekly Report* 2008b;57(45):1229–32.

Centers for Disease Control and Prevention. Disparities in secondhand smoke exposure—United States, 1988–1994 and 1999–2004. *Morbidity and Mortality Weekly Report* 2008c;57(27):744–7.

Centers for Disease Control and Prevention. Smoking-attributable mortality, years of potential life lost, and productivity losses—United States, 2000–2004. *Morbidity and Mortality Weekly Report* 2008d;57(45):1226–48.

Centers for Disease Control and Prevention. State Medicaid coverage for tobacco-dependence treatments—United States, 2006. *Morbidity and Mortality Weekly Report* 2008e;57(5):117–22.

Centers for Disease Control and Prevention. State smoking restrictions for private-sector worksites, restaurants, and bars—United States, 2004 and 2007.

Morbidity and Mortality Weekly Report 2008f; 57(20):549–52.

Centers for Disease Control and Prevention. Cigarette smoking among Adults and trends in smoking cessation—United States, 2008. *Morbidity and Mortality Weekly Report* 2009a;58(44):1227–32.

Centers for Disease Control and Prevention. Federal and state excise taxes—United States, 1995–2009. *Morbidity and Mortality Weekly Report* 2009b;58(19):524–7.

Centers for Disease Control and Prevention. November is Lung Cancer Awareness Month, July 2009c; <http://www.cdc.gov/features/lungcancer/>; accessed: July 17, 2009.

Cokkinides V, Bandi P, McMahon C, Jemal A, Glynn T, Ward E. Tobacco control in the United States—recent progress and opportunities. *CA A Cancer Journal for Clinicians* 2009;59(6):352–65.

Comprehensive Smokeless Tobacco Health Education Act of 1986, Public Law 99-252, *U.S. Statutes at Large* 100 (1986):30.

Cruz TB. Monitoring the tobacco use epidemic IV. The vector: tobacco industry data sources and recommendations for research and evaluation. *Preventive Medicine* 2009;48(1 Suppl):S24–S34.

Delnevo CD, Bauer UE. Monitoring the tobacco use epidemic III. The host: data sources and methodological challenges. *Preventive Medicine* 2009;48(1 Suppl): S16–S23.

Doll R, Peto R, Boreham J, Sutherland I. Mortality in relation to smoking: 50 years' observations on male British doctors. *BMJ (British Medical Journal)* 2004; 328(7455):1519–28.

Doll R, Peto R, Wheatley K, Gray R, Sutherland I. Mortality in relation to smoking: 40 years' observations on male British doctors. *BMJ (British Medical Journal)* 1994;309(6959):901–11.

Dubey S, Powell CA. Update in lung cancer 2007. *American Journal of Respiratory and Critical Care Medicine* 2008;177(9):941–6.

Esteller M. Molecular origins of cancer: epigenetics in cancer. *New England Journal of Medicine* 2008; 358(11):1148–59.

European Commission. *Health Effects of Smokeless Tobacco Products.* Brussels: European Commission, Scientific Committee on Emerging and Newly Identified Health Risks, 2008.

Fagan P, Rigotti NA. Light and intermittent smoking: the road less traveled. *Nicotine & Tobacco Research* 2009;11(2):107–10.

Family Smoking Prevention and Tobacco Control Act, Public Law 111-31, *U.S. Statutes at Large* 123 (2009): 1776.

Farrelly MC. Monitoring the tobacco use epidemic V. The environment: factors that influence tobacco use. *Preventive Medicine* 2009;48(1 Suppl):S35–S43.

Federal Cigarette Labeling and Advertising Act of 1965, Public Law 89-92, *U.S. Statutes at Large 79* (1965):281.

Field JK. Lung cancer risk models come of age. *Cancer Prevention Research* 2008;1(4):226–8.

Field JK, Duffy SW. Lung cancer screening: the way forward. *British Journal of Cancer* 2008;99(4):557–62.

Fiore MC, Jaén CR, Baker TB, Bailey WC, Benowitz NL, Curry SJ, Dorfman SF, Froelicher ES, Goldstein MG, Healton CG, et al. *Treating Tobacco Use and Dependence: 2008 Update.* Clinical Practice Guideline. Rockville (MD): U.S. Department of Health and Human Services, Public Health Service, 2008.

Flanders WD, Lally CA, Zhu B-P, Henley SJ, Thun MJ. Lung cancer mortality in relation to age, duration of smoking, and daily cigarette consumption: results from Cancer Prevention Study II. *Cancer Research* 2003;63(19):6556–62.

Garland C, Barrett-Connor E, Suarez L, Criqui MH, Wingard DL. Effects of passive smoking on ischemic heart disease mortality of nonsmokers: a prospective study. *American Journal of Epidemiology* 1985;121(5): 645–50.

Giovino GA, Biener L, Hartman AM, Marcus SE, Schooley MW, Pechacek TF, Vallone E. Monitoring the tobacco use epidemic. I. Overview: optimizing measurement to facilitate change. *Preventive Medicine* 2009;48 (1 Suppl):S4–S10.

Glantz SA, Parmley WW. Passive smoking and heart disease: epidemiology, physiology, and bio-chemistry. *Circulation* 1991;83(1):1–12.

Glantz SA, Parmley WW. Passive smoking and heart disease: mechanisms and risk. *JAMA: the Journal of the American Medical Association* 1995;273(13):1047–53.

Godtfredsen NS, Holst C, Prescott E, Vestbo J, Osler M. Smoking reduction, smoking cessation, and mortality: a 16-year follow-up of 19,732 men and women from The Copenhagen Centre for Prospective Population Studies. *American Journal of Epidemiology* 2002;156(11):994–1001.

Gonzales D, Rennard SI, Nides M, Oncken C, Azoulay S, Billing CB, Watsky EJ, Gong J, Williams KE, Reeves KR, et al. Varenicline, an α4β2 nicotinic acetylcholine receptor partial agonist, vs sustained-release bupropion and placebo for smoking cessation: a randomized controlled trial. *JAMA: the Journal of the American Medical Association* 2006;296(1):47–55.

Gray N, Henningfield JE, Benowitz NL, Connolly GN, Dresler C, Fagerström K, Jarvis MJ, Boyle P. Toward a comprehensive long term nicotine policy. *Tobacco Control* 2005;14(3):161–5.

Hatsukami DK, Giovino GA, Eissenberg T, Clark PI, Lawrence D, Leischow S. Methods to assess potential reduced exposure products. *Nicotine & Tobacco Research* 2005;7(6):827–44.

Henningfield JE, Benowitz NL, Connolly GN, Davis RM, Gray N, Myers ML, Zeller M. Reducing tobacco addiction through tobacco product regulation. *Tobacco Control* 2004;13(2):132–5.

Henningfield JE, Benowitz NL, Slade J, Houston TP, Davis RM, Deitchman SD. Reducing the addictiveness of cigarettes. *Tobacco Control* 1998;7(3):281–93.

Herbst RS, Heymach JV, Lippman SM. Molecular origins of lung cancer: lung cancer. *New England Journal of Medicine* 2008;359(13):1367–80.

Hirayama T. Lung cancer in Japan: effects of nutrition and passive smoking. In: Mizell M, Correa P, editors. *Lung Cancer: Causes and Prevention*. Deerfield Beach (MA): Verlag Chemie International, 1984:175–95.

International Agency for Research on Cancer. *IARC Monographs on the Evaluation of Carcinogenic Risks to Humans: Tobacco Smoke and Involuntary Smoking*. Vol. 83. Lyon (France): International Agency for Research on Cancer, 2004.

International Agency for Research on Cancer. *Tobacco Control: Reversal of Risk After Quitting Smoking*. IARC Handbooks of Cancer Prevention, Vol. 11. Lyon (France): International Agency for Research on Cancer, 2007a.

International Agency for Research on Cancer. *IARC Monographs on the Evaluation of Carcinogenic Risks to Humans: Smokeless Tobacco and Some Tobacco-specific N-Nitrosamines*. Vol. 89. Lyon (France): International Agency for Research on Cancer, 2007b.

Jemal A, Siegel R, Ward E, Hao Y, Xu J, Murray T, Thun MJ. Cancer statistics, 2008. *CA Cancer Journal for Clinicians* 2008;58(2):71–96.

Jorenby DE, Hays JT, Rigotti NA, Azoulay S, Watsky EJ, Williams KE, Billing CB, Gong J, Reeves KR, Varenicline Phase 3 Study Group. Efficacy of varenicline, an α4β2 nicotinic acetylcholine receptor partial agonist, vs placebo or sustained-release bupropion for smoking cessation: a randomized controlled trial. *JAMA: the Journal of the American Medical Association* 2006;296(1):56–63.

Law MR, Morris JK, Wald NJ. Environmental tobacco smoke exposure and ischaemic heart disease: an evaluation of the evidence. *BMJ (British Medical Journal)* 1997;315(7114):973–80.

Lerman C, Niaura R. Applying genetic approaches to the treatment of nicotine dependence. *Oncogene* 2002; 21(48):7412–20.

Lynch BS, Bonnie RJ, editors. Growing Up Tobacco Free: Preventing Nicotine Addiction in Children and Youths. Washington: National Academy Press, 1994.

Mannino DM, Buist AS. Global burden of COPD: risk factors, prevalence, and future trends. *Lancet* 2007; 370(9589):765–73.

Maciosek MV, Coffield AB, Edwards NM, Flottemesch TJ, Goodman MJ, Solberg LI. Priorities among effective clinical preventive services: results of a systematic review and analysis. *American Journal of Preventive Medicine* 2006;31(1):52–61.

Miller MD, Marty MA, Broadwin R, Johnson KC, Salmon AG, Winder B, Steinmaus C. The association between exposure to environmental tobacco smoke and breast cancer: a review by the California Environmental Protection Agency. *Preventive Medicine* 2007;44(2): 93–106.

National Cancer Institute. *The Role of the Media in Promoting and Reducing Tobacco Use*. Tobacco Control Monograph No. 19. Bethesda (MD): U.S. Department of Health and Human Services, National Institutes of Health, National Cancer Institute, 2008. NIH Publication No. 07-6242.

National Cancer Institute. *Phenotypes and Endophenotypes: Foundations for Genetic Studies of Nicotine Use and Dependence*. Tobacco Control Monograph No. 20. Bethesda (MD): U.S. Department of Health and Human Services, Public Health Service, National Institutes of Health, National Cancer Institute, 2009. NIH Publication No. 08-6366.

NIH State-of-the-Science Panel. National Institutes of Health State-of-the-Science Conference statement: tobacco use: prevention, cessation, and control. *Annals of Internal Medicine* 2006;145(11):839–44.

Nides M, Oncken C, Gonzales D, Rennard S, Watsky EJ, Anziano R, Reeves KR, Varenicline Study Group. Smoking cessation with varenicline, a selective α4β2 nicotinic receptor partial agonist: results from a 7-week, randomized, placebo- and bupropion-controlled trial with 1-year follow-up. *Archives of Internal Medicine* 2006;166(15):1561–8.

NSDUH Report. Cigarette use among pregnant women and recent mothers. *NSDUH Report* February 9, 2007.

Oncken C, Gonzales D, Nides M, Rennard S, Watsky E, Billing CB, Anziano R, Reeves K. Efficacy and safety of the novel selective nicotinic acetylcholine receptor partial agonist, varenicline, for smoking cessation. *Archives of Internal Medicine* 2006;166(15):1571–7.

Partnership for Prevention. *A Call for ACTTION: Access for Cessation Treatment for Tobacco in Our Nation*. Washington: Partnership for Prevention, 2008.

Pentel PR. Vaccines and depot medications for drug addiction: rationale, mechanisms of action, and treatment implications. In: Harwood HJ, Myers TG, editors. *New Treatments for Addiction: Behavioral, Ethical, Legal, and Social Questions*. Washington: National Academies Press, 2004:63–97.

Peto R, Lopez AD, Boreham J, Thun M. Mortality from Smoking in Developed Countries 1950–2000, 2nd ed., revised June 2006. <http://www.ctsu.ox.ac.uk/~tobacco/C4308.pdf>; accessed: March 13, 2008.

Peto R, Lopez AD, Boreham J, Thun M, Heath C Jr. Mortality from smoking in developed countries: indirect estimates from national vital statistics. *Lancet* 1992;339(8804):1268–78.

Phillips DH, Garte S. Smoking and breast cancer: is there really a link? *Cancer Epidemiology, Biomarkers & Prevention* 2008;17(1):1–2.

Reuben SH. *Promoting Healthy Lifestyles: Policy, Program, and Personal Recommendations for Reducing Cancer Risk. 2006–2007 Annual Report: President's Cancer Panel*. Rockville (MD): U.S. Department of Health and Human Services, National Institutes of Health, National Cancer Institute, 2007.

Reuben SH. *Maximizing Our Nation's Investment in Cancer: Three Crucial Actions for America's Health. President's Cancer Panel 2007–2008 Annual Report*. Bethesda (MD): U.S. Department of Health and Human Services, National Institutes of Health, National Cancer Institute, 2008.

Royal College of Physicians of London. Harm Reduction in Nicotine Addiction: Helping People Who Can't Quit. A Report by the Tobacco Advisory Group of the Royal College of Physicians of London. London: Royal College of Physicians of London, 2007.

Spiro SG, Silvestri GA. One hundred years of lung cancer. *American Journal of Respiratory and Critical Care Medicine* 2005;172(5):523–9.

Stellman SD, Djordjevic MV. Monitoring the tobacco use epidemic. II. The agent: current and emerging tobacco products. *Preventive Medicine* 2009;48(1 Suppl):S11–S15.

Stratton K, Shetty P, Wallace R, Bondurant S, editors. *Clearing the Smoke: Assessing the Science Base for Tobacco Harm Reduction*. Washington: National Academy Press, 2001.

Teo KK, Ounpuu S, Hawken S, Pandey MR, Valentin V, Hunt D, Diaz R, Rashed W, Freeman R, Jiang L, et al. Tobacco use and risk of myocardial infarction in 52 countries in the INTERHEART study: a case-control study. *Lancet* 2006;368(9536):647–58.

Tverdal A, Bjartveit K. Health consequences of reduced daily cigarette consumption. *Tobacco Control* 2006;15(6):472–80.

U.S. Department of Health and Human Services. *The Health Benefits of Smoking Cessation: A Report of the Surgeon General*. Atlanta: U.S. Department of Health and Human Services, Centers for Disease Control and Prevention, National Center for Chronic Disease Prevention and Health Promotion, Office on Smoking and Health, 1990.

U.S. Department of Health and Human Services. *Reducing Tobacco Use: A Report of the Surgeon General*. Atlanta: U.S. Department of Health and Human Services, Centers for Disease Control and Prevention, National Center for Chronic Disease Prevention and Health Promotion, Office on Smoking and Health, 2000.

U.S. Department of Health and Human Services. *Women and Smoking. A Report of the Surgeon General*. Rockville (MD): U.S. Department of Health and Human Services, Public Health Service, Office of the Surgeon General, 2001.

U.S. Department of Health and Human Services. *The Health Consequences of Smoking: A Report of the Surgeon General*. Atlanta: U.S. Department of Health and Human Services, Centers for Disease Control and Prevention, National Center for Chronic Disease Prevention and Health Promotion, Office on Smoking and Health, 2004.

U.S. Department of Health and Human Services. *The Health Consequences of Involuntary Exposure to Tobacco Smoke: A Report of the Surgeon General*. Atlanta: U.S. Department of Health and Human Services, Centers for Disease Control and Prevention, National Center for Chronic Disease Prevention and Health Promotion, Office on Smoking and Health, 2006.

U.S. Department of Health, Education, and Welfare. *Smoking and Health: Report of the Advisory Committee to the Surgeon General of the Public Health Service*. Washington: U.S. Department of Health, Education, and Welfare, Public Health Service, Center for Disease Control, 1964. PHS Publication No. 1103.

Wang XL, Scott DA, editors. *Molecular Mechanisms of Tobacco-Induced Diseases*. New York: Nova Biomedical Books, 2005.

World Health Organization. *WHO Report on the Global Tobacco Epidemic, 2008: The MPOWER Package*. Geneva: World Health Organization, 2008.

Zaza S, Briss PA, Harris KW, editors. *The Guide to Community Preventive Services: What Works to Promote Health?* New York: Oxford University Press, 2005.

Zeller M, Hatsukami D, Backinger C, Benowitz N, Biener L, Burns D, Clark P, Connolly G, Djordjevic M, Eissenberg T, et al. The strategic dialogue on tobacco harm reduction: a vision and blueprint for action in the United States. *Tobacco Control* 2009;doi:10.1136/tc.2008.027318.

List of Abbreviations

1-HOP	1-hydroxypyrene	**CDK**	cyclin-dependent kinase
4-ABP	4-aminobiphenyl	**CETP**	cholesterol ester transfer protein
4-HNE	4-hydroxy-2-nonenal	**CHD**	coronary heart disease
8-oxo-dG	7-hydroxy-8-oxo-2′-deoxyguanosine	**CI**	confidence interval
8-OH-dG	8-hydroxy-2′-deoxyguanosine	**CNS**	central nervous system
8-OH-DPAT	8-hydroxy-2-dipropylaminotetralin	**CO**	carbon monoxide
AAT	α1-antitrypsin	**CO$_2$**	carbon dioxide
ACE	angiotensin-converting enzyme	**COPD**	chronic obstructive pulmonary disease
ACh	acetylcholine	**CPS-I**	Cancer Prevention Study I
ACTH	adrenocorticotropic hormone	**CPS-II**	Cancer Prevention Study II
ADMA	asymmetric dimethylarginine	**CREB**	cyclic adenosine monophosphate–response
AGT	O^6-alkylguanine–DNA alkyltransferase		element binding protein
AH	aryl hydrocarbon	**CRP**	C-reactive protein
AHH	aryl hydrocarbon hydroxylase	**CS**	conditioned stimulus
AKT	protein kinase B	**CSE**	cigarette smoke extract
AOR	adjusted odds ratio	**CT**	computed tomography
AP	apurinic/apyrimidinic	**CUZNSOD**	copper zinc superoxide dismutase
AP-1	activator protein-1	**CVD**	cardiovascular disease
APA	American Psychiatric Association	**DEB**	diepoxybutane
APO	apolipoprotein	**DHBMA**	dihydroxybutyl mercapturic acid
APO A-I	apolipoprotein A-I	**DHβE**	[^{3}H]dihydro-beta-erythroidine
APO B	apolipoprotein B	**dL**	deciliter
APO E	apolipoprotein E	**DMBA**	7,12-dimethybenz[*a*]anthracene
ATP	adenosine triphosphate	**DRC**	DNA repair capacity
B[*a*]P	benzo[*a*]pyrene	**DRZ**	diagonal radioactive zone
B[*b*]F	benzo[*b*]fluoranthene	**DSB**	double-strand break
B[*k*]F	benzo[*k*]fluoranthene	**DSBR**	double-strand break repair
BAL	bronchoalveolar lavage	***DSM-III-R***	*Diagnostic and Statistical Manual of Mental*
BER	base excision repair		*Disorders*, 3rd ed. (rev)
BH	BCL-2 homology	***DSM-IV***	*Diagnostic and Statistical Manual of Mental*
BMI	body mass index		*Disorders,* 4th ed.
BPDE	benzo[*a*]pyrene-7,8-diol-9,10-epoxide	**EB**	3,4-epoxybutene
BSID	Bayley Scales of Infant Development	**ECSOD**	extracellular superoxide dismutase
Ca^{2+}	calcium ion	**EF**	etiologic fraction
Cal/EPA	California Environmental Protection Agency	**ELF**	epithelial lining fluid
CAM	chorioallantoic membrane	**ENOS**	endothelial nitric oxide synthase
CaMKII	Ca^{2+} calmodulin-dependent protein kinase II	**EPA**	U.S. Environmental Protection Agency
CAN	Canadian Intense	**EPC**	endothelial progenitor cell
CAT	chloramphenicol acetyltransferase	**EPO**	eosinophil-specific peroxidase
CB$_1$	cannabinoid subtype 1	**ERK**	extracellular signal-regulated kinase
CDC	Centers for Disease Control and Prevention	**F-344**	Fischer-344

FDA	U.S. Food and Drug Administration		**HPG**	hypothalamic-pituitary-gonadal
Fe^{2+}	ferrous ion		**HPLC**	high-performance liquid chromatography
Fe^{3+}	ferric ion		**HR23B**	homologous recombinational repair group 23B
FEV$_1$	forced expiratory volume in one second		**IARC**	International Agency for Research on Cancer
FFA	free fatty acid		**IBF**	intervillous blood flow
FR	fecundability ratio		**ICAM**	intercellular adhesion molecule
FSH	follicle-stimulating hormone		***ICD-10***	*International Statistical Classification of*
FTC	U.S. Federal Trade Commission			*Diseases and Related Health Problems, Tenth*
FTND	Fagerström Test for Nicotine Dependence			*Revision*
FTQ	Fagerström Tolerance Questionnaire		**Ig**	immunoglobulin
FVC	forced vital capacity		**IgM**	immunoglobulin M
g	gram		**IL**	interleukin
GABA	γ-aminobutyric acid		**INOS**	inducible nitric oxide synthase
GC	gas chromatography		**IOM**	Institute of Medicine
GCL	glutamate cysteine ligase		**ISO**	International Organization for
GGR	global genomic nucleotide excision repair			Standardization
GLu-P-1	2-amino-6-methyldipyrido[1,2-*a*:3′,2′-*d*] imidazole		**IUGR**	intrauterine growth restriction
GOLD	Global Initiative for Chronic Obstructive Lung Disease		**IVF**	in vitro fertilization
			kcal	kilocalorie
GPX	glutathione peroxidase		**kg**	kilogram
GRX	glutathione reductase		**L**	liter
GSH	glutathione		**LBW**	low birth weight
GSSG	oxidized glutathione		**LC**	liquid chromotography
GST	glutathione-*S*-transferase		**LDL**	low-density lipoprotein
GTP	guanosine triphosphate		**LDLc**	low-density lipoprotein cholesterol
H/R	hypoxia/reperfusion		**LH**	luteinizing hormone
H$_2$O	water		**LMPCR**	ligation-mediated polymerase chain reaction
H$_2$O$_2$	hydrogen peroxide		**LOD**	logarithm of the odds
H$_2$S	hydrogen sulfide		**LPL**	lipoprotein lipase
HAT	histone acetyltransferase		**LUC**	luciferase
Hb	hemoglobin		**m^3**	cubic meter
HbA$_{1c}$	hemoglobin A$_{1c}$		**MAO**	monoamine oxidase
HBEC	human bronchial epithelial cell		**MAPK**	mitogen-activated protein kinase
HCA	heterocyclic amine		**MDM2**	murine double minute 2
hCG	human chorionic gonadotropin		**MDPH**	Massachusetts Department of Public Health
HCN	hydrogen cyanide		**MEK**	mitogen-activated protein kinase kinase
HCR	host cell reactivation		**mg**	milligram
HDAC	histone deacetylase		**mGluR2/3**	metabotropic glutamate receptor subtype 2/3
HDL	high-density lipoprotein		**mGluR5**	metabotropic glutamate receptor subtype 5
HDLc	high-density lipoprotein cholesterol		**MHBMA**	monohydroxybutenyl mercapturic acid
Hg	mercury		**MI**	myocardial infarction
HIV	human immunodeficiency virus		**mL**	milliliter
HONC	Hooked on Nicotine Checklist		**mm**	millimeter
HOX	hypohalous acids		**MMP**	matrix metalloproteinase

MMR	mismatch repair		**NST**	nonstress test
MMS	methyl methanesulfonate		**NTCA**	*N*-nitrosothiazolidine 4-carboxylic acid
MNSOD	manganese superoxide dismutase		**O₂** O_2	oxygen
MPEP	2-methyl-6-(phenylethynyl)pyridine		**O₂•⁻** $O_2 \bullet^-$	superoxide anion
MPO	myeloperoxidase		**OH**	hydroxyl radical
mRNA	messenger RNA		**ONOO⁻** $ONOO^-$	peroxynitrite
MRP	multidrug-resistance protein		**ONOOH**	peroxynitrous acid
MS	mass spectrometry		**OR**	odds ratio
MSCA	McCarthy Scales of Children's Abilities		**p**	short arm of chromosome
MT1	membrane-type 1		**PAD**	peripheral arterial disease
MTT	3-(4,5-dimethylthiazol-2-yl)-2,5-diphenyltet-razolium bromide		**PAF**	platelet-activating factor
µg	microgram		**PAH**	polycyclic aromatic hydrocarbon
µm	micrometer		**PAI-1**	plasminogen activator inhibitor-1
µmol	micromole		**PARP**	poly (adenosine diphosphate–ribose) polymerase
N₂ N_2	nitrogen		**PAT**	poly AT insertion/deletion polymorphism
NAB	*N'*-nitrosoanabasine		**PCASRM**	Practice Committee of the American Society for Reproductive Medicine
nAChR	nicotinic acetylcholine receptor			
NADPH	reduced nicotinamide adenine dinucleotide phosphate		**PCNA**	proliferating cell nuclear antigen
			p-CREB	phosphorylated CREB
NAT	*N*-acetyltransferase		**PdG**	$1,N^2$-propanodeoxyguanosine
NATB	*N'*-nitrosoanatabine		**PDK1**	3-phosphoinositide–dependent protein kinase-1
NCI	National Cancer Institute			
NDMA	*N*-nitrosodimethylamine		**PET**	positron emission tomography
NER	nucleotide excision repair		**pg**	picogram
NF-κB	nuclear factor-kappa B		**pH**$_{eff}$	effective pH
ng	nanogram		**PhIP**	2-amino-1-methyl-6-phenylimidazo[4,5-*b*]pyridine
NHLBI	National Heart, Lung, and Blood Institute			
NIH	National Institutes of Health		**PHS**	U.S. Public Health Service
NK	natural killer		**PI**	protease inhibitor
nmol	nanomole		**PI-3K**	phosphatidylinositol-3 kinase
NMTCA	*N*-nitroso-2-methylthiazolidine 4-carboxylic acid		**PIP3**	phosphatidylinositol 3,4,5-triphosphate
			PKA	protein kinase A
NNAL	4-(methylnitrosamino)-1-(3-pyridyl)-1-buta-nol		**PKB**	protein kinase B (also known as AKT)
			PKC	protein kinase C
NNK	4-(methylnitrosamino)-1-(3-pyridyl)-1-buta-none		**PK**$_{cs}$	protein kinase catalytic subunit
			PlGF	placental growth factor
NNN	*N'*-nitrosonornicotine		**PMN**	polymorphonuclear neutrophil
NO	nitric oxide		**pmol**	picomole
NO₂ NO_2	nitrogen dioxide		**p-MPPI**	4-(2'-methoxy-phenyl)-1-[2'-(n-2"-pyridinyl)-p-iodobenzamido]ethyl-piperazine
NOS	nitric oxide synthase			
NPRO	*N*-nitrosoproline		**POB**	pyridyloxobutyl
NRC	National Research Council		**pol**	polymerase
NRT	nicotine replacement therapy		**ppm**	parts per million
NSCLC	non-small-cell lung cancer		**PPROM**	preterm premature rupture of membranes

PREP	potential reduced-exposure product
PRX	peroxiredoxin
q	long arm of chromosome
Q•⁻	semiquinone radical
RCT	reverse cholesterol transport
REC	homologous recombination
RI	resistance index
RNS	reactive nitrogen species
ROS	reactive oxygen species
RR	relative risk
S/D	systolic/diastolic
SAB	spontaneous abortion
SARS	severe acute respiratory syndrome
SCC	squamous cell carcinoma
SCE	sister chromatid exchange
SCENIHR	Scientific Commission on Emerging and Newly Identified Health Risks
SCLC	small-cell lung cancer
SD	standard deviation
SES	socioeconomic status
sFlt-1	soluble vascular endothelial growth factor receptor Flt-1
SGA	small for gestational age
sICAM	soluble intercellular adhesion molecule
SIDS	sudden infant death syndrome
SNO	*S*-nitrosothiol
SNP	single nucleotide polymorphism
SOD	superoxide dismutase
***S*-PMA**	*S*-phenylmercapturic acid
STR	short tandem repeat
sVCAM	soluble vascular cell adhesion molecule
TBARS	thiobarbituric acid reactive substances
TCR	transcription-coupled repair
TFIIH	transcription initiation factor IIH
TGFβ	transforming growth factor-beta
TGRL	triglyceride-rich lipoprotein

Th1	helper T-cell subset 1
Th2	helper T-cell subset 2
TIMP	tissue inhibitor of metalloproteinase
T_{max}	time to reach maximum blood concentrations of nicotine
TNFα	tumor necrosis factor-alpha
tPA	tissue plasminogen activator
TPM	total particulate matter
***trans, anti*-PheT**	*r*-1,*t*-2,3,*c*-4-tetrahydroxy-1,2,3,4-tetrahydrophenanthrene
Trp-P-1	3-amino-1,4-dimethyl-5*H*-pyrido[4,3-*b*]indole
Trp-P-2	3-amino-1-methyl-5*H*-pyrido[4,3-*b*]indole
TRX	thioredoxin
TSNA	tobacco-specific nitrosamine
***tt*-MA**	*trans,trans*-muconic acid
TxB_2	thromboxane B_2
TxM	thromboxane metabolite
UCSF	University of California at San Francisco
UGT	uridine-5′-diphosphate-glucuronosyltransferase
US	unconditioned stimulus
USDHEW	U.S. Department of Health, Education, and Welfare
USDHHS	U.S. Department of Health and Human Services
USPSTF	U.S. Preventive Services Task Force
UV	ultraviolet
VCAM	vascular cell adhesion molecule
VEGF	vascular endothelial growth factor
VEGFR	vascular endothelial growth factor receptor
VLDL	very-low-density lipoprotein
V_{max}	maximum velocity
VOC	volatile organic compound
VTA	ventral tegmental area
WHO	World Health Organization
XP (A–G)	xeroderma pigmentosum (groups A–G)
γGT	γ-glutamyltranspeptidase

List of Tables and Figures

**Chapter 5
Cancer**

Chapter 8
Reproductive and Developmental Effects

Chapter 9
A Vision for the Future

Definitions and Alternative Nomenclature of Genetic Symbols Used in This Report

Throughout this report, genes are represented by their abbreviations in italics. In many cases, proteins and enzymes related to these genes have the same abbreviation, presented in roman type. Definitions, alternative genetic symbols, related proteins and enzymes, and polymorphisms and variant genotypes are listed alphabetically by gene abbreviation.

Gene symbol used in this report	Definition	Alternative gene symbol	Related protein/enzyme	Polymorphism/variant genotype
5HTT	serotonin transporter	*SLC6A4, 5HTTLPR*	5HTT, SERT, SLC6A4	*LPR; VNTR*; 5HTTLPR
ADPRT	poly (ADP-ribose) polymerase family, member 1	*PARP1*	ADPRT; PARP1	*VAL762ALA; PRO882LEU; CYS908TYR*
AGT	O^6-alkylguanine–DNA alkyltransferase		AGT	*ILE143VAL; GLY160ARG*
ANKK1	ankyrin repeat and kinase domain containing 1		ANKK1, protein kinase PKK2	*GLU713LYS* (caused by *DRD2 *TAQ1A* system)
APAF1	apoptotic peptidase activating factor 1		APAF1	
APEX1	APEX nuclease (multifunctional DNA repair enzyme) 1		APEX1	*GLU148ASP (T11865G)*
AREG	amphiregulin (schwannoma-derived growth factor)	*SDGF*	AREG, SDGF, CRDGF (colorectum cell-derived growth factor)	
ARP	arginine-rich protein	*ARMET*	ARP, ARMET (arginine-rich mutated in early stage tumors)	
ATM	ataxia telangiectasia mutated	*TEL1*	ATM; TEL1 (telomere maintenance 1)	
BAX	BCL2-associated X protein		BAX	
BRAF	v-raf murine sarcoma viral onco homolog B1		BRAF, B-RAF proto-oncogene serine/threonine-protein kinase (p94)	
BRCA2	breast cancer 2, early onset		BRCA2, breast cancer susceptibility protein	*HIS372ASN (T27113G), ILE3412VAL (G93268A)*
C-FOS	v-fos FBJ murine osteosarcoma viral oncogene homolog	*FOS*	FOS, C-FOS	
C4A	complement component 4A (Rodgers blood group)		C4A	haplotype
C4B	complement component 4B (Childo blood group)		C4B	haplotype
CASPASE-3	cysteine-aspartic acid protease-3		CASPASE-3	
CASPASE-8	cysteine-aspartic acid protease-8		CASPASE-8	

Gene symbol used in this report	Definition	Alternative gene symbol	Related protein/enzyme	Polymorphism/variant genotype
CCK	cholecystokinin		CCK	*C-45T* promoter polymorphism in SP1 binding region of *CCK* gene
CCKAR	cholecystokinin A receptor	*CCK1-R*	CCKAR, CCK1-R (cholecystokinin-1 receptor)	*T779C, VAL365ILE*
CCND1	G1/S-specific cyclin D1		CCND1	*G870A, *A/*A, *G/*A, *G/*G*
CCNH	cyclin H		CCNH, cyclin-dependent kinase-activating kinase	*VAL270ALA*
CD14	CD14 molecule		CD14 molecule; CD14 antigen	*C-159T* (promoter polymorphism)
CDK4	cyclin-dependent kinase 4		CDK4, cell division kinase 4	
CDKN2A	cyclin-dependent kinase inhibitor 2A		CDKN2A, P16	
C-HA-RAS	v-Ha-ras Harvey rat sarcoma viral oncogene homolog	*C-HRAS, HRAS*	C-HRAS, HRAS1 proto-oncoprotein	
CHFR	checkpoint with forkhead and ring finger domains		CHFR, mitotic checkpoint protein	
CHRNA3	cholinergic receptor, nicotinic, α3		CHRNA3	
CHRNA4	cholinergic receptor, nicotinic, α4		CHRNA4, α4 nAChR, nicotinic acetylcholine receptor α4 subunit	SNP *RS3746372* (*1); haplotype
CHRNA5	cholinergic receptor, nicotinic, α5		CHRNA5, nicotinic acetylcholine receptor α5 subunit, α5 nAChR	SNP *RS16969968* (*CHRNA5*); SNPs *RS8023462* and *RS1948* (*CHRNA5/A3/B4* cluster)
CHRNA7	cholinergic receptor, nicotinic, α7		CHRNA7, nicotinic acetylcholine receptor α7 subunit, α7 nAChR	D15S1360 (a microsatellite polymorphic marker in *INTRON 2*) exhibited seven different dinucleotide repeat lengths (99, 109, 111, 113, 115, 117, and 125 bp), the major alleles are *113 and *115 (*113/*113, *113/*115, *115/*115)
CHRNB2	cholinergic receptor, nicotinic, β2 (neuronal)		CHRNB2, nicotinic acetylcholine receptor β2 subunit, β2 nAChR	multiple SNPs; haplotype
CHRNB3	cholinergic receptor, nicotinic, β3		CHRNB3	

Gene symbol used in this report	Definition	Alternative gene symbol	Related protein/enzyme	Polymorphism/variant genotype
CHRNB4	cholinergic receptor, nicotinic, β4		CHRNB4	
C-MYC	avian myelocytomatosis viral oncogene homolog	MYC	C-MYC, myc proto-oncogene protein	
COMT	catechol-O-methyltransferase		COMT	A1947G, *A, *G, VAL158MET
COX-1	cyclooxygenase-1		COX-1	
COX-2	cyclooxygenase-2		COX-2	
CYP17A1	cytochrome P-450, family 17, subfamily A, polypeptide 1		CYP17A1	
CYP1A1	cytochrome P-450, family 1, subfamily A, polypeptide 1		CYP1A1, MSPI	*MSPI (*A/*a, *a/*a), ILE462VAL
CYP2A13	cytochrome P-450, family 2, subfamily A, polypeptide 13		CYP2A13	ARG257CYS (C3375T, *C/*T, *T/*T)
CYP2A6	cytochrome P-450, family 2, subfamily A, polypeptide 6		CYP2A6	*1 (wild type), *1A, *1B, *2, *3, *4, *4A, *4B, *4C, *4D, *5, *6, *7, *8, *9, *10, *12, *16, *NULL, *DEL
CYP2B6	cytochrome P-450, family 2, subfamily B, polypeptide 6		CYP2B6	*5 (C1459T=ARG487CYS); *6 (G516T=GLN172HIS); *2 (C64T=ARG22CYS); *3 (C777A=SER259ARG); *4 (A785G=LYS262ARG)
CYP2D6	cytochrome P-450, family 2, subfamily D, polypeptide 6		CYP2D6	*3, *4A, *5
CYP2E1	cytochrome P-450, family 2, subfamily E, polypeptide 1		CYP2E1	*1C, *1D, *DRA1, *RSA1
DAPK1	death-associated protein kinase 1	DAPK	DAPK1, DAPK	
DAT	dopamine transporter	DAT1	DAT, DAT1	VNTR
DDC	dopa decarboxylase (aromatic l-amino acid decarboxylase)	AADC	DDC, AADC	haplotype
DLC1	deleted in liver cancer 1		DLC1	
DRD1	dopamine receptor D1		DRD1	*DDE1
DRD2	dopamine receptor D2		DRD2	*TAQ1A (*A), *TAQ1B, -141C *INS/*DEL, *FOK1, *INTRON 2, *MBO1

Gene symbol used in this report	Definition	Alternative gene symbol	Related protein/enzyme	Polymorphism/variant genotype
DRD4	dopamine receptor D4		DRD4	*VNTR*
DRD5	dopamine receptor D5		DRD5	haplotype
DβH	dopamine beta hydroxylase		DβH	*G1368A, C1021T, *A* allele *(G444A)*
E-CADHERIN	cadherin 1, type 1, E-cadherin (epithelial)		E-CADHERIN, calcium-dependent adhesion protein, epithelial	
EGFR	epidermal growth factor receptor (erythroblastic leukemia viral (v-erb-b) onco homolog, avian)		EGFR	
ELA2	elastase, neutrophil expressed	*ELANE*	ELA2	
EN2	engrailed homeobox 2	*EN-2*	EN2	
ENOS	endothelial nitric oxide synthase	*NOS3*	ENOS, NOS3	*A* allele (a quadruple repeat of a 27 base-pair sequence in *INTRON 4*), *GLU298ASP (*ASP298)*
EPHX1	gene of epoxide hydrolase 1, microsomal (xenobiotic)	*MEH*	EPHX1, MEH microsomal epoxide hydrolase	*EXON 3* SNP, *EXON 4* SNP, *EXONs 3-4* SNP haplotypes, (T → C) *TYR113HIS (*H)*, (A → G) *HIS139ARG*
ERCC1	excision repair cross-complementing rodent repair deficiency, complementation group 1 (includes overlapping antisense sequence)		ERCC1	
ESR1	estrogen receptor 1		estrogen receptor α	*XBAL (c.454-351A → G)*, *PVULL (c.454-397T → C)*
FAS	Fas (TNF receptor superfamily, member 6)		FAS	
FHIT	fragile histidine triad		FHIT, *FRA3B*	
FMS	colony stimulating factor 1 receptor	*CSF1R, C-FMS, CD115, FIM2, CSFR*	CSF1R, C-FMS, CD115, FIM2, CSFR	
GABARAP	GABA receptor-associated protein		GABARAP	
GABA_{B2}	γ-aminobutyric acid type B receptor 2		GABA_{B2}	haplotype

Gene symbol used in this report	Definition	Alternative gene symbol	Related protein/enzyme	Polymorphism/variant genotype
GC	group-specific component (vitamin D binding protein)		GC	*1S (416GLU, 420THR), *1F (416ASP, 420THR), *1S/*1F, *2 (416ASP, 420LYS), haplotype
GPX	glutathione peroxidase		GPX	
GSTA1	glutathione-*S*-transferase 1α		GSTA1	
GSTM1	glutathione-*S*-transferase μ1		GSTM1	*NULL, *DEL
GSTP1	glutathione-*S*-transferase π1		GSTP1	ILE105VAL, *ILE/*ILE, *ILE/*VAL, ALA114VAL, *ALA/*ALA, *ALA/*VAL
GSTT1	glutathione-*S*-transferase θ1		GSTT1	*NULL, *DEL
H-CADHERIN	cadherin 13, H-cadherin (heart)	*CDH13*	H-CADHERIN, CDH13	
HER-2/NEU	v-erb-b2 erythroblastic leukemia viral oncogene homolog 2, neuro/glioblastoma derived oncogene homolog (avian)	*ERBB2*	HER-2/NEU, erb B2 c-erb B2/neu protein, HER-2(human epidermal growth factor receptor 2)	
HPRT	hypoxanthine phosphoribosyltransferase		HPRT	
IL-1β	interleukin-1β		IL-1β	C-31T (TATA Box), *-31C, *-31T
JUN	jun oncogene		JUN	
KRAS	v-Ki-ras2 Kirsten rat sarcoma viral oncogene homolog		KRAS	
LAMA3	laminin, α3		LAMA3	
LAMB3	laminin, β3		LAMB3	
LAMC2	laminin, γ2		LAMC2	
LIG1	ligase I, DNA, ATP-dependent		LIG1	ALA170ALA (A → C), ASP802ASP (C → T), ALA814ALA (C → G)
LIG4	ligase IV, DNA, ATP-dependent		LIG4	ALA3ALA (C8T, cDNA), THR9ILE (C27T, cDNA)
LKB1/STK11	serine/threonine kinase 11		LKB1, STK11	
LMYC	v-myc myelocytomatosis viral onco gene homolog 1, lung carcinoma derived	*L-MYC, MYCL1*	L-MYC, LMYC, MYCL1	
MAOA	monoamine oxidase A		MAOA	silent C1460T (EXON 14), VNTR

Gene symbol used in this report	Definition	Alternative gene symbol	Related protein/enzyme	Polymorphism/variant genotype
MAOB	monoamine oxidase B		MAOB	*A644G (*A,*G)*
MBD4	methyl-CpG binding domain protein 4		MBD4	*SER342PRO (T → C), GLU346LYS (G → A)*
MGMT	O⁶-methylguanine-DNA methyltransferase		MGMT	*LEU84PHE, ILE143VAL*
MMP-1	matrix metallopeptidase 1 (interstitial collagenase)		MMP-1	
MMP-12	matrix metallopeptidase 12 (macrophage elastase)		MMP-12	
MPO	myeloperoxidase		MPO	
MSX1	msh homeobox 1		MSX1	haplotype (intronic *CA* repeat), **X1.3/*X1.3, *X2.4/*X2.4, *2* (rare allele)
MUC5AC	mucin 5AC, oligomeric mucus/gel-forming		MUC5AC	
MUTYH	mutY homolog (*E. coli*)		MUTYH, mutY DNA glycosylase, A/G-specific adenine DNA glycosylase	*GLN335HIS (G → C)*
MYO18B	myosin XVIIIB		MYO18B	
NAT1	*N*-acetyltransferase 1		NAT1, arylamine *N*-acetyltransferase 1	*1088 *A/*A (T1088A), 1095 *A/*A (C1095A)*
NAT2	*N*-acetyltransferase 2		NAT2, arylamine *N*-acetyltransferase 2	*ILE114THR (T → C), LYS161LYS (C → T), LYS268ARG (A → G), ARG197GLN (G → A), TYR94TYR (C → T), GLY286GLU (G → A), *4/*4* (wild type)
NBS1	Nijmegen breakage syndrome 1	*NBN*	NBS1, NBN, nibrin	*GLN185GLU (C → G)*
N-MYC	v-myc myelocytomatosis viral related oncogene, neuroblastoma derived (avian)	*NMYC, MYCN*	N-MYC, NMYC, MYCN, N-myc proto-oncogene protein	
NORE1A	RAS association (RALGDS/AF-6) domain family member 5	*RASFF5*	NORE1A, RASFF5	
NRXN1	neurexin 1		NRXN1	
NRXN3	neurexin 3		NRXN3	
NTRK2	neurotrophic tyrosine kinase, receptor, type 2		NTRK2	

Gene symbol used in this report	Definition	Alternative gene symbol	Related protein/enzyme	Polymorphism/variant genotype
OGG1	8-oxoguanine DNA glycosylase		OGG1	*SER326CYS (C → G), 326*CYS/*CYS, 326*SER/*SER*
OPRM1	opioid receptor, μ1		OPRM1	*ASN40ASP (A118G), *ASP40, *ASN40*
P14^ARF	cyclin-dependent kinase inhibitor 2A (CDKN2A)	*P14*	P14, P14ARF (the alternate reading frame products of CDKN2A gene)	
P16	cyclin-dependent kinase inhibitor 2A (CDKN2A)	*P16INK4A*	P16, P16INK4A (the major product of CDKN2A gene)	
P21	cyclin-dependent kinase inhibitor 1A	*P21, CDNK1A, CIP1, WAF1, SDI1*	P21, CDNK1A, CIP1, WAF1, SDI1	*SER31ARG*
P53	tumor suppressor		P53	*ARG72PRO (G → C), 72*ARG/*PRO, 72*PRO/*PRO, *MSPI (INTRON 6), 16 bp insertion (INTRON 3)*
P73	tumor protein gene 73	*TP73*	P73, TP73	**GC/*GC, *AT/*AT, *GC/*AT (G4A, C14T in EXON 2)*
PARKIN	Parkinson disease (autosomal recessive, juvenile) 2, parkin	*PARK2*	PARKIN (ligase)	
PAX5 α	paired box gene 5	*BSAP (B-cell specific activator) α*	PAX5 α (one of the products of PAX5 gene), BSAP (B-cell specific activator protein) α	
PAX5 β	paired box gene 5	BSAP (B-cell specific activator) β	PAX β (one of the products of PAX5 gene), BSAP (B-cell specific activator protein) β	
PCMVCAT	a plasmid construct containing the reporter gene *CAT* (chloramphenicol acetyltransferase) driven by CMV (cytomegalovirus) promoter		PCMVCAT, chloramphenicol acetyltransferase as a reporter	
PLAP	placental alkaline phosphatase	ALPP	PLAP, ALPP alkaline phosphatase, placental (Regan isozyme)	**1/*1, *2/*2*
POLD1	polymerase (DNA directed), delta 1, catalytic subunit 125kDa		POLD1	*ARG19HIS (G → A), HIS119ARG (A → G), SER173ASN (A → G)*

Gene symbol used in this report	Definition	Alternative gene symbol	Related protein/enzyme	Polymorphism/variant genotype
PTEN	phosphatase and tensin homolog		PTEN, deleted on chromosome 10	this gene may be deleted on chromosome 10 (10q23) with the development of cancers
RAD23B	RAD23 homolog B (*S. cerevisiae*)		RAD23B, UV excision repair protein RAD23 homolog B, XP-C repair complementing protein	*ALA249VAL (C → T)*
RAD4	RAD4 gene of *S. cerevisiae*		RAD4, *S. cerevisiae* DNA damage recognition and repair protein	
RAD50	RAD50 gene homolog (*S. cerevisiae*)		RAD50 (human)	*ARG1111ILE (G3374T, cDNA)*
RAD51	RAD51 homolog (*S. cerevisiae*)		RAD51	
RAD52	RAD52 homolog (*S. cerevisiae*)		RAD52	
RAD54L	RAD54 homolog (*S. cerevisiae*)	*S. cerevisiae* RAD50 gene homolog	RAD54L	*ARG374SER (G1222C, cDNA)*
RASSF1A	Ras association (RalGDS/AF-6) domain family member 1 (A isoform)		RASSF1A	
RASSF2	Ras association (RalGDS/AF-6) domain family member 2		RASSF2	
RASSF4	Ras association (RalGDS/AF-6) domain family member 4		RASSF4, tumor suppressor protein	
RB	retinoblastoma 1 tumor suppressor	RB1	RB, RB1	
SERPINA1	serpin peptidase inhibitor, clade A (α-1 antiproteinase, antitrypsin), member 1		SERPINA1, AAT protein	**M, *S, *Z, *NULL*
SERPINA3	serpin peptidase inhibitor, clade A (α-1 antiproteinase, antitrypsin), member 3		SERPINA3, ACT protein	*PRO229ALA, LEU55PRO, MET389VAL, ALA-15THR (signal peptide), 1258DELAA*
SFTPB	surfactant protein B		SFTPB; surfactant, pulmonary-associated protein B	*A-18C (promoter), A1013C, C1580T, A9306G, INTRON 4 variants, THR131ILE*
STK11	serine/threonine kinase 11		STK11	
TDG	thymine-DNA glycosylase		TDG	
TGFα	transforming growth factor α		TGFα	

Gene symbol used in this report	Definition	Alternative gene symbol	Related protein/enzyme	Polymorphism/variant genotype
TGFβ1	transforming growth factor β1		TGFβ1	SNP *RS1800469* (*C-509T*, promoter), SNP *RS2241712* (*G-10807A*, promoter), SNP *RS6957* (3'UTR), SNP *RS224178* (3'UTR), SNP *RS1982073* (*T29C, LEU10PRO, EXON 1*)
TGFβ3	transforming growth factor β3		TGFβ3	
TH	tyrosine hydroxylase		TH	VNTR
TIMP-3	tissue inhibitor of metalloproteinase 3		TIMP-3	
TNFα	tumor necrosis factor (TNF superfamily, member 2)	TNF	TNFα, TNF	*TNF2* (a promoter SNP, *G-308A*), SNPs *G-376A* and *G-238A* (promoter), *G489A (INTRON)*, SNP *RS3091257 (3'UTR)*, SNP *RS769178 (3'UTR)*
TP	thymidine phosphorylase		TP	
TPH	tryptophan hydroxylase	TPH1	TPH, TPH1	*C218A, A779C*
TP53	tumor protein		TP53	
TRAIL-R1	TNF-related apoptosis inducing ligand receptor 1	TNFRSF10A	TRAIL-R1, TNFRSF10A, death receptor 4	
UGT1A	UDP glucuronosyltransferase 1 family, polypeptide A1		UGT1A	
XPC	xeroderma pigmentosum, complementation group C	XPCC, XP3	XPC, XPCC, XP3	*ALA499VAL (C → T), LYS939GLN (A → C), *PAT* (poly AT ins/del polymorphism)
XPD	xeroderma pigmentosum, complementation group D	ERCC2	XPD, ERCC2	*ASP312ASN (G → A, 312 *G/*A), LYS751GLN (A → C, 751 *A/*C)*
XPF	xeroderma pigmentosum, complementation group F	ERCC4	XPF, ERCC4	*SER662PRO (T → C), ARG415GLN (G1244A, EXON 8* SNP *RS1800067), SER835SER (T2505C, EXON 11* SNP *RS1799801)*
XPG	xeroderma pigmentosum, complementation group G	ERCC5	XPG, ERCC5	*HIS1104ASP (G3507C,* SNP *RS17655), HIS46HIS (T335C,* SNP *RS1047768), CYS529SER* (SNP *RS2227869)*

Gene symbol used in this report	Definition	Alternative gene symbol	Related protein/enzyme	Polymorphism/variant genotype
XPV	polymerase (DNA directed) eta	POLH	XPV POLH, human DNA polymerase η	
XRCC1	x-ray repair complementing defective repair in Chinese hamster cells 1		XRCC1	*ARG194TRP (C → T), ARG280HIS (G → A), ARG399GLN (G → A)*
XRCC2	x-ray repair complementing defective repair in Chinese hamster cells 2		XRCC2	
XRCC3	x-ray repair complementing defective repair in Chinese hamster cells 3		XRCC3	*THR241MET (T → C)*
XRCC4	x-ray repair complementing defective repair in Chinese hamster cells 4		XRCC4	*ALA247SER (G → T)*
XRCC5	x-ray repair complementing defective repair in Chinese hamster cells 5 (double-strand-break rejoining)	KU80	XRCC5, KU80	
XRCC6	x-ray repair complementing defective repair in Chinese hamster cells 6	KU70	XRCC6, KU70	

Index

Note: t following a number refers to a Table; *f* following a number refers to a Figure.

C

S